Using Word 6 for Windows

10 Steps to a Great Memo

You can create this great-looking document in 10 easy steps with Word for Windows.

❶ Choose Memo Wizard

Choose File, New. Choose the Memo Wizard in the list of templates offered and follow its screens. This example uses the Contemporary style.

❷ Apply a Border and Shading

Select the text. Click the Borders button on the formatting toolbar to get the Borders toolbar. Click the Outside Border button. Choose Format, Borders and Shading. Click the Shading tab. In the Background drop-down list, choose Dark Cyan, then click OK.

❸ Format Heading Text

Select the text. Choose Format, Font. In the dialog box, change the typeface to Arial, the type size to 14 point, and the color to Dark Blue.

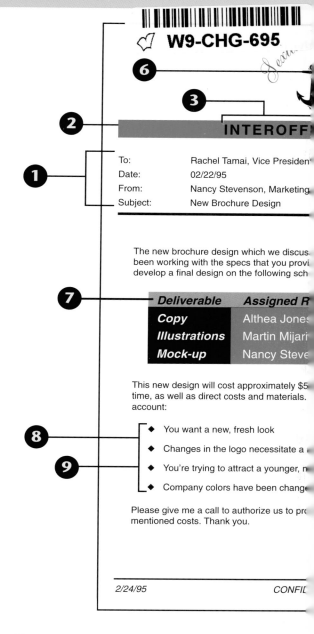

INTEROFF

To:	Rachel Tamai, Vice President
Date:	02/22/95
From:	Nancy Stevenson, Marketing
Subject:	New Brochure Design

The new brochure design which we discus. been working with the specs that you provi develop a final design on the following sch

Deliverable	Assigned R
Copy	Althea Jones
Illustrations	Martin Mijari
Mock-up	Nancy Steve

This new design will cost approximately $5 time, as well as direct costs and materials. account:

- ◆ You want a new, fresh look
- ◆ Changes in the logo necessitate a
- ◆ You're trying to attract a younger, n
- ◆ Company colors have been change

Please give me a call to authorize us to pr mentioned costs. Thank you.

2/24/95   CONFIL

❹ Insert a WordArt Object

Choose Insert, Object. Choose Microsoft WordArt 2.0. Type your text, using the Vivaldi font, make the color Dark Magenta, and select the Arch Up shape. Click in the document window to return to the document.

Outlining

To	Do this in Outline view
Select heading	Click in left margin
Select heading and text	Click heading's icon
Promote heading	Drag icon to left
Demote heading	Drag icon to right
Move heading	Drag icon up or down
Expand/Collapse heading	Double-click heading's button
Display to a level	Click numeric level button
Display all text	Click All button

Double-clicking Hotspots

To	Double-click on
Open GoTo dialog box	Page number in status bar
Make stationary toolbar float	Toolbar background
Make floating toolbar stationary	Toolbar title
Split/restore active window	Split bar
Switch between maximized/tiled window	Title bar
Open application for an embedded object	Object
Open the Page Setup dialog box	Ruler
Open the Record Macro dialog box	The REC indicator in the status bar
Open the Revisions dialog box	The MRK indicator in the status bar
Open WordPerfect Help	The WPH indicator in the status bar
Open footnote window	Footnote reference mark

Mouse Pointer Shapes

Shape	What it means
I	You're ready to move the insertion point or select text; this little I-bar marks the position where the insertion point will be placed.
⇧	You're pointing at the edges of a screen, menu, toolbar, status bar, scroll bar, or ruler—ready to click something.
⇗	You're in the selection bar area at the left edge of the screen; you can click and drag to select a sentence, a paragraph, or the entire document, if you'd like.
⇧?	You've clicked the Help button; move this pointer over anything in your document to get a Help screen for that element.
⇧	You've selected something and you're ready to drag it someplace else in the document.
☝	You're in the Help system, and you can click a word or phrase to see additional or related information.
↔	You're on the edge of a window, a frame, or an object like a picture or an embedded table; if you click and drag in the direction the arrow is pointing, you'll stretch or shrink the object.
⊹	You're on the edge of an item, again, and you can drag it where you want it.
⌛	You (and your mouse) are waiting while your computer performs a function, like saving a file. When the hourglass disappears, command of your screen returns to you.

Word's Best Keyboard Shortcuts

Editing	Shortcut
Undo what I did	Ctrl+Z
Repeat what I did	Ctrl+Y
Select it all	Ctrl+A
Turn bold on/off	Ctrl+B
Turn italic on/off	Ctrl+I
Turn underline on/off	Ctrl+U
Change case	⇧Shift+F3
Find something	Ctrl+F
Replace something	Ctrl+H
GoTo	F5
Return to previous spot	⇧Shift+F5
Delete left word	Ctrl+◆Backspace
Delete right word	Ctrl+Del
Repeat previous command	F4
Insert page break	Ctrl+↵Enter
Insert line break	⇧Shift+↵Enter

Managing Files	Shortcut
Start a new file	Ctrl+N
Open a file	Ctrl+O
Close this file	Ctrl+W
Save this file	Ctrl+S
Print this file	Ctrl+P

Moving & Copying	Shortcut
Cut	Ctrl+X
Copy	Ctrl+C
Paste	Ctrl+V

Formatting	Shortcut
Copy format	Ctrl+⇧Shift+C
Center	Ctrl+E
Justify	Ctrl+J
Left-align	Ctrl+L
Right-align	Ctrl+R
Indent	Ctrl+M
Single-space lines	Ctrl+1
Double-space lines	Ctrl+2
One-and-one-half space lines	Ctrl+5
Apply Normal style	Ctrl+⇧Shift+N

Other Stuff	Shortcut
Print Preview	Ctrl+F2
Repeat Find or GoTo	⇧Shift+F4
Start spell check	F7
Start thesaurus	⇧Shift+F7
Cancel a command	Esc
Get help	F1

Mouse Moves

Selecting

To	Do this
Set the insertion point	Put pointer where you want it and click
Select a word	Point to the word and double-click
Select a sentence	Hold the Ctrl key, point to the sentence, and click
Select a paragraph	Move the mouse pointer to the left margin; when the pointer looks like an arrow, position it beside the paragraph and double-click
Select the whole document	Move the mouse pointer to the left margin; when it turns into an arrow pointer, triple-click
Select an icon or picture	Point at it and click
Select items individually that aren't together	Press and hold the Ctrl key as you click each item
Deselect something	Point outside the selected area and click

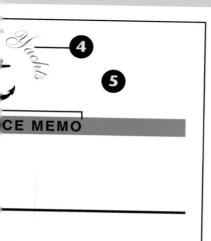

CE MEMO

…ed last Thursday is going well. We have
…ed, and I believe we will be able to
…dule:

…source	Due Date
	3/1/95
	3/5/95
son	3/7/95

…30, taking about 95 hours of resource
…he design will take the following into

…w image for all collateral pieces

…re affluent clientele

…to PMS 1140 and 257

…ed with this schedule and the above

NTIAL   1 ——⑩

201 W. 103rd Street
Indianapolis, IN 46290
(317) 581-3500
Copyright© 1995 Que Corporation

❻ Add a Picture

Choose Insert, Picture. Choose the Anchor
picture and click OK.

❼ Insert a Table

Click the Insert Table button, and drag
to select 4 rows by 3 columns. Enter
text, then choose Table, AutoFormat. Choose
Colorful 3 for the format, and then select Color.

❽ Format a Bulleted List

Select the text, then click the Bullet
button. Click on the right mouse button,
and choose Bullets and Numbering from the
shortcut menu. Select the diamond bullet
shape, and click OK.

❾ Indent Text

Select the text you want to indent. Click
the Increase Indent button.

❿ Add a Footer

Choose View, Header and Footer. Click
the Switch Between Header and Footer
button to move to Footer. Type text; use the
Date and Page Number buttons to enter the
date and page.

❺ Apply Frames

Although invisible, we've
applied frames to the picture
and WordArt object to move them around the
page. Click the Drawing button. Then, with
one of the objects selected, click the Insert
Frame button. Repeat this for the other
object.

Using

Word 6 for Windows

Nancy Stevenson

que

Using Word 6 for Windows

Library of Congress Catalog No.: 95-67677

ISBN: 1-7897-0289-4

97 96 95   4 3 2 1

Interpretation of the printing code: the rightmost double-digit number is the year of the book's printing; the rightmost single-digit number, the number of the book's printing. For example, a printing code of 95-1 shows that the first printing of the book occurred in 1995.

Publisher: *Roland Elgey*

Associate Publisher: *Don Roche, Jr.*

Director of Product Series: *Charles O. Stewart III*

Managing Editor: *Michael Cunningham*

Director of Marketing: *Lynn E. Zingraf*

Credits

Acquisitions Editor
Jenny L. Watson

Product Director
Lorna Gentry

Technical Editor
Gregory A. Dew

Production Editor
Lori A. Lyons

Editor
Nancy E. Sixsmith

Novice Reviewer
Paul Marchesseault

Technical Specialist
Cari Skaggs

Acquisitions Assistant
Tracy M. Williams

Operations Coordinator
Patricia J. Brooks

Editorial Assistant
Jill Pursell

Book Designer
Sandra Stevenson
Schroeder

Cover Designer
Dan Armstrong

Production Team
Claudia Bell
Maxine Dillingham
Karen Gregor
Daryl Kessler
Bob LaRoche
G. Alan Palmore
Jody York

Indexer
Rebecca Mayfield

Composed in *Stone* and *MCPdigital* by Que Corporation

Dedication

This book is dedicated to my parents, who taught me to love all books, and my husband, Graham, for putting up with everything involved in the creation of this one.

About the Author

Nancy Stevenson recently left her position as Publishing Manager at Que to pursue a full-time writing career. She teaches technical writing at Purdue University in Indianapolis, and has had articles published in several national magazines. Prior to this, she was Training Product Manager at Symantec, where she learned a thing or two about how people and computers do—and don't—get along.

Acknowledgments

No book is an island, and none is created by a single person.

Thanks to Dave Ewing for graciously giving me the opportunity to pursue new adventures, including the writing of this book. Thanks, also, to Associate Publisher Don Roche, one of Macmillan's finest, who has both my respect and friendship (whether he wants them or not)!

A special thank you goes to Jenny Watson, Acquisitions Editor. Ironically enough, I taught Jenny everything she knows about acquisitions, and she's becoming a great acquisitions editor in spite of it. Thanks for keeping the communications flowing and blocking those tackles, Jenny!

Two people who worked tirelessly on this project were Lorna Gentry and Lori Lyons. Lorna and I were thrown into the fire together and have emerged with only second-degree burns and this book; Que also ended up with a great Product Development Specialist. Lori used her years of experience as a Que Production Editor to keep this book moving through the process. (Thanks also to Nancy Sixsmith for picking up some of Lori's load when she was on vacation for a few days.)

Ed Bott, whose delightful book *Using Microsoft Office 4* set high standards for this series, deserves credit and thanks for looking over this book and adding his experience and expertise with the series to the final product.

Thanks also to Yael Li-Ron for her eleventh-hour assistance.

There are many others who were involved, from the astute technical editor, Gregory Dew, to the folks in Que design, production, and manufacturing who make all these words into a bound book. Que owes a debt of gratitude to Chuck Stewart for all his hard work developing this series. Finally, there's the Que sales force that puts these books into your hands. Thanks to you all.

Trademarks

All terms mentioned in this book that are known to be trademarks or service marks have been appropriately capitalized. Que cannot attest to the accuracy of this information. Use of a term in this book should not be regarded as affecting the validity of any trademark or service mark.

Microsoft Windows and Word are registered trademarks of Microsoft Corporation.

Screen reproductions in this book were created with Collage Complete from Inner Media, Inc., Hollis, NH.

We'd Like to Hear from You!

As part of our continuing effort to produce books of the highest possible quality, Que would like to hear your comments. To stay competitive, we *really* want you, as a computer book reader and user, to let us know what you like or dislike most about this book or other Que products.

You can mail comments, ideas, or suggestions for improving future editions to the address below, or send us a fax at (317) 581-4663. For the on-line-inclined, Macmillan Computer Publishing has a forum on CompuServe (type **GO QUEBOOKS** at any prompt) through which our staff and authors are available for questions and comments. The address of our Internet site is **http://www.mcp.com** (World Wide Web).

In addition to exploring our forum, please feel free to contact me personally to discuss your opinions of this book: on CompuServe, I'm at 75703,3251, and on the Internet, I'm **lgentry@que.mcp.com**.

Thanks in advance—your comments will help us to continue publishing the best books available on computer topics in today's market.

Lorna Gentry
Product Development Specialist
Que Corporation
201 W. 103rd Street
Indianapolis, IN 46290
USA

Contents at a Glance

{ Table of Contents }

Introduction

*How do I
use this
book?*

see page 2

Part I: Just the Basics

Chapter 1: A Word about Word

Chapter 2: A, B, C: Learning Word Basics

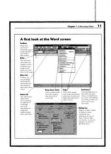

*A first look at the
Word screen*
see page 11

Chapter 2: A, B, C: Learning Word Basics

Close-Up: the Standard toolbar see page 31

Chapter 3: Getting Help in a Pinch

Part II: Making Something from Nothing

Chapter 4: Creating Word Documents

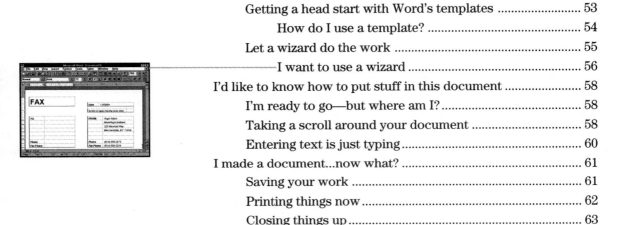

Chapter 5: Secrets of Successful File Management

Where in the world is my file?

see page 68

Chapter 6: Polishing Your Words to Perfection

Chapter 7: Perfect Documents Using Spelling, Grammar, and Thesaurus

How to write good...er, better

see page 103

Chapter 8: Now That I've Made It, I Think I'll Print It

Part III: Dressing Up Documents

Chapter 9: Simple Ways to Make Text Attractive

*Dressing up text
with Word
see page 129*

Chapter 10: Formatting Lines and Paragraphs

Chapter 13: Making Life Easier with Styles

Part IV: Getting Organized

Chapter 14: Organizing Information with Tables

Blueprint of a table
see page 195

Chapter 15: Organize Your Thinking with Outlines

Part V: Desktop Publishing for Everyone

Chapter 16: I Can't Draw, but I Can Desktop Publish

What can I create with WordArt?

see page 266

Part VI: Managing Data and Documents

Chapter 20: Sharing Things

Chapter 21: Mailings for the Masses

*How a mail merge
comes together
see page 297*

*It's alive!
Merging
what you've
created*

see page 306

Chapter 22: Managing Big Documents

Part VII: Getting Fancy with Word

Chapter 23: Making Basic Macros

Chapter 24: Have It Your Way: Customizing Word

Introduction

At the risk of sounding overly confident, I think I know who you are. You're someone who's picked up some pretty useful things in your life. You've probably mastered things like doing your taxes, figuring out the office football pool, and using one of the more complex languages on earth—English.

I know that perfectly intelligent people like you, who have a variety of real-life skills, need to do things like type a memo to your boss, design your first PTA newsletter, or create a fax cover sheet. And since you're reading this book, you must at least be considering using Word 6 for Windows to do these things.

But whenever people are handed a new tool, they naturally need a few questions answered: not obscure, technical questions, but real-life questions, like "How do I put a picture in my newsletter?"

Now, some books would place that under an obscure heading like "Importing Graphics File Formats." Who needs it? Why shouldn't a book just speak your language?

This one does.

How is this book special?

There are at least three different ways to get even the simplest job done in Word, but why should you do the one that involves three trips around the block and a secret password? This book gives you the most direct way to get things done in Word. There are usually other ways, but you want to get productive fast. This book tells you how to do that.

I swear not to bury you in technobabble that keeps you busy looking things up in your computer dictionary as often as you're getting work done in Word.

Finally, I know some of you are executives, secretaries, plumbers, or accountants. You need examples that make sense to anyone, no matter what your occupation or background. The examples and explanations in this book should make sense to you all. And I wrote them to give you the quickest results that you and Word can muster.

How do I use this book?

You could read this book from cover to cover, and I'd be flattered and impressed that it was so entertaining for you. But you don't have to. If you're a first-timer to Word for Windows, you'll want to read Part I, "Just the Basics." You'll get to know the program, how it works, and how you work with it. But if you already know that stuff, feel free to skip Part I and move on to new territory. Browse through the chapters; spot the headings that tell you something you didn't know about Word; pick up a tip here and there.

Feel free to find the chapter that tells you how to do just what you need to do right then, and read just enough to get it done. No need to take time learning about how to draw circles in Word if all you really want to do is type a letter. This book's designed to make it easy for you to learn what you want, when you want.

If you dip into this book often enough to get things done, you'll pick up most of the key features of Word pretty painlessly.

What's between the covers?

A product as big and chock full of features as Word for Windows can be used in different ways and for different jobs. This book is divided into separate parts for all the different ways you might want to use Word: do you want to design fancy documents or just type a basic letter? Do you have to juggle information, or do you need to get that information out to lots of different people? The sections in this book are set up to give you the information you need to get any of those things done, *fast*.

Part I: Just the Basics

Word processing basics include things like opening up a document and learning your way around the toolbars. Simple but essential stuff like that. (If you're already familiar with Word, you can skip this.) Oh, and the chapter on Word's stellar Help system tells you how to get all the help you need to explore other, less basic things.

Part II: Making Something from Nothing

You're here to make documents. Most documents start life the same way and use the same tools for building and editing the stuff in them. From finding your document to printing it, the workings of Word are explored in this section.

Part III: Dressing Up Documents

Beyond basic typing, there are lots of ways Word lets you polish your documents. Things like a great typeface, italic text, bulleted lists, and headers and footers all make for a stylish document. Here's where you learn about using them.

Part IV: Getting Organized

Putting things in tables and outlines are ways of getting your thoughts—and documents—in order. Take advantage of some pretty neat tools and features that make organizing information a cinch. These tools have never been so easy to master as they are in Word 6.

Part V: Desktop Publishing for Everyone

There's a little artist in all of us. And when it's this simple, it's hard to stop yourself from playing around with fancier documents. Try out pictures, drawings, borders, shading, fancy text effects—you get the picture.

Part VI: Managing Data and Documents

When you're ready to get beyond a single document, you can explore sharing information with other programs, doing mass mailings, and building big, beautiful documents. Word has some great (but easy-to-use) features that make it possible to move data around in a variety of ways.

Part VII: Getting Fancy with Word

You don't have to know this stuff in order to use Word. But when you have the time and inclination to learn some of these cool maneuvers, they'll put the icing on the cake of your understanding of Word. Learn how to do things like making macros to automate tasks and customizing Word to work the way you do. The information in this section helps you get the most out of this really power-packed program.

Special book elements

The people who designed this book threw in a lot of great little elements that call your attention to special information or help you out of trouble if you go astray.

(Tip)

> A tip is something you'd tell your best friend to show her something really neat in Word. It might be a shortcut, or a feature you might want to explore when you get a little more comfortable with the program.

{Note}

Notes fill in some important tidbits of information that would be handy for you to know as you try something new.

Sidebars provide a little aside

Sidebars give you a little break from getting things done. They take you on interesting, useful, and (dare I say) sometimes witty excursions outside the realm of "do this, do that."

 There aren't many things you can do in Word that could have really damaging consequences, but there are some. When they come up, a word of caution might help you avoid them.

What's a Q&A?

It's easy to get tangled up sometimes when you're first trying to use Word. Q&As anticipate some common questions you might have when you're working with Word and troubleshoot them before they can trip you up.

 Plain English, please!

Look here for an explanation of a potentially baffling computer term in no-nonsense, straightforward English.

A few more conventions used in this book might be helpful to know about:

- If there are a couple of steps to getting something done through a pull-down menu, they'll be divided by a comma. For example, choose View, Ruler means to pull down the View menu and choose Ruler from the list of choices. Oh—you can also choose View, Ruler by pressing Alt plus the underlined letters: Alt+V, R.

- Two keys separated by a plus sign, like Ctrl+V, means that you should hold down the first key, press the second key, and then let both keys go to get something done.

- When the book tells you to "double-click" something, it means that you should put the mouse pointer over a command, option, toolbar button, or other control and click the left mouse button twice—quickly!

One final note. Word has more buttons than the cockpit of the Space Shuttle. While you can always get things done by pulling down menus, there's often a mouse-click shortcut to get the job done extra-fast. Whenever there's a toolbar button you can click to perform a certain task, you'll see its picture in the margin (like the one you see here) next to the text that tells you how it works.

Part I:

Just the Basics

1

A Word about Word

In this chapter:

- I want to look at Word. Where is it?
- What's all this stuff on the screen?
- Word makes it easy to get to work
- Some of the advanced stuff looks tricky; is it? (Nope...)
- Can I use other programs with Word?

Word for Windows is the luxury sedan of software—fully loaded, yet easy to use.

When you first call on Word for Windows to help you whip up a new document from scratch, it's a lot like sliding into the seat of a fully loaded luxury sedan. All those buttons, controls, and gauges can seem pretty overwhelming at first—especially if you just want to make a quick run to the supermarket. You quickly realize, though, that all you really need to do is turn the key, put the car in Drive, and go. You can learn to adjust the stereo equalizer later.

Well, Microsoft has put a lot of features at your fingertips with Word, too. You can create fancy newsletters, bring in spreadsheets from other programs, add charts and graphs to your documents, and prepare "personalized" letters for 1000 people. No other word processing software beats Word when it comes to advanced, easy-to-use features.

Plain English, please!

Software and **program** are terms that are often used interchangeably (a practice that confuses most of us). Both terms refer to the digitally stored information that tells your computer how to do something.

On the other hand, you may just want to start Word, type a letter, and print it. And like your trip to the grocery in the luxury sedan, you'll find that even when you're doing simple things in Word, you get a really posh ride.

But for now, you want to get to work and learn just what you need to in the most painless way. Fair enough. If you're already familiar with Word, you can skip this stuff and move on to the chapters that deal with the jobs you want to do. But if you're curious about what makes Word, well...Word, read on.

Where is Word and how do I get there?

Where do you start? Well, you can begin by figuring out how to get into Word. If you've used Windows before, you already know how to go through Program Manager to get to Word. If not, here's a quick itinerary.

{Note}

You're going to see the terms **clicking** and **double-clicking** a lot in this book. Clicking means positioning your mouse pointer over something and pressing the left mouse button. Double-clicking is the same process, but you press the left mouse button twice, quickly. You read all about mouse maneuvers in Chapter 2.

Finding Word with Program Manager

The Windows Program Manager is like the port authority for Windows: from here you can launch any program, manage files, and customize the look and feel of Windows and all your Windows programs (see fig. 1.1).

Plain English, please!

It has nothing to do with the space shuttle! **Launching** simply means starting a program. When you launch a program, you tell your computer to run through a *long* list of detailed instructions contained in a special file. It happens at a rate of a few million instructions per second, so all you're likely to notice is that after the whirring stops, you're ready to get to work.

If you prefer words to pictures, use pull-down menus to start programs and work with Windows.

Fig. 1.1

The main Windows screen is controlled by Program Manager, which uses menus and group windows to get things done. Your Program Manager screen probably looks different from the one you see here—it depends on what stuff you have in your computer. But the basics are the same.

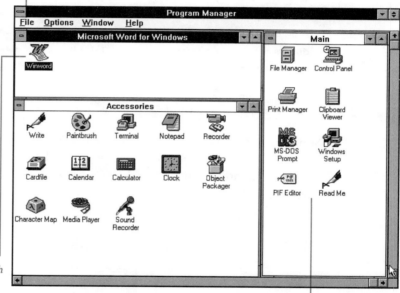

To start a program, you double-click an icon with your mouse.

Each group window includes one or more icons. These icons are shortcuts that Windows uses to keep track of programs.

When you installed Word for Windows, Program Manager created a group window called Word for Windows. A **group window** is a window in Program Manager. The group of icons inside each window are usually related to a particular program or combination of programs. If you installed Word as part of Microsoft Office, the Word icon landed in the Microsoft Office group window. That group contains icons for Word, Excel, and PowerPoint. In some setups, Word may wind up in a group called Applications.

Can't find the right group? Okay, choose <u>W</u>indow from the menu bar and look at the list of groups at the bottom. If you see Word or Microsoft Office, double-click it; if you don't see them, click More Windows. When you do, you see a Select Window dialog box, with a **scroll bar** you can use to move through the list. Find Word or Microsoft Office here, and double-click it to display the group window.

Plain English, please!

What happens when there's too much stuff to fit inside the part of a window or a list box that you can see? You use a special tool called a **scroll bar** to move around. This tool consists of a gray strip with arrows at either end and a little box in between. To move around, click on the arrows to move in the direction they're pointing, or drag the little box in the direction you want to go. (Learn more about moving around in Chapter 4, "Creating Word Documents.")

Now, find the Microsoft Word icon and double-click it. When the Tip of the Day screen pops up, as shown in figure 1.2, click OK or press the Enter key on your keyboard. There you go. You're in a brand new Word document. What's all that stuff around the edges? Well, check out "A first look at the Word screen."

Fig. 1.2
The Tip of the Day helps you learn something new about Word every day.

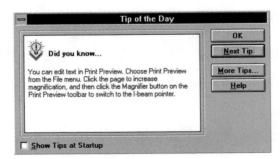

A first look at the Word screen

Toolbars
Many tasks can be performed by simply clicking one of these little buttons.

Ruler
This ruler does more than just measure inches— it helps you put things exactly where you want them on the page.

Menu bar
In Word, you can get things done with the commands you find tucked in these drop-down menus.

Status bar
Get information about what you're working on right here— what page you're on, descriptions of what each toolbar button does, and more.

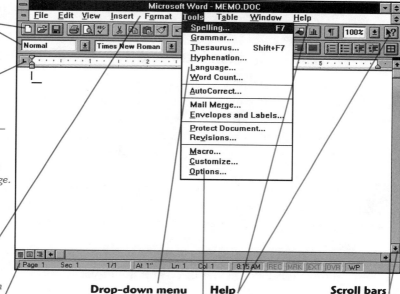

Drop-down menu
Click an item on the menu bar to get a drop-down list of commands.

Help
Word offers several ways to get information about how it works and keeps that information close at hand.

Scroll bars
Click the little boxes in these bars with your mouse, and slide them up, down, and sideways to quickly go where you want to go in your document.

Dialog box
When you click a button or choose a menu command, you sometimes see one of these. This box offers you choices, or asks you questions to help you get things done.

What kind of stuff is packed into Word?

So, Word's got a lot of fancy features. Fortunately, the Microsoft people know that a feature is useless if you don't need it or can't figure out how to use it. That's why they've put useful features in Word *and* made them usable.

Features that are easy to find—and use

Word doesn't think you should have to use a secret code to get to the tools you need to do your job. So, it uses what's called a **GUI**, which is pronounced "gooey" and stands for *graphical user interface*. A GUI works on the principle that you should have all the tools you need within easy reach. Menus, commands, and toolbar controls are all right on your Word screen.

 You may not know where the Print command is in a new program, but you know a printer when you see one! Word understands that a picture's worth a thousand words, so it puts pictures on its buttons to help you locate the tool you need.

If the picture doesn't really clear it up for you, don't worry. Word's also built in something called **ToolTips**—handy little bubbles of information that pop up when you put your mouse pointer over a button.

Want to check out how this GUI works? OK. Type this line:

How do I use the Cut button?

 Place the mouse pointer at the beginning of the line, hold down the mouse button, drag the pointer to the end of the line, and then release the button. The whole sentence is highlighted. Now, move the mouse pointer to rest on the toolbar button that has the picture of scissors on it (the ToolTip tells you this is the Cut button) and click. You've just used the GUI!

Word screens are easy on the eyes and easy to use

No matter how many pretty pictures Word has on its buttons, the other screens you encounter in Word also have to be easy to use. Well, they are. For example:

- **Tabbed file folder dialog boxes** give instant and easy access to various options and settings in Word. They're organized like little sets of index cards you can shuffle through to find exactly what you want. The dialog box in figure 1.3, for example, can be reached by choosing Tools from the menu bar, and then choosing Options from the drop-down menu.

Looking at things in a whole new way

Years ago, I used what was then the most popular word processor, WordPerfect for DOS. When I think back to those days, I'm struck by the amazing turn word processing software has taken.

In those days, WordPerfect had no menus, buttons, or lists on-screen. When you started it up, you saw an almost perfectly blank blue screen. It made for a clutter-free environment, but it wasn't very friendly. You see, to get things done with WordPerfect you used function keys—that row of keys numbered F1 to F12, arranged along the top of most keyboards. If you forgot which function key did what, you needed to look in the manual or on a cheat sheet.

Most word processors today (including Word, of course, and WordPerfect for Windows) now use a **graphical user interface** to visually represent most of your options right on-screen. These little buttons, menus, and boxes put tasks at your fingertips. And once you learn your way around, you'll discover you're just a mouse click away from getting your work done faster!

Fig. 1.3

A lot of power in a small package; Word packs many settings neatly in one place by using these little tabbed pages.

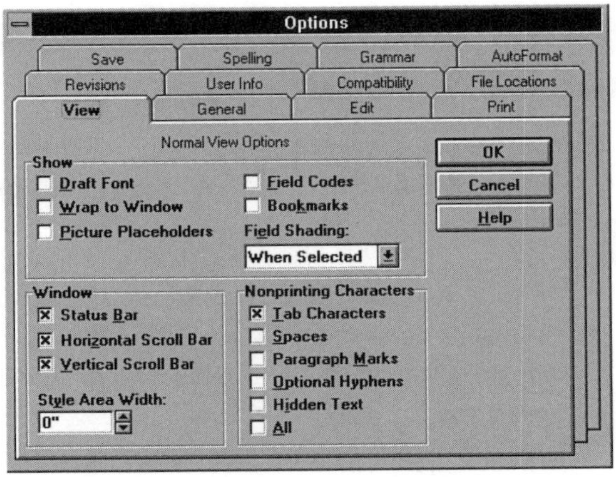

- **Shortcut menus** let you quickly get to the functions you're most likely to need (see fig. 1.4). You get these by placing the mouse pointer over text, a picture, or other on-screen element, then clicking the right mouse button.

Fig. 1.4

Shortcut menus practically guess what you might want to do next.

- **Drag and drop** capabilities let you grab things with your mouse and move them around your screen.

- **Views** let you choose how you want to see your document in Word: Full Screen gets rid of all the clutter and lets you see just what you're working on; Print Preview shows how the printed page will look; and you can Zoom in and out to get a close-up of your work.

All kinds of help—even a Wizard or two!

When you first meet Word's built-in helpers, you might think they're magicians. But there's really nothing magical about what these guys do. **Wizards** help simplify complicated processes, like creating a newsletter or table. The wizard asks questions, you fill in the answers using dialog boxes, and the program does most of the work for you.

That's just one of the many ways Word offers to help you work. In addition to wizards, you get these:

- **Tip of the Day.** As you're learning how to use the software, these simple one-line lessons lend a hand (refer to fig. 1.2).

- The built-in **Help** system offers detailed instructions and information that you can reach through the Help menu, by clicking the Help button, or by pressing the F1 key. You also get on-screen "clues" in the status bar at the bottom of your screen.

- Automatic **Spelling and Grammar checkers** that help make sure you're saying what you want to say, the way you want to say it.

- **"Smart"** features like AutoCorrect and AutoFormat fix things for you—sometimes before you even realize they're broken!

Sophisticated (but not scary) publishing features

There's basic communication, and then there are documents that take their job seriously: they sell, persuade, and inform with lots of powerful images.

With Word, you can break text into columns, place pictures or graphs where you like, make fancy formatting changes to your text, and generally let the artist in you take over—and it's easy.

Here are some of Word's fancier features:

- Built-in document styles and formats provide instant design flair.
- Dozens of ready-made pictures and built-in drawing tools give you the choice of instant art, or help you do it yourself (see fig. 1.5).
- Simple column features make it a snap to publish your own newsletters.

Fig. 1.5

It's easy to get sophisticated design without much effort in Word.

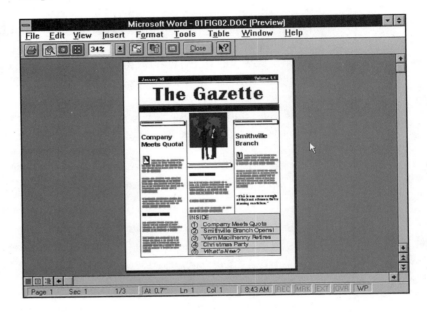

So your boss wants you to put a spreadsheet in your report

You don't do just one kind of work in a day, and if you're like most people you don't use just one kind of software, either. Maybe you push around numbers or you have to do a presentation every now and then.

Microsoft understands, which is why they've come up with a way for Word and other programs to work together. You can snip a piece out of a spreadsheet or a graph, for example, and paste it right into your Word documents. So the next time your boss wants to see the numbers, they'll be right where you both can see them.

Advanced features that give effortless results? Really?

Let's get rid of one misconception right now: just because something is technologically advanced doesn't mean it's more difficult to use. For example, the new fiber optics telephone networks are fairly complex systems, but picking up the phone and calling Mom is still pretty simple.

In the same way, several of the more "advanced" features in Word let you do some pretty spiffy things, but you don't have to be a computer programmer to use them.

- Word's Mail Merge wizard walks you through the steps of creating a personalized mass mailing in minutes.

- You won't need a ruler to draw neat tables in your next report, then fill them with easy-to-read data.

- Stop writing addresses on envelopes and labels by hand! Word handles this stuff without any fuss.

- You can even create your own toolbars and add custom buttons or shortcut keys to make Word work the exact way you do.

Take a deep breath and relax: Word is easy to learn and use, and it's going to make you very productive. Read on.

A, B, C: Learning Word Basics

In this chapter:

- I'm ready to experiment, so tell me how

- My mouse pointer keeps changing! What's up?

- What can I do with Word menus?

- Which tool do I use?

- How do I talk to dialog boxes?

It takes a little time to get familiar with a new place—or new software. Sometimes it's helpful to get a feel for things by taking a quick tour.

When I arrive in a new town, I have to feel my way around for a while. I start by finding downtown and figuring out how the main streets are laid out. Then I discover where to go to get things I need. And, of course, I always learn how to communicate with the locals (believe me, people in Maine and California have very different vocabularies).

It also takes a little time to learn your way around a new piece of software. Chapter 1 gave you a look at Word's map. Now, let's spend some time driving up and down Word's major streets; we'll learn where its major points of interest are located—and how to get to them.

_____ | The information in this chapter deals with fundamental Word features: the mouse techniques, menus, dialog boxes, and so on. If you're familiar with the basics of using Word, you probably don't need to read this chapter. But if you're new in town, this chapter gets you right up to speed.

Start Word and get ready to go

When you find the Microsoft Word icon in the Program Manager, double-click it to launch Word. The next thing you see is the opening screen of Word 6 for Windows. You see this screen for only a few seconds—like a billboard you pass as you move down the highway.

_____ | When you first start Windows, you get a Tip of the Day screen. Just click the OK button to make this screen go away.

When the opening screen passes, you arrive at the main Word screen with a newly created, blank document open. Here we are: Main Street, Word for Windows.

At first glance, this looks like a small town square with all the shops around the outside and an empty lot in the middle. If you've used other word processing programs, or even other Windows programs, like Excel, you may recognize some landmarks.

I suggest that you take a moment to type in some text—take a couple of paragraphs from this book, if you want. Then play around with them by trying out some of the stuff you read about in this chapter.

Getting things done in Word

Menus
A typical menu gives you access to things you can do through commands and tells you keystroke shortcuts to perform some of those commands faster.

Document title bar
Like a street sign, the name of the document you're working on goes here so you always know where you are.

Minimize/Restore buttons
You can shrink the document window so that you have two documents on-screen at once. Or, you can minimize the Word window and work in two programs at once. Restore to bring Word back home.

Toolbars
In addition to standard and formatting toolbars, Word for Windows has several function-specific toolbars.

```
Microsoft Word - Document1
File  Edit  View  Insert  Format  Tools  Table  Window  Help
```

Ruler
Here's where you see information about margins and tabs.

Insertion point
This is where anything you type or insert in your document is going to show up. (You can move this around with the mouse.)

```
Page 1    Sec          At      Ln      Col      11:53 AM  REC  MRK  EXT  OVR  WP
```

Change View buttons
Use these to quickly change between Normal, Page Layout, and Outline views in Word.

Status bar
Like a little town crier, this keeps you up on what's happening in your document and supplies descriptions of Word features.

Selection bar
You can't see this little alleyway, but it's there— a narrow strip along the left edge of your document screen, where you can point and click to select lines of text. (You know you're there when your mouse pointer turns into an upward pointer facing to the right.)

Scroll bars
Think of these as expressways: they allow you get around town quickly and easily.

Mouse moves for working in Word

Before you move on to find out more about Word's features, take a moment to explore how you're going to get around. So, meet your mouse. It takes you almost every place you need to go and does things you never thought a rodent could do.

You may have used computers enough that using a mouse is second nature; or maybe you need a little driver's education. But there are specific ways that the mouse works in Word that everyone should know.

If you need a more basic introduction to the mouse, try running through the Windows Tutorial. It's right in the <u>H</u>elp menu when you're in the Windows Program Manager.

What shape is your mouse in?

You know those machines at amusement parks where you move a lever, and a mechanical claw grabs at toys inside the machine? Working your mouse is like that. You move the mouse on your desk, and something called a **pointer** moves on-screen. This pointer can change shapes, depending on where you are and what you're doing at the time.

The various shapes that the mouse can appear in are important clues about what you can do next.

Deciphering Mouse Pointer Shapes

Pointer shape	What it means
I	You're ready to move the insertion point or select text; this little **I-beam** marks the point where the insertion point will be placed.
▚	You're pointing at the edges of the screen, menu, toolbar, status bar, scroll bar, or ruler—ready to click something.
↱	This appears when you're in what's called the **selection bar**. This is where you click and drag to select things.

Pointer shape	What it means
	Help! The mouse pointer turns to this question mark/arrow when you click the Help button. Move it to the thing you have a question about, click, and the Help screen for that element opens up.
	You see this when you select text or a graphic object (like a picture), then click and hold down the mouse button over the selection. This means you're ready to drag it to someplace else in the document.
	This little hand appears when you're in the Help system. It means you can click this word or phrase to see additional or related information.
	When you're working with a window, frame, or an object like a picture or embedded table, this pointer appears when you're near the edge. It basically says if you click and drag in the direction the arrow is pointing, you'll stretch or shrink the object.
	If you want to move a frame, this special pointer shape appears near the frame border. Just drag to move the frame where you want it.
	When you (and your mouse) are waiting while your computer performs a function, like saving a file, the mouse pointer turns into a little hourglass. When the function is completed, the hourglass disappears and command of the screen returns to you.

Getting around town with your mouse

At first glance, a mouse seems like a pretty simple little beast. It has a right and a left button, and that's pretty much it. But those two buttons, used in different places in Word and combined with keystrokes, allow you to do many more than just two tasks. Here are a few variations on the mouse's basic functions of clicking, dragging, and letting go.

 (Tip)

> Some tasks, like drawing, absolutely require the use of the mouse. Other things can be done with keystrokes or a mouse—whatever seems easier for you.

Clicking your way to success

Most of the time, you'll click on the left button of your mouse to **select** and move things around in Word. Clicking once quickly places your pointer in a particular spot in your document. This is the **insertion point**, which looks like a blinking, vertical line on your screen, and which shows you where you can insert or edit text or graphics.

As you saw in Chapter 1, clicking a toolbar button with your mouse will activate the button's function. Clicking a menu name selects the menu and displays its contents. Clicking in the selection bar on the left side of the screen selects a line of text. Clicking and holding down the left mouse button while you drag the pointer across a block of text selects the text. When you release the left mouse button, you stop selecting text. Go ahead, try some of these mouse moves!

Plain English, please!

When you **select** text in Word, you're preparing the text to be copied, moved, formatted, or deleted entirely. Selected text is highlighted on your screen—for example, it might change to white letters against a black background.

Some mouse functions work differently if you hold down the Ctrl or Shift key while clicking. For example, if you hold down the Ctrl key while clicking in the selection bar, the entire document is selected. Or, select a range of text by clicking once at the beginning of the range and holding the Shift key while you click at the end of the range.

Q&A

I selected some text to delete it, but changed my mind. How do I deselect it?

That's easy. Simply click elsewhere in your document; the text is no longer selected and the insertion point moves where you clicked.

Double-clicking: the just-do-it mouse technique

Double-clicking the Control-menu box in the top left corner of windows and dialog boxes closes them. You can also double-click an option in a list in a dialog box to make the selection, okay it, and close the dialog box all with one action.

 **(Tip)**

> Double-clicking on a word, or to the right or left of it, instantly selects that word so you can perform formatting or editing functions.

Right-click for quick results

The right mouse button can be used to call up **shortcut menus**. These are little on-screen menus that contain the commands you are most likely to need, depending on what you're doing at the moment. For example, with the pointer on the text of a Word document, click on the right mouse button. The shortcut menu in figure 2.1 appears. (To make it go away, click anywhere on-screen outside the menu.)

Fig. 2.1
Shortcut menus appear wherever your mouse pointer is on the page when you right-click.

Shortcut menu

Drag and drop: the direct approach

When you want to rearrange the furniture in your living room, you grab hold of it and slide it across the floor until it's where you want it to be. Windows programs in general—and Word in particular—work the same way.

Instead of straining your back muscles, though, you move things around in Word by using a simple mouse technique called **drag and drop**. First, select the text or object you want to move. Then, click the selection with your mouse and hold down the mouse button until the mouse pointer changes to an arrow with a box. Now, simply drag the pointer to where you want it and drop it by releasing the mouse button.

What can you do with drag and drop?

- After you select text, you can move it by dragging it from one place to another.

- Toolbars can "float" on top of your document windows when you drag them onto the document surface (see "What's a toolbar?" later in this chapter).

- As long as it's not maximized (to fill the whole screen), you can slide a document window or the Word window itself around by clicking the title bar, then dragging and dropping the window where you want it.

- Reset margins and tabs by dragging the indicators on the ruler to a new setting.

What's on the menu?

If you drop into an unfamiliar grocery store, you look up at the signs to find where all the departments are: OK, the produce section's over to the right, the meat counter's in back, frozen foods are right in the middle. The menu names in Word work the same way; if you follow these signs, you'll get a pretty good idea of the type of things you'll find under each one.

Taking a closer look

Any supermarket worth its salt has a produce section, but every one of them is organized a bit differently. The menus in word processing programs are like that, too. The Edit menu in Word, for example, contains the same choices you'll find in other word processing programs, but they're probably organized just a little differently. Learning your way around the menus—and learning which menu to use for which task—takes you a lot closer to feeling at home in Word.

- The File menu lets you open, close, save, and print the files containing your work.

- Use the Edit menu to find things in your document, and to copy, cut, and paste text and objects.

- The View menu offers you different ways to view your document, including Page Layout, Outline, Zoom, and Full Screen views.

- Pull down the Insert menu to bring objects from other programs, or predefined elements, like the date and time, into your document.

- The Format menu lets you change the look of text, add borders, create numbered lists, and reuse collections of formats called **styles**.

- Use the Tools menu to change Word's settings so it works the way you do. You also find writing helpers like Spelling, Thesaurus, and Mail Merge here.

- The Table menu lets you create, rearrange, reformat, and otherwise work with tables.

- The Window menu lets you switch between the different files you've opened or rearrange document windows for easier viewing.

- Finally, the Help menu is your doorway into the Help system described in Chapter 3.

It's worth taking a few minutes to browse around the different menus and check out what's available to you.

When you're ready to order...

To open a menu, simply click the name. It stays open on-screen so that you can make your choice. When you open a menu—say, the File menu (see fig. 2.2)—Word offers you a number of choices.

Fig. 2.2
The File menu opens up a world of possible functions.

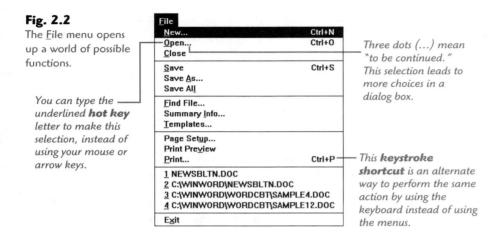

*You can type the underlined **hot key** letter to make this selection, instead of using your mouse or arrow keys.*

Three dots (...) mean "to be continued." This selection leads to more choices in a dialog box.

*This **keystroke shortcut** is an alternate way to perform the same action by using the keyboard instead of using the menus.*

Take a minute now to play around with the Word menus; open up the Format menu and choose some options...don't worry about getting into a jam. If you're messing around in the practice paragraph you typed earlier, you don't need to worry about any changes you make to it. Just explore and enjoy.

Use power tools for the fastest results

Tools give you express options for performing common tasks in Word. They're one-click shortcuts for accomplishing what otherwise would take several clicks in menus and dialog boxes.

What's a toolbar?

A **toolbar** is a predefined or customized set of tools. There's a Standard toolbar, which contains the most commonly used tools. Then there are other toolbars for specific types of activities, such as a Mail Merge toolbar and a Drawing toolbar.

The Standard and Formatting toolbars show by default when you first enter Word. To display other toolbars, choose View, Toolbars. Then click the boxes next to the toolbars you want to display.

Close-Up: the Standard toolbar

 New
Opens a new document

 Paste
Pastes the cut or copied selection into a document

 Columns
Affects column format of document

 Open
Opens an existing document

 Format Painter
Copies formatting from one piece of text to another

 Drawing
Shows or hides drawing toolbar

 Save
Saves the open document

 Undo
Undoes last action

 Insert Chart
Inserts a blank chart

 Print
Prints the open document

 Redo
Redoes last action

 Show/Hide ¶
Shows or hides things that don't print, like paragraph marks

 Print Preview
Shows how the printed document will look

 AutoFormat
Formats the document automatically

 Zoom Control
Makes document appear bigger or smaller

 Spelling
Checks for spelling errors

 Insert AutoText
Creates or inserts an AutoText entry

 Help
Changes cursor so you get help with on-screen items when you click them

 Cut
Cuts the selected item to the Windows Clipboard

 Insert Table
Inserts a blank table

 Copy
Makes a copy of the selected item

 Insert Microsoft Excel Worksheet
Does what it says

Most toolbars appear automatically as soon as you start performing a function that involves them. For example, the Mail Merge toolbar appears when you begin performing a mail merge—you don't have to choose to display it.

Toolbars in Word can **float** (which means you can place them where you want them on-screen). A couple are already floating when you choose to show them. To float a toolbar, click in the space between buttons, drag the toolbar onto the document screen, and let go. To return it to its original position, click and drag it back.

Getting to work with standard tools

The tools on the Standard toolbar perform some of the most commonly used functions in Word. Hold your mouse pointer over each button. Word displays the tool name in a little yellow box called a **ToolTip**, and a brief description appears in the status bar at the bottom of the screen.

Many tools are **toggle** buttons; that is, you click them once to turn them on, and click again to turn them off. The Bold, Italic, and Underline buttons work this way, for example. Others actually start a procedure or launch an **applet**. Then you follow the steps indicated by the dialog box or window that follows.

 Plain English, please!

An **applet** is one of the little free programs that come with Word. These mini-applications help you do things that aren't directly related to word processing, like building charts (Microsoft Graph) and creating fancy text effects (WordArt). You can choose whether or not to install these applications when you install Word. If you've got the space for them, they can be very useful!

Finally, notice that the Standard toolbar also contains some **drop-down lists** (they have arrow buttons next to them). For example, you can use the Zoom Control drop-down list to zoom in for a closer view of your document, or zoom back out again. To see the list of available choices, click the arrow to the right of the Zoom Control.

Holding a dialogue with Word

When Word needs specific details on what you want done, it uses **dialog boxes** to ask you for more details. You make choices from predefined lists or fill in the blanks with information, and Word does the rest.

How do I communicate with my dialog box?

Dialog boxes were designed to be easy to use. The boxes ask you what you want to do and even provide choices for how you want it to be done. All you have to do is choose.

Here's how you make choices in dialog boxes:

- Make choices in drop-down list boxes by clicking the choice or typing in the text box.

- Select a check box by clicking it. To deselect it, click again to remove the check mark.

- If an item's gray, it's not available. You probably need to be performing some other step to make this choice accessible to you.

- To choose measurements, you can use up and down arrows for standard settings, or type in a measurement using decimal points (.25).

- Click OK to accept the changes or Cancel (or hit Esc) to leave the dialog box without saving any changes.

What's in a Word dialog box?

Tabs
In some dialog boxes, you have more than one set of choices. Word makes these look like tabbed file folders. If you want more choices, simply click another tab to see what it offers.

OK and Cancel
Use these buttons to tell Word you've finished. Press OK to tell Word to use the information you filled in, or press Cancel to make like it never happened.

Index and Tables

| Index | Table of Contents | Table of Figures | Table of Authorities |

Type
- Indented
- Run-in

Preview

—A—

Aristotle, 2
Asteroid belt. *See* Jupiter
Atmosphere
   Earth
     exosphere, 4

Formats:
Classic
Fancy
Modern
Bulleted

Columns: 2

☐ Right Align Page Numbers   Tab Leader:

OK
Cancel
Mark Entry...
AutoMark...
Modify...
Help

Additional options
Sometimes more advanced options are available. If so, you'll see extra buttons in the dialog box. Click these, and you probably get another dialog box or choice.

Drop-down list
These scrollable list boxes allow you to make predefined choices.

Help
There's also a Help button in each dialog box to take you directly to a help screen about that particular dialog box.

Option boxes
Click on these circles (called radio buttons) to toggle the function on or off.

Check box
Click in this box to toggle its function on or off.

Description or Preview
In some dialog boxes, you get a preview of what your choice will do to your document, so you can try things out without returning to the screen to see what they look like.

Getting Help in a Pinch

When you yell for help, the last thing you want is a fat dictionary. You just want to know what you're supposed to do and when. Lucky for you, Word tells you just that.

Learning how to use a new piece of software can make you feel like you just touched down in a faraway foreign land. You need to adjust to the language, where familiar words like *window* and *style* don't mean what they meant before. Little pictures arranged on your screen sometimes leave you guessing as to what they stand for. And every so often, a warning sign pops up that lets you know you have a problem, but doesn't seem to tell you what to do.

It's only natural to occasionally feel lost in Word. Don't despair. In this part of the world, you're never far from help—and good help, at that.

Word 6 for Windows offers one of the most sophisticated Help systems ever designed. Microsoft worked long and hard to create a Help system that earns its name—Help! Word has lots of help available for almost any task, no matter how simple or complicated that task may be. And help is always available in a number of ways, no matter where you are in a document or what you're doing there.

How do I find help when I need it?

Even if you've never used a button or a menu choice, you may be able to guess what it does. That's part of Word's **interface** design. The words and icons you see are designed to remind you of objects and concepts in everyday life. For example, see the button on the Word toolbar that contains a pair of scissors (see fig. 3.1)? If you make the connection between scissors and cutting, you'll have no trouble figuring out that this button lets you cut stuff out of your document.

 Plain English, please!

An **interface** is the way software looks to you—the face it presents to you, so to speak. An **intuitive interface** is one that makes sense to most human beings because it resembles other things that are familiar to you. All those pictures and symbols on your toolbar are designed to be more intuitive than obscure computer terms. *99*

Fig. 3.1
Your Word screen can seem pretty cluttered; but once you figure out what all this stuff is for, it's really easy to use.

Scissors—one familiar (inter)face among the crowd!

Put floating toolbars where you want them...or make them go away.

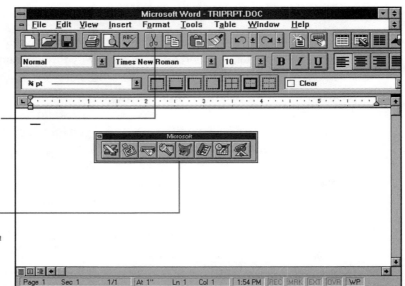

But a pretty interface is only part of what makes software easier to learn and use. A good Help system is essential, and Word has one of the best.

What are all those buttons for?

Until you know the language, getting around a foreign country—or a new piece of software—is difficult. The international community has evolved a visual language of symbols that represent various words, such as "restroom," "airport," and "train."

Word also uses visual markers to tell you of the many tasks it's capable of doing. So what do you do when you can't figure out what the icon on that little button is supposed to mean? Just ask for help.

ToolTips are pop-up labels that tell you what an element on the Word toolbar is for. To reveal a ToolTip, just let the mouse pointer sit on any toolbar element. In a moment, a little yellow box pops up on-screen with the name of the button, and a phrase appears in the status bar at the bottom of your screen to tell you what will happen if you click the button (see fig. 3.2). Move around the screen. Notice that ToolTips work with any button or drop-down list. Now you don't have to memorize a dictionary of buttons just to get going with Word!

Fig. 3.2
Use ToolTips like a foreign language phrase book to give you the quick definitions of on-screen elements.

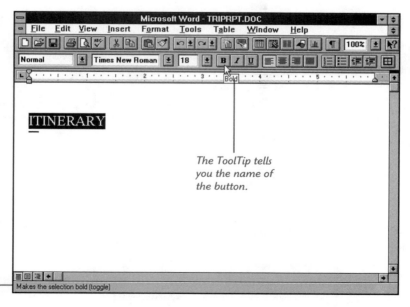

The ToolTip tells you the name of the button.

Read this line to find out what the button does.

I need more than a tip. How do I get to the Help menu?

Knowing what the toolbar buttons represent is a start. But what do you do when you want to add page numbers to a report? There's no "Add Page Numbers" button on the toolbar. Let's see what the Help menu can do for you.

You can get into the Help system a couple of ways. First, if you want details about how to use something you see on-screen, click the Help button. Your pointer changes to a little question mark/arrow symbol. Click the element you want information about, and Word opens the Help system and takes you right to information on that topic.

> If you click the Help button and then click on text in your document, you get a pop-up Paragraph and Font Formatting information box that gives you details of things like indents, fonts used, and spacing (see fig. 3.3). This can help you remember which font or spacing you used. (See Chapters 9 and 10 for more about formatting.)

Fig. 3.3
This little card clues you in to the formats used in this text quickly and easily.

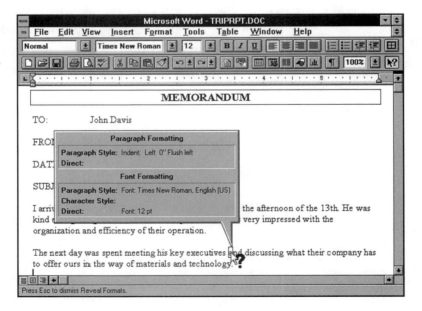

Getting help with the Help tool is fine when there's something on-screen to click, but what if you don't know where to click? If you're not sure where to begin, you may need to do a little research.

Try using the second way to get to Word Help. Choose the Help menu. The first three choices on this menu, Contents, Search for Help On, and Index, are three different ports of entry into the land of Help (see fig. 3.4). Each gets you where you want to be, but in a slightly different way.

Fig. 3.4

The Help menu offers a banquet of help selections.

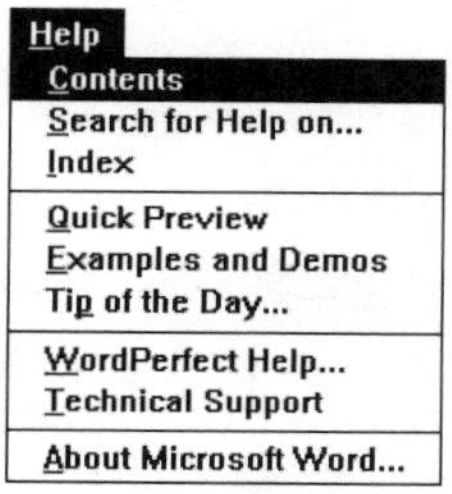

```
Help
Contents
Search for Help on...
Index

Quick Preview
Examples and Demos
Tip of the Day...

WordPerfect Help...
Technical Support

About Microsoft Word...
```

Getting what you need from the Help menu

Choose Help, Contents. The Word Help Contents window appears and gives you an overview of what you can find in Help. In any Help window, the buttons under the menu bar let you move around easily.

The different Help menu options are like different branches of the same system: you can get to the Help Contents window from the Index, you can go instantly from the Index to Search, and you can close the Search dialog box and be right back at the Help Contents.

Check out Help's contents

Shows you the Help Contents window (which you're in now). Use it to return from other Help windows to this main Contents window.

Brings up the Search dialog box, which uses something called **keywords** to find your topic

Like to sit and look at slides of your 1967 vacation? This is for you: History shows a list of topics you've looked at while in Help. You can get back to any topic by double-clicking it.

Takes you to an alphabetical index of Help topics

Takes you back to the last Help item you viewed so you can literally retrace your steps back through your help session

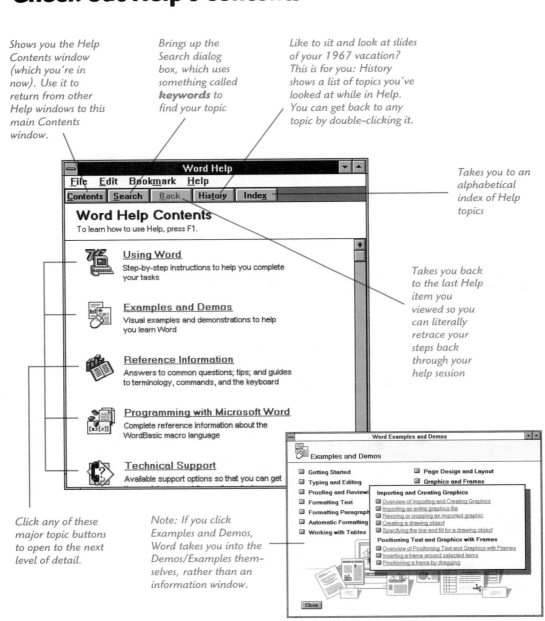

Click any of these major topic buttons to open to the next level of detail.

Note: If you click Examples and Demos, Word takes you into the Demos/Examples them-selves, rather than an information window.

Plain English, please!

A **keyword** is simply a word that the program recognizes for one of its features. When you search by a keyword, Word can run around and find all the topics using that keyword and show them to you so that you can pick just the one you want.

After you choose a general Help topic by clicking it, you'll find that Word takes you by the hand, like the tourist that you are. It leads you through subtopics to deeper and deeper detail, until finally you arrive at the deepest level of detail—a How To window, as shown in figure 3.5. This may take a few clicks of your mouse, but hang in there: the idea is to get to as specific an answer as possible.

Fig. 3.5
The How To window is the final destination in your quest for help.

The Help topic describes a task.

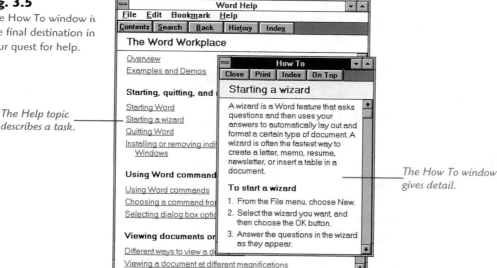

The How To window gives detail.

You know what you want? Search for it!

If you have a specific topic in mind that you need help with, choose Help, Search for Help On. This brings up the Word Help Contents window with the Search dialog box open (see fig. 3.6).

Fig.3.6
The Search dialog box
is flexible; you can type
in a word or choose
from the keyword list.

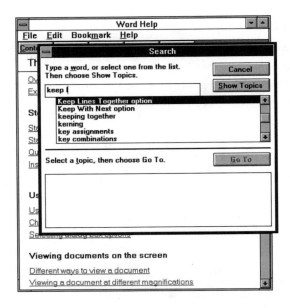

Type the name of the topic you need help with, then click Show Topics; or
double-click a keyword in the list. A list of topics related to your subject
appears in the bottom section of the dialog box. Double-click a topic in this
list to go to its help information.

Q&A

> *I type in a word, but Help doesn't seem to find a*
> *keyword to match!*
>
> You and Help aren't speaking the same language. See if you can think of
> another way to phrase your topic. For example, if you want to find out how
> to capitalize all the letters in a word, you won't find it under `full caps`; try
> `all caps` or `capital letters` instead.

When in doubt, use the Index

Sometimes you know you need help, but you're not sure how to ask for it.
Choose Help, Index. The Index portion of Word Help gives you a detailed list
of topics you can search through. Notice the Index letter buttons in figure
3.7. Clicking one of these buttons takes you to the alphabetical portion of the
list you need. Then, use your scroll bar to browse through the list. When you
find the topic you want, click it to get to a How To or Help topic window.

Fig. 3.7
Find the section of the Index you need by clicking the appropriate letter.

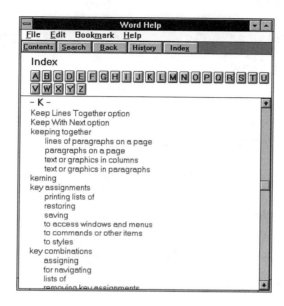

How do I keep Help from vanishing?

All of the above routes should take you to a How To or Help topic window. Notice that the How To window (refer back to fig. 3.5) includes a button called On Top. Because these windows are big on step-by-step information, Word knows you may want to keep them on top of your document, like a big Post-It note, while trying the procedure. Click the On Top button to keep the How To window from vanishing behind other windows; click the Close button to get rid of it.

✱{Note}

As you read some Help topics and How To window information, you'll see words that appear in green with dashed underlines. These are "hot" words. If you click a hot word, you see a pop-up box that contains information related to the current help topic. Click again to remove the pop-up box so that you can continue reading the original topic information.

Word Help is like a little application of its own. To close it, you need to double-click the Control menu button in the upper-left corner.

I'm from Missouri: show me (demos, previews, and tips)

When I first visited Japan, I had to become proficient with chopsticks. I also learned you can't just *tell* someone how to use chopsticks—it's one of those things you really need to demonstrate.

Word knows that one of the best ways to learn something is to actually see somebody else doing it. That's why you'll find examples and demos built into its Help system.

A preview of Word's attractions

To get a broad view of what goes on in Word, choose <u>H</u>elp, <u>Q</u>uick Preview. This takes you into preview demonstrations of three topic areas:

- **Getting Started.** A 10-minute demonstration of the main features of Word.

- **What's New.** Highlights of the features new in Version 6 of Word for Windows, such as AutoCorrect and AutoText.

- **Tips for WordPerfect Users.** This 5-minute demo is meant for people who are used to WordPerfect for DOS, but it includes some tips that are useful to anybody just starting out with Word.

WordPerfect users can also get help on specific functions by choosing <u>H</u>elp, <u>W</u>ordPerfect Help. But note that if you didn't choose this option when you installed Word for Windows, you may get messages that say No Help Message Available—Cannot Open. To enable this feature, select Help for <u>W</u>ordPerfect Users on the General tab in the Options dialog box.

Word struts its stuff in Examples and Demos

Examples are graphic explanations of how to use Word features. **Demos** go even further by performing certain processes in Word (such as formatting and printing letters in mail merge), showing each step on-screen.

You can get to Examples and Demos by choosing <u>H</u>elp, <u>E</u>xamples and Demos. The first screen you see is an index of the available examples and demos (see fig. 3.8).

Fig. 3.8
The list of Examples and Demos topics gives you an overview of what's available (sorry, no chopsticks).

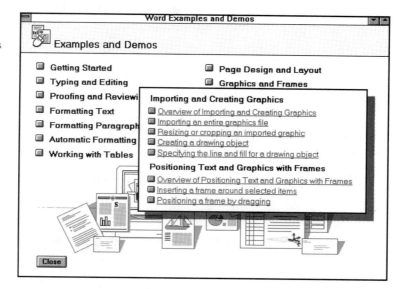

To view an example and demonstration, follow these steps:

1 Click a general topic to get a list of examples.

2 Click one of the examples. Word shows you several views of a sample document going through a process or function in Word (see fig. 3.9). Key steps in the process are pointed to by little labels with check boxes. Click the check box to get a pop-up box with a brief description of that function.

3 In some cases, there is also a <u>D</u>emo button in the lower-right corner. Click it, and Word loads a demonstration of the topic you've chosen.

Fig. 3.9

The example shows you how to perform a task in Word. If the example window has a <u>D</u>emo button, click it to walk through the process step by step.

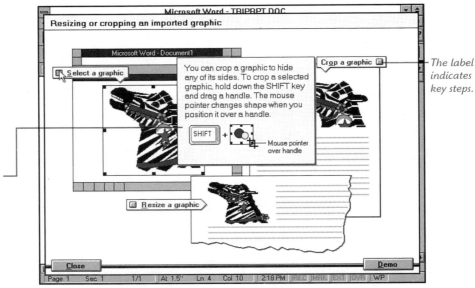

The label indicates key steps.

The pop-up box tells you how to do the job named in the label.

4 After the demo is loaded, you begin it by clicking the <u>S</u>tart button in the Demonstration box in the bottom-right corner of the screen (see fig. 3.10).

Fig. 3.10

The on-screen demonstration is in your control; move to the next step only when you're ready.

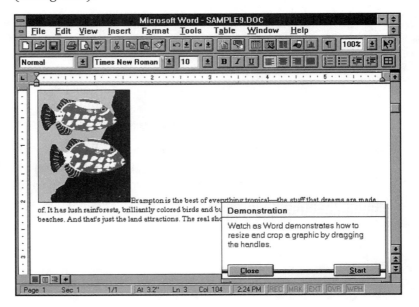

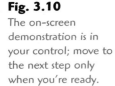

5 When you're ready to move on, click the <u>N</u>ext button.

6 If you want to stop the demo at any time, just click the <u>C</u>lose button, then close the index of Examples and Demos by clicking the Close button in that window.

7 Exit the Word Help Content screen by double-clicking the Control-menu button in the top-left corner.

The Tip of the Day—use it and lose it

Ah...a tip from a native: where's the best place to get seafood on the island? What hotel has the cleanest towels? There's nothing like advice from someone in the know!

One last way of getting help from Word is the Tip of the Day (see fig. 3.11). When you first open Word for Windows, this handy little box appears, giving you one of any number of tips (my favorite is, "It's never too late to learn to play the piano"). It's a good way to just pick up one little thing at a time as you're learning Word.

Fig. 3.11

A tip a day keeps ignorance at bay!

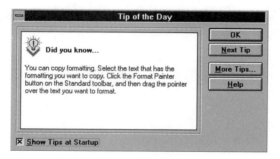

But, if you really don't want to see that perky little tip screen appear every time you start Word, next time it appears, click the little box in the lower-left corner to deselect <u>S</u>how Tips at Startup. That's it!

Part II:

Making Something from Nothing

4 Creating Word Documents

In this chapter:

- How do I begin a new document?

- What can I do with a template?

- What about a wizard?

- How do I put stuff in my document?

- I want to print this document, then close it up

Word gives you tools to build effective documents, and it can provide as much—or as little—of the framework as you want.

Creating documents is what working in Word is all about. Entering text, moving through your document, editing, saving, and printing your work—all the stuff you do to turn out a great-looking letter, memo, or report—are easier than ever with Word 6 for Windows.

Word gives you lots of tools for building effective documents from scratch. But if you're *really* rushed for time, you can choose one of Word's templates or wizards, which are kind of like prefab houses—they go up fast and can be tailored to your own taste.

Laying the foundation

If you're building a house, you pick up your tool belt each morning and head for the lot where your dream house is taking shape. In Word, your work site is the document window.

When you first open Word for Windows, it automatically takes you to a new document window, with a full menu bar and a blank screen (see fig. 4.1). At this point you need to decide just how much of the work you want to do in building your document.

Fig. 4.1

A vacant lot, ready for construction.

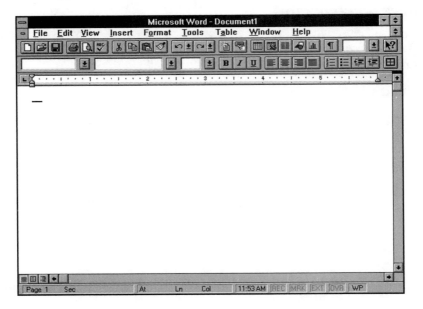

If you have a deadline staring you in the face, putting together a document can be as daunting as preparing to build your dream house. Do you start with a vacant lot and a bulldozer, or opt for an easier route? Why not hire some-one else to lay the foundation and put up the frame? Do you want fixtures and wiring installed? Maybe you just want to hang the wallpaper and paint the baseboards.

Word lets you opt to do as much—or as little—of the work involved in creating a document as you choose. You can choose to build the document yourself from scratch. You can use a template and have Word lay the foundation and put up the document's framework. Or you can have Word create the entire document to your specifications by using a wizard.

Starting your document from scratch

If you want to start from scratch and do all the work on this document yourself, you can just begin typing. Word has attached its default template, NORMAL.DOT, to your document. This template contains all the default settings for standard document text and is fine for most of the stuff you'll do in Word. If you want special fonts, bulleted lists, indented text, or other formats, you can use Word's tools to build in those elements as you go.

In Part III, you learn all about formatting your text and using Word's tools to design your own documents. If you aren't interested in hammering every nail, however, check out Word's templates.

Getting a head start with Word's templates

If you want a head start on creating a great-looking letter, memo, fax cover sheet, or other common document, you can use a **template.** When you choose File, New, Word presents you with its list of ready-made templates (see fig. 4.2).

Fig. 4.2
There are many predefined templates available in Word for a variety of purposes.

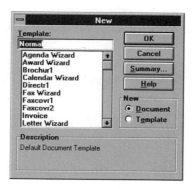

Think of templates as starter kits for your documents. **Templates** are collections of **styles** that provide a ready-made framework for your documents. Word templates can provide as much—or as little—framework as you need. Some templates have placeholders that tell you exactly where to add each element you'll need; a few even include macros or chunks of text and graphics that you can incorporate directly into your document.

 Plain English, please!

A **style** is simply a group of formatting choices saved together and applied to your text all at once. **Character** styles include font formats, such as bold, italic, and small caps. **Paragraph** styles affect blocks of text with formatting such as tab settings, indentation, borders, and shading, in addition to character formats. See more about styles in Chapter 13.

Templates are really just documents with a DOT extension. You can make changes to templates, just as you would any document: edit, delete, add things, format things, and so on. If you're interested in changing a template or creating your own template from scratch, see Chapter 13.

How do I use a template?

If you want to use a standard Word template, like Weektime, shown in figure 4.3, select that template from the list in the New dialog box. When it appears on-screen, replace any placeholders with text that's right for your message, and then add any other words or pictures you need to complete your document. And, if you don't like some of the formats or styles, you can change them for your document.

 If you are unable to make changes to the template, it may be protected. Save the template with a new name, and then choose <u>T</u>ools, Un<u>p</u>rotect Document. You should now be able to modify the template document.

So, if you don't have the time to start with a vacant lot (the NORMAL.DOT template), pick one of these templates and you'll have your document's foundation and framework all in place. Or, if you want Word to do even more of the finish work on your document, you can use wizards—they're located right there in the list of templates in the New dialog box.

Fig. 4.3
Word's weekly time sheet (Weektime) template provides form design and placeholders for text to make document construction easier.

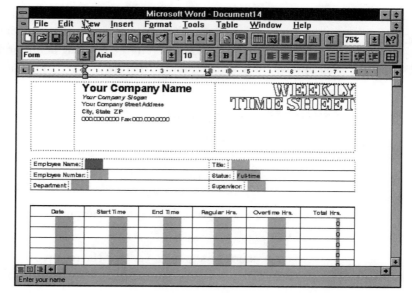

Let a wizard do the work

I went to one of those huge home improvement chain stores last summer because I was thinking about building a deck. The store had a computer terminal for do-it-yourselfers in search of advice. I answered a series of questions about the deck of my dreams, and voilá—I got a little printout with a drawing of the deck and estimated costs for materials.

A **wizard** works pretty much the same way:

- You choose a wizard for the type of document you want to create from the template list.

- The wizard asks you a series of questions (via dialog boxes) about what things you want in the document and how you want it to look. Along the way, it shows you previews of how your document will look based on your decisions.

- Then, using your answers, the wizard creates a document and presents it to you.

Where a template provides you with a document's foundation and framework, you can use a wizard to create the entire document to your specifications. You don't have to do much of the building at all for this dream house; just choose the wallpaper and carpeting, walk in the door, and enjoy!

I want to use a wizard

Let's try using a wizard to create one of the most common business documents around—a fax cover sheet.

1 Choose File, New, select the Fax Wizard, and click OK.

2 Respond to the dialog boxes the wizard presents to you, such as the one in figure 4.4.

    In each dialog box, you can accept the proposed text or setting, or type in any changes or new information.

3 When you finish answering the questions in each dialog box, click Next to move on. If you have to change something you entered in a previous dialog box, just click Back until you reach it.

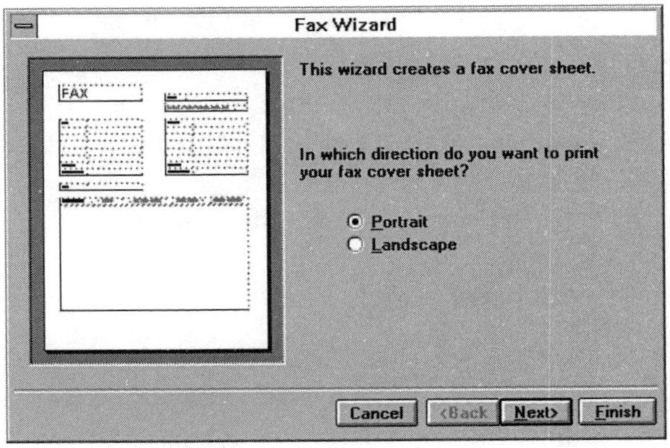

Fig. 4.4
The Fax Wizard asks you to choose the orientation of the document. Do it, then click Next to move to the next question.

4 Enter your name, address, phone, and fax information when asked for it (see fig. 4.5).

Fig. 4.5
Fax Wizard asks you to confirm or enter information for name, company name, address, and phone.

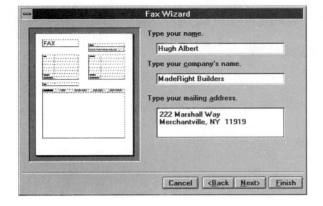

5 When you reach the end of the questions, click <u>F</u>inish and the document appears with your entries filled in, as in figure 4.6.

Fig. 4.6
Fax Wizard has used your answers to build a nicely organized fax cover sheet.

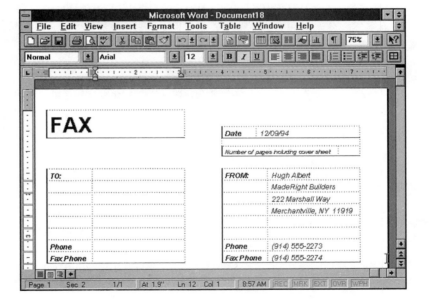

I'd like to know how to put stuff in this document

If you used a template or a wizard to create a document, your framework is all in place. Your screen shows any text and graphics inserted by the template and an insertion point (the blinking line). Now you just need to fill in the details.

To finish the construction of your document, it's time to check your blueprint and figure out how to get everything where it's supposed to go.

I'm ready to go—but where am I?

You know those "You Are Here" arrows on the store-layout diagrams in shopping centers? Your **insertion point**—that little blinking line—in Word is like a "You Are Here" arrow: it tells you where you are and where anything you type is going to appear.

You need to position the insertion point to insert new text or graphics in your document or to **select** text for editing. To do that, simply click wherever you'd like the insertion point to go, and there you are.

 Plain English, please!

To **select** in computerese means to designate something (text, picture, table, etc.) as the item that will be acted on. If you select text and then press Delete, for example, the text is deleted. You select text by clicking and dragging your mouse over it; you can select a picture by clicking on it. You can tell when something's selected because it's highlighted on-screen. (See more about selecting and editing in Chapter 6.) 99

Taking a scroll around your document

Just as you can get someplace on a bike, by car, or on foot, Word gives you some choices about how to move around your document window. The **scroll bars** at the right edge and bottom of your document screen allow you to move through your document in a few different ways (see fig. 4.7):

- The arrows at either end of the scroll bars can be clicked once to move you in the direction the arrow is pointing. Using the vertical scroll bar moves you one line at a time, up or down. The horizontal scroll bar arrows move you over 1/2 inch—left or right—with each click.

- The scroll box can be used in a couple of ways. If you click above or below the scroll box on the side scroll bar, you move up one page or down one page. The bottom scroll bar moves you over by a page's width when you click next to the scroll box.

- You can also click on the scroll box and drag it to move several pages at one time. It's a way to quickly move to an approximate location in the document, but it's hard to gauge exactly how many pages you've moved as you're dragging. When you let go of the box, your new location appears on-screen.

Fig. 4.7
The scroll bars are like little express trains to your destination.

The scroll arrow moves you one line at a time in this direction.

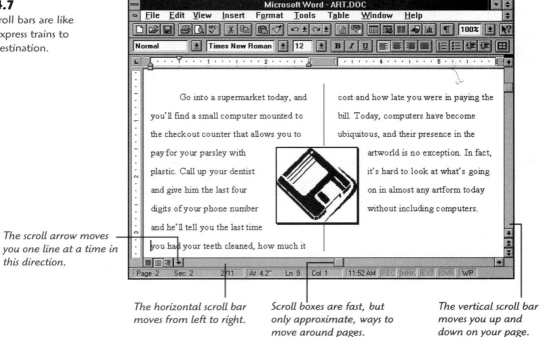

The horizontal scroll bar moves from left to right.

Scroll boxes are fast, but only approximate, ways to move around pages.

The vertical scroll bar moves you up and down on your page.

Okay, now try scrolling around in your fax document. You'll notice that the insertion point doesn't go along with you: it stays where you last clicked in the document or at the end of your last typed line. But don't worry! To make it catch up to you, just click once with your mouse wherever you want the insertion point to appear. There it is!

If you're more comfortable using your keyboard to get around, the Page Up, Page Down, Home, End, Ctrl+Home, Ctrl+End, and arrow keys still work just like they always have. If you use the keyboard to move around, the insertion point does move with you. Only mouse people have to click to move it to the location they've scrolled to.

Entering text is just typing

To enter text, you simply find the right location and type. Using the vertical scroll bar, scroll down in the fax document you created earlier until you reach the Remarks section. Click in the Remarks section, and the insertion point appears there. Begin typing the remarks shown in figure 4.8.

Your fax document template already has preset margins and tabs. The ruler at the top of the screen shows you the edges of the page.

At the right margin of each line, Word automatically wraps to the next line. If you press Enter, Word inserts a paragraph mark at the end of the line and begins a new paragraph. You can see these paragraph marks by clicking the Show/Hide button on the toolbar.

Fig. 4.8
Your fax with nonprinting characters showing, including paragraph marks.

Click the Show/Hide button to see non-printing characters.

These paragraph marks won't appear on your printed document.

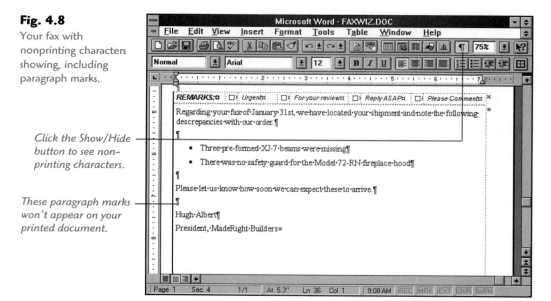

 **{Note}** If you make certain common typing errors, like typing *teh* instead of *the*, you'll notice that they automatically correct themselves on-screen. This Word feature is called AutoCorrect, and you can call up its controls by choosing <u>T</u>ools, <u>A</u>utoCorrect. You'll read more about AutoCorrect in Chapter 7.

I made a document...now what?

The details of saving and printing documents are given in Chapters 6 and 8, respectively. But if you've created a document, you probably need to know how to save, close, or print that document right now. So, here are the basics.

Saving your work

Unless you used substandard building materials in your house, it should be around for some time to come. But Word documents are history if you don't save them or print them.

If you close your document file or exit Word and haven't saved or printed your document, you lose it. Mind you, Word will ask if you're absolutely sure before trashing your document. If that's what you want, fine. But if not, here are the three basic variations on saving documents:

- Save it the first time by choosing <u>F</u>ile, <u>S</u>ave, and giving it a name in the dialog box that appears (see fig. 4.9).

Fig. 4.9
The Save As dialog box appears when you choose to save the first time, or to save after you make changes.

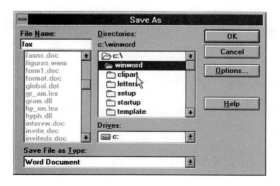

- Save it again under the same name and there are no choices—just choose File, Save or click the Save button on the toolbar.

- Save it again with a different name by choosing File, Save As and typing in a new name in the Save As dialog box.

Why would you change a document's name? Well, let's say you want to have two versions of a letter—the original and a variation. You have to give them two different names if you want to save changes you've made to a document, but not overwrite the original document.

⊛ {Note}

When you first save a new document (or one with a new name), you get a Summary Info dialog box that lets you enter all kinds of details about the file, such as a long descriptive title and the author's name. These details help you ID the file later. You'll learn more about the features in this dialog box in Chapter 5.

① (Tip)

If you don't get a summary dialog box, you can always bring it up yourself. With the document open, choose File, Summary Info, and there it is.

Fig. 4.10
Filling in summary information with more than you can fit in the file name will help you identify files later on.

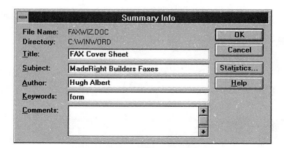

Printing things now

You want to print something, do you? No problem! Printing basics take very little time. Choose File, Print. The Print dialog box appears (see fig. 4.11).

Fig. 4.11
Make your words
concrete by printing
them with the Print
dialog box.

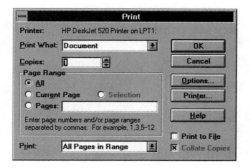

If you click OK to accept the default settings, you will print one copy of the entire document to whatever your default printer is. You can use the settings in the dialog box to print more copies, a range of pages, or print to a different printer. (See Chapter 8 to learn more about printing and its options.)

 (Tip)

To quickly print a file, click the Print button on the toolbar. This bypasses the Print dialog box and prints the entire document with the default settings.

Closing things up

When you're ready to close your document, choose File, Close. If you haven't made any changes to the document since you last saved it, Word closes the document and returns you to a blank screen.

If you've made changes to the document since you last saved it, Word asks if you want to save the changes. Choose Yes, and Word saves the document, then closes it.

If you haven't previously saved your document, Word steps you through the Save process outlined in the previous section, in which you name the file and choose the drive and directory where it is to be stored. When you finish, Word closes the document.

Secrets of Successful File Management

There's nothing more frustrating than spending the day looking for that file you need. That's why Word has a neat system for storing things.

In this chapter:

- How do I find what I was working on yesterday?

- I wrote it in WordPerfect. Now I want to open it in Word

- Can I have more than one document open at once?

- I want my original document—but I want to keep my changes, too!

If you're like me, when you go looking around your house for something that you haven't seen in a few months—maybe that letter from your aunt, or the sweater you haven't worn since last winter, or that crescent wrench you used to fix a leaky faucet—there are a few logical places you look.

You're certain, for example, that you didn't put the letter in your closet, or the sweater in the kitchen. Whether you realize it or not, you've developed a system of storing things in your house that makes sense to you. Word also has a system of storing and retrieving files that's logical. Once you learn the logic, finding and using files will be as natural as finding your way around your own house.

Open that file you created yesterday

Let's face it, the letter you set aside last night is usually easier to find than the wrench you last saw last Christmas. One reason for this is that you tend to keep things handy—say on your desktop—if you know you're going to use them again soon.

Word does something similar. It makes the files you recently used and saved available to you in a "short-term" storage place: right at the bottom of the File menu. By default, this menu shows you the last four files you saved. You can open these files by simply opening the File menu and choosing one of the entries from the list.

 **(Tip)**

> You can change the number of recently used files that Word shows on the File menu. Go to the Tools menu and choose Options. On the General tab, at the bottom, adjust the Recently Used Files list to show up to the last nine files saved.

Find that file you worked with last week

If the kitchen faucet springs a leak (again) and you need to find that wrench in a hurry (again), there are a few logical places you can look. The same is true when you need to open a file that isn't on the recently used file list. Is that wrench in the garage, in the basement, or in a kitchen drawer? Is the file on your hard disk, on a floppy disk, or on a network drive?

Before you begin: file management basics

Computers can keep things in a few different places. You'll hear them called **disks** or **drives** or sometimes even **disk drives**, but they all have a letter name (A-Z) and they're all places to store files.

The hard disk is the drive built into your computer (usually given a drive letter of C). It's where all the information that runs the computer, as well as your software applications, are stored. You also save files here.

You can also save files onto a floppy disk. These removable disks usually have a drive letter of A or B. Floppy disks are handy for storing files, because you can literally divide different kinds of information onto different physical disks. For example, keep all letters on one disk, all spreadsheets on another, and all reports on another.

⊗<*Caution*> If at all possible, avoid opening documents directly from floppy disks. When you work on floppy disks, Word creates a lot of temporary files that can clog things up. And if you take out the floppy while you're still working, you'll get error messages forever. If you have documents on floppy disks, copy them onto your hard drive before you work with them.

The third possibility for file storage is on a network. If your company has your computer hooked into a larger computer system, your computer can get at all the space of that larger system and store files out there. A network drive typically uses letters from F to Z, depending on the way your network is set up.

⊗<*Caution*> Be careful if you store files on a network; other people on the network can get at your files and read, change, or delete them. It is possible to hide them or protect them in certain ways, but there are whole books written about how to do it and you've got this one to get through! When in doubt, ask the person who runs the network in your company.

(Another kind of removable disk—the CD-ROM—doesn't belong in this discussion, because these disks are designed to be read only. You can't save files on a CD.)

The best advice for good file management is the one your investment counselor gives you: diversify! Keep the files you use regularly on your hard disk, with backup copies of important files on floppy disk in case something happens to your hard drive. Save to the network when you actually want to share information with other people (see Chapter 20 for more information about sharing files, and Chapter 22 for more about file management).

Where in the world is my file?

Choose File, Open. As you can see in figure 5.1, Word identifies a file in four ways:

- By the drive the file is stored in

- By the directory that holds the file

- By the file's type (indicated by its extension)

- By the file's name

Fig. 5.1

A place for everything and everything in its place: the File Open dialog box helps you find what you're looking for.

Choose the file name from the list or type a name in this box.

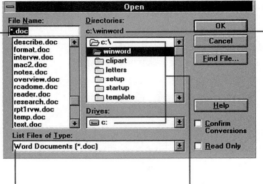

Choose the directory in the Directories list. Double-click the drive letter to see the main directories on that drive.

Select a specific type of file created in a particular software application; or choose All Files to look at every file.

The drive letter is shown at the top of the Directories list; to change drives, use the Drives drop-down list.

 Plain English, please!

Documents are named in two parts: the name you give the file, like REPORT or JONESLTR, and a three-letter **extension**, like DOC, that follows the file name and is separated from it by a period. The extension tells you what software you created the file in, and it's given to your file automatically when you save it. For example, Excel files have an XLS extension, some graphics files have a PCX or BMP extension, and Word documents generally have a DOC extension (unless you choose to save them in another document format; read about that later in this chapter). "

Locating the file you want to open involves narrowing down the search: first find the right drive, then the right directory, then the file in the right format, and bingo—you've found your file. So, let the search begin!

What drive is it in?

The drive list contains any drives that are available to you, including your hard drive, floppy drive(s), and network.

If you just save Word for Windows files with default settings, your documents would be on your C drive in the WINWORD directory (along with a lot of other stuff).

 Q&A

> *I don't see the network drive I need listed here. What do I do now?*
>
> It's possible that your computer isn't connected to the network drive. Trust me, you don't want to learn about this stuff on your own: call your local in-house computer expert and let him/her deal with it.

And then there's the directory

To understand Word's system of directories, think of your closet at home. On one shelf you may store sweaters, on another your T-shirts, and so on.

Think of your closet as a directory. Within the closet directory, you can have **subdirectories**, such as the sweater directory and the T-shirt directory. Each of these is just a more detailed way of dividing things up. Within the WINWORD directory, for example, you might have a directory called REPORTS, with two subdirectories: WEEKLY and PRODUCT for the two types of reports you write.

When you install Word for Windows, it creates a couple of directories with sample documents in them. Just so you don't create duplicate directories, you should take a look at them in the Open file dialog box. For example, there's already one called LETTERS and one called TEMPLATES. If you create a directory called LETTER, you could confuse yourself.

To see all the main directories in a drive, double-click the drive letter at the top of your directory list. All the directories within that drive are displayed in the <u>D</u>irectories list box. You access a directory by double-clicking its name in the <u>D</u>irectories list box. If it has subdirectories, that reveals them; if not, it shows you all the files in the directory in the File <u>N</u>ame list. To get into the subdirectory, such as LETTERS, you double-click WINWORD, then double-click LETTERS. You then see the documents tucked away in that directory in the File <u>N</u>ame list.

There it is!

To locate the file you need, you can scroll down the File <u>N</u>ame list, or you can type the file name in the File <u>N</u>ame text box.

If you still don't see your file, remember to check the File <u>T</u>ype. If it's not a Word document, it won't show in the list of files unless the correct file type or All Files is selected here.

When the correct file name is highlighted in the list or typed in the text box, double-click it to open the file.

Let Word find the file

Okay, I admit it: I'm as guilty of this as anybody. You name a file in haste, and now you can't remember what you called it. Would you have called an agenda AGENDA or MEETING? Or, you've created 27 variations on one name: RPT, RPRT, REPRT, RPT13, MYREPORT, NEWRPT, etc., etc. Yikes!

But don't despair. By clicking the <u>F</u>ind File button in the File Open dialog box, you can look for your files in a variety of ways. The Search dialog box, shown in figure 5.2, allows you to search by name and location. If you've forgotten whether you created this document in another program or Word, type in the name with an asterisk **wild card** (for example, REPORT.*). This tells Word to search for any file named REPORT, regardless of where it was created and how it was saved.

You can also use wild cards with part of a file name. So if you search for REP*.*, you'll find REPORT16.DOC and REPLY12.DOC.

 Plain English, please!

A **wild card** in a computer file name is just like a wild card in poker; it can stand in for anything in any piece of the file name. So, if you search for a file as REPORT.*, the extension for the file could be XLS, DOC, PCX—whatever, and Word would still find it by using the file name as the only search criterion. You could also search *.XLS to get a list of all Excel files, regardless of the file name.

Fig. 5.2

Did you save a file with an obscure name so that your boss (and as it turns out, you) can't find it? Try the Search dialog box.

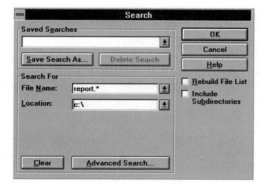

But where <u>F</u>ind File comes in really handy is when you choose <u>A</u>dvanced Search. In this dialog box, shown in figure 5.3, you can choose to search by date and time saved or created, or by summary information, including author and subject. Finally, when you can't begin to think how you saved this monster, you can enter some likely text in the <u>C</u>ontaining Text text box.

Fig. 5.3
The three tabs in the
Advanced Search
dialog box offer
different ways to look
for that long lost
memo.

You can open more than just a single Word document

Now that you know how to find files and open them, you're on a roll. Want to try opening lots of documents at once? How about a document that was created in another word processor? Piece of cake.

What's in a (file) name? Everything!

The first rule of working with file names is to pick a system and stick with it. Over the years, I've run into a few good systems of naming files. Which one is right for you? That depends on your business and how it's organized.

For example, I did some work at a law firm one summer. They had so many important documents, they named each file with a unique number so that there was no chance of duplication. That number was always placed in the footer of the document. They could look at the document

itself and immediately know the file it was printed from.

I also worked for an advertising agency once (I've gotten around). They had a unique abbreviation for each project they worked on, so that abbreviation would always lead off any name for a file associated with that project. For example, the copy for the Acme Travel Brochure might be called ATB-copy.

The important thing is to create a system for yourself that makes sense and stick to it.

Opening several documents at once

Just as you can go into your desk drawer and pull out several files, you can open several files at once in Word for Windows. Just beware of creating too much on-screen clutter!

With hundreds of files open on your desk, you'd never find anything. Same thing with Windows: too many windows, too hard to find anything.

✱ {Note}

> Although Word documents as a rule don't take that much memory to open, if you open too many you'll get a message saying there isn't enough memory available. Rule of thumb: open the files you need, but be a neat housekeeper and close them up when you don't need them any more.

The process of opening multiple files is identical to opening a single file (choose File, Open); you just do it again and again. Each new file will open as a full screen and be placed on top of the other documents. Using the skills you picked up in Chapter 2, "A, B, C: Learning Word Basics," resize the windows or arrange them as necessary for easy access.

❗ (Tip)

> If you want to open several files from the same directory, you can use the Ctrl key and click each name in the File Name list of the Open File dialog box. Then click OK, and they'll all open at once.

What if it's not a Word document?

There are several types of files that Word can open, as shown in figure 5.4. Remember file extensions? You use them to open files created in other programs. We've talked about All Files and Word Documents, but there are a few other types listed here we should mention.

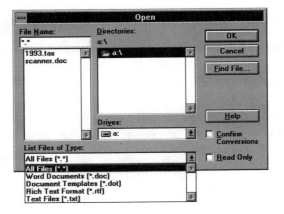

Fig. 5.4
When you have no idea what kind of file it might be, select All Files in the List Files of Type box.

- **Document Templates (*.DOT).** Shows any template files in the File Name list.

- **Rich Text Format (*.RTF).** This Microsoft file format lets a word processed document be saved with all its formatting information intact. This is useful for sharing documents with friends and coworkers who use other word processing programs.

- **Text Files (*.TXT).** This is bare bones stuff: simple typed characters—no formatting or bells and whistles.

The File Name list only displays files of the type selected in the List Files of Type box. If your file is not a Word document, or if it doesn't have a DOC extension, you may not see it in the list right off the bat. The easiest thing to do if you're unsure of your file's extension is to just choose All Files.

After you locate your file, double-click it and Word will open it. There are some variations on how well the file will open up (see Chapter 20, "Sharing Things," to learn more about how Word works with files created in other programs).

Close shop without losing your inventory

When you finally find that wrench you forgot to put away last winter, don't make the mistake of losing it again. Save it in a place where you'll actually be able to find it.

There are three options on the File menu for saving a file: Save, Save As, and Save All.

Saving a document, pure and simple

If you've previously saved the document that you're working on and you want to save it again with the same name, simply choose File, Save.

If you haven't saved the file before, go through the same procedure (choose File, Save), and give it a name in the Save As dialog box, as shown in figure 5.5. Remember, you should give it a logical name so that you can find it again easily.

Fig. 5.5
Simplify your next search for this file now by typing in a slightly more personal name.

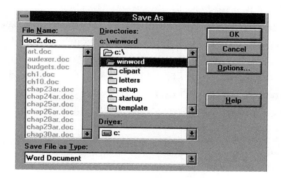

{Note}

You'll notice that when you open a new document, Word gives it a temporary name of Doc1, Doc2, and so on. The number in Doc2 means that this is the second document you've opened (and not saved) since you opened Word.

Summarize your document for future reference

When you choose OK in the Save As dialog box, the Summary Info dialog box shown in figure 5.6 appears. (You can also get to the Summary Info dialog box from the File menu.) Here's where you can enter searchable details about the title, subject, or author, and use keywords to help you locate this file down the road.

Fig. 5.6
Let's see...it was sometime in October, I think I used the phrase "this merger happens over my dead body..."

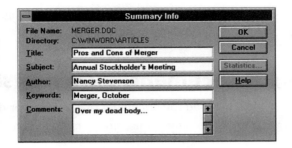

Preserve the record—save changes under a new name

Okay. You've just updated a list of vacation schedules for the entire 150-person department for the coming year. You want to save this, but you also realize you'd like to keep a record of last year's schedule around.

 **<Caution>** If you accidentally give two different files in the same directory the same name, when you save the second file it will wipe out the first. Unless you want to replace an original file, don't use duplicate file names.

Rather than save your changes and **overwrite** the old information, you should save it with a different name; that way both documents will be available to you.

 Plain English, please!

To **overwrite** uses that old law of physics: two pieces of matter cannot occupy the same space. When you put information on a disk, it's saved to a physical location on the disk; the location is designated by the file name. If one piece of information is placed on top of another in that same location, it basically replaces the stuff that was there first. **"**

Choose File, Save As. The Save As dialog box appears and allows you to change the file name, destination drive and directory, and even the file type. In this case, you can simply change the file name.

And don't worry: when Word spots a duplicate file, it lets you know. If you try to save a duplicate file, Word asks if you want to overwrite the existing file. Then, the choice is yours.

(Tip) — If you have several files open at one time and want to save them all, choose File, Save All. If there are some files you haven't saved before, you'll get a Save As dialog box for each of them so that you can name them.

Word can automatically save the day (and your document)

There's a neat way to make sure that all your stuff is saved in case of a power failure, sticky-fingered child, or stray thunderbolt: saving automatically.

You can instruct Word for Windows to save your documents at regular intervals—say, every 5 or 10 minutes. This process saves the file with a different name, so it doesn't overwrite your original file. These files are saved in a temporary directory used by Windows. If something awful happens—for example, if your power fails while you're working—when you come back into Word you'll have a temporary file listed as the last file used at the bottom of your File menu list. (When you save the file, the temp file disappears.)

To use automatic save:

1 Choose Tools, Options

2 Click the Save tab (see fig. 5.7).

3 Choose Automatic Save Every, and select the interval in minutes at which Word should save your document.

Fig. 5.7
The Save tab in
Options sets the
automatic save interval:
automatic peace of
mind!

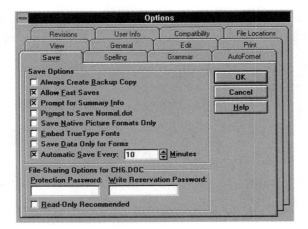

Automatic saving is pretty quick, but it does stop you from working for a couple of seconds while it uses the hard disk. This means that you shouldn't autosave too frequently—it would drive you crazy. Just save often enough that you won't be sorry if lightning strikes.

6 Polishing Your Words to Perfection

Tweak a phrase, replace a word... A few quick clicks of the mouse is all it takes. You can count on Word's editing features to perfect your wording.

In this chapter:

- Where does text go when I delete it?
- What if I delete something and I want it back?
- I want to change several things about my text at once
- I misspelled a name and have to find it and change it

Have you ever seen an old handwritten manuscript—a poem by Keats or a chapter by Dickens? Odds are it's filled with crossed-out words, new phrases are squeezed in between the lines, and even names are changed (I'll bet Tiny Tim was called Little Larry in an early draft of *A Christmas Carol*).

No writer gets it just right the first time. Writing is a continual process of false starts and dead ends. You use the first word or phrase that pops into your head, then realize there's a better way to say the same thing when you reread your draft later. If you put enough energy into editing, you'll end up with a better, more convincing piece of writing.

Word can't make you a better writer, but it can help you make your writing better. With the help of a few tools, Word lets you take charge of every word you write—adding, polishing, rearranging, and deleting words in ways that would dazzle Dickens.

First you select, then you act

If you and Word expect to get along, you'll have to learn how to communicate. It's not that hard, once you learn Word's number-one rule: first you select, then you act.

Before you can do any kind of editing, such as deleting or copying a chunk of text or a picture, you have to **select** the thing you want to change. In essence, you're telling Word, "Hey, I've marked something in this document, and now I'd like to do something with it." As long as you've selected something first, Word will let you do just about anything in its bag of editing tricks.

It's easy to tell when you've selected something; the selection is marked in reverse video, like a photographic negative. If your normal letters are black on white, you'll see a selection as white letters on a black background.

Using the mouse is the easiest way to select things. You can use the invisible selection bar that runs along the left side of the screen to select lines or blocks of text. Try these methods:

- Click once to the left of a line and the whole line is selected.
- Click next to a line of text, hold the mouse button down, and drag—up or down—to select as many lines as you'd like.
- Double-click to the left of a line, and its paragraph is selected.
- Hit Ctrl and click; the whole document is selected.

But you don't have to begin selecting at the start of a line; you can click anywhere in your document and drag your cursor over as much text as you want to select.

If you are more comfortable with the keyboard, you can select text without ever touching the mouse. Just use the arrow keys to position the insertion point where you want the selection to begin, then hold down the Shift key while you use the arrow keys, Home, End, and other keys to extend the selection. When you've marked off the block you want, let go of the Shift key.

**{Note}**

If you check the Automatic <u>W</u>ord Selection setting in the Options dialog box, after you've selected the first word in a sequence of words by dragging your mouse over it, Word selects whole words, rather than individual letters to speed things up. This can be frustrating if you really need to select just a letter or two. With this option selected, however, if you want to delete a single letter or two in a word, place your cursor after them, and hit Backspace.

Finally, to select an object, like a picture, just click it. This selects the object and displays a box around it (see fig. 6.1). See Chapter 16 for more about picture objects.

Fig. 6.1

A picture, when selected, has a box around it with handles that you use to move and resize the picture.

You use these handles to move or resize the picture.

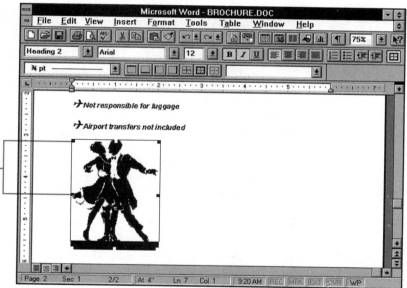

Trash it, or just put it aside for now

Even Dickens tossed off a lame sentence every now and then. When you find one of those, you'll probably want to throw it out right then and there, never to be seen again. But what if that sentence contains a perfectly good thought that's just out of place?

Word lets you cut text—a word, a sentence, even a whole document—and set it aside in a holding place called the Windows **Clipboard**. Think of the

Clipboard as a cork board with exactly one pushpin. When you cut or copy something and place it on the Clipboard, you use that pushpin. If you cut or copy something else, you'll have to throw away whatever's already on the Clipboard before you can pin your new selection there.

 Using Cut takes the text out of your document and places it on the Clipboard. When you decide where you want to put it, you can paste a copy of the cut text in that spot in your document (or even in another document). The text you cut to the Clipboard stays there until you put something else on the Clipboard.

 Be careful. When you cut something to the Clipboard, it replaces anything that's already there. If you aren't going to paste the cut text immediately, put it in a new file and save that file.

If you're not interested in keeping text around, there are several ways to cut out the text and throw it away:

- Selecting something and hitting the Del key on your keyboard clears it.
- Pressing Backspace on your keyboard deletes text one character at a time going backward. If you want to delete a whole word to the left of your insertion point, use Ctrl+Backspace.
- Selecting text and then choosing Edit, Clear deletes it.

When you use these methods, however, whatever you removed isn't on the Clipboard—it's gone. You can get it back, though, by using the Undo feature (more about Undo later in this chapter).

I want to replace *this* with *that*

When you're writing a report, you don't always have every fact at your fingertips. If you're not sure, you'll put a placeholder in a draft, like estimated final sales figures for the year. Later, for the final version, you can replace the estimated figure with the actual numbers.

With Word, exchanging one thing for another is easy. Simply select the text you want to replace, then start typing the new text. Word deletes all selected text and replaces it with the new text.

I didn't mean it! Undoing edits

I've often wished Word's Undo/Redo feature were a built-in feature of life so that we could undo some of our mistakes. For now, though, we'll have to make do with using it in our documents, where we can undo and redo just about anything with the click of a button. Just wrote a sentence you didn't like? Undo it. Did you decide that sentence you just undid wasn't so bad after all? Redo it!

 The Undo button on the toolbar lets you quickly reverse your last action. If you make an editing change, such as adding bold, cutting text, or typing in new text, and you want to undo that change, just click the Undo button.

The best part about Undo is that it doesn't just stop at one level. You can keep pressing the Undo button to roll back the changes you've made, until you're right back where you started.

If you want to undo several things at once and you don't want to click the Undo button over and over, click the Undo button's drop-down arrow to produce a list of editing changes you've made. The last change appears on top, the next to last beneath that, and so on down the list (see fig. 6.2). You can highlight as many items on the list as you want, then click Undo to undo them all at once. You have to undo everything in sequence, however (you can't undo just the third one down on the list and not undo everything leading up to it).

Fig. 6.2

Drag down the list to select however many actions you'd like to undo, then let go of your mouse and they're gone. Use Redo to get them back.

 If you undo a change and then decide you want to put it back in, click the Redo button. Word reinstates the editing change in your document. Like Undo, you can keep clicking the Redo button to return to where you started.

 **{Note}** You can also undo by choosing <u>E</u>dit, <u>U</u>ndo. The command changes depending on your last action; for example, if the last thing you did was make text bold, the command will become Undo Bold.

Sometimes something I say is so brilliant, I just have to use it again and again. Now, this doesn't happen often, but when it does, Word's Copy command comes in handy.

Also, as I revise and craft a document, I find I need to organize things differently. When it's time to move text, you'll once again call on that useful little item, the Clipboard.

The art and craft of cutting and pasting

That paragraph you wrote in your quarterly report would be perfect in this customer proposal. Don't bother to retype it. When you want to take text or a picture out of one place and move it somewhere else, whether it's within one document or from one document to another, you can just use cutting and pasting.

Revisionist thinking

I'll let you in on a little secret: I don't always get things right the first time. In fact, it takes three or four editors to make my work into something you'd want to read. For people like me, there's a handy little feature in Word called revision marking.

When you tell Word to use revision marks (which you do by choosing <u>T</u>ools, Re<u>v</u>isions, <u>M</u>ark Revisions While Editing), everything you do to your original document is marked on-screen and in your printed document. Deletions are marked with strikethrough, and new text is in a different color on-screen (or underlined in a printout).

Why is this so useful? Well, as you make changes in a document that more than one person reviews, they can see just what's been changed, and then accept or cancel the changes. Revision marks are most useful when you're working on a group writing project, or when someone edits your original work.

1 Select the text you want to move.

2 Click the Cut button on the toolbar. Word places the text on the Clipboard.

You can retrieve what you cut from the Clipboard by pasting it.

3 Move your cursor to the place in the document (or even another document) where you want the text to go.

4 Click the Paste button.

Word has taken your information from the Windows Clipboard and placed it in its new setting.

If you're doing a lot of cutting and pasting, it's sometimes easier to use the shortcut menu (fig. 6.3). Select the text, and then click the right mouse button to produce this menu.

Fig. 6.3
The shortcut menu offers several common editing and formatting options.

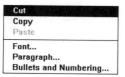

Drag and drop: the direct approach

Drag and drop is one of the simplest ways to move text in Word, and it's all possible because of that wonderful animal called the mouse.

First, you select the text you want to move. Then, click the selection with your mouse and hold down the mouse button until the mouse pointer in figure 6.4 appears.

Fig. 6.4
It may take a second
for this pointer to
appear, but when it
does, you can drag this
text anywhere you
like—even to another
document!

*When you see this
pointer, you know it's
time to do the drag
and drop.*

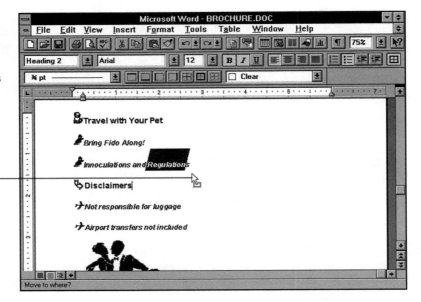

Now, simply drag the pointer to the place where you'd like the text to appear, and let go. That's it.

You can even use drag and drop to drag text between two documents. Just display both documents on-screen, and follow the drag-and-drop procedure.

Copy this and put it there

"It was the best of times, it was the worst of times." That's one of Dickens's more masterful sentences. Maybe you've crafted a sentence that's equally memorable; say you want to use it in the opening remarks, the discussion, and the conclusion of your proposal? No problem. Copying a piece of your document is a simple variation on cutting and pasting. The difference is that the original doesn't disappear.

1 Select the text you want to copy.

2 Click the Copy button.

3 Move your cursor to the place you want to insert the copy of the text.

4 Click the Paste button.

That's it! You can also use drag and drop to copy selected text by simply holding down the Ctrl key as you drag. This even works between documents or applications.

I know that word's there somewhere...

Sometimes you need to track down a word or a phrase. Maybe your report is 42 pages long, and you want to find the section where you talked about Al Jones. Or maybe you just learned that Al prefers to be called Albert, and you'd like to replace every instance of the nickname with the more formal version.

Either way, you're in luck. Word has a full set of powerful tools that let you find and replace text with the greatest of ease. Word offers several variations on finding and replacing text, and they're all controlled through the Edit menu.

I just want to find it

Word can track down a specific chunk of text in any document. This technique is handy when you want to review every place where you've used a certain word or phrase.

When you just want to find something, do this:

1 Choose Edit, Find. The dialog box in figure 6.5 appears.

2 Type the text you want to find in the Find What box.

Use Pattern Matching allows you to search for things like phone numbers by typing ###-#### to find all phone numbers in your document.

Match Case means that searching for Hat won't bring up hat.

Fig. 6.5
When you select Find, the Find box offers you some choices, including changing to the Replace dialog box.

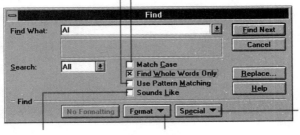

Special looks for special things. For example, if you know the differences between an em dash and an en dash, you can search for either one.

Sounds Like is useful when you're not sure of the spelling; for example, if you search for pattirn with Sounds Like checked, Word finds pattern.

Format lets you search for text with certain formatting; for example, you can find all the bold text in a document.

3 In the Search drop-down list, select All to search the whole document.

4 Make sure Find Whole Words Only is checked; otherwise, if you search for Al, Word will find *Al*, *all*, *align*, etc.

5 Click Find Next to begin the search.

When you've found what you need, click Cancel and do what you like—for example, if you just want to find a particular section in your document to read through it, search for a word you know occurs in it and then click Cancel; or if you want to make changes, go ahead and make them now.

> When you're using the Find and Replace box, you don't have to hit Cancel to work with your text. Just move the dialog box out of the way, click in the document and make your changes, then return to the dialog and look for the next item.

I don't like it: replace it with this

Say that you've agonized over a proposal for a new client, Al Jones. After you've hammered out a first draft, you discover he prefers to be called Albert.

Of course, you're trying to impress your new client—and the last thing you want is to miss just one occurrence of *Al* as you scan your document.

When you want to find every single instance of a word or phrase and replace it with something else, there's a special feature just for you. Use the Replace dialog box (see fig. 6.6). You get to it by choosing Edit, Replace, or by clicking the Replace button in the Find dialog box.

Fig. 6.6

The Replace dialog box is like an expanded Find dialog box with a Replace With box and a Replace All button.

Notice in figure 6.6 that when Word finds matching text, it highlights it in your document so you can see it in context. You have a few choices after Word finds matching text:

- Click the Find Next button to simply find the next occurrence without making any changes.

- Click Replace to replace just this occurrence and move onto the next.

- Click Replace All to replace every occurrence in the document.

⊗<Caution> Although you can undo all the changes made during the Replace All process with the Undo/Redo feature, you have no opportunity to check what Word changes. For example, say your report included a reference to the chemical symbol for aluminum, *Al*. Word would naturally change this *Al* to *Albert*, too, and you'd wind up referring to *Albert foil* instead of *aluminum foil*. The more you narrow your search, using things like Match Case with proper names, the better your chances of avoiding these problems.

I know where it is; I just want to Go To it!

If you want to work with the table on page 7 of your document, you can use the scroll bar or the Page Down key to move there. But why not just go there directly? There's a really slick way to instantly zap yourself from one place to another in a Word document. Just tell Word to go to a specific page, and you're there in a flash.

Ready to beam us up, Scotty? Press F5. The Go To dialog box appears (see fig. 6.7). In this dialog box, you can tell Word to go to a specific page in your document. You also can use this box to go to a bookmark, footnote, picture, object—anything listed in the Go To What list box.

Fig. 6.7

Transport yourself immediately to a page, a footnote, object, table, whatever, using Go To.

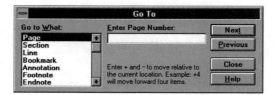

Simply select the type of thing you want to find in the Go To What list, and the Enter box reflects that choice (Enter Page Number becomes Enter Object Name when you select Object, for example). When you enter a page number, section number, etc., the Next button changes to GoTo; click it to get where you want to go. Choose the Next or Previous button to search forward or backward in the document. After you find what you want, click Close.

(Tip)

Homesick? You can always return to the place where you were in your document when you started your "Go to" trip by pressing Shift+F5.

Perfect Documents Using Spelling, Grammar, and Thesaurus

You don't have to memorize a style guide to make your readers think you know everything there is to know about things like spelling and grammar. Word will gladly check these details for you.

Sometimes it's the details that make or break your documents. You wouldn't think of passing around an important report that was dog-eared and covered with coffee stains. So why ruin a perfectly put-together proposal with a big ugly misspelling or a clunky, ungrammatical sentence?

Finding just the right word, spelling it properly, and avoiding the dreaded double negative or dangling participle can make your readers remember your words for all the right reasons.

You'll be glad to hear that you don't need a master's degree in English to master the fine art of spelling and the fine points of grammar. Word has the tools you need: built-in spelling and grammar checkers, plus a thesaurus to help you find a better way to say what you mean. Let these little wonders zip through your document; they'll find and fix most problems for you.

And if you keep making the same mistakes over and over, let Word polish your documents automatically with its built-in clean-up experts, AutoText and AutoCorrect.

Can't spell? That's OK—Word can

To catch all those little spelling bloopers, you can have Word for Windows check the words in your document against built-in dictionaries. It also allows you to create your own dictionaries that contain things like your company or product name, industry-specific jargon, or foreign phrases. Word searches these dictionaries, and if something doesn't match up, it gives you a few different options for making it right.

Unlike your grade school teachers, Word will allow you to leave what seems like an odd spelling alone, or even add it to your dictionary if you want to.

Word's AutoCorrect feature also can correct common spelling errors automatically, as you type.

How do I check my spelling?

Word handles big jobs. After you finish your document, use Word's Spelling tool to compare every single word in your document with the ones in its built-in dictionary.

Word also answers simple questions: if you've typed a word and you're not sure you've spelled it correctly, select it first, then run Spelling to check just that word. In fact, you can check as much or as little of your document as you choose. After it's checked the selection, Word asks whether you want to check the rest of the document or get right back to work. This is a very accommodating (did I spell that right?) feature!

If you want to check the spelling of just a single word, or a section of your document, be sure to select it first. If nothing is selected, Word checks the entire document.

Spelling has its limitations

Even the best speller among us slips up now and then, and the Word Spelling feature is no exception. To get the most of this feature, you need to understand its limitations.

Some correctly spelled words just aren't in Spelling's dictionary, and it will flag them as incorrect. For example, Spelling doesn't recognize many proper names, abbreviations, scientific formulas, words containing punctuation, or acronyms (like NAFTA).

On the other hand, Word sees no problem with a typo that results in another, perfectly legitimate word. If you type *are*, for example, when you meant to type *art*, Word won't warn you (see "Spelling bee," later in this chapter).

The Spelling feature is flexible, however. You can add words to the dictionary (so that Word will stop bothering you every time it sees NAFTA). And if you use Word Spelling along with your own proofreading skills, you can personally make sure that *are* doesn't pass for *art*.

Let's start checking

To begin your spelling check, click the Spelling button on the toolbar. If you have any suspect misspellings, the dialog box in figure 7.1 appears, and the first questionably spelled word shows in the Not in Dictionary box.

Fig. 7.1

When the Spelling feature encounters a word it doesn't recognize, it displays this dialog box.

This drop-down list shows you what dictionaries you can add a spelling to.

Word lists the most likely spelling of the word here. Choose it, choose another from the Suggestions list, or type in your own.

The Spelling dialog box lets you make your own decision about the word it questions. You can:

- Choose to ignore this word or every instance of this word in the document.

- Choose to change this word or every instance of this word in the document to the spelling in the Change To text box.

⊗<Caution> Be careful when choosing to change every instance of a word in a document. Let's say you've used a company name, IBM, throughout a report, and in one instance you've misspelled it IAM. Word finds the error, and you choose to change every instance of IAM to IBM. But if you typed the words I am in another part of the document and missed the space bar, Word will change that to IBM as well, and your sentence will turn to nonsense. Try to use Change All for very specific, unambiguous examples where there's little room for mix-up, like changing Steinfield to Steinfeld.

- Add the word to your dictionary so that Word won't question it again.

- Add the word to AutoCorrect so that Word fixes this particular misspelling every time you type it (we talk about AutoCorrect later in the chapter).

You can also use the Options dialog box to set spelling options, such as whether you want Word to pay attention to capital letters, and which dictionaries to use.

Looking in the dictionary

Even the Master Speller himself, Noah Webster, must have occasionally used his own dictionary to check a word. Dictionaries are the basis of Word's spelling function. They're the rule books that Word checks against, and if something doesn't jibe, it lets you know.

Word's built-in dictionaries

The main dictionary is what Word uses to perform a spelling check. It contains many common words and even some common names. You can also use custom dictionaries in addition to the main dictionary. The main dictionary never changes; when you add a word to a dictionary during a spelling check, it goes into a custom dictionary.

You can control some of the ways Spelling uses your dictionaries by clicking the Options button in the Spelling dialog box. The Options dialog box appears with the Spelling tab on top (see fig. 7.2).

Fig. 7.2
This is where you set the options for your spelling check.

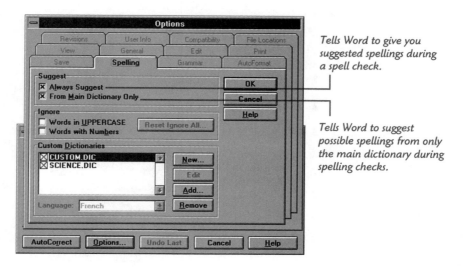

Tells Word to give you suggested spellings during a spell check.

Tells Word to suggest possible spellings from only the main dictionary during spelling checks.

Word always checks your main dictionary first for a match. It's your choice whether or not Word checks the custom dictionaries you create. Just click on any dictionary you want Word to use in addition to your main dictionary in this dialog box.

To create a new dictionary, or to remove or edit an existing one, use the Ne̲w, E̲dit, A̲dd, or R̲emove buttons in the Options dialog box.

You can also define a couple of things that Word should ignore when it runs a spell check. If you use certain terms that always appear in all capital letters, you can avoid having to stop each time Word sees them by clicking Words in UP̲PERCASE. You can also choose to Ignore Words with Numb̲ers. This is a good way to avoid checking formulas or part numbers that show up several times in your document.

The personal touch: write your own dictionary

If you're a lawyer, spelling checks might drive you crazy: every time Word sees a word like *in certio* or *corpus delecti*, it will object. You can overrule the objections one by one, or add each word to your custom dictionary, one at a time, when you run spelling checks. But you're better off creating a custom legal dictionary and filling it with all the legal terms you might use. You can also copy that dictionary and make sure everyone in the firm has access to it.

To create a custom dictionary, do this:

1 Choose T̲ools, O̲ptions.

2 Select the Spelling tab.

3 Click the Ne̲w button, and the dialog box in figure 7.3 comes up.

Fig. 7.3
The Create Custom Dictionary dialog box allows you to designate the name and directory for the dictionary.

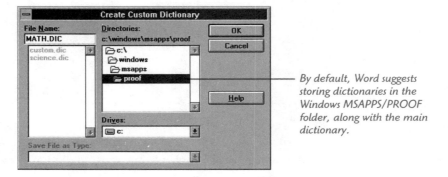

By default, Word suggests storing dictionaries in the Windows MSAPPS/PROOF folder, along with the main dictionary.

4 Enter the name of the dictionary, with a DIC extension.

5 Click OK. You see the name of your new dictionary listed in the Custom Dictionaries drop-down list.

Adding entries to your new dictionary is as easy as editing any Word document:

1 Be sure the dictionary name is selected in the list box, then click the Edit button.

2 Word asks if you want to edit the custom dictionary as a Word document; choose Yes.

Word stores entries for custom dictionaries in a Word document, and editing that document is how you edit a custom dictionary. With a dictionary that you've already put entries into, a document with a list of words appears under the Options dialog box, and you just add to it. With a newly created dictionary, a new, blank document appears.

3 In either case, click OK to close the dialog box, and you're ready to edit (see fig. 7.4).

4 Type an entry, then press Enter to move to the next line. Each line in this document is an entry in your dictionary, and the return after each entry defines its end for Word.

Fig. 7.4
Creating a new dictionary is just a matter of typing entries in a Word document and saving it as a text file.

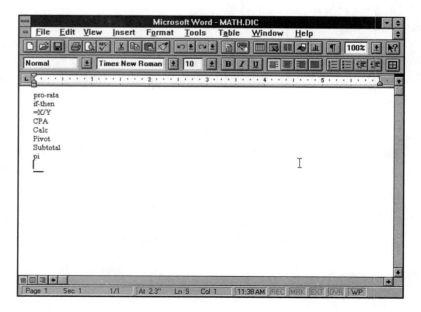

5 After you finish editing, simply save the document as a text file by selecting Text Only in the Save File as Type drop-down list in the Save As dialog box (this is how Word wants to read your dictionaries, so humor it).

6 Close the file to return to your original document.

⊛ *{Note}*_____

In addition to creating your own dictionaries, you can buy special add-on dictionaries from Microsoft—such as legal or medical dictionaries. To use any of these during a spelling check, make sure they are checked in the Custom Dictionaries list of the Spelling dialog box.

❓ *Q&A*_____

I tried to click the Edit button in the Options dialog box, but it's gray and not available to me. How can I edit?

To edit a dictionary, you must enter the Spelling tab of the Options dialog box through the Tools menu. If you go there through the Options button while in the Spelling dialog box, Edit isn't available to you.

Automating with AutoText and AutoCorrect

The sidewalk in front of my house has one crack that I always trip over, and my keyboard has a couple of letter combinations that I just can't type correctly. One of these days the city will get around to repaving the sidewalk, and I'll stop stubbing my toe. Fortunately, it's a lot easier to pave over the stumbling blocks in my typing.

Word includes two features—**AutoText** and **AutoCorrect**—that help even the most fumble-fingered typist produce perfect copy every time. They're two slightly different ways to automatically enter text you use regularly in your documents: AutoCorrect is used mainly to correct common errors, and AutoText stores the text or graphics that you use often. With a simple command, you can insert that information into your document.

What kinds of things can you reuse this way?

- Your company logo
- Your name and address
- The list of people scheduled to get copies of a weekly report

...and so on.

One basic difference between these two methods is that AutoCorrect is entered directly as you type the entry name, and AutoText requires that you confirm its insertion through the menu or by clicking the AutoText tool. Also, AutoText keeps all the original formatting of the text, but AutoCorrect, by default, doesn't.

Let Word do the typing with AutoCorrect

I remember asking my mother how to spell a word, only to have her tell me to look it up in the dictionary. (But, Mom, how can I find it if I don't know how it's spelled?) All I wanted was for her to give me the correct spelling so I could get on with my life. But noooo—I had to learn something in the process.

Well, AutoCorrect in Word does what I want with no questions asked; it just corrects misspellings and doesn't put me through an educational experience.

Using AutoCorrect is a simple two-step process. First you add a pair of words to the list—the one you will type, and the correct version you want Word to replace it with.

To see how this feature works, open a document window and type **teh**. When you hit the space bar at the end of the word, AutoCorrect wastes no time in fixing your spelling to read *the*. You can add entries to AutoCorrect so that it fixes things you commonly misspell.

How does AutoCorrect work?

To reach AutoCorrect, choose Tools, AutoCorrect. The dialog box in figure 7.5 appears.

Fig. 7.5

The items with check boxes at the top of this dialog box are commonly used correcting functions that you may (or may not) want to have happen automatically as you type.

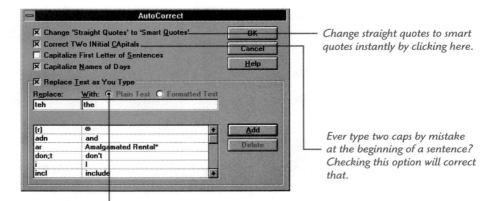

Change straight quotes to smart quotes instantly by clicking here.

Ever type two caps by mistake at the beginning of a sentence? Checking this option will correct that.

When Plain Text is checked, your replacement word takes on the formatting of the rest of the words in your document.

66 *Plain English, please!*

There are plain fries and there are curly fries. **Smart quotes** are the fancy, curled quotation marks that you see in typeset books and magazines. The quotation marks and apostrophe on your keyboard are the straight up and down kind. Usually, you need a keystroke combination to call up smart quotes. Using the AutoFormat setting, you can have Word automatically replace the straight quotes with these curly ones. 99

Notice the entries already there. Some of these are common mistakes already entered into AutoCorrect for you, such as the reversed letters in *and* and the capitalization of *I*. Others, like the entry for Amalgamated Rental, are examples of shortcuts to entering words you type often. Typing **ar** takes a lot less time than typing **Amalgamated Rentals** and gives you much less opportunity to make a typo in the process.

 **<Caution>** Be careful not to use a common word as the name of your AutoCorrect entry. If you use *am* instead of *ar* as your AutoCorrect name, every time you type the word **am**, Word will insert *Amalgamated Rentals*.

Using AutoCorrect

To add an AutoCorrect entry:

1 Type the incorrect version of the word in the Replace text box.

2 Enter the correct spelling in the With text box.

3 The next time you type this misspelling followed by a space, tab, or return, Word corrects it. That's it!

 **{Note}** Suppose your company name is always bold and in a special typeface. You can arrange it so that your AutoCorrect version gets inserted with that formatting. Type the word or phrase and format it in your document window, then select it. Open the AutoCorrect dialog box and click the Formatted Text button. The word, with formatting attached, appears in the With text box. Type whatever replace text, like **AR**, that you want to use in the Replace box. Now every time you type **AR**, AutoCorrect replaces it with the correct text with appropriate formatting intact.

Inserting things with AutoText

When I had my house built, there were certain things I assumed the builder would just do without consulting me—standard wiring, for example. With other things, like paint colors and the style for the kitchen cabinets, I expected him to ask for my input.

Word assumes that an AutoCorrect entry should go into your document without any special confirmation as soon as you type its name. AutoText, on the other hand, requires an additional action to confirm the insertion. It also saves original text formatting and doesn't conform to the text format in your document by default, as AutoCorrect does.

You're likely to use AutoCorrect for things you use all the time, like your name and to correct common misspellings. You'll use AutoText to enter longer blocks of text or graphics used more occasionally.

Creating the AutoText entry

To create an AutoText entry, do this:

1 Type your entry in the document with whatever formatting is appropriate, or insert a picture or graphic.

2 Select the item, then click the Edit AutoText button. (*Note:* If nothing is selected, the tool functions as an insert AutoText button; if something's selected, it's an Edit AutoText button.)

This brings up the AutoText dialog box (see fig. 7.6). You can also get to this by choosing <u>E</u>dit, <u>A</u>utoText.

3 You can name the entry here, then click <u>A</u>dd to add it to the AutoText list.

The name you assign to the selected text; type the name and click <u>A</u>dd to add it to the list beneath it.

Fig. 7.6
The AutoText dialog box can be reached by the AutoText tool or through the <u>E</u>dit menu.

The text that will be inserted into your document

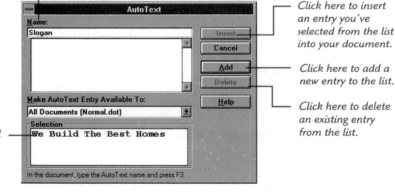

Click here to insert an entry you've selected from the list into your document.

Click here to add a new entry to the list.

Click here to delete an existing entry from the list.

Inserting an AutoText entry in your document

Now, there are a few ways you might go about actually inserting this AutoText entry into a document:

• Type the name of the AutoText in a document, and then click the AutoText button to insert the full entry.

• Another quick and easy way is to type the AutoText name, then just hit F3.

Q&A *I go to the Edit menu and AutoText is gray and not available to me. Is there something wrong?*

Until you create your first AutoText entry, if no text is selected, the AutoText item on the menu is unavailable. You need to select text first, and then AutoText is available through the Edit menu. Also, after you add one entry, the AutoText item in the Edit menu will be available to you whether you have selected text or not.

How to write good...er, better

Teacher: "Who's next?"

Student: "It's me."

Teacher: "It is I."

I walked into that one every single time. Nobody but your 4th grade teacher ever actually says things like "It is I," of course.

But there are some rules of grammar that you do want to follow, because they make your documents more compelling and easier to read. If you haven't thought about grammar since 4th grade, Word's grammar checker can help you polish your writing appropriately.

Checking your grammar

Grammar check works in about the same way as Spelling. Word's Grammar feature has a list of several common rules of grammar—like the words stored in Spelling's dictionaries. If your sentence doesn't fit the rules, Word flags it for you.

These rules pertain to both grammatical structure (like subject-verb agreement and split infinitives) and style (things like wordiness, or use of passive voice). But don't panic. If you've forgotten what a split infinitive is, Word will remind you and it'll fix things for you.

Also, you'll be glad to hear that Word doesn't force its rules upon you. You have the option of checking against all the rules, some of the rules, or ignoring Word when it spots what it thinks is a problem.

Because you write different types of documents, you use different types of grammar. In an informal note, you probably wouldn't write "It is I." In a more formal report or letter, you might. For that reason, Word has three rule groups: formal, business, and casual.

Plain English, please!

A **rule group** is just a subset of rules taken from the main list of rules. Each group matches the way you'd be likely to talk in different types of documents: formal might be used for a client proposal or formal invitation and sticks to every rule in the book; business might work well for your average business letter—it allows for things like jargon or clichés, but sticks pretty close on grammar; and casual is for that note to your brother bragging about your new car—you can get away with things like informal usage and contractions here.

Spelling bee

I'm fascinated by words that are spelled the same but have several, totally different meanings. Sometimes this is compounded by words that are spelled slightly differently, but sound exactly the same.

One of my favorite examples is the identical sounding words fair and fare. Altogether, I can think of eight different meanings for these—maybe you can think of others.

There's a fair complexion (pale), fair weather (good), going to the school fair (a festival), being fair (just). Then there's a bill of fare (goods), the fare you pay to take a bus (fee), times when you fare well (the state of things) and to fare into town (go or travel). This doesn't even include the archaic meanings, like a litter of pigs (honest, it's in my dictionary).

The thing is, Word won't know the difference between words that sound the same, but are spelled differently. Also, if you misspell a word like fare and type far instead, Word doesn't see anything wrong: far is a legitimate, correctly spelled word.

Perhaps in the next version, Word will be able to recognize words in context. Till then, take care as you type, and fare thee well!

What are the rules?

You can select the rule group you want Word to use by choosing Tools, Options. Click the Grammar tab (see fig. 7.7). You can choose and customize your grammar rule sets here. Note that the most formal rule set is the Strictly (All Rules) choice in this list. By default, Word performs a spelling check as part of the grammar check. If you don't want it to, deselect it here.

Fig. 7.7

The Grammar tab in the Options dialog box is where you customize your grammar check.

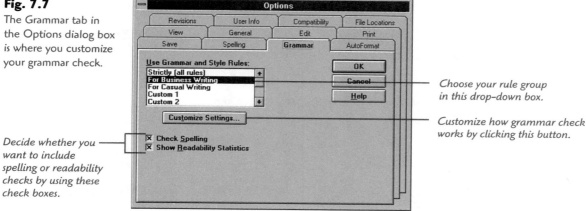

Choose your rule group in this drop-down box.

Customize how grammar check works by clicking this button.

Decide whether you want to include spelling or readability checks by using these check boxes.

To see the list of rules in any given rule group, highlight the name of the group in the Use Grammar and Style Rules list box, then click Customize Settings. The Customize Grammar Settings dialog box appears (see fig. 7.8).

Fig. 7.8

You can customize the grammar rules in any rule group.

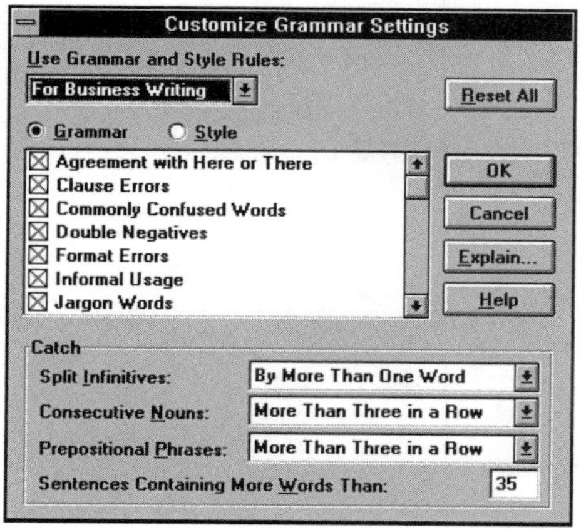

The rules contained in the group are checked—but these rules aren't set in stone. With just a few clicks, you can easily customize any rule group. Just select the group you want to customize, then click the check boxes to select or deselect the rules you want to apply.

(Tip)

> If you ever want to return a rule group to its original state, simply click the Reset All button in this same dialog box.

After you choose the rule set you'd like to use, click OK. You run the grammar check by simply choosing Tools, Grammar.

Performing the grammar check

During the grammar check, if there's a sentence Word doesn't like, it shows you the dialog box in figure 7.9.

Fig. 7.9
Just as with the Spelling check, you can choose to ignore or change problems Word flags during the Grammar check.

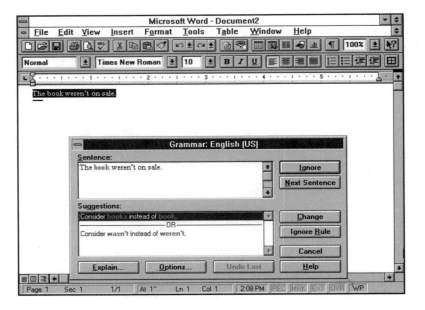

You have a few options here:

- You can ask for a more in-depth explanation of the problem by clicking the Explain button. This gives you the window in figure 7.10.

Fig. 7.10
Scroll through this
window to learn more
about the error of your
ways.

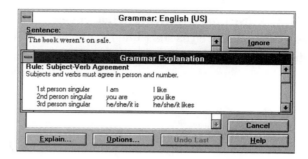

- If you want to ignore the issue that Word's brought up, click <u>I</u>gnore.

- If you want to ignore this rule for the rest of the grammar check, click Ignore <u>R</u>ule.

- If you'd like to make the suggested change, click the <u>C</u>hange button.

- You can also simply skip to the next sentence by clicking <u>N</u>ext Sentence.

- You can undo your last change with the Undo <u>L</u>ast button.

And, as with Spelling, you can go directly to the <u>O</u>ptions dialog box and change the settings for the Grammar tab by clicking <u>O</u>ptions.

At the end of your grammar check (if you haven't deselected it in the Options dialog box), you get a Readability Statistics summary (see fig. 7.11).

Fig. 7.11
If 80% of your
document is passive,
you might want to get
more active in the
future!

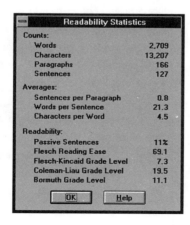

This box gives you a word count that comes in handy if you're getting paid by the word, as well as readability statistics (see "Why you should—or shouldn't—care about readability" in this chapter). Click OK when you're done improving yourself.

 (Tip)

> Another way to get the word count for your document is to choose <u>T</u>ools, <u>W</u>ord Count. Word tells you the number of words, pages, paragraphs, lines—everything you ever wanted to know about how much stuff is in your document.

Using the Thesaurus to find just the right word

I'm sure that you yourself have never been stuck for the right word. But you may know someone who occasionally runs around the office saying things like, "This is driving me crazy. It's a word that means lazy and it starts with an *s*. What IS that word?" This is when Word's Thesaurus comes in handy.

Why you should—or shouldn't—care about readability

What exactly are readability statistics and why should you care? Well, these things use formulas to give you a number that relates to how high a person's reading level should be for them to be comfortable with your writing. Depending on your readers—rocket scientists or third graders—you might rethink your writing style after seeing this rating.

But don't go overboard about this. These formulas basically take into account only two main factors: sentence and word length. The assumption here is that the bigger the word and longer the sentences, the harder the writing is to read.

What's wrong with this? Well, some long words like *announcement* would be easier to understand than a short word like *mor*, depending on whether you're a botanist or not. And a short, disorganized sentence is worse than a lengthy, but well-structured one.

But if you have a tendency to use overly long sentences or words, Word's readability statistics might flag that for you. Also, try to keep the statistic for passive sentences low: active voice ("he hit me," instead of "I was hit by him") is much easier for your reader to understand.

Word's Thesaurus (like any other thesaurus) gives you lists of synonyms and antonyms for selected words. (You know, you learned about this in English: synonyms have the same or similar meaning, antonyms are opposites.)

Word's Thesaurus will either check for the word to the left of the insertion point, or whatever word you have selected. Choose Tools, Thesaurus. The Thesaurus dialog box appears (see fig. 7.12).

The word that was looked up appears in the Looked Up drop-down list.

Fig. 7.12

A rose by any other name...find just the right word in the Thesaurus dialog box.

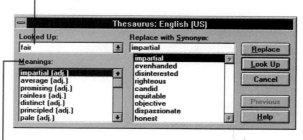

Select the right shade of Meaning here, or choose antonyms.

Because words can take on different shades of meaning (for example, Word says *fair* can mean *promising* or *pale*), use the Meanings list to narrow this down. As you do, the Replace with Synonym/Antonym list changes depending on what meaning you select, or if you request antonyms.

If you find just the right word, Replace the one in your document with it. If you want to look up another word in your list to see more words, select the word and click Look Up.

You can also move around from word to word in the lists in the Thesaurus dialog box. Word gives you slightly different synonym lists that help you narrow down to just the right meaning. Word keeps a list of the words you've looked at in the Looked Up pop-up list, in case you need a reminder.

Now That I've Made It, I Think I'll Print It

You've created a master-piece, and now you want to show it off. Printing in Word is the payoff for all your hard work.

In this chapter:

- I need to print sideways
- How can I see what I'm going to get?
- Can I see all these pages together before I print?
- I just want to print the first two pages—okay?

There's what you see. And then there's what you get. Unfortunately, there's usually a big gap between the two.

Let's be honest. There are very few documents that you create just to look at on-screen. If you want to share the ideas you create in Word with other people, you need to print them out. So how do you keep those documents that look great on-screen from looking...well, *different* when they pop out of the printer?

No problem. Word provides tools that give you a fighting chance at making sure what you see on-screen is what you'll get on the printed page. The secret is to preview your document to determine exactly how the pages will look when they're printed. If you don't like what you see, you can change things before a single drop of ink hits a piece of paper.

Print Preview points the way

You wouldn't take a picture with a camera by just holding it at arm's length and clicking. First, you'd look through the lens to see what you're going to get.

You can do the same thing with your Word documents by using a feature called Print Preview. Print Preview lets you look at the pages in your document—all at once or close up. It's extremely useful for viewing page breaks, margins, and the overall design of your pages.

 Click the Print Preview button on the standard toolbar. You'll notice that everything on your screen changes. The standard and formatting toolbars disappear, and your document appears in Full Screen view with a new toolbar.

Looking at things from every angle

Before you commit words to paper, Word lets you see exactly what your document will look like on the page. There are tools in the Print Preview window that let you jump between pages, look at one, two, or ten pages at once, even move in really close to see whether that's a comma or a semicolon on page 5.

As you're looking around Print Preview, be careful that you don't hit the Print button before you're ready to print. Unlike the Print command in the File menu, you won't get a chance to fuss with options; your entire document will go straight to the printer.

Exploring the Print Preview window

The Print Preview window allows you to see how your printed document will look—
and it lets you make last-minute edits before you print!

Print
Tells Word everything's fine—go ahead and print

Multiple Pages
Shows several pages at once

Zoom Control
Lets you control how the Magnifier works

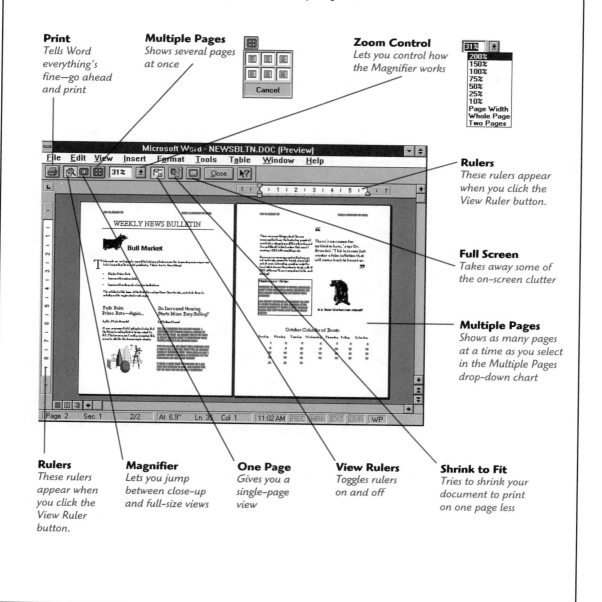

Rulers
These rulers appear when you click the View Ruler button.

Full Screen
Takes away some of the on-screen clutter

Multiple Pages
Shows as many pages at a time as you select in the Multiple Pages drop-down chart

Rulers
These rulers appear when you click the View Ruler button.

Magnifier
Lets you jump between close-up and full-size views

One Page
Gives you a single-page view

View Rulers
Toggles rulers on and off

Shrink to Fit
Tries to shrink your document to print on one page less

Here are your options for moving around and changing your view in the Print Preview window:

- Use the scroll bars to move from page to page within your document.

- If you want to get rid of the menus and title bar so that the preview window gets more space, click the Full Screen button. (Press Esc to bring them back.)

- You can view several pages of your document at once by clicking the Multiple Pages button, holding down the button, and dragging over the squares in the drop-down chart. This option's great if you need to see how text flows from page to page, but don't need to read the text. Figure 8.1 shows eight pages displayed at once in Full Screen view.

Fig. 8.1
Check out the way your text flows in larger documents through the Multiple Pages view.

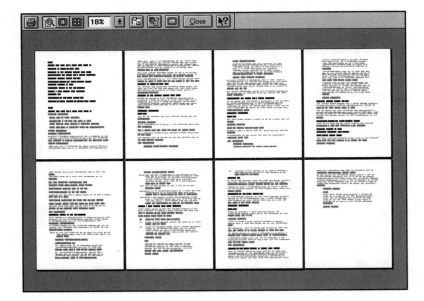

- Use the Zoom Control to zoom in and out of your document pages.

- Shrink to Fit is useful if there's one pesky line hanging around on the last page. Click here, and Word will try to fit that orphan onto the preceding page, saving a piece of paper and making your document look just a bit neater.

- Use the Magnifier button to turn your mouse pointer into a magnifying glass. Just click where you want to see more detail in your document, and Word instantly shows you that section at 100% of the document size. Click again to return to the original magnification.

When I click the Full Screen button, the scroll bars disappear. Do I have to leave Full Screen every time I want to see another page?

Who needs scroll bars? Word lets you use the Page Up and Page Down keys on your keyboard to move around your document. To move to the very first page, use Ctrl+Home; to get to the very last, try Ctrl+End.

Can I make changes from Print Preview?

Let's take a closer look at that Magnifier button. This magnifying glass not only lets you examine things, but it's also your key to editing in the Print Preview window.

Just follow these steps to edit:

1 Display the page you want to edit (if you are using Multiple Page view, click the appropriate page).

2 If your pointer isn't in the shape of a magnifying glass already, click the Magnifier button, then click in the text you'd like to edit.

3 Click the Magnifier button again to return your mouse pointer to normal, then just edit. You can use the menus across the top of the window to change text, format, cut and paste—all the editing stuff you usually do in Word.

4 When you're editing in Print Preview, you can also change margins. Just display the rulers by clicking the View Rulers button, and drag the margin boundaries wherever you want them to be.

5 When you finish editing, click the Magnifier again, then click the page. You return to your original Print Preview view.

 {Note} When you use the ruler to change margins, the change applies to the current section only. If you have several sections, you need to change each one, or make your change through the Page Setup dialog box and choose to apply to the Whole Document (see Chapter 11 for more about sections).

Special print jobs: envelopes, labels, and other page sizes

As you create your document, Word composes your pages based on the settings in the Page Setup dialog box. The default settings are letter size (8 1/2" × 11") and portrait orientation.

If that's what you need, you're all set! But if you're going to print envelopes or labels or a legal-size document—or anything other than the default setup—you need to change some things in Word's Page Setup.

> ❝ *Plain English, please!*
>
> Although it sounds like your first day on a new job, **orientation** is actually Word's way of defining which edge of the paper is at the top of your document. If your text prints out parallel to the short edge of the paper (the way most letters are printed), you're printing in **Portrait orientation**. If the top of the page runs parallel to the long edge of the paper (a good way to present information-packed tables), you're printing in **Landscape orientation**. ❞

Going to the source: knowing your paper

To give Word specific instructions about your paper size and orientation, choose File, Page Setup, and select the Paper Size tab to see the dialog box shown in figure 8.2.

Fig. 8.2
This tab in the Page
Setup dialog box not
only lets you choose
specific paper sizes and
orientation, it lets you
see how your choices
will look.

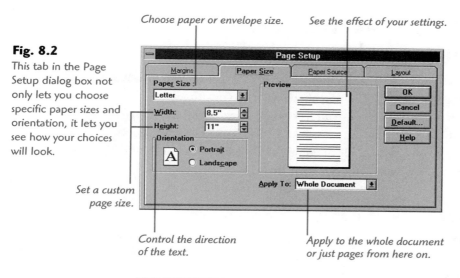

Choose paper or envelope size.

See the effect of your settings.

Set a custom
page size.

Control the direction
of the text.

Apply to the whole document
or just pages from here on.

①(Tip)

> It's a good idea to set your orientation before you begin your document
> because this setting affects your margins and page length. Changing these after
> you've already typed in a lot of text usually involves a lot of extra steps—and
> sometimes a few aspirin.

Use this dialog box to switch from standard paper to legal size (8 1/2" × 14")
or the slightly larger European A5 paper. For labels and envelopes, however,
it's probably easiest to use the <u>T</u>ools menu, which is described in the next
section.

①(Tip)

> You can also change the source for your paper by clicking the <u>P</u>aper Source tab
> in the Page Setup dialog box. You can choose to have a different source for
> the first page of your document, which is handy if you print letters with the first
> page on letterhead stationery. Choose the tray with letterhead paper for the
> first page and the tray with plain paper for the rest of your document.

Envelopes and labels? They're a little different...

If you want to print envelopes or labels, you need to give Word some precise and detailed information about where to position each block of text. If you've got a ruler and a spare afternoon, you can set up each page by hand. Or you can do it the easy way. Choose Tools, Envelopes and Labels, then use the Envelopes and Labels dialog box to enter all the information in a few seconds. You can even print right from this dialog box.

Labels by the sheet or one-by-one

Typically, labels come in sheets designed to slide right through your printer; you can print onto the whole sheet, if you're doing a mass mailing, or pick one label from the sheet if you just want to send out a single package. Simply choose Tools, Envelopes and Labels, and select the Labels tab of the dialog box in figure 8.3.

 **{Note}**

Microsoft has standardized its label choices to the products of a company called Avery. Avery creates about every size label that fits about every need. If you use another label brand, it's very likely to match one of Avery's standard sizes. Just check its dimensions against the Avery labels and you're sure to find a match. If not, you can always create a custom label.

Fig. 8.3
The Labels tab of the Envelopes and Labels dialog box is a simple way to get a whole sheet of labels.

Type the address (or other text) for the label here.

Select here to print a single label or a whole sheet of labels.

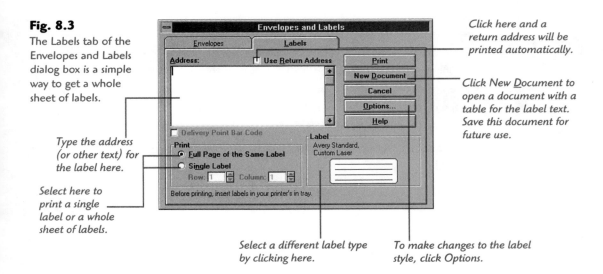

Click here and a return address will be printed automatically.

Click New Document to open a document with a table for the label text. Save this document for future use.

Select a different label type by clicking here.

To make changes to the label style, click Options.

When you click Use Return Address in the Envelopes and Labels dialog box, Word plugs in the information you entered in the User Info section of the Tools, Options dialog box. If you want to use a different return address, click the Envelopes tab and type the new address; when you print, Word will ask whether you want to make this the new default address.

If you want to select a different label style, click Options, which brings up the dialog box in figure 8.4, and then Details, which brings up the dialog box in figure 8.5. With these you can choose a different label product, different label style numbers, or even customize the label size.

Fig. 8.4
This dialog box can be used to change your label size.

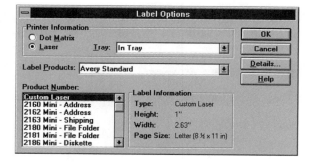

Fig. 8.5
This dialog box can be used to customize your label size.

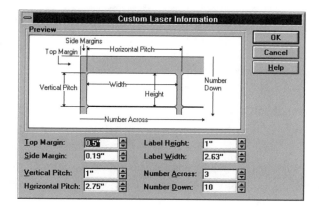

If you have a single blank label left on a sheet, don't throw the sheet away! Choose to print a single label, then designate the row and column location of the blank label and Word will print that specific label only, assuming you've got all the correct information about the label style.

Envelopes in every size and shape

It's amazing how many people stuff their perfectly printed letters into envelopes and then address them by hand. Why? Because they're hopelessly confused by the way most word processors handle envelopes. Not Word. With most laser printers, Word makes it a cinch to print envelopes. You type in the delivery address in the dialog box in figure 8.6. If you don't want a return address, click O<u>m</u>it.

Fig. 8.6
Preview the way your envelope will print from this dialog box.

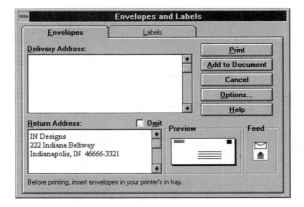

To choose a different envelope size, click <u>O</u>ptions to see the dialog box in figure 8.7.

At the bottom of the Envelope <u>S</u>ize drop-down list is Custom Size. Click this to get one more dialog box where you can type in specific measurements for a custom envelope size.

Fig. 8.7
From here you can choose to print a bar code for the delivery location, change the font you use for either address, and select from a drop-down list of envelope sizes.

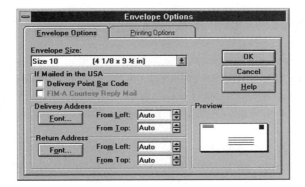

Keeping envelopes and labels under control

Maybe you're worried that there's a special wing in the psychiatric ward of your local hospital reserved especially for people who've snapped under the strain of envelope and label printing. You figure you'll end up there someday, whimpering softly and clutching a fistful of crunched #10's and sheets and sheets of misaligned labels. Printing envelopes and labels isn't all that bad. Trust me.

First of all, you should take advantage of some features in Word that help you get ready to print envelopes or labels. Start with the Mail Merge Helper. If you want to print several envelopes or labels from a list of names and addresses, the Helper can walk you through the process almost painlessly. (See Chapter 21 for more about mail merge.)

If a label sheet is page size (8 1/2" × 11"), just place the sheet in your printer tray. Face up?

Face down? That depends on your printer. You can find out fast by marking one side of a plain piece of paper, putting it in your printer face up, and printing a sample sheet of labels. If they appear on the marked side, you've got it right. If not, remember to feed your labels through the printer upside-down.

For envelopes, click the little picture of an envelope under the word Feed in the Envelopes tab of the Envelopes and Labels dialog box. It gives you a whole dialog box devoted to how you should feed your envelopes into your printer.

Labels and envelopes aren't cheap, so spare yourself some heartache. If you're printing a large quantity of either, always try a test run on plain paper first; that way you can be sure you're set up properly before you do the real print run.

Okay, let's print this thing!

After you've set up everything just right, or if all the default settings suit you just fine, click the Print button from either the main document window or the Print Preview window, and that's it. No options, no dialog boxes—your document goes straight to the printer, probably without any problems.

But what if you want to change a few things first? For example, you might want to print only pages 2 through 6. Or maybe you want to print two copies instead of one. These and other options are found in the Print dialog box.

Talking to the Print dialog box

To set some specific printing choices, choose File, Print to get to the Print dialog box shown in figure 8.8.

Fig. 8.8

Maybe you just want to print one page to make sure everything's working right, or you need more than one copy. You can tell Word what you want, right here.

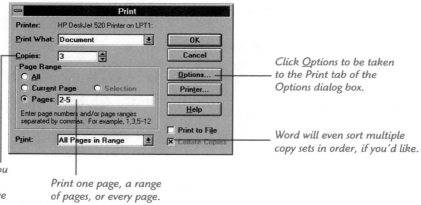

Click Options to be taken to the Print tab of the Options dialog box.

Word will even sort multiple copy sets in order, if you'd like.

Print as many copies as you like; type a number here, or click the arrows to move the number up or down.

Print one page, a range of pages, or every page.

Just select the number of copies you want to print, then the range of pages to print. If you want to print things like hidden text, or the summary information for the document, check out the Print What drop-down list.

Plain English, please!

Hidden is an effect you can apply to text in the Font dialog box. It's useful when you want to add notes that you can see on-screen but don't want to see on the printed page.

You can change some other printing settings by clicking <u>O</u>ptions. This takes you into the Print tab of the Options dialog box, which lets you do things like print the pages in reverse order (so that page 1 comes out on top), or print just the data in forms and not the forms themselves.

 What if I just want to print two paragraphs from the middle of page 7? Do I have to cut and paste those to a new document to do that?

Good question! It's easier than you think. Just select the text you want to print first, then in the Print dialog box, click Selectio<u>n</u>, and just the selected text will print.

Print it!

 If you're in the Print dialog box, just click OK to print. If you're in either the Print Preview or main Word view, just click the Print button, and your document prints.

If you ever have a change of heart about something you've just told your computer to print, quickly double-click on the Print symbol that appears in the status bar—it's where the time usually appears. That will cancel the order.

 All those borders I put in my document aren't printing! What's wrong?

If you choose <u>D</u>raft Output in the Options dialog box, borders and graphics won't print. Or your computer might be low on memory. Graphics take a lot of memory to display or print. If your system runs low on memory, the graphics may not print.

Print Manager: cancel that order!

When you click a button to print something in Word, all the information about the print job is sent to Windows—its local printing company. Now, if you're sitting at your own computer, staring at your own private printer, you know that your job is going to come purring out of the printer right away. But if you share a network and printer with other people, you have to wait your turn.

In Windows, the Print Manager takes the printing information and lines it up in the order it's received. Then each print job is printed as it reaches the front of the line.

If you want to see how your print job is coming, you can go to the Windows Program Manager. You'll find Print Manager hanging out in the Main window. Double-click to open it; it shows you the jobs in a listing called the **print queue**, along with the status of each. To delete your print job from here, click it in the list, and click Delete.

 **{Note}**

If you try to close Print Manager while a job is printing, you'll see a warning message telling you that you're about to cancel all print jobs in progress. If you don't want to interrupt things, just click the Minimize button—the down arrow in the top right corner of the window—and you can get Print Manager out of the way without canceling anything.

Part III:

Dressing Up Documents

Simple Ways to Make Text Attractive

Odds are, you wouldn't attend a board of directors meeting in jeans. Just as clothes make the man—or woman—you can use formatting to make your text attractive and persuasive.

If you expect to be noticed, you'd better pay attention to your appearance, because how you dress sends an unmistakable message to the world. Do you want to blend into the background? Do you want to be taken seriously? Do you want heads to swivel when you walk through the door? What you wear helps create that image.

The documents you create represent you just as surely as the clothes you wear, so why not dress for success here as well? Your wardrobe consists of **formatting**—the art of applying "style" to the numbers and letters in your document. The right font, in the right size, with appropriate use of bold or italic characters or a little underlining, can create just the right impression.

Word for Windows provides an impressive ensemble of fonts and effects you can use to create different looks for different purposes. A business letter looks swell in Times New Roman—the typographical equivalent of a conservative gray suit and dark blue tie. But that sales piece might want to walk through the door with a grand gesture, like the ***Impact font in bold and italic***—just be careful you don't look like you've paired a plaid sports jacket with a paisley tie!

What's a font, anyway?

A **font** is simply a common look applied to all the letters, numbers, symbols, and punctuation marks that make up type. You probably know two or three ways to write the letter *a*. A font, or typeface, gives you dozens or hundreds of ways to present those symbols. Different fonts use different line thicknesses, ornaments, angles, and sizes to represent symbols that you'll recognize as letters and numbers. Think of the difference between a classic Humphrey Bogart-style trench coat (Times New Roman) and a shocking yellow slicker (Benguiat Frisky).

Believe it or not, fonts live in families (see fig. 9.1). Within each of these families, there are fat, skinny, tall, and, distinguished individuals—just like most families you know.

Fig. 9.1
Font families have
distinct personalities.

FAT FONT FAMILY

SKINNY FONT FAMILY

JUST PLAIN FOLKS

THE RICH AND FAMOUS

How to choose the right font

First, a word of advice. If you're like most people, when you first discover fonts, you'll probably go wild, applying too many of them to your document. A document with more than three fonts is sure to make your reader go cross-eyed and dizzy. A font-laden page looks more like a ransom note. Select your fonts judicially. The two most common fonts for business correspondence are Times New Roman or Arial, both available with all versions of Windows. You can buy more fonts (make sure they're TrueType fonts, the type supported by Windows) for documents that need more dressing up, or for your personal correspondence.

Dressing up text with Word

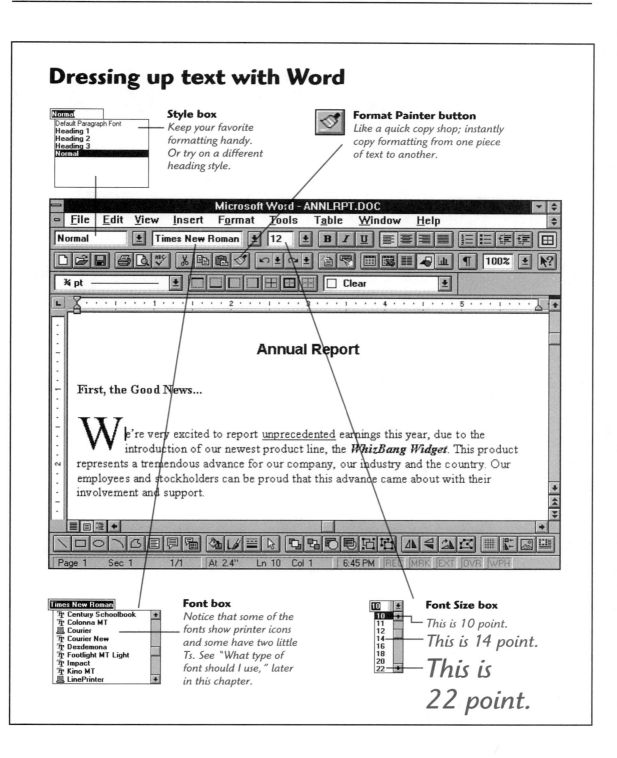

Style box
Keep your favorite formatting handy. Or try on a different heading style.

Format Painter button
Like a quick copy shop; instantly copy formatting from one piece of text to another.

Font box
Notice that some of the fonts show printer icons and some have two little Ts. See "What type of font should I use," later in this chapter.

Font Size box
This is 10 point.
This is 14 point.
This is 22 point.

The following table shows common typefaces in different styles.

Typeface	Regular	Bold	Italic
Times New Roman	Times	**Times**	*Times*
Helvetica	Helvetica	**Helvetica**	*Helvetica*
Courier	Courier	**Courier**	*Courier*

Trying on a font

Applying a font to your text is simple. Open the Font drop-down list on the Formatting toolbar. Notice that the fonts you've used most recently appear in a separate list at the top of the complete font list. Word assumes that if you choose a font once, you'll probably want to use it again as you work, so it makes it easy for you to access it. All the fonts are listed in alphabetical order.

Depending on what you want to format, do one of the following:

- Select the font family you prefer in the Font drop-down list before you begin typing, and your entire document will appear in that font.

- If you want to change the font you're using, you simply select another font from the menu and everything you type from that point on will appear in that font.

- Finally, you might want to change the font for text you've already typed. Simply select the text you want to change, then choose the font you prefer from the drop-down list.

 (Tip)

To try on different fonts quickly, select the text you want to format, go to the Format menu, and choose Font. In the Font dialog box, you can select any font in the Font list (see fig. 9.2). The Preview box shows how the text will look.

Fig. 9.2

To get to this dialog box, also try clicking on the right mouse button and selecting Font; but be sure to select the text first.

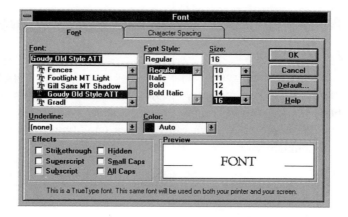

Finding the right size for your text

As we all know, one size does not fit all. Kareem Abdul-Jabbar's sport coat just wouldn't look right on Willie Shoemaker. As you can see in figure 9.3, the same is true of typography. A bold, attention-grabbing heading needs to be set in very large type, while a detailed footnote feels just right in letters you need a magnifying glass to see.

Fig. 9.3

From fine print to text that fairly shouts, type size helps you make text dramatic.

Department Budget

Department Budget

Department Budget

Department Budget

Type size is measured in something called **points**. The typical type size for most business document text is 12 points, but you might want to have titles and headings in a little larger type.

 Plain English, please!

Point is a pretty obscure term. Basically, it's 1/72 of an inch. So, 12 points (commonly abbreviated *pt*) is 1/6 of an inch. Naturally, then, a 72-pt font is 1-inch high, and a 6-pt font is barely legible—perfect for insurance policies.

Making little type bigger, or big type smaller

Now and then for emphasis or design reasons, you'll want to change the size of your type. For example, you might choose to have headings larger than the body text of your document to call attention to them; or you might put a disclaimer about your warranty in very small type so that it can only be read with a magnifying glass.

Changing type size is simple to do in Word:

1 Select the text you'd like to change.

2 Using the font size drop-down list, either type in a custom point size or choose one from the list by clicking it.

3 You can also change type size of selected text in the Font dialog box, and see the effect on the sample text in the Preview box. Just choose F<u>o</u>rmat, <u>F</u>onts.

 **<Caution>**

If you have placed tabs in your document, changing the type size part way through your document may cause your text to realign in odd ways. For that reason, it's recommended that you use paragraph formatting rather than manual tabs in your text. See Chapter 10 for more information about formatting your paragraphs.

Showing off with bold, italic, and underline

Back in the days of typewriters, the best you could do to make your text stand out was to CAPITALIZE IT or <u>underline it</u>. Word offers several ways for you to make a fashion statement with your text. Adding a touch of bold, underline, or italic to your text is a great way to place emphasis on important ideas or words. But remember: the first rule of accessorizing is, never overdo. For example, **boldface can be annoying** when applied to text in the middle of the document. You should reserve this look for headings and titles. *And* *too much italic is a pain in the neck (it can cause the reader to tilt his or her head to read the text).* For the most effective usage of italic, apply it to one word *or* a short phrase.

And, most importantly, use underline only if your company insists on that style for certain types of text (like headings), or for publication titles in bibliographies. Otherwise, this style should remain with typewriters, <u>where it belongs</u>. It's just too low-tech.

How do I change the style of my text?

When you want to make a statement with any of these three effects, you can do it quickly by using the buttons on the toolbar:

1 Click the appropriate button or buttons, then type the text that you want to appear with that effect.

2 Click the button(s) again to turn off the effect(s).

What type of font should I use?

The fonts you see when you are in Word for Windows actually belong to Windows, not Word. Windows comes with a standard wardrobe of fourteen fonts. These are called **TrueType** fonts, and they have a little TT symbol next to them in the Font list in Word. Also, any third-party TrueType font gets that little icon.

You're not limited to TrueType fonts, though. If you have a PostScript printer, you'd probably want to use PostScript fonts. Many printers come with *resident* fonts (i.e., built into the printer) that are available to use from any Windows application once you install the printer driver and accompanying setup disk.

If you have an inkjet or dot-matrix printer, you can either select the resident fonts or regular TrueType fonts. Printing using resident fonts is usually faster. If you have a printer that supports the PCL language (PCL5, PCL4, etc.), there are resident scalable fonts similar to the TrueType offering in Windows. Read your printer's manual to find out what types of resident fonts, if any, it supports.

3 You can also apply the effect to text you've already typed. Just select the text you want to change, and click the appropriate button.

4 To remove the effect, select the text and click the button again.

Most of the buttons on the toolbar are **toggle** buttons. This means that the same action that makes one thing happen can make the thing un-happen; you click once to apply the effect and click again to remove it.

If you feel more comfortable with keyboard operations than with mouse-clicks, try these keystrokes:

Ctrl+B	**Bold**
Ctrl+I	*Italic*
Ctrl+U	<u>Underline</u>

Yikes! I just made my whole document bold, italic, and underlined! How do I get rid of it all?

You can use the Undo tool on the toolbar to take back the effects you just applied. If you did three things in a row (say bold, then italic, then underline), when you click the arrow next to the Undo button, you get a list of your last actions. Select the last three actions (bold, italic, and underline), and the effects are reversed, as though they never happened.

Trying on special effects and color

Clothes serve different functions. Some are purely practical, like warm gloves or work boots. Others are for show: that paisley silk scarf or flashy Mickey Mouse tie your daughter gave you last Father's Day. Flashy effects should be reserved for flyers, newsletters, and personal correspondence. Business documents don't tolerate too much flash, just like you wouldn't wear that tie to a board meeting.

Practical, non-flashy special effects

Some special effects are down-to-earth text accessories; no flair, and just proper enough for business documents. To see these, choose Format, Font to reach the Font dialog box (see fig. 9.4).

Fig. 9.4
This dialog box is your one-stop shopping center for many of your text formatting needs.

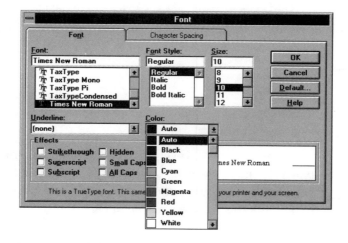

You see a section of choices titled Effects. Here's what they do:

- **Strikethrough.** When you need to see what's changed in a document—maybe one in a series of drafts being reviewed by various people—use ~~strikethrough~~ to indicate text you want to delete.

- **Superscript.** Superscript is used to slightly raise text above the preceding text and make it smaller. This effect is used in equations as in $(a+b)^2$, and with some symbols like copyright or registered trademarks (Copyright $^{\copyright}$ 1995) or the symbol for temperature degrees (32°).

  Subscript. Pretty much the opposite of superscript: this lowers one or more characters below others, as in chemical symbols (H_2O).

- **Hidden.** Say you're printing a memo about the budget and payroll. You may want your supervisors to see every employee's salary, but you don't want the employees to see what their colleagues earn. So you print one version of the document with all the text showing, then select the sensitive text and apply the Hidden effect to it before you print the censored version.

> **¶** When you need to unhide text, select the hidden area, press the right mouse button, select Font, and look at the check box next to Hidden. It's gray, and there's no X in it. Click it once to get an X, and once more to deselect it. For a faster alternative, press Ctrl+Shift+H on the selected area; this is a toggle option, so you can use it to hide or to unhide. To print all the hidden text (even though you can't see it on-screen), choose File, Print, Options, and click the check box next to Hidden text.

- **Small Caps.** This makes every lowercase letter a small capital. It's an interesting effect, which should be reserved for headings and titles, because it Looks Odd Elsewhere.

- **All Caps.** This makes every letter capitalized, LIKE THIS. If you've typed text in all lowercase and realize that it should be in all uppercase, you don't need to erase and re-type. Just select the text and then this option. But this can be achieved much faster by pressing Shift+F3 on the selected text. Press this key combination repeatedly, and it will cycle you through all lowercase, all uppercase, and initial cap.

Color me happy

Color can add life to a document, but it can also fail if you don't use it right. On-screen color makes certain parts of the text stand out. But if you print out a letter with blue, green, and red all over the page, it's sure to look childish.

The only types of documents that beg for color are commonly known as *desktop publishing* documents, such as flyers, newsletters, greeting cards, and so on.

To add color to your text, select it, press the right mouse button, select Font, and click the drop-down arrow next to Color to choose a color. The Preview box gives you a good idea of what the resulting effect will look like.

> Aside from on-screen color, which you can use to make portions of your text stand out, color makes sense only if you have a color printer.

Copy great formats instantly with Format Painter

You've just finished dressing up one paragraph with all kinds of special effects. Before you celebrate, you realize that another paragraph needs to have the same look. But have no fear—you don't need to labor over the second paragraph. Just copy the format. Here's how:

1 Select the text that has the format you want to copy.

2 Click the Format Painter button, which gives you a little paintbrush pointer.

3 Next, select the text you want to change.

That's it! Any formatting you've applied to the first area is applied to the second.

When you want to apply the same format to more than one area, you must repeat the Format Painter process discussed above. But here's a shortcut: double-click the Format Painter button before you apply the format to the target text, and you'll have a paintbrush cursor for as long as you need to apply that format. When you're done copying the format, click the button again to turn it off.

10

Formatting Lines and Paragraphs

Creating a balance of space and text in your document is like decorating a room: get rid of clutter, set special things apart, and give your visitors a place to rest.

In this chapter:

- How can I get my headline to center on the page?
- I'd like to double-space this paragraph
- Is there a way to indent a whole paragraph quickly?
- The last word of this paragraph is printing at the top of the next page—how can I stop it?
- This list would look better with bullets

What if you filled your living room with furniture, floor to ceiling, so that you couldn't even see the walls? You probably wouldn't win an award from *Better Homes and Gardens*. Why? Because the clean white space of your walls is as much a part of your interior design as the furniture. And let's not forget that you want to *live* in your living room, not just look at it, which means you ought to be able to move about freely without bumping into chairs and tables.

An uncluttered, well-designed document should be as comfortable as your living room. Just as a little space around a picture can make it the visual centerpiece of a room, the judicious use of indentation or bullet characters can draw your readers to the most important part of the page.

Word gives you all sorts of tools to help you make your readers feel at home. Breaks between paragraphs add a bit of breathing room between topics. Extra spacing between lines makes long blocks of text easier on the eyes. Neatly indented sections and numbered lists separate special information in a way that's easy for readers to follow.

Putting text in its place

You probably first encountered margins in your notebook in grade school. They had thin blue or red lines down the sides of the pages and you learned to write inside of them. But you also learned to center your title in the middle of the page. See, margins determine how much space you can fill on the page, but **alignment** determines how you fill the space between the margins.

Use alignment differently for different types of documents or pieces of your documents. In an invitation, for example, you want to put all your information center stage. In business documents like reports and letters, you line the main body text up to the left because we read from left to right. And numbers, which all need to add up on the bottom line, fan out from the right margin so that the final digits line up properly. You use text alignment to reflect the kind of information you're conveying and to help readers see that information the way you want them to.

Which alignment should I use?

A single document, like the one in figure 10.1, can have centered, justified, left-aligned, and right-aligned text. You can change your alignment as many times as you like within your document (but you need to stick to one alignment choice per paragraph).

 (Tip)

> If you need different alignments in a single line, use the table feature (each cell of a table can have its own format). See Chapter 14 for more information on tables.

Fig. 10.1
Word understands that different types of text require different alignments. Centered, right-aligned, or left-aligned, it's all easy in Word.

This heading is centered.

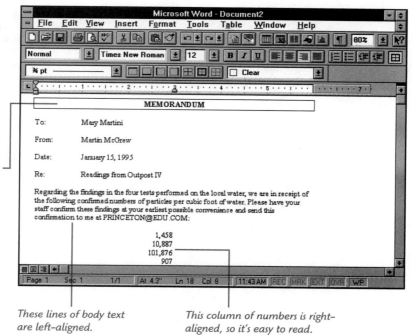

These lines of body text are left-aligned.

This column of numbers is right-aligned, so it's easy to read.

66 *Plain English, please!*

In Word, **justified** text is stretched across the page so that the text completely fills the space between the margins instead of leaving a ragged edge on the right. To make this possible, Word takes the space that would be left at the end of the line and distributes it between words. A paragraph of justified text forms a perfect block on the page, which looks nice in something like a newsletter column, but those unusual letter spacings make text more difficult to read in large blocks like letters. 99

In general, alignment goes like this:

- By default, body text in your Word documents is left-aligned; text is lined up against the left margin, and the ends of lines on the right side of your page form a ragged edge (like the text in this book).

- You often use right-alignment for lining up columns of numbers.

- Justified text looks good in some documents, as shown in figure 10.2.

Fig. 10.2

Some people prefer the look of justified text; Word lets you decide.

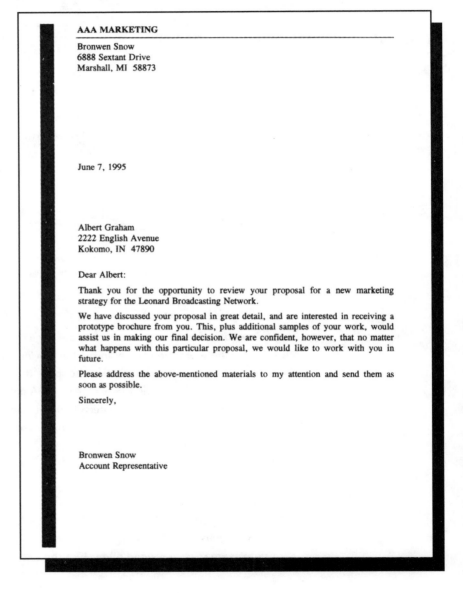

AAA MARKETING

Bronwen Snow
6888 Sextant Drive
Marshall, MI 58873

June 7, 1995

Albert Graham
2222 English Avenue
Kokomo, IN 47890

Dear Albert:

Thank you for the opportunity to review your proposal for a new marketing strategy for the Leonard Broadcasting Network.

We have discussed your proposal in great detail, and are interested in receiving a prototype brochure from you. This, plus additional samples of your work, would assist us in making our final decision. We are confident, however, that no matter what happens with this particular proposal, we would like to work with you in future.

Please address the above-mentioned materials to my attention and send them as soon as possible.

Sincerely,

Bronwen Snow
Account Representative

- Centering is used for headlines, or documents that are completely centered, such as the invitation in figure 10.3.

(Tip)

When shouldn't you use justified text? Those straight blocks give a document a very formal look, so save them for side-by-side columns and boxed text. Also, make sure you have enough text to justify. A good rule of thumb: on average, there should be at least seven words of text per line so that Word has enough gaps in which to distribute the leftover space.

Fig. 10.3
A typical invitation centers all the text.

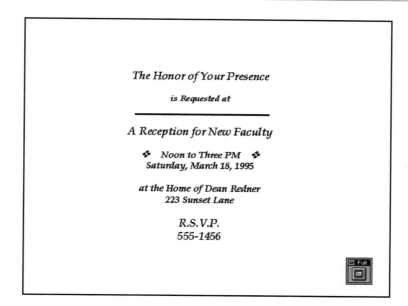

I know what alignment I want; how do I tell Word?

Word handles alignment with four buttons on the toolbar, shown in figure 10.4. These little helpers make aligning text a snap.

Fig. 10.4
Make your alignment changes instantly with these four buttons.

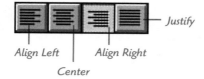

All you do is select the text you want to align, or just put your mouse pointer anywhere in a paragraph if you want to format just that paragraph; then click the appropriate button, and that's it.

⊛ {Note}

You can also use keystroke shortcuts to align text:

Alignment	Keystroke
Center	Ctrl+E
Left	Ctrl+L
Right	Ctrl+R
Justify	Ctrl+J

How can I make a paragraph stand out on the page?

Perhaps you want to give your readers a clue that they're about to read an important block of information that stands apart from the text above and below. You might want to draw attention to a key quote (like the one in fig. 10.5) or a warning, for example. To give a paragraph special placement, use **indenting**—shift one or both sides of the text away from the margin, leaving a little white space.

Some documents identify the start of a new paragraph by indenting the first line, as in figure 10.6. Others set off important information, like a warning, in an indented section.

How to do it

Word offers you a few ways to indent text:

- Use buttons on the toolbar. This is quick and easy, but moves you in automatic increments of 5 spaces at a time and moves only whole paragraphs.

- Manipulate the indent markers that are located on the ruler. This gives you more freedom to set any increment you want, and also to move the first line of a paragraph to the left or right of the rest of the paragraph.

Fig. 10.5
To set off a block of text, such as a long quote, indent it.

The Viability of Rainforests
Third Environmental Conference, 1996

In fact, after careful analysis, our findings confirmed this. There were three occurrences of this which were of any significance at all.

The first occurrence was in March of this year. Dr. Randell and his group had been set up near the river for three weeks when the cloud appeared. Randell recalls the event:

> We had pitched tents so as to get a good view of the stretch of rainforest across the river, thinking that we could observe any pollution cloud activity better from that vantage point. Dr. Cocchiarelli awoke first on the morning of the 15th, and noted some unusual activity among the animals in the forest, as well as a reddish tint to the sky. That was our first clue that something was amiss.

When the cloud appeared, Dr. Randell and his team were able to analyze the ratio of carbon monoxide using the XJ-17 cathode analyzer, which gives readings accurate to within .003 factors.

The results confirmed the earlier findings of the Raintree 7 expedition. All particles appeared as in that study, however the intensity was greater. There are three theories about this:

- The weather at that time of year was drier, so more particles were able to survive in the atmosphere

- The equipment accuracy was not as great as that used by Raintree 7, so a variance must be taken into account

- The proximity of a tree farming operation only 10 miles away, with accompanying machinery and human habitation, could have intensified the findings

Fig. 10.6
Each paragraph begins with an indentation.

GREEN THUMB NURSERIES

4 Nursery Way
Santa Barbara, CA 98890

Green Thumb Opens New Store

A West-side Branch of Green Thumb Opens

For Immediate Release

Thursday, January 05, 1995

**Contact: Mark "Jolly" Harris
Green Thumb Nursery
(805) 933-3333**

Santa Barbara, CA—Today, Green Thumb Nurseries of Montecito announced the opening of a new nursery location on the west side of Santa Barbara.

Says Mark Harris, President of Green Thumb, "we feel we can better serve the needs of our many customers with an additional location. Interest in our landscaping services, begun last Spring, has surprised even us."

With the addition of landscaping services, as well as expanded inventory of trees, gardening supplies and rental equipment, Green Thumb has experienced its most successful year in its 35 years in business.

The store will be located in the 3000 block of West Main Street, opposite the Safeway store, and should open sometime in March.

 Although it's tempting, NEVER use Tab or the space bar to indent text. This can give you uneven alignment when you actually print a document. Also, if you use Tab to indent each line in a paragraph, then add or delete text from the paragraph later, the lines will be out of whack.

Indenting with buttons

 You can use two buttons on the toolbar for indenting paragraphs relative to the left margin: Decrease Indent and Increase Indent. They work on the paragraph you're typing; just stop typing, click one of these buttons, and the paragraph is shifted.

Or, you can select a paragraph or series of paragraphs, then click one of these buttons and it'll shift that paragraph to the left or right.

Indenting using the ruler

 The second way to indent a paragraph is to use the on-screen ruler. There's a little symbol on the left edge of the ruler that looks something like an hourglass standing on a little box. By clicking and dragging parts of this symbol, you can indent the selected paragraph or the paragraph your insertion point is in at the moment. The indent can be as large or as small as you want, depending upon how far you drag the symbol. You can see how the different settings work in figure 10.7. Here's how it works:

- Click and drag the top triangle to indent the first line only to the right of the rest of the paragraph.

- Click and drag the bottom triangle (that and the little block move together) to create a hanging indent, where the first line is to the left of the rest of the paragraph.

- Click and drag the block underneath the "hourglass" (all three pieces move together) to indent the whole paragraph.

Fig. 10.7
The ruler makes it easy
to shift things around.

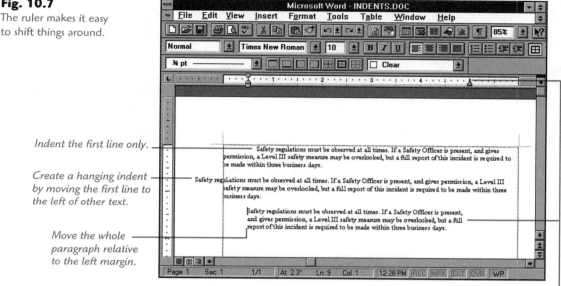

Indent the first line only.

Create a hanging indent
by moving the first line to
the left of other text.

Move the whole
paragraph relative
to the left margin.

Drag this triangle to indent
from the right margin.

You can also use the little triangle on the right side of the ruler to indent your
paragraph in from the right margin.

 **{Note}**

You can also change indentation settings by choosing Format, Paragraph. This
gives you a preview of how your change will look and allows you to set specific
measurements for your indentation.

Spacing out between the lines

In the same way that you need to leave room between rows of chairs so
people can get to their seat easily, you have to leave enough room between
lines of text so that a reader can get around your document easily. You can

adjust the spaces between the lines of your paragraph to make the document easier to read. You can also determine how much line space separates your paragraphs from each other.

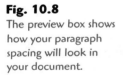

The exact size of line spacing is determined by the size typeface you have. If you're using 10-point type, single line spacing gives you about 10 points between two lines of text, and double line spacing gives you about 20 points. The largest text in a line will determine the size of the space: that's why, if you ever make one word really big in the middle of the paragraph, the spacing around that one line looks different from the rest of the paragraph.

You control line spacing in the Paragraph dialog box; just do the following:

1 Place your insertion point in the paragraph in which you want to change the spacing, or select several paragraphs if you want to adjust more than one.

2 Choose F**o**rmat, **P**aragraph. The Paragraph dialog box appears; make sure the **I**ndents and Spacing tab is displayed (see fig. 10.8).

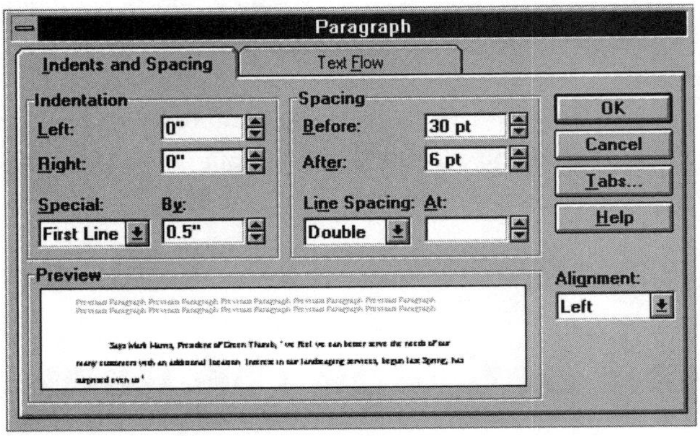

Fig. 10.8
The preview box shows how your paragraph spacing will look in your document.

![Paragraph dialog box with Indents and Spacing tab, showing Indentation (Left: 0", Right: 0"), Special: First Line, By: 0.5", Spacing (Before: 30 pt, After: 6 pt), Line Spacing: Double, Alignment: Left, and a Preview area. Buttons: OK, Cancel, Tabs..., Help]

3 In the Li**n**e Spacing box, click the arrow to produce a drop-down list of options, and then select one of the options (Single, 1.5, Double, At Least, Exactly, Multiple).

If you choose At Least, Exactly, or Multiple, go to the **A**t box and type or select the amount of line spacing you want.

{Note} If you want to set your own spacing, or change spacing before a line but not after it, indicate in the <u>B</u>efore box of the Spacing section the amount of space you want to precede the first line of your paragraph (type in the amount or use the arrows to increase or reduce the number in the box). The Preview box shows how your choice will look. You can do the same thing in the Aft<u>e</u>r box.

Putting in breaks

Now that everything's spaced right, you might want to check one final thing about your paragraphs: are they headed for a messy break-up?

Word automatically breaks your document into pages as you type. But sometimes Word breaks to a new page in a really bad spot—right before the last word of a paragraph, for example, leaving it dangling at the top of a page like a loose muffler on an old Chevy. You can avoid this mess by telling Word where it can and cannot separate your text.

Breaking up paragraphs (or keeping them together)

Word can keep lines of a paragraph together for you. The Text <u>F</u>low tab, shown in figure 10.9, lets you control how page breaks divide your text. You reach this tab by choosing F<u>o</u>rmat, <u>P</u>aragraph, Text <u>F</u>low.

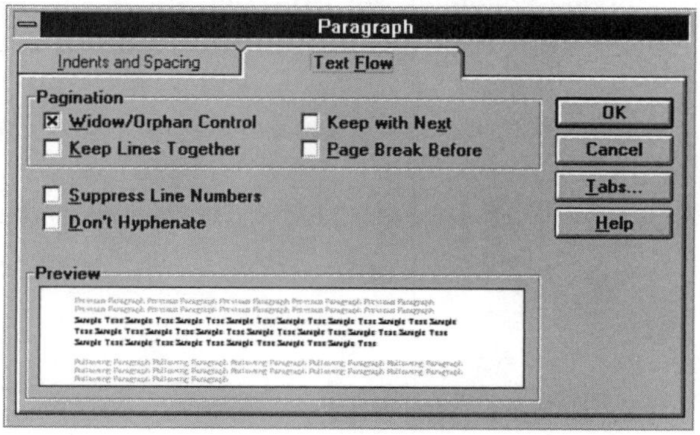

Fig. 10.9
The Text <u>F</u>low tab is your key to controlling how your text is divided in Word.

Here are some ways you can use the options in the Text Flow tab:

- To make sure that at least two lines of a paragraph appear on a single page, click the Widow/Orphan Control option in the Text Flow tab.

Plain English, please!

In typesetting lingo, the terms **widow** and **orphan** refer to one line of a paragraph stranded at the beginning or end of a page, respectively.

- Say you have a paragraph consisting of a several-line quote that you want to keep in one piece on a page. No problem! First, highlight the paragraph you want to preserve as one chunk. Then choose Text Flow and click Keep Lines Together.

- If you want to keep paragraphs together, say a heading and the paragraph that follows it, position the mouse cursor in the first paragraph, choose the Text Flow tab, and then click Keep with Next.

If you want to keep a group of paragraphs together, select all but the last paragraph, choose the Text Flow tab, and click Keep with Next.

Making pages break where you want them to

You can also determine what information stays on one page by inserting your own page break. When you tell Word that you want a page break at a specific point, it inserts the break and adjusts the rest of the document accordingly.

To insert a page break quickly, put the insertion point where you want the break to occur, and press Ctrl+Enter. Word inserts the page break and displays it on-screen. To delete the page break immediately, press Backspace. Or you can select the page break and press Delete.

It's easy to make great-looking lists in Word

Ever notice how, during an argument, if you want to make your point clearly and with emphasis, you resort to lists? "A) I didn't tape over your movie, and B) it's a stupid movie to begin with!" Documents are no different. Lists help you organize and emphasize key points or items.

One way to set off a list is by placing a bullet or number in front of each item. A number or letter tends to indicate some priority or order to the list, whereas a bullet just sets off each item neatly.

Use bullets to make each item stand out

 To create a bulleted list, you simply type the list, then select it. Using the toolbar, click the Bullets button. Round bullets (the default style) appear to the left of each of the items on your list. To remove the bullets, select the list again and click the Bullet button to toggle it off.

If you want to use a different style of bullet, do this:

1 Highlight your bulleted list. Choose F<u>o</u>rmat, Bullets and <u>N</u>umbering. The dialog box in figure 10.10 gives you style choices.

2 Click the style you prefer.

3 Click OK.

Presto! You're back in your document, looking at your cool bulleted list.

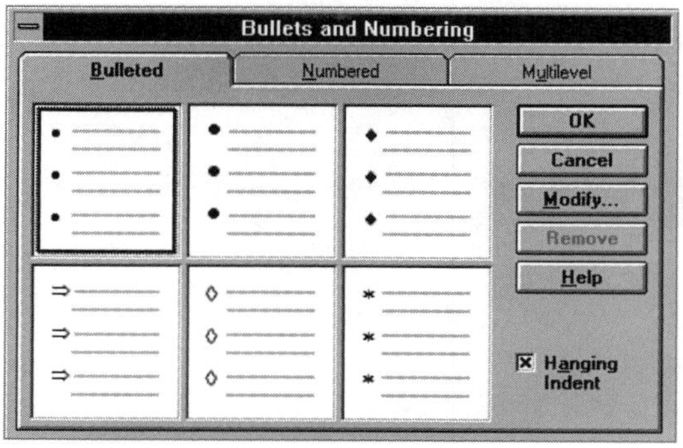

Fig. 10.10
You can choose from six built-in bullet styles.

To be even more creative with your bullets, choose <u>M</u>odify in the Bullets and Numbering dialog box. You get the Modify Bulleted List dialog box. Here you can choose to change the bullets' size, shape, color, and placement.

 (Tip) _____

> If you choose to modify your bullets, click on the button called <u>B</u>ullet in the Modify Bulleted List dialog box. This allows you to choose from any symbol in any available typeface for your bullets, including the Symbol typeface.

Use numbered lists to keep things in order

 Creating numbered lists is very similar to creating bullet lists. Type a list of items, then select it. Click the Numbering button on the toolbar. Your list is numbered with Arabic numerals followed by periods (see fig. 10.11). The Numbering button is also a toggle button; click it again to remove the numbering.

Fig. 10.11
Clicking the Number-
ing button gives your
list simple Arabic
numbers set off with
a period.

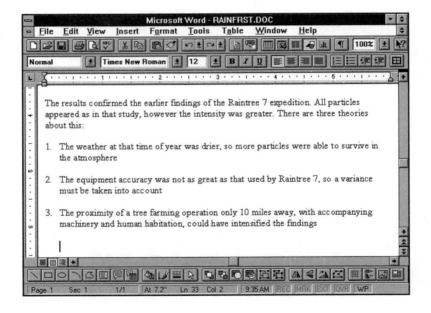

Like bullets, Word offers more than the default style. To choose from a standard list of styles, do this:

1 Highlight your numbered list, then choose F<u>o</u>rmat, Bullets and <u>N</u>umbering. Word puts you into the <u>N</u>umbered tab (see fig. 10.12).

2 Click one of the six numbering styles displayed.

3 Choose OK.

Fig. 10.12

You get a choice of a few different types of numbers or letters in this dialog box. Click <u>M</u>odify to get even more options for customizing numbers.

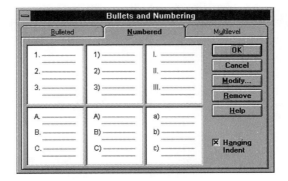

If you want to really spiff up your numbers, click <u>M</u>odify to produce the Modify Numbered List dialog box. In that dialog box you can change the size, font, and placement of numbers. You can also tell Word to place text before or after numbers to create lists that read "Point 1, Point 2," or "First Point, Second Point," and so on.

You can click the M<u>u</u>ltilevel tab in the Bullets and Numbering dialog box and choose numbering styles for outlines (see Chapter 15 for more about outlines).

The Preview section of the Modify Numbered List dialog box lets you see how your choices will look. Try a few combinations until you find just the numbering style you prefer.

{Note}

If you want to put a little more order into your lists, you can sort both bulleted and numbered lists by their content. Select the list you want to sort, and then choose T<u>a</u>ble, Sor<u>t</u> Text. The Sort dialog box appears, where you can choose to sort the list alphabetically, by number, or by date.

11

Setting Things Up: Margins, Tabs, and Hyphens

In most of your documents, margins, tabs, and hyphens just seem to take care of themselves. But when you need to step in, don't worry; Word makes it easy.

In this chapter:

- How do I fit more stuff on a page?
- Okay, I want different margins—but only for this one section
- How do I get rid of all these tabs?
- The right margin is too ragged...I want hyphens!

When you buy something for your house, you can usually just take a standard size off the shelf at Sears. That's because many things in your house come in standard sizes and shapes: windows, plugs, hinges, and so on. But occasionally, you run into something like an oddly sized or shaped window, and you must have custom curtains made.

Margins, tabs, and hyphens are like that. Most of the time, the standard, default settings will fit just fine in your documents. But for some documents that contain specialized information, or when you want to create an extra-special look, you'll have to customize the way Word uses them.

The good news is, it's not difficult to set these up, as long as you know how.

When you design a document, you want to create a balance of text and the white space that falls around or within that text so your reader can get your message quickly and comfortably. Margins, tabs, and hyphens help you arrange text so that it looks good on the page and is easy to read. Margins provide a border around your text, tabs allow you to place text at a particular spot on the page, and hyphens fix lines that have too much white space by automatically breaking up the last word on each line if possible.

Surround your text with margins

Margins are the blank spaces between the text in your document and the edge of your page. If your house were a document, the margins would be the yard that surrounds it. Margin boundaries are usually invisible, but can be shown right on-screen: like the outside walls of your house, they are the lines that mark the beginning of the margins' territory.

Margins have a few purposes:

- They frame your text for a cleaner page design.
- Certain types of text, such as headers and footers and page numbers, are actually placed within the margin itself so they stand out clearly.
- Word places text that you indent relative to margins.

Plain English, please!

Indented text is text that is offset to the left or right of the margin. Sometimes you indent the first line of a paragraph to the right of the rest of the paragraph; you might indent blocks of text such as quotes; or you could indent a note to the left of the left margin boundary, so it actually appears in the margin itself. See Chapter 10 for more about setting indents. 99

The Ruler rules your margins

Your margins are already set at a default 1.25 inches on the sides and 1 inch at the top and bottom when you start a new document. If that's fine with you, just leave them alone.

Looking at rulers, margins, and tabs

The Tab Alignment button sets different styles of tabs.

Header and footer information appears in the margin itself.

Various tabs show as markers along the horizontal ruler.

The horizontal ruler gives you an easy, on-screen way to set side margins and tabs.

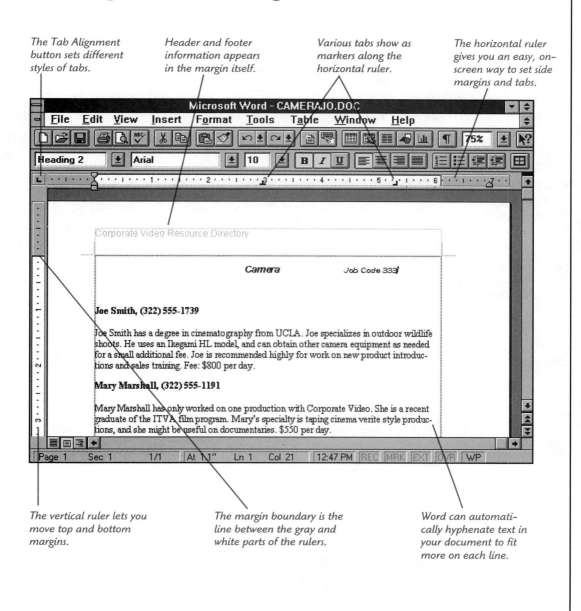

The vertical ruler lets you move top and bottom margins.

The margin boundary is the line between the gray and white parts of the rulers.

Word can automatically hyphenate text in your document to fit more on each line.

But, there are times you might want to change margins. For example:

- To fit more text on a page

- To insert a wide graphic or table

- To set off a block of information

An easy way to set a margin is to use rulers. First, switch to the Page Layout view by clicking the Page Layout View button at the bottom of the Word window. To get the rulers on-screen, choose View, Ruler. You see the horizontal ruler across the top of your document and the vertical ruler down the left side (see fig. 11.1). They have tools for changing both margins and tabs.

Fig. 11.1
Margin settings and tab stops appear right on the ruler.

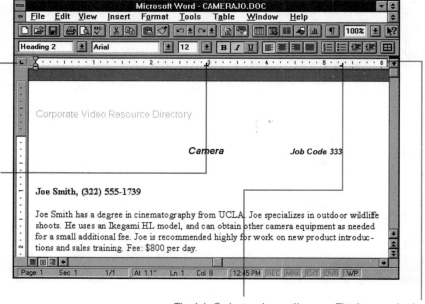

The Tab Alignment button shows what kind of tab you'll create by clicking the ruler.

The heading is placed with a center tab.

The Job Code numbers will line up at the right because of this right tab.

This line marks the right margin boundary.

Getting set

To change the left or right margin, you need to work with the margin boundary markers. Before you can see them, though, you first need to switch to Page Layout view. Now, this part is a little tricky, because the margin boundary markers on the ruler are often hidden by the indent markers—the little triangle shapes on the left and right sides of the ruler.

The margin boundary marker itself is the line between the gray and white portion of the ruler on either side. You'll know you've found it when your mouse pointer turns into a double arrow. Click the margin boundary, drag it to where you want to set the new margin, and release (see fig. 11.2). If a paragraph has been indented to the left or right of the margin, the indented section will move right along and keep its indent relative to the new margin setting.

Fig. 11.2

As you drag the margin boundary marker, a line on the page shows where the new margin boundary will fall.

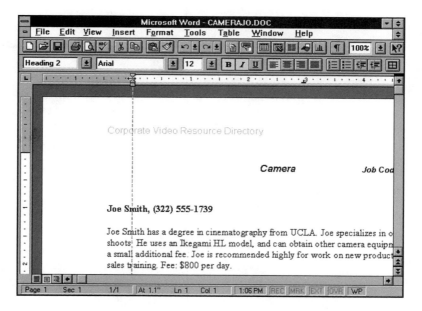

To move the top and bottom margins, use the margin boundary markers on the vertical ruler along the left edge of the Word screen.

 (Tip)

To see the exact measurements while dragging the margin indicator, hold down the Alt key while you drag the two-headed arrow. The tick marks and numbers on the ruler disappear, replaced by indicators that tell you the exact dimensions of the new margin and page width in whatever measurement you've chosen on the General tab in the Options dialog box: inches, picas, points, or centimeters.

Q&A

> **When I drag the left margin, the first line of my paragraph moves over but it doesn't look like the margin's changed at all. What gives?**
>
> The three-piece control on the left side of the horizontal ruler—it looks like an hourglass on a stand (refer to fig. 11.2)—controls indents, not margins, and most of the time it sits on top of the left margin boundary. When you're moving the left margin, be careful to drag the margin boundary and not the indent controls. You can be sure you've clicked the margin boundary by looking for the little two-headed arrow pointer (↔).

Set new margins for one section, or for the whole thing

The **sections** of your Word document are like the rooms in your house: they have some things in common, like doors and walls, but they're each unique. And just as you can decorate each room differently, you can set things like margins and tabs uniquely in each section of your document; the sections of your document can have their own individual settings.

 Plain English, please!

You can set many different **sections** in Word documents. In each section, you can set unique formats, such as margins, headers, and footers. You might want an introductory section of your document to have i, ii, iii, and so on for page numbers, but the main part of the report might have 1, 2, and 3 for page numbers. Or, you might need to include a wide table on one page of your document; you can make it a separate section so that it has extra wide margins. See Chapter 12 for more about sections.

Here's how margins work with sections:

- If your document has no sections, any changes to the margins affect the whole document.

- With sections, a margin change affects the section where your insertion point is resting at the time of the change.

- If you select text and change the margins, Word automatically makes that text a separate section, and the margin change works on just that section.

(Tip)

To fine-tune your margins before printing, you can also change them while in Print Preview. Learn more about making changes in Print Preview in Chapter 8.

Mirrors and Gutters

Many documents have right and left margins that are of equal width. But there are some documents that work better with unequal right and left margins.

Some people prefer a larger outside margin on documents where the pages will face each other—documents with multiple, two-sided pages. In effect, the two margins mirror each other. With **mirror margins**, the left margin on the left-facing page is wider, and the right margin on the right-facing page is wider.

If you're binding a document, you might want to use **gutter margins**. A gutter margin allows extra space on the inside margin (the right side of a left-facing page and the left side of the right-facing page) to allow for the space eaten up by the binding.

Whether you want to use a mirror or a gutter, you get there by choosing File, Page Setup, and choosing the Margins tab of the dialog box.

Tabs, anyone?

The tab stops in your document are preset places you want your insertion point to jump to, so the text you enter will be aligned at that spot. You can also use the Tab key to move between certain elements in your text—for example, to move from column to column in a simple table.

 **{Note}** When should you use a tab and when should you use a table to create a list? A table provides unique cells for each column, like a spreadsheet, and the versatility of formatting each cell uniquely. You can also move from one column to another without having to set or change tab stops. Use tabs for shorter lists or lists with only a few columns. But when the list gets bigger, check into Word's table feature (see Chapter 14 for more on tables).

Tabs come in different varieties

Tab stops are already set every 0.5 inches across the page when you start a new document. To move your cursor to the next tab stop, just hit the Tab key.

To add a tab stop, you can use the ruler in Page Layout or Normal view. There is a little box at the left end of the horizontal ruler. Here you can toggle among four symbols that represent the four kinds of tab stops (the difference between each kind is the way text aligns at the stop):

 • Left-aligned text is pretty much the standard.

 • Right-aligned text is used for something you want to line up on the right margin, like a page number.

 • You can center text at the tab stop. For example, if you want certain headings to always be centered, you can just place a center tab in the middle of the page and hit Tab before typing them.

 • A decimal tab stop is used for columns of numbers; the decimal points all line up on the tab stop.

 **{Note}** It's a big mistake to use tabs to indent each line of an entire paragraph. If you have to go back and add or delete text, the text will shift and your alignment will be completely messed up. To avoid this, use the indent tools on the Formatting toolbar to indent paragraphs (as discussed in Chapter 10). Then, you can change the text all you want without affecting the alignment.

Telling your tab where to stop

To place any of these tabs, simply click the Tab Alignment box on the left end of the ruler until you see the tab style you prefer, then click on the ruler wherever you want the tab to go. That's it! A little tab marker appears on your ruler. If you want to move it, click and drag it elsewhere.

You can change tab settings for a single paragraph or the entire document, depending upon what text you select ahead of time. If you don't select anything before you make tab settings, the settings apply to the paragraph the insertion point currently is in. To apply settings to sections of text, select the text and then make the settings.

Leader. . . . . characters

You also can use something called **leader characters** with your tabs. Leader characters are just a line of dots or dashes that visually connect two pieces of text—for example, we use leader characters to connect chapter names with page numbers in the table of contents for this book.

If you want to use this option, you can choose it in the Tabs dialog box (Format, Tab). You get a choice of three styles of characters: dots, dashes, and a solid line. After you choose one, every time you press Tab, Word leaves a trail of leader characters as your insertion point advances to the next stop.

Clearing everything up

If you need to remove a single tab stop, you can just click it on the ruler and drag it off into the document window. (It doesn't go into the document, of course; it just disappears.)

But at some point you may decide you've become too tab-happy; maybe you just want to get rid of all the tabs so that you can start over. No problem—there's a way to quickly clear all the tab stops at once.

Choose Format, Tabs. The dialog box in figure 11.3 appears.

Fig. 11.3
Clear a single tab or all of them at once.

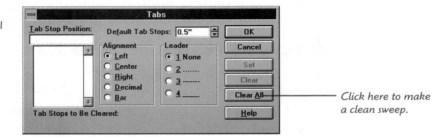

Click here to make a clean sweep.

If you select text before entering this dialog box, clearing tabs will act on just the sections that include the selected text. If you haven't selected anything, tabs in the entire document will be cleared away. In either case, the original default tabs at every 0.5 inches will still be there: this action only takes away new or changed tabs.

Simply click Clear All to remove all the tab stops. Now you can start fresh.

Splitting things up: hyphenation

All good things come to an end, and so do the lines in your document. And sometimes you reach the end of the line when you're in the middle of a word.

By default, Word will simply bump any word that can't fit completely on a line to the beginning of the next line; this feature is called **word wrap**. But if you use lots of big words, or if your margins are narrow, you might wind up with an ugly, jagged right margin. To fix it, let Word hyphenate automatically when it reaches the end of a line. The net effect? More words on the page, and a smoother right-hand margin.

How do I hyphenate?

To get Word to automatically place hyphens, choose Tools, Hyphenation. You see the dialog box in figure 11.4. Click the Automatically Hyphenate Document check box, and Word will take care of the rest.

Fig. 11.4

Apply automatic or manual hyphenation here.

Click here for auto-matic hyphenation.

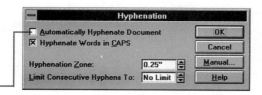

Perhaps you use acronyms in full caps, like UNICEF. If you don't want them to be hyphenated, deselect the Hyphenate Words in CAPS check box.

When you define the Hyphenation Zone, you tell Word how far from the right margin you want it to begin trying to break words. Use a big number if you want Word to fix only big white spaces.

If row upon row of hyphens looks odd to you, you can limit how many consecutive lines can end in a hyphen.

Doing it by hand

So you don't like where Word is breaking a word? Maybe you have some proper names or technical terms that you'd prefer Word hyphenated in a certain way. Okay. Go ahead and manage hyphenation manually.

First, select the word you want to change, then choose Tools, Hyphenation. In the Hyphenation dialog box, click the Manual button. You see the Manual Hyphenation dialog box (see fig. 11.5).

Fig. 11.5

Change hyphenation word-by-word here.

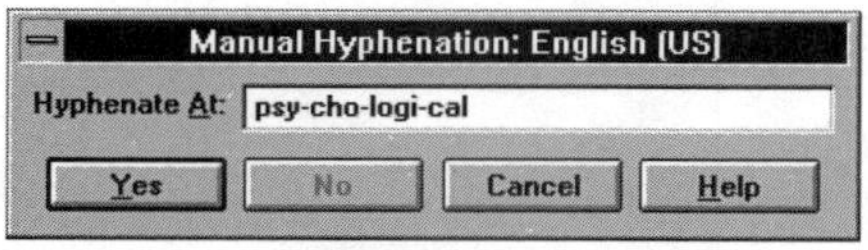

To change where Word inserts a hyphen, just click in the word where you want the hyphen, then click <u>Y</u>es. When Word needs to hyphenate this word, it uses your preference.

If there's a block of text that you don't want hyphenated, select it, and then choose F<u>o</u>rmat, <u>P</u>aragraph. On the Text <u>F</u>low tab of this dialog box, just click <u>D</u>on't Hyphenate.

12

Putting Headers and Footers in Their Place

Word gives you some neat ways to quickly automate headers and footers, including effortless page numbering.

In this chapter:

- Why would I use headers and footers?
- I want to put my company logo in the header
- Can Word take care of page numbering automatically?
- I need to use different page numbering in this part of my report

Y ou see the signs every time you drive down the highway: "Now entering Smallville, pop. 128." Don't blink, or you'll miss the matching "Now leaving Smallville" sign just down the road.

Those signs are helpful reminders of where you are and where you're going. In Word documents, headers and footers are equally reassuring signposts that let your readers know where they are in your document. They're useful for titles and page numbers, draft numbers and company logos, date and time stamps, and *Merry Christmas from the Andersens* at the top of your holiday newsletter.

Headers and footers shouldn't take up too much of your time—which is fine, because Word gives you some neat little tools for automatically creating and editing headers and footers.

What are headers and footers?

If you think of each page of your document as an individual standing upright, the terms **header** and **footer** make perfect sense. Both elements contain repeating information that appears either at the top (header) or the bottom (footer) of the page. The type of information you include in a header or footer is pretty much up to you.

Why should I use headers and footers?

Headers and footers can be used for virtually anything. Here are a few examples:

- The document's title

- The date and time the document was created

- The version number of the document (Draft 3, or 1995 Edition)

- Page numbers

- The section of the document (such as Chapter 5, or Part IV)

- The author's name or the company logo

As the readers of your document move between documents, or within a single document, headers and footers can help them keep track of their whereabouts. (They can also help you put things back together quickly if you spill a stack of loose pages.) Figure 12.1 shows a press release that uses graphics in its header and footer.

What can I put in a header or footer?

There's really no limit to what you can place in a header or footer. Use your imagination:

- Text formatted in virtually any way you like

- Graphics, such as a picture or logo

- A picture you create using Word's drawing tools

- A table or database

In short, anything you can put in Word can be put in a header or footer.

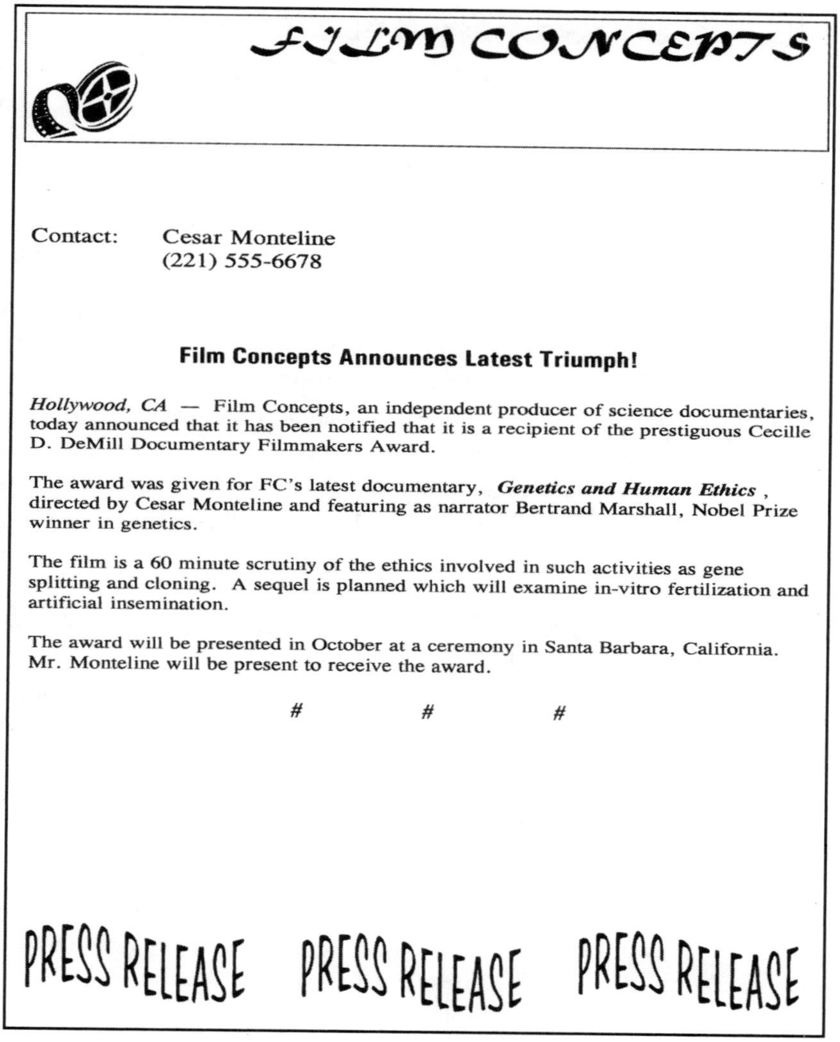

Fig. 12.1

The picture at the top, the company name (actually a WordArt object), and the text at the bottom of this announcement show one way to use headers and footers.

FILM CONCEPTS

Contact: Cesar Monteline
            (221) 555-6678

Film Concepts Announces Latest Triumph!

Hollywood, CA — Film Concepts, an independent producer of science documentaries, today announced that it has been notified that it is a recipient of the prestiguous Cecille D. DeMill Documentary Filmmakers Award.

The award was given for FC's latest documentary, ***Genetics and Human Ethics***, directed by Cesar Monteline and featuring as narrator Bertrand Marshall, Nobel Prize winner in genetics.

The film is a 60 minute scrutiny of the ethics involved in such activities as gene splitting and cloning. A sequel is planned which will examine in-vitro fertilization and artificial insemination.

The award will be presented in October at a ceremony in Santa Barbara, California. Mr. Monteline will be present to receive the award.

\#   \#   \#

PRESS RELEASE   PRESS RELEASE   PRESS RELEASE

 **{Note}**

Although headers and footers are often used for text, such as a document title or page numbers, they're also ideal for repeating graphics, like a company or product logo. See Chapter 16 for more information about how to place pictures in Word, then try that same method to place them in your header or footer.

Does every header and footer have to be the same?

Although headers and footers repeat information, you can vary that information within the same document. For example, you can divide your document into sections and use different headers and footers for items that change, like chapter numbers of a book.

You can also treat odd- and even-page headers and footers differently. Look at this book, for example. The headers always appear on the outside edge of the page—to the right on odd-numbered pages and to the left on even-numbered pages. Also, the header on the right page is the chapter number and title, and the header on the left is the part number and title. If you have a title page or section introductions, you can even choose to eliminate the header and footer on the first page of your document or document sections.

How complicated are headers and footers?

There's not much mystery to using headers and footers. You just place text, graphics—whatever—in the header and footer view and treat it just like you would in the main document.

 ### Plain English, please!

Several of the elements that can be inserted from the Header and Footer toolbar are fields. A **field** is a placeholder for a certain type of information. For ex-ample, the date and time fields tell Word to insert the current date or time at the moment the document is printed. Likewise, a page number field tells Word to count from the beginning of the document and display the appropriate page number.

The header and footer view is where it all happens

To get to the header and footer view in Word, choose Yiew, Header and Footer. Word switches to Page Layout view and shows you a little Header window on top of your document. The text of your document has become shaded in gray, so the Header window stands out.

A floating Header and Footer toolbar also appears that you can move around the screen and use to make changes.

 To move to the Footer view, you simply click the Switch Between Header and Footer button. The Footer window works the same as the Header window; it just appears at the foot of the page.

Close-Up: the Header and Footer toolbar

To bring up header and footer view and the Header and Footer toolbar, choose <u>V</u>iew, <u>H</u>eader and Footer.

 Switch between Header and Footer
Changes the view instantly

 Date
Places current date automatically

 Show Previous
Displays the previous section's header/footer

 Time
Places current time automatically

 Show Next
Shows you the next section's header/footer

 Page Setup
Displays Page Setup dialog box

 Same as Previous
Inserts same header/footer as previous section.

 Show/Hide Document Text
Hides the document, or shows it shaded in gray

 Page Numbers
Inserts a page number field instantly

 Close
Closes Header/Footer View and returns you to your document

Headers and footers are only visible in the Page Layout view. If you want to hide the text of your document, click the Show/Hide Document Text button. To see how your pages will look with the header, footer, and body text all together, choose File, Print Preview.

Getting header and footer text just right

If you know how to type and format text in Word, then you know how to type and format text in a header and footer. But the Header and Footer toolbar offers you some neat little shortcuts. Here's how to create a fancy title that will appear throughout your document.

1 Choose View, Header and Footer.

2 When the Header window appears, type the document title—in this case, **Safety Manual**.

The next thing you want in your header is the date, but you don't have to do anything as mundane as actually typing it!

3 Press Enter to move to the next line. Now click the Date button, and the current date instantly appears. (To add the current time, just click the Time button.)

4 You say you don't want your header on the left side of the page: you want it in the middle? No problem.

Just select the text of the header and click the Center button on the standard toolbar, just as you do to center text in Word.

5 You'd like your header to appear in a different font? You're the boss. Just select the text again and choose Format, Font from the menu bar. Or use the drop-down lists on the Formatting toolbar to change the font to Arial, 12 point.

See. I told you this was easy. You've got a nice little header all formatted and in the right place (see fig. 12.2).

Header window
This little window is where you put the text and
graphics for your header.

Fig. 12.2
Using all the standard
formatting tools to
format headers and
footers, you feel right
at home.

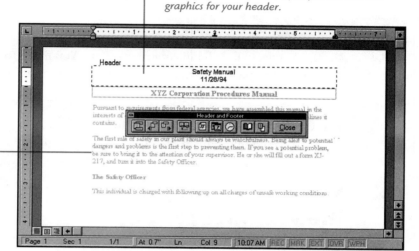

Document text
Notice that the text
of your document is
shaded in gray.

Q&A

When I put a date in a header, it printed out like this:
4/28/95. But my boss decided he wants it spelled out:
April 28, 1995. So I guess I have to always type my date
out, right?

Well, you could, but there's an easier way. Instead of choosing the Date button
on the Header and Footer toolbar, go to the Insert menu. Then choose Date
and Time (see fig. 12.3). When you insert a date or time this way, you have
several formatting options available to you. To set the display format, just click
the Options button and pick a format from the list.

Fig. 12.3
You get more choices
than you'll ever need
when you choose Date
and Time from the
Insert menu.

What's the difference? When things in your document change

Things change, in life and in your documents. You move from chapter to chapter, part to part, even use different page numbering styles for different parts of your documents.

If you start a new section in your document, you need different header and footer information to reflect the new section's content.

Some pages are different: odd/even and the very first page

In many documents, the first page begins with the title of the document and doesn't need a header that repeats that information. And, you sometimes want odd and even pages to have different headers—say if you're using **facing pages**, as in a book.

Here are a few tips for using headers and footers

In longer documents, it's sometimes wise to have unique page numbers for different sections. For example, in a manual, Section 6 might have page numbers like 6.1, 6.2, 6.3, etc. Why? If you ever replace just that section with an updated version, you won't have to renumber and reprint the whole document. You can just reprint the new, renumbered Section 6.

If you place a date or time field in your header or footer, you can get a shortcut menu for them. Place your mouse over the field and click the right mouse button. The shortcut menu includes the ability to manually update the date or time.

Plain English, please!

Facing pages are staring at you right now. This book, and most bound documents, have facing pages. Because the binding (the staples or glue in the middle) eats up margin space, the pages have to be laid out with broader margins on the inside, where the right and left pages meet. On the right page, the left margin is larger, and on the left page, the right margin is larger. Page numbers, or other header and footer information, must stay on the outside of the page, or they would be lost in the binding. So, right-facing pages usually have the page number on the far right, and left-facing pages have it on the far left.

To make either of these format changes, you use the Page Setup dialog box. Here you can tell Word to use different header/footer formats and then define what those differences should be.

1 On the Header and Footer toolbar, click the Page Setup button.

2 In the Page Setup dialog box (see fig. 12.4), you can click Different <u>F</u>irst Page or Different <u>O</u>dd and Even Pages, depending upon which pages you want to change.

Specify where to start the section.

Fig. 12.4
The Page Setup dialog box allows you to make special arrangements for certain pages of your document.

Change headers and footers for odd/even pages.

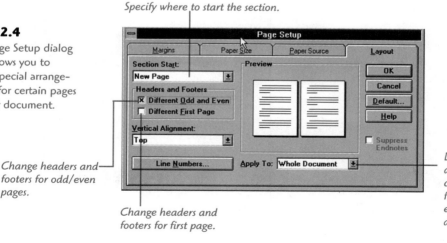

Change headers and footers for first page.

Designate what part of document to apply this change to: going forward only, or to every section of the document.

The Apply To box can apply a setting to the whole document, or just going forward. If your document has separate sections, you will have a choice of applying a setting to that section only.

When you indicate that you want to make changes to the first or odd/even pages of a document header, the header and footer views show you extra header and footer windows that you can customize simply by typing in unique information (see fig. 12.5).

When you're working in your document and you go to Page Layout View (View menu, Page Layout), your headers and footers appear shaded in gray. To instantly go to the Header/Footer window, just double-click the header or footer text itself.

Fig. 12.5
If you want something unique in the first page header, just type it in this special window.

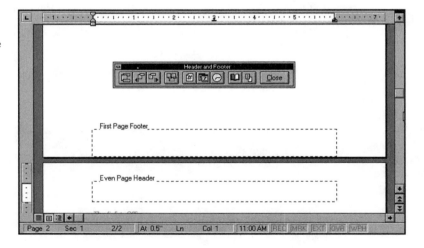

Different sections mean different headers and footers

Many documents need to be divided into parts; a manual, for example, needs sections. And readers of these documents need guideposts to tell them where they are. So, you should know how to create sections. It's—you guessed it— easy to do.

You've already heard a bit about sections in the Page Setup dialog box, where you can choose to apply a setting to one section of your document. Making those sections is simple. Place the insertion point where you want a break and choose Insert, Break. One of the choices (see fig. 12.6) is to create a section break. You have several options for where to begin the section.

You can have any number of sections in your document. Each section can have its own margin, header/footer, and page numbering settings. Just create the section break, and then you can change that section's layout through the Page Setup dialog box, or the section's header/footer content by editing it on the first page of the section.

Fig. 12.6
The Break dialog box is where you create different sections.

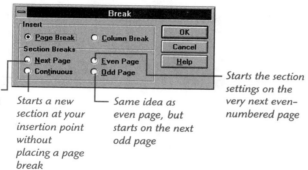

Inserts a page break where your insertion point is and begins section settings with that page

Starts a new section at your insertion point without placing a page break

Same idea as even page, but starts on the next odd page

Starts the section settings on the very next even-numbered page

Let Word take care of page numbering

All that's required of you here is to put the page number field where you want it, tell Word what number to start with, and sit back. You can add and delete text at will in your document; Word adjusts your page numbers to remain accurate.

Putting the numbers on the page

You can place a page number in a header or footer by simply clicking the Page Number button on the Header and Footer toolbar and formatting the page number text as you would any other header/footer text.

However, there's another way to insert page numbers that offers you several page number format options all in one place. Choose Insert, Page Numbers. You see the dialog box in figure 12.7.

Fig. 12.7
A neat way to make all your page number settings at once.

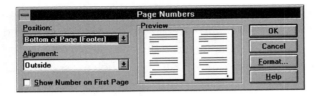

In this dialog box, you can choose to show or not show page numbers on the first page. Also, you can position the page number in either the header or footer by choosing Bottom Of Page or Top Of Page in the Position drop-down list.

Finally, you can automatically align the page numbers on the left, center, or right of the page, or choose inside or outside if you have facing pages. The preview in this box shows you what each choice will look like in your document.

Page numbers deserve formats, too

One more thing in your Page Numbers dialog box is the option to format the page numbers. Click the Format button, and you see the Page Number Format dialog box (see fig. 12.8).

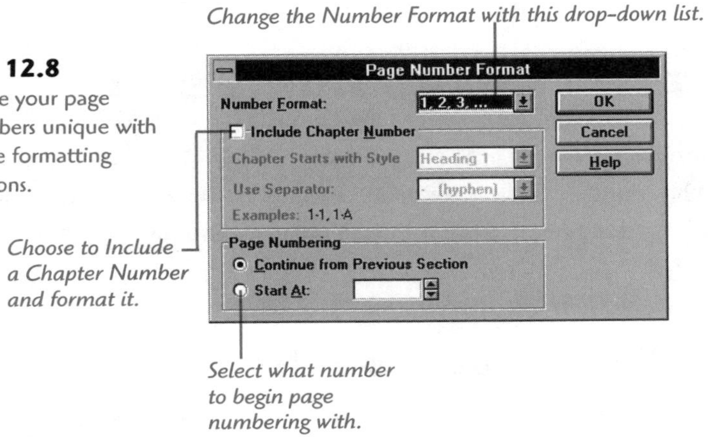

Change the Number Format with this drop-down list.

Fig. 12.8
Make your page numbers unique with these formatting options.

Choose to Include a Chapter Number and format it.

Select what number to begin page numbering with.

Notice that you have a lot more formatting options here than you did in the header/footer view, all in one place.

Making Life Easier with Styles

Word styles are like wigs; they're reusable, time-saving tools that can give you a different look for every occasion.

I know a woman who owns dozens of wigs, one for each occasion. There's the short-coifed one for business meetings, and the long, curly one for when she goes dancing; and, of course, the Tina Turner model for those days when nothing goes her way and she wants people to stop her at the mall and ask for her autograph.

My friend loves wigs because she enjoys changing her look without spending hours in front of the mirror. Word *styles* are like wigs. They're reusable, time-saving tools for crafting just the right look in your Word documents.

How do I use styles?

For examples of styles, look at this book. Notice how there are certain consistencies in headings and body text throughout? Different level headings are bold and some text appears out in the margin. All the headings at the beginning of each chapter also have certain features: font, font size, italic, bold, and so on. Each of these "chunks" of text was **formatted** with a style—and there are dozens of styles in this book.

Plain English, please!

A **format** is a setting that affects how text appears on a page, such as its size, shape, thickness, or location relative to the margins. See more about text formats in Chapter 10.

Your styles reside in the Style box on the Formatting toolbar (see fig. 13.1). There are two kinds of styles:

- **Paragraph Styles** affect an entire paragraph. This is a great shortcut, because you don't need to select the paragraph, only place your cursor anywhere within it, and the style applies to the whole paragraph. Paragraph styles take into consideration issues such as line spacing, indentation, and other paragraph-related formatting attributes. Paragraph styles appear in bold in the style list.

- **Character Styles** affect selected text—for those occasions when you need to apply a style to just one word or any part of your text.

There are several ways to apply styles to your text:

- To select a style before you start typing, just click the drop-down arrow next to the Style box, find the style you need, and click it.

- To apply a **paragraph style** to existing text, click somewhere within the paragraph you want to format and select the style.

- To apply a **character style** to existing text, first select the text and then select the style.

Word considers a paragraph any chunk of text that ends with a paragraph mark—the code inserted when you press Enter. Even a single line, such as a heading, is considered a paragraph if it ends in a paragraph mark. Paragraph marks are often called **hard returns**.

Fig. 13.1
Window shopping for the right style. This drop-down list shows you all the available styles.

Microsoft Word - RESULTS.DOC
File Edit View Insert Format Tools Table Window Help
Heading 1
Arial
14
Default Paragraph Font
Heading 1
Heading 2
Heading 3
Normal
Steel has seen significant growth in the past few years, and the recent quarter was no exception.
Contracts from major car companies have been a major contributing factor. In addition, two new products contributed significantly:
-Allright Alloy Mix (R)
-Allright Hardy Tensile (TM)
II. International
The International division has had a weak quarter, mainly because of the extreme fluctuation of European currencies in the current economic climate.
Other factors include the delay in getting approval for certain export rights to Asian destinations, such as
Page 1 Sec 1 1/1 At 3.3" Ln 14 Col 1 10:01 AM REC MRK EXT OVR WP

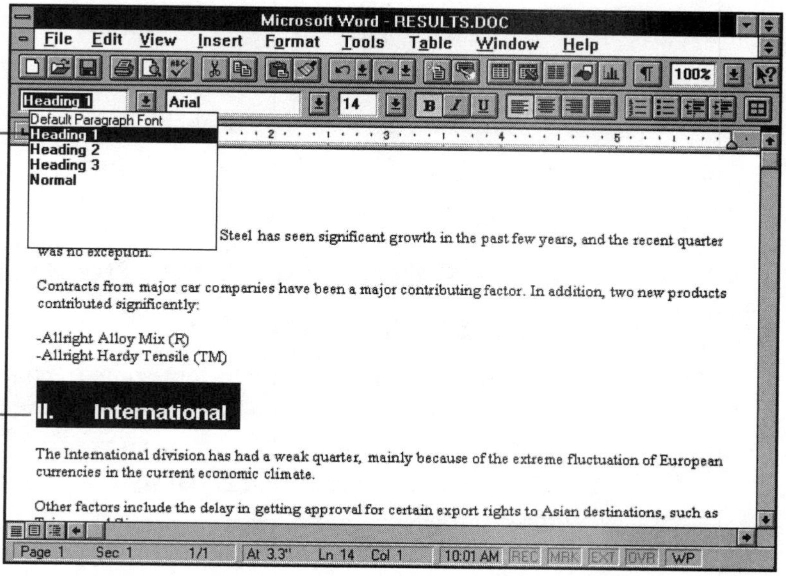

The style name appears here.

The style as it looks applied to text.

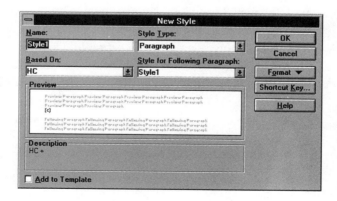

How do I create a style?

Many companies have text standards. Let's say your company's heading standard is 14 pt bold, underlined. To create that style, do the following:

1 Choose Format, Style, and click New. The dialog box in figure 13.2 appears.

2 In the Name box, type a name like **Std Heading**.

Fig. 13.2
After you create a style, you can use it again and again.

New Style
Name:
Style1
Style Type:
Paragraph
Based On:
HC
Style for Following Paragraph:
Style1
OK
Cancel
Format
Shortcut Key...
Help
Preview
Description
HC +
Add to Template

3 Click the Format button, and choose Font.

4 Select the right font, size, and font style, and click OK.

5 Click the Add to Template check box.

6 Click OK and then click Close; the style has been created.

I don't like the way these headings have turned out!

Company standards, just like fashion, tend to change by the season. So now your boss thinks that the standard headings are dated and don't reflect the company's younger spirit. Will you have to apply new formatting to each heading? Not likely. Just modify the style and all the affected text will change before your eyes:

1 Choose Format, Style.

2 From the Styles box on the left, select the format you need to change.

3 Click Modify, then Format, and apply the new formatting you want from the drop-down list.

When you return to the document, the text will have that new Spring look.

Creating a style by example

With the new Spring look comes a new haircut. You can tell your hairdresser exactly how you want it done ("Trim a bit off the back, keep the sides, dye it red...") or simply point to the latest tabloid and ask for the Princess Di look. Many people opt for the second option, because it's easier to explain (though some of us prefer the Michael Jordan style, for obvious reasons). Word styles are no different. Rather than create a new style from scratch, you can tell Word to use an existing format from your document. Just do this:

1 Select the text you want to use as an example.

2 Select the current style name showing in the Style box and type another name over it.

3 Press Enter, and your style is saved with that name.

All about templates

A Word document has an interesting foundation called a **template**. The default Word template is called Normal, and it's a bare-bones document, with a few preset formatting attributes, such as margins (1 inch from the top and bottom, and 1.25 inch from the left and the right), default fonts (Times New Roman 10 pt), and so on. You can easily create your own custom templates, with your favorite formatting and more.

 Plain English, please!

A **template** is a ready-made Word document that has style sets, macros, and even text stored in it. You can change a template by adding styles to it or by changing the styles it contains.

Templates are excellent tools for forms, such as invoices or surveys. But they also come in handy when you use such "boilerplate" (meaning, fill-in-the-blanks) documents as fax cover sheets, memos, and so on. You can become more efficient by using templates for many of your regular documents.

How do I create a template?

You create a template much the same way you create a regular document. Apply all your formatting, and type in the boilerplate text. For example, let's create an invoice template:

1 Type the company's logo, address, and phone number at the top of the page, as shown in figure 13.3.

2 Type **Invoice No. #** as a centered heading.

3 Create a table for the invoice itself, with all the appropriate column headings (see Chapter 14 for information on creating tables). Don't type any data into the table. Remember, this is only a template, not a "live" document.

4 Choose File, Save As, and click the drop-down arrow next to Save File As Type. Select Document Template and type a name in the File Name box. (If you name this file INVOICE, be aware that you will overwrite the INVOICE.DOT template that comes with Word.) Notice that the file receives the DOT extension, and is automatically placed in the \WINWORD\TEMPLATE directory.

Fig. 13.3
After you create this
handy form, it's always
at your disposal.

ACME WIDGETS INC.

5555 NORTH WASHINGTON BLVD. ANYTOWN, CA 94444

INVOICE NO.

QTY	DESCRIPTION	PRICE	DISCOUNT	TOTAL

How do I use a template?

To use a template, choose <u>F</u>ile, <u>N</u>ew, and choose the appropriate template from the resulting dialog box. From now on, whenever you need to issue an invoice, just select the Invoice template, fill in the blanks, and print. Any style you create gets saved in the current document.

 **<Caution>** There can be only one style with a particular name attached to the template you're working on. Template names are case-sensitive, so it's okay to have two styles named the same if one is capitalized and the other isn't.

To apply styles that already exist in Word's templates, the first thing you should do is start with a template that has most of the styles you might want in a document. Try using the Style Gallery to help you choose a likely template. After you open a document based on a template, you can modify it to suit your needs by adding all the styles of another template to the open document, or by applying styles from the Style dialog box. To move styles around, you use Word's Style Organizer (see "Copying styles between templates," later in this chapter).

Let's begin this process by exploring the different templates available in the Style Gallery.

**{Note}**_____ Templates are divided into families, indicated by a number in a template's name. For example, there's a Letter1, Letter2, and Letter3 template. The 1 family of template is in a Classic mode, 2 is Contemporary, 3 is a Typewriter style, and 4 is Elegant. These family numbers give you a clue as to that family's style.

What does that style do? Look in the Gallery

The Style Gallery is like going to a costume store where all the costumes are on display. The Style Gallery allows you to see, all in one place, which styles are available in a given template and what they can do for your documents.

Choose F̲ormat, Style G̲allery. The dialog box in figure 13.4 appears, giving you a large preview area for viewing different styles.

Most templates are in Word's T̲emplate directory, which is what appears here when you enter the Gallery. Look through the list of templates to find the one you want.

Preview how this template would look if used on the current document, or with a sample Word document, or in a document that previews the different styles using the style names as placeholders.

Fig. 13.4
The Style Gallery lets you browse through templates all in one place.

*Choose the **template** you want to view here.*

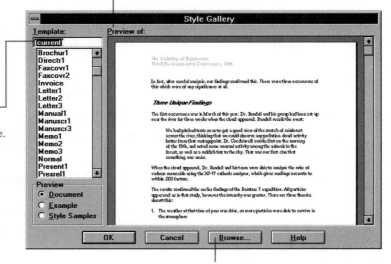

Browse lets you open other directories for other templates.

Making changes to styles

You can modify styles in Word either in just the current document, or save the changes permanently so that the modified style is saved with a template. For example, the Normal template always opens a document with a Normal style that includes 10-point type. But I prefer 12-point type, so why should I always have to change the type size before I start typing?

You can modify the Normal style and save it as part of the Normal template through the Style dialog box, seen in figure 13.5.

Paragraph Preview
Shows how the selected style would affect your paragraph

Fig. 13.5
Add a style using the Style dialog box.

Styles
Lists the styles you have selected in the List box

List
Gives you a choice of Styles in Use, All Styles, or just User-defined Styles

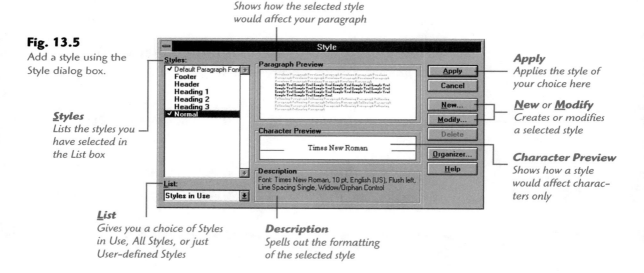

Apply
Applies the style of your choice here

New or Modify
Creates or modifies a selected style

Character Preview
Shows how a style would affect characters only

Description
Spells out the formatting of the selected style

To modify the Normal style, do this:

1 Choose F<u>o</u>rmat, <u>S</u>tyle.

2 Select the Normal style in the <u>S</u>tyles list, and then click the <u>M</u>odify button.

3 The dialog box in figure 13.6 is where you can make changes.

You can choose to make changes to specific elements of the style in the F<u>o</u>rmat drop-down list. To change the font size, for example, select <u>F</u>ont in the list. That brings up the Font dialog box, where you can change any font format, including its size. After you make those changes, click OK twice to return to the Style dialog box and close it.

Fig. 13.6
Preview how your
changes to a style will
look here.

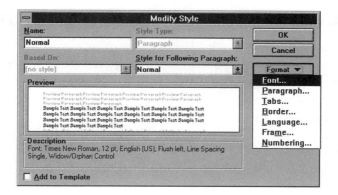

So far, the changes you've made are to the style as you use it in this document only. To change the style in the template itself, click Add to Template in the Modify Style dialog box. Then, whenever you open this template, the changed style will be available.

Naming styles

When you create a new style, you can use up to 253 characters for its name, which gives you a lot of room to get into trouble. Don't get carried away: choose a simple name that you can remember easily.

Although you can use spaces and commas in the name, you can't use a backslash, braces, or semicolons.

Because a new style would overwrite an old one if you give it the same name, it's important to know that style names are case sensitive. That means you're allowed two separate styles called XYZ Company Style, as long as the capitalization between the two varies—for example, XYZ company style and the other XYZ Company Style.

Word won't let you change the name of a built-in style, such as Normal or Heading 1; if you modify a built-in style by typing in a new name, Word doesn't change it, it creates what's called an **alias**. This basically copies the style with a new name but leaves the first one alone. So if it's easier for you to remember that the style you always use with your weekly report heading is named WEEKREPHEAD, go ahead and make an alias.

If styles will be used by others in your workgroup, make sure the names make sense to everyone.

Copying styles between templates

The only problem with styles is that they're "stuck" to the template in which they were created. So you labor over a template with many styles that your company requires, but when a colleague asks for a couple of the styles, you don't want to make a copy of that template (there may be some personal styles or macros in it). But there's a way.

To copy selected styles between templates, you use the Organizer. Here's how:

1   Choose F<u>o</u>rmat, <u>S</u>tyle, and click <u>O</u>rganizer. The dialog box in figure 13.7 appears.

2   The <u>I</u>n box shows the available styles in the template attached to the current document, and the T<u>o</u> box shows the styles stored in the Normal template. If you want to copy those styles to or from a different template or an existing document, click Clos<u>e</u> File, which then becomes Open File. Click that button and select the target file from the disk.

3   Mark the style you want to copy in the <u>I</u>n box by clicking it. If you want to select several styles, press Ctrl while you click each additional style. (Note that you can also copy styles in the other direction.)

4   Click <u>C</u>opy, and you're done.

5   To exit, click Close.

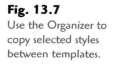

Fig. 13.7
Use the Organizer to copy selected styles between templates.

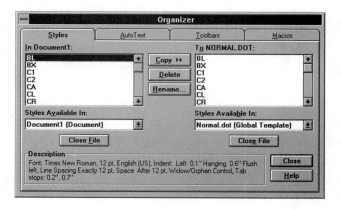

Opting for manual formatting

There are times when you'll want to apply a single format to text, even though it may override formatting contained in styles you used to format most of the document. For example, if you use a company name in a heading and you want it to be in the company-approved font, you can change the formatting for that text alone.

If you'd like to apply manual formatting that overrides a style, it's easy to do. But, you should know how manual formatting works with styles.

Let's say you manually format a word in your paragraph, and then apply a paragraph style to your document again later. A few things could happen, depending on whether the style that's applied to that text involved the type of format you're applying manually:

- If the manual formatting involves a category of formatting also addressed by the paragraph style, the style overrides it. For example, if you manually made the paragraph flush left, and the paragraph style aligns to the right, the style wins.

- If the manual formatting isn't a formatting element that's used by the style, the style won't touch it. For example, let's say you add a border manually and the style doesn't involve borders at all. Your border won't be touched by the style.

Remember that some effects, such as bold, are toggles (click once to turn on, click again to turn off). So, if you manually make text bold, and then apply a style that also includes bold, the style toggles off the bold you applied manually.

Part IV:

Getting Organized

14

Organizing Information with Tables

If you want to present information in a way that your reader can under-stand at a glance, try tables. They're short, sweet, and very effective.

Every year, those friendly folks at the IRS send you and me a perfect example of how to communicate a lot of information in a very small space. You know the table: it's right there in the Form 1040 booklet, with headings that describe your marital status—Married, Married Filing Separately, Single, and so on—across the top, and your salary range—$25,000–$25,050 or $95,850–$95,900, depending on your luck that year—down the side.

Although government documents aren't normally known for their clarity, this one is a winner. Trying to present all this information in ordinary text, without the help of a table, would add insult to the injury of paying taxes. The table format keeps the information concise and adds order. It shows you a relationship between the salary and tax without any further rhetoric.

Word tables make it easy to create and edit rows and columns of information. Just type in text and let Word deal with resizing rows to accommodate it. Align all the numbers in a column with a single mouse click. Add or delete rows, columns, or individual cells without all the other columns suddenly shifting into another dimension.

In other words, get ready to organize information for your reader without organizing yourself into a nervous breakdown.

What is a table? And why would I use one?

A **table** simply divides information into rows and columns to organize it and present it in a way that's immediately understandable to your reader. Presenting information this way can often be more persuasive and powerful than burying the pertinent information in the middle of a paragraph.

When you have information that speaks for itself—numbers, statistics, names of things, dates, symbols—anything that doesn't need a long explanation, consider a table. Also, if your reader might need only one or two pieces of information in a collection of data—like that tax amount from the IRS—this format lets him find just the number or date he needs and move on without having to read through paragraphs of information. And, of course, typing those concise facts into the cells of a table saves you from typing paragraphs of information, too!

 Plain English, please!

Tables are like spreadsheets, which is where the term cell comes from. In a table, a cell is the point where a row and column intersect. The information in that cell often describes a relationship between that row and column (like sales by month). Each cell in a Word table can contain graphics, text, or even a formula that performs a calculation on stuff in other cells.

If you've ever created tables with tabs, you probably remember hitting Enter and then tab, tab, tab, tab to add a second line to the fifth column. One of the nice things about table cells is that as you type in more information, they automatically wrap around and expand to accommodate it.

Blueprint of a table

Shading
Makes rows and columns stand out, which can make your table easier to read

Column
Made up of cells stacked on top of each other

Heading
Can span across several cells and repeat on every page

Row
Consists of cells running in a line from left to right

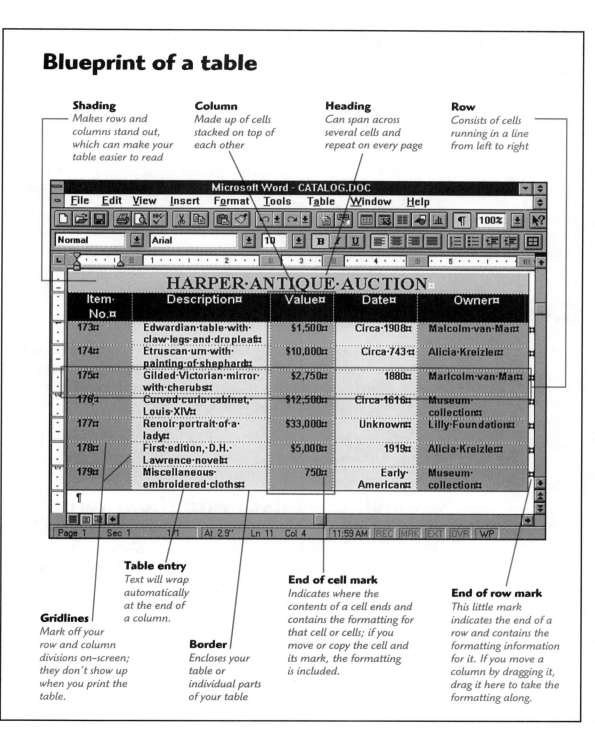

Gridlines
Mark off your row and column divisions on-screen; they don't show up when you print the table.

Table entry
Text will wrap automatically at the end of a column.

Border
Encloses your table or individual parts of your table

End of cell mark
Indicates where the contents of a cell ends and contains the formatting for that cell or cells; if you move or copy the cell and its mark, the formatting is included.

End of row mark
This little mark indicates the end of a row and contains the formatting information for it. If you move a column by dragging it, drag it here to take the formatting along.

How can I organize information with tables?

Tables in Word allow you to do certain things with information:

- Place information side-by-side in neat columns and rows

- Show a relationship between two types of information; for example, at the intersection of a row listing "Profits" and column listing "January," you can show how much money you made in that month

- Place text and graphics next to each other, as in a catalog of products

- Build neat-looking forms

Give me a basic table

Word gives you several features to help you work with tables. For example, if you like to use menus, there's a whole menu in Word devoted to tables. However, Word lets you get most things done without ever opening the Table menu by using the toolbar, mouse, or shortcut menus.

And Word's even got a Table wizard to get the basics of your table set up right away with minimal effort.

Fast and easy tables with the wizard

Table wizard walks you through the steps of creating a table, presenting you with options that help define its contents. Use this if you want help getting the structure and some basic formatting for your table set right up front.

You get to the wizard by choosing Table, Insert Table. In the Insert Table dialog box, click Wizard (see fig. 14.1).

Fig. 14.1
Get the Table Wizard
going through this
dialog box.

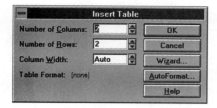

Table Wizard walks you through the following choices:

- Choose a table layout (the default one is a good choice for most common tables).

- Designate column and row headings, and whether headings should repeat on every page.

- Select the most common alignment (numbers are usually right-aligned; text is generally aligned to the left or centered).

- Decide whether your table should be oriented as portrait (up and down) or landscape (sideways).

Move through each step and make your choices, clicking Next to move to the next step. After you've made all your choices for your table, click Finish. Word then displays the Table AutoFormat dialog box, in which you can choose a design look for your table (we'll get into AutoFormat a little later in the chapter).

For now, click OK. You end up with something like the table in figure 14.2.

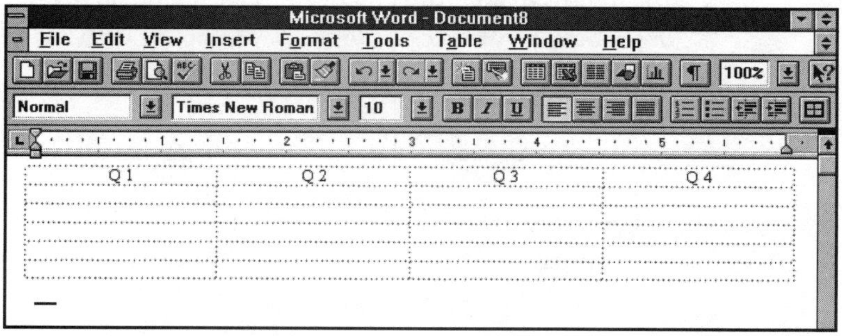

Fig. 14.2
After only a few
choices, Wizard delivers
a table with column
headings and cell
alignment already in
place.

Faster and easier tables: the Table Insert button

 The Table Insert button is a great way to get a plain generic version of a blank table quickly and easily. If you need minimal formatting, or prefer to format things yourself, try this instead of using the Table Wizard. The only choice you have to make is how many rows and columns you want in your table. They'll show up on the page separated by faint gridlines.

 Plain English, please!

A **gridline** is a faint dotted line that appears on-screen and shows you where the edges of the cells are. You can turn them on and off by clicking Gridlines in the Table menu. When I'm working with tables, I leave gridlines showing on-screen at all times so I don't lose my way. Remember, though, that gridlines don't print; if you want to see lines around the cells in your table, you'll need to add borders.

 Click the Insert Table button. A drop-down grid contains blocks that represent rows and columns. You drag your mouse to select the size table you want.

Notice that you've got more space than you might think: you can drag beyond the original 5-column by 4-row boundaries of the drop-down box. As you drag, the number of rows and columns is listed at the bottom of the box.!

 (Tip)

The Insert Table button limits you to a certain number of columns and rows, depending on your computer display setup. If you want a larger table, try choosing Table, Insert Table, and select a larger number in the dialog box that appears.

When you release the mouse button, a basic table appears, with no headings or formatting settings.

Need another row or column?
No problem!

You can always add more rows or columns (or delete them, for that matter) at any time after you've created your table. Just do this:

1 Select a row or column.

To select a row, move the mouse pointer into the selection bar to the left of the row and click. To select a column, point to the top of the column (look for the pointer to turn into a downward-pointing arrow) and click.

2 Click on the right mouse button to pop up a shortcut menu. Depending on what you've selected, you'll be able to choose from Insert Row and Delete Row or Insert Column and Delete Column.

3 To add (or delete) more rows or columns, repeat the process. To work with more than one row or column at a time, just select more than one.

New rows appear above the selected row, and new columns appear to the left of the selected column.

 *{Note}*

Word allows you to create tables with up to 31 columns and more than 32,000 rows. For most jobs, that should be plenty of table. What if your information needs more room? It's time to open a spreadsheet program (like Microsoft Excel) to manage your table.

How do I turn this text into a table?

You thought this would be an easy job, didn't you? You've already typed in projected profits for the next three months, and now your boss wants a 12-month projection? You don't have to toss what you've already typed; just transform it into a table and add the rest of the data in the new table.

Word converts text into a table by making a few assumptions: that commas or tabs in your text mark the end of cells and paragraph marks (you get these when you hit Enter at the end of a line) define the ends of rows. Just be sure your text doesn't have any extra tabs or commas before you start; these would give you extra columns you don't need.

So let's do it:

1 Select the text and choose Table, Convert Text to Table.

2 Accept the settings in the Convert Text to Table dialog box.

That's it!

To do this in reverse and make a table into text:

1 Select the table and choose Table—the command is now Convert Table to Text.

2 Word asks you if you want to leave tabs for the column dividers; say yes, and you've got your text back the way it was.

Setting your table

When you place a table in Word, your insertion point appears in the first cell. To enter information, you can just start typing. After you've entered information, you can also make formatting choices, like alignment or font, or type size.

An important thing to understand about tables is that you can format by individual cell, by row, column, or the whole table at once. This means that columns of numbers, for example, can be aligned to the right of their cells, while text columns align left; heading text can be set off in a large bold typeface; or a single cell can contain a picture or symbol, while the next cell in the same row contains text.

Moving around

To enter information into your table and format it, you should get the hang of moving around a table. Table 14.1 lists how to use the movement keys to move around a table.

Table 14.1   Getting around Tables

To make this move	Do this
To a particular cell	Click it with your mouse
One cell to the right	Press Tab⇄ or →
Back one cell	Press ⬆Shift + Tab⇄
Up, down, or left	Use the ↑, ↓ or ←
To first cell in a row	Alt + Home
To last cell in a row	Alt + End
To top cell in a column	Alt + PgUp
To bottom cell in a column	Alt + PgDn

{Note}_____ When you press Tab while in a cell, you move to the next cell. To add a tab character within a cell, you have to use Ctrl+Tab. However, if your cursor is already at the right edge of the cell, Ctrl+Tab will wrap to the next line, expanding the cell's height by one line—just as if you were typing text and the text wrapped to the next line.

Selecting things

To format, add, or delete parts of a table, you should also practice selecting things, as shown in table 14.2.

Table 14.2   Selecting Things in Tables

To select this	Do this
A row	Click to the left of the first cell in the row.
A single cell	Move your mouse to the cell's left boundary until the pointer becomes an arrow, then click.
A column	Move your mouse over the top border of the column until you get a black downward-pointing arrow, then click.
A range of cells	Select the first cell in the range, then drag down and over to highlight the cells you want to select.

> You can also quickly select the whole table with a keyboard shortcut. Hold
> down the Alt key and press the number 5 on the numeric keypad found to
> the right of most keyboards.

To move something you've selected, like a row or column, place your cursor
in the middle of the selected column or row until you get a left pointing
cursor. Now just click, drag it to the new location, and let go!

Making it look nice

Now that you know how to get around and select things, you can go where
you like and enter information. Then, after the content of your columns is in
place, you can format it to give your table a polished look.

You can format individual elements by simply selecting them and applying
the formatting you want, such as font or font size or alignment (Refer to
Chapter 9 for more about formatting text.) If you want to apply a format to a
whole row, column, or the whole table, select it first, then apply the format.

AutoFormat: an easy way to elegant tables

The fastest way to create a "look" for a whole table all at once is by using the
AutoFormat feature. AutoFormat gives you several predefined styles for your
tables, with things like borders, shading, alignment, and so on already
formatted.

Click your table using your right mouse button and the Table shortcut menu
appears. Select Table AutoFormat from it, and the dialog box in figure 14.3
appears.

In figure 14.4, you can see the same table before and after AutoFormat did its
thing.

> Using the AutoText feature, you can save a table with its formatting and
> headings as an entry. Any time you need to use that style of table, just insert it.
> See Chapter 7 for more about AutoText.

In the **Formats** list you can choose what type of border and shading style you want in your table.

Preview gives you a glimpse of what your choices will look like when you apply them to the table.

Fig. 14.3
Table AutoFormat lets you make a variety of settings all in one place.

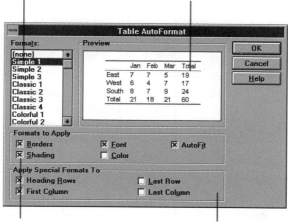

Formats to Apply is where you can keep or get rid of certain formats that belong to these predefined designs (for example, you might not want to use color if you don't have a color printer).

Apply Special Formats To allows you to apply or remove formatting for a particular row or column in your table.

Fig. 14.4
Shading and font settings make your table more attractive.

	February	March	April	May
East	223	321	43	223
West	333	45	98	133
South	431	276	102	178
North	112	656	33	233
Central	556	45	778	890

	February	March	April	May
East	223	321	43	223
West	333	45	98	133
South	431	276	102	178
North	112	656	33	233
Central	556	45	778	890

Stretching and shrinking columns and rows

When you create a table, Word automatically assigns equal widths to each of your columns, based on the width of your page from the left to the right margin. When you type in a cell and reach the edge of the column, Word automatically wraps your text to the next line. When one line in a row wraps to a second line, the entire row expands to accommodate that second line.

But what if you have a mix of information in your table, with one column that needs plenty of space for descriptions, and another that shows only three-digit item numbers, as in figure 14.5? This table will be much more readable if you widen the description column and shrink the column of numbers.

The simplest way to change a column's width is to use the mouse, which changes shape when placed on a table gridline. Drag the column boundary, as in figure 14.6, to an approximate location, and let go.

 **(Tip)**

To see exact measurements while dragging a gridline, hold down the Alt key.

 To make your table easier to read, you might also want to expand the size of your rows. You can do this with the vertical ruler in the Page Layout view. Click the Page Layout View button at the bottom of the screen, and use the individual row markers, which you can see in figure 14.6, to move row dividers.

 {Note}

If you want all your rows or columns to change height or width to an exact specification, with the cell you want to adjust selected, hold down the right mouse button. Select Cell Height and Width in the shortcut menu. Make specific settings on the row and column tabs of the dialog box that appears.

Q&A

I typed something but the end of it disappeared. Where did it go?

If a row is set to be an exact size, your entry will just stop where the row ends. Choose Table, Cell Height and Width to change from exact to auto size. Your rows will now grow as much as you need as you type.

Fig. 14.5
In this table, the description column is too narrow. Each entry requires extra lines to accommodate the wrapped text.

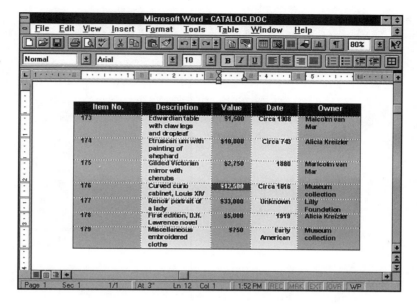

Fig. 14.6
Drag the double-headed arrow to the new location for the gridline.

Drag row markers on the vertical ruler to change row height.

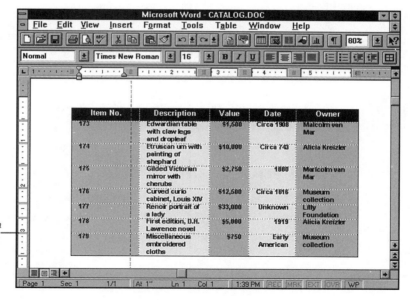

Finishing touches: borders and titles

The most common tables consist of simple rows and columns of data, but you can create elaborate tables with the help of borders and titles. You can even have information that spans across several cells. When you use these features in combination, you can design attractive forms that make you more efficient no matter what your business.

Use borders to make things clearer

Adding a border to your table is like putting up walls where before you only had lines drawn on the floor; borders make these guidelines solid and printable. This can make your table much easier to read.

You can add an outside border around the edges of the table, or inside borders for the column and row dividers, or both (see Chapter 17 for more about borders).

1 Select the entire table, and click the Borders button on the Formatting toolbar. The borders toolbar appears.

2 Select a border line width in the line style box.

3 Click the Outside Border and Inside Border buttons to place a border both around the outside and on the internal gridlines of the table.

Give your table a title

The quickest way to tell your readers what's in a table is to give it an informative heading. If your column headings are in the top row of the table, the first step is to add a new top row that can hold the title. Select the top row, then click the right mouse button and choose Insert Rows from the pop-up menu.

So far so good, but you don't want to cram your title into one of those cells—you want it to stretch over all the columns. To pull off that trick, you'll need to **merge** the cells into a single cell that goes from margin to margin. To merge the cells, you first have to select them (in this case, select the whole new row you've just inserted). Then choose Table, Merge Cells.

Now just type your title, format the text as needed, and center it over your table (see fig. 14.7).

Fig. 14.7
Use the Center tool
to make your selected
text line up in the
middle of your table.

Unit Sales By Region				
	February	March	April	May
East	223	321	43	223
West	333	45	98	133
South	431	276	102	178
North	112	656	33	233
Central	556	45	778	890

> If you want to split the merged cells back up, just select them again and choose T̲able, S̲plit Cells.

If your table spreads over several pages, you might want a title to be repeated automatically at the beginning of each page of your document. Just do this:

1 Select the row you want to repeat.

2 Choose T̲able, H̲eadings.

   A check mark now appears by Headings whenever you select this particular row, which designates this row as your headings row.

Make changes to the heading, and they're also made automatically in the headings at the top of each page. (However, don't insert a manual page break, or your heading stops repeating!)

When a table becomes a form

You might be perfectly happy just using tables to list quarterly profits. But if you're more adventurous, you can also turn Word tables into slick-looking forms: invoices, time sheets, work orders, whatever you like.

How do tables fit together to make a form?

Take a look at figure 14.8. It combines several tables to make an attractive and functional form.

The Invoice title information fits in a three-column table and includes a WordArt object in the first column. Without borders, it has a clean, contemporary look.

Fig. 14.8
Mix and match tables to build impressive forms.

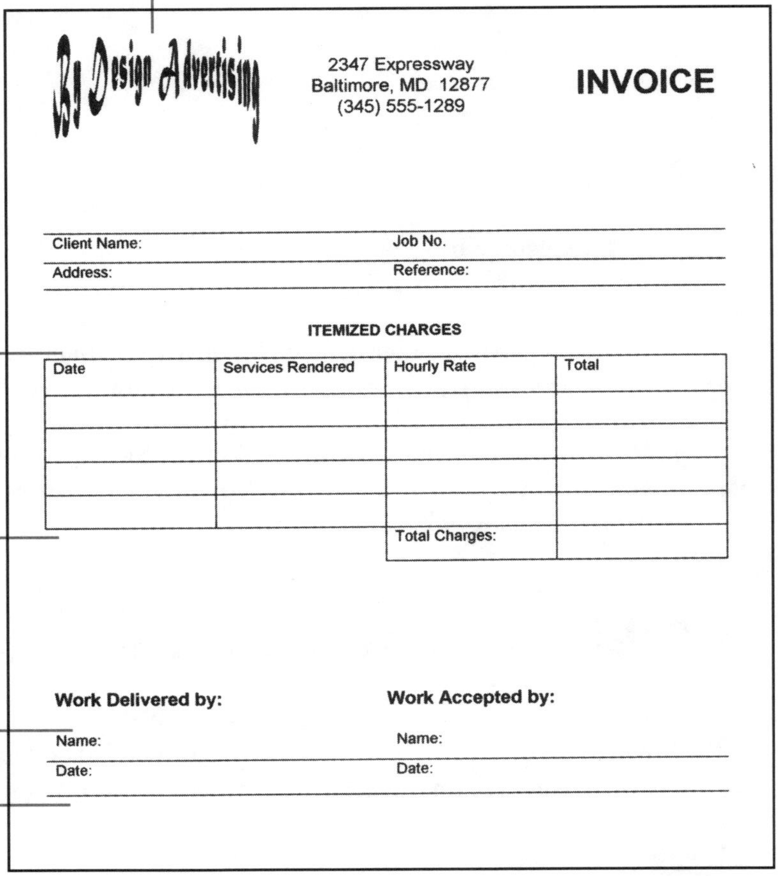

By Design Advertising

2347 Expressway
Baltimore, MD 12877
(345) 555-1289

INVOICE

Client Name: _____   Job No. _____

Address: _____   Reference: _____

ITEMIZED CHARGES

The list of itemized charges spans four columns and uses borders to help the user enter information easily. The bottom two columns on the left have been set up with no borders, so they're invisible.

Date	Services Rendered	Hourly Rate	Total
		Total Charges:	

The signature and date lines are really a simple two-column table, where a bottom border forms the line where people can sign their names.

Work Delivered by: **Work Accepted by:**

Name: _____   Name: _____

Date: _____   Date: _____

Designing your form

Form design is the sort of stuff people go to graduate school for, so I'm not about to give you a course in it. But there are some basics to keep in mind:

- Try sketching your form before starting to build it in Word so that you understand the different pieces and know that you've got all the information your form needs.

- Test your form content on people who will use it every day to make sure it covers all the bases.

- Leave some space between the tables you use as the building blocks for a form; that way it's uncrowded and easy to read.

- If you expect people to fill in your form using a pen or pencil, make sure you leave enough room to hold the information they'll add.

- Stick with similar typefaces and font sizes; watch out for forms that look like ransom notes!

- Experiment with different ways to use borders. For example, with signature lines, use just a bottom border for that cell.

 **{Note}** If you're seriously into building forms, Word even has a Forms toolbar that collects things like the Table tool and some others to help you out, but it still basically builds on the basic concepts of using tables. Check it out.

15

Organize Your Thinking with Outlines

An outline helps the least organized of us turn the bare bones of an idea into a fully fleshed-out treatise. Word makes this transformation a pleasure.

Your house has to stand up to all sorts of natural stresses. You might have to deal with hurricanes, tornadoes, ice storms, earthquakes, or mudslides. When those gale-force gusts start blowing, it doesn't matter how gorgeous the outside is; underneath, you'd better have a strong, solid foundation or the whole thing will be gone with the wind.

You don't add a foundation as an afterthought. It's the mandatory starting point for a strong house, and it's equally important for a convincing document. You start with a few strong, well-anchored arguments. Then you add a few supporting beams, and tie it all together so that every piece reinforces the others. By the time you get around to filling in the details with words and graphics, it's a simple task.

The best way to build a solid document in Word is to start with a strong outline. Fortunately, Word takes to outlining like a fish to water. There's even a special Outline view in Word, with its own toolbar and pre-set formatting for text. Once you're in Outline view, you can arrange and view your outline so that you see all the details, or only the high points. With a well-constructed outline, you can see how your document is put together from the inside out. When you strip away all those distracting details, you can see how strong your argument really is. Get your thoughts organized instantly.

Organize your thoughts instantly

You remember outlining from freshman English. There are different levels of headings, starting at the highest level of detail, and rambling down the page with farther and farther right indents as you get into more detailed levels.

A lot of what Word outlining lets you do is instantly **promote** or **demote** headings to different levels in your outline, using the Outlining toolbar.

 Plain English, please!

In outline lingo, to **promote** a heading means to move it to a higher level of detail—in other words, to move it back toward the left margin. To **demote** a heading is to make it a detail under another heading—in other words, to move it farther to the right on the page.

What do I need to know to use outlines in Word?

Creating outlines in Word is easy. Basically, Word applies special **styles**, created especially for use with outlines, to different levels of headings. All you have to do is let Word know which level of heading you want the text to occupy, and it provides the structure.

 Plain English, please!

Styles are simply sets of formatting commands saved together. When you apply a style, what you're really doing is applying several formats to selected text all at once. (See Chapter 13 for more about styles.)

Close-Up: the Outlining toolbar

 To get to the Outlining toolbar, click the Outline View button at the bottom of the Word screen.

 Promote
Moves heading out one level.

 Demote
Moves heading in one level.

 Demote to Body Text
Changes a heading to body text level.

 Move Up
Moves headings up in the outline.

Move Down
Moves headings down in the outline.

Expand
Opens (expands) the outline to show more detail.

 Collapse
Collapses the outline to show higher-level headings only.

 Show Headings
Numbered 1–8, these buttons reveal some, but not all, the headings in your outline.

 All
Shows all levels of headings and body text.

 Show First Line Only
Sometimes, to save space and make the outline more read-able, you just want to show the heading and first line of text.

 Show Formatting
If you don't want to see bold, italic, and larger point sizes (lets you fit more on-screen), click here.

 Master Document view
You can use this view to pull together several documents into one large document; it uses outlines to help you do this. This process can be complicated, so make sure you have backup copies of all your work.

In addition to the important information about indentation that helps make an outline look like an outline, outline styles also include text formatting such as bold, italic, point size, font, and so on.

Exploring the Outlining toolbar

 In Word, you work with outlines in the Outline view. Click the Outline View button in the lower left side of the screen to get there.

The Outlining toolbar appears when you enter Outline view. These buttons allow you to do the following types of things:

- Promote or demote a heading

- Move sections of the outline up or down

- Show different amounts of detail by expanding or collapsing the outline's structure

- Change the formatting to take away bold, italic, and larger point size, but leave the indentation of the outline intact.

- Switch to Master Document view

Order, please! (or: Outlining 101)

 There are several things that make a good outline. But above all else, a really good outline presents information in a logical order. This gives you—and your readers— a structure that's easy to follow.

For example, if you're writing about the rise and fall of the Roman Empire, your outline should follow chronological order. If you're writing a repair manual, on the other hand, you may want to structure your outline to present easy, minor repairs first, and the "travel at your own risk" repairs last. You'll want to divide each major repair section into subsections that take the reader through the process, step by step.

But, always keep in mind how your audience will use the document. A manual on defusing a bomb had better call out the most urgent actions and warnings right off the bat, or you won't have a reader at all!

 **{Note}** Basically, the Master Document is used to assemble several smaller documents into one large document. To do this, Word for Windows uses outlining features. For more on Master Document, see Chapter 22, "Managing Big Documents."

Rearrange it 'til you get it right

The brutal truth is that Word can't help you determine what information to put in your outline. But, once you've done your research and know what facts to include, Word's outlining feature is so flexible that it makes the process of creating an outline relatively painless. And once you've created the outline, reorganizing and rearranging things is a snap.

You have to start somewhere

To create your outline in Word, you can type in the details in any view, such as Normal or Page Layout. The outline structure can be added after you enter all the information, or as you go along, by working in the Outline view. You use the Outlining toolbar to assign outline levels to text, then use other tools to rearrange or display selected portions of the outline.

Try entering some text for your outline in the Outline view. Type three headings, as in figure 15.1.

When you first enter text in Outline view, Word automatically assigns the Heading 1 style to that text (the font and point size are part of that style). The minus sign to the left of the text indicates that it has no **subordinate** headings.

 Plain English, please!

Think of the way an organizational chart looks: one boss with several subordinates under her. A **subordinate heading** is simply a heading in an outline that's indented beneath a higher-level heading. Usually, most of the headings in an outline are subordinate, just as there are more workers than managers in the world.

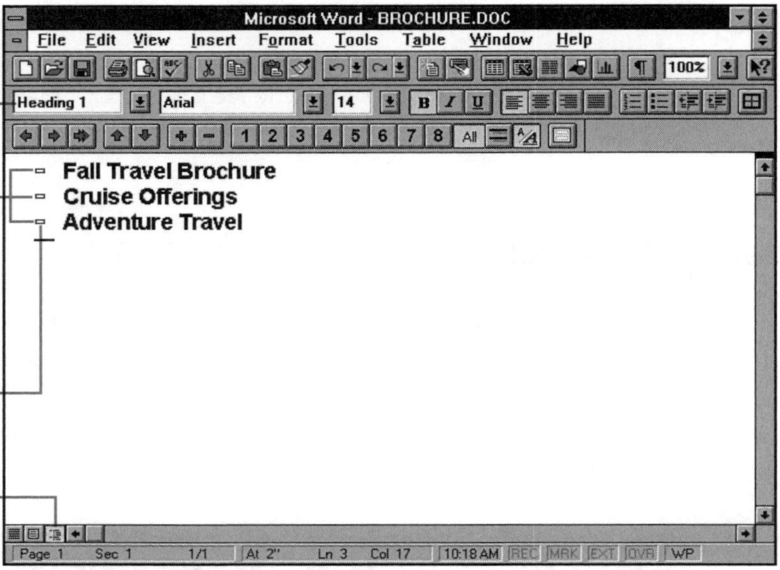

Fig. 15.1
Here are the contents
of an outline entered
in Outline view before
you've promoted or
demoted anybody.

*Heading 1 style
automatically applied
to all level 1 headings.*

*The Minus icon
indicates no
subordinate
headings.*

Outline View button

Demoting, promoting, and generally moving things around

To begin to give structure to your outline, click in the selection bar to the left of the second and third headings to highlight them, and then click the Demote button on the toolbar. The headings move to the right and become subordinate headings.

> To quickly promote or demote a heading, click with the mouse on the plus or minus icon next to the heading, and drag the heading to whatever level you want.

In figure 15.2, the higher heading now has a plus icon next to it to show that it has subordinate headings. The two subordinates, with no lowlier headings to boss around, have the minus icon beside them. When you change heading levels, the outlining feature automatically assigns a new style for each level (which just happens to be one of Word's best outlining tricks).

Fig. 15.2
After you demote
these headings, your
list begins to look
like an outline.

*Heading 2 style is
automatically applied
to second-level
headings.*

*A plus icon indicates
that there are sub-
ordinate headings.*

As you start to add to an outline and you get closer to turning it into a document, you'll probably want to use body text for the sentences and paragraphs that grow beneath your headings. One variation on demoting is that you can quickly demote any heading to body text, no matter where it is in the hierarchy, by clicking the Demote To Body Text button (see fig. 15.3).

Fig. 15.3
Body Text has a little
box to its left, rather
than a plus or minus
icon.

*Body text has the Normal
style applied to it.*

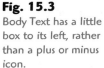

You can easily assemble a table of contents for an existing document by switching to Outline view, organizing the headings at different levels, and hiding the body text.

After you type a few more headings in your outline, it's also very simple to move a heading alone, or along with its subordinate headings, to another place in the outline.

  Select a heading (or a heading and its subordinate headings), and then click the Move Up or Move Down button to move the selected text up or down in the outline. Notice that this doesn't change the heading's outline level—just moves it up or down, not in or out.

 An outline can help you edit and reorganize an entire document. By collapsing your document so that only the headings show, you can easily move and rearrange entire sections of text—headings, subheadings, and any body text.

Roman numerals or letters?

Remember those endless series of Roman numerals, letters, and Arabic numerals that used to drive you crazy when you created outlines? I don't know about you, but I always got lost at about level 4—am I supposed to use a tiny a), or am I on tiny numbers now?

Word takes the number/letter drudgery out of outlining by keeping track of where you are and applying numbering or letters automatically. To apply a heading numbering style, either before you enter your outline or at any point along the way, choose F*o*rmat, *H*eading Numbering. The Heading Numbering dialog box appears, offering you several standard numbering options, including some letter styles (see fig. 15.4).

Fig. 15.4
Forget figuring out
those Roman numerals
and capital letters—
let Word apply these
heading patterns
instantly!

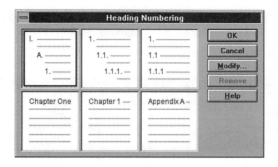

Just click the number style you like, and when you click OK, your entire
outline is numbered automatically (see fig. 15.5).

Fig. 15.5
This pattern will be
carried out through all
levels of headings
without you having to
lift another finger.

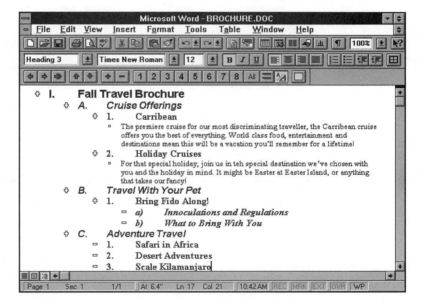

You can get pretty fancy with customized numbering for your outlines, like
the example in figure 15.6. Click Modify to get various options for numbering.
One of these is a pop-up for bullet or number choice. One of these choices,
New Bullet, lets you choose any kind of character or symbol you like for your
bullets.

The best way to figure out the possibilities here is to play around with them—when you don't have a deadline staring you in the face. (See more about custom bullets and numbering in Chapter 10.)

Fig. 15.6

You can use custom bullets to make your outline special.

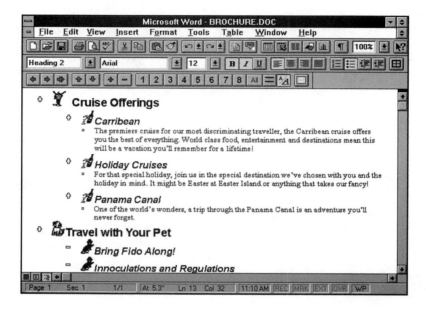

Q&A

I changed the font on one of my headings by mistake and then closed the document. I can't undo it anymore, so how do I get my original heading style back?

When you manually change the heading formatting, the original heading style is still listed in the style box on your toolbar when you choose the heading. In essence, you've made a manual modification to the style, not gotten rid of it. Select the heading, then choose the heading style again in the style box. You get a dialog box asking if you'd like to redefine the style or put it back the way it was. Put it back.

Part V:

Desktop Publishing for Everyone

16

I Can't Draw, but I Can Desktop Publish

Want an eye-catching résumé, a great looking newsletter, or a really unique party invitation? Word can create them all!

You may wear sneakers (or even go barefoot) all weekend, but for most of us the casual clothes go back in the closet as soon as Monday rolls around. For business meetings, a well-polished pair of dress shoes is far more appropriate.

Your everyday memos and laundry lists may be as casual as a pair of old Keds, but certain documents—résumés, for example, or newsletters, invitations, and brochures—call for a little extra design polish. When you start to pay this much attention to structure and design, you've stepped into the realm of **desktop publishing**.

Scared? You needn't be. Even if you can't draw a straight line, you can do some surprisingly sophisticated desktop publishing with Word. Start by learning how to divide text into neat columns, then add pictures, and pretty soon, piece by piece, you'll find you've built the perfect page without even trying.

I'll take one from Column A...

Pick up your local newspaper; you see columns of text and pictures arranged in a way that fits the message. The newspaper, with multiple stories of different types and a wide page format, may use 6, 7, or 8 columns. On the other hand, your dictionary, with a single type of content, probably has only two columns.

Both the newspaper and the dictionary give the reader a sense of order and structure at first glance because of those neat columns. They're also easier to read because the eye can scan a narrow column much more quickly than it can move from side to side across an entire newspaper page.

Word columns behave exactly the way you expect them to behave; text flows automatically from the bottom of one column to the top of the next, just as your text flows from one page to the next in your document.

How can columns make my documents easier to read?

Columns are a versatile design tool. They can be different widths and lengths. You can even mix and match different styles of columns right on the same page. And you can use columns for a number of things in your documents:

- Use two, unequal columns to make dates stand out in a stylish, well-organized résumé.

- Try a three-column design for a newsletter; the multicolumn format gives you the flexibility to arrange stories in a variety of ways.

- Use two equal columns to organize the definitions in a glossary at the end of a manual.

Or you might use a combination of these. Figure 16.1 shows some examples of documents designed with columns.

Fig. 16.1
A résumé, travel brochure, and newsletter all make good use of columns.

The top half of this page is formatted in two columns. You can use columns to hold graphic images, as we've done here.

Newsletters typically hold three columns. This layout looks good and makes text easier to read.

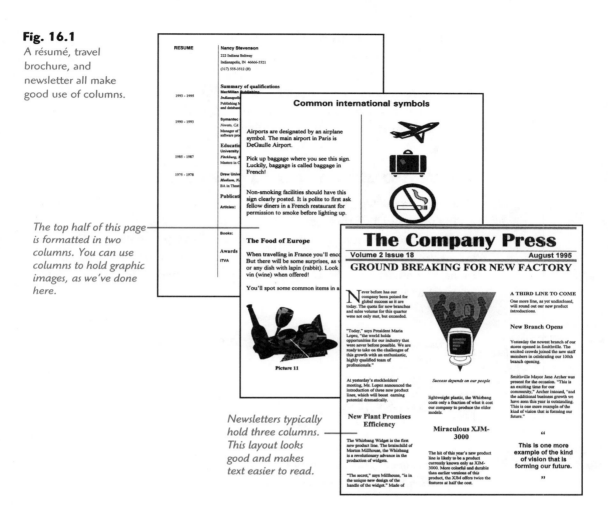

Creating columns takes hardly any effort. But before you create them, you should think about how many columns make sense for your document. Take a moment to consider the following points:

- **Physical space.** What size paper you will be using, and whether your document is in landscape or portrait orientation.

- **Layout decisions.** Remember that you need to allow room for white space—0.5 inches is the standard width. And your columns must be wide enough to keep the text legible; skinny little columns may be filled with half words and hyphens that just confuse the reader.

- **Matching form to function.** Finally, consider how much of a "break" you want your columns to give to the information in your document. A newsletter succeeds with multiple columns because it consists of different stories—the reader's attention is broken up frequently by change in content, and the columns reflect that. But with a single topic, too many breaks just become distracting.

Click a button, build some columns

 When you're ready to create your columns, you can use the Columns button on the toolbar. Click this button and drag the mouse pointer through the graphic representation of columns that drops down (see figure 16.2). If you select three columns, for example, the current section (or your entire document, if you haven't defined any sections) will be divided into three columns of equal width.

Fig. 16.2
Drag across this graphic representation to select the number of columns for your document.

 The number of columns you can create using the columns drop-down varies, depending on the page size and whether you're using portrait or landscape orientation.

There are a few variations on how this column selection will work, depending on what you've selected:

- If you select text and then click the Columns button, just the selected text is arranged in columns.

- If you have created different sections and don't select anything, the column setting affects only the section where your insertion point is at the time you set the columns (see Chapter 12 for more about sections).

That's all you have to do; your text will automatically flow from column to column and page to page without any further effort on your part.

I selected my text and set my document up with two columns, but instead I get one column down the left side of the screen.

To see multiple columns, you need to be in Page Layout view or Print Preview. In Normal view, you see one very long column when you format your document with columns.

I don't want all my columns to be the same

Although perfectly even columns give a nice order to your documents, sometimes you need both wide and narrow columns on the same page. Think of a résumé: you might place the dates of employment in the left column, and then use the second column for job descriptions. Not only is the actual information about the job more lengthy than the dates, it's also more important to the reader; so, you make it the larger of the two columns.

The Columns dialog box, shown in figure 16.3, offers you a lot of options for customizing columns. To open this dialog box, choose Format, Columns.

If any of these Presets look like the column design you want, click one for a quick setup.

Fig. 16.3
You can create or modify your columns right here.

Choose the number of columns you want here.

You can enter a specific width for each column.

Columns
Presets
One   Two   Three   Left   Right
OK
Cancel
Help
Number of Columns: [2]
☐ Line Between
Width and Spacing
Col #:   Width: Spacing:
1:   [2.81"]   [0.38"]
2:   [2.81"]
☒ Equal Column Width
Preview
Apply To: [This Section]
☐ Start New Column

Click here to put a line between columns.

Preview shows you how the columns you're choosing will look.

You have to turn off this selection to set up columns of varying widths.

Maybe you don't want unequal columns in every part of your document. That's fine; you can change some of the columns:

1 Create a two-column setup at the beginning of your document.

2 With your cursor at the bottom of the two-column section, choose Format, Columns. The Columns dialog box appears.

3 Use the Apply To drop-down box to apply a new column setup to This Point Forward, and choose three columns.

The new column setup will apply to everything past your insertion point.

When you're ready to change the column setup again, use the same method. You can apply a column setup to the whole document or by section, as well as using the from This Point Forward option.

 **(Tip)**

> If you choose to apply the settings in the Columns dialog box to This Point Forward, Word automatically inserts a section break at the point where the new column setting begins.

When you click OK to return to your document, notice that the column marker on your ruler is slightly different (see fig. 16.4). There's a little gray patch in the middle. You can use this marker to adjust column widths right on-screen. It's a little quicker than using the dialog box, and it lets you see the effect right on your document as you manipulate the ruler. Just point at the marker until a two-headed arrow appears, then drag the marker to the column width you want.

Fig. 16.4

Drag this little gray box to change the width of the two columns.

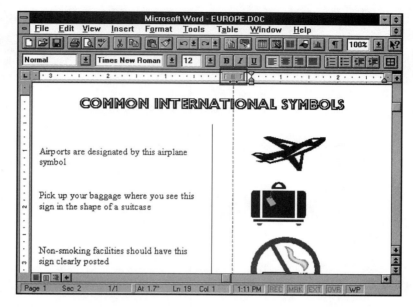

How much space do I need between columns?

In designing documents, all space counts. Don't look at just the columns and pictures; the white space, where there's nothing at all, is important, too. Intelligently used, white space keeps the page from getting cluttered and helps to break up lines of text to give readers a mental "break."

If the space between columns looks too narrow (making things feel cluttered) or too wide (which wastes space and upsets the balance of the page), change it. You can do it directly using the column markers on the ruler, shown in figure 16.5.

Fig. 16.5
Drag column markers—the lines at either edge of this block—to change the space between columns.

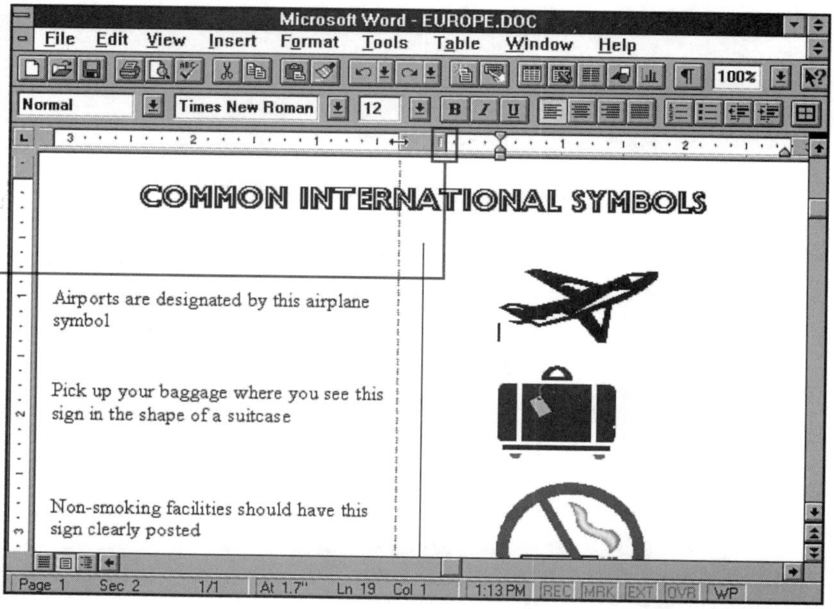
Column marker
Microsoft Word - EUROPE.DOC
File Edit View Insert Format Tools Table Window Help
Normal
Times New Roman
12
100%
COMMON INTERNATIONAL SYMBOLS
Airports are designated by this airplane symbol
Pick up your baggage where you see this sign in the shape of a suitcase
Non-smoking facilities should have this sign clearly posted
Page 1 Sec 2 1/1 At 1.7" Ln 19 Col 1 1:13 PM REC MRK EXT OVR WP

If necessary, choose View, Ruler to make the ruler visible. To adjust the space between columns, put your pointer on either edge of the gray column marker, and drag one way or the other. With columns of equal width, the column sizes stay equal as the space between them changes.

Putting pictures alongside your words

Breaking your text into columns makes it more readable. That's good. But it doesn't necessarily communicate your ideas with all the force they deserve. For that, you need to add graphics.

> ***Plain English, please!***
>
> **Graphics** is a catch-all term for computer-generated art. This category includes a wide range of visuals, from elaborate scanned-in photographs, to logos, to simple line drawings and cartoons.

Pictures in your document serve a few purposes. They add visual interest, giving you a chance to hook your audience before they've read a single word.

They can also help you tell your story, and help your reader remember it. The Chinese proverb said a picture is worth 10,000 words. Well, the Information Age and the MTV generation combined have probably sent that number into the stratosphere, for good reason. Pictures increase the amount of information people retain. Word provides you with a nice supply of ready-made pictures, and with the tools to arrange pictures and text in documents to create everything from nifty newsletters to beautiful brochures.

How Word handles pictures

If you're in charge of producing the company's new safety manual, you might be tempted to paste in some Polaroid pictures to help define different sections: a fire extinguisher for the fire-safety section, a red cross for the first-aid section, and so on.

With Word, you can keep the Scotch tape in your desk drawer. There's a built-in collection of **clip art**, pictures you can paste into your document. You can also **import** graphic files from other programs into your Word documents.

Plain English, please!

To **import** a graphic object into Word means to use a file that was originally created using another program. You do this using one of the choices from the Insert menu.

The clip-art files provided with Word use the extension WMF (see Chapter 5 for more about file extensions), which means they follow the "Windows meta-file" format. If you've installed the proper graphics options, Word can also handle an alphabet soup of other graphics file formats, like TIF, CGM, EPS, PIC, BMP, and more. If you want to import one of these graphics files, just open the Insert Picture dialog box, choose All Files (*.*) under List Files of Type, and locate your file in the directory listing. Word will let you know if it can't handle the file.

To get to Word's stash of pictures, choose Insert, Picture. The Insert Picture dialog box appears (see fig. 16.6).

Fig. 16.6
By default, Word places you in the clip-art directory.

Choose a file name in this list.

This defaults to all graphics files, but you can narrow down to a specific file format here.

Click either place to preview the picture before inserting it in your document.

You can do a few things here to find just the right image for your document:

- Look for the file in the Dri_v_es list. Maybe it's on your main hard disk (C drive) or a floppy disk (A or B).

- If your graphic is in another directory, just click different _D_irectories and file names until you find the one you like. Make sure the right file format is selected, or you won't see your file.

- You wouldn't buy a painting without looking at it first, so Word lets you look at the picture in the Preview box before inserting it.

②Q&A

When my picture comes in, I only see a small part of it. Where'd the rest of it go?

If you have line spacing set at Exactly in the Indents and Spacing tab of the Paragraph dialog box, you only see part of your picture. Choose F_o_rmat, _P_aragraph, and change the line spacing to Single. When you click OK, your entire figure appears.

I want this picture right here

Half the fun of having pictures in your documents is playing around with them. You can move them around, make them bigger or smaller, and combine them with words in different ways.

In order to do things with a graphic, you have to know about two things: selection handles and frames. **Selection handles** are part of your graphic object; they're the little black boxes connected by a thin line that surrounds the object when you click on it. You use them to resize a picture.

A **frame** can be added to a graphic object once you've imported it into Word. Frames place a shaded gray line around the picture and allow you to move it around your document freely. And, the frame encloses the object, so text can wrap around it. Without the frame, text just stops when it hits a graphic, then starts again on the other side. (Chapter 17 gives you more information on frames.)

Plain English, please!

An **object** is a hundred-dollar word for a pretty simple concept: a chunk of information you create and edit in another program and then plop into a Word document. Objects usually can't be edited in Word, but they can be resized or moved. A **graphic object** is usually a picture or drawing that was created with a graphics program.

I want this picture over there

Just as it's easier to hang a canvas that's been framed, the easiest way to move a picture around in your document is to give it a Word frame.

Use the Pictures shortcut menu for this one:

1 In Page Layout view, click the picture with your right mouse button. The menu in figure 16.7 appears.

Fig. 16.7
The shortcut menu provides quick access to common functions.

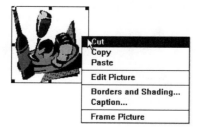

2 Choose Frame Picture. The frame, a shaded gray border with black handles, surrounds the picture (see fig. 16.8).

3 Place your mouse pointer over the picture, and you get a positioning pointer. Now just click, and you can move the picture where you want it on the page.

Fig. 16.8

A four-way pointing arrow now appears next to the arrow, indicating you can move the picture.

 A frame stores information about the object's location. If you remove a frame after moving it, the object will move back to its original position.

I want this picture much bigger (or smaller)

If one picture is worth 10,000 words, is a really big picture worth 100,000 words? Maybe your picture only merits about 500 words. At any rate, sometimes you need to make a picture bigger or smaller. Changing the size of a picture in Word is incredibly easy.

Remember those selection handles that surround the picture object? You use those handles to resize the picture. Click on the top handle, and drag up. Your box becomes a dotted line, as shown in figure 16.9. Your mouse pointer changes to a crosshair as you drag to resize the picture. When you let go, your picture snaps to the new size.

Fig. 16.9

Drag on the handle that's on the side of the box you want to stretch.

⚠(Tip) _____

> Dragging these handles in different directions can distort your picture, kind of like what happens to the picture on a balloon when you stretch it. If you want to resize your picture but keep it in proportion, drag it by a corner handle. To put the picture back to the proportions it originally had when you inserted it, choose Format, Picture, Reset.

Capping off your picture with words

Some pictures say it all, but others need a few words of explanation. You want to identify the parts of a diagram in your report on plant biology, or give a brief description of an illustration of a procedure in a safety manual? That's when you need **callouts** or **captions**.

 Plain English, please!

A **caption** is usually placed right beneath or above a figure. It gives a title that you can reference in your text, such as *Figure 10* or *Table B* (see captions used to identify the figures in this book, for example).

Callouts literally call out points of interest in the picture, directing the reader to a specific point or object and describing or naming it. 🙷

Creating captions

Click the picture with your right mouse button to get the shortcut menu. Choose Caption, and you see the dialog box in figure 16.10.

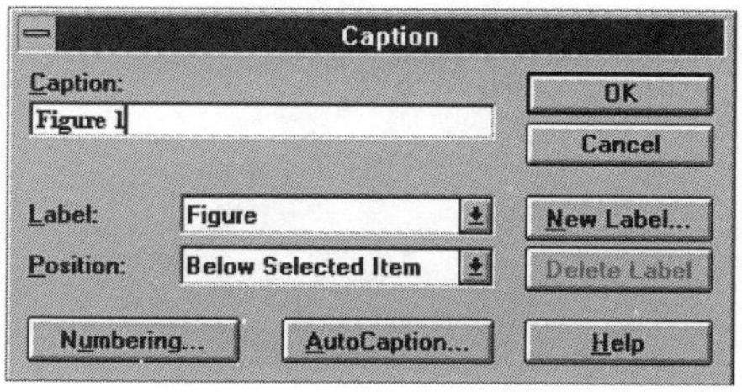

Fig. 16.10
Simply select the label that's most appropriate, and whether you want it above or below your picture.

Caption	
<u>C</u>aption:	[OK]
Figure 1	[Cancel]
<u>L</u>abel: Figure ⬇	[<u>N</u>ew Label...]
<u>P</u>osition: Below Selected Item ⬇	Delete Label
[<u>N</u>umbering...] [<u>A</u>utoCaption...]	[<u>H</u>elp]

The predefined labels listed here are pretty ho-hum. You can change to a different preset label by selecting it from the Label drop-down list. Add to this drop-down list by clicking New Label and typing another label, such as *Picture* or *Element*. Word gives the label a number and automatically assigns consecutive numbers to all captions with the same label in your document.

You place the caption above or below your figure using the Position drop-down list. Click OK, and the caption appears. For those times when you want to add to the label with a descriptive sentence, that's easy, too. You can change the whole caption by highlighting it and typing anything you want—even get rid of the label, if you like. Or you can place your insertion point at the end of the label and type additional text right on-screen.

Call out your most important points

Callouts draw attention to important elements in your figures. For example, this book uses callouts throughout to point out parts of Word screens, toolbars, or dialog boxes.

To place callouts, you're going to use the drawing tools (you'll explore more about drawing in Chapter 18):

1 Click the Drawing button to see this toolbar (see fig. 16.11).

Fig. 16.11
Add callouts easily with the click of a button.

As you draw the callout, you get a box, ready for callout text.

Format your callout by clicking here.

Add a callout by clicking on this button, then dragging your cursor on-screen.

The Drawing toolbar

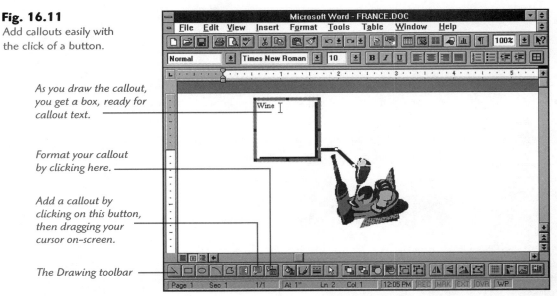

2 Click the Callout button on the Drawing toolbar.

3 Move your pointer over the picture and the pointer changes to a crosshair.

4 Just click the part of the picture that you want the callout to point to, then drag to place the callout somewhere outside the picture.

5 Now just type the information you want in the callout box, as in figure 16.12.

You can format this text by selecting it and using all the common text formatting tools to change its size, font, make it bold, and so on. You can also click the callout and move it around the page to get it in the perfect position.

Fig. 16.12
The callout should tell the reader something about the item that the callout line points to.

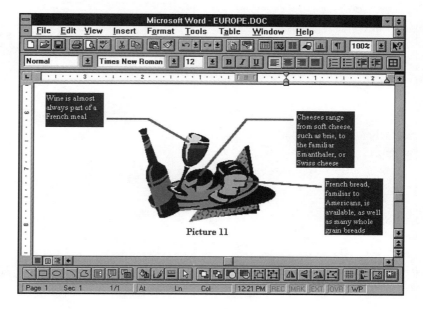

If you want to adjust the way the callout box is drawn, or the space between the text and callout box, try the Format Callout button. Click this, and a dialog box appears that lets you fine-tune callouts (see fig. 16.13).

Fig. 16.13
Beyond regular text formatting, you can format the shape and arrangement of your callouts right here.

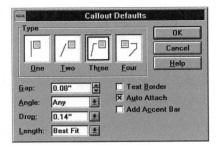

Let the Wizard do it!

Word offers the would-be desktop publisher some handy shortcuts in the person of some creative little wizards. If you're all thumbs when it comes to designing documents any more complicated than a business letter, give them a try.

For example, there's the Newsletter Wizard. Follow this guy's lead, and you'll end up with something very like the documents shown here with no effort at all.

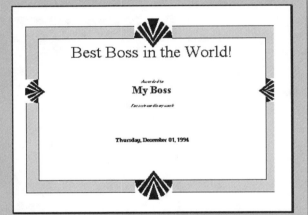

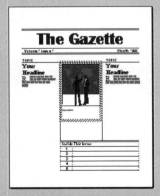

If it's time to give your co-worker or spouse some recognition, just fill in the appropriate name and reason for celebration in the Award Wizard, and Word does the rest.

Just select the wizard of your choice from the template list Word offers you when you're opening a new documen, and follow his lead.

There are also others: Calender Wizard, Resume Wizard, and Fax Wizard, for example. They all give you a nicely designed document that you can modify with text and pictures specific to your needs.

17

Word's Picture Shop: Frames and Borders

Frames make moving things around a snap, and borders help your words or pictures practically jump out at the reader.

In this chapter:

- I want to move this picture here...no, over there
- If I put the picture here, where will the text go?
- I want this text to *really* stand out
- Can I put this block of text in a gray box?

There's more to some documents than just words. Sometimes, to make a point, you use pictures, tables, or charts. You might even take a paragraph out of your document and treat it as a special element, like the quotes we highlight at the beginning of each chapter in this book. Anything in your document that you use for something other than the main text is an object. When you work with objects, you usually want to position them precisely on the page. You might also want to set them off from the rest of the document with a line, or even add a hint of color to the background. That's where frames and borders come in.

Frames and borders sound like the same thing—something that surrounds something else. Well, in Word, frames and borders are both used to surround objects, but they have very different purposes. A frame is just a container that makes it easy to move elements around your page. But a border is a visual element that surrounds text or graphics and appears in your printed document.

Frames and borders: what do I do with them?

Frames are strictly practical, like the plain plastic bag you use to carry around a bunch of apples or to keep them from getting mixed up with the broccoli. Frames help you position and resize objects, and they define the physical boundaries of the object so that text knows how to move around it. But frames don't show up on the printed page.

Borders, on the other hand, are mostly decorative, like a pretty ceramic bowl you'd keep those apples in. You wouldn't lug your produce home from the market in a big bowl; likewise, borders are no good for moving stuff around. Borders *do* show up when you print; by separating and highlighting text and pictures, they make your document look cool and can help get your point across more effectively.

You can place a frame around text, pictures, tables—just about anything you can put in a Word document. You can even put more than one thing—like a picture and its caption—in the same frame. Move the frame, and you move everything that's in it, too.

Borders, on the other hand, are more artistic. When you put a border around text, pictures, tables, or any combination of those things, you surround them with a visible boundary that will print out as a design element. And, if you want it all, you can add a frame to a bordered object so that you can move the whole thing around by just clicking and dragging (see fig. 17.1).

Fig. 17.1
A bordered picture, framed picture, and framed picture selected and ready to be moved.

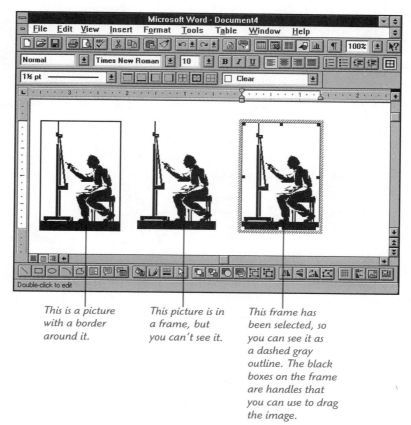

This is a picture with a border around it.

This picture is in a frame, but you can't see it.

This frame has been selected, so you can see it as a dashed gray outline. The black boxes on the frame are handles that you can use to drag the image.

Putting text and pictures in a frame

Which came first—the picture or the frame? Well, just like the chicken and the egg, it really doesn't matter. You can insert a frame, then put something in it; or you can create the text or picture first, and then put a frame around it.

I want to jump in frame first

To draw a frame first, switch to Page Layout view, then do this:

1 Click the Drawing button to put the Drawing toolbar on-screen.

2 Click the Insert Frame button. Your pointer changes to a crosshair pointer.

3 Position the pointer where you want any corner of the frame, and then click and drag to stretch the frame to the size and shape you need.

4 Let your mouse button go, and you've inserted a frame.

After you've created the frame, you can click inside the frame and simply begin typing text, or select existing text and cut and paste it into the frame. To put a picture in the frame, click the frame, and then choose Insert, Picture.

? Q&A

I inserted a picture into the frame, and it's very small. Is there something wrong?

Not at all. When you insert a picture into a frame, Word sizes the picture to fit the frame. You can resize the picture by dragging its frame handles; the frame resizes right along with it.

I want to frame something that's already there

So you already have a picture in your document and now you decide you'd like to move it to the left margin? No problem. To put a frame around existing text or a picture, select the item, then click the Insert Frame button. The frame appears in just the right size to fit the object. Now when you click the object, you see a gray shaded frame around the outside.

✴ {Note}

When you apply a frame to text, you automatically give it a border. You can change or remove the border if you like. To remove it, display the border toolbar by clicking the Border button, then click the No Border button.

How about the text that goes around my frame?

Frames don't just help you get a handle on inserted objects; a frame also automatically forces text to flow around it, the way water flows around a rock in a stream. If you inserted a picture into your document and didn't frame it, it would be like water flowing over the rock: text would appear above and below the picture, but wouldn't wrap around the side of it. Figure 17.2 shows how text wraps around a framed picture.

Fig. 17.2

Text will wrap around a framed picture or text.

This object has a frame, so text wraps around it. It also has a border, so there's a printed line surrounding it.

This object is framed, so text wraps around it. Because there's no border, it appears to "float" on the page.

This picture is bordered, but has no frame: text won't go near it.

Of course, if you don't want text to wrap around your framed object, Word is happy to oblige. You can change how text flows around your framed object by selecting the object, then choosing Format, Frame. Use the Frame dialog box, shown in figure 17.3, to specify that you don't want text to wrap around the object. Besides this setting, and the Remove Frame button, the rest of this box is pretty much used to set a framed object's position.

The Frame dialog box is a great way to position objects when you need real precision—for forms and desktop publishing grids, for example. But when the overall "look" of your document is the most important thing, moving objects around on-screen and judging their position with the on-screen rulers is much easier.

Fig. 17.3
Let text wrap around the edges of a framed object or have it steer clear.

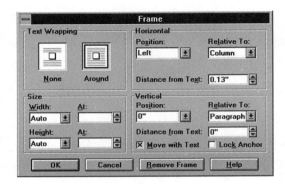

Getting rid of a frame

But what if you decide you want some text you framed to go right back into the body of your document, so you just don't need the frame after all? To delete a frame, simply click the Remove Frame button in the Frame dialog box.

 **<Caution>** The information about the position of a framed object is stored with the frame. If you move the object around, then delete the frame, the object will lose its new position, too.

Of course, if you want to throw out the baby with the bath water—that is, get rid of an object and its frame both—you can. Select the framed object in the Page Layout view and just hit the Delete key on your keyboard. It's history!

Let's change things around

The whole point of framing an object is to make it easier to place objects exactly where you want them on your page. After the frame's in place, you can move an object just by clicking and dragging.

And remember: just because you've framed something, that doesn't mean it's cast in bronze. You can change the size of things or add text to frames just like any other part of your document.

I want to move this frame

There's really nothing to moving a frame around. Just put your mouse on its edges, and you get a positioning pointer. Click and drag the framed object anywhere you like.

 (Tip)

> Most printers won't print within 1/4 inch or so of the edge of the paper. If you drag a framed object into the margin, be sure to leave enough space to allow for this unprintable area.

Here's an important thing to know about frames. Framed objects are automatically **anchored** to a paragraph in your document. Think of each object as having an invisible rope attached to it; as you move a framed object from one place to another, it uses that rope to attach itself to the paragraph that's nearest its new position.

Should you care about this relationship between the framed object and a paragraph? You don't need to, unless you want to make sure that the paragraph and the framed object remain on the same page. For example, you might want to keep a picture of your new company logo attached to the paragraph that contains your company's mission statement. In this case, you'll need to lock the anchor, so that when you move the frame it stays on the same page as that paragraph.

To lock the anchor, select the frame, bring up the Frame dialog box by choosing F<u>o</u>rmat, <u>F</u>rame, then check the box labeled Loc<u>k</u> Anchor. Now, although you can move the frame so it appears next to different paragraphs, Word won't let you actually move it off the page where the paragraph it's anchored to is located.

If you don't want a framed object to move with the paragraph it's anchored to, go to the Frame dialog box (refer to fig. 17.3). Here you can deselect the <u>M</u>ove with Text option.

⚠ (Tip) _____

From the Frame dialog box, you can also choose to lock the framed object to a page or margin, rather than a paragraph. Use the Relative To drop-down list in the Vertical positioning section and choose page or margin.

This frame isn't the right size

Word lets you stretch and shrink frames. With a picture, simply grab onto one of the little handles that appear when the object is selected, and then drag. When you do this, the frame expands or shrinks to the new size of the picture.

If you have text in the frame, you can click inside the frame to get an insertion point, then type, and the frame will automatically grow longer to accommodate the lines of type. To add a new line, just hit Shift+Enter.

I've been framed (and I'm easier to read)! Putting things in interesting places

In real estate, they say the three most important things are location, location, and location. The same is true for your documents. When you put important elements in the right place, you communicate more effectively. With the ability to move things around in a frame, a world of possibilities is open to you.

Try putting a picture in the middle of two columns and letting the words wrap around it to help break up the text.

Got a great quote in your report? Magazine and book designers take an intriguing phrase, make it bigger and bolder, then place it in the middle of other text to attract the reader.

Try creating a matted picture frame effect. First insert one frame and give it a border. Shade the border in dark gray. Then create another, smaller frame and place it over the first. Insert a picture in the inside frame, and you've got an interesting frame, like the one we show here.

Head for the border

Look through this book for a moment. It's crawling with borders. Some are thin lines forming a box around something like a Tip. Others just have a left border, like Cautions. There are also shaded borders, used at the beginning of each chapter and for sidebars. Borders set off text or pictures in a way that adds emphasis and sets the bordered material apart.

You can use a Word border for different things in your documents:

- Put text for a caution or warning in a box so that readers notice it right away.

- Border a heading on a page for design impact.

- Mark the boundaries between the individual cells in a Word table.

- Use a one-sided border to place a line under text. That line automatically moves with that text, and you can modify its thickness with the border tools, which you can't do with underlining.

Create borders that go beyond boxes

 To work with borders, click the Borders button on the Formatting toolbar to get the Borders toolbar.

Select the text or graphic image you want to place a border around, then click the border button of your choice. If your insertion point is within a paragraph when you click a border button, the entire paragraph will be bordered. To place a border around more than one paragraph, select the paragraphs you want in the border, then click the border button of your choice.

Close-Up: the Borders toolbar

To bring up the Borders toolbar, click the Borders button in the Formatting toolbar.

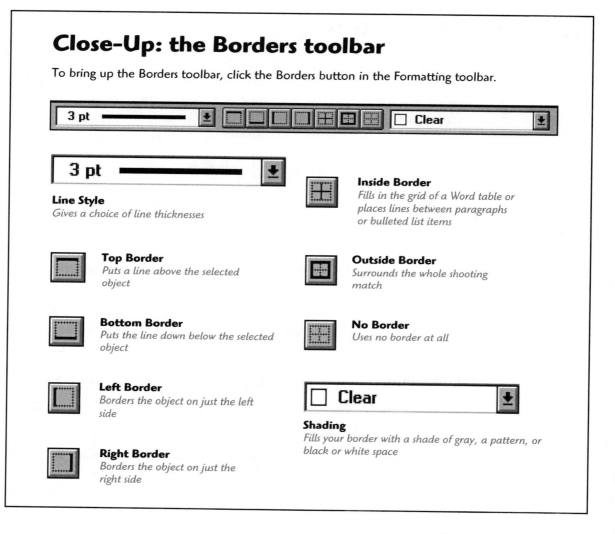

Line Style
Gives a choice of line thicknesses

Top Border
Puts a line above the selected object

Bottom Border
Puts the line down below the selected object

Left Border
Borders the object on just the left side

Right Border
Borders the object on just the right side

Inside Border
Fills in the grid of a Word table or places lines between paragraphs or bulleted list items

Outside Border
Surrounds the whole shooting match

No Border
Uses no border at all

Shading
Fills your border with a shade of gray, a pattern, or black or white space

To create a boxed effect, place a full border around something, which places all four sides around your object. This works great for notes, warnings, or sidebars that you want to set apart from other text. Try using just top and bottom or just right and left borders for an interesting, contemporary effect, as in figure 17.4. And a bottom border can be used along with the various line styles on the Border toolbar to place a thick, double, or dotted line under your text.

Fig. 17.4
Set off a heading with
a top and bottom
border only.

MEMORANDUM

TO: All Staff

FROM: Supervisor

DATE: September 3, 1995

Please post this memorandum on all employee bulletin boards as soon as possible

When you choose a full outside border, notice that Word automatically shows
the four side Border buttons as chosen. If you change your mind and want to
get rid of individual sides, you can click each to deselect them one by one.
Or, get rid of the full outside border by clicking the No Border button. Now
you can start over with any combination of the top, bottom, right, and left
border buttons you want.

{Note} If you have more than one paragraph selected, the Inside Border button adds a
line between paragraphs; in a table, it adds lines between the cells, as in figure
17.5. See Chapter 14 for more about tables.

Fig. 17.5
This table has no
outside borders at all,
but the inside bor-
ders appear as lines
between each cell,
making the table
easier to read.

	Sales by Region, 1995			
	Q 1	Q 2	Q 3	Q 4
1. East Coast	$34,111	$43,199	$55,934	$47,112
2. West Coast	$22,234	$19,888	$24,118	$30,107
3. South	$15,543	$17,087	$17,991	$19,772
4. Canada	$55,137	$54,987	$40,337	$47,331
5. Mid-West	$98,876	$77,129	$87,112	$78,087

Now that you know how to get a basic border, it's time to expand into more
creative realms. Once again, Word makes it easy to play Michelangelo, by
giving you lots of ways to create really dazzling border effects.

Create blazing borderlines

Maybe you want a thin, dark line surrounding your picture, and maybe you want something that screams LOOK AT ME; one's as easy as the other, in Word.

When you first click a border button, the border appears with the line style showing in the line style box. But you're not stuck with that style; choose a new line style from the drop-down list, then click the border button again to apply the new style. Take a look at the options in the line style drop-down list in figure 17.6.

Fig. 17.6
Choose the line style that suits your border's personality.

Maybe you want one line style on the top and bottom border, and another style for the sides of your border. Choose the line style you want, then click the Top, Bottom, Left, or Right Border button to apply the style where you want it. For example, maybe your bordered object is a coupon that fills the bottom third of your document. For the top edge, use a dashed line to indicate that the reader can cut along that line.

Throw some shade inside your border

Sometimes shading or a pattern can make a bordered object more distinctive. You can fill it with a shade of gray or black, or even a pattern by using the Shading drop-down list on the Border toolbar (see fig. 17.7). Choose Clear for no shading at all, or scroll all the way to the bottom of this list and you'll find some interesting shading patterns you can use, such as a dark trellis pattern, or a light grid.

Fig. 17.7
Choose percentages
of black, from none
(Clear) to 100%
(black) or from an
assortment of patterns.

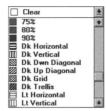

 **<Caution>** You're really the final judge of which shade or pattern works best, but be careful: too dark a shade or too busy a pattern behind text can make it unreadable. A light shading, say around 20%, is usually a good choice.

Click the bordered object, then choose a shade from this list. You can see some different border and shading styles combined in figure 17.8. You can even play around with adding color to your shading by choosing from the Background pop-up list in this dialog box.

Fig. 17.8
Make use of different
shadings for different
elements in your
document.

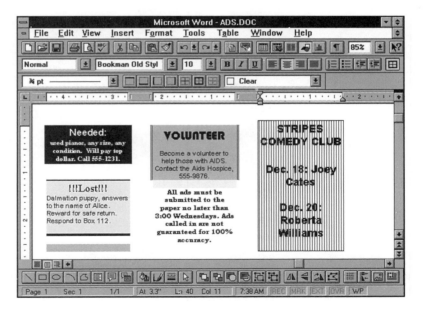

 (Tip) You can change the color of your text to white in the Font dialog box, then shade your border box in black. The letters jump out in white against the black background.

Do-It-Yourself Drawing

18

In this chapter:

- I just need to draw one line; but I want to make it really wide!

- Okay, I've drawn this box, but now what can I do to make it look really neat?

- Can I flip this drawing sideways?

- I want words on top of my drawing

You'd be amazed what you can add to your document by just drawing a simple box, circle, or line. Add color or shading, and you've got a lot of impact for very little effort.

You know that Word has a collection of really cool features that let you add pictures, clip art, and graphic effects in your documents. But what happens when you can't find the right piece of ready-made art? In that case, you may want to create your own masterpiece. That's when you need Word's drawing tools.

You don't have to be an artist to get creative with these tools. Although you may not use them often, you'll be surprised at how easily you can create great graphics with them. And let's face it—they're a lot of fun to play with.

Use Word's built-in collection of pens, paintbrushes, and stencils to build graphics out of basic shapes. Finish your work with great line effects, colors, and patterns. The drawing tools also let you create your own **freeform** drawings—something you really can't do with the other features.

Plain English, please!

Freeform drawing is the kind of drawing you do when you doodle while talking on the phone, except in Word you use a mouse instead of a pencil. With some of its other drawing tools, Word lends a hand to influence the final look; with freeform drawing, though, what you draw is exactly what you get. **99**

What can you do with the Drawing toolbar?

At first glance, the Drawing toolbar can be pretty overwhelming (see fig. 18.1). But you don't need to know how to use every tool to get going. I'll focus in this chapter on the few tools you need to get a lot done quickly. After you're familiar with the basic drawing tools, you can explore the other possibilities on your own.

Fig 18.1
You can use many of the Drawing tools to easily create impressive graphics.

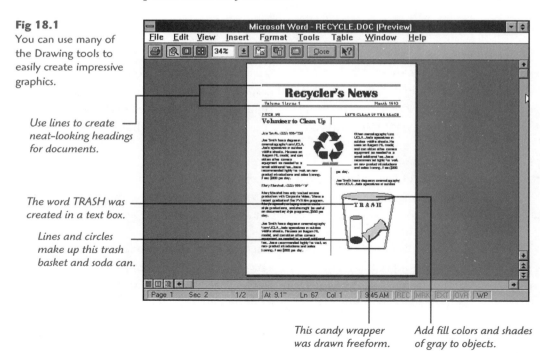

Use lines to create neat-looking headings for documents.

The word TRASH was created in a text box.

Lines and circles make up this trash basket and soda can.

This candy wrapper was drawn freeform.

Add fill colors and shades of gray to objects.

Close-Up: the Drawing toolbar

 To see this toolbar, just click the Drawing button on the Standard toolbar.

 Line
Draw a line in any direction.

 Rectangle
Draw rectangles and squares.

 Ellipse
Make circles and ovals.

 Arc
Make a variety of angles.

 Freeform
Draw your own thing.

 Text box
Place text here and move it around the page easily.

 Callout
Explain elements of your picture.

 Format Callout
Get callouts just the way you want them.

 Fill Color
Fill any drawing object with a variety of colors.

 Line Color
Draw lines in many colors, too.

 Line Style
Make it thicker or thinner? Or maybe dashed?

 Select Drawing Object
Choose an object to make a change to it.

 Bring to Front
Place the selected object in front of others.

 Send to Back
Place the selected object behind others.

 Bring in Front of Text
Put a drawing object in front of text.

 Send Behind
Send the drawing object behind text.

 Group
Select several objects and click here to make them one.

 Ungroup
Break those objects into separate pieces again.

 Flip Horizontal
Flip your object left to right.

 Flip Vertical
Flip your object top to bottom.

 Rotate Right
Turn the object to the right.

 Reshape
Change the shape of selected objects.

 Snap to Grid
Align objects to Word's grid.

 Align Drawing Objects
Center your drawing on the page.

 Create Picture
Open a special drawing window to create new objects.

Insert Frame
Add a frame to the selected object.

Let Word build your picture

In Word, you don't really draw a picture; most of the time it's more accurate to say you *build* a picture. Think of a Word drawing as a collage, with all the shapes and text objects you create lying on the workspace like so many pieces of construction paper. Word does all the work. Click a button, Word draws a line; click another button, Word draws a circle. Keep clicking to make the line thicker or fill the circle with color. It's that easy to build a picture in Word.

Start with lines and shapes

Lines and shapes are the basic building blocks of your drawings. A triangle perched on a long, thin rectangle becomes a Christmas tree. A circle gives you a smiling face when you add two smaller circles for eyes and an arc for a mouth. Want to build a boat? Try an arc object for the hull, a couple of thick lines for masts, and triangle sails on the deck.

Remember the filled trash can from the newsletter shown earlier in this chapter? Look at the close-up in figure 18.2 and you'll notice it's largely made up of lines and shapes. You can create most of it by using a combination of the methods below.

Fig. 18.2

You can easily create this trash can by using a few tools from the Drawing toolbar.

 The first thing you have to do to start drawing is get the Drawing toolbar on-screen. To do that, just click the Drawing button on the Standard toolbar. Next, move into Page Layout view: this gives you the best view of how your drawings will really look.

In a nutshell, here's how you draw various objects:

- To draw a line, click the Line button, then click on your document and drag your mouse in any direction. When the line is as long as you want it to be, let go. Your line appears, with a handle at either end, which you can drag to resize it.

- To draw a box or circle, click the Rectangle or Ellipse button. Click somewhere in your document, then drag until the object is the size and shape you want.

- To draw an arc, click the Arc button, then drag in any direction you want.

(Tip)

> To draw a perfect square, hold down the Shift key while drawing with the Rectangle tool. Same thing works with the Ellipse tool if you want a perfect circle. With the Arc tool, using the Shift key keeps the arc to a quarter-circle.

So maybe you're unlikely to ever want to draw a trash can in Word. But the best way to become familiar with—and adept at—using the Word drawing tools is to play around with them. You can use the information in this section to do just that.

Try creating a few of the shapes shown in figure 18.2:

1 Click the Ellipse button, and draw two ellipses.

2 Select one; when you get the move cursor, drag it to a position relative to the other ellipse.

3 Once they're in the right position for the top and bottom of the can, click the Line button.

4 Now, draw a line between the two circles on the right side. Then repeat this to draw the left side of the can.

Every time you want to select any object so that you can change its appearance or move it around the screen, use the Select Drawing Object tool. When it's selected, the object shows little black boxes, called **handles**, around it. These are used to change the size of the object, as you'll see later.

Add fills and color and widen those lines

Part of the fun of working with drawing in Word is changing the stuff you've drawn. You know how to change the size and shape of drawn objects, but Word has other special effects you can add to your drawings. You can add color to lines, you can change the thickness of lines, and you can fill in objects with color. If you want to doctor up one of your drawn objects, you start any of the following steps by clicking on the object first to select it:

- To fill an object—like our soda can top or bottom—with color, select it, then click the Fill Color button; you see the palette in figure 18.3. Click the color you prefer, and Word changes the object's color.

Fig. 18.3
This palette offers several colors; click None if you want an object with no color.

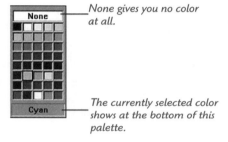

None gives you no color at all.

The currently selected color shows at the bottom of this palette.

 {Note}

After you select a Fill Color, that selection remains for any new objects you create. If you have a few objects that you'd like to be the same color, save time by drawing them one right after another, and they'll automatically have the right fill color. To change the fill color, just select an object and apply a new color.

- To change the thickness of object lines, click the Line Style button to get the choices in figure 18.4.

Fig. 18.4
You can use these line styles to change a simple line, or to change the outer lines of objects like circles and squares.

- To change the color of a line, including those that make up object shapes like circles and arcs, click the Line Color button, and select a color from a pop-up palette that looks just like the one in figure 18.3.

The line color affects the outer line that defines an object, like a circle. The fill color affects what goes inside that line. Try combining one fill color with a different line color in a single object to get a colorful border effect.

I selected a circle, then the line style pop-up, but there were no arrows. Who took my arrows?

Depending on what you've selected, you may get different choices in the line style pop-up. Since an ellipse, rectangle, and arc technically have no line ends to place arrows on, you don't get that choice with them. Check out what's available with different selections: they usually make sense for what you're working with.

Making layers

When you draw a couple of objects on top of each other, it's like placing one piece of paper above another. They are still separate pieces, and you can pull the bottom one out and put it on top of the other. For example, say you want to draw a few computer disks, stacked one on top of the other. You only want the top one to show completely, and the ones beneath it to stay behind, as in figure 18.5. Easy. But you need to know how to grab that disk (or square, or circle) in a Word drawing and put it on top.

Fig. 18.5
Stacks of things are good candidates for the Send To Back/Send To Front tools.

To move the object on the bottom to the top:

1 Click the object on top.

2 Click the Send to Back button, and it's moved under the other object.

3 Or, if you can see a piece of the bottom object, you can click that, then click the Send to Front button to move it on top.

That's it!

I drew a circle around some text and filled it with blue. Now I can't see the text, and the Send to Back button doesn't do the trick.

There are special tools to use when trying to get text and drawing objects to switch places. Click the object, then click the Send Behind Text button. With all but the darkest fill colors, you should be able to make out your text right through the object, as in figure 18.6.

Fig. 18.6
On the left, the text is behind the object; on the right, the text is in front of the object, so you can read it.

Drawing on your own

Freeform drawing is a little like learning how to ski: at first you feel wobbly and unsure, and you take a few spills while you learn. Some people never get that good at it. But once you've mastered the basic techniques, you'll probably enjoy it.

Start out practicing with simple shapes, like triangles or hearts. The lines may not look quite right at first, but you'll get better—and there's always Undo! Anyway, sometimes the best use for freeform drawing (especially the second method, below) is for things that should look a little more primitive, as if drawn by hand. For example, look at the candy wrapper in the trash can. It doesn't even try to be a fancy shape, but it serves its purpose just fine.

Drawing a freeform object requires a couple of steps and can be done in one of two ways. The first way draws straight lines for you, but you choose how many lines to draw, and where they begin and end. This technique is great for drawing regular objects like stars, top hats, and kitchen tables.

Look at the star drawn in figure 18.7. The callouts show the order to draw these lines to form a simple star.

Fig. 18.7
This method of freeform drawing is better for geometric forms, like this star.

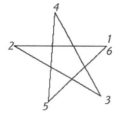

1. *Click the Freeform button, then click here to begin*
2. *Drag to here and click*
3. *Drag down here; click again*
4. *Up to the top and click*
5. *Almost there: click once more down here*
6. *Finish where you started with a double-click*

When you're done with all the points of the star, double-click to get out of freeform drawing mode. You can also click once back on the original point to get out of freeform drawing mode.

With the second method of using freeform drawing, you hold down your mouse and drag your cursor, rather than clicking at different points. Using this method, you get a truly free line—with all the accompanying jiggles and bumps that occur as your hand moves your mouse. When you're in this freeform drawing mode, you don't click on different points; just keep your mouse button depressed, shift direction, and keep dragging to keep drawing. When you're done, double-click to finish. Try this with the candy wrapper shape in the trash can example. Just draw a basic rectangle, but allow it to have the ragged edges a crumpled up piece of paper would have.

 **{Note}**

The second kind of freeform drawing can be tricky to get the hang of. Every little movement of the mouse ends up in your lines. Be patient with yourself if you want to explore this kind of drawing. And remember, you can reshape the object after it's drawn to take out the little slips of the mouse (see the next section, "These shapes are *almost* right...").

These shapes are *almost* right...

Your Word drawing objects have a lot of the flexibility of Silly Putty. Once you've drawn something, you can easily change its size and shape by pulling and tugging it in different directions.

I want to resize this shape

Use the sizing handles to resize any object. Simply click the object to select it, then drag the handle on the corner or side where you'd like the object to expand or shrink. Figures 18.8, 18.9, and 18.10 show how this works.

Fig. 18.8

Drag and let go, and the object changes both shape and size, growing in the direction you've dragged.

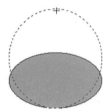

Drawing on experience

There are plenty of things to do with drawing objects to pep up your documents. Try some of these:

- Place text in a drawing object, like a circle, to highlight a special offer in a brochure or circular. If you have a color printer, fill the circle with red and send it behind the text for real impact!

- Play around with changing your text's color to white (Format, Font), and putting it in front of a black-filled object. Called reverse type, this is a useful design tool for a headline or warning note.

- Choose Format, Drawing Objects and fuse the dialog box to add a shadow or rounded edges to any objects you draw that have a fill color.

Fig. 18.9

To resize so the object grows (or shrinks) equally on both sides, hold down Ctrl and drag the object's handle.

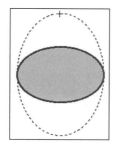

Fig. 18.10

To resize and keep the object proportionately the same shape (only larger or smaller), hold down the Shift key and drag by a corner handle.

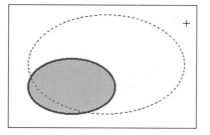

I want to smooth out this shape

So you didn't draw that freeform star perfectly the first time? I'll tell you a secret: neither did I. Freeform drawing isn't the easiest thing to get the hang of. But the good news is that once you've drawn a freeform object, you can reshape it and fix whatever little bumps or odd shapes you created.

 Just select an object, then click the Reshape button, which remains active until you choose another tool or click outside your drawings. You get a whole lot of little handles, as in figure 18.11.

Fig. 18.11

Drag on these little handles one by one to edit the shape of a freeform object.

To change the object's shape, just click and drag any or all of its handles, as shown in figure 18.12.

Fig. 18.12
Word shows you a dotted line representing the new position as you drag.

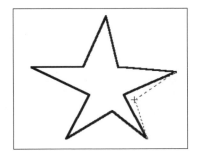

I want to rotate this shape

Ever look at a piece of modern art in a magazine and turn it every which way trying to figure out which way is up? Sometimes a drawing just looks better upside down; or it might fit in with another element of your document better if you turn it just a little to the right. This technique is a great way to make one drawing play a bunch of roles: try drawing one flower, then make copies of it; flip one vertically, rotate one a bit to the right, and so on to create a bunch of different flowers (see fig. 18.13).

Fig. 18.13
Make the same object look different using the flip and rotation tools.

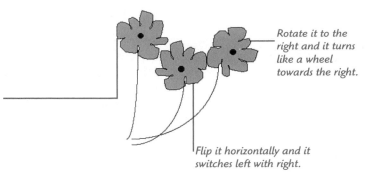

Here's the original flower.

Rotate it to the right and it turns like a wheel towards the right.

Flip it horizontally and it switches left with right.

Click an object, then use the Flip Horizontal, Flip Vertical, or Rotate Right tools to get it the way you want it.

(Tip)

 If you'd like to flip all the objects you've drawn together, use a handy tool called Group. Click an object, then hold down the Shift key and click all the other objects. When they're all selected, click the Group button. Now the objects are one unit, and will move, resize, and rotate as one piece. To ungroup them, use the Ungroup tool.

19

Weird and Wonderful Things to Do with Text

WordArt is like opening a toy box filled with fun things to make your text practically jump off the page!

Have you ever seen a medieval manuscript—maybe one of those hand-lettered Bibles, say, from the days before the printing press was invented? They're absolutely fascinating documents, filled with color and elaborate decorations wrapped around the first letter of each chapter and verse. They'd probably be extremely readable, too, if you could understand medieval Latin.

Some monk spent a few weeks or months getting those letters looking just so. You, on the other hand, can accomplish nearly the same thing with a few mouse clicks and keystrokes, and the help of Word.

If you're really into making your Word documents look fancy, try treating text—the numbers, letters, and symbols you type—as a piece of art you can sculpt and decorate as much as you like. Word includes a small program called **WordArt** that lets you stretch and realign words and letters so that they're distinctive. Word also contains tools that let you blow up the first letter of a paragraph to create a drop cap. You can even add special text characters and symbols.

What can I create with WordArt?

WordArt is like a tiny application of its own (called an **applet**) that's tucked inside Word for Windows. With WordArt, you create what's called an **object** and put it in your document using a process called **embedding**. These text objects can be manipulated while in the WordArt editing window, then transferred to your main Word window and moved around and resized like any other object in your document (see Chapter 16 for more on moving and sizing objects).

 Plain English, please!

Object refers to something that you create in one application and move into another as a single unit. You may create a fancy headline in WordArt, for example, and then place it in a Word document. That fancy headline is no longer separate letters, it's one text object. Objects can consist of text, pictures, a table—whatever.

Embedded objects are entire files that you stuff into Word. They look and act like part of the document, but if you want to change them, you need to use the application where they were created. The file "lives" completely inside Word and travels along wherever the Word document file goes. See Chapter 20, "Sharing Things," for more information on embedding.

Using text effects for emphasis

Just as the raised lettering on an alphabet block makes that letter look special, WordArt lets you add special effects to text in Word by using different design effects (see fig. 19.1). With the many choices available, you can get pretty fancy.

Use WordArt effects sparingly for maximum impact:

- Effects do well in headings, titles, or to make a product name stand out.

- One on a page is usually sufficient.

- Never manipulate a WordArt object in a way that makes it illegible.

Fig. 19.1
With WordArt, you can play around with text to your heart's content. But be careful of overdoing it!

⊗<Caution> Certain things make it hard to read a WordArt object. Stretching text out too far, making a thick font bold so that all the letters run into each other, or adding a shadow to certain fonts are all things that can make your letters hard to read. If you're not sure whether your WordArt object is still readable, get a friend or coworker to take a look at it.

A prize in every package

Remember Cracker Jacks—the snack that comes with a tiny plastic toy inside the box? Kids buy the snack, but some of them appreciate the toy even more.

When you bought Word for Windows, whether you know it or not, you hit the jackpot. Word includes a collection of **applets**—tiny programs that do a specialized job—and they're considerably more valuable than anything you'll find in a Cracker Jack box.

WordArt is just one of the applets available to you. There's also Microsoft Graph, which allows you to turn data into graphs almost instantly; and ClipArt Gallery, which offers hundreds of pictures for you to use in your Word documents.

Some of the applets appear as toolbar buttons, but you get to most of them by choosing Insert, Object. Browse through the Object list and see what prizes Word has to offer.

Close-Up: the WordArt toolbar

The WordArt toolbar buttons are the building blocks of WordArt objects: mix and match, and just have fun!

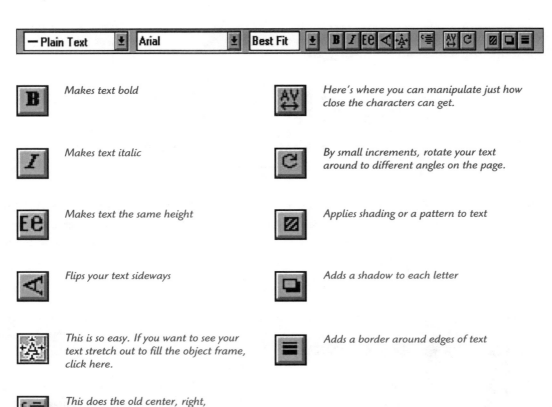

B — Makes text bold

AV — Here's where you can manipulate just how close the characters can get.

I — Makes text italic

C — By small increments, rotate your text around to different angles on the page.

Ee — Makes text the same height

— Applies shading or a pattern to text

— Flips your text sideways

— Adds a shadow to each letter

— This is so easy. If you want to see your text stretch out to fill the object frame, click here.

— Adds a border around edges of text

— This does the old center, right, left, and justify alignment game with your text.

How do I get to WordArt?

You get into the WordArt screen by choosing Insert, Object. The Object dialog box appears (see fig. 19.2).

Fig. 19.2
The Object dialog box is a treasure chest that includes WordArt.

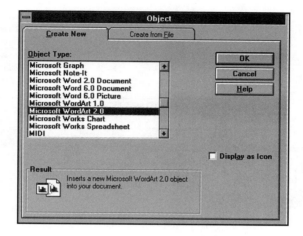

To see the WordArt option, scroll down the Object Type list box. Notice that the Result area at the bottom of the dialog box describes what will happen when you make a selection in the Object Type box. Click Microsoft WordArt 2.0, and then click OK.

 **{Note}**

Depending on what you chose to install when you put Word on your computer, you might have different items listed in the Object Type list.

The WordArt edit window appears, with a text box titled Enter Your Text Here, and a box with the text as it's currently formatted.

 Q&A

I go to the Insert menu and choose Object, but WordArt isn't listed. What happened to it?

If you chose the Typical Installation option when you installed Word for Windows, the WordArt program was also installed. If you chose a different installation, WordArt wasn't installed. You can use the Word setup program to add just that program. If you're not comfortable reinstalling your software, find a sympathetic friend to do it instead.

WordArt's toy box

WordArt menus
Different menus help you format and view the object.

Your Text Here
This text object will magically modify every time you update the display.

WordArt toolbar
These buttons and drop-down lists let you play around with text.

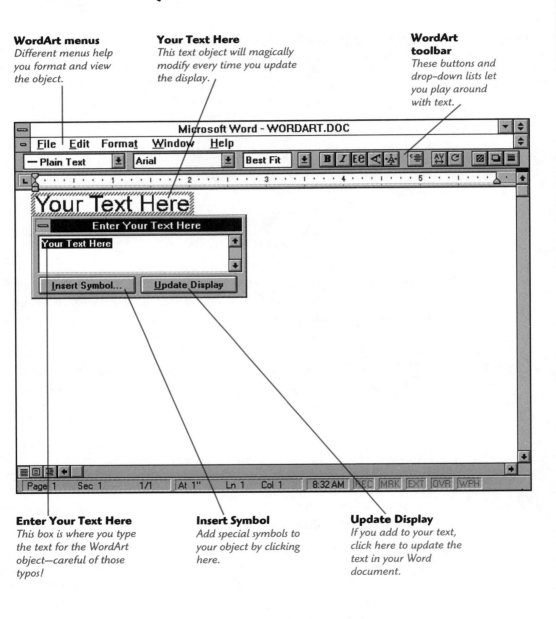

Enter Your Text Here
This box is where you type the text for the WordArt object—careful of those typos!

Insert Symbol
Add special symbols to your object by clicking here.

Update Display
If you add to your text, click here to update the text in your Word document.

 **{Note}**___

If you choose to display WordArt as an icon by selecting that option in the Object dialog box, you will get a different screen. With this option, the different WordArt functions are all shown in one dialog box, rather than on a full screen with toolbars along the top. You also get a WordArt icon when you go back to Word, which you can double-click to get back to this dialog box.

How do I create a WordArt object?

It's easy to create the curved WordArt object shown later in figure 19.6:

1 Type the text **Save the Rainforest**.

2 From the Font drop-down list on the toolbar, select the font Brush Script MT.

3 Open the Shape box (to the left of the Font box) to produce the shape palette (see fig. 19.3). Select the button curve shape (second row down, fourth from the left).

Fig. 19.3
The Shape palette lets you choose a cool new shape for your plain old text.

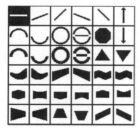

4 In the Font Size drop-down list, leave the selection of Best Fit. Word will adjust the size of the object automatically.

 5 Click the Shadow button, and from the drop-down palette, choose the shadow effect in the second row down on the far left.

6 Click anywhere outside the Enter Your Text Here box to return to your document and place the WordArt object, as in figure 19.4.

 **<Caution>**

WordArt only works with TrueType fonts. Word recognizes other font varieties, so TrueType fonts are indicated by a TT symbol in the drop-down Font list. The font list in WordArt contains only TrueType fonts.

Fig. 19.4
Here's your WordArt
object placed back in
your Word document.

How do I flip that WordArt thing over?

If you're feeling particularly artistic, you can rotate text in WordArt—it's
child's play.

1 Right-click the WordArt object to get a shortcut menu, and choose Edit
WordArt.

2 To rotate the text, click the Rotate button. A dialog box appears as in
figure 19.5. Click the arrow under Rotation until the rotation reads 20+.

3 Click OK. Figure 19.6 shows how the rotated text gives a nice balance
to the heading of a brochure.

4 Click the screen outside the object to return to Word.

Fig. 19.5
Click on these up or
down arrows until the
amount of rotation
suits you.

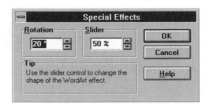

Fig. 19.6
Rotating this figure makes the WordArt object fit nicely with the other elements of the Word document.

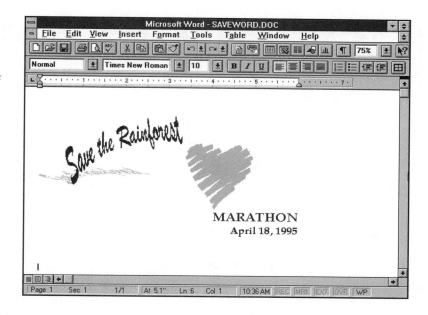

Time to experiment!

You can begin to see the possibilities available with WordArt by looking at the toolbar buttons—your WordArt building blocks. The best way to learn what each button can do is to experiment and see what effects different combinations create. Check out the use of shading, stretched out text, and letters of the same height in figure 19.7.

Fig. 19.7
Mix and match effects until you find the ones that work for you.

Shading and a border have been applied here.

Making lowercase letters all the same height makes for a fun look.

These letters have been stretched out and combined with a jazzy shape.

Other ways to dress up plain text

There are a couple of other simple text effects that can add a dramatic visual touch to your documents. Drop caps let you emphasize the beginning of a new paragraph, while expanded and condensed text let you fit a word or phrase precisely in a given space.

Drop cap—the ultimate accessory

Ever noticed how sometimes the first letter in a newspaper or magazine article is much larger than the rest of the text? That effect is called **drop cap**, and it's easy to create in Word. Here's how:

1 Just type your text, then go back to the first letter and carefully select it.

2 Choose For̲mat, D̲rop Cap. The dialog box in figure 19.8 appears.

3 Select D̲ropped Cap.

4 In the Distance From Te̲xt box, type **.05** so that the surrounding text won't be too close to the drop-capped letter.

   You can even select a different font here, for extra pizzazz.

Fig. 19.8
The D̲ropped effect is the standard business look, while In M̲argin is a unique look to be used in flyers.

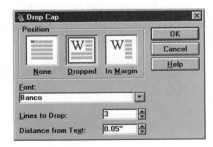

5 Click OK, and you'll see the result.

   If you're not happy with what you see, you can always re-select that letter, and repeat the process. Think of this as a brilliant pin on an otherwise boring gray business suit. However, don't overuse drop caps or they'll lose their impact.

Expanding and condensing text

In the Font dialog box, there's a simple procedure for stretching out your text, or shrinking it. Expanding and shrinking text can produce neat design effects, or they can help you fit text into a certain size space. (See, I have a practical side, too.)

Go to the Font dialog box by choosing F̲ormat, F̲ont. Select the Cha̲racter Spacing "file folder" tab. You see the options shown in figure 19.9.

Fig. 19.9
The Character Spacing tab on the Font dialog box opens up options for stretching out your letters.

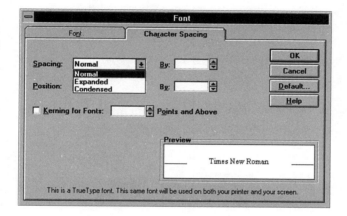

The choices here are simple. The S̲pacing drop-down list offers preset normal, expanded, or condensed text settings. With the arrows to the right, you can customize how much you'd like to expand or condense text.

The P̲osition drop-down list allows you to ʳᵃⁱˢᵉ or ₗₒwₑᵣ text. These settings work differently than superscript or subscript, because they also affect the size of the type. With P̲osition, the text stays the same except for its position.

⊛ {Note}

The K̲erning for Fonts option that appears in this dialog box has to do with fine-tuning the spacing between individual characters. With some typefaces, certain letters tend to 'bump up' against each other when placed together. Desktop publishers use kerning, but you probably never will.

Special characters and symbols you'll want to meet

Man does not live by letters and numbers alone. Most of us also run across certain special symbols that we need to include in documents now and then, like in equations or scientific formulas.

But on the other end of the spectrum are those swell little smiley faces, or a grape leaf, or some other useless but fun little symbol that can liven up your next invitation.

Symbols are used for all sorts of things, from the practical to the frivolous. For example:

- If you use a product name, you might need a registered trademark symbol (®).

- If you're an Aquarian, like me, you might need your astrological symbol (≅)—don't ask why.

- Belong to the Omega Fraternity? (Ω)

- Or maybe you're a bridge champion (♣).

How do you get hold of them?

This procedure is simplicity itself. Choose Insert, Symbol. The box in figure 19.10 appears.

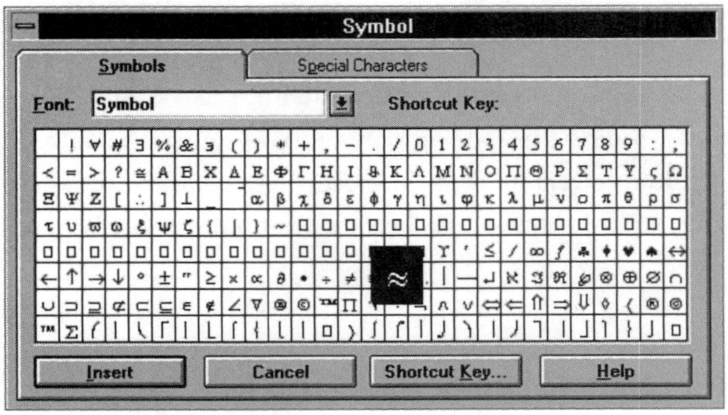

Fig. 19.10
A virtual cornucopia full of symbols, common and not so common, is at your disposal.

If you click a symbol, you get an enlarged view of it. When you find the one you want, simply click Insert, and it appears in your document wherever your cursor is.

But the first set of symbols you see isn't all you get: change the font by selecting another one in the drop-down Font list. If you choose Milestone or WingDings, you get a whole other category of symbols: little pictures of useful things like bells and footballs, mailboxes and mouses (mice?).

❋{Note}

Notice the second tab in the Symbol dialog box, Special Characters. This tab offers commonly used special characters, like the em dash (—) or quotation marks (") preferred by typesetters. Just click on the one you want and click Insert. When there's a shortcut key for inserting these characters, it's noted next to the character name.

You can do stuff to symbols

There's one simple thing to remember about these special characters: they're really just typefaces with symbols instead of letters or numbers. You can do pretty much anything to them that you can do to regular text.

For example, you can select one of these characters and resize it by using the Font Size drop-down list.

Try changing the color of the symbol by selecting it, going to the Font dialog box (choose Format, Font), and using the color pop-up list.

❓Q&A

I selected a symbol and tried to change it to small caps. Nothing happened!

Some effects don't work on certain typefaces. For example, although super-script and strikethrough work on a picture or symbol, capitalization won't. But why are you trying to capitalize a picture of a basketball, anyway? If you can't do it, you probably don't really need it.

Part VI:

Managing Data and Documents

20
Sharing Things

In this chapter:

- How do I get stuff from one Word document into another?

- Can I bring a paragraph from this WordPerfect document into my Word document?

- I want to use a picture that comes from another program

- Can I save my Word document so other programs can use it?

Word is a team player. Word lets documents work together and share a variety of things: text, graphics, spreadsheets— you name it.

You can't work in an office these days without feeling like you've stepped into a broadcast booth at the Super Bowl. There's an incredible amount of talk about teamwork, most of it couched in obscure sports analogies. If you're not a football fan, you might have trouble keeping up.

Of course, you don't need to be a sports fanatic to know why teamwork pays off in the office. It's all about sharing things: ideas, information, office supplies—whatever.

And when it comes to sharing things, Word for Windows is the most valuable player on the all-star team. Word lets documents work together and share a variety of things: text, graphics, spreadsheets—you name it. In fact, Word's team spirit extends beyond its own team of documents. Word even shares with files created by other programs.

How do I share data between documents?

One of Word's biggest time- and labor-saving features is its willingness to help you quickly copy information between documents. You can move or copy chunks of text, tables, and other information between individual Word documents. You can also shuttle information gracefully between Word documents and files created in other software programs, including Microsoft Mail.

Word uses the Windows Clipboard as a temporary holding area for cutting, copying, and pasting stuff. With two Word files open, it's easy to literally cut a brilliant quote or statistic out of one document and paste it into the other. So, the first thing to do is to open two Word documents at once.

Opening a second Word document

People in offices work side-by-side to get things done, and so do Word documents. Word lets you open several Word documents and look at them side by side, or one on top of the other. Just open one file after another using the procedures you learned in Chapter 5, "Secrets of Successful File Management."

Each new document you open covers the one beneath it. To let your documents share the Word window, you can choose <u>W</u>indow, <u>A</u>rrange All and show several document windows stacked one on top of the other (see fig. 20.1).

⊛ {Note} You can also customize the size of windows yourself. With one or more windows arranged on-screen, place the mouse on the edge or corner of the window. A double-headed arrow appears. Drag the top or bottom edge to make the window longer; drag the sides to make it wider; or drag a corner to shrink or stretch the whole window. When it's the right size, release the mouse button.

Fig. 20.1

Want to easily share information? Start by arranging two or more documents in the Word window.

Opening a document created in another program

Does everyone in your circle use Word? Maybe not. You might find yourself around other people who use other word processors—WordPerfect, for example. Fortunately, Word makes it easy to exchange documents with people who use other word processing programs. The trick is to use one of Word's built-in **converters**.

 Plain English, please!

A **converter** works just like a translator at the United Nations. When Word encounters a file that's in some language other than its own, it hands it to the converter, which quickly reads the document and translates it—text, formats, and all—into Word. The converter leaves the original file intact. Believe me, if you share files with people who use other word processing programs, converters will make your life a lot easier.

Word includes converters for most of the popular word processing, spreadsheet, and graphics file formats. (You select which converters to install when you install Word.) When you try to open a document created in another program through the File Open dialog box (see fig. 20.2), Word looks the file over to see if it recognizes the format. If there's a converter that can handle the foreign format, it joins Word's team as a converted Word document.

Fig. 20.2
This dialog box is control central for converting and opening files of all kinds.

In the File list, only files of this type will appear.

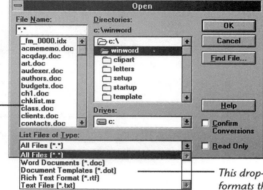

This drop-down list offers several options for formats that the incoming file might be in.

⊛ {Note}

To see the file you want to open in the File Name list, you can enter the extension (such as *.xls, for Excel files) if you know it. This asks Word to show all files in the selected directory with this extension (make sure you're in the correct directory). If you don't know the extension, select All Files in the List Files of Type list.

When you click OK to open a document, if Word doesn't recognize the format, or if you've clicked the Confirm Conversions check box in the open dialog box, you'll get a Convert File dialog box (see fig. 20.3). This box asks how you want to handle the format of the file you want to open.

Fig. 20.3
Word asks you to tell it which file converter it should use.

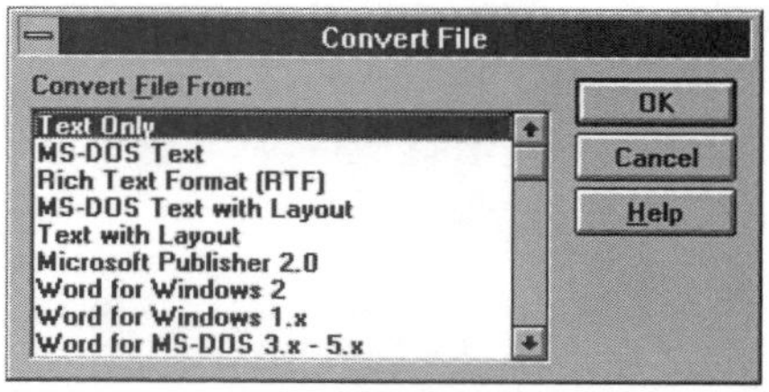

Word has chosen what it thinks would be the best converter already. With common formats, like WordPerfect, the file should come up pretty seamlessly, appearing like a regular Word document. But if Word suggests a less common converter, like Text Only or Rich Text Format, you should be aware that these formats might give you something that ranges from a little strange to unreadable. For example, it could bring in the document missing things like line breaks, or it might show some strange codes for formatting instead of the formatting itself. Still, accepting whatever format Word suggests in this conversion box is really the only way to go.

However, there are a couple of things that you should be aware of. If there's a graphic in the document you're bringing in, Word needs to find either the original graphic file, or have an appropriate graphics converter. If neither is true, the document may appear minus the graphic. If you don't need the graphic, don't worry. If you do, try to have a copy of the original graphic on your hard drive; then Word can refer to it and open the document with graphics intact.

Also, if the original document uses a typeface not available to Word, Word will substitute a typeface of its choosing. Don't worry: if you don't agree with Word's choice, you can always change the typeface to one that you prefer.

Cutting and pasting between documents

Your office is filled with the tools you need to share information with your coworkers. A photocopy machine, routing slips, Scotch tape, paper clips, etc.

Word gives you the electronic tools you need to share bits and pieces of documents easily: the cut, copy, and paste functions. (For more details about cutting and pasting, see Chapter 6.) The main difference between cutting and pasting between electronic documents and paper is that with Word, you don't make such a mess.

Just between Word documents

Moving text between two Word documents isn't much more difficult than moving text from one page to another within a single Word document. Just do this:

1 Open a couple of documents that were either created in or converted to Word.

2 Choose <u>W</u>indow, <u>A</u>rrange All to display the two documents.

3 Select the text you want to move, and use the Cut tool to cut it out of the first document;

or, select the text you want to move, then use the Copy tool to copy it from the first document.

4 Use the Paste tool to paste it in the second document. It's that simple.

 **<Caution>** Use Copy, rather than Cut, if you want to leave the original document intact. If you cut something from one document and paste it in another, the original document no longer contains the cut material. If you copy the material, it exists in both documents.

Now, how about between applications?

You can also open two application windows—say, Word and Microsoft Publisher—and cut and paste things directly between the documents in both windows. This works particularly well with the other Microsoft applications included with Word in the Microsoft Office suite—Excel, PowerPoint, and Access.

The quickest way to open other Microsoft applications from Word is with the Microsoft toolbar. Choose <u>V</u>iew, <u>T</u>oolbars. Click the Microsoft toolbar and click OK. The floating toolbar in figure 20.4 appears. Click any of these tools to instantly open the other application.

(Tip) If you have Word installed as part of the Microsoft Office suite, you can also use the Microsoft Office Manager toolbar in the menu bar to switch between applications.

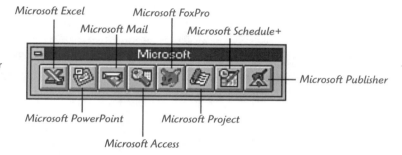

Fig. 20.4
The Microsoft toolbar gives you immediate access to other Microsoft programs.

Microsoft Excel

Microsoft Mail

Microsoft FoxPro

Microsoft Schedule+

Microsoft Publisher

Microsoft PowerPoint

Microsoft Access

Microsoft Project

The Suite revolution

When Microsoft Word showed up on your hard disk, did it bring along a few friends? If you got it as part of a package called the Microsoft Office, those friends included a spreadsheet called Microsoft Excel, a presentation graphics program called Microsoft PowerPoint, and a database manager called Microsoft Access.

Microsoft isn't the only company selling these all-in-one "suites" of software, but it's by far the most successful. In addition to a word processor, spreadsheet, and graphics or presentation software, there might also be an electronic mail or calendar and personal information manager included.

The idea of a suite is that all these applications have similar interfaces and common tools that work together like a well-oiled machine. A suite saves you the headache of trying to share information among applications that don't understand each other's obscure file formats. In theory, it's like a big office in which every department is designed with exactly the same layout. That way, you can zip around and get work done without having to learn a new way of working in each new department.

Of course, these suites take up humonguous amounts of memory and disk space, and you need a separate bookcase just for the disks and documentation that come with them. But if you use at least two of the applications for your everyday work, the Microsoft Office might be a great deal. And you can always use the box for a spare filing cabinet.

Minimize and adjust the two windows so that they fit on-screen together, as in figure 20.5. Now, just select what you want to move from one document, and cut (or copy) and paste it into the other document window.

Fig. 20.5

Sharing across the back fence; simply cut and paste between application windows.

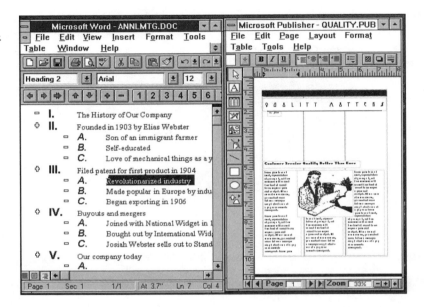

Working with other programs

Besides using a simple cut and paste to move something from one document to another, Word has a few other ways to play ball with other applications on your computer.

Every file is an object—on a larger scale than a single graphic object, perhaps, but an object nevertheless. Through something called **object linking and embedding** (OLE in computerese), you can create lasting relationships between your Word documents and other kinds of data.

 Plain English, please!

Whether it's an Excel worksheet, PowerPoint slide, Paintbrush picture, or Access database, something embedded in your document is always called an **object**. When you click on an embedded object, you can see small handles around the edges. Use these handles to move or resize the objects.

You can stick a copy of an entire file, or a piece of a file—like a picture or a spreadsheet range—into a Word file, the same way you'd make a photocopy of a paper document and put it into a manila folder. That's the **embedding** part of OLE.

You can also create a connection between the Word document and the external object without actually making a copy of the object. The effect is the same as if you put a piece of paper in your manila folder telling your coworkers where to locate another piece of related information. That's the **linking** part of OLE.

When you embed information from one Microsoft Office application in another, double-clicking on the embedded object causes a startling change. Word's menus and toolbars vanish, to be replaced by those of the originating application. You can now edit the embedded object directly; the Word menus and tools come back as soon as you click outside the embedded object.

To embed, or not to embed?

When you embed an object in your document, you're basically making a copy of a file or something from a file created in another Windows application and placing it in Word. It can then be edited and changed, and it doesn't affect the object in the other document.

Beware the memory monster: when you embed something, a full copy of it (taking up the associated memory for that object) is made part of your document. With a graphics file in particular, that could be sizeable.

Embedding an object in Word

If you've already read other chapters in this book, you've already done some embedding. When you created a WordArt object in Chapter 19, for example, you opened the WordArt applet, created an object, then inserted it into your document.

Several applets that you can use in this way are attached to Word. Applets and applications available to you for creating objects are listed in the Object dialog box (see fig. 20.6). You can access this dialog box by choosing Insert, Object.

Fig. 20.6
Some of these are applets, others are full-blown programs, but they're all willing to open up to you.

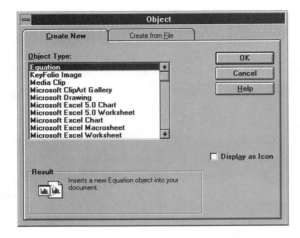

You also use the mail merge function in Chapter 21 to get database information from a file and embed it in a Word document.

 Let's run through this play one more time with Excel. Click the Insert Microsoft Excel Worksheet button on the standard toolbar.

A new Excel worksheet appears wherever your insertion point was in your Word document (see fig. 20.7). Also, notice that in the spirit of cooperation, Word's even put on the Excel team uniform: your Word window now displays Excel toolbars and menus.

 Not every type of object has a convenient tool you can use to insert it on the Word toolbar. For other types of objects, use the Insert menu and choose Object.

After you've entered information into the worksheet, just click outside it. Your spreadsheet appears in your Word document, as in figure 20.8.

Fig. 20.7

When you first insert an Excel worksheet object into a Word document, it appears in edit mode, with Excel toolbars and menus on-screen.

Excel toolbars appear when the embedded object is in edit mode.

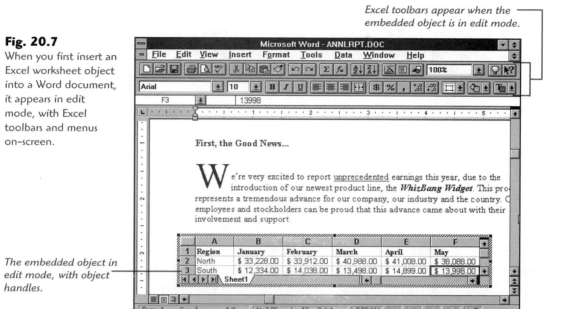

The embedded object in edit mode, with object handles.

Fig. 20.8

A finished spreadsheet appears as part of your Word document, and the toolbars are once again Word's.

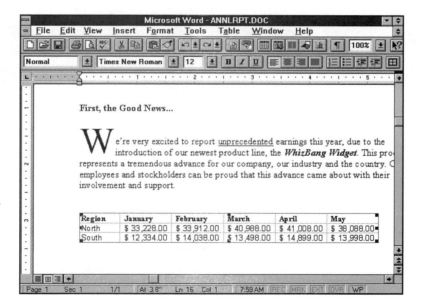

 **{Note}**

Inserting an object with the Insert Excel Worksheet tool or through the Insert menu usually gives you a new, empty object, like the blank Excel spreadsheet. To insert an existing object, like a completed Excel spreadsheet, from another file into your Word file, try <u>I</u>nsert, <u>F</u>ile.

Editing an embedded object

Because Excel and Word are such buddies, when you want to edit an embedded object, you just have to double-click it. Word hollers to Excel, which immediately opens up and places its tools and menus on the Word screen so that you can edit the object. When you're done editing, click anywhere outside the object itself, and you're back to home base: your Word screen.

 Q&A

When I open Paintbrush, I get both a Word and Paintbrush window, not Paintbrush tools on the Word screen like you said. What gives?

It's not that Paintbrush doesn't want to play ball. But if you're using an application that uses an older version of object linking and embedding (OLE), the rules are a little different. The second application actually opens up in its own window, and you just edit your object there. When you're done editing, choose to Exit or Quit the application, and say you want to update the object in the Word window. Then you're back at the Word screen.

Saving in other formats

Teamwork isn't a one-way street. If Word can borrow from other applications, it should also share its documents with them. It does. The converters in Word allow you to save Word documents to common program formats, such as Microsoft Excel, dBASE, Microsoft Word for DOS and Macintosh, and WordPerfect. You can also get converters from Microsoft for Lotus 1-2-3, WordStar, and Microsoft Publisher, and others by calling the Microsoft Sales Information Center at (800) 426-9400.

To save a Word file in another format, choose <u>F</u>ile, Save <u>A</u>s. In the Save As dialog box in figure 20.9, select the File Type you want to use to save your document.

Fig. 20.9
You might want to
save a document in
WordPerfect format
so that your coworker
can use it on her
computer.

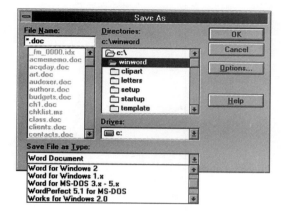

Then, proceed to save it with the name and in the directory you prefer. (See
Chapter 5 for more information about saving files.)

②Q&A

> ### Word doesn't save in a file format my coworker needs. What do I do?
>
> Don't worry, you have an out. Almost all Windows programs can handle Rich
> Text Format (RTF). Try saving your file in the RTF format and let your
> coworker's application convert it.

21 Mailings for the Masses

In this chapter:

- How do I send a personalized letter to a lot of different people?

- How do I tell Word where to put stuff in my letter?

- Can I use the same addresses in a lot of different letters?

- I need to print a lot of envelopes, too

- I want to sort my mailing by last name

With Word's mail-merge feature, you can create effective form letters that look like they were hand-crafted, one-by-one.

Imagine that you're the poor soul at General Motors who has to send out the letters notifying people their cars have been recalled. You have enough problems. You certainly don't want to type 5,000 individual letters. Well, if you have a list on your computer of all the lucky people who bought that model, Word mail merge can use it to make the process of sending personalized letters to them a breeze.

Maybe you just want all 5,000 of those folks to feel good about you when they all get identical letters that don't *look* like a form letter. Or maybe you need to make subtle changes in the information available to each of them, like the phone number they're supposed to call to make a service appointment.

Word has the tools to handle either situation. You put together a list of names and addresses and other details, then mix that information into your master letter. When your reader opens the letter, it looks like you spent hours on it, even if each letter actually took only a few milliseconds to work its way through Word.

How does mail get merged?

The idea behind mail merge is that you have a lot of similar, well-organized information called a **data source**, and you want to use some or all of that stuff in a document.

Plain English, please!

Besides being a character on *Star Trek: The Next Generation*, **data** is basically pieces of information: names, phone numbers, dates, etc. The set of data that you use as the source for your mail merge is called the **data source** for that mail merge.

A **field** is one type of information. For example, in a table of names and addresses, one field is City, one is First Name, and another is Postal Code. The field's name is the name of the column in your data source.

The document in a mail merge might be a customer invoice that includes frequently changing customer information, like balance due. Or, it could be a set of letters and labels for a mass mailing. The data source could be a typed list or table in Word, or a database or spreadsheet that was created in dBASE or Excel. You can also build a database as you go along when you use Word's Mail Merge Helper.

Your challenge is to add each separate entry in your data source to a blank copy of your document. Think of Word as a freeway where fresh, new copies of your letter roll by at regular intervals. Each record in your data source file sits on the on ramp, and one at a time they merge into the document flow to fill in a blank letter—hence the name, *mail merge*.

Building a mail merge (getting the pieces in place)

So how do you get this data and your documents together? Easy. Imagine you've got a table of names and addresses. Each piece of information is in its own column: all the first names in one column, all the street addresses and ZIP codes in their own columns, and so on.

How a mail merge comes together

Mail merge is not a complex process, and you needn't be a techno-guru to use it. You just take some unique pieces of information—like names—and put them in individual copies of the same document—say, a letter.

Merge field
This field sends Word looking for a corresponding piece of data in the data source.

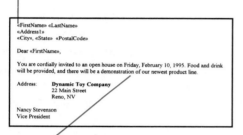

Data source
A table, list, spreadsheet, or other source of information

FirstName	LastName	Company	Address1	City	State	PostalCode
Nellie	Wright	ABC Toys	10 "R" St.	Reno	NV	55555
P.G.	Stier	Gregory's	2 Elm Dr.	Napa	CA	92222
Elvis	Ricardo	Zen Toys	17 Oak Lane	Reno	NV	55554
Sam	Sumi	PlayShop	3A Rt. 117	Elko	NV	55444

Main document
Take a form letter, invoice, invitation— whatever—and customize it.

Headers
The Headings of your data source columns are the field names.

The first copy of your letter uses the first row of data, the second uses the second row, and so on.

Merge field
On a letter, the address goes here, corresponding to the merge fields in your main document.

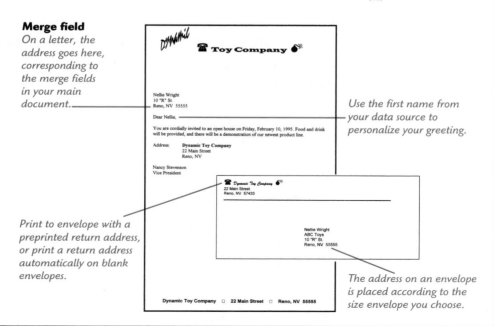

Use the first name from your data source to personalize your greeting.

Print to envelope with a preprinted return address, or print a return address automatically on blank envelopes.

The address on an envelope is placed according to the size envelope you choose.

You simply place codes for those columns of data in a document as something called **merge fields**. Merge fields basically are place holders for specific types of data in your source. Word goes to the database, takes a piece of information from the First Name column, and puts it where the FirstName merge field is in the document. The top name in that column goes in your first copy of the document, the second name goes in the second copy of the document, and so on.

Meet Mail Merge Helper

To start your mail merge, you need to create a document and put in the merge fields. Let's say, for example, that you've been in business five years and you've decided to throw an open house for all your loyal customers. You'll need to get together a list of their names and addresses and create an invitation. For this, you need help—and fortunately, Word's Mail Merge Helper is standing by to help you create your invitation and envelopes.

To create a mail merge, you can use either an existing data source and document, or you can create them as you go along. We'll start by creating a new document (choose File, New). Next, type the invitation:

Dear ,

You are cordially invited to an open house on Friday, February 10, 1995. Food and drink will be provided, and there will be a demonstration of our newest product line.

Address: Dynamic Toy Company
             22 Main Street
             Reno, NV

[Your Name]
Vice President

Save the file with the name **Invite**. Now it's time to put Mail Merge Helper to work. Choose Tools, Mail Merge. You see the dialog box in figure 21.1.

Step-by-step guidance
through the process

Fig. 21.1
Mail Merge Helper
walks you through the
three steps of a mail
merge (*if only it could
lick stamps!*).

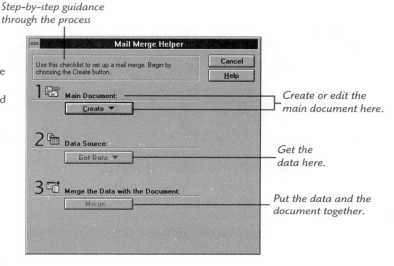

Create or edit the
main document here.

Get the
data here.

Put the data and the
document together.

Getting to the main document

The first thing you need to do is tell Mail Merge Helper where to find your
invitation. Click the Create button. Word gives you common document
options, such as form letters and envelopes (see fig. 21.2). Because the open
house invitation is a form letter, click Form Letters.

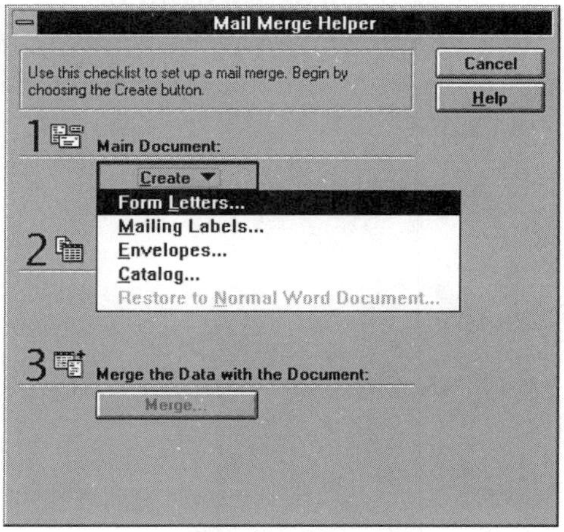

Fig. 21.2
The Main Document is
where you'll place your
merge fields.

Mail Merge Helper has a question (see fig. 21.3): do you want to create a new document or use the document you have open? In this case, you've already typed your invitation, so choose to use the Active Window, where it's waiting patiently for you.

Fig. 21.3
Answer the question: go with what you've got, or start a new main document.

{Note}

If you have one document window open and you choose to create a new main document with Mail Merge Helper, a new, blank Word document opens. Don't worry. Your first document is still there, under this new document. It's no different than pulling out a clean sheet of paper and placing it on top of the other papers on your desk.

Gotta have a data source to merge

After you've told the Helper that the active window is the main document, Word returns you to the Mail Merge Helper dialog box. Notice in figure 21.4 that there's now some information under the Create button: the merge type—Form Letters—and the name of your main document file, C:\WINWORD\INVITE.DOC.

Fig. 21.4
See how Mail Merge Helper holds your hand each step of the way? Now it's time to get the data.

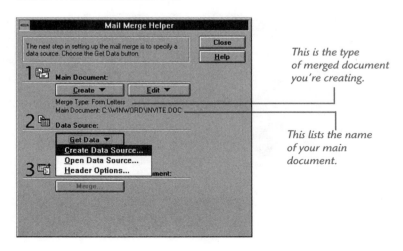

This is the type of merged document you're creating.

This lists the name of your main document.

Notice also that the Get Data button is now available to you—a subtle hint from Mail Merge Helper that it's time to get the data.

Telling Word what type of information to use

Let's create a list of the clients you are going to invite to come gorge themselves on all that free food. Choose Create Data Source.

> You could choose to open an existing data source here, in which case you'd see the Open Data Source dialog box (which pretty much resembles every other Open File dialog box), and you'd simply choose the file you want to use.

The Create Data Source dialog box appears (see fig. 21.5). The first step in creating a data source is to tell Word what field names you want to use—things like FirstName, Address, and so on. Word uses these field names like you use the labels on recycling bins—just as you put glass in the bin labeled *Glass*, Word puts FirstName data from the data source into the FirstName merge field in the main document.

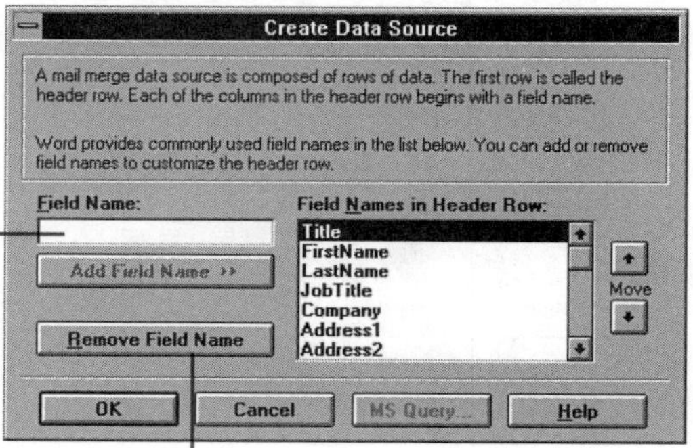

Fig. 21.5

Of course, if you address your clients by title (Dr., Mr., Your Eminence, etc.) you'd keep the title field; but for now, let's go informal.

Need a unique field name? Write your own!

Remove the field names you don't need.

Mail Merge Helper has already put several common field names in the list for you. For the invitations, you only need FirstName, LastName, Company, Address, City, State, and PostalCode, so start by removing all the other field names. Select Title (if it's not already highlighted) and then click Remove Field Name. Repeat this for JobTitle, Company, Address2, Country, HomePhone, and WorkPhone field names.

Q&A

> **I want to use a field name that isn't on the list. What do I do?**
>
> To add a field name, you simply type the new name in the Field Name text box and then click the Add Field Name button. The new name is added to the end of the Field Names in the Header Row list.

Saving the data source for future use

When you click OK to save this list of field names, Word asks you to save the data source file. Save it with the name CLIENTS.DOC (you can use it again to send out Christmas cards) and click OK once to save the file and click OK again to accept the file summary information.

The cast of characters: adding data to your data source

Mail Merge Helper is no slouch: it noticed that your data source has no data. That's pretty useless, so it prompts you with the dialog box in figure 21.6. Click Edit Data Source so that you can begin to enter your customers' names and addresses.

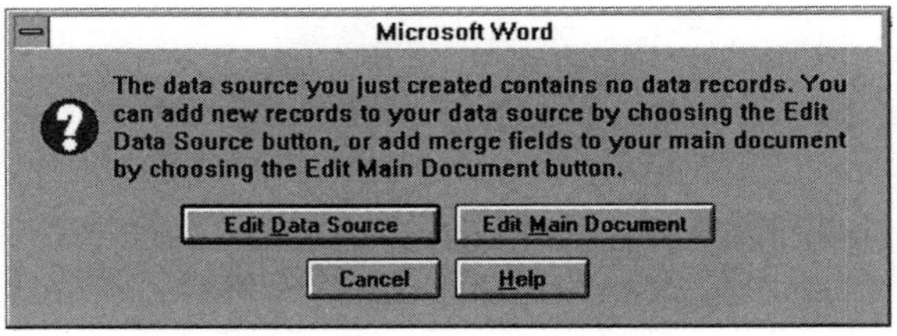

Fig. 21.6

What's a data source without data? Edit the data source.

Microsoft Word

The data source you just created contains no data records. You can add new records to your data source by choosing the Edit Data Source button, or add merge fields to your main document by choosing the Edit Main Document button.

[Edit Data Source]   [Edit Main Document]
[Cancel]   [Help]

A Data Form appears (see fig. 21.7). Just enter your top four clients for now. Fill in these forms by typing in each of the following **records**, pressing Enter to move to the next field. Click Add New when you finish one record and want to move on to the next.

Field	Record 1	Record 2	Record 3	Record 4
FirstName:	Nellie	P.G.	Elvis	Sam
LastName:	Wright	Stier	Ricardo	Sumi
Company:	ABC Toys	Gregory's	Zen Toys	PlayShop
Address1:	10 "R" St.	2 Elm Dr.	17 Oak Lane	3A Rt. 117
City:	Reno	Napa	Reno	Elko
State:	NV	CA	NV	NV
PostalCode:	55555	92222	55554	55444

Plain English, please!

A **record** is a single set of information. In your client database, one client's name, address, city, state, and zip information is a single record. Each client has his own record. Each record will be used to generate a single copy of your document in the mail merge.

Fig. 21.7
The data forms already have your chosen field names; just fill them in to provide data for your mail merge.

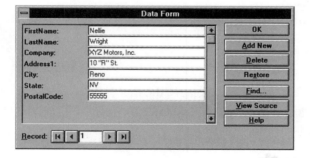

To move from field to field in a data record, you can use your Tab key. To move backwards one field at a time, use Shift+Tab.

After you enter the last record, click OK. Mail Merge Helper takes you back to the main document—your invitation—which has been waiting patiently all this time.

Preparing the document with merge fields

Now that you have a main document and a data source, you need to make the connection between them. It's kind of like hooking up a doorbell to the ringer: once you've done that, every time you push the doorbell button, you hear a ring. Once you've placed the merge fields, every time you print or view the merge, Word makes the connection between the data source and your document.

You make this connection by placing the merge fields in your document that correspond to the fields in your data source using the Mail Merge toolbar.

Preparing your document with merge fields

It's time to place those merge fields you've heard so much about. Begin with the name and address that will appear at the top of your invitation. Put your cursor immediately before the word *Dear*. Click the Insert Merge Field button and a pop-up list appears (see fig. 21.8).

Fig. 21.8
Voila! All the field names you designated for your data source automatically appear in the Insert Merge Field list.

Click FirstName. Word places the merge field code for FirstName in your document. Add a space, then click the Insert Merge Field button again, and select LastName. Hit Enter.

Repeat this procedure to place the rest of the fields in your document to match the example in figure 21.9. It's up to you to put a space between first and last names, a comma and space between city and state, and a space between the state and the postal code fields.

Finally, add a blank line between the address and greeting, and insert a space and the FirstName field after *Dear*, followed by a comma.

Close-Up: the Mail Merge toolbar

You use this toolbar to add merge fields to your document that tell Word where to put your data source information. It's also used to actually print your mail merge.

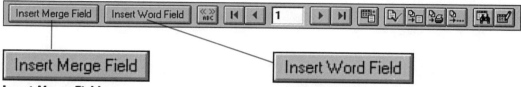

Insert Merge Field
Has a list of all the data source field names (so you can insert them in the main document)

Insert Word Field
This is pretty complicated stuff. It lets you set all kinds of parameters like "If...then" statements for your mail merge. DO NOT OPEN UNTIL YOU'RE MORE EXPERIENCED WITH MAIL MERGE.

 View Merged Data
Shows you how the merged records would look in your document one by one using the arrow navigator to the right of it

 First, Previous, Next, and Last Record
These buttons display the first, previous, next, and last record, respectively, in the active mail merge data source.

 Mail Merge Helper
Help is never far away—click here to return to it.

 Check for Errors
Does just that in your mail merge fields

 Merge to New Document
Saves the individual documents created by the mail merge to a file

 Merge to Printer
Prints the personalized documents

 Mail Merge
Brings up a dialog box that gives you some options in creating your mail merge

 Find Record
Gives you the Find Record dialog box so you can search for a particular record

 Edit Data Source
Made a mistake? Got a new client? This takes you to the data forms to edit records.

Fig. 21.9

It may look funny, but these little merge field codes are going to save you a lot of work creating your invitations.

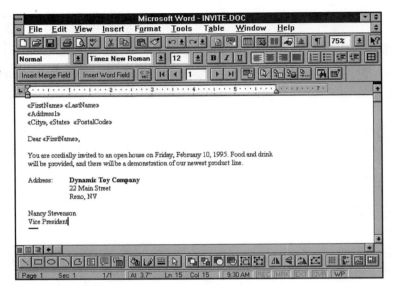

It's alive! Merging what you've created

Now that you have merge fields in place, the actual merge is all set. When you ask Word to print or display the individual invitations, Word performs the merge while printing, matching each merge field with each field in your data source. You can take a look at your merged documents on-screen, and print them to a file or to a printer using your Mail Merge toolbar.

Take a look at what you've done!

You can view the merged documents by clicking the View Merged Data button. Your first record appears, and Word has magically merged everything just as promised. Move through these previews of your merged documents by using the arrows to the right of the View Merged Data button.

I see a mistake in one of my records: I typed Nelly instead of Nellie. What can I do at this late date to fix it?

  Don't panic! Use the Edit Data Source button. This brings up the data forms for the individual records so that you can make any changes quickly and easily before you print your invitations. Just click the arrow keys to move from record to record until you find the one you want. If you've got a really large database, you might want to click the Find Record button to search for it instead.

Get ready to print

There are a couple of possibilities at this point. One is that you want to go ahead and print everything right now.

Another possibility is to create and then save a document that contains all the merged invitations. You might do this if you have some reason to save these invitations and either print them at a later time, print them more than once, or just save a record of them in a file.

You can put the results in a document...

 To merge your invitations to a document now, you simply click the Merge to New Document button on the toolbar. Notice that your merged letters have been created as Form Letters1—a document with four invitations in it. Word has thoughtfully placed a page break between each invitation.

You still need to save this document. Close it, saving it as PARTY.DOC.

...Or you can print it now!

 To print the invitations now, simply click the Merge to Printer button. The Print dialog box lets you set the usual options: how many pages to print, which printer to print to, and so on.

(Tip) You might want to review Chapter 8 for more information on printing. Since you are potentially printing hundreds of documents at a time with a mail merge, it's important to get everything set up right. Try printing just the first page of your merge to make sure everything looks right, or use the Check for Errors button on the Mail Merge toolbar before printing.

What if you want to make some special adjustments to how your invitations will print?

Customizing how your merge will print

 Click the Mail Merge button, and use the Merge dialog box to choose different mail merge options (see fig. 21.10).

Fig. 21.10
It's practically party time: handle all the variables of printing your mail merge right from this dialog box.

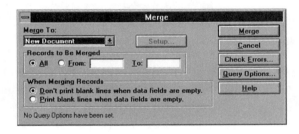

This is how you use the stuff in the Merge dialog box:

- **Merge To.** This drop-down list is where you choose to merge to a new document or a printer.

- **Records to be Merged.** Select a range of records, or print them all.

- **When Merging Records**. You get an option here. If you have a field— say Suite Number—that may or may not have data in it, you can choose to print the blank line when the field is empty, or not to print it.

- **Check Errors.** It's always a good idea to use this feature if you're printing a lengthy mail merge; Word checks for mail merge errors (like merge field codes that are wrong).

- **Query Options.** You can print just certain records or sort the records before printing.

Decide exactly what you want to print

I know you're ready to party, but let's look briefly at the Query Options dialog box. This dialog box gives you the opportunity to customize your mailing. Want to send a special mailing to people from a single town or company? Or do you want to sort the mailing in a specific order? This dialog box is where you do it.

Filter out what you don't need

Click Query Options in the Merge dialog box, and select Filter Records. Use the Filter Records tab to create a mailing for only certain records in your list (for example, only those records having the same City field).

You can print party invitations, for example, to only those in Reno, Nevada:

1 Click on the Field drop-down list in the Filter Records tab, and select the field called City.

2 The default Comparison is Equals, which is what you want. Go to the Compare To box and type **Reno**.

3 Click OK. Word only prints merge documents where the City field equals Reno.

Using this method, you can filter in lots of ways. You might choose records where the number of days that a payment is late is greater than 90. Or, you might choose to send letters at tax time to those whose company field is blank, asking them to confirm whether they are a corporation.

Sort things before you print

Sort lets you produce mailings in a specific order; for example, sorting by ZIP code, which the Post Office requires for large mailings. You can sort by up to three categories. To sort by last name:

1 Choose the Sort Records tab (see fig. 21.11), then click the Sort By drop-down box.

2 Choose LastName.

3 Click the Merge button to perform the merge right from here.

Fig. 21.11
Sort your documents so that they print in the order you want: alphabetical by last name, by postal code for mass mailings, etc.

Can't mail the letter without envelopes (or labels)!

Now that you've finished setting up your mail merge, it's simple to generate addressed envelopes using the same data source. (It had better be: it's practically party time and you haven't even ordered the cake!)

Setting up the envelope

Click the Mail Merge Helper button on the toolbar. Basically, what you're going to do is choose a different main document type for your data source to merge with. Click the Create button and choose Envelopes.

⊛{Note} If you want to merge this list to labels, you would just choose labels as the main document. The steps that follow very closely resemble those for envelopes. Just follow Mail Merge Helper's lead, and be sure to put a label sheet in your printer before you print!

Mail Merge Helper asks another question (see fig. 21.12): do you want to change the document INVITE.DOC to envelopes, or do you want to create a new main document?

Fig. 21.12
Here's where
you change to
envelopes...can't send
those invitations
without envelopes!

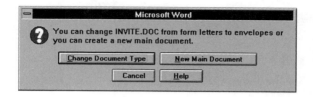

Let's keep working with the current document: choose Change Document
Type. Word returns you to the Mail Merge Helper screen, and the Merge Type
now reads Envelopes. Now you also have a Setup button available; click it to
select your envelope options (see fig. 21.13). These include what size envelope to use, how they should print, and if you want to use a different font on
your envelopes.

⊛ {Note} _____ A return address is automatically generated for your envelopes using information from the User Info tab of the Options dialog box.

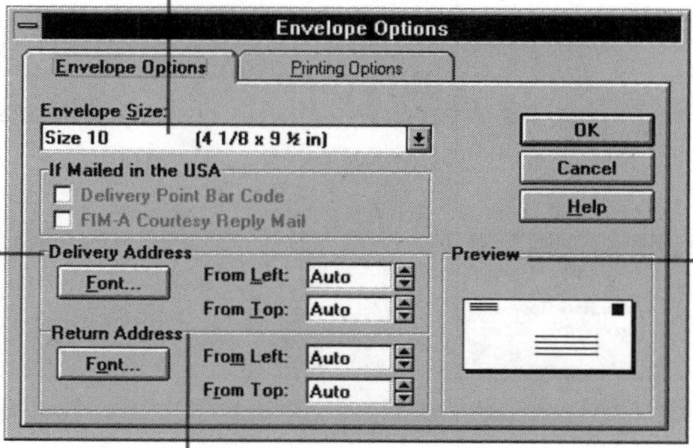

*Choose from a variety of
envelope sizes.*

Fig. 21.13
Business letters or
invitations; Courier or
Roman font? Envelope
Options and Printing
Options let you cus-
tomize the look of the
final printed enve-
lopes.

*A sneak peak at
what the envelopes
will look like*

*You can adjust the
font and placement
of the address.*

*Adjust the formatting of
the return address, too.*

After you make your choices, click OK. The next dialog box, shown in figure
21.14, is where you enter your merge field codes for the envelopes. Using the
Insert Merge Field button, select the codes for FirstName, LastName, Company, Address1, City, State, and PostalCode as you did earlier for your
invitation, adding spaces and commas where they're needed.

Fig. 21.14

The Envelope Address dialog box is the place for envelope merge field codes.

When you click OK, Word asks whether you want this information to replace the existing document (your invitation). Because you already saved your invitations to a new document (PARTY.DOC), go ahead and replace the original document with the envelope document.

I'm ready: print those envelopes

You return to the Mail Merge Helper dialog box. It's now time to merge. Click Merge, then click Merge once again in the final dialog box to merge your information to a new document (you could also have chosen to merge to printer in the Merge To drop-down list). Congratulations! Your envelopes appear on-screen as a document (see fig. 21.15).

Fig. 21.15

Time to order the champagne; your invitations and envelopes are ready to go!

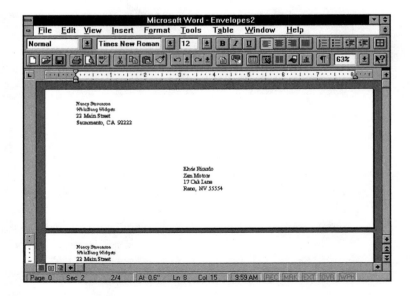

To print the envelopes, simply load envelopes into the printer and print them as you would any document (for more details about printing envelopes, see Chapter 8).

Now, get to a post office, and watch those party animals come running!

> ### *I want to do another mail merge, but I want to create a new document and source.*
>
> When you go to the Mail Merge Helper after having used it once, there's a simple way to clear it. Click the <u>C</u>reate button, and select a document type. Then, click <u>N</u>ew Main Document, and you've got a fresh start.

Managing Big Documents

Sometimes the best way to handle a big writing project is to break it into smaller pieces. Fortunately, Word juggles those smaller pieces for you with ease.

Don't imagine for one minute that the deluxe desktop encyclopedia that I own—all 2,662 pages of it—was assembled by one person. The early riser got *aardvark* to *Aztec*, while someone who came along a little later handled *oaf* to *ozone*.

And when it came time to put all those sections together into one book, you can bet the publishers didn't go in and number every page by hand—they had a system to make the process easier.

What do you do when you want to chop a big document into small pieces, so that a group of people can work on it or you can manage it more easily? Use Word's built-in tools to stitch all those small, manageable parts into one big ensemble called a **master document**.

What is a master document?

Think of the most complicated document you worked on last year. Maybe it was your company's safety manual, in which case you had to pull together detailed notes on mandatory procedures, a large table with information on hazardous materials, and three different supervisors' reports on equipment safety. Because all that information was in separate documents, you had to cut and paste each piece into place, then laboriously create a table of contents for the whole thing.

Master documents automate that process by letting you assemble several **subdocuments** into one compact file. The actual contents of each subdocument remain in their own file; the master document contains a pointer that tells Word where it can find each piece. Each subdocument works just like a section of an outline—you can move it around, use styles to format all the pieces consistently, and open or close each part to see more or less detail on-screen at any one time (see Chapter 15 for more about outlines).

 Plain English, please!

A **subdocument** is just an ordinary Word document that has been inserted into a master document. You can create it from scratch from inside the master document, or you can bring it in from a document that you or someone else has already created. You can split a subdocument into smaller pieces, or merge a group of them into a single subdocument.

Individuals can work on separate pieces of a master document—for example, when you need input from three or four departments for a proposal. When they make their revisions, master document can then pull their changes together again easily. And, things like tables of contents, cross-references, and indexing are far easier for large documents created with a master document.

To be honest, working with master documents can get tricky. If you find you need to use the master document feature frequently, or for extremely large documents, you might want to get more detailed information about this feature from Que's *Special Edition, Using Word 6 for Windows*. But here are the basics.

Is my project right for a master document?

Large documents sometimes have a life of their own, so there's no hard and fast rule about exactly when to use master documents. Say you have a Human Resources manual with six 10-page chapters, each written by a different author. This would be a perfect time to use a master document. Or maybe you've created several documents before you realize they can be combined into a larger one. For large projects, you can plan to use a master document from the beginning. Word is flexible, so you can easily start on a master document at any stage of the process.

So, in place of hard-and-fast rules for deciding whether or not to use a master document, let me provide some hypothetical situations in which you may not want to use this feature:

- A document that includes financial disclosure statements and legal disclaimers is a toss-up. You might be better off using OLE links instead. See Chapter 20 for information on OLE.

- You're collaborating on a two-page memo. Don't use master docs. Just use the Clipboard to cut and paste these small pieces together. See Chapter 6 for information about using the Clipboard.

- You're the primary author, but five others will be reviewing this document. Try using revision marking instead of master documents for this project. See Chapter 6 for information on using revision marks.

Bottom line—master documents are the right choice when documents are so big that simply scrolling through them is a pain, or when three or more individuals have nearly complete responsibility for individual sections.

Bringing it all together

The master document is like a receptacle where all the subdocuments can be placed.

Each document is created in or inserted into the master document.

The Master Document view shows your subdocuments as parts of an outline.

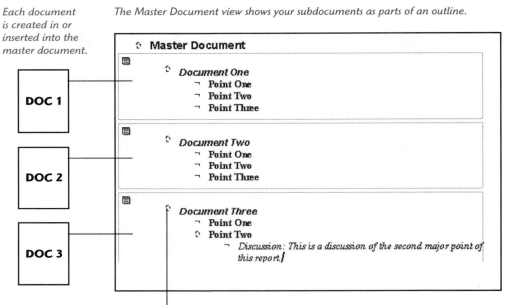

Double-click this icon to open the subdocument and work with it in a new window.

The subdocuments appear as part of the larger document.

How do I create a master document?

A master document is, in fact, just a special sort of outline that works on a very large scale. In master document view, each main section of the outline consists of a subdocument, rather than single phrases or points.

You can select a part of any document, designate it as a subdocument, and then manipulate it within the outline structure. Or you can take a separate Word document and bring it into your master document as a subdocument.

Either way, after you have identified the subdocuments in a master document, you can make global changes easily: change heading formats, create a single header or footer, and so on.

Looking at Master Document view

Word's View menu includes a choice called Master Document. It looks a lot like Outline view, with a little more—specifically, a Master Document toolbar that allows you to create and insert subdocuments, then rearrange the individual pieces that make up a master document.

You can actually create your subdocuments right in Master Document view; just type the information in as one section of the outline. Or, you can insert subdocuments that you've created elsewhere using a tool on the Master View toolbar. Finally, you can split one document into further subdocuments, or merge subdocuments together into one, all within the Master Document view.

Let's begin by opening a new document, and moving to the Master Document view by choosing View, Master Document.

Creating the master document from scratch

  You create an outline by typing its headings in Master Document view, then using the outlining buttons to promote or demote selected headings to different levels (see fig. 22.1). Be sure to use the built-in heading styles (Heading 1 through Heading 9) for the different heading levels in your outline (see Chapter 13 for more about styles). The Promote and Demote tools automatically apply these styles when you move a heading in or out in your outline.

Why do you need to be so concerned with Heading styles? Well, Word uses the headings as flags that indicate where to create new subdocuments. You tell Word, "I want all headings with Heading 3 style to be at the beginning of a new subdocument." Word looks through the selected text and, wherever it encounters a Heading 3 style, creates a subdocument made up of that heading and the stuff included under it.

Fig. 22.1
A Word outline indicates with a plus symbol that a heading has more headings underneath it, and a minus sign indicates a solitary heading.

A plus symbol indicates there is more detail beneath this heading.

— The heading styles are shown in the style drop-down list.

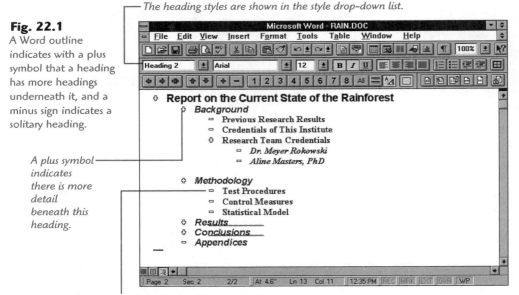

A minus symbol tells you there are no more headings subordinate to this one.

How does Word know which Heading style to look for? You have to select the headings and text that you want Word to divide into subdocuments. The first heading you select sets the stage by telling Word, "This is the style to look for." Of course, this means that when you create your outline you have to be sure to apply the same Heading style to every heading that you want to begin a new subdocument. It doesn't matter what Heading style you use, but you have to be consistent (like Word).

Close-Up: the Master Document toolbar

The outlining tools and Master Document tools are side-by-side on this toolbar.

Outlining tools (see Chapter 15)

 Create Subdocument
Makes any part of your outline into a subdocument

 Merge Subdocument
Makes two subdocuments into one

 Remove Subdocument
Changes part of your outline back into part of the master document, rather than a subdocument

 Split Subdocument
Breaks up a subdocument into smaller subdocuments

 Insert Subdocument
Allows you to get existing files and insert them as subdocuments

 Lock Document
Keeps anyone other than the original document author from changing it

In figure 22.2, for example, Background is the first heading in the selected group of headings. Because Background has a Heading 2 style, selecting it first designates that each section beginning with a Heading 2-style heading will begin a new subdocument.

It doesn't matter what heading level you decide to use as the beginning of a subdocument. You just have to be sure that you apply the same Heading style to every heading that marks a section you want to make into a subdocument.

 After you click the Create Subdocument button, you can see the results in the selected headings. All level 2 headings start a new subdocument, and each has a small subdocument icon and gray box around it (see fig. 22.3).

You can also rearrange subdocuments easily in Master Document view. You do this by clicking the subdocument icon, then dragging it to a new place in the master document and letting go.

Fig. 22.2
Select all headings you
want to include as
subdocuments.

*The first heading
chosen has
Heading 2 style
applied.*

*All selected headings
with Heading 2 style
will begin new
subdocuments.*

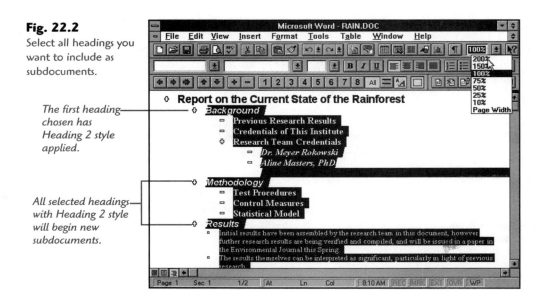

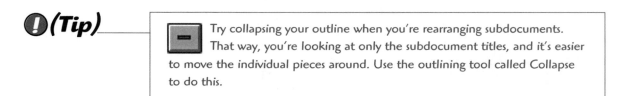

(Tip)

Try collapsing your outline when you're rearranging subdocuments.
That way, you're looking at only the subdocument titles, and it's easier
to move the individual pieces around. Use the outlining tool called Collapse
to do this.

Fig. 22.3
Word creates
subdocuments based
on your selection.

*Every subdocument
gets its own
subdocument icon.*

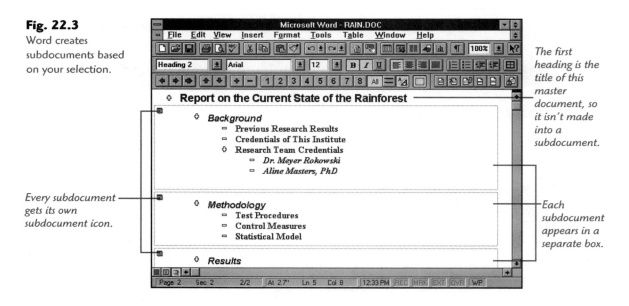

*The first
heading is the
title of this
master
document, so
it isn't made
into a
subdocument.*

*Each
subdocument
appears in a
separate box.*

The documents exist: just bring them all together!

Besides creating subdocuments in the master document, you can also assemble existing documents into a master document, or use a combination.

 Make sure you're in Master Document view. Type a heading for a document title (if it doesn't already have one). With your cursor still at the end of the first heading, click the Insert Subdocument button. In the dialog box shown in figure 22.4, enter the name of the file you'd like to add.

Fig. 22.4

Just insert files into your master document as subdocuments to assemble existing documents into one big document.

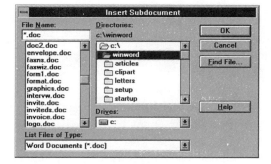

To insert a new subdocument beneath another subdocument, make sure the insertion point is in a blank heading right after the subdocument, then use the Insert Subdocument button. Repeat this process to assemble all the files you want to include as subdocuments.

 Be careful! If the insertion point is within another subdocument when you click the Insert Subdocument button, you'll end up with a subdocument inside the first subdocument, and the first subdocument will turn into its own master document. If you invented Rubik's Cube, this kind of complexity may appeal to you. For most of us, though, it's too confusing.

The subdocument will appear with appropriate outline heading styles applied automatically by Word. If you move the headings around, they'll automatically take on the headings styles based on their position.

 If you've already created a large document and you want to break it down into subdocuments so you can work with its sections more easily, you can. Just open the file, move into Master Document view, and make sure the different pieces are at the right place in the outline (see Chapter 15 for information about outlining existing documents). Then, select the whole document, and click the Create Subdocument button. Don't forget the importance of the heading style of the first heading selected, though!

Working with subdocuments

When I began keeping a Rolodex (back in the days before I had 20,000 people to track), I made do with one that had dividers for A–C, D–F, and so on. Nowadays, I have one that's broken down into a section for every single letter of the alphabet.

Your subdocuments will evolve like that. You'll start with three, then want to break them down into six, then back to five—you get the idea.

With a master document, you can easily split up a subdocument into two subdocuments or merge two subdocuments into one subdocument.

 After you create subdocuments, you can get into each one by just double-clicking the subdocument icon in Master Document view. Word opens the subdocument on top of the master document. Make any changes, then close and save the document.

Make one subdocument into two

 Sometimes you start writing about one topic, and discover it's taken on a life of its own. When one of those subtopics suddenly becomes three, you can break them into separate subdocuments to make them easier to handle. To break up one subdocument into two, just place your insertion point in the place where you'd like to split a subdocument, and click the Split Subdocument button.

How a group can master master documents

There's a special feature built into the master document that makes working on a large document in a group easier.

Each subdocument retains the name of its author; this information comes from the file summary information dialog box that appears when the author first created the file.

If you open the master document, only the subdocuments that have your name as author attached—that is, any documents you created— are available to you to edit. Subdocuments created by others can be read, but not changed.

These have a little lock symbol next to the heading, as in the figure below. This lock has nothing to do with any read-only setting you may have made when you saved a file: it's master document's own little security system.

But this lock isn't really a heavy-duty security measure—it's really just a little caution sign for other people in the group. You can easily unlock documents you didn't create so that you can make changes to them. Just look on the Master Document toolbar, select the locked section, and click the Lock Document button.

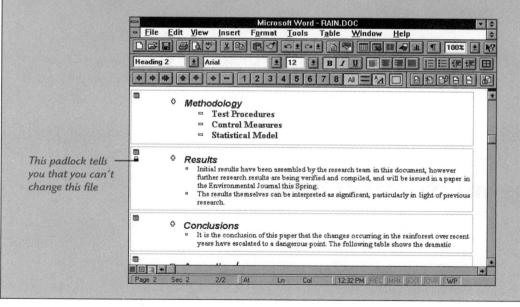

This padlock tells you that you can't change this file

 **{Note}** — | After you split up a subdocument, the next time you save the master document, Word will save each piece as a separate file with a unique name.

Make two subdocuments into one

Say that you have a separate document with each quarter's results, but as you're working on your document, you decide you want one section that covers all results for the year in one place. Just merge the four documents into one. To merge two or more subdocuments, first make sure they're next to each other in the outline. Then, do this:

1 Select the first subdocument by clicking its subdocument icon.

2 Hold down the Shift key, and click any other subdocument icons you want to combine.

 3 Click the Merge Subdocument button, and they become one subdocument.

That's it!

 (Tip) — | If you want to move just selected text or graphics from one subdocument to another, open the master document and go to Normal view. Select the text or graphics, then drag them around the master document to the place where you want them to appear.

Saving master documents

When you save the master document, all the little subdocuments are saved into their own files. Word gives them each a name that's based on the text of the beginning heading. So, if your heading is Part IV, Word might name the document PARTIV.DOC.

But, there can be variations on this. If you already have another document with that name, Word might add some other designation to the heading to make it unique. Maybe Word will name it PARTIV07.DOC. If you need to know a particular subdocument name, open the master document, then open the subdocument by double-clicking the subdocument icon. The title bar reveals how Word chose to name it.

You can open each individual subdocument, or open the master document and work on them all at once. If you're making a change that will impact the whole master document—say renaming or moving a subdocument—do it from within the master document so changes will be saved with the master document.

 If you rename, move, or delete subdocuments using File Manager, you break the link to your master document. When you try to open the master document, you'll get an error message that says your subdoc is among the missing!

Printing it all at once

One reason master document is such a cool feature is that you can print all those subdocuments with a single print command.

To print your whole master document, go into Normal view, then choose File, Print to print as usual (see Chapter 8 for more about printing).

If you'd prefer a printout of your outline, you can do that, too. Simply move to the Master Document view first, open or close sections of your document to show the heading levels you prefer, then print.

Part VII:

Getting Fancy with Word

Making Basic Macros

Ever think, "I'll go crazy if I have to do this once more!"? It's time to teach Word to handle those repetitive tasks for you.

In this chapter:

- What is a macro?

- I keep doing the same things over and over. Isn't there an easier way?

- How do I make a macro?

- I want to use this macro with all my documents

- I made a mistake when I was recording this macro; am I stuck with it?

You could stumble out of bed every Thursday at 2:30 am and punch the record button on your VCR to add to your collection of old *Get Smart* episodes, but why lose sleep over it? Your VCR is smart enough to handle that trivial job for you (assuming that you're smart enough to program it).

The word *programming* may scare you—don't let it. There are all kinds of of programming in the world, and the simplest is no more complicated than a VCR. You show Word how you typically handle a tedious process—mouse clicks, typing, and all. The next time you want to get that boring old job done, you ask Word to handle the drudgery.

What can a Word macro do?

- Open a certain file you use all the time
- Change a setting in the Options dialog box
- Format documents you bring in from another application

The possibilities are endless.

What's a macro, anyway?

A **macro** is a recorded list of commands that are stored together as one. If you have a certain computer task that you do repeatedly throughout the day, you can record a macro of all the commands you use in doing that task. And forever after, whenever you want to play back the commands to complete that task, all you need to do is run the macro.

 Plain English, please!

To **record** in computerese means that your PC creates and saves a list of a precise series of commands you perform, in the order you perform them. Word goes a step further, interpreting the *results* of your actions rather than just the steps that got you there.

To **run** a macro means that your PC plays back that series of commands, the way a tape recorder plays back a series of sentences. Because you recorded all those commands under one macro command, you only have to choose the macro command and leave the rest to Word.

Here's an example of a good candidate for a macro. Let's say that you run a home business, and you often address and print envelopes from your computer. Sometimes these are personal letters, so you use your home address. But when you're sending business letters, you have to add the business name to the return address.

To change the return address for envelopes, you open the Options dialog box, click the User Info tab, and type the alternate address. After you've done this a few times, you'll get thoroughly sick of this repetitive job. Time for a macro!

Record your own macro

Recording a macro is pretty simple: you tell Word that you want to record a macro, and then you give the macro a name and assign it to a toolbar, menu, or keyboard shortcut. Next, you go through the series of commands and keystrokes you want to record. Finally, you tell Word to stop recording and save the results.

You begin this whole process by choosing <u>T</u>ools, <u>M</u>acro to reach the Macro dialog box; then, click the Re<u>c</u>ord button. You see the Record Macro dialog box, shown in figure 23.1.

> You can also double-click the REC indicator on the status bar at the bottom of the Word screen to begin recording a macro. This indicator is gray, not black, so it doesn't stand out a lot; but it's located to the right of the box that displays the time.

Fig. 23.1
This is where you list your macro's vital statistics. Be sure to give your macro a name that reflects what it does.

Describe what the macro does; if you haven't used it in a while, this reminds you of its purpose.

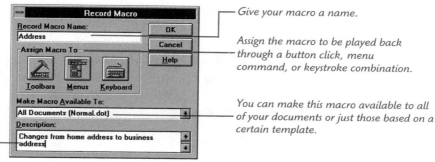

Give your macro a name.

Assign the macro to be played back through a button click, menu command, or keystroke combination.

You can make this macro available to all of your documents or just those based on a certain template.

Tell Word all about your macro

Before you begin recording, you have to name and describe your macro. Word volunteers the rather vague name of Macro1 for your new macro. You can replace that name with one of your own; just begin typing the new name. Next, type a description of what it does. Do you want to use this macro in all, or just some, of your files? In the Make Macros <u>A</u>vailable To list box, choose which files you want the macro available to (based on the template the files were created in).

⊛ {Note} _____

Give your macro a name that in some way describes what the macro does. A macro name can be as many as 36 characters long. But you can't use spaces, commas, or periods—which is why macros end up with names like ChangeReturnAddress. Of course, if you prefer to use the name that Word proposes, you can omit this step.

Now you have to decide how you want to issue the macro command. Do you want to run it by clicking a button, choosing from a menu, or using a keystroke combination?

⊛ {Note} _____

Keyboard combinations are convenient, but Word already uses a lot of them for its own commands. If you choose this method, you'll either have to replace one of Word's built-in assignments or keep trying combinations until you find one that's not already taken. Word will tell you when you choose a combination that's currently unassigned.

For now, let's assume you're going to assign a macro to a button on the toolbar:

1 Click the Toolbars button in the Assign Macro To area, and you get the Customize dialog box with the Toolbars tab open (see fig. 23.2).

Fig. 23.2

You assign your macro to a command source in the Customize dialog box.

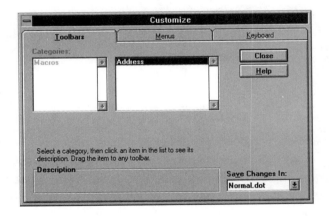

2 The highlighted name of your macro appears in the commands list. Put your pointer on the name and click and hold the mouse button. A tool button outline appears under your cursor; drag this to the toolbar where you want the button to be located.

3 When you release the mouse button, a blank tool button appears on the toolbar and you get the Custom Button dialog box (see fig. 23.3). Click the button face of your choice, then click Assign (or just click Assign to get a button with a text name).

4 When you return to the Customize dialog box, click Close and you are ready to begin recording your macro.

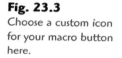

Fig. 23.3
Choose a custom icon for your macro button here.

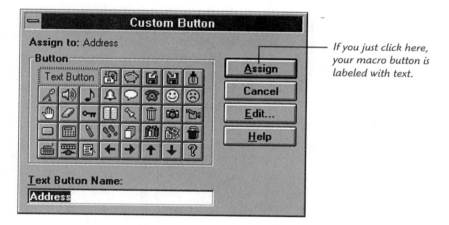

If you just click here, your macro button is labeled with text.

That's it! Now when you want to run the macro, you'll just have to click the tool button you've just created.

Record it, pause it, or stop it

As soon as you close the Macros dialog box, you're in recording mode. A little floating toolbar appears with two functions on it: stop and pause. Also, so you'll remember that you're on the air, your mouse cursor looks like a little cassette tape while you're recording (see fig. 23.4).

Fig. 23.4

This toolbar and cursor are little reminders that everything you're doing is being recorded!

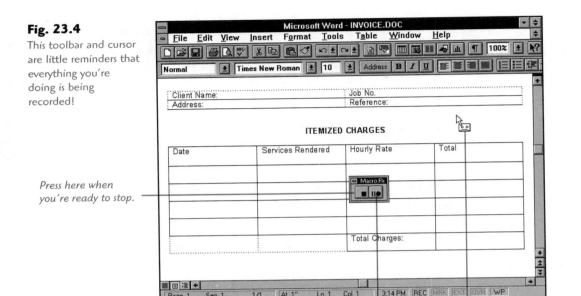

Press here when you're ready to stop.

This button toggles between pausing and restarting the recording.

When you see this pointer, you're recording.

Now—very carefully—go through all the steps of the job you want the macro to perform: every keystroke, menu command, and button you'd use to get the job done. If you were making the return address macro discussed earlier, for example, you'd have to change the User Info Options dialog box, like so:

1 Choose Tools, Options.

2 Click the User Info tab.

3 Click before the address, type your company name, and then press Enter to move the address down one line, as in fig. 23.5.

4 Click OK.

5 Click the Macro Record stop button to stop recording the macro.

Fig. 23.5
When you record a macro, you go through the steps of completing a task and Word copies them down. Next time, you just use the macro and let Word do the work.

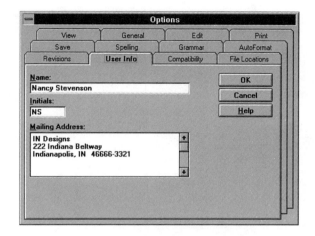

⊛ {Note} When entering text in Options dialog boxes, Word doesn't actually record the keystrokes of the text, it just "memorizes" how the text looks when you accept the dialog box. Word will make sure that's how things are when you run the macro. That way, no matter what's entered in this dialog box, when you run the macro, you'll get just what you asked for. If you already have your company name typed in the return address and run the macro, you won't get two company names. But if it's not there, it will get added.

❓ Q&A *What about typos? I left out a letter in my name. I guess I really should stop recording now, right?*

Nope. If you're in the middle of recording a macro and you make a small mistake—say you choose the wrong menu or make a typing mistake—you don't have to stop recording. Just correct the mistake and go forward. When the macro runs, it will make the same correction every time and it will happen so *fast* you won't even notice it when you run the macro. Perfectionists may want to redo the macro, but for most of us, it's the results that count.

Now that you've made a macro, use it!

There's nothing quite so satisfying as playing back a macro and seeing it do your work for you. You can run them in a few different ways, and they're all easy.

When you're ready to run your macro, just click its button on the toolbar. Word whips through the macro. Don't believe me? If you created the Address macro, run it, and then check it out by going back to the User Info tab; you'll see what your macro did.

Are you ready to macro?

Being an extrovert, a microphone never frightened me. But plenty of people get understandably nervous when their every word or action is being recorded.

Cut down on possible errors while recording your macro by preparing things ahead of time:

- If your macro is going to add or delete text, as in the Address example, make sure that what you're adding isn't already typed in, and that what you're deleting is typed in before you start recording.

- If your macro opens a file, make sure the file is available to you before you start. For example, if it's on a network, connect your computer to the network before you start recording. But remember: for your macro to work right, you have to be set up the same way you were when you recorded it. If you later try to run the macro when

you're not on the network, you may get an error message.

- Say you create a macro to print a report. Make sure the printer is on and ready to print; otherwise, you'll get a printer message and have to run and get it set up while in recording mode. You can always hit pause and do this, but why cause yourself the aggravation?

- And unlike many recordings, a macro just records your actions, not the time between them. Take all the time you need to check your spelling and search for typos. Fixing them now may be better than going back to them later.

- If you're truly chicken, try a practice run through the steps, and even write them down for yourself so you know exactly how to proceed once you're recording.

If you use an address macro, you might want to create two macros: name one Home and the other Office. The Home one can reverse the action of the first one; that is, change from the business address to the home address. Then, depending on which name you need, just run the appropriate macro and you can be sure things are the way you want them.

So you made a mistake? Edit it

If you're like me, there's always the chance that you made a small typo when you typed in your macro. No big deal. If you catch the mistake while you're recording the macro, you can correct it right then. But chances are you won't catch the mistake until you run the macro.

If you notice a small mistake when you run the macro, it's still no big deal to fix it. You can do one of two things: you can either re-record the macro—which might be the easiest fix if your macro is ultra-simple—or you can open the macro and edit it.

Editing macros can be tricky—it actually borders on programming. I only recommend editing the macro if you have a really simple problem, like a typo, to fix. For any larger problems, just re-record the macro.

To edit the macro, choose Tools, Macro. The Macro dialog box appears (see fig. 23.6). As you can see, this dialog box is sort of like command central for macros. You can record, run, edit, and even delete macros in this box. For this situation, though, just select the name of the macro you want to edit, then click the Edit button.

Fig. 23.6
Besides editing macros, you can control all the macro functions from right here.

Select the macro you want from this list.

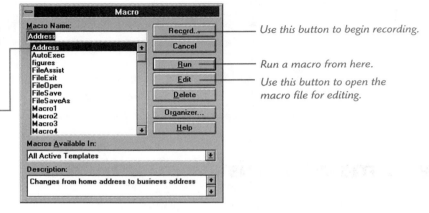

Use this button to begin recording.

Run a macro from here.

Use this button to open the macro file for editing.

The text you typed during the macro is in quotation marks, as shown in figure 23.7. In this figure, I want to take the *s* off *Designs*. Find the text, fix the typo, then close the file. And make sure you choose Yes when Word asks you if you want to save the changes.

Fig. 23.7
To fix simple mistakes, you can edit the macro language just like you edit any Word text. The weird-looking text is programming language. Avoid it and you'll be all right.

This stuff is programming language.

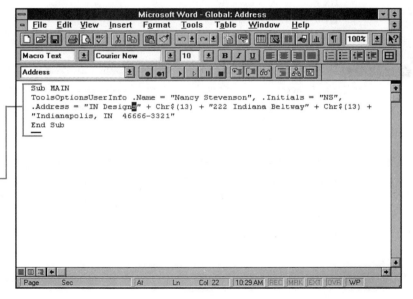

24

Have It Your Way: Customizing Word

Word is your workspace. If you spend a lot of time here, customize it so that things you need are right at hand and stuff happens the way that's easiest for you.

In this chapter:

- When my screen feels cluttered, can I get rid of some of this stuff?

- Can I change the way Word edits or prints things?

- I want to add a button to my toolbar for something I do all the time

- How do I create a shortcut key of my own?

started working from my home recently. In setting up my home workspace, I had to analyze and organize the stuff in that room. I didn't need the broken sewing machine at all, so I got rid of it. I look at my high school yearbook once in a while, but not often, so I stored it away. I needed a desk calendar and didn't have one, so I got one. Well, you can do the same things with Word.

Word allows you to display or hide various things on-screen while you're working so that what's useful to you is what's available.

Word also lets you set things up to operate the way you prefer. Just like I set my answering machine to answer on the first ring, you can change Word's built-in settings. You can even create your own shortcut keys and toolbar buttons so that the commands YOU need are available for your work.

Setting up your workspace

Word uses certain settings by default, and the default settings match the way many people work. But we're all unique, and Word recognizes that. To accommodate us all, Word provides the Customize and Options choices on the Tools menu, some different perspectives from the View menu, and the Show/Hide button on the Standard toolbar; you use them to customize how things look and operate in Word.

Customizing what's on-screen

If you don't need a ruler, for example, you can hide it for now by choosing View, and clicking Ruler to take away the check mark next to it. Then, when you do need it, you pull it out (select it again on the menu) and use it.

These are several other things you can choose to hide or display in Word:

- **Scroll bars, status bar, specific nonprinting characters.** Choose Tools, Options, then go to the View tab seen in figure 24.1. Select or deselect check boxes in the Window and Nonprinting Characters sections.

Fig. 24.1
The View tab in the Options dialog box lets you show it all or hide it away.

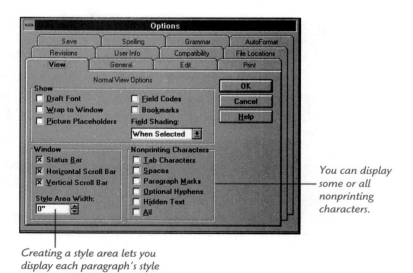

You can display some or all nonprinting characters.

Creating a style area lets you display each paragraph's style name in the left margin.

- **Toolbars.** Choose View, Toolbars. In the Toolbars dialog box, shown in figure 24.2, you can choose which toolbars are displayed and how they are displayed (with large buttons, or color buttons, and whether ToolTips will show or not).

Fig. 24.2
Word offers a lot of toolbars, and you can work with some or all of them on-screen. Hide, display, or customize toolbars in this dialog box.

(Tip)

Don't forget that you can also drag toolbars onto your document window and let them float wherever you like on-screen.

- **Ruler.** Choose View, and click Ruler to select or deselect that option. With a check mark by it, the ruler will show; with no check mark, it doesn't show.

- **All nonprinting characters.** To hide or display all nonprinting characters (tabs, paragraphs marks, etc.), click the Show/Hide button on the Standard toolbar (if the button's light gray, it shows characters; if it's dark gray, it hides them).

- **Everything.** Finally, to make a clean sweep, choose View, Full Screen. You get a screen with only your document and a full screen icon (see fig. 24.3). Click this icon to return to the regular Word screen.

Fig. 24.3
The Full Screen view
gets rid of tools,
menus, and so on, but
retains the character-
istics of the view
you had on screen:
Normal, Page Layout,
or Outline.

Full Screen icon

 Q&A

> *I go to Full Screen view, but there's no button in the
> lower right to get out. What do I do now?*

The short answer is: to get out of Full Screen view without the button, press
Esc. You return to your familiar, tool-laden screen, with all your text in place.
But for future reference, you need to keep a couple of things in mind:

- The Full Screen view has its own toolbar, which by default has only one
  button—the one you use to get out of Full Screen view. Somehow the
  toolbar must have been toggled off. You have to be in Full Screen view
  before this toolbar even appears on the View menu's toolbar list; then,
  press Alt+V to get to the View menu. Select Toolbars, then click Full
  Screen. The button should appear.

- Your menus don't "go away" when you're in Full Screen view; they're just
  hiding off-screen. You can press Alt+V to pull up the View menu; for that
  matter, you can press Alt+F to pull up the File menu, then use the right-
  arrow key to pull up each menu, one at a time.

Do it my way: changing Word's settings

The designers of Word understand the benefits of flexibility in the workplace, so they designed a program that accommodates different working styles. Word allows you to change standard settings of its workspace to ones that work better for you, and you do this by changing options.

 **{Note}**

Word includes the topic of Customizing the Word Screen in its Examples and Demos in the Help menu. Run this demo to get an idea of what's possible.

You saw in figure 24.1 that the Options dialog box is made up of several tabs. You've already changed selections in some of these tabs while you were working through this book, so this process isn't entirely new to you. These Option tabs contain Word's default settings—like how it edits or prints documents—many of which you'll never need to mess with. On the other hand, when you do get around to customizing things, they offer some interesting options.

Here are what the different tabs have to offer:

- **AutoFormat** settings determine how formatting is applied to your document, including the automatic replacement of certain characters, such as smart quotes.

 Plain English, please!

There are plain fries and there are curly fries. Smart quotes are the fancy, curled quotation marks that you see in typeset books and magazines. The quotation marks and apostrophe on your keyboard are the straight up and down kind. Usually, you need a keystroke combination to call up smart quotes. Using the AutoFormat setting, you can have Word automatically replace the straight quotes with these curly ones.

- **Compatibility** gives you several options for working with other file and font formats.

- **Edit** options include drag-and-drop, text selection, and overtype mode.

- **File Locations** lists and allows you to modify default file locations.

(Tip) If you change the location where Word keeps certain files, you should probably move any previously created files of that type into the new location so you don't end up searching for them in two places.

- **General** contains a variety of basic settings, such as measurement units, automatic repagination, and how WordPerfect users can interact with Word.

- **Grammar** contains the sets of rules you use to analyze your document's grammar; you can also customize rules here.

- **Print** includes settings for how your document will print, as well as what elements will print by default, such as annotations or hidden text.

- **Revisions** settings let you determine how changes will appear in your document when you choose to display revision marks.

- **Save** settings include those that control how often Word performs automatic saves and whether or not it creates automatic backup files.

- **Spelling** settings modify the spelling check and designate dictionaries used in the check.

- **View** lets you control what elements appear on-screen.

- **User Info** is where you list the name, company, and address information that Word uses when inserting your return address in places like Mail Merge Wizard.

Making toolbars and shortcut keys your own

One of the first things I did to my home office was get rid of things I wouldn't use on a regular basis and bring in the things that I need. Out went the little TV (no "Oprah" for this worker bee). In came a phone and bookcase.

You can also add and take things away from toolbars in Word so that you're displaying what you use most often. And you can customize shortcut keys so that the functions you use most are easy to get to.

Put the right tools at hand

It would be pretty stupid for me to have a ruler, T-square, and screwdriver on my desk if I spend most of my day making phone calls. All I need is my Rolodex, a notepad, and a pencil (or their computer equivalents).

In Word, when you want to get just the right buttons on your toolbars, it's easy to put away what you don't need and add what you do.

First, display the toolbar you'd like to customize. Then, choose <u>T</u>ools, <u>C</u>ustomize. The dialog box in figure 24.4 appears.

Fig. 24.4

The Customize dialog box offers ways to customize your toolbars, menus, and keyboard shortcuts with three different tabs.

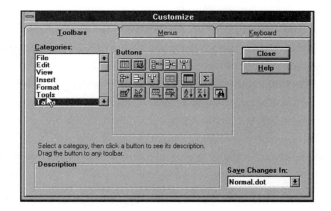

Choose the category of tool you'd like to add in the <u>C</u>ategories drop-down list. Each category has a corresponding set of possible buttons that appear to the right of this list. To determine what the button does, click its name in this list. In the description box at the bottom of the dialog box, Word tells you what the button does.

When you find a button that you want to add, simply click it and drag it where you'd like it to be on the toolbar on your screen.

⊛ {Note}

Let's say you always use either Times New Roman or Arial fonts in your documents. If you choose Fonts as a category in the Customize dialog box, Word shows you a list of font names. To be able to quickly move back and forth, you might want to make a button for both Arial and Times New Roman by just dragging their names one by one up to the toolbar. Now, move back and forth between the two fonts with the click of a button!

On the other hand, if there's a button on an on-screen toolbar that you don't want to display, you can get rid of it. With this dialog box open, click the unwanted button on the toolbar and drag it onto the document window.

You can also adjust the spaces between buttons on displayed toolbars when this dialog box is open. You know how you have to wiggle around a little to get people on a bench to slide over and give you some room? Same principle: click the button and drag it one way or the other slightly. Word adds space between it and the button next to it.

Having fun in your workspace: a manifesto

Let's face it. In today's office, the way your computer works is as personal as the family pictures and knick-knacks that you need to feel comfortable in your little bit of corporate space.

So, try to find fun ways to personalize your computer time. There's a lot more you can do besides fiddling with the way Word works. You can also add software that makes computing more fun.

Screen savers are an example. These programs bring a moving image up on your screen if you leave your computer inactive for a certain amount of time. Originally, these programs

"saved" your screen by preventing static images from burning into the monitor. Today's VGA monitors don't burn, but screen-savers still serve a key function: they protect your on-screen work from the scrutiny of everyone who passes by your computer. That's the reason many screen savers have password protection available as an option. And, they give you something entertaining to watch when you're on those long, drawn out phone calls with your clients.

Isn't it nice to know that the little cartoon with the duck and cow hitting each other over the head is really practical?

①(Tip)

You can create a new toolbar with all your favorite buttons on it. Choose View, Toolbars. In the dialog box, click New. Word lets you name the toolbar, then brings up the Customize dialog box so that you can drag the buttons you want onto the new, floating toolbar.

②Q&A

I changed my toolbars all around, but when I open a new document, they're back the way they were. What gives?

Notice that when you are in the Customize dialog box, there's a Save Changes In selection. It lets you save these toolbar changes to any templates currently attached to active document windows. You can select one of these template styles; or, if you want these changes available to all documents, you need to select the Normal template.

Creating shortcut keys

If you like to use keystroke combinations as shortcuts to perform certain functions, you might want to check into creating some shortcuts of your own. For example, let's say you regularly work with long, complex documents filled with different sections. You could assign a shortcut key to the "move to next section" command and then jump quickly from section to section by just hitting that combination.

These shortcuts are convenient, like being able to dial a number on your phone by hitting a pre-programmed button. And assigning new shortcut keys is not that difficult to do.

Choose Tools, Customize. Select the Keyboard tab, and watch the tab in figure 24.5 appear.

Fig. 24.5

Pick your own shortcut with the Keyboard tab of the Customize dialog box.

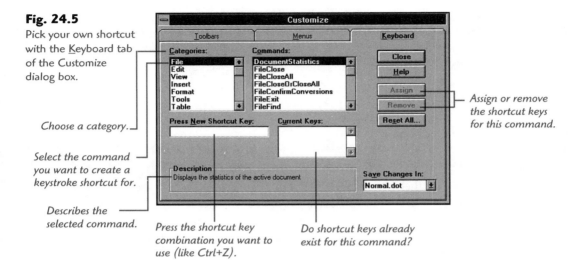

Choose a category.

Select the command you want to create a keystroke shortcut for.

Describes the selected command.

Assign or remove the shortcut keys for this command.

Press the shortcut key combination you want to use (like Ctrl+Z).

Do shortcut keys already exist for this command?

First, select a category like Edit. Then click the command you want (say GoToNextSection). If there is any current keystroke shortcut assigned to that command, Word shows it to you in the Current Keys box.

To assign a key combination, simply press the keys, such as Alt+N, and the combination appears in the Press New Shortcut Key box. If that combination is currently assigned to some other function, a little note will appear under this box with that information.

To make the assignment, click Assign.

 **<Caution>**

Remember that if you replace a keystroke combination with a new one, information about the original function will stay the same in on-screen messages and help screens, which could confuse you later on. Try to use only new keystroke combinations to avoid confusion.

That's it! Play around with all these customizing features to get them the way you prefer. And remember that you can reset your menus and keyboards back the way they were by using the Reset All buttons in the Customize dialog box.

{ Index }

Symbols

* (asterisk) wild card, 71

¶ (paragraph marks), *see* nonprinting characters

A

addresses
envelopes, 119, 121
labels, 119
see also data sources (mail merge)
Advanced Search dialog boxes, 71
alignment
graphics, 255
text, 140
applying, 143-144
centered, 140-143
justified, 140-143
left-alignment, 140-143
right-alignment, 140-143
All tool (Outlining toolbar), 213
anchors (frames), 245
angles, drawing, 255
antonyms, 108-109
applets
ClipArt Gallery, 267
Microsoft Graph, 267
WordArt, 265-266, 269-271
arcs, drawing, 255, 257
Arrange All command (Window menu), 282, 286

arranging windows, 43, 282
arrow pointers, *see* mouse pointer
arrowheads (graphics), 259
assigning
toolbar buttons to macros, 334-335
keystroke combinations to macros, 334-335
shortcut keys to commands, 349-350
asterisk (*) wild card, 71
author information (subdocuments), 325
AutoCorrect, 17, 61, 98-101
AutoCorrect command (Tools menu), 61, 99
AutoCorrect dialog box, 99-100
AutoFormat tool (Standard toolbar), 31
AutoFormats, 17, 31
customizing, 345
tables, 202
automatic features
hyphenation, 165
saves, 77-78
word selection, 81
AutoText, 98-99, 101-103
inserting, 31
troubleshooting, 103
AutoText command (Edit menu), 103

AutoText dialog box, 102
Avery labels, printing, 118
Award wizard, 238

B

backups, 67
bar codes (envelopes), 121
body text (outlines), 216-218
boilerplates, *see* templates
boldfacing text, 132-134

borders, 240-241, 247
colors, 251
drawing, 247-249
frames (text), 242
line styles, 248
patterns, 250-251
shading, 250-251
styles, 248, 250
tables, 206
Borders toolbar, 247-248
Bottom Border tool (Borders toolbar), 248
boxes (text boxes), 255
Break command (Insert menu), 177
breaks
columns, 226
pages, 150
paragraphs, 149-150

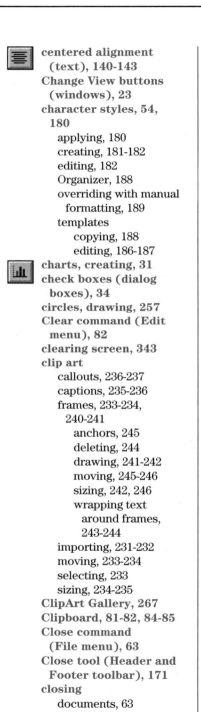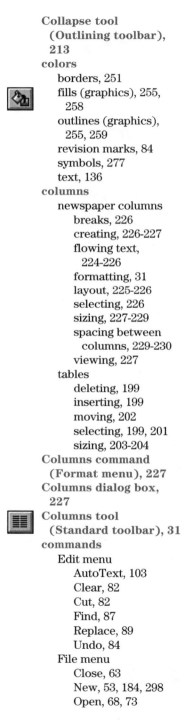

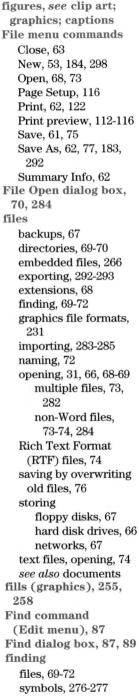

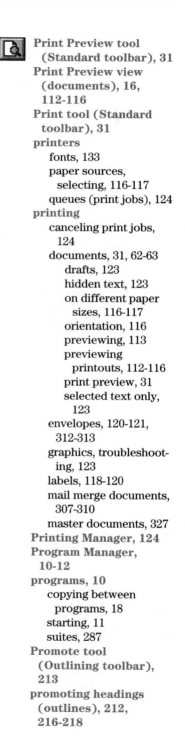

X-Y-Z

Data Structures and Algorithms in Java™

Sixth Edition

Michael T. Goodrich
Department of Computer Science
University of California, Irvine

Roberto Tamassia
Department of Computer Science
Brown University

Michael H. Goldwasser
Department of Mathematics and Computer Science
Saint Louis University

WILEY

Vice President and Executive Publisher	Don Fowley
Executive Editor	Beth Lang Golub
Assistant Marketing Manager	Debbie Martin
Sponsoring Editor	Mary O'Sullivan
Project Editor	Ellen Keohane
Associate Production Manager	Joyce Poh
Cover Designer	Kenji Ngieng

This book was set in LaTeX by the authors, and printed and bound by RR Donnelley. The cover was printed by RR Donnelley.

Trademark Acknowledgments: *Java is a trademark of Oracle Corporation. Unix® is a registered trademark in the United States and other countries, licensed through X/Open Company, Ltd. PowerPoint® is a trademark of Microsoft Corporation. All other product names mentioned herein are the trademarks of their respective owners.*

This book is printed on acid free paper.

Founded in 1807, John Wiley & Sons, Inc. has been a valued source of knowledge and understanding for more than 200 years, helping people around the world meet their needs and fulfill their aspirations. Our company is built on a foundation of principles that include responsibility to the communities we serve and where we live and work. In 2008, we launched a Corporate Citizenship Initiative, a global effort to address the environmental, social, economic, and ethical challenges we face in our business. Among the issues we are addressing are carbon impact, paper specifications and procurement, ethical conduct within our business and among our vendors, and community and charitable support. For more information, please visit our website: www.wiley.com/go/citizenship.

ISBN: 978-1-118-77133-4 (paperback)

Printed in the United States of America

10 9 8 7 6 5 4 3 2

To Karen, Paul, Anna, and Jack
    – *Michael T. Goodrich*

To Isabel
    – *Roberto Tamassia*

To Susan, Calista, and Maya
    – *Michael H. Goldwasser*

Preface to the Sixth Edition

Data Structures and Algorithms in Java provides an introduction to data structures and algorithms, including their design, analysis, and implementation. The major changes in this sixth edition include the following:

- We redesigned the entire code base to increase clarity of presentation and consistency in style and convention, including reliance on *type inference*, as introduced in Java 7, to reduce clutter when instantiating generic types.
- We added 38 new figures, and redesigned 144 existing figures.
- We revised and expanded exercises, bringing the grand total to 794 exercises! We continue our approach of dividing them into reinforcement, creativity, and project exercises. However, we have chosen not to reset the numbering scheme with each new category, thereby avoiding possible ambiguity between exercises such as R-7.5, C-7.5, P-7.5.
- The introductory chapters contain additional examples of classes and inheritance, increased discussion of Java's generics framework, and expanded coverage of cloning and equivalence testing in the context of data structures.
- A new chapter, dedicated to the topic of recursion, provides comprehensive coverage of material that was previously divided within Chapters 3, 4, and 9 of the fifth edition, while newly introducing the use of recursion when processing file systems.
- We provide a new empirical study of the efficiency of Java's StringBuilder class relative to the repeated concatenation of strings, and then discuss the theoretical underpinnings of its amortized performance.
- We provide increased discussion of iterators, contrasting between so-called *lazy iterators* and *snapshot iterators*, with examples of both styles of implementation for several data structures.
- We have increased the use of abstract base classes to reduce redundancy when providing multiple implementations of a common interface, and the use of nested classes to provide greater encapsulation for our data structures.
- We have included complete Java implementations for many data structures and algorithms that were only described with pseudocode in earlier editions. These new implementations include both array-based and linked-list-based queue implementations, a heap-based *adaptable* priority queue, a bottom-up heap construction, hash tables with either separate chaining or linear probing, splay trees, dynamic programming for the least-common subsequence problem, a union-find data structure with path compression, breadth-first search of a graph, the Floyd-Warshall algorithm for computing a graph's transitive closure, topological sorting of a DAG, and both the Prim-Jarník and Kruskal algorithms for computing a minimum spanning tree.

Prerequisites

We assume that the reader is at least vaguely familiar with a high-level programming language, such as C, C++, Python, or Java, and that he or she understands the main constructs from such a high-level language, including:

- Variables and expressions
- Methods (also known as functions or procedures)
- Decision structures (such as if-statements and switch-statements)
- Iteration structures (for-loops and while-loops)

For readers who are familiar with these concepts, but not with how they are expressed in Java, we provide a primer on the Java language in Chapter 1. Still, this book is primarily a data structures book, not a Java book; hence, it does not provide a comprehensive treatment of Java. Nevertheless, we do not assume that the reader is necessarily familiar with object-oriented design or with linked structures, such as linked lists, for these topics are covered in the core chapters of this book.

In terms of mathematical background, we assume the reader is somewhat familiar with topics from high-school mathematics. Even so, in Chapter 4, we discuss the seven most-important functions for algorithm analysis. In fact, sections that use something other than one of these seven functions are considered optional, and are indicated with a star ($\star$).

Online Resources

This book is accompanied by an extensive set of online resources, which can be found at the following website:

www.wiley.com/college/goodrich

Included on this website is a collection of educational aids that augment the topics of this book, for both students and instructors. For all readers, and especially for students, we include the following resources:

- All Java source code presented in this book
- An appendix of useful mathematical facts
- PDF handouts of PowerPoint slides (four-per-page)
- A study guide with hints to exercises, indexed by problem number

For instructors using this book, we include the following additional teaching aids:

- Solutions to hundreds of the book's exercises
- Color versions of all figures and illustrations from the book
- Slides in PowerPoint and PDF (one-per-page) format

The slides are fully editable, so as to allow an instructor using this book full freedom in customizing his or her presentations.

Use as a Textbook

The design and analysis of efficient data structures has long been recognized as a core subject in computing. We feel that the central role of data structure design and analysis in the curriculum is fully justified, given the importance of efficient data structures and algorithms in most software systems, including the Web, operating systems, databases, compilers, and scientific simulation systems.

This book is designed for use in a beginning-level data structures course, or in an intermediate-level introduction to algorithms course. The chapters for this book are organized to provide a pedagogical path that starts with the basics of Java programming and object-oriented design. We then discuss concrete structures including arrays and linked lists, and foundational techniques like algorithm analysis and recursion. In the main portion of the book we present fundamental data structures and algorithms, concluding with a discussion of memory management. A detailed table of contents follows this preface, beginning on page x.

To assist instructors in designing a course in the context of the IEEE/ACM 2013 Computing Curriculum, the following table describes curricular knowledge units that are covered within this book.

Knowledge Unit	Relevant Material
AL/Basic Analysis	Chapter 4 and Sections 5.2 & 12.1.4
AL/Algorithmic Strategies	Sections 5.3.3, 12.1.1, 13.2.1, 13.4.2, 13.5, 14.6.2 & 14.7
AL/Fundamental Data Structures and Algorithms	Sections 3.1.2, 5.1.3, 9.3, 9.4.1, 10.2, 11.1, 13.2, and Chapters 12 & 14
AL/Advanced Data Structures	Sections 7.2.1, 10.4, 11.2–11.6, 12.2.1, 13.3, 14.5.1 & 15.3
AR/Memory System Organization and Architecture	Chapter 15
DS/Sets, Relations, and Functions	Sections 9.2.2 & 10.5
DS/Proof Techniques	Sections 4.4, 5.2, 7.2.3, 9.3.4 & 12.3.1
DS/Basics of Counting	Sections 2.2.3, 6.2.2, 8.2.2 & 12.1.4.
DS/Graphs and Trees	Chapters 8 and 14
DS/Discrete Probability	Sections 3.1.3, 10.2, 10.4.2 & 12.2.1
PL/Object-Oriented Programming	Chapter 2 and Sections 7.3, 9.5.1 & 11.2.1
SDF/Algorithms and Design	Sections 2.1, 4.3 & 12.1.1
SDF/Fundamental Programming Concepts	Chapters 1 & 5
SDF/Fundamental Data Structures	Chapters 3 & 6, and Sections 1.3, 9.1 & 10.1
SDF/Developmental Methods	Sections 1.9 & 2.4
SE/Software Design	Section 2.1

Mapping the *IEEE/ACM 2013 Computing Curriculum* knowledge units to coverage within this book.

About the Authors

Michael Goodrich received his Ph.D. in Computer Science from Purdue University in 1987. He is currently a Chancellor's Professor in the Department of Computer Science at University of California, Irvine. Previously, he was a professor at Johns Hopkins University. He is a Fulbright Scholar and a Fellow of the American Association for the Advancement of Science (AAAS), Association for Computing Machinery (ACM), and Institute of Electrical and Electronics Engineers (IEEE). He is a recipient of the IEEE Computer Society Technical Achievement Award, the ACM Recognition of Service Award, and the Pond Award for Excellence in Undergraduate Teaching.

Roberto Tamassia received his Ph.D. in Electrical and Computer Engineering from the University of Illinois at Urbana–Champaign in 1988. He is the Plastech Professor of Computer Science and the Chair of the Department of Computer Science at Brown University. He is also the Director of Brown's Center for Geometric Computing. His research interests include information security, cryptography, analysis, design, and implementation of algorithms, graph drawing, and computational geometry. He is a Fellow of the American Association for the Advancement of Science (AAAS), Association for Computing Machinery (ACM) and Institute for Electrical and Electronic Engineers (IEEE). He is a recipient of the IEEE Computer Society Technical Achievement Award.

Michael Goldwasser received his Ph.D. in Computer Science from Stanford University in 1997. He is currently Professor and Director of the Computer Science program in the Department of Mathematics and Computer Science at Saint Louis University. He was previously a faculty member in the Department of Computer Science at Loyola University Chicago. His research interests focus on the design and implementation of algorithms, having published work involving approximation algorithms, online computation, computational biology, and computational geometry. He is also active in the computer science education community.

Additional Books by These Authors

- Di Battista, Eades, Tamassia, and Tollis, *Graph Drawing*, Prentice Hall
- Goodrich, Tamassia, and Goldwasser, *Data Structures and Algorithms in Python*, Wiley
- Goodrich, Tamassia, and Mount, *Data Structures and Algorithms in C++*, Wiley
- Goodrich and Tamassia, *Algorithm Design: Foundations, Analysis, and Internet Examples*, Wiley
- Goodrich and Tamassia, *Introduction to Computer Security*, Addison-Wesley
- Goldwasser and Letscher, *Object-Oriented Programming in Python*, Prentice Hall

Acknowledgments

There are so many individuals who have made contributions to the development of this book over the past decade, it is difficult to name them all. We wish to reiterate our thanks to the many research collaborators and teaching assistants whose feedback shaped the previous versions of this material. The benefits of those contributions carry forward to this book.

For the sixth edition, we are indebted to the outside reviewers and readers for their copious comments, emails, and constructive criticisms. We therefore thank the following people for their comments and suggestions: Sameer O. Abufardeh (North Dakota State University), Mary Boelk (Marquette University), Frederick Crabbe (United States Naval Academy), Scot Drysdale (Dartmouth College), David Eisner, Henry A. Etlinger (Rochester Institute of Technology), Chun-Hsi Huang (University of Connecticut), John Lasseter (Hobart and William Smith Colleges), Yupeng Lin, Suely Oliveira (University of Iowa), Vincent van Oostrom (Utrecht University), Justus Piater (University of Innsbruck), Victor I. Shtern (Boston University), Tim Soethout, and a number of additional anonymous reviewers.

There have been a number of friends and colleagues whose comments have led to improvements in the text. We are particularly thankful to Erin Chambers, Karen Goodrich, David Letscher, David Mount, and Ioannis Tollis for their insightful comments. In addition, contributions by David Mount to the coverage of recursion and to several figures are gratefully acknowledged.

We appreciate the wonderful team at Wiley, including our editor, Beth Lang Golub, for her enthusiastic support of this project from beginning to end, and the Product Solutions Group editors, Mary O'Sullivan and Ellen Keohane, for carrying the project to its completion. The quality of this book is greatly enhanced as a result of the attention to detail demonstrated by our copyeditor, Julie Kennedy. The final months of the production process were gracefully managed by Joyce Poh.

Finally, we would like to warmly thank Karen Goodrich, Isabel Cruz, Susan Goldwasser, Giuseppe Di Battista, Franco Preparata, Ioannis Tollis, and our parents for providing advice, encouragement, and support at various stages of the preparation of this book, and Calista and Maya Goldwasser for offering their advice regarding the artistic merits of many illustrations. More importantly, we thank all of these people for reminding us that there are things in life beyond writing books.

Michael T. Goodrich
Roberto Tamassia
Michael H. Goldwasser

Contents

Chapter

1

Java Primer

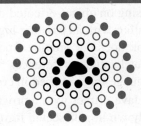

Contents

1.1 Getting Started

Building data structures and algorithms requires that we communicate detailed instructions to a computer. An excellent way to perform such communication is using a high-level computer language, such as Java. In this chapter, we provide an overview of the Java programming language, and we continue this discussion in the next chapter, focusing on object-oriented design principles. We assume that readers are somewhat familiar with an existing high-level language, although not necessarily Java. This book does not provide a complete description of the Java language (there are numerous language references for that purpose), but it does introduce all aspects of the language that are used in code fragments later in this book.

We begin our Java primer with a program that prints "Hello Universe!" on the screen, which is shown in a dissected form in Figure 1.1.

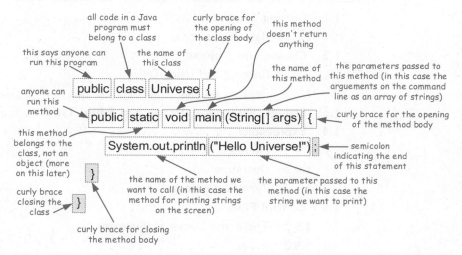

Figure 1.1: A "Hello Universe!" program.

In Java, executable statements are placed in functions, known as ***methods***, that belong to ***class*** definitions. The Universe class, in our first example, is extremely simple; its only method is a static one named main, which is the first method to be executed when running a Java program. Any set of statements between the braces "{" and "}" define a program ***block***. Notice that the entire Universe class definition is delimited by such braces, as is the body of the main method.

The name of a class, method, or variable in Java is called an ***identifier***, which can be any string of characters as long as it begins with a letter and consists of letters, numbers, and underscore characters (where "letter" and "number" can be from any written language defined in the Unicode character set). We list the exceptions to this general rule for Java identifiers in Table 1.1.

Reserved Words				
abstract	default	goto	package	synchronized
assert	do	if	private	this
boolean	double	implements	protected	throw
break	else	import	public	throws
byte	enum	instanceof	return	transient
case	extends	int	short	true
catch	false	interface	static	try
char	final	long	strictfp	void
class	finally	native	super	volatile
const	float	new	switch	while
continue	for	null		

Table 1.1: A listing of the reserved words in Java. These names cannot be used as class, method, or variable names.

Comments

In addition to executable statements and declarations, Java allows a programmer to embed comments, which are annotations provided for human readers that are not processed by the Java compiler. Java allows two kinds of comments: inline comments and block comments. Java uses a "//" to begin an inline comment, ignoring everything subsequently on that line. For example:

```
// This is an inline comment.
```

We will intentionally color all comments in blue in this book, so that they are not confused with executable code.

While inline comments are limited to one line, Java allows multiline comments in the form of block comments. Java uses a "/*" to begin a block comment and a "*/" to close it. For example:

```
/*
 * This is a block comment.
 */
```

Block comments that begin with "/**" (note the second asterisk) have a special purpose, allowing a program, called Javadoc, to read these comments and automatically generate software documentation. We discuss the syntax and interpretation of Javadoc comments in Section 1.9.4.

1.1.1   Base Types

For the most commonly used data types, Java provides the following *base types* (also called *primitive types*):

boolean	a boolean value: true or false
char	16-bit Unicode character
byte	8-bit signed two's complement integer
short	16-bit signed two's complement integer
int	32-bit signed two's complement integer
long	64-bit signed two's complement integer
float	32-bit floating-point number (IEEE 754-1985)
double	64-bit floating-point number (IEEE 754-1985)

A variable having one of these types simply stores a value of that type. Integer constants, like 14 or 195, are of type **int**, unless followed immediately by an 'L' or 'l', in which case they are of type **long**. Floating-point constants, like 3.1416 or 6.022e23, are of type **double**, unless followed immediately by an 'F' or 'f', in which case they are of type **float**. Code Fragment 1.1 demonstrates the declaration, and initialization in some cases, of various base-type variables.

```
1   boolean flag = true;
2   boolean verbose, debug;          // two variables declared, but not yet initialized
3   char grade = 'A';
4   byte b = 12;
5   short s = 24;
6   int i, j, k = 257;               // three variables declared; only k initialized
7   long l = 890L;                   // note the use of "L" here
8   float pi = 3.1416F;              // note the use of "F" here
9   double e = 2.71828, a = 6.022e23;  // both variables are initialized
```

Code Fragment 1.1: Declarations and initializations of several base-type variables.

Note that it is possible to declare (and initialize) multiple variables of the same type in a single statement, as done on lines 2, 6, and 9 of this example. In this code fragment, variables verbose, debug, i, and j remain uninitialized. Variables declared locally within a block of code must be initialized before they are first used.

A nice feature of Java is that when base-type variables are declared as instance variables of a class (see next section), Java ensures initial default values if not explicitly initialized. In particular, all numeric types are initialized to zero, a boolean is initialized to false, and a character is initialized to the null character by default.

1.2 Classes and Objects

In more complex Java programs, the primary "actors" are *objects*. Every object is an *instance* of a class, which serves as the *type* of the object and as a blueprint, defining the data which the object stores and the methods for accessing and modifying that data. The critical *members* of a class in Java are the following:

- *Instance variables*, which are also called *fields*, represent the data associated with an object of a class. Instance variables must have a *type*, which can either be a base type (such as **int**, **float**, or **double**) or any class type (also known as a *reference type* for reasons we soon explain).

- *Methods* in Java are blocks of code that can be called to perform actions (similar to functions and procedures in other high-level languages). Methods can accept parameters as arguments, and their behavior may depend on the object upon which they are invoked and the values of any parameters that are passed. A method that returns information to the caller without changing any instance variables is known as an *accessor method*, while an *update method* is one that may change one or more instance variables when called.

For the purpose of illustration, Code Fragment 1.2 provides a complete definition of a very simple class named Counter, to which we will refer during the remainder of this section.

```
1  public class Counter {
2    private int count;                              // a simple integer instance variable
3    public Counter() { }                            // default constructor (count is 0)
4    public Counter(int initial) { count = initial; }      // an alternate constructor
5    public int getCount() { return count; }              // an accessor method
6    public void increment() { count++; }                 // an update method
7    public void increment(int delta) { count += delta; }  // an update method
8    public void reset() { count = 0; }                   // an update method
9  }
```

Code Fragment 1.2: A Counter class for a simple counter, which can be queried, incremented, and reset.

This class includes one instance variable, named count, which is declared at line 2. As noted on the previous page, the count will have a default value of zero, unless we otherwise initialize it.

The class includes two special methods known as constructors (lines 3 and 4), one accessor method (line 5), and three update methods (lines 6–8). Unlike the original Universe class from page 2, our Counter class does not have a main method, and so it cannot be run as a complete program. Instead, the purpose of the Counter class is to create instances that might be used as part of a larger program.

1.2.1   Creating and Using Objects

Before we explore the intricacies of the syntax for our Counter class definition, we prefer to describe how Counter instances can be created and used. To this end, Code Fragment 1.3 presents a new class named CounterDemo.

```
1   public class CounterDemo {
2     public static void main(String[ ] args) {
3       Counter c;                          // declares a variable; no counter yet constructed
4       c = new Counter( );                 // constructs a counter; assigns its reference to c
5       c.increment( );                     // increases its value by one
6       c.increment(3);                     // increases its value by three more
7       int temp = c.getCount( );           // will be 4
8       c.reset( );                         // value becomes 0
9       Counter d = new Counter(5);         // declares and constructs a counter having value 5
10      d.increment( );                     // value becomes 6
11      Counter e = d;                      // assigns e to reference the same object as d
12      temp = e.getCount( );               // will be 6 (as e and d reference the same counter)
13      e.increment(2);                     // value of e (also known as d) becomes 8
14    }
15  }
```

Code Fragment 1.3: A demonstration of the use of Counter instances.

There is an important distinction in Java between the treatment of base-type variables and class-type variables. At line 3 of our demonstration, a new variable c is declared with the syntax:

   Counter c;

This establishes the identifier, c, as a variable of type Counter, but it does not create a Counter instance. Classes are known as *reference types* in Java, and a variable of that type (such as c in our example) is known as a *reference variable*. A reference variable is capable of storing the location (i.e., *memory address*) of an object from the declared class. So we might assign it to reference an existing instance or a newly constructed instance. A reference variable can also store a special value, **null**, that represents the lack of an object.

In Java, a new object is created by using the **new** operator followed by a call to a constructor for the desired class; a constructor is a method that always shares the same name as its class. The **new** operator returns a *reference* to the newly created instance; the returned reference is typically assigned to a variable for further use.

In Code Fragment 1.3, a new Counter is constructed at line 4, with its reference assigned to the variable c. That relies on a form of the constructor, Counter( ), that takes no arguments between the parentheses. (Such a zero-parameter constructor is known as a *default constructor*.) At line 9 we construct another counter using a one-parameter form that allows us to specify a nonzero initial value for the counter.

Three events occur as part of the creation of a new instance of a class:

- A new object is dynamically allocated in memory, and all instance variables are initialized to standard default values. The default values are **null** for reference variables and 0 for all base types except **boolean** variables (which are **false** by default).
- The constructor for the new object is called with the parameters specified. The constructor may assign more meaningful values to any of the instance variables, and perform any additional computations that must be done due to the creation of this object.
- After the constructor returns, the **new** operator returns a reference (that is, a memory address) to the newly created object. If the expression is in the form of an assignment statement, then this address is stored in the object variable, so the object variable *refers* to this newly created object.

The Dot Operator

One of the primary uses of an object reference variable is to access the members of the class for this object, an instance of its class. That is, an object reference variable is useful for accessing the methods and instance variables associated with an object. This access is performed with the dot (".") operator. We call a method associated with an object by using the reference variable name, following that by the dot operator and then the method name and its parameters. For example, in Code Fragment 1.3, we call c.increment( ) at line 5, c.increment(3) at line 6, c.getCount( ) at line 7, and c.reset( ) at line 8. If the dot operator is used on a reference that is currently **null**, the Java runtime environment will throw a NullPointerException.

If there are several methods with this same name defined for a class, then the Java runtime system uses the one that matches the actual number of parameters sent as arguments, as well as their respective types. For example, our Counter class supports two methods named increment: a zero-parameter form and a one-parameter form. Java determines which version to call when evaluating commands such as c.increment( ) versus c.increment(3). A method's name combined with the number and types of its parameters is called a method's *signature*, for it takes all of these parts to determine the actual method to perform for a certain method call. Note, however, that the signature of a method in Java does not include the type that the method returns, so Java does not allow two methods with the same signature to return different types.

A reference variable v can be viewed as a "pointer" to some object o. It is as if the variable is a holder for a remote control that can be used to control the newly created object (the device). That is, the variable has a way of pointing at the object and asking it to do things or give us access to its data. We illustrate this concept in Figure 1.2. Using the remote control analogy, a **null** reference is a remote control holder that is empty.

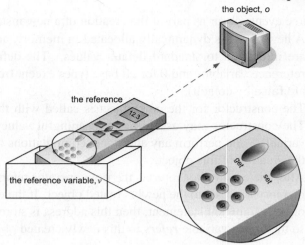

Figure 1.2: Illustrating the relationship between objects and object reference variables. When we assign an object reference (that is, memory address) to a reference variable, it is as if we are storing that object's remote control at that variable.

There can, in fact, be many references to the same object, and each reference to a specific object can be used to call methods on that object. Such a situation would correspond to our having many remote controls that all work on the same device. Any of the remotes can be used to make a change to the device (like changing a channel on a television). Note that if one remote control is used to change the device, then the (single) object pointed to by all the remotes changes. Likewise, if one object reference variable is used to change the state of the object, then its state changes for all the references to it. This behavior comes from the fact that there are many references, but they all point to the same object.

Returning to our CounterDemo example, the instance constructed at line 9 as

Counter d = **new** Counter(5);

is a distinct instance from the one identified as c. However, the command at line 11,

Counter e = d;

does not result in the construction of a new Counter instance. This declares a new *reference variable* named e, and assigns that variable a reference to the existing counter instance currently identified as d. At that point, both variables d and e are aliases for the same object, and so the call to d.getCount( ) behaves just as would e.getCount( ). Similarly, the call to update method e.increment(2) is affecting the same object identified by d.

It is worth noting, however, that the aliasing of two reference variables to the same object is not permanent. At any point in time, we may reassign a reference variable to a new instance, to a different existing instance, or to **null**.

1.2.2 Defining a Class

Thus far, we have provided definitions for two simple classes: the Universe class on page 2 and the Counter class on page 5. At its core, a class definition is a block of code, delimited by braces "{" and "}" , within which is included declarations of instance variables and methods that are the members of the class. In this section, we will undertake a deeper examination of class definitions in Java.

Modifiers

Immediately before the definition of a class, instance variable, or method in Java, keywords known as *modifiers* can be placed to convey additional stipulations about that definition.

Access Control Modifiers

The first set of modifiers we discuss are known as *access control modifiers*, as they control the level of access (also known as *visibility*) that the defining class grants to other classes in the context of a larger Java program. The ability to limit access among classes supports a key principle of object-orientation known as encapsulation (see Section 2.1). In general, the different access control modifiers and their meaning are as follows:

- The **public** class modifier designates that all classes may access the defined aspect. For example, line 1 of of Code Fragment 1.2 designates

  public class Counter {

  and therefore all other classes (such as CounterDemo) are allowed to construct new instances of the Counter class, as well as to declare variables and parameters of type Counter. In Java, each public class must be defined in a separate file named *classname*.java, where "*classname*" is the name of the class (for example, file Counter.java for the Counter class definition).

  The designation of **public** access for a particular *method* of a class allows any other class to make a call to that method. For example, line 5 of Code Fragment 1.2 designates

  public int getCount( ) { **return** count; }

  which is why the CounterDemo class may call c.getCount( ).

  If an instance variable is declared as public, dot notation can be used to directly access the variable by code in any other class that possesses a reference to an instance of this class. For example, were the count variable of Counter to be declared as public (which it is not), then the CounterDemo would be allowed to read or modify that variable using a syntax such as c.count.

- The **protected** class modifier designates that access to the defined aspect is only granted to the following groups of other classes:
  - Classes that are designated as *subclasses* of the given class through inheritance. (We will discuss inheritance as the focus of Section 2.2.)
  - Classes that belong to the same *package* as the given class. (We will discuss packages within Section 1.8.)
- The **private** class modifier designates that access to a defined member of a class be granted only to code within that class. Neither subclasses nor any other classes have access to such members.

  For example, we defined the count instance variable of the Counter class to have private access level. We were allowed to read or edit its value from within methods of that class (such as getCount, increment, and reset), but other classes such as CounterDemo cannot directly access that field. Of course, we did provide other public methods to grant outside classes with behaviors that depended on the current count value.

- Finally, we note that if no explicit access control modifier is given, the defined aspect has what is known as *package-private* access level. This allows other classes in the same package (see Section 1.8) to have access, but not any classes or subclasses from other packages.

The **static** Modifier

The **static** modifier in Java can be declared for any variable or method of a class (or for a nested class, as we will introduce in Section 2.6).

When a variable of a class is declared as **static**, its value is associated with the class as a whole, rather than with each individual instance of that class. Static variables are used to store "global" information about a class. (For example, a static variable could be used to maintain the total number of instances of that class that have been created.) Static variables exist even if no instance of their class exists.

When a method of a class is declared as **static**, it too is associated with the class itself, and not with a particular instance of the class. That means that the method is not invoked on a particular instance of the class using the traditional dot notation. Instead, it is typically invoked using the name of the class as a qualifier.

As an example, in the java.lang package, which is part of the standard Java distribution, there is a Math class that provides many static methods, including one named sqrt that computes square roots of numbers. To compute a square root, you do not need to create an instance of the Math class; that method is called using a syntax such as Math.sqrt(2), with the class name Math as the qualifier before the dot operator.

Static methods can be useful for providing utility behaviors related to a class that need not rely on the state of any particular instance of that class.

The **abstract** Modifier

A method of a class may be declared as **abstract**, in which case its signature is provided but without an implementation of the method body. Abstract methods are an advanced feature of object-oriented programming to be combined with inheritance, and the focus of Section 2.3.3. In short, any subclass of a class with abstract methods is expected to provide a concrete implementation for each abstract method.

A class with one or more abstract methods must also be formally declared as **abstract**, because it is essentially incomplete. (It is also permissible to declare a class as abstract even if it does not contain any abstract methods.) As a result, Java will not allow any instances of an abstract class to be constructed, although reference variables may be declared with an abstract type.

The **final** Modifier

A variable that is declared with the **final** modifier can be initialized as part of that declaration, but can never again be assigned a new value. If it is a base type, then it is a constant. If a reference variable is **final**, then it will always refer to the same object (even if that object changes its internal state). If a member variable of a class is declared as **final**, it will typically be declared as **static** as well, because it would be unnecessarily wasteful to have every instance store the identical value when that value can be shared by the entire class.

Designating a method or an entire class as **final** has a completely different consequence, only relevant in the context of inheritance. A final method cannot be overridden by a subclass, and a final class cannot even be subclassed.

Declaring Instance Variables

When defining a class, we can declare any number of instance variables. An important principle of object-orientation is that each instance of a class maintains its own individual set of instance variables (that is, in fact, why they are called *instance* variables). So in the case of the Counter class, each instance will store its own (independent) value of count.

The general syntax for declaring one or more instance variables of a class is as follows (with optional portions bracketed):

[*modifiers*] *type identifier*$_1$ [=*initialValue*$_1$], *identifier*$_2$[=*initialValue*$_2$];

In the case of the Counter class, we declared

private int count;

where **private** is the modifier, **int** is the type, and count is the identifier. Because we did not declare an initial value, it automatically receives the default of zero as a base-type integer.

Declaring Methods

A method definition has two parts: the ***signature***, which defines the name and parameters for a method, and the ***body***, which defines what the method does. The method signature specifies how the method is called, and the method body specifies what the object will do when it is called. The syntax for defining a method is as follows:

[*modifiers*] *returnType methodName*(*type*$_1$ *param*$_1$, ..., *type*$_n$ *param*$_n$) {
    // method body . . .
}

Each of the pieces of this declaration has an important purpose. We have already discussed the significance of *modifiers* such as **public**, **private**, and **static**. The *returnType* designation defines the type of value returned by the method. The *methodName* can be any valid Java identifier. The list of parameters and their types declares the local variables that correspond to the values that are to be passed as arguments to this method. Each type declaration *type*$_i$ can be any Java type name and each *param*$_i$ can be any distinct Java identifier. This list of parameters and their types can be empty, which signifies that there are no values to be passed to this method when it is invoked. These parameter variables, as well as the instance variables of the class, can be used inside the body of the method. Likewise, other methods of this class can be called from inside the body of a method.

When a (nonstatic) method of a class is called, it is invoked on a specific instance of that class and can change the state of that object. For example, the following method of the Counter class increases the counter's value by the given amount.

public void increment(**int** delta) {
    count += delta;
}

Notice that the body of this method uses count, which is an instance variable, and delta, which is a parameter.

Return Types

A method definition must specify the type of value the method will return. If the method does not return a value (as with the increment method of the Counter class), then the keyword **void** must be used. To return a value in Java, the body of the method must use the **return** keyword, followed by a value of the appropriate return type. Here is an example of a method (from the Counter class) with a nonvoid return type:

public int getCount() {
    return count;
}

Java methods can return only one value. To return multiple values in Java, we should instead combine all the values we want to return in a *compound object*, whose instance variables include all the values we want to return, and then return a reference to that compound object. In addition, we can change the internal state of an object that is passed to a method as another way of "returning" multiple results.

Parameters

A method's parameters are defined in a comma-separated list enclosed in parentheses after the name of the method. A parameter consists of two parts, the parameter type and the parameter name. If a method has no parameters, then only an empty pair of parentheses is used.

All parameters in Java are passed *by value*, that is, any time we pass a parameter to a method, a copy of that parameter is made for use within the method body. So if we pass an **int** variable to a method, then that variable's integer value is copied. The method can change the copy but not the original. If we pass an object reference as a parameter to a method, then the reference is copied as well. Remember that we can have many different variables that all refer to the same object. Reassigning the internal reference variable inside a method will not change the reference that was passed in.

For the sake of demonstration, we will assume that the following two methods were added to an arbitrary class (such as CounterDemo).

```
public static void badReset(Counter c) {
    c = new Counter();          // reassigns local name c to a new counter
}
```

```
public static void goodReset(Counter c) {
    c.reset();                  // resets the counter sent by the caller
}
```

Now we will assume that variable strikes refers to an existing Counter instance in some context, and that it currently has a value of 3.

If we were to call badReset(strikes), this has *no* effect on the Counter known as strikes. The body of the badReset method reassigns the (local) parameter variable c to reference a newly created Counter instance; but this does not change the state of the existing counter that was sent by the caller (i.e., strikes).

In contrast, if we were to call goodReset(strikes), this does indeed reset the caller's counter back to a value of zero. That is because the variables c and strikes are both reference variables that refer to the same Counter instance. So when c.reset() is called, that is effectively the same as if strikes.reset() were called.

Defining Constructors

A *constructor* is a special kind of method that is used to initialize a newly created instance of the class so that it will be in a consistent and stable initial state. This is typically achieved by initializing each instance variable of the object (unless the default value will suffice), although a constructor can perform more complex computation. The general syntax for declaring a constructor in Java is as follows:

$$modifiers\ name(type_0\ parameter_0,\ \ldots,\ type_{n-1}\ parameter_{n-1})\ \{$$
```
    // constructor body . . .
}
```

Constructors are defined in a very similar way as other methods of a class, but there are a few important distinctions:

1. Constructors cannot be **static**, **abstract**, or **final**, so the only modifiers that are allowed are those that affect visibility (i.e., **public**, **protected**, **private**, or the default package-level visibility).

2. The name of the constructor must be identical to the name of the class it constructs. For example, when defining the Counter class, a constructor must be named Counter as well.

3. We don't specify a return type for a constructor (not even **void**). Nor does the body of a constructor explicitly return anything. When a user of a class creates an instance using a syntax such as

   ```
   Counter d = new Counter(5);
   ```

   the **new** operator is responsible for returning a reference to the new instance to the caller; the responsibility of the constructor method is only to initialize the state of the new instance.

A class can have many constructors, but each must have a different *signature*, that is, each must be distinguished by the type and number of the parameters it takes. If no constructors are explicitly defined, Java provides an implicit *default constructor* for the class, having zero arguments and leaving all instance variables initialized to their default values. However, if a class defines one or more nondefault constructors, no default constructor will be provided.

As an example, our Counter class defines the following pair of constructors:

```
public Counter() { }
public Counter(int initial) { count = initial; }
```

The first of these has a trivial body, { }, as the goal for this default constructor is to create a counter with value zero, and that is already the default value of the integer instance variable, count. However, it is still important that we declared such an explicit constructor, because otherwise none would have been provided, given the existence of the nondefault constructor. In that scenario, a user would have been unable to use the syntax, **new** Counter( ).

The Keyword **this**

Within the body of a (nonstatic) meth~~
defined as a reference to the instanc~~
is, if a caller uses a syntax such
method foo for that call, the key~~
the caller's context. There are th~~
from within a method body:

1. To store the referenc~~
   method that expects an m~~

2. To differentiate between an instance ,
   same name. If a local variable is declareu ~~
   name as an instance variable for the class, that nam~~
   variable within that method body. (We say that the local v~~
   instance variable.) In this case, the instance variable can still be ~~
   by explicitly using the dot notation with **this** as the qualifier. For examp~~
   some programmers prefer to use the following style for a constructor, with a
   parameter having the same name as the underlying variable.

   ```
   public Counter(int count) {
     this.count = count;   // set the instance variable equal to parameter
   }
   ```

3. To allow one constructor body to invoke another constructor body. When one
   method of a class invokes another method of that same class on the current
   instance, that is typically done by using the (unqualified) name of the other
   method. But the syntax for calling a constructor is special. Java allows use of
   the keyword **this** to be used as a method within the body of one constructor,
   so as to invoke another constructor with a different signature.

   This is often useful because all of the initialization steps of one constructor
   can be reused with appropriate parameterization. As a trivial demonstration of the syntax, we could reimplement the zero-argument version of our
   Counter constructor to have it invoke the one-argument version sending 0 as
   an explicit parameter. This would be written as follows:

   ```
   public Counter() {
     this(0);          // invoke one-parameter constructor with value zero
   }
   ```

   We will provide a more meaningful demonstration of this technique in a later
   example of a CreditCard class in Section 1.7.

ethod

classes, such as our Counter class, are meant to be used by other classes,
not intended to serve as a self-standing program. The primary control for an
ation in Java must begin in some class with the execution of a special method
ed main. This method must be declared as follows:

```java
public static void main(String[ ] args) {
    // main method body...
}
```

The args parameter is an array of String objects, that is, a collection of indexed
strings, with the first string being args[0], the second being args[1], and so on. (We
say more about strings and arrays in Section 1.3.) Those represent what are known
as *command-line arguments* that are given by a user when the program is executed.

Java programs can be called from the command line using the java command
(in a Windows, Linux, or Unix shell), followed by the name of the Java class whose
main method we want to run, plus any optional arguments. For example, to execute the main method of a class named Aquarium, we could issue the following
command:

```
java Aquarium
```

In this case, the Java runtime system looks for a compiled version of the Aquarium
class, and then invokes the special main method in that class.

If we had defined the Aquarium program to take an optional argument that
specifies the number of fish in the aquarium, then we might invoke the program by
typing the following in a shell window:

```
java Aquarium 45
```

to specify that we want an aquarium with 45 fish in it. In this case, args[0] would
refer to the string "45". It would be up to the body of the main method to interpret
that string as the desired number of fish.

Programmers who use an integrated development environment (IDE), such as
Eclipse, can optionally specify command-line arguments when executing the program through the IDE.

Unit Testing

When defining a class, such as Counter, that is meant to be used by other classes
rather than as a self-standing program, there is no need to define a main method.
However, a nice feature of Java's design is that we could provide such a method
as a way to test the functionality of that class in isolation, knowing that it would
not be run unless we specifically invoke the java command on that isolated class.
However, for more robust testing, frameworks such as JUnit are preferred.

1.3 Strings, Wrappers, Arrays, and Enum Types

The String Class

Java's **char** base type stores a value that represents a single text *character*. In Java, the set of all possible characters, known as an *alphabet*, is the Unicode international character set, a 16-bit character encoding that covers most used written languages. (Some programming languages use the smaller ASCII character set, which is a proper subset of the Unicode alphabet based on a 7-bit encoding.) The form for expressing a character literal in Java is using single quotes, such as 'G'.

Because it is common to work with sequences of text characters in programs (e.g., for user interactions or data processing), Java provides support in the form of a **String** *class*. A string instance represents a sequence of zero or more characters. The class provides extensive support for various text-processing tasks, and in Chapter 13 we will examine several of the underlying algorithms for text processing. For now, we will only highlight the most central aspects of the String class. Java uses double quotes to designate string literals. Therefore, we might declare and initialize a String instance as follows:

```
String title = "Data Structures & Algorithms in Java"
```

Character Indexing

Each character c within a string s can be referenced by using an *index*, which is equal to the number of characters that come before c in s. By this convention, the first character is at index 0, and the last is at index $n - 1$, where n is the length of the string. For example, the string title, defined above, has length 36. The character at index 2 is 't' (the third character), and the character at index 4 is ' ' (the space character). Java's String class supports a method length( ), which returns the length of a string instance, and a method charAt(k), which returns the character at index k.

Concatenation

The primary operation for combining strings is called *concatenation*, which takes a string P and a string Q combines them into a new string, denoted $P + Q$, which consists of all the characters of P followed by all the characters of Q. In Java, the "+" operation performs concatenation when acting on two strings, as follows:

```
String term = "over" + "load";
```

This statement defines a variable named term that references a string with value "overload". (We will discuss assignment statements and expressions such as that above in more detail later in this chapter.)

The StringBuilder Class

An important trait of Java's String class is that its instances are *immutable*; once an instance is created and initialized, the value of that instance cannot be changed. This is an intentional design, as it allows for great efficiencies and optimizations within the Java Virtual Machine.

However, because String is a class in Java, it is a reference type. Therefore, variables of type String can be reassigned to another string instance (even if the current string instance cannot be changed), as in the following:

```
String greeting = "Hello";
greeting = "Ciao";                  // we changed our mind
```

It is also quite common in Java to use string concatenation to build a new string that is subsequently used to replace one of the operands of concatenation, as in:

```
greeting = greeting + '!';          // now it is "Ciao!"
```

However, it is important to remember that this operation does create a new string instance, copying all the characters of the existing string in the process. For long string (such as DNA sequences), this can be very time consuming. (In fact, we will experiment with the efficiency of string concatenation to begin Chapter 4.)

In order to support more efficient editing of character strings, Java provides a **StringBuilder** *class*, which is effectively a *mutable* version of a string. This class combines some of the accessor methods of the String class, while supporting additional methods including the following (and more):

setCharAt(k, c): Change the character at index k to character c.

insert(k, s): Insert a copy of string s starting at index k of the sequence, shifting existing characters further back to make room.

append(s): Append string s to the end of the sequence.

reverse$()$: Reverse the current sequence.

toString$()$: Return a traditional String instance based on the current character sequence.

An error condition occurs, for both String and StringBuilder classes, if an index k is out of the bounds of the indices of the character sequence.

The StringBuilder class can be very useful, and it serves as an interesting case study for data structures and algorithms. We will further explore the empirical efficiency of the StringBuilder class in Section 4.1 and the theoretical underpinnings of its implementation in Section 7.2.4.

Wrapper Types

There are many data structures and algorithms in Java's libraries that are specifically designed so that they only work with object types (not primitives). To get around this obstacle, Java defines a *wrapper class* for each base type. An instance of each wrapper type stores a single value of the corresponding base type. In Table 1.2, we show the base types and their corresponding wrapper class, along with examples of how objects are created and accessed.

Base Type	Class Name	Creation Example	Access Example
boolean	Boolean	obj = new Boolean(true);	obj.booleanValue()
char	Character	obj = new Character('Z');	obj.charValue()
byte	Byte	obj = new Byte((byte) 34);	obj.byteValue()
short	Short	obj = new Short((short) 100);	obj.shortValue()
int	Integer	obj = new Integer(1045);	obj.intValue()
long	Long	obj = new Long(10849L);	obj.longValue()
float	Float	obj = new Float(3.934F);	obj.floatValue()
double	Double	obj = new Double(3.934);	obj.doubleValue()

Table 1.2: Java's wrapper classes. Each class is given with its corresponding base type and example expressions for creating and accessing such objects. For each row, we assume the variable obj is declared with the corresponding class name.

Automatic Boxing and Unboxing

Java provides additional support for implicitly converting between base types and their wrapper types through a process known as automatic boxing and unboxing.

In any context for which an Integer is expected (for example, as a parameter), an **int** value k can be expressed, in which case Java automatically *boxes* the **int**, with an implicit call to **new** Integer(k). In reverse, in any context for which an **int** is expected, an Integer value v can be given in which case Java automatically *unboxes* it with an implicit call to v.intValue(). Similar conversions are made with the other base-type wrappers. Finally, all of the wrapper types provide support for converting back and forth between string literals. Code Fragment 1.4 demonstrates many such features.

```
1  int j = 8;
2  Integer a = new Integer(12);
3  int k = a;                        // implicit call to a.intValue()
4  int m = j + a;                    // a is automatically unboxed before the addition
5  a = 3 * m;                        // result is automatically boxed before assignment
6  Integer b = new Integer("-135");  // constructor accepts a String
7  int n = Integer.parseInt("2013"); // using static method of Integer class
```

Code Fragment 1.4: A demonstration of the use of the Integer wrapper class.

Arrays

A common programming task is to keep track of an ordered sequence of related values or objects. For example, we may want a video game to keep track of the top ten scores for that game. Rather than using ten different variables for this task, we would prefer to use a single name for the group and use index numbers to refer to the high scores in that group. Similarly, we may want a medical information system to keep track of the patients currently assigned to beds in a certain hospital. Again, we would rather not have to introduce 200 variables in our program just because the hospital has 200 beds.

In such cases, we can save programming effort by using an ***array***, which is a sequenced collection of variables all of the same type. Each variable, or ***cell***, in an array has an ***index***, which uniquely refers to the value stored in that cell. The cells of an array a are numbered 0, 1, 2, and so on. We illustrate an array of high scores for a video game in Figure 1.3.

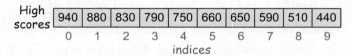

Figure 1.3: An illustration of an array of ten (**int**) high scores for a video game.

Array Elements and Capacities

Each value stored in an array is called an ***element*** of that array. Since the length of an array determines the maximum number of things that can be stored in the array, we will sometimes refer to the length of an array as its ***capacity***. In Java, the length of an array named a can be accessed using the syntax a.length. Thus, the cells of an array a are numbered 0, 1, 2, and so on, up through a.length−1, and the cell with index k can be accessed with syntax $a[k]$.

Out of Bounds Errors

It is a dangerous mistake to attempt to index into an array a using a number outside the range from 0 to a.length−1. Such a reference is said to be ***out of bounds***. Out of bounds references have been exploited numerous times by hackers using a method called the ***buffer overflow attack*** to compromise the security of computer systems written in languages other than Java. As a safety feature, array indices are always checked in Java to see if they are ever out of bounds. If an array index is out of bounds, the runtime Java environment signals an error condition. The name of this condition is the ArrayIndexOutOfBoundsException. This check helps Java avoid a number of security problems, such as buffer overflow attacks.

Declaring and Constructing Arrays

Arrays in Java are somewhat unusual, in that they are not technically a base type nor are they instances of a particular class. With that said, an instance of an array is treated as an object by Java, and variables of an array type are *reference variables*.

To declare a variable (or parameter) to have an array type, we use an empty pair of square brackets just after the type of element that the array will store. For example, we might declare:

int[ ] primes;

Because arrays are a reference type, this declares the variable primes to be a reference to an array of integer values, but it does not immediately construct any such array. There are two ways for creating an array.

The first way to create an array is to use an assignment to a literal form when initially declaring the array, using a syntax as:

elementType[] *arrayName* = {*initialValue*$_0$, *initialValue*$_1$, ..., *initialValue*$_{N-1}$};

The *elementType* can be any Java base type or class name, and *arrayName* can be any valid Java identifier. The initial values must be of the same type as the array. For example, we could initialize the array of primes to contain the first ten prime numbers as:

int[ ] primes = {2, 3, 5, 7, 11, 13, 17, 19, 23, 29};

When using an initializer, an array is created having precisely the capacity needed to store the indicated values.

The second way to create an array is to use the **new** operator. However, because an array is not an instance of a class, we do not use a typical constructor syntax. Instead we use the syntax:

new *elementType*[*length*]

where *length* is a positive integer denoting the length of the new array. The **new** operator returns a reference to the new array, and typically this would be assigned to an array variable. For example, the following statement declares an array variable named measurements, and immediately assigns it a new array of 1000 cells.

double[ ] measurements = **new double**[1000];

When arrays are created using the **new** operator, all of their elements are automatically assigned the default value for the element type. That is, if the element type is numeric, all cells of the array are initialized to zero, if the element type is boolean, all cells are **false**, and if the element type is a reference type (such as with an array of String instances), all cells are initialized to **null**.

Enum Types

In olden times, programmers would often define a series of constant integer values to be used for representing a finite set of choices. For example, in representing a day of the week, they might declare variable today as an **int** and then set it with value 0 for Monday, 1 for Tuesday, and so on.

A slightly better programming style is to define static constants (with the **final** keyword), to make the associations, such as:

static final int MON = 0;
static final int TUE = 1;
static final int WED = 2;
...

because then it becomes possible to make assignments such as today = TUE, rather than the more obscure today = 1. Unfortunately, the variable today is still declared as an **int** using such a programming style, and it may not be clear that you intend for it to represent a day of the week when storing it as an instance variable or sending it as a parameter.

Java supports a more elegant approach to representing choices from a finite set by defining what is known as an enumerated type, or enum for short. These are types that are only allowed to take on values that come from a specified set of names. They are declared as follows:

modifier **enum** *name* { *valueName*$_0$, *valueName*$_1$, ..., *valueName*$_{n-1}$ };

where the *modifier* can be blank, **public**, **protected**, or **private**. The name of this enum, *name*, can be any legal Java identifier. Each of the value identifiers, *valueName*$_i$, is the name of a possible value that variables of this enum type can take on. Each of these name values can also be any legal Java identifier, but the Java convention is that these should usually be capitalized words. For example, an enumerated type definition for days of the weak might appear as:

public enum Day { MON, TUE, WED, THU, FRI, SAT, SUN };

Once defined, Day becomes an official type and we may declare variables or parameters with type Day. A variable of that type can be declared as:

Day today;

and an assignment of a value to that variable can appear as:

today = Day.TUE;

1.4   Expressions

Variables and constants are used in *expressions* to define new values and to modify variables. In this section, we discuss how expressions work in Java in more detail. Expressions involve the use of *literals*, *variables*, and *operators*. Since we have already discussed variables, let us briefly focus on literals and then discuss operators in some detail.

1.4.1   Literals

A *literal* is any "constant" value that can be used in an assignment or other expression. Java allows the following kinds of literals:

- The **null** object reference (this is the only object literal, and it is allowed to be any reference type).

- Boolean: **true** and **false**.

- Integer: The default for an integer like 176, or -52 is that it is of type **int**, which is a 32-bit integer. A long integer literal must end with an "L" or "l", for example, 176L or -52l, and defines a 64-bit integer.

- Floating Point: The default for floating-point numbers, such as 3.1415 and 135.23, is that they are **double**. To specify that a literal is a **float**, it must end with an "F" or "f". Floating-point literals in exponential notation are also allowed, such as 3.14E2 or .19e10; the base is assumed to be 10.

- Character: In Java, character constants are assumed to be taken from the Unicode alphabet. Typically, a character is defined as an individual symbol enclosed in single quotes. For example, 'a' and '?' are character constants. In addition, Java defines the following special character constants:

'\n'	(newline)	'\t'	(tab)
'\b'	(backspace)	'\r'	(return)
'\f'	(form feed)	'\\'	(backslash)
'\''	(single quote)	'\"'	(double quote).

- String Literal: A string literal is a sequence of characters enclosed in double quotes, for example, the following is a string literal:

  ```
  "dogs cannot climb trees"
  ```

1.4.2   Operators

Java expressions involve composing literals and variables with operators. We will survey the operators in Java in this section.

Arithmetic Operators

The following are binary arithmetic operators in Java:

$+$	addition
$-$	subtraction
$*$	multiplication
$/$	division
$\%$	the modulo operator

This last operator, modulo, is also known as the "remainder" operator, because it is the remainder left after an integer division. We often use "mod" to denote the modulo operator, and we define it formally as

$$n \bmod m = r,$$

such that

$$n = mq + r,$$

for an integer q and $0 \le r < m$.

Java also provides a unary minus $(-)$, which can be placed in front of an arithmetic expression to invert its sign. Parentheses can be used in any expression to define the order of evaluation. Java also uses a fairly intuitive operator precedence rule to determine the order of evaluation when parentheses are not used. Unlike C++, Java does not allow operator overloading for class types.

String Concatenation

With strings, the $(+)$ operator performs ***concatenation***, so that the code

```
String rug = "carpet";
String dog = "spot";
String mess = rug + dog;
String answer = mess + " will cost me " + 5 + " hours!";
```

would have the effect of making answer refer to the string

```
"carpetspot will cost me 5 hours!"
```

This example also shows how Java converts nonstring values (such as 5) into strings, when they are involved in a string concatenation operation.

Increment and Decrement Operators

Like C and C++, Java provides increment and decrement operators. Specifically, it provides the plus-one increment (++) and decrement (−−) operators. If such an operator is used in front of a variable reference, then 1 is added to (or subtracted from) the variable and its value is read into the expression. If it is used after a variable reference, then the value is first read and then the variable is incremented or decremented by 1. So, for example, the code fragment

```
int i = 8;
int j = i++;              // j becomes 8 and then i becomes 9
int k = ++i;              // i becomes 10 and then k becomes 10
int m = i--;              // m becomes 10 and then i becomes 9
int n = 9 + --i;          // i becomes 8 and then n becomes 17
```

assigns 8 to j, 10 to k, 10 to m, 17 to n, and returns *i* to value 8, as noted.

Logical Operators

Java supports the standard comparisons operators between numbers:

<	less than
<=	less than or equal to
==	equal to
!=	not equal to
>=	greater than or equal to
>	greater than

The type of the result of any of these comparison is a **boolean**. Comparisons may also be performed on **char** values, with inequalities determined according to the underlying character codes.

For reference types, it is important to know that the operators == and != are defined so that expression a == b is true if a and b both refer to the identical object (or are both **null**). Most object types support an equals method, such that a.equals(b) is true if a and b refer to what are deemed as "equivalent" instances for that class (even if not the same instance); see Section 3.5 for further discussion.

Operators defined for **boolean** values are the following:

!	not (prefix)
&&	conditional and
||	conditional or

The boolean operators && and || will not evaluate the second operand (to the right) in their expression if it is not needed to determine the value of the expression. This *"short circuiting"* feature is useful for constructing boolean expressions where we first test that a certain condition holds (such as an array index being valid) and then test a condition that could have otherwise generated an error condition had the prior test not succeeded.

Bitwise Operators

Java also provides the following bitwise operators for integers and booleans:

~	bitwise complement (prefix unary operator)
&	bitwise and
|	bitwise or
^	bitwise exclusive-or
<<	shift bits left, filling in with zeros
>>	shift bits right, filling in with sign bit
>>>	shift bits right, filling in with zeros

The Assignment Operator

The standard assignment operator in Java is "=". It is used to assign a value to an instance variable or local variable. Its syntax is as follows:

variable = expression

where *variable* refers to a variable that is allowed to be referenced by the statement block containing this expression. The value of an assignment operation is the value of the expression that was assigned. Thus, if j and k are both declared as type **int**, it is correct to have an assignment statement like the following:

```
j = k = 25;     // works because '=' operators are evaluated right-to-left
```

Compound Assignment Operators

Besides the standard assignment operator (=), Java also provides a number of other assignment operators that combine a binary operation with an assignment. These other kinds of operators are of the following form:

variable op= expression

where *op* is any binary operator. The above expression is generally equivalent to

variable = variable op expression

so that x *= 2 is equivalent to x = x * 2. However, if *variable* contains an expression (for example, an array index), the expression is evaluated only once. Thus, the code fragment

```
a[5] = 10;
j = 5;
a[j++] += 2;              // not the same as a[j++] = a[j++] + 2
```

leaves a[5] with value 12 and j with value 6.

Operator Precedence

Operators in Java are given preferences, or precedence, that determine the order in which operations are performed when the absence of parentheses brings up evaluation ambiguities. For example, we need a way of deciding if the expression, "5+2*3," has value 21 or 11 (Java says it is 11). We show the precedence of the operators in Java (which, incidentally, is the same as in C and C++) in Table 1.3.

	Operator Precedence	
	Type	**Symbols**
1	array index method call dot operator	[ ] ( ) .
2	postfix ops prefix ops cast	*exp*++ *exp*−− ++*exp* −−*exp* +*exp* −*exp* ~*exp* !*exp* (*type*) *exp*
3	mult./div.	* / %
4	add./subt.	+ −
5	shift	<< >> >>>
6	comparison	< <= > >= **instanceof**
7	equality	== !=
8	bitwise-and	&
9	bitwise-xor	^
10	bitwise-or	|
11	and	&&
12	or	||
13	conditional	*booleanExpression* ? *valueIfTrue* : *valueIfFalse*
14	assignment	= += −= *= /= %= <<= >>= >>>= &= ^= |=

Table 1.3: The Java precedence rules. Operators in Java are evaluated according to the ordering above if parentheses are not used to determine the order of evaluation. Operators on the same line are evaluated in left-to-right order (except for assignment and prefix operations, which are evaluated in right-to-left order), subject to the conditional evaluation rule for boolean && and || operations. The operations are listed from highest to lowest precedence (we use *exp* to denote an atomic or parenthesized expression). Without parenthesization, higher precedence operators are performed before lower precedence operators.

We have now discussed almost all of the operators listed in Table 1.3. A notable exception is the conditional operator, which involves evaluating a boolean expression and then taking on the appropriate value depending on whether this boolean expression is true or false. (We discuss the use of the **instanceof** operator in the next chapter.)

1.4.3   Type Conversions

Casting is an operation that allows us to change the type of a value. In essence, we can take a value of one type and *cast* it into an equivalent value of another type. There are two forms of casting in Java: *explicit casting* and *implicit casting*.

Explicit Casting

Java supports an explicit casting syntax with the following form:

   (*type*) *exp*

where *type* is the type that we would like the expression *exp* to have. This syntax may only be used to cast from one primitive type to another primitive type, or from one reference type to another reference type. We will discuss its use between primitives here, and between reference types in Section 2.5.1.

Casting from an **int** to a **double** is known as a *widening* cast, as the **double** type is more broad than the **int** type, and a conversion can be performed without losing information. But a cast from a **double** to an **int** is a *narrowing* cast; we may lose precision, as any fractional portion of the value will be truncated. For example, consider the following:

```
double d1 = 3.2;
double d2 = 3.9999;
int i1 = (int) d1;                          // i1 gets value 3
int i2 = (int) d2;                          // i2 gets value 3
double d3 = (double) i2;                    // d3 gets value 3.0
```

Although explicit casting cannot directly convert a primitive type to a reference type, or vice versa, there are other means for performing such type conversions. We already discussed, as part of Section 1.3, conversions between Java's primitive types and corresponding wrapper classes (such as **int** and Integer). For convenience, those wrapper classes also provide static methods that convert between their corresponding primitive type and String values.

For example, the Integer.toString method accepts an **int** parameter and returns a String representation of that integer, while the Integer.parseInt method accepts a String as a parameter and returns the corresponding **int** value that the string represents. (If that string does not represent an integer, a NumberFormatException results.) We demonstrate their use as follows:

```
String s1 = "2014";
int i1 = Integer.parseInt(s1);              // i1 gets value 2014
int i2 = −35;
String s2 = Integer.toString(i2);           // s2 gets value "-35"
```

Similar methods are supported by other wrapper types, such as Double.

Implicit Casting

There are cases where Java will perform an ***implicit cast*** based upon the context of an expression. For example, you can perform a *widening* cast between primitive types (such as from an **int** to a **double**), without explicit use of the casting operator. However, if attempting to do an implicit *narrowing* cast, a compiler error results. For example, the following demonstrates both a legal and an illegal implicit cast via assignment statements:

```
int i1 = 42;
double d1 = i1;        // d1 gets value 42.0
i1 = d1;               // compile error: possible loss of precision
```

Implicit casting also occurs when performing arithmetic operations involving a mixture of numeric types. Most notably, when performing an operation with an integer type as one operand and a floating-point type as the other operand, the integer value is implicitly converted to a floating-point type before the operation is performed. For example, the expression 3 + 5.7 is implicitly converted to 3.0 + 5.7 before computing the resulting **double** value of 8.7.

It is common to combine an explicit cast and an implicit cast to perform a floating-point division on two integer operands. The expression (**double**) 7 / 4 produces the result 1.75, because operator precedence dictates that the cast happens first, as ((**double**) 7) / 4, and thus 7.0 / 4, which implicitly becomes 7.0 / 4.0. Note however that the expression, (**double**) (7 / 4) produces the result 1.0.

Incidentally, there is one situation in Java when only implicit casting is allowed, and that is in string concatenation. Any time a string is concatenated with any object or base type, that object or base type is automatically converted to a string. Explicit casting of an object or base type to a string is not allowed, however. Thus, the following assignments are incorrect:

```
String s = 22;                              // this is wrong!
String t = (String) 4.5;                    // this is wrong!
String u = "Value = " + (String) 13;        // this is wrong!
```

To perform a conversion to a string, we must use the appropriate toString method or perform an implicit cast via the concatenation operation. Thus, the following statements are correct:

```
String s = Integer.toString(22);            // this is good
String t = "" + 4.5;                        // correct, but poor style
String u = "Value = " + 13;                 // this is good
```

1.5 Control Flow

Control flow in Java is similar to that of other high-level languages. We review the basic structure and syntax of control flow in Java in this section, including method returns, **if** statements, **switch** statements, loops, and restricted forms of "jumps" (the **break** and **continue** statements).

1.5.1 The If and Switch Statements

In Java, conditionals work similarly to the way they work in other languages. They provide a way to make a decision and then execute one or more different statement blocks based on the outcome of that decision.

The If Statement

The syntax of a simple **if** statement is as follows:

> **if** (*booleanExpression*)
>   *trueBody*
> **else**
>   *falseBody*

where *booleanExpression* is a boolean expression and *trueBody* and *falseBody* are each either a single statement or a block of statements enclosed in braces ("{" and "}"). Note that, unlike some similar languages, the value tested by an **if** statement in Java must be a boolean expression. In particular, it is definitely not an integer expression. Nevertheless, as in other similar languages, the **else** part (and its associated statement) in a Java **if** statement is optional. There is also a way to group a number of boolean tests, as follows:

> **if** (*firstBooleanExpression*)
>   *firstBody*
> **else if** (*secondBooleanExpression*)
>   *secondBody*
> **else**
>   *thirdBody*

If the first boolean expression is false, the second boolean expression will be tested, and so on. An **if** statement can have an arbitrary number of **else if** parts. Braces can be used for any or all statement bodies to define their extent.

As a simple example, a robot controller might have the following logic:

```
if (door.isClosed( ))
  door.open( );
advance( );
```

Notice that the final command, advance( ), is not part of the conditional body; it will be executed unconditionally (although after opening a closed door).

We may nest one control structure within another, relying on explicit braces to mark the extent of the various bodies if needed. Revisiting our robot example, here is a more complex control that accounts for unlocking a closed door.

```
if (door.isClosed( )) {
  if (door.isLocked( ))
    door.unlock( );
  door.open( );
}
advance( );
```

The logic expressed by this example can be diagrammed as a traditional *flowchart*, as portrayed in Figure 1.4.

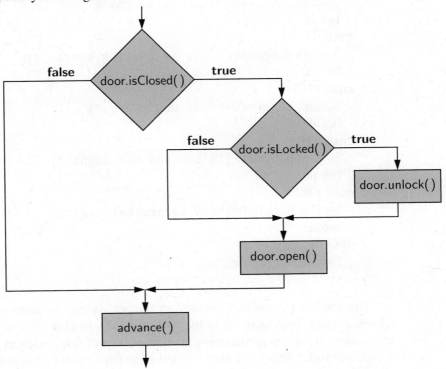

Figure 1.4: A flowchart describing the logic of nested conditional statements.

The following is an example of the nesting of **if** and **else** clauses.

```java
if (snowLevel < 2) {
    goToClass( );
    comeHome( );
} else if (snowLevel < 5) {
    goSledding( );
    haveSnowballFight( );
} else
    stayAtHome( );              // single-statement body needs no { } braces
```

Switch Statements

Java provides for multiple-value control flow using the **switch** statement, which is especially useful with enum types. The following is an indicative example (based on a variable d of the Day enum type of Section 1.3).

```java
switch (d) {
    case MON:
        System.out.println("This is tough.");
        break;
    case TUE:
        System.out.println("This is getting better.");
        break;
    case WED:
        System.out.println("Half way there.");
        break;
    case THU:
        System.out.println("I can see the light.");
        break;
    case FRI:
        System.out.println("Now we are talking.");
        break;
    default:
        System.out.println("Day off!");
}
```

The **switch** statement evaluates an integer, string, or enum expression and causes control flow to jump to the code location labeled with the value of this expression. If there is no matching label, then control flow jumps to the location labeled "**default**." This is the only explicit jump performed by the **switch** statement, however, so flow of control "falls through" to the next case if the code for a case is not ended with a **break** statement (which causes control flow to jump to the end).

1.5.2 Loops

Another important control flow mechanism in a programming language is looping. Java provides for three types of loops.

While Loops

The simplest kind of loop in Java is a **while** loop. Such a loop tests that a certain condition is satisfied and will perform the body of the loop each time this condition is evaluated to be **true**. The syntax for such a conditional test before a loop body is executed is as follows:

> **while** (*booleanExpression*)
> *loopBody*

As with an **if** statement, *booleanExpression*, can be an arbitrary boolean expression, and the body of the loop can be an arbitrary block of code (including nested control structures). The execution of a **while** loop begins with a test of the boolean condition. If that condition evaluates to **true**, the body of the loop is performed. After each execution of the body, the loop condition is retested and if it evaluates to **true**, another iteration of the body is performed. If the condition evaluates to **false** when tested (assuming it ever does), the loop is exited and the flow of control continues just beyond the body of the loop.

As an example, here is a loop that advances an index through an array named data until finding an entry with value target or reaching the end of the array.

```
int j = 0;
while ((j < data.length) && (data[j] != target))
    j++;
```

When this loop terminates, variable j's value will be the index of the leftmost occurrence of target, if found, or otherwise the length of the array (which is recognizable as an invalid index to indicate failure of the search). The correctness of the loop relies on the short-circuiting behavior of the logical && operator, as described on page 25. We intentionally test j < data.length to ensure that j is a valid index, prior to accessing element data[j]. Had we written that compound condition with the opposite order, the evaluation of data[j] would eventually throw an ArrayIndexOutOfBoundsException if the target is not found. (See Section 2.4 for discussion of exceptions.)

We note that a **while** loop will execute its body zero times in the case that the initial condition fails. For example, our above loop will not increment the value of j if data[0] matches the target (or if the array has length 0).

Do-While Loops

Java has another form of the **while** loop that allows the boolean condition to be checked at the *end* of each pass of the loop rather than before each pass. This form is known as a **do-while** loop, and has syntax shown below:

> **do**
>> *loopBody*
>
> **while** (*booleanExpression*)

A consequence of the **do-while** loop is that its body always executes at least once. (In contrast, a **while** loop will execute zero times if the initial condition fails.) This form is most useful for a situation in which the condition is ill-defined until after at least one pass. Consider, for example, that we want to prompt the user for input and then do something useful with that input. (We discuss Java input and output in more detail in Section 1.6.) A possible condition, in this case, for exiting the loop is when the user enters an empty string. However, even in this case, we may want to handle that input and inform the user that he or she has quit. The following example illustrates this case:

```java
String input;
do {
  input = getInputString( );
  handleInput(input);
} while (input.length( ) > 0);
```

For Loops

Another kind of loop is the **for** loop. Java supports two different styles of **for** loop. The first, which we will refer to as the "traditional" style, is patterned after a similar syntax as **for** loops in the C and C++ languages. The second style, which is known as the "for-each" loop, was introduced into Java in 2004 as part of the SE 5 release. This style provides a more succinct syntax for iterating through elements of an array or an appropriate container type.

The traditional **for**-loop syntax consists of four sections—an initialization, a boolean condition, an increment statement, and the body—although any of those can be empty. The structure is as follows:

> **for** (*initialization*; *booleanCondition*; *increment*)
>> *loopBody*

For example, the most common use of a **for** loop provides repetition based on an integer index, such as the following:

```java
for (int j=0; j < n; j++)
  // do something
```

The behavior of a **for** loop is very similar to the following **while** loop equivalent:

```
{
    initialization;
    while (booleanCondition) {
        loopBody;
        increment;
    }
}
```

The *initialization* section will be executed once, before any other portion of the loop begins. Traditionally, it is used to either initialize existing variables, or to declare and initialize new variables. Note that any variables declared in the initialization section only exist in scope for the duration of the **for** loop.

The *booleanCondition* will be evaluated immediately before each potential iteration of the loop. It should be expressed similar to a **while**-loop condition, in that if it is **true**, the loop body is executed, and if **false**, the loop is exited and the program continues to the next statement beyond the **for**-loop body.

The *increment* section is executed immediately after each iteration of the formal loop body, and is traditionally used to update the value of the primary loop variable. However, the incrementing statement can be any legal statement, allowing significant flexibility in coding.

As a concrete example, here is a method that computes the sum of an array of **double** values using a **for** loop:

```
public static double sum(double[ ] data) {
    double total = 0;
    for (int j=0; j < data.length; j++)      // note the use of length
        total += data[j];
    return total;
}
```

As one further example, the following method computes the maximum value within a (nonempty) array.

```
public static double max(double[ ] data) {
    double currentMax = data[0];        // assume first is biggest (for now)
    for (int j=1; j < data.length; j++)      // consider all other entries
        if (data[j] > currentMax)          // if data[j] is biggest thus far...
            currentMax = data[j];          // record it as the current max
    return currentMax;
}
```

Notice that a conditional statement is nested within the body of the loop, and that no explicit "{" and "}" braces are needed for the loop body, as the entire conditional construct serves as a single statement.

For-Each Loop

Since looping through elements of a collection is such a common construct, Java provides a shorthand notation for such loops, called the *for-each loop*. The syntax for such a loop is as follows:

> **for** (*elementType name* : *container*)
>   *loopBody*

where *container* is an array of the given *elementType* (or a collection that implements the Iterable interface, as we will later discuss in Section 7.4.1).

Revisiting a previous example, the traditional loop for computing the sum of elements in an array of **double** values can be written as:

```
public static double sum(double[ ] data) {
  double total = 0;
  for (double val : data)                    // Java's for-each loop style
    total += val;
  return total;
}
```

When using a for-each loop, there is no explicit use of array indices. The loop variable represents one particular element of the array. However, within the body of the loop, there is no designation as to which element it is.

It is also worth emphasizing that making an assignment to the loop variable has no effect on the underlying array. Therefore, the following method is an invalid attempt to scale all values of a numeric array.

```
public static void scaleBad(double[ ] data, double factor) {
  for (double val : data)
    val *= factor;                           // changes local variable only
}
```

In order to overwrite the values in the cells of an array, we must make use of indices. Therefore, this task is best solved with a traditional **for** loop, such as the following:

```
public static void scaleGood(double[ ] data, double factor) {
  for (int j=0; j < data.length; j++)
    data[j] *= factor;                       // overwrites cell of the array
}
```

1.5.3 Explicit Control-Flow Statements

Java also provides statements that cause explicit change in the flow of control of a program.

Returning from a Method

If a Java method is declared with a return type of **void**, then flow of control returns when it reaches the last line of code in the method or when it encounters a **return** statement (with no argument). If a method is declared with a return type, however, the method must exit by returning an appropriate value as an argument to a **return** statement. It follows that the **return** statement *must* be the last statement executed in a method, as the rest of the code will never be reached.

Note that there is a significant difference between a statement being the last line of code that is *executed* in a method and the last line of code in the method itself. The following (correct) example illustrates returning from a method:

```java
public double abs(double value) {
    if (value < 0)          // value is negative,
        return −value;      // so return its negation
    return value;           // return the original nonnegative value
}
```

In the example above, the line **return** −value; is clearly not the last line of code that is written in the method, but it may be the last line that is executed (if the original value is negative). Such a statement explicitly interrupts the flow of control in the method. There are two other such explicit control-flow statements, which are used in conjunction with loops and switch statements.

The break Statement

We first introduced use of the **break** command, in Section 1.5.1, to exit from the body of a switch statement. More generally, it can be used to "break" out of the innermost **switch, for, while,** or **do-while** statement body. When it is executed, a break statement causes the flow of control to jump to the next line after the loop or **switch** to the body containing the **break**.

The continue Statement

A **continue** statement can be used within a loop. It causes the execution to skip over the remaining steps of the *current iteration* of the loop body, but then, unlike the **break** statement, the flow of control returns to the top of the loop, assuming its condition remains satisfied.

1.6   Simple Input and Output

Java provides a rich set of classes and methods for performing input and output within a program. There are classes in Java for doing graphical user interface design, complete with pop-up windows and pull-down menus, as well as methods for the display and input of text and numbers. Java also provides methods for dealing with graphical objects, images, sounds, Web pages, and mouse events (such as clicks, mouse overs, and dragging). Moreover, many of these input and output methods can be used in either stand-alone programs or in applets.

Unfortunately, going into the details on how all of the methods work for constructing sophisticated graphical user interfaces is beyond the scope of this book. Still, for the sake of completeness, we describe how simple input and output can be done in Java in this section.

Simple input and output in Java occurs within the Java console window. Depending on the Java environment we are using, this window is either a special pop-up window that can be used for displaying and inputting text, or a window used to issue commands to the operating system (such windows are referred to as shell windows, command windows, or terminal windows).

Simple Output Methods

Java provides a built-in static object, called System.out, that performs output to the "standard output" device. Most operating system shells allow users to redirect standard output to files or even as input to other programs, but the default output is to the Java console window. The System.out object is an instance of the java.io.PrintStream class. This class defines methods for a buffered output stream, meaning that characters are put in a temporary location, called a **buffer**, which is then emptied when the console window is ready to print characters.

Specifically, the java.io.PrintStream class provides the following methods for performing simple output (we use *baseType* here to refer to any of the possible base types):

print(String *s*):   **Print the string *s*.**

print(Object *o*):   **Print the object *o* using its toString method.**

print(*baseType b*):   **Print the base type value *b*.**

println(String *s*):   **Print the string *s*, followed by the newline character.**

println(Object *o*):   **Similar to print(*o*), followed by the newline character.**

println(*baseType b*):   **Similar to print(*b*), followed by the newline character.**

An Output Example

Consider, for example, the following code fragment:

```
System.out.print("Java values: ");
System.out.print(3.1416);
System.out.print(',');
System.out.print(15);
System.out.println(" (double,char,int).");
```

When executed, this fragment will output the following in the Java console window:
```
Java values: 3.1416,15 (double,char,int).
```

Simple Input Using the java.util.Scanner Class

Just as there is a special object for performing output to the Java console window, there is also a special object, called System.in, for performing input from the Java console window. Technically, the input is actually coming from the "standard input" device, which by default is the computer keyboard echoing its characters in the Java console. The System.in object is an object associated with the standard input device. A simple way of reading input with this object is to use it to create a Scanner object, using the expression

new Scanner(System.in)

The Scanner class has a number of convenient methods that read from the given input stream, one of which is demonstrated in the following program:

```
import java.util.Scanner;              // loads Scanner definition for our use

public class InputExample {
  public static void main(String[ ] args) {
    Scanner input = new Scanner(System.in);
    System.out.print("Enter your age in years: ");
    double age = input.nextDouble();
    System.out.print("Enter your maximum heart rate: ");
    double rate = input.nextDouble();
    double fb = (rate − age) * 0.65;
    System.out.println("Your ideal fat-burning heart rate is " + fb);
  }
}
```

When executed, this program could produce the following on the Java console:
```
Enter your age in years: 21
Enter your maximum heart rate: 220
Your ideal fat-burning heart rate is 129.35
```

java.util.Scanner Methods

The Scanner class reads the input stream and divides it into *tokens*, which are strings of characters separated by *delimiters*. A delimiter is a special separating string, and the default delimiter is whitespace. That is, tokens are separated by strings of spaces, tabs, and newlines, by default. Tokens can either be read immediately as strings or a Scanner object can convert a token to a base type, if the token has the right form. Specifically, the Scanner class includes the following methods for dealing with tokens:

hasNext( ): Return **true** if there is another token in the input stream.

next( ): Return the next token string in the input stream; generate an error if there are no more tokens left.

hasNext*Type*( ): Return **true** if there is another token in the input stream and it can be interpreted as the corresponding base type, *Type*, where *Type* can be Boolean, Byte, Double, Float, Int, Long, or Short.

next*Type*( ): Return the next token in the input stream, returned as the base type corresponding to *Type*; generate an error if there are no more tokens left or if the next token cannot be interpreted as a base type corresponding to *Type*.

Additionally, Scanner objects can process input line by line, ignoring delimiters, and even look for patterns within lines while doing so. The methods for processing input in this way include the following:

hasNextLine( ): Returns **true** if the input stream has another line of text.

nextLine( ): Advances the input past the current line ending and returns the input that was skipped.

findInLine(String *s*): Attempts to find a string matching the (regular expression) pattern *s* in the current line. If the pattern is found, it is returned and the scanner advances to the first character after this match. If the pattern is not found, the scanner returns **null** and doesn't advance.

These methods can be used with those above, as in the following:

```
Scanner input = new Scanner(System.in);
System.out.print("Please enter an integer: ");
while (!input.hasNextInt()) {
  input.nextLine();
  System.out.print("Invalid integer; please enter an integer: ");
}
int i = input.nextInt();
```

1.7 An Example Program

In this section, we present another example of a Java class, which illustrates many of the constructs defined thus far in this chapter. This CreditCard class defines credit card objects that model a simplified version of traditional credit cards. They store information about the customer, issuing bank, account identifier, credit limit, and current balance. They do not charge interest or late payments, but they do restrict charges that would cause a card's balance to go over its credit limit. We also provide a static main method as part of this class to demonstrate its use.

The primary definition of the CreditCard class is given in Code Fragment 1.5. We defer until Code Fragment 1.6 the presentation of the main method, and in Code Fragment 1.7 we show the output produced by the main method. Highlights of this class, and underlying techniques that are demonstrated, include:

- The class defines five instance variables (lines 3–7), four of which are declared as **private** and one that is **protected**. (We will take advantage of the **protected** balance member when introducing inheritance in the next chapter.)

- The class defines two different constructor forms. The first version (beginning at line 9) requires five parameters, including an explicit initial balance for the account. The second constructor (beginning at line 16) accepts only four parameters; it relies on use of the special **this** keyword to invoke the five-parameter version, with an explicit initial balance of zero (a reasonable default for most new accounts).

- The class defines five basic accessor methods (lines 20–24), and two update methods (charge and makePayment). The charge method relies on conditional logic to ensure that a charge is rejected if it would have resulted in the balance exceeding the credit limit on the card.

- We provide a **static** utility method, named printSummary, in lines 37–43.

- The main method includes an array, named wallet, storing CreditCard instances. The main method also demonstrates a **while** loop, a traditional **for** loop, and a for-each loop over the contents of the wallet.

- The main method demonstrates the syntax for calling traditional (nonstatic) methods—charge, getBalance, and makePayment—as well as the syntax for invoking the static printSummary method.

```
1   public class CreditCard {
2     // Instance variables:
3     private String customer;        // name of the customer (e.g., "John Bowman")
4     private String bank;            // name of the bank (e.g., "California Savings")
5     private String account;         // account identifier (e.g., "5391 0375 9387 5309")
6     private int limit;              // credit limit (measured in dollars)
7     protected double balance;       // current balance (measured in dollars)
8     // Constructors:
9     public CreditCard(String cust, String bk, String acnt, int lim, double initialBal) {
10        customer = cust;
11        bank = bk;
12        account = acnt;
13        limit = lim;
14        balance = initialBal;
15    }
16    public CreditCard(String cust, String bk, String acnt, int lim) {
17      this(cust, bk, acnt, lim, 0.0);                    // use a balance of zero as default
18    }
19    // Accessor methods:
20    public String getCustomer() { return customer; }
21    public String getBank() { return bank; }
22    public String getAccount() { return account; }
23    public int getLimit() { return limit; }
24    public double getBalance() { return balance; }
25    // Update methods:
26    public boolean charge(double price) {               // make a charge
27      if (price + balance > limit)                      // if charge would surpass limit
28        return false;                                   // refuse the charge
29      // at this point, the charge is successful
30      balance += price;                                 // update the balance
31      return true;                                      // announce the good news
32    }
33    public void makePayment(double amount) {            // make a payment
34      balance -= amount;
35    }
36    // Utility method to print a card's information
37    public static void printSummary(CreditCard card) {
38      System.out.println("Customer = " + card.customer);
39      System.out.println("Bank = " + card.bank);
40      System.out.println("Account = " + card.account);
41      System.out.println("Balance = " + card.balance);   // implicit cast
42      System.out.println("Limit = " + card.limit);       // implicit cast
43    }
44    // main method shown on next page...
45  }
```

Code Fragment 1.5: The CreditCard class.

```
1   public static void main(String[ ] args) {
2     CreditCard[ ] wallet = new CreditCard[3];
3     wallet[0] = new CreditCard("John Bowman", "California Savings",
4                        "5391 0375 9387 5309", 5000);
5     wallet[1] = new CreditCard("John Bowman", "California Federal",
6                        "3485 0399 3395 1954", 3500);
7     wallet[2] = new CreditCard("John Bowman", "California Finance",
8                        "5391 0375 9387 5309", 2500, 300);
9
10    for (int val = 1; val <= 16; val++) {
11      wallet[0].charge(3*val);
12      wallet[1].charge(2*val);
13      wallet[2].charge(val);
14    }
15
16    for (CreditCard card : wallet) {
17      CreditCard.printSummary(card);        // calling static method
18      while (card.getBalance( ) > 200.0) {
19        card.makePayment(200);
20        System.out.println("New balance = " + card.getBalance( ));
21      }
22    }
23  }
```

Code Fragment 1.6: The main method of the CreditCard class.

```
Customer = John Bowman
Bank = California Savings
Account = 5391 0375 9387 5309
Balance = 408.0
Limit = 5000
New balance = 208.0
New balance = 8.0
Customer = John Bowman
Bank = California Federal
Account = 3485 0399 3395 1954
Balance = 272.0
Limit = 3500
New balance = 72.0
Customer = John Bowman
Bank = California Finance
Account = 5391 0375 9387 5309
Balance = 436.0
Limit = 2500
New balance = 236.0
New balance = 36.0
```

Code Fragment 1.7: Output from the Test class.

1.8   Packages and Imports

The Java language takes a general and useful approach to the organization of classes into programs. Every stand-alone public class defined in Java must be given in a separate file. The file name is the name of the class with a `.java` extension. So a class declared as **public class** Window is defined in a file `Window.java`. That file may contain definitions for other stand-alone classes, but none of them may be declared with public visibility.

To aid in the organization of large code repository, Java allows a group of related type definitions (such as classes and enums) to be grouped into what is known as a ***package***. For types to belong to a package named *packageName*, their source code must all be located in a directory named *packageName* and each file must begin with the line:

> **package** *packageName*;

By convention, most package names are lowercased. For example, we might define an architecture package that defines classes such as Window, Door, and Room. Public definitions within a file that does not have an explicit **package** declaration are placed into what is known as the ***default package***.

To refer to a type within a named package, we may use a fully qualified name based on dot notation, with that type treated as an attribute of the package. For example, we might declare a variable with architecture.Window as its type.

Packages can be further organized hierarchically into ***subpackages***. Code for classes in a subpackage must be located within a subdirectory of the package's directory, and qualified names for subpackages rely on further use of dot notation. For example, there is a java.util.zip subpackage (with support for working with ZIP compression) within the java.util package, and the Deflater class within that subpackage is fully qualified as java.util.zip.Deflater.

There are many advantages to organizing classes into packages, most notably:

- Packages help us avoid the pitfalls of name conflicts. If all type definitions were in a single package, there could be only one public class named Window. But with packages, we can have an architecture.Window class that is independent from a gui.Window class for graphical user interfaces.

- It is much easier to distribute a comprehensive set of classes for other programmers to use when those classes are packaged.

- When type definitions have a related purpose, it is often easier for other programmers to find them in a large library and to better understand their coordinated use when they are grouped as a package.

- Classes within the same package have access to any of each others' members having **public**, **protected**, or default visibility (i.e., anything but **private**).

Import Statements

As noted on the previous page, we may refer to a type within a package using its fully qualified name. For example, the Scanner class, introduced in Section 1.6, is defined in the java.util package, and so we may refer to it as java.util.Scanner. We could declare and construct a new instance of that class in a project using the following statement:

java.util.Scanner input = **new** java.util.Scanner(System.in);

However, all the extra typing needed to refer to a class outside of the current package can get tiring. In Java, we can use the **import** keyword to include external classes or entire packages in the current file. To import an individual class from a specific package, we type the following at the beginning of the file:

import *packageName.className*;

For example, in Section 1.6 we imported the Scanner class from the java.util package with the command:

import java.util.Scanner;

and then we were allowed to use the less burdensome syntax:

Scanner input = **new** Scanner(System.in);

Note that it is illegal to import a class with the above syntax if a similarly named class is defined elsewhere in the current file, or has already been imported from another package. For example, we could not simultaneously import both architecture.Window and gui.Window to use with the unqualified name Window.

Importing a Whole Package

If we know we will be using many definitions from the same package, we can import all of them using an asterisk character (∗) to denote a wildcard, as in the following syntax:

import *packageName*.∗;

If a locally defined name conflicts with one in a package being imported in this way, the locally defined one retains the unqualified name. If there is a name conflict between definitions in two different packages being imported this way, *neither* of the conflicting names can be used without qualification. For example, if we import the following hypothetical packages:

import architecture.∗;   // which we assume includes a Window class
import gui.∗;   // which we assume includes a Window class

we must still use the qualified names architecture.Window and gui.Window in the rest of our program.

1.9   Software Development

Traditional software development involves several phases. Three major steps are:

1. Design
2. Coding
3. Testing and Debugging

In this section, we briefly discuss the role of these phases, and we introduce several good practices for programming in Java, including coding style, naming conventions, formal documentation, and testing.

1.9.1   Design

For object-oriented programming, the design step is perhaps the most important phase in the process of developing software. It is in the design step that we decide how to divide the workings of our program into classes, when we decide how these classes will interact, what data each will store, and what actions each will perform. Indeed, one of the main challenges that beginning programmers face is deciding what classes to define to do the work of their program. While general prescriptions are hard to come by, there are some rules of thumb that we can apply when determining how to define our classes:

- **Responsibilities**: Divide the work into different **actors**, each with a different responsibility. Try to describe responsibilities using action verbs. These actors will form the classes for the program.

- **Independence**: Define the work for each class to be as independent from other classes as possible. Subdivide responsibilities between classes so that each class has autonomy over some aspect of the program. Give data (as instance variables) to the class that has jurisdiction over the actions that require access to this data.

- **Behaviors**: Define the behaviors for each class carefully and precisely, so that the consequences of each action performed by a class will be well understood by other classes that interact with it. These behaviors will define the methods that this class performs, and the set of behaviors for a class form the **protocol** by which other pieces of code will interact with objects from the class.

Defining the classes, together with their instance variables and methods, are key to the design of an object-oriented program. A good programmer will naturally develop greater skill in performing these tasks over time, as experience teaches him or her to notice patterns in the requirements of a program that match patterns that he or she has seen before.

A common tool for developing an initial high-level design for a project is the use of ***CRC cards***. Class-Responsibility-Collaborator (CRC) cards are simple index cards that subdivide the work required of a program. The main idea behind this tool is to have each card represent a component, which will ultimately become a class in the program. We write the name of each component on the top of an index card. On the left-hand side of the card, we begin writing the responsibilities for this component. On the right-hand side, we list the collaborators for this component, that is, the other components that this component will have to interact with to perform its duties.

The design process iterates through an action/actor cycle, where we first identify an action (that is, a responsibility), and we then determine an actor (that is, a component) that is best suited to perform that action. The design is complete when we have assigned all actions to actors. In using index cards for this process (rather than larger pieces of paper), we are relying on the fact that each component should have a small set of responsibilities and collaborators. Enforcing this rule helps keep the individual classes manageable.

As the design takes form, a standard approach to explain and document the design is the use of UML (Unified Modeling Language) diagrams to express the organization of a program. UML diagrams are a standard visual notation to express object-oriented software designs. Several computer-aided tools are available to build UML diagrams. One type of UML figure is known as a ***class diagram***.

An example of a class diagram is given in Figure 1.5, corresponding to our CreditCard class from Section 1.7. The diagram has three portions, with the first designating the name of the class, the second designating the recommended instance variables, and the third designating the recommended methods of the class. The type declarations of variables, parameters, and return values are specified in the appropriate place following a colon, and the visibility of each member is designated on its left, with the "+" symbol for **public** visibility, the "#" symbol for **protected** visibility, and the "−" symbol for **private** visibility.

class:	CreditCard	
fields:	− customer : String − bank : String − account : String	− limit : int # balance : double
methods:	+ getCustomer( ) : String + getBank( ) : String + charge(price : double) : boolean + makePayment(amount : double)	+ getAccount( ) : String + getLimit( ) : int + getBalance( ) : double

Figure 1.5: A UML Class diagram for the CreditCard class from Section 1.7.

1.9.2   Pseudocode

As an intermediate step before the implementation of a design, programmers are often asked to describe algorithms in a way that is intended for human eyes only. Such descriptions are called *pseudocode*. Pseudocode is not a computer program, but is more structured than usual prose. It is a mixture of natural language and high-level programming constructs that describe the main ideas behind a generic implementation of a data structure or algorithm. Because pseudocode is designed for a human reader, not a computer, we can communicate high-level ideas without being burdened by low-level implementation details. At the same time, we should not gloss over important steps. Like many forms of human communication, finding the right balance is an important skill that is refined through practice.

There really is no precise definition of the pseudocode language. At the same time, to help achieve clarity, pseudocode mixes natural language with standard programming language constructs. The programming language constructs that we choose are those consistent with modern high-level languages such as C, C++, and Java. These constructs include the following:

- *Expressions:* We use standard mathematical symbols to express numeric and boolean expressions. To be consistent with Java, we use the equal sign "=" as the assignment operator in assignment statements, and the "==" relation to test equivalence in boolean expressions.

- *Method declarations:* **Algorithm** name($param1, param2, \ldots$) declares new method "name" and its parameters.

- *Decision structures:* **if** condition **then** true-actions [**else** false-actions]. We use indentation to indicate what actions should be included in the true-actions and false-actions.

- *While-loops:* **while** condition **do** actions. We use indentation to indicate what actions should be included in the loop actions.

- *Repeat-loops:* **repeat** actions **until** condition. We use indentation to indicate what actions should be included in the loop actions.

- *For-loops:* **for** variable-increment-definition **do** actions. We use indentation to indicate what actions should be included among the loop actions.

- *Array indexing:* $A[i]$ represents the ith cell in the array A. The cells of an n-celled array A are indexed from $A[0]$ to $A[n-1]$ (consistent with Java).

- *Method calls:* object.method(args); object is optional if it is understood.

- *Method returns:* **return** value. This operation returns the value specified to the method that called this one.

- *Comments:* { Comment goes here. }. We enclose comments in braces.

1.9.3 Coding

One of the key steps in implementing an object-oriented program is coding the descriptions of classes and their respective data and methods. In order to accelerate the development of this skill, we will discuss various ***design patterns*** for designing object-oriented programs (see Section 2.1.3) at various points throughout this text. These patterns provide templates for defining classes and the interactions between these classes.

Once we have settled on a design for the classes or our program and their responsibilities, and perhaps drafted pseudocode for their behaviors, we are ready to begin the actual coding on a computer. We type the Java source code for the classes of our program by using either an independent text editor (such as emacs, WordPad, or vi), or the editor embedded in an ***integrated development environment*** (IDE), such as Eclipse.

Once we have completed coding for a class (or package), we compile this file into working code by invoking a compiler. If we are not using an IDE, then we compile our program by calling a program, such as `javac`, on our file. If we are using an IDE, then we compile our program by clicking the appropriate compilation button. If we are fortunate, and our program has no syntax errors, then this compilation process will create files with a ".`class`" extension.

If our program contains syntax errors, then these will be identified, and we will have to go back into our editor to fix the offending lines of code. Once we have eliminated all syntax errors, and created the appropriate compiled code, we can run our program by either invoking a command, such as "`java`" (outside an IDE), or by clicking on the appropriate "run" button (within an IDE). When a Java program is run in this way, the runtime environment locates the directories containing the named class and any other classes that are referenced from this class according to a special operating system environment variable named "CLASSPATH." This variable defines an order of directories in which to search, given as a list of directories, which are separated by colons in Unix/Linux or semicolons in DOS/Windows. An example CLASSPATH assignment in the DOS/Windows operating system could be the following:

```
SET CLASSPATH=.;C:\java;C:\Program Files\Java\
```

Whereas an example CLASSPATH assignment in the Unix/Linux operating system could be the following:

```
setenv CLASSPATH ".:/usr/local/java/lib:/usr/netscape/classes"
```

In both cases, the dot (".") refers to the current directory in which the runtime environment is invoked.

1.9.4   Documentation and Style

Javadoc

In order to encourage good use of block comments and the automatic production of documentation, the Java programming environment comes with a documentation production program called **javadoc**. This program takes a collection of Java source files that have been commented using certain keywords, called **tags**, and it produces a series of HTML documents that describe the classes, methods, variables, and constants contained in these files. As an example, Figure 1.6 shows a portion of the documentation generated for our CreditCard class.

Each javadoc comment is a block comment that starts with "/**" and ends with "*/", and each line between these two can begin with a single asterisk, "*", which is ignored. The block comment is assumed to start with a descriptive sentence, which is followed by special lines that begin with javadoc tags. A block comment that comes just before a class definition, instance variable declaration, or method definition is processed by javadoc into a comment about that class, variable, or method. The primary javadoc tags that we use are the following:

- @author *text*: Identifies each author (one per line) for a class.
- @throws *exceptionName description*: Identifies an error condition that is signaled by this method (see Section 2.4).
- @param *parameterName description*: Identifies a parameter accepted by this method.
- @return *description*: Describes the return type and its range of values for a method.

There are other tags as well; the interested reader is referred to online documentation for javadoc for further information. For space reasons, we cannot always include javadoc-style comments in all the example programs included in this book, but we include such a sample in Code Fragment 1.8, and within the online code at the website that accompanies this book.

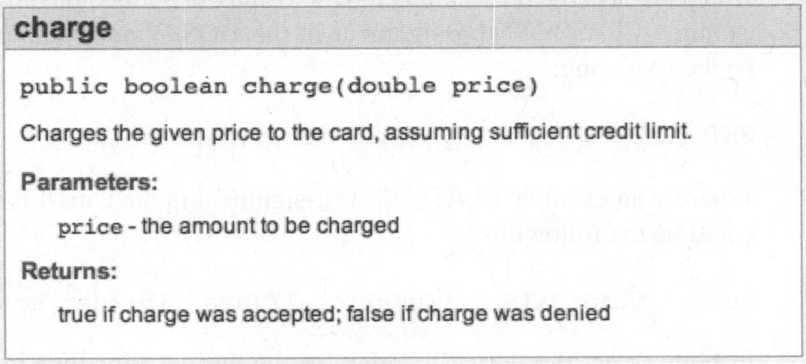

---

charge

```
public boolean charge(double price)
```

Charges the given price to the card, assuming sufficient credit limit.

Parameters:

    price - the amount to be charged

Returns:

    true if charge was accepted; false if charge was denied

Figure 1.6: Documentation rendered by javadoc for the CreditCard.charge method.

```
 1  /**
 2   * A simple model for a consumer credit card.
 3   *
 4   * @author Michael T. Goodrich
 5   * @author Roberto Tamassia
 6   * @author Michael H. Goldwasser
 7   */
 8  public class CreditCard {
 9    /**
10     * Constructs a new credit card instance.
11     * @param cust        the name of the customer (e.g., "John Bowman")
12     * @param bk          the name of the bank (e.g., "California Savings")
13     * @param acnt        the account identifier (e.g., "5391 0375 9387 5309")
14     * @param lim         the credit limit (measured in dollars)
15     * @param initialBal  the initial balance (measured in dollars)
16     */
17    public CreditCard(String cust, String bk, String acnt, int lim, double initialBal) {
18      customer = cust;
19      bank = bk;
20      account = acnt;
21      limit = lim;
22      balance = initialBal;
23    }
24
25    /**
26     * Charges the given price to the card, assuming sufficient credit limit.
27     * @param price   the amount to be charged
28     * @return true    if charge was accepted; false if charge was denied
29     */
30    public boolean charge(double price) {          // make a charge
31      if (price + balance > limit)                 // if charge would surpass limit
32        return false;                              // refuse the charge
33      // at this point, the charge is successful
34      balance += price;                            // update the balance
35      return true;                                 // announce the good news
36    }
37
38    /**
39     * Processes customer payment that reduces balance.
40     * @param amount  the amount of payment made
41     */
42    public void makePayment(double amount) {   // make a payment
43      balance -= amount;
44    }
45    // remainder of class omitted...
```

Code Fragment 1.8: A portion of the CreditCard class definition, originally from Code Fragment 1.5, with javadoc-style comments included.

Readability and Programming Conventions

Programs should be made easy to read and understand. Good programmers should therefore be mindful of their coding style, and develop a style that communicates the important aspects of a program's design for both humans and computers. Much has been written about good coding style, with some of the main principles being the following:

- Use meaningful names for identifiers. Try to choose names that can be read aloud, and choose names that reflect the action, responsibility, or data each identifier is naming. The tradition in most Java circles is to capitalize the first letter of each word in an identifier, except for the first word for a variable or method name. By this convention, "Date," "Vector," "DeviceManager" would identify classes, and "isFull( )," "insertItem( )," "studentName," and "studentHeight" would respectively identify methods and variables.
- Use named constants or enum types instead of literals. Readability, robustness, and modifiability are enhanced if we include a series of definitions of named constant values in a class definition. These can then be used within this class and others to refer to special values for this class. The tradition in Java is to fully capitalize such constants, as shown below:

```java
public class Student {
  public static final int MIN_CREDITS = 12;  // min credits per term
  public static final int MAX_CREDITS = 24;  // max credits per term
  public enum Year {FRESHMAN, SOPHOMORE, JUNIOR, SENIOR};

  // Instance variables, constructors, and method definitions go here...
}
```

- Indent statement blocks. Typically programmers indent each statement block by 4 spaces; in this book we typically use 2 spaces, however, to avoid having our code overrun the book's margins.
- Organize each class in the following order:
    1. Constants
    2. Instance variables
    3. Constructors
    4. Methods

  We note that some Java programmers prefer to put instance variable definitions last. We put them earlier so that we can read each class sequentially and understand the data each method is working with.
- Use comments that add meaning to a program and explain ambiguous or confusing constructs. In-line comments are good for quick explanations and do not need to be sentences. Block comments are good for explaining the purpose of a method and complex code sections.

1.9.5   Testing and Debugging

Testing is the process of experimentally checking the correctness of a program, while debugging is the process of tracking the execution of a program and discovering the errors in it. Testing and debugging are often the most time-consuming activity in the development of a program.

Testing

A careful testing plan is an essential part of writing a program. While verifying the correctness of a program over all possible inputs is usually infeasible, we should aim at executing the program on a representative subset of inputs. At the very minimum, we should make sure that every method of a program is tested at least once (method coverage). Even better, each code statement in the program should be executed at least once (statement coverage).

Programs often tend to fail on *special cases* of the input. Such cases need to be carefully identified and tested. For example, when testing a method that sorts (that is, puts in order) an array of integers, we should consider the following inputs:

- The array has zero length (no elements).
- The array has one element.
- All the elements of the array are the same.
- The array is already sorted.
- The array is reverse sorted.

In addition to special inputs to the program, we should also consider special conditions for the structures used by the program. For example, if we use an array to store data, we should make sure that boundary cases, such as inserting or removing at the beginning or end of the subarray holding data, are properly handled.

While it is essential to use handcrafted test suites, it is also advantageous to run the program on a large collection of randomly generated inputs. The Random class in the `java.util` package provides several means for generating pseudorandom numbers.

There is a hierarchy among the classes and methods of a program induced by the caller-callee relationship. Namely, a method *A* is above a method *B* in the hierarchy if *A* calls *B*. There are two main testing strategies, *top-down* testing and *bottom-up* testing, which differ in the order in which methods are tested.

Top-down testing proceeds from the top to the bottom of the program hierarchy. It is typically used in conjunction with *stubbing*, a boot-strapping technique that replaces a lower-level method with a *stub*, a replacement for the method that simulates the functionality of the original. For example, if method *A* calls method *B* to get the first line of a file, when testing *A* we can replace *B* with a stub that returns a fixed string.

Bottom-up testing proceeds from lower-level methods to higher-level methods. For example, bottom-level methods, which do not invoke other methods, are tested first, followed by methods that call only bottom-level methods, and so on. Similarly a class that does not depend upon any other classes can be tested before another class that depends on the former. This form of testing is usually described as ***unit testing***, as the functionality of a specific component is tested in isolation of the larger software project. If used properly, this strategy better isolates the cause of errors to the component being tested, as lower-level components upon which it relies should have already been thoroughly tested.

Java provides several forms of support for automated testing. We have already discussed how a class's static main method can be repurposed to perform tests of the functionality of that class (as was done in Code 1.6 for the CreditCard class). Such a test can be executed by invoking the Java virtual machine directly on this secondary class, rather than on the primary class for the entire application. When Java is started on the primary class, any code within such secondary main methods will be ignored.

More robust support for automation of unit testing is provided by the JUnit framework, which is not part of the standard Java toolkit but freely available at www.junit.org. This framework allows the grouping of individual test cases into larger test suites, and provides support for executing those suites, and reporting or analyzing the results of those tests. As software is maintained, ***regression testing*** should be performed, whereby automation is used to re-execute all previous tests to ensure that changes to the software do not introduce new bugs in previously tested components.

Debugging

The simplest debugging technique consists of using ***print statements*** to track the values of variables during the execution of the program. A problem with this approach is that eventually the print statements need to be removed or commented out, so they are not executed when the software is finally released.

A better approach is to run the program within a ***debugger***, which is a specialized environment for controlling and monitoring the execution of a program. The basic functionality provided by a debugger is the insertion of ***breakpoints*** within the code. When the program is executed within the debugger, it stops at each breakpoint. While the program is stopped, the current value of variables can be inspected. In addition to fixed breakpoints, advanced debuggers allow specification of ***conditional breakpoints***, which are triggered only if a given expression is satisfied.

The standard Java toolkit includes a basic debugger named jdb, which has a command-line interface. Most IDEs for Java programming provide advanced debugging environments with graphical user interfaces.

1.10   Exercises

Reinforcement

R-1.1   Write a short Java method, inputAllBaseTypes, that inputs a different value of each base type from the standard input device and prints it back to the standard output device.

R-1.2   Suppose that we create an array A of GameEntry objects, which has an integer scores field, and we clone A and store the result in an array B. If we then immediately set $A[4]$.score equal to 550, what is the score value of the GameEntry object referenced by $B[4]$?

R-1.3   Write a short Java method, isMultiple, that takes two **long** values, n and m, and returns true if and only if n is a multiple of m, that is, $n = mi$ for some integer i.

R-1.4   Write a short Java method, isEven, that takes an **int** i and returns true if and only if i is even. Your method cannot use the multiplication, modulus, or division operators, however.

R-1.5   Write a short Java method that takes an integer n and returns the sum of all positive integers less than or equal to n.

R-1.6   Write a short Java method that takes an integer n and returns the sum of all the odd positive integers less than or equal to n.

R-1.7   Write a short Java method that takes an integer n and returns the sum of the squares of all positive integers less than or equal to n.

R-1.8   Write a short Java method that counts the number of vowels in a given character string.

R-1.9   Write a short Java method that uses a StringBuilder instance to remove all the punctuation from a string s storing a sentence, for example, transforming the string "Let's try, Mike!" to "Lets try Mike".

R-1.10   Write a Java class, Flower, that has three instance variables of type **String**, **int**, and **float**, which respectively represent the name of the flower, its number of petals, and price. Your class must include a constructor method that initializes each variable to an appropriate value, and your class should include methods for setting the value of each type, and getting the value of each type.

R-1.11   Modify the CreditCard class from Code Fragment 1.5 to include a method that updates the credit limit.

R-1.12   Modify the CreditCard class from Code Fragment 1.5 so that it ignores any request to process a negative payment amount.

R-1.13   Modify the declaration of the first **for** loop in the main method in Code Fragment 1.6 so that its charges will cause exactly one of the three credit cards to attempt to go over its credit limit. Which credit card is it?

Creativity

C-1.14   Write a pseudocode description of a method that reverses an array of n integers, so that the numbers are listed in the opposite order than they were before, and compare this method to an equivalent Java method for doing the same thing.

C-1.15   Write a pseudocode description of a method for finding the smallest and largest numbers in an array of integers and compare that to a Java method that would do the same thing.

C-1.16   Write a short program that takes as input three integers, a, b, and c, from the Java console and determines if they can be used in a correct arithmetic formula (in the given order), like "$a + b = c$," "$a = b - c$," or "$a * b = c$."

C-1.17   Write a short Java method that takes an array of **int** values and determines if there is a pair of distinct elements of the array whose product is even.

C-1.18   The *p-norm* of a vector $v = (v_1, v_2, \ldots, v_n)$ in n-dimensional space is defined as

$$\|v\| = \sqrt[p]{v_1^p + v_2^p + \cdots + v_n^p}.$$

For the special case of $p = 2$, this results in the traditional *Euclidean norm*, which represents the length of the vector. For example, the Euclidean norm of a two-dimensional vector with coordinates $(4, 3)$ has a Euclidean norm of $\sqrt{4^2 + 3^2} = \sqrt{16 + 9} = \sqrt{25} = 5$. Give an implementation of a method named norm such that norm(v, p) returns the p-norm value of v and norm(v) returns the Euclidean norm of v, where v is represented as an array of coordinates.

C-1.19   Write a Java program that can take a positive integer greater than 2 as input and write out the number of times one must repeatedly divide this number by 2 before getting a value less than 2.

C-1.20   Write a Java method that takes an array of **float** values and determines if all the numbers are different from each other (that is, they are distinct).

C-1.21   Write a Java method that takes an array containing the set of all integers in the range 1 to 52 and shuffles it into random order. Your method should output each possible order with equal probability.

C-1.22   Write a short Java program that outputs all possible strings formed by using the characters 'c', 'a', 't', 'd', 'o', and 'g' exactly once.

C-1.23   Write a short Java program that takes two arrays a and b of length n storing **int** values, and returns the dot product of a and b. That is, it returns an array c of length n such that $c[i] = a[i] \cdot b[i]$, for $i = 0, \ldots, n - 1$.

C-1.24   Modify the CreditCard class from Code Fragment 1.5 so that printSummary becomes a *nonstatic* method, and modify the main method from Code Fragment 1.6 accordingly.

C-1.25   Modify the CreditCard class to add a toString() method that returns a String representation of the card (rather than printing it to the console, as done by printSummary). Modify the main method from Code Fragment 1.6 accordingly to use the standard println command.

Projects

P-1.26 Write a short Java program that takes all the lines input to standard input and writes them to standard output in reverse order. That is, each line is output in the correct order, but the ordering of the lines is reversed.

P-1.27 Write a Java program that can simulate a simple calculator, using the Java console as the exclusive input and output device. That is, each input to the calculator, be it a number, like 12.34 or 1034, or an operator, like + or =, can be done on a separate line. After each such input, you should output to the Java console what would be displayed on your calculator.

P-1.28 A common punishment for school children is to write out a sentence multiple times. Write a Java stand-alone program that will write out the following sentence one hundred times: "I will never spam my friends again." Your program should number each of the sentences and it should make eight different random-looking typos.

P-1.29 The *birthday paradox* says that the probability that two people in a room will have the same birthday is more than half, provided n, the number of people in the room, is more than 23. This property is not really a paradox, but many people find it surprising. Design a Java program that can test this paradox by a series of experiments on randomly generated birthdays, which test this paradox for $n = 5, 10, 15, 20, \ldots, 100$.

P-1.30 *(For those who know Java graphical user interface methods:)* Define a GraphicalTest class that tests the functionality of the CreditCard class from Code Fragment 1.5 using text fields and buttons.

Chapter Notes

For more detailed information about the Java programming language, we refer the reader to the Java website (http://www.java.com), as well as some of the fine books about Java, including the books by Arnold, Gosling and Holmes [8], Flanagan [33], and Horstmann and Cornell [47, 48].

Chapter

2

Object-Oriented Design

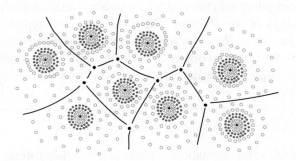

Contents

2.1   Goals, Principles, and Patterns

As the name implies, the main "actors" in the object-oriented paradigm are called ***objects***. Each object is an ***instance*** of a ***class***. Each class presents to the outside world a concise and consistent view of the objects that are instances of this class, without going into too much unnecessary detail or giving others access to the inner workings of the objects. The class definition typically specifies the ***data fields***, also known as ***instance variables***, that an object contains, as well as the ***methods*** (operations) that an object can execute. This view of computing fulfill several goals and incorporates design principles, which we will discuss in this chapter.

2.1.1   Object-Oriented Design Goals

Software implementations should achieve ***robustness***, ***adaptability***, and ***reusability***. (See Figure 2.1.)

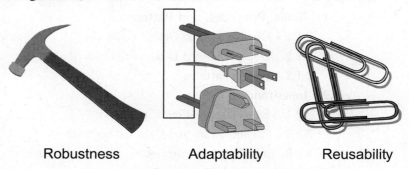

| Robustness | Adaptability | Reusability |

Figure 2.1: Goals of object-oriented design.

Robustness

Every good programmer wants to develop software that is correct, which means that a program produces the right output for all the anticipated inputs in the program's application. In addition, we want software to be ***robust***, that is, capable of handling unexpected inputs that are not explicitly defined for its application. For example, if a program is expecting a positive integer (perhaps representing the price of an item) and instead is given a negative integer, then the program should be able to recover gracefully from this error. More importantly, in ***life-critical applications***, where a software error can lead to injury or loss of life, software that is not robust could be deadly. This point was driven home in the late 1980s in accidents involving Therac-25, a radiation-therapy machine, which severely overdosed six patients between 1985 and 1987, some of whom died from complications resulting from their radiation overdose. All six accidents were traced to software errors.

Adaptability

Modern software applications, such as Web browsers and Internet search engines, typically involve large programs that are used for many years. Software, therefore, needs to be able to evolve over time in response to changing conditions in its environment. Thus, another important goal of quality software is that it achieves *adaptability* (also called *evolvability*). Related to this concept is *portability*, which is the ability of software to run with minimal change on different hardware and operating system platforms. An advantage of writing software in Java is the portability provided by the language itself.

Reusability

Going hand in hand with adaptability is the desire that software be reusable, that is, the same code should be usable as a component of different systems in various applications. Developing quality software can be an expensive enterprise, and its cost can be offset somewhat if the software is designed in a way that makes it easily reusable in future applications. Such reuse should be done with care, however, for one of the major sources of software errors in the Therac-25 came from inappropriate reuse of Therac-20 software (which was not object-oriented and not designed for the hardware platform used with the Therac-25).

2.1.2 Object-Oriented Design Principles

Chief among the principles of the object-oriented approach, which are intended to facilitate the goals outlined above, are the following (see Figure 2.2):

- Abstraction
- Encapsulation
- Modularity

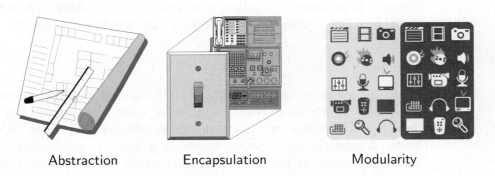

Abstraction   Encapsulation   Modularity

Figure 2.2: Principles of object-oriented design.

Abstraction

The notion of *abstraction* is to distill a complicated system down to its most funda-mental parts. Typically, describing the parts of a system involves naming them and explaining their functionality. Applying the abstraction paradigm to the design of data structures gives rise to *abstract data types* (ADTs). An ADT is a mathematical model of a data structure that specifies the type of data stored, the operations sup-ported on them, and the types of parameters of the operations. An ADT specifies *what* each operation does, but not *how* it does it. In Java, an ADT can be expressed by an *interface*, which is simply a list of method declarations, where each method has an empty body. (We will say more about Java interfaces in Section 2.3.1.)

An ADT is realized by a concrete data structure, which is modeled in Java by a *class*. A class defines the data being stored and the operations supported by the objects that are instances of the class. Also, unlike interfaces, classes specify *how* the operations are performed in the body of each method. A Java class is said to *implement an interface* if its methods include all the methods declared in the interface, thus providing a body for them. However, a class can have more methods than those of the interface.

Encapsulation

Another important principle of object-oriented design is *encapsulation*; different components of a software system should not reveal the internal details of their respective implementations. One of the main advantages of encapsulation is that it gives one programmer freedom to implement the details of a component, without concern that other programmers will be writing code that intricately depends on those internal decisions. The only constraint on the programmer of a component is to maintain the public interface for the component, as other programmers will be writing code that depends on that interface. Encapsulation yields robustness and adaptability, for it allows the implementation details of parts of a program to change without adversely affecting other parts, thereby making it easier to fix bugs or add new functionality with relatively local changes to a component.

Modularity

Modern software systems typically consist of several different components that must interact correctly in order for the entire system to work properly. Keeping these interactions straight requires that these different components be well orga-nized. *Modularity* refers to an organizing principle in which different compo-nents of a software system are divided into separate functional units. Robustness is greatly increased because it is easier to test and debug separate components before they are integrated into a larger software system.

2.1.3 Design Patterns

Object-oriented design facilitates reusable, robust, and adaptable software. Designing good code takes more than simply understanding object-oriented methodologies, however. It requires the effective use of object-oriented design techniques.

Computing researchers and practitioners have developed a variety of organizational concepts and methodologies for designing quality object-oriented software that is concise, correct, and reusable. Of special relevance to this book is the concept of a ***design pattern***, which describes a solution to a "typical" software design problem. A pattern provides a general template for a solution that can be applied in many different situations. It describes the main elements of a solution in an abstract way that can be specialized for a specific problem at hand. It consists of a name, which identifies the pattern; a context, which describes the scenarios for which this pattern can be applied; a template, which describes how the pattern is applied; and a result, which describes and analyzes what the pattern produces.

We present several design patterns in this book, and we show how they can be consistently applied to implementations of data structures and algorithms. These design patterns fall into two groups—patterns for solving algorithm design problems and patterns for solving software engineering problems. Some of the algorithm design patterns we discuss include the following:

- Recursion (Chapter 5)
- Amortization (Sections 7.2.3, 11.4.4, and 14.7.3)
- Divide-and-conquer (Section 12.1.1)
- Prune-and-search, also known as decrease-and-conquer (Section 12.5.1)
- Brute force (Section 13.2.1)
- The greedy method (Sections 13.4.2, 14.6.2, and 14.7)
- Dynamic programming (Section 13.5)

Likewise, some of the software engineering design patterns we discuss include:
- Template method (Sections 2.3.3, 10.5.1, and 11.2.1)
- Composition (Sections 2.5.2, 2.6, and 9.2.1)
- Adapter (Section 6.1.3)
- Position (Sections 7.3, 8.1.2, and 14.7.3)
- Iterator (Section 7.4)
- Factory Method (Sections 8.3.1 and 11.2.1)
- Comparator (Sections 9.2.2, 10.3, and Chapter 12)
- Locator (Section 9.5.1)

Rather than explain each of these concepts here, however, we will introduce them throughout the text as noted above. For each pattern, be it for algorithm engineering or software engineering, we explain its general use and we illustrate it with at least one concrete example.

2.2   Inheritance

A natural way to organize various structural components of a software package is in a ***hierarchical*** fashion, with similar abstract definitions grouped together in a level-by-level manner that goes from specific to more general as one traverses up the hierarchy. An example of such a hierarchy is shown in Figure 2.3. Using mathematical notations, the set of houses is a ***subset*** of the set of buildings, but a ***superset*** of the set of ranches. The correspondence between levels is often referred to as an ***"is a" relationship***, as a house is a building, and a ranch is a house.

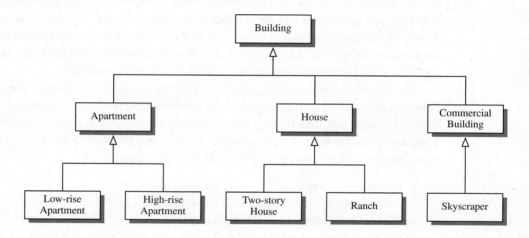

Figure 2.3: An example of an "is a" hierarchy involving architectural buildings.

A hierarchical design is useful in software development, as common functionality can be grouped at the most general level, thereby promoting reuse of code, while differentiated behaviors can be viewed as extensions of the general case. In object-oriented programming, the mechanism for a modular and hierarchical organization is a technique known as ***inheritance***. This allows a new class to be defined based upon an existing class as the starting point. In object-oriented terminology, the existing class is typically described as the ***base class***, ***parent class***, or ***superclass***, while the newly defined class is known as the ***subclass*** or ***child class***. We say that the subclass ***extends*** the superclass.

When inheritance is used, the subclass automatically inherits, as its starting point, all methods from the superclass (other than constructors). The subclass can differentiate itself from its superclass in two ways. It may ***augment*** the superclass by adding new fields and new methods. It may also ***specialize*** existing behaviors by providing a new implementation that ***overrides*** an existing method.

2.2.1 Extending the CreditCard Class

As an introduction to the use of inheritance, we revisit the CreditCard class of Section 1.7, designing a new subclass that, for lack of a better name, we name PredatoryCreditCard. The new class will differ from the original in two ways: (1) if an attempted charge is rejected because it would have exceeded the credit limit, a $5 fee will be charged, and (2) there will be a mechanism for assessing a monthly interest charge on the outstanding balance, using an annual percentage rate (APR) specified as a constructor parameter.

Figure 2.4 provides a UML diagram that serves as an overview of our design for the new PredatoryCreditCard class as a subclass of the existing CreditCard class. The hollow arrow in that diagram indicates the use of inheritance, with the arrow oriented from the subclass to the superclass.

The PredatoryCreditCard class *augments* the original CreditCard class, adding a new instance variable named apr to store the annual percentage rate, and adding a new method named processMonth that will assess interest charges. The new class also *specializes* its superclass by *overriding* the original charge method in order to provide a new implementation that assess a $5 fee for an attempted overcharge.

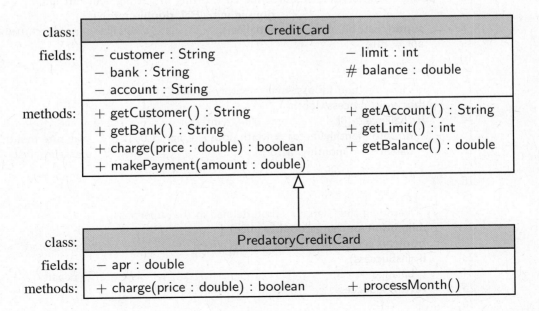

Figure 2.4: A UML diagram showing PredatoryCreditCard as a subclass of CreditCard. (See Figure 1.5 for the original CreditCard design.)

To demonstrate the mechanisms for inheritance in Java, Code Fragment 2.1 presents a complete implementation of the new PredatoryCreditCard class. We wish to draw attention to several aspects of the Java implementation.

We begin with the first line of the class definition, which indicates that the new class inherits from the existing CreditCard class by using Java's **extends** keyword followed by the name of its superclass. In Java, each class can extend exactly one other class. Because of this property, Java is said to allow only *single inheritance* among classes. We should also note that even if a class definition makes no explicit use of the **extends** clause, it automatically inherits from a class, java.lang.Object, which serves as the universal superclass in Java.

We next consider the declaration of the new apr instance variable, at line 3 of the code. Each instance of the PredatoryCreditCard class will store each of the variables inherited from the CreditCard definition (customer, bank, account, limit, and balance) in addition to the new apr variable. Yet we are only responsible for declaring the new instance variable within the subclass definition.

```java
 1  public class PredatoryCreditCard extends CreditCard {
 2    // Additional instance variable
 3    private double apr;                                    // annual percentage rate
 4
 5    // Constructor for this class
 6    public PredatoryCreditCard(String cust, String bk, String acnt, int lim,
 7                               double initialBal, double rate) {
 8      super(cust, bk, acnt, lim, initialBal);              // initialize superclass attributes
 9      apr = rate;
10    }
11
12    // A new method for assessing monthly interest charges
13    public void processMonth( ) {
14      if (balance > 0) {    // only charge interest on a positive balance
15        double monthlyFactor = Math.pow(1 + apr, 1.0/12); // compute monthly rate
16        balance *= monthlyFactor;                         // assess interest
17      }
18    }
19
20    // Overriding the charge method defined in the superclass
21    public boolean charge(double price) {
22      boolean isSuccess = super.charge(price);            // call inherited method
23      if (!isSuccess)
24        balance += 5;                                     // assess a $5 penalty
25      return isSuccess;
26    }
27  }
```

Code Fragment 2.1: A subclass of CreditCard that assesses interest and fees.

Constructors are never inherited in Java. Lines 6–10 of Code Fragment 2.1 define a constructor for the new class. When a PredatoryCreditCard instance is created, all of its fields must be properly initialized, including any inherited fields. For this reason, the first operation performed within the body of a constructor must be to invoke a constructor of the superclass, which is responsible for properly initializing the fields defined in the superclass.

In Java, a constructor of the superclass is invoked by using the keyword **super** with appropriate parameterization, as demonstrated at line 8 of our implementation:

    super(cust, mk, acnt, lim, initialBal);

This use of the **super** keyword is very similar to use of the keyword **this** when invoking a different constructor within the same class (as described on page 15 of Section 1.2.2). If a constructor for a subclass does not make an explicit call to **super** or **this** as its first command, then an implicit call to **super**( ), the zero-parameter version of the superclass constructor, will be made. Returning our attention to the constructor for PredatoryCreditCard, after calling the superclass constructor with appropriate parameters, line 9 initializes the newly declared apr field. (That field was unknown to the superclass.)

The processMonth method is a new behavior, so there is no inherited version upon which to rely. In our model, this method should be invoked by the bank, once each month, to add new interest charges to the customer's balance. From a technical aspect, we note that this method accesses the value of the inherited balance field (at line 14), and potentially modifies that balance at line 16. This is permitted precisely because the balance attributed was declared with **protected** visibility in the original CreditCard class. (See Code Fragment 1.5.)

The most challenging aspect in implementing the processMonth method is making sure we have working knowledge of how an annual percentage rate translates to a monthly rate. We do not simply divide the annual rate by twelve to get a monthly rate (that would be too predatory, as it would result in a higher APR than advertised). The correct computation is to take the twelfth-root of $1 + \mathsf{apr}$, and use that as a multiplicative factor. For example, if the APR is 0.0825 (representing 8.25%), we compute $\sqrt[12]{1.0825} \approx 1.006628$, and therefore charge 0.6628% interest per month. In this way, each \$100 of debt will amass \$8.25 of compounded interest in a year. Notice that we use the Math.pow method from Java's libraries.

Finally, we consider the new implementation of the charge method provided for the PredatoryCreditCard class (lines 21–27). This definition *overrides* the inherited method. Yet, our implementation of the new method relies on a call to the inherited method, with syntax **super**.charge(price) at line 22. The return value of that call designates whether the charge was successful. We examine that return value to decide whether to assess a fee, and in either case return that boolean to the caller, so that the new version of charge maintains a similar outward interface as the original.

2.2.2   Polymorphism and Dynamic Dispatch

The word ***polymorphism*** literally means "many forms." In the context of object-oriented design, it refers to the ability of a reference variable to take different forms. Consider, for example, the declaration of a variable having CreditCard as its type:

    CreditCard card;

Because this is a reference variable, the statement declares the new variable, which does not yet refer to any card instance. While we have already seen that we can assign it to a newly constructed instance of the CreditCard class, Java also allows us to assign that variable to refer to an instance of the PredatoryCreditCard subclass. That is, we can do the following:

    CreditCard card = **new** PredatoryCreditCard(...);   // parameters omitted

This is a demonstration of what is known as the ***Liskov Substitution Principle***, which states that a variable (or parameter) with a declared type can be assigned an instance from any direct or indirect subclass of that type. Informally, this is a manifestation of the "is a" relationship modeled by inheritance, as a predatory credit card is a credit card (but a credit card is not necessarily predatory).

We say that the variable, card, is ***polymorphic***; it may take one of many forms, depending on the specific class of the object to which it refers. Because card has been declared with type CreditCard, that variable may only be used to call methods that are declared as part of the CreditCard definition. So we can call card.makePayment(50) and card.charge(100), but a compilation error would be reported for the call card.processMonth( ) because a CreditCard is not guaranteed to have such a behavior. (That call could be made if the variable were originally declared to have PredatoryCreditCard as its type.)

An interesting (and important) issue is how Java handles a call such as card.charge(100) when the variable card has a declared type of CreditCard. Recall that the object referenced by card might be an instance of the CreditCard class or an instance of the PredatoryCreditCard class, and that there are distinct implementations of the charge method: CreditCard.charge and PredatoryCreditCard.charge. Java uses a process known as ***dynamic dispatch***, deciding at runtime to call the version of the method that is most specific to the *actual* type of the referenced object (not the declared type). So, if the object is a PredatoryCreditCard instance, it will execute the PredatoryCreditCard.charge method, even if the reference variable has a declared type of CreditCard.

Java also provides an **instanceof** operator that tests, at runtime, whether an instance satisfies as a particular type. For example, the evaluation of the boolean condition, (card **instanceof** PredatoryCreditCard), produces **true** if the object currently referenced by the variable card belongs to the PredatoryCreditCard class, or any further subclass of that class. (See Section 2.5.1 for further discusion.)

2.2.3 Inheritance Hierarchies

Although a subclass may not inherit from multiple superclasses in Java, a superclass may have many subclasses. In fact, it is quite common in Java to develop complex inheritance hierarchies to maximize the reusability of code.

As a second example of the use of inheritance, we develop a hierarchy of classes for iterating numeric progressions. A numeric progression is a sequence of numbers, where each number depends on one or more of the previous numbers. For example, an *arithmetic progression* determines the next number by adding a fixed constant to the previous value, and a *geometric progression* determines the next number by multiplying the previous value by a fixed constant. In general, a progression requires a first value, and a way of identifying a new value based on one or more previous values.

Our hierarchy stems from a general base class that we name Progression. This class produces the progression of whole numbers: 0, 1, 2, ... More importantly, this class has been designed so that it can easily be specialized by other progression types, producing a hierarchy given in Figure 2.5.

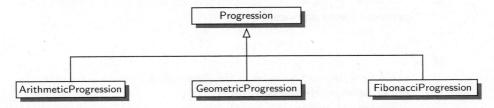

Figure 2.5: An overview of our hierarchy of progression classes.

Our implementation of the basic Progression class is provided in Code Fragment 2.2. This class has a single field, named current. It defines two constructors, one accepting an arbitrary starting value for the progression and the other using 0 as the default value. The remainder of the class includes three methods:

nextValue( ): A public method that returns the next value of the progression, implicitly advancing the value each time.

advance( ): A protected method that is responsible for advancing the value of current in the progression.

printProgression(n): A public utility that advances the progression n times while displaying each value.

Our decision to factor out the protected advance( ) method, which is called during the execution of nextValue( ), is to minimize the burden on subclasses, which are solely responsible for overriding the advance method to update the current field.

```
 1   /** Generates a simple progression. By default: 0, 1, 2, ... */
 2   public class Progression {
 3
 4     // instance variable
 5     protected long current;
 6
 7     /** Constructs a progression starting at zero. */
 8     public Progression( ) { this(0); }
 9
10     /** Constructs a progression with given start value. */
11     public Progression(long start) { current = start; }
12
13     /** Returns the next value of the progression. */
14     public long nextValue( ) {
15       long answer = current;
16       advance( );       // this protected call is responsible for advancing the current value
17       return answer;
18     }
19
20     /** Advances the current value to the next value of the progression. */
21     protected void advance( ) {
22       current++;
23     }
24
25     /** Prints the next n values of the progression, separated by spaces. */
26     public void printProgression(int n) {
27       System.out.print(nextValue( ));                  // print first value without leading space
28       for (int j=1; j < n; j++)
29         System.out.print(" " + nextValue( )); // print leading space before others
30       System.out.println( );                            // end the line
31     }
32   }
```

Code Fragment 2.2: General numeric progression class.

The body of the nextValue method temporarily records the current value of the progression, which will soon be returned, and then calls the protected advance method in order to update the value in preparation for a subsequent call.

The implementation of the advance method in our Progression class simply increments the current value. This method is the one that will be overridden by our specialized subclasses in order to alter the progression of numbers.

In the remainder of this section, we present three subclasses of the Progression class—ArithmeticProgression, GeometricProgression, and FibonacciProgression–which respectively produce arithmetic, geometric, and Fibonacci progressions.

An Arithmetic Progression Class

Our first example of a specialized progression is an arithmetic progression. While the default progression increases its value by one in each step, an arithmetic progression adds a fixed constant to one term of the progression to produce the next. For example, using an increment of 4 for an arithmetic progression that starts at 0 results in the sequence $0, 4, 8, 12, \ldots$.

Code Fragment 2.3 presents our implementation of an ArithmeticProgression class, which relies on Progression as its base class. We include three constructor forms, with the most general (at lines 12–15) accepting an increment value and a start value, such that ArithmeticProgression(4, 2) produces the sequence $2, 6, 10, 14, \ldots$. The body of that constructor invokes the superclass constructor, with syntax **super**(start), to initialize current to the given start value, and then it initializes the increment field introduced by this subclass.

For convenience, we offer two additional constructors, so that the default progression produces $0, 1, 2, 3, \ldots$, and a one-parameter constructor produces an arithmetic progression with a given increment value (but a default starting value of 0).

Finally (and most importantly), we override the protected advance method so that the given increment is added to each successive value of the progression.

```
1  public class ArithmeticProgression extends Progression {
2
3    protected long increment;
4
5    /** Constructs progression 0, 1, 2, ... */
6    public ArithmeticProgression() { this(1, 0); }        // start at 0 with increment of 1
7
8    /** Constructs progression 0, stepsize, 2*stepsize, ... */
9    public ArithmeticProgression(long stepsize) { this(stepsize, 0); }      // start at 0
10
11   /** Constructs arithmetic progression with arbitrary start and increment. */
12   public ArithmeticProgression(long stepsize, long start) {
13     super(start);
14     increment = stepsize;
15   }
16
17   /** Adds the arithmetic increment to the current value. */
18   protected void advance() {
19     current += increment;
20   }
21 }
```

Code Fragment 2.3: Class for arithmetic progressions, which inherits from the general progression class shown in Code Fragment 2.2.

A Geometric Progression Class

Our second example of a specialized progression is a geometric progression, in which each value is produced by multiplying the preceding value by a fixed constant, known as the *base* of the geometric progression. The starting point of a geometric progression is traditionally 1, rather than 0, because multiplying 0 by any factor results in 0. As an example, a geometric progression with base 2, starting at value 1, produces the sequence $1, 2, 4, 8, 16, \ldots$.

Code Fragment 2.4 presents our implementation of a GeometricProgression class. It is quite similar to the ArithmeticProgression class in terms of the programming techniques used. In particular, it introduces one new field (the base of the geometric progression), provides three forms of a constructor for convenience, and overrides the protected advance method so that the current value of the progression is multiplied by the base at each step.

In the case of a geometric progression, we have chosen to have the default (zero-parameter) constructor use a starting value of 1 and a base of 2 so that it produces the progression $1, 2, 4, 8, \ldots$. The one-parameter version of the constructor accepts an arbitrary base and uses 1 as the starting value, thus GeometricProgression(3) produces the sequence $1, 3, 9, 27, \ldots$. Finally, we offer a two-parameter version accepting both a base and start value, such that GeometricProgression(3,2) produces the sequence $2, 6, 18, 54, \ldots$.

```
 1  public class GeometricProgression extends Progression {
 2
 3    protected long base;
 4
 5    /** Constructs progression 1, 2, 4, 8, 16, ... */
 6    public GeometricProgression( ) { this(2, 1); }              // start at 1 with base of 2
 7
 8    /** Constructs progression 1, b, b^2, b^3, b^4, ... for base b. */
 9    public GeometricProgression(long b) { this(b, 1); }                    // start at 1
10
11    /** Constructs geometric progression with arbitrary base and start. */
12    public GeometricProgression(long b, long start) {
13      super(start);
14      base = b;
15    }
16
17    /** Multiplies the current value by the geometric base. */
18    protected void advance( ) {
19      current *= base;                           // multiply current by the geometric base
20    }
21  }
```

Code Fragment 2.4: Class for geometric progressions.

A Fibonacci Progression Class

As our final example, we demonstrate how to use our progression framework to produce a ***Fibonacci progression***. Each value of a Fibonacci series is the sum of the two most recent values. To begin the series, the first two values are conventionally 0 and 1, leading to the Fibonacci series $0, 1, 1, 2, 3, 5, 8, \ldots$. More generally, such a series can be generated from any two starting values. For example, if we start with values 4 and 6, the series proceeds as $4, 6, 10, 16, 26, 42, \ldots$.

Code Fragment 2.5 presents an implementation of the FibonacciProgression class. This class is markedly different from those for the arithmetic and geometric progressions because we cannot determine the next value of a Fibonacci series solely from the current one. We must maintain knowledge of the two most recent values. Our FibonacciProgression class introduces a new member, named prev, to store the value that proceeded the current one (which is stored in the inherited current field).

However, the question arises as to how to initialize the previous value in the constructor, when provided with the desired first and second values as parameters. The first should be stored as current so that it is reported by the first call to nextValue( ). Within that method call, an assignment will set the new current value (which will be the second value reported) equal to the first value plus the "previous." By initializing the previous value to (second − first), the initial advancement will set the new current value to first + (second − first) = second, as desired.

```
1  public class FibonacciProgression extends Progression {
2
3    protected long prev;
4
5    /** Constructs traditional Fibonacci, starting 0, 1, 1, 2, 3, ... */
6    public FibonacciProgression( ) { this(0, 1); }
7
8    /** Constructs generalized Fibonacci, with give first and second values. */
9    public FibonacciProgression(long first, long second) {
10     super(first);
11     prev = second − first;        // fictitious value preceding the first
12   }
13
14   /** Replaces (prev,current) with (current, current+prev). */
15   protected void advance( ) {
16     long temp = prev;
17     prev = current;
18     current += temp;
19   }
20 }
```

Code Fragment 2.5: Class for the Fibonacci progression.

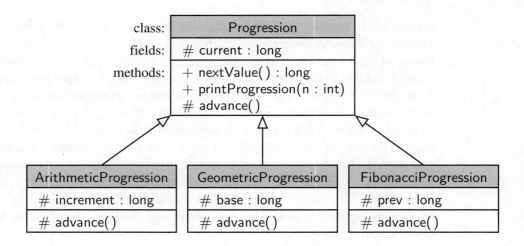

Figure 2.6: Detailed inheritance diagram for class Progression and its subclasses.

As a summary, Figure 2.6 presents a more detailed version of our inheritance design than was originally given in Figure 2.5. Notice that each of these classes introduces an additional field that allows it to properly implement the advance() method in an appropriate manner for its progression.

Testing Our Progression Hierarchy

To complete our example, we define a class TestProgression, shown in Code Fragment 2.6, which performs a simple test of each of the three classes. In this class, variable prog is polymorphic during the execution of the main method, since it references objects of class ArithmeticProgression, GeometricProgression, and FibonacciProgression in turn. When the main method of the TestProgression class is invoked by the Java runtime system, the output shown in Code Fragment 2.7 is produced.

The example presented in this section is admittedly simple, but it provides an illustration of an inheritance hierarchy in Java. As an interesting aside, we consider how quickly the numbers grow in the three progressions, and how long it would be before the long integers used for computations overflow. With the default increment of one, an arithmetic progression would not overflow for 2^{63} steps (that is approximately 10 billion billions). In contrast, a geometric progression with base $b = 3$ will overflow a long integer after 40 iterations, as $3^{40} > 2^{63}$. Likewise, the 94th Fibonacci number is greater than 2^{63}; hence, the Fibonacci progression will overflow a long integer after 94 iterations.

```
 1  /** Test program for the progression hierarchy. */
 2  public class TestProgression {
 3    public static void main(String[ ] args) {
 4      Progression prog;
 5      // test ArithmeticProgression
 6      System.out.print("Arithmetic progression with default increment: ");
 7      prog = new ArithmeticProgression( );
 8      prog.printProgression(10);
 9      System.out.print("Arithmetic progression with increment 5: ");
10      prog = new ArithmeticProgression(5);
11      prog.printProgression(10);
12      System.out.print("Arithmetic progression with start 2: ");
13      prog = new ArithmeticProgression(5, 2);
14      prog.printProgression(10);
15      // test GeometricProgression
16      System.out.print("Geometric progression with default base: ");
17      prog = new GeometricProgression( );
18      prog.printProgression(10);
19      System.out.print("Geometric progression with base 3: ");
20      prog = new GeometricProgression(3);
21      prog.printProgression(10);
22      // test FibonacciProgression
23      System.out.print("Fibonacci progression with default start values: ");
24      prog = new FibonacciProgression( );
25      prog.printProgression(10);
26      System.out.print("Fibonacci progression with start values 4 and 6: ");
27      prog = new FibonacciProgression(4, 6);
28      prog.printProgression(8);
29    }
30  }
```

Code Fragment 2.6: Program for testing the progression classes.

Arithmetic progression with default increment: 0 1 2 3 4 5 6 7 8 9
Arithmetic progression with increment 5: 0 5 10 15 20 25 30 35 40 45
Arithmetic progression with start 2: 2 7 12 17 22 27 32 37 42 47
Geometric progression with default base: 1 2 4 8 16 32 64 128 256 512
Geometric progression with base 3: 1 3 9 27 81 243 729 2187 6561 19683
Fibonacci progression with default start values: 0 1 1 2 3 5 8 13 21 34
Fibonacci progression with start values 4 and 6: 4 6 10 16 26 42 68 110

Code Fragment 2.7: Output of the TestProgression program of Code Fragment 2.6.

2.3   Interfaces and Abstract Classes

In order for two objects to interact, they must "know" about the various messages that each will accept, that is, the methods each object supports. To enforce this "knowledge," the object-oriented design paradigm asks that classes specify the **application programming interface** (API), or simply **interface**, that their objects present to other objects. In the **ADT-based** approach (see Section 2.1.2) to data structures followed in this book, an interface defining an ADT is specified as a type definition and a collection of methods for this type, with the arguments for each method being of specified types. This specification is, in turn, enforced by the compiler or runtime system, which requires that the types of parameters that are actually passed to methods rigidly conform with the type specified in the interface. This requirement is known as **strong typing**. Having to define interfaces and then having those definitions enforced by strong typing admittedly places a burden on the programmer, but this burden is offset by the rewards it provides, for it enforces the encapsulation principle and often catches programming errors that would otherwise go unnoticed.

2.3.1   Interfaces in Java

The main structural element in Java that enforces an API is an **interface**. An interface is a collection of method declarations with no data and no bodies. That is, the methods of an interface are always empty; they are simply method signatures. Interfaces do not have constructors and they cannot be directly instantiated.

When a class implements an interface, it must implement all of the methods declared in the interface. In this way, interfaces enforce requirements that an implementing class has methods with certain specified signatures.

Suppose, for example, that we want to create an inventory of antiques we own, categorized as objects of various types and with various properties. We might, for instance, wish to identify some of our objects as sellable, in which case they could implement the Sellable interface shown in Code Fragment 2.8.

We can then define a concrete class, Photograph, shown in Code Fragment 2.9, that implements the Sellable interface, indicating that we would be willing to sell any of our Photograph objects. This class defines an object that implements each of the methods of the Sellable interface, as required. In addition, it adds a method, isColor, which is specialized for Photograph objects.

Another kind of object in our collection might be something we could transport. For such objects, we define the interface shown in Code Fragment 2.10.

```
1   /** Interface for objects that can be sold. */
2   public interface Sellable {
3
4     /** Returns a description of the object. */
5     public String description( );
6
7     /** Returns the list price in cents. */
8     public int listPrice( );
9
10    /** Returns the lowest price in cents we will accept. */
11    public int lowestPrice( );
12  }
```

Code Fragment 2.8: Interface Sellable.

```
1   /** Class for photographs that can be sold. */
2   public class Photograph implements Sellable {
3     private String descript;                          // description of this photo
4     private int price;                                // the price we are setting
5     private boolean color;                            // true if photo is in color
6
7     public Photograph(String desc, int p, boolean c) {   // constructor
8       descript = desc;
9       price = p;
10      color = c;
11    }
12
13    public String description( ) { return descript; }
14    public int listPrice( ) { return price; }
15    public int lowestPrice( ) { return price/2; }
16    public boolean isColor( ) { return color; }
17  }
```

Code Fragment 2.9: Class Photograph implementing the Sellable interface.

```
1   /** Interface for objects that can be transported. */
2   public interface Transportable {
3     /** Returns the weight in grams. */
4     public int weight( );
5     /** Returns whether the object is hazardous. */
6     public boolean isHazardous( );
7   }
```

Code Fragment 2.10: Interface Transportable.

We could then define the class BoxedItem, shown in Code Fragment 2.11, for miscellaneous antiques that we can sell, pack, and ship. Thus, the class BoxedItem implements the methods of the Sellable interface and the Transportable interface, while also adding specialized methods to set an insured value for a boxed shipment and to set the dimensions of a box for shipment.

```
1   /** Class for objects that can be sold, packed, and shipped. */
2   public class BoxedItem implements Sellable, Transportable {
3     private String descript;        // description of this item
4     private int price;              // list price in cents
5     private int weight;             // weight in grams
6     private boolean haz;            // true if object is hazardous
7     private int height=0;           // box height in centimeters
8     private int width=0;            // box width in centimeters
9     private int depth=0;            // box depth in centimeters
10    /** Constructor */
11    public BoxedItem(String desc, int p, int w, boolean h) {
12      descript = desc;
13      price = p;
14      weight = w;
15      haz = h;
16    }
17    public String description() { return descript; }
18    public int listPrice() { return price; }
19    public int lowestPrice() { return price/2;      }
20    public int weight() { return weight; }
21    public boolean isHazardous() { return haz; }
22    public int insuredValue() { return price*2; }
23    public void setBox(int h, int w, int d) {
24      height = h;
25      width = w;
26      depth = d;
27    }
28  }
```

Code Fragment 2.11: Class BoxedItem.

The class BoxedItem shows another feature of classes and interfaces in Java, as well—that a class can implement multiple interfaces (even though it may only extend one other class). This allows us a great deal of flexibility when defining classes that should conform to multiple APIs.

2.3.2 Multiple Inheritance for Interfaces

The ability of extending from more than one type is known as ***multiple inheritance***. In Java, multiple inheritance is allowed for interfaces but not for classes. The reason for this rule is that interfaces do not define fields or method bodies, yet classes typically do. Thus, if Java were to allow multiple inheritance for classes, there could be a confusion if a class tried to extend from two classes that contained fields with the same name or methods with the same signatures. Since there is no such confusion for interfaces, and there are times when multiple inheritance of interfaces is useful, Java allows interfaces to use multiple inheritance.

One use for multiple inheritance of interfaces is to approximate a multiple inheritance technique called the ***mixin***. Unlike Java, some object-oriented languages, such as Smalltalk and C++, allow multiple inheritance of concrete classes, not just interfaces. In such languages, it is common to define classes, called ***mixin*** classes, that are never intended to be created as stand-alone objects, but are instead meant to provide additional functionality to existing classes. Such inheritance is not allowed in Java, however, so programmers must approximate it with interfaces. In particular, we can use multiple inheritance of interfaces as a mechanism for "mixing" the methods from two or more unrelated interfaces to define an interface that combines their functionality, possibly adding more methods of its own. Returning to our example of the antique objects, we could define an interface for insurable items as follows:

```
public interface Insurable extends Sellable, Transportable {
    /** Returns insured value in cents */
    public int insuredValue( );
}
```

This interface combines the methods of the Transportable interface with the methods of the Sellable interface, and adds an extra method, insuredValue. Such an interface could allow us to define the BoxedItem alternately as follows:

```
public class BoxedItem2 implements Insurable {

    // ... same code as class BoxedItem
}
```

In this case, note that the method insuredValue is not optional, whereas it was optional in the declaration of BoxedItem given previously.

Java interfaces that approximate the mixin include java.lang.Cloneable, which adds a copy feature to a class; java.lang.Comparable, which adds a comparability feature to a class (imposing a natural order on its instances); and java.util.Observer, which adds an update feature to a class that wishes to be notified when certain "observable" objects change state.

2.3.3 Abstract Classes

In Java, an ***abstract class*** serves a role somewhat between that of a traditional class and that of an interface. Like an interface, an abstract class may define signatures for one or more methods without providing an implementation of those method bodies; such methods are known as ***abstract methods***. However, unlike an interface, an abstract class may define one or more fields and any number of methods with implementation (so-called ***concrete methods***). An abstract class may also extend another class and be extended by further subclasses.

As is the case with interfaces, an abstract class may not be instantiated, that is, no object can be created directly from an abstract class. In a sense, it remains an incomplete class. A subclass of an abstract class must provide an implementation for the abstract methods of its superclass, or else remain abstract. To distinguish from abstract classes, we will refer to nonabstract classes as ***concrete classes***.

In comparing the use of interfaces and abstract classes, it is clear that abstract classes are more powerful, as they can provide some concrete functionality. However, the use of abstract classes in Java is limited to ***single inheritance***, so a class may have at most one superclass, whether concrete or abstract (see Section 2.3.2).

We will take great advantage of abstract classes in our study of data structures, as they support greater reusability of code (one of our object-oriented design goals from Section 2.1.1). The commonality between a family of classes can be placed within an abstract class, which serves as a superclass to multiple concrete classes. In this way, the concrete subclasses need only implement the additional functionality that differentiates themselves from each other.

As a tangible example, we reconsider the progression hierarchy introduced in Section 2.2.3. Although we did not formally declare the Progression base class as abstract in that presentation, it would have been a reasonable design to have done so. We did not intend for users to directly create instances of the Progression class; in fact, the sequence that it produces is simply a special case of an arithmetic progression with increment one. The primary purpose of the Progression class is to provide common functionality to all three subclasses: the declaration and initialization of the current field, and the concrete implementations of the nextValue and printProgression methods.

The most important aspect in specializing that class was in overriding the protected advance method. Although we gave a simple implementation of that method within the Progression class to increment the current value, none of our three subclasses rely on that behavior. On the next page, we demonstrate the mechanics of abstract classes in Java by redesigning the progression base class into an AbstractProgression base class. In that design, we leave the advance method as truly abstract, leaving the burden of an implementation to the various subclasses.

Mechanics of Abstract Classes in Java

In Code Fragment 2.12, we give a Java implementation of a new abstract base class for our progression hierarchy. We name the new class AbstractProgression rather than Progression, only to differentiate it in our discussion. The definitions are almost identical; there are only two key differences that we highlight. The first is the use of the **abstract** modifier on line 1, when declaring the class. (See Section 1.2.2 for a discussion of class modifiers.)

As with our original class, the new class declares the current field and provides constructors that initialize it. Although our abstract class cannot be instantiated, the constructors can be invoked within the subclass constructors using the **super** keyword. (We do just that, within all three of our progression subclasses.)

The new class has the same concrete implementations of methods nextValue and printProgression as did our original. However, we explicitly define the advance method with the **abstract** modifier at line 19, and without any method body.

Even though we have not implemented the advance method as part of the AbstractProgression class, it is legal to call it from within the body of nextValue. This is an example of an object-oriented design pattern known as the ***template method pattern***, in which an abstract base class provides a concrete behavior that relies upon calls to other abstract behaviors. Once a subclass provides definitions for the missing abstract behaviors, the inherited concrete behavior is well defined.

```java
 1  public abstract class AbstractProgression {
 2    protected long current;
 3    public AbstractProgression( ) { this(0); }
 4    public AbstractProgression(long start) { current = start; }
 5
 6    public long nextValue( ) {                    // this is a concrete method
 7      long answer = current;
 8      advance( );      // this protected call is responsible for advancing the current value
 9      return answer;
10    }
11
12    public void printProgression(int n) {        // this is a concrete method
13      System.out.print(nextValue( ));            // print first value without leading space
14      for (int j=1; j < n; j++)
15        System.out.print(" " + nextValue( ));    // print leading space before others
16      System.out.println( );                     // end the line
17    }
18
19    protected abstract void advance( );          // notice the lack of a method body
20  }
```

Code Fragment 2.12: An abstract version of the progression base class, originally given in Code Fragment 2.2. (We omit documentation for brevity.)

2.4   Exceptions

Exceptions are unexpected events that occur during the execution of a program. An exception might result due to an unavailable resource, unexpected input from a user, or simply a logical error on the part of the programmer. In Java, exceptions are objects that can be ***thrown*** by code that encounters an unexpected situation, or by the Java Virtual Machine, for example, if running out of memory. An exception may also be ***caught*** by a surrounding block of code that "handles" the problem in an appropriate fashion. If uncaught, an exception causes the virtual machine to stop executing the program and to report an appropriate message to the console. In this section, we discuss common exception types in Java, as well as the syntax for throwing and catch exceptions within user-defined blocks of code.

2.4.1   Catching Exceptions

If an exception occurs and is not handled, then the Java runtime system will termi-nate the program after printing an appropriate message together with a trace of the runtime stack. The stack trace shows the series of nested method calls that were active at the time the exception occurred, as in the following example:

```
Exception in thread "main" java.lang.NullPointerException
   at java.util.ArrayList.toArray(ArrayList.java:358)
   at net.datastructures.HashChainMap.bucketGet(HashChainMap.java:35)
   at net.datastructures.AbstractHashMap.get(AbstractHashMap.java:62)
   at dsaj.design.Demonstration.main(Demonstration.java:12)
```

However, before a program is terminated, each method on the stack trace has an opportunity to ***catch*** the exception. Starting with the most deeply nested method in which the exception occurs, each method may either catch the exception, or allow it to pass through to the method that called it. For example, in the above stack trace, the ArrayList.java method had the first opportunity to catch the exception. Since it did not do so, the exception was passed upward to the HashChainMap.bucketGet method, which in turn ignored the exception, causing it to pass further upward to the AbstractHashMap.get method. The final opportunity to catch the exception was in the Demonstration.main method, but since it did not do so, the program terminated with the above diagnostic message.

The general methodology for handling exceptions is a ***try-catch*** construct in which a guarded fragment of code that might throw an exception is executed. If it throws an exception, then that exception is ***caught*** by having the flow of control jump to a predefined **catch** block that contains the code to analyze the exception and apply an appropriate resolution. If no exception occurs in the guarded code, all catch blocks are ignored.

A typical syntax for a *try-catch statement* in Java is as follows:

```
try {
    guardedBody
} catch (exceptionType₁ variable₁) {
    remedyBody₁
} catch (exceptionType₂ variable₂) {
    remedyBody₂
} ...
    ...
```

Each *exceptionType$_i$* is the type of some exception, and each *variable$_i$* is a valid Java variable name.

The Java runtime environment begins performing a try-catch statement such as this by executing the block of statements, *guardedBody*. If no exceptions are generated during this execution, the flow of control continues with the first statement beyond the last line of the entire try-catch statement.

If, on the other hand, the block, guardedBody, generates an exception at some point, the execution of that block immediate terminates and execution jumps to the **catch** block whose *exceptionType* most closely matches the exception thrown (if any). The *variable* for this catch statement references the exception object itself, which can be used in the block of the matching **catch** statement. Once execution of that **catch** block completes, control flow continues with the first statement beyond the entire try-catch construct.

If an exception occurs during the execution of the block, guardedBody, that does not match any of the exception types declared in the catch statements, that exception is rethrown in the surrounding context.

There are several possible reactions when an exception is caught. One possibility is to print out an error message and terminate the program. There are also some interesting cases in which the best way to handle an exception is to quietly catch and ignore it (this can be done by having an empty body as a **catch** block). Another legitimate way of handling exceptions is to create and throw another exception, possibly one that specifies the exceptional condition more precisely.

We note briefly that try-catch statements in Java support a few advanced techniques that we will not use in this book. There can be an optional **finally** clause with a body that will be executed whether or not an exception happens in the original guarded body; this can be useful, for example, to close a file before proceeding onward. Java SE 7 introduced a new syntax known as a "try with resource" that provides even more advanced cleanup techniques for resources such as open files that must be properly cleaned up. Also as of Java SE 7, each catch statement can designate multiple exception types that it handles; previously, a separate clause would be needed for each one, even if the same remedy were applied in each case.

```
1  public static void main(String[ ] args) {
2    int n = DEFAULT;
3    try {
4      n = Integer.parseInt(args[0]);
5      if (n <= 0) {
6        System.out.println("n must be positive. Using default.");
7        n = DEFAULT;
8      }
9    } catch (ArrayIndexOutOfBoundsException e) {
10     System.out.println("No argument specified for n. Using default.");
11   } catch (NumberFormatException e) {
12     System.out.println("Invalid integer argument. Using default.");
13   }
14 }
```

Code Fragment 2.13: A demonstration of catching an exception.

As a tangible example of a try-catch statement, we consider the simple application presented in Code Fragment 2.13. This main method attempts to interpret the first command-line argument as a positive integer. (Command-line arguments were introduced on page 16.)

The statement at risk of throwing an exception, at line 4, is the command n = Integer.parseInt(args[0]). That command may fail for one of two reasons. First, the attempt to access args[0] will fail if the user did not specify any arguments, and thus, the array args is empty. An ArrayIndexOutOfBoundsException will be thrown in that case (and caught by us at line 9). The second potential exception is when calling the Integer.parseInt method. That command succeeds so long as the parameter is a string that is a legitimate integer representation, such as "2013". Of course, since a command-line argument can be any string, the user might provide an invalid integer representation, in which case the parseInt method throws a NumberFormatException (caught by us at line 11).

A final condition we wish to enforce is that the integer specified by the user is positive. To test this property, we rely on a traditional conditional statement (lines 5–8). However, notice that we have placed that conditional statement within the primary body of the try-catch statement. That conditional statement will only be evaluated if the command at line 4 succeeded without exception; had an exception occurred at line 4, the primary try block is terminated, and control proceeds directly to the exception handling for the appropriate catch statement.

As an aside, if we had been willing to use the same error message for the two exceptional cases, we can use a single catch clause with the following syntax:

```
} catch (ArrayIndexOutOfBoundsException | NumberFormatException e) {
  System.out.println("Using default value for n.");
}
```

2.4.2 Throwing Exceptions

Exceptions originate when a piece of Java code finds some sort of problem during execution and *throws* an exception object. This is done by using the **throw** keyword followed by an instance of the exception type to be thrown. It is often convenient to instantiate an exception object at the time the exception has to be thrown. Thus, a **throw** statement is typically written as follows:

> **throw new** *exceptionType*(*parameters*);

where *exceptionType* is the type of the exception and the parameters are sent to that type's constructor; most exception types offer a version of a constructor that accepts an error message string as a parameter.

As an example, the following method takes an integer parameter, which it expects to be positive. If a negative integer is sent, an IllegalArgumentException is thrown.

```
public void ensurePositive(int n) {
  if (n < 0)
    throw new IllegalArgumentException("That's not positive!");
  // ...
}
```

The execution of a **throw** statement immediately terminates the body of a method.

The Throws Clause

When a method is declared, it is possible to explicitly declare, as part of its signature, the possibility that a particular exception type may be thrown during a call to that method. It does not matter whether the exception is directly from a **throw** statement in that method body, or propagated upward from a secondary method call made from within the body.

The syntax for declaring possible exceptions in a method signature relies on the keyword **throws** (not to be confused with an actual **throw** statement). For example, the parseInt method of the Integer class has the following formal signature:

> **public static int** parseInt(String s) **throws** NumberFormatException;

The designation "**throws** NumberFormatException" warns users about the possibility of an exceptional case, so that they might be better prepared to handle an exception that may arise. If one of many exception types may possibly be thrown, all such types can be listed, separated with commas. Alternatively, it may be possible to list an appropriate superclass that encompasses all specific exceptions that may be thrown.

The use of a **throws** clause in a method signature does not take away the responsibility of properly documenting all possible exceptions through the use of the @throws tag within a javadoc comment (see Section 1.9.4). The type and reasons for any potential exceptions should always be properly declared in the documentation for a method.

In contrast, the use of the **throws** clause in a method signature is optional for many types of exceptions. For example, the documentation for the nextInt( ) method of the Scanner class makes clear that three different exception types may arise:

- An IllegalStateException, if the scanner has been closed
- A NoSuchElementException, if the scanner is active, but there is currently no token available for input
- An InputMismatchException, if the next available token does not represent an integer

However, no potential exceptions are formally declared within the method signature; they are only noted in the documentation.

To better understand the functional purpose of the **throws** declaration in a method signature, it is helpful to know more about the way Java organizes its hierarchy of exception types.

2.4.3   Java's Exception Hierarchy

Java defines a rich inheritance hierarchy of all objects that are deemed Throwable. We show a small portion of this hierarchy in Figure 2.7. The hierarchy is intentionally divided into two subclasses: Error and Exception. *Errors* are typically thrown only by the Java Virtual Machine and designate the most serious situations that are unlikely to be recoverable, such as when the virtual machine is asked to execute a corrupt class file, or when the system runs out of memory. In contrast, *exceptions* designate situations in which a running program might reasonably be able to recover, for example, when unable to open a data file.

Checked and Unchecked Exceptions

Java provides further refinement by declaring the RuntimeException class as an important subclass of Exception. All subtypes of RuntimeException in Java are officially treated as *unchecked exceptions*, and any exception type that is not part of the RuntimeException is a *checked exception*.

The intent of the design is that runtime exceptions occur entirely due to mistakes in programming logic, such as using a bad index with an array, or sending an inappropriate value as a parameter to a method. While such programming errors

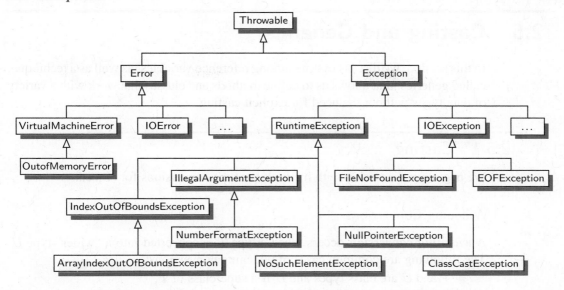

Figure 2.7: A small portion of Java's hierarchy of Throwable types.

will certainly occur as part of the software development process, they should presumably be resolved before software reaches production quality. Therefore, it is not in the interest of efficiency to explicitly check for each such mistake at runtime, and thus these are designated as "unchecked" exceptions.

In contrast, other exceptions occur because of conditions that cannot easily be detected until a program is executing, such as an unavailable file or a failed network connection. Those are typically designated as "checked" exceptions in Java (and thus, not a subtype of RuntimeException).

The designation between checked and unchecked exceptions plays a significant role in the syntax of the language. In particular, ***all checked exceptions that might propagate upward from a method must be explicitly declared in its signature.***

A consequence is that if one method calls a second method declaring checked exceptions, then the call to that second method must either be guarded within a try-catch statement, or else the calling method must itself declare the checked exceptions in its signature, since there is risk that such an exception might propagate upward from the calling method.

Defining New Exception Types

In this book, we will rely entirely on existing RuntimeException types to designate various requirements on the use of our data structures. However, some libraries define new classes of exceptions to describe more specific conditions. Specialized exceptions should inherit either from the Exception class (if checked), from the RuntimeException class (if unchecked), or from an existing Exception subtype that is more relevant.

2.5 Casting and Generics

In this section, we discuss casting among reference variables, as well as a technique, called generics, that allows us to define methods and classes that work with a variety of data types without the need for explicit casting.

2.5.1 Casting

We begin our discussion with methods for type conversions for objects.

Widening Conversions

A *widening conversion* occurs when a type T is converted into a "wider" type U. The following are common cases of widening conversions:
- T and U are class types and U is a superclass of T.
- T and U are interface types and U is a superinterface of T.
- T is a class that implements interface U.

Widening conversions are automatically performed to store the result of an expression into a variable, without the need for an explicit cast. Thus, we can directly assign the result of an expression of type T into a variable v of type U when the conversion from T to U is a widening conversion. When discussing polymorphism on page 68, we gave the following example of an implicit widening cast, assigning an instance of the narrower PredatoryCreditCard class to a variable of the wider CreditCard type:

```
CreditCard card = new PredatoryCreditCard(...);   // parameters omitted
```

The correctness of a widening conversion can be checked by the compiler and its validity does not require testing by the Java runtime environment during program execution.

Narrowing Conversions

A *narrowing conversion* occurs when a type T is converted into a "narrower" type S. The following are common cases of narrowing conversions:
- T and S are class types and S is a subclass of T.
- T and S are interface types and S is a subinterface of T.
- T is an interface implemented by class S.

In general, a narrowing conversion of reference types requires an explicit cast. Also, the correctness of a narrowing conversion may not be verifiable by the compiler. Thus, its validity should be tested by the Java runtime environment during program execution.

The example code fragment below shows how to use a cast to perform a narrowing conversion from type PredatoryCreditCard to type CreditCard.

```
CreditCard card = new PredatoryCreditCard(...);        // widening
PredatoryCreditCard pc = (PredatoryCreditCard) card;   // narrowing
```

Although variable card happens to reference an instance of a PredatoryCreditCard, the variable has declared type, CreditCard. Therefore, the assignment pc = card is a narrowing conversion and requires an explicit cast that will be evaluated at runtime (as not all cards are predatory).

Casting Exceptions

In Java, we can cast an object reference o of type T into a type S, provided the object o is referring to is actually of type S. If, on the other hand, object o is not also of type S, then attempting to cast o to type S will throw an exception called ClassCastException. We illustrate this rule in the following code fragment, using Java's Number abstract class, which is a superclass of both Integer and Double.

```
Number n;
Integer i;
n = new Integer(3);
i = (Integer) n;              // This is legal
n = new Double(3.1415);
i = (Integer) n;              // This is illegal
```

To avoid problems such as this and to avoid peppering our code with try-catch blocks every time we perform a cast, Java provides a way to make sure an object cast will be correct. Namely, it provides an operator, **instanceof**, that allows us to test whether an object variable is referring to an object that belongs to a particular type. The syntax for this operator is *objectReference* **instanceof** *referenceType*, where *objectReference* is an expression that evaluates to an object reference and *referenceType* is the name of some existing class, interface, or enum (Section 1.3). If *objectReference* is indeed an instance satisfying *referenceType*, then the operator returns **true**; otherwise, it returns **false**. Thus, we can avoid a ClassCastException from being thrown in the code fragment above by modifying it as follows:

```
Number n;
Integer i;
n = new Integer(3);
if (n instanceof Integer)
    i = (Integer) n;          // This is legal
n = new Double(3.1415);
if (n instanceof Integer)
    i = (Integer) n;          // This will not be attempted
```

Casting with Interfaces

Interfaces allow us to enforce that objects implement certain methods, but using interface variables with concrete objects sometimes requires casting. Suppose we declare a Person interface as shown in Code Fragment 2.14. Note that method equals of the Person interface takes one parameter of type Person. Thus, we can pass an object of any class implementing the Person interface to this method.

```
1   public interface Person {
2     public boolean equals(Person other);         // is this the same person?
3     public String getName( );                     // get this person's name
4     public int getAge( );                         // get this person's age
5   }
```

Code Fragment 2.14: Interface Person.

In Code Fragment 2.15, we show a class, Student, that implements Person. Because the parameter to equals is a Person, the implementation must not assume that it is necessarily of type Student. Instead, it first uses the **instanceof** operator at line 15, returning **false** if the argument is not a student (since it surely is not the student in question). Only after verifying that the parameter is a student, is it explicitly cast to a Student, at which point its id field can be accessed.

```
1    public class Student implements Person {
2      String id;
3      String name;
4      int age;
5      public Student(String i, String n, int a) {      // simple constructor
6        id = i;
7        name = n;
8        age = a;
9      }
10     protected int studyHours( ) { return age/2;}     // just a guess
11     public String getID( ) { return id;}             // ID of the student
12     public String getName( ) { return name; }        // from Person interface
13     public int getAge( ) { return age; }             // from Person interface
14     public boolean equals(Person other) {            // from Person interface
15       if (!(other instanceof Student)) return false; // cannot possibly be equal
16       Student s = (Student) other;                   // explicit cast now safe
17       return id.equals(s.id);                        // compare IDs
18     }
19     public String toString( ) {                      // for printing
20       return "Student(ID:" + id + ", Name:" + name + ", Age:" + age + ")";
21     }
22   }
```

Code Fragment 2.15: Class Student implementing interface Person.

2.5.2 Generics

Java includes support for writing *generic* classes and methods that can operate on a variety of data types while often avoiding the need for explicit casts. The generics framework allows us to define a class in terms of a set of *formal type parameters*, which can then be used as the declared type for variables, parameters, and return values within the class definition. Those formal type parameters are later specified when using the generic class as a type elsewhere in a program.

To better motivate the use of generics, we consider a simple case study. Often, we wish to treat a pair of related values as a single object, for example, so that the pair can be returned from a method. A solution is to define a new class whose instances store both values. This is our first example of an object-oriented design pattern known as the *composition design pattern*. If we know, for example, that we want a pair to store a string and a floating-point number, perhaps to store a stock ticker label and a price, we could easily design a custom class for that purpose. However, for another purpose, we might want to store a pair that consists of a Book object and an integer that represents a quantity. The goal of generic programming is to be able to write a single class that can represent all such pairs.

The generics framework was not a part of the original Java language; it was added as part of Java SE 5. Prior to that, generic programming was implemented by relying heavily on Java's Object class, which is the universal supertype of all objects (including the wrapper types corresponding to primitives). In that "classic" style, a generic pair might be implemented as shown in Code Fragment 2.16.

```
1  public class ObjectPair {
2    Object first;
3    Object second;
4    public ObjectPair(Object a, Object b) {        // constructor
5      first = a;
6      second = b;
7    }
8    public Object getFirst( ) { return first; }
9    public Object getSecond( ) { return second;}
10 }
```

Code Fragment 2.16: Representing a generic pair of objects using a classic style.

An ObjectPair instance stores the two objects that are sent to the constructor, and provides individual accessors for each component of the pair. With this definition, a pair can be declared and instantiated with the following command:

    ObjectPair bid = new ObjectPair("ORCL", 32.07);

This instantiation is legal because the parameters to the constructor undergo widening conversions. The first parameter, "ORCL", is a String, and thus also an Object.

The second parameter is a **double**, but it is automatically boxed into a Double, which then qualifies as an Object. (For the record, this is not quite the "classic" style, as automatic boxing was not introduced until Java SE 5.)

The drawback of the classic approach involves use of the accessors, both of which formally return an Object reference. Even if we know that the first object is a string in our application, we cannot legally make the following assignment:

```
String stock = bid.getFirst( );          // illegal; compile error
```

This represents a narrowing conversion from the declared return type of Object to the variable of type String. Instead, an explicit cast is required, as follows:

```
String stock = (String) bid.getFirst( ); // narrowing cast: Object to String
```

With the classic style for generics, code became rampant with such explicit casts.

Using Java's Generics Framework

With Java's generics framework, we can implement a pair class using formal type parameters to represent the two relevant types in our composition. An implementation using this framework is given in Code Fragment 2.17.

```
1  public class Pair<A,B> {
2    A first;
3    B second;
4    public Pair(A a, B b) {                    // constructor
5      first = a;
6      second = b;
7    }
8    public A getFirst( ) { return first; }
9    public B getSecond( ) { return second;}
10 }
```

Code Fragment 2.17: Representing a pair of objects with generic type parameters.

Angle brackets are used at line 1 to enclose the sequence of formal type parameters. Although any valid identifier can be used for a formal type parameter, single-letter uppercase names are conventionally used (in this example, A and B). We may then use these type parameters within the body of the class definition. For example, we declare instance variable, first, to have type A; we similarly use A as the declared type for the first constructor parameter and for the return type of method, getFirst.

When subsequently declaring a variable with such a parameterize type, we must explicitly specify *actual type parameters* that will take the place of the generic formal type parameters. For example, to declare a variable that is a pair holding a stock-ticker string and a price, we write the following:

```
Pair<String,Double> bid;
```

Effectively, we have stated that we wish to have String serve in place of type A, and Double serve in place of type B for the pair known as bid. The actual types for generic programming must be object types, which is why we use the wrapper class Double instead of the primitive type **double**. (Fortunately, the automatic boxing and unboxing will work in our favor.)

We can subsequently instantiate the generic class using the following syntax:

bid = **new** Pair<>("ORCL", 32.07);   // rely on type inference

After the **new** operator, we provide the name of the generic class, then an empty set of angle brackets (known as the "diamond"), and finally the parameters to the constructor. An instance of the generic class is created, with the actual types for the formal type parameters determined based upon the original declaration of the variable to which it is assigned (bid in this example). This process is known as *type inference*, and was introduced to the generics framework in Java SE 7.

It is also possible to use a style that existed prior to Java SE 7, in which the generic type parameters are explicitly specified between angle brackets during instantiation. Using that style, our previous example would be implemented as:

bid = **new** Pair<String,Double>("ORCL", 32.07);   // give explicit types

However, it is important that one of the two above styles be used. If angle brackets are entirely omitted, as in the following example,

bid = **new** Pair("ORCL", 32.07);   // classic style

this reverts to the classic style, with Object automatically used for all generic type parameters, and resulting in a compiler warning when assigning to a variable with more specific types.

Although the syntax for the declaration and instantiation of objects using the generics framework is slightly more cluttered than the classic style, the advantage is that there is no longer any need for explicit narrowing casts from Object to a more specific type. Continuing with our example, since bid was declared with actual type parameters <String,Double>, the return type of the getFirst() method is String, and the return type of the getSecond() method is Double. Unlike the classic style, we can make the following assignments without any explicit casting (although there is still an automatic unboxing of the Double):

```
String stock = bid.getFirst();
double price = bid.getSecond();
```

Generics and Arrays

There is an important caveat related to generic types and the use of arrays. Although Java allows the declaration of an array storing a parameterized type, it does not technically allow the instantiation of new arrays involving those types. Fortunately, it allows an array defined with a parameterized type to be initialized with a newly created, nonparametric array, which can then be cast to the parameterized type. Even so, this latter mechanism causes the Java compiler to issue a warning, because it is not 100% type-safe.

We will see this issue arise in two ways:

- Code outside a generic class may wish to declare an array storing instances of the generic class with actual type parameters.

- A generic class may wish to declare an array storing objects that belong to one of the formal parameter types.

As an example of the first use case, we continue with our stock market example and presume that we would like to keep an array of Pair<String,Double> objects. Such an array can be declared with a parameterized type, but it must be instantiated with an *unparameterized* type and then cast back to the parameterized type. We demonstrate this usage in the following:

```
Pair<String,Double>[ ] holdings;
holdings = new Pair<String,Double>[25];     // illegal; compile error
holdings = new Pair[25];     // correct, but warning about unchecked cast
holdings[0] = new Pair<>("ORCL", 32.07);   // valid element assignment
```

As an example of the second use case, assume that we want to create a generic Portfolio class that can store a fixed number of generic entries in an array. If the class uses <T> as a parameterized type, it can declare an array of type T[ ], but it cannot directly instantiate such an array. Instead, a common approach is to instantiate an array of type Object[ ], and then make a narrowing cast to type T[ ], as shown in the following:

```
public class Portfolio<T> {
  T[ ] data;
  public Portfolio(int capacity) {
    data = new T[capacity];              // illegal; compiler error
    data = (T[ ]) new Object[capacity];   // legal, but compiler warning
  }
  public T get(int index) { return data[index]; }
  public void set(int index, T element) { data[index] = element; }
}
```

Generic Methods

The generics framework allows us to define generic versions of individual methods (as opposed to generic versions of entire classes). To do so, we include a generic formal type declaration among the method modifiers.

For example, we show below a nonparametric GenericDemo class with a parameterized static method that can reverse an array containing elements of any object type.

```java
public class GenericDemo {
    public static <T> void reverse(T[ ] data) {
        int low = 0, high = data.length − 1;
        while (low < high) {                    // swap data[low] and data[high]
            T temp = data[low];
            data[low++] = data[high];           // post-increment of low
            data[high−−] = temp;                // post-decrement of high
        }
    }
}
```

Note the use of the <T> modifier to declare the method to be generic, and the use of the type T within the method body, when declaring the local variable, temp.

The method can be called using the syntax, GenericDemo.reverse(books), with type inference determining the generic type, assuming books is an array of some object type. (This generic method cannot be applied to primitive arrays, because autoboxing does not apply to entire arrays.)

As an aside, we note that we could have implemented a reverse method equally well using a classic style, acting upon an Object[ ] array.

Bounded Generic Types

By default, when using a type name such as T in a generic class or method, a user can specify any object type as the actual type of the generic. A formal parameter type can be restricted by using the **extends** keyword followed by a class or interface. In that case, only a type that satisfies the stated condition is allowed to substitute for the parameter. The advantage of such a bounded type is that it becomes possible to call any methods that are guaranteed by the stated bound.

As an example, we might declare a generic ShoppingCart that could only be instantiated with a type that satisfied the Sellable interface (from Code Fragment 2.8 on page 77). Such a class would be declared beginning with the line:

```java
public class ShoppingCart<T extends Sellable> {
```

Within that class definition, we would then be allowed to call methods such as description( ) and lowestPrice( ) on any instances of type T.

2.6　Nested Classes

Java allows a class definition to be *nested* inside the definition of another class. The main use for nesting classes is when defining a class that is strongly affili- ated with another class. This can help increase encapsulation and reduce undesired name conflicts. Nested classes are a valuable technique when implementing data structures, as an instance of a nested use can be used to represent a small portion of a larger data structure, or an auxiliary class that helps navigate a primary data structure. We will use nested classes in many implementations within this book.

To demonstrate the mechanics of a nested class, we consider a new Transaction class to support logging of transactions associated with a credit card. That new class definition can be nested within the CreditCard class using a style as follows:

```java
public class CreditCard {
    private static class Transaction { /* details omitted */ }

    // instance variable for a CreditCard
    Transaction[ ] history;          // keep log of all transactions for this card
}
```

The containing class is known as the *outer class*. The *nested class* is formally a member of the outer class, and its fully qualified name is *OuterName.NestedName*. For example, with the above definition the nested class is CreditCard.Transaction, although we may refer to it simply as Transaction from within the CreditCard class.

Much like packages (see Section 1.8), the use of nested classes can help re- duce name collisions, as it is perfectly acceptable to have another class named Transaction nested within some other class (or as a self-standing class).

A nested class has an independent set of modifiers from the outer class. Visi- bility modifiers (e.g., **public**, **private**) effect whether the nested class definition is accessible beyond the outer class definition. For example, a **private** nested class can be used by the outer class, but by no other classes.

A nested class can also be designated as either **static** or (by default) nonstatic, with significant consequences. A **static** nested class is most like a traditional class; its instances have no association with any specific instance of the outer class.

A nonstatic nested class is more commonly known as an *inner class* in Java. An instance of an inner class can only be created from within a nonstatic method of the outer class, and that inner instance becomes associated with the outer instance that creates it. Each instance of an inner class implicitly stores a reference to its associated outer instance, accessible from within the inner class methods using the syntax *OuterName*.**this** (as opposed to **this**, which refers to the inner instance). The inner instance also has private access to all members of its associated outer instance, and can rely on the formal type parameters of the outer class, if generic.

2.7 Exercises

Reinforcement

R-2.1 Give three examples of life-critical software applications.

R-2.2 Give an example of a software application in which adaptability can mean the difference between a prolonged lifetime of sales and bankruptcy.

R-2.3 Describe a component from a text-editor GUI and the methods that it encapsulates.

R-2.4 Assume that we change the CreditCard class (see Code Fragment 1.5) so that instance variable balance has **private** visibility. Why is the following implementation of the PredatoryCreditCard.charge method flawed?

```java
public boolean charge(double price) {
    boolean isSuccess = super.charge(price);
    if (!isSuccess)
        charge(5);              // the penalty
    return isSuccess;
}
```

R-2.5 Assume that we change the CreditCard class (see Code Fragment 1.5) so that instance variable balance has **private** visibility. Why is the following implementation of the PredatoryCreditCard.charge method flawed?

```java
public boolean charge(double price) {
    boolean isSuccess = super.charge(price);
    if (!isSuccess)
        super.charge(5);        // the penalty
    return isSuccess;
}
```

R-2.6 Give a short fragment of Java code that uses the progression classes from Section 2.2.3 to find the eighth value of a Fibonacci progression that starts with 2 and 2 as its first two values.

R-2.7 If we choose an increment of 128, how many calls to the nextValue method from the ArithmeticProgression class of Section 2.2.3 can we make before we cause a long-integer overflow?

R-2.8 Can two interfaces mutually extend each other? Why or why not?

R-2.9 What are some potential efficiency disadvantages of having very deep inheritance trees, that is, a large set of classes, A, B, C, and so on, such that B extends A, C extends B, D extends C, etc.?

R-2.10 What are some potential efficiency disadvantages of having very shallow inheritance trees, that is, a large set of classes, A, B, C, and so on, such that all of these classes extend a single class, Z?

R-2.11 Consider the following code fragment, taken from some package:

```java
public class Maryland extends State {
  Maryland() { /* null constructor */ }
  public void printMe() { System.out.println("Read it."); }
  public static void main(String[ ] args) {
    Region east = new State();
    State md = new Maryland();
    Object obj = new Place();
    Place usa = new Region();
    md.printMe();
    east.printMe();
    ((Place) obj).printMe();
    obj = md;
    ((Maryland) obj).printMe();
    obj = usa;
    ((Place) obj).printMe();
    usa = md;
    ((Place) usa).printMe();
  }
}
class State extends Region {
  State() { /* null constructor */ }
  public void printMe() { System.out.println("Ship it."); }
}
class Region extends Place {
  Region() { /* null constructor */ }
  public void printMe() { System.out.println("Box it."); }
}
class Place extends Object {
  Place() { /* null constructor */ }
  public void printMe() { System.out.println("Buy it."); }
}
```

What is the output from calling the main( ) method of the Maryland class?

R-2.12 Draw a class inheritance diagram for the following set of classes:

- Class Goat extends Object and adds an instance variable tail and methods milk( ) and jump( ).
- Class Pig extends Object and adds an instance variable nose and methods eat(food) and wallow( ).
- Class Horse extends Object and adds instance variables height and color, and methods run( ) and jump( ).
- Class Racer extends Horse and adds a method race( ).
- Class Equestrian extends Horse and adds instance variable weight and is-Trained, and methods trot( ) and isTrained( ).

R-2.13 Consider the inheritance of classes from Exercise R-2.12, and let *d* be an object variable of type Horse. If *d* refers to an actual object of type Equestrian, can it be cast to the class Racer? Why or why not?

R-2.14 Give an example of a Java code fragment that performs an array reference that is possibly out of bounds, and if it is out of bounds, the program catches that exception and prints the following error message:
"Don't try buffer overflow attacks in Java!"

R-2.15 If the parameter to the makePayment method of the CreditCard class (see Code Fragment 1.5) were a negative number, that would have the effect of *raising* the balance on the account. Revise the implementation so that it throws an IllegalArgumentException if a negative amount is sent as a parameter.

Creativity

C-2.16 Suppose you are on the design team for a new e-book reader. What are the primary classes and methods that the Java software for your reader will need? You should include an inheritance diagram for this code, but you don't need to write any actual code. Your software architecture should at least include ways for customers to buy new books, view their list of purchased books, and read their purchased books.

C-2.17 Most modern Java compilers have optimizers that can detect simple cases when it is logically impossible for certain statements in a program to ever be executed. In such cases, the compiler warns the programmer about the useless code. Write a short Java method that contains code for which it is provably impossible for that code to ever be executed, yet the Java compiler does not detect this fact.

C-2.18 The PredatoryCreditCard class provides a processMonth( ) method that models the completion of a monthly cycle. Modify the class so that once a customer has made ten calls to charge during a month, each additional call to that method in the current month results in an additional $1 surcharge.

C-2.19 Modify the PredatoryCreditCard class so that a customer is assigned a minimum monthly payment, as a percentage of the balance, and so that a late fee is assessed if the customer does not subsequently pay that minimum amount before the next monthly cycle.

C-2.20 Assume that we change the CreditCard class (see Code Fragment 1.5) so that instance variable balance has **private** visibility, but a new **protected** method is added, with signature setBalance(newBalance). Show how to properly implement the method PredatoryCreditCard.processMonth( ) in this setting.

C-2.21 Write a program that consists of three classes, *A*, *B*, and *C*, such that *B* extends *A* and that *C* extends *B*. Each class should define an instance variable named "*x*" (that is, each has its own variable named *x*). Describe a way for a method in *C* to access and set *A*'s version of *x* to a given value, without changing *B* or *C*'s version.

C-2.22 Explain why the Java dynamic dispatch algorithm, which looks for the method to invoke for a call obj.foo( ), will never get into an infinite loop.

C-2.23 Modify the advance method of the FibonacciProgression class so as to avoid use of any temporary variable.

C-2.24 Write a Java class that extends the Progression class so that each value in the progression is the absolute value of the difference between the previous two values. You should include a default constructor that starts with 2 and 200 as the first two values and a parametric constructor that starts with a specified pair of numbers as the first two values.

C-2.25 Redesign the Progression class to be abstract and generic, producing a sequence of values of generic type T, and supporting a single constructor that accepts an initial value. Make all corresponding modifications to the rest of the classes in our hierarchy so that they remain as nongeneric classes, while inheriting from the new generic Progression class.

C-2.26 Use a solution to Exercise C-2.25 to create a new progression class for which each value is the square root of the previous value, represented as a Double. You should include a default constructor that has $65,536$ as the first value and a parametric constructor that starts with a specified number as the first value.

C-2.27 Use a solution to Exercise C-2.25 to reimplement the FibonacciProgression subclass to rely on the BigInteger class, in order to avoid overflows all together.

C-2.28 Write a set of Java classes that can simulate an Internet application in which one party, Alice, is periodically creating a set of packets that she wants to send to Bob. An Internet process is continually checking if Alice has any packets to send, and if so, it delivers them to Bob's computer; Bob is periodically checking if his computer has a packet from Alice, and if so, he reads and deletes it.

C-2.29 Write a Java program that inputs a polynomial in standard algebraic notation and outputs the first derivative of that polynomial.

Projects

P-2.30 Write a Java program that inputs a document and then outputs a bar-chart plot of the frequencies of each alphabet character that appears within that document.

P-2.31 Write a Java program to simulate an ecosystem containing two types of creatures, *bears* and *fish*. The ecosystem consists of a river, which is modeled as a relatively large array. Each cell of the array should contain an Animal object, which can be a Bear object, a Fish object, or **null**. In each time step, based on a random process, each animal either attempts to move into an adjacent array cell or stay where it is. If two animals of the same type are about to collide in the same cell, then they stay where they are, but they create a new instance of that type of animal, which is placed in a random empty (i.e., previously **null**) cell in the array. If a bear and a fish collide, however, then the fish dies (i.e., it disappears). Use actual object creation, via the **new** operator, to model the creation of new objects, and provide a visualization of the array after each time step.

P-2.32 Write a simulator as in the previous project, but add a boolean gender field and a floating-point strength field to each Animal object. Now, if two animals of the same type try to collide, then they only create a new instance of that type of animal if they are of different genders. Otherwise, if two animals of the same type and gender try to collide, then only the one of larger strength survives.

P-2.33 Write a Java program that simulates a system that supports the functions of an e-book reader. You should include methods for users of your system to "buy" new books, view their list of purchased books, and read their purchased books. Your system should use actual books, which have expired copyrights and are available on the Internet, to populate your set of available books for users of your system to "purchase" and read.

P-2.34 Define a Polygon interface that has methods area( ) and perimeter( ). Then implement classes for Triangle, Quadrilateral, Pentagon, Hexagon, and Octagon, which implement this interface, with the obvious meanings for the area( ) and perimeter( ) methods. Also implement classes, IsoscelesTriangle, Equilateral-Triangle, Rectangle, and Square, which have the appropriate inheritance relationships. Finally, write a simple user interface, which allows users to create polygons of the various types, input their geometric dimensions, and then output their area and perimeter. For extra effort, allow users to input polygons by specifying their vertex coordinates and be able to test if two such polygons are similar.

P-2.35 Write a Java program that inputs a list of words, separated by whitespace, and outputs how many times each word appears in the list. You need not worry about efficiency at this point, however, as this topic is something that will be addressed later in this book.

P-2.36 Write a Java program that can "make change." Your program should take two numbers as input, one that is a monetary amount charged and the other that is a monetary amount given. It should then return the number of each kind of bill and coin to give back as change for the difference between the amount given and the amount charged. The values assigned to the bills and coins can be based on the monetary system of any current or former government. Try to design your program so that it returns the fewest number of bills and coins as possible.

Chapter Notes

For a broad overview of developments in computer science and engineering, we refer the reader to *The Computer Science and Engineering Handbook* [89]. For more information about the Therac-25 incident, please see the paper by Leveson and Turner [65].

The reader interested in studying object-oriented programming further is referred to the books by Booch [16], Budd [19], and Liskov and Guttag [67]. Liskov and Guttag also provide a nice discussion of abstract data types, as does the book chapter by Demurjian [28] in the *The Computer Science and Engineering Handbook* [89]. Design patterns are described in the book by Gamma *et al.* [37].

Chapter 3

Fundamental Data Structures

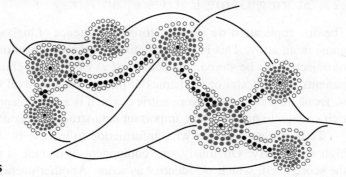

Contents

3.1 Using Arrays

In this section, we explore a few applications of arrays—the concrete data structures introduced in Section 1.3 that access their entries using integer indices.

3.1.1 Storing Game Entries in an Array

The first application we study is storing a sequence of high score entries for a video game in an array. This is representative of many applications in which a sequence of objects must be stored. We could just as easily have chosen to store records for patients in a hospital or the names of players on a football team. Nevertheless, let us focus on storing high score entries, which is a simple application that is already rich enough to present some important data-structuring concepts.

To begin, we consider what information to include in an object representing a high score entry. Obviously, one component to include is an integer representing the score itself, which we identify as score. Another useful thing to include is the name of the person earning this score, which we identify as name. We could go on from here, adding fields representing the date the score was earned or game statistics that led to that score. However, we omit such details to keep our example simple. A Java class, GameEntry, representing a game entry, is given in Code Fragment 3.1.

```
 1  public class GameEntry {
 2    private String name;                        // name of the person earning this score
 3    private int score;                          // the score value
 4    /** Constructs a game entry with given parameters.. */
 5    public GameEntry(String n, int s) {
 6      name = n;
 7      score = s;
 8    }
 9    /** Returns the name field. */
10    public String getName() { return name; }
11    /** Returns the score field. */
12    public int getScore() { return score; }
13    /** Returns a string representation of this entry. */
14    public String toString() {
15      return "(" + name + ", " + score + ")";
16    }
17  }
```

Code Fragment 3.1: Java code for a simple GameEntry class. Note that we include methods for returning the name and score for a game entry object, as well as a method for returning a string representation of this entry.

A Class for High Scores

To maintain a sequence of high scores, we develop a class named Scoreboard. A scoreboard is limited to a certain number of high scores that can be saved; once that limit is reached, a new score only qualifies for the scoreboard if it is strictly higher than the lowest "high score" on the board. The length of the desired scoreboard may depend on the game, perhaps 10, 50, or 500. Since that limit may vary, we allow it to be specified as a parameter to our Scoreboard constructor.

Internally, we will use an array named board to manage the GameEntry instances that represent the high scores. The array is allocated with the specified maximum capacity, but all entries are initially **null**. As entries are added, we will maintain them from highest to lowest score, starting at index 0 of the array. We illustrate a typical state of the data structure in Figure 3.1, and give Java code to construct such a data structure in Code Fragment 3.2.

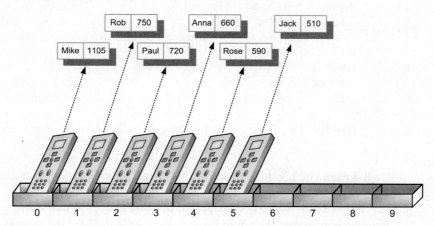

Figure 3.1: An illustration of an array of length ten storing references to six GameEntry objects in the cells with indices 0 to 5; the rest are **null** references.

```
1   /** Class for storing high scores in an array in nondecreasing order. */
2   public class Scoreboard {
3     private int numEntries = 0;            // number of actual entries
4     private GameEntry[ ] board;            // array of game entries (names & scores)
5     /** Constructs an empty scoreboard with the given capacity for storing entries. */
6     public Scoreboard(int capacity) {
7       board = new GameEntry[capacity];
8     }
...   // more methods will go here
36  }
```

Code Fragment 3.2: The beginning of a Scoreboard class for maintaining a set of scores as GameEntry objects. (Completed in Code Fragments 3.3 and 3.4.)

Adding an Entry

One of the most common updates we might want to make to a Scoreboard is to add a new entry. Keep in mind that not every entry will necessarily qualify as a high score. If the board is not yet full, any new entry will be retained. Once the board is full, a new entry is only retained if it is strictly better than one of the other scores, in particular, the last entry of the scoreboard, which is the lowest of the high scores.

Code Fragment 3.3 provides an implementation of an update method for the Scoreboard class that considers the addition of a new game entry.

```
 9   /** Attempt to add a new score to the collection (if it is high enough) */
10   public void add(GameEntry e) {
11     int newScore = e.getScore();
12     // is the new entry e really a high score?
13     if (numEntries < board.length || newScore > board[numEntries−1].getScore()) {
14       if (numEntries < board.length)              // no score drops from the board
15         numEntries++;                             // so overall number increases
16       // shift any lower scores rightward to make room for the new entry
17       int j = numEntries − 1;
18       while (j > 0 && board[j−1].getScore() < newScore) {
19         board[j] = board[j−1];                    // shift entry from j-1 to j
20         j−−;                                      // and decrement j
21       }
22       board[j] = e;                               // when done, add new entry
23     }
24   }
```

Code Fragment 3.3: Java code for inserting a GameEntry object into a Scoreboard.

When a new score is considered, the first goal is to determine whether it qualifies as a high score. This will be the case (see line 13) if the scoreboard is below its capacity, or if the new score is strictly higher than the lowest score on the board.

Once it has been determined that a new entry should be kept, there are two remaining tasks: (1) properly update the number of entries, and (2) place the new entry in the appropriate location, shifting entries with inferior scores as needed.

The first of these tasks is easily handled at lines 14 and 15, as the total number of entries can only be increased if the board is not yet at full capacity. (When full, the addition of a new entry will be counteracted by the removal of the entry with lowest score.)

The placement of the new entry is implemented by lines 17–22. Index j is initially set to numEntries − 1, which is the index at which the last GameEntry will reside after completing the operation. Either j is the correct index for the newest entry, or one or more immediately before it will have lesser scores. The while loop checks the compound condition, shifting entries rightward and decrementing j, as long as there is another entry at index $j − 1$ with a score less than the new score.

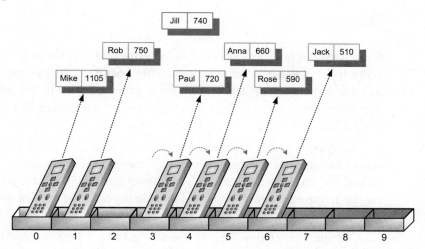

Figure 3.2: Preparing to add Jill's GameEntry object to the board array. In order to make room for the new reference, we have to shift any references to game entries with smaller scores than the new one to the right by one cell.

Figure 3.2 shows an example of the process, just after the shifting of existing entries, but before adding the new entry. When the loop completes, j will be the correct index for the new entry. Figure 3.3 shows the result of a complete operation, after the assignment of board[j] = e, accomplished by line 22 of the code.

In Exercise C-3.19, we explore how game entry addition might be simplified for the case when we don't need to preserve relative orders.

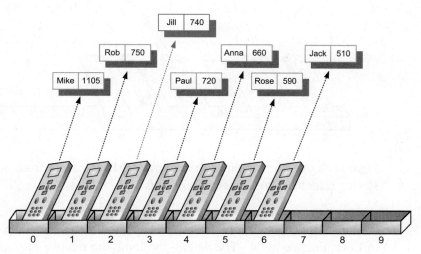

Figure 3.3: Adding a reference to Jill's GameEntry object to the board array. The reference can now be inserted at index 2, since we have shifted all references to GameEntry objects with scores less than the new one to the right.

Removing an Entry

Suppose some hot shot plays our video game and gets his or her name on our high score list, but we later learn that cheating occurred. In this case, we might want to have a method that lets us remove a game entry from the list of high scores. Therefore, let us consider how we might remove a reference to a GameEntry object from a Scoreboard.

We choose to add a method to the Scoreboard class, with signature remove(i), where i designates the current index of the entry that should be removed and returned. When a score is removed, any lower scores will be shifted upward, to fill in for the removed entry. If index i is outside the range of current entries, the method will throw an IndexOutOfBoundsException.

Our implementation for remove will involve a loop for shifting entries, much like our algorithm for addition, but in reverse. To remove the reference to the object at index i, we start at index i and move all the references at indices higher than i one cell to the left. (See Figure 3.4.)

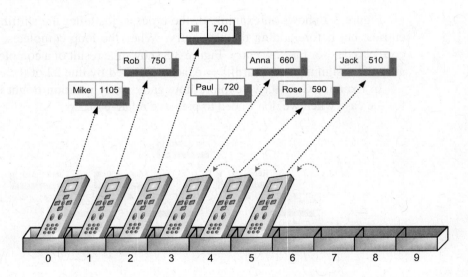

Figure 3.4: An illustration of the removal of Paul's score from index 3 of an array storing references to GameEntry objects.

Our implementation of the remove method for the Scoreboard class is given in Code Fragment 3.4. The details for doing the remove operation contain a few subtle points. The first is that, in order to remove and return the game entry (let's call it e) at index i in our array, we must first save e in a temporary variable. We will use this variable to return e when we are done removing it.

```
25    /** Remove and return the high score at index i. */
26    public GameEntry remove(int i) throws IndexOutOfBoundsException {
27      if (i < 0 || i >= numEntries)
28        throw new IndexOutOfBoundsException("Invalid index: " + i);
29      GameEntry temp = board[i];              // save the object to be removed
30      for (int j = i; j < numEntries − 1; j++)   // count up from i (not down)
31        board[j] = board[j+1];                // move one cell to the left
32      board[numEntries −1 ] = null;           // null out the old last score
33      numEntries−−;
34      return temp;                            // return the removed object
35    }
```

Code Fragment 3.4: Java code for performing the Scoreboard.remove operation.

The second subtle point is that, in moving references higher than i one cell to the left, we don't go all the way to the end of the array. First, we base our loop on the number of current entries, not the capacity of the array, because there is no reason for "shifting" a series of **null** references that may be at the end of the array. We also carefully define the loop condition, j < numEntries − 1, so that the last iteration of the loop assigns board[numEntries−2] = board[numEntries−1]. There is no entry to shift into cell board[numEntries−1], so we return that cell to **null** just after the loop. We conclude by returning a reference to the removed entry (which no longer has any reference pointing to it within the board array).

Conclusions

In the version of the Scoreboard class that is available online, we include an implementation of the toString( ) method, which allows us to display the contents of the current scoreboard, separated by commas. We also include a main method that performs a basic test of the class.

The methods for adding and removing objects in an array of high scores are simple. Nevertheless, they form the basis of techniques that are used repeatedly to build more sophisticated data structures. These other structures may be more general than the array structure above, of course, and often they will have a lot more operations that they can perform than just add and remove. But studying the concrete array data structure, as we are doing now, is a great starting point to understanding these other structures, since every data structure has to be implemented using concrete means.

In fact, later in this book, we will study a Java collections class, ArrayList, which is more general than the array structure we are studying here. The ArrayList has methods to operate on an underlying array; yet it also eliminates the error that occurs when adding an object to a full array by automatically copying the objects into a larger array when necessary. We will discuss the ArrayList class in far more detail in Section 7.2.

3.1.2 Sorting an Array

In the previous subsection, we considered an application for which we added an object to an array at a given position while shifting other elements so as to keep the previous order intact. In this section, we use a similar technique to solve the **sorting** problem, that is, starting with an unordered array of elements and rearranging them into nondecreasing order.

The Insertion-Sort Algorithm

We study several sorting algorithms in this book, most of which are described in Chapter 12. As a warm-up, in this section we describe a simple sorting algorithm known as **insertion-sort**. The algorithm proceeds by considering one element at a time, placing the element in the correct order relative to those before it. We start with the first element in the array, which is trivially sorted by itself. When considering the next element in the array, if it is smaller than the first, we swap them. Next we consider the third element in the array, swapping it leftward until it is in its proper order relative to the first two elements. We continue in this manner with the fourth element, the fifth, and so on, until the whole array is sorted. We can express the insertion-sort algorithm in pseudocode, as shown in Code Fragment 3.5.

Algorithm InsertionSort(A):
  Input: An array A of n comparable elements
  Output: The array A with elements rearranged in nondecreasing order
  for k from 1 to $n - 1$ **do**
    Insert $A[k]$ at its proper location within $A[0], A[1], \ldots, A[k]$.

Code Fragment 3.5: High-level description of the insertion-sort algorithm.

This is a simple, high-level description of insertion-sort. If we look back to Code Fragment 3.3 in Section 3.1.1, we see that the task of inserting a new entry into the list of high scores is almost identical to the task of inserting a newly considered element in insertion-sort (except that game scores were ordered from high to low). We provide a Java implementation of insertion-sort in Code Fragment 3.6, using an outer loop to consider each element in turn, and an inner loop that moves a newly considered element to its proper location relative to the (sorted) subarray of elements that are to its left. We illustrate an example run of the insertion-sort algorithm in Figure 3.5.

We note that if an array is already sorted, the inner loop of insertion-sort does only one comparison, determines that there is no swap needed, and returns back to the outer loop. Of course, we might have to do a lot more work than this if the input array is extremely out of order. In fact, we will have to do the most work if the input array is in decreasing order.

```
1    /** Insertion-sort of an array of characters into nondecreasing order */
2    public static void insertionSort(char[ ] data) {
3      int n = data.length;
4      for (int k = 1; k < n; k++) {             // begin with second character
5        char cur = data[k];                     // time to insert cur=data[k]
6        int j = k;                              // find correct index j for cur
7        while (j > 0 && data[j−1] > cur) {      // thus, data[j-1] must go after cur
8          data[j] = data[j−1];                  // slide data[j-1] rightward
9          j−−;                                  // and consider previous j for cur
10       }
11       data[j] = cur;                          // this is the proper place for cur
12     }
13   }
```

Code Fragment 3.6: Java code for performing insertion-sort on a character array.

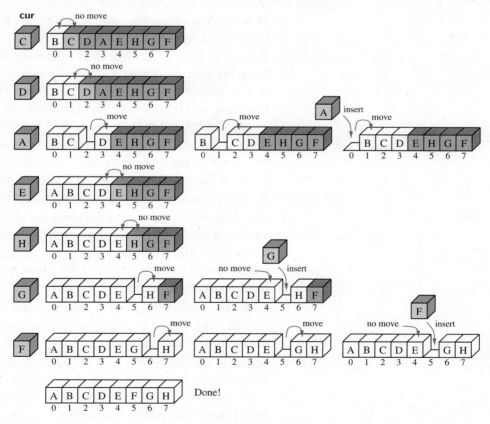

Figure 3.5: Execution of the insertion-sort algorithm on an array of eight characters. Each row corresponds to an iteration of the outer loop, and each copy of the sequence in a row corresponds to an iteration of the inner loop. The current element that is being inserted is highlighted in the array, and shown as the cur value.

3.1.3   java.util Methods for Arrays and Random Numbers

Because arrays are so important, Java provides a class, java.util.Arrays, with a number of built-in static methods for performing common tasks on arrays. Later in this book, we will describe the algorithms that several of these methods are based upon. For now, we provide an overview of the most commonly used methods of that class, as follows (more discussion is in Section 3.5.1):

equals(A, B): Returns true if and only if the array A and the array B are equal. Two arrays are considered equal if they have the same number of elements and every corresponding pair of elements in the two arrays are equal. That is, A and B have the same values in the same order.

fill(A, x): Stores value x in every cell of array A, provided the type of array A is defined so that it is allowed to store the value x.

copyOf(A, n): Returns an array of size n such that the first k elements of this array are copied from A, where $k = \min\{n, A.\text{length}\}$. If $n > A.\text{length}$, then the last $n - A.\text{length}$ elements in this array will be padded with default values, e.g., 0 for an array of **int** and **null** for an array of objects.

copyOfRange(A, s, t): Returns an array of size $t - s$ such that the elements of this array are copied in order from $A[s]$ to $A[t-1]$, where $s < t$, padded as with copyOf( ) if $t > A.\text{length}$.

toString(A): Returns a String representation of the array A, beginning with [, ending with], and with elements of A displayed separated by string ", ". The string representation of an element $A[i]$ is obtained using String.valueOf($A[i]$), which returns the string "null" for a **null** reference and otherwise calls $A[i]$.toString( ).

sort(A): Sorts the array A based on a natural ordering of its elements, which must be comparable. Sorting algorithms are the focus of Chapter 12.

binarySearch(A, x): Searches the *sorted* array A for value x, returning the index where it is found, or else the index of where it could be inserted while maintaining the sorted order. The binary-search algorithm is described in Section 5.1.3.

As static methods, these are invoked directly on the java.util.Arrays class, not on a particular instance of the class. For example, if data were an array, we could sort it with syntax, java.util.Arrays.sort(data), or with the shorter syntax Arrays.sort(data) if we first import the Arrays class (see Section 1.8).

PseudoRandom Number Generation

Another feature built into Java, which is often useful when testing programs dealing with arrays, is the ability to generate pseudorandom numbers, that is, numbers that appear to be random (but are not necessarily truly random). In particular, Java has a built-in class, java.util.Random, whose instances are ***pseudorandom number generators***, that is, objects that compute a sequence of numbers that are statistically random. These sequences are not actually random, however, in that it is possible to predict the next number in the sequence given the past list of numbers. Indeed, a popular pseudorandom number generator is to generate the next number, next, from the current number, cur, according to the formula (in Java syntax):

$$next = (a * cur + b) \% n;$$

where a, b, and n are appropriately chosen integers, and % is the modulus operator. Something along these lines is, in fact, the method used by java.util.Random objects, with $n = 2^{48}$. It turns out that such a sequence can be proven to be statistically uniform, which is usually good enough for most applications requiring random numbers, such as games. For applications, such as computer security settings, where unpredictable random sequences are needed, this kind of formula should not be used. Instead, ideally a sample from a source that is actually random should be used, such as radio static coming from outer space.

Since the next number in a pseudorandom generator is determined by the previous number(s), such a generator always needs a place to start, which is called its *seed*. The sequence of numbers generated for a given seed will always be the same. The seed for an instance of the java.util.Random class can be set in its constructor or with its setSeed( ) method.

One common trick to get a different sequence each time a program is run is to use a seed that will be different for each run. For example, we could use some timed input from a user or we could set the seed to the current time in milliseconds since January 1, 1970 (provided by method System.currentTimeMillis).

Methods of the java.util.Random class include the following:

nextBoolean( ): Returns the next pseudorandom **boolean** value.

nextDouble( ): Returns the next pseudorandom **double** value, between 0.0 and 1.0.

nextInt( ): Returns the next pseudorandom **int** value.

nextInt(n): Returns the next pseudorandom **int** value in the range from 0 up to but not including n.

setSeed(s): Sets the seed of this pseudorandom number generator to the **long** s.

An Illustrative Example

We provide a short (but complete) illustrative program in Code Fragment 3.7.

```
1  import java.util.Arrays;
2  import java.util.Random;
3  /** Program showing some array uses. */
4  public class ArrayTest {
5    public static void main(String[ ] args) {
6      int data[ ] = new int[10];
7      Random rand = new Random( );                 // a pseudo-random number generator
8      rand.setSeed(System.currentTimeMillis( ));        // use current time as a seed
9      // fill the data array with pseudo-random numbers from 0 to 99, inclusive
10     for (int i = 0; i < data.length; i++)
11       data[i] = rand.nextInt(100);                   // the next pseudo-random number
12     int[ ] orig = Arrays.copyOf(data, data.length); // make a copy of the data array
13     System.out.println("arrays equal before sort: "+Arrays.equals(data, orig));
14     Arrays.sort(data);                       // sorting the data array (orig is unchanged)
15     System.out.println("arrays equal after sort: " + Arrays.equals(data, orig));
16     System.out.println("orig = " + Arrays.toString(orig));
17     System.out.println("data = " + Arrays.toString(data));
18   }
19 }
```

Code Fragment 3.7: A simple test of some built-in methods in java.util.Arrays.

We show a sample output of this program below:

```
arrays equal before sort: true
arrays equal after sort: false
orig = [41, 38, 48, 12, 28, 46, 33, 19, 10, 58]
data = [10, 12, 19, 28, 33, 38, 41, 46, 48, 58]
```

In another run, we got the following output:

```
arrays equal before sort: true
arrays equal after sort: false
orig = [87, 49, 70, 2, 59, 37, 63, 37, 95, 1]
data = [1, 2, 37, 37, 49, 59, 63, 70, 87, 95]
```

By using a pseudorandom number generator to determine program values, we get a different input to our program each time we run it. This feature is, in fact, what makes pseudorandom number generators useful for testing code, particularly when dealing with arrays. Even so, we should not use random test runs as a replacement for reasoning about our code, as we might miss important special cases in test runs. Note, for example, that there is a slight chance that the orig and data arrays will be equal even after data is sorted, namely, if orig is already ordered. The odds of this occurring are less than 1 in 3 million, so it's unlikely to happen during even a few thousand test runs; however, we need to reason that this is possible.

3.1.4 Simple Cryptography with Character Arrays

An important application of character arrays and strings is *cryptography*, which is the science of secret messages. This field involves the process of *encryption*, in which a message, called the *plaintext*, is converted into a scrambled message, called the *ciphertext*. Likewise, cryptography studies corresponding ways of performing *decryption*, turning a ciphertext back into its original plaintext.

Arguably the earliest encryption scheme is the *Caesar cipher*, which is named after Julius Caesar, who used this scheme to protect important military messages. (All of Caesar's messages were written in Latin, of course, which already makes them unreadable for most of us!) The Caesar cipher is a simple way to obscure a message written in a language that forms words with an alphabet.

The Caesar cipher involves replacing each letter in a message with the letter that is a certain number of letters after it in the alphabet. So, in an English message, we might replace each A with D, each B with E, each C with F, and so on, if shifting by three characters. We continue this approach all the way up to W, which is replaced with Z. Then, we let the substitution pattern *wrap around*, so that we replace X with A, Y with B, and Z with C.

Converting Between Strings and Character Arrays

Given that strings are immutable, we cannot directly edit an instance to encrypt it. Instead, our goal will be to generate a new string. A convenient technique for performing string transformations is to create an equivalent array of characters, edit the array, and then reassemble a (new) string based on the array.

Java has support for conversions from strings to character arrays and vice versa. Given a string S, we can create a new character array matching S by using the method, S.toCharArray( ). For example, if s="bird", the method returns the character array A={'b', 'i', 'r', 'd'}. Conversely, there is a form of the String constructor that accepts a character array as a parameter. For example, with character array A={'b', 'i', 'r', 'd'}, the syntax **new** String(A) produces "bird".

Using Character Arrays as Replacement Codes

If we were to number our letters like array indices, so that A is 0, B is 1, C is 2, then we can represent the replacement rule as a character array, encoder, such that A is mapped to encoder[0], B is mapped to encoder[1], and so on. Then, in order to find a replacement for a character in our Caesar cipher, we need to map the characters from A to Z to the respective numbers from 0 to 25. Fortunately, we can rely on the fact that characters are represented in Unicode by integer code points, and the code points for the uppercase letters of the Latin alphabet are consecutive (for simplicity, we restrict our encryption to uppercase letters).

Java allows us to "subtract" two characters from each other, with an integer result equal to their separation distance in the encoding. Given a variable c that is known to be an uppercase letter, the Java computation, $j = $ c $-$ 'A' produces the desired index j. As a sanity check, if character c is 'A', then $j = 0$. When c is 'B', the difference is 1. In general, the integer j that results from such a calculation can be used as an index into our precomputed encoder array, as illustrated in Figure 3.6.

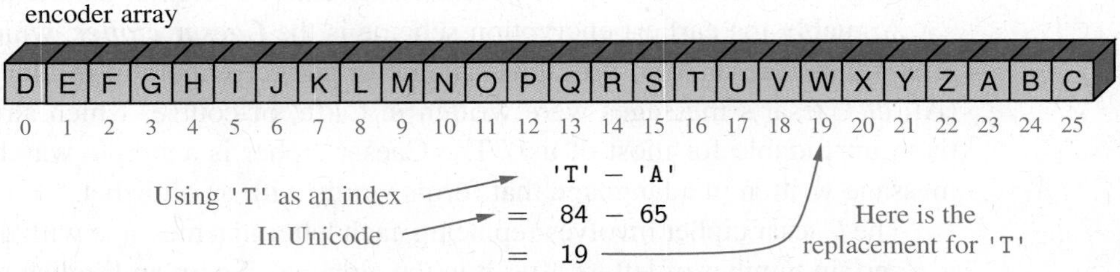

Figure 3.6: Illustrating the use of uppercase characters as indices, in this case to perform the replacement rule for Caesar cipher encryption.

The process of ***decrypting*** the message can be implemented by simply using a different character array to represent the replacement rule—one that effectively shifts characters in the opposite direction.

In Code Fragment 3.8, we present a Java class that performs the Caesar cipher with an arbitrary rotational shift. The constructor for the class builds the encoder and decoder translation arrays for the given rotation. We rely heavily on modular arithmetic, as a Caesar cipher with a rotation of r encodes the letter having index k with the letter having index $(k + r)$ mod 26, where mod is the ***modulo*** operator, which returns the remainder after performing an integer division. This operator is denoted with % in Java, and it is exactly the operator we need to easily perform the wraparound at the end of the alphabet, for 26 mod 26 is 0, 27 mod 26 is 1, and 28 mod 26 is 2. The decoder array for the Caesar cipher is just the opposite— we replace each letter with the one r places before it, with wraparound; to avoid subtleties involving negative numbers and the modulus operator, we will replace the letter having code k with the letter having code $(k - r + 26)$ mod 26.

With the encoder and decoder arrays in hand, the encryption and decryption algorithms are essentially the same, and so we perform both by means of a private utility method named transform. This method converts a string to a character array, performs the translation diagrammed in Figure 3.6 for any uppercase alphabet symbols, and finally returns a new string, constructed from the updated array.

The main method of the class, as a simple test, produces the following output:

```
Encryption code = DEFGHIJKLMNOPQRSTUVWXYZABC
Decryption code = XYZABCDEFGHIJKLMNOPQRSTUVW
Secret:  WKH HDJOH LV LQ SODB; PHHW DW MRH'V.
Message: THE EAGLE IS IN PLAY; MEET AT JOE'S.
```

```java
 1  /** Class for doing encryption and decryption using the Caesar Cipher. */
 2  public class CaesarCipher {
 3    protected char[ ] encoder = new char[26];          // Encryption array
 4    protected char[ ] decoder = new char[26];          // Decryption array
 5    /** Constructor that initializes the encryption and decryption arrays */
 6    public CaesarCipher(int rotation) {
 7      for (int k=0; k < 26; k++) {
 8        encoder[k] = (char) ('A' + (k + rotation) % 26);
 9        decoder[k] = (char) ('A' + (k − rotation + 26) % 26);
10      }
11    }
12    /** Returns String representing encrypted message. */
13    public String encrypt(String message) {
14      return transform(message, encoder);              // use encoder array
15    }
16    /** Returns decrypted message given encrypted secret. */
17    public String decrypt(String secret) {
18      return transform(secret, decoder);               // use decoder array
19    }
20    /** Returns transformation of original String using given code. */
21    private String transform(String original, char[ ] code) {
22      char[ ] msg = original.toCharArray( );
23      for (int k=0; k < msg.length; k++)
24        if (Character.isUpperCase(msg[k])) {           // we have a letter to change
25          int j = msg[k] − 'A';                        // will be value from 0 to 25
26          msg[k] = code[j];                            // replace the character
27        }
28      return new String(msg);
29    }
30    /** Simple main method for testing the Caesar cipher */
31    public static void main(String[ ] args) {
32      CaesarCipher cipher = new CaesarCipher(3);
33      System.out.println("Encryption code = " + new String(cipher.encoder));
34      System.out.println("Decryption code = " + new String(cipher.decoder));
35      String message = "THE EAGLE IS IN PLAY; MEET AT JOE'S.";
36      String coded = cipher.encrypt(message);
37      System.out.println("Secret:   " + coded);
38      String answer = cipher.decrypt(coded);
39      System.out.println("Message: " + answer);        // should be plaintext again
40    }
41  }
```

Code Fragment 3.8: A complete Java class for performing the Caesar cipher.

3.1.5   Two-Dimensional Arrays and Positional Games

Many computer games, be they strategy games, simulation games, or first-person conflict games, involve objects that reside in a two-dimensional space. Software for such **positional games** needs a way of representing objects in a two-dimensional space. A natural way to do this is with a **two-dimensional array**, where we use two indices, say *i* and *j*, to refer to the cells in the array. The first index usually refers to a row number and the second to a column number. Given such an array, we can maintain two-dimensional game boards and perform other kinds of computations involving data stored in rows and columns.

Arrays in Java are one-dimensional; we use a single index to access each cell of an array. Nevertheless, there is a way we can define two-dimensional arrays in Java—we can create a two-dimensional array as an array of arrays. That is, we can define a two-dimensional array to be an array with each of its cells being another array. Such a two-dimensional array is sometimes also called a **matrix**. In Java, we may declare a two-dimensional array as follows: .

```
int[ ][ ] data = new int[8][10];
```

This statement creates a two-dimensional "array of arrays," data, which is 8×10, having 8 rows and 10 columns. That is, data is an array of length 8 such that each element of data is an array of length 10 of integers. (See Figure 3.7.) The following would then be valid uses of array data and **int** variables i, j, and k:

```
data[i][i+1] = data[i][i] + 3;
j = data.length;             // j is 8
k = data[4].length;          // k is 10
```

Two-dimensional arrays have many applications to numerical analysis. Rather than going into the details of such applications, however, we explore an application of two-dimensional arrays for implementing a simple positional game.

	0	1	2	3	4	5	6	7	8	9
0	22	18	709	5	33	10	4	56	82	440
1	45	32	830	120	750	660	13	77	20	105
2	4	880	45	66	61	28	650	7	510	67
3	940	12	36	3	20	100	306	590	0	500
4	50	65	42	49	88	25	70	126	83	288
5	398	233	5	83	59	232	49	8	365	90
6	33	58	632	87	94	5	59	204	120	829
7	62	394	3	4	102	140	183	390	16	26

Figure 3.7: Illustration of a two-dimensional integer array, data, which has 8 rows and 10 columns. The value of data[3][5] is 100 and the value of data[6][2] is 632.

Tic-Tac-Toe

As most school children know, ***Tic-Tac-Toe*** is a game played in a three-by-three board. Two players—X and O—alternate in placing their respective marks in the cells of this board, starting with player X. If either player succeeds in getting three of his or her marks in a row, column, or diagonal, then that player wins.

This is admittedly not a sophisticated positional game, and it's not even that much fun to play, since a good player O can always force a tie. Tic-Tac-Toe's saving grace is that it is a nice, simple example showing how two-dimensional arrays can be used for positional games. Software for more sophisticated positional games, such as checkers, chess, or the popular simulation games, are all based on the same approach we illustrate here for using a two-dimensional array for Tic-Tac-Toe.

The basic idea is to use a two-dimensional array, board, to maintain the game board. Cells in this array store values that indicate if that cell is empty or stores an X or O. That is, board is a three-by-three matrix, whose middle row consists of the cells board[1][0], board[1][1], and board[1][2]. In our case, we choose to make the cells in the board array be integers, with a 0 indicating an empty cell, a 1 indicating an X, and a -1 indicating an O. This encoding allows us to have a simple way of testing if a given board configuration is a win for X or O, namely, if the values of a row, column, or diagonal add up to 3 or -3, respectively. We illustrate this approach in Figure 3.8.

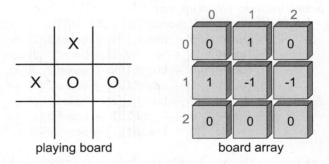

Figure 3.8: An illustration of a Tic-Tac-Toe board and the two-dimensional integer array, board, representing it.

We give a complete Java class for maintaining a Tic-Tac-Toe board for two players in Code Fragments 3.9 and 3.10. We show a sample output in Figure 3.9. Note that this code is just for maintaining the Tic-Tac-Toe board and registering moves; it doesn't perform any strategy or allow someone to play Tic-Tac-Toe against the computer. The details of such a program are beyond the scope of this chapter, but it might nonetheless make a good course project (see Exercise P-8.67).

```
 1  /** Simulation of a Tic-Tac-Toe game (does not do strategy). */
 2  public class TicTacToe {
 3    public static final int X = 1, O = −1;          // players
 4    public static final int EMPTY = 0;              // empty cell
 5    private int board[ ][ ] = new int[3][3];        // game board
 6    private int player;                             // current player
 7    /** Constructor */
 8    public TicTacToe( ) { clearBoard( ); }
 9    /** Clears the board */
10    public void clearBoard( ) {
11      for (int i = 0; i < 3; i++)
12        for (int j = 0; j < 3; j++)
13          board[i][j] = EMPTY;                      // every cell should be empty
14      player = X;                                   // the first player is 'X'
15    }
16    /** Puts an X or O mark at position i,j. */
17    public void putMark(int i, int j) throws IllegalArgumentException {
18      if ((i < 0) || (i > 2) || (j < 0) || (j > 2))
19        throw new IllegalArgumentException("Invalid board position");
20      if (board[i][j] != EMPTY)
21        throw new IllegalArgumentException("Board position occupied");
22      board[i][j] = player;          // place the mark for the current player
23      player = − player;             // switch players (uses fact that O = - X)
24    }
25    /** Checks whether the board configuration is a win for the given player. */
26    public boolean isWin(int mark) {
27      return ((board[0][0] + board[0][1] + board[0][2] == mark*3)    // row 0
28          || (board[1][0] + board[1][1] + board[1][2] == mark*3)    // row 1
29          || (board[2][0] + board[2][1] + board[2][2] == mark*3)    // row 2
30          || (board[0][0] + board[1][0] + board[2][0] == mark*3)    // column 0
31          || (board[0][1] + board[1][1] + board[2][1] == mark*3)    // column 1
32          || (board[0][2] + board[1][2] + board[2][2] == mark*3)    // column 2
33          || (board[0][0] + board[1][1] + board[2][2] == mark*3)    // diagonal
34          || (board[2][0] + board[1][1] + board[0][2] == mark*3));  // rev diag
35    }
36    /** Returns the winning player's code, or 0 to indicate a tie (or unfinished game).*/
37    public int winner( ) {
38      if (isWin(X))
39        return(X);
40      else if (isWin(O))
41        return(O);
42      else
43        return(0);
44    }
```

Code Fragment 3.9: A simple, complete Java class for playing Tic-Tac-Toe between two players. (Continues in Code Fragment 3.10.)

```
45    /** Returns a simple character string showing the current board. */
46    public String toString( ) {
47      StringBuilder sb = new StringBuilder( );
48      for (int i=0; i<3; i++) {
49        for (int j=0; j<3; j++) {
50          switch (board[i][j]) {
51          case X:       sb.append("X"); break;
52          case O:       sb.append("O"); break;
53          case EMPTY:   sb.append(" "); break;
54          }
55          if (j < 2) sb.append("|");              // column boundary
56        }
57        if (i < 2) sb.append("\n-----\n");        // row boundary
58      }
59      return sb.toString( );
60    }
61    /** Test run of a simple game */
62    public static void main(String[ ] args) {
63      TicTacToe game = new TicTacToe( );
64      /* X moves: */              /* O moves: */
65      game.putMark(1,1);          game.putMark(0,2);
66      game.putMark(2,2);          game.putMark(0,0);
67      game.putMark(0,1);          game.putMark(2,1);
68      game.putMark(1,2);          game.putMark(1,0);
69      game.putMark(2,0);
70      System.out.println(game);
71      int winningPlayer = game.winner( );
72      String[ ] outcome = {"O wins", "Tie", "X wins"};  // rely on ordering
73      System.out.println(outcome[1 + winningPlayer]);
74    }
75  }
```

Code Fragment 3.10: A simple, complete Java class for playing Tic-Tac-Toe between two players. (Continued from Code Fragment 3.9.)

```
O|X|O
-----
O|X|X
-----
X|O|X
Tie
```

Figure 3.9: Sample output of a Tic-Tac-Toe game.

3.2   Singly Linked Lists

In the previous section, we presented the array data structure and discussed some of its applications. Arrays are great for storing things in a certain order, but they have drawbacks. The capacity of the array must be fixed when it is created, and insertions and deletions at interior positions of an array can be time consuming if many elements must be shifted.

In this section, we introduce a data structure known as a ***linked list***, which provides an alternative to an array-based structure. A linked list, in its simplest form, is a collection of ***nodes*** that collectively form a linear sequence. In a ***singly linked list***, each node stores a reference to an object that is an element of the sequence, as well as a reference to the next node of the list (see Figure 3.10).

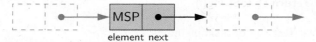

Figure 3.10: Example of a node instance that forms part of a singly linked list. The node's element field refers to an object that is an element of the sequence (the airport code MSP, in this example), while the next field refers to the subsequent node of the linked list (or null if there is no further node).

A linked list's representation relies on the collaboration of many objects (see Figure 3.11). Minimally, the linked list instance must keep a reference to the first node of the list, known as the ***head***. Without an explicit reference to the head, there would be no way to locate that node (or indirectly, any others). The last node of the list is known as the ***tail***. The tail of a list can be found by ***traversing*** the linked list— starting at the head and moving from one node to another by following each node's next reference. We can identify the tail as the node having **null** as its next reference. This process is also known as ***link hopping*** or ***pointer hopping***. However, storing an explicit reference to the tail node is a common efficiency to avoid such a traversal. In similar regard, it is common for a linked list instance to keep a count of the total number of nodes that comprise the list (also known as the ***size*** of the list), to avoid traversing the list to count the nodes.

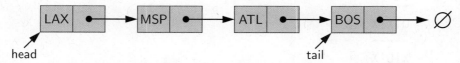

Figure 3.11: Example of a singly linked list whose elements are strings indicating airport codes. The list instance maintains a member named head that refers to the first node of the list, and another member named tail that refers to the last node of the list. The **null** value is denoted as Ø.

Inserting an Element at the Head of a Singly Linked List

An important property of a linked list is that it does not have a predetermined fixed size; it uses space proportional to its current number of elements. When using a singly linked list, we can easily insert an element at the head of the list, as shown in Figure 3.12, and described with pseudocode in Code Fragment 3.11. The main idea is that we create a new node, set its element to the new element, set its next link to refer to the current head, and set the list's head to point to the new node.

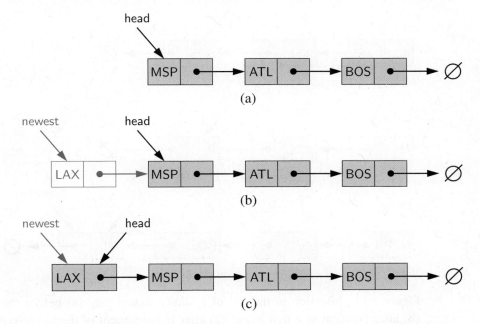

Figure 3.12: Insertion of an element at the head of a singly linked list: (a) before the insertion; (b) after a new node is created and linked to the existing head; (c) after reassignment of the head reference to the newest node.

Algorithm addFirst(*e*):

    newest = Node(*e*) {create new node instance storing reference to element *e*}

    newest.next = head   {set new node's next to reference the old head node}

    head = newest   {set variable head to reference the new node}

    size = size + 1   {increment the node count}

Code Fragment 3.11: Inserting a new element at the beginning of a singly linked list. Note that we set the next pointer of the new node *before* we reassign variable head to it. If the list were initially empty (i.e., head is null), then a natural consequence is that the new node has its next reference set to null.

Inserting an Element at the Tail of a Singly Linked List

We can also easily insert an element at the tail of the list, provided we keep a reference to the tail node, as shown in Figure 3.13. In this case, we create a new node, assign its next reference to null, set the next reference of the tail to point to this new node, and then update the tail reference itself to this new node. We give pseudocode for the process in Code Fragment 3.12.

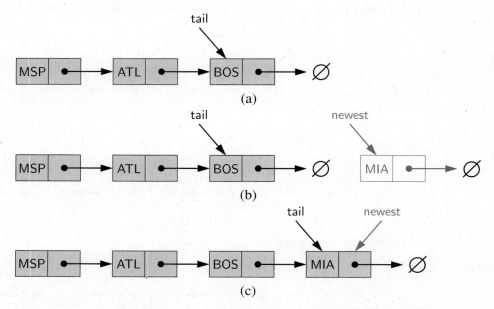

Figure 3.13: Insertion at the tail of a singly linked list: (a) before the insertion; (b) after creation of a new node; (c) after reassignment of the tail reference. Note that we must set the next link of the tail node in (b) before we assign the tail variable to point to the new node in (c).

Algorithm addLast(e):

    newest = Node(e)   {create new node instance storing reference to element e}

    newest.next = null   {set new node's next to reference the null object}

    tail.next = newest   {make old tail node point to new node}

    tail = newest   {set variable tail to reference the new node}

    size = size + 1   {increment the node count}

Code Fragment 3.12: Inserting a new node at the end of a singly linked list. Note that we set the next pointer for the old tail node *before* we make variable tail point to the new node. This code would need to be adjusted for inserting onto an empty list, since there would not be an existing tail node.

Removing an Element from a Singly Linked List

Removing an element from the *head* of a singly linked list is essentially the reverse operation of inserting a new element at the head. This operation is illustrated in Figure 3.14 and described in detail in Code Fragment 3.13.

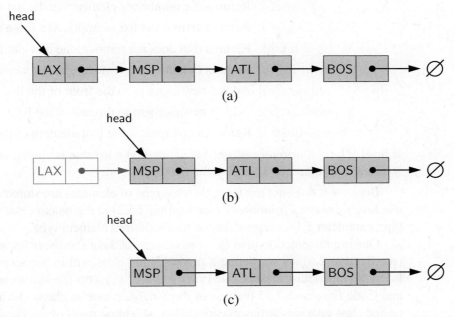

Figure 3.14: Removal of an element at the head of a singly linked list: (a) before the removal; (b) after "linking out" the old head; (c) final configuration.

Algorithm removeFirst( ):
    if head == null **then**
       the list is empty.
    head = head.next   {make head point to next node (or null)}
    size = size − 1   {decrement the node count}

Code Fragment 3.13: Removing the node at the beginning of a singly linked list.

Unfortunately, we cannot easily delete the last node of a singly linked list. Even if we maintain a tail reference directly to the last node of the list, we must be able to access the node *before* the last node in order to remove the last node. But we cannot reach the node before the tail by following next links from the tail. The only way to access this node is to start from the head of the list and search all the way through the list. But such a sequence of link-hopping operations could take a long time. If we want to support such an operation efficiently, we will need to make our list *doubly linked* (as we do in Section 3.4).

3.2.1   Implementing a Singly Linked List Class

In this section, we present a complete implementation of a SinglyLinkedList class, supporting the following methods:

size( ): Returns the number of elements in the list.

isEmpty( ): Returns **true** if the list is empty, and **false** otherwise.

first( ): Returns (but does not remove) the first element in the list.

last( ): Returns (but does not remove) the last element in the list.

addFirst(e): Adds a new element to the front of the list.

addLast(e): Adds a new element to the end of the list.

removeFirst( ): Removes and returns the first element of the list.

If first( ), last( ), or removeFirst( ) are called on a list that is empty, we will simply return a **null** reference and leave the list unchanged.

Because it does not matter to us what type of elements are stored in the list, we use Java's **_generics framework_** (see Section 2.5.2) to define our class with a formal type parameter E that represents the user's desired element type.

Our implementation also takes advantage of Java's support for **_nested classes_** (see Section 2.6), as we define a private Node class within the scope of the public SinglyLinkedList class. Code Fragment 3.14 presents the Node class definition, and Code Fragment 3.15 the rest of the SinglyLinkedList class. Having Node as a nested class provides strong encapsulation, shielding users of our class from the underlying details about nodes and links. This design also allows Java to differentiate this node type from forms of nodes we may define for use in other structures.

```
1   public class SinglyLinkedList<E> {
2     //---------------- nested Node class ----------------
3     private static class Node<E> {
4       private E element;                // reference to the element stored at this node
5       private Node<E> next;             // reference to the subsequent node in the list
6       public Node(E e, Node<E> n) {
7         element = e;
8         next = n;
9       }
10      public E getElement() { return element; }
11      public Node<E> getNext() { return next; }
12      public void setNext(Node<E> n) { next = n; }
13    } //----------- end of nested Node class -----------
      ... rest of SinglyLinkedList class will follow ...
```

Code Fragment 3.14: A nested Node class within the SinglyLinkedList class. (The remainder of the SinglyLinkedList class will be given in Code Fragment 3.15.)

```
1   public class SinglyLinkedList<E> {
...    (nested Node class goes here)
14    // instance variables of the SinglyLinkedList
15    private Node<E> head = null;        // head node of the list (or null if empty)
16    private Node<E> tail = null;        // last node of the list (or null if empty)
17    private int size = 0;               // number of nodes in the list
18    public SinglyLinkedList() { }       // constructs an initially empty list
19    // access methods
20    public int size() { return size; }
21    public boolean isEmpty() { return size == 0; }
22    public E first() {                  // returns (but does not remove) the first element
23      if (isEmpty()) return null;
24      return head.getElement();
25    }
26    public E last() {                   // returns (but does not remove) the last element
27      if (isEmpty()) return null;
28      return tail.getElement();
29    }
30    // update methods
31    public void addFirst(E e) {         // adds element e to the front of the list
32      head = new Node<>(e, head);       // create and link a new node
33      if (size == 0)
34        tail = head;                    // special case: new node becomes tail also
35      size++;
36    }
37    public void addLast(E e) {          // adds element e to the end of the list
38      Node<E> newest = new Node<>(e, null);   // node will eventually be the tail
39      if (isEmpty())
40        head = newest;                  // special case: previously empty list
41      else
42        tail.setNext(newest);           // new node after existing tail
43      tail = newest;                    // new node becomes the tail
44      size++;
45    }
46    public E removeFirst() {            // removes and returns the first element
47      if (isEmpty()) return null;       // nothing to remove
48      E answer = head.getElement();
49      head = head.getNext();            // will become null if list had only one node
50      size--;
51      if (size == 0)
52        tail = null;                    // special case as list is now empty
53      return answer;
54    }
55  }
```

Code Fragment 3.15: The SinglyLinkedList class definition (when combined with the nested Node class of Code Fragment 3.14).

3.3 Circularly Linked Lists

Linked lists are traditionally viewed as storing a sequence of items in a linear order, from first to last. However, there are many applications in which data can be more naturally viewed as having a *cyclic order*, with well-defined neighboring relationships, but no fixed beginning or end.

For example, many multiplayer games are turn-based, with player A taking a turn, then player B, then player C, and so on, but eventually back to player A again, and player B again, with the pattern repeating. As another example, city buses and subways often run on a continuous loop, making stops in a scheduled order, but with no designated first or last stop per se. We next consider another important example of a cyclic order in the context of computer operating systems.

3.3.1 Round-Robin Scheduling

One of the most important roles of an operating system is in managing the many processes that are currently active on a computer, including the scheduling of those processes on one or more central processing units (CPUs). In order to support the responsiveness of an arbitrary number of concurrent processes, most operating systems allow processes to effectively share use of the CPUs, using some form of an algorithm known as *round-robin scheduling*. A process is given a short turn to execute, known as a *time slice*, but it is interrupted when the slice ends, even if its job is not yet complete. Each active process is given its own time slice, taking turns in a cyclic order. New processes can be added to the system, and processes that complete their work can be removed.

A round-robin scheduler could be implemented with a traditional linked list, by repeatedly performing the following steps on linked list L (see Figure 3.15):

1. process $p = L$.removeFirst( )
2. Give a time slice to process p
3. L.addLast(p)

Unfortunately, there are drawbacks to the use of a traditional linked list for this purpose. It is unnecessarily inefficient to repeatedly throw away a node from one end of the list, only to create a new node for the same element when reinserting it, not to mention the various updates that are performed to decrement and increment the list's size and to unlink and relink nodes.

In the remainder of this section, we demonstrate how a slight modification to our singly linked list implementation can be used to provide a more efficient data structure for representing a cyclic order.

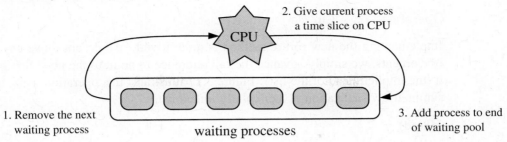

Figure 3.15: The three iterative steps for round-robin scheduling.

3.3.2 Designing and Implementing a Circularly Linked List

In this section, we design a structure known as a ***circularly linked list***, which is essentially a singularly linked list in which the next reference of the tail node is set to refer back to the head of the list (rather than **null**), as shown in Figure 3.16.

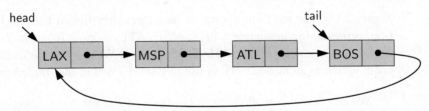

Figure 3.16: Example of a singly linked list with circular structure.

We use this model to design and implement a new CircularlyLinkedList class, which supports all of the public behaviors of our SinglyLinkedList class and one additional update method:

rotate( ): Moves the first element to the end of the list.

With this new operation, round-robin scheduling can be efficiently implemented by repeatedly performing the following steps on a circularly linked list C:

1. Give a time slice to process C.first( )
2. C.rotate( )

Additional Optimization

In implementing a new class, we make one additional optimization—we no longer explicitly maintain the head reference. So long as we maintain a reference to the tail, we can locate the head as tail.getNext( ). Maintaining only the tail reference not only saves a bit on memory usage, it makes the code simpler and more efficient, as it removes the need to perform additional operations to keep a head reference current. In fact, our new implementation is arguably superior to our original singly linked list implementation, even if we are not interested in the new rotate method.

Operations on a Circularly Linked List

Implementing the new rotate method is quite trivial. We do not move any nodes or elements, we simply advance the tail reference to point to the node that follows it (the implicit head of the list). Figure 3.17 illustrates this operation using a more symmetric visualization of a circularly linked list.

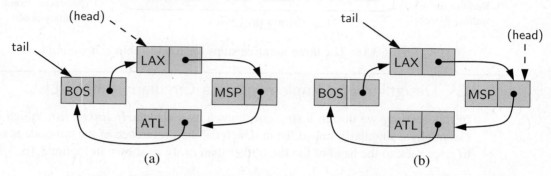

(a)   (b)

Figure 3.17: The rotation operation on a circularly linked list: (a) before the rotation, representing sequence { LAX, MSP, ATL, BOS }; (b) after the rotation, representing sequence { MSP, ATL, BOS, LAX }. We display the implicit head reference, which is identified only as tail.getNext( ) within the implementation.

We can add a new element at the front of the list by creating a new node and linking it just *after* the tail of the list, as shown in Figure 3.18. To implement the addLast method, we can rely on the use of a call to addFirst and then immediately advance the tail reference so that the newest node becomes the last.

Removing the first node from a circularly linked list can be accomplished by simply updating the next field of the tail node to bypass the implicit head. A Java implementation of all methods of the CircularlyLinkedList class is given in Code Fragment 3.16.

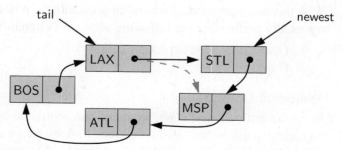

Figure 3.18: Effect of a call to addFirst(STL) on the circularly linked list of Figure 3.17(b). The variable newest has local scope during the execution of the method. Notice that when the operation is complete, STL is the first element of the list, as it is stored within the implicit head, tail.getNext( ).

```
1    public class CircularlyLinkedList<E> {
...       (nested node class identical to that of the SinglyLinkedList class)
14   // instance variables of the CircularlyLinkedList
15     private Node<E> tail = null;              // we store tail (but not head)
16     private int size = 0;                     // number of nodes in the list
17     public CircularlyLinkedList() { }         // constructs an initially empty list
18   // access methods
19     public int size() { return size; }
20     public boolean isEmpty() { return size == 0; }
21     public E first() {                        // returns (but does not remove) the first element
22       if (isEmpty()) return null;
23       return tail.getNext().getElement();     // the head is *after* the tail
24     }
25     public E last() {                         // returns (but does not remove) the last element
26       if (isEmpty()) return null;
27       return tail.getElement();
28     }
29   // update methods
30     public void rotate() {                    // rotate the first element to the back of the list
31       if (tail != null)                       // if empty, do nothing
32         tail = tail.getNext();                // the old head becomes the new tail
33     }
34     public void addFirst(E e) {               // adds element e to the front of the list
35       if (size == 0) {
36         tail = new Node<>(e, null);
37         tail.setNext(tail);                   // link to itself circularly
38       } else {
39         Node<E> newest = new Node<>(e, tail.getNext());
40         tail.setNext(newest);
41       }
42       size++;
43     }
44     public void addLast(E e) {                // adds element e to the end of the list
45       addFirst(e);                            // insert new element at front of list
46       tail = tail.getNext();                  // now new element becomes the tail
47     }
48     public E removeFirst() {                  // removes and returns the first element
49       if (isEmpty()) return null;             // nothing to remove
50       Node<E> head = tail.getNext();
51       if (head == tail) tail = null;          // must be the only node left
52       else tail.setNext(head.getNext());      // removes "head" from the list
53       size--;
54       return head.getElement();
55     }
56   }
```

Code Fragment 3.16: Implementation of the CircularlyLinkedList class.

3.4   Doubly Linked Lists

In a singly linked list, each node maintains a reference to the node that is immediately after it. We have demonstrated the usefulness of such a representation when managing a sequence of elements. However, there are limitations that stem from the asymmetry of a singly linked list. In Section 3.2, we demonstrated that we can efficiently insert a node at either end of a singly linked list, and can delete a node at the head of a list, but we are unable to efficiently delete a node at the tail of the list. More generally, we cannot efficiently delete an arbitrary node from an interior position of the list if only given a reference to that node, because we cannot determine the node that immediately *precedes* the node to be deleted (yet, that node needs to have its next reference updated).

To provide greater symmetry, we define a linked list in which each node keeps an explicit reference to the node before it and a reference to the node after it. Such a structure is known as a ***doubly linked list***. These lists allow a greater variety of $O(1)$-time update operations, including insertions and deletions at arbitrary positions within the list. We continue to use the term "next" for the reference to the node that follows another, and we introduce the term "prev" for the reference to the node that precedes it.

Header and Trailer Sentinels

In order to avoid some special cases when operating near the boundaries of a doubly linked list, it helps to add special nodes at both ends of the list: a ***header*** node at the beginning of the list, and a ***trailer*** node at the end of the list. These "dummy" nodes are known as ***sentinels*** (or guards), and they do not store elements of the primary sequence. A doubly linked list with such sentinels is shown in Figure 3.19.

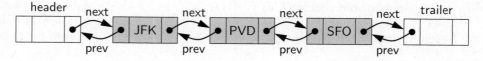

Figure 3.19: A doubly linked list representing the sequence { JFK, PVD, SFO }, using sentinels header and trailer to demarcate the ends of the list.

When using sentinel nodes, an empty list is initialized so that the next field of the header points to the trailer, and the prev field of the trailer points to the header; the remaining fields of the sentinels are irrelevant (presumably null, in Java). For a nonempty list, the header's next will refer to a node containing the first real element of a sequence, just as the trailer's prev references the node containing the last element of a sequence.

Advantage of Using Sentinels

Although we could implement a doubly linked list without sentinel nodes (as we did with our singly linked list in Section 3.2), the slight extra memory devoted to the sentinels greatly simplifies the logic of our operations. Most notably, the header and trailer nodes never change—only the nodes between them change. Furthermore, we can treat all insertions in a unified manner, because a new node will always be placed between a pair of existing nodes. In similar fashion, every element that is to be deleted is guaranteed to be stored in a node that has neighbors on each side.

For contrast, we look at our SinglyLinkedList implementation from Section 3.2. Its addLast method required a conditional (lines 39–42 of Code Fragment 3.15) to manage the special case of inserting into an empty list. In the general case, the new node was linked after the existing tail. But when adding to an empty list, there is no existing tail; instead it is necessary to reassign head to reference the new node. The use of a sentinel node in that implementation would eliminate the special case, as there would always be an existing node (possibly the header) before a new node.

Inserting and Deleting with a Doubly Linked List

Every insertion into our doubly linked list representation will take place between a pair of existing nodes, as diagrammed in Figure 3.20. For example, when a new element is inserted at the front of the sequence, we will simply add the new node *between* the header and the node that is currently after the header. (See Figure 3.21.)

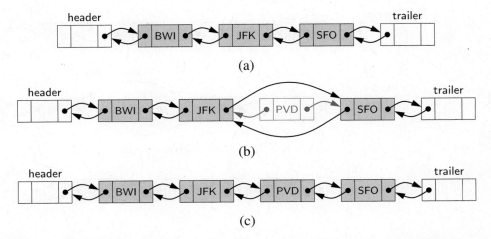

Figure 3.20: Adding an element to a doubly linked list with header and trailer sentinels: (a) before the operation; (b) after creating the new node; (c) after linking the neighbors to the new node.

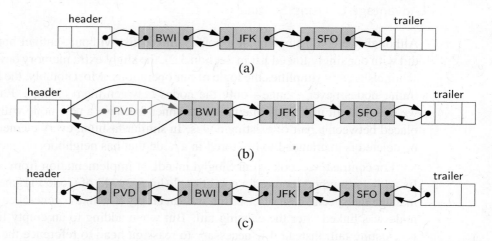

Figure 3.21: Adding an element to the front of a sequence represented by a doubly linked list with header and trailer sentinels: (a) before the operation; (b) after creating the new node; (c) after linking the neighbors to the new node.

The deletion of a node, portrayed in Figure 3.22, proceeds in the opposite fashion of an insertion. The two neighbors of the node to be deleted are linked directly to each other, thereby bypassing the original node. As a result, that node will no longer be considered part of the list and it can be reclaimed by the system. Because of our use of sentinels, the same implementation can be used when deleting the first or the last element of a sequence, because even such an element will be stored at a node that lies between two others.

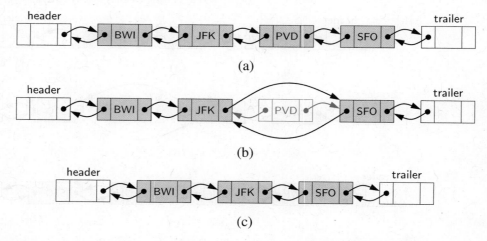

Figure 3.22: Removing the element PVD from a doubly linked list: (a) before the removal; (b) after linking out the old node; (c) after the removal (and garbage collection).

3.4.1 Implementing a Doubly Linked List Class

In this section, we present a complete implementation of a DoublyLinkedList class, supporting the following public methods:

size( ): Returns the number of elements in the list.

isEmpty( ): Returns **true** if the list is empty, and **false** otherwise.

first( ): Returns (but does not remove) the first element in the list.

last( ): Returns (but does not remove) the last element in the list.

addFirst(e): Adds a new element to the front of the list.

addLast(e): Adds a new element to the end of the list.

removeFirst( ): Removes and returns the first element of the list.

removeLast( ): Removes and returns the last element of the list.

If first( ), last( ), removeFirst( ), or removeLast( ) are called on a list that is empty, we will return a **null** reference and leave the list unchanged.

Although we have seen that it is possible to add or remove an element at an internal position of a doubly linked list, doing so requires knowledge of one or more nodes, to identify the position at which the operation should occur. In this chapter, we prefer to maintain encapsulation, with a private, nested Node class. In Chapter 7, we will revisit the use of doubly linked lists, offering a more advanced interface that supports internal insertions and deletions while maintaining encapsulation.

Code Fragments 3.17 and 3.18 present the DoublyLinkedList class implementation. As we did with our SinglyLinkedList class, we use the generics framework to accept any type of element. The nested Node class for the doubly linked list is similar to that of the singly linked list, except with support for an additional prev reference to the preceding node.

Our use of sentinel nodes, header and trailer, impacts the implementation in several ways. We create and link the sentinels when constructing an empty list (lines 25–29). We also keep in mind that the first element of a nonempty list is stored in the node just *after* the header (not in the header itself), and similarly that the last element is stored in the node just *before* the trailer.

The sentinels greatly ease our implementation of the various update methods. We will provide a private method, addBetween, to handle the general case of an insertion, and then we will rely on that utility as a straightforward method to implement both addFirst and addLast. In similar fashion, we will define a private remove method that can be used to easily implement both removeFirst and removeLast.

```
1   /** A basic doubly linked list implementation. */
2   public class DoublyLinkedList<E> {
3     //--------------- nested Node class ----------------
4     private static class Node<E> {
5       private E element;                    // reference to the element stored at this node
6       private Node<E> prev;                 // reference to the previous node in the list
7       private Node<E> next;                 // reference to the subsequent node in the list
8       public Node(E e, Node<E> p, Node<E> n) {
9         element = e;
10        prev = p;
11        next = n;
12      }
13      public E getElement() { return element; }
14      public Node<E> getPrev() { return prev; }
15      public Node<E> getNext() { return next; }
16      public void setPrev(Node<E> p) { prev = p; }
17      public void setNext(Node<E> n) { next = n; }
18    } //----------- end of nested Node class -----------
19
20    // instance variables of the DoublyLinkedList
21    private Node<E> header;                         // header sentinel
22    private Node<E> trailer;                        // trailer sentinel
23    private int size = 0;                           // number of elements in the list
24    /** Constructs a new empty list. */
25    public DoublyLinkedList() {
26      header = new Node<>(null, null, null);        // create header
27      trailer = new Node<>(null, header, null);     // trailer is preceded by header
28      header.setNext(trailer);                      // header is followed by trailer
29    }
30    /** Returns the number of elements in the linked list. */
31    public int size() { return size; }
32    /** Tests whether the linked list is empty. */
33    public boolean isEmpty() { return size == 0; }
34    /** Returns (but does not remove) the first element of the list. */
35    public E first() {
36      if (isEmpty()) return null;
37      return header.getNext().getElement();         // first element is beyond header
38    }
39    /** Returns (but does not remove) the last element of the list. */
40    public E last() {
41      if (isEmpty()) return null;
42      return trailer.getPrev().getElement();        // last element is before trailer
43    }
```

Code Fragment 3.17: Implementation of the DoublyLinkedList class. (Continues in Code Fragment 3.18.)

```
44    // public update methods
45    /** Adds element e to the front of the list. */
46    public void addFirst(E e) {
47      addBetween(e, header, header.getNext( ));        // place just after the header
48    }
49    /** Adds element e to the end of the list. */
50    public void addLast(E e) {
51      addBetween(e, trailer.getPrev( ), trailer);       // place just before the trailer
52    }
53    /** Removes and returns the first element of the list. */
54    public E removeFirst( ) {
55      if (isEmpty( )) return null;                     // nothing to remove
56      return remove(header.getNext( ));               // first element is beyond header
57    }
58    /** Removes and returns the last element of the list. */
59    public E removeLast( ) {
60      if (isEmpty( )) return null;                     // nothing to remove
61      return remove(trailer.getPrev( ));              // last element is before trailer
62    }
63
64    // private update methods
65    /** Adds element e to the linked list in between the given nodes. */
66    private void addBetween(E e, Node<E> predecessor, Node<E> successor) {
67      // create and link a new node
68      Node<E> newest = new Node<>(e, predecessor, successor);
69      predecessor.setNext(newest);
70      successor.setPrev(newest);
71      size++;
72    }
73    /** Removes the given node from the list and returns its element. */
74    private E remove(Node<E> node) {
75      Node<E> predecessor = node.getPrev( );
76      Node<E> successor = node.getNext( );
77      predecessor.setNext(successor);
78      successor.setPrev(predecessor);
79      size--;
80      return node.getElement( );
81    }
82  } //----------- end of DoublyLinkedList class -----------
```

Code Fragment 3.18: Implementation of the public and private update methods for the DoublyLinkedList class. (Continued from Code Fragment 3.17.)

3.5   Equivalence Testing

When working with reference types, there are many different notions of what it means for one expression to be equal to another. At the lowest level, if a and b are reference variables, then expression a == b tests whether a and b refer to the same object (or if both are set to the **null** value).

However, for many types there is a higher-level notion of two variables being considered "equivalent" even if they do not actually refer to the same instance of the class. For example, we typically want to consider two String instances to be equivalent to each other if they represent the identical sequence of characters.

To support a broader notion of equivalence, all object types support a method named **equals**. Users of reference types should rely on the syntax a.equals(b), unless they have a specific need to test the more narrow notion of identity. The equals method is formally defined in the Object class, which serves as a superclass for all reference types, but that implementation reverts to returning the value of expression a == b. Defining a more meaningful notion of equivalence requires knowledge about a class and its representation.

The author of each class has a responsibility to provide an implementation of the equals method, which overrides the one inherited from Object, if there is a more relevant definition for the equivalence of two instances. For example, Java's String class redefines equals to test character-for-character equivalence.

Great care must be taken when overriding the notion of equality, as the consistency of Java's libraries depends upon the equals method defining what is known as an *equivalence relation* in mathematics, satisfying the following properties:

Treatment of null: For any nonnull reference variable x, the call x.equals(**null**) should return **false** (that is, nothing equals **null** except **null**).

Reflexivity: For any nonnull reference variable x, the call x.equals(x) should return **true** (that is, an object should equal itself).

Symmetry: For any nonnull reference variables x and y, the calls x.equals(y) and y.equals(x) should return the same value.

Transitivity: For any nonnull reference variables x, y, and z, if both calls x.equals(y) and y.equals(z) return **true**, then call x.equals(z) must return **true** as well.

While these properties may seem intuitive, it can be challenging to properly implement equals for some data structures, especially in an object-oriented context, with inheritance and generics. For most of the data structures in this book, we omit the implementation of a valid equals method (leaving it as an exercise). However, in this section, we consider the treatment of equivalence testing for both arrays and linked lists, including a concrete example of a proper implementation of the equals method for our SinglyLinkedList class.

3.5.1 Equivalence Testing with Arrays

As we mentioned in Section 1.3, arrays are a reference type in Java, but not technically a class. However, the java.util.Arrays class, introduced in Section 3.1.3, provides additional static methods that are useful when processing arrays. The following provides a summary of the treatment of equivalence for arrays, assuming that variables a and b refer to array objects:

a == b: Tests if a and b refer to the same underlying array instance.

a.equals(b): Interestingly, this is identical to a == b. Arrays are not a true class type and do not override the Object.equals method.

Arrays.equals(a,b): This provides a more intuitive notion of equivalence, returning **true** if the arrays have the same length and all pairs of corresponding elements are "equal" to each other. More specifically, if the array elements are primitives, then it uses the standard == to compare values. If elements of the arrays are a reference type, then it makes pairwise comparisons a[k].equals(b[k]) in evaluating the equivalence.

For most applications, the Arrays.equals behavior captures the appropriate notion of equivalence. However, there is an additional complication when using multidimensional arrays. The fact that two-dimensional arrays in Java are really one-dimensional arrays nested inside a common one-dimensional array raises an interesting issue with respect to how we think about *compound objects*, which are objects—like a two-dimensional array—that are made up of other objects. In particular, it brings up the question of where a compound object begins and ends.

Thus, if we have a two-dimensional array, a, and another two-dimensional array, b, that has the same entries as a, we probably want to think that a is equal to b. But the one-dimensional arrays that make up the rows of a and b (such as a[0] and b[0]) are stored in different memory locations, even though they have the same internal content. Therefore, a call to the method java.util.Arrays.equals(a,b) will return **false** in this case, because it tests a[k].equals(b[k]), which invokes the Object class's definition of equals.

To support the more natural notion of multidimensional arrays being equal if they have equal contents, the class provides an additional method:

Arrays.deepEquals(a,b): Identical to Arrays.equals(a,b) except when the elements of a and b are themselves arrays, in which case it calls Arrays.deepEquals(a[k],b[k]) for corresponding entries, rather than a[k].equals(b[k]).

3.5.2   Equivalence Testing with Linked Lists

In this section, we develop an implementation of the equals method in the context of the SinglyLinkedList class of Section 3.2.1. Using a definition very similar to the treatment of arrays by the java.util.Arrays.equals method, we consider two lists to be equivalent if they have the same length and contents that are element-by-element equivalent. We can evaluate such equivalence by simultaneously traversing two lists, verifying that x.equals(y) for each pair of corresponding elements x and y.

The implementation of the SinglyLinkedList.equals method is given in Code Fragment 3.19. Although we are focused on comparing two singly linked lists, the equals method must take an arbitrary Object as a parameter. We take a conservative approach, demanding that two objects be instances of the same class to have any possibility of equivalence. (For example, we do not consider a singly linked list to be equivalent to a doubly linked list with the same sequence of elements.) After ensuring, at line 2, that parameter o is nonnull, line 3 uses the getClass( ) method supported by all objects to test whether the two instances belong to the same class.

When reaching line 4, we have ensured that the parameter was an instance of the SinglyLinkedList class (or an appropriate subclass), and so we can safely cast it to a SinglyLinkedList, so that we may access its instance variables size and head. There is subtlety involving the treatment of Java's generics framework. Although our SinglyLinkedList class has a declared formal type parameter $<E>$, we cannot detect at runtime whether the other list has a matching type. (For those interested, look online for a discussion of *erasure* in Java.) So we revert to using a more classic approach with nonparameterized type SinglyLinkedList at line 4, and nonparameterized Node declarations at lines 6 and 7. If the two lists have incompatible types, this will be detected when calling the equals method on corresponding elements.

```
 1    public boolean equals(Object o) {
 2       if (o == null) return false;
 3       if (getClass( ) != o.getClass( )) return false;
 4       SinglyLinkedList other = (SinglyLinkedList) o;        // use nonparameterized type
 5       if (size != other.size) return false;
 6       Node walkA = head;                                    // traverse the primary list
 7       Node walkB = other.head;                              // traverse the secondary list
 8       while (walkA != null) {
 9          if (!walkA.getElement( ).equals(walkB.getElement( ))) return false; //mismatch
10          walkA = walkA.getNext( );
11          walkB = walkB.getNext( );
12       }
13       return true;      // if we reach this, everything matched successfully
14    }
```

Code Fragment 3.19: Implementation of the SinglyLinkedList.equals method.

3.6 Cloning Data Structures

The beauty of object-oriented programming is that abstraction allows for a data structure to be treated as a single object, even though the encapsulated implementation of the structure might rely on a more complex combination of many objects. In this section, we consider what it means to make a copy of such a structure.

In a programming environment, a common expectation is that a copy of an object has its own state and that, once made, the copy is independent of the original (for example, so that changes to one do not directly affect the other). However, when objects have fields that are reference variables pointing to auxiliary objects, it is not always obvious whether a copy should have a corresponding field that refers to the same auxiliary object, or to a new copy of that auxiliary object.

For example, if a hypothetical AddressBook class has instances that represent an electronic address book—with contact information (such as phone numbers and email addresses) for a person's friends and acquaintances—how might we envision a copy of an address book? Should an entry added to one book appear in the other? If we change a person's phone number in one book, would we expect that change to be synchronized in the other?

There is no one-size-fits-all answer to questions like this. Instead, each class in Java is responsible for defining whether its instances can be copied, and if so, precisely how the copy is constructed. The universal Object superclass defines a method named **clone**, which can be used to produce what is known as a *shallow copy* of an object. This uses the standard assignment semantics to assign the value of each field of the new object equal to the corresponding field of the existing object that is being copied. The reason this is known as a shallow copy is because if the field is a reference type, then an initialization of the form duplicate.field = original.field causes the field of the new object to refer to the same underlying instance as the field of the original object.

A shallow copy is not always appropriate for all classes, and therefore, Java intentionally disables use of the clone( ) method by declaring it as **protected**, and by having it throw a CloneNotSupportedException when called. The author of a class must explicitly declare support for cloning by formally declaring that the class implements the Cloneable interface, and by declaring a public version of the clone( ) method. That public method can simply call the protected one to do the field-by-field assignment that results in a shallow copy, if appropriate. However, for many classes, the class may choose to implement a deeper version of cloning, in which some of the referenced objects are themselves cloned.

For most of the data structures in this book, we omit the implementation of a valid clone method (leaving it as an exercise). However, in this section, we consider approaches for cloning both arrays and linked lists, including a concrete implementation of the clone method for the SinglyLinkedList class.

3.6.1   Cloning Arrays

Although arrays support some special syntaxes such as a[k] and a.length, it is important to remember that they are objects, and that array variables are reference variables. This has important consequences. As a first example, consider the following code:

```
int[ ] data = {2, 3, 5, 7, 11, 13, 17, 19};
int[ ] backup;
backup = data;                              // warning; not a copy
```

The assignment of variable backup to data does not create any new array; it simply creates a new alias for the same array, as portrayed in Figure 3.23.

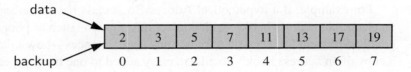

Figure 3.23: The result of the command backup = data for **int** arrays.

Instead, if we want to make a copy of the array, data, and assign a reference to the new array to variable, backup, we should write:

```
backup = data.clone( );
```

The clone method, when executed on an array, initializes each cell of the new array to the value that is stored in the corresponding cell of the original array. This results in an independent array, as shown in Figure 3.24.

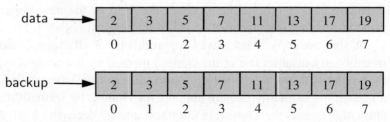

Figure 3.24: The result of the command backup = data.clone( ) for **int** arrays.

If we subsequently make an assignment such as data[4] = 23 in this configuration, the backup array is unaffected.

There are more considerations when copying an array that stores reference types rather than primitive types. The clone( ) method produces a ***shallow copy*** of the array, producing a new array whose cells refer to the same objects referenced by the first array.

For example, if the variable contacts refers to an array of hypothetical Person instances, the result of the command guests = contacts.clone( ) produces a shallow copy, as portrayed in Figure 3.25.

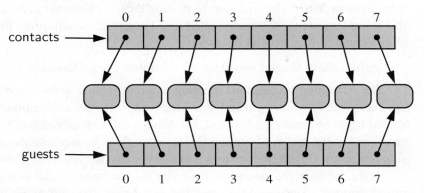

Figure 3.25: A shallow copy of an array of objects, resulting from the command guests = contacts.clone( ).

A *deep copy* of the contact list can be created by iteratively cloning the individual elements, as follows, but only if the Person class is declared as Cloneable.

```
Person[ ] guests = new Person[contacts.length];
for (int k=0; k < contacts.length; k++)
  guests[k] = (Person) contacts[k].clone( );        // returns Object type
```

Because a two-dimensional array is really a one-dimensional array storing other one-dimensional arrays, the same distinction between a shallow and deep copy exists. Unfortunately, the java.util.Arrays class does not provide any "deepClone" method. However, we can implement our own method by cloning the individual rows of an array, as shown in Code Fragment 3.20, for a two-dimensional array of integers.

```
1 public static int[ ][ ] deepClone(int[ ][ ] original) {
2   int[ ][ ] backup = new int[original.length][ ];      // create top-level array of arrays
3   for (int k=0; k < original.length; k++)
4     backup[k] = original[k].clone( );                 // copy row k
5   return backup;
6 }
```

Code Fragment 3.20: A method for creating a deep copy of a two-dimensional array of integers.

3.6.2   Cloning Linked Lists

In this section, we add support for cloning instances of the SinglyLinkedList class from Section 3.2.1. The first step to making a class cloneable in Java is declaring that it implements the Cloneable interface. Therefore, we adjust the first line of the class definition to appear as follows:

public class SinglyLinkedList<E> **implements** Cloneable {

The remaining task is implementing a public version of the clone( ) method of the class, which we present in Code Fragment 3.21. By convention, that method should begin by creating a new instance using a call to **super**.clone( ), which in our case invokes the method from the Object class (line 3). Because the inherited version returns an Object, we perform a narrowing cast to type SinglyLinkedList<E>.

At this point in the execution, the other list has been created as a shallow copy of the original. Since our list class has two fields, size and head, the following assignments have been made:

other.size = **this**.size;
other.head = **this**.head;

While the assignment of the size variable is correct, we cannot allow the new list to share the same head value (unless it is **null**). For a nonempty list to have an independent state, it must have an entirely new chain of nodes, each storing a reference to the corresponding element from the original list. We therefore create a new head node at line 5 of the code, and then perform a walk through the remainder of the original list (lines 8–13) while creating and linking new nodes for the new list.

```
 1   public SinglyLinkedList<E> clone( ) throws CloneNotSupportedException {
 2     // always use inherited Object.clone() to create the initial copy
 3     SinglyLinkedList<E> other = (SinglyLinkedList<E>) super.clone(); // safe cast
 4     if (size > 0) {                               // we need independent chain of nodes
 5       other.head = new Node<>(head.getElement( ), null);
 6       Node<E> walk = head.getNext( );   // walk through remainder of original list
 7       Node<E> otherTail = other.head;   // remember most recently created node
 8       while (walk != null) {             // make a new node storing same element
 9         Node<E> newest = new Node<>(walk.getElement( ), null);
10         otherTail.setNext(newest);       // link previous node to this one
11         otherTail = newest;
12         walk = walk.getNext( );
13       }
14     }
15     return other;
16   }
```

Code Fragment 3.21: Implementation of the SinglyLinkedList.clone method.

3.7 Exercises

Reinforcement

R-3.1 Give the next five pseudorandom numbers generated by the process described on page 113, with a = 12, b = 5, and n = 100, and 92 as the seed for cur.

R-3.2 Write a Java method that repeatedly selects and removes a random entry from an array until the array holds no more entries.

R-3.3 Explain the changes that would have to be made to the program of Code Fragment 3.8 so that it could perform the Caesar cipher for messages that are written in an alphabet-based language other than English, such as Greek, Russian, or Hebrew.

R-3.4 The TicTacToe class of Code Fragments 3.9 and 3.10 has a flaw, in that it allows a player to place a mark even after the game has already been won by someone. Modify the class so that the putMark method throws an IllegalStateException in that case.

R-3.5 The removeFirst method of the SinglyLinkedList class includes a special case to reset the tail field to **null** when deleting the last node of a list (see lines 51 and 52 of Code Fragment 3.15). What are the consequences if we were to remove those two lines from the code? Explain why the class would or would not work with such a modification.

R-3.6 Give an algorithm for finding the second-to-last node in a singly linked list in which the last node is indicated by a null next reference.

R-3.7 Consider the implementation of CircularlyLinkedList.addFirst, in Code Fragment 3.16. The else body at lines 39 and 40 of that method relies on a locally declared variable, newest. Redesign that clause to avoid use of any local variable.

R-3.8 Describe a method for finding the middle node of a doubly linked list with header and trailer sentinels by "link hopping," and without relying on explicit knowledge of the size of the list. In the case of an even number of nodes, report the node slightly left of center as the "middle." What is the running time of this method?

R-3.9 Give an implementation of the size( ) method for the SingularlyLinkedList class, assuming that we did not maintain size as an instance variable.

R-3.10 Give an implementation of the size( ) method for the CircularlyLinkedList class, assuming that we did not maintain size as an instance variable.

R-3.11 Give an implementation of the size( ) method for the DoublyLinkedList class, assuming that we did not maintain size as an instance variable.

R-3.12 Implement a rotate( ) method in the SinglyLinkedList class, which has semantics equal to addLast(removeFirst( )), yet without creating any new node.

R-3.13 What is the difference between a shallow equality test and a deep equality test between two Java arrays, A and B, if they are one-dimensional arrays of type **int**? What if the arrays are two-dimensional arrays of type **int**?

R-3.14 Give three different examples of a single Java statement that assigns variable, backup, to a new array with copies of all **int** entries of an existing array, original.

R-3.15 Implement the equals( ) method for the CircularlyLinkedList class, assuming that two lists are equal if they have the same sequence of elements, with corresponding elements currently at the front of the list.

R-3.16 Implement the equals( ) method for the DoublyLinkedList class.

Creativity

C-3.17 Let A be an array of size $n \geq 2$ containing integers from 1 to $n-1$ inclusive, one of which is repeated. Describe an algorithm for finding the integer in A that is repeated.

C-3.18 Let B be an array of size $n \geq 6$ containing integers from 1 to $n-5$ inclusive, five of which are repeated. Describe an algorithm for finding the five integers in B that are repeated.

C-3.19 Give Java code for performing add(e) and remove(i) methods for the Scoreboard class, as in Code Fragments 3.3 and 3.4, except this time, don't maintain the game entries in order. Assume that we still need to keep n entries stored in indices 0 to $n-1$. You should be able to implement the methods without using any loops, so that the number of steps they perform does not depend on n.

C-3.20 Give examples of values for a and b in the pseudorandom generator given on page 113 of this chapter such that the result is not very random looking, for n = 1000.

C-3.21 Suppose you are given an array, A, containing 100 integers that were generated using the method r.nextInt(10), where r is an object of type java.util.Random. Let x denote the product of the integers in A. There is a single number that x will equal with probability at least 0.99. What is that number and what is a formula describing the probability that x is equal to that number?

C-3.22 Write a method, shuffle(A), that rearranges the elements of array A so that every possible ordering is equally likely. You may rely on the nextInt(n) method of the java.util.Random class, which returns a random number between 0 and $n-1$ inclusive.

C-3.23 Suppose you are designing a multiplayer game that has $n \geq 1000$ players, numbered 1 to n, interacting in an enchanted forest. The winner of this game is the first player who can meet all the other players at least once (ties are allowed). Assuming that there is a method meet(i, j), which is called each time a player i meets a player j (with $i \neq j$), describe a way to keep track of the pairs of meeting players and who is the winner.

C-3.24 Write a Java method that takes two three-dimensional integer arrays and adds them componentwise.

C-3.25 Describe an algorithm for concatenating two singly linked lists L and M, into a single list L' that contains all the nodes of L followed by all the nodes of M.

C-3.26 Give an algorithm for concatenating two doubly linked lists L and M, with header and trailer sentinel nodes, into a single list L'.

C-3.27 Describe in detail how to swap two nodes x and y (and not just their contents) in a singly linked list L given references only to x and y. Repeat this exercise for the case when L is a doubly linked list. Which algorithm takes more time?

C-3.28 Describe in detail an algorithm for reversing a singly linked list L using only a constant amount of additional space.

C-3.29 Suppose you are given two circularly linked lists, L and M. Describe an algorithm for telling if L and M store the same sequence of elements (but perhaps with different starting points).

C-3.30 Given a circularly linked list L containing an even number of nodes, describe how to split L into two circularly linked lists of half the size.

C-3.31 Our implementation of a doubly linked list relies on two sentinel nodes, header and trailer, but a single sentinel node that guards both ends of the list should suffice. Reimplement the DoublyLinkedList class using only one sentinel node.

C-3.32 Implement a circular version of a doubly linked list, without any sentinels, that supports all the public behaviors of the original as well as two new update methods, rotate( ) and rotateBackward( ).

C-3.33 Solve the previous problem using inheritance, such that a DoublyLinkedList class inherits from the existing CircularlyLinkedList, and the DoublyLinkedList.Node nested class inherits from CircularlyLinkedList.Node.

C-3.34 Implement the clone( ) method for the CircularlyLinkedList class.

C-3.35 Implement the clone( ) method for the DoublyLinkedList class.

Projects

P-3.36 Write a Java program for a matrix class that can add and multiply arbitrary two-dimensional arrays of integers.

P-3.37 Write a class that maintains the top ten scores for a game application, implementing the add and remove methods of Section 3.1.1, but using a singly linked list instead of an array.

P-3.38 Perform the previous project, but use a doubly linked list. Moreover, your implementation of remove(i) should make the fewest number of pointer hops to get to the game entry at index i.

P-3.39 Write a program that can perform the Caesar cipher for English messages that include both upper- and lowercase characters.

P-3.40 Implement a class, SubstitutionCipher, with a constructor that takes a string with the 26 uppercase letters in an arbitrary order and uses that as the encoder for a cipher (that is, A is mapped to the first character of the parameter, B is mapped to the second, and so on.) You should derive the decoding map from the forward version.

P-3.41 Redesign the CaesarCipher class as a subclass of the SubstitutionCipher from the previous problem.

P-3.42 Design a RandomCipher class as a subclass of the SubstitutionCipher from Exercise P-3.40, so that each instance of the class relies on a random permutation of letters for its mapping.

P-3.43 In the children's game, Duck, Duck, Goose, a group of children sit in a circle. One of them is elected "it" and that person walks around the outside of the circle. The person who is "it" pats each child on the head, saying "Duck" each time, until randomly reaching a child that the "it" person identifies as "Goose." At this point there is a mad scramble, as the "Goose" and the "it" person race around the circle. Whoever returns to the Goose's former place first gets to remain in the circle. The loser of this race is the "it" person for the next round of play. The game continues like this until the children get bored or an adult tells them it's snack time. Write software that simulates a game of Duck, Duck, Goose.

Chapter Notes

The fundamental data structures of arrays and linked lists discussed in this chapter belong to the folklore of computer science. They were first chronicled in the computer science literature by Knuth in his seminal book on *Fundamental Algorithms* [60].

Chapter

4

Algorithm Analysis

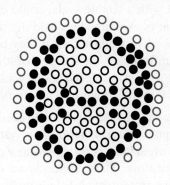

Contents

In a classic story, the famous mathematician Archimedes was asked to determine if a golden crown commissioned by the king was indeed pure gold, and not part silver, as an informant had claimed. Archimedes discovered a way to perform this analysis while stepping into a bath. He noted that water spilled out of the bath in proportion to the amount of him that went in. Realizing the implications of this fact, he immediately got out of the bath and ran naked through the city shouting, "Eureka, eureka!" for he had discovered an analysis tool (displacement), which, when combined with a simple scale, could determine if the king's new crown was good or not. That is, Archimedes could dip the crown and an equal-weight amount of gold into a bowl of water to see if they both displaced the same amount. This discovery was unfortunate for the goldsmith, however, for when Archimedes did his analysis, the crown displaced more water than an equal-weight lump of pure gold, indicating that the crown was not, in fact, pure gold.

In this book, we are interested in the design of "good" data structures and algorithms. Simply put, a *data structure* is a systematic way of organizing and accessing data, and an *algorithm* is a step-by-step procedure for performing some task in a finite amount of time. These concepts are central to computing, but to be able to classify some data structures and algorithms as "good," we must have precise ways of analyzing them.

The primary analysis tool we will use in this book involves characterizing the running times of algorithms and data structure operations, with space usage also being of interest. Running time is a natural measure of "goodness," since time is a precious resource—computer solutions should run as fast as possible. In general, the running time of an algorithm or data structure operation increases with the input size, although it may also vary for different inputs of the same size. Also, the running time is affected by the hardware environment (e.g., the processor, clock rate, memory, disk) and software environment (e.g., the operating system, programming language) in which the algorithm is implemented and executed. All other factors being equal, the running time of the same algorithm on the same input data will be smaller if the computer has, say, a much faster processor or if the implementation is done in a program compiled into native machine code instead of an interpreted implementation run on a virtual machine. We begin this chapter by discussing tools for performing experimental studies, yet also limitations to the use of experiments as a primary means for evaluating algorithm efficiency.

Focusing on running time as a primary measure of goodness requires that we be able to use a few mathematical tools. In spite of the possible variations that come from different environmental factors, we would like to focus on the relationship between the running time of an algorithm and the size of its input. We are interested in characterizing an algorithm's running time as a function of the input size. But what is the proper way of measuring it? In this chapter, we "roll up our sleeves" and develop a mathematical way of analyzing algorithms.

4.1 Experimental Studies

One way to study the efficiency of an algorithm is to implement it and experiment by running the program on various test inputs while recording the time spent during each execution. A simple mechanism for collecting such running times in Java is based on use of the currentTimeMillis method of the System class. That method reports the number of milliseconds that have passed since a benchmark time known as the epoch (January 1, 1970 UTC). It is not that we are directly interested in the time since the epoch; the key is that if we record the time immediately before executing the algorithm and then immediately after, we can measure the *elapsed* time of an algorithm's execution by computing the difference of those times. A typical way to automate this process is shown in Code Fragment 4.1.

```
1  long startTime = System.currentTimeMillis( );      // record the starting time
2  /* (run the algorithm) */
3  long endTime = System.currentTimeMillis( );        // record the ending time
4  long elapsed = endTime − startTime;                // compute the elapsed time
```

Code Fragment 4.1: Typical approach for timing an algorithm in Java.

Measuring elapsed time in this fashion provides a reasonable reflection of an algorithm's efficiency; for extremely quick operations, Java provides a method, nanoTime, that measures in nanoseconds rather than milliseconds.

Because we are interested in the general dependence of running time on the size and structure of the input, we should perform independent experiments on many different test inputs of various sizes. We can then visualize the results by plotting the performance of each run of the algorithm as a point with x-coordinate equal to the input size, n, and y-coordinate equal to the running time, t. Such a visualization provides some intuition regarding the relationship between problem size and execution time for the algorithm. This may be followed by a statistical analysis that seeks to fit the best function of the input size to the experimental data. To be meaningful, this analysis requires that we choose good sample inputs and test enough of them to be able to make sound statistical claims about the algorithm's running time.

However, the measured times reported by both methods currentTimeMillis and nanoTime will vary greatly from machine to machine, and may likely vary from trial to trial, even on the same machine. This is because many processes share use of a computer's **central processing unit** (or **CPU**) and memory system; therefore, the elapsed time will depend on what other processes are running on the computer when a test is performed. While the precise running time may not be dependable, experiments are quite useful when comparing the efficiency of two or more algorithms, so long as they gathered under similar circumstances.

As a tangible example of experimental analysis, we consider two algorithms for constructing long strings in Java. Our goal will be to have a method, with a calling signature such as repeat('*', 40), that produces a string composed of 40 asterisks: "**".

The first algorithm we consider performs repeated string concatenation, based on the + operator. It is implemented as method repeat1 in Code Fragment 4.2. The second algorithm relies on Java's StringBuilder class (see Section 1.3), and is implemented as method repeat2 in Code Fragment 4.2.

```java
 1  /** Uses repeated concatenation to compose a String with n copies of character c. */
 2  public static String repeat1(char c, int n) {
 3    String answer = "";
 4    for (int j=0; j < n; j++)
 5      answer += c;
 6    return answer;
 7  }
 8
 9  /** Uses StringBuilder to compose a String with n copies of character c. */
10  public static String repeat2(char c, int n) {
11    StringBuilder sb = new StringBuilder();
12    for (int j=0; j < n; j++)
13      sb.append(c);
14    return sb.toString();
15  }
```

Code Fragment 4.2: Two algorithms for composing a string of repeated characters.

As an experiment, we used System.currentTimeMillis( ), in the style of Code Fragment 4.1, to measure the efficiency of both repeat1 and repeat2 for very large strings. We executed trials to compose strings of increasing lengths to explore the relationship between the running time and the string length. The results of our experiments are shown in Table 4.1 and charted on a log-log scale in Figure 4.1.

n	repeat1 (in ms)	repeat2 (in ms)
50,000	2,884	1
100,000	7,437	1
200,000	39,158	2
400,000	170,173	3
800,000	690,836	7
1,600,000	2,874,968	13
3,200,000	12,809,631	28
6,400,000	59,594,275	58
12,800,000	265,696,421	135

Table 4.1: Results of timing experiment on the methods from Code Fragment 4.2.

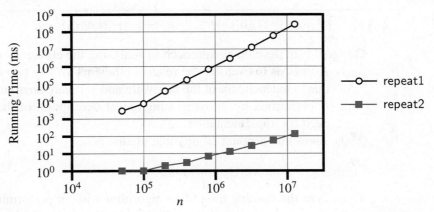

Figure 4.1: Chart of the results of the timing experiment from Code Fragment 4.2, displayed on a log-log scale. The divergent slopes demonstrate an order of magnitude difference in the growth of the running times.

The most striking outcome of these experiments is how much faster the repeat2 algorithm is relative to repeat1. While repeat1 is already taking more than 3 *days* to compose a string of 12.8 million characters, repeat2 is able to do the same in a fraction of a *second*. We also see some interesting trends in how the running times of the algorithms each depend upon the size of n. As the value of n is doubled, the running time of repeat1 typically increases more than fourfold, while the running time of repeat2 approximately doubles.

Challenges of Experimental Analysis

While experimental studies of running times are valuable, especially when fine-tuning production-quality code, there are three major limitations to their use for algorithm analysis:

- Experimental running times of two algorithms are difficult to directly compare unless the experiments are performed in the same hardware and software environments.
- Experiments can be done only on a limited set of test inputs; hence, they leave out the running times of inputs not included in the experiment (and these inputs may be important).
- An algorithm must be fully implemented in order to execute it to study its running time experimentally.

This last requirement is the most serious drawback to the use of experimental studies. At early stages of design, when considering a choice of data structures or algorithms, it would be foolish to spend a significant amount of time implementing an approach that could easily be deemed inferior by a higher-level analysis.

4.1.1   Moving Beyond Experimental Analysis

Our goal is to develop an approach to analyzing the efficiency of algorithms that:

1. Allows us to evaluate the relative efficiency of any two algorithms in a way that is independent of the hardware and software environment.
2. Is performed by studying a high-level description of the algorithm without need for implementation.
3. Takes into account all possible inputs.

Counting Primitive Operations

To analyze the running time of an algorithm without performing experiments, we perform an analysis directly on a high-level description of the algorithm (either in the form of an actual code fragment, or language-independent pseudocode). We define a set of ***primitive operations*** such as the following:

- Assigning a value to a variable
- Following an object reference
- Performing an arithmetic operation (for example, adding two numbers)
- Comparing two numbers
- Accessing a single element of an array by index
- Calling a method
- Returning from a method

Formally, a primitive operation corresponds to a low-level instruction with an execution time that is constant. Ideally, this might be the type of basic operation that is executed by the hardware, although many of our primitive operations may be translated to a small number of instructions. Instead of trying to determine the specific execution time of each primitive operation, we will simply count how many primitive operations are executed, and use this number t as a measure of the running time of the algorithm.

This operation count will correlate to an actual running time in a specific computer, for each primitive operation corresponds to a constant number of instructions, and there are only a fixed number of primitive operations. The implicit assumption in this approach is that the running times of different primitive operations will be fairly similar. Thus, the number, t, of primitive operations an algorithm performs will be proportional to the actual running time of that algorithm.

Measuring Operations as a Function of Input Size

To capture the order of growth of an algorithm's running time, we will associate, with each algorithm, a function $f(n)$ that characterizes the number of primitive operations that are performed as a function of the input size n. Section 4.2 will introduce the seven most common functions that arise, and Section 4.3 will introduce a mathematical framework for comparing functions to each other.

Focusing on the Worst-Case Input

An algorithm may run faster on some inputs than it does on others of the same size. Thus, we may wish to express the running time of an algorithm as the function of the input size obtained by taking the average over all possible inputs of the same size. Unfortunately, such an ***average-case*** analysis is typically quite challenging. It requires us to define a probability distribution on the set of inputs, which is often a difficult task. Figure 4.2 schematically shows how, depending on the input distribution, the running time of an algorithm can be anywhere between the worst-case time and the best-case time. For example, what if inputs are really only of types "A" or "D"?

An average-case analysis usually requires that we calculate expected running times based on a given input distribution, which usually involves sophisticated probability theory. Therefore, for the remainder of this book, unless we specify otherwise, we will characterize running times in terms of the ***worst case***, as a function of the input size, n, of the algorithm.

Worst-case analysis is much easier than average-case analysis, as it requires only the ability to identify the worst-case input, which is often simple. Also, this approach typically leads to better algorithms. Making the standard of success for an algorithm to perform well in the worst case necessarily requires that it will do well on ***every*** input. That is, designing for the worst case leads to stronger algorithmic "muscles," much like a track star who always practices by running up an incline.

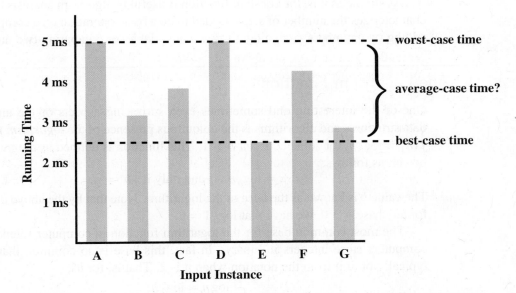

Figure 4.2: The difference between best-case and worst-case time. Each bar represents the running time of some algorithm on a different possible input.

4.2   The Seven Functions Used in This Book

In this section, we will briefly discuss the seven most important functions used in the analysis of algorithms. We will use only these seven simple functions for almost all the analysis we do in this book. In fact, a section that uses a function other than one of these seven will be marked with a star ($\star$) to indicate that it is optional. In addition to these seven fundamental functions, an appendix (available on the companion website) contains a list of other useful mathematical facts that apply in the analysis of data structures and algorithms.

The Constant Function

The simplest function we can think of is the ***constant function***, that is,

$$f(n) = c,$$

for some fixed constant c, such as $c = 5$, $c = 27$, or $c = 2^{10}$. That is, for any argument n, the constant function $f(n)$ assigns the value c. In other words, it does not matter what the value of n is; $f(n)$ will always be equal to the constant value c.

Because we are most interested in integer functions, the most fundamental constant function is $g(n) = 1$, and this is the typical constant function we use in this book. Note that any other constant function, $f(n) = c$, can be written as a constant c times $g(n)$. That is, $f(n) = cg(n)$ in this case.

As simple as it is, the constant function is useful in algorithm analysis because it characterizes the number of steps needed to do a basic operation on a computer, like adding two numbers, assigning a value to a variable, or comparing two numbers.

The Logarithm Function

One of the interesting and sometimes even surprising aspects of the analysis of data structures and algorithms is the ubiquitous presence of the ***logarithm function***, $f(n) = \log_b n$, for some constant $b > 1$. This function is defined as the inverse of a power, as follows:

$$x = \log_b n \quad \text{if and only if} \quad b^x = n.$$

The value b is known as the ***base*** of the logarithm. Note that by the above definition, for any base $b > 0$, we have that $\log_b 1 = 0$.

The most common base for the logarithm function in computer science is 2 as computers store integers in binary. In fact, this base is so common that we will typically omit it from the notation when it is 2. That is, for us,

$$\log n = \log_2 n.$$

We note that most handheld calculators have a button marked LOG, but this is typically for calculating the logarithm base-10, not base-two.

Computing the logarithm function exactly for any integer n involves the use of calculus, but we can use an approximation that is good enough for our purposes without calculus. We recall that the **ceiling** of a real number, x, is the smallest integer greater than or equal to x, denoted with $\lceil x \rceil$. The ceiling of x can be viewed as an integer approximation of x since we have $x \leq \lceil x \rceil < x + 1$. For a positive integer, n, we repeatedly divide n by b and stop when we get a number less than or equal to 1. The number of divisions performed is equal to $\lceil \log_b n \rceil$. We give below three examples of the computation of $\lceil \log_b n \rceil$ by repeated divisions:

- $\lceil \log_3 27 \rceil = 3$, because $((27/3)/3)/3 = 1$;
- $\lceil \log_4 64 \rceil = 3$, because $((64/4)/4)/4 = 1$;
- $\lceil \log_2 12 \rceil = 4$, because $(((12/2)/2)/2)/2 = 0.75 \leq 1$.

The following proposition describes several important identities that involve logarithms for any base greater than 1.

Proposition 4.1 (Logarithm Rules): *Given real numbers* $a > 0$, $b > 1$, $c > 0$, *and* $d > 1$, *we have:*

1. $\log_b(ac) = \log_b a + \log_b c$
2. $\log_b(a/c) = \log_b a - \log_b c$
3. $\log_b(a^c) = c \log_b a$
4. $\log_b a = \log_d a / \log_d b$
5. $b^{\log_d a} = a^{\log_d b}$

By convention, the unparenthesized notation $\log n^c$ denotes the value $\log(n^c)$. We use a notational shorthand, $\log^c n$, to denote the quantity, $(\log n)^c$, in which the result of the logarithm is raised to a power.

The above identities can be derived from converse rules for exponentiation that we will present on page 161. We illustrate these identities with a few examples.

Example 4.2: *We demonstrate below some interesting applications of the logarithm rules from Proposition 4.1 (using the usual convention that the base of a logarithm is 2 if it is omitted).*

- $\log(2n) = \log 2 + \log n = 1 + \log n$, *by rule 1*
- $\log(n/2) = \log n - \log 2 = \log n - 1$, *by rule 2*
- $\log n^3 = 3 \log n$, *by rule 3*
- $\log 2^n = n \log 2 = n \cdot 1 = n$, *by rule 3*
- $\log_4 n = (\log n)/\log 4 = (\log n)/2$, *by rule 4*
- $2^{\log n} = n^{\log 2} = n^1 = n$, *by rule 5*.

As a practical matter, we note that rule 4 gives us a way to compute the base-two logarithm on a calculator that has a base-10 logarithm button, LOG, *for*

$$\log_2 n = \text{LOG } n / \text{LOG } 2.$$

The Linear Function

Another simple yet important function is the ***linear function***,

$$f(n) = n.$$

That is, given an input value n, the linear function f assigns the value n itself.

This function arises in algorithm analysis any time we have to do a single basic operation for each of n elements. For example, comparing a number x to each element of an array of size n will require n comparisons. The linear function also represents the best running time we can hope to achieve for any algorithm that processes each of n objects that are not already in the computer's memory, because reading in the n objects already requires n operations.

The *N*-Log-*N* Function

The next function we discuss in this section is the ***n-log-n function***,

$$f(n) = n \log n,$$

that is, the function that assigns to an input n the value of n times the logarithm base-two of n. This function grows a little more rapidly than the linear function and a lot less rapidly than the quadratic function; therefore, we would greatly prefer an algorithm with a running time that is proportional to $n \log n$, than one with quadratic running time. We will see several important algorithms that exhibit a running time proportional to the n-log-n function. For example, the fastest possible algorithms for sorting n arbitrary values require time proportional to $n \log n$.

The Quadratic Function

Another function that appears often in algorithm analysis is the ***quadratic function***,

$$f(n) = n^2.$$

That is, given an input value n, the function f assigns the product of n with itself (in other words, "n squared").

The main reason why the quadratic function appears in the analysis of algorithms is that there are many algorithms that have nested loops, where the inner loop performs a linear number of operations and the outer loop is performed a linear number of times. Thus, in such cases, the algorithm performs $n \cdot n = n^2$ operations.

Nested Loops and the Quadratic Function

The quadratic function can also arise in the context of nested loops where the first iteration of a loop uses one operation, the second uses two operations, the third uses three operations, and so on. That is, the number of operations is

$$1 + 2 + 3 + \cdots + (n-2) + (n-1) + n.$$

In other words, this is the total number of operations that will be performed by the nested loop if the number of operations performed inside the loop increases by one with each iteration of the outer loop. This quantity also has an interesting history.

In 1787, a German schoolteacher decided to keep his 9- and 10-year-old pupils occupied by adding up the integers from 1 to 100. But almost immediately one of the children claimed to have the answer! The teacher was suspicious, for the student had only the answer on his slate. But the answer, 5050, was correct and the student, Carl Gauss, grew up to be one of the greatest mathematicians of his time. We presume that young Gauss used the following identity.

Proposition 4.3: *For any integer $n \geq 1$, we have:*

$$1 + 2 + 3 + \cdots + (n-2) + (n-1) + n = \frac{n(n+1)}{2}.$$

We give two "visual" justifications of Proposition 4.3 in Figure 4.3.

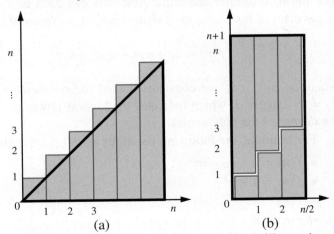

(a)	(b)

Figure 4.3: Visual justifications of Proposition 4.3. Both illustrations visualize the identity in terms of the total area covered by n unit-width rectangles with heights $1, 2, \ldots, n$. In (a), the rectangles are shown to cover a big triangle of area $n^2/2$ (base n and height n) plus n small triangles of area $1/2$ each (base 1 and height 1). In (b), which applies only when n is even, the rectangles are shown to cover a big rectangle of base $n/2$ and height $n+1$.

The lesson to be learned from Proposition 4.3 is that if we perform an algorithm with nested loops such that the operations in the inner loop increase by one each time, then the total number of operations is quadratic in the number of times, n, we perform the outer loop. To be fair, the number of operations is $n^2/2 + n/2$, and so this is just over half the number of operations than an algorithm that uses n operations each time the inner loop is performed. But the order of growth is still quadratic in n.

The Cubic Function and Other Polynomials

Continuing our discussion of functions that are powers of the input, we consider the **cubic function**,

$$f(n) = n^3,$$

which assigns to an input value n the product of n with itself three times.

The cubic function appears less frequently in the context of algorithm analysis than the constant, linear, and quadratic functions previously mentioned, but it does appear from time to time.

Polynomials

The linear, quadratic and cubic functions can each be viewed as being part of a larger class of functions, the **polynomials**. A **polynomial** function has the form,

$$f(n) = a_0 + a_1 n + a_2 n^2 + a_3 n^3 + \cdots + a_d n^d,$$

where $a_0, a_1, \ldots, a_d$ are constants, called the **coefficients** of the polynomial, and $a_d \neq 0$. Integer d, which indicates the highest power in the polynomial, is called the **degree** of the polynomial.

For example, the following functions are all polynomials:

- $f(n) = 2 + 5n + n^2$
- $f(n) = 1 + n^3$
- $f(n) = 1$
- $f(n) = n$
- $f(n) = n^2$

Therefore, we could argue that this book presents just four important functions used in algorithm analysis, but we will stick to saying that there are seven, since the constant, linear, and quadratic functions are too important to be lumped in with other polynomials. Running times that are polynomials with small degree are generally better than polynomial running times with larger degree.

Summations

A notation that appears again and again in the analysis of data structures and algorithms is the **summation**, which is defined as follows:

$$\sum_{i=a}^{b} f(i) = f(a) + f(a+1) + f(a+2) + \cdots + f(b),$$

where a and b are integers and $a \leq b$. Summations arise in data structure and algorithm analysis because the running times of loops naturally give rise to summations.

Using a summation, we can rewrite the formula of Proposition 4.3 as

$$\sum_{i=1}^{n} i = \frac{n(n+1)}{2}.$$

Likewise, we can write a polynomial $f(n)$ of degree d with coefficients $a_0, \ldots, a_d$ as

$$f(n) = \sum_{i=0}^{d} a_i n^i.$$

Thus, the summation notation gives us a shorthand way of expressing sums of increasing terms that have a regular structure.

The Exponential Function

Another function used in the analysis of algorithms is the **exponential function**,
$$f(n) = b^n,$$
where b is a positive constant, called the **base**, and the argument n is the **exponent**. That is, function $f(n)$ assigns to the input argument n the value obtained by multiplying the base b by itself n times. As was the case with the logarithm function, the most common base for the exponential function in algorithm analysis is $b = 2$. For example, an integer word containing n bits can represent all the nonnegative integers less than 2^n. If we have a loop that starts by performing one operation and then doubles the number of operations performed with each iteration, then the number of operations performed in the nth iteration is 2^n.

We sometimes have other exponents besides n, however; hence, it is useful for us to know a few handy rules for working with exponents. In particular, the following **exponent rules** are quite helpful.

Proposition 4.4 (Exponent Rules): *Given positive integers a, b, and c, we have*
1. $(b^a)^c = b^{ac}$
2. $b^a b^c = b^{a+c}$
3. $b^a / b^c = b^{a-c}$

For example, we have the following:

- $256 = 16^2 = (2^4)^2 = 2^{4 \cdot 2} = 2^8 = 256$ (Exponent Rule 1)
- $243 = 3^5 = 3^{2+3} = 3^2 3^3 = 9 \cdot 27 = 243$ (Exponent Rule 2)
- $16 = 1024/64 = 2^{10}/2^6 = 2^{10-6} = 2^4 = 16$ (Exponent Rule 3)

We can extend the exponential function to exponents that are fractions or real numbers and to negative exponents, as follows. Given a positive integer k, we define $b^{1/k}$ to be k^{th} root of b, that is, the number r such that $r^k = b$. For example, $25^{1/2} = 5$, since $5^2 = 25$. Likewise, $27^{1/3} = 3$ and $16^{1/4} = 2$. This approach allows us to define any power whose exponent can be expressed as a fraction, for $b^{a/c} = (b^a)^{1/c}$, by Exponent Rule 1. For example, $9^{3/2} = (9^3)^{1/2} = 729^{1/2} = 27$. Thus, $b^{a/c}$ is really just the cth root of the integral exponent b^a.

We can further extend the exponential function to define b^x for any real number x, by computing a series of numbers of the form $b^{a/c}$ for fractions a/c that get progressively closer and closer to x. Any real number x can be approximated arbitrarily closely by a fraction a/c; hence, we can use the fraction a/c as the exponent of b to get arbitrarily close to b^x. For example, the number 2^π is well defined. Finally, given a negative exponent d, we define $b^d = 1/b^{-d}$, which corresponds to applying Exponent Rule 3 with $a = 0$ and $c = -d$. For example, $2^{-3} = 1/2^3 = 1/8$.

Geometric Sums

Suppose we have a loop for which each iteration takes a multiplicative factor longer than the previous one. This loop can be analyzed using the following proposition.

Proposition 4.5: *For any integer $n \geq 0$ and any real number a such that $a > 0$ and $a \neq 1$, consider the summation*

$$\sum_{i=0}^{n} a^i = 1 + a + a^2 + \cdots + a^n$$

(remembering that $a^0 = 1$ if $a > 0$). This summation is equal to

$$\frac{a^{n+1} - 1}{a - 1}.$$

Summations as shown in Proposition 4.5 are called **geometric** summations, because each term is geometrically larger than the previous one if $a > 1$. For example, everyone working in computing should know that

$$1 + 2 + 4 + 8 + \cdots + 2^{n-1} = 2^n - 1,$$

for this is the largest unsigned integer that can be represented in binary notation using n bits.

4.2.1 Comparing Growth Rates

To sum up, Table 4.2 shows, in order, each of the seven common functions used in algorithm analysis.

constant	logarithm	linear	n-log-n	quadratic	cubic	exponential
1	$\log n$	n	$n \log n$	n^2	n^3	a^n

Table 4.2: Seven functions commonly used in the analysis of algorithms. We recall that $\log n = \log_2 n$. Also, we denote with a a constant greater than 1.

Ideally, we would like data structure operations to run in times proportional to the constant or logarithm function, and we would like our algorithms to run in linear or n-log-n time. Algorithms with quadratic or cubic running times are less practical, and algorithms with exponential running times are infeasible for all but the smallest sized inputs. Plots of the seven functions are shown in Figure 4.4.

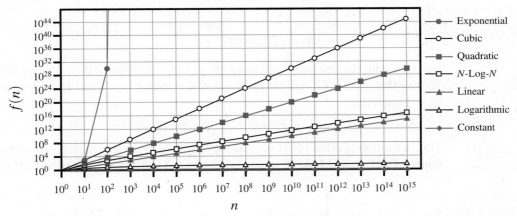

Figure 4.4: Growth rates for the seven fundamental functions used in algorithm analysis. We use base $a = 2$ for the exponential function. The functions are plotted on a log-log chart to compare the growth rates primarily as slopes. Even so, the exponential function grows too fast to display all its values on the chart.

The Ceiling and Floor Functions

When discussing logarithms, we noted that the value is generally not an integer, yet the running time of an algorithm is usually expressed by means of an integer quantity, such as the number of operations performed. Thus, the analysis of an algorithm may sometimes involve the use of the **floor function** and **ceiling function**, which are defined respectively as follows:

- $\lfloor x \rfloor$ = the largest integer less than or equal to x. (e.g., $\lfloor 3.7 \rfloor = 3$.)
- $\lceil x \rceil$ = the smallest integer greater than or equal to x. (e.g., $\lceil 5.2 \rceil = 6$.)

4.3   Asymptotic Analysis

In algorithm analysis, we focus on the growth rate of the running time as a function of the input size n, taking a "big-picture" approach. For example, it is often enough just to know that the running time of an algorithm ***grows proportionally to*** n.

   We analyze algorithms using a mathematical notation for functions that disregards constant factors. Namely, we characterize the running times of algorithms by using functions that map the size of the input, n, to values that correspond to the main factor that determines the growth rate in terms of n. This approach reflects that each basic step in a pseudocode description or a high-level language implementation may correspond to a small number of primitive operations. Thus, we can perform an analysis of an algorithm by estimating the number of primitive operations executed up to a constant factor, rather than getting bogged down in language-specific or hardware-specific analysis of the exact number of operations that execute on the computer.

4.3.1   The "Big-Oh" Notation

Let $f(n)$ and $g(n)$ be functions mapping positive integers to positive real numbers. We say that $f(n)$ is $O(g(n))$ if there is a real constant $c > 0$ and an integer constant $n_0 \geq 1$ such that

$$f(n) \leq c \cdot g(n), \quad \text{for} \quad n \geq n_0.$$

This definition is often referred to as the "big-Oh" notation, for it is sometimes pronounced as "$f(n)$ is ***big-Oh*** of $g(n)$." Figure 4.5 illustrates the general definition.

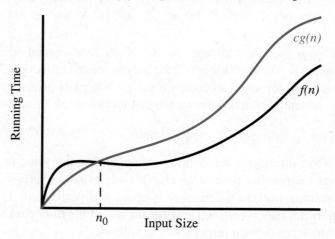

Figure 4.5: Illustrating the "big-Oh" notation. The function $f(n)$ is $O(g(n))$, since $f(n) \leq c \cdot g(n)$ when $n \geq n_0$.

Example 4.6: *The function $8n + 5$ is $O(n)$.*

Justification: By the big-Oh definition, we need to find a real constant $c > 0$ and an integer constant $n_0 \geq 1$ such that $8n + 5 \leq cn$ for every integer $n \geq n_0$. It is easy to see that a possible choice is $c = 9$ and $n_0 = 5$. Indeed, this is one of infinitely many choices available because there is a trade-off between c and n_0. For example, we could rely on constants $c = 13$ and $n_0 = 1$. ∎

The big-Oh notation allows us to say that a function $f(n)$ is "less than or equal to" another function $g(n)$ up to a constant factor and in the ***asymptotic*** sense as n grows toward infinity. This ability comes from the fact that the definition uses "$\leq$" to compare $f(n)$ to a $g(n)$ times a constant, c, for the asymptotic cases when $n \geq n_0$. However, it is considered poor taste to say "$f(n) \leq O(g(n))$," since the big-Oh already denotes the "less-than-or-equal-to" concept. Likewise, although common, it is not fully correct to say "$f(n) = O(g(n))$," with the usual understanding of the "$=$" relation, because there is no way to make sense of the symmetric statement, "$O(g(n)) = f(n)$." It is best to say, "$f(n)$ *is* $O(g(n))$."

Alternatively, we can say "$f(n)$ is ***order of*** $g(n)$." For the more mathematically inclined, it is also correct to say, "$f(n) \in O(g(n))$," for the big-Oh notation, technically speaking, denotes a whole collection of functions. In this book, we will stick to presenting big-Oh statements as "$f(n)$ *is* $O(g(n))$." Even with this interpretation, there is considerable freedom in how we can use arithmetic operations with the big-Oh notation, and with this freedom comes a certain amount of responsibility.

Some Properties of the Big-Oh Notation

The big-Oh notation allows us to ignore constant factors and lower-order terms and focus on the main components of a function that affect its growth.

Example 4.7: $5n^4 + 3n^3 + 2n^2 + 4n + 1$ is $O(n^4)$.

Justification: Note that $5n^4 + 3n^3 + 2n^2 + 4n + 1 \leq (5 + 3 + 2 + 4 + 1)n^4 = cn^4$, for $c = 15$, when $n \geq n_0 = 1$. ∎

In fact, we can characterize the growth rate of any polynomial function.

Proposition 4.8: *If $f(n)$ is a polynomial of degree d, that is,*

$$f(n) = a_0 + a_1 n + \cdots + a_d n^d,$$

and $a_d > 0$, then $f(n)$ is $O(n^d)$.

Justification: Note that, for $n \geq 1$, we have $1 \leq n \leq n^2 \leq \cdots \leq n^d$; hence,

$$a_0 + a_1 n + a_2 n^2 + \cdots + a_d n^d \leq (|a_0| + |a_1| + |a_2| + \cdots + |a_d|)\, n^d.$$

We show that $f(n)$ is $O(n^d)$ by defining $c = |a_0| + |a_1| + \cdots + |a_d|$ and $n_0 = 1$. ∎

Thus, the highest-degree term in a polynomial is the term that determines the asymptotic growth rate of that polynomial. We consider some additional properties of the big-Oh notation in the exercises. Let us consider some further examples here, focusing on combinations of the seven fundamental functions used in algorithm design. We rely on the mathematical fact that $\log n \le n$ for $n \ge 1$.

Example 4.9: $5n^2 + 3n\log n + 2n + 5$ *is* $O(n^2)$.

Justification: $5n^2 + 3n\log n + 2n + 5 \le (5 + 3 + 2 + 5)n^2 = cn^2$, for $c = 15$, when $n \ge n_0 = 1$. ∎

Example 4.10: $20n^3 + 10n\log n + 5$ *is* $O(n^3)$.

Justification: $20n^3 + 10n\log n + 5 \le 35n^3$, for $n \ge 1$. ∎

Example 4.11: $3\log n + 2$ *is* $O(\log n)$.

Justification: $3\log n + 2 \le 5\log n$, for $n \ge 2$. Note that $\log n$ is zero for $n = 1$. That is why we use $n \ge n_0 = 2$ in this case. ∎

Example 4.12: 2^{n+2} *is* $O(2^n)$.

Justification: $2^{n+2} = 2^n \cdot 2^2 = 4 \cdot 2^n$; hence, we can take $c = 4$ and $n_0 = 1$ in this case. ∎

Example 4.13: $2n + 100\log n$ *is* $O(n)$.

Justification: $2n + 100\log n \le 102n$, for $n \ge n_0 = 1$; hence, we can take $c = 102$ in this case. ∎

Characterizing Functions in Simplest Terms

In general, we should use the big-Oh notation to characterize a function as closely as possible. While it is true that the function $f(n) = 4n^3 + 3n^2$ is $O(n^5)$ or even $O(n^4)$, it is more accurate to say that $f(n)$ is $O(n^3)$. Consider, by way of analogy, a scenario where a hungry traveler driving along a long country road happens upon a local farmer walking home from a market. If the traveler asks the farmer how much longer he must drive before he can find some food, it may be truthful for the farmer to say, "certainly no longer than 12 hours," but it is much more accurate (and helpful) for him to say, "you can find a market just a few minutes drive up this road." Thus, even with the big-Oh notation, we should strive as much as possible to tell the whole truth.

It is also considered poor taste to include constant factors and lower-order terms in the big-Oh notation. For example, it is not fashionable to say that the function $2n^2$ is $O(4n^2 + 6n\log n)$, although this is completely correct. We should strive instead to describe the function in the big-Oh in ***simplest terms***.

The seven functions listed in Section 4.2 are the most common functions used in conjunction with the big-Oh notation to characterize the running times and space usage of algorithms. Indeed, we typically use the names of these functions to refer to the running times of the algorithms they characterize. So, for example, we would say that an algorithm that runs in worst-case time $4n^2 + n \log n$ is a *quadratic-time* algorithm, since it runs in $O(n^2)$ time. Likewise, an algorithm running in time at most $5n + 20 \log n + 4$ would be called a *linear-time* algorithm.

Big-Omega

Just as the big-Oh notation provides an asymptotic way of saying that a function is "less than or equal to" another function, the following notations provide an asymptotic way of saying that a function grows at a rate that is "greater than or equal to" that of another.

Let $f(n)$ and $g(n)$ be functions mapping positive integers to positive real numbers. We say that $f(n)$ is $\Omega(g(n))$, pronounced "$f(n)$ is big-Omega of $g(n)$," if $g(n)$ is $O(f(n))$, that is, there is a real constant $c > 0$ and an integer constant $n_0 \geq 1$ such that

$$f(n) \geq cg(n), \quad \text{for} \quad n \geq n_0.$$

This definition allows us to say asymptotically that one function is greater than or equal to another, up to a constant factor.

Example 4.14: $3n \log n - 2n$ *is* $\Omega(n \log n)$.

Justification: $3n \log n - 2n = n \log n + 2n(\log n - 1) \geq n \log n$ for $n \geq 2$; hence, we can take $c = 1$ and $n_0 = 2$ in this case. ∎

Big-Theta

In addition, there is a notation that allows us to say that two functions grow at the same rate, up to constant factors. We say that $f(n)$ is $\Theta(g(n))$, pronounced "$f(n)$ is big-Theta of $g(n)$," if $f(n)$ is $O(g(n))$ and $f(n)$ is $\Omega(g(n))$, that is, there are real constants $c' > 0$ and $c'' > 0$, and an integer constant $n_0 \geq 1$ such that

$$c'g(n) \leq f(n) \leq c''g(n), \quad \text{for} \quad n \geq n_0.$$

Example 4.15: $3n \log n + 4n + 5 \log n$ *is* $\Theta(n \log n)$.

Justification: $3n \log n \leq 3n \log n + 4n + 5 \log n \leq (3 + 4 + 5)n \log n$ for $n \geq 2$. ∎

4.3.2 Comparative Analysis

The big-Oh notation is widely used to characterize running times and space bounds in terms of some parameter n, which is defined as a chosen measure of the "size" of the problem. Suppose two algorithms solving the same problem are available: an algorithm A, which has a running time of $O(n)$, and an algorithm B, which has a running time of $O(n^2)$. Which algorithm is better? We know that n is $O(n^2)$, which implies that algorithm A is ***asymptotically better*** than algorithm B, although for a small value of n, B may have a lower running time than A.

We can use the big-Oh notation to order classes of functions by asymptotic growth rate. Our seven functions are ordered by increasing growth rate in the following sequence, such that $f(n)$ is $O(g(n))$ if function $f(n)$ precedes function $g(n)$:

$$1, \quad \log n, \quad n, \quad n\log n, \quad n^2, \quad n^3, \quad 2^n.$$

We illustrate the growth rates of the seven functions in Table 4.3. (See also Figure 4.4 from Section 4.2.1.)

n	$\log n$	n	$n\log n$	n^2	n^3	2^n
8	3	8	24	64	512	256
16	4	16	64	256	4,096	65,536
32	5	32	160	1,024	32,768	4,294,967,296
64	6	64	384	4,096	262,144	1.84×10^{19}
128	7	128	896	16,384	2,097,152	3.40×10^{38}
256	8	256	2,048	65,536	16,777,216	1.15×10^{77}
512	9	512	4,608	262,144	134,217,728	1.34×10^{154}

Table 4.3: Selected values of fundamental functions in algorithm analysis.

We further illustrate the importance of the asymptotic viewpoint in Table 4.4. This table explores the maximum size allowed for an input instance that is processed by an algorithm in 1 second, 1 minute, and 1 hour. It shows the importance of good algorithm design, because an asymptotically slow algorithm is beaten in the long run by an asymptotically faster algorithm, even if the constant factor for the asymptotically faster algorithm is worse.

Running	Maximum Problem Size (n)		
Time (μs)	1 second	1 minute	1 hour
$400n$	2,500	150,000	9,000,000
$2n^2$	707	5,477	42,426
2^n	19	25	31

Table 4.4: Maximum size of a problem that can be solved in 1 second, 1 minute, and 1 hour, for various running times measured in microseconds.

The importance of good algorithm design goes beyond just what can be solved effectively on a given computer, however. As shown in Table 4.5, even if we achieve a dramatic speedup in hardware, we still cannot overcome the handicap of an asymptotically slow algorithm. This table shows the new maximum problem size achievable for any fixed amount of time, assuming algorithms with the given running times are now run on a computer 256 times faster than the previous one.

Running Time	New Maximum Problem Size
$400n$	$256m$
$2n^2$	$16m$
2^n	$m+8$

Table 4.5: Increase in the maximum size of a problem that can be solved in a fixed amount of time, by using a computer that is 256 times faster than the previous one. Each entry is a function of m, the previous maximum problem size.

Some Words of Caution

A few words of caution about asymptotic notation are in order at this point. First, note that the use of the big-Oh and related notations can be somewhat misleading should the constant factors they "hide" be very large. For example, while it is true that the function $10^{100}n$ is $O(n)$, if this is the running time of an algorithm being compared to one whose running time is $10n\log n$, we should prefer the $O(n\log n)$-time algorithm, even though the linear-time algorithm is asymptotically faster. This preference is because the constant factor, 10^{100}, which is called "one googol," is believed by many astronomers to be an upper bound on the number of atoms in the observable universe. So we are unlikely to ever have a real-world problem that has this number as its input size.

The observation above raises the issue of what constitutes a "fast" algorithm. Generally speaking, any algorithm running in $O(n\log n)$ time (with a reasonable constant factor) should be considered efficient. Even an $O(n^2)$-time function may be fast enough in some contexts, that is, when n is small. But an algorithm whose running time is an exponential function, e.g., $O(2^n)$, should almost never be considered efficient.

Exponential Running Times

To see how fast the function 2^n grows, consider the famous story about the inventor of the game of chess. He asked only that his king pay him 1 grain of rice for the first square on the board, 2 grains for the second, 4 grains for the third, 8 for the fourth, and so on. The number of grains in the 64th square would be

$$2^{63} = 9,223,372,036,854,775,808,$$

which is about nine billion billions!

If we must draw a line between efficient and inefficient algorithms, therefore, it is natural to make this distinction be that between those algorithms running in polynomial time and those running in exponential time. That is, make the distinction between algorithms with a running time that is $O(n^c)$, for some constant $c > 1$, and those with a running time that is $O(b^n)$, for some constant $b > 1$. Like so many notions we have discussed in this section, this too should be taken with a "grain of salt," for an algorithm running in $O(n^{100})$ time should probably not be considered "efficient." Even so, the distinction between polynomial-time and exponential-time algorithms is considered a robust measure of tractability.

4.3.3 Examples of Algorithm Analysis

Now that we have the big-Oh notation for doing algorithm analysis, let us give some examples by characterizing the running time of some simple algorithms using this notation. Moreover, in keeping with our earlier promise, we will illustrate below how each of the seven functions given earlier in this chapter can be used to characterize the running time of an example algorithm.

Constant-Time Operations

All of the primitive operations, originally described on page 154, are assumed to run in constant time; formally, we say they run in $O(1)$ time. We wish to emphasize several important constant-time operations that involve arrays. Assume that variable A is an array of n elements. The expression A.length in Java is evaluated in constant time, because arrays are represented internally with an explicit variable that records the length of the array. Another central behavior of arrays is that for any valid index j, the individual element, $A[j]$, can be accessed in constant time. This is because an array uses a consecutive block of memory. The jth element can be found, not by iterating through the array one element at a time, but by validating the index, and using it as an offset from the beginning of the array in determining the appropriate memory address. Therefore, we say that the expression $A[j]$ is evaluated in $O(1)$ time for an array.

Finding the Maximum of an Array

As a classic example of an algorithm with a running time that grows proportional to n, we consider the goal of finding the largest element of an array. A typical strategy is to loop through elements of the array while maintaining as a variable the largest element seen thus far. Code Fragment 4.3 presents a method named arrayMax implementing this strategy.

```
1   /** Returns the maximum value of a nonempty array of numbers. */
2   public static double arrayMax(double[ ] data) {
3     int n = data.length;
4     double currentMax = data[0];           // assume first entry is biggest (for now)
5     for (int j=1; j < n; j++)               // consider all other entries
6       if (data[j] > currentMax)             // if data[j] is biggest thus far...
7         currentMax = data[j];               // record it as the current max
8     return currentMax;
9   }
```

Code Fragment 4.3: A method that returns the maximum value of an array.

Using the big-Oh notation, we can write the following mathematically precise statement on the running time of algorithm arrayMax for *any* computer.

Proposition 4.16: *The algorithm,* arrayMax, *for computing the maximum element of an array of n numbers, runs in $O(n)$ time.*

Justification: The initialization at lines 3 and 4 and the **return** statement at line 8 require only a constant number of primitive operations. Each iteration of the loop also requires only a constant number of primitive operations, and the loop executes $n-1$ times. Therefore, we account for the number of primitive operations being $c' \cdot (n-1) + c''$ for appropriate constants c' and c'' that reflect, respectively, the work performed inside and outside the loop body. Because each primitive operation runs in constant time, we have that the running time of algorithm arrayMax on an input of size n is at most $c' \cdot (n-1) + c'' = c' \cdot n + (c''-c') \leq c' \cdot n$ if we assume, without loss of generality, that $c'' \leq c'$. We conclude that the running time of algorithm arrayMax is $O(n)$.   ■

Further Analysis of the Maximum-Finding Algorithm

A more interesting question about arrayMax is how many times we might update the current "biggest" value. In the worst case, if the data is given to us in increasing order, the biggest value is reassigned $n-1$ times. But what if the input is given to us in random order, with all orders equally likely; what would be the expected number of times we update the biggest value in this case? To answer this question, note that we update the current biggest in an iteration of the loop only if the current element is bigger than all the elements that precede it. If the sequence is given to us in random order, the probability that the jth element is the largest of the first j elements is $1/j$ (assuming uniqueness). Hence, the expected number of times we update the biggest (including initialization) is $H_n = \sum_{j=1}^{n} 1/j$, which is known as the nth ***Harmonic number***. It can be shown that H_n is $O(\log n)$. Therefore, the expected number of times the biggest value is updated by arrayMax on a randomly ordered sequence is $O(\log n)$.

Composing Long Strings

As our next example, we revisit the experimental study from Section 4.1, in which we examined two different implementations for composing a long string (see Code Fragment 4.2). Our first algorithm was based on repeated use of the string concatenation operator; for convenience, that method is also given in Code Fragment 4.4.

```
1  /** Uses repeated concatenation to compose a String with n copies of character c. */
2  public static String repeat1(char c, int n) {
3    String answer = "";
4    for (int j=0; j < n; j++)
5      answer += c;
6    return answer;
7  }
```

Code Fragment 4.4: Composing a string using repeated concatenation.

The most important aspect of this implementation is that strings in Java are *immutable* objects. Once created, an instance cannot be modified. The command, answer += c, is shorthand for answer = (answer + c). This command does not cause a new character to be added to the existing String instance; instead it produces a new String with the desired sequence of characters, and then it reassigns the variable, answer, to refer to that new string.

In terms of efficiency, the problem with this interpretation is that the creation of a new string as a result of a concatenation, requires time that is proportional to the length of the resulting string. The first time through this loop, the result has length 1, the second time through the loop the result has length 2, and so on, until we reach the final string of length n. Therefore, the overall time taken by this algorithm is proportional to

$$1 + 2 + \cdots + n,$$

which we recognize as the familiar $O(n^2)$ summation from Proposition 4.3. Therefore, the total time complexity of the repeat1 algorithm is $O(n^2)$.

We see this theoretical analysis reflected in the experimental results. The running time of a quadratic algorithm should theoretically quadruple if the size of the problem doubles, as $(2n)^2 = 4 \cdot n^2$. (We say "theoretically," because this does not account for lower-order terms that are hidden by the asymptotic notation.) We see such an approximate fourfold increase in the running time of repeat1 in Table 4.1 on page 152.

In contrast, the running times in that table for the repeat2 algorithm, which uses Java's StringBuilder class, demonstrate a trend of approximately *doubling* each time the problem size doubles. The StringBuilder class relies on an advanced technique with a worst-case running time of $O(n)$ for composing a string of length n; we will later explore that technique as the focus of Section 7.2.1.

Three-Way Set Disjointness

Suppose we are given three sets, A, B, and C, stored in three different integer arrays. We will assume that no individual set contains duplicate values, but that there may be some numbers that are in two or three of the sets. The ***three-way set disjointness*** problem is to determine if the intersection of the three sets is empty, namely, that there is no element x such that $x \in A$, $x \in B$, and $x \in C$. A simple Java method to determine this property is given in Code Fragment 4.5.

```
1  /** Returns true if there is no element common to all three arrays. */
2  public static boolean disjoint1(int[ ] groupA, int[ ] groupB, int[ ] groupC) {
3    for (int a : groupA)
4      for (int b : groupB)
5        for (int c : groupC)
6          if ((a == b) && (b == c))
7            return false;                      // we found a common value
8    return true;                               // if we reach this, sets are disjoint
9  }
```

Code Fragment 4.5: Algorithm disjoint1 for testing three-way set disjointness.

This simple algorithm loops through each possible triple of values from the three sets to see if those values are equivalent. If each of the original sets has size n, then the worst-case running time of this method is $O(n^3)$.

We can improve upon the asymptotic performance with a simple observation. Once inside the body of the loop over B, if selected elements a and b do not match each other, it is a waste of time to iterate through all values of C looking for a matching triple. An improved solution to this problem, taking advantage of this observation, is presented in Code Fragment 4.6.

```
1   /** Returns true if there is no element common to all three arrays. */
2   public static boolean disjoint2(int[ ] groupA, int[ ] groupB, int[ ] groupC) {
3     for (int a : groupA)
4       for (int b : groupB)
5         if (a == b)                // only check C when we find match from A and B
6           for (int c : groupC)
7             if (a == c)            // and thus b == c as well
8               return false;        // we found a common value
9     return true;                   // if we reach this, sets are disjoint
10  }
```

Code Fragment 4.6: Algorithm disjoint2 for testing three-way set disjointness.

In the improved version, it is not simply that we save time if we get lucky. We claim that the *worst-case* running time for disjoint2 is $O(n^2)$. There are quadratically many pairs (a,b) to consider. However, if A and B are each sets of distinct elements, there can be at most $O(n)$ such pairs with a equal to b. Therefore, the innermost loop, over C, executes at most n times.

To account for the overall running time, we examine the time spent executing each line of code. The management of the for loop over A requires $O(n)$ time. The management of the for loop over B accounts for a total of $O(n^2)$ time, since that loop is executed n different times. The test a $==$ b is evaluated $O(n^2)$ times. The rest of the time spent depends upon how many matching (a, b) pairs exist. As we have noted, there are at most n such pairs; therefore, the management of the loop over C and the commands within the body of that loop use at most $O(n^2)$ time. By our standard application of Proposition 4.8, the total time spent is $O(n^2)$.

Element Uniqueness

A problem that is closely related to the three-way set disjointness problem is the **element uniqueness problem**. In the former, we are given three sets and we presumed that there were no duplicates within a single set. In the element uniqueness problem, we are given an array with n elements and asked whether all elements of that collection are distinct from each other.

Our first solution to this problem uses a straightforward iterative algorithm. The unique1 method, given in Code Fragment 4.7, solves the element uniqueness problem by looping through all distinct pairs of indices $j < k$, checking if any of those pairs refer to elements that are equivalent to each other. It does this using two nested for loops, such that the first iteration of the outer loop causes $n - 1$ iterations of the inner loop, the second iteration of the outer loop causes $n - 2$ iterations of the inner loop, and so on. Thus, the worst-case running time of this method is proportional to

$$(n-1) + (n-2) + \cdots + 2 + 1,$$

which we recognize as the familiar $O(n^2)$ summation from Proposition 4.3.

```
1  /** Returns true if there are no duplicate elements in the array. */
2  public static boolean unique1(int[ ] data) {
3    int n = data.length;
4    for (int j=0; j < n−1; j++)
5      for (int k=j+1; k < n; k++)
6        if (data[j] == data[k])
7          return false;              // found duplicate pair
8    return true;                     // if we reach this, elements are unique
9  }
```

Code Fragment 4.7: Algorithm unique1 for testing element uniqueness.

Using Sorting as a Problem-Solving Tool

An even better algorithm for the element uniqueness problem is based on using sorting as a problem-solving tool. In this case, by sorting the array of elements, we are guaranteed that any duplicate elements will be placed next to each other. Thus, to determine if there are any duplicates, all we need to do is perform a single pass over the sorted array, looking for *consecutive* duplicates.

A Java implementation of this algorithm is given in Code Fragment 4.8. (See Section 3.1.3 for discussion of the java.util.Arrays class.)

```
1  /** Returns true if there are no duplicate elements in the array. */
2  public static boolean unique2(int[ ] data) {
3    int n = data.length;
4    int[ ] temp = Arrays.copyOf(data, n);       // make copy of data
5    Arrays.sort(temp);                          // and sort the copy
6    for (int j=0; j < n−1; j++)
7      if (temp[j] == temp[j+1])                 // check neighboring entries
8        return false;                           // found duplicate pair
9    return true;                                // if we reach this, elements are unique
10 }
```

Code Fragment 4.8: Algorithm unique2 for testing element uniqueness.

Sorting algorithms will be the focus of Chapter 12. The best sorting algorithms (including those used by Array.sort in Java) guarantee a worst-case running time of $O(n\log n)$. Once the data is sorted, the subsequent loop runs in $O(n)$ time, and so the entire unique2 algorithm runs in $O(n\log n)$ time. Exercise C-4.35 explores the use of sorting to solve the three-way set disjointness problem in $O(n\log n)$ time.

Prefix Averages

The next problem we consider is computing what are known as **prefix averages** of a sequence of numbers. Namely, given a sequence x consisting of n numbers, we want to compute a sequence a such that a_j is the average of elements $x_0,\ldots,x_j$, for $j = 0,\ldots,n-1$, that is,

$$a_j = \frac{\sum_{i=0}^{j} x_i}{j+1}.$$

Prefix averages have many applications in economics and statistics. For example, given the year-by-year returns of a mutual fund, ordered from recent to past, an investor will typically want to see the fund's average annual returns for the most recent year, the most recent three years, the most recent five years, and so on. Likewise, given a stream of daily Web usage logs, a website manager may wish to track average usage trends over various time periods. We present two implementation for computing prefix averages, yet with significantly different running times.

A Quadratic-Time Algorithm

Our first algorithm for computing prefix averages, denoted as prefixAverage1, is shown in Code Fragment 4.9. It computes each element a_j independently, using an inner loop to compute that partial sum.

```
1  /** Returns an array a such that, for all j, a[j] equals the average of x[0], ..., x[j]. */
2  public static double[ ] prefixAverage1(double[ ] x) {
3    int n = x.length;
4    double[ ] a = new double[n];              // filled with zeros by default
5    for (int j=0; j < n; j++) {
6      double total = 0;                       // begin computing x[0] + ... + x[j]
7      for (int i=0; i <= j; i++)
8        total += x[i];
9      a[j] = total / (j+1);                   // record the average
10   }
11   return a;
12 }
```

Code Fragment 4.9: Algorithm prefixAverage1.

Let us analyze the prefixAverage1 algorithm.

- The initialization of n = x.length at line 3 and the eventual return of a reference to array a at line 11 both execute in $O(1)$ time.
- Creating and initializing the new array, a, at line 4 can be done with in $O(n)$ time, using a constant number of primitive operations per element.
- There are two nested **for** loops, which are controlled, respectively, by counters j and i. The body of the outer loop, controlled by counter j, is executed n times, for $j = 0, \ldots, n-1$. Therefore, statements total = 0 and a[j] = total / (j+1) are executed n times each. This implies that these two statements, plus the management of counter j in the loop, contribute a number of primitive operations proportional to n, that is, $O(n)$ time.
- The body of the inner loop, which is controlled by counter i, is executed $j+1$ times, depending on the current value of the outer loop counter j. Thus, statement total += x[i], in the inner loop, is executed $1 + 2 + 3 + \cdots + n$ times. By recalling Proposition 4.3, we know that $1 + 2 + 3 + \cdots + n = n(n+1)/2$, which implies that the statement in the inner loop contributes $O(n^2)$ time. A similar argument can be done for the primitive operations associated with maintaining counter i, which also take $O(n^2)$ time.

The running time of implementation prefixAverage1 is given by the sum of these terms. The first term is $O(1)$, the second and third terms are $O(n)$, and the fourth term is $O(n^2)$. By a simple application of Proposition 4.8, the running time of prefixAverage1 is $O(n^2)$.

A Linear-Time Algorithm

An intermediate value in the computation of the prefix average is the ***prefix sum*** $x_0 + x_1 + \cdots + x_j$, denoted as total in our first implementation; this allows us to compute the prefix average a[j] = total / (j + 1). In our first algorithm, the prefix sum is computed anew for each value of j. That contributed $O(j)$ time for each j, leading to the quadratic behavior.

For greater efficiency, we can maintain the current prefix sum dynamically, effectively computing $x_0 + x_1 + \cdots + x_j$ as total + x_j, where value total is equal to the sum $x_0 + x_1 + \cdots + x_{j-1}$, when computed by the previous pass of the loop over j. Code Fragment 4.10 provides a new implementation, denoted as prefixAverage2, using this approach.

```
 1  /** Returns an array a such that, for all j, a[j] equals the average of x[0], ..., x[j]. */
 2  public static double[ ] prefixAverage2(double[ ] x) {
 3    int n = x.length;
 4    double[ ] a = new double[n];          // filled with zeros by default
 5    double total = 0;                      // compute prefix sum as x[0] + x[1] + ...
 6    for (int j=0; j < n; j++) {
 7      total += x[j];                       // update prefix sum to include x[j]
 8      a[j] = total / (j+1);                // compute average based on current sum
 9    }
10    return a;
11  }
```

Code Fragment 4.10: Algorithm prefixAverage2.

The analysis of the running time of algorithm prefixAverage2 follows:

- Initializing variables n and total uses $O(1)$ time.

- Initializing the array a uses $O(n)$ time.

- There is a single **for** loop, which is controlled by counter j. The maintenance of that loop contributes a total of $O(n)$ time.

- The body of the loop is executed n times, for $j = 0, \ldots, n - 1$. Thus, statements total += x[j] and a[j] = total / (j+1) are executed n times each. Since each of these statements uses $O(1)$ time per iteration, their overall contribution is $O(n)$ time.

- The eventual return of a reference to array A uses $O(1)$ time.

The running time of algorithm prefixAverage2 is given by the sum of the five terms. The first and last are $O(1)$ and the remaining three are $O(n)$. By a simple application of Proposition 4.8, the running time of prefixAverage2 is $O(n)$, which is much better than the quadratic time of algorithm prefixAverage1.

4.4   Simple Justification Techniques

Sometimes, we will want to make claims about an algorithm, such as showing that it is correct or that it runs fast. In order to rigorously make such claims, we must use mathematical language, and in order to back up such claims, we must justify or **prove** our statements. Fortunately, there are several simple ways to do this.

4.4.1   By Example

Some claims are of the generic form, "There is an element x in a set S that has property P." To justify such a claim, we only need to produce a particular x in S that has property P. Likewise, some hard-to-believe claims are of the generic form, "Every element x in a set S has property P." To justify that such a claim is false, we only need to produce a particular x from S that does not have property P. Such an instance is called a **counterexample**.

Example 4.17: *Professor Amongus claims that every number of the form $2^i - 1$ is a prime, when i is an integer greater than* 1. *Professor Amongus is wrong.*

Justification: To prove Professor Amongus is wrong, we find a counterexample. Fortunately, we need not look too far, for $2^4 - 1 = 15 = 3 \cdot 5$.   ∎

4.4.2   The "Contra" Attack

Another set of justification techniques involves the use of the negative. The two primary such methods are the use of the **contrapositive** and the **contradiction**. To justify the statement "if p is true, then q is true," we establish that "if q is not true, then p is not true" instead. Logically, these two statements are the same, but the latter, which is called the **contrapositive** of the first, may be easier to think about.

Example 4.18: *Let a and b be integers. If ab is even, then a is even or b is even.*

Justification: To justify this claim, consider the contrapositive, "If a is odd and b is odd, then ab is odd." So, suppose $a = 2j + 1$ and $b = 2k + 1$, for some integers j and k. Then $ab = 4jk + 2j + 2k + 1 = 2(2jk + j + k) + 1$; hence, ab is odd.   ∎

Besides showing a use of the contrapositive justification technique, the previous example also contains an application of **de Morgan's law**. This law helps us deal with negations, for it states that the negation of a statement of the form "p or q" is "not p and not q." Likewise, it states that the negation of a statement of the form "p and q" is "not p or not q."

Contradiction

Another negative justification technique is justification by ***contradiction***, which also often involves using de Morgan's law. In applying the justification by contradiction technique, we establish that a statement q is true by first supposing that q is false and then showing that this assumption leads to a contradiction (such as $2 \neq 2$ or $1 > 3$). By reaching such a contradiction, we show that no consistent situation exists with q being false, so q must be true. Of course, in order to reach this conclusion, we must be sure our situation is consistent before we assume q is false.

Example 4.19: *Let a and b be integers. If ab is odd, then a is odd and b is odd.*

Justification: Let ab be odd. We wish to show that a is odd and b is odd. So, with the hope of leading to a contradiction, let us assume the opposite, namely, suppose a is even or b is even. In fact, without loss of generality, we can assume that a is even (since the case for b is symmetric). Then $a = 2j$ for some integer j. Hence, $ab = (2j)b = 2(jb)$, that is, ab is even. But this is a contradiction: ab cannot simultaneously be odd and even. Therefore, a is odd and b is odd. ∎

4.4.3 Induction and Loop Invariants

Most of the claims we make about a running time or a space bound involve an integer parameter n (usually denoting an intuitive notion of the "size" of the problem). Moreover, most of these claims are equivalent to saying some statement $q(n)$ is true "for all $n \geq 1$." Since this is making a claim about an infinite set of numbers, we cannot justify this exhaustively in a direct fashion.

Induction

We can often justify claims such as those above as true, however, by using the technique of ***induction***. This technique amounts to showing that, for any particular $n \geq 1$, there is a finite sequence of implications that starts with something known to be true and ultimately leads to showing that $q(n)$ is true. Specifically, we begin a justification by induction by showing that $q(n)$ is true for $n = 1$ (and possibly some other values $n = 2, 3, \ldots, k$, for some constant k). Then we justify that the inductive "step" is true for $n > k$, namely, we show "if $q(j)$ is true for all $j < n$, then $q(n)$ is true." The combination of these two pieces completes the justification by induction.

Proposition 4.20: *Consider the Fibonacci function $F(n)$, which is defined such that $F(1) = 1$, $F(2) = 2$, and $F(n) = F(n-2) + F(n-1)$ for $n > 2$. (See Section 2.2.3.) We claim that $F(n) < 2^n$.*

Justification: We will show our claim is correct by induction.
Base cases: *($n \leq 2$).* $F(1) = 1 < 2 = 2^1$ and $F(2) = 2 < 4 = 2^2$.
Induction step: *($n > 2$).* Suppose our claim is true for all $j < n$. Since both $n - 2$ and $n - 1$ are less than n, we can apply the inductive assumption (sometimes called the "inductive hypothesis") to imply that

$$F(n) = F(n-2) + F(n-1) < 2^{n-2} + 2^{n-1}.$$

Since

$$2^{n-2} + 2^{n-1} < 2^{n-1} + 2^{n-1} = 2 \cdot 2^{n-1} = 2^n,$$

we have that $F(n) < 2^n$, thus showing the inductive hypothesis for n.   ∎

Let us do another inductive argument, this time for a fact we have seen before.

Proposition 4.21: *(which is the same as Proposition 4.3)*

$$\sum_{i=1}^{n} i = \frac{n(n+1)}{2}.$$

Justification: We will justify this equality by induction.
Base case: $n = 1$. Trivial, for $1 = n(n+1)/2$, if $n = 1$.
Induction step: $n \geq 2$. Assume the inductive hypothesis is true for any $j < n$. Therefore, for $j = n - 1$, we have

$$\sum_{i=1}^{n-1} i = \frac{(n-1)(n-1+1)}{2} = \frac{(n-1)n}{2}.$$

Hence, we obtain

$$\sum_{i=1}^{n} i = n + \sum_{i=1}^{n-1} i = n + \frac{(n-1)n}{2} = \frac{2n + n^2 - n}{2} = \frac{n^2 + n}{2} = \frac{n(n+1)}{2},$$

thereby proving the inductive hypothesis for n.   ∎

We may sometimes feel overwhelmed by the task of justifying something true for *all $n \geq 1$*. We should remember, however, the concreteness of the inductive technique. It shows that, for any particular n, there is a finite step-by-step sequence of implications that starts with something true and leads to the truth about n. In short, the inductive argument is a template for building a sequence of direct justifications.

Loop Invariants

The final justification technique we discuss in this section is the **loop invariant**. To prove some statement $\mathcal{L}$ about a loop is correct, define $\mathcal{L}$ in terms of a series of smaller statements $\mathcal{L}_0, \mathcal{L}_1, \ldots, \mathcal{L}_k$, where:

1. The **initial** claim, $\mathcal{L}_0$, is true before the loop begins.
2. If $\mathcal{L}_{j-1}$ is true before iteration j, then $\mathcal{L}_j$ will be true after iteration j.
3. The final statement, $\mathcal{L}_k$, implies the desired statement $\mathcal{L}$ to be true.

Let us give a simple example of using a loop-invariant argument to justify the correctness of an algorithm. In particular, we use a loop invariant to justify that the method arrayFind (see Code Fragment 4.11) finds the smallest index at which element val occurs in array A.

```
1   /** Returns index j such that data[j] == val, or −1 if no such element. */
2   public static int arrayFind(int[ ] data, int val) {
3     int n = data.length;
4     int j = 0;
5     while (j < n) {  // val is not equal to any of the first j elements of data
6       if (data[j] == val)
7         return j;                           // a match was found at index j
8       j++;                                  // continue to next index
9       // val is not equal to any of the first j elements of data
10    }
11    return −1;                              // if we reach this, no match found
12  }
```

Code Fragment 4.11: Algorithm arrayFind for finding the first index at which a given element occurs in an array.

To show that arrayFind is correct, we inductively define a series of statements, $\mathcal{L}_j$, that lead to the correctness of our algorithm. Specifically, we claim the following is true at the beginning of iteration j of the **while** loop:

$\mathcal{L}_j$: val is not equal to any of the first j elements of data.

This claim is true at the beginning of the first iteration of the loop, because j is 0 and there are no elements among the first 0 in data (this kind of a trivially true claim is said to hold **vacuously**). In iteration j, we compare element val to element data[j]; if these two elements are equivalent, we return the index j, which is clearly correct since no earlier elements equal val. If the two elements val and data[j] are not equal, then we have found one more element not equal to val and we increment the index j. Thus, the claim $\mathcal{L}_j$ will be true for this new value of j; hence, it is true at the beginning of the next iteration. If the while loop terminates without ever returning an index in data, then we have $j = n$. That is, $\mathcal{L}_n$ is true—there are no elements of data equal to val. Therefore, the algorithm correctly returns −1 to indicate that val is not in data.

4.5   Exercises

Reinforcement

R-4.1 Graph the functions $8n$, $4n\log n$, $2n^2$, n^3, and 2^n using a logarithmic scale for the x- and y-axes; that is, if the function value $f(n)$ is y, plot this as a point with x-coordinate at $\log n$ and y-coordinate at $\log y$.

R-4.2 The number of operations executed by algorithms A and B is $8n\log n$ and $2n^2$, respectively. Determine n_0 such that A is better than B for $n \geq n_0$.

R-4.3 The number of operations executed by algorithms A and B is $40n^2$ and $2n^3$, respectively. Determine n_0 such that A is better than B for $n \geq n_0$.

R-4.4 Give an example of a function that is plotted the same on a log-log scale as it is on a standard scale.

R-4.5 Explain why the plot of the function n^c is a straight line with slope c on a log-log scale.

R-4.6 What is the sum of all the even numbers from 0 to $2n$, for any integer $n \geq 1$?

R-4.7 Show that the following two statements are equivalent:
(a) The running time of algorithm A is always $O(f(n))$.
(b) In the worst case, the running time of algorithm A is $O(f(n))$.

R-4.8 Order the following functions by asymptotic growth rate.

$$4n\log n + 2n \quad 2^{10} \quad 2^{\log n}$$
$$3n + 100\log n \quad 4n \quad 2^n$$
$$n^2 + 10n \quad n^3 \quad n\log n$$

R-4.9 Give a big-Oh characterization, in terms of n, of the running time of the example1 method shown in Code Fragment 4.12.

R-4.10 Give a big-Oh characterization, in terms of n, of the running time of the example2 method shown in Code Fragment 4.12.

R-4.11 Give a big-Oh characterization, in terms of n, of the running time of the example3 method shown in Code Fragment 4.12.

R-4.12 Give a big-Oh characterization, in terms of n, of the running time of the example4 method shown in Code Fragment 4.12.

R-4.13 Give a big-Oh characterization, in terms of n, of the running time of the example5 method shown in Code Fragment 4.12.

R-4.14 Show that if $d(n)$ is $O(f(n))$, then $ad(n)$ is $O(f(n))$, for any constant $a > 0$.

R-4.15 Show that if $d(n)$ is $O(f(n))$ and $e(n)$ is $O(g(n))$, then the product $d(n)e(n)$ is $O(f(n)g(n))$.

R-4.16 Show that if $d(n)$ is $O(f(n))$ and $e(n)$ is $O(g(n))$, then $d(n) + e(n)$ is $O(f(n) + g(n))$.

```
1    /** Returns the sum of the integers in given array. */
2    public static int example1(int[ ] arr) {
3      int n = arr.length, total = 0;
4      for (int j=0; j < n; j++)                      // loop from 0 to n-1
5        total += arr[j];
6      return total;
7    }
8
9    /** Returns the sum of the integers with even index in given array. */
10   public static int example2(int[ ] arr) {
11     int n = arr.length, total = 0;
12     for (int j=0; j < n; j += 2)                   // note the increment of 2
13       total += arr[j];
14     return total;
15   }
16
17   /** Returns the sum of the prefix sums of given array. */
18   public static int example3(int[ ] arr) {
19     int n = arr.length, total = 0;
20     for (int j=0; j < n; j++)                      // loop from 0 to n-1
21       for (int k=0; k <= j; k++)                   // loop from 0 to j
22         total += arr[j];
23     return total;
24   }
25
26   /** Returns the sum of the prefix sums of given array. */
27   public static int example4(int[ ] arr) {
28     int n = arr.length, prefix = 0, total = 0;
29     for (int j=0; j < n; j++) {                    // loop from 0 to n-1
30       prefix += arr[j];
31       total += prefix;
32     }
33     return total;
34   }
35
36   /** Returns the number of times second array stores sum of prefix sums from first. */
37   public static int example5(int[ ] first, int[ ] second) { // assume equal-length arrays
38     int n = first.length, count = 0;
39     for (int i=0; i < n; i++) {                    // loop from 0 to n-1
40       int total = 0;
41       for (int j=0; j < n; j++)                    // loop from 0 to n-1
42         for (int k=0; k <= j; k++)                 // loop from 0 to j
43           total += first[k];
44       if (second[i] == total) count++;
45     }
46     return count;
47   }
```

Code Fragment 4.12: Some sample algorithms for analysis.

R-4.17 Show that if $d(n)$ is $O(f(n))$ and $e(n)$ is $O(g(n))$, then $d(n) - e(n)$ is **not necessarily** $O(f(n) - g(n))$.

R-4.18 Show that if $d(n)$ is $O(f(n))$ and $f(n)$ is $O(g(n))$, then $d(n)$ is $O(g(n))$.

R-4.19 Show that $O(\max\{f(n), g(n)\}) = O(f(n) + g(n))$.

R-4.20 Show that $f(n)$ is $O(g(n))$ if and only if $g(n)$ is $\Omega(f(n))$.

R-4.21 Show that if $p(n)$ is a polynomial in n, then $\log p(n)$ is $O(\log n)$.

R-4.22 Show that $(n+1)^5$ is $O(n^5)$.

R-4.23 Show that 2^{n+1} is $O(2^n)$.

R-4.24 Show that n is $O(n \log n)$.

R-4.25 Show that n^2 is $\Omega(n \log n)$.

R-4.26 Show that $n \log n$ is $\Omega(n)$.

R-4.27 Show that $\lceil f(n) \rceil$ is $O(f(n))$, if $f(n)$ is a positive nondecreasing function that is always greater than 1.

R-4.28 For each function $f(n)$ and time t in the following table, determine the largest size n of a problem P that can be solved in time t if the algorithm for solving P takes $f(n)$ microseconds (one entry is already completed).

	1 Second	1 Hour	1 Month	1 Century
$\log n$	$\approx 10^{300000}$			
n				
$n \log n$				
n^2				
2^n				

R-4.29 Algorithm A executes an $O(\log n)$-time computation for each entry of an array storing n elements. What is its worst-case running time?

R-4.30 Given an n-element array X, Algorithm B chooses $\log n$ elements in X at random and executes an $O(n)$-time calculation for each. What is the worst-case running time of Algorithm B?

R-4.31 Given an n-element array X of integers, Algorithm C executes an $O(n)$-time computation for each even number in X, and an $O(\log n)$-time computation for each odd number in X. What are the best-case and worst-case running times of Algorithm C?

R-4.32 Given an n-element array X, Algorithm D calls Algorithm E on each element $X[i]$. Algorithm E runs in $O(i)$ time when it is called on element $X[i]$. What is the worst-case running time of Algorithm D?

R-4.33 Al and Bob are arguing about their algorithms. Al claims his $O(n\log n)$-time method is *always* faster than Bob's $O(n^2)$-time method. To settle the issue, they perform a set of experiments. To Al's dismay, they find that if $n < 100$, the $O(n^2)$-time algorithm runs faster, and only when $n \geq 100$ is the $O(n\log n)$-time one better. Explain how this is possible.

R-4.34 There is a well-known city (which will go nameless here) whose inhabitants have the reputation of enjoying a meal only if that meal is the best they have ever experienced in their life. Otherwise, they hate it. Assuming meal quality is distributed uniformly across a person's life, describe the expected number of times inhabitants of this city are happy with their meals?

Creativity

C-4.35 Assuming it is possible to sort n numbers in $O(n\log n)$ time, show that it is possible to solve the three-way set disjointness problem in $O(n\log n)$ time.

C-4.36 Describe an efficient algorithm for finding the ten largest elements in an array of size n. What is the running time of your algorithm?

C-4.37 Give an example of a positive function $f(n)$ such that $f(n)$ is neither $O(n)$ nor $\Omega(n)$.

C-4.38 Show that $\sum_{i=1}^{n} i^2$ is $O(n^3)$.

C-4.39 Show that $\sum_{i=1}^{n} i/2^i < 2$.

C-4.40 Determine the total number of grains of rice requested by the inventor of chess.

C-4.41 Show that $\log_b f(n)$ is $\Theta(\log f(n))$ if $b > 1$ is a constant.

C-4.42 Describe an algorithm for finding both the minimum and maximum of n numbers using fewer than $3n/2$ comparisons.

C-4.43 Bob built a website and gave the URL only to his n friends, which he numbered from 1 to n. He told friend number i that he/she can visit the website at most i times. Now Bob has a counter, C, keeping track of the total number of visits to the site (but not the identities of who visits). What is the minimum value for C such that Bob can know that one of his friends has visited his/her maximum allowed number of times?

C-4.44 Draw a visual justification of Proposition 4.3 analogous to that of Figure 4.3(b) for the case when n is odd.

C-4.45 An array A contains $n - 1$ unique integers in the range $[0, n - 1]$, that is, there is one number from this range that is not in A. Design an $O(n)$-time algorithm for finding that number. You are only allowed to use $O(1)$ additional space besides the array A itself.

C-4.46 Perform an asymptotic analysis of the insertion-sort algorithm given in Section 3.1.2. What are the worst-case and best-case running times?

C-4.47 Communication security is extremely important in computer networks, and one way many network protocols achieve security is to encrypt messages. Typical *cryptographic* schemes for the secure transmission of messages over such networks are based on the fact that no efficient algorithms are known for factoring large integers. Hence, if we can represent a secret message by a large prime number p, we can transmit, over the network, the number $r = p \cdot q$, where $q > p$ is another large prime number that acts as the *encryption key*. An eavesdropper who obtains the transmitted number r on the network would have to factor r in order to figure out the secret message p.

Using factoring to figure out a message is hard without knowing the encryption key q. To understand why, consider the following naive factoring algorithm:

```
for (int p=2; p < r; p++)
  if (r % p == 0)
    return "The secret message is p!";
```

a. Suppose the eavesdropper's computer can divide two 100-bit integers in μs (1 millionth of a second). Estimate the worst-case time to decipher the secret message p if the transmitted message r has 100 bits.

b. What is the worst-case time complexity of the above algorithm? Since the input to the algorithm is just one large number r, assume that the input size n is the number of bytes needed to store r, that is, $n = \lfloor (\log_2 r)/8 \rfloor + 1$, and that each division takes time $O(n)$.

C-4.48 Al says he can prove that all sheep in a flock are the same color:

Base case: One sheep. It is clearly the same color as itself.

Induction step: A flock of n sheep. Take a sheep, a, out. The remaining $n-1$ are all the same color by induction. Now put sheep a back in and take out a different sheep, b. By induction, the $n-1$ sheep (now with a) are all the same color. Therefore, all the sheep in the flock are the same color. What is wrong with Al's "justification"?

C-4.49 Consider the following "justification" that the Fibonacci function, $F(n)$ is $O(n)$:
Base case ($n \le 2$): $F(1) = 1$ and $F(2) = 2$.
Induction step ($n > 2$): Assume claim true for $n' < n$. Consider n. $F(n) = F(n-2) + F(n-1)$. By induction, $F(n-2)$ is $O(n-2)$ and $F(n-1)$ is $O(n-1)$. Then, $F(n)$ is $O((n-2) + (n-1))$, by the identity presented in Exercise R-4.16. Therefore, $F(n)$ is $O(n)$.
What is wrong with this "justification"?

C-4.50 Consider the Fibonacci function, $F(n)$ (see Proposition 4.20). Show by induction that $F(n)$ is $\Omega((3/2)^n)$.

C-4.51 Let S be a set of n lines in the plane such that no two are parallel and no three meet in the same point. Show, by induction, that the lines in S determine $\Theta(n^2)$ intersection points.

C-4.52 Show that the summation $\sum_{i=1}^{n} \log i$ is $O(n \log n)$.

C-4.53 Show that the summation $\sum_{i=1}^{n} \log i$ is $\Omega(n \log n)$.

C-4.54 Let $p(x)$ be a polynomial of degree n, that is, $p(x) = \sum_{i=0}^{n} a_i x^i$.

    a. Describe a simple $O(n^2)$-time algorithm for computing $p(x)$.

    b. Describe an $O(n \log n)$-time algorithm for computing $p(x)$, based upon a more efficient calculation of x^i.

    c. Now consider a rewriting of $p(x)$ as

$$p(x) = a_0 + x(a_1 + x(a_2 + x(a_3 + \cdots + x(a_{n-1} + xa_n) \cdots))),$$

which is known as **Horner's method**. Using the big-Oh notation, characterize the number of arithmetic operations this method executes.

C-4.55 An evil king has n bottles of wine, and a spy has just poisoned one of them. Unfortunately, they do not know which one it is. The poison is very deadly; just one drop diluted even a billion to one will still kill. Even so, it takes a full month for the poison to take effect. Design a scheme for determining exactly which one of the wine bottles was poisoned in just one month's time while expending $O(\log n)$ taste testers.

C-4.56 An array A contains n integers taken from the interval $[0, 4n]$, with repetitions allowed. Describe an efficient algorithm for determining an integer value k that occurs the most often in A. What is the running time of your algorithm?

C-4.57 Given an array A of n positive integers, each represented with $k = \lceil \log n \rceil + 1$ bits, describe an $O(n)$-time method for finding a k-bit integer not in A.

C-4.58 Argue why any solution to the previous problem must run in $\Omega(n)$ time.

C-4.59 Given an array A of n arbitrary integers, design an $O(n)$-time method for finding an integer that cannot be formed as the sum of two integers in A.

Projects

P-4.60 Perform an experimental analysis of the two algorithms prefixAverage1 and prefixAverage2, from Section 4.3.3. Visualize their running times as a function of the input size with a log-log chart.

P-4.61 Perform an experimental analysis that compares the relative running times of the methods shown in Code Fragment 4.12.

P-4.62 Perform an experimental analysis to test the hypothesis that Java's Array.sort method runs in $O(n \log n)$ time on average.

P-4.63 For each of the algorithms unique1 and unique2, which solve the element uniqueness problem, perform an experimental analysis to determine the largest value of n such that the given algorithm runs in one minute or less.

Chapter Notes

The big-Oh notation has prompted several comments about its proper use [18, 43, 59]. Knuth [60, 59] defines it using the notation $f(n) = O(g(n))$, but says this "equality" is only "one way." We have chosen to take a more standard view of equality and view the big-Oh notation as a set, following Brassard [18]. The reader interested in studying average-case analysis is referred to the book chapter by Vitter and Flajolet [93].

Chapter
5

Recursion

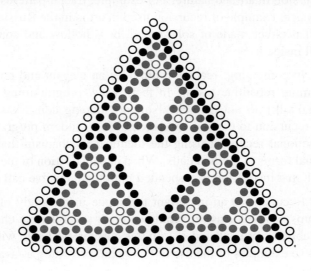

Contents

One way to describe repetition within a computer program is the use of loops, such as Java's while-loop and for-loop constructs described in Section 1.5.2. An entirely different way to achieve repetition is through a process known as *recursion*.

Recursion is a technique by which a method makes one or more calls to itself during execution, or by which a data structure relies upon smaller instances of the very same type of structure in its representation. There are many examples of recursion in art and nature. For example, fractal patterns are naturally recursive. A physical example of recursion used in art is in the Russian Matryoshka dolls. Each doll is either made of solid wood, or is hollow and contains another Matryoshka doll inside it.

In computing, recursion provides an elegant and powerful alternative for performing repetitive tasks. In fact, a few programming languages (e.g., Scheme, Smalltalk) do not explicitly support looping constructs and instead rely directly on recursion to express repetition. Most modern programming languages support functional recursion using the identical mechanism that is used to support traditional forms of method calls. When one invocation of the method makes a recursive call, that invocation is suspended until the recursive call completes.

Recursion is an important technique in the study of data structures and algorithms. We will use it prominently in several later chapters of this book (most notably, Chapters 8 and 12). In this chapter, we begin with the following four illustrative examples of the use of recursion, providing a Java implementation for each.

- The *factorial function* (commonly denoted as $n!$) is a classic mathematical function that has a natural recursive definition.

- An *English ruler* has a recursive pattern that is a simple example of a fractal structure.

- *Binary search* is among the most important computer algorithms. It allows us to efficiently locate a desired value in a data set with upwards of billions of entries.

- The *file system* for a computer has a recursive structure in which directories can be nested arbitrarily deeply within other directories. Recursive algorithms are widely used to explore and manage these file systems.

We then describe how to perform a formal analysis of the running time of a recursive algorithm, and we discuss some potential pitfalls when defining recursions. In the balance of the chapter, we provide many more examples of recursive algorithms, organized to highlight some common forms of design.

5.1 Illustrative Examples

5.1.1 The Factorial Function

To demonstrate the mechanics of recursion, we begin with a simple mathematical example of computing the value of the ***factorial function***. The factorial of a positive integer n, denoted $n!$, is defined as the product of the integers from 1 to n. If $n = 0$, then $n!$ is defined as 1 by convention. More formally, for any integer $n \geq 0$,

$$n! = \begin{cases} 1 & \text{if } n = 0 \\ n \cdot (n-1) \cdot (n-2) \cdots 3 \cdot 2 \cdot 1 & \text{if } n \geq 1. \end{cases}$$

For example, $5! = 5 \cdot 4 \cdot 3 \cdot 2 \cdot 1 = 120$. The factorial function is important because it is known to equal the number of ways in which n distinct items can be arranged into a sequence, that is, the number of ***permutations*** of n items. For example, the three characters a, b, and c can be arranged in $3! = 3 \cdot 2 \cdot 1 = 6$ ways: abc, acb, bac, bca, cab, and cba.

There is a natural recursive definition for the factorial function. To see this, observe that $5! = 5 \cdot (4 \cdot 3 \cdot 2 \cdot 1) = 5 \cdot 4!$. More generally, for a positive integer n, we can define $n!$ to be $n \cdot (n-1)!$. This ***recursive definition*** can be formalized as

$$n! = \begin{cases} 1 & \text{if } n = 0 \\ n \cdot (n-1)! & \text{if } n \geq 1. \end{cases}$$

This definition is typical of many recursive definitions of functions. First, we have one or more ***base cases***, which refer to fixed values of the function. The above definition has one base case stating that $n! = 1$ for $n = 0$. Second, we have one or more ***recursive cases***, which define the function in terms of itself. In the above definition, there is one recursive case, which indicates that $n! = n \cdot (n-1)!$ for $n \geq 1$.

A Recursive Implementation of the Factorial Function

Recursion is not just a mathematical notation; we can use recursion to design a Java implementation of the factorial function, as shown in Code Fragment 5.1.

```java
1  public static int factorial(int n) throws IllegalArgumentException {
2    if (n < 0)
3      throw new IllegalArgumentException();      // argument must be nonnegative
4    else if (n == 0)
5      return 1;                                  // base case
6    else
7      return n * factorial(n−1);                 // recursive case
8  }
```

Code Fragment 5.1: A recursive implementation of the factorial function.

This method does not use any explicit loops. Repetition is achieved through repeated recursive invocations of the method. The process is finite because each time the method is invoked, its argument is smaller by one, and when a base case is reached, no further recursive calls are made.

We illustrate the execution of a recursive method using a ***recursion trace***. Each entry of the trace corresponds to a recursive call. Each new recursive method call is indicated by a downward arrow to a new invocation. When the method returns, an arrow showing this return is drawn and the return value may be indicated alongside this arrow. An example of such a trace for the factorial function is shown in Figure 5.1.

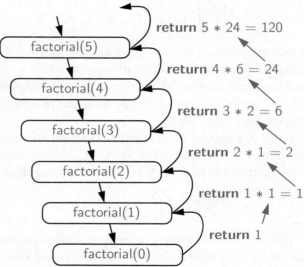

Figure 5.1: A recursion trace for the call factorial(5).

A recursion trace closely mirrors a programming language's execution of the recursion. In Java, each time a method (recursive or otherwise) is called, a structure known as an ***activation record*** or ***activation frame*** is created to store information about the progress of that invocation of the method. This frame stores the parameters and local variables specific to a given call of the method, and information about which command in the body of the method is currently executing.

When the execution of a method leads to a nested method call, the execution of the former call is suspended and its frame stores the place in the source code at which the flow of control should continue upon return of the nested call. A new frame is then created for the nested method call. This process is used both in the standard case of one method calling a different method, or in the recursive case where a method invokes itself. The key point is to have a separate frame for each active call.

5.1.2   Drawing an English Ruler

In the case of computing the factorial function, there is no compelling reason for preferring recursion over a direct iteration with a loop. As a more complex example of the use of recursion, consider how to draw the markings of a typical English ruler. For each inch, we place a tick with a numeric label. We denote the length of the tick designating a whole inch as the ***major tick length***. Between the marks for whole inches, the ruler contains a series of ***minor ticks***, placed at intervals of 1/2 inch, 1/4 inch, and so on. As the size of the interval decreases by half, the tick length decreases by one. Figure 5.2 demonstrates several such rulers with varying major tick lengths (although not drawn to scale).

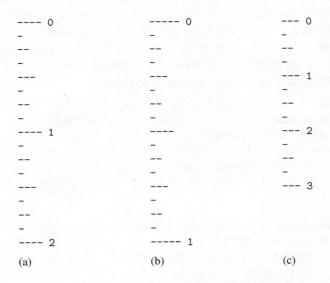

Figure 5.2: Three sample outputs of an English ruler drawing: (a) a 2-inch ruler with major tick length 4; (b) a 1-inch ruler with major tick length 5; (c) a 3-inch ruler with major tick length 3.

A Recursive Approach to Ruler Drawing

The English ruler pattern is a simple example of a ***fractal***, that is, a shape that has a self-recursive structure at various levels of magnification. Consider the rule with major tick length 5 shown in Figure 5.2(b). Ignoring the lines containing 0 and 1, let us consider how to draw the sequence of ticks lying between these lines. The central tick (at 1/2 inch) has length 4. Observe that the two patterns of ticks above and below this central tick are identical, and each has a central tick of length 3.

In general, an interval with a central tick length $L \geq 1$ is composed of:
- An interval with a central tick length $L - 1$
- A single tick of length L
- An interval with a central tick length $L - 1$

Although it is possible to draw such a ruler using an iterative process (see Exercise P-5.29), the task is considerably easier to accomplish with recursion. Our implementation consists of three methods, as shown in Code Fragment 5.2.

The main method, drawRuler, manages the construction of the entire ruler. Its arguments specify the total number of inches in the ruler and the major tick length. The utility method, drawLine, draws a single tick with a specified number of dashes (and an optional integer label that is printed to the right of the tick).

The interesting work is done by the recursive drawInterval method. This method draws the sequence of minor ticks within some interval, based upon the length of the interval's central tick. We rely on the intuition shown at the top of this page, and with a base case when $L = 0$ that draws nothing. For $L \geq 1$, the first and last steps are performed by recursively calling drawInterval($L - 1$). The middle step is performed by calling method drawLine(L).

```
1  /** Draws an English ruler for the given number of inches and major tick length. */
2  public static void drawRuler(int nInches, int majorLength) {
3    drawLine(majorLength, 0);                    // draw inch 0 line and label
4    for (int j = 1; j <= nInches; j++) {
5      drawInterval(majorLength − 1);            // draw interior ticks for inch
6      drawLine(majorLength, j);                  // draw inch j line and label
7    }
8  }
9  private static void drawInterval(int centralLength) {
10   if (centralLength >= 1) {                     // otherwise, do nothing
11     drawInterval(centralLength − 1);           // recursively draw top interval
12     drawLine(centralLength);                    // draw center tick line (without label)
13     drawInterval(centralLength − 1);           // recursively draw bottom interval
14   }
15 }
16 private static void drawLine(int tickLength, int tickLabel) {
17   for (int j = 0; j < tickLength; j++)
18     System.out.print("-");
19   if (tickLabel >= 0)
20     System.out.print(" " + tickLabel);
21   System.out.print("\n");
22 }
23 /** Draws a line with the given tick length (but no label). */
24 private static void drawLine(int tickLength) {
25   drawLine(tickLength, −1);
26 }
```

Code Fragment 5.2: A recursive implementation of a method that draws a ruler.

Illustrating Ruler Drawing Using a Recursion Trace

The execution of the recursive drawInterval method can be visualized using a recursion trace. The trace for drawInterval is more complicated than in the factorial example, however, because each instance makes two recursive calls. To illustrate this, we will show the recursion trace in a form that is reminiscent of an outline for a document. See Figure 5.3.

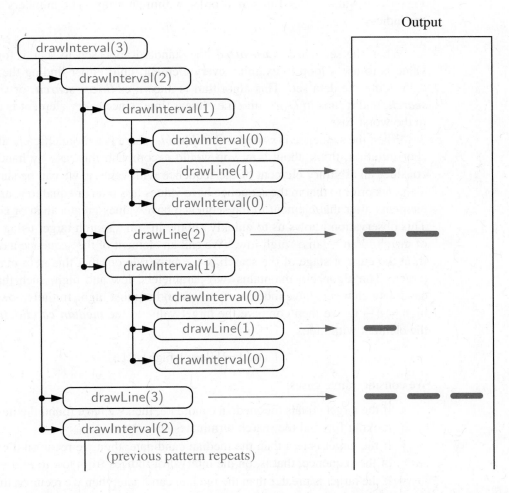

Figure 5.3: A partial recursion trace for the call drawInterval(3). The second pattern of calls for drawInterval(2) is not shown, but it is identical to the first.

5.1.3 Binary Search

In this section, we describe a classic recursive algorithm, **binary search**, used to efficiently locate a target value within a sorted sequence of n elements stored in an array. This is among the most important of computer algorithms, and it is the reason that we so often store data in sorted order (as in Figure 5.4).

0	1	2	3	4	5	6	7	8	9	10	11	12	13	14	15
2	4	5	7	8	9	12	14	17	19	22	25	27	28	33	37

Figure 5.4: Values stored in sorted order within an array. The numbers at top are the indices.

When the sequence is **unsorted**, the standard approach to search for a target value is to use a loop to examine every element, until either finding the target or exhausting the data set. This algorithm is known as **linear search**, or **sequential search**, and it runs in $O(n)$ time (i.e., linear time) since every element is inspected in the worst case.

When the sequence is **sorted** and **indexable**, there is a more efficient algorithm. (For intuition, think about how you would accomplish this task by hand!) If we consider an arbitrary element of the sequence with value v, we can be sure that all elements prior to that in the sequence have values less than or equal to v, and that all elements after that element in the sequence have values greater than or equal to v. This observation allows us to quickly "home in" on a search target using a variant of the children's game "high-low." We call an element of the sequence a **candidate** if, at the current stage of the search, we cannot rule out that this item matches the target. The algorithm maintains two parameters, low and high, such that all the candidate elements have index at least low and at most high. Initially, low $= 0$ and high $= n - 1$. We then compare the target value to the **median candidate**, that is, the element with index

$$\mathsf{mid} = \lfloor (\mathsf{low} + \mathsf{high})/2 \rfloor .$$

We consider three cases:

- If the target equals the median candidate, then we have found the item we are looking for, and the search terminates successfully.
- If the target is less than the median candidate, then we recur on the first half of the sequence, that is, on the interval of indices from low to mid $- 1$.
- If the target is greater than the median candidate, then we recur on the second half of the sequence, that is, on the interval of indices from mid $+ 1$ to high.

An unsuccessful search occurs if low $>$ high, as the interval [low, high] is empty.

This algorithm is known as ***binary search***. We give a Java implementation in Code Fragment 5.3, and an illustration of the execution of the algorithm in Figure 5.5. Whereas sequential search runs in $O(n)$ time, the more efficient binary search runs in $O(\log n)$ time. This is a significant improvement, given that if n is 1 billion, $\log n$ is only 30. (We defer our formal analysis of binary search's running time to Proposition 5.2 in Section 5.2.)

```java
1  /**
2   * Returns true if the target value is found in the indicated portion of the data array.
3   * This search only considers the array portion from data[low] to data[high] inclusive.
4   */
5  public static boolean binarySearch(int[ ] data, int target, int low, int high) {
6    if (low > high)
7      return false;                                    // interval empty; no match
8    else {
9      int mid = (low + high) / 2;
10     if (target == data[mid])
11       return true;                                   // found a match
12     else if (target < data[mid])
13       return binarySearch(data, target, low, mid − 1);   // recur left of the middle
14     else
15       return binarySearch(data, target, mid + 1, high);  // recur right of the middle
16   }
17 }
```

Code Fragment 5.3: An implementation of the binary search algorithm on a sorted array.

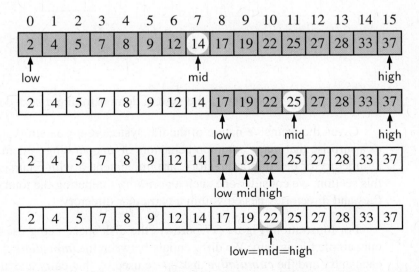

Figure 5.5: Example of a binary search for target value 22 on a sorted array with 16 elements.

5.1.4   File Systems

Modern operating systems define file-system directories (also called "folders") in a recursive way. Namely, a file system consists of a top-level directory, and the contents of this directory consists of files and other directories, which in turn can contain files and other directories, and so on. The operating system allows directories to be nested arbitrarily deeply (as long as there is enough memory), although by necessity there must be some base directories that contain only files, not further subdirectories. A representation of a portion of such a file system is given in Figure 5.6.

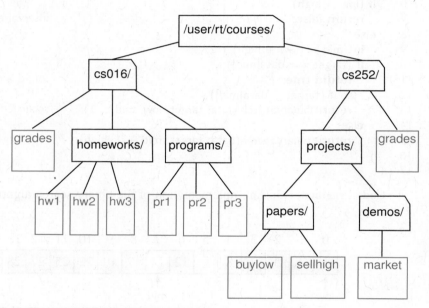

Figure 5.6: A portion of a file system demonstrating a nested organization.

Given the recursive nature of the file-system representation, it should not come as a surprise that many common behaviors of an operating system, such as copying a directory or deleting a directory, are implemented with recursive algorithms. In this section, we consider one such algorithm: computing the total disk usage for all files and directories nested within a particular directory.

For illustration, Figure 5.7 portrays the disk space being used by all entries in our sample file system. We differentiate between the *immediate* disk space used by each entry and the *cumulative* disk space used by that entry and all nested features. For example, the cs016 directory uses only 2K of immediate space, but a total of 249K of cumulative space.

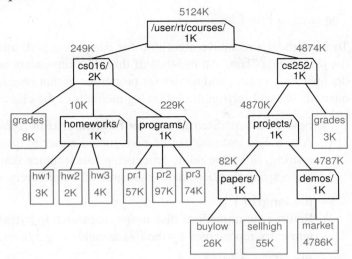

Figure 5.7: The same portion of a file system given in Figure 5.6, but with additional annotations to describe the amount of disk space that is used. Within the icon for each file or directory is the amount of space directly used by that artifact. Above the icon for each directory is an indication of the cumulative disk space used by that directory and all its (recursive) contents.

The cumulative disk space for an entry can be computed with a simple recursive algorithm. It is equal to the immediate disk space used by the entry plus the sum of the cumulative disk space usage of any entries that are stored directly within the entry. For example, the cumulative disk space for cs016 is 249K because it uses 2K itself, 8K cumulatively in grades, 10K cumulatively in homeworks, and 229K cumulatively in programs. Pseudocode for this algorithm is given in Code Fragment 5.4.

Algorithm DiskUsage(*path*):

   Input: A string designating a path to a file-system entry

   Output: The cumulative disk space used by that entry and any nested entries

   total = size(*path*)   {immediate disk space used by the entry}

   if *path* represents a directory **then**

      for each *child* entry stored within directory *path* **do**

         total = *total* + DiskUsage(*child*)   {recursive call}

   return *total*

Code Fragment 5.4: An algorithm for computing the cumulative disk space usage nested at a file-system entry. We presume that method size returns the immediate disk space of an entry.

The java.io.File Class

To implement a recursive algorithm for computing disk usage in Java, we rely on the java.io.File class. An instance of this class represents an abstract pathname in the operating system and allows for properties of that operating system entry to be queried. We will rely on the following methods of the class:

- **new File(pathString)** or **new File(parentFile, childString)**
  A new File instance can be constructed either by providing the full path as a string, or by providing an existing File instance that represents a directory and a string that designates the name of a child entry within that directory.

- **file.length( )**
  Returns the immediate disk usage (measured in bytes) for the operating system entry represented by the File instance (e.g., /user/rt/courses).

- **file.isDirectory( )**
  Returns true if the File instance represents a directory; false otherwise.

- **file.list( )**
  Returns an array of strings designating the names of all entries within the given directory. In our sample file system, if we call this method on the File associated with path /user/rt/courses/cs016, it returns an array with contents: {"grades", "homeworks", "programs"}.

Java Implementation

With use of the File class, we now convert the algorithm from Code Fragment 5.4 into the Java implementation of Code Fragment 5.5.

```
1  /**
2   * Calculates the total disk usage (in bytes) of the portion of the file system rooted
3   * at the given path, while printing a summary akin to the standard 'du' Unix tool.
4   */
5  public static long diskUsage(File root) {
6    long total = root.length( );                        // start with direct disk usage
7    if (root.isDirectory( )) {                          // and if this is a directory,
8      for (String childname : root.list( )) {           // then for each child
9        File child = new File(root, childname);         // compose full path to child
10       total += diskUsage(child);                      // add child's usage to total
11     }
12   }
13   System.out.println(total + "\t" + root);            // descriptive output
14   return total;                                       // return the grand total
15 }
```

Code Fragment 5.5: A recursive method for reporting disk usage of a file system.

Recursion Trace

To produce a different form of a recursion trace, we have included an extraneous print statement within our Java implementation (line 13 of Code Fragment 5.5). The precise format of that output intentionally mirrors the output that is produced by a classic Unix/Linux utility named du (for "disk usage"). It reports the amount of disk space used by a directory and all contents nested within, and can produce a verbose report, as given in Figure 5.8.

When executed on the sample file system portrayed in Figure 5.7, our implementation of the diskUsage method produces the result given in Figure 5.8. During the execution of the algorithm, exactly one recursive call is made for each entry in the portion of the file system that is considered. Because each line is printed just before returning from a recursive call, the lines of output reflect the order in which the recursive calls are *completed*. Notice that it computes and reports the cumulative disk space for a nested entry before computing and reporting the cumulative disk space for the directory that contains it. For example, the recursive calls regarding entries grades, homeworks, and programs are computed before the cumulative total for the directory /user/rt/courses/cs016 that contains them.

```
   8   /user/rt/courses/cs016/grades
   3   /user/rt/courses/cs016/homeworks/hw1
   2   /user/rt/courses/cs016/homeworks/hw2
   4   /user/rt/courses/cs016/homeworks/hw3
  10   /user/rt/courses/cs016/homeworks
  57   /user/rt/courses/cs016/programs/pr1
  97   /user/rt/courses/cs016/programs/pr2
  74   /user/rt/courses/cs016/programs/pr3
 229   /user/rt/courses/cs016/programs
 249   /user/rt/courses/cs016
  26   /user/rt/courses/cs252/projects/papers/buylow
  55   /user/rt/courses/cs252/projects/papers/sellhigh
  82   /user/rt/courses/cs252/projects/papers
4786   /user/rt/courses/cs252/projects/demos/market
4787   /user/rt/courses/cs252/projects/demos
4870   /user/rt/courses/cs252/projects
   3   /user/rt/courses/cs252/grades
4874   /user/rt/courses/cs252
5124   /user/rt/courses/
```

Figure 5.8: A report of the disk usage for the file system shown in Figure 5.7, as generated by our diskUsage method from Code Fragment 5.5, or equivalently by the Unix/Linux command du with option -a (which lists both directories and files).

5.2   Analyzing Recursive Algorithms

In Chapter 4, we introduced mathematical techniques for analyzing the efficiency of an algorithm, based upon an estimate of the number of primitive operations that are executed by the algorithm. We use notations such as big-Oh to summarize the relationship between the number of operations and the input size for a problem. In this section, we demonstrate how to perform this type of running-time analysis to recursive algorithms.

With a recursive algorithm, we will account for each operation that is performed based upon the particular ***activation*** of the method that manages the flow of control at the time it is executed. Stated another way, for each invocation of the method, we only account for the number of operations that are performed within the body of that activation. We can then account for the overall number of operations that are executed as part of the recursive algorithm by taking the sum, over all activations, of the number of operations that take place during each individual activation. (As an aside, this is also the way we analyze a nonrecursive method that calls other methods from within its body.)

To demonstrate this style of analysis, we revisit the four recursive algorithms presented in Sections 5.1.1 through 5.1.4: factorial computation, drawing an English ruler, binary search, and computation of the cumulative size of a file system. In general, we may rely on the intuition afforded by a ***recursion trace*** in recognizing how many recursive activations occur, and how the parameterization of each activation can be used to estimate the number of primitive operations that occur within the body of that activation. However, each of these recursive algorithms has a unique structure and form.

Computing Factorials

It is relatively easy to analyze the efficiency of our method for computing factorials, as described in Section 5.1.1. A sample recursion trace for our factorial method was given in Figure 5.1. To compute factorial(n), we see that there are a total of $n+1$ activations, as the parameter decreases from n in the first call, to $n-1$ in the second call, and so on, until reaching the base case with parameter 0.

It is also clear, given an examination of the method body in Code Fragment 5.1, that each individual activation of factorial executes a constant number of operations. Therefore, we conclude that the overall number of operations for computing factorial(n) is $O(n)$, as there are $n+1$ activations, each of which accounts for $O(1)$ operations.

Drawing an English Ruler

In analyzing the English ruler application from Section 5.1.2, we consider the fundamental question of how many total lines of output are generated by an initial call to drawInterval(c), where c denotes the center length. This is a reasonable benchmark for the overall efficiency of the algorithm as each line of output is based upon a call to the drawLine utility, and each recursive call to drawInterval with nonzero parameter makes exactly one direct call to drawLine.

Some intuition may be gained by examining the source code and the recursion trace. We know that a call to drawInterval(c) for $c > 0$ spawns two calls to drawInterval($c - 1$) and a single call to drawLine. We will rely on this intuition to prove the following claim.

Proposition 5.1: *For $c \geq 0$, a call to* drawInterval(c) *results in precisely $2^c - 1$ lines of output.*

Justification: We provide a formal proof of this claim by ***induction*** (see Section 4.4.3). In fact, induction is a natural mathematical technique for proving the correctness and efficiency of a recursive process. In the case of the ruler, we note that an application of drawInterval(0) generates no output, and that $2^0 - 1 = 1 - 1 = 0$. This serves as a base case for our claim.

More generally, the number of lines printed by drawInterval(c) is one more than twice the number generated by a call to drawInterval($c - 1$), as one center line is printed between two such recursive calls. By induction, we have that the number of lines is thus $1 + 2 \cdot (2^{c-1} - 1) = 1 + 2^c - 2 = 2^c - 1$. ∎

This proof is indicative of a more mathematically rigorous tool, known as a ***recurrence equation***, that can be used to analyze the running time of a recursive algorithm. That technique is discussed in Section 12.1.4, in the context of recursive sorting algorithms.

Performing a Binary Search

When considering the running time of the binary search algorithm, as presented in Section 5.1.3, we observe that a constant number of primitive operations are executed during each recursive call of the binary search method. Hence, the running time is proportional to the number of recursive calls performed. We will show that at most $\lfloor \log n \rfloor + 1$ recursive calls are made during a binary search of a sequence having n elements, leading to the following claim.

Proposition 5.2: *The binary search algorithm runs in $O(\log n)$ time for a sorted array with n elements.*

Justification: To prove this claim, a crucial fact is that with each recursive call the number of candidate elements still to be searched is given by the value

$$\text{high} - \text{low} + 1.$$

Moreover, the number of remaining candidates is reduced by at least one-half with each recursive call. Specifically, from the definition of mid, the number of remaining candidates is either

$$(\text{mid} - 1) - \text{low} + 1 = \left\lfloor \frac{\text{low} + \text{high}}{2} \right\rfloor - \text{low} \le \frac{\text{high} - \text{low} + 1}{2}$$

or

$$\text{high} - (\text{mid} + 1) + 1 = \text{high} - \left\lfloor \frac{\text{low} + \text{high}}{2} \right\rfloor \le \frac{\text{high} - \text{low} + 1}{2}.$$

Initially, the number of candidates is n; after the first call in a binary search, it is at most $n/2$; after the second call, it is at most $n/4$; and so on. In general, after the jth call in a binary search, the number of candidate elements remaining is at most $n/2^j$. In the worst case (an unsuccessful search), the recursive calls stop when there are no more candidate elements. Hence, the maximum number of recursive calls performed, is the smallest integer r such that

$$\frac{n}{2^r} < 1.$$

In other words (recalling that we omit a logarithm's base when it is 2), r is the smallest integer such that $r > \log n$. Thus, we have

$$r = \lfloor \log n \rfloor + 1,$$

which implies that binary search runs in $O(\log n)$ time.   ■

Computing Disk Space Usage

Our final recursive algorithm from Section 5.1 was that for computing the overall disk space usage in a specified portion of a file system. To characterize the "problem size" for our analysis, we let n denote the number of file-system entries in the portion of the file system that is considered. (For example, the file system portrayed in Figure 5.6 has $n = 19$ entries.)

To characterize the cumulative time spent for an initial call to diskUsage, we must analyze the total number of recursive invocations that are made, as well as the number of operations that are executed within those invocations.

We begin by showing that there are precisely n recursive invocations of the method, in particular, one for each entry in the relevant portion of the file system. Intuitively, this is because a call to diskUsage for a particular entry e of the file system is only made from within the for loop of Code Fragment 5.5 when processing the entry for the unique directory that contains e, and that entry will only be explored once.

To formalize this argument, we can define the ***nesting level*** of each entry such that the entry on which we begin has nesting level 0, entries stored directly within it have nesting level 1, entries stored within those entries have nesting level 2, and so on. We can prove by induction that there is exactly one recursive invocation of diskUsage upon each entry at nesting level k. As a base case, when $k = 0$, the only recursive invocation made is the initial one. As the inductive step, once we know there is exactly one recursive invocation for each entry at nesting level k, we can claim that there is exactly one invocation for each entry e at nesting level $k + 1$, made within the for loop for the entry at level k that contains e.

Having established that there is one recursive call for each entry of the file system, we return to the question of the overall computation time for the algorithm. It would be great if we could argue that we spend $O(1)$ time in any single invocation of the method, but that is not the case. While there is a constant number of steps reflected in the call to root.length( ) to compute the disk usage directly at that entry, when the entry is a directory, the body of the diskUsage method includes a for loop that iterates over all entries that are contained within that directory. In the worst case, it is possible that one entry includes $n - 1$ others.

Based on this reasoning, we could conclude that there are $O(n)$ recursive calls, each of which runs in $O(n)$ time, leading to an overall running time that is $O(n^2)$. While this upper bound is technically true, it is not a tight upper bound. Remarkably, we can prove the stronger bound that the recursive algorithm for diskUsage completes in $O(n)$ time! The weaker bound was pessimistic because it assumed a worst-case number of entries for each directory. While it is possible that some directories contain a number of entries proportional to n, they cannot all contain that many. To prove the stronger claim, we choose to consider the *overall* number of iterations of the for loop across all recursive calls. We claim there are precisely $n - 1$ such iterations of that loop overall. We base this claim on the fact that each iteration of that loop makes a recursive call to diskUsage, and yet we have already concluded that there are a total of n calls to diskUsage (including the original call). We therefore conclude that there are $O(n)$ recursive calls, each of which uses $O(1)$ time outside the loop, and that the *overall* number of operations due to the loop is $O(n)$. Summing all of these bounds, the overall number of operations is $O(n)$.

The argument we have made is more advanced than with the earlier examples of recursion. The idea that we can sometimes get a tighter bound on a series of operations by considering the cumulative effect, rather than assuming that each achieves a worst case is a technique called ***amortization***; we will see another example of such analysis in Section 7.2.3. Furthermore, a file system is an implicit example of a data structure known as a ***tree***, and our disk usage algorithm is really a manifestation of a more general algorithm known as a ***tree traversal***. Trees will be the focus of Chapter 8, and our argument about the $O(n)$ running time of the disk usage algorithm will be generalized for tree traversals in Section 8.4.

5.3 Further Examples of Recursion

In this section, we provide additional examples of the use of recursion. We organize our presentation by considering the maximum number of recursive calls that may be started from within the body of a single activation.

- If a recursive call starts at most one other, we call this a ***linear recursion***.
- If a recursive call may start two others, we call this a ***binary recursion***.
- If a recursive call may start three or more others, this is ***multiple recursion***.

5.3.1 Linear Recursion

If a recursive method is designed so that each invocation of the body makes at most one new recursive call, this is know as ***linear recursion***. Of the recursions we have seen so far, the implementation of the factorial method (Section 5.1.1) is a clear example of linear recursion. More interestingly, the binary search algorithm (Section 5.1.3) is also an example of *linear recursion*, despite the term "binary" in the name. The code for binary search (Code Fragment 5.3) includes a case analysis, with two branches that lead to a further recursive call, but only one branch is followed during a particular execution of the body.

A consequence of the definition of linear recursion is that any recursion trace will appear as a single sequence of calls, as we originally portrayed for the factorial method in Figure 5.1 of Section 5.1.1. Note that the *linear recursion* terminology reflects the structure of the recursion trace, not the asymptotic analysis of the running time; for example, we have seen that binary search runs in $O(\log n)$ time.

Summing the Elements of an Array Recursively

Linear recursion can be a useful tool for processing a sequence, such as a Java array. Suppose, for example, that we want to compute the sum of an array of n integers. We can solve this summation problem using linear recursion by observing that if $n = 0$ the sum is trivially 0, and otherwise it is the sum of the first $n - 1$ integers in the array plus the last value in the array. (See Figure 5.9.)

0	1	2	3	4	5	6	7	8	9	10	11	12	13	14	15
4	3	6	2	8	9	3	2	8	5	1	7	2	8	3	7

Figure 5.9: Computing the sum of a sequence recursively, by adding the last number to the sum of the first $n - 1$.

A recursive algorithm for computing the sum of an array of integers based on this intuition is implemented in Code Fragment 5.6.

```
1  /** Returns the sum of the first n integers of the given array. */
2  public static int linearSum(int[ ] data, int n) {
3    if (n == 0)
4      return 0;
5    else
6      return linearSum(data, n−1) + data[n−1];
7  }
```

Code Fragment 5.6: Summing an array of integers using linear recursion.

A recursion trace of the linearSum method for a small example is given in Figure 5.10. For an input of size n, the linearSum algorithm makes $n+1$ method calls. Hence, it will take $O(n)$ time, because it spends a constant amount of time performing the nonrecursive part of each call. Moreover, we can also see that the memory space used by the algorithm (in addition to the array) is also $O(n)$, as we use a constant amount of memory space for each of the $n+1$ frames in the trace at the time we make the final recursive call (with $n=0$).

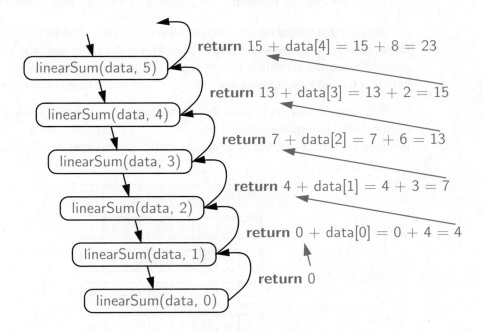

Figure 5.10: Recursion trace for an execution of linearSum(data, 5) with input parameter data = 4, 3, 6, 2, 8.

Reversing a Sequence with Recursion

Next, let us consider the problem of reversing the n elements of an array, so that the first element becomes the last, the second element becomes second to the last, and so on. We can solve this problem using linear recursion, by observing that the reversal of a sequence can be achieved by swapping the first and last elements and then recursively reversing the remaining elements. We present an implementation of this algorithm in Code Fragment 5.7, using the convention that the first time we call this algorithm we do so as reverseArray(data, 0, n−1).

```
1  /** Reverses the contents of subarray data[low] through data[high] inclusive. */
2  public static void reverseArray(int[ ] data, int low, int high) {
3    if (low < high) {                            // if at least two elements in subarray
4      int temp = data[low];                      // swap data[low] and data[high]
5      data[low] = data[high];
6      data[high] = temp;
7      reverseArray(data, low + 1, high − 1);     // recur on the rest
8    }
9  }
```

Code Fragment 5.7: Reversing the elements of an array using linear recursion.

We note that whenever a recursive call is made, there will be two fewer elements in the relevant portion of the array. (See Figure 5.11.) Eventually a base case is reached when the condition low < high fails, either because low == high in the case that n is odd, or because low == high + 1 in the case that n is even.

The above argument implies that the recursive algorithm of Code Fragment 5.7 is guaranteed to terminate after a total of $1 + \lfloor \frac{n}{2} \rfloor$ recursive calls. Because each call involves a constant amount of work, the entire process runs in $O(n)$ time.

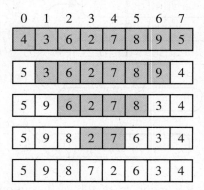

Figure 5.11: A trace of the recursion for reversing a sequence. The highlighted portion has yet to be reversed.

Recursive Algorithms for Computing Powers

As another interesting example of the use of linear recursion, we consider the problem of raising a number x to an arbitrary nonnegative integer n. That is, we wish to compute the **power function**, defined as $power(x, n) = x^n$. (We use the name "power" for this discussion, to differentiate from the pow method of the Math class, which provides such functionality.) We will consider two different recursive formulations for the problem that lead to algorithms with very different performance.

A trivial recursive definition follows from the fact that $x^n = x \cdot x^{n-1}$ for $n > 0$.

$$power(x, n) = \begin{cases} 1 & \text{if } n = 0 \\ x \cdot power(x, n-1) & \text{otherwise.} \end{cases}$$

This definition leads to a recursive algorithm shown in Code Fragment 5.8.

```
1  /** Computes the value of x raised to the nth power, for nonnegative integer n. */
2  public static double power(double x, int n) {
3    if (n == 0)
4      return 1;
5    else
6      return x * power(x, n−1);
7  }
```

Code Fragment 5.8: Computing the power function using trivial recursion.

A recursive call to this version of $power(x, n)$ runs in $O(n)$ time. Its recursion trace has structure very similar to that of the factorial function from Figure 5.1, with the parameter decreasing by one with each call, and constant work performed at each of $n + 1$ levels.

However, there is a much faster way to compute the power function using an alternative definition that employs a squaring technique. Let $k = \left\lfloor \frac{n}{2} \right\rfloor$ denote the floor of the integer division (equivalent to n/2 in Java when n is an int). We consider the expression $\left(x^k \right)^2$. When n is even, $\left\lfloor \frac{n}{2} \right\rfloor = \frac{n}{2}$ and therefore $\left(x^k \right)^2 = \left(x^{\frac{n}{2}} \right)^2 = x^n$. When n is odd, $\left\lfloor \frac{n}{2} \right\rfloor = \frac{n-1}{2}$ and $\left(x^k \right)^2 = x^{n-1}$, and therefore $x^n = \left(x^k \right)^2 \cdot x$, just as $2^{13} = \left(2^6 \cdot 2^6 \right) \cdot 2$. This analysis leads to the following recursive definition:

$$power(x, n) = \begin{cases} 1 & \text{if } n = 0 \\ \left(power\left(x, \left\lfloor \frac{n}{2} \right\rfloor \right) \right)^2 \cdot x & \text{if } n > 0 \text{ is odd} \\ \left(power\left(x, \left\lfloor \frac{n}{2} \right\rfloor \right) \right)^2 & \text{if } n > 0 \text{ is even} \end{cases}$$

If we were to implement this recursion making *two* recursive calls to compute $power(x, \left\lfloor \frac{n}{2} \right\rfloor) \cdot power(x, \left\lfloor \frac{n}{2} \right\rfloor)$, a trace of the recursion would demonstrate $O(n)$ calls. We can perform significantly fewer operations by computing $power(x, \left\lfloor \frac{n}{2} \right\rfloor)$ and storing it in a variable as a partial result, and then multiplying it by itself. An implementation based on this recursive definition is given in Code Fragment 5.9.

```
1   /** Computes the value of x raised to the nth power, for nonnegative integer n. */
2   public static double power(double x, int n) {
3     if (n == 0)
4       return 1;
5     else {
6       double partial = power(x, n/2);          // rely on truncated division of n
7       double result = partial * partial;
8       if (n % 2 == 1)                          // if n odd, include extra factor of x
9         result *= x;
10      return result;
11    }
12  }
```

Code Fragment 5.9: Computing the power function using repeated squaring.

To illustrate the execution of our improved algorithm, Figure 5.12 provides a recursion trace of the computation power(2, 13).

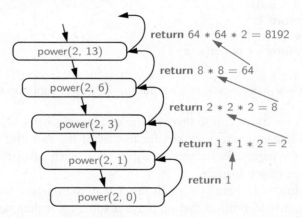

Figure 5.12: Recursion trace for an execution of power(2, 13).

To analyze the running time of the revised algorithm, we observe that the exponent in each recursive call of method power(x,n) is at most half of the preceding exponent. As we saw with the analysis of binary search, the number of times that we can divide n by two before getting to one or less is $O(\log n)$. Therefore, our new formulation of power results in $O(\log n)$ recursive calls. Each individual activation of the method uses $O(1)$ operations (excluding the recursive call), and so the total number of operations for computing power(x,n) is $O(\log n)$. This is a significant improvement over the original $O(n)$-time algorithm.

The improved version also provides significant saving in reducing the memory usage. The first version has a recursive depth of $O(n)$, and therefore, $O(n)$ frames are simultaneously stored in memory. Because the recursive depth of the improved version is $O(\log n)$, its memory usage is $O(\log n)$ as well.

5.3.2 Binary Recursion

When a method makes two recursive calls, we say that it uses ***binary recursion***. We have already seen an example of binary recursion when drawing the English ruler (Section 5.1.2). As another application of binary recursion, let us revisit the problem of summing the n integers of an array. Computing the sum of one or zero values is trivial. With two or more values, we can recursively compute the sum of the first half, and the sum of the second half, and add those sums together. Our implementation of such an algorithm, in Code Fragment 5.10, is initially invoked as binarySum(data, 0, n−1).

```
1  /** Returns the sum of subarray data[low] through data[high] inclusive. */
2  public static int binarySum(int[ ] data, int low, int high) {
3    if (low > high)                              // zero elements in subarray
4      return 0;
5    else if (low == high)                        // one element in subarray
6      return data[low];
7    else {
8      int mid = (low + high) / 2;
9      return binarySum(data, low, mid) + binarySum(data, mid+1, high);
10   }
11 }
```

Code Fragment 5.10: Summing the elements of a sequence using binary recursion.

To analyze algorithm binarySum, we consider, for simplicity, the case where n is a power of two. Figure 5.13 shows the recursion trace of an execution of binarySum(data, 0, 7). We label each box with the values of parameters low and high for that call. The size of the range is divided in half at each recursive call, and so the depth of the recursion is $1 + \log_2 n$. Therefore, binarySum uses $O(\log n)$ amount of additional space, which is a big improvement over the $O(n)$ space used by the linearSum method of Code Fragment 5.6. However, the running time of binarySum is $O(n)$, as there are $2n - 1$ method calls, each requiring constant time.

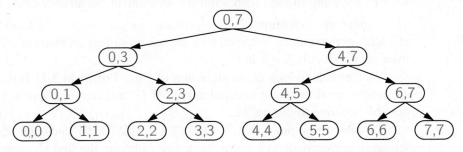

Figure 5.13: Recursion trace for the execution of binarySum(data, 0, 7).

5.3.3 Multiple Recursion

Generalizing from binary recursion, we define ***multiple recursion*** as a process in which a method may make more than two recursive calls. Our recursion for analyzing the disk space usage of a file system (see Section 5.1.4) is an example of multiple recursion, because the number of recursive calls made during one invocation was equal to the number of entries within a given directory of the file system.

Another common application of multiple recursion is when we want to enumerate various configurations in order to solve a combinatorial puzzle. For example, the following are all instances of what are known as ***summation puzzles***:

$$pot + pan = bib$$
$$dog + cat = pig$$
$$boy + girl = baby$$

To solve such a puzzle, we need to assign a unique digit (that is, $0, 1, \ldots, 9$) to each letter in the equation, in order to make the equation true. Typically, we solve such a puzzle by using our human observations of the particular puzzle we are trying to solve to eliminate configurations (that is, possible partial assignments of digits to letters) until we can work through the feasible configurations that remain, testing for the correctness of each one.

If the number of possible configurations is not too large, however, we can use a computer to simply enumerate all the possibilities and test each one, without employing any human observations. Such an algorithm can use multiple recursion to work through the configurations in a systematic way. To keep the description general enough to be used with other puzzles, we consider an algorithm that enumerates and tests all k-length sequences, without repetitions, chosen from a given universe U. We show pseudocode for such an algorithm in Code Fragment 5.11, building the sequence of k elements with the following steps:

1. Recursively generating the sequences of $k - 1$ elements
2. Appending to each such sequence an element not already contained in it.

Throughout the execution of the algorithm, we use a set U to keep track of the elements not contained in the current sequence, so that an element e has not been used yet if and only if e is in U.

Another way to look at the algorithm of Code Fragment 5.11 is that it enumerates every possible size-k ordered subset of U, and tests each subset for being a possible solution to our puzzle.

For summation puzzles, $U = \{0, 1, 2, 3, 4, 5, 6, 7, 8, 9\}$ and each position in the sequence corresponds to a given letter. For example, the first position could stand for b, the second for o, the third for y, and so on.

Algorithm PuzzleSolve(k, S, U):

    Input: An integer k, sequence S, and set U

    Output: An enumeration of all k-length extensions to S using elements in U
       without repetitions

   for each e in U **do**

      Add e to the end of S

      Remove e from U {e is now being used}

      if k == 1 **then**

         Test whether S is a configuration that solves the puzzle

         if S solves the puzzle **then**

            add S to output   {a solution}

      else

         PuzzleSolve($k - 1$, S, U)   {a recursive call}

      Remove e from the end of S

      Add e back to U {e is now considered as unused}

Code Fragment 5.11: Solving a combinatorial puzzle by enumerating and testing all possible configurations.

In Figure 5.14, we show a recursion trace of a call to PuzzleSolve(3, S, U), where S is empty and $U = \{a,b,c\}$. During the execution, all the permutations of the three characters are generated and tested. Note that the initial call makes three recursive calls, each of which in turn makes two more. If we had executed PuzzleSolve(3, S, U) on a set U consisting of four elements, the initial call would have made four recursive calls, each of which would have a trace looking like the one in Figure 5.14.

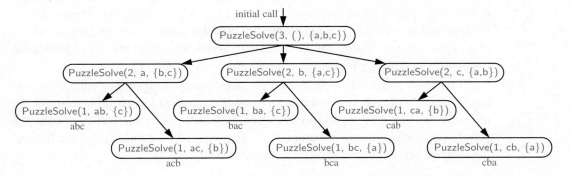

Figure 5.14: Recursion trace for an execution of PuzzleSolve(3, S, U), where S is empty and $U = \{a,b,c\}$. This execution generates and tests all permutations of a, b, and c. We show the permutations generated directly below their respective boxes.

5.4   Designing Recursive Algorithms

An algorithm that uses recursion typically has the following form:

- ***Test for base cases.*** We begin by testing for a set of base cases (there should be at least one). These base cases should be defined so that every possible chain of recursive calls will eventually reach a base case, and the handling of each base case should not use recursion.

- ***Recur.*** If not a base case, we perform one or more recursive calls. This recursive step may involve a test that decides which of several possible recursive calls to make. We should define each possible recursive call so that it makes progress towards a base case.

Parameterizing a Recursion

To design a recursive algorithm for a given problem, it is useful to think of the different ways we might define subproblems that have the same general structure as the original problem. If one has difficulty finding the repetitive structure needed to design a recursive algorithm, it is sometimes useful to work out the problem on a few concrete examples to see how the subproblems should be defined.

A successful recursive design sometimes requires that we redefine the original problem to facilitate similar-looking subproblems. Often, this involved reparameterizing the signature of the method. For example, when performing a binary search in an array, a natural method signature for a caller would appear as binarySearch(data, target). However, in Section 5.1.3, we defined our method with calling signature binarySearch(data, target, low, high), using the additional parameters to demarcate subarrays as the recursion proceeds. This change in parameterization is critical for binary search. Several other examples in this chapter (e.g., reverseArray, linearSum, binarySum) also demonstrated the use of additional parameters in defining recursive subproblems.

If we wish to provide a cleaner public interface to an algorithm without exposing the user to the recursive parameterization, a standard technique is to make the recursive version private, and to introduce a cleaner public method (that calls the private one with appropriate parameters). For example, we might offer the following simpler version of binarySearch for public use:

```
/** Returns true if the target value is found in the data array. */
public static boolean binarySearch(int[ ] data, int target) {
  return binarySearch(data, target, 0, data.length − 1);  // use parameterized version
}
```

5.5 Recursion Run Amok

Although recursion is a very powerful tool, it can easily be misused in various ways. In this section, we examine several cases in which a poorly implemented recursion causes drastic inefficiency, and we discuss some strategies for recognizing and avoid such pitfalls.

We begin by revisiting the ***element uniqueness problem***, defined on page 174 of Section 4.3.3. We can use the following recursive formulation to determine if all n elements of a sequence are unique. As a base case, when $n = 1$, the elements are trivially unique. For $n \geq 2$, the elements are unique if and only if the first $n - 1$ elements are unique, the last $n - 1$ items are unique, and the first and last elements are different (as that is the only pair that was not already checked as a subcase). A recursive implementation based on this idea is given in Code Fragment 5.12, named unique3 (to differentiate it from unique1 and unique2 from Chapter 4).

```
1  /** Returns true if there are no duplicate values from data[low] through data[high].*/
2  public static boolean unique3(int[ ] data, int low, int high) {
3    if (low >= high) return true;                        // at most one item
4    else if (!unique3(data, low, high−1)) return false;  // duplicate in first n−1
5    else if (!unique3(data, low+1, high)) return false;  // duplicate in last n−1
6    else return (data[low] != data[high]);               // do first and last differ?
7  }
```

Code Fragment 5.12: Recursive unique3 for testing element uniqueness.

Unfortunately, this is a terribly inefficient use of recursion. The nonrecursive part of each call uses $O(1)$ time, so the overall running time will be proportional to the total number of recursive invocations. To analyze the problem, we let n denote the number of entries under consideration, that is, let $n = 1 + \text{high} - \text{low}$.

If $n = 1$, then the running time of unique3 is $O(1)$, since there are no recursive calls for this case. In the general case, the important observation is that a single call to unique3 for a problem of size n may result in two recursive calls on problems of size $n - 1$. Those two calls with size $n - 1$ could in turn result in four calls (two each) with a range of size $n - 2$, and thus eight calls with size $n - 3$ and so on. Thus, in the worst case, the total number of method calls is given by the geometric summation

$$1 + 2 + 4 + \cdots + 2^{n-1},$$

which is equal to $2^n - 1$ by Proposition 4.5. Thus, the running time of method unique3 is $O(2^n)$. This is an incredibly inefficient method for solving the element uniqueness problem. Its inefficiency comes not from the fact that it uses recursion—it comes from the fact that it uses recursion poorly, which is something we address in Exercise C-5.12.

An Inefficient Recursion for Computing Fibonacci Numbers

In Section 2.2.3, we introduced a process for generating the progression of Fibonacci numbers, which can be defined recursively as follows:

$$F_0 = 0$$
$$F_1 = 1$$
$$F_n = F_{n-2} + F_{n-1} \quad \text{for } n > 1.$$

Ironically, a recursive implementation based directly on this definition results in the method fibonacciBad shown in Code Fragment 5.13, which computes a Fibonacci number by making two recursive calls in each non-base case.

```
1  /** Returns the nth Fibonacci number (inefficiently). */
2  public static long fibonacciBad(int n) {
3    if (n <= 1)
4      return n;
5    else
6      return fibonacciBad(n−2) + fibonacciBad(n−1);
7  }
```

Code Fragment 5.13: Computing the nth Fibonacci number using binary recursion.

Unfortunately, such a direct implementation of the Fibonacci formula results in a terribly inefficient method. Computing the nth Fibonacci number in this way requires an exponential number of calls to the method. Specifically, let c_n denote the number of calls performed in the execution of fibonacciBad(n). Then, we have the following values for the c_n's:

$$c_0 = 1$$
$$c_1 = 1$$
$$c_2 = 1 + c_0 + c_1 = 1 + 1 + 1 = 3$$
$$c_3 = 1 + c_1 + c_2 = 1 + 1 + 3 = 5$$
$$c_4 = 1 + c_2 + c_3 = 1 + 3 + 5 = 9$$
$$c_5 = 1 + c_3 + c_4 = 1 + 5 + 9 = 15$$
$$c_6 = 1 + c_4 + c_5 = 1 + 9 + 15 = 25$$
$$c_7 = 1 + c_5 + c_6 = 1 + 15 + 25 = 41$$
$$c_8 = 1 + c_6 + c_7 = 1 + 25 + 41 = 67$$

If we follow the pattern forward, we see that the number of calls more than doubles for each two consecutive indices. That is, c_4 is more than twice c_2, c_5 is more than twice c_3, c_6 is more than twice c_4, and so on. Thus, $c_n > 2^{n/2}$, which means that fibonacciBad(n) makes a number of calls that is exponential in n.

An Efficient Recursion for Computing Fibonacci Numbers

We were tempted into using the bad recursive formulation because of the way the nth Fibonacci number, F_n, depends on the two previous values, F_{n-2} and F_{n-1}. But notice that after computing F_{n-2}, the call to compute F_{n-1} requires its own recursive call to compute F_{n-2}, as it does not have knowledge of the value of F_{n-2} that was computed at the earlier level of recursion. That is duplicative work. Worse yet, both of those calls will need to (re)compute the value of F_{n-3}, as will the computation of F_{n-1}. This snowballing effect is what leads to the exponential running time of fibonacciBad.

We can compute F_n much more efficiently using a recursion in which each invocation makes only one recursive call. To do so, we need to redefine the expectations of the method. Rather than having the method return a single value, which is the nth Fibonacci number, we define a recursive method that returns an array with two consecutive Fibonacci numbers $\{F_n, F_{n-1}\}$, using the convention $F_{-1} = 0$. Although it seems to be a greater burden to report two consecutive Fibonacci numbers instead of one, passing this extra information from one level of the recursion to the next makes it much easier to continue the process. (It allows us to avoid having to recompute the second value that was already known within the recursion.) An implementation based on this strategy is given in Code Fragment 5.14.

```
1  /** Returns array containing the pair of Fibonacci numbers, F(n) and F(n−1). */
2  public static long[ ] fibonacciGood(int n) {
3    if (n <= 1) {
4      long[ ] answer = {n, 0};
5      return answer;
6    } else {
7      long[ ] temp = fibonacciGood(n − 1);      // returns {F_{n-1}, F_{n-2}}
8      long[ ] answer = {temp[0] + temp[1], temp[0]};   // we want {F_n, F_{n-1}}
9      return answer;
10   }
11 }
```

Code Fragment 5.14: Computing the nth Fibonacci number using linear recursion.

In terms of efficiency, the difference between the bad and good recursions for this problem is like night and day. The fibonacciBad method uses exponential time. We claim that the execution of method fibonacciGood(n) runs in $O(n)$ time. Each recursive call to fibonacciGood decreases the argument n by 1; therefore, a recursion trace includes a series of n method calls. Because the nonrecursive work for each call uses constant time, the overall computation executes in $O(n)$ time.

5.5.1 Maximum Recursive Depth in Java

Another danger in the misuse of recursion is known as ***infinite recursion***. If each recursive call makes another recursive call, without ever reaching a base case, then we have an infinite series of such calls. This is a fatal error. An infinite recursion can quickly swamp computing resources, not only due to rapid use of the CPU, but because each successive call creates a frame requiring additional memory. A blatant example of an ill-formed recursion is the following:

```
1  /** Don't call this (infinite) version. */
2  public static int fibonacci(int n) {
3    return fibonacci(n);                        // After all F_n does equal F_n
4  }
```

However, there are far more subtle errors that can lead to an infinite recursion. Revisiting our implementation of binary search (Code Fragment 5.3), when we make a recursive call on the right portion of the sequence (line 15), we specify the subarray from index mid+1 to high. Had that line instead been written as

```
    return binarySearch(data, target, mid, high);   // sending mid, not mid+1
```

this could result in an infinite recursion. In particular, when searching a range of two elements, it becomes possible to make a recursive call on the identical range.

A programmer should ensure that each recursive call is in some way progressing toward a base case (for example, by having a parameter value that decreases with each call). To combat against infinite recursions, the designers of Java made an intentional decision to limit the overall space used to store activation frames for simultaneously active method calls. If this limit is reached, the Java Virtual Machine throws a StackOverflowError. (We will further discuss the "stack" data structure in Section 6.1.) The precise value of this limit depends upon the Java installation, but a typical value might allow upward of 1000 simultaneous calls.

For many applications of recursion, allowing up to 1000 nested calls suffices. For example, our binarySearch method (Section 5.1.3) has $O(\log n)$ recursive depth, and so for the default recursive limit to be reached, there would need to be 2^{1000} elements (far, far more than the estimated number of atoms in the universe). However, we have seen several linear recursions that have recursive depth proportional to n. Java's limit on the recursive depth might disrupt such computations.

It is possible to reconfigure the Java Virtual Machine so that it allows for greater space to be devoted to nested method calls. This is done by setting the -Xss runtime option when starting Java, either as a command-line option or through the settings of an IDE. But it often possible to rely upon the intuition of a recursive algorithm, yet to reimplement it more directly using traditional loops rather than method calls to express the necessary repetition. We discuss just such an approach to conclude the chapter.

5.6   Eliminating Tail Recursion

The main benefit of a recursive approach to algorithm design is that it allows us to succinctly take advantage of a repetitive structure present in many problems. By making our algorithm description exploit the repetitive structure in a recursive way, we can often avoid complex case analyses and nested loops. This approach can lead to more readable algorithm descriptions, while still being quite efficient.

However, the usefulness of recursion comes at a modest cost. In particular, the Java Virtual Machine must maintain frames that keep track of the state of each nested call. When computer memory is at a premium, it can be beneficial to derive nonrecursive implementations of recursive algorithms.

In general, we can use the stack data structure, which we will introduce in Section 6.1, to convert a recursive algorithm into a nonrecursive algorithm by managing the nesting of the recursive structure ourselves, rather than relying on the interpreter to do so. Although this only shifts the memory usage from the interpreter to our stack, we may be able to further reduce the memory usage by storing the minimal information necessary.

Even better, some forms of recursion can be eliminated without any use of auxiliary memory. One such form is known as ***tail recursion***. A recursion is a tail recursion if any recursive call that is made from one context is the very last operation in that context, with the return value of the recursive call (if any) immediately returned by the enclosing recursion. By necessity, a tail recursion must be a linear recursion (since there is no way to make a second recursive call if you must immediately return the result of the first).

Of the recursive methods demonstrated in this chapter, the binarySearch method of Code Fragment 5.3 and the reverseArray method of Code Fragment 5.7 are examples of tail recursion. Several others of our linear recursions are almost like tail recursion, but not technically so. For example, our factorial method of Code Fragment 5.1 is *not* a tail recursion. It concludes with the command:

> **return** n * factorial(n−1);

This is not a tail recursion because an additional multiplication is performed after the recursive call is completed, and the result returned is not the same. For similar reasons, the linearSum method of Code Fragment 5.6, both power methods from Code Fragments 5.8 and 5.9, and the fibonacciGood method of Code Fragment 5.13 fail to be tail recursions.

Tail recursions are special, as they can be automatically reimplemented nonrecursively by enclosing the body in a loop for repetition, and replacing a recursive call with new parameters by a reassignment of the existing parameters to those values. In fact, many programming language implementations may convert tail recursions in this way as an optimization.

```
1   /** Returns true if the target value is found in the data array. */
2   public static boolean binarySearchIterative(int[ ] data, int target) {
3     int low = 0;
4     int high = data.length − 1;
5     while (low <= high) {
6       int mid = (low + high) / 2;
7       if (target == data[mid])                    // found a match
8         return true;
9       else if (target < data[mid])
10        high = mid − 1;                           // only consider values left of mid
11      else
12        low = mid + 1;                            // only consider values right of mid
13    }
14    return false;                                 // loop ended without success
15  }
```

Code Fragment 5.15: A nonrecursive implementation of binary search.

As a tangible example, our binarySearch method can be reimplemented as shown in Code Fragment 5.15. We initialize variables low and high to represent the full extent of the array just prior to our while loop. Then, during each pass of the loop, we either find the target, or we narrow the range of the candidate subarray. Where we made the recursive call binarySearch(data, target, low, mid −1) in the original version, we simply replace high = mid − 1 in our new version and then continue to the next iteration of the loop. Our original base case condition of low > high has simply been replaced by the opposite loop condition, while low <= high. In our new implementation, we return false to designate a failed search if the while loop ends without having ever returned true from within.

Most other linear recursions can be expressed quite efficiently with iteration, even if they were not formally tail recursions. For example, there are trivial nonrecursive implementations for computing factorials, computing Fibonacci numbers, summing elements of an array, or reversing the contents of an array. For example, Code Fragment 5.16 provides a nonrecursive method to reverse the contents of an array (as compared to the earlier recursive method from Code Fragment 5.7).

```
1   /** Reverses the contents of the given array. */
2   public static void reverseIterative(int[ ] data) {
3     int low = 0, high = data.length − 1;
4     while (low < high) {                          // swap data[low] and data[high]
5       int temp = data[low];
6       data[low++] = data[high];                   // post-increment of low
7       data[high−−] = temp;                        // post-decrement of high
8     }
9   }
```

Code Fragment 5.16: Reversing the elements of a sequence using iteration.

5.7   Exercises

Reinforcement

R-5.1 Describe a recursive algorithm for finding the maximum element in an array, A, of n elements. What is your running time and space usage?

R-5.2 Explain how to modify the recursive binary search algorithm so that it returns the index of the target in the sequence or -1 (if the target is not found).

R-5.3 Draw the recursion trace for the computation of $power(2,5)$, using the traditional algorithm implemented in Code Fragment 5.8.

R-5.4 Draw the recursion trace for the computation of $power(2,18)$, using the repeated squaring algorithm, as implemented in Code Fragment 5.9.

R-5.5 Draw the recursion trace for the execution of reverseArray(data, 0, 4), from Code Fragment 5.7, on array data = 4, 3, 6, 2, 6.

R-5.6 Draw the recursion trace for the execution of method PuzzleSolve$(3, S, U)$, from Code Fragment 5.11, where S is empty and $U = \{a, b, c, d\}$.

R-5.7 Describe a recursive algorithm for computing the nth ***Harmonic number***, defined as $H_n = \sum_{k=1}^{n} 1/k$.

R-5.8 Describe a recursive algorithm for converting a string of digits into the integer it represents. For example, '13531' represents the integer $13,531$.

R-5.9 Develop a nonrecursive implementation of the version of the power method from Code Fragment 5.9 that uses repeated squaring.

R-5.10 Describe a way to use recursion to compute the sum of all the elements in an $n \times n$ (two-dimensional) array of integers.

Creativity

C-5.11 Describe a recursive algorithm to compute the integer part of the base-two logarithm of n using only addition and integer division.

C-5.12 Describe an efficient recursive algorithm for solving the element uniqueness problem, which runs in time that is at most $O(n^2)$ in the worst case without using sorting.

C-5.13 Give a recursive algorithm to compute the product of two positive integers, m and n, using only addition and subtraction.

C-5.14 In Section 5.2 we prove by induction that the number of *lines* printed by a call to drawInterval(c) is $2^c - 1$. Another interesting question is how many *dashes* are printed during that process. Prove by induction that the number of dashes printed by drawInterval(c) is $2^{c+1} - c - 2$.

C-5.15 Write a recursive method that will output all the subsets of a set of n elements (without repeating any subsets).

C-5.16 In the ***Towers of Hanoi*** puzzle, we are given a platform with three pegs, a, b, and c, sticking out of it. On peg a is a stack of n disks, each larger than the next, so that the smallest is on the top and the largest is on the bottom. The puzzle is to move all the disks from peg a to peg c, moving one disk at a time, so that we never place a larger disk on top of a smaller one. See Figure 5.15 for an example of the case $n = 4$. Describe a recursive algorithm for solving the Towers of Hanoi puzzle for arbitrary n. (Hint: Consider first the subproblem of moving all but the nth disk from peg a to another peg using the third as "temporary storage.")

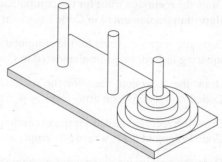

Figure 5.15: An illustration of the Towers of Hanoi puzzle.

C-5.17 Write a short recursive Java method that takes a character string s and outputs its reverse. For example, the reverse of `'pots&pans'` would be `'snap&stop'`.

C-5.18 Write a short recursive Java method that determines if a string s is a palindrome, that is, it is equal to its reverse. Examples of palindromes include `'racecar'` and `'gohangasalamiimalasagnahog'`.

C-5.19 Use recursion to write a Java method for determining if a string s has more vowels than consonants.

C-5.20 Write a short recursive Java method that rearranges an array of integer values so that all the even values appear before all the odd values.

C-5.21 Given an unsorted array, A, of integers and an integer k, describe a recursive algorithm for rearranging the elements in A so that all elements less than or equal to k come before any elements larger than k. What is the running time of your algorithm on an array of n values?

C-5.22 Suppose you are given an array, A, containing n distinct integers that are listed in increasing order. Given a number k, describe a recursive algorithm to find two integers in A that sum to k, if such a pair exists. What is the running time of your algorithm?

C-5.23 Describe a recursive algorithm that will check if an array A of integers contains an integer $A[i]$ that is the sum of two integers that appear earlier in A, that is, such that $A[i] = A[j] + A[k]$ for $j, k < i$.

C-5.24 Isabel has an interesting way of summing up the values in an array A of n integers, where n is a power of two. She creates an array B of half the size of A and sets $B[i] = A[2i] + A[2i + 1]$, for $i = 0, 1, \ldots, (n/2) - 1$. If B has size 1, then she outputs $B[0]$. Otherwise, she replaces A with B, and repeats the process. What is the running time of her algorithm?

C-5.25 Describe a fast recursive algorithm for reversing a singly linked list L, so that the ordering of the nodes becomes opposite of what it was before.

C-5.26 Give a recursive definition of a singly linked list class that does not use any Node class.

Projects

P-5.27 Implement a recursive method with calling signature find(path, filename) that reports all entries of the file system rooted at the given path having the given file name.

P-5.28 Write a program for solving summation puzzles by enumerating and testing all possible configurations. Using your program, solve the three puzzles given in Section 5.3.3.

P-5.29 Provide a nonrecursive implementation of the drawInterval method for the English ruler project of Section 5.1.2. There should be precisely $2^c - 1$ lines of output if c represents the length of the center tick. If incrementing a counter from 0 to $2^c - 2$, the number of dashes for each tick line should be exactly one more than the number of consecutive 1's at the end of the binary representation of the counter.

P-5.30 Write a program that can solve instances of the Tower of Hanoi problem (from Exercise C-5.16).

Chapter Notes

The use of recursion in programs belongs to the folklore of computer science (for example, see the article of Dijkstra [31]). It is also at the heart of functional programming languages (for example, see the book by Abelson, Sussman, and Sussman [1]). Interestingly, binary search was first published in 1946, but was not published in a fully correct form until 1962. For further discussions on lessons learned, see papers by Bentley [13] and Lesuisse [64].

Chapter 6

Stacks, Queues, and Deques

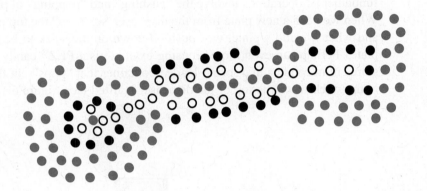

Contents

6.1   Stacks

A *stack* is a collection of objects that are inserted and removed according to the *last-in, first-out* (*LIFO*) principle. A user may insert objects into a stack at any time, but may only access or remove the most recently inserted object that remains (at the so-called "top" of the stack). The name "stack" is derived from the metaphor of a stack of plates in a spring-loaded, cafeteria plate dispenser. In this case, the fundamental operations involve the "pushing" and "popping" of plates on the stack. When we need a new plate from the dispenser, we "pop" the top plate off the stack, and when we add a plate, we "push" it down on the stack to become the new top plate. Perhaps an even more amusing example is a PEZ® candy dispenser, which stores mint candies in a spring-loaded container that "pops" out the topmost candy in the stack when the top of the dispenser is lifted (see Figure 6.1).

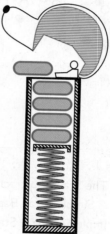

Figure 6.1: A schematic drawing of a PEZ® dispenser; a physical implementation of the stack ADT. (PEZ® is a registered trademark of PEZ Candy, Inc.)

Stacks are a fundamental data structure. They are used in many applications, including the following.

Example 6.1: *Internet Web browsers store the addresses of recently visited sites on a stack. Each time a user visits a new site, that site's address is "pushed" onto the stack of addresses. The browser then allows the user to "pop" back to previously visited sites using the "back" button.*

Example 6.2: *Text editors usually provide an "undo" mechanism that cancels recent editing operations and reverts to former states of a document. This undo operation can be accomplished by keeping text changes in a stack.*

6.1.1   The Stack Abstract Data Type

Stacks are the simplest of all data structures, yet they are also among the most important, as they are used in a host of different applications, and as a tool for many more sophisticated data structures and algorithms. Formally, a stack is an abstract data type (ADT) that supports the following two update methods:

push(*e*): Adds element *e* to the top of the stack.

pop( ): Removes and returns the top element from the stack
(or null if the stack is empty).

Additionally, a stack supports the following accessor methods for convenience:

top( ): Returns the top element of the stack, without removing it
(or null if the stack is empty).

size( ): Returns the number of elements in the stack.

isEmpty( ): Returns a boolean indicating whether the stack is empty.

By convention, we assume that elements added to the stack can have arbitrary type and that a newly created stack is empty.

Example 6.3: *The following table shows a series of stack operations and their effects on an initially empty stack S of integers.*

Method	Return Value	Stack Contents
push(5)	–	(5)
push(3)	–	(5, 3)
size( )	2	(5, 3)
pop( )	3	(5)
isEmpty( )	false	(5)
pop( )	5	( )
isEmpty( )	true	( )
pop( )	null	( )
push(7)	–	(7)
push(9)	–	(7, 9)
top( )	9	(7, 9)
push(4)	–	(7, 9, 4)
size( )	3	(7, 9, 4)
pop( )	4	(7, 9)
push(6)	–	(7, 9, 6)
push(8)	–	(7, 9, 6, 8)
pop( )	8	(7, 9, 6)

A Stack Interface in Java

In order to formalize our abstraction of a stack, we define what is known as its *application programming interface* (API) in the form of a Java *interface*, which describes the names of the methods that the ADT supports and how they are to be declared and used. This interface is defined in Code Fragment 6.1.

We rely on Java's *generics framework* (described in Section 2.5.2), allowing the elements stored in the stack to belong to any object type <E>. For example, a variable representing a stack of integers could be declared with type Stack<Integer>. The formal type parameter is used as the parameter type for the push method, and the return type for both pop and top.

Recall, from the discussion of Java interfaces in Section 2.3.1, that the interface serves as a type definition but that it cannot be directly instantiated. For the ADT to be of any use, we must provide one or more concrete classes that implement the methods of the interface associated with that ADT. In the following subsections, we will give two such implementations of the Stack interface: one that uses an array for storage and another that uses a linked list.

The java.util.Stack Class

Because of the importance of the stack ADT, Java has included, since its original version, a concrete class named java.util.Stack that implements the LIFO semantics of a stack. However, Java's Stack class remains only for historic reasons, and its interface is not consistent with most other data structures in the Java library. In fact, the current documentation for the Stack class recommends that it not be used, as LIFO functionality (and more) is provided by a more general data structure known as a double-ended queue (which we describe in Section 6.3).

For the sake of comparison, Table 6.1 provides a side-by-side comparison of the interface for our stack ADT and the `java.util.Stack` class. In addition to some differences in method names, we note that methods pop and peek of the java.util.Stack class throw a custom EmptyStackException if called when the stack is empty (whereas null is returned in our abstraction).

Our Stack ADT	Class java.util.Stack	
size( )	size( )	
isEmpty( )	empty( )	⇐
push(*e*)	push(*e*)	
pop( )	pop( )	
top( )	peek( )	⇐

Table 6.1: Methods of our stack ADT and corresponding methods of the class java.util.Stack, with differences highlighted in the right margin.

```
 1  /**
 2   * A collection of objects that are inserted and removed according to the last-in
 3   * first-out principle. Although similar in purpose, this interface differs from
 4   * java.util.Stack.
 5   *
 6   * @author Michael T. Goodrich
 7   * @author Roberto Tamassia
 8   * @author Michael H. Goldwasser
 9   */
10  public interface Stack<E> {
11
12    /**
13     * Returns the number of elements in the stack.
14     * @return number of elements in the stack
15     */
16    int size( );
17
18    /**
19     * Tests whether the stack is empty.
20     * @return true if the stack is empty, false otherwise
21     */
22    boolean isEmpty( );
23
24    /**
25     * Inserts an element at the top of the stack.
26     * @param e   the element to be inserted
27     */
28    void push(E e);
29
30    /**
31     * Returns, but does not remove, the element at the top of the stack.
32     * @return top element in the stack (or null if empty)
33     */
34    E top( );
35
36    /**
37     * Removes and returns the top element from the stack.
38     * @return element removed (or null if empty)
39     */
40    E pop( );
41  }
```

Code Fragment 6.1: Interface Stack documented with comments in Javadoc style (Section 1.9.4). Note also the use of the generic parameterized type, E, which allows a stack to contain elements of any specified (reference) type.

6.1.2 A Simple Array-Based Stack Implementation

As our first implementation of the stack ADT, we store elements in an array, named data, with capacity N for some fixed N. We oriented the stack so that the bottom element of the stack is always stored in cell data[0], and the top element of the stack in cell data[t] for index t that is equal to one less than the current size of the stack. (See Figure 6.2.)

Figure 6.2: Representing a stack with an array; the top element is in cell data[t].

Recalling that arrays start at index 0 in Java, when the stack holds elements from data[0] to data[t] inclusive, it has size $t + 1$. By convention, when the stack is empty it will have t equal to -1 (and thus has size $t + 1$, which is 0). A complete Java implementation based on this strategy is given in Code Fragment 6.2 (with Javadoc comments omitted due to space considerations).

```java
 1  public class ArrayStack<E> implements Stack<E> {
 2    public static final int CAPACITY=1000;    // default array capacity
 3    private E[ ] data;                         // generic array used for storage
 4    private int t = −1;                        // index of the top element in stack
 5    public ArrayStack( ) { this(CAPACITY); }   // constructs stack with default capacity
 6    public ArrayStack(int capacity) {          // constructs stack with given capacity
 7      data = (E[ ]) new Object[capacity];      // safe cast; compiler may give warning
 8    }
 9    public int size( ) { return (t + 1); }
10    public boolean isEmpty( ) { return (t == −1); }
11    public void push(E e) throws IllegalStateException {
12      if (size( ) == data.length) throw new IllegalStateException("Stack is full");
13      data[++t] = e;                           // increment t before storing new item
14    }
15    public E top( ) {
16      if (isEmpty( )) return null;
17      return data[t];
18    }
19    public E pop( ) {
20      if (isEmpty( )) return null;
21      E answer = data[t];
22      data[t] = null;                          // dereference to help garbage collection
23      t−−;
24      return answer;
25    }
26  }
```

Code Fragment 6.2: Array-based implementation of the Stack interface.

A Drawback of This Array-Based Stack Implementation

The array implementation of a stack is simple and efficient. Nevertheless, this implementation has one negative aspect—it relies on a fixed-capacity array, which limits the ultimate size of the stack.

For convenience, we allow the user of a stack to specify the capacity as a parameter to the constructor (and offer a default constructor that uses capacity of $1,000$). In cases where a user has a good estimate on the number of items needing to go in the stack, the array-based implementation is hard to beat. However, if the estimate is wrong, there can be grave consequences. If the application needs much less space than the reserved capacity, memory is wasted. Worse yet, if an attempt is made to push an item onto a stack that has already reached its maximum capacity, the implementation of Code Fragment 6.2 throws an IllegalStateException, refusing to store the new element. Thus, even with its simplicity and efficiency, the array-based stack implementation is not necessarily ideal.

Fortunately, we will later demonstrate two approaches for implementing a stack without such a size limitation and with space always proportional to the actual number of elements stored in the stack. One approach, given in the next subsection uses a singly linked list for storage; in Section 7.2.1, we will provide a more advanced array-based approach that overcomes the limit of a fixed capacity.

Analyzing the Array-Based Stack Implementation

The correctness of the methods in the array-based implementation follows from our definition of index t. Note well that when pushing an element, t is incremented before placing the new element, so that it uses the first available cell.

Table 6.2 shows the running times for methods of this array-based stack implementation. Each method executes a constant number of statements involving arithmetic operations, comparisons, and assignments, or calls to size and isEmpty, which both run in constant time. Thus, in this implementation of the stack ADT, each method runs in constant time, that is, they each run in $O(1)$ time.

Method	Running Time
size	$O(1)$
isEmpty	$O(1)$
top	$O(1)$
push	$O(1)$
pop	$O(1)$

Table 6.2: Performance of a stack realized by an array. The space usage is $O(N)$, where N is the size of the array, determined at the time the stack is instantiated, and independent from the number $n \leq N$ of elements that are actually in the stack.

Garbage Collection in Java

We wish to draw attention to one interesting aspect involving the implementation of the pop method in Code Fragment 6.2. We set a local variable, answer, to reference the element that is being popped, and then we intentionally reset data[t] to **null** at line 22, before decrementing t. The assignment to **null** was not technically required, as our stack would still operate correctly without it.

Our reason for returning the cell to a null reference is to assist Java's *garbage collection* mechanism, which searches memory for objects that are no longer actively referenced and reclaims their space for future use. (For more details, see Section 15.1.3.) If we continued to store a reference to the popped element in our array, the stack class would ignore it (eventually overwriting the reference if more elements get added to the stack). But, if there were no other active references to the element in the user's application, that spurious reference in the stack's array would stop Java's garbage collector from reclaiming the element.

Sample Usage

We conclude this section by providing a demonstration of code that creates and uses an instance of the ArrayStack class. In this example, we declare the parameterized type of the stack as the Integer wrapper class. This causes the signature of the push method to accept an Integer instance as a parameter, and for the return type of both top and pop to be an Integer. Of course, with Java's autoboxing and unboxing (see Section 1.3), a primitive **int** can be sent as a parameter to push.

```
Stack<Integer> S = new ArrayStack<>();   // contents: ()
S.push(5);                               // contents: (5)
S.push(3);                               // contents: (5, 3)
System.out.println(S.size());            // contents: (5, 3)      outputs 2
System.out.println(S.pop());             // contents: (5)         outputs 3
System.out.println(S.isEmpty());         // contents: (5)         outputs false
System.out.println(S.pop());             // contents: ()          outputs 5
System.out.println(S.isEmpty());         // contents: ()          outputs true
System.out.println(S.pop());             // contents: ()          outputs null
S.push(7);                               // contents: (7)
S.push(9);                               // contents: (7, 9)
System.out.println(S.top());             // contents: (7, 9)      outputs 9
S.push(4);                               // contents: (7, 9, 4)
System.out.println(S.size());            // contents: (7, 9, 4)   outputs 3
System.out.println(S.pop());             // contents: (7, 9)      outputs 4
S.push(6);                               // contents: (7, 9, 6)
S.push(8);                               // contents: (7, 9, 6, 8)
System.out.println(S.pop());             // contents: (7, 9, 6)   outputs 8
```

Code Fragment 6.3: Sample usage of our ArrayStack class.

6.1.3 Implementing a Stack with a Singly Linked List

In this section, we demonstrate how the Stack interface can be easily implemented using a singly linked list for storage. Unlike our array-based implementation, the linked-list approach has memory usage that is always proportional to the number of actual elements currently in the stack, and without an arbitrary capacity limit.

In designing such an implementation, we need to decide if the top of the stack is at the front or back of the list. There is clearly a best choice here, however, since we can insert and delete elements in constant time only at the front. With the top of the stack stored at the front of the list, all methods execute in constant time.

The Adapter Pattern

The *adapter* design pattern applies to any context where we effectively want to modify an existing class so that its methods match those of a related, but different, class or interface. One general way to apply the adapter pattern is to define a new class in such a way that it contains an instance of the existing class as a hidden field, and then to implement each method of the new class using methods of this hidden instance variable. By applying the adapter pattern in this way, we have created a new class that performs some of the same functions as an existing class, but repackaged in a more convenient way.

In the context of the stack ADT, we can adapt our SinglyLinkedList class of Section 3.2.1 to define a new LinkedStack class, shown in Code Fragment 6.4. This class declares a SinglyLinkedList named list as a private field, and uses the following correspondences:

Stack Method	*Singly Linked List Method*
size( )	list.size( )
isEmpty( )	list.isEmpty( )
push(e)	list.addFirst(e)
pop( )	list.removeFirst( )
top( )	list.first( )

```
1  public class LinkedStack<E> implements Stack<E> {
2    private SinglyLinkedList<E> list = new SinglyLinkedList<>();   // an empty list
3    public LinkedStack() { }                        // new stack relies on the initially empty list
4    public int size() { return list.size(); }
5    public boolean isEmpty() { return list.isEmpty(); }
6    public void push(E element) { list.addFirst(element); }
7    public E top() { return list.first(); }
8    public E pop() { return list.removeFirst(); }
9  }
```

Code Fragment 6.4: Implementation of a Stack using a SinglyLinkedList as storage.

6.1.4   Reversing an Array Using a Stack

As a consequence of the LIFO protocol, a stack can be used as a general toll to reverse a data sequence. For example, if the values 1, 2, and 3 are pushed onto a stack in that order, they will be popped from the stack in the order 3, 2, and then 1.

We demonstrate this concept by revisiting the problem of reversing the elements of an array. (We provided a recursive algorithm for this task in Section 5.3.1.) We create an empty stack for auxiliary storage, push all of the array elements onto the stack, and then pop those elements off of the stack while overwriting the cells of the array from beginning to end. In Code Fragment 6.5, we give a Java implementation of this algorithm. We show an example use of this method in Code Fragment 6.6.

```java
1   /** A generic method for reversing an array. */
2   public static <E> void reverse(E[ ] a) {
3     Stack<E> buffer = new ArrayStack<>(a.length);
4     for (int i=0; i < a.length; i++)
5       buffer.push(a[i]);
6     for (int i=0; i < a.length; i++)
7       a[i] = buffer.pop( );
8   }
```

Code Fragment 6.5: A generic method that reverses the elements in an array with objects of type E, using a stack declared with the interface Stack<E> as its type.

```java
1   /** Tester routine for reversing arrays */
2   public static void main(String args[ ]) {
3     Integer[ ] a = {4, 8, 15, 16, 23, 42};        // autoboxing allows this
4     String[ ] s = {"Jack", "Kate", "Hurley", "Jin", "Michael"};
5     System.out.println("a = " + Arrays.toString(a));
6     System.out.println("s = " + Arrays.toString(s));
7     System.out.println("Reversing...");
8     reverse(a);
9     reverse(s);
10    System.out.println("a = " + Arrays.toString(a));
11    System.out.println("s = " + Arrays.toString(s));
12  }
```

The output from this method is the following:

```
a = [4, 8, 15, 16, 23, 42]
s = [Jack, Kate, Hurley, Jin, Michael]
Reversing...
a = [42, 23, 16, 15, 8, 4]
s = [Michael, Jin, Hurley, Kate, Jack]
```

Code Fragment 6.6: A test of the reverse method using two arrays.

6.1.5 Matching Parentheses and HTML Tags

In this subsection, we explore two related applications of stacks, both of which involve testing for pairs of matching delimiters. In our first application, we consider arithmetic expressions that may contain various pairs of grouping symbols, such as

- Parentheses: "(" and ")"
- Braces: "{" and "}"
- Brackets: "[" and "]"

Each opening symbol must match its corresponding closing symbol. For example, a left bracket, "[," must match a corresponding right bracket, "]," as in the following expression

$$[(5+x) - (y+z)].$$

The following examples further illustrate this concept:

- Correct: ()(()){([()])}
- Correct: ((()(()){([()])}))
- Incorrect:)(()){([()])}
- Incorrect: ({[])}
- Incorrect: (

We leave the precise definition of a matching group of symbols to Exercise R-6.6.

An Algorithm for Matching Delimiters

An important task when processing arithmetic expressions is to make sure their delimiting symbols match up correctly. We can use a stack to perform this task with a single left-to-right scan of the original string.

Each time we encounter an opening symbol, we push that symbol onto the stack, and each time we encounter a closing symbol, we pop a symbol from the stack (assuming it is not empty) and check that these two symbols form a valid pair. If we reach the end of the expression and the stack is empty, then the original expression was properly matched. Otherwise, there must be an opening delimiter on the stack without a matching symbol. If the length of the original expression is n, the algorithm will make at most n calls to push and n calls to pop. Code Fragment 6.7 presents a Java implementation of such an algorithm. It specifically checks for delimiter pairs ( ), { }, and [ ], but could easily be changed to accommodate further symbols. Specifically, we define two fixed strings, "({[" and ")}]", that are intentionally coordinated to reflect the symbol pairs. When examining a character of the expression string, we call the indexOf method of the String class on these special strings to determine if the character matches a delimiter and, if so, which one. Method indexOf returns the the index at which a given character is first found in a string (or −1 if the character is not found).

```
1  /** Tests if delimiters in the given expression are properly matched. */
2  public static boolean isMatched(String expression) {
3    final String opening    = "({[";          // opening delimiters
4    final String closing    = ")}]";          // respective closing delimiters
5    Stack<Character> buffer = new LinkedStack<>();
6    for (char c : expression.toCharArray()) {
7      if (opening.indexOf(c) != −1)            // this is a left delimiter
8        buffer.push(c);
9      else if (closing.indexOf(c) != −1) {     // this is a right delimiter
10       if (buffer.isEmpty())                  // nothing to match with
11         return false;
12       if (closing.indexOf(c) != opening.indexOf(buffer.pop()))
13         return false;                        // mismatched delimiter
14     }
15   }
16   return buffer.isEmpty();                   // were all opening delimiters matched?
17 }
```

Code Fragment 6.7: Method for matching delimiters in an arithmetic expression.

Matching Tags in a Markup Language

Another application of matching delimiters is in the validation of markup languages such as HTML or XML. HTML is the standard format for hyperlinked documents on the Internet and XML is an extensible markup language used for a variety of structured data sets. We show a sample HTML document in Figure 6.3.

```
<body>
<center>
<h1> The Little Boat </h1>
</center>
<p> The storm tossed the little
boat like a cheap sneaker in an
old washing machine.  The three
drunken fishermen were used to
such treatment, of course, but
not the tree salesman, who even as
a stowaway now felt that he
had overpaid for the voyage. </p>
<ol>
<li> Will the salesman die? </li>
<li> What color is the boat? </li>
<li> And what about Naomi? </li>
</ol>
</body>
```

The Little Boat

The storm tossed the little boat like a cheap sneaker in an old washing machine. The three drunken fishermen were used to such treatment, of course, but not the tree salesman, who even as a stowaway now felt that he had overpaid for the voyage.

1. Will the salesman die?
2. What color is the boat?
3. And what about Naomi?

(a)   (b)

Figure 6.3: Illustrating (a) an HTML document and (b) its rendering.

In an HTML document, portions of text are delimited by *HTML tags*. A simple opening HTML tag has the form "<name>" and the corresponding closing tag has the form "</name>". For example, we see the <body> tag on the first line of Figure 6.3a, and the matching </body> tag at the close of that document. Other commonly used HTML tags that are used in this example include:

- <body>: document body
- <h1>: section header
- <center>: center justify
- <p>: paragraph
- <ol>: numbered (ordered) list
- <li>: list item

Ideally, an HTML document should have matching tags, although most browsers tolerate a certain number of mismatching tags. In Code Fragment 6.8, we give a Java method that matches tags in a string representing an HTML document.

We make a left-to-right pass through the raw string, using index j to track our progress. The indexOf method of the String class, which optionally accepts a starting index as a second parameter, locates the '<' and '>' characters that define the tags. Method substring, also of the String class, returns the substring starting at a given index and optionally ending right before another given index. Opening tags are pushed onto the stack, and matched against closing tags as they are popped from the stack, just as we did when matching delimiters in Code Fragment 6.7.

```
1   /** Tests if every opening tag has a matching closing tag in HTML string. */
2   public static boolean isHTMLMatched(String html) {
3     Stack<String> buffer = new LinkedStack<>();
4     int j = html.indexOf('<');                  // find first '<' character (if any)
5     while (j != −1) {
6       int k = html.indexOf('>', j+1);           // find next '>' character
7       if (k == −1)
8         return false;                           // invalid tag
9       String tag = html.substring(j+1, k);      // strip away < >
10      if (!tag.startsWith("/"))                 // this is an opening tag
11        buffer.push(tag);
12      else {                                    // this is a closing tag
13        if (buffer.isEmpty())
14          return false;                         // no tag to match
15        if (!tag.substring(1).equals(buffer.pop()))
16          return false;                         // mismatched tag
17      }
18      j = html.indexOf('<', k+1);               // find next '<' character (if any)
19    }
20    return buffer.isEmpty();                     // were all opening tags matched?
21  }
```

Code Fragment 6.8: Method for testing if an HTML document has matching tags.

6.2   Queues

Another fundamental data structure is the *queue*. It is a close "cousin" of the stack, but a queue is a collection of objects that are inserted and removed according to the *first-in, first-out* (*FIFO*) principle. That is, elements can be inserted at any time, but only the element that has been in the queue the longest can be next removed.

We usually say that elements enter a queue at the back and are removed from the front. A metaphor for this terminology is a line of people waiting to get on an amusement park ride. People waiting for such a ride enter at the back of the line and get on the ride from the front of the line. There are many other applications of queues (see Figure 6.4). Stores, theaters, reservation centers, and other similar services typically process customer requests according to the FIFO principle. A queue would therefore be a logical choice for a data structure to handle calls to a customer service center, or a wait-list at a restaurant. FIFO queues are also used by many computing devices, such as a networked printer, or a Web server responding to requests.

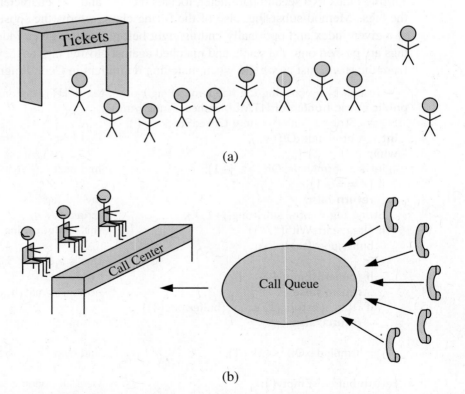

(a)

(b)

Figure 6.4: Real-world examples of a first-in, first-out queue. (a) People waiting in line to purchase tickets; (b) phone calls being routed to a customer service center.

6.2.1 The Queue Abstract Data Type

Formally, the queue abstract data type defines a collection that keeps objects in a sequence, where element access and deletion are restricted to the *first* element in the queue, and element insertion is restricted to the back of the sequence. This restriction enforces the rule that items are inserted and deleted in a queue according to the first-in, first-out (FIFO) principle. The *queue* abstract data type (ADT) supports the following two update methods:

> enqueue(*e*): Adds element *e* to the back of queue.
>
> dequeue( ): Removes and returns the first element from the queue (or null if the queue is empty).

The queue ADT also includes the following accessor methods (with first being analogous to the stack's top method):

> first( ): Returns the first element of the queue, without removing it (or null if the queue is empty).
>
> size( ): Returns the number of elements in the queue.
>
> isEmpty( ): Returns a boolean indicating whether the queue is empty.

By convention, we assume that elements added to the queue can have arbitrary type and that a newly created queue is empty. We formalize the queue ADT with the Java interface shown in Code Fragment 6.9.

```
1  public interface Queue<E> {
2    /** Returns the number of elements in the queue. */
3    int size( );
4    /** Tests whether the queue is empty. */
5    boolean isEmpty( );
6    /** Inserts an element at the rear of the queue. */
7    void enqueue(E e);
8    /** Returns, but does not remove, the first element of the queue (null if empty). */
9    E first( );
10   /** Removes and returns the first element of the queue (null if empty). */
11   E dequeue( );
12  }
```

Code Fragment 6.9: A Queue interface defining the queue ADT, with a standard FIFO protocol for insertions and removals.

Example 6.4: *The following table shows a series of queue operations and their effects on an initially empty queue Q of integers.*

Method	Return Value	first ← Q ← last
enqueue(5)	–	(5)
enqueue(3)	–	(5, 3)
size( )	2	(5, 3)
dequeue( )	5	(3)
isEmpty( )	false	(3)
dequeue( )	3	( )
isEmpty( )	true	( )
dequeue( )	null	( )
enqueue(7)	–	(7)
enqueue(9)	–	(7, 9)
first( )	7	(7, 9)
enqueue(4)	–	(7, 9, 4)

The java.util.Queue Interface in Java

Java provides a type of queue interface, java.util.Queue, which has functionality similar to the traditional queue ADT, given above, but the documentation for the java.util.Queue interface does not insist that it support only the FIFO principle. When supporting the FIFO principle, the methods of the java.util.Queue interface have the equivalences with the queue ADT shown in Table 6.3.

The java.util.Queue interface supports two styles for most operations, which vary in the way that they treat exceptional cases. When a queue is empty, the remove( ) and element( ) methods throw a NoSuchElementException, while the corresponding methods poll( ) and peek( ) return **null**. For implementations with a bounded capacity, the add method will throw an IllegalStateException when full, while the offer method ignores the new element and returns **false** to signal that the element was not accepted.

Our Queue ADT	Interface java.util.Queue	
	throws exceptions	returns special value
enqueue(*e*)	add(*e*)	offer(*e*)
dequeue( )	remove( )	poll( )
first( )	element( )	peek( )
size( )	size( )	
isEmpty( )	isEmpty( )	

Table 6.3: Methods of the queue ADT and corresponding methods of the interface java.util.Queue, when supporting the FIFO principle.

6.2.2 Array-Based Queue Implementation

In Section 6.1.2, we implemented the LIFO semantics of the Stack ADT using an array (albeit, with a fixed capacity), such that every operation executes in constant time. In this section, we will consider how to use an array to efficiently support the FIFO semantics of the Queue ADT.

Let's assume that as elements are inserted into a queue, we store them in an array such that the first element is at index 0, the second element at index 1, and so on. (See Figure 6.5.)

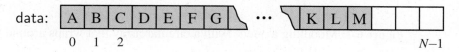

Figure 6.5: Using an array to store elements of a queue, such that the first element inserted, "A", is at cell 0, the second element inserted, "B", at cell 1, and so on.

With such a convention, the question is how we should implement the dequeue operation. The element to be removed is stored at index 0 of the array. One strategy is to execute a loop to shift all other elements of the queue one cell to the left, so that the front of the queue is again aligned with cell 0 of the array. Unfortunately, the use of such a loop would result in an $O(n)$ running time for the dequeue method.

We can improve on the above strategy by avoiding the loop entirely. We will replace a dequeued element in the array with a null reference, and maintain an explicit variable f to represent the index of the element that is currently at the front of the queue. Such an algorithm for dequeue would run in $O(1)$ time. After several dequeue operations, this approach might lead to the configuration portrayed in Figure 6.6.

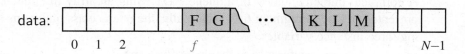

Figure 6.6: Allowing the front of the queue to drift away from index 0. In this representation, index f denotes the location of the front of the queue.

However, there remains a challenge with the revised approach. With an array of capacity N, we should be able to store up to N elements before reaching any exceptional case. If we repeatedly let the front of the queue drift rightward over time, the back of the queue would reach the end of the underlying array even when there are fewer than N elements currently in the queue. We must decide how to store additional elements in such a configuration.

Using an Array Circularly

In developing a robust queue implementation, we allow both the front and back of the queue to drift rightward, with the contents of the queue "wrapping around" the end of an array, as necessary. Assuming that the array has fixed length N, new elements are enqueued toward the "end" of the current queue, progressing from the front to index $N-1$ and continuing at index 0, then 1. Figure 6.7 illustrates such a queue with first element F and last element R.

data:

| Q | R | | | | F | G |

0   1   2 f

... K | L | M | N | O | P

$N-1$

Figure 6.7: Modeling a queue with a circular array that wraps around the end.

Implementing such a circular view is relatively easy with the ***modulo*** operator, denoted with the symbol % in Java. Recall that the modulo operator is computed by taking the remainder after an integral division. For example, 14 divided by 3 has a quotient of 4 with remainder 2, that is, $\frac{14}{3} = 4\frac{2}{3}$. So in Java, 14 / 3 evaluates to the quotient 4, while 14 % 3 evaluates to the remainder 2.

The modulo operator is ideal for treating an array circularly. When we dequeue an element and want to "advance" the front index, we use the arithmetic $f = (f+1)$ % N. As a concrete example, if we have an array of length 10, and a front index 7, we can advance the front by formally computing (7+1) % 10, which is simply 8, as 8 divided by 10 is 0 with a remainder of 8. Similarly, advancing index 8 results in index 9. But when we advance from index 9 (the last one in the array), we compute (9+1) % 10, which evaluates to index 0 (as 10 divided by 10 has a remainder of zero).

A Java Queue Implementation

A complete implementation of a queue ADT using an array in circular fashion is presented in Code Fragment 6.10. Internally, the queue class maintains the following three instance variables:

> data: a reference to the underlying array.
>
> f: an integer that represents the index, within array data, of the first element of the queue (assuming the queue is not empty).
>
> sz: an integer representing the current number of elements stored in the queue (not to be confused with the length of the array).

We allow the user to specify the capacity of the queue as an optional parameter to the constructor.

The implementations of methods size and isEmpty are trivial, given the sz field, and the implementation of first is simple, given index f. A discussion of update methods enqueue and dequeue follows the presentation of the code.

```
 1  /** Implementation of the queue ADT using a fixed-length array. */
 2  public class ArrayQueue<E> implements Queue<E> {
 3    // instance variables
 4    private E[ ] data;                       // generic array used for storage
 5    private int f = 0;                       // index of the front element
 6    private int sz = 0;                      // current number of elements
 7
 8    // constructors
 9    public ArrayQueue() {this(CAPACITY);}    // constructs queue with default capacity
10    public ArrayQueue(int capacity) {        // constructs queue with given capacity
11      data = (E[ ]) new Object[capacity];    // safe cast; compiler may give warning
12    }
13
14    // methods
15    /** Returns the number of elements in the queue. */
16    public int size() { return sz; }
17
18    /** Tests whether the queue is empty. */
19    public boolean isEmpty() { return (sz == 0); }
20
21    /** Inserts an element at the rear of the queue. */
22    public void enqueue(E e) throws IllegalStateException {
23      if (sz == data.length) throw new IllegalStateException("Queue is full");
24      int avail = (f + sz) % data.length;    // use modular arithmetic
25      data[avail] = e;
26      sz++;
27    }
28
29    /** Returns, but does not remove, the first element of the queue (null if empty). */
30    public E first() {
31      if (isEmpty()) return null;
32      return data[f];
33    }
34
35    /** Removes and returns the first element of the queue (null if empty). */
36    public E dequeue() {
37      if (isEmpty()) return null;
38      E answer = data[f];
39      data[f] = null;                        // dereference to help garbage collection
40      f = (f + 1) % data.length;
41      sz--;
42      return answer;
43    }
```

Code Fragment 6.10: Array-based implementation of a queue.

Adding and Removing Elements

The goal of the enqueue method is to add a new element to the back of the queue. We need to determine the proper index at which to place the new element. Although we do not explicitly maintain an instance variable for the back of the queue, we compute the index of the next opening based on the formula:

avail = (f + sz) % data.length;

Note that we are using the size of the queue as it exists *prior* to the addition of the new element. As a sanity check, for a queue with capacity 10, current size 3, and first element at index 5, its three elements are stored at indices 5, 6, and 7, and the next element should be added at index 8, computed as (5+3) % 10. As a case with wraparound, if the queue has capacity 10, current size 3, and first element at index 8, its three elements are stored at indices 8, 9, and 0, and the next element should be added at index 1, computed as (8+3) % 10.

When the dequeue method is called, the current value of f designates the index of the value that is to be removed and returned. We keep a local reference to the element that will be returned, before setting its cell of the array back to **null**, to aid the garbage collector. Then the index f is updated to reflect the removal of the first element, and the presumed promotion of the second element to become the new first. In most cases, we simply want to increment the index by one, but because of the possibility of a wraparound configuration, we rely on modular arithmetic, computing f = (f+1) % data.length, as originally described on page 242.

Analyzing the Efficiency of an Array-Based Queue

Table 6.4 shows the running times of methods in a realization of a queue by an array. As with our array-based stack implementation, each of the queue methods in the array realization executes a constant number of statements involving arithmetic operations, comparisons, and assignments. Thus, each method in this implementation runs in $O(1)$ time.

Method	Running Time
size	$O(1)$
isEmpty	$O(1)$
first	$O(1)$
enqueue	$O(1)$
dequeue	$O(1)$

Table 6.4: Performance of a queue realized by an array. The space usage is $O(N)$, where N is the size of the array, determined at the time the queue is created, and independent from the number $n < N$ of elements that are actually in the queue.

6.2.3   Implementing a Queue with a Singly Linked List

As we did for the stack ADT, we can easily adapt a singly linked list to implement the queue ADT while supporting worst-case $O(1)$-time for all operations, and without any artificial limit on the capacity. The natural orientation for a queue is to align the front of the queue with the front of the list, and the back of the queue with the tail of the list, because the only update operation that singly linked lists support at the back end is an insertion. Our Java implementation of a LinkedQueue class is given in Code 6.11.

```
1  /** Realization of a FIFO queue as an adaptation of a SinglyLinkedList. */
2  public class LinkedQueue<E> implements Queue<E> {
3    private SinglyLinkedList<E> list = new SinglyLinkedList<>();   // an empty list
4    public LinkedQueue() { }                    // new queue relies on the initially empty list
5    public int size() { return list.size(); }
6    public boolean isEmpty() { return list.isEmpty(); }
7    public void enqueue(E element) { list.addLast(element); }
8    public E first() { return list.first(); }
9    public E dequeue() { return list.removeFirst(); }
10 }
```

Code Fragment 6.11: Implementation of a Queue using a SinglyLinkedList.

Analyzing the Efficiency of a Linked Queue

Although we had not yet introduced asymptotic analysis when we presented our SinglyLinkedList implementation in Chapter 3, it is clear upon reexamination that each method of that class runs in $O(1)$ worst-case time. Therefore, each method of our LinkedQueue adaptation also runs in $O(1)$ worst-case time.

We also avoid the need to specify a maximum size for the queue, as was done in the array-based queue implementation. However, this benefit comes with some expense. Because each node stores a next reference, in addition to the element reference, a linked list uses more space per element than a properly sized array of references.

Also, although all methods execute in constant time for both implementations, it seems clear that the operations involving linked lists have a large number of primitive operations per call. For example, adding an element to an array-based queue consists primarily of calculating an index with modular arithmetic, storing the element in the array cell, and incrementing the size counter. For a linked list, an insertion includes the instantiation and initialization of a new node, relinking an existing node to the new node, and incrementing the size counter. In practice, this makes the linked-list method more expensive than the array-based method.

6.2.4 A Circular Queue

In Section 3.3, we implemented a *circularly linked list* class that supports all behaviors of a singly linked list, and an additional rotate( ) method that efficiently moves the first element to the end of the list. We can generalize the Queue interface to define a new CircularQueue interface with such a behavior, as shown in Code Fragment 6.12.

```
1  public interface CircularQueue<E> extends Queue<E> {
2    /**
3     * Rotates the front element of the queue to the back of the queue.
4     * This does nothing if the queue is empty.
5     */
6    void rotate( );
7  }
```

Code Fragment 6.12: A Java interface, CircularQueue, that extends the Queue ADT with a new rotate( ) method.

This interface can easily be implemented by adapting the CircularlyLinkedList class of Section 3.3 to produce a new LinkedCircularQueue class. This class has an advantage over the traditional LinkedQueue, because a call to Q.rotate( ) is implemented more efficiently than the combination of calls, Q.enqueue(Q.dequeue( )), because no nodes are created, destroyed, or relinked by the implementation of a rotate operation on a circularly linked list.

A circular queue is an excellent abstraction for applications in which elements are cyclically arranged, such as for multiplayer, turn-based games, or round-robin scheduling of computing processes. In the remainder of this section, we provide a demonstration of the use of a circular queue.

The Josephus Problem

In the children's game "hot potato," a group of n children sit in a circle passing an object, called the "potato," around the circle. The potato begins with a starting child in the circle, and the children continue passing the potato until a leader rings a bell, at which point the child holding the potato must leave the game after handing the potato to the next child in the circle. After the selected child leaves, the other children close up the circle. This process is then continued until there is only one child remaining, who is declared the winner. If the leader always uses the strategy of ringing the bell so that every k^{th} person is removed from the circle, for some fixed value k, then determining the winner for a given list of children is known as the *Josephus problem* (named after an ancient story with far more severe consequences than in the children's game).

Solving the Josephus Problem Using a Queue

We can solve the Josephus problem for a collection of n elements using a circular queue, by associating the potato with the element at the front of the queue and storing elements in the queue according to their order around the circle. Thus, passing the potato is equivalent to rotating the first element to the back of the queue. After this process has been performed $k - 1$ times, we remove the front element by dequeuing it from the queue and discarding it. We show a complete Java program for solving the Josephus problem using this approach in Code Fragment 6.13, which describes a solution that runs in $O(nk)$ time. (We can solve this problem faster using techniques beyond the scope of this book.)

```
1   public class Josephus {
2     /** Computes the winner of the Josephus problem using a circular queue. */
3     public static <E> E Josephus(CircularQueue<E> queue, int k) {
4       if (queue.isEmpty()) return null;
5       while (queue.size() > 1) {
6         for (int i=0; i < k−1; i++)      // skip past k-1 elements
7           queue.rotate();
8         E e = queue.dequeue();            // remove the front element from the collection
9         System.out.println("     " + e + " is out");
10       }
11      return queue.dequeue();            // the winner
12    }
13
14    /** Builds a circular queue from an array of objects. */
15    public static <E> CircularQueue<E> buildQueue(E a[ ]) {
16      CircularQueue<E> queue = new LinkedCircularQueue<>();
17      for (int i=0; i<a.length; i++)
18        queue.enqueue(a[i]);
19      return queue;
20    }
21
22    /** Tester method */
23    public static void main(String[ ] args) {
24      String[ ] a1 = {"Alice", "Bob", "Cindy", "Doug", "Ed", "Fred"};
25      String[ ] a2 = {"Gene", "Hope", "Irene", "Jack", "Kim", "Lance"};
26      String[ ] a3 = {"Mike", "Roberto"};
27      System.out.println("First winner is " + Josephus(buildQueue(a1), 3));
28      System.out.println("Second winner is " + Josephus(buildQueue(a2), 10));
29      System.out.println("Third winner is " + Josephus(buildQueue(a3), 7));
30    }
31  }
```

Code Fragment 6.13: A complete Java program for solving the Josephus problem using a circular queue.

6.3   Double-Ended Queues

We next consider a queue-like data structure that supports insertion and deletion at both the front and the back of the queue. Such a structure is called a ***double-ended queue***, or ***deque***, which is usually pronounced "deck" to avoid confusion with the dequeue method of the regular queue ADT, which is pronounced like the abbreviation "D.Q."

The deque abstract data type is more general than both the stack and the queue ADTs. The extra generality can be useful in some applications. For example, we described a restaurant using a queue to maintain a waitlist. Occasionally, the first person might be removed from the queue only to find that a table was not available; typically, the restaurant will reinsert the person at the *first* position in the queue. It may also be that a customer at the end of the queue may grow impatient and leave the restaurant. (We will need an even more general data structure if we want to model customers leaving the queue from other positions.)

6.3.1   The Deque Abstract Data Type

The deque abstract data type is richer than both the stack and the queue ADTs. To provide a symmetrical abstraction, the deque ADT is defined to support the following update methods:

addFirst(e): Insert a new element e at the front of the deque.

addLast(e): Insert a new element e at the back of the deque.

removeFirst( ): Remove and return the first element of the deque (or null if the deque is empty).

removeLast( ): Remove and return the last element of the deque (or null if the deque is empty).

Additionally, the deque ADT will include the following accessors:

first( ): Returns the first element of the deque, without removing it (or null if the deque is empty).

last( ): Returns the last element of the deque, without removing it (or null if the deque is empty).

size( ): Returns the number of elements in the deque.

isEmpty( ): Returns a boolean indicating whether the deque is empty.

We formalize the deque ADT with the Java interface shown in Code Fragment 6.14.

```
1  /**
2   * Interface for a double-ended queue: a collection of elements that can be inserted
3   * and removed at both ends; this interface is a simplified version of java.util.Deque.
4   */
5  public interface Deque<E> {
6    /** Returns the number of elements in the deque. */
7    int size( );
8    /** Tests whether the deque is empty. */
9    boolean isEmpty( );
10   /** Returns, but does not remove, the first element of the deque (null if empty). */
11   E first( );
12   /** Returns, but does not remove, the last element of the deque (null if empty). */
13   E last( );
14   /** Inserts an element at the front of the deque. */
15   void addFirst(E e);
16   /** Inserts an element at the back of the deque. */
17   void addLast(E e);
18   /** Removes and returns the first element of the deque (null if empty). */
19   E removeFirst( );
20   /** Removes and returns the last element of the deque (null if empty). */
21   E removeLast( );
22 }
```

Code Fragment 6.14: A Java interface, Deque, describing the double-ended queue ADT. Note the use of the generic parameterized type, E, allowing a deque to contain elements of any specified class.

Example 6.5: *The following table shows a series of operations and their effects on an initially empty deque D of integers.*

Method	Return Value	D
addLast(5)	–	(5)
addFirst(3)	–	(3, 5)
addFirst(7)	–	(7, 3, 5)
first( )	7	(7, 3, 5)
removeLast( )	5	(7, 3)
size( )	2	(7, 3)
removeLast( )	3	(7)
removeFirst( )	7	( )
addFirst(6)	–	(6)
last( )	6	(6)
addFirst(8)	–	(8, 6)
isEmpty( )	false	(8, 6)
last( )	6	(8, 6)

6.3.2 Implementing a Deque

We can implement the deque ADT efficiently using either an array or a linked list for storing elements.

Implementing a Deque with a Circular Array

If using an array, we recommend a representation similar to the ArrayQueue class, treating the array in circular fashion and storing the index of the first element and the current size of the deque as fields; the index of the last element can be calculated, as needed, using modular arithmetic.

One extra concern is avoiding use of negative values with the modulo operator. When removing the first element, the front index is advanced in circular fashion, with the assignment $f = (f+1) \% N$. But when an element is inserted at the front, the first index must effectively be decremented in circular fashion and it is a mistake to assign $f = (f-1) \% N$. The problem is that when f is 0, the goal should be to "decrement" it to the other end of the array, and thus to index $N-1$. However, a calculation such as $-1 \% 10$ in Java results in the value -1. A standard way to decrement an index circularly is instead to assign $f = (f-1+N) \% N$. Adding the additional term of N before the modulus is calculated assures that the result is a positive value. We leave details of this approach to Exercise P-6.40.

Implementing a Deque with a Doubly Linked List

Because the deque requires insertion and removal at both ends, a doubly linked list is most appropriate for implementing all operations efficiently. In fact, the DoublyLinkedList class from Section 3.4.1 already implements the entire Deque interface; we simply need to add the declaration "**implements** Deque<E>" to that class definition in order to use it as a deque.

Performance of the Deque Operations

Table 6.5 shows the running times of methods for a deque implemented with a doubly linked list. Note that every method runs in $O(1)$ time.

Method	Running Time
size, isEmpty	$O(1)$
first, last	$O(1)$
addFirst, addLast	$O(1)$
removeFirst, removeLast	$O(1)$

Table 6.5: Performance of a deque realized by either a circular array or a doubly linked list. The space usage for the array-based implementation is $O(N)$, where N is the size of the array, while the space usage of the doubly linked list is $O(n)$ where $n < N$ is the actual number of elements in the deque.

6.3.3 Deques in the Java Collections Framework

The Java Collections Framework includes its own definition of a deque, as the java.util.Deque interface, as well as several implementations of the interface including one based on use of a circular array (java.util.ArrayDeque) and one based on use of a doubly linked list (java.util.LinkedList). So, if we need to use a deque and would rather not implement one from scratch, we can simply use one of those built-in classes.

As is the case with the java.util.Queue class (see page 240), the java.util.Deque provides duplicative methods that use different techniques to signal exceptional cases. A summary of those methods is given in Table 6.6.

Our Deque ADT	Interface java.util.Deque	
	throws exceptions	returns special value
first( )	getFirst( )	peekFirst( )
last( )	getLast( )	peekLast( )
addFirst(e)	addFirst(e)	offerFirst(e)
addLast(e)	addLast(e)	offerLast(e)
removeFirst( )	removeFirst( )	pollFirst( )
removeLast( )	removeLast( )	pollLast( )
size( )	size( )	
isEmpty( )	isEmpty( )	

Table 6.6: Methods of our deque ADT and the corresponding methods of the java.util.Deque interface.

When attempting to access or remove the first or last element of an *empty* deque, the methods in the middle column of Table 6.6—that is, getFirst( ), getLast( ), removeFirst( ), and removeLast( )—throw a NoSuchElementException. The methods in the rightmost column—that is, peekFirst( ), peekLast( ), pollFirst( ), and pollLast( )—simply return the null reference when a deque is empty. In similar manner, when attempting to add an element to an end of a deque with a capacity limit, the addFirst and addLast methods throw an exception, while the offerFirst and offerLast methods return false.

The methods that handle bad situations more gracefully (i.e., without throwing exceptions) are useful in applications, known as producer-consumer scenarios, in which it is common for one component of software to look for an element that may have been placed in a queue by another program, or in which it is common to try to insert an item into a fixed-sized buffer that might be full. However, having methods return null when empty are not appropriate for applications in which null might serve as an actual element of a queue.

6.4   Exercises

Reinforcement

R-6.1   Suppose an initially empty stack S has performed a total of 25 push operations, 12 top operations, and 10 pop operations, 3 of which returned null to indicate an empty stack. What is the current size of S?

R-6.2   Had the stack of the previous problem been an instance of the ArrayStack class, from Code Fragment 6.2, what would be the final value of the instance variable t?

R-6.3   What values are returned during the following series of stack operations, if executed upon an initially empty stack? push(5), push(3), pop(), push(2), push(8), pop(), pop(), push(9), push(1), pop(), push(7), push(6), pop(), pop(), push(4), pop(), pop().

R-6.4   Implement a method with signature transfer(S, T) that transfers all elements from stack S onto stack T, so that the element that starts at the top of S is the first to be inserted onto T, and the element at the bottom of S ends up at the top of T.

R-6.5   Give a recursive method for removing all the elements from a stack.

R-6.6   Give a precise and complete definition of the concept of matching for grouping symbols in an arithmetic expression. Your definition may be recursive.

R-6.7   Suppose an initially empty queue Q has performed a total of 32 enqueue operations, 10 first operations, and 15 dequeue operations, 5 of which returned null to indicate an empty queue. What is the current size of Q?

R-6.8   Had the queue of the previous problem been an instance of the ArrayQueue class, from Code Fragment 6.10, with capacity 30 never exceeded, what would be the final value of the instance variable f?

R-6.9   What values are returned during the following sequence of queue operations, if executed on an initially empty queue? enqueue(5), enqueue(3), dequeue(), enqueue(2), enqueue(8), dequeue(), dequeue(), enqueue(9), enqueue(1), dequeue(), enqueue(7), enqueue(6), dequeue(), dequeue(), enqueue(4), dequeue(), dequeue().

R-6.10   Give a simple adapter that implements the stack ADT while using an instance of a deque for storage.

R-6.11   Give a simple adapter that implements the queue ADT while using an instance of a deque for storage.

R-6.12   What values are returned during the following sequence of deque ADT operations, on an initially empty deque? addFirst(3), addLast(8), addLast(9), addFirst(1), last( ), isEmpty( ), addFirst(2), removeLast( ), addLast(7), first( ), last( ), addLast(4), size( ), removeFirst( ), removeFirst( ).

R-6.13 Suppose you have a deque D containing the numbers $(1,2,3,4,5,6,7,8)$, in this order. Suppose further that you have an initially empty queue Q. Give a code fragment that uses only D and Q (and no other variables) and results in D storing the elements in the order $(1,2,3,5,4,6,7,8)$.

R-6.14 Repeat the previous problem using the deque D and an initially empty stack S.

R-6.15 Augment the ArrayQueue implementation with a new rotate( ) method having semantics identical to the combination, enqueue(dequeue( )). But, your implementation should be more efficient than making two separate calls (for example, because there is no need to modify the size).

Creativity

C-6.16 Suppose Alice has picked three distinct integers and placed them into a stack S in random order. Write a short, straightline piece of pseudocode (with no loops or recursion) that uses only one comparison and only one variable x, yet that results in variable x storing the largest of Alice's three integers with probability $2/3$. Argue why your method is correct.

C-6.17 Show how to use the transfer method, described in Exercise R-6.4, and two temporary stacks, to replace the contents of a given stack S with those same elements, but in reversed order.

C-6.18 In Code Fragment 6.8 we assume that opening tags in HTML have form `<name>`, as with `<li>`. More generally, HTML allows optional attributes to be expressed as part of an opening tag. The general form used for expressing an attribute is `<name attribute1="value1" attribute2="value2">`; for example, a table can be given a border and additional padding by using an opening tag of `<table border="3" cellpadding="5">`. Modify Code Fragment 6.8 so that it can properly match tags, even when an opening tag may include one or more such attributes.

C-6.19 **Postfix notation** is an unambiguous way of writing an arithmetic expression without parentheses. It is defined so that if "(exp_1) **op** (exp_2)" is a normal fully parenthesized expression whose operation is **op**, the postfix version of this is "$pexp_1$ $pexp_2$ **op**", where $pexp_1$ is the postfix version of exp_1 and $pexp_2$ is the postfix version of exp_2. The postfix version of a single number or variable is just that number or variable. So, for example, the postfix version of "$((5+2)*(8-3))/4$" is "5 2 + 8 3 $-$ * 4 /". Describe a nonrecursive way of evaluating an expression in postfix notation.

C-6.20 Suppose you have three nonempty stacks R, S, and T. Describe a sequence of operations that results in S storing all elements originally in T below all of S's original elements, with both sets of those elements in their original order. The final configuration for R should be the same as its original configuration. For example, if $R = (1,2,3)$, $S = (4,5)$, and $T = (6,7,8,9)$, when ordered from bottom to top, then the final configuration should have $R = (1,2,3)$ and $S = (6,7,8,9,4,5)$.

C-6.21 Describe a nonrecursive algorithm for enumerating all permutations of the numbers $\{1, 2, \ldots, n\}$ using an explicit stack.

C-6.22 Alice has three array-based stacks, A, B, and C, such that A has capacity 100, B has capacity 5, and C has capacity 3. Initially, A is full, and B and C are empty. Unfortunately, the person who programmed the class for these stacks made the push and pop methods private. The only method Alice can use is a static method, dump(S, T), which transfers (by iteratively applying the private pop and push methods) elements from stack S to stack T until either S becomes empty or T becomes full. So, for example, starting from our initial configuration and performing dump(A, C) results in A now holding 97 elements and C holding 3. Describe a sequence of dump operations that starts from the initial configuration and results in B holding 4 elements at the end.

C-6.23 Show how to use a stack S and a queue Q to generate all possible subsets of an n-element set T nonrecursively.

C-6.24 Suppose you have a stack S containing n elements and a queue Q that is initially empty. Describe how you can use Q to scan S to see if it contains a certain element x, with the additional constraint that your algorithm must return the elements back to S in their original order. You may only use S, Q, and a constant number of other primitive variables.

C-6.25 Describe how to implement the stack ADT using a single queue as an instance variable, and only constant additional local memory within the method bodies. What is the running time of the push(), pop(), and top() methods for your design?

C-6.26 When implementing the ArrayQueue class, we initialized $f = 0$ (at line 5 of Code Fragment 6.10). What would happen had we initialized that field to some other positive value? What if we had initialized it to -1?

C-6.27 Implement the clone( ) method for the ArrayStack class. (See Section 3.6 for a discussion of cloning data structures.)

C-6.28 Implement the clone( ) method for the ArrayQueue class. (See Section 3.6 for a discussion of cloning data structures.)

C-6.29 Implement a method with signature concatenate(LinkedQueue<E> Q2) for the LinkedQueue<E> class that takes all elements of Q2 and appends them to the end of the original queue. The operation should run in $O(1)$ time and should result in Q2 being an empty queue.

C-6.30 Give a pseudocode description for an array-based implementation of the double-ended queue ADT. What is the running time for each operation?

C-6.31 Describe how to implement the deque ADT using two stacks as the only instance variables. What are the running times of the methods?

C-6.32 Suppose you have two nonempty stacks S and T and a deque D. Describe how to use D so that S stores all the elements of T below all of its original elements, with both sets of elements still in their original order.

C-6.33 Alice has two circular queues, C and D, which can store integers. Bob gives Alice 50 odd integers and 50 even integers and insists that she stores all 100 integers in C and D. They then play a game where Bob picks C or D at random and then applies the rotate( ) method to the chosen queue a random number of times. If the last number to be rotated at the end of this game is odd, Bob wins. Otherwise, Alice wins. How can Alice allocate integers to queues to optimize her chances of winning? What is her chance of winning?

C-6.34 Suppose Bob has four cows that he wants to take across a bridge, but only one yoke, which can hold up to two cows, side by side, tied to the yoke. The yoke is too heavy for him to carry across the bridge, but he can tie (and untie) cows to it in no time at all. Of his four cows, Mazie can cross the bridge in 2 minutes, Daisy can cross it in 4 minutes, Crazy can cross it in 10 minutes, and Lazy can cross it in 20 minutes. Of course, when two cows are tied to the yoke, they must go at the speed of the slower cow. Describe how Bob can get all his cows across the bridge in 34 minutes.

Projects

P-6.35 Implement a program that can input an expression in postfix notation (see Exercise C-6.19) and output its value.

P-6.36 When a share of common stock of some company is sold, the *capital gain* (or, sometimes, loss) is the difference between the share's selling price and the price originally paid to buy it. This rule is easy to understand for a single share, but if we sell multiple shares of stock bought over a long period of time, then we must identify the shares actually being sold. A standard accounting principle for identifying which shares of a stock were sold in such a case is to use a FIFO protocol—the shares sold are the ones that have been held the longest (indeed, this is the default method built into several personal finance software packages). For example, suppose we buy 100 shares at $20 each on day 1, 20 shares at $24 on day 2, 200 shares at $36 on day 3, and then sell 150 shares on day 4 at $30 each. Then applying the FIFO protocol means that of the 150 shares sold, 100 were bought on day 1, 20 were bought on day 2, and 30 were bought on day 3. The capital gain in this case would therefore be $100 \cdot 10 + 20 \cdot 6 + 30 \cdot (-6)$, or $940. Write a program that takes as input a sequence of transactions of the form "buy x share(s) at $y each" or "sell x share(s) at $y each," assuming that the transactions occur on consecutive days and the values x and y are integers. Given this input sequence, the output should be the total capital gain (or loss) for the entire sequence, using the FIFO protocol to identify shares.

P-6.37 Design an ADT for a two-color, double-stack ADT that consists of two stacks— one "red" and one "blue"—and has as its operations color-coded versions of the regular stack ADT operations. For example, this ADT should support both a redPush operation and a bluePush operation. Give an efficient implementation of this ADT using a single array whose capacity is set at some value N that is assumed to always be larger than the sizes of the red and blue stacks combined.

P-6.38 The introduction of Section 6.1 notes that stacks are often used to provide "undo" support in applications like a Web browser or text editor. While support for undo can be implemented with an unbounded stack, many applications provide only *limited* support for such an undo history, with a fixed-capacity stack. When push is invoked with the stack at full capacity, rather than throwing an exception, a more typical semantic is to accept the pushed element at the top while "leaking" the oldest element from the bottom of the stack to make room. Give an implementation of such a LeakyStack abstraction, using a circular array.

P-6.39 Repeat the previous problem using a singly linked list for storage, and a maximum capacity specified as a parameter to the constructor.

P-6.40 Give a complete implementation of the Deque ADT using a fixed-capacity array, so that each of the update methods runs in $O(1)$ time.

Chapter Notes

We were introduced to the approach of defining data structures first in terms of their ADTs and then in terms of concrete implementations by the classic books by Aho, Hopcroft, and Ullman [5, 6]. Exercises C-6.22, C-6.33, and C-6.34 are similar to interview questions said to be from a well-known software company. For further study of abstract data types, see Liskov and Guttag [67] and Demurjian [28].

Chapter

7

List and Iterator ADTs

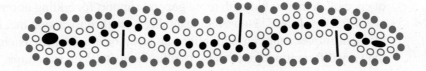

Contents

7.1   The List ADT

In Chapter 6, we introduced the stack, queue, and deque abstract data types, and discussed how either an array or a linked list could be used for storage in an efficient concrete implementation of each. Each of those ADTs represents a linearly ordered sequence of elements. The deque is the most general of the three, yet even so, it only allows insertions and deletions at the front or back of a sequence.

In this chapter, we explore several abstract data types that represent a linear sequence of elements, but with more general support for adding or removing elements at arbitrary positions. However, designing a single abstraction that is well suited for efficient implementation with either an array or a linked list is challenging, given the very different nature of these two fundamental data structures.

Locations within an array are easily described with an integer *index*. Recall that an index of an element e in a sequence is equal to the number of elements before e in that sequence. By this definition, the first element of a sequence has index 0, and the last has index $n - 1$, assuming that n denotes the total number of elements. The notion of an element's index is well defined for a linked list as well, although we will see that it is not as convenient of a notion, as there is no way to efficiently access an element at a given index without traversing a portion of the linked list that depends upon the magnitude of the index.

With that said, Java defines a general interface, java.util.List, that includes the following index-based methods (and more):

size( ):   Returns the number of elements in the list.

isEmpty( ):   Returns a boolean indicating whether the list is empty.

get(i):   Returns the element of the list having index i; an error condition occurs if i is not in range $[0, \text{size}() - 1]$.

set(i, e):   Replaces the element at index i with e, and returns the old element that was replaced; an error condition occurs if i is not in range $[0, \text{size}() - 1]$.

add(i, e):   Inserts a new element e into the list so that it has index i, moving all subsequent elements one index later in the list; an error condition occurs if i is not in range $[0, \text{size}()]$.

remove(i):   Removes and returns the element at index i, moving all subsequent elements one index earlier in the list; an error condition occurs if i is not in range $[0, \text{size}() - 1]$.

We note that the index of an existing element may change over time, as other elements are added or removed in front of it. We also draw attention to the fact that the range of valid indices for the add method includes the current size of the list, in which case the new element becomes the last.

Example 7.1 demonstrates a series of operations on a list instance, and Code Fragment 7.1 below provides a formal definition of our simplified version of the List interface; we use an IndexOutOfBoundsException to signal an invalid index argument.

Example 7.1: *We demonstrate operations on an initially empty list of characters.*

Method	Return Value	List Contents
add(0, A)	–	(A)
add(0, B)	–	(B, A)
get(1)	A	(B, A)
set(2, C)	"error"	(B, A)
add(2, C)	–	(B, A, C)
add(4, D)	"error"	(B, A, C)
remove(1)	A	(B, C)
add(1, D)	–	(B, D, C)
add(1, E)	–	(B, E, D, C)
get(4)	"error"	(B, E, D, C)
add(4, F)	–	(B, E, D, C, F)
set(2, G)	D	(B, E, G, C, F)
get(2)	G	(B, E, G, C, F)

```
1   /** A simplified version of the java.util.List interface. */
2   public interface List<E> {
3     /** Returns the number of elements in this list. */
4     int size( );
5
6     /** Returns whether the list is empty. */
7     boolean isEmpty( );
8
9     /** Returns (but does not remove) the element at index i. */
10    E get(int i) throws IndexOutOfBoundsException;
11
12    /** Replaces the element at index i with e, and returns the replaced element. */
13    E set(int i, E e) throws IndexOutOfBoundsException;
14
15    /** Inserts element e to be at index i, shifting all subsequent elements later. */
16    void add(int i, E e) throws IndexOutOfBoundsException;
17
18    /** Removes/returns the element at index i, shifting subsequent elements earlier. */
19    E remove(int i) throws IndexOutOfBoundsException;
20  }
```

Code Fragment 7.1: A simple version of the List interface.

7.2   Array Lists

An obvious choice for implementing the list ADT is to use an array A, where $A[i]$ stores (a reference to) the element with index i. We will begin by assuming that we have a fixed-capacity array, but in Section 7.2.1 describe a more advanced technique that effectively allows an array-based list to have unbounded capacity. Such an unbounded list is known as an ***array list*** in Java (or a ***vector*** in C++ and in the earliest versions of Java).

With a representation based on an array A, the get(i) and set(i, e) methods are easy to implement by accessing $A[i]$ (assuming i is a legitimate index). Methods add(i, e) and remove(i) are more time consuming, as they require shifting elements up or down to maintain our rule of always storing an element whose list index is i at index i of the array. (See Figure 7.1.) Our initial implementation of the ArrayList class follows in Code Fragments 7.2 and 7.3.

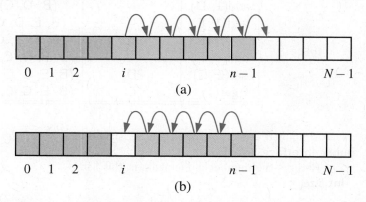

Figure 7.1: Array-based implementation of an array list that is storing n elements: (a) shifting up for an insertion at index i; (b) shifting down for a removal at index i.

```
1   public class ArrayList<E> implements List<E> {
2     // instance variables
3     public static final int CAPACITY=16;      // default array capacity
4     private E[ ] data;                         // generic array used for storage
5     private int size = 0;                      // current number of elements
6     // constructors
7     public ArrayList() { this(CAPACITY); }     // constructs list with default capacity
8     public ArrayList(int capacity) {           // constructs list with given capacity
9       data = (E[ ]) new Object[capacity];      // safe cast; compiler may give warning
10    }
```

Code Fragment 7.2: An implementation of a simple ArrayList class with bounded capacity. (Continues in Code Fragment 7.3.)

```
11    // public methods
12    /** Returns the number of elements in the array list. */
13    public int size( ) { return size; }
14    /** Returns whether the array list is empty. */
15    public boolean isEmpty( ) { return size == 0; }
16    /** Returns (but does not remove) the element at index i. */
17    public E get(int i) throws IndexOutOfBoundsException {
18      checkIndex(i, size);
19      return data[i];
20    }
21    /** Replaces the element at index i with e, and returns the replaced element. */
22    public E set(int i, E e) throws IndexOutOfBoundsException {
23      checkIndex(i, size);
24      E temp = data[i];
25      data[i] = e;
26      return temp;
27    }
28    /** Inserts element e to be at index i, shifting all subsequent elements later. */
29    public void add(int i, E e) throws IndexOutOfBoundsException,
30                                         IllegalStateException {
31      checkIndex(i, size + 1);
32      if (size == data.length)              // not enough capacity
33        throw new IllegalStateException("Array is full");
34      for (int k=size−1; k >= i; k−−)       // start by shifting rightmost
35        data[k+1] = data[k];
36      data[i] = e;                          // ready to place the new element
37      size++;
38    }
39    /** Removes/returns the element at index i, shifting subsequent elements earlier. */
40    public E remove(int i) throws IndexOutOfBoundsException {
41      checkIndex(i, size);
42      E temp = data[i];
43      for (int k=i; k < size−1; k++)        // shift elements to fill hole
44        data[k] = data[k+1];
45      data[size−1] = null;                  // help garbage collection
46      size−−;
47      return temp;
48    }
49    // utility method
50    /** Checks whether the given index is in the range [0, n−1]. */
51    protected void checkIndex(int i, int n) throws IndexOutOfBoundsException {
52      if (i < 0 || i >= n)
53        throw new IndexOutOfBoundsException("Illegal index: " + i);
54    }
55  }
```

Code Fragment 7.3: An implementation of a simple ArrayList class with bounded capacity. (Continued from Code Fragment 7.2.)

The Performance of a Simple Array-Based Implementation

Table 7.1 shows the worst-case running times of the methods of an array list with n elements realized by means of an array. Methods isEmpty, size, get and set clearly run in $O(1)$ time, but the insertion and removal methods can take much longer than this. In particular, add(i, e) runs in time $O(n)$. Indeed, the worst case for this operation occurs when i is 0, since all the existing n elements have to be shifted forward. A similar argument applies to method remove(i), which runs in $O(n)$ time, because we have to shift backward $n - 1$ elements in the worst case, when i is 0. In fact, assuming that each possible index is equally likely to be passed as an argument to these operations, their average running time is $O(n)$, for we will have to shift $n/2$ elements on average.

Method	Running Time
size( )	$O(1)$
isEmpty( )	$O(1)$
get(i)	$O(1)$
set(i, e)	$O(1)$
add(i, e)	$O(n)$
remove(i)	$O(n)$

Table 7.1: Performance of an array list with n elements realized by a fixed-capacity array.

Looking more closely at add(i, e) and remove(i), we note that they each run in time $O(n - i + 1)$, for only those elements at index i and higher have to be shifted up or down. Thus, inserting or removing an item at the end of an array list, using the methods add(n, e) and remove($n - 1$) respectively, takes $O(1)$ time each. Moreover, this observation has an interesting consequence for the adaptation of the array list ADT to the deque ADT from Section 6.3.1. If we do the "obvious" thing and store elements of a deque so that the first element is at index 0 and the last element at index $n - 1$, then methods addLast and removeLast of the deque each run in $O(1)$ time. However, methods addFirst and removeFirst of the deque each run in $O(n)$ time.

Actually, with a little effort, we can produce an array-based implementation of the array list ADT that achieves $O(1)$ time for insertions and removals at index 0, as well as insertions and removals at the end of the array list. Achieving this requires that we give up on our rule that an element at index i is stored in the array at index i, however, as we would have to use a circular array approach like the one we used in Section 6.2 to implement a queue. We leave the details of this implementation as Exercise C-7.25.

7.2.1 Dynamic Arrays

The ArrayList implementation in Code Fragments 7.2 and 7.3 (as well as those for a stack, queue, and deque from Chapter 6) has a serious limitation; it requires that a fixed maximum capacity be declared, throwing an exception if attempting to add an element once full. This is a major weakness, because if a user is unsure of the maximum size that will be reached for a collection, there is risk that either too large of an array will be requested, causing an inefficient waste of memory, or that too small of an array will be requested, causing a fatal error when exhausting that capacity.

Java's ArrayList class provides a more robust abstraction, allowing a user to add elements to the list, with no apparent limit on the overall capacity. To provide this abstraction, Java relies on an algorithmic sleight of hand that is known as a ***dynamic array***.

In reality, elements of an ArrayList are stored in a traditional array, and the precise size of that traditional array must be internally declared in order for the system to properly allocate a consecutive piece of memory for its storage. For example, Figure 7.2 displays an array with 12 cells that might be stored in memory locations 2146 through 2157 on a computer system.

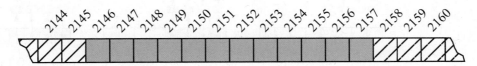

Figure 7.2: An array of 12 cells, allocated in memory locations 2146 through 2157.

Because the system may allocate neighboring memory locations to store other data, the capacity of an array cannot be increased by expanding into subsequent cells.

The first key to providing the semantics of an unbounded array is that an array list instance maintains an internal array that often has greater capacity than the current length of the list. For example, while a user may have created a list with five elements, the system may have reserved an underlying array capable of storing eight object references (rather than only five). This extra capacity makes it easy to add a new element to the end of the list by using the next available cell of the array.

If a user continues to add elements to a list, all reserved capacity in the underlying array will eventually be exhausted. In that case, the class requests a new, larger array from the system, and copies all references from the smaller array into the beginning of the new array. At that point in time, the old array is no longer needed, so it can be reclaimed by the system. Intuitively, this strategy is much like that of the hermit crab, which moves into a larger shell when it outgrows its previous one.

7.2.2   Implementing a Dynamic Array

We now demonstrate how our original version of the ArrayList, from Code Fragments 7.2 and 7.3, can be transformed to a dynamic-array implementation, having unbounded capacity. We rely on the same internal representation, with a traditional array A, that is initialized either to a default capacity or to one specified as a parameter to the constructor.

The key is to provide means to "grow" the array A, when more space is needed. Of course, we cannot actually grow that array, as its capacity is fixed. Instead, when a call to add a new element risks ***overflowing*** the current array, we perform the following additional steps:

1. Allocate a new array B with larger capacity.
2. Set $B[k] = A[k]$, for $k = 0, \ldots, n-1$, where n denotes current number of items.
3. Set $A = B$, that is, we henceforth use the new array to support the list.
4. Insert the new element in the new array.

An illustration of this process is shown in Figure 7.3.

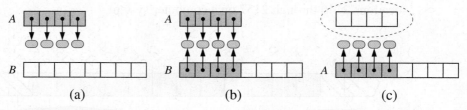

Figure 7.3: An illustration of "growing" a dynamic array: (a) create new array B; (b) store elements of A in B; (c) reassign reference A to the new array. Not shown is the future garbage collection of the old array, or the insertion of a new element.

Code Fragment 7.4 provides a concrete implementation of a resize method, which should be included as a protected method within the original ArrayList class. The instance variable data corresponds to array A in the above discussion, and local variable temp corresponds to array B.

```
/** Resizes internal array to have given capacity >= size. */
protected void resize(int capacity) {
  E[ ] temp = (E[ ]) new Object[capacity]; // safe cast; compiler may give warning
  for (int k=0; k < size; k++)
    temp[k] = data[k];
  data = temp;                             // start using the new array
}
```

Code Fragment 7.4: An implementation of the ArrayList.resize method.

The remaining issue to consider is how large of a new array to create. A commonly used rule is for the new array to have twice the capacity of the existing array that has been filled. In Section 7.2.3, we will provide a mathematical analysis to justify such a choice.

To complete the revision to our original ArrayList implementation, we redesign the add method so that it calls the new resize utility when detecting that the current array is filled (rather than throwing an exception). The revised version appears in Code Fragment 7.5.

```
28  /** Inserts element e to be at index i, shifting all subsequent elements later. */
29  public void add(int i, E e) throws IndexOutOfBoundsException {
30    checkIndex(i, size + 1);
31    if (size == data.length)              // not enough capacity
32      resize(2 * data.length);            // so double the current capacity
...   // rest of method unchanged...
```

Code Fragment 7.5: A revision to the ArrayList.add method, originally from Code Fragment 7.3, which calls the resize method of Code Fragment 7.4 when more capacity is needed.

Finally, we note that our original implementation of the ArrayList class includes two constructors: a default constructor that uses an initial capacity of 16, and a parameterized constructor that allows the caller to specify a capacity value. With the use of dynamic arrays, that capacity is no longer a fixed limit. Still, greater efficiency is achieved when a user selects an initial capacity that matches the actual size of a data set, as this can avoid time spent on intermediate array reallocations and potential space that is wasted by having too large of an array.

7.2.3 Amortized Analysis of Dynamic Arrays

In this section, we will perform a detailed analysis of the running time of operations on dynamic arrays. As a shorthand notation, let us refer to the insertion of an element to be the last element in an array list as a ***push*** operation.

The strategy of replacing an array with a new, larger array might at first seem slow, because a single push operation may require $\Omega(n)$ time to perform, where n is the current number of elements in the array. (Recall, from Section 4.3.1, that big-Omega notation, describes an asymptotic lower bound on the running time of an algorithm.) However, by doubling the capacity during an array replacement, our new array allows us to add n further elements before the array must be replaced again. In this way, there are many simple push operations for each expensive one (see Figure 7.4). This fact allows us to show that a series of push operations on an initially empty dynamic array is efficient in terms of its total running time.

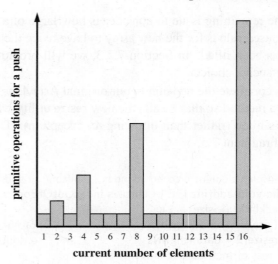

Figure 7.4: Running times of a series of push operations on a dynamic array.

Using an algorithmic design pattern called ***amortization***, we show that performing a sequence of push operations on a dynamic array is actually quite efficient. To perform an ***amortized analysis***, we use an accounting technique where we view the computer as a coin-operated appliance that requires the payment of one ***cyber-dollar*** for a constant amount of computing time. When an operation is executed, we should have enough cyber-dollars available in our current "bank account" to pay for that operation's running time. Thus, the total amount of cyber-dollars spent for any computation will be proportional to the total time spent on that computation. The beauty of using this analysis method is that we can overcharge some operations in order to save up cyber-dollars to pay for others.

Proposition 7.2: *Let L be an initially empty array list with capacity one, implemented by means of a dynamic array that doubles in size when full. The total time to perform a series of n push operations in L is $O(n)$.*

Justification: Let us assume that one cyber-dollar is enough to pay for the execution of each push operation in L, excluding the time spent for growing the array. Also, let us assume that growing the array from size k to size $2k$ requires k cyber-dollars for the time spent initializing the new array. We shall charge each push operation three cyber-dollars. Thus, we overcharge each push operation that does not cause an overflow by two cyber-dollars. Think of the two cyber-dollars profited in an insertion that does not grow the array as being "stored" with the cell in which the element was inserted. An overflow occurs when the array L has 2^i elements, for some integer $i \geq 0$, and the size of the array used by the array representing L is 2^i. Thus, doubling the size of the array will require 2^i cyber-dollars. Fortunately, these cyber-dollars can be found stored in cells 2^{i-1} through $2^i - 1$. (See Figure 7.5.)

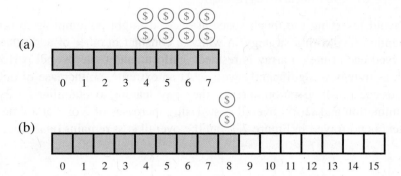

Figure 7.5: Illustration of a series of push operations on a dynamic array: (a) an 8-cell array is full, with two cyber-dollars "stored" at cells 4 through 7; (b) a push operation causes an overflow and a doubling of capacity. Copying the eight old elements to the new array is paid for by the cyber-dollars already stored in the table. Inserting the new element is paid for by one of the cyber-dollars charged to the current push operation, and the two cyber-dollars profited are stored at cell 8.

Note that the previous overflow occurred when the number of elements became larger than 2^{i-1} for the first time, and thus the cyber-dollars stored in cells 2^{i-1} through $2^i - 1$ have not yet been spent. Therefore, we have a valid amortization scheme in which each operation is charged three cyber-dollars and all the computing time is paid for. That is, we can pay for the execution of n push operations using $3n$ cyber-dollars. In other words, the amortized running time of each push operation is $O(1)$; hence, the total running time of n push operations is $O(n)$. ∎

Geometric Increase in Capacity

Although the proof of Proposition 7.2 relies on the array being doubled each time it is expanded, the $O(1)$ amortized bound per operation can be proven for any geometrically increasing progression of array sizes. (See Section 2.2.3 for discussion of geometric progressions.) When choosing the geometric base, there exists a trade-off between runtime efficiency and memory usage. If the last insertion causes a resize event, with a base of 2 (i.e., doubling the array), the array essentially ends up twice as large as it needs to be. If we instead increase the array by only 25% of its current size (i.e., a geometric base of 1.25), we do not risk wasting as much memory in the end, but there will be more intermediate resize events along the way. Still it is possible to prove an $O(1)$ amortized bound, using a constant factor greater than the 3 cyber-dollars per operation used in the proof of Proposition 7.2 (see Exercise R-7.7). The key to the performance is that the amount of additional space is proportional to the current size of the array.

Beware of Arithmetic Progression

To avoid reserving too much space at once, it might be tempting to implement a dynamic array with a strategy in which a constant number of additional cells are reserved each time an array is resized. Unfortunately, the overall performance of such a strategy is significantly worse. At an extreme, an increase of only one cell causes each push operation to resize the array, leading to a familiar $1 + 2 + 3 + \cdots + n$ summation and $\Omega(n^2)$ overall cost. Using increases of 2 or 3 at a time is slightly better, as portrayed in Figure 7.4, but the overall cost remains quadratic.

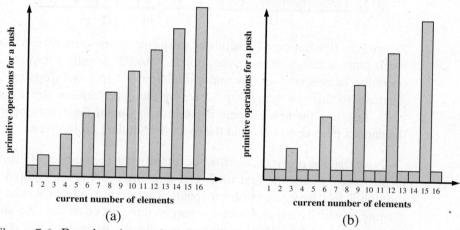

Figure 7.6: Running times of a series of push operations on a dynamic array using arithmetic progression of sizes. Part (a) assumes an increase of 2 in the size of the array, while part (b) assumes an increase of 3.

Using a *fixed* increment for each resize, and thus an arithmetic progression of intermediate array sizes, results in an overall time that is quadratic in the number of operations, as shown in the following proposition. In essence, even an increase in 10,000 cells per resize will become insignificant for large data sets.

Proposition 7.3: *Performing a series of n push operations on an initially empty dynamic array using a fixed increment with each resize takes $\Omega(n^2)$ time.*

Justification: Let $c > 0$ represent the fixed increment in capacity that is used for each resize event. During the series of n push operations, time will have been spent initializing arrays of size $c, 2c, 3c, \ldots, mc$ for $m = \lceil n/c \rceil$, and therefore, the overall time is proportional to $c + 2c + 3c + \cdots + mc$. By Proposition 4.3, this sum is

$$\sum_{i=1}^{m} ci = c \cdot \sum_{i=1}^{m} i = c \frac{m(m+1)}{2} \geq c \frac{\frac{n}{c}(\frac{n}{c}+1)}{2} \geq \frac{1}{2c} \cdot n^2.$$

Therefore, performing the n push operations takes $\Omega(n^2)$ time.   ■

Memory Usage and Shrinking an Array

Another consequence of the rule of a geometric increase in capacity when adding to a dynamic array is that the final array size is guaranteed to be proportional to the overall number of elements. That is, the data structure uses $O(n)$ memory. This is a very desirable property for a data structure.

If a container, such as an array list, provides operations that cause the removal of one or more elements, greater care must be taken to ensure that a dynamic array guarantees $O(n)$ memory usage. The risk is that repeated insertions may cause the underlying array to grow arbitrarily large, and that there will no longer be a proportional relationship between the actual number of elements and the array capacity after many elements are removed.

A robust implementation of such a data structure will shrink the underlying array, on occasion, while maintaining the $O(1)$ amortized bound on individual operations. However, care must be taken to ensure that the structure cannot rapidly oscillate between growing and shrinking the underlying array, in which case the amortized bound would not be achieved. In Exercise C-7.29, we explore a strategy in which the array capacity is halved whenever the number of actual element falls below one-fourth of that capacity, thereby guaranteeing that the array capacity is at most four times the number of elements; we explore the amortized analysis of such a strategy in Exercises C-7.30 and C-7.31.

7.2.4 Java's StringBuilder class

Near the beginning of Chapter 4, we described an experiment in which we compared two algorithms for composing a long string (Code Fragment 4.2). The first of those relied on repeated concatenation using the String class, and the second relied on use of Java's StringBuilder class. We observed the StringBuilder was significantly faster, with empirical evidence that suggested a quadratic running time for the algorithm with repeated concatenations, and a linear running time for the algorithm with the StringBuilder. We are now able to explain the theoretical underpinning for those observations.

The StringBuilder class represents a mutable string by storing characters in a dynamic array. With analysis similar to Proposition 7.2, it guarantees that a series of append operations resulting in a string of length n execute in a combined time of $O(n)$. (Insertions at positions other than the end of a string builder do not carry this guarantee, just as they do not for an ArrayList.)

In contrast, the repeated use of string concatenation requires quadratic time. We originally analyzed that algorithm on page 172 of Chapter 4. In effect, that approach is akin to a dynamic array with an arithmetic progression of size one, repeatedly copying all characters from one array to a new array with size one greater than before.

7.3   Positional Lists

When working with array-based sequences, integer indices provide an excellent means for describing the location of an element, or the location at which an insertion or deletion should take place. However, numeric indices are not a good choice for describing positions within a linked list because, knowing only an element's index, the only way to reach it is to traverse the list incrementally from its beginning or end, counting elements along the way.

Furthermore, indices are not a good abstraction for describing a more local view of a position in a sequence, because the index of an entry changes over time due to insertions or deletions that happen earlier in the sequence. For example, it may not be convenient to describe the location of a person waiting in line based on the index, as that requires knowledge of precisely how far away that person is from the front of the line. We prefer an abstraction, as characterized in Figure 7.7, in which there is some other means for describing a position.

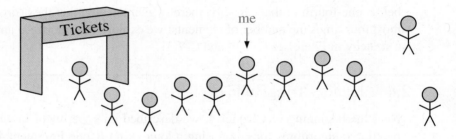

Figure 7.7: We wish to be able to identify the position of an element in a sequence without the use of an integer index. The label "me" represents some abstraction that identifies the position.

Our goal is to design an abstract data type that provides a user a way to refer to elements anywhere in a sequence, and to perform arbitrary insertions and deletions. This would allow us to efficiently describe actions such as a person deciding to leave the line before reaching the front, or allowing a friend to "cut" into line right behind him or her.

As another example, a text document can be viewed as a long sequence of characters. A word processor uses the abstraction of a ***cursor*** to describe a position within the document without explicit use of an integer index, allowing operations such as "delete the character at the cursor" or "insert a new character just after the cursor." Furthermore, we may be able to refer to an inherent position within a document, such as the beginning of a particular chapter, without relying on a character index (or even a chapter number) that may change as the document evolves.

For these reasons, we temporarily forego the index-based methods of Java's formal List interface, and instead develop our own abstract data type that we denote as a ***positional list***. Although a positional list is an abstraction, and need not rely on a linked list for its implementation, we certainly have a linked list in mind as we design the ADT, ensuring that it takes best advantage of particular capabilities of a linked list, such as $O(1)$-time insertions and deletions at arbitrary positions (something that is not possible with an array-based sequence).

We face an immediate challenge in designing the ADT; to achieve constant time insertions and deletions at arbitrary locations, we effectively need a reference to the node at which an element is stored. It is therefore very tempting to develop an ADT in which a node reference serves as the mechanism for describing a position. In fact, our DoublyLinkedList class of Section 3.4.1 has methods addBetween and remove that accept node references as parameters; however, we intentionally declared those methods as private.

Unfortunately, the public use of nodes in the ADT would violate the object-oriented design principles of abstraction and encapsulation, which were introduced in Chapter 2. There are several reasons to prefer that we encapsulate the nodes of a linked list, for both our sake and for the benefit of users of our abstraction:

- It will be simpler for users of our data structure if they are not bothered with unnecessary details of our implementation, such as low-level manipulation of nodes, or our reliance on the use of sentinel nodes. Notice that to use the addBetween method of our DoublyLinkedList class to add a node at the beginning of a sequence, the header sentinel must be sent as a parameter.

- We can provide a more robust data structure if we do not permit users to directly access or manipulate the nodes. We can then ensure that users do not invalidate the consistency of a list by mismanaging the linking of nodes. A more subtle problem arises if a user were allowed to call the addBetween or remove method of our DoublyLinkedList class, sending a node that does not belong to the given list as a parameter. (Go back and look at that code and see why it causes a problem!)

- By better encapsulating the internal details of our implementation, we have greater flexibility to redesign the data structure and improve its performance. In fact, with a well-designed abstraction, we can provide a notion of a nonnumeric position, even if using an array-based sequence. (See Exercise C-7.43.)

Therefore, in defining the positional list ADT, we also introduce the concept of a ***position***, which formalizes the intuitive notion of the "location" of an element relative to others in the list. (When we do use a linked list for the implementation, we will later see how we can privately use node references as natural manifestations of positions.)

7.3.1   Positions

To provide a general abstraction for the location of an element within a structure, we define a simple ***position*** abstract data type. A position supports the following single method:

getElement( ): Returns the element stored at this position.

A position acts as a marker or token within a broader positional list. A position p, which is associated with some element e in a list L, does not change, even if the index of e changes in L due to insertions or deletions elsewhere in the list. Nor does position p change if we replace the element e stored at p with another element. The only way in which a position becomes invalid is if that position (and its element) are explicitly removed from the list.

Having a formal definition of a position type allows positions to serve as parameters to some methods and return values from other methods of the positional list ADT, which we next describe.

7.3.2   The Positional List Abstract Data Type

We now view a ***positional list*** as a collection of positions, each of which stores an element. The accessor methods provided by the positional list ADT include the following, for a list L:

first( ): Returns the position of the first element of L (or null if empty).

last( ): Returns the position of the last element of L (or null if empty).

before(p): Returns the position of L immediately before position p (or null if p is the first position).

after(p): Returns the position of L immediately after position p (or null if p is the last position).

isEmpty( ): Returns true if list L does not contain any elements.

size( ): Returns the number of elements in list L.

An error occurs if a position p, sent as a parameter to a method, is not a valid position for the list.

Note well that the first( ) and last( ) methods of the positional list ADT return the associated *positions*, not the *elements*. (This is in contrast to the corresponding first and last methods of the deque ADT.) The first element of a positional list can be determined by subsequently invoking the getElement method on that position, as first( ).getElement. The advantage of receiving a position as a return value is that we can subsequently use that position to traverse the list.

As a demonstration of a typical traversal of a positional list, Code Fragment 7.6 traverses a list, named guests, that stores string elements, and prints each element while traversing from the beginning of the list to the end.

```
1   Position<String> cursor = guests.first( );
2   while (cursor != null) {
3     System.out.println(cursor.getElement( ));
4     cursor = guests.after(cursor);              // advance to the next position (if any)
5   }
```

Code Fragment 7.6: A traversal of a positional list.

This code relies on the convention that the null reference is returned when the after method is called upon the last position. (That return value is clearly distinguishable from any legitimate position.) The positional list ADT similarly indicates that the null value is returned when the before method is invoked at the front of the list, or when first or last methods are called upon an empty list. Therefore, the above code fragment works correctly even if the guests list is empty.

Updated Methods of a Positional List

The positional list ADT also includes the following *update* methods:

addFirst(e): Inserts a new element e at the front of the list, returning the position of the new element.

addLast(e): Inserts a new element e at the back of the list, returning the position of the new element.

addBefore(p, e): Inserts a new element e in the list, just before position p, returning the position of the new element.

addAfter(p, e): Inserts a new element e in the list, just after position p, returning the position of the new element.

set(p, e): Replaces the element at position p with element e, returning the element formerly at position p.

remove(p): Removes and returns the element at position p in the list, invalidating the position.

There may at first seem to be redundancy in the above repertoire of operations for the positional list ADT, since we can perform operation addFirst(e) with addBefore(first( ), e), and operation addLast(e) with addAfter(last( ), e). But these substitutions can only be done for a nonempty list.

Example 7.4: *The following table shows a series of operations on an initially empty positional list storing integers. To identify position instances, we use variables such as p and q. For ease of exposition, when displaying the list contents, we use subscript notation to denote the position storing an element.*

Method	Return Value	List Contents
addLast(8)	p	(8_p)
first( )	p	(8_p)
addAfter(p, 5)	q	$(8_p, 5_q)$
before(q)	p	$(8_p, 5_q)$
addBefore(q, 3)	r	$(8_p, 3_r, 5_q)$
r.getElement( )	3	$(8_p, 3_r, 5_q)$
after(p)	r	$(8_p, 3_r, 5_q)$
before(p)	null	$(8_p, 3_r, 5_q)$
addFirst(9)	s	$(9_s, 8_p, 3_r, 5_q)$
remove(last( ))	5	$(9_s, 8_p, 3_r)$
set(p, 7)	8	$(9_s, 7_p, 3_r)$
remove(q)	"error"	$(9_s, 7_p, 3_r)$

Java Interface Definitions

We are now ready to formalize the position ADT and positional list ADT. A Java Position interface, representing the position ADT, is given in Code Fragment 7.7. Following that, Code Fragment 7.8 presents a Java definition for our PositionalList interface. If the getElement( ) method is called on a Position instance that has previously been removed from its list, an IllegalStateException is thrown. If an invalid Position instance is sent as a parameter to a method of a PositionalList, an IllegalArgumentException is thrown. (Both of those exception types are defined in the standard Java hierarchy.)

```java
public interface Position<E> {
  /**
   * Returns the element stored at this position.
   *
   * @return the stored element
   * @throws IllegalStateException if position no longer valid
   */
  E getElement() throws IllegalStateException;
}
```

Code Fragment 7.7: The Position interface.

```
1   /** An interface for positional lists. */
2   public interface PositionalList<E> {
3
4     /** Returns the number of elements in the list. */
5     int size( );
6
7     /** Tests whether the list is empty. */
8     boolean isEmpty( );
9
10    /** Returns the first Position in the list (or null, if empty). */
11    Position<E> first( );
12
13    /** Returns the last Position in the list (or null, if empty). */
14    Position<E> last( );
15
16    /** Returns the Position immediately before Position p (or null, if p is first). */
17    Position<E> before(Position<E> p) throws IllegalArgumentException;
18
19    /** Returns the Position immediately after Position p (or null, if p is last). */
20    Position<E> after(Position<E> p) throws IllegalArgumentException;
21
22    /** Inserts element e at the front of the list and returns its new Position. */
23    Position<E> addFirst(E e);
24
25    /** Inserts element e at the back of the list and returns its new Position. */
26    Position<E> addLast(E e);
27
28    /** Inserts element e immediately before Position p and returns its new Position. */
29    Position<E> addBefore(Position<E> p, E e)
30      throws IllegalArgumentException;
31
32    /** Inserts element e immediately after Position p and returns its new Position. */
33    Position<E> addAfter(Position<E> p, E e)
34      throws IllegalArgumentException;
35
36    /** Replaces the element stored at Position p and returns the replaced element. */
37    E set(Position<E> p, E e) throws IllegalArgumentException;
38
39    /** Removes the element stored at Position p and returns it (invalidating p). */
40    E remove(Position<E> p) throws IllegalArgumentException;
41  }
```

Code Fragment 7.8: The PositionalList interface.

7.3.3   Doubly Linked List Implementation

Not surprisingly, our preferred implementation of the PositionalList interface relies on a doubly linked list. Although we implemented a DoublyLinkedList class in Chapter 3, that class does not adhere to the PositionalList interface.

In this section, we develop a concrete implementation of the PositionalList interface using a doubly linked list. The low-level details of our new linked-list representation, such as the use of header and trailer sentinels, will be identical to our earlier version; we refer the reader to Section 3.4 for a discussion of the doubly linked list operations. What differs in this section is our management of the positional abstraction.

The obvious way to identify locations within a linked list are node references. Therefore, we declare the nested Node class of our linked list so as to implement the Position interface, supporting the required getElement method. So the nodes *are* the positions. Yet, the Node class is declared as private, to maintain proper encapsulation. All of the public methods of the positional list rely on the Position type, so although we know we are sending and receiving nodes, these are only known to be positions from the outside; as a result, users of our class cannot call any method other than getElement( ).

In Code Fragments 7.9–7.12, we define a LinkedPositionalList class, which implements the positional list ADT. We provide the following guide to that code:

- Code Fragment 7.9 contains the definition of the nested Node<E> class, which implements the Position<E> interface. Following that are the declaration of the instance variables of the outer LinkedPositionalList class and its constructor.
- Code Fragment 7.10 begins with two important utility methods that help us robustly cast between the Position and Node types. The validate(p) method is called anytime the user sends a Position instance as a parameter. It throws an exception if it determines that the position is invalid, and otherwise returns that instance, implicitly cast as a Node, so that methods of the Node class can subsequently be called. The private position(node) method is used when about to return a Position to the user. Its primary purpose is to make sure that we do not expose either sentinel node to a caller, returning a **null** reference in such a case. We rely on both of these private utility methods in the public accessor methods that follow.
- Code Fragment 7.11 provides most of the public update methods, relying on a private addBetween method to unify the implementations of the various insertion operations.
- Code Fragment 7.12 provides the public remove method. Note that it sets all fields of the removed node back to null—a condition we can later detect to recognize a defunct position.

```java
1  /** Implementation of a positional list stored as a doubly linked list. */
2  public class LinkedPositionalList<E> implements PositionalList<E> {
3    //---------------- nested Node class ----------------
4    private static class Node<E> implements Position<E> {
5      private E element;                    // reference to the element stored at this node
6      private Node<E> prev;                 // reference to the previous node in the list
7      private Node<E> next;                 // reference to the subsequent node in the list
8      public Node(E e, Node<E> p, Node<E> n) {
9        element = e;
10       prev = p;
11       next = n;
12     }
13     public E getElement() throws IllegalStateException {
14       if (next == null)                   // convention for defunct node
15         throw new IllegalStateException("Position no longer valid");
16       return element;
17     }
18     public Node<E> getPrev() {
19       return prev;
20     }
21     public Node<E> getNext() {
22       return next;
23     }
24     public void setElement(E e) {
25       element = e;
26     }
27     public void setPrev(Node<E> p) {
28       prev = p;
29     }
30     public void setNext(Node<E> n) {
31       next = n;
32     }
33   } //----------- end of nested Node class -----------
34
35   // instance variables of the LinkedPositionalList
36   private Node<E> header;                 // header sentinel
37   private Node<E> trailer;                // trailer sentinel
38   private int size = 0;                   // number of elements in the list
39
40   /** Constructs a new empty list. */
41   public LinkedPositionalList() {
42     header = new Node<>(null, null, null);        // create header
43     trailer = new Node<>(null, header, null);     // trailer is preceded by header
44     header.setNext(trailer);                      // header is followed by trailer
45   }
```

Code Fragment 7.9: An implementation of the LinkedPositionalList class.
(Continues in Code Fragments 7.10–7.12.)

```java
46    // private utilities
47    /** Validates the position and returns it as a node. */
48    private Node<E> validate(Position<E> p) throws IllegalArgumentException {
49      if (!(p instanceof Node)) throw new IllegalArgumentException("Invalid p");
50      Node<E> node = (Node<E>) p;      // safe cast
51      if (node.getNext() == null)        // convention for defunct node
52        throw new IllegalArgumentException("p is no longer in the list");
53      return node;
54    }
55
56    /** Returns the given node as a Position (or null, if it is a sentinel). */
57    private Position<E> position(Node<E> node) {
58      if (node == header || node == trailer)
59        return null;      // do not expose user to the sentinels
60      return node;
61    }
62
63    // public accessor methods
64    /** Returns the number of elements in the linked list. */
65    public int size() { return size; }
66
67    /** Tests whether the linked list is empty. */
68    public boolean isEmpty() { return size == 0; }
69
70    /** Returns the first Position in the linked list (or null, if empty). */
71    public Position<E> first() {
72      return position(header.getNext());
73    }
74
75    /** Returns the last Position in the linked list (or null, if empty). */
76    public Position<E> last() {
77      return position(trailer.getPrev());
78    }
79
80    /** Returns the Position immediately before Position p (or null, if p is first). */
81    public Position<E> before(Position<E> p) throws IllegalArgumentException {
82      Node<E> node = validate(p);
83      return position(node.getPrev());
84    }
85
86    /** Returns the Position immediately after Position p (or null, if p is last). */
87    public Position<E> after(Position<E> p) throws IllegalArgumentException {
88      Node<E> node = validate(p);
89      return position(node.getNext());
90    }
```

Code Fragment 7.10: An implementation of the LinkedPositionalList class.
(Continued from Code Fragment 7.9; continues in Code Fragments 7.11 and 7.12.)

```
91    // private utilities
92    /** Adds element e to the linked list between the given nodes. */
93    private Position<E> addBetween(E e, Node<E> pred, Node<E> succ) {
94      Node<E> newest = new Node<>(e, pred, succ);  // create and link a new node
95      pred.setNext(newest);
96      succ.setPrev(newest);
97      size++;
98      return newest;
99    }
100
101   // public update methods
102   /** Inserts element e at the front of the linked list and returns its new Position. */
103   public Position<E> addFirst(E e) {
104     return addBetween(e, header, header.getNext( ));        // just after the header
105   }
106
107   /** Inserts element e at the back of the linked list and returns its new Position. */
108   public Position<E> addLast(E e) {
109     return addBetween(e, trailer.getPrev( ), trailer);        // just before the trailer
110   }
111
112   /** Inserts element e immediately before Position p, and returns its new Position.*/
113   public Position<E> addBefore(Position<E> p, E e)
114                                      throws IllegalArgumentException {
115     Node<E> node = validate(p);
116     return addBetween(e, node.getPrev( ), node);
117   }
118
119   /** Inserts element e immediately after Position p, and returns its new Position. */
120   public Position<E> addAfter(Position<E> p, E e)
121                                      throws IllegalArgumentException {
122     Node<E> node = validate(p);
123     return addBetween(e, node, node.getNext( ));
124   }
125
126   /** Replaces the element stored at Position p and returns the replaced element. */
127   public E set(Position<E> p, E e) throws IllegalArgumentException {
128     Node<E> node = validate(p);
129     E answer = node.getElement( );
130     node.setElement(e);
131     return answer;
132   }
```

Code Fragment 7.11: An implementation of the LinkedPositionalList class. (Continued from Code Fragments 7.9 and 7.10; continues in Code Fragment 7.12.)

```
133   /** Removes the element stored at Position p and returns it (invalidating p). */
134   public E remove(Position<E> p) throws IllegalArgumentException {
135     Node<E> node = validate(p);
136     Node<E> predecessor = node.getPrev();
137     Node<E> successor = node.getNext();
138     predecessor.setNext(successor);
139     successor.setPrev(predecessor);
140     size--;
141     E answer = node.getElement();
142     node.setElement(null);                   // help with garbage collection
143     node.setNext(null);                      // and convention for defunct node
144     node.setPrev(null);
145     return answer;
146   }
147 }
```

Code Fragment 7.12: An implementation of the LinkedPositionalList class.
(Continued from Code Fragments 7.9–7.11.)

The Performance of a Linked Positional List

The positional list ADT is ideally suited for implementation with a doubly linked
list, as all operations run in worst-case constant time, as shown in Table 7.2. This is
in stark contrast to the ArrayList structure (analyzed in Table 7.1), which requires
linear time for insertions or deletions at arbitrary positions, due to the need for a
loop to shift other elements.

Of course, our positional list does not support the index-based methods of the
official List interface of Section 7.1. It is possible to add support for those methods
by traversing the list while counting nodes (see Exercise C-7.38), but that requires
time proportional to the sublist that is traversed.

Method	Running Time
size()	$O(1)$
isEmpty()	$O(1)$
first(), last()	$O(1)$
before(p), after(p)	$O(1)$
addFirst(e), addLast(e)	$O(1)$
addBefore(p, e), addAfter(p, e)	$O(1)$
set(p, e)	$O(1)$
remove(p)	$O(1)$

Table 7.2: Performance of a positional list with n elements realized by a doubly
linked list. The space usage is $O(n)$.

Implementing a Positional List with an Array

We can implement a positional list L using an array A for storage, but some care is necessary in designing objects that will serve as positions. At first glance, it would seem that a position p need only store the index i at which its associated element is stored within the array. We can then implement method getElement(p) simply by returning $A[i]$. The problem with this approach is that the index of an element e changes when other insertions or deletions occur before it. If we have already returned a position p associated with element e that stores an outdated index i to a user, the wrong array cell would be accessed when the position was used. (Remember that positions in a positional list should always be defined relative to their neighboring positions, not their indices.)

Hence, if we are going to implement a positional list with an array, we need a different approach. We recommend the following representation. Instead of storing the elements of L directly in array A, we store a new kind of position object in each cell of A. A position p stores the element e as well as the current index i of that element within the list. Such a data structure is illustrated in Figure 7.8.

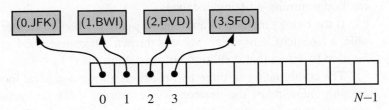

Figure 7.8: An array-based representation of a positional list.

With this representation, we can determine the index currently associated with a position, and we can determine the position currently associated with a specific index. We can therefore implement an accessor, such as before(p), by finding the index of the given position and using the array to find the neighboring position.

When an element is inserted or deleted somewhere in the list, we can loop through the array to update the index variable stored in all later positions in the list that are shifted during the update.

Efficiency Trade-Offs with an Array-Based Sequence

In this array implementation of a sequence, the addFirst, addBefore, addAfter, and remove methods take $O(n)$ time, because we have to shift position objects to make room for the new position or to fill in the hole created by the removal of the old position (just as in the insert and remove methods based on index). All the other position-based methods take $O(1)$ time.

7.4   Iterators

An ***iterator*** is a software design pattern that abstracts the process of scanning through a sequence of elements, one element at a time. The underlying elements might be stored in a container class, streaming through a network, or generated by a series of computations.

In order to unify the treatment and syntax for iterating objects in a way that is independent from a specific organization, Java defines the java.util.Iterator interface with the following two methods:

hasNext( ): Returns true if there is at least one additional element in the sequence, and false otherwise.

next( ): Returns the next element in the sequence.

The interface uses Java's generic framework, with the next( ) method returning a parameterized element type. For example, the Scanner class (described in Section 1.6) formally implements the Iterator<String> interface, with its next( ) method returning a String instance.

If the next( ) method of an iterator is called when no further elements are available, a NoSuchElementException is thrown. Of course, the hasNext( ) method can be used to detect that condition before calling next( ).

The combination of these two methods allows a general loop construct for processing elements of the iterator. For example, if we let variable, iter, denote an instance of the Iterator<String> type, then we can write the following:

```
while (iter.hasNext()) {
  String value = iter.next();
  System.out.println(value);
}
```

The java.util.Iterator interface contains a third method, which is *optionally* supported by some iterators:

remove( ): Removes from the collection the element returned by the most recent call to next( ). Throws an IllegalStateException if next has not yet been called, or if remove was already called since the most recent call to next.

This method can be used to filter a collection of elements, for example to discard all negative numbers from a data set.

For the sake of simplicity, we will not implement the remove method for most data structures in this book, but we will give two tangible examples later in this section. If removal is not supported, an UnsupportedOperationException is conventionally thrown.

7.4.1   The Iterable Interface and Java's For-Each Loop

A single iterator instance supports only one pass through a collection; calls to next can be made until all elements have been reported, but there is no way to "reset" the iterator back to the beginning of the sequence.

However, a data structure that wishes to allow repeated iterations can support a method that returns a *new* iterator, each time it is called. To provide greater standardization, Java defines another parameterized interface, named Iterable, that includes the following single method:

iterator( ): Returns an iterator of the elements in the collection.

An instance of a typical collection class in Java, such as an ArrayList, is *iterable* (but not itself an *iterator*); it produces an iterator for its collection as the return value of the iterator( ) method. Each call to iterator( ) returns a new iterator instance, thereby allowing multiple (even simultaneous) traversals of a collection.

Java's Iterable class also plays a fundamental role in support of the "for-each" loop syntax (described in Section 1.5.2). The loop syntax,

```
for (ElementType variable : collection) {
    loopBody                                    // may refer to "variable"
}
```

is supported for any instance, *collection*, of an iterable class. *ElementType* must be the type of object returned by its iterator, and *variable* will take on element values within the *loopBody*. Essentially, this syntax is shorthand for the following:

```
Iterator<ElementType> iter = collection.iterator( );
while (iter.hasNext( )) {
    ElementType variable = iter.next( );
    loopBody                                    // may refer to "variable"
}
```

We note that the iterator's remove method cannot be invoked when using the for-each loop syntax. Instead, we must explicitly use an iterator. As an example, the following loop can be used to remove all negative numbers from an ArrayList of floating-point values.

```
ArrayList<Double> data;    // populate with random numbers (not shown)
Iterator<Double> walk = data.iterator( );
while (walk.hasNext( ))
  if (walk.next( ) < 0.0)
    walk.remove( );
```

7.4.2   Implementing Iterators

There are two general styles for implementing iterators that differ in terms of what work is done when the iterator instance is first created, and what work is done each time the iterator is advanced with a call to next( ).

A *snapshot iterator* maintains its own private copy of the sequence of elements, which is constructed at the time the iterator object is created. It effectively records a "snapshot" of the sequence of elements at the time the iterator is created, and is therefore unaffected by any subsequent changes to the primary collection that may occur. Implementing snapshot iterators tends to be very easy, as it requires a simple traversal of the primary structure. The downside of this style of iterator is that it requires $O(n)$ time and $O(n)$ auxiliary space, upon construction, to copy and store a collection of n elements.

A *lazy iterator* is one that does not make an upfront copy, instead performing a piecewise traversal of the primary structure only when the next( ) method is called to request another element. The advantage of this style of iterator is that it can typically be implemented so the iterator requires only $O(1)$ space and $O(1)$ construction time. One downside (or feature) of a lazy iterator is that its behavior is affected if the primary structure is modified (by means other than by the iterator's own remove method) before the iteration completes. Many of the iterators in Java's libraries implement a "fail-fast" behavior that immediately invalidates such an iterator if its underlying collection is modified unexpectedly.

We will demonstrate how to implement iterators for both the ArrayList and LinkedPositionalList classes as examples. We implement lazy iterators for both, including support for the remove operation (but without any fail-fast guarantee).

Iterations with the ArrayList class

We begin by discussing iteration for the ArrayList<E> class. We will have it implement the Iterable<E> interface. (In fact, that requirement is already part of Java's List interface.) Therefore, we must add an iterator( ) method to that class definition, which returns an instance of an object that implements the Iterator<E> interface. For this purpose, we define a new class, ArrayIterator, as a nonstatic nested class of ArrayList (i.e., an *inner class*, as described in Section 2.6). The advantage of having the iterator as an inner class is that it can access private fields (such as the array A) that are members of the containing list.

Our implementation is given in Code Fragment 7.13. The iterator( ) method of ArrayList returns a new instance of the inner ArrayIterator class. Each iterator maintains a field j that represents the index of the next element to be returned. It is initialized to 0, and when j reaches the size of the list, there are no more elements to return. In order to support element removal through the iterator, we also maintain a boolean variable that denotes whether a call to remove is currently permissible.

```
1    //--------------- nested ArrayIterator class ----------------
2    /**
3     * A (nonstatic) inner class. Note well that each instance contains an implicit
4     * reference to the containing list, allowing it to access the list's members.
5     */
6    private class ArrayIterator implements Iterator<E> {
7      private int j = 0;                    // index of the next element to report
8      private boolean removable = false;    // can remove be called at this time?
9
10     /**
11      * Tests whether the iterator has a next object.
12      * @return true if there are further objects, false otherwise
13      */
14     public boolean hasNext() { return j < size; }  // size is field of outer instance
15
16     /**
17      * Returns the next object in the iterator.
18      *
19      * @return next object
20      * @throws NoSuchElementException if there are no further elements
21      */
22     public E next() throws NoSuchElementException {
23       if (j == size) throw new NoSuchElementException("No next element");
24       removable = true;    // this element can subsequently be removed
25       return data[j++];    // post-increment j, so it is ready for future call to next
26     }
27
28     /**
29      * Removes the element returned by most recent call to next.
30      * @throws IllegalStateException if next has not yet been called
31      * @throws IllegalStateException if remove was already called since recent next
32      */
33     public void remove() throws IllegalStateException {
34       if (!removable) throw new IllegalStateException("nothing to remove");
35       ArrayList.this.remove(j−1);    // that was the last one returned
36       j−−;                           // next element has shifted one cell to the left
37       removable = false;             // do not allow remove again until next is called
38     }
39   } //------------ end of nested ArrayIterator class ------------
40
41   /** Returns an iterator of the elements stored in the list. */
42   public Iterator<E> iterator() {
43     return new ArrayIterator();    // create a new instance of the inner class
44   }
```

Code Fragment 7.13: Code providing support for ArrayList iterators. (This should be nested within the ArrayList class definition of Code Fragments 7.2 and 7.3.)

Iterations with the LinkedPositionalList class

In support the concept of iteration with the LinkedPositionalList class, a first question is whether to support iteration of the *elements* of the list or the *positions* of the list. If we allow a user to iterate through all positions of the list, those positions could be used to access the underlying elements, so support for position iteration is more general. However, it is more standard for a container class to support iteration of the core elements, by default, so that the for-each loop syntax could be used to write code such as the following,

> **for** (String guest : waitlist)

assuming that variable waitlist has type LinkedPositionalList<String>.

For maximum convenience, we will support *both* forms of iteration. We will have the standard iterator( ) method return an iterator of the elements of the list, so that our list class formally implements the Iterable interface for the declared element type.

For those wishing to iterate through the positions of a list, we will provide a new method, positions( ). At first glance, it would seem a natural choice for such a method to return an Iterator. However, we prefer for the return type of that method to be an instance that is Iterable (and hence, has its own iterator( ) method that returns an iterator of positions). Our reason for the extra layer of complexity is that we wish for users of our class to be able to use a for-each loop with a simple syntax such as the following:

> **for** (Position<String> p : waitlist.positions( ))

For this syntax to be legal, the return type of positions( ) must be Iterable.

Code Fragment 7.14 presents our new support for the iteration of positions and elements of a LinkedPositionalList. We define three new inner classes. The first of these is PositionIterator, providing the core functionality of our list iterations. Whereas the array list iterator maintained the index of the next element to be returned as a field, this class maintains the position of the next element to be returned (as well as the position of the most recently returned element, to support removal).

To support our goal of the positions( ) method returning an Iterable object, we define a trivial PositionIterable inner class, which simply constructs and returns a new PositionIterator object each time its iterator( ) method is called. The positions( ) method of the top-level class returns a new PositionIterable instance. Our framework relies heavily on these being inner classes, not static nested classes.

Finally, we wish to have the top-level iterator( ) method return an iterator of elements (not positions). Rather than reinvent the wheel, we trivially adapt the PositionIterator class to define a new ElementIterator class, which lazily manages a position iterator instance, while returning the element stored at each position when next( ) is called.

```
1    //---------------- nested PositionIterator class ----------------
2    private class PositionIterator implements Iterator<Position<E>> {
3      private Position<E> cursor = first();      // position of the next element to report
4      private Position<E> recent = null;         // position of last reported element
5      /** Tests whether the iterator has a next object. */
6      public boolean hasNext() { return (cursor != null);      }
7      /** Returns the next position in the iterator. */
8      public Position<E> next() throws NoSuchElementException {
9        if (cursor == null) throw new NoSuchElementException("nothing left");
10       recent = cursor;                    // element at this position might later be removed
11       cursor = after(cursor);
12       return recent;
13     ' }
14     /** Removes the element returned by most recent call to next. */
15     public void remove() throws IllegalStateException {
16       if (recent == null) throw new IllegalStateException("nothing to remove");
17       LinkedPositionalList.this.remove(recent);       // remove from outer list
18       recent = null;                  // do not allow remove again until next is called
19     }
20   } //------------- end of nested PositionIterator class ------------
21
22   //---------------- nested PositionIterable class ----------------
23   private class PositionIterable implements Iterable<Position<E>> {
24     public Iterator<Position<E>> iterator() { return new PositionIterator(); }
25   } //------------- end of nested PositionIterable class ------------
26
27   /** Returns an iterable representation of the list's positions. */
28   public Iterable<Position<E>> positions() {
29     return new PositionIterable();          // create a new instance of the inner class
30   }
31
32   //---------------- nested ElementIterator class ----------------
33   /* This class adapts the iteration produced by positions() to return elements. */
34   private class ElementIterator implements Iterator<E> {
35     Iterator<Position<E>> posIterator = new PositionIterator();
36     public boolean hasNext() { return posIterator.hasNext(); }
37     public E next() { return posIterator.next().getElement(); } // return element!
38     public void remove() { posIterator.remove(); }
39   }
40
41   /** Returns an iterator of the elements stored in the list. */
42   public Iterator<E> iterator() { return new ElementIterator(); }
```

Code Fragment 7.14: Support for providing iterations of positions and elements of a LinkedPositionalList. (This should be nested within the LinkedPositionalList class definition of Code Fragments 7.9–7.12.)

7.5   The Java Collections Framework

Java provides many data structure interfaces and classes, which together form the **Java Collections Framework**. This framework, which is part of the java.util package, includes versions of several of the data structures discussed in this book, some of which we have already discussed and others of which we will discuss later in this book. The root interface in the Java collections framework is named Collection. This is a general interface for any data structure, such as a list, that represents a collection of elements. The Collection interface includes many methods, including some we have already seen (e.g., size( ), isEmpty( ), iterator( )). It is a superinterface for other interfaces in the Java Collections Framework that can hold elements, including the java.util interfaces Deque, List, and Queue, and other subinterfaces discussed later in this book, including Set (Section 10.5.1) and Map (Section 10.1).

The Java Collections Framework also includes concrete classes implementing various interfaces with a combination of properties and underlying representations. We summarize but a few of those classes in Table 7.3. For each, we denote which of the Queue, Deque, or List interfaces are implemented (possibly several). We also discuss several behavioral properties. Some classes enforce, or allow, a fixed capacity limit. Robust classes provide support for **concurrency**, allowing multiple processes to share use of a data structure in a thread-safe manner. If the structure is designated as **blocking**, a call to retrieve an element from an empty collection waits until some other process inserts an element. Similarly, a call to insert into a full blocking structure must wait until room becomes available.

Class	Interfaces			Properties			Storage	
	Queue	Deque	List	Capacity Limit	Thread-Safe	Blocking	Array	Linked List
ArrayBlockingQueue	✓			✓	✓	✓	✓	
LinkedBlockingQueue	✓			✓	✓	✓		✓
ConcurrentLinkedQueue	✓				✓		✓	
ArrayDeque	✓	✓					✓	
LinkedBlockingDeque	✓	✓		✓	✓	✓		✓
ConcurrentLinkedDeque	✓	✓			✓			✓
ArrayList			✓				✓	
LinkedList	✓	✓	✓					✓

Table 7.3: Several classes in the Java Collections Framework.

7.5.1 List Iterators in Java

The java.util.LinkedList class does not expose a position concept to users in its API, as we do in our positional list ADT. Instead, the preferred way to access and update a LinkedList object in Java, without using indices, is to use a ListIterator that is returned by the list's listIterator() method. Such an iterator provides forward and backward traversal methods as well as local update methods. It views its current position as being before the first element, between two elements, or after the last element. That is, it uses a list *cursor*, much like a screen cursor is viewed as being located between two characters on a screen. Specifically, the java.util.ListIterator interface includes the following methods:

add(e): Adds the element e at the current position of the iterator.

hasNext(): Returns true if there is an element after the current position of the iterator.

hasPrevious(): Returns true if there is an element before the current position of the iterator.

previous(): Returns the element e before the current position and sets the current position to be before e.

next(): Returns the element e after the current position and sets the current position to be after e.

nextIndex(): Returns the index of the next element.

previousIndex(): Returns the index of the previous element.

remove(): Removes the element returned by the most recent next or previous operation.

set(e): Replaces the element returned by the most recent call to the next or previous operation with e.

It is risky to use multiple iterators over the same list while modifying its contents. If insertions, deletions, or replacements are required at multiple "places" in a list, it is safer to use positions to specify these locations. But the java.util.LinkedList class does not expose its position objects to the user. So, to avoid the risks of modifying a list that has created multiple iterators, the iterators have a "fail-fast" feature that invalidates such an iterator if its underlying collection is modified unexpectedly. For example, if a java.util.LinkedList object L has returned five different iterators and one of them modifies L, a ConcurrentModificationException is thrown if any of the other four is subsequently used. That is, Java allows many list iterators to be traversing a linked list L at the same time, but if one of them modifies L (using an add, set, or remove method), then all the other iterators for L become invalid. Likewise, if L is modified by one of its own update methods, then all existing iterators for L immediately become invalid.

7.5.2   Comparison to Our Positional List ADT

Java provides functionality similar to our array list and positional lists ADT in the java.util.List interface, which is implemented with an array in java.util.ArrayList and with a linked list in java.util.LinkedList.

Moreover, Java uses iterators to achieve a functionality similar to what our positional list ADT derives from positions. Table 7.4 shows corresponding methods between our (array and positional) list ADTs and the java.util interfaces List and ListIterator interfaces, with notes about their implementations in the java.util classes ArrayList and LinkedList.

Positional List ADT Method	java.util.List Method	ListIterator Method	Notes
size( )	size( )		$O(1)$ time
isEmpty( )	isEmpty( )		$O(1)$ time
	get(i)		A is $O(1)$, L is $O(\min\{i, n-i\})$
first( )	listIterator( )		first element is next
last( )	listIterator(size( ))		last element is previous
before(p)		previous( )	$O(1)$ time
after(p)		next( )	$O(1)$ time
set(p, e)		set(e)	$O(1)$ time
	set(i, e)		A is $O(1)$, L is $O(\min\{i, n-i\})$
	add(i, e)		$O(n)$ time
addFirst(e)	add(0, e)		A is $O(n)$, L is $O(1)$
addFirst(e)	addFirst(e)		only exists in L, $O(1)$
addLast(e)	add(e)		$O(1)$ time
addLast(e)	addLast(e)		only exists in L, $O(1)$
addAfter(p, e)		add(e)	insertion is at cursor; A is $O(n)$, L is $O(1)$
addBefore(p, e)		add(e)	insertion is at cursor; A is $O(n)$, L is $O(1)$
remove(p)		remove( )	deletion is at cursor; A is $O(n)$, L is $O(1)$
	remove(i)		A is $O(1)$, L is $O(\min\{i, n-i\})$

Table 7.4: Correspondences between methods in our positional list ADT and the java.util interfaces List and ListIterator. We use A and L as abbreviations for java.util.ArrayList and java.util.LinkedList (or their running times).

7.5.3   List-Based Algorithms in the Java Collections Framework

In addition to the classes that are provided in the Java Collections Framework, there are a number of simple algorithms that it provides as well. These algorithms are implemented as static methods in the java.util.Collections class (not to be confused with the java.util.Collection interface) and they include the following methods:

copy(L_{dest}, L_{src}): Copies all elements of the L_{src} list into corresponding indices of the L_{dest} list.

disjoint(C, D): Returns a boolean value indicating whether the collections C and D are disjoint.

fill(L, e): Replaces each element of the list L with element e.

frequency(C, e): Returns the number of elements in the collection C that are equal to e.

max(C): Returns the maximum element in the collection C, based on the natural ordering of its elements.

min(C): Returns the minimum element in the collection C, based on the natural ordering of its elements.

replaceAll(L, e, f): Replaces each element in L that is equal to e with element f.

reverse(L): Reverses the ordering of elements in the list L.

rotate(L, d): Rotates the elements in the list L by the distance d (which can be negative), in a circular fashion.

shuffle(L): Pseudorandomly permutes the ordering of the elements in the list L.

sort(L): Sorts the list L, using the natural ordering of its elements.

swap(L, i, j): Swap the elements at indices i and j of list L.

Converting Lists into Arrays

Lists are a beautiful concept and they can be applied in a number of different contexts, but there are some instances where it would be useful if we could treat a list like an array. Fortunately, the java.util.Collection interface includes the following helpful methods for generating an array that has the same elements as the given collection:

toArray( ): Returns an array of elements of type Object containing all the elements in this collection.

toArray(A): Returns an array of elements of the same element type as A containing all the elements in this collection.

If the collection is a list, then the returned array will have its elements stored in the same order as that of the original list. Thus, if we have a useful array-based method that we want to use on a list or other type of collection, then we can do so by simply using that collection's toArray( ) method to produce an array representation of that collection.

Converting Arrays into Lists

In a similar vein, it is often useful to be able to convert an array into an equivalent list. Fortunately, the java.util.Arrays class includes the following method:

asList(A): Returns a list representation of the array A, with the same element type as the elements of A.

The list returned by this method uses the array A as its internal representation for the list. So this list is guaranteed to be an array-based list and any changes made to it will automatically be reflected in A. Because of these types of side effects, use of the asList method should always be done with caution, so as to avoid unintended consequences. But, used with care, this method can often save us a lot of work. For instance, the following code fragment could be used to randomly shuffle an array of Integer objects, arr:

```
Integer[ ] arr = {1, 2, 3, 4, 5, 6, 7, 8};        // allowed by autoboxing
List<Integer> listArr = Arrays.asList(arr);
Collections.shuffle(listArr);                     // this has side effect of shuffling arr
```

It is worth noting that the array A sent to the asList method should be a reference type (hence, our use of Integer rather than **int** in the above example). This is because the List interface is generic, and requires that the element type be an object.

7.6 Sorting a Positional List

In Section 3.1.2, we introduced the *insertion-sort* algorithm in the context of an array-based sequence. In this section, we develop an implementation that operates on a PositionalList, relying on the same high-level algorithm in which each element is placed relative to a growing collection of previously sorted elements.

We maintain a variable named marker that represents the rightmost position of the currently sorted portion of a list. During each pass, we consider the position just past the marker as the pivot and consider where the pivot's element belongs relative to the sorted portion; we use another variable, named walk, to move leftward from the marker, as long as there remains a preceding element with value larger than the pivot's. A typical configuration of these variables is diagrammed in Figure 7.9. A Java implementation of this strategy is given in Code 7.15.

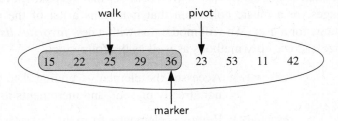

Figure 7.9: Overview of one step of our insertion-sort algorithm. The shaded elements, those up to and including marker, have already been sorted. In this step, the pivot's element should be relocated immediately before the walk position.

```
1   /** Insertion-sort of a positional list of integers into nondecreasing order */
2   public static void insertionSort(PositionalList<Integer> list) {
3       Position<Integer> marker = list.first();        // last position known to be sorted
4       while (marker != list.last()) {
5           Position<Integer> pivot = list.after(marker);
6           int value = pivot.getElement();              // number to be placed
7           if (value > marker.getElement())             // pivot is already sorted
8               marker = pivot;
9           else {                                        // must relocate pivot
10              Position<Integer> walk = marker;         // find leftmost item greater than value
11              while (walk != list.first() && list.before(walk).getElement() > value)
12                  walk = list.before(walk);
13              list.remove(pivot);                       // remove pivot entry and
14              list.addBefore(walk, value);              // reinsert value in front of walk
15          }
16      }
17  }
```

Code Fragment 7.15: Java code for performing insertion-sort on a positional list.

7.7 Case Study: Maintaining Access Frequencies

The positional list ADT is useful in a number of settings. For example, a program that simulates a game of cards could model each person's hand as a positional list (Exercise P-7.60). Since most people keep cards of the same suit together, inserting and removing cards from a person's hand could be implemented using the methods of the positional list ADT, with the positions being determined by a natural order of the suits. Likewise, a simple text editor embeds the notion of positional insertion and deletion, since such editors typically perform all updates relative to a ***cursor***, which represents the current position in the list of characters of text being edited.

In this section, we will consider maintaining a collection of elements while keeping track of the number of times each element is accessed. Keeping such access counts allows us to know which elements are among the most popular. Examples of such scenarios include a Web browser that keeps track of a user's most accessed pages, or a music collection that maintains a list of the most frequently played songs for a user. We will model this with a new ***favorites list ADT*** that supports the size and isEmpty methods as well as the following:

access(e): Accesses the element e, adding it to the favorites list if it is not already present, and increments its access count.

remove(e): Removes element e from the favorites list, if present.

getFavorites(k): Returns an iterable collection of the k most accessed elements.

7.7.1 Using a Sorted List

Our first approach for managing a list of favorites is to store elements in a linked list, keeping them in nonincreasing order of access counts. We access or remove an element by searching the list from the most frequently accessed to the least frequently accessed. Reporting the k most accessed elements is easy, as they are the first k entries of the list.

To maintain the invariant that elements are stored in nonincreasing order of access counts, we must consider how a single access operation may affect the order. The accessed element's count increases by one, and so it may become larger than one or more of its preceding neighbors in the list, thereby violating the invariant.

Fortunately, we can reestablish the sorted invariant using a technique similar to a single pass of the insertion-sort algorithm, introduced in the previous section. We can perform a backward traversal of the list, starting at the position of the element whose access count has increased, until we locate a valid position after which the element can be relocated.

Using the Composition Pattern

We wish to implement a favorites list by making use of a PositionalList for storage. If elements of the positional list were simply elements of the favorites list, we would be challenged to maintain access counts and to keep the proper count with the associated element as the contents of the list are reordered. We use a general object-oriented design pattern, the ***composition pattern***, in which we define a single object that is composed of two or more other objects. (See, for example, Section 2.5.2.)

Specifically, we define a nonpublic nested class, Item, that stores the element and its access count as a single instance. We then maintain our favorites list as a PositionalList of *item* instances, so that the access count for a user's element is embedded alongside it in our representation. (An Item is never exposed to a user of a FavoritesList.)

```
1  /** Maintains a list of elements ordered according to access frequency. */
2  public class FavoritesList<E> {
3    // ---------------- nested Item class ----------------
4    protected static class Item<E> {
5      private E value;
6      private int count = 0;
7      /** Constructs new item with initial count of zero. */
8      public Item(E val) { value = val; }
9      public int getCount() { return count; }
10     public E getValue() { return value; }
11     public void increment() { count++; }
12   } //----------- end of nested Item class -----------
13
14   PositionalList<Item<E>> list = new LinkedPositionalList<>();    // list of Items
15   public FavoritesList() { }                          // constructs initially empty favorites list
16
17   // nonpublic utilities
18   /** Provides shorthand notation to retrieve user's element stored at Position p. */
19   protected E value(Position<Item<E>> p) { return p.getElement().getValue(); }
20
21   /** Provides shorthand notation to retrieve count of item stored at Position p. */
22   protected int count(Position<Item<E>> p) {return p.getElement().getCount();}
23
24   /** Returns Position having element equal to e (or null if not found). */
25   protected Position<Item<E>> findPosition(E e) {
26     Position<Item<E>> walk = list.first();
27     while (walk != null && !e.equals(value(walk)))
28       walk = list.after(walk);
29     return walk;
30   }
```

Code Fragment 7.16: Class FavoritesList. (Continues in Code Fragment 7.17.)

```
31    /** Moves item at Position p earlier in the list based on access count. */
32    protected void moveUp(Position<Item<E>> p) {
33      int cnt = count(p);                              // revised count of accessed item
34      Position<Item<E>> walk = p;
35      while (walk != list.first( ) && count(list.before(walk)) < cnt)
36        walk = list.before(walk);                      // found smaller count ahead of item
37      if (walk != p)
38        list.addBefore(walk, list.remove(p));          // remove/reinsert item
39    }
40
41    // public methods
42    /** Returns the number of items in the favorites list. */
43    public int size( ) { return list.size( ); }
44
45    /** Returns true if the favorites list is empty. */
46    public boolean isEmpty( ) { return list.isEmpty( ); }
47
48    /** Accesses element e (possibly new), increasing its access count. */
49    public void access(E e) {
50      Position<Item<E>> p = findPosition(e);           // try to locate existing element
51      if (p == null)
52        p = list.addLast(new Item<E>(e));              // if new, place at end
53      p.getElement( ).increment( );                    // always increment count
54      moveUp(p);                                       // consider moving forward
55    }
56
57    /** Removes element equal to e from the list of favorites (if found). */
58    public void remove(E e) {
59      Position<Item<E>> p = findPosition(e);           // try to locate existing element
60      if (p != null)
61        list.remove(p);
62    }
63
64    /** Returns an iterable collection of the k most frequently accessed elements. */
65    public Iterable<E> getFavorites(int k) throws IllegalArgumentException {
66      if (k < 0 || k > size( ))
67        throw new IllegalArgumentException("Invalid k");
68      PositionalList<E> result = new LinkedPositionalList<>( );
69      Iterator<Item<E>> iter = list.iterator( );
70      for (int j=0; j < k; j++)
71        result.addLast(iter.next( ).getValue( ));
72      return result;
73    }
74  }
```

Code Fragment 7.17: Class FavoritesList. (Continued from Code Fragment 7.16.)

7.7.2   Using a List with the Move-to-Front Heuristic

The previous implementation of a favorites list performs the access(e) method in time proportional to the index of e in the favorites list. That is, if e is the kth most popular element in the favorites list, then accessing it takes $O(k)$ time. In many real-life access sequences (e.g., Web pages visited by a user), once an element is accessed it is more likely to be accessed again in the near future. Such scenarios are said to possess *locality of reference*.

A *heuristic*, or rule of thumb, that attempts to take advantage of the locality of reference that is present in an access sequence is the *move-to-front heuristic*. To apply this heuristic, each time we access an element we move it all the way to the front of the list. Our hope, of course, is that this element will be accessed again in the near future. Consider, for example, a scenario in which we have n elements and the following series of n^2 accesses:

- element 1 is accessed n times.
- element 2 is accessed n times.
- ...
- element n is accessed n times.

If we store the elements sorted by their access counts, inserting each element the first time it is accessed, then

- each access to element 1 runs in $O(1)$ time.
- each access to element 2 runs in $O(2)$ time.
- ...
- each access to element n runs in $O(n)$ time.

Thus, the total time for performing the series of accesses is proportional to

$$n + 2n + 3n + \cdots + n \cdot n = n(1 + 2 + 3 + \cdots + n) = n \cdot \frac{n(n+1)}{2},$$

which is $O(n^3)$.

On the other hand, if we use the move-to-front heuristic, inserting each element the first time it is accessed, then

- each subsequent access to element 1 takes $O(1)$ time.
- each subsequent access to element 2 takes $O(1)$ time.
- ...
- each subsequent access to element n runs in $O(1)$ time.

So the running time for performing all the accesses in this case is $O(n^2)$. Thus, the move-to-front implementation has faster access times for this scenario. Still, the move-to-front approach is just a heuristic, for there are access sequences where using the move-to-front approach is slower than simply keeping the favorites list ordered by access counts.

The Trade-Offs with the Move-to-Front Heuristic

If we no longer maintain the elements of the favorites list ordered by their access counts, when we are asked to find the k most accessed elements, we need to search for them. We will implement the getFavorites(k) method as follows:

1. We copy all entries of our favorites list into another list, named temp.

2. We scan the temp list k times. In each scan, we find the entry with the largest access count, remove this entry from temp, and add it to the results.

This implementation of method getFavorites(k) takes $O(kn)$ time. Thus, when k is a constant, method getFavorites(k) runs in $O(n)$ time. This occurs, for example, when we want to get the "top ten" list. However, if k is proportional to n, then the method getFavorites(k) runs in $O(n^2)$ time. This occurs, for example, when we want a "top 25%" list.

In Chapter 9 we will introduce a data structure that will allow us to implement getFavorites in $O(n + k \log n)$ time (see Exercise P-9.51), and more advanced techniques could be used to perform getFavorites in $O(n + k \log k)$ time.

We could easily achieve $O(n \log n)$ time if we use a standard sorting algorithm to reorder the temporary list before reporting the top k (see Chapter 12); this approach would be preferred to the original in the case that k is $\Omega(\log n)$. (Recall the big-Omega notation introduced in Section 4.3.1 to give an asymptotic lower bound on the running time of an algorithm.) There is a specialized sorting algorithm (see Section 12.3.2) that can take advantage of the fact that access counts are integers in order to achieve $O(n)$ time for getFavorites, for any value of k.

Implementing the Move-to-Front Heuristic in Java

We give an implementation of a favorites list using the move-to-front heuristic in Code Fragment 7.18. The new FavoritesListMTF class inherits most of its functionality from the original FavoritesList as a base class.

By our original design, the access method of the original class relies on a protected utility named moveUp to enact the potential shifting of an element forward in the list, after its access count had been incremented. Therefore, we implement the move-to-front heuristic by simply overriding the moveUp method so that each accessed element is moved directly to the front of the list (if not already there). This action is easily implemented by means of the positional list ADT.

The more complex portion of our FavoritesListMTF class is the new definition for the getFavorites method. We rely on the first of the approaches outlined above, inserting copies of the items into a temporary list and then repeatedly finding, reporting, and removing an element that has the largest access count of those remaining.

```
1   /** Maintains a list of elements ordered with move-to-front heuristic. */
2   public class FavoritesListMTF<E> extends FavoritesList<E> {
3
4     /** Moves accessed item at Position p to the front of the list. */
5     protected void moveUp(Position<Item<E>> p) {
6       if (p != list.first())
7         list.addFirst(list.remove(p));                          // remove/reinsert item
8     }
9
10    /** Returns an iterable collection of the k most frequently accessed elements. */
11    public Iterable<E> getFavorites(int k) throws IllegalArgumentException {
12      if (k < 0 || k > size())
13        throw new IllegalArgumentException("Invalid k");
14
15      // we begin by making a copy of the original list
16      PositionalList<Item<E>> temp = new LinkedPositionalList<>();
17      for (Item<E> item : list)
18        temp.addLast(item);
19
20      // we repeated find, report, and remove element with largest count
21      PositionalList<E> result = new LinkedPositionalList<>();
22      for (int j=0; j < k; j++) {
23        Position<Item<E>> highPos = temp.first();
24        Position<Item<E>> walk = temp.after(highPos);
25        while (walk != null) {
26          if (count(walk) > count(highPos))
27            highPos = walk;
28          walk = temp.after(walk);
29        }
30        // we have now found element with highest count
31        result.addLast(value(highPos));
32        temp.remove(highPos);
33      }
34      return result;
35    }
36  }
```

Code Fragment 7.18: Class FavoritesListMTF implementing the move-to-front heuristic. This class extends FavoritesList (Code Fragments 7.16 and 7.17) and overrides methods moveUp and getFavorites.

7.8   Exercises

Reinforcement

R-7.1   Draw a representation, akin to Example 7.1, of an initially empty list L after performing the following sequence of operations: add(0, 4), add(0, 3), add(0, 2), add(2, 1), add(1, 5), add(1, 6), add(3, 7), add(0, 8).

R-7.2   Give an implementation of the stack ADT using an array list for storage.

R-7.3   Give an implementation of the deque ADT using an array list for storage.

R-7.4   Give a justification of the running times shown in Table 7.1 for the methods of an array list implemented with a (nonexpanding) array.

R-7.5   The java.util.ArrayList includes a method, trimToSize( ), that replaces the underlying array with one whose capacity precisely equals the number of elements currently in the list. Implement such a method for our dynamic version of the ArrayList class from Section 7.2.

R-7.6   Redo the justification of Proposition 7.2 assuming that the the cost of growing the array from size k to size $2k$ is $3k$ cyber-dollars. How much should each push operation be charged to make the amortization work?

R-7.7   Consider an implementation of the array list ADT using a dynamic array, but instead of copying the elements into an array of double the size (that is, from N to $2N$) when its capacity is reached, we copy the elements into an array with $\lceil N/4 \rceil$ additional cells, going from capacity N to $N + \lceil N/4 \rceil$. Show that performing a sequence of n push operations (that is, insertions at the end) still runs in $O(n)$ time in this case.

R-7.8   Suppose we are maintaining a collection C of elements such that, each time we add a new element to the collection, we copy the contents of C into a new array list of just the right size. What is the running time of adding n elements to an initially empty collection C in this case?

R-7.9   The add method for a dynamic array, as described in Code Fragment 7.5, has the following inefficiency. In the case when a resize occurs, the resize operation takes time to copy all the elements from the old array to a new array, and then the subsequent loop in the body of add shifts some of them to make room for a new element. Give an improved implementation of the add method, so that, in the case of a resize, the elements are copied into their final place in the new array (that is, no shifting is done).

R-7.10   Reimplement the ArrayStack class, from Section 6.1.2, using dynamic arrays to support unlimited capacity.

R-7.11   Describe an implementation of the positional list methods addLast and addBefore realized by using only methods in the set {isEmpty, first, last, before, after, addAfter, addFirst}.

R-7.12 Suppose we want to extend the PositionalList abstract data type with a method, indexOf(p), that returns the current index of the element stored at position p. Show how to implement this method using only other methods of the Positional-List interface (not details of our LinkedPositionalList implementation).

R-7.13 Suppose we want to extend the PositionalList abstract data type with a method, findPosition(e), that returns the first position containing an element equal to e (or null if no such position exists). Show how to implement this method using only existing methods of the PositionalList interface (not details of our LinkedPositionalList implementation).

R-7.14 The LinkedPositionalList implementation of Code Fragments 7.9–7.12 does not do any error checking to test if a given position p is actually a member of the relevant list. Give a detailed explanation of the effect of a call L.addAfter(p, e) on a list L, yet with a position p that belongs to some other list M.

R-7.15 To better model a FIFO queue in which entries may be deleted before reaching the front, design a LinkedPositionalQueue class that supports the complete queue ADT, yet with enqueue returning a position instance and support for a new method, remove(p), that removes the element associated with position p from the queue. You may use the adapter design pattern (Section 6.1.3), using a LinkedPositionalList as your storage.

R-7.16 Describe how to implement a method, alternateIterator( ), for a positional list that returns an iterator that reports only those elements having even index in the list.

R-7.17 Redesign the Progression class, from Section 2.2.3, so that it formally implements the Iterator<long> interface.

R-7.18 The java.util.Collection interface includes a method, contains(o), that returns true if the collection contains any object that equals Object o. Implement such a method in the ArrayList class of Section 7.2.

R-7.19 The java.util.Collection interface includes a method, clear( ), that removes all elements from a collection. Implement such a method in the ArrayList class of Section 7.2.

R-7.20 Demonstrate how to use the java.util.Colletions.reverse method to reverse an array of objects.

R-7.21 Given the set of element $\{a,b,c,d,e,f\}$ stored in a list, show the final state of the list, assuming we use the move-to-front heuristic and access the elements according to the following sequence: $(a,b,c,d,e,f,a,c,f,b,d,e)$.

R-7.22 Suppose that we have made kn total accesses to the elements in a list L of n elements, for some integer $k \geq 1$. What are the minimum and maximum number of elements that have been accessed fewer than k times?

R-7.23 Let L be a list of n items maintained according to the move-to-front heuristic. Describe a series of $O(n)$ accesses that will reverse L.

R-7.24 Implement a resetCounts( ) method for the FavoritesList class that resets all elements' access counts to zero (while leaving the order of the list unchanged).

Creativity

C-7.25　Give an array-based list implementation, with fixed capacity, treating the array circularly so that it achieves $O(1)$ time for insertions and removals at index 0, as well as insertions and removals at the end of the array list. Your implementation should also provide for a constant-time get method.

C-7.26　Complete the previous exercise, except using a dynamic array to provide unbounded capacity.

C-7.27　Modify our ArrayList implementation to support the Cloneable interface, as described in Section 3.6.

C-7.28　In Section 7.5.3, we demonstrated how the Collections.shuffle method can be adapted to shuffle a reference-type array. Give a direct implementation of a shuffle method for an array of **int** values. You may use the method, nextInt(n) of the Random class, which returns a random number between 0 and $n - 1$, inclusive. Your method should guarantee that every possible ordering is equally likely. What is the running time of your method?

C-7.29　Revise the array list implementation given in Section 7.2.1 so that when the actual number of elements, n, in the array goes below $N/4$, where N is the array capacity, the array shrinks to half its size.

C-7.30　Prove that when using a dynamic array that grows and shrinks as in the previous exercise, the following series of $2n$ operations takes $O(n)$ time: n insertions at the end of an initially empty list, followed by n deletions, each from the end of the list.

C-7.31　Give a formal proof that any sequence of n push or pop operations (that is, insertions or deletions at the end) on an initially empty dynamic array takes $O(n)$ time, if using the strategy described in Exercise C-7.29.

C-7.32　Consider a variant of Exercise C-7.29, in which an array of capacity N is resized to capacity precisely that of the number of elements, any time the number of elements in the array goes strictly below $N/4$. Give a formal proof that any sequence of n push or pop operations on an initially empty dynamic array takes $O(n)$ time.

C-7.33　Consider a variant of Exercise C-7.29, in which an array of capacity N, is resized to capacity precisely that of the number of elements, any time the number of elements in the array goes strictly below $N/2$. Show that there exists a sequence of n push and pop operations that requires $\Omega(n^2)$ time to execute.

C-7.34　Describe how to implement the queue ADT using two stacks as instance variables, such that all queue operations execute in amortized $O(1)$ time. Give a formal proof of the amortized bound.

C-7.35　Reimplement the ArrayQueue class, from Section 6.2.2, using dynamic arrays to support unlimited capacity. Be especially careful about the treatment of a circular array when resizing.

C-7.36 Suppose we want to extend the PositionalList interface to include a method, positionAtIndex(i), that returns the position of the element having index i (or throws an IndexOutOfBoundsException, if warranted). Show how to implement this method, using only existing methods of the PositionalList interface, by traversing the appropriate number of steps from the front of the list.

C-7.37 Repeat the previous problem, but use knowledge of the size of the list to traverse from the end of the list that is closest to the desired index.

C-7.38 Explain how any implementation of the PositionalList ADT can be made to support all methods of the List ADT, described in Section 7.1, assuming an implementation is given for the positionAtIndex(i) method, proposed in Exercise C-7.36.

C-7.39 Suppose we want to extend the PositionalList abstract data type with a method, moveToFront(p), that moves the element at position p to the front of a list (if not already there), while keeping the relative order of the remaining elements unchanged. Show how to implement this method using only existing methods of the PositionalList interface (not details of our LinkedPositionalList implementation).

C-7.40 Redo the previous problem, but providing an implementation within the class LinkedPositionalList that does not create or destroy any nodes.

C-7.41 Modify our LinkedPositionalList implementation to support the Cloneable interface, as described in Section 3.6.

C-7.42 Describe a nonrecursive method for reversing a positional list represented with a doubly linked list using a single pass through the list.

C-7.43 Page 281 describes an *array-based* representation for implementing the positional list ADT. Give a pseudocode description of the addBefore method for that representation.

C-7.44 Describe a method for performing a ***card shuffle*** of a list of $2n$ elements, by converting it into two lists. A card shuffle is a permutation where a list L is cut into two lists, L_1 and L_2, where L_1 is the first half of L and L_2 is the second half of L, and then these two lists are merged into one by taking the first element in L_1, then the first element in L_2, followed by the second element in L_1, the second element in L_2, and so on.

C-7.45 How might the LinkedPositionalList class be redesigned to detect the error described in Exercise R-7.14.

C-7.46 Modify the LinkedPositionalList class to support a method swap(p, q) that causes the underlying nodes referenced by positions p and q to be exchanged for each other. Relink the existing nodes; do not create any new nodes.

C-7.47 An array is ***sparse*** if most of its entries are **null**. A list L can be used to implement such an array, A, efficiently. In particular, for each nonnull cell $A[i]$, we can store a pair (i, e) in L, where e is the element stored at $A[i]$. This approach allows us to represent A using $O(m)$ storage, where m is the number of nonnull entries in A. Describe and analyze efficient ways of performing the methods of the array list ADT on such a representation.

C-7.48 Design a circular positional list ADT that abstracts a circularly linked list in the same way that the positional list ADT abstracts a doubly linked list.

C-7.49 Provide an implementation of the listiterator( ) method, in the context of the class LinkedPositionalList, that returns an object that supports the java.util.ListIterator interface described in Section 7.5.1.

C-7.50 Describe a scheme for creating list iterators that *fail fast*, that is, they all become invalid as soon as the underlying list changes.

C-7.51 There is a simple algorithm, called ***bubble-sort***, for sorting a list L of n comparable elements. This algorithm scans the list $n-1$ times, where, in each scan, the algorithm compares the current element with the next one and swaps them if they are out of order. Give a pseudocode description of bubble-sort that is as efficient as possible assuming L is implemented with a doubly linked list. What is the running time of this algorithm?

C-7.52 Redo Exercise C-7.51 assuming L is implemented with an array list.

C-7.53 Describe an efficient method for maintaining a favorites list L, with the move-to-front heuristic, such that elements that have not been accessed in the most recent n accesses are automatically purged from the list.

C-7.54 Suppose we have an n-element list L maintained according to the move-to-front heuristic. Describe a sequence of n^2 accesses that is guaranteed to take $\Omega(n^3)$ time to perform on L.

C-7.55 A useful operation in databases is the ***natural join***. If we view a database as a list of *ordered* pairs of objects, then the natural join of databases A and B is the list of all ordered triples (x, y, z) such that the pair (x, y) is in A and the pair (y, z) is in B. Describe and analyze an efficient algorithm for computing the natural join of a list A of n pairs and a list B of m pairs.

C-7.56 When Bob wants to send Alice a message M on the Internet, he breaks M into n ***data packets***, numbers the packets consecutively, and injects them into the network. When the packets arrive at Alice's computer, they may be out of order, so Alice must assemble the sequence of n packets in order before she can be sure she has the entire message. Describe an efficient scheme for Alice to do this. What is the running time of this algorithm?

C-7.57 Implement the FavoritesList class using an array list.

Projects

P-7.58 Develop an experiment, using techniques similar to those in Section 4.1, to test the efficiency of n successive calls to the add method of an ArrayList, for various n, under each of the following three scenarios:

    a. Each add takes place at index 0.
    b. Each add takes place at index size( )/2.
    c. Each add takes place at index size( ).

Analyze your empirical results.

P-7.59 Reimplement the LinkedPositionalList class so that an invalid position is reported in a scenario such as the one described in Exercise R-7.14.

P-7.60 Implement a CardHand class that supports a person arranging a group of cards in his or her hand. The simulator should represent the sequence of cards using a single positional list ADT so that cards of the same suit are kept together. Implement this strategy by means of four "fingers" into the hand, one for each of the suits of hearts, clubs, spades, and diamonds, so that adding a new card to the person's hand or playing a correct card from the hand can be done in constant time. The class should support the following methods:

- addCard(r, s): Add a new card with rank r and suit s to the hand.
- play(s): Remove and return a card of suit s from the player's hand; if there is no card of suit s, then remove and return an arbitrary card from the hand.
- iterator( ): Return an iterator for all cards currently in the hand.
- suitIterator(s): Return an iterator for all cards of suit s that are currently in the hand.

P-7.61 Write a simple text editor, which stores and displays a string of characters using the positional list ADT, together with a cursor object that highlights a position in the string. The editor must support the following operations:

- left: Move cursor left one character (do nothing if at beginning).
- right: Move cursor right one character (do nothing if at end).
- insert c: Insert the character c just after the cursor.
- delete: Delete the character just after the cursor (if not at end).

Chapter Notes

The treatment of data structures as collections (and other principles of object-oriented design) can be found in object-oriented design books by Booch [16], Budd [19], and Liskov and Guttag [67]. Lists and iterators are pervasive concepts in the Java Collections Framework. Our positional list ADT is derived from the "position" abstraction introduced by Aho, Hopcroft, and Ullman [6], and the list ADT of Wood [96]. Implementations of lists via arrays and linked lists are discussed by Knuth [60].

Chapter
8

Trees

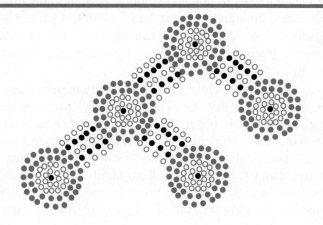

Contents

8.1   General Trees

Productivity experts say that breakthroughs come by thinking "nonlinearly." In this chapter, we will discuss one of the most important nonlinear data structures in computing—***trees***. Tree structures are indeed a breakthrough in data organization, for they allow us to implement a host of algorithms much faster than when using linear data structures, such as arrays or linked lists. Trees also provide a natural organization for data, and consequently have become ubiquitous structures in file systems, graphical user interfaces, databases, websites, and many other computer systems.

It is not always clear what productivity experts mean by "nonlinear" thinking, but when we say that trees are "nonlinear," we are referring to an organizational relationship that is richer than the simple "before" and "after" relationships between objects in sequences. The relationships in a tree are ***hierarchical***, with some objects being "above" and some "below" others. Actually, the main terminology for tree data structures comes from family trees, with the terms "parent," "child," "ancestor," and "descendant" being the most common words used to describe relationships. We show an example of a family tree in Figure 8.1.

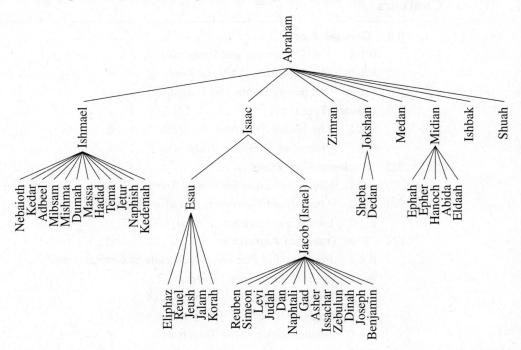

Figure 8.1: A family tree showing some descendants of Abraham, as recorded in Genesis, chapters 25–36.

8.1.1 Tree Definitions and Properties

A *tree* is an abstract data type that stores elements hierarchically. With the exception of the top element, each element in a tree has a *parent* element and zero or more *children* elements. A tree is usually visualized by placing elements inside ovals or rectangles, and by drawing the connections between parents and children with straight lines. (See Figure 8.2.) We typically call the top element the *root* of the tree, but it is drawn as the highest element, with the other elements being connected below (just the opposite of a botanical tree).

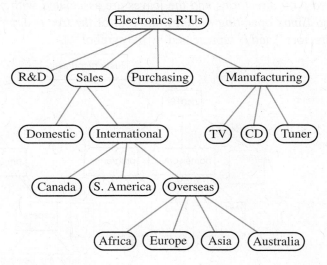

Figure 8.2: A tree with 17 nodes representing the organization of a fictitious corporation. The root stores *Electronics R'Us*. The children of the root store *R&D*, *Sales*, *Purchasing*, and *Manufacturing*. The internal nodes store *Sales*, *International*, *Overseas*, *Electronics R'Us*, and *Manufacturing*.

Formal Tree Definition

Formally, we define a *tree* T as a set of *nodes* storing elements such that the nodes have a *parent-child* relationship that satisfies the following properties:

- If T is nonempty, it has a special node, called the *root* of T, that has no parent.
- Each node v of T different from the root has a unique *parent* node w; every node with parent w is a *child* of w.

Note that according to our definition, a tree can be empty, meaning that it does not have any nodes. This convention also allows us to define a tree recursively such that a tree T is either empty or consists of a node r, called the root of T, and a (possibly empty) set of subtrees whose roots are the children of r.

Other Node Relationships

Two nodes that are children of the same parent are **siblings**. A node v is **external** if v has no children. A node v is **internal** if it has one or more children. External nodes are also known as **leaves**.

Example 8.1: *In Section 5.1.4, we discussed the hierarchical relationship between files and directories in a computer's file system, although at the time we did not emphasize the nomenclature of a file system as a tree. In Figure 8.3, we revisit an earlier example. We see that the internal nodes of the tree are associated with directories and the leaves are associated with regular files. In the Unix and Linux operating systems, the root of the tree is appropriately called the "root directory," and is represented by the symbol "/."*

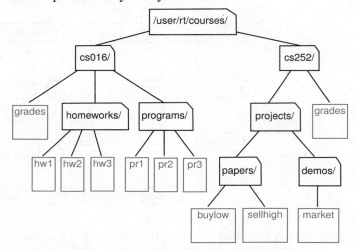

Figure 8.3: Tree representing a portion of a file system.

A node u is an **ancestor** of a node v if $u = v$ or u is an ancestor of the parent of v. Conversely, we say that a node v is a **descendant** of a node u if u is an ancestor of v. For example, in Figure 8.3, cs252/ is an ancestor of papers/, and pr3 is a descendant of cs016/. The **subtree** of T **rooted** at a node v is the tree consisting of all the descendants of v in T (including v itself). In Figure 8.3, the subtree rooted at cs016/ consists of the nodes cs016/, grades, homeworks/, programs/, hw1, hw2, hw3, pr1, pr2, and pr3.

Edges and Paths in Trees

An **edge** of tree T is a pair of nodes (u, v) such that u is the parent of v, or vice versa. A **path** of T is a sequence of nodes such that any two consecutive nodes in the sequence form an edge. For example, the tree in Figure 8.3 contains the path (cs252/, projects/, demos/, market).

Ordered Trees

A tree is ***ordered*** if there is a meaningful linear order among the children of each node; that is, we purposefully identify the children of a node as being the first, second, third, and so on. Such an order is usually visualized by arranging siblings left to right, according to their order.

Example 8.2: *The components of a structured document, such as a book, are hierarchically organized as a tree whose internal nodes are parts, chapters, and sections, and whose leaves are paragraphs, tables, figures, and so on. (See Figure 8.4.) The root of the tree corresponds to the book itself. We could, in fact, consider expanding the tree further to show paragraphs consisting of sentences, sentences consisting of words, and words consisting of characters. Such a tree is an example of an ordered tree, because there is a well-defined order among the children of each node.*

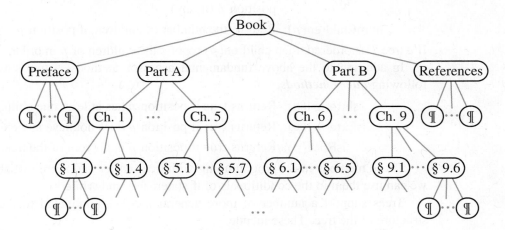

Figure 8.4: An ordered tree associated with a book.

Let's look back at the other examples of trees that we have described thus far, and consider whether the order of children is significant. A family tree that describes generational relationships, as in Figure 8.1, is often modeled as an ordered tree, with siblings ordered according to their birth.

In contrast, an organizational chart for a company, as in Figure 8.2, is typically considered an unordered tree. Likewise, when using a tree to describe an inheritance hierarchy, as in Figure 2.7, there is no particular significance to the order among the subclasses of a parent class. Finally, we consider the use of a tree in modeling a computer's file system, as in Figure 8.3. Although an operating system often displays entries of a directory in a particular order (e.g., alphabetical, chronological), such an order is not typically inherent to the file system's representation.

8.1.2   The Tree Abstract Data Type

As we did with positional lists in Section 7.3, we define a tree ADT using the concept of a *position* as an abstraction for a node of a tree. An element is stored at each position, and positions satisfy parent-child relationships that define the tree structure. A position object for a tree supports the method:

getElement( ): Returns the element stored at this position.

The tree ADT then supports the following *accessor methods*, allowing a user to navigate the various positions of a tree T:

root( ): Returns the position of the root of the tree (or null if empty).

parent(p): Returns the position of the parent of position p (or null if p is the root).

children(p): Returns an iterable collection containing the children of position p (if any).

numChildren(p): Returns the number of children of position p.

If a tree T is ordered, then children(p) reports the children of p in order.

In addition to the above fundamental accessor methods, a tree supports the following *query methods*:

isInternal(p): Returns true if position p has at least one child.

isExternal(p): Returns true if position p does not have any children.

isRoot(p): Returns true if position p is the root of the tree.

These methods make programming with trees easier and more readable, since we can use them in the conditionals of **if** statements and **while** loops.

Trees support a number of more general methods, unrelated to the specific structure of the tree. These incude:

size( ): Returns the number of positions (and hence elements) that are contained in the tree.

isEmpty( ): Returns true if the tree does not contain any positions (and thus no elements).

iterator( ): Returns an iterator for all elements in the tree (so that the tree itself is Iterable).

positions( ): Returns an iterable collection of all positions of the tree.

If an invalid position is sent as a parameter to any method of a tree, then an IllegalArgumentException is thrown.

We do not define any methods for creating or modifying trees at this point. We prefer to describe different tree update methods in conjunction with specific implementations of the tree interface, and specific applications of trees.

A Tree Interface in Java

In Code Fragment 8.1, we formalize the Tree ADT by defining the Tree interface in Java. We rely upon the same definition of the Position interface as introduced for positional lists in Section 7.3.2. Note well that we declare the Tree interface to formally extend Java's Iterable interface (and we include a declaration of the required iterator( ) method).

```
1  /** An interface for a tree where nodes can have an arbitrary number of children. */
2  public interface Tree<E> extends Iterable<E> {
3    Position<E> root( );
4    Position<E> parent(Position<E> p) throws IllegalArgumentException;
5    Iterable<Position<E>> children(Position<E> p)
6                                        throws IllegalArgumentException;
7    int numChildren(Position<E> p) throws IllegalArgumentException;
8    boolean isInternal(Position<E> p) throws IllegalArgumentException;
9    boolean isExternal(Position<E> p) throws IllegalArgumentException;
10   boolean isRoot(Position<E> p) throws IllegalArgumentException;
11   int size( );
12   boolean isEmpty( );
13   Iterator<E> iterator( );
14   Iterable<Position<E>> positions( );
15  }
```

Code Fragment 8.1: Definition of the Tree interface.

An AbstractTree Base Class in Java

In Section 2.3, we discussed the role of interfaces and abstract classes in Java. While an interface is a type definition that includes public declarations of various methods, an interface cannot include definitions for any of those methods. In contrast, an ***abstract class*** may define concrete implementations for some of its methods, while leaving other abstract methods without definition.

An abstract class is designed to serve as a base class, through inheritance, for one or more concrete implementations of an interface. When some of the functionality of an interface is implemented in an abstract class, less work remains to complete a concrete implementation. The standard Java libraries include many such abstract classes, including several within the Java Collections Framework. To make their purpose clear, those classes are conventionally named beginning with the word Abstract. For example, there is an AbstractCollection class that implements some of the functionality of the Collection interface, an AbstractQueue class that implements some of the functionality of the Queue interface, and an AbstractList class that implements some of the functionality of the List interface.

In the case of our Tree interface, we will define an AbstractTree base class, demonstrating how many tree-based algorithms can be described independently of the low-level representation of a tree data structure. In fact, if a concrete implementation provides three fundamental methods—root( ), parent(p), and children(p)—all other behaviors of the Tree interface can be derived within the AbstractTree base class.

Code Fragment 8.2 presents an initial implementation of an AbstractTree base class that provides the most trivial methods of the Tree interface. We will defer until Section 8.4 a discussion of general tree-traversal algorithms that can be used to produced the positions( ) iteration within the AbstractTree class. As with our positional list ADT in Chapter 7, the iteration of *positions* of the tree can easily be adapted to produce an iteration of the *elements* of a tree, or even to determine the size of a tree (although our concrete tree implementations will provide more direct means for reporting the size).

```
1  /** An abstract base class providing some functionality of the Tree interface. */
2  public abstract class AbstractTree<E> implements Tree<E> {
3    public boolean isInternal(Position<E> p) { return numChildren(p) > 0; }
4    public boolean isExternal(Position<E> p) { return numChildren(p) == 0; }
5    public boolean isRoot(Position<E> p) { return p == root(); }
6    public boolean isEmpty() { return size() == 0; }
7  }
```

Code Fragment 8.2: An initial implementation of the AbstractTree base class. (We add additional functionality to this class as the chapter continues.)

8.1.3 Computing Depth and Height

Let p be a position within tree T. The **depth** of p is the number of ancestors of p, other than p itself. For example, in the tree of Figure 8.2, the node storing *International* has depth 2. Note that this definition implies that the depth of the root of T is 0. The depth of p can also be recursively defined as follows:

- If p is the root, then the depth of p is 0.
- Otherwise, the depth of p is one plus the depth of the parent of p.

Based on this definition, we present a simple recursive algorithm, depth, in Code Fragment 8.3, for computing the depth of a position p in tree T. This method calls itself recursively on the parent of p, and adds 1 to the value returned.

The running time of depth(p) for position p is $O(d_p + 1)$, where d_p denotes the depth of p in the tree, because the algorithm performs a constant-time recursive step for each ancestor of p. Thus, algorithm depth(p) runs in $O(n)$ worst-case time, where n is the total number of positions of T, because a position of T may have depth $n - 1$ if all nodes form a single branch. Although such a running time is a function of the input size, it is more informative to characterize the running time in terms of the parameter d_p, as this parameter may be much smaller than n.

```
1    /** Returns the number of levels separating Position p from the root. */
2    public int depth(Position<E> p) {
3        if (isRoot(p))
4            return 0;
5        else
6            return 1 + depth(parent(p));
7    }
```

Code Fragment 8.3: Method depth, as implemented within the AbstractTree class.

Height

We next define the ***height*** of a tree to be equal to the maximum of the depths of its positions (or zero, if the tree is empty). For example, the tree of Figure 8.2 has height 4, as the node storing *Africa* (and its siblings) has depth 4. It is easy to see that the position with maximum depth must be a leaf.

In Code Fragment 8.4, we present a method that computes the height of a tree based on this definition. Unfortunately, such an approach is not very efficient, and so name the algorithm heightBad and declare it as a private method of the AbstractTree class (so that it cannot be used by others).

```
1    /** Returns the height of the tree. */
2    private int heightBad() {               // works, but quadratic worst-case time
3        int h = 0;
4        for (Position<E> p : positions())
5            if (isExternal(p))              // only consider leaf positions
6                h = Math.max(h, depth(p));
7        return h;
8    }
```

Code Fragment 8.4: Method heightBad of the AbstractTree class. Note that this method calls the depth method from Code Fragment 8.3.

Although we have not yet defined the positions() method, we will see that it can be implemented such that the entire iteration runs in $O(n)$ time, where n is the number of positions of T. Because heightBad calls algorithm depth(p) on each leaf of T, its running time is $O(n + \sum_{p \in L}(d_p + 1))$, where L is the set of leaf positions of T. In the worst case, the sum $\sum_{p \in L}(d_p + 1)$ is proportional to n^2. (See Exercise C-8.31.) Thus, algorithm heightBad runs in $O(n^2)$ worst-case time.

We can compute the height of a tree more efficiently, in $O(n)$ worst-case time, by considering a recursive definition. To do this, we will parameterize a function based on a position within the tree, and calculate the height of the subtree rooted at that position. Formally, we define the ***height*** of a position p in a tree T as follows:

- If p is a leaf, then the height of p is 0.
- Otherwise, the height of p is one more than the maximum of the heights of p's children.

The following proposition relates our original definition of the height of a tree to the height of the *root* position using this recursive formula.

Proposition 8.3: *The height of the root of a nonempty tree T, according to the recursive definition, equals the maximum depth among all leaves of tree T.*

We leave the justification of this proposition as Exercise R-8.3.

An implementation of a recursive algorithm to compute the height of a subtree rooted at a given position p is presented in Code Fragment 8.5. The overall height of a nonempty tree can be computed by sending the root of the tree as a parameter.

```
1  /** Returns the height of the subtree rooted at Position p. */
2  public int height(Position<E> p) {
3    int h = 0;                              // base case if p is external
4    for (Position<E> c : children(p))
5      h = Math.max(h, 1 + height(c));
6    return h;
7  }
```

Code Fragment 8.5: Method height for computing the height of a subtree rooted at a position p of an AbstractTree.

It is important to understand why method height is more efficient than method heightBad. The algorithm is recursive, and it progresses in a top-down fashion. If the method is initially called on the root of T, it will eventually be called once for each position of T. This is because the root eventually invokes the recursion on each of its children, which in turn invokes the recursion on each of their children, and so on.

We can determine the running time of the recursive height algorithm by summing, over all the positions, the amount of time spent on the nonrecursive part of each call. (Review Section 5.2 for analyses of recursive processes.) In our implementation, there is a constant amount of work per position, plus the overhead of computing the maximum over the iteration of children. Although we do not yet have a concrete implementation of children(p), we assume that such an iteration is executed in $O(c_p + 1)$ time, where c_p denotes the number of children of p. Algorithm height(p) spends $O(c_p + 1)$ time at each position p to compute the maximum, and its overall running time is $O(\sum_p (c_p + 1)) = O(n + \sum_p c_p)$. In order to complete the analysis, we make use of the following property.

Proposition 8.4: *Let T be a tree with n positions, and let c_p denote the number of children of a position p of T. Then, summing over the positions of T, $\sum_p c_p = n - 1$.*

Justification: Each position of T, with the exception of the root, is a child of another position, and thus contributes one unit to the above sum. ∎

By Proposition 8.4, the running time of algorithm height, when called on the root of T, is $O(n)$, where n is the number of positions of T.

8.2 Binary Trees

A ***binary tree*** is an ordered tree with the following properties:

1. Every node has at most two children.
2. Each child node is labeled as being either a ***left child*** or a ***right child***.
3. A left child precedes a right child in the order of children of a node.

The subtree rooted at a left or right child of an internal node *v* is called a ***left subtree*** or ***right subtree***, respectively, of *v*. A binary tree is ***proper*** if each node has either zero or two children. Some people also refer to such trees as being ***full*** binary trees. Thus, in a proper binary tree, every internal node has exactly two children. A binary tree that is not proper is ***improper***.

Example 8.5: *An important class of binary trees arises in contexts where we wish to represent a number of different outcomes that can result from answering a series of yes-or-no questions. Each internal node is associated with a question. Starting at the root, we go to the left or right child of the current node, depending on whether the answer to the question is "Yes" or "No." With each decision, we follow an edge from a parent to a child, eventually tracing a path in the tree from the root to a leaf. Such binary trees are known as* **decision trees**, *because a leaf position p in such a tree represents a decision of what to do if the questions associated with p's ancestors are answered in a way that leads to p. A decision tree is a proper binary tree. Figure 8.5 illustrates a decision tree that provides recommendations to a prospective investor.*

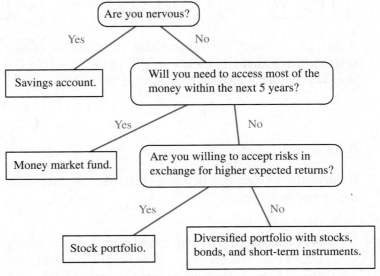

Figure 8.5: A decision tree providing investment advice.

Example 8.6: *An arithmetic expression can be represented by a binary tree whose leaves are associated with variables or constants, and whose internal nodes are associated with one of the operators +, −, ∗, and /, as demonstrated in Figure 8.6. Each node in such a tree has a value associated with it.*

- *If a node is leaf, then its value is that of its variable or constant.*
- *If a node is internal, then its value is defined by applying its operation to the values of its children.*

A typical arithmetic expression tree is a proper binary tree, since each operator +, −, ∗, and / takes exactly two operands. Of course, if we were to allow unary operators, like negation (−), as in "−x," then we could have an improper binary tree.

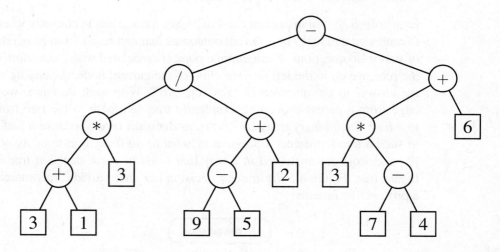

Figure 8.6: A binary tree representing an arithmetic expression. This tree represents the expression $((((3+1)*3)/((9-5)+2))-((3*(7-4))+6))$. The value associated with the internal node labeled "/" is 2.

A Recursive Binary Tree Definition

Incidentally, we can also define a binary tree in a recursive way. In that case, a binary tree is either:

- An empty tree.
- A nonempty tree having a root node r, which stores an element, and two binary trees that are respectively the left and right subtrees of r. We note that one or both of those subtrees can be empty by this definition.

8.2.1   The Binary Tree Abstract Data Type

As an abstract data type, a binary tree is a specialization of a tree that supports three additional accessor methods:

left(p): Returns the position of the left child of p
(or null if p has no left child).

right(p): Returns the position of the right child of p
(or null if p has no right child).

sibling(p): Returns the position of the sibling of p
(or null if p has no sibling).

Just as in Section 8.1.2 for the tree ADT, we do not define specialized update methods for binary trees here. Instead, we will consider some possible update methods when we describe specific implementations and applications of binary trees.

Defining a BinaryTree Interface

Code Fragment 8.6 formalizes the binary tree ADT by defining a BinaryTree interface in Java. This interface extends the Tree interface that was given in Section 8.1.2 to add the three new behaviors. In this way, a binary tree is expected to support all the functionality that was defined for general trees (e.g., root, isExternal, parent), and the new behaviors left, right, and sibling.

```
1  /** An interface for a binary tree, in which each node has at most two children. */
2  public interface BinaryTree<E> extends Tree<E> {
3    /** Returns the Position of p's left child (or null if no child exists). */
4    Position<E> left(Position<E> p) throws IllegalArgumentException;
5    /** Returns the Position of p's right child (or null if no child exists). */
6    Position<E> right(Position<E> p) throws IllegalArgumentException;
7    /** Returns the Position of p's sibling (or null if no sibling exists). */
8    Position<E> sibling(Position<E> p) throws IllegalArgumentException;
9  }
```

Code Fragment 8.6: A BinaryTree interface that extends the Tree interface from Code Fragment 8.1.

Defining an AbstractBinaryTree Base Class

We continue our use of abstract base classes to promote greater reusability within our code. The AbstractBinaryTree class, presented in Code Fragment 8.7, inherits from the AbstractTree class from Section 8.1.2. It provides additional concrete methods that can be derived from the newly declared left and right methods (which remain abstract).

The new sibling method is derived from a combination of left, right, and parent. Typically, we identify the sibling of a position *p* as the "other" child of *p*'s parent. However, *p* does not have a sibling if it is the root, or if it is the only child of its parent.

We can also use the presumed left and right methods to provide concrete implementations of the numChildren and children methods, which are part of the original Tree interface. Using the terminology of Section 7.4, the implementation of the children method relies on producing a **snapshot**. We create an empty java.util.ArrayList, which qualifies as being an iterable container, and then add any children that exist, ordered so that a left child is reported before a right child.

```
 1  /** An abstract base class providing some functionality of the BinaryTree interface.*/
 2  public abstract class AbstractBinaryTree<E> extends AbstractTree<E>
 3                                          implements BinaryTree<E> {
 4    /** Returns the Position of p's sibling (or null if no sibling exists). */
 5    public Position<E> sibling(Position<E> p) {
 6      Position<E> parent = parent(p);
 7      if (parent == null) return null;            // p must be the root
 8      if (p == left(parent))                      // p is a left child
 9        return right(parent);                     // (right child might be null)
10      else                                        // p is a right child
11        return left(parent);                      // (left child might be null)
12    }
13    /** Returns the number of children of Position p. */
14    public int numChildren(Position<E> p) {
15      int count=0;
16      if (left(p) != null)
17        count++;
18      if (right(p) != null)
19        count++;
20      return count;
21    }
22    /** Returns an iterable collection of the Positions representing p's children. */
23    public Iterable<Position<E>> children(Position<E> p) {
24      List<Position<E>> snapshot = new ArrayList<>(2);   // max capacity of 2
25      if (left(p) != null)
26        snapshot.add(left(p));
27      if (right(p) != null)
28        snapshot.add(right(p));
29      return snapshot;
30    }
31  }
```

Code Fragment 8.7: An AbstractBinaryTree class that extends the AbstractTree class of Code Fragment 8.2 and implements the BinaryTree interface of Code Fragment 8.6.

8.2.2 Properties of Binary Trees

Binary trees have several interesting properties dealing with relationships between their heights and number of nodes. We denote the set of all nodes of a tree T at the same depth d as *level d* of T. In a binary tree, level 0 has at most one node (the root), level 1 has at most two nodes (the children of the root), level 2 has at most four nodes, and so on. (See Figure 8.7.) In general, level d has at most 2^d nodes.

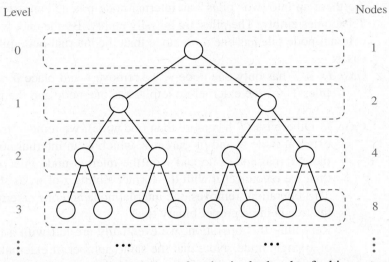

Figure 8.7: Maximum number of nodes in the levels of a binary tree.

We can see that the maximum number of nodes on the levels of a binary tree grows exponentially as we go down the tree. From this simple observation, we can derive the following properties relating the height of a binary tree T with its number of nodes. A detailed justification of these properties is left as Exercise R-8.8.

Proposition 8.7: *Let T be a nonempty binary tree, and let n, n_E, n_I, and h denote the number of nodes, number of external nodes, number of internal nodes, and height of T, respectively. Then T has the following properties:*

1. $h + 1 \leq n \leq 2^{h+1} - 1$
2. $1 \leq n_E \leq 2^h$
3. $h \leq n_I \leq 2^h - 1$
4. $\log(n+1) - 1 \leq h \leq n - 1$

Also, if T is proper, then T has the following properties:

1. $2h + 1 \leq n \leq 2^{h+1} - 1$
2. $h + 1 \leq n_E \leq 2^h$
3. $h \leq n_I \leq 2^h - 1$
4. $\log(n+1) - 1 \leq h \leq (n-1)/2$

Relating Internal Nodes to External Nodes in a Proper Binary Tree

In addition to the earlier binary tree properties, the following relationship exists between the number of internal nodes and external nodes in a proper binary tree.

Proposition 8.8: *In a nonempty proper binary tree T, with n_E external nodes and n_I internal nodes, we have $n_E = n_I + 1$.*

Justification: We justify this proposition by removing nodes from T and dividing them up into two "piles," an internal-node pile and an external-node pile, until T becomes empty. The piles are initially empty. By the end, we will show that the external-node pile has one more node than the internal-node pile. We consider two cases:

Case 1: If T has only one node v, we remove v and place it on the external-node pile. Thus, the external-node pile has one node and the internal-node pile is empty.

Case 2: Otherwise (T has more than one node), we remove from T an (arbitrary) external node w and its parent v, which is an internal node. We place w on the external-node pile and v on the internal-node pile. If v has a parent u, then we reconnect u with the former sibling z of w, as shown in Figure 8.8. This operation, removes one internal node and one external node, and leaves the tree being a proper binary tree.

Repeating this operation, we eventually are left with a final tree consisting of a single node. Note that the same number of external and internal nodes have been removed and placed on their respective piles by the sequence of operations leading to this final tree. Now, we remove the node of the final tree and we place it on the external-node pile. Thus, the external-node pile has one more node than the internal-node pile. ∎

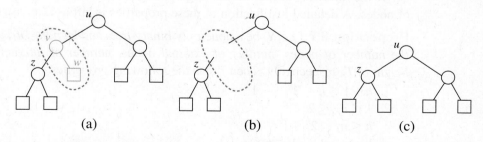

(a)   (b)   (c)

Figure 8.8: Operation that removes an external node and its parent node, used in the justification of Proposition 8.8.

Note that the above relationship does not hold, in general, for improper binary trees and nonbinary trees, although there are other interesting relationships that do hold. (See Exercises C-8.30 through C-8.32.)

8.3 Implementing Trees

The AbstractTree and AbstractBinaryTree classes that we have defined thus far in this chapter are both *abstract base classes*. Although they provide a great deal of support, neither of them can be directly instantiated. We have not yet defined key implementation details for how a tree will be represented internally, and how we can effectively navigate between parents and children.

There are several choices for the internal representation of trees. We describe the most common representations in this section. We begin with the case of a *binary tree*, since its shape is more strictly defined.

8.3.1 Linked Structure for Binary Trees

A natural way to realize a binary tree T is to use a *linked structure*, with a node (see Figure 8.9a) that maintains references to the element stored at a position p and to the nodes associated with the children and parent of p. If p is the root of T, then the parent field of p is null. Likewise, if p does not have a left child (respectively, right child), the associated field is null. The tree itself maintains an instance variable storing a reference to the root node (if any), and a variable, called size, that represents the overall number of nodes of T. We show such a linked structure representation of a binary tree in Figure 8.9b.

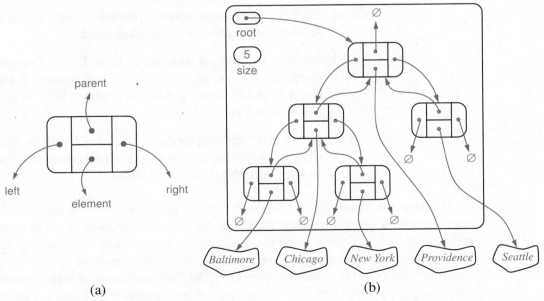

Figure 8.9: A linked structure for representing: (a) a single node; (b) a binary tree.

Operations for Updating a Linked Binary Tree

The Tree and BinaryTree interfaces define a variety of methods for inspecting an existing tree, yet they do not declare any update methods. Presuming that a newly constructed tree is empty, we would like to have means for changing the structure of content of a tree.

Although the principle of encapsulation suggests that the outward behaviors of an abstract data type need not depend on the internal representation, the *efficiency* of the operations depends greatly upon the representation. We therefore prefer to have each concrete implementation of a tree class support the most suitable behaviors for updating a tree. In the case of a linked binary tree, we suggest that the following update methods be supported:

addRoot(e): Creates a root for an empty tree, storing e as the element, and returns the position of that root; an error occurs if the tree is not empty.

addLeft(p, e): Creates a left child of position p, storing element e, and returns the position of the new node; an error occurs if p already has a left child.

addRight(p, e): Creates a right child of position p, storing element e, and returns the position of the new node; an error occurs if p already has a right child.

set(p, e): Replaces the element stored at position p with element e, and returns the previously stored element.

attach(p, T_1, T_2): Attaches the internal structure of trees T_1 and T_2 as the respective left and right subtrees of leaf position p and resets T_1 and T_2 to empty trees; an error condition occurs if p is not a leaf.

remove(p): Removes the node at position p, replacing it with its child (if any), and returns the element that had been stored at p; an error occurs if p has two children.

We have specifically chosen this collection of operations because each can be implemented in $O(1)$ worst-case time with our linked representation. The most complex of these are attach and remove, due to the case analyses involving the various parent-child relationships and boundary conditions, yet there remains only a constant number of operations to perform. (The implementation of both methods could be greatly simplified if we used a tree representation with a sentinel node, akin to our treatment of positional lists; see Exercise C-8.38.)

Java Implementation of a Linked Binary Tree Structure

We now present a concrete implementation of a LinkedBinaryTree class that implements the binary tree ADT, and supports the update methods described on the previous page. The new class formally extends the AbstractBinaryTree base class, inheriting several concrete implementations of methods from that class (as well as the formal designation that it implements the BinaryTree interface).

The low-level details of our linked tree implementation are reminiscent of techniques used when implementing the LinkedPositionalList class in Section 7.3.3. We define a nonpublic nested Node class to represent a node, and to serve as a Position for the public interface. As was portrayed in Figure 8.9, a node maintains a reference to an element, as well as references to its parent, its left child, and its right child (any of which might be null). The tree instance maintains a reference to the root node (possibly null), and a count of the number of nodes in the tree.

We also provide a validate utility that is called anytime a Position is received as a parameter, to ensure that it is a valid node. In the case of a linked tree, we adopt a convention in which we set a node's parent pointer to itself when it is removed from a tree, so that we can later recognize it as an invalid position.

The entire LinkedBinaryTree class is presented in Code Fragments 8.8–8.11. We provide the following guide to that code:

- Code Fragment 8.8 contains the definition of the nested Node class, which implements the Position interface. It also defines a method, createNode, that returns a new node instance. Such a design uses what is known as the *factory method pattern*, allowing us to later subclass our tree in order to use a specialized node type. (See Section 11.2.1.) Code Fragment 8.8 concludes with the declaration of the instance variables of the outer LinkedBinaryTree class and its constructor.

- Code Fragment 8.9 includes the protected validate(p) method, followed by the accessors size, root, left, and right. We note that all other methods of the Tree and BinaryTree interfaces are derived from these four concrete methods, via the AbstractTree and AbstractBinaryTree base classes.

- Code Fragments 8.10 and 8.11 provide the six update methods for a linked binary tree, as described on the preceding page. We note that the three methods—addRoot, addLeft, and addRight—each rely on use of the factory method, createNode, to produce a new node instance.

The remove method, given at the end of Code Fragment 8.11, intentionally sets the parent field of a deleted node to refer to itself, in accordance with our conventional representation of a defunct node (as detected within the validate method). It resets all other fields to null, to aid in garbage collection.

```
1   /** Concrete implementation of a binary tree using a node-based, linked structure. */
2   public class LinkedBinaryTree<E> extends AbstractBinaryTree<E> {
3
4     //--------------- nested Node class ----------------
5     protected static class Node<E> implements Position<E> {
6       private E element;                        // an element stored at this node
7       private Node<E> parent;                   // a reference to the parent node (if any)
8       private Node<E> left;                     // a reference to the left child (if any)
9       private Node<E> right;                    // a reference to the right child (if any)
10      /** Constructs a node with the given element and neighbors. */
11      public Node(E e, Node<E> above, Node<E> leftChild, Node<E> rightChild) {
12        element = e;
13        parent = above;
14        left = leftChild;
15        right = rightChild;
16      }
17      // accessor methods
18      public E getElement() { return element; }
19      public Node<E> getParent() { return parent; }
20      public Node<E> getLeft() { return left; }
21      public Node<E> getRight() { return right; }
22      // update methods
23      public void setElement(E e) { element = e; }
24      public void setParent(Node<E> parentNode) { parent = parentNode; }
25      public void setLeft(Node<E> leftChild) { left = leftChild; }
26      public void setRight(Node<E> rightChild) { right = rightChild; }
27    } //----------- end of nested Node class -----------
28
29    /** Factory function to create a new node storing element e. */
30    protected Node<E> createNode(E e, Node<E> parent,
31                                 Node<E> left, Node<E> right) {
32      return new Node<E>(e, parent, left, right);
33    }
34
35    // LinkedBinaryTree instance variables
36    protected Node<E> root = null;              // root of the tree
37    private int size = 0;                       // number of nodes in the tree
38
39    // constructor
40    public LinkedBinaryTree() { }               // constructs an empty binary tree
```

Code Fragment 8.8: An implementation of the LinkedBinaryTree class.
(Continues in Code Fragments 8.9–8.11.)

```
41   // nonpublic utility
42   /** Validates the position and returns it as a node. */
43   protected Node<E> validate(Position<E> p) throws IllegalArgumentException {
44     if (!(p instanceof Node))
45       throw new IllegalArgumentException("Not valid position type");
46     Node<E> node = (Node<E>) p;                    // safe cast
47     if (node.getParent() == node)                  // our convention for defunct node
48       throw new IllegalArgumentException("p is no longer in the tree");
49     return node;
50   }
51
52   // accessor methods (not already implemented in AbstractBinaryTree)
53   /** Returns the number of nodes in the tree. */
54   public int size() {
55     return size;
56   }
57
58   /** Returns the root Position of the tree (or null if tree is empty). */
59   public Position<E> root() {
60     return root;
61   }
62
63   /** Returns the Position of p's parent (or null if p is root). */
64   public Position<E> parent(Position<E> p) throws IllegalArgumentException {
65     Node<E> node = validate(p);
66     return node.getParent();
67   }
68
69   /** Returns the Position of p's left child (or null if no child exists). */
70   public Position<E> left(Position<E> p) throws IllegalArgumentException {
71     Node<E> node = validate(p);
72     return node.getLeft();
73   }
74
75   /** Returns the Position of p's right child (or null if no child exists). */
76   public Position<E> right(Position<E> p) throws IllegalArgumentException {
77     Node<E> node = validate(p);
78     return node.getRight();
79   }
```

Code Fragment 8.9: An implementation of the LinkedBinaryTree class.
(Continued from Code Fragment 8.8; continues in Code Fragments 8.10 and 8.11.)

```
80    // update methods supported by this class
81    /** Places element e at the root of an empty tree and returns its new Position. */
82    public Position<E> addRoot(E e) throws IllegalStateException {
83      if (!isEmpty()) throw new IllegalStateException("Tree is not empty");
84      root = createNode(e, null, null, null);
85      size = 1;
86      return root;
87    }
88
89    /** Creates a new left child of Position p storing element e; returns its Position. */
90    public Position<E> addLeft(Position<E> p, E e)
91                              throws IllegalArgumentException {
92      Node<E> parent = validate(p);
93      if (parent.getLeft() != null)
94        throw new IllegalArgumentException("p already has a left child");
95      Node<E> child = createNode(e, parent, null, null);
96      parent.setLeft(child);
97      size++;
98      return child;
99    }
100
101   /** Creates a new right child of Position p storing element e; returns its Position. */
102   public Position<E> addRight(Position<E> p, E e)
103                             throws IllegalArgumentException {
104     Node<E> parent = validate(p);
105     if (parent.getRight() != null)
106       throw new IllegalArgumentException("p already has a right child");
107     Node<E> child = createNode(e, parent, null, null);
108     parent.setRight(child);
109     size++;
110     return child;
111   }
112
113   /** Replaces the element at Position p with e and returns the replaced element. */
114   public E set(Position<E> p, E e) throws IllegalArgumentException {
115     Node<E> node = validate(p);
116     E temp = node.getElement();
117     node.setElement(e);
118     return temp;
119   }
```

Code Fragment 8.10: An implementation of the LinkedBinaryTree class.
(Continued from Code Fragments 8.8 and 8.9; continues in Code Fragment 8.11.)

```
120     /** Attaches trees t1 and t2 as left and right subtrees of external p. */
121     public void attach(Position<E> p, LinkedBinaryTree<E> t1,
122                         LinkedBinaryTree<E> t2) throws IllegalArgumentException {
123       Node<E> node = validate(p);
124       if (isInternal(p)) throw new IllegalArgumentException("p must be a leaf");
125       size += t1.size() + t2.size();
126       if (!t1.isEmpty()) {                       // attach t1 as left subtree of node
127         t1.root.setParent(node);
128         node.setLeft(t1.root);
129         t1.root = null;
130         t1.size = 0;
131       }
132       if (!t2.isEmpty()) {                       // attach t2 as right subtree of node
133         t2.root.setParent(node);
134         node.setRight(t2.root);
135         t2.root = null;
136         t2.size = 0;
137       }
138     }
139     /** Removes the node at Position p and replaces it with its child, if any. */
140     public E remove(Position<E> p) throws IllegalArgumentException {
141       Node<E> node = validate(p);
142       if (numChildren(p) == 2)
143         throw new IllegalArgumentException("p has two children");
144       Node<E> child = (node.getLeft() != null ? node.getLeft() : node.getRight() );
145       if (child != null)
146         child.setParent(node.getParent());    // child's grandparent becomes its parent
147       if (node == root)
148         root = child;                          // child becomes root
149       else {
150         Node<E> parent = node.getParent();
151         if (node == parent.getLeft())
152           parent.setLeft(child);
153         else
154           parent.setRight(child);
155       }
156       size--;
157       E temp = node.getElement();
158       node.setElement(null);                   // help garbage collection
159       node.setLeft(null);
160       node.setRight(null);
161       node.setParent(node);                    // our convention for defunct node
162       return temp;
163     }
164   } //----------- end of LinkedBinaryTree class -----------
```

Code Fragment 8.11: An implementation of the LinkedBinaryTree class.
(Continued from Code Fragments 8.8–8.10.)

Performance of the Linked Binary Tree Implementation

To summarize the efficiencies of the linked structure representation, we analyze the running times of the LinkedBinaryTree methods, including derived methods that are inherited from the AbstractTree and AbstractBinaryTree classes:

- The size method, implemented in LinkedBinaryTree, uses an instance variable storing the number of nodes of a tree and therefore takes $O(1)$ time. Method isEmpty, inherited from AbstractTree, relies on a single call to size and thus takes $O(1)$ time.

- The accessor methods root, left, right, and parent are implemented directly in LinkedBinaryTree and take $O(1)$ time each. The sibling, children, and numChildren methods are derived in AbstractBinaryTree using on a constant number of calls to these other accessors, so they run in $O(1)$ time as well.

- The isInternal and isExternal methods, inherited from the AbstractTree class, rely on a call to numChildren, and thus run in $O(1)$ time as well. The isRoot method, also implemented in AbstractTree, relies on a comparison to the result of the root method and runs in $O(1)$ time.

- The update method, set, clearly runs in $O(1)$ time. More significantly, all of the methods addRoot, addLeft, addRight, attach, and remove run in $O(1)$ time, as each involves relinking only a constant number of parent-child relationships per operation.

- Methods depth and height were each analyzed in Section 8.1.3. The depth method at position p runs in $O(d_p + 1)$ time where d_p is its depth; the height method on the root of the tree runs in $O(n)$ time.

The overall space requirement of this data structure is $O(n)$, for a tree with n nodes, as there is an instance of the Node class for every node, in addition to the top-level size and root fields. Table 8.1 summarizes the performance of the linked structure implementation of a binary tree.

Method	Running Time
size, isEmpty	$O(1)$
root, parent, left, right, sibling, children, numChildren	$O(1)$
isInternal, isExternal, isRoot	$O(1)$
addRoot, addLeft, addRight, set, attach, remove	$O(1)$
depth(p)	$O(d_p + 1)$
height	$O(n)$

Table 8.1: Running times for the methods of an n-node binary tree implemented with a linked structure. The space usage is $O(n)$.

8.3.2   Array-Based Representation of a Binary Tree

An alternative representation of a binary tree T is based on a way of numbering the positions of T. For every position p of T, let $f(p)$ be the integer defined as follows.

- If p is the root of T, then $f(p) = 0$.
- If p is the left child of position q, then $f(p) = 2f(q) + 1$.
- If p is the right child of position q, then $f(p) = 2f(q) + 2$.

The numbering function f is known as a ***level numbering*** of the positions in a binary tree T, for it numbers the positions on each level of T in increasing order from left to right. (See Figure 8.10.) Note well that the level numbering is based on *potential* positions within a tree, not the actual shape of a specific tree, so they are not necessarily consecutive. For example, in Figure 8.10(b), there are no nodes with level numbering 13 or 14, because the node with level numbering 6 has no children.

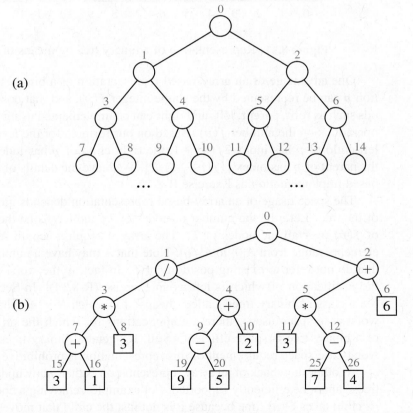

Figure 8.10: Binary tree level numbering: (a) general scheme; (b) an example.

The level numbering function f suggests a representation of a binary tree T by means of an array-based structure A, with the element at position p of T stored at index $f(p)$ of the array. We show an example of an array-based representation of a binary tree in Figure 8.11.

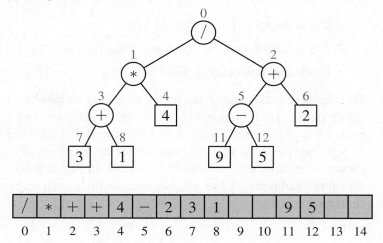

Figure 8.11: Representation of a binary tree by means of an array.

One advantage of an array-based representation of a binary tree is that a position p can be represented by the single integer $f(p)$, and that position-based methods such as root, parent, left, and right can be implemented using simple arithmetic operations on the number $f(p)$. Based on our formula for the level numbering, the left child of p has index $2f(p) + 1$, the right child of p has index $2f(p) + 2$, and the parent of p has index $\lfloor (f(p) - 1)/2 \rfloor$. We leave the details of a complete array-based implementation as Exercise R-8.16.

The space usage of an array-based representation depends greatly on the shape of the tree. Let n be the number of nodes of T, and let f_M be the maximum value of $f(p)$ over all the nodes of T. The array A requires length $N = 1 + f_M$, since elements range from $A[0]$ to $A[f_M]$. Note that A may have a number of empty cells that do not refer to existing positions of T. In fact, in the worst case, $N = 2^n - 1$, the justification of which is left as an exercise (R-8.14). In Section 9.3, we will see a class of binary trees, called "heaps" for which $N = n$. Thus, in spite of the worst-case space usage, there are applications for which the array representation of a binary tree is space efficient. Still, for general binary trees, the exponential worst-case space requirement of this representation is prohibitive.

Another drawback of an array representation is that many update operations for trees cannot be efficiently supported. For example, removing a node and promoting its child takes $O(n)$ time because it is not just the child that moves locations within the array, but all descendants of that child.

8.3.3 Linked Structure for General Trees

When representing a binary tree with a linked structure, each node explicitly maintains fields left and right as references to individual children. For a general tree, there is no a priori limit on the number of children that a node may have. A natural way to realize a general tree T as a linked structure is to have each node store a single *container* of references to its children. For example, a children field of a node can be an array or list of references to the children of the node (if any). Such a linked representation is schematically illustrated in Figure 8.12.

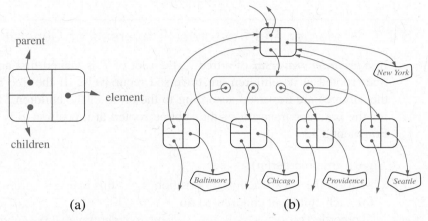

(a)   (b)

Figure 8.12: The linked structure for a general tree: (a) the structure of a node; (b) a larger portion of the data structure associated with a node and its children.

Table 8.2 summarizes the performance of the implementation of a general tree using a linked structure. The analysis is left as an exercise (R-8.13), but we note that, by using a collection to store the children of each position p, we can implement children(p) by simply iterating that collection.

Method	Running Time
size, isEmpty	$O(1)$
root, parent, isRoot, isInternal, isExternal	$O(1)$
numChildren(p)	$O(1)$
children(p)	$O(c_p + 1)$
depth(p)	$O(d_p + 1)$
height	$O(n)$

Table 8.2: Running times of the accessor methods of an n-node general tree implemented with a linked structure. We let c_p denote the number of children of a position p, and d_p its depth. The space usage is $O(n)$.

8.4   Tree Traversal Algorithms

A *traversal* of a tree T is a systematic way of accessing, or "visiting," all the positions of T. The specific action associated with the "visit" of a position p depends on the application of this traversal, and could involve anything from incrementing a counter to performing some complex computation for p. In this section, we describe several common traversal schemes for trees, implement them in the context of our various tree classes, and discuss several common applications of tree traversals.

8.4.1   Preorder and Postorder Traversals of General Trees

In a *preorder traversal* of a tree T, the root of T is visited first and then the subtrees rooted at its children are traversed recursively. If the tree is ordered, then the subtrees are traversed according to the order of the children. The pseudocode for the preorder traversal of the subtree rooted at a position p is shown in Code Fragment 8.12.

Algorithm preorder(p):

    perform the "visit" action for position p { this happens before any recursion }
    for each child c in children(p) **do**
        preorder(c)   { recursively traverse the subtree rooted at c }

Code Fragment 8.12: Algorithm preorder for performing the preorder traversal of a subtree rooted at position p of a tree.

Figure 8.13 portrays the order in which positions of a sample tree are visited during an application of the preorder traversal algorithm.

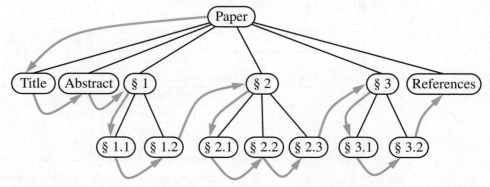

Figure 8.13: Preorder traversal of an ordered tree, where the children of each position are ordered from left to right.

Postorder Traversal

Another important tree traversal algorithm is the ***postorder traversal***. In some sense, this algorithm can be viewed as the opposite of the preorder traversal, because it recursively traverses the subtrees rooted at the children of the root first, and then visits the root (hence, the name "postorder"). Pseudocode for the postorder traversal is given in Code Fragment 8.13, and an example of a postorder traversal is portrayed in Figure 8.14.

Algorithm postorder(p):
    for each child c in children(p) **do**
        postorder(c)   { recursively traverse the subtree rooted at c }
    perform the "visit" action for position p { this happens after any recursion }

Code Fragment 8.13: Algorithm postorder for performing the postorder traversal of a subtree rooted at position p of a tree.

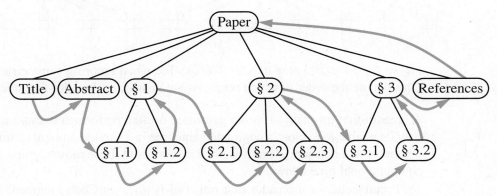

Figure 8.14: Postorder traversal of the ordered tree of Figure 8.13.

Running-Time Analysis

Both preorder and postorder traversal algorithms are efficient ways to access all the positions of a tree. The analysis of either of these traversal algorithms is similar to that of algorithm height, given in Code Fragment 8.5 of Section 8.1.3. At each position p, the nonrecursive part of the traversal algorithm requires time $O(c_p + 1)$, where c_p is the number of children of p, under the assumption that the "visit" itself takes $O(1)$ time. By Proposition 8.4, the overall running time for the traversal of tree T is $O(n)$, where n is the number of positions in the tree. This running time is asymptotically optimal since the traversal must visit all n positions of the tree.

8.4.2 Breadth-First Tree Traversal

Although the preorder and postorder traversals are common ways of visiting the positions of a tree, another approach is to traverse a tree so that we visit all the positions at depth d before we visit the positions at depth $d + 1$. Such an algorithm is known as a ***breadth-first traversal***.

A breadth-first traversal is a common approach used in software for playing games. A ***game tree*** represents the possible choices of moves that might be made by a player (or computer) during a game, with the root of the tree being the initial configuration for the game. For example, Figure 8.15 displays a partial game tree for Tic-Tac-Toe.

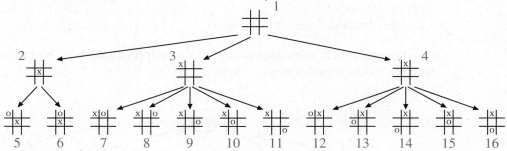

Figure 8.15: Partial game tree for Tic-Tac-Toe when ignoring symmetries; annotations denote the order in which positions are visited in a breadth-first tree traversal.

A breadth-first traversal of such a game tree is often performed because a computer may be unable to explore a complete game tree in a limited amount of time. So the computer will consider all moves, then responses to those moves, going as deep as computational time allows.

Pseudocode for a breadth-first traversal is given in Code Fragment 8.14. The process is not recursive, since we are not traversing entire subtrees at once. We use a queue to produce a FIFO (i.e., first-in first-out) semantics for the order in which we visit nodes. The overall running time is $O(n)$, due to the n calls to enqueue and n calls to dequeue.

Algorithm breadthfirst( ):
    Initialize queue Q to contain root( )
    while Q not empty **do**
        $p = Q$.dequeue( )   { p is the oldest entry in the queue }
        perform the "visit" action for position p
        for each child c in children(p) **do**
            Q.enqueue(c)   { add p's children to the end of the queue for later visits }

Code Fragment 8.14: Algorithm for performing a breadth-first traversal of a tree.

8.4.3 Inorder Traversal of a Binary Tree

The standard preorder, postorder, and breadth-first traversals that were introduced for general trees can be directly applied to binary trees. In this section, we will introduce another common traversal algorithm specifically for a binary tree.

During an ***inorder traversal***, we visit a position between the recursive traversals of its left and right subtrees. The inorder traversal of a binary tree T can be informally viewed as visiting the nodes of T "from left to right." Indeed, for every position p, the inorder traversal visits p after all the positions in the left subtree of p and before all the positions in the right subtree of p. Pseudocode for the inorder traversal algorithm is given in Code Fragment 8.15, and an example of an inorder traversal is portrayed in Figure 8.16.

Algorithm inorder(p):
 if p has a left child lc **then**
  inorder(lc)   { recursively traverse the left subtree of p }
 perform the "visit" action for position p
 if p has a right child rc **then**
  inorder(rc)   { recursively traverse the right subtree of p }

Code Fragment 8.15: Algorithm inorder for performing an inorder traversal of a subtree rooted at position p of a binary tree.

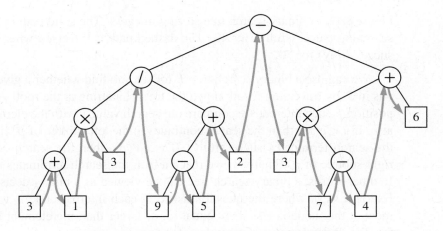

Figure 8.16: Inorder traversal of a binary tree.

The inorder traversal algorithm has several important applications. When using a binary tree to represent an arithmetic expression, as in Figure 8.16, the inorder traversal visits positions in a consistent order with the standard representation of the expression, as in $3 + 1 \times 3/9 - 5 + 2 \dots$ (albeit without parentheses).

Binary Search Trees

An important application of the inorder traversal algorithm arises when we store an ordered sequence of elements in a binary tree, defining a structure we call a ***binary search tree***. Let S be a set whose unique elements have an order relation. For example, S could be a set of integers. A binary search tree for S is a proper binary tree T such that, for each internal position p of T:

- Position p stores an element of S, denoted as $e(p)$.
- Elements stored in the left subtree of p (if any) are less than $e(p)$.
- Elements stored in the right subtree of p (if any) are greater than $e(p)$.

An example of a binary search tree is shown in Figure 8.17. The above properties assure that an inorder traversal of a binary search tree T visits the elements in nondecreasing order.

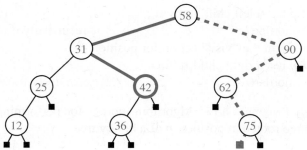

Figure 8.17: A binary search tree storing integers. The solid path is traversed when searching (successfully) for 42. The dashed path is traversed when searching (unsuccessfully) for 70.

We can use a binary search tree T for set S to find whether a given search value v is in S, by traversing a path down the tree T, starting at the root. At each internal position p encountered, we compare our search value v with the element $e(p)$ stored at p. If $v < e(p)$, then the search continues in the left subtree of p. If $v = e(p)$, then the search terminates successfully. If $v > e(p)$, then the search continues in the right subtree of p. Finally, if we reach a leaf, the search terminates unsuccessfully. In other words, a binary search tree can be viewed as a binary decision tree (recall Example 8.5), where the question asked at each internal node is whether the element at that node is less than, equal to, or larger than the element being searched for. We illustrate several examples of the search operation in Figure 8.17.

Note that the running time of searching in a binary search tree T is proportional to the height of T. Recall from Proposition 8.7 that the height of a binary tree with n nodes can be as small as $\log(n+1) - 1$ or as large as $n - 1$. Thus, binary search trees are most efficient when they have small height. Chapter 11 is devoted to the study of search trees.

8.4.4   Implementing Tree Traversals in Java

When first defining the tree ADT in Section 8.1.2, we stated that tree T must include the following supporting methods:

> iterator( ): Returns an iterator for all elements in the tree.

> positions( ): Returns an iterable collection of all positions of the tree.

At that time, we did not make any assumption about the order in which these iterations report their results. In this section, we will demonstrate how any of the tree traversal algorithms we have introduced can be used to produce these iterations as concrete implementations within the AbstractTree or AbstractBinaryTree base classes.

First, we note that an iteration of all *elements* of a tree can easily be produced if we have an iteration of all *positions* of that tree. Code Fragment 8.16 provides an implementation of the iterator( ) method by adapting an iteration produced by the positions( ) method. In fact, this is the identical approach we used in Code Fragment 7.14 of Section 7.4.2 for the LinkedPositionalList class.

```
1    //---------------- nested ElementIterator class ----------------
2    /* This class adapts the iteration produced by positions() to return elements. */
3    private class ElementIterator implements Iterator<E> {
4      Iterator<Position<E>> posIterator = positions().iterator();
5      public boolean hasNext() { return posIterator.hasNext(); }
6      public E next() { return posIterator.next().getElement(); } // return element!
7      public void remove() { posIterator.remove(); }
8    }
9
10   /** Returns an iterator of the elements stored in the tree. */
11   public Iterator<E> iterator() { return new ElementIterator(); }
```

Code Fragment 8.16: Iterating all elements of an AbstractTree instance, based upon an iteration of the positions of the tree.

To implement the positions( ) method, we have a choice of tree traversal algorithms. Given that there are advantages to each of those traversal orders, we provide public implementations of each strategy that can be called directly by a user of our class. We can then trivially adapt one of those as a default order for the positions method of the AbstractTree class. For example, on the following page we will define a public method, preorder( ), that returns an iteration of the positions of a tree in preorder; Code Fragment 8.17 demonstrates how the positions( ) method can be trivially defined to rely on that order.

```
public Iterable<Position<E>> positions() { return preorder(); }
```

Code Fragment 8.17: Defining preorder as the default traversal algorithm for the public positions method of an abstract tree.

Preorder Traversals

We begin by considering the ***preorder traversal*** algorithm. Our goal is to provide a public method preorder( ), as part of the AbstractTree class, which returns an iterable container of the positions of the tree in preorder. For ease of implementation, we choose to produce a ***snapshot iterator***, as defined in Section 7.4.2, returning a list of all positions. (Exercise C-8.47 explores the goal of implementing a ***lazy iterator*** that reports positions in preorder.)

We begin by defining a private utility method, preorderSubtree, given in Code Fragment 8.18, which allows us to parameterize the recursive process with a specific position of the tree that serves as the root of a subtree to traverse. (We also pass a list as a parameter that serves as a buffer to which "visited" positions are added.)

```
1   /** Adds positions of the subtree rooted at Position p to the given snapshot. */
2   private void preorderSubtree(Position<E> p, List<Position<E>> snapshot) {
3     snapshot.add(p);        // for preorder, we add position p before exploring subtrees
4     for (Position<E> c : children(p))
5       preorderSubtree(c, snapshot);
6   }
```

Code Fragment 8.18: A recursive subroutine for performing a preorder traversal of the subtree rooted at position *p* of a tree. This code should be included within the body of the AbstractTree class.

The preorderSubtree method follows the high-level algorithm originally described as pseudocode in Code Fragment 8.12. It has an implicit base case, as the **for** loop body never executes if a position has no children.

The public preorder method, shown in Code Fragment 8.19, has the responsibility of creating an empty list for the snapshot buffer, and invoking the recursive method at the root of the tree (assuming the tree is nonempty). We rely on a java.util.ArrayList instance as an Iterable instance for the snapshot buffer.

```
1   /** Returns an iterable collection of positions of the tree, reported in preorder. */
2   public Iterable<Position<E>> preorder() {
3     List<Position<E>> snapshot = new ArrayList<>();
4     if (!isEmpty())
5       preorderSubtree(root(), snapshot);       // fill the snapshot recursively
6     return snapshot;
7   }
```

Code Fragment 8.19: A public method that performs a preorder traversal of an entire tree. This code should be included within the body of the AbstractTree class.

Postorder Traversal

We implement a ***postorder traversal*** using a similar design as we used for a pre-order traversal. The only difference is that a "visited" position is not added to a postorder snapshot until *after* all of its subtrees have been traversed. Both the recursive utility and the top-level public method are given in Code Fragment 8.20.

```
 1   /** Adds positions of the subtree rooted at Position p to the given snapshot. */
 2   private void postorderSubtree(Position<E> p, List<Position<E>> snapshot) {
 3     for (Position<E> c : children(p))
 4       postorderSubtree(c, snapshot);
 5     snapshot.add(p);        // for postorder, we add position p after exploring subtrees
 6   }
 7   /** Returns an iterable collection of positions of the tree, reported in postorder. */
 8   public Iterable<Position<E>> postorder() {
 9     List<Position<E>> snapshot = new ArrayList<>();
10     if (!isEmpty())
11       postorderSubtree(root(), snapshot);      // fill the snapshot recursively
12     return snapshot;
13   }
```

Code Fragment 8.20: Support for performing a postorder traversal of a tree. This code should be included within the body of the AbstractTree class.

Breadth-First Traversal

On the following page, we will provide an implementation of the breadth-first traversal algorithm in the context of our AbstractTree class (Code Fragment 8.21). Recall that the breadth-first traversal algorithm is not recursive; it relies on a queue of positions to manage the traversal process. We will use the LinkedQueue class from Section 6.2.3, although any implementation of the queue ADT would suffice.

Inorder Traversal for Binary Trees

The preorder, postorder, and breadth-first traversal algorithms are applicable to all trees. The inorder traversal algorithm, because it explicitly relies on the notion of a left and right child of a node, only applies to binary trees. We therefore include its definition within the body of the AbstractBinaryTree class. We use a similar design to our preorder and postorder traversals, with a private recursive utility for traversing subtrees. (See Code Fragment 8.22.)

For many applications of binary trees (for example, see Chapter 11), an inorder traversal is the most natural order. Therefore, Code Fragment 8.22 makes it the default for the AbstractBinaryTree class by overriding the positions method that was inherited from the AbstractTree class. Because the iterator( ) method relies on positions( ), it will also use inorder when reporting the elements of a binary tree.

```
1   /** Returns an iterable collection of positions of the tree in breadth-first order. */
2   public Iterable<Position<E>> breadthfirst() {
3     List<Position<E>> snapshot = new ArrayList<>();
4     if (!isEmpty()) {
5       Queue<Position<E>> fringe = new LinkedQueue<>();
6       fringe.enqueue(root());                    // start with the root
7       while (!fringe.isEmpty()) {
8         Position<E> p = fringe.dequeue();        // remove from front of the queue
9         snapshot.add(p);                         // report this position
10        for (Position<E> c : children(p))
11          fringe.enqueue(c);                     // add children to back of queue
12      }
13    }
14    return snapshot;
15  }
```

Code Fragment 8.21: An implementation of a breadth-first traversal of a tree. This code should be included within the body of the AbstractTree class.

```
1   /** Adds positions of the subtree rooted at Position p to the given snapshot. */
2   private void inorderSubtree(Position<E> p, List<Position<E>> snapshot) {
3     if (left(p) != null)
4       inorderSubtree(left(p), snapshot);
5     snapshot.add(p);
6     if (right(p) != null)
7       inorderSubtree(right(p), snapshot);
8   }
9   /** Returns an iterable collection of positions of the tree, reported in inorder. */
10  public Iterable<Position<E>> inorder() {
11    List<Position<E>> snapshot = new ArrayList<>();
12    if (!isEmpty())
13      inorderSubtree(root(), snapshot);          // fill the snapshot recursively
14    return snapshot;
15  }
16  /** Overrides positions to make inorder the default order for binary trees. */
17  public Iterable<Position<E>> positions() {
18    return inorder();
19  }
```

Code Fragment 8.22: Support for performing an inorder traversal of a binary tree, and for making that order the default traversal for binary trees. This code should be included within the body of the AbstractBinaryTree class.

8.4.5 Applications of Tree Traversals

In this section, we demonstrate several representative applications of tree traversals, including some customizations of the standard traversal algorithms.

Table of Contents

When using a tree to represent the hierarchical structure of a document, a preorder traversal of the tree can be used to produce a table of contents for the document. For example, the table of contents associated with the tree from Figure 8.13 is displayed in Figure 8.18. Part (a) of that figure gives a simple presentation with one element per line; part (b) shows a more attractive presentation, produced by indenting each element based on its depth within the tree.

```
Paper                      Paper
Title                      Title
Abstract                   Abstract
§1                         §1
    §1.1                       §1.1
    §1.2                       §1.2
§2                         §2
§2.1                           §2.1
...                        ...

(a)                        (b)
```

Figure 8.18: Table of contents for a document represented by the tree in Figure 8.13: (a) without indentation; (b) with indentation based on depth within the tree.

The unindented version of the table of contents can be produced with the following code, given a tree T supporting the preorder( ) method:

```
for (Position<E> p : T.preorder())
    System.out.println(p.getElement());
```

To produce the presentation of Figure 8.18(b), we indent each element with a number of spaces equal to twice the element's depth in the tree (hence, the root element was unindented). If we assume that method, spaces(n), produces a string of n spaces, we could replace the body of the above loop with the statement System.out.println(spaces(2*T.depth(p)) + p.getElement()). Unfortunately, although the work to produce the preorder traversal runs in $O(n)$ time, based on the analysis of Section 8.4.1, the calls to depth incur a hidden cost. Making a call to depth from every position of the tree results in $O(n^2)$ worst-case time, as noted when analyzing the algorithm heightBad in Section 8.1.3.

A preferred approach to producing an indented table of contents is to redesign a top-down recursion that includes the current depth as an additional parameter. Such an implementation is provided in Code Fragment 8.23. This implementation runs in worst-case $O(n)$ time (except, technically, the time it takes to print strings of increasing lengths).

```java
1  /** Prints preorder representation of subtree of T rooted at p having depth d. */
2  public static <E> void printPreorderIndent(Tree<E> T, Position<E> p, int d) {
3    System.out.println(spaces(2*d) + p.getElement());       // indent based on d
4    for (Position<E> c : T.children(p))
5      printPreorderIndent(T, c, d+1);                        // child depth is d+1
6  }
```

Code Fragment 8.23: Efficient recursion for printing indented version of a preorder traversal. To print an entire tree T, the recursion should be started with form printPreorderIndent(T, T.root(), 0).

In the example of Figure 8.18, we were fortunate in that the numbering was embedded within the elements of the tree. More generally, we might be interested in using a preorder traversal to display the structure of a tree, with indentation and also explicit numbering that was not present in the tree. For example, we might display the tree from Figure 8.2 beginning as:

```
Electronics R'Us
    1 R&D
    2 Sales
        2.1 Domestic
        2.2 International
            2.2.1 Canada
            2.2.2 S. America
```

This is more challenging, because the numbers used as labels are implicit in the structure of the tree. A label depends on the path from the root to the current position. To accomplish our goal, we add an additional parameter to the recursive signature. We send a list of integers representing the labels leading to a particular position. For example, when visiting the node *Domestic* above, we will send the list of values $\{2, 1\}$ that comprise its label.

At the implementation level, we wish to avoid the inefficiency of duplicating such lists when sending a new parameter from one level of the recursion to the next. A standard solution is to pass the same list instance throughout the recursion. At one level of the recursion, a new entry is temporarily added to the end of the list before making further recursive calls. In order to "leave no trace," the extraneous entry must later be removed from the list by the same recursive call that added it. An implementation based on this approach is given in Code Fragment 8.24.

```
1   /** Prints labeled representation of subtree of T rooted at p having depth d. */
2   public static <E>
3   void printPreorderLabeled(Tree<E> T, Position<E> p, ArrayList<Integer> path) {
4     int d = path.size( );                      // depth equals the length of the path
5     System.out.print(spaces(2*d));             // print indentation, then label
6     for (int j=0; j < d; j++) System.out.print(path.get(j) + (j == d−1 ? " " : ".")));
7     System.out.println(p.getElement( ));
8     path.add(1);                               // add path entry for first child
9     for (Position<E> c : T.children(p)) {
10      printPreorderLabeled(T, c, path);
11      path.set(d, 1 + path.get(d));            // increment last entry of path
12    }
13    path.remove(d);                            // restore path to its incoming state
14  }
```

Code Fragment 8.24: Efficient recursion for printing an indented and *labeled* presentation of a preorder traversal.

Computing Disk Space

In Example 8.1, we considered the use of a tree as a model for a file-system structure, with internal positions representing directories and leaves representing files. In fact, when introducing the use of recursion back in Chapter 5, we specifically examined the topic of file systems (see Section 5.1.4). Although we did not explicitly model it as a tree at that time, we gave an implementation of an algorithm for computing the disk usage (Code Fragment 5.5).

The recursive computation of disk space is emblematic of a *postorder* traversal, as we cannot effectively compute the total space used by a directory until *after* we know the space that is used by its children directories. Unfortunately, the formal implementation of postorder, as given in Code Fragment 8.20, does not suffice for this purpose. We would like to have a mechanism for children to return information to the parent as part of the traversal process. A custom solution to the disk space problem, with each level of recursion providing a return value to the (parent) caller, is provided in Code Fragment 8.25.

```
1   /** Returns total disk space for subtree of T rooted at p. */
2   public static int diskSpace(Tree<Integer> T, Position<Integer> p) {
3     int subtotal = p.getElement( );        // we assume element represents space usage
4     for (Position<Integer> c : T.children(p))
5       subtotal += diskSpace(T, c);
6     return subtotal;
7   }
```

Code Fragment 8.25: Recursive computation of disk space for a tree. We assume that each tree element reports the local space used at that position.

Parenthetic Representations of a Tree

It is not possible to reconstruct a general tree, given only the preorder sequence of elements, as in Figure 8.18a. Some additional context is necessary for the structure of the tree to be well defined. The use of indentation or numbered labels provides such context, with a very human-friendly presentation. However, there are more concise string representations of trees that are computer-friendly.

In this section, we explore one such representation. The ***parenthetic string representation*** $P(T)$ of tree T is recursively defined. If T consists of a single position p, then $P(T) = p.\text{getElement}()$. Otherwise, it is defined recursively as,

$$P(T) = p.\text{getElement}() + "(" + P(T_1) + ", \ " + \cdots + ", \ " + P(T_k) + ")"$$

where p is the root of T and $T_1, T_2, \ldots, T_k$ are the subtrees rooted at the children of p, which are given in order if T is an ordered tree. We are using "+" here to denote string concatenation. As an example, the parenthetic representation of the tree of Figure 8.2 would appear as follows (line breaks are cosmetic):

```
Electronics R'Us (R&D, Sales (Domestic, International (Canada,
S. America, Overseas (Africa, Europe, Asia, Australia))),
Purchasing, Manufacturing (TV, CD, Tuner))
```

Although the parenthetic representation is essentially a preorder traversal, we cannot easily produce the additional punctuation using the formal implementation of preorder. The opening parenthesis must be produced just before the loop over a position's children, the separating commas between children, and the closing parenthesis just after the loop completes. The Java method parenthesize, shown in Code Fragment 8.26, is a custom traversal that prints such a parenthetic string representation of a tree T.

```
1  /** Prints parenthesized representation of subtree of T rooted at p. */
2  public static <E> void parenthesize(Tree<E> T, Position<E> p) {
3    System.out.print(p.getElement());
4    if (T.isInternal(p)) {
5      boolean firstTime = true;
6      for (Position<E> c : T.children(p)) {
7        System.out.print( (firstTime ? " (" : ", ") ); // determine proper punctuation
8        firstTime = false;                              // any future passes will get comma
9        parenthesize(T, c);                             // recur on child
10     }
11     System.out.print(")");
12   }
13 }
```

Code Fragment 8.26: Method that prints parenthetic string representation of a tree.

Using Inorder Traversal for Tree Drawing

An inorder traversal can be applied to the problem of computing a graphical layout of a binary tree, as shown in Figure 8.19. We assume the convention, common to computer graphics, that x-coordinates increase left to right and y-coordinates increase top to bottom, so that the origin is in the upper left corner of the drawing.

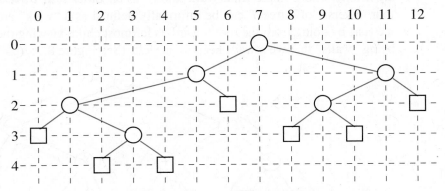

Figure 8.19: An inorder drawing of a binary tree.

The geometry is determined by an algorithm that assigns x- and y-coordinates to each position p of a binary tree T using the following two rules:

- $x(p)$ is the number of positions visited before p in an inorder traversal of T.
- $y(p)$ is the depth of p in T.

Code Fragment 8.27 provides an implementation of a recursive method that assigns x- and y-coordinates to positions of a tree in this manner. Depth information is passed from one level of the recursion to another, as done in our earlier example for indentation. To maintain an accurate value for the x-coordinate as the traversal proceeds, the method must be provided with the value of x that should be assigned to the leftmost node of the current subtree, and it must return to its parent a revised value of x that is appropriate for the first node drawn to the right of the subtree.

```
1   public static <E> int layout(BinaryTree<E> T, Position<E> p, int d, int x) {
2     if (T.left(p) != null)
3       x = layout(T, T.left(p), d+1, x);        // resulting x will be increased
4     p.getElement().setX(x++);                   // post-increment x
5     p.getElement().setY(d);
6     if (T.right(p) != null)
7       x = layout(T, T.right(p), d+1, x);        // resulting x will be increased
8     return x;
9   }
```

Code Fragment 8.27: Recursive method for computing coordinates at which to draw positions of a binary tree. We assume that the element type for the tree supports setX and setY methods. The initial call should be layout(T, T.root(), 0, 0).

8.4.6   Euler Tours

The various applications described in Section 8.4.5 demonstrate the great power of recursive tree traversals, but they also show that not every application strictly fits the mold of a preorder, postorder, or inorder traversal. We can unify the tree-traversal algorithms into a single framework known as an ***Euler tour traversal***. The Euler tour traversal of a tree T can be informally defined as a "walk" around T, where we start by going from the root toward its leftmost child, viewing the edges of T as being "walls" that we always keep to our left. (See Figure 8.20.)

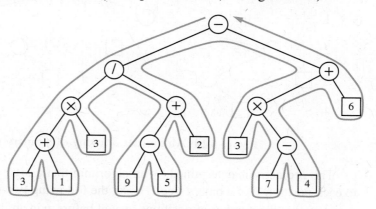

Figure 8.20: Euler tour traversal of a tree.

The complexity of the walk is $O(n)$, for a tree with n nodes, because it progresses exactly two times along each of the $n - 1$ edges of the tree—once going downward along the edge, and later going upward along the edge. To unify the concept of preorder and postorder traversals, we can view there being two notable "visits" to each position p:

- A "pre visit" occurs when first reaching the position, that is, when the walk passes immediately *left* of the node in our visualization.
- A "post visit" occurs when the walk later proceeds upward from that position, that is, when the walk passes to the *right* of the node in our visualization.

The process of an Euler tour can be naturally viewed as recursive. In between the "pre visit" and "post visit" of a given position will be a recursive tour of each of its subtrees. Looking at Figure 8.20 as an example, there is a contiguous portion of the entire tour that is itself an Euler tour of the subtree of the node with element "/". That tour contains two contiguous subtours, one traversing that position's left subtree and another traversing the right subtree.

In the special case of a binary tree, we can designate the time when the walk passes immediately *below* a node as an "in visit" event. This will be just after the tour of its left subtree (if any), but before the tour of its right subtree (if any).

The pseudocode for an Euler tour traversal of a subtree rooted at a position p is shown in Code Fragment 8.28.

Algorithm eulerTour(T, p):

    perform the "pre visit" action for position p

    for each child c in T.children(p) **do**

        eulerTour(T, c)   { recursively tour the subtree rooted at c }

    perform the "post visit" action for position p

Code Fragment 8.28: Algorithm eulerTour for performing an Euler tour traversal of a subtree rooted at position p of a tree.

The Euler tour traversal extends the preorder and postorder traversals, but it can also perform other kinds of traversals. For example, suppose we wish to compute the number of descendants of each position p in an n-node binary tree. We start an Euler tour by initializing a counter to 0, and then increment the counter during the "pre visit" for each position. To determine the number of descendants of a position p, we compute the difference between the values of the counter from when the pre-visit occurs and when the post-visit occurs, and add 1 (for p). This simple rule gives us the number of descendants of p, because each node in the subtree rooted at p is counted between p's visit on the left and p's visit on the right. Therefore, we have an $O(n)$-time method for computing the number of descendants of each node.

For the case of a binary tree, we can customize the algorithm to include an explicit "in visit" action, as shown in Code Fragment 8.29.

Algorithm eulerTourBinary(T, p):

    perform the "pre visit" action for position p

    if p has a left child lc **then**

        eulerTourBinary(T, lc)   { recursively tour the left subtree of p }

    perform the "in visit" action for position p

    if p has a right child rc **then**

        eulerTourBinary(T, rc)   { recursively tour the right subtree of p }

    perform the "post visit" action for position p

Code Fragment 8.29: Algorithm eulerTourBinary for performing an Euler tour traversal of a subtree rooted at position p of a binary tree.

For example, a binary Euler tour can produce a traditional parenthesized arithmetic expression, such as `"(((( 3+1)x3)/((9-5)+2))-((3x(7-4))+6))"` for the tree in Figure 8.20, as follows:

- "Pre visit" action: if the position is internal, print "(".
- "In visit" action: print the value or operator stored at the position.
- "Post visit" action: if the position is internal, print ")".

8.5 Exercises

Reinforcement

R-8.1 The following questions refer to the tree of Figure 8.3.

    a. Which node is the root?

    b. What are the internal nodes?

    c. How many descendants does node cs016/ have?

    d. How many ancestors does node cs016/ have?

    e. What are the siblings of node homeworks/?

    f. Which nodes are in the subtree rooted at node projects/?

    g. What is the depth of node papers/?

    h. What is the height of the tree?

R-8.2 Show a tree achieving the worst-case running time for algorithm depth.

R-8.3 Give a justification of Proposition 8.3.

R-8.4 What is the running time of a call to T.height(p) when called on a position p distinct from the root of tree T? (See Code Fragment 8.5.)

R-8.5 Describe an algorithm, relying only on the BinaryTree operations, that counts the number of leaves in a binary tree that are the *left* child of their respective parent.

R-8.6 Let T be an n-node binary tree that may be improper. Describe how to represent T by means of a ***proper*** binary tree T' with $O(n)$ nodes.

R-8.7 What are the minimum and maximum number of internal and external nodes in an improper binary tree with n nodes?

R-8.8 Answer the following questions so as to justify Proposition 8.7.

    a. What is the minimum number of external nodes for a proper binary tree with height h? Justify your answer.

    b. What is the maximum number of external nodes for a proper binary tree with height h? Justify your answer.

    c. Let T be a proper binary tree with height h and n nodes. Show that

$$\log(n+1) - 1 \le h \le (n-1)/2.$$

    d. For which values of n and h can the above lower and upper bounds on h be attained with equality?

R-8.9 Give a proof by induction of Proposition 8.8.

R-8.10 Find the value of the arithmetic expression associated with each subtree of the binary tree of Figure 8.6.

R-8.11 Draw an arithmetic expression tree that has four external nodes, storing the numbers 1, 5, 6, and 7 (with each number stored in a distinct external node, but not necessarily in this order), and has three internal nodes, each storing an operator from the set $\{+, -, *, /\}$, so that the value of the root is 21. The operators may return and act on fractions, and an operator may be used more than once.

R-8.12 Draw the binary tree representation of the following arithmetic expression:
"$(((5+2)*(2-1))/((2+9)+((7-2)-1))*8)$".

R-8.13 Justify Table 8.2, summarizing the running time of the methods of a tree represented with a linked structure, by providing, for each method, a description of its implementation, and an analysis of its running time.

R-8.14 Let T be a binary tree with n nodes, and let $f()$ be the level numbering function of the positions of T, as given in Section 8.3.2.

    a. Show that, for every position p of T, $f(p) \leq 2^n - 2$.

    b. Show an example of a binary tree with seven nodes that attains the above upper bound on $f(p)$ for some position p.

R-8.15 Show how to use an Euler tour traversal to compute the level number $f(p)$, as defined in Section 8.3.2, of each position in a binary tree T.

R-8.16 Let T be a binary tree with n positions that is realized with an array representation A, and let $f()$ be the level numbering function of the positions of T, as given in Section 8.3.2. Give pseudocode descriptions of each of the methods root, parent, left, right, isExternal, and isRoot.

R-8.17 Our definition of the level numbering function $f(p)$, as given in Section 8.3.2, begins with the root having number 0. Some people prefer to use a level numbering $g(p)$ in which the root is assigned number 1, because it simplifies the arithmetic for finding neighboring positions. Redo Exercise R-8.16, but assuming that we use a level numbering $g(p)$ in which the root is assigned number 1.

R-8.18 In what order are positions visited during a preorder traversal of the tree of Figure 8.6?

R-8.19 In what order are positions visited during a postorder traversal of the tree of Figure 8.6?

R-8.20 Let T be an ordered tree with more than one node. Is it possible that the preorder traversal of T visits the nodes in the same order as the postorder traversal of T? If so, give an example; otherwise, explain why this cannot occur. Likewise, is it possible that the preorder traversal of T visits the nodes in the reverse order of the postorder traversal of T? If so, give an example; otherwise, explain why this cannot occur.

R-8.21 Answer the previous question for the case when T is a proper binary tree with more than one node.

R-8.22 Draw a binary tree T that simultaneously satisfies the following:

- Each internal node of T stores a single character.
- A *preorder* traversal of T yields EXAMFUN.
- An *inorder* traversal of T yields MAFXUEN.

R-8.23 Consider the example of a breadth-first traversal given in Figure 8.15. Using the annotated numbers from that figure, describe the contents of the queue before each pass of the while loop in Code Fragment 8.14. To get started, the queue has contents $\{1\}$ before the first pass, and contents $\{2,3,4\}$ before the second pass.

R-8.24 Give the output of the method parenthesize(T, T.root()), as described in Code Fragment 8.26, when T is the tree of Figure 8.6.

R-8.25 Describe a modification to parenthesize, from Code Fragment 8.26, that relies on the length( ) method for the String class to output the parenthetic representation of a tree with line breaks added to display the tree in a text window that is 80 characters wide.

R-8.26 What is the running time of parenthesize(T, T.root()), as given in Code Fragment 8.26, for a tree T with n nodes?

Creativity

C-8.27 Describe an efficient algorithm for converting a fully balanced string of parentheses into an equivalent tree. The tree associated with such a string is defined recursively. The outermost pair of balanced parentheses is associated with the root and each substring inside this pair, defined by the substring between two balanced parentheses, is associated with a subtree of this root.

C-8.28 The *path length* of a tree T is the sum of the depths of all positions in T. Describe a linear-time method for computing the path length of a tree T.

C-8.29 Define the *internal path length*, $I(T)$, of a tree T to be the sum of the depths of all the internal positions in T. Likewise, define the *external path length*, $E(T)$, of a tree T to be the sum of the depths of all the external positions in T. Show that if T is a proper binary tree with n positions, then $E(T) = I(T) + n - 1$.

C-8.30 Let T be a (not necessarily proper) binary tree with n nodes, and let D be the sum of the depths of all the external nodes of T. Show that if T has the minimum number of external nodes possible, then D is $O(n)$ and if T has the maximum number of external nodes possible, then D is $O(n \log n)$.

C-8.31 Let T be a (possibly improper) binary tree with n nodes, and let D be the sum of the depths of all the external nodes of T. Describe a configuration for T such that D is $\Omega(n^2)$. Such a tree would be the worst case for the asymptotic running time of method heightBad (Code Fragment 8.4).

C-8.32 For a tree T, let n_I denote the number of its internal nodes, and let n_E denote the number of its external nodes. Show that if every internal node in T has exactly 3 children, then $n_E = 2n_I + 1$.

C-8.33 Two ordered trees T' and T'' are said to be *isomorphic* if one of the following holds:

- Both T' and T'' are empty.
- Both T' and T'' consist of a single node
- The roots of T' and T'' have the same number $k \geq 1$ of subtrees, and the ith such subtree of T' is isomorphic to the ith such subtree of T'' for $i = 1, \ldots, k$.

Design an algorithm that tests whether two given ordered trees are isomorphic. What is the running time of your algorithm?

C-8.34 Show that there are more than 2^n improper binary trees with n internal nodes such that no pair are isomorphic (see Exercise C-8.33).

C-8.35 If we exclude isomorphic trees (see Exercise C-8.33), exactly how many proper binary trees exist with exactly 4 leaves?

C-8.36 Add support in LinkedBinaryTree for a method, pruneSubtree(p), that removes the entire subtree rooted at position p, making sure to maintain an accurate count of the size of the tree. What is the running time of your implementation?

C-8.37 Add support in LinkedBinaryTree for a method, swap(p, q), that has the effect of restructuring the tree so that the node referenced by p takes the place of the node referenced by q, and vice versa. Make sure to properly handle the case when the nodes are adjacent.

C-8.38 We can simplify parts of our LinkedBinaryTree implementation if we make use of of a single sentinel node, such that the sentinel is the parent of the real root of the tree, and the root is referenced as the left child of the sentinel. Furthermore, the sentinel will take the place of null as the value of the left or right member for a node without such a child. Give a new implementation of the update methods remove and attach, assuming such a representation.

C-8.39 Describe how to clone a LinkedBinaryTree instance representing a proper binary tree, with use of the attach method.

C-8.40 Describe how to clone a LinkedBinaryTree instance representing a (not necessarily proper) binary tree, with use of the addLeft and addRight methods.

C-8.41 Modify the LinkedBinaryTree class to formally support the Cloneable interface, as described in Section 3.6.

C-8.42 Give an efficient algorithm that computes and prints, for every position p of a tree T, the element of p followed by the height of p's subtree.

C-8.43 Give an $O(n)$-time algorithm for computing the depths of all positions of a tree T, where n is the number of nodes of T.

C-8.44 The ***balance factor*** of an internal position p of a proper binary tree is the difference between the heights of the right and left subtrees of p. Show how to specialize the Euler tour traversal of Section 8.4.6 to print the balance factors of all the internal nodes of a proper binary tree.

C-8.45 Design algorithms for the following operations for a binary tree T:
- preorderNext(p): Return the position visited after p in a preorder traversal of T (or null if p is the last node visited).
- inorderNext(p): Return the position visited after p in an inorder traversal of T (or null if p is the last node visited).
- postorderNext(p): Return the position visited after p in a postorder traversal of T (or null if p is the last node visited).

What are the worst-case running times of your algorithms?

C-8.46 Describe, in pseudocode, a nonrecursive method for performing an inorder traversal of a binary tree in linear time.

C-8.47 To implement the preorder method of the AbstractTree class, we relied on the convenience of creating a snapshot. Reimplement a preorder method that creates a *lazy iterator*. (See Section 7.4.2 for discussion of iterators.)

C-8.48 Repeat Exercise C-8.47, implementing the postorder method of the AbstractTree class.

C-8.49 Repeat Exercise C-8.47, implementing the AbstractBinaryTree's inorder method.

C-8.50 Algorithm preorderDraw draws a binary tree T by assigning x- and y-coordinates to each position p such that $x(p)$ is the number of nodes preceding p in the preorder traversal of T and $y(p)$ is the depth of p in T.

    a. Show that the drawing of T produced by preorderDraw has no pairs of crossing edges.

    b. Redraw the binary tree of Figure 8.19 using preorderDraw.

C-8.51 Redo the previous problem for the algorithm postorderDraw that is similar to preorderDraw except that it assigns $x(p)$ to be the number of nodes preceding position p in the postorder traversal.

C-8.52 We can define a ***binary tree representation*** T' for an ordered general tree T as follows (see Figure 8.21):

- For each position p of T, there is an associated position p' of T'.
- If p is a leaf of T, then p' in T' does not have a left child; otherwise the left child of p' is q', where q is the first child of p in T.
- If p has a sibling q ordered immediately after it in T, then q' is the right child of p' in T; otherwise p' does not have a right child.

Given such a representation T' of a general ordered tree T, answer each of the following questions:

    a. Is a preorder traversal of T' equivalent to a preorder traversal of T?

    b. Is a postorder traversal of T' equivalent to a postorder traversal of T?

    c. Is an inorder traversal of T' equivalent to one of the standard traversals of T? If so, which one?

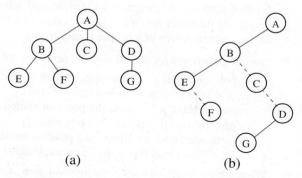

(a)   (b)

Figure 8.21: Representation of a tree with a binary tree: (a) tree T; (b) binary tree T' for T. The dashed edges connect nodes of T' that are siblings in T.

C-8.53 Design an algorithm for drawing *general* trees, using a style similar to the inorder traversal approach for drawing binary trees.

C-8.54 Let the **rank** of a position p during a traversal be defined such that the first element visited has rank 1, the second element visited has rank 2, and so on. For each position p in a tree T, let $\text{pre}(p)$ be the rank of p in a preorder traversal of T, let $\text{post}(p)$ be the rank of p in a postorder traversal of T, let $\text{depth}(p)$ be the depth of p, and let $\text{desc}(p)$ be the number of descendants of p, including p itself. Derive a formula defining $\text{post}(p)$ in terms of $\text{desc}(p)$, $\text{depth}(p)$, and $\text{pre}(p)$, for each node p in T.

C-8.55 Let T be a tree with n positions. Define the **lowest common ancestor** (LCA) between two positions p and q as the lowest position in T that has both p and q as descendants (where we allow a position to be a descendant of itself). Given two positions p and q, describe an efficient algorithm for finding the LCA of p and q. What is the running time of your algorithm?

C-8.56 Suppose each position p of a binary tree T is labeled with its value $f(p)$ in a level numbering of T. Design a fast method for determining $f(a)$ for the lowest common ancestor (LCA), a, of two positions p and q in T, given $f(p)$ and $f(q)$. You do not need to find position a, just value $f(a)$.

C-8.57 Let T be a binary tree with n positions, and, for any position p in T, let d_p denote the depth of p in T. The **distance** between two positions p and q in T is $d_p + d_q - 2d_a$, where a is the lowest common ancestor (LCA) of p and q. The **diameter** of T is the maximum distance between two positions in T. Describe an efficient algorithm for finding the diameter of T. What is the running time of your algorithm?

C-8.58 The **indented parenthetic representation** of a tree T is a variation of the parenthetic representation of T (see Code Fragment 8.26) that uses indentation and line breaks as illustrated in Figure 8.22. Give an algorithm that prints this representation of a tree.

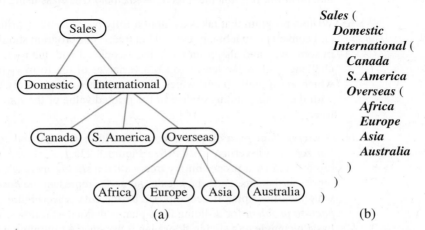

Figure 8.22: (a) Tree T; (b) indented parenthetic representation of T.

C-8.59 As mentioned in Exercise C-6.19, ***postfix notation*** is an unambiguous way of writing an arithmetic expression without parentheses. It is defined so that if "$(exp_1)\,\textbf{op}\,(exp_2)$" is a normal (infix) fully parenthesized expression with operation **op**, then its postfix equivalent is "$pexp_1\ pexp_2\ \textbf{op}$", where $pexp_1$ is the postfix version of exp_1 and $pexp_2$ is the postfix version of exp_2. The postfix version of a single number or variable is just that number or variable. So, for example, the postfix version of the infix expression "$((5+2)*(8-3))/4$" is "$5\ 2+8\ 3-*$ $4\ /$". Give an efficient algorithm for converting an infix arithmetic expression to its equivalent postfix notation. (Hint: First convert the infix expression into its equivalent binary tree representation.)

C-8.60 Let T be a binary tree with n positions. Define a ***Roman position*** to be a position p in T, such that the number of descendants in p's left subtree differ from the number of descendants in p's right subtree by at most 5. Describe a linear-time method for finding each position p of T, such that p is not a Roman position, but all of p's descendants are Roman.

Projects

P-8.61 Implement the binary tree ADT using the array-based representation described in Section 8.3.2.

P-8.62 Implement the tree ADT using a linked structure as described in Section 8.3.3. Provide a reasonable set of update methods for your tree.

P-8.63 Implement the tree ADT using the binary tree representation described in Exercise C-8.52. You may adapt the LinkedBinaryTree implementation.

P-8.64 The memory usage for the LinkedBinaryTree class can be streamlined by removing the parent reference from each node, and instead implementing a Position as an object that keeps a list of nodes representing the entire path from the root to that position. Reimplement the LinkedBinaryTree class using this strategy.

P-8.65 Write a program that takes as input a fully parenthesized, arithmetic expression and converts it to a binary expression tree. Your program should display the tree in some way and also print the value associated with the root. For an additional challenge, allow the leaves to store variables of the form x_1, x_2, x_3, and so on, which are initially 0 and which can be updated interactively by your program, with the corresponding update in the printed value of the root of the expression tree.

P-8.66 A ***slicing floor plan*** divides a rectangle with horizontal and vertical sides using horizontal and vertical ***cuts***. (See Figure 8.23a.) A slicing floor plan can be represented by a proper binary tree, called a ***slicing tree***, whose internal nodes represent the cuts, and whose external nodes represent the ***basic rectangles*** into which the floor plan is decomposed by the cuts. (See Figure 8.23b.) The ***compaction problem*** for a slicing floor plan is defined as follows. Assume that each basic rectangle of a slicing floor plan is assigned a minimum width w and a minimum height h. The compaction problem is to find the smallest possible height

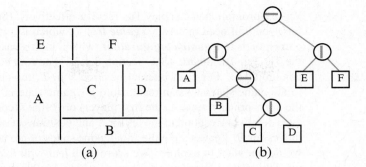

Figure 8.23: (a) Slicing floor plan; (b) slicing tree associated with the floor plan.

and width for each rectangle of the slicing floor plan that is compatible with the minimum dimensions of the basic rectangles. Namely, this problem requires the assignment of values $h(p)$ and $w(p)$ to each position p of the slicing tree such that:

$$
w(p) = \begin{cases}
w & \text{if } p \text{ is a leaf whose basic rectangle has minimum width } w \\[2ex]
\max(w(\ell), w(r)) & \text{if } p \text{ is an internal position, associated with a horizontal cut, with left child } \ell \text{ and right child } r \\[2ex]
w(\ell) + w(r) & \text{if } p \text{ is an internal position, associated with a vertical cut, with left child } \ell \text{ and right child } r
\end{cases}
$$

$$
h(p) = \begin{cases}
h & \text{if } p \text{ is a leaf node whose basic rectangle has minimum height } h \\[2ex]
h(\ell) + h(r) & \text{if } p \text{ is an internal position, associated with a horizontal cut, with left child } \ell \text{ and right child } r \\[2ex]
\max(h(\ell), h(r)) & \text{if } p \text{ is an internal position, associated with a vertical cut, with left child } \ell \text{ and right child } r
\end{cases}
$$

Design a data structure for slicing floor plans that supports the operations:

- Create a floor plan consisting of a single basic rectangle.
- Decompose a basic rectangle by means of a horizontal cut.
- Decompose a basic rectangle by means of a vertical cut.
- Assign minimum height and width to a basic rectangle.
- Draw the slicing tree associated with the floor plan.
- Compact and draw the floor plan.

P-8.67 Write a program that can play Tic-Tac-Toe effectively. (See Section 3.1.5.) To do this, you will need to create a **game tree** T, which is a tree where each position corresponds to a **game configuration**, which, in this case, is a representation of the Tic-Tac-Toe board. (See Section 8.4.2.) The root corresponds to the initial configuration. For each internal position p in T, the children of p correspond to the game states we can reach from p's game state in a single legal move for the appropriate player, A (the first player) or B (the second player). Positions at even depths correspond to moves for A and positions at odd depths correspond to moves for B. Leaves are either final game states or are at a depth beyond which we do not want to explore. We score each leaf with a value that indicates how good this state is for player A. In large games, like chess, we have to use a heuristic scoring function, but for small games, like Tic-Tac-Toe, we can construct the entire game tree and score leaves as $+1$, 0, -1, indicating whether player A has a win, draw, or lose in that configuration. A good algorithm for choosing moves is **minimax**. In this algorithm, we assign a score to each internal position p in T, such that if p represents A's turn, we compute p's score as the maximum of the scores of p's children (which corresponds to A's optimal play from p). If an internal node p represents B's turn, then we compute p's score as the minimum of the scores of p's children (which corresponds to B's optimal play from p).

P-8.68 Write a program that takes as input a general tree T and a position p of T and converts T to another tree with the same set of position adjacencies, but now with p as its root.

P-8.69 Write a program that draws a binary tree.

P-8.70 Write a program that draws a general tree.

P-8.71 Write a program that can input and display a person's family tree.

P-8.72 Write a program that visualizes an Euler tour traversal of a proper binary tree, including the movements from node to node and the actions associated with visits on the left, from below, and on the right. Illustrate your program by having it compute and display preorder labels, inorder labels, postorder labels, ancestor counts, and descendant counts for each node in the tree (not necessarily all at the same time).

Chapter Notes

Discussions of the classic preorder, inorder, and postorder tree traversal methods can be found in Knuth's *Fundamental Algorithms* book [60]. The Euler tour traversal technique comes from the parallel algorithms community; it is introduced by Tarjan and Vishkin [86] and is discussed by JáJá [50] and by Karp and Ramachandran [55]. The algorithm for drawing a tree is generally considered to be a part of the "folklore" of graph-drawing algorithms. The reader interested in graph drawing is referred to the book by Di Battista, Eades, Tamassia, and Tollis [29] and the survey by Tamassia and Liotta [85]. The puzzle in Exercise R-8.11 was communicated by Micha Sharir.

Chapter
9

Priority Queues

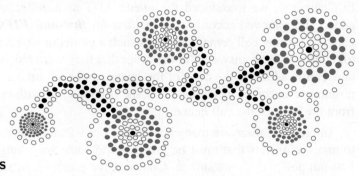

Contents

9.1   The Priority Queue Abstract Data Type

9.1.1 Priorities

In Chapter 6, we introduced the queue ADT as a collection of objects that are added and removed according to the *first-in, first-out* (*FIFO*) principle. A company's customer call center embodies such a model in which waiting customers are told "calls will be answered in the order that they were received." In that setting, a new call is added to the back of the queue, and each time a customer service representative becomes available, he or she is connected with the call that is removed from the front of the call queue.

In practice, there are many applications in which a queue-like structure is used to manage objects that must be processed in some way, but for which the first-in, first-out policy does not suffice. Consider, for example, an air-traffic control center that has to decide which flight to clear for landing from among many approaching the airport. This choice may be influenced by factors such as each plane's distance from the runway, time spent waiting in a holding pattern, or amount of remaining fuel. It is unlikely that the landing decisions are based purely on a FIFO policy.

There are other situations in which a "first come, first serve" policy might seem reasonable, yet for which other priorities come into play. To use another airline analogy, suppose a certain flight is fully booked an hour prior to departure. Because of the possibility of cancellations, the airline maintains a queue of standby passengers hoping to get a seat. Although the priority of a standby passenger is influenced by the check-in time of that passenger, other considerations include the fare paid and frequent-flyer status. So it may be that an available seat is given to a passenger who has arrived *later* than another, if such a passenger is assigned a better priority by the airline agent.

In this chapter, we introduce a new abstract data type known as a ***priority queue***. This is a collection of prioritized elements that allows arbitrary element insertion, and allows the removal of the element that has first priority. When an element is added to a priority queue, the user designates its priority by providing an associated ***key***. The element with the *minimal* key will be the next to be removed from the queue (thus, an element with key 1 will be given priority over an element with key 2). Although it is quite common for priorities to be expressed numerically, any Java object may be used as a key, as long as there exists means to compare any two instances a and b, in a way that defines a natural order of the keys. With such generality, applications may develop their own notion of priority for each element. For example, different financial analysts may assign different ratings (i.e., priorities) to a particular asset, such as a share of stock.

9.1.2 The Priority Queue ADT

We model an element and its priority as a key-value composite known as an *entry*. (However, we defer until Section 9.2.1 the technical definition of the Entry type.)

We define the priority queue ADT to support the following methods:

insert(k, v): Creates an entry with key k and value v in the priority queue.

min( ): Returns (but does not remove) a priority queue entry (k,v) having minimal key; returns null if the priority queue is empty.

removeMin( ): Removes and returns an entry (k,v) having minimal key from the priority queue; returns null if the priority queue is empty.

size( ): Returns the number of entries in the priority queue.

isEmpty( ): Returns a boolean indicating whether the priority queue is empty.

A priority queue may have multiple entries with equivalent keys, in which case methods min and removeMin may report an arbitrary choice among those entry having minimal key. Values may be any type of object.

In our initial model for a priority queue, we assume that an element's key remains fixed once it has been added to a priority queue. In Section 9.5, we consider an extension that allows a user to update an element's key within the priority queue.

Example 9.1: *The following table shows a series of operations and their effects on an initially empty priority queue. The "Priority Queue Contents" column is somewhat deceiving since it shows the entries sorted by key. Such an internal representation is not required of a priority queue.*

Method	Return Value	Priority Queue Contents
insert(5,A)		{ (5,A) }
insert(9,C)		{ (5,A), (9,C) }
insert(3,B)		{ (3,B), (5,A), (9,C) }
min( )	(3,B)	{ (3,B), (5,A), (9,C) }
removeMin( )	(3,B)	{ (5,A), (9,C) }
insert(7,D)		{ (5,A), (7,D), (9,C) }
removeMin( )	(5,A)	{ (7,D), (9,C) }
removeMin( )	(7,D)	{ (9,C) }
removeMin( )	(9,C)	{ }
removeMin( )	null	{ }
isEmpty( )	true	{ }

9.2   Implementing a Priority Queue

In this section, we discuss several technical issues involving the implementation of the priority queue ADT in Java, and we define an abstract base class that provides functionality that is shared by all priority queue implementations in this chapter. We then provide two concrete priority queue implementations using a positional list L (see Section 7.3) for storage. They differ in whether or not entries are maintained in sorted order according to their keys.

9.2.1   The Entry Composite

One challenge in implementing a priority queue is that we must keep track of both an element and its key, even as entries are relocated within a data structure. This is reminiscent of a case study from Section 7.7 in which we maintain a list of elements with access frequencies. In that setting, we introduced the **composition design pattern**, defining an Item class that paired each element with its associated count in our primary data structure. For priority queues, we use composition to pair a key k and a value v as a single object. To formalize this, we define the public interface, Entry, shown in Code Fragment 9.1.

```
1  /** Interface for a key-value pair. */
2  public interface Entry<K,V> {
3    K getKey( );                          // returns the key stored in this entry
4    V getValue( );                        // returns the value stored in this entry
5  }
```

Code Fragment 9.1: Java interface for an entry storing a key-value pair.

We then use the Entry type in the formal interface for the priority queue, shown in Code Fragment 9.2. This allows us to return both a key and value as a single object from methods such as min and removeMin. We also define the insert method to return an entry; in a more advanced **adaptable priority queue** (see Section 9.5), that entry can be subsequently updated or removed.

```
1  /** Interface for the priority queue ADT. */
2  public interface PriorityQueue<K,V> {
3    int size( );
4    boolean isEmpty( );
5    Entry<K,V> insert(K key, V value) throws IllegalArgumentException;
6    Entry<K,V> min( );
7    Entry<K,V> removeMin( );
8  }
```

Code Fragment 9.2: Java interface for the priority queue ADT.

9.2.2   Comparing Keys with Total Orders

In defining the priority queue ADT, we can allow any type of object to serve as a key, but we must be able to compare keys to each other in a meaningful way. More so, the results of the comparisons must not be contradictory. For a comparison rule, which we denote by $\leq$, to be self-consistent, it must define a **total order** relation, which is to say that it satisfies the following properties for any keys k_1, k_2, and k_3:

- **Comparability property:** $k_1 \leq k_2$ or $k_2 \leq k_1$.
- **Antisymmetric property**: if $k_1 \leq k_2$ and $k_2 \leq k_1$, then $k_1 = k_2$.
- **Transitive property**: if $k_1 \leq k_2$ and $k_2 \leq k_3$, then $k_1 \leq k_3$.

The comparability property states that comparison rule is defined for every pair of keys. Note that this property implies the following one:

- **Reflexive property**: $k \leq k$.

A comparison rule, $\leq$, that defines a total order relation will never lead to a contradiction. Such a rule defines a linear ordering among a set of keys; hence, if a (finite) set of elements has a total order defined for it, then the notion of a **minimal** key, $k_{\min}$, is well defined, as a key in which $k_{\min} \leq k$, for any other key k in our set.

The Comparable Interface

Java provides two means for defining comparisons between object types. The first of these is that a class may define what is known as the **natural ordering** of its instances by formally implementing the java.lang.Comparable interface, which includes a single method, compareTo. The syntax a.compareTo(b) must return an integer i with the following meaning:

- $i < 0$ designates that $a < b$.
- $i = 0$ designates that $a = b$.
- $i > 0$ designates that $a > b$.

For example, the compareTo method of the String class defines the natural ordering of strings to be **lexicographic**, which is a case-sensitive extension of the alphabetic ordering to Unicode.

The Comparator Interface

In some applications, we may want to compare objects according to some notion other than their natural ordering. For example, we might be interested in which of two strings is the shortest, or in defining our own complex rules for judging which of two stocks is more promising. To support generality, Java defines the java.util.Comparator interface. A **comparator** is an object that is external to the class of the keys it compares. It provides a method with the signature compare(a, b) that returns an integer with similar meaning to the compareTo method described above.

As a concrete example, Code Fragment 9.3 defines a comparator that evaluates strings based on their length (rather than their natural lexicographic order).

```
1  public class StringLengthComparator implements Comparator<String> {
2    /** Compares two strings according to their lengths. */
3    public int compare(String a, String b) {
4      if (a.length() < b.length()) return −1;
5      else if (a.length() == b.length()) return 0;
6      else return 1;
7    }
8  }
```

Code Fragment 9.3: A comparator that evaluates strings based on their lengths.

Comparators and the Priority Queue ADT

For a general and reusable form of a priority queue, we allow a user to choose any key type and to send an appropriate comparator instance as a parameter to the priority queue constructor. The priority queue will use that comparator anytime it needs to compare two keys to each other.

For convenience, we also allow a default priority queue to instead rely on the natural ordering for the given keys (assuming those keys come from a comparable class). In that case, we build our own instance of a DefaultComparator class, shown in Code Fragment 9.4.

```
1  public class DefaultComparator<E> implements Comparator<E> {
2    public int compare(E a, E b) throws ClassCastException {
3      return ((Comparable<E>) a).compareTo(b);
4    }
5  }
```

Code Fragment 9.4: A DefaultComparator class that implements a comparator based upon the natural ordering of its element type.

9.2.3 The AbstractPriorityQueue Base Class

To manage technical issues common to all our priority queue implementations, we define an abstract base class named AbstractPriorityQueue in Code Fragment 9.5. (See Section 2.3.3 for a discussion of abstract base classes.) This includes a nested PQEntry class that implements the public Entry interface.

Our abstract class also declares and initializes an instance variable, comp, that stores the comparator being used for the priority queue. We then provide a protected method, compare, that invokes the comparator on the keys of two given entries.

```
1   /** An abstract base class to assist implementations of the PriorityQueue interface.*/
2   public abstract class AbstractPriorityQueue<K,V>
3                                                implements PriorityQueue<K,V> {
4     //---------------- nested PQEntry class ----------------
5     protected static class PQEntry<K,V> implements Entry<K,V> {
6       private K k;   // key
7       private V v;   // value
8       public PQEntry(K key, V value) {
9         k = key;
10        v = value;
11      }
12      // methods of the Entry interface
13      public K getKey() { return k; }
14      public V getValue() { return v; }
15      // utilities not exposed as part of the Entry interface
16      protected void setKey(K key) { k = key; }
17      protected void setValue(V value) { v = value; }
18    } //----------- end of nested PQEntry class -----------
19
20    // instance variable for an AbstractPriorityQueue
21    /** The comparator defining the ordering of keys in the priority queue. */
22    private Comparator<K> comp;
23    /** Creates an empty priority queue using the given comparator to order keys. */
24    protected AbstractPriorityQueue(Comparator<K> c) { comp = c; }
25    /** Creates an empty priority queue based on the natural ordering of its keys. */
26    protected AbstractPriorityQueue() { this(new DefaultComparator<K>()); }
27    /** Method for comparing two entries according to key */
28    protected int compare(Entry<K,V> a, Entry<K,V> b) {
29      return comp.compare(a.getKey(), b.getKey());
30    }
31    /** Determines whether a key is valid. */
32    protected boolean checkKey(K key) throws IllegalArgumentException {
33      try {
34        return (comp.compare(key,key) == 0);  // see if key can be compared to itself
35      } catch (ClassCastException e) {
36        throw new IllegalArgumentException("Incompatible key");
37      }
38    }
39    /** Tests whether the priority queue is empty. */
40    public boolean isEmpty() { return size() == 0; }
41  }
```

Code Fragment 9.5: The AbstractPriorityQueue class. This provides a nested PQEntry class that composes a key and a value into a single object, and support for managing a comparator. For convenience, we also provide an implementation of isEmpty based on a presumed size method.

9.2.4   Implementing a Priority Queue with an Unsorted List

In our first concrete implementation of a priority queue, we store entries within an *unsorted* linked list. Code Fragment 9.6 presents our UnsortedPriorityQueue class as a subclass of the AbstractPriorityQueue class (from Code Fragment 9.5). For internal storage, key-value pairs are represented as composites, using instances of the inherited PQEntry class. These entries are stored within a PositionalList that is an instance variable. We assume that the positional list is implemented with a doubly linked list, as in Section 7.3, so that all operations of that ADT execute in $O(1)$ time.

We begin with an empty list when a new priority queue is constructed. At all times, the size of the list equals the number of key-value pairs currently stored in the priority queue. For this reason, our priority queue size method simply returns the length of the internal list. By the design of our AbstractPriorityQueue class, we inherit a concrete implementation of the isEmpty method that relies on a call to our size method.

Each time a key-value pair is added to the priority queue, via the insert method, we create a new PQEntry composite for the given key and value, and add that entry to the end of the list. Such an implementation takes $O(1)$ time.

The remaining challenge is that when min or removeMin is called, we must locate the entry with minimal key. Because the entries are not sorted, we must inspect all entries to find one with a minimal key. For convenience, we define a private findMin utility that returns the *position* of an entry with minimal key. Knowledge of the position allows the removeMin method to invoke the remove method on the positional list. The min method simply uses the position to retrieve the entry when preparing a key-value tuple to return. Due to the loop for finding the minimal key, both min and removeMin methods run in $O(n)$ time, where n is the number of entries in the priority queue.

A summary of the running times for the UnsortedPriorityQueue class is given in Table 9.1.

Method	Running Time
size	$O(1)$
isEmpty	$O(1)$
insert	$O(1)$
min	$O(n)$
removeMin	$O(n)$

Table 9.1: Worst-case running times of the methods of a priority queue of size n, realized by means of an unsorted, doubly linked list. The space requirement is $O(n)$.

```
1   /** An implementation of a priority queue with an unsorted list. */
2   public class UnsortedPriorityQueue<K,V> extends AbstractPriorityQueue<K,V> {
3     /** primary collection of priority queue entries */
4     private PositionalList<Entry<K,V>> list = new LinkedPositionalList<>();
5
6     /** Creates an empty priority queue based on the natural ordering of its keys. */
7     public UnsortedPriorityQueue() { super(); }
8     /** Creates an empty priority queue using the given comparator to order keys. */
9     public UnsortedPriorityQueue(Comparator<K> comp) { super(comp); }
10
11    /** Returns the Position of an entry having minimal key. */
12    private Position<Entry<K,V>> findMin() {     // only called when nonempty
13      Position<Entry<K,V>> small = list.first();
14      for (Position<Entry<K,V>> walk : list.positions())
15        if (compare(walk.getElement(), small.getElement()) < 0)
16          small = walk;          // found an even smaller key
17      return small;
18    }
19
20    /** Inserts a key-value pair and returns the entry created. */
21    public Entry<K,V> insert(K key, V value) throws IllegalArgumentException {
22      checkKey(key);      // auxiliary key-checking method (could throw exception)
23      Entry<K,V> newest = new PQEntry<>(key, value);
24      list.addLast(newest);
25      return newest;
26    }
27
28    /** Returns (but does not remove) an entry with minimal key. */
29    public Entry<K,V> min() {
30      if (list.isEmpty()) return null;
31      return findMin().getElement();
32    }
33
34    /** Removes and returns an entry with minimal key. */
35    public Entry<K,V> removeMin() {
36      if (list.isEmpty()) return null;
37      return list.remove(findMin());
38    }
39
40    /** Returns the number of items in the priority queue. */
41    public int size() { return list.size(); }
42  }
```

Code Fragment 9.6: An implementation of a priority queue using an unsorted list. The parent class AbstractPriorityQueue is given in Code Fragment 9.5, and the LinkedPositionalList class is from Section 7.3.

9.2.5   Implementing a Priority Queue with a Sorted List

Our next implementation of a priority queue also uses a positional list, yet maintains entries sorted by nondecreasing keys. This ensures that the first element of the list is an entry with the smallest key.

Our SortedPriorityQueue class is given in Code Fragment 9.7. The implementation of min and removeMin are rather straightforward given knowledge that the first element of a list has a minimal key. We rely on the first method of the positional list to find the position of the first entry, and the remove method to remove the entry from the list. Assuming that the list is implemented with a doubly linked list, operations min and removeMin take $O(1)$ time.

This benefit comes at a cost, however, for method insert now requires that we scan the list to find the appropriate position to insert the new entry. Our implementation starts at the end of the list, walking backward until the new key is smaller than that of an existing entry; in the worst case, it progresses until reaching the front of the list. Therefore, the insert method takes $O(n)$ worst-case time, where n is the number of entries in the priority queue at the time the method is executed. In summary, when using a sorted list to implement a priority queue, insertion runs in linear time, whereas finding and removing the minimum can be done in constant time.

Comparing the Two List-Based Implementations

Table 9.2 compares the running times of the methods of a priority queue realized by means of a sorted and unsorted list, respectively. We see an interesting trade-off when we use a list to implement the priority queue ADT. An unsorted list supports fast insertions but slow queries and deletions, whereas a sorted list allows fast queries and deletions, but slow insertions.

Method	Unsorted List	Sorted List
size	$O(1)$	$O(1)$
isEmpty	$O(1)$	$O(1)$
insert	$O(1)$	$O(n)$
min	$O(n)$	$O(1)$
removeMin	$O(n)$	$O(1)$

Table 9.2: Worst-case running times of the methods of a priority queue of size n, realized by means of an unsorted or sorted list, respectively. We assume that the list is implemented by a doubly linked list. The space requirement is $O(n)$.

```
1    /** An implementation of a priority queue with a sorted list. */
2    public class SortedPriorityQueue<K,V> extends AbstractPriorityQueue<K,V> {
3      /** primary collection of priority queue entries */
4      private PositionalList<Entry<K,V>> list = new LinkedPositionalList<>();
5
6      /** Creates an empty priority queue based on the natural ordering of its keys. */
7      public SortedPriorityQueue() { super(); }
8      /** Creates an empty priority queue using the given comparator to order keys. */
9      public SortedPriorityQueue(Comparator<K> comp) { super(comp); }
10
11     /** Inserts a key-value pair and returns the entry created. */
12     public Entry<K,V> insert(K key, V value) throws IllegalArgumentException {
13       checkKey(key);      // auxiliary key-checking method (could throw exception)
14       Entry<K,V> newest = new PQEntry<>(key, value);
15       Position<Entry<K,V>> walk = list.last();
16       // walk backward, looking for smaller key
17       while (walk != null && compare(newest, walk.getElement()) < 0)
18         walk = list.before(walk);
19       if (walk == null)
20         list.addFirst(newest);                          // new key is smallest
21       else
22         list.addAfter(walk, newest);                    // newest goes after walk
23       return newest;
24     }
25
26     /** Returns (but does not remove) an entry with minimal key. */
27     public Entry<K,V> min() {
28       if (list.isEmpty()) return null;
29       return list.first().getElement();
30     }
31
32     /** Removes and returns an entry with minimal key. */
33     public Entry<K,V> removeMin() {
34       if (list.isEmpty()) return null;
35       return list.remove(list.first());
36     }
37
38     /** Returns the number of items in the priority queue. */
39     public int size() { return list.size(); }
40   }
```

Code Fragment 9.7: An implementation of a priority queue using a sorted list. The parent class AbstractPriorityQueue is given in Code Fragment 9.5, and the LinkedPositionalList class is from Section 7.3.

9.3   Heaps

The two strategies for implementing a priority queue ADT in the previous section demonstrate an interesting trade-off. When using an *unsorted* list to store entries, we can perform insertions in $O(1)$ time, but finding or removing an element with minimal key requires an $O(n)$-time loop through the entire collection. In contrast, if using a *sorted* list, we can trivially find or remove the minimal element in $O(1)$ time, but adding a new element to the queue may require $O(n)$ time to restore the sorted order.

In this section, we provide a more efficient realization of a priority queue using a data structure called a ***binary heap***. This data structure allows us to perform both insertions and removals in logarithmic time, which is a significant improvement over the list-based implementations discussed in Section 9.2. The fundamental way the heap achieves this improvement is to use the structure of a binary tree to find a compromise between elements being entirely unsorted and perfectly sorted.

9.3.1   The Heap Data Structure

A heap (see Figure 9.1) is a binary tree T that stores entries at its positions, and that satisfies two additional properties: a relational property defined in terms of the way keys are stored in T and a structural property defined in terms of the shape of T itself. The relational property is the following:

Heap-Order Property: In a heap T, for every position p other than the root, the key stored at p is greater than or equal to the key stored at p's parent.

As a consequence of the heap-order property, the keys encountered on a path from the root to a leaf of T are in nondecreasing order. Also, a minimal key is always stored at the root of T. This makes it easy to locate such an entry when min or removeMin is called, as it is informally said to be "at the top of the heap" (hence, the name "heap" for the data structure). By the way, the heap data structure defined here has nothing to do with the memory heap (Section 15.1.2) used in the runtime environment supporting a programming language like Java.

For the sake of efficiency, as will become clear later, we want the heap T to have as small a height as possible. We enforce this requirement by insisting that the heap T satisfy an additional structural property; it must be what we term ***complete***.

Complete Binary Tree Property: A heap T with height h is a ***complete*** binary tree if levels $0, 1, 2, \ldots, h-1$ of T have the maximal number of nodes possible (namely, level i has 2^i nodes, for $0 \leq i \leq h-1$) and the remaining nodes at level h reside in the leftmost possible positions at that level.

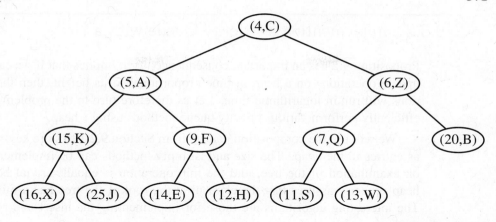

Figure 9.1: Example of a heap storing 13 entries with integer keys. The last position is the one storing entry $(13, W)$.

The tree in Figure 9.1 is complete because levels 0, 1, and 2 are full, and the six nodes in level 3 are in the six leftmost possible positions at that level. In formalizing what we mean by the leftmost possible positions, we refer to the discussion of *level numbering* from Section 8.3.2, in the context of an array-based representation of a binary tree. (In fact, in Section 9.3.2 we will discuss the use of an array to represent a heap.) A complete binary tree with n elements is one that has positions with level numbering 0 through $n - 1$. For example, in an array-based representation of the above tree, its 13 entries would be stored consecutively from $A[0]$ to $A[12]$.

The Height of a Heap

Let h denote the height of T. Insisting that T be complete also has an important consequence, as shown in Proposition 9.2.

Proposition 9.2: *A heap T storing n entries has height $h = \lfloor \log n \rfloor$.*

Justification: From the fact that T is complete, we know that the number of nodes in levels 0 through $h - 1$ of T is precisely $1 + 2 + 4 + \cdots + 2^{h-1} = 2^h - 1$, and that the number of nodes in level h is at least 1 and at most 2^h. Therefore

$$n \geq 2^h - 1 + 1 = 2^h \quad \text{and} \quad n \leq 2^h - 1 + 2^h = 2^{h+1} - 1.$$

By taking the logarithm of both sides of inequality $n \geq 2^h$, we see that height $h \leq \log n$. By rearranging terms and taking the logarithm of both sides of inequality $n \leq 2^{h+1} - 1$, we see that $h \geq \log(n + 1) - 1$. Since h is an integer, these two inequalities imply that $h = \lfloor \log n \rfloor$. ∎

9.3.2   Implementing a Priority Queue with a Heap

Proposition 9.2 has an important consequence, for it implies that if we can perform update operations on a heap in time proportional to its height, then those operations will run in logarithmic time. Let us therefore turn to the problem of how to efficiently perform various priority queue methods using a heap.

We will use the composition pattern from Section 9.2.1 to store key-value pairs as entries in the heap. The size and isEmpty methods can be implemented based on examination of the tree, and the min operation is equally trivial because the heap property assures that the element at the root of the tree has a minimal key. The interesting algorithms are those for implementing the insert and removeMin methods.

Adding an Entry to the Heap

Let us consider how to perform insert(k, v) on a priority queue implemented with a heap T. We store the pair (k, v) as an entry at a new node of the tree. To maintain the ***complete binary tree property***, that new node should be placed at a position p just beyond the rightmost node at the bottom level of the tree, or as the leftmost position of a new level, if the bottom level is already full (or if the heap is empty).

Up-Heap Bubbling After an Insertion

After this action, the tree T is complete, but it may violate the ***heap-order property***. Hence, unless position p is the root of T (that is, the priority queue was empty before the insertion), we compare the key at position p to that of p's parent, which we denote as q. If key $k_p \geq k_q$, the heap-order property is satisfied and the algorithm terminates. If instead $k_p < k_q$, then we need to restore the heap-order property, which can be locally achieved by swapping the entries stored at positions p and q. (See Figure 9.2c and d.) This swap causes the new entry to move up one level. Again, the heap-order property may be violated, so we repeat the process, going up in T until no violation of the heap-order property occurs. (See Figure 9.2e and h.)

The upward movement of the newly inserted entry by means of swaps is conventionally called ***up-heap bubbling***. A swap either resolves the violation of the heap-order property or propagates it one level up in the heap. In the worst case, up-heap bubbling causes the new entry to move all the way up to the root of heap T. Thus, in the worst case, the number of swaps performed in the execution of method insert is equal to the height of T. By Proposition 9.2, that bound is $\lfloor \log n \rfloor$.

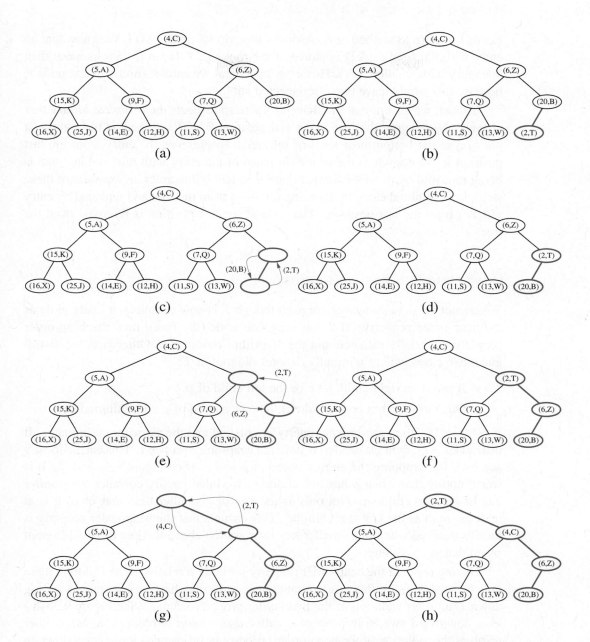

Figure 9.2: Insertion of a new entry with key 2 into the heap of Figure 9.1: (a) initial heap; (b) after adding a new node; (c and d) swap to locally restore the partial order property; (e and f) another swap; (g and h) final swap.

Removing the Entry with Minimal Key

Let us now turn to method removeMin of the priority queue ADT. We know that an entry with the smallest key is stored at the root r of T (even if there is more than one entry with smallest key). However, in general we cannot simply delete node r, because this would leave two disconnected subtrees.

Instead, we ensure that the shape of the heap respects the **complete binary tree property** by deleting the leaf at the *last* position p of T, defined as the rightmost position at the bottommost level of the tree. To preserve the entry from the last position p, we copy it to the root r (in place of the entry with minimal key that is being removed by the operation). Figure 9.3a and b illustrates an example of these steps, with minimal entry $(4, C)$ being removed from the root and replaced by entry $(13, W)$ from the last position. The node at the last position is removed from the tree.

Down-Heap Bubbling After a Removal

We are not yet done, however, for even though T is now complete, it likely violates the heap-order property. If T has only one node (the root), then the heap-order property is trivially satisfied and the algorithm terminates. Otherwise, we distinguish two cases, where p initially denotes the root of T:

- If p has no right child, let c be the left child of p.
- Otherwise (p has both children), let c be a child of p with minimal key.

If key $k_p \leq k_c$, the heap-order property is satisfied and the algorithm terminates. If instead $k_p > k_c$, then we need to restore the heap-order property. This can be locally achieved by swapping the entries stored at p and c. (See Figure 9.3c and d.) It is worth noting that when p has two children, we intentionally consider the *smaller* key of the two children. Not only is the key of c smaller than that of p, it is at least as small as the key at c's sibling. This ensures that the heap-order property is locally restored when that smaller key is promoted above the key that had been at p and that at c's sibling.

Having restored the heap-order property for node p relative to its children, there may be a violation of this property at c; hence, we may have to continue swapping down T until no violation of the heap-order property occurs. (See Figure 9.3e–h.) This downward swapping process is called **down-heap bubbling**. A swap either resolves the violation of the heap-order property or propagates it one level down in the heap. In the worst case, an entry moves all the way down to the bottom level. (See Figure 9.3.) Thus, the number of swaps performed in the execution of method removeMin is, in the worst case, equal to the height of heap T, that is, it is $\lfloor \log n \rfloor$ by Proposition 9.2.

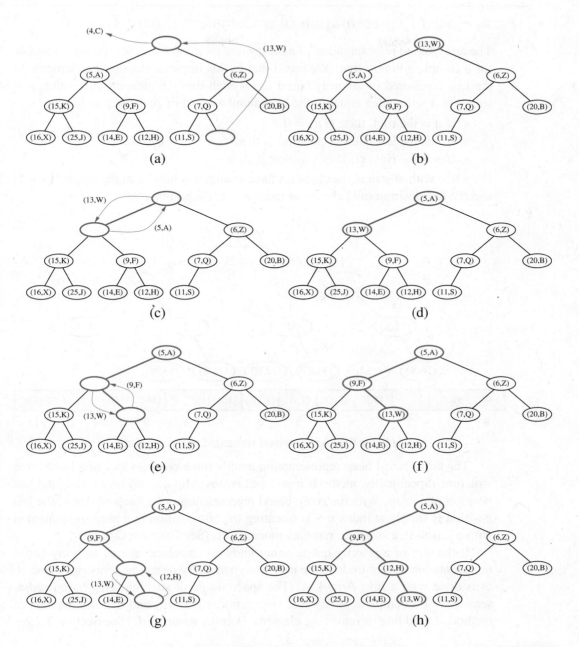

Figure 9.3: Removal of the entry with the smallest key from a heap: (a and b) deletion of the last node, whose entry gets stored into the root; (c and d) swap to locally restore the heap-order property; (e and f) another swap; (g and h) final swap.

Array-Based Representation of a Complete Binary Tree

The array-based representation of a binary tree (Section 8.3.2) is especially suitable for a complete binary tree. We recall that in this implementation, the elements of the tree are stored in an array-based list A such that the element at position p is stored in A with index equal to the level number $f(p)$ of p, defined as follows:

- If p is the root, then $f(p) = 0$.
- If p is the left child of position q, then $f(p) = 2f(q) + 1$.
- If p is the right child of position q, then $f(p) = 2f(q) + 2$.

For a tree with of size n, the elements have contiguous indices in the range $[0, n-1]$ and the last position of is always at index $n - 1$. (See Figure 9.4.)

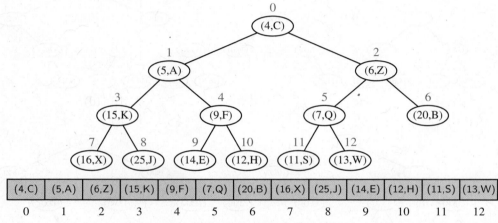

Figure 9.4: Array-based representation of a heap.

The array-based heap representation avoids some complexities of a linked tree structure. Specifically, methods insert and removeMin depend on locating the last position of a heap. With the array-based representation of a heap of size n, the last position is simply at index $n - 1$. Locating the last position in a heap implemented with a linked tree structure requires more effort. (See Exercise C-9.33.)

If the size of a priority queue is not known in advance, use of an array-based representation does introduce the need to dynamically resize the array on occasion, as is done with a Java ArrayList. The space usage of such an array-based representation of a complete binary tree with n nodes is $O(n)$, and the time bounds of methods for adding or removing elements become ***amortized***. (See Section 7.2.2.)

Java Heap Implementation

In Code Fragments 9.8 and 9.9, we provide a Java implementation of a heap-based priority queue. Although we think of our heap as a binary tree, we do not formally use the binary tree ADT. We prefer to use the more efficient array-based representation of a tree, maintaining a Java ArrayList of entry composites. To allow us to formalize our algorithms using tree-like terminology of *parent*, *left*, and *right*, the class includes protected utility methods that compute the level numbering of a parent or child of another position (lines 10–14 of Code Fragment 9.8). However, the "positions" in this representation are simply integer indices into the array-list.

Our class also has protected utilities swap, upheap, and downheap for the low-level movement of entries within the array-list. A new entry is added the end of the array-list, and then repositioned as needed with upheap. To remove the entry with minimal key (which resides at index 0), we move the last entry of the array-list from index $n - 1$ to index 0, and then invoke downheap to reposition it.

```java
1   /** An implementation of a priority queue using an array-based heap. */
2   public class HeapPriorityQueue<K,V> extends AbstractPriorityQueue<K,V> {
3     /** primary collection of priority queue entries */
4     protected ArrayList<Entry<K,V>> heap = new ArrayList<>( );
5     /** Creates an empty priority queue based on the natural ordering of its keys. */
6     public HeapPriorityQueue( ) { super( ); }
7     /** Creates an empty priority queue using the given comparator to order keys. */
8     public HeapPriorityQueue(Comparator<K> comp) { super(comp); }
9     // protected utilities
10    protected int parent(int j) { return (j−1) / 2; }         // truncating division
11    protected int left(int j) { return 2*j + 1; }
12    protected int right(int j) { return 2*j + 2; }
13    protected boolean hasLeft(int j) { return left(j) < heap.size( ); }
14    protected boolean hasRight(int j) { return right(j) < heap.size( ); }
15    /** Exchanges the entries at indices i and j of the array list. */
16    protected void swap(int i, int j) {
17      Entry<K,V> temp = heap.get(i);
18      heap.set(i, heap.get(j));
19      heap.set(j, temp);
20    }
21    /** Moves the entry at index j higher, if necessary, to restore the heap property. */
22    protected void upheap(int j) {
23      while (j > 0) {                        // continue until reaching root (or break statement)
24        int p = parent(j);
25        if (compare(heap.get(j), heap.get(p)) >= 0) break;    // heap property verified
26        swap(j, p);
27        j = p;                               // continue from the parent's location
28      }
29    }
```

Code Fragment 9.8: Priority queue that uses an array-based heap and extends AbstractPriorityQueue (Code Fragment 9.5). (Continues in Code Fragment 9.9.)

```
30    /** Moves the entry at index j lower, if necessary, to restore the heap property. */
31    protected void downheap(int j) {
32      while (hasLeft(j)) {                         // continue to bottom (or break statement)
33        int leftIndex = left(j);
34        int smallChildIndex = leftIndex;           // although right may be smaller
35        if (hasRight(j)) {
36            int rightIndex = right(j);
37            if (compare(heap.get(leftIndex), heap.get(rightIndex)) > 0)
38              smallChildIndex = rightIndex;         // right child is smaller
39        }
40        if (compare(heap.get(smallChildIndex), heap.get(j)) >= 0)
41          break;                                   // heap property has been restored
42        swap(j, smallChildIndex);
43        j = smallChildIndex;                       // continue at position of the child
44      }
45    }
46
47    // public methods
48    /** Returns the number of items in the priority queue. */
49    public int size() { return heap.size(); }
50    /** Returns (but does not remove) an entry with minimal key (if any). */
51    public Entry<K,V> min() {
52      if (heap.isEmpty()) return null;
53      return heap.get(0);
54    }
55    /** Inserts a key-value pair and returns the entry created. */
56    public Entry<K,V> insert(K key, V value) throws IllegalArgumentException {
57      checkKey(key);          // auxiliary key-checking method (could throw exception)
58      Entry<K,V> newest = new PQEntry<>(key, value);
59      heap.add(newest);                            // add to the end of the list
60      upheap(heap.size() − 1);                     // upheap newly added entry
61      return newest;
62    }
63    /** Removes and returns an entry with minimal key (if any). */
64    public Entry<K,V> removeMin() {
65      if (heap.isEmpty()) return null;
66      Entry<K,V> answer = heap.get(0);
67      swap(0, heap.size() − 1);                     // put minimum item at the end
68      heap.remove(heap.size() − 1);                 // and remove it from the list;
69      downheap(0);                                  // then fix new root
70      return answer;
71    }
72  }
```

Code Fragment 9.9: Priority queue implemented with an array-based heap (continued from Code Fragment 9.8).

9.3.3 Analysis of a Heap-Based Priority Queue

Table 9.3 shows the running time of the priority queue ADT methods for the heap implementation of a priority queue, assuming that two keys can be compared in $O(1)$ time and that the heap T is implemented with an array-based or linked-based tree representation.

In short, each of the priority queue ADT methods can be performed in $O(1)$ or in $O(\log n)$ time, where n is the number of entries at the time the method is executed. The analysis of the running time of the methods is based on the following:

- The heap T has n nodes, each storing a reference to a key-value entry.
- The height of heap T is $O(\log n)$, since T is complete (Proposition 9.2).
- The min operation runs in $O(1)$ because the root of the tree contains such an element.
- Locating the last position of a heap, as required for insert and removeMin, can be performed in $O(1)$ time for an array-based representation, or $O(\log n)$ time for a linked-tree representation. (See Exercise C-9.33.)
- In the worst case, up-heap and down-heap bubbling perform a number of swaps equal to the height of T.

Method	Running Time
size, isEmpty	$O(1)$
min	$O(1)$
insert	$O(\log n)^*$
removeMin	$O(\log n)^*$

*amortized, if using dynamic array

Table 9.3: Performance of a priority queue realized by means of a heap. We let n denote the number of entries in the priority queue at the time an operation is executed. The space requirement is $O(n)$. The running time of operations min and removeMin are amortized for an array-based representation, due to occasional resizing of a dynamic array; those bounds are worst case with a linked tree structure.

We conclude that the heap data structure is a very efficient realization of the priority queue ADT, independent of whether the heap is implemented with a linked structure or an array. The heap-based implementation achieves fast running times for both insertion and removal, unlike the implementations that were based on using an unsorted or sorted list.

9.3.4   Bottom-Up Heap Construction ⋆

If we start with an initially empty heap, n successive calls to the insert operation will run in $O(n \log n)$ time in the worst case. However, if all n key-value pairs to be stored in the heap are given in advance, such as during the first phase of the heap-sort algorithm (introduced in Section 9.4.2), there is an alternative **bottom-up** construction method that runs in $O(n)$ time.

In this section, we describe the bottom-up heap construction, and provide an implementation that can be used by the constructor of a heap-based priority queue.

For simplicity of exposition, we describe this bottom-up heap construction assuming the number of keys, n, is an integer such that $n = 2^{h+1} - 1$. That is, the heap is a complete binary tree with every level being full, so the heap has height $h = \log(n+1) - 1$. Viewed nonrecursively, bottom-up heap construction consists of the following $h + 1 = \log(n+1)$ steps:

1. In the first step (see Figure 9.5b), we construct $(n+1)/2$ elementary heaps storing one entry each.

2. In the second step (see Figure 9.5c–d), we form $(n+1)/4$ heaps, each storing three entries, by joining pairs of elementary heaps and adding a new entry. The new entry is placed at the root and may have to be swapped with the entry stored at a child to preserve the heap-order property.

3. In the third step (see Figure 9.5e–f), we form $(n+1)/8$ heaps, each storing 7 entries, by joining pairs of 3-entry heaps (constructed in the previous step) and adding a new entry. The new entry is placed initially at the root, but may have to move down with a down-heap bubbling to preserve the heap-order property.

   $\vdots$

i. In the generic ith step, $2 \leq i \leq h$, we form $(n+1)/2^i$ heaps, each storing $2^i - 1$ entries, by joining pairs of heaps storing $(2^{i-1} - 1)$ entries (constructed in the previous step) and adding a new entry. The new entry is placed initially at the root, but may have to move down with a down-heap bubbling to preserve the heap-order property.

   $\vdots$

$h+1$. In the last step (see Figure 9.5g–h), we form the final heap, storing all the n entries, by joining two heaps storing $(n-1)/2$ entries (constructed in the previous step) and adding a new entry. The new entry is placed initially at the root, but may have to move down with a down-heap bubbling to preserve the heap-order property.

We illustrate bottom-up heap construction in Figure 9.5 for $h = 3$.

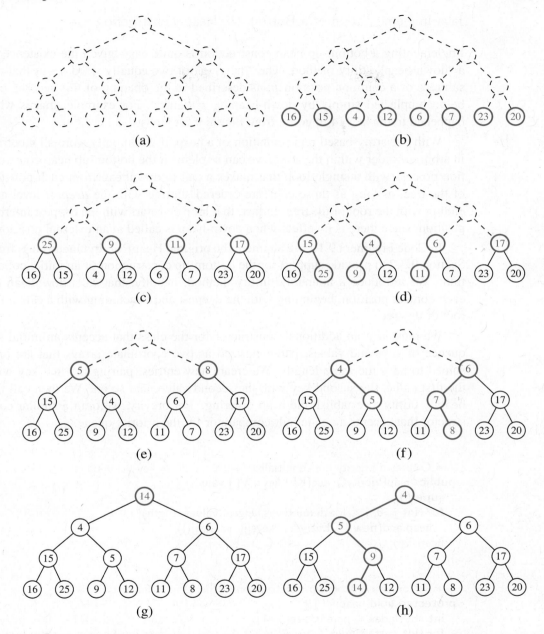

Figure 9.5: Bottom-up construction of a heap with 15 entries: (a and b) we begin by constructing 1-entry heaps on the bottom level; (c and d) we combine these heaps into 3-entry heaps; (e and f) we build 7-entry heaps; (g and h) we create the final heap. The paths of the down-heap bubblings are highlighted in (d, f, and h). For simplicity, we only show the key within each node instead of the entire entry.

Java Implementation of a Bottom-Up Heap Construction

Implementing a bottom-up heap construction is quite easy, given the existence of a "down-heap" utility method. The "merging" of two equally sized heaps that are subtrees of a common position p, as described in the opening of this section, can be accomplished simply by down-heaping p's entry. For example, that is what happened to the key 14 in going from Figure 9.5(f) to (g).

With our array-based representation of a heap, if we initially store all n entries in arbitrary order within the array, we can implement the bottom-up heap construction process with a single loop that makes a call to downheap from each position of the tree, as long as those calls are ordered starting with the *deepest* level and ending with the root of the tree. In fact, that loop can start with the deepest internal position, since there is no effect when down-heap is called at an external position.

In Code Fragment 9.10, we augment the original HeapPriorityQueue class from Section 9.3.2 to provide support for the bottom-up construction of an initial collection. We introduce a nonpublic utility method, heapify, that calls downheap on each nonleaf position, beginning with the deepest and concluding with a call at the root of the tree.

We introduce an additional constructor for the class that accepts an initial sequence of keys and values, parameterized as two coordinate arrays that are presumed to have the same length. We create new entries, pairing the first key with the first value, the second key with the second value, and so on. We then call the heapify utility to establish the heap ordering. For brevity, we omit a similar constructor that accepts a nondefault comparator for the priority queue.

```java
/** Creates a priority queue initialized with the given key-value pairs. */
public HeapPriorityQueue(K[ ] keys, V[ ] values) {
  super();
  for (int j=0; j < Math.min(keys.length, values.length); j++)
    heap.add(new PQEntry<>(keys[j], values[j]));
  heapify();
}
```

```java
/** Performs a bottom-up construction of the heap in linear time. */
protected void heapify() {
  int startIndex = parent(size()-1);          // start at PARENT of last entry
  for (int j=startIndex; j >= 0; j--)          // loop until processing the root
    downheap(j);
}
```

Code Fragment 9.10: Revision to the HeapPriorityQueue class of Code Fragments 9.8 and 9.9, supporting linear-time construction given an initial collection of key-value pairs.

Asymptotic Analysis of Bottom-Up Heap Construction

Bottom-up heap construction is asymptotically faster than incrementally inserting n entries into an initially empty heap. Intuitively, we are performing a single down-heap operation at each position in the tree, rather than a single up-heap operation from each. Since more nodes are closer to the bottom of a tree than the top, the sum of the downward paths is linear, as shown in the following proposition.

Proposition 9.3: *Bottom-up construction of a heap with n entries takes $O(n)$ time, assuming two keys can be compared in $O(1)$ time.*

Justification: The primary cost of the construction is due to the down-heap steps performed at each nonleaf position. Let π_v denote the path of T from nonleaf node v to its "inorder successor" leaf, that is, the path that starts at v, goes to the right child of v, and then goes down leftward until it reaches a leaf. Although, π_v is not necessarily the path followed by the down-heap bubbling step from v, its number of edges $\|\pi_v\|$ is proportional to the height of the subtree rooted at v, and thus a bound on the complexity of the down-heap operation at v. The total running time of the bottom-up heap construction algorithm is therefore bounded by the sum $\sum_v \|\pi_v\|$. For intuition, Figure 9.6 illustrates the justification "visually," marking each edge with the label of the nonleaf node v whose path π_v contains that edge.

We claim that the paths π_v for all nonleaf v are edge-disjoint, and thus the sum of the path lengths is bounded by the number of total edges in the tree, hence $O(n)$. To show this, we consider what we term "right-leaning" and "left-leaning" edges (i.e., those going from a parent to a right, respectively left, child). A particular right-leaning edge e can only be part of the path π_v for node v that is the parent in the relationship represented by e. Left-leaning edges can be partitioned by considering the leaf that is reached if continuing down leftward until reaching a leaf. Each nonleaf node only uses left-leaning edges in the group leading to that nonleaf node's inorder successor. Since each nonleaf node must have a different inorder successor, no two such paths can contain the same left-leaning edge. We conclude that the bottom-up construction of heap T takes $O(n)$ time. ∎

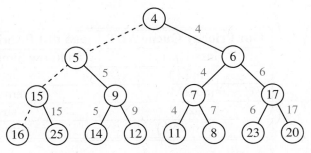

Figure 9.6: Visual justification of the linear running time of bottom-up heap construction. Each edge e is labeled with a node v for which π_v contains e (if any).

9.3.5   Using the java.util.PriorityQueue Class

There is no priority queue interface built into Java, but Java does include a class, java.util.PriorityQueue, which implements the java.util.Queue interface. Instead of adding and removing elements according to the standard FIFO policy used by most queues, the java.util.PriorityQueue class processes its entries according to a priority The "front" of the queue will always be a minimal element, with priorities based either on the natural ordering of the elements, or in accordance with a comparator object sent as a parameter when constructing the priority queue.

The most notable difference between the java.util.PriorityQueue class and our own priority queue ADT is the model for managing keys and values. Whereas our public interface distinguishes between keys and values, the java.util.PriorityQueue class relies on a single element type. That element is effectively treated as a key.

If a user wishes to insert distinct keys and values, the burden is on the user to define and insert appropriate composite objects, and to ensure that those objects can be compared based on their keys. (The Java Collections Framework does include its own entry interface, java.util.Map.Entry, and a concrete implementation in the java.util.AbstractMap.SimpleEntry class; we discuss the map ADT in the next chapter.)

Table 9.4 shows the correspondance between methods of our priority queue ADT and those of the java.util.PriorityQueue class. The java.util.PriorityQueue class is implemented with a heap, so it guarantees $O(\log n)$-time performance for methods add and remove, and constant-time performance for accessors peek, size, and isEmpty. In addition, it provides a parameterized method, remove(e), that removes a specific element e from the priority queue. However, that method runs in $O(n)$ time, performing a sequential search to locate the element within the heap. (In Section 9.5, we extend our heap-based priority queue implementation to support a more efficient means for removing an arbitrary entry, or for updating the priority of an existing entry.)

Our Priority Queue ADT	java.util.PriorityQueue Class
insert(k,v)	add(**new** SimpleEntry(k,v))
min( )	peek( )
removeMin( )	remove( )
size( )	size( )
isEmpty( )	isEmpty( )

Table 9.4: Methods of our priority queue ADT and the corresponding methods when using the java.util.PriorityQueue class.

9.4 Sorting with a Priority Queue

One application of priority queues is sorting, where we are given a sequence of elements that can be compared according to a total order relation, and we want to rearrange them in increasing order (or at least in nondecreasing order if there are ties). The algorithm for sorting a sequence S with a priority queue P is quite simple and consists of the following two phases:

1. In the first phase, we insert the elements of S as keys into an initially empty priority queue P by means of a series of n insert operations, one for each element.

2. In the second phase, we extract the elements from P in nondecreasing order by means of a series of n removeMin operations, putting them back into S in that order.

A Java implementation of this algorithm is given in Code Fragment 9.11, assuming that the sequence is stored as a positional list. (Code for a different type of collection, such as an array or an array list, would be similar.)

The algorithm works correctly for any priority queue P, no matter how P is implemented. However, the running time of the algorithm is determined by the running times of operations insert and removeMin, which do depend on how P is implemented. Indeed, pqSort should be considered more a sorting "scheme" than a sorting "algorithm," because it does not specify how the priority queue P is implemented. The pqSort scheme is the paradigm of several popular sorting algorithms, including selection-sort, insertion-sort, and heap-sort, which we will discuss in this section.

```
1  /** Sorts sequence S, using initially empty priority queue P to produce the order. */
2  public static <E> void pqSort(PositionalList<E> S, PriorityQueue<E,?> P) {
3    int n = S.size( );
4    for (int j=0; j < n; j++) {
5      E element = S.remove(S.first( ));
6      P.insert(element, null);       // element is key; null value
7    }
8    for (int j=0; j < n; j++) {
9      E element = P.removeMin( ).getKey( );
10     S.addLast(element);            // the smallest key in P is next placed in S
11   }
12 }
```

Code Fragment 9.11: An implementation of a pqSort method that sorts elements of a positional list using an initially empty priority queue to produce the ordering.

9.4.1   Selection-Sort and Insertion-Sort

We next demonstrate how the pqSort scheme results in two classic sorting algorithms when using an unsorted or sorted list for a priority queue.

Selection-Sort

In Phase 1 of the pqSort scheme, we insert all elements into a priority queue P; in Phase 2 we repeatedly remove the minimal element from P using the removeMin method. If we implement P with an unsorted list, then Phase 1 of pqSort takes $O(n)$ time, for we can insert each element in $O(1)$ time. In Phase 2, the running time of each removeMin operation is proportional to the size of P. Thus, the bottleneck computation is the repeated "selection" of the minimum element in Phase 2. For this reason, this algorithm is better known as *selection-sort*. (See Figure 9.7.)

		Sequence S	**Priority Queue P**
Input		(7, 4, 8, 2, 5, 3, 9)	()
Phase 1	(a)	(4, 8, 2, 5, 3, 9)	(7)
	(b)	(8, 2, 5, 3, 9)	(7, 4)
	⋮	⋮	⋮
	(g)	()	(7, 4, 8, 2, 5, 3, 9)
Phase 2	(a)	(2)	(7, 4, 8, 5, 3, 9)
	(b)	(2, 3)	(7, 4, 8, 5, 9)
	(c)	(2, 3, 4)	(7, 8, 5, 9)
	(d)	(2, 3, 4, 5)	(7, 8, 9)
	(e)	(2, 3, 4, 5, 7)	(8, 9)
	(f)	(2, 3, 4, 5, 7, 8)	(9)
	(g)	(2, 3, 4, 5, 7, 8, 9)	()

Figure 9.7: Execution of selection-sort on sequence $S = (7, 4, 8, 2, 5, 3, 9)$.

As noted above, the bottleneck is in Phase 2 where we repeatedly remove an entry with smallest key from the priority queue P. The size of P starts at n and incrementally decreases with each removeMin until it becomes 0. Thus, the first removeMin operation takes time $O(n)$, the second one takes time $O(n-1)$, and so on, until the last (n^{th}) operation takes time $O(1)$. Therefore, the total time needed for the second phase is

$$O(n + (n-1) + \cdots + 2 + 1) = O\left(\sum_{i=1}^{n} i\right).$$

By Proposition 4.3, we have $\sum_{i=1}^{n} i = n(n+1)/2$. Thus, Phase 2 takes time $O(n^2)$, as does the entire selection-sort algorithm.

Insertion-Sort

If we implement the priority queue P using a sorted list, then the running time of Phase 2 improves to $O(n)$, for each operation removeMin on P now takes $O(1)$ time. Unfortunately, Phase 1 now becomes the bottleneck for the running time, since, in the worst case, each insert operation takes time proportional to the size of P. This sorting algorithm is therefore better known as *insertion-sort* (see Figure 9.8), for the bottleneck in this sorting algorithm involves the repeated "insertion" of a new element at the appropriate position in a sorted list.

		Sequence S	Priority Queue P
Input		(7, 4, 8, 2, 5, 3, 9)	( )
Phase 1	(a)	(4, 8, 2, 5, 3, 9)	(7)
	(b)	(8, 2, 5, 3, 9)	(4, 7)
	(c)	(2, 5, 3, 9)	(4, 7, 8)
	(d)	(5, 3, 9)	(2, 4, 7, 8)
	(e)	(3, 9)	(2, 4, 5, 7, 8)
	(f)	(9)	(2, 3, 4, 5, 7, 8)
	(g)	( )	(2, 3, 4, 5, 7, 8, 9)
Phase 2	(a)	(2)	(3, 4, 5, 7, 8, 9)
	(b)	(2, 3)	(4, 5, 7, 8, 9)
	⋮	⋮	⋮
	(g)	(2, 3, 4, 5, 7, 8, 9)	( )

Figure 9.8: Execution of insertion-sort on sequence $S = (7, 4, 8, 2, 5, 3, 9)$. In Phase 1, we repeatedly remove the first element of S and insert it into P. In Phase 2, we repeatedly perform the removeMin operation on P and add the returned element to the end of S.

Analyzing the running time of Phase 1 of insertion-sort, we note that it is

$$O(1 + 2 + \ldots + (n-1) + n) = O\left(\sum_{i=1}^{n} i\right).$$

Again, by recalling Proposition 4.3, Phase 1 runs in $O(n^2)$ time, and hence, so does the entire insertion-sort algorithm.

Alternatively, we could change our definition of insertion-sort so that we insert elements starting from the end of the priority-queue list in Phase 1, in which case performing insertion-sort on a sequence that is already sorted would run in $O(n)$ time. Indeed, the running time of insertion-sort in this case is $O(n + I)$, where I is the number of *inversions* in the sequence, that is, the number of pairs of elements that start out in the input sequence in the wrong relative order.

9.4.2 Heap-Sort

As we have previously observed, realizing a priority queue with a heap has the advantage that all the methods in the priority queue ADT run in logarithmic time or better. Hence, this realization is suitable for applications where fast running times are sought for all the priority queue methods. Therefore, let us again consider the pqSort scheme, this time using a heap-based implementation of the priority queue.

During Phase 1, the ith insert operation takes $O(\log i)$ time, since the heap has i entries after the operation is performed. Therefore, this phase takes $O(n \log n)$ time. (It could be improved to $O(n)$ with the bottom-up heap construction described in Section 9.3.4.)

During the second phase of method pqSort, the jth removeMin operation runs in $O(\log(n - j + 1))$, since the heap has $n - j + 1$ entries at the time the operation is performed. Summing over all j, this phase takes $O(n \log n)$ time, so the entire priority-queue sorting algorithm runs in $O(n \log n)$ time when we use a heap to implement the priority queue. This sorting algorithm is better known as ***heap-sort***, and its performance is summarized in the following proposition.

Proposition 9.4: *The heap-sort algorithm sorts a sequence S of n elements in $O(n \log n)$ time, assuming two elements of S can be compared in $O(1)$ time.*

Let us stress that the $O(n \log n)$ running time of heap-sort is considerably better than the $O(n^2)$ running time of selection-sort and insertion-sort.

Implementing Heap-Sort In-Place

If the sequence S to be sorted is implemented by means of an array-based sequence, such as an ArrayList in Java, we can speed up heap-sort and reduce its space requirement by a constant factor by using a portion of the array itself to store the heap, thus avoiding the use of an auxiliary heap data structure. This is accomplished by modifying the algorithm as follows:

1. We redefine the heap operations to be a *maximum-oriented* heap, with each position key being at least as *large* as its children. This can be done by re-coding the algorithm, or by providing a new comparator that reverses the outcome of each comparison. At any time during the execution of the algorithm, we use the left portion of S, up to a certain index $i - 1$, to store the entries of the heap, and the right portion of S, from index i to $n - 1$, to store the elements of the sequence. Thus, the first i elements of S (at indices $0, \ldots, i - 1$) provide the array-list representation of the heap.

2. In the first phase of the algorithm, we start with an empty heap and move the boundary between the heap and the sequence from left to right, one step at a time. In step i, for $i = 1, \ldots, n$, we expand the heap by adding the element at index $i - 1$.

3. In the second phase of the algorithm, we start with an empty sequence and move the boundary between the heap and the sequence from right to left, one step at a time. At step i, for $i = 1, \ldots, n$, we remove a maximal element from the heap and store it at index $n - i$.

In general, we say that a sorting algorithm is **in-place** if it uses only a small amount of memory in addition to the sequence storing the objects to be sorted. The variation of heap-sort above qualifies as in-place; instead of transferring elements out of the sequence and then back in, we simply rearrange them. We illustrate the second phase of in-place heap-sort in Figure 9.9.

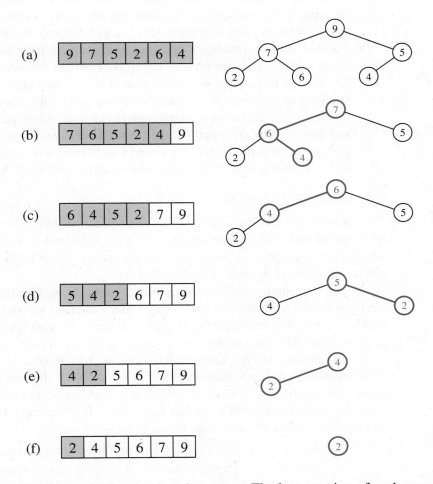

Figure 9.9: Phase 2 of an in-place heap-sort. The heap portion of each sequence representation is highlighted. The binary tree that each sequence (implicitly) represents is diagrammed with the most recent path of down-heap bubbling highlighted.

9.5   Adaptable Priority Queues

The methods of the priority queue ADT given in Section 9.1.2 are sufficient for most basic applications of priority queues, such as sorting. However, there are situations in which additional methods would be useful, as shown by the scenarios below involving the standby airline passenger application.

- A standby passenger with a pessimistic attitude may become tired of waiting and decide to leave ahead of the boarding time, requesting to be removed from the waiting list. Thus, we would like to remove from the priority queue the entry associated with this passenger. Operation removeMin does not suffice since the passenger leaving does not necessarily have first priority. Instead, we want a new operation, remove, that removes an arbitrary entry.

- Another standby passenger finds her gold frequent-flyer card and shows it to the agent. Thus, her priority has to be modified accordingly. To achieve this change of priority, we would like to have a new operation replaceKey allowing us to replace the key of an existing entry with a new key.

- Finally, a third standby passenger notices her name is misspelled on the ticket and asks it to be corrected. To perform this change, we need to update the passenger's record. Hence, we would like to have a new operation replaceValue, allowing us to replace the value of an existing entry with a new value.

The Adaptable Priority Queue ADT

The above scenarios motivate the definition of a new **adaptable priority queue** ADT that extends the priority queue ADT with additional functionality. We will see another application of adaptable priority queues when implementing certain graph algorithms in Sections 14.6.2 and 14.7.1.

In order to implement methods remove, replaceKey, and replaceValue efficiently, we need a mechanism for finding a user's element within a priority queue, ideally in a way that avoids performing a linear search through the entire collection. In the original definition of the priority queue ADT, a call to insert(k, v) formally returns an instance of type Entry to the user. In order to be able to update or remove an entry in our new adaptable priority queue ADT, the user must retain that Entry object as a token that can be sent back as a parameter to identify the relevant entry. Formally, the adaptable priority queue ADT includes the following methods (in addition to those of the standard priority queue):

remove(e): Removes entry e from the priority queue.

replaceKey(e, k): Replaces the key of existing entry e with k.

replaceValue(e, v): Replaces the value of existing entry e with v.

An error occurs with each of these methods if parameter e is invalid (for example, because it had previously been removed from the priority queue).

9.5.1 Location-Aware Entries

To allow an entry instance to encode a location within a priority queue, we extend the PQEntry class (originally defined with the AbstractPriorityQueue base class), adding a third field that designates the current index of an entry within the array-based representation of the heap, as shown in Figure 9.10. (This approach is similar to our recommendation, on page 281, for implementing the positional list abstraction with an array.)

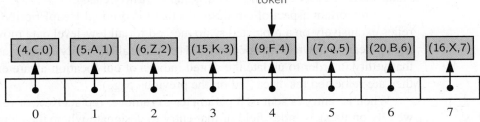

Figure 9.10: Representing a heap using an array of location-aware entries. The third field of each entry instance corresponds to the index of that entry within the array. Identifier token is presumed to be an entry reference in the user's scope.

When we perform priority queue operations on our heap, causing entries to be relocated within our structure, we must make sure to update the third field of each affected entry to reflect its new index within the array. As an example, Figure 9.11 shows the state of the above heap after a call to removeMin( ). The heap operation causes the minimal entry, (4,C), to be removed, and the last entry, (16,X), to be temporarily moved from the last position to the root, followed by a down-heap bubble phase. During the down-heap, element (16,X) is swapped with its left child, (5,A), at index 1 of the list, then swapped with its right child, (9,F), at index 4 of the list. In the final configuration, the last field for all affected entries has been modified to reflect their new location.

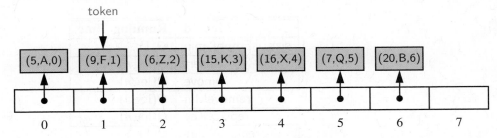

Figure 9.11: The result of a call to removeMin( ) on the heap originally portrayed in Figure 9.10. Identifier token continues to reference the same entry as in the original configuration, but the placement of that entry in the array has changed, as has the third field of the entry.

9.5.2   Implementing an Adaptable Priority Queue

Code Fragments 9.12 and 9.13 present a Java implementation of an adaptable priority queue, as a subclass of the HeapPriorityQueue class from Section 9.3.2. We begin by defining a nested AdaptablePQEntry class (lines 5–15) that extends the inherited PQEntry class, augmenting it with an additional index field. The inherited insert method is overridden, so that we create and initialize an instance of the AdaptablePQEntry class (not the original PQEntry class).

An important aspect of our design is that the original HeapPriorityQueue class relies exclusively on a protected swap method for all low-level data movement during up-heap or down-heap operations. The AdaptablePriorityQueue class overrides that utility in order to update the stored indices of our location-aware entries when they are relocated (as discussed on the previous page).

When an entry is sent as a parameter to remove, replaceKey, or replaceValue, we rely on the new index field of that entry to designate where the element resides in the heap (a fact that is easily validated). When a key of an existing entry is replaced, that new key may violate the heap-order property by being either too big or too small. We provide a new bubble utility that determines whether an up-heap or down-heap bubbling step is warranted. When removing an arbitrary entry, we replace it with the last entry in the heap (to maintain the complete binary tree property) and perform the bubbling step, since the displaced element may have a key that is too large or too small for its new location.

Performance of Adaptable Priority Queue Implementations

The performance of an adaptable priority queue by means of our location-aware heap structure is summarized in Table 9.5. The new class provides the same asymptotic efficiency and space usage as the nonadaptive version, and provides logarithmic performance for the new locator-based remove and replaceKey methods, and constant-time performance for the new replaceValuemethod.

Method	Running Time
size, isEmpty, min	$O(1)$
insert	$O(\log n)$
remove	$O(\log n)$
removeMin	$O(\log n)$
replaceKey	$O(\log n)$
replaceValue	$O(1)$

Table 9.5: Running times of the methods of an adaptable priority queue with size n, realized by means of our array-based heap representation. The space requirement is $O(n)$.

```
1   /** An implementation of an adaptable priority queue using an array-based heap. */
2   public class HeapAdaptablePriorityQueue<K,V> extends HeapPriorityQueue<K,V>
3                                      implements AdaptablePriorityQueue<K,V> {
4
5     //---------------- nested AdaptablePQEntry class ----------------
6     /** Extension of the PQEntry to include location information. */
7     protected static class AdaptablePQEntry<K,V> extends PQEntry<K,V> {
8       private int index;                      // entry's current index within the heap
9       public AdaptablePQEntry(K key, V value, int j) {
10        super(key, value);                    // this sets the key and value
11        index = j;                            // this sets the new field
12      }
13      public int getIndex() { return index; }
14      public void setIndex(int j) { index = j; }
15    } //----------- end of nested AdaptablePQEntry class -----------
16
17    /** Creates an empty adaptable priority queue using natural ordering of keys. */
18    public HeapAdaptablePriorityQueue() { super(); }
19    /** Creates an empty adaptable priority queue using the given comparator. */
20    public HeapAdaptablePriorityQueue(Comparator<K> comp) { super(comp);}
21
22    // protected utilites
23    /** Validates an entry to ensure it is location-aware. */
24    protected AdaptablePQEntry<K,V> validate(Entry<K,V> entry)
25                                      throws IllegalArgumentException {
26      if (!(entry instanceof AdaptablePQEntry))
27        throw new IllegalArgumentException("Invalid entry");
28      AdaptablePQEntry<K,V> locator = (AdaptablePQEntry<K,V>) entry;  // safe
29      int j = locator.getIndex();
30      if (j >= heap.size() || heap.get(j) != locator)
31        throw new IllegalArgumentException("Invalid entry");
32      return locator;
33    }
34
35    /** Exchanges the entries at indices i and j of the array list. */
36    protected void swap(int i, int j) {
37      super.swap(i,j);                                        // perform the swap
38      ((AdaptablePQEntry<K,V>) heap.get(i)).setIndex(i);     // reset entry's index
39      ((AdaptablePQEntry<K,V>) heap.get(j)).setIndex(j);     // reset entry's index
40    }
```

Code Fragment 9.12: An implementation of an adaptable priority queue. (Continues in Code Fragment 9.13.) This extends the HeapPriorityQueue class of Code Fragments 9.8 and 9.9.

```
41    /** Restores the heap property by moving the entry at index j upward/downward.*/
42    protected void bubble(int j) {
43      if (j > 0 && compare(heap.get(j), heap.get(parent(j))) < 0)
44        upheap(j);
45      else
46        downheap(j);                              // although it might not need to move
47    }
48
49    /** Inserts a key-value pair and returns the entry created. */
50    public Entry<K,V> insert(K key, V value) throws IllegalArgumentException {
51      checkKey(key);                              // might throw an exception
52      Entry<K,V> newest = new AdaptablePQEntry<>(key, value, heap.size( ));
53      heap.add(newest);                           // add to the end of the list
54      upheap(heap.size( ) − 1);                   // upheap newly added entry
55      return newest;
56    }
57
58    /** Removes the given entry from the priority queue. */
59    public void remove(Entry<K,V> entry) throws IllegalArgumentException {
60      AdaptablePQEntry<K,V> locator = validate(entry);
61      int j = locator.getIndex( );
62      if (j == heap.size( ) − 1)                  // entry is at last position
63        heap.remove(heap.size( ) − 1);            // so just remove it
64      else {
65        swap(j, heap.size( ) − 1);                // swap entry to last position
66        heap.remove(heap.size( ) − 1);            // then remove it
67        bubble(j);                                // and fix entry displaced by the swap
68      }
69    }
70
71    /** Replaces the key of an entry. */
72    public void replaceKey(Entry<K,V> entry, K key)
73                          throws IllegalArgumentException {
74      AdaptablePQEntry<K,V> locator = validate(entry);
75      checkKey(key);                              // might throw an exception
76      locator.setKey(key);                        // method inherited from PQEntry
77      bubble(locator.getIndex( ));                // with new key, may need to move entry
78    }
79
80    /** Replaces the value of an entry. */
81    public void replaceValue(Entry<K,V> entry, V value)
82                            throws IllegalArgumentException {
83      AdaptablePQEntry<K,V> locator = validate(entry);
84      locator.setValue(value);                    // method inherited from PQEntry
85    }
```

Code Fragment 9.13: An implementation of an adaptable priority queue (continued from Code Fragment 9.12).

9.6   Exercises

Reinforcement

R-9.1 How long would it take to remove the $\lceil \log n \rceil$ smallest elements from a heap that contains n entries, using the removeMin operation?

R-9.2 Suppose you set the key for each position p of a binary tree T equal to its preorder rank. Under what circumstances is T a heap?

R-9.3 What does each removeMin call return within the following sequence of priority queue ADT operations: insert(5, A), insert(4, B), insert(7, F), insert(1, D), removeMin( ), insert(3, J), insert(6, L), removeMin( ), removeMin( ), insert(8, G), removeMin( ), insert(2, H), removeMin( ), removeMin( )?

R-9.4 An airport is developing a computer simulation of air-traffic control that handles events such as landings and takeoffs. Each event has a *time stamp* that denotes the time when the event will occur. The simulation program needs to efficiently perform the following two fundamental operations:

- Insert an event with a given time stamp (that is, add a future event).
- Extract the event with smallest time stamp (that is, determine the next event to process).

Which data structure should be used for the above operations? Why?

R-9.5 The min method for the UnsortedPriorityQueue class executes in $O(n)$ time, as analyzed in Table 9.2. Give a simple modification to the class so that min runs in $O(1)$ time. Explain any necessary modifications to other methods of the class.

R-9.6 Can you adapt your solution to the previous problem to make removeMin run in $O(1)$ time for the UnsortedPriorityQueue class? Explain your answer.

R-9.7 Illustrate the execution of the selection-sort algorithm on the following input sequence: (22, 15, 36, 44, 10, 3, 9, 13, 29, 25).

R-9.8 Illustrate the execution of the insertion-sort algorithm on the input sequence of the previous problem.

R-9.9 Give an example of a worst-case sequence with n elements for insertion-sort, and show that insertion-sort runs in $\Omega(n^2)$ time on such a sequence.

R-9.10 At which positions of a heap might the third smallest key be stored?

R-9.11 At which positions of a heap might the largest key be stored?

R-9.12 Consider a situation in which a user has numeric keys and wishes to have a priority queue that is *maximum-oriented*. How could a standard (min-oriented) priority queue be used for such a purpose?

R-9.13 Illustrate the execution of the in-place heap-sort algorithm on the following input sequence: (2, 5, 16, 4, 10, 23, 39, 18, 26, 15).

R-9.14 Let T be a complete binary tree such that position p stores an element with key $f(p)$, where $f(p)$ is the level number of p (see Section 8.3.2). Is tree T a heap? Why or why not?

R-9.15 Explain why the description of down-heap bubbling does not consider the case in which position p has a right child but not a left child.

R-9.16 Is there a heap H storing seven entries with distinct keys such that a preorder traversal of H yields the entries of H in increasing or decreasing order by key? How about an inorder traversal? How about a postorder traversal? If so, give an example; if not, say why.

R-9.17 Let H be a heap storing 15 entries using the array-based representation of a complete binary tree. What is the sequence of indices of the array that are visited in a preorder traversal of H? What about an inorder traversal of H? What about a postorder traversal of H?

R-9.18 Show that the sum $\sum_{i=1}^{n} \log i$, appearing in the analysis of heap-sort, is $\Omega(n \log n)$.

R-9.19 Bill claims that a preorder traversal of a heap will list its keys in nondecreasing order. Draw an example of a heap that proves him wrong.

R-9.20 Hillary claims that a postorder traversal of a heap will list its keys in nonincreasing order. Draw an example of a heap that proves her wrong.

R-9.21 Illustrate all the steps of the adaptable priority queue call remove(e) for entry e storing (16,X) in the heap of Figure 9.1.

R-9.22 Illustrate all the steps of the adaptable priority queue call replaceKey(e, 18) for entry e storing (5, A) in the heap of Figure 9.1.

R-9.23 Draw an example of a heap whose keys are all the odd numbers from 1 to 59 (with no repeats), such that the insertion of an entry with key 32 would cause up-heap bubbling to proceed all the way up to a child of the root (replacing that child's key with 32).

R-9.24 Describe a sequence of n insertions in a heap that requires $\Omega(n \log n)$ time to process.

Creativity

C-9.25 Show how to implement the stack ADT using only a priority queue and one additional integer instance variable.

C-9.26 Show how to implement the FIFO queue ADT using only a priority queue and one additional integer instance variable.

C-9.27 Professor Idle suggests the following solution to the previous problem. Whenever an entry is inserted into the queue, it is assigned a key that is equal to the current size of the queue. Does such a strategy result in FIFO semantics? Prove that it is so or provide a counterexample.

C-9.28 Reimplement the SortedPriorityQueue using a Java array. Make sure to maintain removeMin's $O(1)$ performance.

C-9.29 Give an alternative implementation of the HeapPriorityQueue's upheap method that uses recursion (and no loop).

C-9.30 Give an implementation of the HeapPriorityQueue's downheap method that uses recursion (and no loop).

C-9.31 Assume that we are using a linked representation of a complete binary tree T, and an extra reference to the last node of that tree. Show how to update the reference to the last node after operations insert or remove in $O(\log n)$ time, where n is the current number of nodes of T. Be sure to handle all possible cases, as illustrated in Figure 9.12.

C-9.32 When using a linked-tree representation for a heap, an alternative method for finding the last node during an insertion in a heap T is to store, in the last node and each leaf node of T, a reference to the leaf node immediately to its right (wrapping to the first node in the next lower level for the rightmost leaf node). Show how to maintain such references in $O(1)$ time per operation of the priority queue ADT assuming that T is implemented with a linked structure.

C-9.33 We can represent a path from the root to a given node of a binary tree by means of a binary string, where 0 means "go to the left child" and 1 means "go to the right child." For example, the path from the root to the node storing $(8, W)$ in the heap of Figure 9.12a is represented by "101." Design an $O(\log n)$-time algorithm for finding the last node of a complete binary tree with n nodes, based on the above representation. Show how this algorithm can be used in the implementation of a complete binary tree by means of a linked structure that does not keep an explicit reference to the last node instance.

C-9.34 Given a heap H and a key k, give an algorithm to compute all the entries in H having a key less than or equal to k. For example, given the heap of Figure 9.12a and query $k = 7$, the algorithm should report the entries with keys 2, 4, 5, 6, and 7 (but not necessarily in this order). Your algorithm should run in time proportional to the number of entries returned, and should *not* modify the heap.

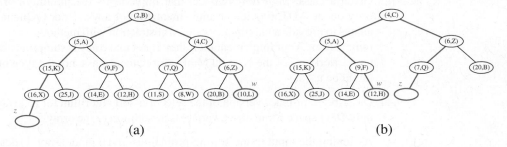

(a)   (b)

Figure 9.12: Two cases of updating the last node in a complete binary tree after operation insert or remove. Node w is the last node before operation insert or after operation remove. Node z is the last node after operation insert or before operation remove.

C-9.35　Provide a justification of the time bounds in Table 9.5.

C-9.36　Give an alternative analysis of bottom-up heap construction by showing the following summation is $O(1)$, for any positive integer h:

$$\sum_{i=1}^{h} \left(i/2^i\right).$$

C-9.37　Suppose two binary trees, T_1 and T_2, hold entries satisfying the heap-order property (but not necessarily the complete binary tree property). Describe a method for combining T_1 and T_2 into a binary tree T, whose nodes hold the union of the entries in T_1 and T_2 and also satisfy the heap-order property. Your algorithm should run in time $O(h_1 + h_2)$ where h_1 and h_2 are the respective heights of T_1 and T_2.

C-9.38　Tamarindo Airlines wants to give a first-class upgrade coupon to their top $\log n$ frequent flyers, based on the number of miles accumulated, where n is the total number of the airlines' frequent flyers. The algorithm they currently use, which runs in $O(n \log n)$ time, sorts the flyers by the number of miles flown and then scans the sorted list to pick the top $\log n$ flyers. Describe an algorithm that identifies the top $\log n$ flyers in $O(n)$ time.

C-9.39　Explain how the k largest elements from an unordered collection of size n can be found in time $O(n + k \log n)$ using a maximum-oriented heap.

C-9.40　Explain how the k largest elements from an unordered collection of size n can be found in time $O(n \log k)$ using $O(k)$ auxiliary space.

C-9.41　Write a comparator for nonnegative integers that determines order based on the number of 1's in each integer's binary expansion, so that $i < j$ if the number of 1's in the binary representation of i is less than the number of 1's in the binary representation of j.

C-9.42　Implement the binarySearch algorithm (see Section 5.1.3) using a Comparator for an array with elements of generic type E.

C-9.43　Given a class, MinPriorityQueue, that implements the minimum-oriented priority queue ADT, provide an implementation of a MaxPriorityQueue class that adapts to provide a maximum-oriented abstraction with methods insert, max, and removeMax. Your implementation should not make any assumption about the internal workings of the original MinPriorityQueue class, nor the type of keys that might be used.

C-9.44　Describe an in-place version of the selection-sort algorithm for an array that uses only $O(1)$ space for instance variables in addition to the array.

C-9.45　Assuming the input to the sorting problem is given in an array A, describe how to implement the insertion-sort algorithm using only the array A and at most six additional (base-type) variables.

C-9.46　Give an alternate description of the in-place heap-sort algorithm using the standard minimum-oriented priority queue (instead of a maximum-oriented one).

C-9.47 A group of children want to play a game, called ***Unmonopoly***, where in each turn the player with the most money must give half of his/her money to the player with the least amount of money. What data structure(s) should be used to play this game efficiently? Why?

C-9.48 An online computer system for trading stocks needs to process orders of the form "buy 100 shares at $x each" or "sell 100 shares at $y each." A buy order for $x can only be processed if there is an existing sell order with price $y such that $y \leq x$. Likewise, a sell order for $y can only be processed if there is an existing buy order with price $x such that $y \leq x$. If a buy or sell order is entered but cannot be processed, it must wait for a future order that allows it to be processed. Describe a scheme that allows buy and sell orders to be entered in $O(\log n)$ time, independent of whether or not they can be immediately processed.

C-9.49 Extend a solution to the previous problem so that users are allowed to update the prices for their buy or sell orders that have yet to be processed.

Projects

P-9.50 Implement the in-place heap-sort algorithm. Experimentally compare its running time with that of the standard heap-sort that is not in-place.

P-9.51 Use the approach of either Exercise C-9.39 or C-9.40 to reimplement the method getFavorites of the FavoritesListMTF class from Section 7.7.2. Make sure that results are generated from largest to smallest.

P-9.52 Develop a Java implementation of an adaptable priority queue that is based on an unsorted list and supports location-aware entries.

P-9.53 Write an applet or stand-alone graphical program that animates a heap. Your program should support all the priority queue operations and should visualize the swaps in the up-heap and down-heap bubblings. (Extra: Visualize bottom-up heap construction as well.)

P-9.54 Write a program that can process a sequence of stock buy and sell orders as described in Exercise C-9.48.

P-9.55 One of the main applications of priority queues is in operating systems—for ***scheduling jobs*** on a CPU. In this project you are to build a program that schedules simulated CPU jobs. Your program should run in a loop, each iteration of which corresponds to a ***time slice*** for the CPU. Each job is assigned a priority, which is an integer between -20 (highest priority) and 19 (lowest priority), inclusive. From among all jobs waiting to be processed in a time slice, the CPU must work on a job with highest priority. In this simulation, each job will also come with a ***length*** value, which is an integer between 1 and 100, inclusive, indicating the number of time slices that are needed to process this job. For simplicity, you may assume jobs cannot be interrupted—once it is scheduled on the CPU, a job runs for a number of time slices equal to its length. Your simulator must output the name of the job running on the CPU in each time slice and must process a sequence of commands, one per time slice, each of which is of the form "add job *name* with length n and priority p" or "no new job this slice".

P-9.56 Let S be a set of n points in the plane with distinct integer x- and y-coordinates. Let T be a complete binary tree storing the points from S at its external nodes, such that the points are ordered left to right by increasing x-coordinates. For each node v in T, let $S(v)$ denote the subset of S consisting of points stored in the subtree rooted at v. For the root r of T, define $top(r)$ to be the point in $S = S(r)$ with maximal y-coordinate. For every other node v, define $top(r)$ to be the point in S with highest y-coordinate in $S(v)$ that is not also the highest y-coordinate in $S(u)$, where u is the parent of v in T (if such a point exists). Such labeling turns T into a **priority search tree**. Describe a linear-time algorithm for turning T into a priority search tree. Implement this approach.

Chapter Notes

Knuth's book on sorting and searching [61] describes the motivation and history for the selection-sort, insertion-sort, and heap-sort algorithms. The heap-sort algorithm is due to Williams [95], and the linear-time heap construction algorithm is due to Floyd [35]. Additional algorithms and analyses for heaps and heap-sort variations can be found in papers by Bentley [14], Carlsson [21], Gonnet and Munro [39], McDiarmid and Reed [69], and Schaffer and Sedgewick [82].

Chapter

10 Maps, Hash Tables, and Skip Lists

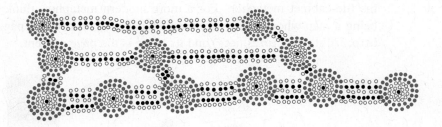

Contents

10.1   Maps

A *map* is an abstract data type designed to efficiently store and retrieve values based upon a uniquely identifying *search key* for each. Specifically, a map stores key-value pairs (k, v), which we call *entries*, where k is the key and v is its corresponding value. Keys are required to be unique, so that the association of keys to values defines a mapping. Figure 10.1 provides a conceptual illustration of a map using the file-cabinet metaphor. For a more modern metaphor, think about the web as being a map whose entries are the web pages. The key of a page is its URL (e.g., http://datastructures.net/) and its value is the page content.

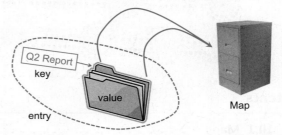

Figure 10.1: A conceptual illustration of the map ADT. Keys (labels) are assigned to values (folders) by a user. The resulting entries (labeled folders) are inserted into the map (file cabinet). The keys can be used later to retrieve or remove values.

Maps are also known as *associative arrays*, because the entry's key serves somewhat like an index into the map, in that it assists the map in efficiently locating the associated entry. However, unlike a standard array, a key of a map need not be numeric, and is does not directly designate a position within the structure. Common applications of maps include the following:

- A university's information system relies on some form of a student ID as a key that is mapped to that student's associated record (such as the student's name, address, and course grades) serving as the value.

- The domain-name system (DNS) maps a host name, such as www.wiley.com, to an Internet-Protocol (IP) address, such as 208.215.179.146.

- A social media site typically relies on a (nonnumeric) username as a key that can be efficiently mapped to a particular user's associated information.

- A company's customer base may be stored as a map, with a customer's account number or unique user ID as a key, and a record with the customer's information as a value. The map would allow a service representative to quickly access a customer's record, given the key.

- A computer graphics system may map a color name, such as 'turquoise', to the triple of numbers that describes the color's RGB (red-green-blue) representation, such as (64, 224, 208).

10.1.1   The Map ADT

Since a map stores a collection of objects, it should be viewed as a collection of key-value pairs. As an ADT, a **map** M supports the following methods:

size( ): Returns the number of entries in M.

isEmpty( ): Returns a boolean indicating whether M is empty.

get(k): Returns the value v associated with key k, if such an entry exists; otherwise returns null.

put(k, v): If M does not have an entry with key equal to k, then adds entry (k, v) to M and returns null; else, replaces with v the existing value of the entry with key equal to k and returns the old value.

remove(k): Removes from M the entry with key equal to k, and returns its value; if M has no such entry, then returns null.

keySet( ): Returns an iterable collection containing all the keys stored in M.

values( ): Returns an iterable collection containing all the *values* of entries stored in M (with repetition if multiple keys map to the same value).

entrySet( ): Returns an iterable collection containing all the key-value entries in M.

Maps in the java.util Package

Our definition of the map ADT is a simplified version of the java.util.Map interface. For the elements of the iteration returned by entrySet, we will rely on the composite Entry interface introduced in Section 9.2.1 (the java.util.Map relies on the nested java.util.Map.Entry interface).

Notice that each of the operations get(k), put(k, v), and remove(k) returns the existing value associated with key k, if the map has such an entry, and otherwise returns null. This introduces ambiguity in an application for which null is allowed as a natural value associated with a key k. That is, if an entry (k, null) exists in a map, then the operation get(k) will return null, not because it couldn't find the key, but because it found the key and is returning its associated value.

Some implementations of the java.util.Map interface explicitly forbid use of a null value (and null keys, for that matter). However, to resolve the ambiguity when null is allowable, the interface contains a boolean method, containsKey(k) to definitively check whether k exists as a key. (We leave implementation of such a method as an exercise.)

Example 10.1: *In the following, we show the effect of a series of operations on an initially empty map storing entries with integer keys and single-character values.*

Method	Return Value	Map
isEmpty()	true	{}
put(5,A)	null	{(5,A)}
put(7,B)	null	{(5,A),(7,B)}
put(2,C)	null	{(5,A),(7,B),(2,C)}
put(8,D)	null	{(5,A),(7,B),(2,C),(8,D)}
put(2,E)	C	{(5,A),(7,B),(2,E),(8,D)}
get(7)	B	{(5,A),(7,B),(2,E),(8,D)}
get(4)	null	{(5,A),(7,B),(2,E),(8,D)}
get(2)	E	{(5,A),(7,B),(2,E),(8,D)}
size()	4	{(5,A),(7,B),(2,E),(8,D)}
remove(5)	A	{(7,B),(2,E),(8,D)}
remove(2)	E	{(7,B),(8,D)}
get(2)	null	{(7,B),(8,D)}
remove(2)	null	{(7,B),(8,D)}
isEmpty()	false	{(7,B),(8,D)}
entrySet()	{(7,B),(8,D)}	{(7,B),(8,D)}
keySet()	{7,8}	{(7,B),(8,D)}
values()	{B,D}	{(7,B),(8,D)}

A Java Interface for the Map ADT

A formal definition of a Java interface for our version of the map ADT is given in Code Fragment 10.1. It uses the generics framework (Section 2.5.2), with K designating the key type and V designating the value type.

```java
1   public interface Map<K,V> {
2     int size();
3     boolean isEmpty();
4     V get(K key);
5     V put(K key, V value);
6     V remove(K key);
7     Iterable<K> keySet();
8     Iterable<V> values();
9     Iterable<Entry<K,V>> entrySet();
10  }
```

Code Fragment 10.1: Java interface for our simplified version of the map ADT.

10.1.2 Application: Counting Word Frequencies

As a case study for using a map, consider the problem of counting the number of occurrences of words in a document. This is a standard task when performing a statistical analysis of a document, for example, when categorizing an email or news article. A map is an ideal data structure to use here, for we can use words as keys and word counts as values. We show such an application in Code Fragment 10.2.

We begin with an empty map, mapping words to their integer frequencies. (We rely on the ChainHashMap class that will be introduced in Section 10.2.4.) We first scan through the input, considering adjacent alphabetic characters to be words, which we then convert to lowercase. For each word found, we attempt to retrieve its current frequency from the map using the get method, with a yet unseen word having frequency zero. We then (re)set its frequency to be one more to reflect the current occurrence of the word. After processing the entire input, we loop through the entrySet( ) of the map to determine which word has the most occurrences.

```java
1  /** A program that counts words in a document, printing the most frequent. */
2  public class WordCount {
3    public static void main(String[ ] args) {
4      Map<String,Integer> freq = new ChainHashMap<>();   // or any concrete map
5      // scan input for words, using all nonletters as delimiters
6      Scanner doc = new Scanner(System.in).useDelimiter("[^a-zA-Z]+");
7      while (doc.hasNext()) {
8        String word = doc.next().toLowerCase();   // convert next word to lowercase
9        Integer count = freq.get(word);           // get the previous count for this word
10       if (count == null)
11         count = 0;                              // if not in map, previous count is zero
12       freq.put(word, 1 + count);                // (re)assign new count for this word
13     }
14     int maxCount = 0;
15     String maxWord = "no word";
16     for (Entry<String,Integer> ent : freq.entrySet())        // find max-count word
17       if (ent.getValue() > maxCount) {
18         maxWord = ent.getKey();
19         maxCount = ent.getValue();
20       }
21     System.out.print("The most frequent word is '" + maxWord);
22     System.out.println("' with " + maxCount + " occurrences.");
23   }
24 }
```

Code Fragment 10.2: A program for counting word frequencies in a document, printing the most frequent word. The document is parsed using the Scanner class, for which we change the delimiter for separating tokens from whitespace to any nonletter. We also convert words to lowercase.

10.1.3 An AbstractMap Base Class

In the remainder of this chapter (and the next), we will be providing many different implementations of the map ADT using a variety of data structures, each with its own trade-off of advantages and disadvantages. As we have done in earlier chapters, we rely on a combination of abstract and concrete classes in the interest of greater code reuse. Figure 10.2 provides a preview of those classes.

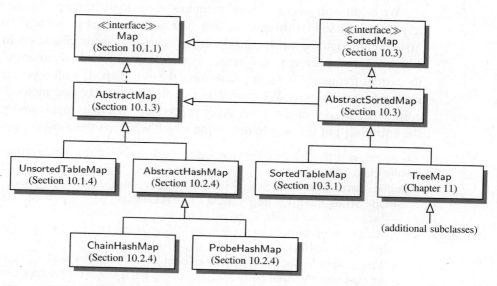

Figure 10.2: Our hierarchy of map types (with references to where they are defined).

We begin, in this section, by designing an AbstractMap base class that provides functionality that is shared by all of our map implementations. More specifically, the base class (given in Code Fragment 10.3) provides the following support:

- An implementation of the isEmpty method, based upon the presumed implementation of the size method.

- A nested MapEntry class that implements the public Entry interface, while providing a composite for storing key-value entries in a map data structure.

- Concrete implementations of the keySet and values methods, based upon an adaption to the entrySet method. In this way, concrete map classes need only implement the entrySet method to provide all three forms of iteration.

We implement the iterations using the technique introduced in Section 7.4.2 (at that time providing an iteration of all elements of a positional list given an iteration of all positions of the list).

```
1   public abstract class AbstractMap<K,V> implements Map<K,V> {
2     public boolean isEmpty( ) { return size( ) == 0; }
3     //---------------- nested MapEntry class ----------------
4     protected static class MapEntry<K,V> implements Entry<K,V> {
5       private K k;    // key
6       private V v;    // value
7       public MapEntry(K key, V value) {
8         k = key;
9         v = value;
10      }
11      // public methods of the Entry interface
12      public K getKey( ) { return k; }
13      public V getValue( ) { return v; }
14      // utilities not exposed as part of the Entry interface
15      protected void setKey(K key) { k = key; }
16      protected V setValue(V value) {
17        V old = v;
18        v = value;
19        return old;
20      }
21    } //----------- end of nested MapEntry class -----------
22
23    // Support for public keySet method...
24    private class KeyIterator implements Iterator<K> {
25      private Iterator<Entry<K,V>> entries = entrySet( ).iterator( ); // reuse entrySet
26      public boolean hasNext( ) { return entries.hasNext( ); }
27      public K next( ) { return entries.next( ).getKey( ); }              // return key!
28      public void remove( ) { throw new UnsupportedOperationException( ); }
29    }
30    private class KeyIterable implements Iterable<K> {
31      public Iterator<K> iterator( ) { return new KeyIterator( ); }
32    }
33    public Iterable<K> keySet( ) { return new KeyIterable( ); }
34
35    // Support for public values method...
36    private class ValueIterator implements Iterator<V> {
37      private Iterator<Entry<K,V>> entries = entrySet( ).iterator( ); // reuse entrySet
38      public boolean hasNext( ) { return entries.hasNext( ); }
39      public V next( ) { return entries.next( ).getValue( ); }            // return value!
40      public void remove( ) { throw new UnsupportedOperationException( ); }
41    }
42    private class ValueIterable implements Iterable<V> {
43      public Iterator<V> iterator( ) { return new ValueIterator( ); }
44    }
45    public Iterable<V> values( ) { return new ValueIterable( ); }
46  }
```

Code Fragment 10.3: Implementation of the AbstractMap base class.

10.1.4   A Simple Unsorted Map Implementation

We demonstrate the use of the AbstractMap class with a very simple concrete implementation of the map ADT that relies on storing key-value pairs in arbitrary order within a Java ArrayList. The presentation of such an UnsortedTableMap class is given in Code Fragments 10.4 and 10.5.

Each of the fundamental methods get(k), put(k, v), and remove(k) requires an initial scan of the array to determine whether an entry with key equal to k exists. For this reason, we provide a nonpublic utility, findIndex(key), that returns the index at which such an entry is found, or -1 if no such entry is found. (See Code Fragment 10.4.)

The rest of the implementation is rather simple. One subtlety worth mentioning is the way in which we remove an entry from the array list. Although we could use the remove method of the ArrayList class, that would result in an unnecessary loop to shift all subsequent entries to the left. Because the map is unordered, we prefer to fill the vacated cell of the array by relocating the last entry to that location. Such an update step runs in constant time.

Unfortunately, the UnsortedTableMap class on the whole is not very efficient. On a map with n entries, each of the fundamental methods takes $O(n)$ time in the worst case because of the need to scan through the entire list when searching for an existing entry. Fortunately, as we discuss in the next section, there is a much faster strategy for implementing the map ADT.

```
 1  public class UnsortedTableMap<K,V> extends AbstractMap<K,V> {
 2    /** Underlying storage for the map of entries. */
 3    private ArrayList<MapEntry<K,V>> table = new ArrayList<>();
 4
 5    /** Constructs an initially empty map. */
 6    public UnsortedTableMap() { }
 7
 8    // private utility
 9    /** Returns the index of an entry with equal key, or −1 if none found. */
10    private int findIndex(K key) {
11      int n = table.size();
12      for (int j=0; j < n; j++)
13        if (table.get(j).getKey().equals(key))
14          return j;
15      return −1;                           // special value denotes that key was not found
16    }
```

Code Fragment 10.4: An implementation of a map using a Java ArrayList as an unsorted table. (Continues in Code Fragment 10.5.) The parent class AbstractMap is given in Code Fragment 10.3.

```
17    /** Returns the number of entries in the map. */
18    public int size() { return table.size(); }
19    /** Returns the value associated with the specified key (or else null). */
20    public V get(K key) {
21      int j = findIndex(key);
22      if (j == −1) return null;                    // not found
23      return table.get(j).getValue();
24    }
25    /** Associates given value with given key, replacing a previous value (if any). */
26    public V put(K key, V value) {
27      int j = findIndex(key);
28      if (j == −1) {
29        table.add(new MapEntry<>(key, value));     // add new entry
30        return null;
31      } else                                       // key already exists
32        return table.get(j).setValue(value);       // replaced value is returned
33    }
34    /** Removes the entry with the specified key (if any) and returns its value. */
35    public V remove(K key) {
36      int j = findIndex(key);
37      int n = size();
38      if (j == −1) return null;                    // not found
39      V answer = table.get(j).getValue();
40      if (j != n − 1)
41        table.set(j, table.get(n−1));   // relocate last entry to 'hole' created by removal
42      table.remove(n−1);                           // remove last entry of table
43      return answer;
44    }
45    // Support for public entrySet method...
46    private class EntryIterator implements Iterator<Entry<K,V>> {
47      private int j=0;
48      public boolean hasNext() { return j < table.size(); }
49      public Entry<K,V> next() {
50        if (j == table.size()) throw new NoSuchElementException();
51        return table.get(j++);
52      }
53      public void remove() { throw new UnsupportedOperationException(); }
54    }
55    private class EntryIterable implements Iterable<Entry<K,V>> {
56      public Iterator<Entry<K,V>> iterator() { return new EntryIterator(); }
57    }
58    /** Returns an iterable collection of all key-value entries of the map. */
59    public Iterable<Entry<K,V>> entrySet() { return new EntryIterable(); }
60  }
```

Code Fragment 10.5: An implementation of a map using a Java ArrayList as an unsorted table (continued from Code Fragment 10.4).

10.2   Hash Tables

In this section, we introduce one of the most efficient data structures for implementing a map, and the one that is used most in practice. This structure is known as a ***hash table***.

Intuitively, a map M supports the abstraction of using keys as "addresses" that help locate an entry. As a mental warm-up, consider a restricted setting in which a map with n entries uses keys that are known to be integers in a range from 0 to $N - 1$ for some $N \geq n$. In this case, we can represent the map using a ***lookup table*** of length N, as diagrammed in Figure 10.3.

0	1	2	3	4	5	6	7	8	9	10
	D		Z			C	Q			

Figure 10.3: A lookup table with length 11 for a map containing entries (1,D), (3,Z), (6,C), and (7,Q).

In this representation, we store the value associated with key k at index k of the table (presuming that we have a distinct way to represent an empty slot). Basic map operations get, put, and remove can be implemented in $O(1)$ worst-case time.

There are two challenges in extending this framework to the more general setting of a map. First, we may not wish to devote an array of length N if it is the case that $N \gg n$. Second, we do not in general require that a map's keys be integers. The novel concept for a hash table is the use of a ***hash function*** to map general keys to corresponding indices in a table. Ideally, keys will be well distributed in the range from 0 to $N - 1$ by a hash function, but in practice there may be two or more distinct keys that get mapped to the same index. As a result, we will conceptualize our table as a ***bucket array***, as shown in Figure 10.4, in which each bucket may manage a collection of entries that are sent to a specific index by the hash function. (To save space, an empty bucket may be replaced by a null reference.)

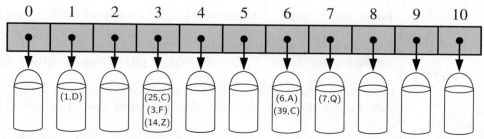

Figure 10.4: A bucket array of capacity 11 with entries (1,D), (25,C), (3,F), (14,Z), (6,A), (39,C), and (7,Q), using a simple hash function.

10.2.1 Hash Functions

The goal of a *hash function*, h, is to map each key k to an integer in the range $[0, N-1]$, where N is the capacity of the bucket array for a hash table. Equipped with such a hash function, h, the main idea of this approach is to use the hash function value, $h(k)$, as an index into our bucket array, A, instead of the key k (which may not be appropriate for direct use as an index). That is, we store the entry (k, v) in the bucket $A[h(k)]$.

If there are two or more keys with the same hash value, then two different entries will be mapped to the same bucket in A. In this case, we say that a *collision* has occurred. To be sure, there are ways of dealing with collisions, which we will discuss later, but the best strategy is to try to avoid them in the first place. We say that a hash function is "good" if it maps the keys in our map so as to sufficiently minimize collisions. For practical reasons, we also would like a hash function to be fast and easy to compute.

It is common to view the evaluation of a hash function, $h(k)$, as consisting of two portions—a *hash code* that maps a key k to an integer, and a *compression function* that maps the hash code to an integer within a range of indices, $[0, N-1]$, for a bucket array. (See Figure 10.5.)

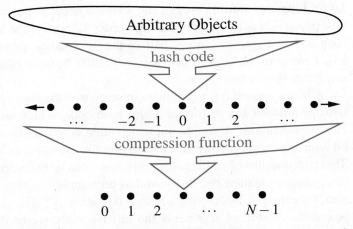

Figure 10.5: Two parts of a hash function: a hash code and a compression function.

The advantage of separating the hash function into two such components is that the hash code portion of that computation is independent of a specific hash table size. This allows the development of a general hash code for each object that can be used for a hash table of any size; only the compression function depends upon the table size. This is particularly convenient, because the underlying bucket array for a hash table may be dynamically resized, depending on the number of entries currently stored in the map. (See Section 10.2.3.)

Hash Codes

The first action that a hash function performs is to take an arbitrary key k in our map and compute an integer that is called the ***hash code*** for k; this integer need not be in the range $[0, N-1]$, and may even be negative. We desire that the set of hash codes assigned to our keys should avoid collisions as much as possible. For if the hash codes of our keys cause collisions, then there is no hope for our compression function to avoid them. In this subsection, we begin by discussing the theory of hash codes. Following that, we discuss practical implementations of hash codes in Java.

Treating the Bit Representation as an Integer

To begin, we note that, for any data type X that is represented using at most as many bits as our integer hash codes, we can simply take as a hash code for X an integer interpretation of its bits. Java relies on 32-bit hash codes, so for base types **byte**, **short**, **int**, and **char**, we can achieve a good hash code simply by casting a value to **int**. Likewise, for a variable x of base type **float**, we can convert x to an integer using a call to Float.floatToIntBits(x), and then use this integer as x's hash code.

For a type whose bit representation is longer than a desired hash code (such as Java's **long** and **double** types), the above scheme is not immediately applicable. One possibility is to use only the high-order 32 bits (or the low-order 32 bits). This hash code, of course, ignores half of the information present in the original key, and if many of the keys in our map only differ in these bits, then they will collide using this simple hash code.

A better approach is to combine in some way the high-order and low-order portions of a 64-bit key to form a 32-bit hash code, which takes all the original bits into consideration. A simple implementation is to add the two components as 32-bit numbers (ignoring overflow), or to take the exclusive-or of the two components. These approaches of combining components can be extended to any object x whose binary representation can be viewed as an n-tuple $(x_0, x_1, \ldots, x_{n-1})$ of 32-bit integers, for example, by forming a hash code for x as $\sum_{i=0}^{n-1} x_i$, or as $x_0 \oplus x_1 \oplus \cdots \oplus x_{n-1}$, where the $\oplus$ symbol represents the bitwise exclusive-or operation (which is the ^ operator in Java).

Polynomial Hash Codes

The summation and exclusive-or hash codes, described above, are not good choices for character strings or other variable-length objects that can be viewed as tuples of the form $(x_0, x_1, \ldots, x_{n-1})$, where the order of the x_i's is significant. For example, consider a 16-bit hash code for a character string s that sums the Unicode values of the characters in s. This hash code unfortunately produces lots of unwanted collisions for common groups of strings. In particular, `"temp01"` and `"temp10"` collide using this function, as do `"stop"`, `"tops"`, `"pots"`, and `"spot"`. A better hash code should somehow take into consideration the positions of the x_i's. An alternative hash code, which does exactly this, is to choose a nonzero constant, $a \neq 1$, and use as a hash code the value

$$x_0 a^{n-1} + x_1 a^{n-2} + \cdots + x_{n-2} a + x_{n-1}.$$

Mathematically speaking, this is simply a polynomial in a that takes the components $(x_0, x_1, \ldots, x_{n-1})$ of an object x as its coefficients. This hash code is therefore called a ***polynomial hash code***. By Horner's rule (see Exercise C-4.54), this polynomial can be computed as

$$x_{n-1} + a(x_{n-2} + a(x_{n-3} + \cdots + a(x_2 + a(x_1 + ax_0)) \cdots)).$$

Intuitively, a polynomial hash code uses multiplication by different powers as a way to spread out the influence of each component across the resulting hash code.

Of course, on a typical computer, evaluating a polynomial will be done using the finite bit representation for a hash code; hence, the value will periodically overflow the bits used for an integer. Since we are more interested in a good spread of the object x with respect to other keys, we simply ignore such overflows. Still, we should be mindful that such overflows are occurring and choose the constant a so that it has some nonzero, low-order bits, which will serve to preserve some of the information content even as we are in an overflow situation.

We have done some experimental studies that suggest that 33, 37, 39, and 41 are particularly good choices for a when working with character strings that are English words. In fact, in a list of over 50,000 English words formed as the union of the word lists provided in two variants of Unix, we found that taking a to be 33, 37, 39, or 41 produced fewer than 7 collisions in each case!

Cyclic-Shift Hash Codes

A variant of the polynomial hash code replaces multiplication by a with a cyclic shift of a partial sum by a certain number of bits. For example, a 5-bit cyclic shift of the 32-bit value 00111101100101101010100010101000 is achieved by taking the leftmost five bits and placing those on the rightmost side of the representation, resulting in 10110010110101010001010100000111. While this operation has little natural meaning in terms of arithmetic, it accomplishes the goal of varying the bits of the calculation. In Java, a cyclic shift of bits can be accomplished through careful use of the bitwise shift operators.

An implementation of a cyclic-shift hash code computation for a character string in Java appears as follows:

```java
static int hashCode(String s) {
  int h=0;
  for (int i=0; i<s.length( ); i++) {
    h = (h << 5) | (h >>> 27);        // 5-bit cyclic shift of the running sum
    h += (int) s.charAt(i);           // add in next character
  }
  return h;
}
```

As with the traditional polynomial hash code, fine-tuning is required when using a cyclic-shift hash code, as we must wisely choose the amount to shift by for each new character. Our choice of a 5-bit shift is justified by experiments run on a list of just over 230,000 English words, comparing the number of collisions for various shift amounts (see Table 10.1).

Shift	Collisions Total	Collisions Max
0	234735	623
1	165076	43
2	38471	13
3	7174	5
4	1379	3
5	190	3
6	502	2
7	560	2
8	5546	4
9	393	3
10	5194	5
11	11559	5
12	822	2
13	900	4
14	2001	4
15	19251	8
16	211781	37

Table 10.1: Comparison of collision behavior for the cyclic-shift hash code as applied to a list of 230,000 English words. The "Total" column records the total number of words that collide with at least one other, and the "Max" column records the maximum number of words colliding at any one hash code. Note that with a cyclic shift of 0, this hash code reverts to the one that simply sums all the characters.

Hash Codes in Java

The notion of hash codes are an integral part of the Java language. The Object class, which serves as an ancestor of all object types, includes a default hashCode( ) method that returns a 32-bit integer of type **int**, which serves as an object's hash code. The default version of hashCode( ) provided by the Object class is often just an integer representation derived from the object's memory address.

However, we must be careful if relying on the default version of hashCode( ) when authoring a class. For hashing schemes to be reliable, it is imperative that any two objects that are viewed as "equal" to each other have the same hash code. This is important because if an entry is inserted into a map, and a later search is performed on a key that is considered equivalent to that entry's key, the map must recognize this as a match. (See, for example, the UnsortedTableMap.findIndex method in Code Fragment 10.4.) Therefore, when using a hash table to implement a map, we want equivalent keys to have the same hash code so that they are guaranteed to map to the same bucket. More formally, if a class defines equivalence through the equals method (see Section 3.5), then that class should also provide a consistent implementation of the hashCode method, such that if x.equals(y) then x.hashCode( ) == y.hashCode( ).

As an example, Java's String class defines the equals method so that two instances are equivalent if they have precisely the same sequence of characters. That class also overrides the hashCode method to provide consistent behavior. In fact, the implementation of hash codes for the String class is excellent. If we repeat the experiment from the previous page using Java's implementation of hash codes, there are only 12 collisions among more than 230,000 words. Java's primitive wrapper classes also define hashCode, using techniques described on page 412.

As an example of how to properly implement hashCode for a user-defined class, we will revisit the SinglyLinkedList class from Chapter 3. We defined the equals method for that class, in Section 3.5.2, so that two lists are equivalent if they represent equal-length sequences of elements that are pairwise equivalent. We can compute a robust hash code for a list by taking the exclusive-or of its elements' hash codes, while performing a cyclic shift. (See Code Fragment 10.6.)

```
1  public int hashCode( ) {
2    int h = 0;
3    for (Node walk=head; walk != null; walk = walk.getNext()) {
4      h ^= walk.getElement().hashCode();   // bitwise exclusive-or with element's code
5      h = (h << 5) | (h >>> 27);           // 5-bit cyclic shift of composite code
6    }
7    return h;
8  }
```

Code Fragment 10.6: A robust implementation of the hashCode method for the SinglyLinkedList class from Chapter 3.

Compression Functions

The hash code for a key k will typically not be suitable for immediate use with a bucket array, because the integer hash code may be negative or may exceed the capacity of the bucket array. Thus, once we have determined an integer hash code for a key object k, there is still the issue of mapping that integer into the range $[0, N-1]$. This computation, known as a *compression function*, is the second action performed as part of an overall hash function. A good compression function is one that minimizes the number of collisions for a given set of distinct hash codes.

The Division Method

A simple compression function is the *division method*, which maps an integer i to

$$i \bmod N,$$

where N, the size of the bucket array, is a fixed positive integer. Additionally, if we take N to be a prime number, then this compression function helps "spread out" the distribution of hashed values. Indeed, if N is not prime, then there is greater risk that patterns in the distribution of hash codes will be repeated in the distribution of hash values, thereby causing collisions. For example, if we insert keys with hash codes $\{200, 205, 210, 215, 220, \ldots, 600\}$ into a bucket array of size 100, then each hash code will collide with three others. But if we use a bucket array of size 101, then there will be no collisions. If a hash function is chosen well, it should ensure that the probability of two different keys getting hashed to the same bucket is $1/N$. Choosing N to be a prime number is not always enough, however, for if there is a repeated pattern of hash codes of the form $pN + q$ for several different p's, then there will still be collisions.

The MAD Method

A more sophisticated compression function, which helps eliminate repeated patterns in a set of integer keys, is the *Multiply-Add-and-Divide* (or "MAD") method. This method maps an integer i to

$$[(ai + b) \bmod p] \bmod N,$$

where N is the size of the bucket array, p is a prime number larger than N, and a and b are integers chosen at random from the interval $[0, p-1]$, with $a > 0$. This compression function is chosen in order to eliminate repeated patterns in the set of hash codes and get us closer to having a "good" hash function, that is, one such that the probability any two different keys collide is $1/N$. This good behavior would be the same as we would have if these keys were "thrown" into A uniformly at random.

10.2.2   Collision-Handling Schemes

The main idea of a hash table is to take a bucket array, A, and a hash function, h, and use them to implement a map by storing each entry (k, v) in the "bucket" $A[h(k)]$. This simple idea is challenged, however, when we have two distinct keys, k_1 and k_2, such that $h(k_1) = h(k_2)$. The existence of such *collisions* prevents us from simply inserting a new entry (k, v) directly into the bucket $A[h(k)]$. It also complicates our procedure for performing insertion, search, and deletion operations.

Separate Chaining

A simple and efficient way for dealing with collisions is to have each bucket $A[j]$ store its own secondary container, holding all entries (k, v) such that $h(k) = j$. A natural choice for the secondary container is a small map instance implemented using an unordered list, as described in Section 10.1.4. This *collision resolution* rule is known as *separate chaining*, and is illustrated in Figure 10.6.

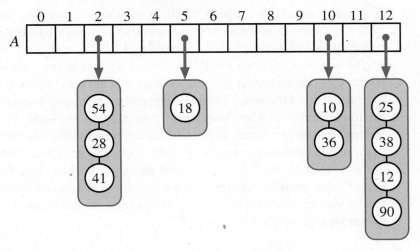

Figure 10.6: A hash table of size 13, storing 10 entries with integer keys, with collisions resolved by separate chaining. The compression function is $h(k) = k \bmod 13$. For simplicity, we do not show the values associated with the keys.

In the worst case, operations on an individual bucket take time proportional to the size of the bucket. Assuming we use a good hash function to index the n entries of our map in a bucket array of capacity N, the expected size of a bucket is n/N. Therefore, if given a good hash function, the core map operations run in $O(\lceil n/N \rceil)$. The ratio $\lambda = n/N$, called the *load factor* of the hash table, should be bounded by a small constant, preferably below 1. As long as λ is $O(1)$, the core operations on the hash table run in $O(1)$ expected time.

Open Addressing

The separate chaining rule has many nice properties, such as affording simple implementations of map operations, but it nevertheless has one slight disadvantage: It requires the use of an auxiliary data structure to hold entries with colliding keys. If space is at a premium (for example, if we are writing a program for a small hand-held device), then we can use the alternative approach of storing each entry directly in a table slot. This approach saves space because no auxiliary structures are employed, but it requires a bit more complexity to properly handle collisions. There are several variants of this approach, collectively referred to as *open addressing* schemes, which we discuss next. Open addressing requires that the load factor is always at most 1 and that entries are stored directly in the cells of the bucket array itself.

Linear Probing and Its Variants

A simple method for collision handling with open addressing is *linear probing*. With this approach, if we try to insert an entry (k, v) into a bucket $A[j]$ that is already occupied, where $j = h(k)$, then we next try $A[(j+1) \bmod N]$. If $A[(j+1) \bmod N]$ is also occupied, then we try $A[(j+2) \bmod N]$, and so on, until we find an empty bucket that can accept the new entry. Once this bucket is located, we simply insert the entry there. Of course, this collision resolution strategy requires that we change the implementation when searching for an existing key—the first step of all get, put, or remove operations. In particular, to attempt to locate an entry with key equal to k, we must examine consecutive slots, starting from $A[h(k)]$, until we either find an entry with an equal key or we find an empty bucket. (See Figure 10.7.) The name "linear probing" comes from the fact that accessing a cell of the bucket array can be viewed as a "probe," and that consecutive probes occur in neighboring cells (when viewed circularly).

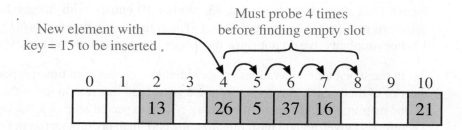

Figure 10.7: Insertion into a hash table with integer keys using linear probing. The hash function is $h(k) = k \bmod 11$. Values associated with keys are not shown.

To implement a deletion, we cannot simply remove a found entry from its slot in the array. For example, after the insertion of key 15 portrayed in Figure 10.7, if the entry with key 37 were trivially deleted, a subsequent search for 15 would fail because that search would start by probing at index 4, then index 5, and then index 6, at which an empty cell is found. A typical way to get around this difficulty is to replace a deleted entry with a special "defunct" sentinel object. With this special marker possibly occupying spaces in our hash table, we modify our search algorithm so that the search for a key k will skip over cells containing the defunct sentinel and continue probing until reaching the desired entry or an empty bucket (or returning back to where we started from). Additionally, our algorithm for put should remember a defunct location encountered during the search for k, since this is a valid place to put a new entry (k, v), if no existing entry is found beyond it.

Although use of an open addressing scheme can save space, linear probing suffers from an additional disadvantage. It tends to cluster the entries of a map into contiguous runs, which may even overlap (particularly if more than half of the cells in the hash table are occupied). Such contiguous runs of occupied hash cells cause searches to slow down considerably.

Another open addressing strategy, known as *quadratic probing*, iteratively tries the buckets $A[(h(k) + f(i)) \bmod N]$, for $i = 0, 1, 2, \ldots$, where $f(i) = i^2$, until finding an empty bucket. As with linear probing, the quadratic probing strategy complicates the removal operation, but it does avoid the kinds of clustering patterns that occur with linear probing. Nevertheless, it creates its own kind of clustering, called *secondary clustering*, where the set of filled array cells still has a nonuniform pattern, even if we assume that the original hash codes are distributed uniformly. When N is prime and the bucket array is less than half full, the quadratic probing strategy is guaranteed to find an empty slot. However, this guarantee is not valid once the table becomes at least half full, or if N is not chosen as a prime number; we explore the cause of this type of clustering in an exercise (C-10.42).

An open addressing strategy that does not cause clustering of the kind produced by linear probing or the kind produced by quadratic probing is the *double hashing* strategy. In this approach, we choose a secondary hash function, h', and if h maps some key k to a bucket $A[h(k)]$ that is already occupied, then we iteratively try the buckets $A[(h(k) + f(i)) \bmod N]$ next, for $i = 1, 2, 3, \ldots$, where $f(i) = i \cdot h'(k)$. In this scheme, the secondary hash function is not allowed to evaluate to zero; a common choice is $h'(k) = q - (k \bmod q)$, for some prime number $q < N$. Also, N should be a prime.

Another approach to avoid clustering with open addressing is to iteratively try buckets $A[(h(k) + f(i)) \bmod N]$ where $f(i)$ is based on a pseudorandom number generator, providing a repeatable, but somewhat arbitrary, sequence of subsequent probes that depends upon bits of the original hash code.

10.2.3   Load Factors, Rehashing, and Efficiency

In the hash table schemes described thus far, it is important that the load factor, $\lambda = n/N$, be kept below 1. With separate chaining, as λ gets very close to 1, the probability of a collision greatly increases, which adds overhead to our operations, since we must revert to linear-time list-based methods in buckets that have collisions. Experiments and average-case analyses suggest that we should maintain $\lambda < 0.9$ for hash tables with separate chaining. (By default, Java's implementation uses separate chaining with $\lambda < 0.75$.)

With open addressing, on the other hand, as the load factor λ grows beyond 0.5 and starts approaching 1, clusters of entries in the bucket array start to grow as well. These clusters cause the probing strategies to "bounce around" the bucket array for a considerable amount of time before they find an empty slot. In Exercise C-10.42, we explore the degradation of quadratic probing when $\lambda \geq 0.5$. Experiments suggest that we should maintain $\lambda < 0.5$ for an open addressing scheme with linear probing, and perhaps only a bit higher for other open addressing schemes.

If an insertion causes the load factor of a hash table to go above the specified threshold, then it is common to resize the table (to regain the specified load factor) and to reinsert all objects into this new table. Although we need not define a new hash code for each object, we do need to reapply a new compression function that takes into consideration the size of the new table. Rehashing will generally scatter the entries throughout the new bucket array. When rehashing to a new table, it is a good requirement for the new array's size to be a prime number approximately double the previous size (see Exercise C-10.32). In that way, the cost of rehashing all the entires in the table can be amortized against the time used to insert them in the first place (as with dynamic arrays; see Section 7.2.1).

Efficiency of Hash Tables

Although the details of the average-case analysis of hashing are beyond the scope of this book, its probabilistic basis is quite intuitive. If our hash function is good, then we expect the entries to be uniformly distributed in the N cells of the bucket array. Thus, to store n entries, the expected number of keys in a bucket would be $\lceil n/N \rceil$, which is $O(1)$ if n is $O(N)$.

The costs associated with a periodic rehashing (when resizing a table after occasional insertions or deletions) can be accounted for separately, leading to an additional $O(1)$ amortized cost for put and remove.

In the worst case, a poor hash function could map every entry to the same bucket. This would result in linear-time performance for the core map operations with separate chaining, or with any open addressing model in which the secondary sequence of probes depends only on the hash code. A summary of these costs is given in Table 10.2.

Method	Unsorted List	Hash Table expected	worst case
get	$O(n)$	$O(1)$	$O(n)$
put	$O(n)$	$O(1)$	$O(n)$
remove	$O(n)$	$O(1)$	$O(n)$
size, isEmpty	$O(1)$	$O(1)$	$O(1)$
entrySet, keySet, values	$O(n)$	$O(n)$	$O(n)$

Table 10.2: Comparison of the running times of the methods of a map realized by means of an unsorted list (as in Section 10.1.4) or a hash table. We let n denote the number of entries in the map, and we assume that the bucket array supporting the hash table is maintained such that its capacity is proportional to the number of entries in the map.

An Anecdote About Hashing and Computer Security

In a 2003 academic paper, researchers discuss the possibility of exploiting a hash table's worst-case performance to cause a denial-of-service (DoS) attack of Internet technologies. Since many published algorithms compute hash codes with a deterministic function, an attacker could precompute a very large number of moderate-length strings that all hash to the identical 32-bit hash code. (Recall that by any of the hashing schemes we describe, other than double hashing, if two keys are mapped to the same hash code, they will be inseparable in the collision resolution.) This concern was brought to the attention of the Java development team, and that of many other programming languages, but deemed an insignificant risk at the time by most. (Kudos to the Perl team for implementing a fix in 2003.)

In late 2011, another team of researchers demonstrated an implementation of just such an attack. Web servers allow a series of key-value parameters to be embedded in a URL using a syntax such as `?key1=val1&key2=val2&key3=val3`. Those key-value pairs are strings and a typical Web server immediately stores them in a hash-map. Servers already place a limit on the length and number of such parameters, to avoid overload, but they presume that the total insertion time in the map will be linear in the number of entries, given the expected constant-time operations. However, if all keys were to collide, the insertions into the map will require quadratic time, causing the server to perform an inordinate amount of work.

In 2012, the OpenJDK team announced the following resolution: they distributed a security patch that includes an alternative hash function that introduces randomization into the computation of hash codes, making it less tractable to reverse engineer a set of colliding strings. However, to avoid breaking existing code, the new feature is disabled by default in Java SE 7 and, when enabled, is only used for hashing strings and only when a table size grows beyond a certain threshold. Enhanced hashing will be enabled in Java SE 8 for all types and uses.

10.2.4   Java Hash Table Implementation

In this section, we develop two implementations of a hash table, one using separate chaining and the other using open addressing with linear probing. While these approaches to collision resolution are quite different, there are many higher-level commonalities to the two hashing algorithms. For that reason, we extend the AbstractMap class (from Code Fragment 10.3) to define a new AbstractHashMap class (see Code Fragment 10.7), which provides much of the functionality common to our two hash table implementations.

We will begin by discussing what this abstract class does *not* do—it does not provide any concrete representation of a table of "buckets." With separate chaining, each bucket will be a secondary map. With open addressing, however, there is no tangible container for each bucket; the "buckets" are effectively interleaved due to the probing sequences. In our design, the AbstractHashMap class presumes the following to be abstract methods—to be implemented by each concrete subclass:

createTable( ): This method should create an initially empty table having size equal to a designated capacity instance variable.

bucketGet(h, k): This method should mimic the semantics of the public get method, but for a key k that is known to hash to bucket h.

bucketPut(h, k, v): This method should mimic the semantics of the public put method, but for a key k that is known to hash to bucket h.

bucketRemove(h, k): This method should mimic the semantics of the public remove method, but for a key k known to hash to bucket h.

entrySet( ): This standard map method iterates through *all* entries of the map. We do not delegate this on a per-bucket basis because "buckets" in open addressing are not inherently disjoint.

What the AbstractHashMap class does provide is mathematical support in the form of a hash compression function using a randomized Multiply-Add-and-Divide (MAD) formula, and support for automatically resizing the underlying hash table when the load factor reaches a certain threshold.

The hashValue method relies on an original key's hash code, as returned by its hashCode( ) method, followed by MAD compression based on a prime number and the scale and shift parameters that are randomly chosen in the constructor.

To manage the load factor, the AbstractHashMap class declares a protected member, n, which should equal the current number of entries in the map; however, it must rely on the subclasses to update this field from within methods bucketPut and bucketRemove. If the load factor of the table increases beyond 0.5, we request a bigger table (using the createTable method) and reinsert all entries into the new table. (For simplicity, this implementation uses tables of size $2^k + 1$, even though these are not generally prime.)

```
1   public abstract class AbstractHashMap<K,V> extends AbstractMap<K,V> {
2     protected int n = 0;                    // number of entries in the dictionary
3     protected int capacity;                 // length of the table
4     private int prime;                      // prime factor
5     private long scale, shift;              // the shift and scaling factors
6     public AbstractHashMap(int cap, int p) {
7       prime = p;
8       capacity = cap;
9       Random rand = new Random();
10      scale = rand.nextInt(prime−1) + 1;
11      shift = rand.nextInt(prime);
12      createTable();
13    }
14    public AbstractHashMap(int cap) { this(cap, 109345121); }  // default prime
15    public AbstractHashMap() { this(17); }                     // default capacity
16    // public methods
17    public int size() { return n; }
18    public V get(K key) { return bucketGet(hashValue(key), key); }
19    public V remove(K key) { return bucketRemove(hashValue(key), key); }
20    public V put(K key, V value) {
21      V answer = bucketPut(hashValue(key), key, value);
22      if (n > capacity / 2)                  // keep load factor <= 0.5
23        resize(2 * capacity − 1);            // (or find a nearby prime)
24      return answer;
25    }
26    // private utilities
27    private int hashValue(K key) {
28      return (int) ((Math.abs(key.hashCode()*scale + shift) % prime) % capacity);
29    }
30    private void resize(int newCap) {
31      ArrayList<Entry<K,V>> buffer = new ArrayList<>(n);
32      for (Entry<K,V> e : entrySet())
33        buffer.add(e);
34      capacity = newCap;
35      createTable();                         // based on updated capacity
36      n = 0;                                 // will be recomputed while reinserting entries
37      for (Entry<K,V> e : buffer)
38        put(e.getKey(), e.getValue());
39    }
40    // protected abstract methods to be implemented by subclasses
41    protected abstract void createTable();
42    protected abstract V bucketGet(int h, K k);
43    protected abstract V bucketPut(int h, K k, V v);
44    protected abstract V bucketRemove(int h, K k);
45  }
```

Code Fragment 10.7: A base class for our hash table implementations, extending the AbstractMap class from Code Fragment 10.3.

Separate Chaining

To represent each bucket for separate chaining, we use an instance of the simpler UnsortedTableMap class from Section 10.1.4. This technique, in which we use a simple solution to a problem to create a new, more advanced solution, is known as **bootstrapping**. The advantage of using a map for each bucket is that it becomes easy to delegate responsibilities for top-level map operations to the appropriate bucket.

The entire hash table is then represented as a fixed-capacity array A of the secondary maps. Each cell, $A[h]$, is initially a null reference; we only create a secondary map when an entry is first hashed to a particular bucket.

As a general rule, we implement bucketGet(h, k) by calling $A[h]$.get(k), we implement bucketPut(h, k, v) by calling $A[h]$.put(k, v), and bucketRemove(h, k) by calling $A[h]$.remove(k). However, care is needed for two reasons.

First, because we choose to leave table cells as null until a secondary map is needed, each of these fundamental operations must begin by checking to see if $A[h]$ is null. In the case of bucketGet and bucketRemove, if the bucket does not yet exist, we can simply return null as there can not be any entry matching key k. In the case of bucketPut, a new entry must be inserted, so we instantiate a new UnsortedTableMap for $A[h]$ before continuing.

The second issue is that, in our AbstractHashMap framework, the subclass has the responsibility to properly maintain the instance variable n when an entry is newly inserted or deleted. Remember that when put(k, v) is called on a map, the size of the map only increases if key k is new to the map (otherwise, the value of an existing entry is reassigned). Similarly, a call to remove(k) only decreases the size of the map when an entry with key equal to k is found. In our implementation, we determine the change in the overall size of the map, by determining if there is any change in the size of the relevant secondary map before and after an operation.

Code Fragment 10.8 provides a complete definition for our ChainHashMap class, which implements a hash table with separate chaining. If we assume that the hash function performs well, a map with n entries and a table of capacity N will have an expected bucket size of n/N (recall, this is its **load factor**). So even though the individual buckets, implemented as UnsortedTableMap instances, are not particularly efficient, each bucket has expected $O(1)$ size, provided that n is $O(N)$, as in our implementation. Therefore, the expected running time of operations get, put, and remove for this map is $O(1)$. The entrySet method (and thus the related keySet and values) runs in $O(n+N)$ time, as it loops through the length of the table (with length N) and through all buckets (which have cumulative lengths n).

```
1   public class ChainHashMap<K,V> extends AbstractHashMap<K,V> {
2     // a fixed capacity array of UnsortedTableMap that serve as buckets
3     private UnsortedTableMap<K,V>[ ] table;   // initialized within createTable
4     public ChainHashMap( ) { super( ); }
5     public ChainHashMap(int cap) { super(cap); }
6     public ChainHashMap(int cap, int p) { super(cap, p); }
7     /** Creates an empty table having length equal to current capacity. */
8     protected void createTable( ) {
9       table = (UnsortedTableMap<K,V>[ ]) new UnsortedTableMap[capacity];
10    }
11    /** Returns value associated with key k in bucket with hash value h, or else null. */
12    protected V bucketGet(int h, K k) {
13      UnsortedTableMap<K,V> bucket = table[h];
14      if (bucket == null) return null;
15      return bucket.get(k);
16    }
17    /** Associates key k with value v in bucket with hash value h; returns old value. */
18    protected V bucketPut(int h, K k, V v) {
19      UnsortedTableMap<K,V> bucket = table[h];
20      if (bucket == null)
21        bucket = table[h] = new UnsortedTableMap<>( );
22      int oldSize = bucket.size( );
23      V answer = bucket.put(k,v);
24      n += (bucket.size( ) − oldSize);      // size may have increased
25      return answer;
26    }
27    /** Removes entry having key k from bucket with hash value h (if any). */
28    protected V bucketRemove(int h, K k) {
29      UnsortedTableMap<K,V> bucket = table[h];
30      if (bucket == null) return null;
31      int oldSize = bucket.size( );
32      V answer = bucket.remove(k);
33      n −= (oldSize − bucket.size( ));      // size may have decreased
34      return answer;
35    }
36    /** Returns an iterable collection of all key-value entries of the map. */
37    public Iterable<Entry<K,V>> entrySet( ) {
38      ArrayList<Entry<K,V>> buffer = new ArrayList<>( );
39      for (int h=0; h < capacity; h++)
40        if (table[h] != null)
41          for (Entry<K,V> entry : table[h].entrySet( ))
42            buffer.add(entry);
43      return buffer;
44    }
45  }
```

Code Fragment 10.8: A concrete hash map implementation using separate chaining.

Linear Probing

Our implementation of a ProbeHashMap class, using open addressing with linear probing, is given in Code Fragments 10.9 and 10.10. In order to support deletions, we use a technique described in Section 10.2.2 in which we place a special marker in a table location at which an entry has been deleted, so that we can distinguish between it and a location that has always been empty. To this end, we create a fixed entry instance, DEFUNCT, as a sentinel (disregarding any key or value stored within), and use references to that instance to mark vacated cells.

The most challenging aspect of open addressing is to properly trace the series of probes when collisions occur during a search for an existing entry, or placement of a new entry. To this end, the three primary map operations each rely on a utility, findSlot, that searches for an entry with key k in "bucket" h (that is, where h is the index returned by the hash function for key k). When attempting to retrieve the value associated with a given key, we must continue probing until we find the key, or until we reach a table slot with a null reference. We cannot stop the search upon reaching an DEFUNCT sentinel, because it represents a location that may have been filled at the time the desired entry was once inserted.

When a key-value pair is being placed in the map, we must first attempt to find an existing entry with the given key, so that we might overwrite its value. Therefore, we must search beyond any occurrences of the DEFUNCT sentinel when inserting. However, if no match is found, we prefer to repurpose the first slot marked with DEFUNCT, if any, when placing the new element in the table. The findSlot method enacts this logic, continuing an unsuccessful search until finding a truly empty slot, and returning the index of the first available slot for an insertion.

When deleting an existing entry within bucketRemove, we intentionally set the table entry to the DEFUNCT sentinel in accordance with our strategy.

```
1  public class ProbeHashMap<K,V> extends AbstractHashMap<K,V> {
2    private MapEntry<K,V>[ ] table;       // a fixed array of entries (all initially null)
3    private MapEntry<K,V> DEFUNCT = new MapEntry<>(null, null);   //sentinel
4    public ProbeHashMap( ) { super( ); }
5    public ProbeHashMap(int cap) { super(cap); }
6    public ProbeHashMap(int cap, int p) { super(cap, p); }
7    /** Creates an empty table having length equal to current capacity. */
8    protected void createTable( ) {
9      table = (MapEntry<K,V>[ ]) new MapEntry[capacity];   // safe cast
10   }
11   /** Returns true if location is either empty or the "defunct" sentinel. */
12   private boolean isAvailable(int j) {
13     return (table[j] == null || table[j] == DEFUNCT);
14   }
```

Code Fragment 10.9: Concrete ProbeHashMap class that uses linear probing for collision resolution. (Continues in Code Fragment 10.10.)

```
15    /** Returns index with key k, or −(a+1) such that k could be added at index a. */
16    private int findSlot(int h, K k) {
17      int avail = −1;                          // no slot available (thus far)
18      int j = h;                               // index while scanning table
19      do {
20        if (isAvailable(j)) {                  // may be either empty or defunct
21          if (avail == −1) avail = j;          // this is the first available slot!
22          if (table[j] == null) break;         // if empty, search fails immediately
23        } else if (table[j].getKey().equals(k))
24          return j;                            // successful match
25        j = (j+1) % capacity;                  // keep looking (cyclically)
26      } while (j != h);                        // stop if we return to the start
27      return −(avail + 1);                     // search has failed
28    }
29    /** Returns value associated with key k in bucket with hash value h, or else null. */
30    protected V bucketGet(int h, K k) {
31      int j = findSlot(h, k);
32      if (j < 0) return null;                  // no match found
33      return table[j].getValue();
34    }
35    /** Associates key k with value v in bucket with hash value h; returns old value. */
36    protected V bucketPut(int h, K k, V v) {
37      int j = findSlot(h, k);
38      if (j >= 0)                              // this key has an existing entry
39        return table[j].setValue(v);
40      table[−(j+1)] = new MapEntry<>(k, v);    // convert to proper index
41      n++;
42      return null;
43    }
44    /** Removes entry having key k from bucket with hash value h (if any). */
45    protected V bucketRemove(int h, K k) {
46      int j = findSlot(h, k);
47      if (j < 0) return null;                  // nothing to remove
48      V answer = table[j].getValue();
49      table[j] = DEFUNCT;                      // mark this slot as deactivated
50      n−−;
51      return answer;
52    }
53    /** Returns an iterable collection of all key-value entries of the map. */
54    public Iterable<Entry<K,V>> entrySet() {
55      ArrayList<Entry<K,V>> buffer = new ArrayList<>();
56      for (int h=0; h < capacity; h++)
57        if (!isAvailable(h)) buffer.add(table[h]);
58      return buffer;
59    }
60  }
```

Code Fragment 10.10: Concrete ProbeHashMap class that uses linear probing for collision resolution (continued from Code Fragment 10.9).

10.3   Sorted Maps

The traditional map ADT allows a user to look up the value associated with a given key, but the search for that key is a form known as an *exact search*. In this section, we will introduce an extension known as the *sorted map* ADT that includes all behaviors of the standard map, plus the following:

firstEntry( ): Returns the entry with smallest key value (or null, if the map is empty).

lastEntry( ): Returns the entry with largest key value (or null, if the map is empty).

ceilingEntry(k): Returns the entry with the least key value greater than or equal to k (or null, if no such entry exists).

floorEntry(k): Returns the entry with the greatest key value less than or equal to k (or null, if no such entry exists).

lowerEntry(k): Returns the entry with the greatest key value strictly less than k (or null, if no such entry exists).

higherEntry(k): Returns the entry with the least key value strictly greater than k (or null if no such entry exists).

subMap(k_1, k_2): Returns an iteration of all entries with key greater than or equal to k_1, but strictly less than k_2.

We note that the above methods are included within the java.util.NavigableMap interface (which extends the simpler java.util.SortedMap interface).

To motivate the use of a sorted map, consider a computer system that maintains information about events that have occurred (such as financial transactions), with a *time stamp* marking the occurrence of each event. If the time stamps were unique for a particular system, we could organize a map with a time stamp serving as a key, and a record about the event that occurred at that time as the value. A particular time stamp could serve as a reference ID for an event, in which case we can quickly retrieve information about that event from the map. However, the (unsorted) map ADT does not provide any way to get a list of all events ordered by the time at which they occur, or to search for which event occurred closest to a particular time. In fact, hash-based implementations of the map ADT intentionally scatter keys that may seem very "near" to each other in the original domain, so that they are more uniformly distributed in a hash table.

10.3.1 Sorted Search Tables

Several data structures can efficiently support the sorted map ADT, and we will examine some advanced techniques in Section 10.4 and Chapter 11. In this section, we will begin by exploring a simple implementation of a sorted map. We store the map's entries in an array list A so that they are in increasing order of their keys. (See Figure 10.8.) We refer to this implementation as a *sorted search table*.

0	1	2	3	4	5	6	7	8	9	10	11	12	13	14	15
2	4	5	7	8	9	12	14	17	19	22	25	27	28	33	37

Figure 10.8: Realization of a map by means of a sorted search table. We show only the keys for this map, so as to highlight their ordering.

As was the case with the unsorted table map of Section 10.1.4, the sorted search table has a space requirement that is $O(n)$. The primary advantage of this representation, and our reason for insisting that A be array-based, is that it allows us to use the *binary search* algorithm for a variety of efficient operations.

Binary Search and Inexact Searches

We originally presented the binary search algorithm in Section 5.1.3, as a means for detecting whether a given target is stored within a sorted sequence. In our original presentation (Code Fragment 5.3 on page 197), a binarySearch method returned true or false to designate whether the desired target was found.

The important realization is that, while performing a binary search, we can instead return the index at or near where a target might be found. During a successful search, the standard implementation determines the precise index at which the target is found. During an unsuccessful search, although the target is not found, the algorithm will effectively determine a pair of indices designating elements of the collection that are just less than or just greater than the missing target.

In Code Fragments 10.11 and 10.12, we present a complete implementation of a class, SortedTableMap, that supports the sorted map ADT. The most notable feature of our design is the inclusion of a findIndex utility method. This method uses the recursive binary search algorithm, but returns the *index* of the leftmost entry in the search range having key greater than or equal to k; if no entry in the search range has such a key, we return the index just beyond the end of the search range. By this convention, if an entry has the target key, the search returns the index of that entry. (Recall that keys are unique in a map.) If the key is absent, the method returns the index at which a new entry with that key would be inserted.

```
1   public class SortedTableMap<K,V> extends AbstractSortedMap<K,V> {
2     private ArrayList<MapEntry<K,V>> table = new ArrayList<>();
3     public SortedTableMap() { super(); }
4     public SortedTableMap(Comparator<K> comp) { super(comp); }
5     /** Returns the smallest index for range table[low..high] inclusive storing an entry
6         with a key greater than or equal to k (or else index high+1, by convention). */
7     private int findIndex(K key, int low, int high) {
8       if (high < low) return high + 1;              // no entry qualifies
9       int mid = (low + high) / 2;
10      int comp = compare(key, table.get(mid));
11      if (comp == 0)
12        return mid;                                 // found exact match
13      else if (comp < 0)
14        return findIndex(key, low, mid − 1);  // answer is left of mid (or possibly mid)
15      else
16        return findIndex(key, mid + 1, high); // answer is right of mid
17    }
18    /** Version of findIndex that searches the entire table */
19    private int findIndex(K key) { return findIndex(key, 0, table.size() − 1); }
20    /** Returns the number of entries in the map. */
21    public int size() { return table.size(); }
22    /** Returns the value associated with the specified key (or else null). */
23    public V get(K key) {
24      int j = findIndex(key);
25      if (j == size() || compare(key, table.get(j)) != 0) return null;   // no match
26      return table.get(j).getValue();
27    }
28    /** Associates the given value with the given key, returning any overridden value.*/
29    public V put(K key, V value) {
30      int j = findIndex(key);
31      if (j < size() && compare(key, table.get(j)) == 0)        // match exists
32        return table.get(j).setValue(value);
33      table.add(j, new MapEntry<K,V>(key,value));              // otherwise new
34      return null;
35    }
36    /** Removes the entry having key k (if any) and returns its associated value. */
37    public V remove(K key) {
38      int j = findIndex(key);
39      if (j == size() || compare(key, table.get(j)) != 0) return null;   // no match
40      return table.remove(j).getValue();
41    }
```

Code Fragment 10.11: An implementation of the SortedTableMap class. (Continues in Code Fragment 10.12.) The AbstractSortedMap base class (available online), provides the utility method, compare, based on a given comparator.

```
42    /** Utility returns the entry at index j, or else null if j is out of bounds. */
43    private Entry<K,V> safeEntry(int j) {
44      if (j < 0 || j >= table.size()) return null;
45      return table.get(j);
46    }
47    /** Returns the entry having the least key (or null if map is empty). */
48    public Entry<K,V> firstEntry() { return safeEntry(0); }
49    /** Returns the entry having the greatest key (or null if map is empty). */
50    public Entry<K,V> lastEntry() { return safeEntry(table.size()-1); }
51    /** Returns the entry with least key greater than or equal to given key (if any). */
52    public Entry<K,V> ceilingEntry(K key) {
53      return safeEntry(findIndex(key));
54    }
55    /** Returns the entry with greatest key less than or equal to given key (if any). */
56    public Entry<K,V> floorEntry(K key) {
57      int j = findIndex(key);
58      if (j == size() || ! key.equals(table.get(j).getKey()))
59        j--;    // look one earlier (unless we had found a perfect match)
60      return safeEntry(j);
61    }
62    /** Returns the entry with greatest key strictly less than given key (if any). */
63    public Entry<K,V> lowerEntry(K key) {
64      return safeEntry(findIndex(key) − 1);      // go strictly before the ceiling entry
65    }
66    public Entry<K,V> higherEntry(K key) {
67    /** Returns the entry with least key strictly greater than given key (if any). */
68      int j = findIndex(key);
69      if (j < size() && key.equals(table.get(j).getKey()))
70        j++;    // go past exact match
71      return safeEntry(j);
72    }
73    // support for snapshot iterators for entrySet() and subMap() follow
74    private Iterable<Entry<K,V>> snapshot(int startIndex, K stop) {
75      ArrayList<Entry<K,V>> buffer = new ArrayList<>();
76      int j = startIndex;
77      while (j < table.size() && (stop == null || compare(stop, table.get(j)) > 0))
78        buffer.add(table.get(j++));
79      return buffer;
80    }
81    public Iterable<Entry<K,V>> entrySet() { return snapshot(0, null); }
82    public Iterable<Entry<K,V>> subMap(K fromKey, K toKey) {
83      return snapshot(findIndex(fromKey), toKey);
84    }
85  }
```

Code Fragment 10.12: An implementation of the SortedTableMap class (continued from Code Fragment 10.11).

Analysis

We conclude by analyzing the performance of our SortedTableMap implementation. A summary of the running times for all methods of the sorted map ADT (including the traditional map operations) is given in Table 10.3. It should be clear that the size, firstEntry, and lastEntry methods run in $O(1)$ time, and that iterating the keys of the table in either direction can be performed in $O(n)$ time.

The analysis for the various forms of search all depend on the fact that a binary search on a table with n entries runs in $O(\log n)$ time. This claim was originally shown as Proposition 5.2 in Section 5.2, and that analysis clearly applies to our findIndex method as well. We therefore claim an $O(\log n)$ worst-case running time for methods get, ceilingEntry, floorEntry, lowerEntry, and higherEntry. Each of these makes a single call to findIndex, followed by a constant number of additional steps to determine the appropriate answer based on the index. The analysis of subMap is a bit more interesting. It begins with a binary search to find the first item within the range (if any). After that, it executes a loop that takes $O(1)$ time per iteration to gather subsequent values until reaching the end of the range. If there are s items reported in the range, the total running time is $O(s + \log n)$.

In contrast to the efficient search operations, update operations for a sorted table may take considerable time. Although binary search can help identify the index at which an update occurs, both insertions and deletions require, in the worst case, that linearly many existing elements be shifted in order to maintain the sorted order of the table. Specifically, the potential call to table.add from within put and table.remove from within remove lead to $O(n)$ worst-case time. (See the discussion of corresponding operations of the ArrayList class in Section 7.2.)

In conclusion, sorted tables are primarily used in situations where we expect many searches but relatively few updates.

Method	Running Time
size	$O(1)$
get	$O(\log n)$
put	$O(n)$; $O(\log n)$ if map has entry with given key
remove	$O(n)$
firstEntry, lastEntry	$O(1)$
ceilingEntry, floorEntry, lowerEntry, higherEntry	$O(\log n)$
subMap	$O(s + \log n)$ where s items are reported
entrySet, keySet, values	$O(n)$

Table 10.3: Performance of a sorted map, as implemented with SortedTableMap. We use n to denote the number of items in the map at the time the operation is performed. The space requirement is $O(n)$.

10.3.2 Two Applications of Sorted Maps

In this section, we explore applications in which there is particular advantage to using a *sorted* map rather than a traditional (unsorted) map. To apply a sorted map, keys must come from a domain that is totally ordered. Furthermore, to take advantage of the inexact or range searches afforded by a sorted map, there should be some reason why nearby keys have relevance to a search.

Flight Databases

There are several websites on the Internet that allow users to perform queries on flight databases to find flights between various cities, typically with the intent to buy a ticket. To make a query, a user specifies origin and destination cities, a departure date, and a departure time. To support such queries, we can model the flight database as a map, where keys are Flight objects that contain fields corresponding to these four parameters. That is, a key is a tuple

$$k = (\text{origin}, \text{destination}, \text{date}, \text{time}).$$

Additional information about a flight, such as the flight number, the number of seats still available in first (F) and coach (Y) class, the flight duration, and the fare, can be stored in the value object.

Finding a requested flight is not simply a matter of finding an exact match for a requested query. Although a user typically wants to exactly match the origin and destination cities, he or she may have flexibility for the departure date, and certainly will have some flexibility for the departure time on a specific day. We can handle such a query by ordering our keys lexicographically. Then, an efficient implementation for a sorted map would be a good way to satisfy users' queries. For instance, given a user query key k, we could call ceilingEntry(k) to return the first flight between the desired cities, having a departure date and time matching the desired query or later. Better yet, with well-constructed keys, we could use subMap(k_1, k_2) to find all flights within a given range of times. For example, if $k1 = (\text{ORD, PVD, 05May, 09:30})$, and $k2 = (\text{ORD, PVD, 05May, 20:00})$, a respective call to subMap(k_1, k_2) might result in the following sequence of key-value pairs:

```
(ORD, PVD, 05May, 09:53)  :  (AA 1840, F5, Y15, 02:05, $251),
(ORD, PVD, 05May, 13:29)  :  (AA 600, F2, Y0, 02:16, $713),
(ORD, PVD, 05May, 17:39)  :  (AA 416, F3, Y9, 02:09, $365),
(ORD, PVD, 05May, 19:50)  :  (AA 1828, F9, Y25, 02:13, $186)
```

Maxima Sets

Life is full of trade-offs. We often have to trade off a desired performance measure against a corresponding cost. Suppose, for the sake of an example, we are interested in maintaining a database rating automobiles by their maximum speeds and their cost. We would like to allow someone with a certain amount of money to query our database to find the fastest car they can possibly afford.

We can model such a trade-off problem as this by using a key-value pair to model the two parameters that we are trading off, which in this case would be the pair (cost, speed) for each car. Notice that some cars are strictly better than other cars using this measure. For example, a car with cost-speed pair $(30000, 100)$ is strictly better than a car with cost-speed pair $(40000, 90)$. At the same time, there are some cars that are not strictly dominated by another car. For example, a car with cost-speed pair $(30000, 100)$ may be better or worse than a car with cost-speed pair $(40000, 120)$, depending on how much money we have to spend. (See Figure 10.9.)

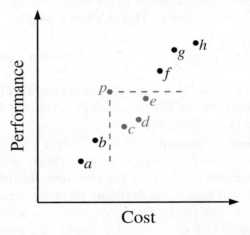

Figure 10.9: Illustrating the cost-performance trade-off with pairs represented by points in the plane. Notice that point p is strictly better than points c, d, and e, but may be better or worse than points a, b, f, g, and h, depending on the price we are willing to pay. Thus, if we were to add p to our set, we could remove the points c, d, and e, but not the others.

Formally, we say a cost-performance pair (a, b) **dominates** pair $(c, d) \neq (a, b)$ if $a \leq c$ and $b \geq d$, that is, if the first pair has no greater cost and at least as good performance. A pair (a, b) is called a **maximum** pair if it is not dominated by any other pair. We are interested in maintaining the set of maxima of a collection of cost-performance pairs. That is, we would like to add new pairs to this collection (for example, when a new car is introduced), and to query this collection for a given dollar amount, d, to find the fastest car that costs no more than d dollars.

Maintaining a Maxima Set with a Sorted Map

We can store the set of maxima pairs in a sorted map so that the cost is the key field and performance (speed) is the value. We can then implement operations add(c, p), which adds a new cost-performance entry (c, p), and best(c), which returns the entry having best performance of those with cost at most c. Code Fragment 10.13 provides an implementation of such a CostPerformanceDatabase class.

```java
 1  /** Maintains a database of maximal (cost,performance) pairs. */
 2  public class CostPerformanceDatabase {
 3
 4    SortedMap<Integer,Integer> map = new SortedTableMap<>();
 5
 6    /** Constructs an initially empty database. */
 7    public CostPerformanceDatabase( ) { }
 8
 9    /** Returns the (cost,performance) entry with largest cost not exceeding c.
10     * (or null if no entry exist with cost c or less).
11     */
12    public Entry<Integer,Integer> best(int cost) {
13      return map.floorEntry(cost);
14    }
15
16    /** Add a new entry with given cost c and performance p. */
17    public void add(int c, int p) {
18      Entry<Integer,Integer> other = map.floorEntry(c); // other is at least as cheap
19      if (other != null && other.getValue( ) >= p)    // if its performance is as good,
20        return;                                       // (c,p) is dominated, so ignore
21      map.put(c, p);                                  // else, add (c,p) to database
22      // and now remove any entries that are dominated by the new one
23      other = map.higherEntry(c);                     // other is more expensive than c
24      while (other != null && other.getValue( ) <= p) { // if not better performance
25        map.remove(other.getKey( ));                  // remove the other entry
26        other = map.higherEntry(c);
27      }
28    }
29  }
```

Code Fragment 10.13: An implementation of a class maintaining a set of maximal cost-performance entries using a sorted map.

Unfortunately, if we implement the sorted map using the SortedTableMap class, the add behavior has $O(n)$ worst-case running time. If, on the other hand, we implement the map using a skip list, which we next describe, we can perform best(c) queries in $O(\log n)$ expected time and add(c, p) updates in $O((1 + r) \log n)$ expected time, where r is the number of points removed.

10.4   Skip Lists

In Section 10.3.1, we saw that a sorted table will allow $O(\log n)$-time searches via the binary search algorithm. Unfortunately, update operations on a sorted table have $O(n)$ worst-case running time because of the need to shift elements. In Chapter 7 we demonstrated that linked lists support very efficient update operations, as long as the position within the list is identified. Unfortunately, we cannot perform fast searches on a standard linked list; for example, the binary search algorithm requires an efficient means for direct accessing an element of a sequence by index.

An interesting data structure for efficiently realizing the sorted map ADT is the **skip list**. Skip lists provide a clever compromise to efficiently support search and update operations; they are implemented as the java.util.ConcurrentSkipListMap class. A **skip list** S for a map M consists of a series of lists $\{S_0, S_1, \ldots, S_h\}$. Each list S_i stores a subset of the entries of M sorted by increasing keys, plus entries with two sentinel keys denoted $-\infty$ and $+\infty$, where $-\infty$ is smaller than every possible key that can be inserted in M and $+\infty$ is larger than every possible key that can be inserted in M. In addition, the lists in S satisfy the following:

- List S_0 contains every entry of the map M (plus sentinels $-\infty$ and $+\infty$).
- For $i = 1, \ldots, h-1$, list S_i contains (in addition to $-\infty$ and $+\infty$) a randomly generated subset of the entries in list S_{i-1}.
- List S_h contains only $-\infty$ and $+\infty$.

An example of a skip list is shown in Figure 10.10. It is customary to visualize a skip list S with list S_0 at the bottom and lists $S_1, \ldots, S_h$ above it. Also, we refer to h as the **height** of skip list S.

Intuitively, the lists are set up so that S_{i+1} contains roughly alternate entries of S_i. However, the halving of the number of entries from one list to the next is not enforced as an explicit property of skip lists; instead, randomization is used. As

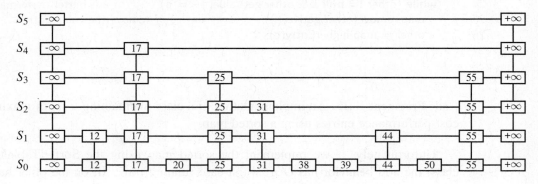

Figure 10.10: Example of a skip list storing 10 entries. For simplicity, we show only the entries' keys, not their associated values.

we shall see in the details of the insertion method, the entries in S_{i+1} are chosen at random from the entries in S_i by picking each entry from S_i to also be in S_{i+1} with probability $1/2$. That is, in essence, we "flip a coin" for each entry in S_i and place that entry in S_{i+1} if the coin comes up "heads." Thus, we expect S_1 to have about $n/2$ entries, S_2 to have about $n/4$ entries, and, in general, S_i to have about $n/2^i$ entries. As a consequence, we expect the height h of S to be about $\log n$.

Functions that generate random-like numbers are built into most modern computers, because they are used extensively in computer games, cryptography, and computer simulations. Some functions, called ***pseudorandom number generators***, generate such numbers, starting with an initial ***seed***. (See discussion of the java.util.Random class in Section 3.1.3.) Other methods use hardware devices to extract "true" random numbers from nature. In any case, we will assume that our computer has access to numbers that are sufficiently random for our analysis.

An advantage of using ***randomization*** in data structure and algorithm design is that the structures and methods that result can be simple and efficient. The skip list has the same logarithmic time bounds for searching as is achieved by the binary search algorithm, yet it extends that performance to update methods when inserting or deleting entries. Nevertheless, the bounds are ***expected*** for the skip list, while binary search of a sorted table has a ***worst-case*** bound.

A skip list makes random choices in arranging its structure in such a way that search and update times are $O(\log n)$ ***on average***, where n is the number of entries in the map. Interestingly, the notion of average time complexity used here does not depend on the probability distribution of the keys in the input. Instead, it depends on the use of a random-number generator in the implementation of the insertions to help decide where to place the new entry. The running time is averaged over all possible outcomes of the random numbers used when inserting entries.

As with the position abstraction used for lists and trees, we view a skip list as a two-dimensional collection of positions arranged horizontally into ***levels*** and vertically into ***towers***. Each level is a list S_i and each tower contains positions storing the same entry across consecutive lists. The positions in a skip list can be traversed using the following operations:

next(p): Returns the position following p on the same level.

prev(p): Returns the position preceding p on the same level.

above(p): Returns the position above p in the same tower.

below(p): Returns the position below p in the same tower.

We conventionally assume that these operations return null if the position requested does not exist. Without going into the details, we note that we can easily implement a skip list by means of a linked structure such that the individual traversal methods each take $O(1)$ time, given a skip-list position p. Such a linked structure is essentially a collection of h doubly linked lists aligned at towers, which are also doubly linked lists.

10.4.1   Search and Update Operations in a Skip List

The skip-list structure affords simple map search and update algorithms. In fact, all of the skip-list search and update algorithms are based on an elegant SkipSearch method that takes a key k and finds the position p of the entry in list S_0 that has the largest key less than or equal to k (which is possibly $-\infty$).

Searching in a Skip List

Suppose we are given a search key k. We begin the SkipSearch method by setting a position variable p to the topmost, left position in the skip list S, called the ***start position*** of S. That is, the start position is the position of S_h storing the special entry with key $-\infty$. We then perform the following steps (see Figure 10.11), where $\text{key}(p)$ denotes the key of the entry at position p:

1. If $S.\text{below}(p)$ is null, then the search terminates—we are ***at the bottom*** and have located the entry in S with the largest key less than or equal to the search key k. Otherwise, we ***drop down*** to the next lower level in the present tower by setting $p = S.\text{below}(p)$.
2. Starting at position p, we move p forward until it is at the rightmost position on the present level such that $\text{key}(p) \leq k$. We call this the ***scan forward*** step. Note that such a position always exists, since each level contains the keys $+\infty$ and $-\infty$. It may be that p remains where it started after we perform such a forward scan for this level.
3. Return to step 1.

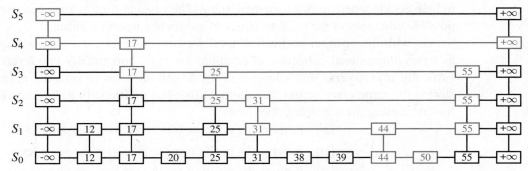

Figure 10.11: Example of a search in a skip list. The positions examined when searching for key 50 are highlighted.

We give a pseudocode description of the skip-list search algorithm, SkipSearch, in Code Fragment 10.14. Given this method, we perform the map operation $\text{get}(k)$ by computing $p = \text{SkipSearch}(k)$ and testing whether or not $\text{key}(p) = k$. If these two keys are equal, we return the associated value; otherwise, we return null.

Algorithm SkipSearch(k):

> *Input:* A search key k
>
> *Output:* Position p in the bottom list S_0 with the largest key having key$(p) \leq k$
>
> $p = s$ {begin at start position}
>
> **while** below$(p) \neq$ null **do**
>
> $p =$ below(p) {drop down}
>
>   **while** $k \geq$ key$($next$(p))$ **do**
>
> $p =$ next(p) {scan forward}
>
> **return** p

Code Fragment 10.14: Algorithm to search a skip list S for key k. Variable s holds the start position of S.

As it turns out, the expected running time of algorithm SkipSearch on a skip list with n entries is $O(\log n)$. We postpone the justification of this fact, however, until after we discuss the implementation of the update methods for skip lists. Navigation starting at the position identified by SkipSearch(k) can be easily used to provide the additional forms of searches in the sorted map ADT (e.g., ceilingEntry, subMap).

Insertion in a Skip List

The execution of the map operation put(k, v) begins with a call to SkipSearch(k). This gives us the position p of the bottom-level entry with the largest key less than or equal to k (note that p may hold the special entry with key $-\infty$). If key$(p) = k$, the associated value is overwritten with v. Otherwise, we need to create a new tower for entry (k, v). We insert (k, v) immediately after position p within S_0. After inserting the new entry at the bottom level, we use randomization to decide the height of the tower for the new entry. We "flip" a coin, and if the flip comes up tails, then we stop here. Else (the flip comes up heads), we backtrack to the previous (next higher) level and insert (k, v) in this level at the appropriate position. We again flip a coin; if it comes up heads, we go to the next higher level and repeat. Thus, we continue to insert the new entry (k, v) in lists until we finally get a flip that comes up tails. We link together all the references to the new entry (k, v) created in this process to create its tower. A fair coin flip can be simulated with Java's built-in pseudorandom number generator java.util.Random by calling nextBoolean( ), which returns true or false, each with probability $1/2$.

We give the insertion algorithm for a skip list S in Code Fragment 10.15 and we illustrate it in Figure 10.12. The algorithm uses an insertAfterAbove$(p, q, (k, v))$ method that inserts a position storing the entry (k, v) after position p (on the same level as p) and above position q, returning the new position r (and setting internal references so that next, prev, above, and below methods will work correctly for p, q, and r). The expected running time of the insertion algorithm on a skip list with n entries is $O(\log n)$, as we show in Section 10.4.2.

Algorithm SkipInsert(k, v):

   Input: Key k and value v

   Output: Topmost position of the entry inserted in the skip list

   p = SkipSearch(k)   {position in bottom list with largest key less than k}
   q = null   {current node of new entry's tower}
   i = -1 {current height of new entry's tower}
   repeat
      i = i +1   {increase height of new entry's tower}
      if $i \geq h$ **then**
         h = h +1   {add a new level to the skip list}
         t = next(s)
         s = insertAfterAbove(null, s, $(-\infty,$ null$)$)   {grow leftmost tower}
         insertAfterAbove(s, t, $(+\infty,$ null$)$)   {grow rightmost tower}
      q = insertAfterAbove(p, q, (k,v))   {add node to new entry's tower}
      while above(p) == null **do**
         p = prev(p)   {scan backward}
      p = above(p)   {jump up to higher level}
   until coinFlip( ) == tails
   n = n +1
   return q {top node of new entry's tower}

Code Fragment 10.15: Insertion in a skip list of entry (k,v) We assume the skip list does not have an entry with key k. Method coinFlip( ) returns "heads" or "tails", each with probability $1/2$. Instance variables n, h, and s respectively hold the number of entries, the height, and the start node of the skip list.

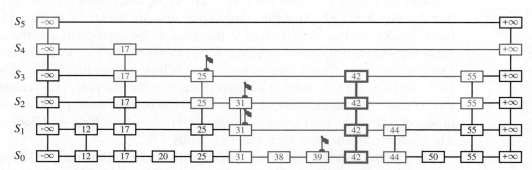

Figure 10.12: Insertion of an entry with key 42 into the skip list of Figure 10.10 using method SkipInsert (Code Fragment 10.15). We assume that the random "coin flips" for the new entry came up heads three times in a row, followed by tails. The positions visited are highlighted in blue. The positions of the tower of the new entry (variable q) are drawn with thick lines, and the positions preceding them (variable p) are flagged.

Removal in a Skip List

Like the search and insertion algorithms, the removal algorithm for a skip list is quite simple. In fact, it is even easier than the insertion algorithm. To perform the map operation remove(k), we will begin by executing method SkipSearch(k). If the returned position p stores an entry with key different from k, we return null. Otherwise, we remove p and all the positions above p, which are easily accessed by using above operations to climb up the tower of this entry in S starting at position p. While removing levels of the tower, we reestablish links between the horizontal neighbors of each removed position. The removal algorithm is illustrated in Figure 10.13 and a detailed description of it is left as an exercise (R-10.24). As we show in the next subsection, the remove operation in a skip list with n entries has $O(\log n)$ expected running time.

Before we give this analysis, however, there are some minor improvements to the skip-list data structure we would like to discuss. First, we do not actually need to store references to values at the levels of the skip list above the bottom level, because all that is needed at these levels are references to keys. In fact, we can more efficiently represent a tower as a single object, storing the key-value pair, and maintaining j previous references and j next references if the tower reaches level S_j. Second, for the horizontal axes, it is possible to keep the list singly linked, storing only the next references. We can perform insertions and removals in strictly a top-down, scan-forward fashion. We explore the details of this optimization in Exercise C-10.55. Neither of these optimizations improve the asymptotic performance of skip lists by more than a constant factor, but these improvements can, nevertheless, be meaningful in practice. In fact, experimental evidence suggests that optimized skip lists are faster in practice than AVL trees and other balanced search trees, which are discussed in Chapter 11.

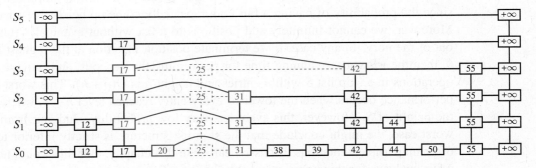

Figure 10.13: Removal of the entry with key 25 from the skip list of Figure 10.12. The positions visited after the search for the position of S_0 holding the entry are highlighted in blue. The positions removed are drawn with dashed lines.

Maintaining the Topmost Level

A skip list S must maintain a reference to the start position (the topmost, leftmost position in S) as an instance variable, and must have a policy for any insertion that wishes to continue growing the tower for a new entry past the top level of S. There are two possible courses of action we can take, both of which have their merits.

One possibility is to restrict the top level, h, to be kept at some fixed value that is a function of n, the number of entries currently in the map (from the analysis we will see that $h = \max\{10, 2\lceil \log n \rceil\}$ is a reasonable choice, and picking $h = 3\lceil \log n \rceil$ is even safer). Implementing this choice means that we must modify the insertion algorithm to stop inserting a new position once we reach the topmost level (unless $\lceil \log n \rceil < \lceil \log(n+1) \rceil$, in which case we can now go at least one more level, since the bound on the height is increasing).

The other possibility is to let an insertion continue growing a tower as long as heads keep getting returned from the random number generator. This is the approach taken by algorithm SkipInsert of Code Fragment 10.15. As we show in the analysis of skip lists, the probability that an insertion will go to a level that is more than $O(\log n)$ is very low, so this design choice should also work.

Either choice will still result in the expected $O(\log n)$ time to perform search, insertion, and removal, as we will show in the next section.

10.4.2 Probabilistic Analysis of Skip Lists ⋆

As we have shown above, skip lists provide a simple implementation of a sorted map. In terms of worst-case performance, however, skip lists are not a superior data structure. In fact, if we do not officially prevent an insertion from continuing significantly past the current highest level, then the insertion algorithm can go into what is almost an infinite loop (it is not actually an infinite loop, however, since the probability of having a fair coin repeatedly come up heads forever is 0). Moreover, we cannot infinitely add positions to a list without eventually running out of memory. In any case, if we terminate position insertion at the highest level h, then the **worst-case** running time for performing the get, put, and remove map operations in a skip list S with n entries and height h is $O(n+h)$. This worst-case performance occurs when the tower of every entry reaches level $h-1$, where h is the height of S. However, this event has very low probability. Judging from this worst case, we might conclude that the skip-list structure is strictly inferior to the other map implementations discussed earlier in this chapter. But this would not be a fair analysis, for this worst-case behavior is a gross overestimate.

---

*We use a star ($\star$) to indicate sections containing material more advanced than the material in the rest of the chapter; this material can be considered optional in a first reading.

Bounding the Height of a Skip List

Because the insertion step involves randomization, a more accurate analysis of skip lists involves a bit of probability. At first, this might seem like a major undertaking, for a complete and thorough probabilistic analysis could require deep mathematics (and, indeed, there are several such deep analyses that have appeared in data structures research literature). Fortunately, such an analysis is not necessary to understand the expected asymptotic behavior of skip lists. The informal and intuitive probabilistic analysis we give below uses only basic concepts of probability theory.

Let us begin by determining the expected value of the height h of a skip list S with n entries (assuming that we do not terminate insertions early). The probability that a given entry has a tower of height $i \geq 1$ is equal to the probability of getting i consecutive heads when flipping a coin, that is, this probability is $1/2^i$. Hence, the probability P_i that level i has at least one position is at most

$$P_i \leq \frac{n}{2^i},$$

because the probability that any one of n different events occurs is at most the sum of the probabilities that each occurs.

The probability that the height h of S is larger than i is equal to the probability that level i has at least one position, that is, it is no more than P_i. This means that h is larger than, say, $3 \log n$ with probability at most

$$
\begin{aligned}
P_{3\log n} &\leq \frac{n}{2^{3\log n}} \\
&= \frac{n}{n^3} = \frac{1}{n^2}.
\end{aligned}
$$

For example, if $n = 1000$, this probability is a one-in-a-million long shot. More generally, given a constant $c > 1$, h is larger than $c \log n$ with probability at most $1/n^{c-1}$. That is, the probability that h is smaller than $c \log n$ is at least $1 - 1/n^{c-1}$. Thus, with high probability, the height h of S is $O(\log n)$.

Analyzing Search Time in a Skip List

Next, consider the running time of a search in skip list S, and recall that such a search involves two nested **while** loops. The inner loop performs a scan forward on a level of S as long as the next key is no greater than the search key k, and the outer loop drops down to the next level and repeats the scan forward iteration. Since the height h of S is $O(\log n)$ with high probability, the number of drop-down steps is $O(\log n)$ with high probability.

So we have yet to bound the number of scan-forward steps we make. Let n_i be the number of keys examined while scanning forward at level i. Observe that, after the key at the starting position, each additional key examined in a scan-forward at level i cannot also belong to level $i+1$. If any of these keys were on the previous level, we would have encountered them in the previous scan-forward step. Thus, the probability that any key is counted in n_i is $1/2$. Therefore, the expected value of n_i is exactly equal to the expected number of times we must flip a fair coin before it comes up heads. This expected value is 2. Hence, the expected amount of time spent scanning forward at any level i is $O(1)$. Since S has $O(\log n)$ levels with high probability, a search in S takes expected time $O(\log n)$. By a similar analysis, we can show that the expected running time of an insertion or a removal is $O(\log n)$.

Space Usage in a Skip List

Finally, let us turn to the space requirement of a skip list S with n entries. As we observed above, the expected number of positions at level i is $n/2^i$, which means that the expected total number of positions in S is

$$\sum_{i=0}^{h} \frac{n}{2^i} = n \sum_{i=0}^{h} \frac{1}{2^i}.$$

Using Proposition 4.5 on geometric summations, we have

$$\sum_{i=0}^{h} \frac{1}{2^i} = \frac{\left(\frac{1}{2}\right)^{h+1} - 1}{\frac{1}{2} - 1} = 2 \cdot \left(1 - \frac{1}{2^{h+1}}\right) < 2 \quad \text{for all } h \geq 0.$$

Hence, the expected space requirement of S is $O(n)$.

Table 10.4 summarizes the performance of a sorted map realized by a skip list.

Method	Running Time
size, isEmpty	$O(1)$
get	$O(\log n)$ expected
put	$O(\log n)$ expected
remove	$O(\log n)$ expected
firstEntry, lastEntry	$O(1)$
ceilingEntry, floorEntry lowerEntry, higherEntry	$O(\log n)$ expected
subMap	$O(s + \log n)$ expected, with s entries reported
entrySet, keySet, values	$O(n)$

Table 10.4: Performance of a sorted map implemented with a skip list. We use n to denote the number of entries in the dictionary at the time the operation is performed. The expected space requirement is $O(n)$.

10.5 Sets, Multisets, and Multimaps

We conclude this chapter by examining several additional abstractions that are closely related to the map ADT, and that can be implemented using data structures similar to those for a map.

- A *set* is an unordered collection of elements, without duplicates, that typically supports efficient membership tests. In essence, elements of a set are like keys of a map, but without any auxiliary values.

- A *multiset* (also known as a *bag*) is a set-like container that allows duplicates.

- A *multimap* is similar to a traditional map, in that it associates values with keys; however, in a multimap the same key can be mapped to multiple values. For example, the index of this book (page 714) maps a given term to one or more locations at which the term occurs elsewhere in the book.

10.5.1 The Set ADT

The Java Collections Framework defines the java.util.Set interface, which includes the following fundamental methods:

add(e): Adds the element e to S (if not already present).

remove(e): Removes the element e from S (if it is present).

contains(e): Returns whether e is an element of S.

iterator( ): Returns an iterator of the elements of S.

There is also support for the traditional mathematical set operations of *union*, *intersection*, and *subtraction* of two sets S and T:

$$S \cup T = \{e : e \text{ is in } S \text{ or } e \text{ is in } T\},$$
$$S \cap T = \{e : e \text{ is in } S \text{ and } e \text{ is in } T\},$$
$$S - T = \{e : e \text{ is in } S \text{ and } e \text{ is not in } T\}.$$

In the java.util.Set interface, these operations are provided through the following methods, if executed on a set S:

addAll(T): Updates S to also include all elements of set T, effectively replacing S by $S \cup T$.

retainAll(T): Updates S so that it only keeps those elements that are also elements of set T, effectively replacing S by $S \cap T$.

removeAll(T): Updates S by removing any of its elements that also occur in set T, effectively replacing S by $S - T$.

The *template method pattern* can be applied to implement each of the methods addAll, retainAll, and removeAll using only calls to the more fundamental methods add, remove, contains, and iterator. In fact, the java.util.AbstractSet class provides such implementations. To demonstrate the technique, we could implement the addAll method in the context of a set class as follows:

```
public void addAll(Set<E> other) {
    for (E element : other)              // rely on iterator( ) method of other
        add(element);                    // duplicates will be ignored by add
}
```

The removeAll and retailAll methods can be implemented with similar techniques, although a bit more care is needed for retainAll, to avoid removing elements while iterating over the same set (see Exercise C-10.59). The efficiency of these methods for a concrete set implementation will depend on the underlying efficiency of the fundamental methods upon which they rely.

Sorted Sets

For the standard set abstraction, there is no explicit notion of keys being ordered; all that is assumed is that the equals method can detect equivalent elements.

If, however, elements come from a Comparable class (or a suitable Comparator object is provided), we can extend the notion of a set to define the *sorted set ADT*, including the following additional methods:

first( ):	Returns the smallest element in S.
last( ):	Returns the largest element in S.
ceiling(e):	Returns the smallest element greater than or equal to e.
floor(e):	Returns the largest element less than or equal to e.
lower(e):	Returns the largest element strictly less than e.
higher(e):	Returns the smallest element strictly greater than e.
subSet(e_1, e_2):	Returns an iteration of all elements greater than or equal to e_1, but strictly less than e_2.
pollFirst( ):	Returns and removes the smallest element in S.
pollLast( ):	Returns and removes the largest element in S.

In the Java Collection Framework, the above methods are included in a combination of the java.util.SortedSet and java.util.NavigableSet interfaces.

Implementing Sets

Although a set is a completely different abstraction than a map, the techniques used to implement the two can be quite similar. In effect, a set is simply a map in which (unique) keys do not have associated values.

Therefore, any data structure used to implement a map can be modified to implement the set ADT with similar performance guarantees. As a trivial adaption of a map, each set element can be stored as a key, and the null reference can be stored as an (irrelevant) value. Of course, such an implementation is unnecessarily wasteful; a more efficient set implementation should abandon the Entry composite and store set elements directly in a data structure.

The Java Collections Framework includes the following set implementations, mirroring similar data structures used for maps:

- java.util.HashSet provides an implementation of the (unordered) set ADT with a hash table.
- java.util.concurrent.ConcurrentSkipListSet provides an implementation of the sorted set ADT using a skip list.
- java.util.TreeSet provides an implementation of the sorted set ADT using a balanced search tree. (Search trees are the focus of Chapter 11.)

10.5.2 The Multiset ADT

Before discussing models for a multiset abstraction, we must carefully consider the notion of "duplicate" elements. Throughout the Java Collections Framework, objects are considered equivalent to each other based on the standard equals method (see Section 3.5). For example, keys of a map must be unique, but the notion of uniqueness allows distinct yet equivalent objects to be matched. This is important for many typical uses of maps. For example, when strings are used as keys, the instance of the string "October" that is used when inserting an entry may not be the same instance of "October" that is used when later retrieving the associated value. The call birthstones.get("October") will succeed in such a scenario because strings are considered equal to each other.

In the context of multisets, if we represent a collection that appears through the notion of equivalence as $\{a,a,a,a,b,c,c\}$, we must decide if we want a data structure to explicitly maintain each instance of a (because each might be distinct though equivalent), or just that there exist four occurrences. In either case, a multiset can be implemented by directly adapting a map. We can use one element from a group of equivalent occurrences as the key in a map, with the associated value either a secondary container containing all of the equivalent instances, or a count of the number of occurrences. Note that our word-frequency application in Section 10.1.2 uses just such a map, associating strings with counts.

The Java Collections Framework does not include any form of a multiset. However, implementations exist in several widely used, open source Java collections libraries. The Apache Commons defines Bag and SortedBag interfaces that correspond respectively to unsorted and sorted multisets. The Google Core Libraries for Java (named *Guava*) includes Multiset and SortedMultiset interfaces for these abstractions. Both of those libraries take the approach of modeling a multiset as a collection of elements having multiplicities, and both offer several concrete implementations using standard data structures. In formalizing the abstract data type, the Multiset interface of the Guava library includes the following behaviors (and more):

add(e): Adds a single occurrences of e to the multiset.

contains(e): Returns true if the multiset contains an element equal to e.

count(e): Returns the number of occurrences of e in the multiset.

remove(e): Removes a single occurrence of e from the multiset.

remove(e, n): Removes n occurrences of e from the multiset.

size( ): Returns the number of elements of the multiset (including duplicates).

iterator( ): Returns an iteration of all elements of the multiset (repeating those with multiplicity greater than one).

The multiset ADT also includes the notion of an immutable Entry that represents an element and its count, and the SortedMultiset interface includes additional methods such as firstEntry and lastEntry.

10.5.3   The Multimap ADT

Like a map, a multimap stores entries that are key-value pairs (k, v), where k is the key and v is the value. Whereas a map insists that entries have unique keys, a multimap allows multiple entries to have the same key, much like an English dictionary, which allows multiple definitions for the same word. That is, we will allow a multimap to contain entries (k, v) and (k, v') having the same key.

There are two standard approaches for representing a multimap as a variation of a traditional map. One is to redesign the underlying data structure to allow separate entries to be stored for pairs such as (k, v) and (k, v'). The other is to map key k to a secondary container of all values associated with that key (e.g., $\{v, v'\}$).

Much as it is missing a formal abstraction for a multiset, the Java Collections Framework does not include any multiset interface nor implementations. However, as we will soon demonstrate, it is easy to represent a multiset by adapting other collection classes that are included in the java.util package.

To formalize the multimap abstract data type, we consider a simplified version of the Multimap interface included in Google's Guava library. Among its methods are the following:

get(k): Returns a collection of all values associated with key k in the multimap.

put(k, v): Adds a new entry to the multimap associating key k with value v, without overwriting any existing mappings for key k.

remove(k, v): Removes an entry mapping key k to value v from the multimap (if one exists).

removeAll(k): Removes all entries having key equal to k from the multimap.

size(): Returns the number of entries of the multiset (including multiple associations).

entries(): Returns a collection of all entries in the multimap.

keys(): Returns a collection of keys for all entries in the multimap (including duplicates for keys with multiple bindings).

keySet(): Returns a nonduplicative collection of keys in the multimap.

values(): Returns a collection of values for all entries in the multimap.

In Code Fragments 10.16 and 10.17, we provide an implementation of a class, HashMultimap, that uses a java.util.HashMap to map each key to a secondary ArrayList of all values that are associated with the key. For brevity, we omit the formality of defining a Multimap interface, and we provide the entries() method as the only form of iteration.

```
1  public class HashMultimap<K,V> {
2    Map<K,List<V>> map = new HashMap<>();   // the primary map
3    int total = 0;                          // total number of entries in the multimap
4    /** Constructs an empty multimap. */
5    public HashMultimap() { }
6    /** Returns the total number of entries in the multimap. */
7    public int size() { return total; }
8    /** Returns whether the multimap is empty. */
9    public boolean isEmpty() { return (total == 0); }
10   /** Returns a (possibly empty) iteration of all values associated with the key. */
11   Iterable<V> get(K key) {
12     List<V> secondary = map.get(key);
13     if (secondary != null)
14       return secondary;
15     return new ArrayList<>();              // return an empty list of values
16   }
```

Code Fragment 10.16: An implementation of a multimap as an adaptation of classes from the java.util package. (Continues in Code Fragment 10.17.)

```
17    /** Adds a new entry associating key with value. */
18    void put(K key, V value) {
19      List<V> secondary = map.get(key);
20      if (secondary == null) {
21        secondary = new ArrayList<>();
22        map.put(key, secondary);          // begin using new list as secondary structure
23      }
24      secondary.add(value);
25      total++;
26    }
27    /** Removes the (key,value) entry, if it exists. */
28    boolean remove(K key, V value) {
29      boolean wasRemoved = false;
30      List<V> secondary = map.get(key);
31      if (secondary != null) {
32        wasRemoved = secondary.remove(value);
33        if (wasRemoved) {
34          total--;
35          if (secondary.isEmpty())
36            map.remove(key);               // remove secondary structure from primary map
37        }
38      }
39      return wasRemoved;
40    }
41    /** Removes all entries with the given key. */
42    Iterable<V> removeAll(K key) {
43      List<V> secondary = map.get(key);
44      if (secondary != null) {
45        total -= secondary.size();
46        map.remove(key);
47      } else
48        secondary = new ArrayList<>();     // return empty list of removed values
49      return secondary;
50    }
51    /** Returns an iteration of all entries in the multimap. */
52    Iterable<Map.Entry<K,V>> entries() {
53      List<Map.Entry<K,V>> result = new ArrayList<>();
54      for (Map.Entry<K,List<V>> secondary : map.entrySet()) {
55        K key = secondary.getKey();
56        for (V value : secondary.getValue())
57          result.add(new AbstractMap.SimpleEntry<K,V>(key,value));
58      }
59      return result;
60    }
61  }
```

Code Fragment 10.17: An implementation of a multimap as an adaptation of classes from the java.util package. (Continued from Code Fragment 10.16.)

10.6 Exercises

Reinforcement

R-10.1 What is the worst-case running time for inserting n key-value pairs into an initially empty map M that is implemented with the UnsortedTableMap class?

R-10.2 Reimplement the UnsortedTableMap class using the PositionalList class from Section 7.3 rather than an ArrayList.

R-10.3 The use of null values in a map is problematic, as there is then no way to differentiate whether a null value returned by the call get(k) represents the legitimate value of an entry (k, null), or designates that key k was not found. The java.util.Map interface includes a boolean method, containsKey(k), that resolves any such ambiguity. Implement such a method for the UnsortedTableMap class.

R-10.4 Which of the hash table collision-handling schemes could tolerate a load factor above 1 and which could not?

R-10.5 What would be a good hash code for a vehicle identification number that is a string of numbers and letters of the form "9X9XX99X9XX999999," where a "9" represents a digit and an "X" represents a letter?

R-10.6 Draw the 11-entry hash table that results from using the hash function, $h(i) = (3i + 5) \bmod 11$, to hash the keys 12, 44, 13, 88, 23, 94, 11, 39, 20, 16, and 5, assuming collisions are handled by chaining.

R-10.7 What is the result of the previous exercise, assuming collisions are handled by linear probing?

R-10.8 Show the result of Exercise R-10.6, assuming collisions are handled by quadratic probing, up to the point where the method fails.

R-10.9 What is the result of Exercise R-10.6 when collisions are handled by double hashing using the secondary hash function $h'(k) = 7 - (k \bmod 7)$?

R-10.10 What is the worst-case time for putting n entries in an initially empty hash table, with collisions resolved by chaining? What is the best case?

R-10.11 Show the result of rehashing the hash table shown in Figure 10.6 into a table of size 19 using the new hash function $h(k) = 3k \bmod 17$.

R-10.12 Modify the Pair class from Code Fragment 2.17 on page 92 so that it provides a natural definition for both the equals( ) and hashCode( ) methods.

R-10.13 Consider lines 31–33 of Code Fragment 10.8 in our implementation of the class ChainHashMap. We use the difference in the size of a secondary bucket before and after a call to bucket.remove(k) to update the variable n. If we replace those three lines with the following, does the class behave properly? Explain.

```
V answer = bucket.remove(k);          // value of removed entry
if (answer != null)                   // size has decreased
    n−−;
```

R-10.14 Our AbstractHashMap class maintains a load factor $\lambda \leq 0.5$. Reimplement that class to allow the user to specify the maximum load, and adjust the concrete subclasses accordingly.

R-10.15 Give a pseudocode description of an insertion into a hash table that uses quadratic probing to resolve collisions, assuming we also use the trick of replacing deleted entries with a special "available" object.

R-10.16 Modify our ProbeHashMap to use quadratic probing.

R-10.17 Explain why a hash table is not suited to implement a sorted map.

R-10.18 What is the worst-case asymptotic running time for performing n deletions from a SortedTableMap instance that initially contains $2n$ entries?

R-10.19 Implement the containKey(k) method, as described in Exercise R-10.3, for the SortedTableClass.

R-10.20 Describe how a sorted list implemented as a doubly linked list could be used to implement the sorted map ADT.

R-10.21 Consider the following variant of the findIndex method of the SortedTableMap class, originally given in Code Fragment 10.11:

```
1    private int findIndex(K key, int low, int high) {
2      if (high < low) return high + 1;
3      int mid = (low + high) / 2;
4      if (compare(key, table.get(mid)) < 0)
5        return findIndex(key, low, mid − 1);
6      else
7        return findIndex(key, mid + 1, high);
8    }
```

Does this always produce the same result as the original version? Justify your answer.

R-10.22 What is the expected running time of the methods for maintaining a maxima set if we insert n pairs such that each pair has lower cost and performance than one before it? What is contained in the sorted map at the end of this series of operations? What if each pair had a lower cost and higher performance than the one before it?

R-10.23 Draw the result after performing the following series of operations on the skip list shown in Figure 10.13: remove(38), put(48, x), put(24, y), remove(55). Use an actual coin flip to generate random bits as needed (and report your sequence of flips).

R-10.24 Give a pseudocode description of the remove map operation for a skip list.

R-10.25 Give a description, in pseudocode, for implementing the removeAll method for the set ADT, using only the other fundamental methods of the set.

R-10.26 Give a description, in pseudocode, for implementing the retainAll method for the set ADT, using only the other fundamental methods of the set.

R-10.27 If we let n denote the size of set S, and m denote the size of set T, what would be the running time of the operation S.addAll(T), as implemented on page 446, if both sets were implemented as skip lists?

R-10.28 If we let n denote the size of set S, and m denote the size of set T, what would be the running time of the operation S.addAll(T), as implemented on page 446, if both sets were implemented using hashing?

R-10.29 If we let n denote the size of set S, and m denote the size of set T, what would be the running time of the operation S.removeAll(T) when both sets are implemented using hashing?

R-10.30 If we let n denote the size of set S, and m denote the size of set T, what would be the running time of the operation S.retainAll(T) when both sets are implemented using hashing?

R-10.31 What abstraction would you use to manage a database of friends' birthdays in order to support efficient queries such as "find all friends whose birthday is today" and "find the friend who will be the next to celebrate a birthday"?

Creativity

C-10.32 For an ideal compression function, the capacity of the bucket array for a hash table should be a prime number. Therefore, we consider the problem of locating a prime number in a range $[M, 2M]$. Implement a method for finding such a prime by using the *sieve algorithm*. In this algorithm, we allocate a $2M$ cell boolean array A, such that cell i is associated with the integer i. We then initialize the array cells to all be "true" and we "mark off" all the cells that are multiples of 2, 3, 5, 7, and so on. This process can stop after it reaches a number larger than $\sqrt{2M}$. (Hint: Consider a bootstrapping method for finding the primes up to $\sqrt{2M}$.)

C-10.33 Consider the goal of adding entry (k, v) to a map only if there does not yet exist some other entry with key k. For a map M (without null values), this might be accomplished as follows.

    if (M.get(k) == **null**)
      M.put(k, v);

While this accomplishes the goal, its efficiency is less than ideal, as time will be spent on the failed search during the get call, and again during the put call (which always begins by trying to locate an existing entry with the given key). To avoid this inefficiency, some map implementations support a custom method putIfAbsent(k, v) that accomplishes this goal. Given such an implementation of putIfAbsent for the UnsortedTableMap class.

C-10.34 Repeat Exercise C-10.33 for the ChainHashMap class.

C-10.35 Repeat Exercise C-10.33 for the ProbeHashMap class.

C-10.36 Describe how to redesign the AbstractHashMap framework to include support for a method, containsKey, as described in Exercise R-10.3.

C-10.37 Modify the ChainHashMap class in accordance with your design for the previous exercise.

C-10.38 Modify the ProbeHashMap class in accordance with Exercise C-10.36.

C-10.39 Redesign the AbstractHashMap class so that it halves the capacity of the table if the load factor falls below 0.25. Your solution must not involve any changes to the concrete ProbeHashMap and ChainHashMap classes.

C-10.40 The java.util.HashMap class uses separate chaining, but without any explicit secondary structures. The table is an array of entries, and each entry has an additional next field that can reference another entry in that bucket. In this way, the entry instances can be threaded as a singly linked list. Reimplement our ChainHashMap class using such an approach.

C-10.41 Describe how to perform a removal from a hash table that uses linear probing to resolve collisions where we do not use a special marker to represent deleted elements. That is, we must rearrange the contents so that it appears that the removed entry was never inserted in the first place.

C-10.42 The quadratic probing strategy has a clustering problem related to the way it looks for open slots. Namely, when a collision occurs at bucket $h(k)$, it checks buckets $A[(h(k) + i^2) \bmod N]$, for $i = 1, 2, \ldots, N - 1$.

   a. Show that $i^2 \bmod N$ will assume at most $(N + 1)/2$ distinct values, for N prime, as i ranges from 1 to $N - 1$. As a part of this justification, note that $i^2 \bmod N = (N - i)^2 \bmod N$ for all i.

   b. A better strategy is to choose a prime N such that $N \bmod 4 = 3$ and then to check the buckets $A[(h(k) \pm i^2) \bmod N]$ as i ranges from 1 to $(N - 1)/2$, alternating between plus and minus. Show that this alternate version is guaranteed to check every bucket in A.

C-10.43 Redesign our ProbeHashMap class so that the sequence of secondary probes for collision resolution can be more easily customized. Demonstrate your new design by providing separate concrete subclasses for linear probing and quadratic probing.

C-10.44 The java.util.LinkedHashMap class is a subclass of the standard HashMap class that retains the expected $O(1)$ performance for the primary map operations while guaranteeing that iterations report entries of the map according to first-in, first-out (FIFO) principle. That is, the key that has been in the map the longest is reported first. (The order is unaffected when the value for an existing key is changed.) Describe an algorithmic approach for achieving such performance.

C-10.45 Develop a location-aware version of the UnsortedTableMap class so that an operation remove(e) for existing Entry e can be implemented in $O(1)$ time.

C-10.46 Repeat the previous exercise for the ProbeHashMap class.

C-10.47 Repeat Exercise C-10.45 for the ChainHashMap class.

C-10.48 Although keys in a map are distinct, the binary search algorithm can be applied in a more general setting in which an array stores possibly duplicative elements in nondecreasing order. Consider the goal of identifying the index of the *leftmost* element with key greater than or equal to given k. Does the findIndex method as given in Code Fragment 10.11 guarantee such a result? Does the findIndex method as given in Exercise R-10.21 guarantee such a result? Justify your answers.

C-10.49 Suppose we are given two sorted search tables S and T, each with n entries (with S and T being implemented with arrays). Describe an $O(\log^2 n)$-time algorithm for finding the kth smallest key in the union of the keys from S and T (assuming no duplicates).

C-10.50 Give an $O(\log n)$-time solution for the previous problem.

C-10.51 Give an alternative implementation of the SortedTableMap's entrySet method that creates a *lazy iterator* rather than a snapshot. (See Section 7.4.2 for discussion of iterators.)

C-10.52 Repeat the previous exercise for the ChainHashMap class.

C-10.53 Repeat Exercise C-10.51 for the ProbeHashMap class.

C-10.54 Given a database D of n cost-performance pairs (c, p), describe an algorithm for finding the maxima pairs of C in $O(n \log n)$ time.

C-10.55 Show that the methods above(p) and before(p) are not actually needed to efficiently implement a map using a skip list. That is, we can implement insertions and deletions in a skip list using a strictly top-down, scan-forward approach, without ever using the above or before methods. (Hint: In the insertion algorithm, first repeatedly flip the coin to determine the level where you should start inserting the new entry.)

C-10.56 Describe how to modify the skip-list data structure to support the method median( ), which returns the position of the element in the "bottom" list S_0 at index $\lfloor n/2 \rfloor$, Show that your implementation of this method runs in $O(\log n)$ expected time.

C-10.57 Describe how to modify a skip-list representation so that index-based operations, such as retrieving the entry at index j, can be performed in $O(\log n)$ expected time.

C-10.58 Suppose that each row of an $n \times n$ array A consists of 1's and 0's such that, in any row of A, all the 1's come before any 0's in that row. Assuming A is already in memory, describe a method running in $O(n \log n)$ time (not $O(n^2)$ time) for counting the number of 1's in A.

C-10.59 Give a concrete implementation of the retainAll method for the set ADT, using only the other fundamental methods of the set. You are to assume that the underlying set implementation uses *fail-fast iterators* (see Section 7.4.2).

C-10.60 Consider sets whose elements are integers in the range $[0, N-1]$. A popular scheme for representing a set A of this type is by means of a boolean array, B, where we say that x is in A if and only if $B[x] =$ **true**. Since each cell of B can be represented with a single bit, B is sometimes referred to as a *bit vector*. Describe and analyze efficient algorithms for performing the methods of the set ADT assuming this representation.

C-10.61 An *inverted file* is a critical data structure for implementing applications such an index of a book or a search engine. Given a document D, which can be viewed as an unordered, numbered list of words, an inverted file is an ordered list of words, L, such that, for each word w in L, we store the indices of the places in D where w appears. Design an efficient algorithm for constructing L from D.

C-10.62 The operation get(k) for our multimap ADT is responsible for returning a collection of *all* values currently associated with key k. Design a variation of binary search for performing this operation on a sorted search table that includes duplicates, and show that it runs in time $O(s + \log n)$, where n is the number of elements in the dictionary and s is the number of entries with given key k.

C-10.63 Describe an efficient multimap structure for storing n entries that have an associated set of $r < n$ keys that come from a total order. That is, the set of keys is smaller than the number of entries. Your structure should perform operation getAll in $O(\log r + s)$ expected time, where s is the number of entries returned, operation entrySet() in $O(n)$ time, and the remaining operations of the multimap ADT in $O(\log r)$ expected time.

C-10.64 Describe an efficient multimap structure for storing n entries whose $r < n$ keys have distinct hash codes. Your structure should perform operation getAll in $O(1 + s)$ expected time, where s is the number of entries returned, operation entrySet() in $O(n)$ time, and the remaining operations of the multimap ADT in $O(1)$ expected time.

Projects

P-10.65 An interesting strategy for hashing with open addressing is known as *cuckoo hashing*. Two independent hash functions are computed for each key, and an element is always stored in one of the two cells indicated by those hash functions. When a new element is inserted, if either of those two cells is available, it is placed there. Otherwise, it is placed into one of its choice of locations, evicting another entry. The evicted entry is then placed in its alternate choice of cells, potentially evicting yet another entry. This continues until an open cell is found, or an infinite loop is detected (in which case, two new hash functions are chosen and all entries are deleted and reinserted). It can be shown that as long as the load factor of the table remains below 0.5, then an insertion succeeds in expected constant time. Notice that a search can be performed in *worst-case* constant time, because it can only be stored in one of two possible locations. Give a complete map implementation based on this strategy.

P-10.66 An interesting strategy for hashing with separate chaining is known as ***power-of-two-choices hashing***. Two independent hash functions are computed for each key, and a newly inserted element is placed into the choice of the two indicated buckets that currently has the fewest entries. Give a complete map implementation based on this strategy.

P-10.67 Implement a LinkedHashMap class, as described in Exercise C-10.44, ensuring that the primary map operations run in $O(1)$ expected time.

P-10.68 Perform experiments on our ChainHashMap and ProbeHashMap classes to measure its efficiency using random key sets and varying limits on the load factor (see Exercise R-10.14).

P-10.69 Perform a comparative analysis that studies the collision rates for various hash codes for character strings, such as polynomial hash codes for different values of the parameter a. Use a hash table to determine collisions, but only count collisions where different strings map to the same hash code (not if they map to the same location in this hash table). Test these hash codes on text files found on the Internet.

P-10.70 Perform a comparative analysis as in the previous exercise, but for 10-digit telephone numbers instead of character strings.

P-10.71 Design a Java class that implements the skip-list data structure. Use this class to create a complete implementation of the sorted map ADT.

P-10.72 Extend the previous project by providing a graphical animation of the skip-list operations. Visualize how entries move up the skip list during insertions and are linked out of the skip list during removals. Also, in a search operation, visualize the scan-forward and drop-down actions.

P-10.73 Describe how to use a skip list to implement the array list ADT, so that index-based insertions and removals both run in $O(\log n)$ expected time.

P-10.74 Write a spell-checker class that stores a lexicon of words, W, in a set, and implements a method, check(s), which performs a ***spell check*** on the string s with respect to the set of words, W. If s is in W, then the call to check(s) returns a list containing only s, as it is assumed to be spelled correctly in this case. If s is not in W, then the call to check(s) returns a list of every word in W that might be a correct spelling of s. Your program should be able to handle all the common ways that s might be a misspelling of a word in W, including swapping adjacent characters in a word, inserting a single character in between two adjacent characters in a word, deleting a single character from a word, and replacing a character in a word with another character. For an extra challenge, consider phonetic substitutions as well.

Chapter Notes

Hashing is a well-studied technique. The reader interested in further study is encouraged to explore the book by Knuth [61], as well as the book by Vitter and Chen [92]. The denial-of-service vulnerability exploiting the worst-case performance of hash tables was first described by Crosby and Wallach [27], and later demonstrated by Klink and Wälde [58]. The remedy adopted by the OpenJDK team for Java is described in [76].

Skip lists were introduced by Pugh [80]. Our analysis of skip lists is a simplification of a presentation given by Motwani and Raghavan [75]. For a more in-depth analysis of skip lists, please see the various research papers on skip lists that have appeared in the data structures literature [56, 77, 78]. Exercise C-10.42 was contributed by James Lee.

Chapter

11

Search Trees

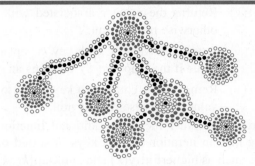

Contents

11.1   Binary Search Trees

In Chapter 8 we introduced the tree data structure and demonstrated a variety of applications. One important use is as a *search tree* (as described on page 338). In this chapter, we use a search-tree structure to efficiently implement a *sorted map*. The three most fundamental methods of of a map (see Section 10.1.1) are:

get(k): Returns the value v associated with key k, if such an entry exists; otherwise returns null.

put(k, v): Associates value v with key k, replacing and returning any existing value if the map already contains an entry with key equal to k.

remove(k): Removes the entry with key equal to k, if one exists, and returns its value; otherwise returns null.

The sorted map ADT includes additional functionality (see Section 10.3), guaranteeing that an iteration reports keys in sorted order, and supporting additional searches such as higherEntry(k) and subMap(k_1, k_2).

Binary trees are an excellent data structure for storing entries of a map, assuming we have an order relation defined on the keys. In this chapter, we define a *binary search tree* as a *proper binary tree* (see Section 8.2) such that each internal position p stores a key-value pair (k, v) such that:

- Keys stored in the left subtree of p are less than k.
- Keys stored in the right subtree of p are greater than k.

An example of such a binary search tree is given in Figure 11.1. Notice that the leaves of the tree serve only as "placeholders." Their use as sentinels simplifies the presentation of several of our search and update algorithms. With care, they can be represented as null references in practice, thereby reducing the number of nodes in half (since there are more leaves than internal nodes in a proper binary tree).

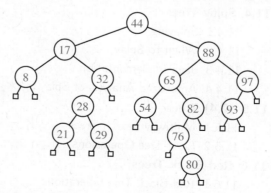

Figure 11.1: A binary search tree with integer keys. We omit the display of associated values in this chapter, since they are not relevant to the order of entries within a search tree.

11.1.1 Searching Within a Binary Search Tree

The most important consequence of the structural property of a binary search tree is its namesake search algorithm. We can attempt to locate a particular key in a binary search tree by viewing it as a decision tree (recall Figure 8.5). In this case, the question asked at each internal position p is whether the desired key k is less than, equal to, or greater than the key stored at position p, which we denote as key(p). If the answer is "less than," then the search continues in the left subtree. If the answer is "equal," then the search terminates successfully. If the answer is "greater than," then the search continues in the right subtree. Finally, if we reach a leaf, then the search terminates unsuccessfully. (See Figure 11.2.)

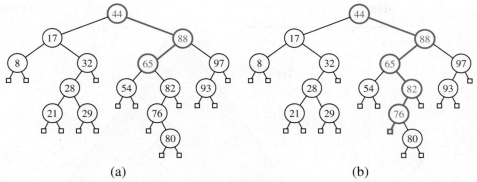

(a)   (b)

Figure 11.2: (a) A successful search for key 65 in a binary search tree; (b) an unsuccessful search for key 68 that terminates at the leaf to the left of the key 76.

We describe this approach in Code Fragment 11.1. If key k occurs in a subtree rooted at p, a call to TreeSearch(p, k) results in the position at which the key is found. For an unsuccessful search, the TreeSearch algorithm returns the final leaf explored on the search path (which we will later make use of when determining where to insert a new entry in a search tree).

Algorithm TreeSearch(p, k):

    if p is external **then**

        return p {unsuccessful search}

    else if k == key(p) **then**

        return p {successful search}

    else if $k <$ key(p) **then**

        return TreeSearch(left(p), k)   {recur on left subtree}

    else {we know that $k >$ key(p)}

        return TreeSearch(right(p), k)   {recur on right subtree}

Code Fragment 11.1: Recursive search in a binary search tree.

Analysis of Binary Tree Searching

The analysis of the worst-case running time of searching in a binary search tree T is simple. Algorithm TreeSearch is recursive and executes a constant number of primitive operations for each recursive call. Each recursive call of TreeSearch is made on a child of the previous position. That is, TreeSearch is called on the positions of a path of T that starts at the root and goes down one level at a time. Thus, the number of such positions is bounded by $h+1$, where h is the height of T. In other words, since we spend $O(1)$ time per position encountered in the search, the overall search runs in $O(h)$ time, where h is the height of the binary search tree T. (See Figure 11.3.)

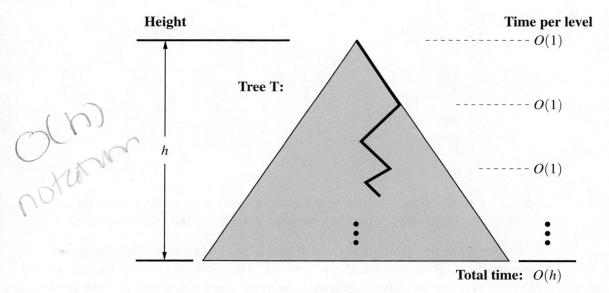

Figure 11.3: Illustrating the running time of searching in a binary search tree. The figure uses a standard visualization shortcut of a binary search tree as a big triangle and a path from the root as a zig-zag line.

In the context of the sorted map ADT, the search will be used as a subroutine for implementing the get method, as well as for the put and remove methods, since each of these begins by trying to locate an existing entry with the given key. We will later demonstrate how to implement sorted map operations, such as lowerEntry and higherEntry, by navigating within the tree after performing a standard search. All of these operations will run in worst-case $O(h)$ time for a tree with height h.

Admittedly, the height h of T can be as large as the number of entries, n, but we expect that it is usually much smaller. Later in this chapter we will show various strategies to maintain an upper bound of $O(\log n)$ on the height of a search tree T.

11.1.2 Insertions and Deletions

Binary search trees allow implementations of the put and remove operations using algorithms that are fairly straightforward, although not trivial.

Insertion

The map operation put(k, v) begins with a search for an entry with key k. If found, that entry's existing value is reassigned. Otherwise, the new entry can be inserted into the underlying tree by expanding the leaf that was reached at the end of the failed search into an internal node. The binary search-tree property is sustained by that placement (note that it is placed exactly where a search would expect it). Let us assume a proper binary tree supports the following update operation:

expandExternal(p, e): Stores entry e at the external position p, and expands p to be internal, having two new leaves as children.

We can then describe the TreeInsert algorithm with the pseudocode given in in Code Fragment 11.2. An example of insertion into a binary search tree is shown in Figure 11.4.

Algorithm TreeInsert(k, v):

    Input: A search key k to be associated with value v

    p = TreeSearch(root(), k)

    if k == key(p) **then**

        Change p's value to (v)

    else

        expandExternal(p, (k, v))

Code Fragment 11.2: Algorithm for inserting a key-value pair into a map that is represented as a binary search tree.

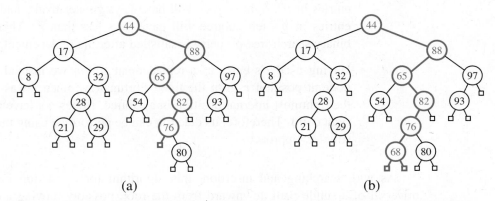

(a)   (b)

Figure 11.4: Insertion of an entry with key 68 into the search tree of Figure 11.2. Finding the position to insert is shown in (a), and the resulting tree is shown in (b).

Deletion

Deleting an entry from a binary search tree is a bit more complex than inserting a new entry because the position of an entry to be deleted might be anywhere in the tree (as opposed to insertions, which always occur at a leaf). To delete an entry with key k, we begin by calling TreeSearch(root(), k) to find the position p storing an entry with key equal to k (if any). If the search returns an external node, then there is no entry to remove. Otherwise, we distinguish between two cases (of increasing difficulty):

- If at most one of the children of position p is internal, the deletion of the entry at position p is easily implemented (see Figure 11.5). Let position r be a child of p that is internal (or an arbitrary child, if both are leaves). We will remove p and the leaf that is r's sibling, while promoting r upward to take the place of p. We note that all remaining ancestor-descendant relationships that remain in the tree after the operation existed before the operation; therefore, the binary search-tree property is maintained.

- If position p has two children, we cannot simply remove the node from the tree since this would create a "hole" and two orphaned children. Instead, we proceed as follows (see Figure 11.6):

  ○ We locate position r containing the entry having the greatest key that is strictly less than that of position p (its so-called *predecessor* in the ordering of keys). That predecessor will always be located in the right-most internal position of the left subtree of position p.

  ○ We use r's entry as a replacement for the one being deleted at position p. Because r has the immediately preceding key in the map, any entries in p's right subtree will have keys greater than r and any other entries in p's left subtree will have keys less than r. Therefore, the binary search-tree property is satisfied after the replacement.

  ○ Having used r's entry as a replacement for p, we instead delete the node at position r from the tree. Fortunately, since r was located as the rightmost internal position in a subtree, r does not have an internal right child. Therefore, its deletion can be performed using the first (and simpler) approach.

As with searching and insertion, this algorithm for a deletion involves the traversal of a single path downward from the root, possibly moving an entry between two positions of this path, and removing a node from that path and promoting its child. Therefore, it executes in time $O(h)$ where h is the height of the tree.

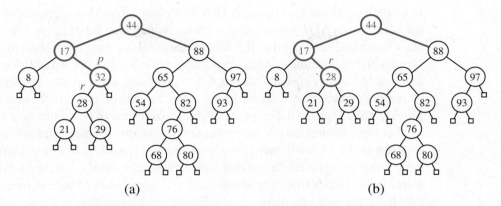

Figure 11.5: Deletion from the binary search tree of Figure 11.4b, where the entry to delete (with key 32) is stored at a position p with one child r: (a) before the deletion; (b) after the deletion.

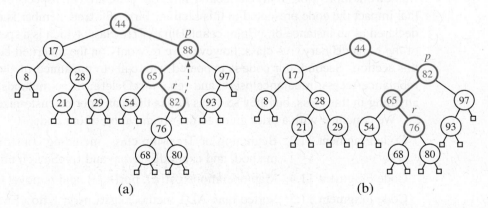

Figure 11.6: Deletion from the binary search tree of Figure 11.5b, where the entry to delete (with key 88) is stored at a position p with two children, and replaced by its predecessor r: (a) before the deletion; (b) after the deletion.

11.1.3   Java Implementation

In Code Fragments 11.3 through 11.6 we define a TreeMap class that implements the sorted map ADT while using a binary search tree for storage. The TreeMap class is declared as a child of the AbstractSortedMap base class, thereby inheriting support for performing comparisons based upon a given (or default) Comparator, a nested MapEntry class for storing key-value pairs, and concrete implementations of methods keySet and values based upon the entrySet method, which we will provide. (See Figure 10.2 on page 406 for an overview of our entire map hierarchy.)

For representing the tree structure, our TreeMap class maintains an instance of a subclass of the LinkedBinaryTree class from Section 8.3.1. In this implementation, we choose to represent the search tree as a *proper* binary tree, with explicit leaf nodes in the binary tree as sentinels, and map entries stored only at internal nodes. (We leave the task of a more space-efficient implementation to Exercise P-11.55.)

The TreeSearch algorithm of Code Fragment 11.1 is implemented as a private recursive method, treeSearch(p, k). That method either returns a position with an entry equal to key k, or else the last position that is visited on the search path. The method is not only used for all of the primary map operations, get(k), put(k, v), and remove(k), but for most of the sorted map methods, as the final internal position visited during an unsuccessful search has either the greatest key less than k or the least key greater than k.

Finally, we note that our TreeMap class is designed so that it can be subclassed to implement various forms of *balanced* search trees. We discuss the balancing framework more thoroughly in Section 11.2, but there are two aspects of the design that impact the code presented in this section. First, our tree member is technically declared as an instance of a BalanceableBinaryTree class, which is a specialization of the LinkedBinaryTree class; however, we rely only on the inherited behaviors in this section. Second, our code is peppered with calls to presumed methods named rebalanceAccess, rebalanceInsert, and rebalanceDelete; these methods do not do anything in this class, but they serve as **hooks** that can later be customized.

We conclude with a brief guide to the organization of our code.

Code Fragment 11.3: Beginning of TreeMap class, including constructors, size method, and expandExternal and treeSearch utilities.

Code Fragment 11.4: Map operations get(k), put(k, v), and remove(k).

Code Fragment 11.5: Sorted map ADT methods lastEntry( ), floorEntry(k), and lowerEntry(k), and protected utility treeMax. Symmetric methods firstEntry( ), ceilingEntry(k), higherEntry(k), and treeMin are provided online.

Code Fragment 11.6: Support for producing an iteration of all entries (method entrySet of the map ADT), or of a selected range of entries (method subMap(k_1, k_2) of the sorted map ADT).

```
1   /** An implementation of a sorted map using a binary search tree. */
2   public class TreeMap<K,V> extends AbstractSortedMap<K,V> {
3     // To represent the underlying tree structure, we use a specialized subclass of the
4     // LinkedBinaryTree class that we name BalanceableBinaryTree (see Section 11.2).
5     protected BalanceableBinaryTree<K,V> tree = new BalanceableBinaryTree<>();
6
7     /** Constructs an empty map using the natural ordering of keys. */
8     public TreeMap() {
9       super();                              // the AbstractSortedMap constructor
10      tree.addRoot(null);                   // create a sentinel leaf as root
11    }
12    /** Constructs an empty map using the given comparator to order keys. */
13    public TreeMap(Comparator<K> comp) {
14      super(comp);                          // the AbstractSortedMap constructor
15      tree.addRoot(null);                   // create a sentinel leaf as root
16    }
17    /** Returns the number of entries in the map. */
18    public int size() {
19      return (tree.size() − 1) / 2;         // only internal nodes have entries
20    }
21    /** Utility used when inserting a new entry at a leaf of the tree */
22    private void expandExternal(Position<Entry<K,V>> p, Entry<K,V> entry) {
23      tree.set(p, entry);                   // store new entry at p
24      tree.addLeft(p, null);                // add new sentinel leaves as children
25      tree.addRight(p, null);
26    }
27
28    // Omitted from this code fragment, but included in the online version of the code,
29    // are a series of protected methods that provide notational shorthands to wrap
30    // operations on the underlying linked binary tree. For example, we support the
31    // protected syntax root() as shorthand for tree.root() with the following utility:
32    protected Position<Entry<K,V>> root() { return tree.root(); }
33
34    /** Returns the position in p's subtree having given key (or else the terminal leaf).*/
35    private Position<Entry<K,V>> treeSearch(Position<Entry<K,V>> p, K key) {
36      if (isExternal(p))
37        return p;                           // key not found; return the final leaf
38      int comp = compare(key, p.getElement());
39      if (comp == 0)
40        return p;                           // key found; return its position
41      else if (comp < 0)
42        return treeSearch(left(p), key);    // search left subtree
43      else
44        return treeSearch(right(p), key);   // search right subtree
45    }
```

Code Fragment 11.3: Beginning of a TreeMap class based on a binary search tree.

```
46    /** Returns the value associated with the specified key (or else null). */
47    public V get(K key) throws IllegalArgumentException {
48      checkKey(key);                                  // may throw IllegalArgumentException
49      Position<Entry<K,V>> p = treeSearch(root(), key);
50      rebalanceAccess(p);                             // hook for balanced tree subclasses
51      if (isExternal(p)) return null;                 // unsuccessful search
52      return p.getElement().getValue();               // match found
53    }
54    /** Associates the given value with the given key, returning any overridden value.*/
55    public V put(K key, V value) throws IllegalArgumentException {
56      checkKey(key);                                  // may throw IllegalArgumentException
57      Entry<K,V> newEntry = new MapEntry<>(key, value);
58      Position<Entry<K,V>> p = treeSearch(root(), key);
59      if (isExternal(p)) {                            // key is new
60        expandExternal(p, newEntry);
61        rebalanceInsert(p);                           // hook for balanced tree subclasses
62        return null;
63      } else {                                        // replacing existing key
64        V old = p.getElement().getValue();
65        set(p, newEntry);
66        rebalanceAccess(p);                           // hook for balanced tree subclasses
67        return old;
68      }
69    }
70    /** Removes the entry having key k (if any) and returns its associated value. */
71    public V remove(K key) throws IllegalArgumentException {
72      checkKey(key);                                  // may throw IllegalArgumentException
73      Position<Entry<K,V>> p = treeSearch(root(), key);
74      if (isExternal(p)) {                            // key not found
75        rebalanceAccess(p);                           // hook for balanced tree subclasses
76        return null;
77      } else {
78        V old = p.getElement().getValue();
79        if (isInternal(left(p)) && isInternal(right(p))) { // both children are internal
80          Position<Entry<K,V>> replacement = treeMax(left(p));
81          set(p, replacement.getElement());
82          p = replacement;
83        } // now p has at most one child that is an internal node
84        Position<Entry<K,V>> leaf = (isExternal(left(p)) ? left(p) : right(p));
85        Position<Entry<K,V>> sib = sibling(leaf);
86        remove(leaf);
87        remove(p);                                    // sib is promoted in p's place
88        rebalanceDelete(sib);                         // hook for balanced tree subclasses
89        return old;
90      }
91    }
```

Code Fragment 11.4: Primary map operations for the TreeMap class.

```
92    /** Returns the position with the maximum key in subtree rooted at Position p. */
93    protected Position<Entry<K,V>> treeMax(Position<Entry<K,V>> p) {
94      Position<Entry<K,V>> walk = p;
95      while (isInternal(walk))
96        walk = right(walk);
97      return parent(walk);                        // we want the parent of the leaf
98    }
99    /** Returns the entry having the greatest key (or null if map is empty). */
100   public Entry<K,V> lastEntry() {
101     if (isEmpty()) return null;
102     return treeMax(root()).getElement();
103   }
104   /** Returns the entry with greatest key less than or equal to given key (if any). */
105   public Entry<K,V> floorEntry(K key) throws IllegalArgumentException {
106     checkKey(key);                              // may throw IllegalArgumentException
107     Position<Entry<K,V>> p = treeSearch(root(), key);
108     if (isInternal(p)) return p.getElement();   // exact match
109     while (!isRoot(p)) {
110       if (p == right(parent(p)))
111         return parent(p).getElement();          // parent has next lesser key
112       else
113         p = parent(p);
114     }
115     return null;                                // no such floor exists
116   }
117   /** Returns the entry with greatest key strictly less than given key (if any). */
118   public Entry<K,V> lowerEntry(K key) throws IllegalArgumentException {
119     checkKey(key);                              // may throw IllegalArgumentException
120     Position<Entry<K,V>> p = treeSearch(root(), key);
121     if (isInternal(p) && isInternal(left(p)))
122       return treeMax(left(p)).getElement();  // this is the predecessor to p
123     // otherwise, we had failed search, or match with no left child
124     while (!isRoot(p)) {
125       if (p == right(parent(p)))
126         return parent(p).getElement();          // parent has next lesser key
127       else
128         p = parent(p);
129     }
130     return null;                                // no such lesser key exists
131   }
```

Code Fragment 11.5: A sample of the sorted map operations for the TreeMap class. The symmetrical utility, treeMin, and public methods firstEntry, ceilingEntry, and higherEntry are available online.

```
132      /** Returns an iterable collection of all key-value entries of the map. */
133      public Iterable<Entry<K,V>> entrySet( ) {
134        ArrayList<Entry<K,V>> buffer = new ArrayList<>(size( ));
135        for (Position<Entry<K,V>> p : tree.inorder( ))
136          if (isInternal(p)) buffer.add(p.getElement( ));
137        return buffer;
138      }
139      /** Returns an iterable of entries with keys in range [fromKey, toKey). */
140      public Iterable<Entry<K,V>> subMap(K fromKey, K toKey) {
141        ArrayList<Entry<K,V>> buffer = new ArrayList<>(size( ));
142        if (compare(fromKey, toKey) < 0)                  // ensure that fromKey < toKey
143          subMapRecurse(fromKey, toKey, root( ), buffer);
144        return buffer;
145      }
146      private void subMapRecurse(K fromKey, K toKey, Position<Entry<K,V>> p,
147                                  ArrayList<Entry<K,V>> buffer) {
148        if (isInternal(p))
149          if (compare(p.getElement( ), fromKey) < 0)
150            // p's key is less than fromKey, so any relevant entries are to the right
151            subMapRecurse(fromKey, toKey, right(p), buffer);
152          else {
153            subMapRecurse(fromKey, toKey, left(p), buffer); // first consider left subtree
154            if (compare(p.getElement( ), toKey) < 0) {      // p is within range
155              buffer.add(p.getElement( ));                  // so add it to buffer, and consider
156              subMapRecurse(fromKey, toKey, right(p), buffer); // right subtree as well
157            }
158          }
159      }
```

Code Fragment 11.6: TreeMap operations supporting iteration of the entire map, or a portion of the map with a given key range.

11.1.4   Performance of a Binary Search Tree

An analysis of the operations of our TreeMap class is given in Table 11.1. Almost all operations have a worst-case running time that depends on h, where h is the height of the current tree. This is because most operations rely on traversing a path from the root of the tree, and the maximum path length within a tree is proportional to the height of the tree. Most notably, our implementations of map operations get, put, and remove, and most of the sorted map operations, each begins with a call to the treeSearch utility. Similar paths are traced when searching for the minimum or maximum entry in a subtree, a task used when finding a replacement during a deletion or in finding the overall first or last entry in the map. An iteration of the entire map is accomplished in $O(n)$ time using an inorder traversal of the underlying tree, and the recursive subMap implementation can be shown to run in $O(s+h)$ worst-case bound for a call that reports s results (see Exercise C-11.34).

Method	Running Time
size, isEmpty	$O(1)$
get, put, remove	$O(h)$
firstEntry, lastEntry	$O(h)$
ceilingEntry, floorEntry, lowerEntry, higherEntry	$O(h)$
subMap	$O(s+h)$
entrySet, keySet, values	$O(n)$

Table 11.1: Worst-case running times of the operations for a TreeMap. We denote the current height of the tree with h, and the number of entries reported by subMap as s. The space usage is $O(n)$, where n is the number of entries stored in the map.

A binary search tree T is therefore an efficient implementation of a map with n entries only if its height is small. In the best case, T has height $h = \lceil \log(n+1) \rceil - 1$, which yields logarithmic-time performance for most of the map operations. In the worst case, however, T has height n, in which case it would look and feel like an ordered list implementation of a map. Such a worst-case configuration arises, for example, if we insert entries with keys in increasing or decreasing order. (See Figure 11.7.)

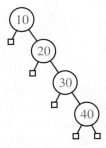

Figure 11.7: Example of a binary search tree with linear height, obtained by inserting entries in increasing order of their keys.

We can nevertheless take comfort that, on average, a binary search tree with n keys generated from a random series of insertions and removals of keys has expected height $O(\log n)$; the justification of this statement is beyond the scope of the book, requiring careful mathematical language to precisely define what we mean by a random series of insertions and removals, and sophisticated probability theory.

In applications where one cannot guarantee the random nature of updates, it is better to rely on variations of search trees, presented in the remainder of this chapter, that guarantee a ***worst-case*** height of $O(\log n)$, and thus $O(\log n)$ worst-case time for searches, insertions, and deletions.

11.2   Balanced Search Trees

In the closing of the previous section, we noted that if we could assume a random series of insertions and removals, the standard binary search tree supports $O(\log n)$ expected running times for the basic map operations. However, we may only claim $O(n)$ worst-case time, because some sequences of operations may lead to an unbalanced tree with height proportional to n.

In the remainder of this chapter, we will explore four search-tree algorithms that provide stronger performance guarantees. Three of the four data structures (AVL trees, splay trees, and red-black trees) are based on augmenting a standard binary search tree with occasional operations to reshape the tree and reduce its height.

The primary operation to rebalance a binary search tree is known as a ***rotation***. During a rotation, we "rotate" a child to be above its parent, as diagrammed in Figure 11.8.

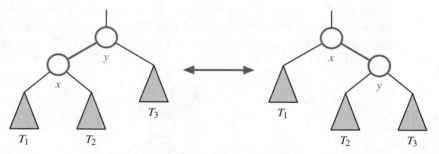

Figure 11.8: A rotation operation in a binary search tree. A rotation can be performed to transform the left formation into the right, or the right formation into the left. Note that all keys in subtree T_1 have keys less than that of position x, all keys in subtree T_2 have keys that are between those of positions x and y, and all keys in subtree T_3 have keys that are greater than that of position y.

To maintain the binary search-tree property through a rotation, we note that if position x was a left child of position y prior to a rotation (and therefore the key of x is less than the key of y), then y becomes the *right* child of x after the rotation, and vice versa. Furthermore, we must relink the subtree of entries with keys that lie between the keys of the two positions that are being rotated. For example, in Figure 11.8 the subtree labeled T_2 represents entries with keys that are known to be greater than that of position x and less than that of position y. In the first configuration of that figure, T_2 is the right subtree of position x; in the second configuration, it is the left subtree of position y.

Because a single rotation modifies a constant number of parent-child relationships, it can be implemented in $O(1)$ time with a linked binary tree representation.

In the context of a tree-balancing algorithm, a rotation allows the shape of a tree to be modified while maintaining the search-tree property. If used wisely, this operation can be performed to avoid highly unbalanced tree configurations. For example, a rightward rotation from the first formation of Figure 11.8 to the second reduces the depth of each node in subtree T_1 by one, while increasing the depth of each node in subtree T_3 by one. (Note that the depth of nodes in subtree T_2 are unaffected by the rotation.)

One or more rotations can be combined to provide broader rebalancing within a tree. One such compound operation we consider is a ***trinode restructuring***. For this manipulation, we consider a position x, its parent y, and its grandparent z. The goal is to restructure the subtree rooted at z in order to reduce the overall path length to x and its subtrees. Pseudocode for a restructure(x) method is given in Code Fragment 11.7 and illustrated in Figure 11.9. In describing a trinode restructuring, we temporarily rename the positions x, y, and z as a, b, and c, so that a precedes b and b precedes c in an inorder traversal of T. There are four possible orientations mapping x, y, and z to a, b, and c, as shown in Figure 11.9, which are unified into one case by our relabeling. The trinode restructuring replaces z with the node identified as b, makes the children of this node be a and c, and makes the children of a and c be the four previous children of x, y, and z (other than x and y), while maintaining the inorder relationships of all the nodes in T.

Algorithm restructure(x):

    Input: A position x of a binary search tree T that has both a parent y and a grandparent z

    Output: Tree T after a trinode restructuring (which corresponds to a single or double rotation) involving positions x, y, and z

1: Let (a, b, c) be a left-to-right (inorder) listing of the positions x, y, and z, and let (T_1, T_2, T_3, T_4) be a left-to-right (inorder) listing of the four subtrees of x, y, and z not rooted at x, y, or z.

2: Replace the subtree rooted at z with a new subtree rooted at b.

3: Let a be the left child of b and let T_1 and T_2 be the left and right subtrees of a, respectively.

4: Let c be the right child of b and let T_3 and T_4 be the left and right subtrees of c, respectively.

Code Fragment 11.7: The trinode restructuring operation in a binary search tree.

In practice, the modification of a tree T caused by a trinode restructuring operation can be implemented through case analysis either as a single rotation (as in Figure 11.9a and b) or as a double rotation (as in Figure 11.9c and d). The double rotation arises when position x has the middle of the three relevant keys and is first rotated above its parent, and then above what was originally its grandparent. In any of the cases, the trinode restructuring is completed with $O(1)$ running time.

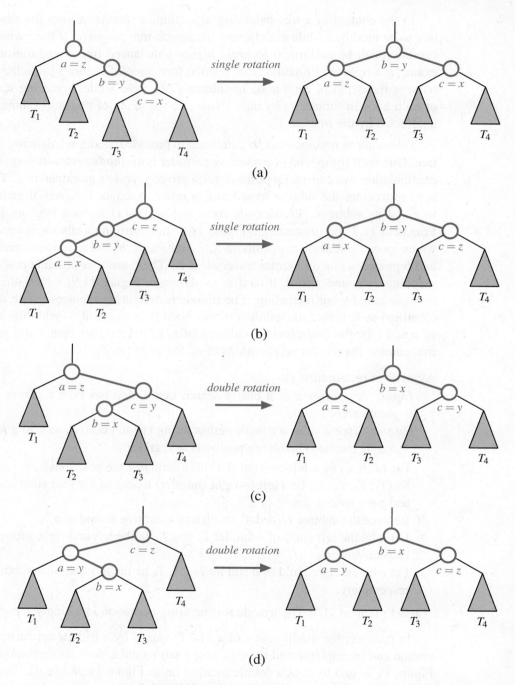

Figure 11.9: Schematic illustration of a trinode restructuring operation: (a and b) require a single rotation; (c and d) require a double rotation.

11.2.1   Java Framework for Balancing Search Trees

Our TreeMap class (introduced in Section 11.1.3) is a fully functional map implementation. However, the running time for its operations depend on the height of the tree, and in the worst-case, that height may be $O(n)$ for a map with n entries. Therefore, we have intentionally designed the TreeMap class in a way that allows it to be easily extended to provide more advanced tree-balancing strategies. In later sections of this chapter, we will implement subclasses AVLTreeMap, SplayTreeMap, and RBTreeMap. In this section, we describe three important forms of support that the TreeMap class offers these subclasses.

Hooks for Rebalancing Operations

Our implementation of the basic map operations in Section 11.1.3 includes strategic calls to three nonpublic methods that serve as **hooks** for rebalancing algorithms:

- A call to rebalanceInsert(p) is made from within the put method, after a new node is added to the tree at position p (line 61 of Code Fragment 11.4).

- A call to rebalanceDelete(p) is made from within the remove method, after a node is deleted from the tree (line 88 of Code Fragment 11.4); position p identifies the child of the removed node that was promoted in its place.

- A call to rebalanceAccess(p) is made by any call to get, put, or remove that does *not* result in a structural change. Position p, which could be internal or external, represents the deepest node of the tree that was accessed during the operation. This hook is specifically used by the **splay tree** structure (see Section 11.4) to restructure a tree so that more frequently accessed nodes are brought closer to the root.

Within our TreeMap class, we provide the trivial declarations of these three methods, having bodies that do nothing, as shown in Code Fragment 11.8. A subclass of TreeMap may override any of these methods to implement a nontrivial action to rebalance a tree. This is another example of the **template method design pattern**, as originally discussed in Section 2.3.3.

```
protected void rebalanceInsert(Position<Entry<K,V>> p) { }
protected void rebalanceDelete(Position<Entry<K,V>> p) { }
protected void rebalanceAccess(Position<Entry<K,V>> p) { }
```

Code Fragment 11.8: Trivial definitions of TreeMap methods that serve as hooks for our rebalancing framework. These methods may be overridden by subclasses in order to perform appropriate rebalancing operations.

Protected Methods for Rotating and Restructuring

To support common restructuring operations, our TreeMap class relies on storing the tree as an instance of a new nested class, BalanceableBinaryTree (shown in Code Fragments 11.9 and 11.10). That class is a specialization of the original LinkedBinaryTree class from Section 8.3.1. This new class provides protected utility methods rotate and restructure that, respectively, implement a single rotation and a trinode restructuring (described at the beginning of Section 11.2). Although these methods are not invoked by the standard TreeMap operations, their inclusion supports greater code reuse, as they are available to all balanced-tree subclasses.

These methods are implemented in Code Fragment 11.10. To simplify the code, we define an additional relink utility that properly links parent and child nodes to each other. The focus of the rotate method then becomes redefining the relationship between the parent and child, relinking a rotated node directly to its original grandparent, and shifting the "middle" subtree (that labeled as T_2 in Figure 11.8) between the rotated nodes.

For the trinode restructuring, we determine whether to perform a single or double rotation, as originally described in Figure 11.9. The four cases in that figure demonstrate a downward path z to y to x that are respectively right-right, left-left, right-left, and left-right. The first two patterns, with matching orientation, warrant a single rotation moving y upward, while the last two patterns, with opposite orientations, warrant a double rotation moving x upward.

Specialized Nodes with an Auxiliary Data Member

Many tree-balancing strategies require that some form of auxiliary "balancing" information be stored at nodes of a tree. To ease the burden on the balanced-tree subclasses, we choose to add an auxiliary integer value to every node within the BalanceableSearchTree class. This is accomplished by defining a new BSTNode class, which itself inherits from the nested LinkedBinaryTree.Node class. The new class declares the auxiliary variable, and provides methods for getting and setting its value.

We draw attention to an important subtlety in our design, including that of the original LinkedBinaryTree subclass. Whenever a low-level operation on an underlying linked tree requires a new node, we must ensure that the correct type of node is created. That is, for our balanceable tree, we need each node to be a BTNode, which includes the auxiliary field. However, the creation of nodes occurs within low-level operations, such as addLeft and addRight, that reside in the original LinkedBinaryTree class.

We rely on a technique known as the *factory method design pattern*. The LinkedBinaryTree class includes a protected method, createNode (originally given at lines 30–33 of Code Fragment 8.8), that is responsible for instantiating a new node of the appropriate type. The rest of the code in that class makes sure to always use the createNode method when a new node is needed.

In the LinkedBinaryTree class, the createNode method returns a simple Node instance. In our new BalanceableBinaryTree class, we override the createNode method (see lines 22–27 in Code Fragment 11.9), so that a new instance of the BSTNode class is returned. In this way, we effectively change the behavior of the low-level operations in the LinkedBinaryTree class so that it uses instances of our specialized node class, and therefore, that every node in our balanced trees includes support for the new auxiliary field.

```
1  /** A specialized version of LinkedBinaryTree with support for balancing. */
2  protected static class BalanceableBinaryTree<K,V>
3                            extends LinkedBinaryTree<Entry<K,V>> {
4    //-------------- nested BSTNode class --------------
5    // this extends the inherited LinkedBinaryTree.Node class
6    protected static class BSTNode<E> extends Node<E> {
7      int aux=0;
8      BSTNode(E e, Node<E> parent, Node<E> leftChild, Node<E> rightChild) {
9        super(e, parent, leftChild, rightChild);
10     }
11     public int getAux() { return aux; }
12     public void setAux(int value) { aux = value; }
13   } //--------- end of nested BSTNode class ---------
14
15   // positional-based methods related to aux field
16   public int getAux(Position<Entry<K,V>> p) {
17     return ((BSTNode<Entry<K,V>>) p).getAux();
18   }
19   public void setAux(Position<Entry<K,V>> p, int value) {
20     ((BSTNode<Entry<K,V>>) p).setAux(value);
21   }
22   // Override node factory function to produce a BSTNode (rather than a Node)
23   protected
24   Node<Entry<K,V>> createNode(Entry<K,V> e, Node<Entry<K,V>> parent,
25                       Node<Entry<K,V>> left, Node<Entry<K,V>> right) {
26     return new BSTNode<>(e, parent, left, right);
27   }
```

Code Fragment 11.9: The BalanceableBinaryTree class, which is nested within the TreeMap class definition. (Continues in Code Fragment 11.10.)

```
28   /** Relinks a parent node with its oriented child node. */
29   private void relink(Node<Entry<K,V>> parent, Node<Entry<K,V>> child,
30                       boolean makeLeftChild) {
31     child.setParent(parent);
32     if (makeLeftChild)
33       parent.setLeft(child);
34     else
35       parent.setRight(child);
36   }
37   /** Rotates Position p above its parent. */
38   public void rotate(Position<Entry<K,V>> p) {
39     Node<Entry<K,V>> x = validate(p);
40     Node<Entry<K,V>> y = x.getParent();          // we assume this exists
41     Node<Entry<K,V>> z = y.getParent();          // grandparent (possibly null)
42     if (z == null) {
43       root = x;                                  // x becomes root of the tree
44       x.setParent(null);
45     } else
46       relink(z, x, y == z.getLeft());            // x becomes direct child of z
47     // now rotate x and y, including transfer of middle subtree
48     if (x == y.getLeft()) {
49       relink(y, x.getRight(), true);             // x's right child becomes y's left
50       relink(x, y, false);                       // y becomes x's right child
51     } else {
52       relink(y, x.getLeft(), false);             // x's left child becomes y's right
53       relink(x, y, true);                        // y becomes left child of x
54     }
55   }
56   /** Performs a trinode restructuring of Position x with its parent/grandparent. */
57   public Position<Entry<K,V>> restructure(Position<Entry<K,V>> x) {
58     Position<Entry<K,V>> y = parent(x);
59     Position<Entry<K,V>> z = parent(y);
60     if ((x == right(y)) == (y == right(z))) {    // matching alignments
61       rotate(y);                                 // single rotation (of y)
62       return y;                                  // y is new subtree root
63     } else {                                     // opposite alignments
64       rotate(x);                                 // double rotation (of x)
65       rotate(x);
66       return x;                                  // x is new subtree root
67     }
68   }
69 }
```

Code Fragment 11.10: The BalanceableBinaryTree class, which is nested within the TreeMap class definition (continued from Code Fragment 11.9).

11.3 AVL Trees

The TreeMap class, which uses a standard binary search tree as its data structure, should be an efficient map data structure, but its worst-case performance for the various operations is linear time, because it is possible that a series of operations results in a tree with linear height. In this section, we describe a simple balancing strategy that guarantees worst-case logarithmic running time for all the fundamental map operations.

Definition of an AVL Tree

The simple correction is to add a rule to the binary search-tree definition that will maintain a logarithmic height for the tree. Recall that we defined the height of a subtree rooted at position p of a tree to be the number of *edges* on the longest path from p to a leaf (see Section 8.1.3). By this definition, a leaf position has height 0.

In this section, we consider the following ***height-balance property***, which characterizes the structure of a binary search tree T in terms of the heights of its nodes.

> ***Height-Balance Property***: For every internal position p of T, the heights of the children of p differ by at most 1.

Any binary search tree T that satisfies the height-balance property is said to be an **AVL tree**, named after the initials of its inventors: Adel'son-Vel'skii and Landis. An example of an AVL tree is shown in Figure 11.10.

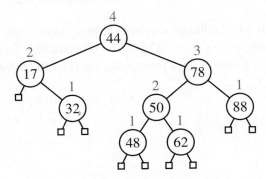

Figure 11.10: An example of an AVL tree. The keys of the entries are shown inside the nodes, and the heights of the nodes are shown above the nodes (all leaves have height 0).

An immediate consequence of the height-balance property is that a subtree of an AVL tree is itself an AVL tree. The height-balance property also has the important consequence of keeping the height small, as shown in the following proposition.

Proposition 11.1: *The height of an AVL tree storing n entries is $O(\log n)$.*

Justification: Instead of trying to find an upper bound on the height of an AVL tree directly, it turns out to be easier to work on the "inverse problem" of finding a lower bound on the minimum number of *internal* nodes, denoted as $n(h)$, of an AVL tree with height h. We will show that $n(h)$ grows at least exponentially. From this, it will be an easy step to derive that the height of an AVL tree storing n entries is $O(\log n)$.

We begin by noting that $n(1) = 1$ and $n(2) = 2$, because an AVL tree of height 1 must have exactly one internal node and an AVL tree of height 2 must have at least two internal nodes. Now, an AVL tree with the minimum number of nodes having height h for $h \geq 3$, is such that both its subtrees are AVL trees with the minimum number of nodes: one with height $h-1$ and the other with height $h-2$. Taking the root into account, we obtain the following formula that relates $n(h)$ to $n(h-1)$ and $n(h-2)$, for $h \geq 3$:

$$n(h) = 1 + n(h-1) + n(h-2). \tag{11.1}$$

At this point, the reader familiar with the properties of Fibonacci progressions (Sections 2.2.3 and 5.5) will already see that $n(h)$ is a function exponential in h. To formalize that observation, we proceed as follows.

Formula 11.1 implies that $n(h)$ is a strictly increasing function of h. Thus, we know that $n(h-1) > n(h-2)$. Replacing $n(h-1)$ with $n(h-2)$ in Formula 11.1 and dropping the 1, we get, for $h \geq 3$,

$$n(h) \; > \; 2 \cdot n(h-2). \tag{11.2}$$

Formula 11.2 indicates that $n(h)$ at least doubles each time h increases by 2, which intuitively means that $n(h)$ grows exponentially. To show this fact in a formal way, we apply Formula 11.2 repeatedly, yielding the following series of inequalities:

$$\begin{aligned} n(h) \; &> \; 2 \cdot n(h-2) \\ &> \; 4 \cdot n(h-4) \\ &> \; 8 \cdot n(h-6) \\ &\;\; \vdots \\ &> \; 2^i \cdot n(h-2i). \end{aligned} \tag{11.3}$$

That is, $n(h) > 2^i \cdot n(h-2i)$, for any integer i, such that $h - 2i \geq 1$. Since we already know the values of $n(1)$ and $n(2)$, we pick i so that $h - 2i$ is equal to either 1 or 2.

That is, we pick

$$i = \left\lceil \frac{h}{2} \right\rceil - 1.$$

By substituting the above value of i in Formula 11.3, we obtain, for $h \geq 3$,

$$
\begin{aligned}
n(h) \quad &> \quad 2^{\left\lceil \frac{h}{2} \right\rceil - 1} \cdot n\left(h - 2\left\lceil \frac{h}{2} \right\rceil + 2\right) \\
&\geq \quad 2^{\left\lceil \frac{h}{2} \right\rceil - 1} n(1) \\
&\geq \quad 2^{\frac{h}{2} - 1}.
\end{aligned}
\tag{11.4}
$$

By taking logarithms of both sides of Formula 11.4, we obtain

$$\log(n(h)) > \frac{h}{2} - 1,$$

from which we get

$$h < 2\log(n(h)) + 2, \tag{11.5}$$

which implies that an AVL tree storing n entries has height at most $2\log n + 2$. ∎

By Proposition 11.1 and the analysis of binary search trees given in Section 11.1, the operation get, in a map implemented with an AVL tree, runs in time $O(\log n)$, where n is the number of entries in the map. Of course, we still have to show how to maintain the height-balance property after an insertion or deletion.

11.3.1 Update Operations

Given a binary search tree T, we say that a position is **balanced** if the absolute value of the difference between the heights of its children is at most 1, and we say that it is **unbalanced** otherwise. Thus, the height-balance property characterizing AVL trees is equivalent to saying that every position is balanced.

The insertion and deletion operations for AVL trees begin similarly to the corresponding operations for (standard) binary search trees, but with post-processing for each operation to restore the balance of any portions of the tree that are adversely affected by the change.

Insertion

Suppose that tree T satisfies the height-balance property, and hence is an AVL tree, prior to the insertion of a new entry. An insertion of a new entry in a binary search tree, as described in Section 11.1.2, results in a leaf position p being expanded to become internal, with two new external children. This action may violate the height-balance property (see, for example, Figure 11.11a), yet the only positions that may become unbalanced are ancestors of p, because those are the only positions whose subtrees have changed. Therefore, let us describe how to restructure T to fix any unbalance that may have occurred.

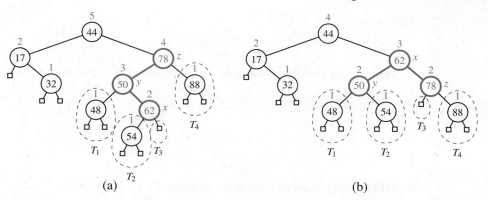

Figure 11.11: An example insertion of an entry with key 54 in the AVL tree of Figure 11.10: (a) after adding a new node for key 54, the nodes storing keys 78 and 44 become unbalanced; (b) a trinode restructuring restores the height-balance property. We show the heights of nodes above them, and we identify the nodes x, y, and z and subtrees T_1, T_2, T_3, and T_4 participating in the trinode restructuring.

We restore the balance of the nodes in the binary search tree T by a simple "search-and-repair" strategy. In particular, let z be the first position we encounter in going up from p toward the root of T such that z is unbalanced (see Figure 11.11a.) Also, let y denote the child of z with greater height (and note that y must be an ancestor of p). Finally, let x be the child of y with greater height (there cannot be a tie and position x must also be an ancestor of p, possibly p itself). We rebalance the subtree rooted at z by calling the ***trinode restructuring*** method, restructure(x), originally described in Section 11.2. An example of such a restructuring in the context of an AVL insertion is portrayed in Figure 11.11.

To formally argue the correctness of this process in reestablishing the AVL height-balance property, we consider the implication of z being the nearest ancestor of p that became unbalanced after the insertion of p. It must be that the height of y increased by one due to the insertion and that it is now 2 greater than its sibling. Since y remains balanced, it must be that it formerly had subtrees with equal heights, and that the subtree containing x has increased its height by one. That subtree increased either because $x = p$, and thus its height changed from 0 to 1, or because x previously had equal-height subtrees and the height of the one containing p has increased by 1. Letting $h \geq 0$ denote the height of the tallest child of x, this scenario might be portrayed as in Figure 11.12.

After the trinode restructuring, each of x, y, and z is balanced. Furthermore, the root of the subtree after the restructuring has height $h + 2$, which is precisely the height that z had before the insertion of the new entry. Therefore, any ancestor of z that became temporarily unbalanced becomes balanced again, and this one restructuring restores the height-balance property ***globally***.

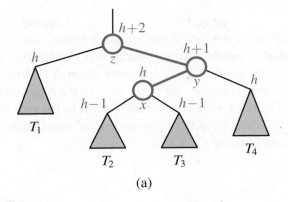

(a)

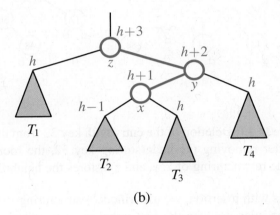

(b)

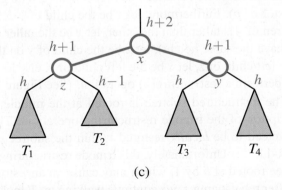

(c)

Figure 11.12: Rebalancing of a subtree during a typical insertion into an AVL tree: (a) before the insertion; (b) after an insertion in subtree T_3 causes imbalance at z; (c) after restoring balance with trinode restructuring. Notice that the overall height of the subtree after the insertion is the same as before the insertion.

Deletion

Recall that a deletion from a regular binary search tree results in the structural removal of a node having either zero or one internal children. Such a change may violate the height-balance property in an AVL tree. In particular, if position p represents a (possibly external) child of the removed node in tree T, there may be an unbalanced node on the path from p to the root of T. (See Figure 11.13a.) In fact, there can be at most one such unbalanced node. (The justification of this fact is left as Exercise C-11.41.)

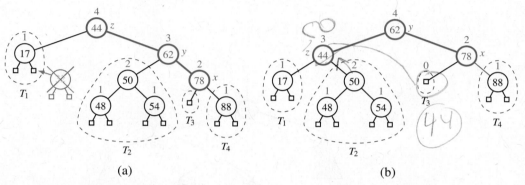

Figure 11.13: Deletion of the entry with key 32 from the AVL tree of Figure 11.11b: (a) after removing the node storing key 32, the root becomes unbalanced; (b) a trinode restructuring of x, y, and z restores the height-balance property.

As with insertion, we use trinode restructuring to restore balance in the tree T. In particular, let z be the first unbalanced position encountered going up from p toward the root of T, and let y be that child of z with greater height (y will not be an ancestor of p). Furthermore, let x be the child of y defined as follows: if one of the children of y is taller than the other, let x be the taller child of y; else (both children of y have the same height), let x be the child of y on the same side as y (that is, if y is the left child of z, let x be the left child of y, else let x be the right child of y). We then perform a restructure(x) operation. (See Figure 11.13b.)

The restructured subtree is rooted at the middle position denoted as b in the description of the trinode restructuring operation. The height-balance property is guaranteed to be **locally** restored within the subtree of b. (See Exercises R-11.11 and R-11.12.) Unfortunately, this trinode restructuring may reduce the height of the subtree rooted at b by 1, which may cause an ancestor of b to become unbalanced. So, after rebalancing z, we continue walking up T looking for unbalanced positions. If we find another, we perform a restructure operation to restore its balance, and continue marching up T looking for more, all the way to the root. Since the height of T is $O(\log n)$, where n is the number of entries, by Proposition 11.1, $O(\log n)$ trinode restructurings are sufficient to restore the height-balance property.

Performance of AVL Trees

By Proposition 11.1, the height of an AVL tree with n entries is guaranteed to be $O(\log n)$. Because the standard binary search-tree operation had running times bounded by the height (see Table 11.1), and because the additional work in maintaining balance factors and restructuring an AVL tree can be bounded by the length of a path in the tree, the traditional map operations run in worst-case logarithmic time with an AVL tree. We summarize these results in Table 11.2, and illustrate this performance in Figure 11.14.

Method	Running Time
size, isEmpty	$O(1)$
get, put, remove	$O(\log n)$
firstEntry, lastEntry	$O(\log n)$
ceilingEntry, floorEntry, lowerEntry, higherEntry	$O(\log n)$
subMap	$O(s + \log n)$
entrySet, keySet, values	$O(n)$

Table 11.2: Worst-case running times of operations for an n-entry sorted map realized as an AVL tree T, with s denoting the number of entries reported by subMap.

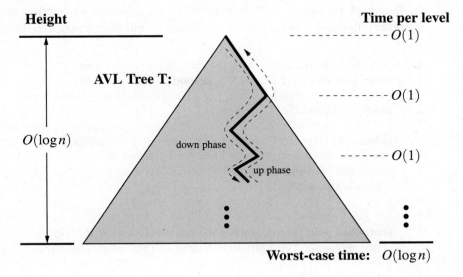

Figure 11.14: Illustrating the running time of searches and updates in an AVL tree. The time performance is $O(1)$ per level, broken into a down phase, which typically involves searching, and an up phase, which typically involves updating height values and performing local trinode restructurings (rotations).

11.3.2   Java Implementation

A complete implementation of an AVLTreeMap class is provided in Code Fragments 11.11 and 11.12. It inherits from the standard TreeMap class and relies on the balancing framework described in Section 11.2.1. We highlight two important aspects of our implementation. First, the AVLTreeMap uses the node's auxiliary balancing variable to store the height of the subtree rooted at that node, with leaves having a balance factor of 0 by default. We also provide several utilities involving heights of nodes (see Code Fragment 11.11).

To implement the core logic of the AVL balancing strategy, we define a utility, named rebalance, that suffices to restore the height-balance property after an insertion or a deletion (see Code Fragment 11.11). Although the inherited behaviors for insertion and deletion are quite different, the necessary post-processing for an AVL tree can be unified. In both cases, we trace an upward path from the position p at which the change took place, recalculating the height of each position based on the (updated) heights of its children. We perform a trinode restructuring operation if an imbalanced position is reached. The upward march from p continues until we reach an ancestor with height that was unchanged by the map operation, or with height that was restored to its previous value by a trinode restructuring operation, or until reaching the root of the tree (in which case the overall height of the tree has increased by one). To easily detect the stopping condition, we record the "old" height of a position, as it existed before the insertion or deletion operation begin, and compare that to the newly calculated height after a possible restructuring.

```
1   /** An implementation of a sorted map using an AVL tree. */
2   public class AVLTreeMap<K,V> extends TreeMap<K,V> {
3     /** Constructs an empty map using the natural ordering of keys. */
4     public AVLTreeMap( ) { super( ); }
5     /** Constructs an empty map using the given comparator to order keys. */
6     public AVLTreeMap(Comparator<K> comp) { super(comp); }
7     /** Returns the height of the given tree position. */
8     protected int height(Position<Entry<K,V>> p) {
9       return tree.getAux(p);
10    }
11    /** Recomputes the height of the given position based on its children's heights. */
12    protected void recomputeHeight(Position<Entry<K,V>> p) {
13      tree.setAux(p, 1 + Math.max(height(left(p)), height(right(p))));
14    }
15    /** Returns whether a position has balance factor between −1 and 1 inclusive. */
16    protected boolean isBalanced(Position<Entry<K,V>> p) {
17      return Math.abs(height(left(p)) − height(right(p))) <= 1;
18    }
```

Code Fragment 11.11: AVLTreeMap class. (Continues in Code Fragment 11.12.)

```
19    /** Returns a child of p with height no smaller than that of the other child. */
20    protected Position<Entry<K,V>> tallerChild(Position<Entry<K,V>> p) {
21      if (height(left(p)) > height(right(p))) return left(p);         // clear winner
22      if (height(left(p)) < height(right(p))) return right(p);        // clear winner
23      // equal height children; break tie while matching parent's orientation
24      if (isRoot(p)) return left(p);                  // choice is irrelevant
25      if (p == left(parent(p))) return left(p);       // return aligned child
26      else return right(p);
27    }
28    /**
29     * Utility used to rebalance after an insert or removal operation. This traverses the
30     * path upward from p, performing a trinode restructuring when imbalance is found,
31     * continuing until balance is restored.
32     */
33    protected void rebalance(Position<Entry<K,V>> p) {
34      int oldHeight, newHeight;
35      do {
36        oldHeight = height(p);                        // not yet recalculated if internal
37        if (!isBalanced(p)) {                         // imbalance detected
38          // perform trinode restructuring, setting p to resulting root,
39          // and recompute new local heights after the restructuring
40          p = restructure(tallerChild(tallerChild(p)));
41          recomputeHeight(left(p));
42          recomputeHeight(right(p));
43        }
44        recomputeHeight(p);
45        newHeight = height(p);
46        p = parent(p);
47      } while (oldHeight != newHeight && p != null);
48    }
49    /** Overrides the TreeMap rebalancing hook that is called after an insertion. */
50    protected void rebalanceInsert(Position<Entry<K,V>> p) {
51      rebalance(p);
52    }
53    /** Overrides the TreeMap rebalancing hook that is called after a deletion. */
54    protected void rebalanceDelete(Position<Entry<K,V>> p) {
55      if (!isRoot(p))
56        rebalance(parent(p));
57    }
58  }
```

Code Fragment 11.12: AVLTreeMap class (continued from Code Fragment 11.11).

11.4 Splay Trees

The next search-tree structure we study is known as a a *splay tree*. This structure is conceptually quite different from the other balanced search trees we will discuss in this chapter, for a splay tree does not strictly enforce a logarithmic upper bound on the height of the tree. In fact, no additional height, balance, or other auxiliary data need be stored with the nodes of this tree.

The efficiency of splay trees is due to a certain move-to-root operation, called *splaying*, that is performed at the bottommost position p reached during every insertion, deletion, or even a search. (In essence, this is a variant of the move-to-front heuristic that we explored for lists in Section 7.7.2.) Intuitively, a splay operation causes more frequently accessed elements to remain nearer to the root, thereby reducing the typical search times. The surprising thing about splaying is that it allows us to guarantee a logarithmic amortized running time, for insertions, deletions, and searches.

11.4.1 Splaying

Given a node x of a binary search tree T, we *splay* x by moving x to the root of T through a sequence of restructurings. The particular restructurings we perform are important, for it is not sufficient to move x to the root of T by just any sequence of restructurings. The specific operation we perform to move x up depends upon the relative positions of x, its parent y, and x's grandparent z (if it exists). There are three cases that we will consider.

zig-zig: The node x and its parent y are both left children or both right children. (See Figure 11.15.) We promote x, making y a child of x and z a child of y, while maintaining the inorder relationships of the nodes in T.

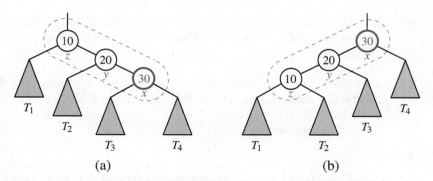

(a)   (b)

Figure 11.15: Zig-zig: (a) before; (b) after. There is another symmetric configuration where x and y are left children.

zig-zag: One of x and y is a left child and the other is a right child. (See Figure 11.16.) In this case, we promote x by making x have y and z as its children, while maintaining the inorder relationships of the nodes in T.

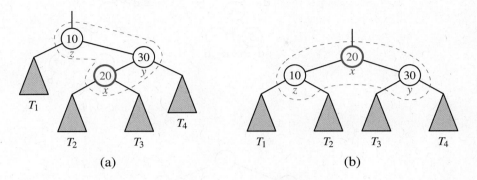

| (a) | (b) |

Figure 11.16: Zig-zag: (a) before; (b) after. There is another symmetric configuration where x is a right child and y is a left child.

zig: x does not have a grandparent. (See Figure 11.17.) In this case, we perform a single rotation to promote x over y, making y a child of x, while maintaining the relative inorder relationships of the nodes in T.

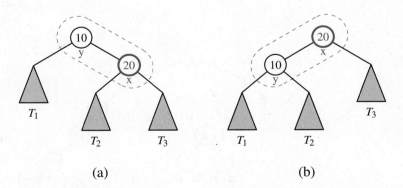

| (a) | (b) |

Figure 11.17: Zig: (a) before; (b) after. There is another symmetric configuration where x is originally a left child of y.

We perform a zig-zig or a zig-zag when x has a grandparent, and we perform a zig when x has a parent but not a grandparent. A ***splaying*** step consists of repeating these restructurings at x until x becomes the root of T. An example of the splaying of a node is shown in Figures 11.18 and 11.19.

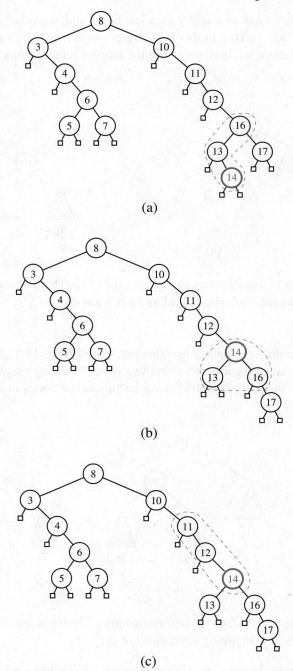

Figure 11.18: Example of splaying a node: (a) splaying the node storing 14 starts with a zig-zag; (b) after the zig-zag; (c) the next step will be a zig-zig. (Continues in Figure 11.19.)

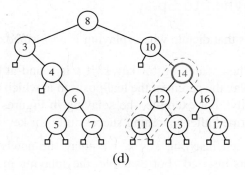

(d)

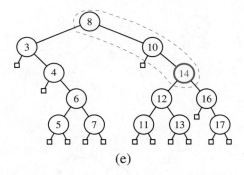

(e)

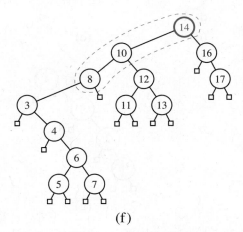

(f)

Figure 11.19: Example of splaying a node:(d) after the zig-zig; (e) the next step is again a zig-zig; (f) after the zig-zig. (Continued from Figure 11.18.)

11.4.2 When to Splay

The rules that dictate when splaying is performed are as follows:

- When searching for key k, if k is found at position p, we splay p, else we splay the parent of the leaf position at which the search terminates unsuccessfully. For example, the splaying in Figures 11.18 and 11.19 would be performed after searching successfully for key 14 or unsuccessfully for key 15.

- When inserting key k, we splay the newly created internal node where k gets inserted. For example, the splaying in Figures 11.18 and 11.19 would be performed if 14 were the newly inserted key. We show a sequence of insertions in a splay tree in Figure 11.20.

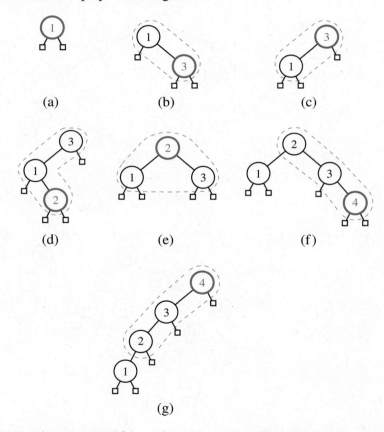

Figure 11.20: A sequence of insertions in a splay tree: (a) initial tree; (b) after inserting 3, but before a zig step; (c) after splaying; (d) after inserting 2, but before a zig-zag step; (e) after splaying; (f) after inserting 4, but before a zig-zig step; (g) after splaying.

- When deleting a key k, we splay the position p that is the parent of the removed node; recall that by the removal algorithm for binary search trees, the
  removed node may be that originally containing k, or a descendant node with
  a replacement key. An example of splaying following a deletion is shown in
  Figure 11.21.

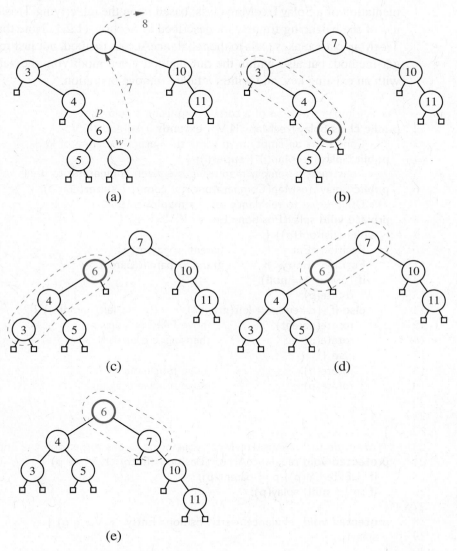

Figure 11.21: Deletion from a splay tree: (a) the deletion of 8 from the root node
is performed by moving to the root the key of its inorder predecessor w, deleting
w, and splaying the parent p of w; (b) splaying p starts with a zig-zig; (c) after the
zig-zig; (d) the next step is a zig; (e) after the zig.

11.4.3   Java Implementation

Although the mathematical analysis of a splay tree's performance is complex (see Section 11.4.4), the *implementation* of splay trees is a rather simple adaptation to a standard binary search tree. Code Fragment 11.13 provides a complete implementation of a SplayTreeMap class, based upon the underlying TreeMap class and use of the balancing framework described in Section 11.2.1. Note that the original TreeMap class makes calls to the rebalanceAccess method, not just from within the get method, but also within the put method when modifying the value associated with an existing key, and within a failed remove operation.

```java
1  /** An implementation of a sorted map using a splay tree. */
2  public class SplayTreeMap<K,V> extends TreeMap<K,V> {
3    /** Constructs an empty map using the natural ordering of keys. */
4    public SplayTreeMap( ) { super( ); }
5    /** Constructs an empty map using the given comparator to order keys. */
6    public SplayTreeMap(Comparator<K> comp) { super(comp); }
7    /** Utility used to rebalance after a map operation. */
8    private void splay(Position<Entry<K,V>> p) {
9      while (!isRoot(p)) {
10       Position<Entry<K,V>> parent = parent(p);
11       Position<Entry<K,V>> grand = parent(parent);
12       if (grand == null)                                            // zig case
13         rotate(p);
14       else if ((parent == left(grand)) == (p == left(parent))) {    // zig-zig case
15         rotate(parent);          // move PARENT upward
16         rotate(p);               // then move p upward
17       } else {                                                      // zig-zag case
18         rotate(p);               // move p upward
19         rotate(p);               // move p upward again
20       }
21     }
22   }
23   // override the various TreeMap rebalancing hooks to perform the appropriate splay
24   protected void rebalanceAccess(Position<Entry<K,V>> p) {
25     if (isExternal(p)) p = parent(p);
26     if (p != null) splay(p);
27   }
28   protected void rebalanceInsert(Position<Entry<K,V>> p) {
29     splay(p);
30   }
31   protected void rebalanceDelete(Position<Entry<K,V>> p) {
32     if (!isRoot(p)) splay(parent(p));
33   }
34 }
```

Code Fragment 11.13: A complete implementation of the SplayTreeMap class.

11.4.4 Amortized Analysis of Splaying ★

After a zig-zig or zig-zag, the depth of position p decreases by two, and after a zig the depth of p decreases by one. Thus, if p has depth d, splaying p consists of a sequence of $\lfloor d/2 \rfloor$ zig-zigs and/or zig-zags, plus one final zig if d is odd. Since a single zig-zig, zig-zag, or zig affects a constant number of nodes, it can be done in $O(1)$ time. Thus, splaying a position p in a binary search tree T takes time $O(d)$, where d is the depth of p in T. In other words, the time for performing a splaying step for a position p is asymptotically the same as the time needed just to reach that position in a top-down search from the root of T.

Worst-Case Time

In the worst case, the overall running time of a search, insertion, or deletion in a splay tree of height h is $O(h)$, since the position we splay might be the deepest position in the tree. Moreover, it is possible for h to be as large as n, as shown in Figure 11.20. Thus, from a worst-case point of view, a splay tree is not an attractive data structure.

In spite of its poor worst-case performance, a splay tree performs well in an amortized sense. That is, in a sequence of intermixed searches, insertions, and deletions, each operation takes on average logarithmic time. We perform the amortized analysis of splay trees using the accounting method.

Amortized Performance of Splay Trees

For our analysis, we note that the time for performing a search, insertion, or deletion is proportional to the time for the associated splaying. So let us consider only splaying time.

Let T be a splay tree with n keys, and let w be a node of T. We define the *size* $n(w)$ of w as the number of nodes in the subtree rooted at w. Note that this definition implies that the size of an internal node is one more than the sum of the sizes of its children. We define the *rank* $r(w)$ of a node w as the logarithm in base 2 of the size of w, that is, $r(w) = \log(n(w))$. Clearly, the root of T has the maximum size, n, and the maximum rank, $\log n$, while each leaf has size 1 and rank 0.

We use cyber-dollars to pay for the work we perform in splaying a position p in T, and we assume that one cyber-dollar pays for a zig, while two cyber-dollars pay for a zig-zig or a zig-zag. Hence, the cost of splaying a position at depth d is d cyber-dollars. We keep a virtual account storing cyber-dollars at each position of T. Note that this account exists only for the purpose of our amortized analysis, and does not need to be included in a data structure implementing the splay tree T.

An Accounting Analysis of Splaying

When we perform a splaying, we pay a certain number of cyber-dollars (the exact value of the payment will be determined at the end of our analysis). We distinguish three cases:

- If the payment is equal to the splaying work, then we use it all to pay for the splaying.

- If the payment is greater than the splaying work, we deposit the excess in the accounts of several nodes.

- If the payment is less than the splaying work, we make withdrawals from the accounts of several nodes to cover the deficiency.

We show below that a payment of $O(\log n)$ cyber-dollars per operation is sufficient to keep the system working, that is, to ensure that each node keeps a nonnegative account balance.

An Accounting Invariant for Splaying

We use a scheme in which transfers are made between the accounts of the nodes to ensure that there will always be enough cyber-dollars to withdraw for paying for splaying work when needed.

In order to use the accounting method to perform our analysis of splaying, we maintain the following invariant:

> **Before and after a splaying, each node w of T has $r(w)$ cyber-dollars in its account.**

Note that the invariant is "financially sound," since it does not require us to make a preliminary deposit to endow a tree with zero keys.

Let $r(T)$ be the sum of the ranks of all the nodes of T. To preserve the invariant after a splaying, we must make a payment equal to the splaying work plus the total change in $r(T)$. We refer to a single zig, zig-zig, or zig-zag operation in a splaying as a splaying **substep**. Also, we denote the rank of a node w of T before and after a splaying substep with $r(w)$ and $r'(w)$, respectively. The following proposition gives an upper bound on the change of $r(T)$ caused by a single splaying substep. We will repeatedly use this lemma in our analysis of a full splaying of a node to the root.

Proposition 11.2: Let δ be the variation of $r(T)$ caused by a single splaying substep (a zig, zig-zig, or zig-zag) for a node x in T. We have the following:

- $\delta \leq 3(r'(x) - r(x)) - 2$ if the substep is a zig-zig or zig-zag.
- $\delta \leq 3(r'(x) - r(x))$ if the substep is a zig.

Justification: We use the fact that, if $a > 0$, $b > 0$, and $c > a + b$,
$$\log a + \log b < 2 \log c - 2. \tag{11.6}$$

Let us consider the change in $r(T)$ caused by each type of splaying substep.

zig-zig: (Recall Figure 11.15.) Since the size of each node is one more than the size of its two children, note that only the ranks of x, y, and z change in a zig-zig operation, where y is the parent of x and z is the parent of y. Also, $r'(x) = r(z)$, $r'(y) \leq r'(x)$, and $r(x) \leq r(y)$. Thus,

$$
\begin{aligned}
\delta &= r'(x) + r'(y) + r'(z) - r(x) - r(y) - r(z) \\
&= r'(y) + r'(z) - r(x) - r(y) \\
&\leq r'(x) + r'(z) - 2r(x). \tag{11.7}
\end{aligned}
$$

Note that $n(x) + n'(z) < n'(x)$. Thus, $r(x) + r'(z) < 2r'(x) - 2$, as per Formula 11.6; that is,

$$r'(z) < 2r'(x) - r(x) - 2.$$

This inequality and Formula 11.7 imply

$$
\begin{aligned}
\delta &\leq r'(x) + (2r'(x) - r(x) - 2) - 2r(x) \\
&\leq 3(r'(x) - r(x)) - 2.
\end{aligned}
$$

zig-zag: (Recall Figure 11.16.) Again, by the definition of size and rank, only the ranks of x, y, and z change, where y denotes the parent of x and z denotes the parent of y. Also, $r(x) < r(y) < r(z) = r'(x)$. Thus,

$$
\begin{aligned}
\delta &= r'(x) + r'(y) + r'(z) - r(x) - r(y) - r(z) \\
&= r'(y) + r'(z) - r(x) - r(y) \\
&\leq r'(y) + r'(z) - 2r(x). \tag{11.8}
\end{aligned}
$$

Note that $n'(y) + n'(z) < n'(x)$; hence, $r'(y) + r'(z) < 2r'(x) - 2$, as per Formula 11.6. Thus,

$$
\begin{aligned}
\delta &\leq 2r'(x) - 2 - 2r(x) \\
&= 2(r'(x) - r(x)) - 2 \leq 3(r'(x) - r(x)) - 2.
\end{aligned}
$$

zig: (Recall Figure 11.17.) In this case, only the ranks of x and y change, where y denotes the parent of x. Also, $r'(y) \leq r(y)$ and $r'(x) \geq r(x)$. Thus,

$$
\begin{aligned}
\delta &= r'(y) + r'(x) - r(y) - r(x) \\
&\leq r'(x) - r(x) \\
&\leq 3(r'(x) - r(x)).
\end{aligned}
$$

∎

Proposition 11.3: *Let T be a splay tree with root t, and let Δ be the total variation of $r(T)$ caused by splaying a node x at depth d. We have*

$$\Delta \le 3(r(t) - r(x)) - d + 2.$$

Justification: Splaying node x consists of $c = \lceil d/2 \rceil$ splaying substeps, each of which is a zig-zig or a zig-zag, except possibly the last one, which is a zig if d is odd. Let $r_0(x) = r(x)$ be the initial rank of x, and for $i = 1, \ldots, c$, let $r_i(x)$ be the rank of x after the ith substep and δ_i be the variation of $r(T)$ caused by the ith substep. By Proposition 11.2, the total variation Δ of $r(T)$ caused by splaying x is

$$
\begin{aligned}
\Delta &= \sum_{i=1}^{c} \delta_i \\
&\le 2 + \sum_{i=1}^{c} 3(r_i(x) - r_{i-1}(x)) - 2 \\
&= 3(r_c(x) - r_0(x)) - 2c + 2 \\
&\le 3(r(t) - r(x)) - d + 2.
\end{aligned}
$$

∎

By Proposition 11.3, if we make a payment of $3(r(t) - r(x)) + 2$ cyber-dollars towards the splaying of node x, we have enough cyber-dollars to maintain the invariant, keeping $r(w)$ cyber-dollars at each node w in T, and pay for the entire splaying work, which costs d cyber-dollars. Since the size of the root t is n, its rank $r(t) = \log n$. Given that $r(x) \ge 0$, the payment to be made for splaying is $O(\log n)$ cyber-dollars. To complete our analysis, we have to compute the cost for maintaining the invariant when a node is inserted or deleted.

When inserting a new node w into a splay tree with n keys, the ranks of all the ancestors of w are increased. Namely, let $w_0, w_1, \ldots, w_d$ be the ancestors of w, where $w_0 = w$, w_i is the parent of w_{i-1}, and w_d is the root. For $i = 1, \ldots, d$, let $n'(w_i)$ and $n(w_i)$ be the size of w_i before and after the insertion, respectively, and let $r'(w_i)$ and $r(w_i)$ be the rank of w_i before and after the insertion. We have

$$n'(w_i) = n(w_i) + 1.$$

Also, since $n(w_i) + 1 \le n(w_{i+1})$, for $i = 0, 1, \ldots, d-1$, we have the following for each i in this range:

$$r'(w_i) = \log(n'(w_i)) = \log(n(w_i) + 1) \le \log(n(w_{i+1})) = r(w_{i+1}).$$

Thus, the total variation of $r(T)$ caused by the insertion is

$$
\begin{aligned}
\sum_{i=1}^{d} (r'(w_i) - r(w_i)) &\le r'(w_d) + \sum_{i=1}^{d-1} (r(w_{i+1}) - r(w_i)) \\
&= r'(w_d) - r(w_0) \\
&\le \log n.
\end{aligned}
$$

Therefore, a payment of $O(\log n)$ cyber-dollars is sufficient to maintain the invariant when a new node is inserted.

When deleting a node w from a splay tree with n keys, the ranks of all the ancestors of w are decreased. Thus, the total variation of $r(T)$ caused by the deletion is negative, and we do not need to make any payment to maintain the invariant when a node is deleted. Therefore, we may summarize our amortized analysis in the following proposition (which is sometimes called the "balance proposition" for splay trees):

Proposition 11.4: *Consider a sequence of m operations on a splay tree, each one a search, insertion, or deletion, starting from a splay tree with zero keys. Also, let n_i be the number of keys in the tree after operation i, and n be the total number of insertions. The total running time for performing the sequence of operations is*

$$O\left(m + \sum_{i=1}^{m} \log n_i\right),$$

which is $O(m \log n)$.

In other words, the amortized running time of performing a search, insertion, or deletion in a splay tree is $O(\log n)$, where n is the size of the splay tree at the time. Thus, a splay tree can achieve logarithmic-time amortized performance for implementing a sorted map ADT. This amortized performance matches the worst-case performance of AVL trees, $(2,4)$ trees, and red-black trees, but it does so using a simple binary tree that does not need any extra balance information stored at each of its nodes. In addition, splay trees have a number of other interesting properties that are not shared by these other balanced search trees. We explore one such additional property in the following proposition (which is sometimes called the "Static Optimality" proposition for splay trees):

Proposition 11.5: *Consider a sequence of m operations on a splay tree, each one a search, insertion, or deletion, starting from a splay tree T with zero keys. Also, let $f(i)$ denote the number of times the entry i is accessed in the splay tree, that is, its frequency, and let n denote the total number of entries. Assuming that each entry is accessed at least once, then the total running time for performing the sequence of operations is*

$$O\left(m + \sum_{i=1}^{n} f(i) \log(m/f(i))\right).$$

We omit the proof of this proposition, but it is not as hard to justify as one might imagine. The remarkable thing is that this proposition states that the amortized running time of accessing an entry i is $O(\log(m/f(i)))$.

11.5   (2,4) Trees

In this section, we will consider a data structure known as a *(2,4) tree*. It is a particular example of a more general structure known as a *multiway search tree*, in which internal nodes may have more than two children. Other forms of multiway search trees will be discussed in Section 15.3.

11.5.1   Multiway Search Trees

Recall that general trees are defined so that internal nodes may have many children. In this section, we discuss how general trees can be used as multiway search trees. Map entries stored in a search tree are pairs of the form (k, v), where k is the *key* and v is the *value* associated with the key.

Definition of a Multiway Search Tree

Let w be a node of an ordered tree. We say that w is a *d-node* if w has d children. We define a multiway search tree to be an ordered tree T that has the following properties, which are illustrated in Figure 11.22a:

- Each internal node of T has at least two children. That is, each internal node is a d-node such that $d \geq 2$.
- Each internal d-node w of T with children $c_1, \ldots, c_d$ stores an ordered set of $d - 1$ key-value pairs $(k_1, v_1), \ldots, (k_{d-1}, v_{d-1})$, where $k_1 \leq \cdots \leq k_{d-1}$.
- Let us conventionally define $k_0 = -\infty$ and $k_d = +\infty$. For each entry (k, v) stored at a node in the subtree of w rooted at c_i, $i = 1, \ldots, d$, we have that $k_{i-1} \leq k \leq k_i$.

That is, if we think of the set of keys stored at w as including the special fictitious keys $k_0 = -\infty$ and $k_d = +\infty$, then a key k stored in the subtree of T rooted at a child node c_i must be "in between" two keys stored at w. This simple viewpoint gives rise to the rule that a d-node stores $d - 1$ regular keys, and it also forms the basis of the algorithm for searching in a multiway search tree.

By the above definition, the external nodes of a multiway search do not store any data and serve only as "placeholders." As with our convention for binary search trees (Section 11.1), these can be replaced by null references in practice. A binary search tree can be viewed as a special case of a multiway search tree, where each internal node stores one entry and has two children.

Whether internal nodes of a multiway tree have two children or many, however, there is an interesting relationship between the number of key-value pairs and the number of external nodes in a multiway search tree.

Proposition 11.6: *An n-entry multiway search tree has $n + 1$ external nodes.*

We leave the justification of this proposition as an exercise (C-11.49).

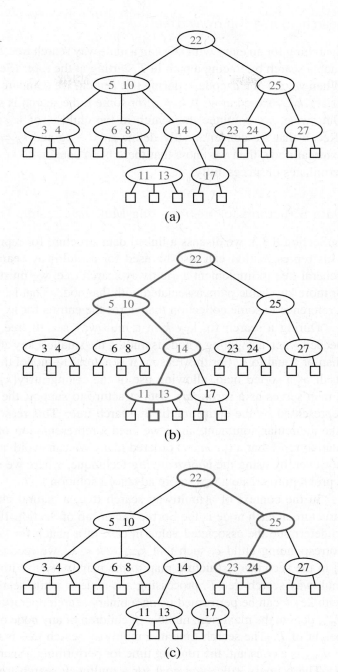

Figure 11.22: (a) A multiway search tree T; (b) search path in T for key 12 (unsuccessful search); (c) search path in T for key 24 (successful search).

Searching in a Multiway Tree

Searching for an entry with key k in a multiway search tree T is simple. We perform such a search by tracing a path in T starting at the root. (See Figure 11.22b and c.) When we are at a d-node w during this search, we compare the key k with the keys $k_1, \ldots, k_{d-1}$ stored at w. If $k = k_i$ for some i, the search is successfully completed. Otherwise, we continue the search in the child c_i of w such that $k_{i-1} < k < k_i$. (Recall that we conventionally define $k_0 = -\infty$ and $k_d = +\infty$.) If we reach an external node, then we know that there is no entry with key k in T, and the search terminates unsuccessfully.

Data Structures for Representing Multiway Search Trees

In Section 8.3.3, we discuss a linked data structure for representing a general tree. This representation can also be used for a multiway search tree. When using a general tree to implement a multiway search tree, we must store at each node one or more key-value pairs associated with that node. That is, we need to store with w a reference to some collection that stores the entries for w.

During a search for key k in a multiway search tree, the primary operation needed when navigating a node is finding the smallest key at that node that is greater than or equal to k. For this reason, it is natural to model the information at a node itself as a sorted map, allowing use of the ceilingEntry(k) method. We say such a map serves as a **secondary** data structure to support the **primary** data structure represented by the entire multiway search tree. This reasoning may at first seem like a circular argument, since we need a representation of a (secondary) ordered map to represent a (primary) ordered map. We can avoid any circular dependence, however, by using the **bootstrapping** technique, where we use a simple solution to a problem to create a new, more advanced solution.

In the context of a multiway search tree, a natural choice for the secondary structure at each node is the SortedTableMap of Section 10.3.1. Because we want to determine the associated value in case of a match for key k, and otherwise the corresponding child c_i such that $k_{i-1} < k < k_i$, we recommend having each key k_i in the secondary structure map to the pair (v_i, c_i). With such a realization of a multiway search tree T, processing a d-node w while searching for an entry of T with key k can be performed using a binary search operation in $O(\log d)$ time. Let $d_{\max}$ denote the maximum number of children of any node of T, and let h denote the height of T. The search time in a multiway search tree is therefore $O(h \log d_{\max})$. If $d_{\max}$ is a constant, the running time for performing a search is $O(h)$.

The primary efficiency goal for a multiway search tree is to keep the height as small as possible. We will next discuss a strategy that caps $d_{\max}$ at 4 while guaranteeing a height h that is logarithmic in n, the total number of entries stored in the map.

11.5.2 (2,4)-Tree Operations

One form of a multiway search tree that keeps the tree balanced while using small secondary data structures at each node is the (**2,4**) *tree*, also known as a 2-4 tree or 2-3-4 tree. This data structure achieves these goals by maintaining two simple properties (see Figure 11.23):

Size Property: Every internal node has at most four children.

Depth Property: All the external nodes have the same depth.

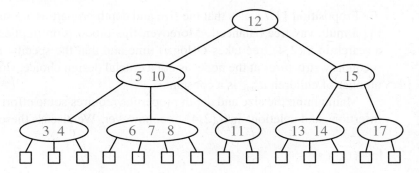

Figure 11.23: A (2,4) tree.

Again, we assume that external nodes are empty and, for the sake of simplicity, we describe our search and update methods assuming that external nodes are real nodes, although this latter requirement is not strictly needed.

Enforcing the size property for (2,4) trees keeps the nodes in the multiway search tree simple. It also gives rise to the alternative name "2-3-4 tree," since it implies that each internal node in the tree has 2, 3, or 4 children. Another implication of this rule is that we can represent the secondary map stored at each internal node using an unordered list or an ordered array, and still achieve $O(1)$-time performance for all operations (since $d_{\max} = 4$). The depth property, on the other hand, enforces an important bound on the height of a (2,4) tree.

Proposition 11.7: *The height of a (2,4) tree storing n entries is $O(\log n)$.*

Justification: Let h be the height of a (2,4) tree T storing n entries. We justify the proposition by showing the claim

$$\frac{1}{2}\log(n+1) \leq h \leq \log(n+1).\qquad(11.9)$$

To justify this claim note first that, by the size property, we can have at most 4 nodes at depth 1, at most 4^2 nodes at depth 2, and so on. Thus, the number of external nodes in T is at most 4^h. Likewise, by the depth property and the definition of a $(2,4)$ tree, we must have at least 2 nodes at depth 1, at least 2^2 nodes at depth 2, and so on. Thus, the number of external nodes in T is at least 2^h. In addition, by Proposition 11.6, the number of external nodes in T is $n+1$. Therefore, we obtain

$$2^h \leq n+1 \leq 4^h.$$

Taking the logarithm in base 2 of the terms for the above inequalities, we get that

$$h \leq \log(n+1) \leq 2h,$$

which justifies our claim (Formula 11.9) when terms are rearranged.   ∎

Proposition 11.7 states that the size and depth properties are sufficient for keeping a multiway tree balanced. Moreover, this proposition implies that performing a search in a $(2,4)$ tree takes $O(\log n)$ time and that the specific realization of the secondary structures at the nodes is not a crucial design choice, since the maximum number of children d_{max} is a constant.

Maintaining the size and depth properties requires some effort after performing insertions and deletions in a $(2,4)$ tree, however. We discuss these operations next.

Insertion

To insert a new entry (k,v), with key k, into a $(2,4)$ tree T, we first perform a search for k. Assuming that T has no entry with key k, this search terminates unsuccessfully at an external node z. Let w be the parent of z. We insert the new entry into node w and add a new child y (an external node) to w on the left of z.

Our insertion method preserves the depth property, since we add a new external node at the same level as existing external nodes. Nevertheless, it may violate the size property. Indeed, if a node w was previously a 4-node, then it would become a 5-node after the insertion, which causes the tree T to no longer be a $(2,4)$ tree. This type of violation of the size property is called an **overflow** at node w, and it must be resolved in order to restore the properties of a $(2,4)$ tree. Let $c_1, \ldots, c_5$ be the children of w, and let $k_1, \ldots, k_4$ be the keys stored at w. To remedy the overflow at node w, we perform a **split** operation on w as follows (see Figure 11.24):

- Replace w with two nodes w' and w'', where
  - w' is a 3-node with children c_1, c_2, c_3 storing keys k_1 and k_2.
  - w'' is a 2-node with children c_4, c_5 storing key k_4.
- If w is the root of T, create a new root node u; else, let u be the parent of w.
- Insert key k_3 into u and make w' and w'' children of u, so that if w was child i of u, then w' and w'' become children i and $i+1$ of u, respectively.

As a consequence of a split operation on node w, a new overflow may occur at the parent u of w. If such an overflow occurs, it triggers in turn a split at node u. (See Figure 11.25.) A split operation either eliminates the overflow or propagates it into the parent of the current node. We show a sequence of insertions in a $(2,4)$ tree in Figure 11.26.

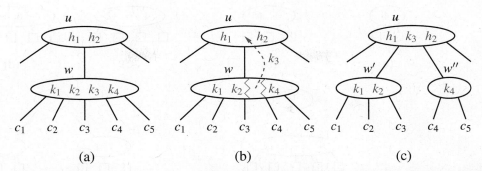

Figure 11.24: A node split: (a) overflow at a 5-node w; (b) the third key of w inserted into the parent u of w; (c) node w replaced with a 3-node w' and a 2-node w''.

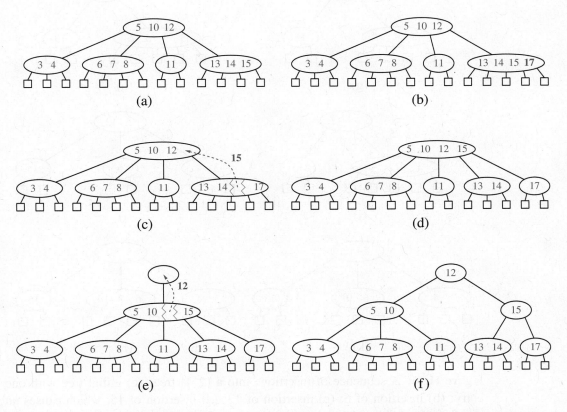

Figure 11.25: An insertion in a (2,4) tree that causes a cascading split: (a) before the insertion; (b) insertion of 17, causing an overflow; (c) a split; (d) after the split a new overflow occurs; (e) another split, creating a new root node; (f) final tree.

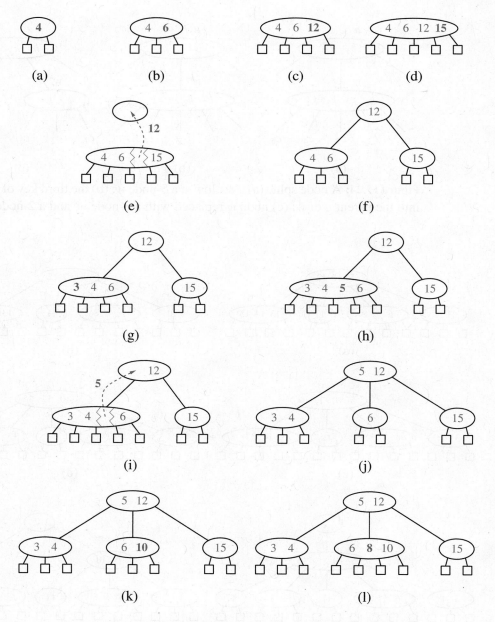

Figure 11.26: A sequence of insertions into a (2,4) tree: (a) initial tree with one entry; (b) insertion of 6; (c) insertion of 12; (d) insertion of 15, which causes an overflow; (e) split, which causes the creation of a new root node; (f) after the split; (g) insertion of 3; (h) insertion of 5, which causes an overflow; (i) split; (j) after the split; (k) insertion of 10; (l) insertion of 8.

Analysis of Insertion in a (2,4) Tree

Because $d_{\max}$ is at most 4, the original search for the placement of new key k uses $O(1)$ time at each level, and thus $O(\log n)$ time overall, since the height of the tree is $O(\log n)$ by Proposition 11.7.

The modifications to a single node to insert a new key and child can be implemented to run in $O(1)$ time, as can a single split operation. The number of cascading split operations is bounded by the height of the tree, and so that phase of the insertion process also runs in $O(\log n)$ time. Therefore, the total time to perform an insertion in a $(2,4)$ tree is $O(\log n)$.

Deletion

Let us now consider the removal of an entry with key k from a $(2,4)$ tree T. We begin such an operation by performing a search in T for an entry with key k. Removing an entry from a $(2,4)$ tree can always be reduced to the case where the entry to be removed is stored at a node w whose children are external nodes. Suppose, for instance, that the entry with key k that we wish to remove is stored in the ith entry (k_i, v_i) at a node z that has internal children. In this case, we swap the entry (k_i, v_i) with an appropriate entry that is stored at a node w with external children as follows (see Figure 11.27d):

1. We find the rightmost internal node w in the subtree rooted at the ith child of z, noting that the children of node w are all external nodes.
2. We swap the entry (k_i, v_i) at z with the last entry of w.

Once we ensure that the entry to remove is stored at a node w with only external children (because either it was already at w or we swapped it into w), we simply remove the entry from w and remove the external node that is the ith child of w.

Removing an entry (and a child) from a node w as described above preserves the depth property, for we always remove an external child from a node w with only external children. However, in removing such an external node, we may violate the size property at w. Indeed, if w was previously a 2-node, then it becomes a 1-node with no entries after the removal (Figure 11.27a and d), which is not allowed in a $(2,4)$ tree. This type of violation of the size property is called an **underflow** at node w. To remedy an underflow, we check whether an immediate sibling of w is a 3-node or a 4-node. If we find such a sibling s, then we perform a **transfer** operation, in which we move a child of s to w, a key of s to the parent u of w and s, and a key of u to w. (See Figure 11.27b and c.) If w has only one sibling, or if both immediate siblings of w are 2-nodes, then we perform a **fusion** operation, in which we merge w with a sibling, creating a new node w', and move a key from the parent u of w to w'. (See Figure 11.27e and f.)

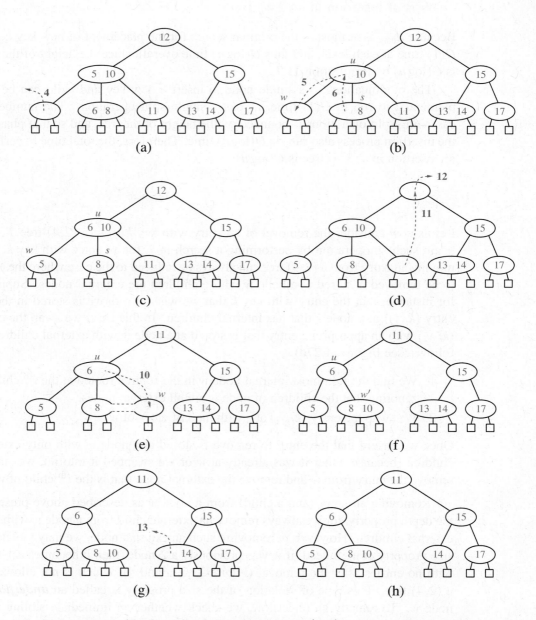

Figure 11.27: A sequence of removals from a (2,4) tree: (a) removal of 4, causing an underflow; (b) a transfer operation; (c) after the transfer operation; (d) removal of 12, causing an underflow; (e) a fusion operation; (f) after the fusion operation; (g) removal of 13; (h) after removing 13.

A fusion operation at node w may cause a new underflow to occur at the parent u of w, which in turn triggers a transfer or fusion at u. (See Figure 11.28.) Hence, the number of fusion operations is bounded by the height of the tree, which is $O(\log n)$ by Proposition 11.7. If an underflow propagates all the way up to the root, then the root is simply deleted. (See Figure 11.28c and d.)

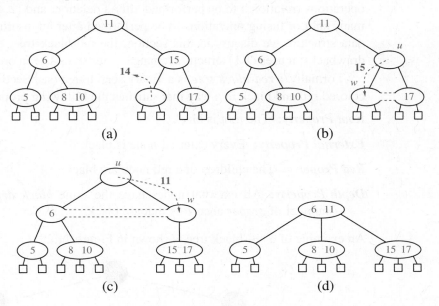

Figure 11.28: A propagating sequence of fusions in a $(2,4)$ tree: (a) removal of 14, which causes an underflow; (b) fusion, which causes another underflow; (c) second fusion operation, which causes the root to be removed; (d) final tree.

Performance of (2,4) Trees

The asymptotic performance of a $(2,4)$ tree is identical to that of an AVL tree (see Table 11.2) in terms of the sorted map ADT, with guaranteed logarithmic bounds for most operations. The time complexity analysis for a $(2,4)$ tree having n key-value pairs is based on the following:

- The height of a $(2,4)$ tree storing n entries is $O(\log n)$, by Proposition 11.7.
- A split, transfer, or fusion operation takes $O(1)$ time.
- A search, insertion, or removal of an entry visits $O(\log n)$ nodes.

Thus, $(2,4)$ trees provide for fast map search and update operations. $(2,4)$ trees also have an interesting relationship to the data structure we discuss next.

11.6   Red-Black Trees

Although AVL trees and $(2,4)$ trees have a number of nice properties, they also have some disadvantages. For instance, AVL trees may require many restructure operations (rotations) to be performed after a deletion, and $(2,4)$ trees may require many split or fusing operations to be performed after an insertion or removal. The data structure we discuss in this section, the red-black tree, does not have these drawbacks; it uses $O(1)$ structural changes after an update in order to stay balanced.

Formally, a ***red-black tree*** is a binary search tree (see Section 11.1) with nodes colored red and black in a way that satisfies the following properties:

Root Property: The root is black.

External Property: Every external node is black.

Red Property: The children of a red node are black.

Depth Property: All external nodes have the same ***black depth***, defined as the number of *proper* ancestors that are black.

An example of a red-black tree is shown in Figure 11.29.

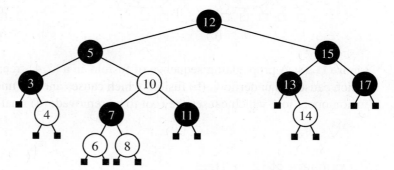

Figure 11.29: An example of a red-black tree, with "red" nodes drawn in white. The common black depth for this tree is 3.

We can make the red-black tree definition more intuitive by noting an interesting correspondence between red-black trees and $(2,4)$ trees. Namely, given a red-black tree, we can construct a corresponding $(2,4)$ tree by merging every red node w into its parent, storing the entry from w at its parent, and with the children of w becoming ordered children of the parent. For example, the red-black tree in Figure 11.29 corresponds to the $(2,4)$ tree from Figure 11.23, as illustrated in Figure 11.30. The depth property of the red-black tree corresponds to the depth property of the $(2,4)$ tree since exactly one black node of the red-black tree contributes to each node of the corresponding $(2,4)$ tree.

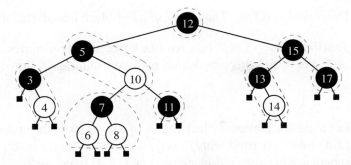

Figure 11.30: An illustration of the correspondance between the red-black tree of Figure 11.29 and the (2,4) tree of Figure 11.23, based on the highlighted grouping of red nodes with their black parents.

Conversely, we can transform any (2,4) tree into a corresponding red-black tree by coloring each node w black and then performing the following transformations, as illustrated in Figure 11.31.

- If w is a 2-node, then keep the (black) children of w as is.

- If w is a 3-node, then create a new red node y, give w's last two (black) children to y, and make the first child of w and y be the two children of w.

- If w is a 4-node, then create two new red nodes y and z, give w's first two (black) children to y, give w's last two (black) children to z, and make y and z be the two children of w.

Notice that a red node always has a black parent in this construction.

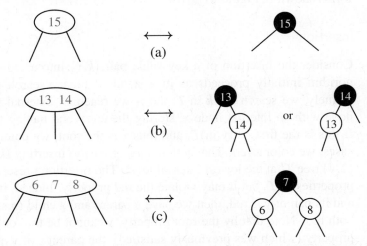

Figure 11.31: Correspondence between nodes of a (2,4) tree and a red-black tree: (a) 2-node; (b) 3-node; (c) 4-node.

Proposition 11.8: *The height of a red-black tree storing n entries is $O(\log n)$.*

Justification: Let T be a red-black tree storing n entries, and let h be the height of T. We justify this proposition by establishing the following fact:

$$\log(n+1) \le h \le 2\log(n+1).$$

Let d be the common black depth of all the external nodes of T. Let T' be the $(2,4)$ tree associated with T, and let h' be the height of T'. Because of the correspondence between red-black trees and $(2,4)$ trees, we know that $h' = d$. Hence, by Proposition 11.7, $d = h' \le \log(n+1)$. By the red property, $h \le 2d$. Thus, we obtain $h \le 2\log(n+1)$. The other inequality, $\log(n+1) \le h$, follows from Proposition 8.7 and the fact that T has n internal nodes. ∎

11.6.1 Red-Black Tree Operations

The algorithm for searching in a red-black tree T is the same as that for a standard binary search tree (Section 11.1). Thus, searching in a red-black tree takes time proportional to the height of the tree, which is $O(\log n)$ by Proposition 11.8.

The correspondence between $(2,4)$ trees and red-black trees provides important intuition that we will use in our discussion of how to perform updates in red-black trees; in fact, the update algorithms for red-black trees can seem mysteriously complex without this intuition. Split and fuse operations of a $(2,4)$ tree will be effectively mimicked by recoloring neighboring red-black tree nodes. A rotation within a red-black tree will be used to change orientations of a 3-node between the two forms shown in Figure 11.31(b).

Insertion

Consider the insertion of a key-value pair (k,v) into a red-black tree T. The algorithm initially proceeds as in a standard binary search tree (Section 11.1.2). Namely, we search for k in T and if we reach an external node, we replace this node with an internal node x, storing the entry and having two external children. If this is the first entry in T, and thus x is the root, we color it black. In all other cases, we color x red. That action corresponds to inserting (k,v) into a node of the $(2,4)$ tree T' at the lowest internal level. The insertion preserves the root and depth properties of T, but it may violate the red property. Indeed, if x is not the root of T and its parent y is red, then we have a parent and a child (namely, y and x) that are both red. Note that by the root property, y cannot be the root of T, and by the red property (which was previously satisfied), the parent z of y must be black. Since x and its parent are red, but x's grandparent z is black, we call this violation of the red property a **double red** at node x. To remedy a double red, we consider two cases.

Case 1: *The Sibling s of y is Black.* (See Figure 11.32.) In this case, the double red denotes the fact that we have added the new node to a corresponding 3-node of the $(2,4)$ tree T', effectively creating a malformed 4-node. This formation has one red node, y, that is the parent of another red node, x; we want the two red nodes to be siblings instead. To fix this problem, we perform a ***trinode restructuring*** of T. The trinode restructuring (introduced in Section 11.2) is done by the operation restructure(x), which consists of the following steps (see again Figure 11.32):

- Take node x, its parent y, and grandparent z, and temporarily relabel them as a, b, and c, in left-to-right order, so that a, b, and c will be visited in this order by an inorder tree traversal.
- Replace the grandparent z with the node labeled b, and make nodes a and c the children of b, keeping inorder relationships unchanged.

After performing the restructure(x) operation, we color b black and we color a and c red. Thus, the restructuring eliminates the double-red problem. Notice that the portion of any path through the restructured part of the tree is incident to exactly one black node, both before and after the trinode restructuring. Therefore, the black depth of the tree is unaffected.

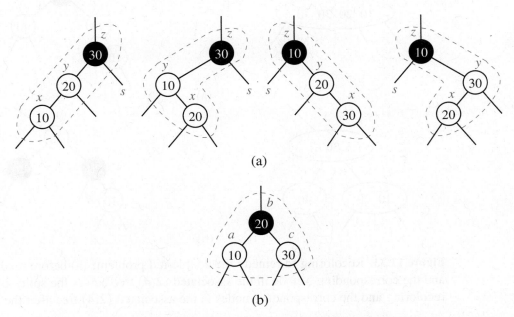

(a)

(b)

Figure 11.32: Restructuring a red-black tree to remedy a double red: (a) the four configurations for x, y, and z before restructuring; (b) after restructuring.

Case 2: *The Sibling s of y is Red*. (See Figure 11.33.) In this case, the double red denotes an overflow in the corresponding $(2,4)$ tree T'. To fix the problem, we perform the equivalent of a split operation. Namely, we do a ***recoloring***: we color y and s black and their parent z red (unless z is the root, in which case, it remains black). Notice that unless z is the root, the portion of any path through the affected part of the tree is incident to exactly one black node, both before and after the recoloring. Therefore, the black depth of the tree is unaffected by the recoloring unless z is the root, in which case it is increased by one.

However, it is possible that the double-red problem reappears after such a recoloring, albeit higher up in the tree T, since z may have a red parent. If the double-red problem reappears at z, then we repeat the consideration of the two cases at z. Thus, a recoloring either eliminates the double-red problem at node x, or propagates it to the grandparent z of x. We continue going up T performing recolorings until we finally resolve the double-red problem (with either a final recoloring or a trinode restructuring). Thus, the number of recolorings caused by an insertion is no more than half the height of tree T, that is, $O(\log n)$ by Proposition 11.8.

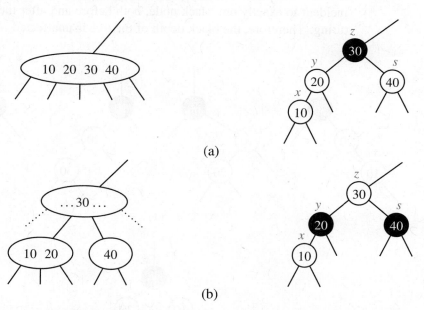

(a)

(b)

Figure 11.33: Recoloring to remedy the double-red problem: (a) before recoloring and the corresponding 5-node in the associated $(2,4)$ tree before the split; (b) after recoloring and the corresponding nodes in the associated $(2,4)$ tree after the split.

As further examples, Figures 11.34 and 11.35 show a sequence of insertion operations in a red-black tree.

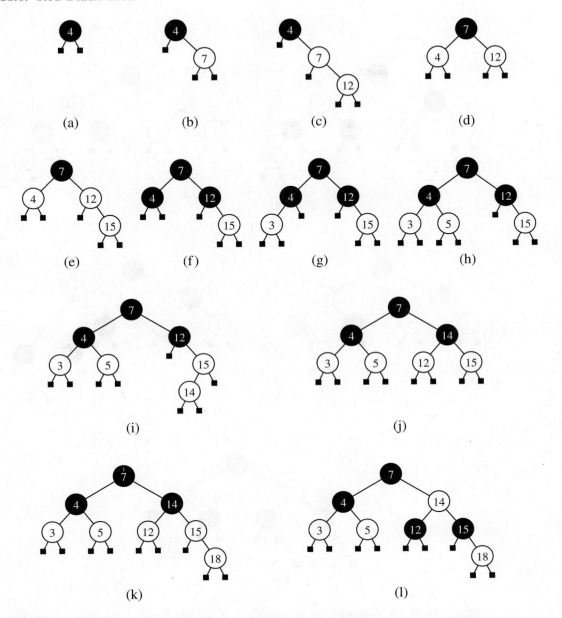

Figure 11.34: A sequence of insertions in a red-black tree: (a) initial tree; (b) insertion of 7; (c) insertion of 12, which causes a double red; (d) after restructuring; (e) insertion of 15, which causes a double red; (f) after recoloring (the root remains black); (g) insertion of 3; (h) insertion of 5; (i) insertion of 14, which causes a double red; (j) after restructuring; (k) insertion of 18, which causes a double red; (l) after recoloring. (Continues in Figure 11.35.)

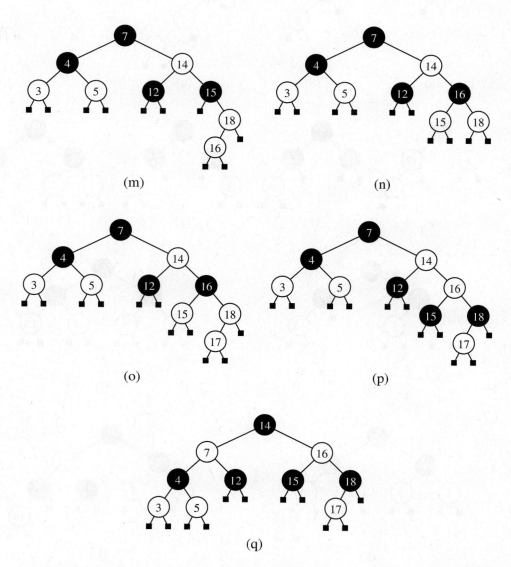

Figure 11.35: A sequence of insertions in a red-black tree (continued from Figure 11.34): (m) insertion of 16, which causes a double red; (n) after restructuring; (o) insertion of 17, which causes a double red; (p) after recoloring there is again a double red, to be handled by a restructuring; (q) after restructuring.

Deletion

Deleting an entry with key k from a red-black tree T initially proceeds as for a binary search tree (Section 11.1.2). Structurally, the process results in the removal of an internal node (either that originally containing key k or its inorder predecessor) together with a child that is external, and the promotion of its other child.

If the removed internal node was red, this structural change does not affect the black depths of any paths in the tree, nor introduce any red violations, and so the resulting tree remains a valid red-black tree. In the corresponding $(2,4)$ tree T', this case denotes the shrinking of a 4-node or 3-node. If the removed internal node was black, it must have had black height 1, and therefore either both of its children were external, or it had one red child that was an internal node with two external children. In the latter case, the removed node represents the black part of a corresponding 3-node, and we restore the red-black properties by recoloring the promoted child to be black.

The most complex case is when the removed node was black and had two external children. In the corresponding $(2,4)$ tree, this denotes the removal of an entry from a 2-node. Without rebalancing, such a change results in a deficit of one for the black depth of the external position p that is the promoted child of the deleted internal node. To preserve the depth property, we temporarily assign the promoted leaf a fictitious ***double black*** color. A double black in T denotes an underflow in the corresponding $(2,4)$ tree T'. To remedy a double-black problem at an arbitrary position p, we will consider three cases.

Case 1: *The Sibling y of p is Black and has a Red Child x.* (See Figure 11.36.)

We perform a ***trinode restructuring***, as originally described in Section 11.2. The operation restructure(x) takes the node x, its parent y, and grandparent z, labels them temporarily left to right as a, b, and c, and replaces z with the node labeled b, making it the parent of the other two. We color a and c black, and give b the former color of z.

Notice that the path to p in the result includes one additional black node after the restructure, while the number of black nodes on paths to any of the other three subtrees illustrated in Figure 11.36 remains unchanged. Therefore, we return p to be colored (regular) black, and the double-black problem is eliminated.

Resolving this case corresponds to a transfer operation in the $(2,4)$ tree T' between two children of node z. The fact that y has a red child assures us that it represents either a 3-node or a 4-node. In effect, the entry previously stored at z is demoted to become a new 2-node to resolve the deficiency, while an entry stored at y or its child is promoted to take the place of the entry previously stored at z.

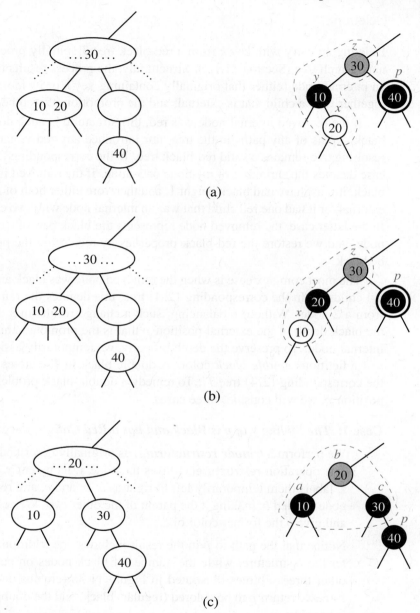

(a)

(b)

(c)

Figure 11.36: Restructuring of a red-black tree to remedy the double-black problem: (a) and (b) configurations before the restructuring, where p is a right child and the associated nodes in the corresponding $(2,4)$ tree before the transfer (two other symmetric configurations where p is a left child are possible); (c) configuration after the restructuring and the associated nodes in the corresponding $(2,4)$ tree after the transfer. The gray color for node z in parts (a) and (b) and for node b in part (c) denotes the fact that this node may be colored either red or black.

Case 2: *The Sibling y of p is Black and Both Children of y are Black.*

We do a ***recoloring***, beginning by changing the color of p from double black to black and the color of y from black to red. This does not create any red violation, because both children of y are black. To counteract the decrease in black depth for paths passing through y or p, we consider the common parent of p and y, which we denote as z. If z is red, we color it black and the problem has been resolved (see Figure 11.37a). If z is black, we color it ***double black***, thereby propagating the problem higher up the tree (see Figure 11.37b).

Resolving this case corresponds to a fusion operation in the corresponding $(2, 4)$ tree T', as y must represent a 2-node. The case where the problem propagates upward is when parent z also represents a 2-node.

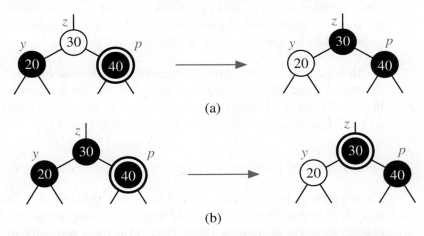

Figure 11.37: A recoloring operation, which has neutral effect on the black depth for paths: (a) when z is originally red, the recoloring resolves the double-black problem, ending the process; (b) when z is originally black, it becomes double-black, requiring a cascading remedy.

Case 3: *Sibling y of p is Red.* (See Figure 11.38.)

Let z denote the common parent of y and p, and note that z must be black, because y is red. The combination of y and z represents a 3-node in the corresponding $(2, 4)$ tree T'. In this case, we perform a rotation about y and z, and then recolor y black and z red. This denotes a reorientation of a 3-node in the corresponding $(2, 4)$ tree T'.

We now reconsider the double-black problem at p. After the adjustment, the sibling of p is black, and either Case 1 or Case 2 applies. Furthermore, the next application will be the last, because Case 1 is always terminal and Case 2 will be terminal given that the parent of p is now red.

Figure 11.38: A rotation and recoloring about red node y and black node z in the presence of a double-black problem (a symmetric configuration is possible). This amounts to a change of orientation in the corresponding 3-node of a $(2,4)$ tree. This operation does not affect the black depth of any paths through this portion of the tree, but after the operation, one of the other resolutions to the double-black problem may be applied, as the sibling of p will be black.

In Figure 11.39, we show a sequence of deletions on a red-black tree. We illustrate a Case 1 restructuring in parts (c) and (d). We illustrate a Case 2 recoloring in parts (f) and (g). Finally, we show an example of a Case 3 rotation between parts (i) and (j), concluding with a Case 2 recoloring in part (k).

Performance of Red-Black Trees

The asymptotic performance of a red-black tree is identical to that of an AVL tree or a $(2,4)$ tree in terms of the sorted map ADT, with guaranteed logarithmic time bounds for most operations. (See Table 11.2 for a summary of the AVL performance.) The primary advantage of a red-black tree is that an insertion or deletion requires only a ***constant number of restructuring operations***. (This is in contrast to AVL trees and $(2,4)$ trees, both of which require a logarithmic number of structural changes per map operation in the worst case.) That is, an insertion or deletion in a red-black tree requires logarithmic time for a search, and may require a logarithmic number of recoloring operations that cascade upward. We formalize these facts with the following propositions.

Proposition 11.9: *The insertion of an entry in a red-black tree storing n entries can be done in $O(\log n)$ time and requires $O(\log n)$ recolorings and at most one trinode restructuring.*

Proposition 11.10: *The algorithm for deleting an entry from a red-black tree with n entries takes $O(\log n)$ time and performs $O(\log n)$ recolorings and at most two restructuring operations.*

The proofs of these propositions are left as Exercises R-11.26 and R-11.27.

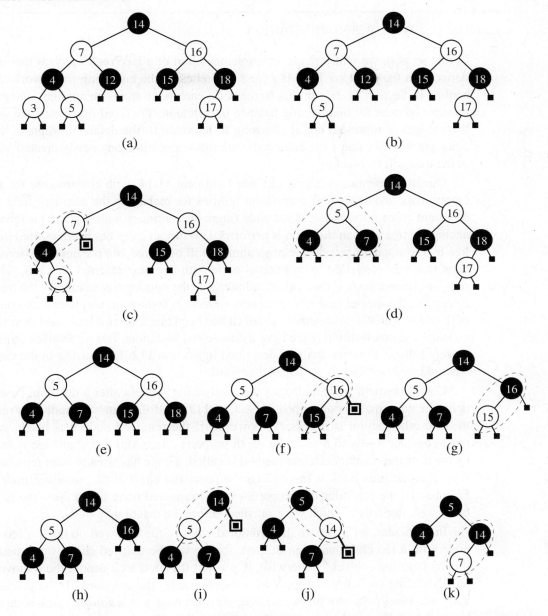

Figure 11.39: A sequence of deletions from a red-black tree: (a) initial tree; (b) removal of 3; (c) removal of 12, causing a black deficit to the right of 7 (handled by restructuring); (d) after restructuring; (e) removal of 17; (f) removal of 18, causing a black deficit to the right of 16 (handled by recoloring); (g) after recoloring; (h) removal of 15; (i) removal of 16, causing a black deficit to the right of 14 (handled initially by a rotation); (j) after the rotation the black deficit needs to be handled by a recoloring; (k) after the recoloring.

11.6.2   Java Implementation

In this section, we will provide an implementation of a RBTreeMap class that inherits from the standard TreeMap class and relies on the balancing framework described in Section 11.2.1. In that framework, each node stores an auxiliary integer that can be used for maintaining balance information. For a red-black tree, we use that integer to represent color, choosing to let value 0 (the default) designate the color black, and value 1 the color red; with this convention, any newly created leaf in the tree will be black.

Our implementation begins in Code Fragment 11.14, with constructors for an empty map, and a series of convenient utilities for managing the auxiliary field to represent color information. That code fragment continues with support for rebalancing the tree after an insertion is performed. When an entry has been inserted in a tree by the standard search-tree algorithm, it will be stored at a previously external node that was converted to an internal node with two new external children. The rebalanceInsert hook is then called, allowing us the opportunity to modify the tree. Except for the special case where the new element is at the root, we change the color of the node with the new element to red (it had been black when a leaf), and then we consider the possibility that we have a double-red violation. The resolveRed utility closely follows the case analysis described in Section 11.6.1, recurring in the case when the red violation is propagated upward.

Code Fragment 11.15 manages the rebalancing process after a deletion, based upon the case analysis described in Section 11.6.1. If the removed node was red, then no other action is necessary; however, if the removed node was black, we must consider a way to restore the depth property. An additional challenge is that by the time the rebalanceDelete method is called, a node has already been removed from the tree (this hook is invoked on the promoted *child* of that removed node). Fortunately, we can infer the properties of the removed node based upon the red-black tree properties, which were satisfied before the deletion.

In particular, let p denote the promoted child of the removed node. If a black node with a red child has been deleted, then p will be that red child; we remedy this by coloring p black. Otherwise, if p is not the root, let s denote the removed node's sibling (which will appear as p's sibling after the deletion). If the deleted node was black with two black children, we must treat p as a ***double black*** node to be remedied. This is the case if, and only if, its sibling's subtree has a black internal node (because the red-black depth property was satisfied prior to the deletion). We therefore test whether s is a black internal node, or a red internal node with an internal node as a child (which must be black due to the red property of the tree).

We are able to detect the double-black problem within the rebalanceDelete method of Code Fragment 11.15, and we rely on the recursive remedyDoubleBlack method of that code fragment to resolve the problem.

```
1   /** An implementation of a sorted map using a red-black tree. */
2   public class RBTreeMap<K,V> extends TreeMap<K,V> {
3     /** Constructs an empty map using the natural ordering of keys. */
4     public RBTreeMap() { super(); }
5     /** Constructs an empty map using the given comparator to order keys. */
6     public RBTreeMap(Comparator<K> comp) { super(comp); }
7     // we use the inherited aux field with convention that 0=black and 1=red
8     // (note that new leaves will be black by default, as aux=0)
9     private boolean isBlack(Position<Entry<K,V>> p) { return tree.getAux(p)==0;}
10    private boolean isRed(Position<Entry<K,V>> p) { return tree.getAux(p)==1; }
11    private void makeBlack(Position<Entry<K,V>> p) { tree.setAux(p, 0); }
12    private void makeRed(Position<Entry<K,V>> p) { tree.setAux(p, 1); }
13    private void setColor(Position<Entry<K,V>> p, boolean toRed) {
14      tree.setAux(p, toRed ? 1 : 0);
15    }
16    /** Overrides the TreeMap rebalancing hook that is called after an insertion. */
17    protected void rebalanceInsert(Position<Entry<K,V>> p) {
18      if (!isRoot(p)) {
19        makeRed(p);                          // the new internal node is initially colored red
20        resolveRed(p);                       // but this may cause a double-red problem
21      }
22    }
23    /** Remedies potential double-red violation above red position p. */
24    private void resolveRed(Position<Entry<K,V>> p) {
25      Position<Entry<K,V>> parent,uncle,middle,grand; // used in case analysis
26      parent = parent(p);
27      if (isRed(parent)) {                              // double-red problem exists
28        uncle = sibling(parent);
29        if (isBlack(uncle)) {                           // Case 1: misshapen 4-node
30          middle = restructure(p);                      // do trinode restructuring
31          makeBlack(middle);
32          makeRed(left(middle));
33          makeRed(right(middle));
34        } else {                                        // Case 2: overfull 5-node
35          makeBlack(parent);                            // perform recoloring
36          makeBlack(uncle);
37          grand = parent(parent);
38          if (!isRoot(grand)) {
39            makeRed(grand);                             // grandparent becomes red
40            resolveRed(grand);                          // recur at red grandparent
41          }
42        }
43      }
44    }
```

Code Fragment 11.14: The RBTreeMap class. (Continues in Code Fragment 11.15.)

```
45   /** Overrides the TreeMap rebalancing hook that is called after a deletion. */
46   protected void rebalanceDelete(Position<Entry<K,V>> p) {
47     if (isRed(p))                                          // deleted parent was black
48       makeBlack(p);                                        // so this restores black depth
49     else if (!isRoot(p)) {
50       Position<Entry<K,V>> sib = sibling(p);
51       if (isInternal(sib) && (isBlack(sib) || isInternal(left(sib))))
52         remedyDoubleBlack(p);              // sib's subtree has nonzero black height
53     }
54   }
55
56   /** Remedies a presumed double-black violation at the given (nonroot) position. */
57   private void remedyDoubleBlack(Position<Entry<K,V>> p) {
58     Position<Entry<K,V>> z = parent(p);
59     Position<Entry<K,V>> y = sibling(p);
60     if (isBlack(y)) {
61       if (isRed(left(y)) || isRed(right(y))) {            // Case 1: trinode restructuring
62         Position<Entry<K,V>> x = (isRed(left(y)) ? left(y) : right(y));
63         Position<Entry<K,V>> middle = restructure(x);
64         setColor(middle, isRed(z)); // root of restructured subtree gets z's old color
65         makeBlack(left(middle));
66         makeBlack(right(middle));
67       } else {                                             // Case 2: recoloring
68         makeRed(y);
69         if (isRed(z))
70           makeBlack(z);                                    // problem is resolved
71         else if (!isRoot(z))
72           remedyDoubleBlack(z);                            // propagate the problem
73       }
74     } else {                                               // Case 3: reorient 3-node
75       rotate(y);
76       makeBlack(y);
77       makeRed(z);
78       remedyDoubleBlack(p);                                // restart the process at p
79     }
80   }
81 }
```

Code Fragment 11.15: Support for deletion in the RBTreeMap class (continued from Code Fragment 11.14).

11.7   Exercises

Reinforcement

R-11.1   If we insert the entries $(1,A)$, $(2,B)$, $(3,C)$, $(4,D)$, and $(5,E)$, in this order, into an initially empty binary search tree, what will it look like?

R-11.2   Insert, into an empty binary search tree, entries with keys 30, 40, 24, 58, 48, 26, 11, 13 (in this order). Draw the tree after each insertion.

R-11.3   How many different binary search trees can store the keys $\{1,2,3\}$?

R-11.4   Dr. Amongus claims that the order in which a fixed set of entries is inserted into a binary search tree does not matter—the same tree results every time. Give a small example that proves he is wrong.

R-11.5   Dr. Amongus claims that the order in which a fixed set of entries is inserted into an AVL tree does not matter—the same AVL tree results every time. Give a small example that proves he is wrong.

R-11.6   Our implementation of the treeSearch utility, from Code Fragment 11.3, relies on recursion. For a large unbalanced tree, it is possible that Java's call stack will reach its limit due to the recursive depth. Give an alternative implementation of that method that does not rely on the use of recursion.

R-11.7   Does the trinode restructuring in Figure 11.11 rely on a single or double rotation? What about the restructuring in Figure 11.13?

R-11.8   Draw the AVL tree resulting from the insertion of an entry with key 52 into the AVL tree of Figure 11.13b.

R-11.9   Draw the AVL tree resulting from the removal of the entry with key 62 from the AVL tree of Figure 11.13b.

R-11.10   Explain why performing a rotation in an n-node binary tree when using the array-based representation of Section 8.3.2 takes $\Omega(n)$ time.

R-11.11   Consider a deletion operation in an AVL tree that triggers a trinode restructuring for the case in which both children of the node denoted as y have equal heights. Give a schematic figure, in the style of Figure 11.12, showing the tree before and after the deletion. What is the net effect of the height of the rebalanced subtree due to the operation?

R-11.12   Repeat the previous problem, considering the case in which y's children start with different heights.

R-11.13   The rules for a deletion in an AVL tree specifically require that when the two subtrees of the node denoted as y have equal height, child x should be chosen to be "aligned" with y (so that x and y are both left children or both right children). To better understand this requirement, repeat Exercise R-11.11 assuming we picked the misaligned choice of x. Why might there be a problem in restoring the AVL property with that choice?

R-11.14 What does a splay tree look like if its entries are accessed in increasing order by their keys?

R-11.15 Perform the following sequence of operations in an initially empty splay tree and draw the tree after each set of operations.

    a. Insert keys 0, 2, 4, 6, 8, 10, 12, 14, 16, 18, in this order.
    b. Search for keys 1, 3, 5, 7, 9, 11, 13, 15, 17, 19, in this order.
    c. Delete keys 0, 2, 4, 6, 8, 10, 12, 14, 16, 18, in this order.

R-11.16 The splay tree does not have good performance for the sorted map operations, because those methods lack calls to the rebalanceAccess hook. Reimplement TreeMap to include such calls.

R-11.17 Is the search tree of Figure 11.22(a) a $(2,4)$ tree? Why or why not?

R-11.18 An alternative way of performing a split at a node w in a $(2,4)$ tree is to partition w into w' and w'', with w' being a 2-node and w'' a 3-node. Which of the keys k_1, k_2, k_3, or k_4 do we store at w's parent? Why?

R-11.19 Dr. Amongus claims that a $(2,4)$ tree storing a set of entries will always have the same structure, regardless of the order in which the entries are inserted. Show that he is wrong.

R-11.20 Draw four different red-black trees that correspond to the same $(2,4)$ tree.

R-11.21 Consider the set of keys $K = \{1,2,3,4,5,6,7,8,9,10,11,12,13,14,15\}$.

    a. Draw a $(2,4)$ tree storing K as its keys using the fewest number of nodes.
    b. Draw a $(2,4)$ tree storing K as its keys using the greatest number of nodes.

R-11.22 Consider the sequence of keys $(5,16,22,45,2,10,18,30,50,12,1)$. Draw the result of inserting entries with these keys (in the given order) into

    a. An initially empty $(2,4)$ tree.
    b. An initially empty red-black tree.

R-11.23 For the following statements about red-black trees, provide a justification for each true statement and a counterexample for each false one.

    a. A subtree of a red-black tree is itself a red-black tree.
    b. The sibling of an external node is either external or it is red.
    c. There is a unique $(2,4)$ tree associated with a given red-black tree.
    d. There is a unique red-black tree associated with a given $(2,4)$ tree.

R-11.24 Consider a tree T storing 100,000 entries. What is the worst-case height of T in the following cases?

    a. T is a binary search tree.
    b. T is an AVL tree.
    c. T is a splay tree.
    d. T is a $(2,4)$ tree.
    e. T is a red-black tree.

R-11.25 Draw an example of a red-black tree that is not an AVL tree.

R-11.26 Give a proof of Proposition 11.9

R-11.27 Give a proof of Proposition 11.10

Creativity

C-11.28 Explain why you would get the same output in an inorder listing of the entries in a binary search tree, T, independent of whether T is maintained to be an AVL tree, splay tree, or red-black tree.

C-11.29 Explain how to use an AVL tree or a red-black tree to sort n comparable elements in $O(n \log n)$ time in the worst case.

C-11.30 Can we use a splay tree to sort n comparable elements in $O(n \log n)$ time in the **worst case**? Why or why not?

C-11.31 Implement a putIfAbsent method, as originally described in Exercise C-10.33, for the TreeMap class.

C-11.32 Show that any n-node binary tree can be converted to any other n-node binary tree using $O(n)$ rotations.

C-11.33 For a key k that is not found in binary search tree T, prove that both the greatest key less than k and the least key greater than k lie on the path traced by the search for k.

C-11.34 In Section 11.1.4 we claim that the subMap method of a binary search tree, as implemented in Code Fragment 11.6, executes in $O(s + h)$ time where s is the number of entries contained within the submap and h is the height of the tree. Prove this result, by arguing about the maximum number of times the recursive submethod can be called on positions that are not included within the submap.

C-11.35 Consider a sorted map that is implemented with a standard binary search tree T. Describe how to perform an operation removeSubMap(k_1, k_2) that removes all the entries whose keys fall within subMap(k_1, k_2), in worst-case time $O(s + h)$, where s is the number of entries removed and h is the height of T.

C-11.36 Repeat the previous problem using an AVL tree, achieving a running time of $O(s \log n)$. Why doesn't the solution to the previous problem trivially result in an $O(s + \log n)$ algorithm for AVL trees?

C-11.37 Suppose we wish to support a new method countRange(k_1, k_2) that determines how many keys of a sorted map fall in the specified range. We could clearly implement this in $O(s + h)$ time by adapting our approach to subMap. Describe how to modify the search-tree structure to support $O(h)$ worst-case time for countRange.

C-11.38 If the approach described in the previous problem were implemented as part of the TreeMap class, what additional modifications (if any) would be necessary to a subclass such as AVLTreeMap in order to maintain support for the new method?

C-11.39 Draw a schematic of an AVL tree such that a single remove operation could require $\Omega(\log n)$ trinode restructurings (or rotations) from a leaf to the root in order to restore the height-balance property.

C-11.40 Show that the nodes that become temporarily unbalanced in an AVL tree during an insertion may be nonconsecutive on the path from the newly inserted node to the root.

C-11.41 Show that at most one node in an AVL tree becomes temporarily unbalanced after the immediate deletion of a node as part of the standard remove map operation.

C-11.42 In our AVL implementation, each node stores the height of its subtree, which is an arbitrarily large integer. The space usage for an AVL tree can be reduced by instead storing the *balance factor* of a node, which is defined as the height of its left subtree minus the height of its right subtree. Thus, the balance factor of a node is always equal to -1, 0, or 1, except during an insertion or removal, when it may become *temporarily* equal to -2 or $+2$. Reimplement the AVLTreeMap class storing balance factors rather than subtree heights.

C-11.43 If we maintain a reference to the position of the leftmost node of a binary search tree, then operation firstEntry can be performed in $O(1)$ time. Describe how the implementation of the other map methods need to be modified to maintain a reference to the leftmost position.

C-11.44 If the approach described in the previous problem were implemented as part of the TreeMap class, what additional modifications (if any) would be necessary to a subclass such as AVLTreeMap in order to accurately maintain the reference to the leftmost position?

C-11.45 Describe a modification to the binary search-tree data structure that would support the following two index-based operations for a sorted map in $O(h)$ time, where h is the height of the tree.

atIndex(i): Return the position p of the entry at index i of a sorted map.

indexOf(p): Return the index i of the entry at position p of a sorted map.

C-11.46 Draw a splay tree, T_1, together with the sequence of updates that produced it, and a red-black tree, T_2, on the same set of ten entries, such that a preorder traversal of T_1 would be the same as a preorder traversal of T_2.

C-11.47 Let T and U be $(2,4)$ trees storing n and m entries, respectively, such that all the entries in T have keys less than the keys of all the entries in U. Describe an $O(\log n + \log m)$-time method for *joining* T and U into a single tree that stores all the entries in T and U.

C-11.48 Let T be a red-black tree storing n entries, and let k be the key of an entry in T. Show how to construct from T, in $O(\log n)$ time, two red-black trees T' and T'', such that T' contains all the keys of T less than k, and T'' contains all the keys of T greater than k. This operation destroys T.

C-11.49 Prove that an n-entry multiway search tree has $n + 1$ external nodes.

C-11.50 The boolean indicator used to mark nodes in a red-black tree as being "red" or "black" is not strictly needed when we have distinct keys. Describe a scheme for implementing a red-black tree without adding any extra space to standard binary search-tree nodes.

C-11.51 Show that the nodes of any AVL tree T can be colored "red" and "black" so that T becomes a red-black tree.

C-11.52 The standard splaying step requires two passes, one downward pass to find the node x to splay, followed by an upward pass to splay the node x. Describe a method for splaying and searching for x in one downward pass. Each substep now requires that you consider the next two nodes in the path down to x, with a possible zig substep performed at the end. Describe how to perform the zig-zig, zig-zag, and zig steps.

C-11.53 Consider a variation of splay trees, called **_half-splay trees_**, where splaying a node at depth d stops as soon as the node reaches depth $\lfloor d/2 \rfloor$. Perform an amortized analysis of half-splay trees.

C-11.54 Describe a sequence of accesses to an n-node splay tree T, where n is odd, that results in T consisting of a single chain of nodes such that the path down T alternates between left children and right children.

Projects

P-11.55 Reimplement the TreeMap class using null references in place of explicit sentinels for the leaves of a tree.

P-11.56 Modify the TreeMap implementation to support location-aware entries. Provide methods firstEntry( ), lastEntry( ), findEntry(k), before(e), after(e), and remove(e), with all but the last of these returning an Entry instance, and the latter three accepting an Entry e as a parameter.

P-11.57 Perform an experimental study to compare the speed of our AVL tree, splay tree, and red-black tree implementations for various sequences of operations.

P-11.58 Redo the previous exercise, including an implementation of skip lists. (See Exercise P-10.71.)

P-11.59 Implement the Sorted Map ADT using a $(2,4)$ tree. (See Section 10.3.)

P-11.60 Write a Java class that can take any red-black tree and convert it into its corresponding $(2,4)$ tree and can take any $(2,4)$ tree and convert it into its corresponding red-black tree.

P-11.61 In describing multisets and multimaps in Section 10.5.3, we describe a general approach for adapting a traditional map by storing all duplicates within a secondary container as a value in the map. Give an alternative implementation of a multimap using a binary search tree such that each entry of the map is stored at a distinct node of the tree. With the existence of duplicates, we redefine the search-tree property so that all entries in the left subtree of a position p with key k have keys that are less than _or equal to k_, while all entries in the right subtree of p have keys that are greater than _or equal to k_. Use the public interface given in Section 10.5.3.

P-11.62 Prepare an implementation of splay trees that uses top-down splaying as described in Exercise C-11.52. Perform extensive experimental studies to compare its performance to the standard bottom-up splaying implemented in this chapter.

P-11.63 The **mergeable heap** ADT is an extension of the priority queue ADT consisting of operations insert(k, v), min( ), removeMin( ), and merge(h), where the merge(h) operations performs a union of the mergeable heap h with the present one, incorporating all entries into the current one while emptying h. Describe a concrete implementation of the mergeable heap ADT that achieves $O(\log n)$ performance for all its operations, where n denotes the size of the resulting heap for the merge operation.

P-11.64 Write a program that performs a simple n-body simulation, called "Jumping Leprechauns." This simulation involves n leprechauns, numbered 1 to n. It maintains a gold value g_i for each leprechaun i, which begins with each leprechaun starting out with a million dollars worth of gold, that is, $g_i = 1,000,000$ for each $i = 1, 2, \ldots, n$. In addition, the simulation also maintains, for each leprechaun, i, a place on the horizon, which is represented as a double-precision floating-point number, x_i. In each iteration of the simulation, the simulation processes the leprechauns in order. Processing a leprechaun i during this iteration begins by computing a new place on the horizon for i, which is determined by the assignment

$$x_i = x_i + rg_i,$$

where r is a random floating-point number between -1 and 1. The leprechaun i then steals half the gold from the nearest leprechauns on either side of him and adds this gold to his gold value, g_i. Write a program that can perform a series of iterations in this simulation for a given number, n, of leprechauns. You must maintain the set of horizon positions using a sorted map data structure described in this chapter.

Chapter Notes

Some of the data structures discussed in this chapter are extensively covered by Knuth in his *Sorting and Searching* book [61], and by Mehlhorn in [71]. AVL trees are due to Adel'son-Vel'skii and Landis [2], who invented this class of balanced search trees in 1962. Binary search trees, AVL trees, and hashing are described in Knuth's *Sorting and Searching* [61] book. Average-height analyses for binary search trees can be found in the books by Aho, Hopcroft, and Ullman [6] and Cormen, Leiserson, Rivest and Stein [25]. The handbook by Gonnet and Baeza-Yates [38] contains a number of theoretical and experimental comparisons among map implementations. Aho, Hopcroft, and Ullman [5] discuss $(2, 3)$ trees, which are similar to $(2, 4)$ trees. Red-black trees were defined by Bayer [10]. Variations and interesting properties of red-black trees are presented in a paper by Guibas and Sedgewick [42]. The reader interested in learning more about different balanced tree data structures is referred to the books by Mehlhorn [71] and Tarjan [88], and the book chapter by Mehlhorn and Tsakalidis [73]. Knuth [61] is excellent additional reading that includes early approaches to balancing trees. Splay trees were invented by Sleator and Tarjan [83] (see also [88]).

Chapter

12

Sorting and Selection

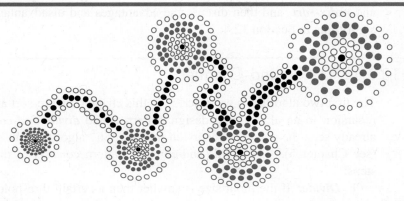

Contents

12.1   Merge-Sort

We have introduced several sorting algorithms thus far, including insertion-sort (see Sections 3.1.2, 7.6, and 9.4.1); selection-sort (see Section 9.4.1); bubble-sort (see Exercise C-7.51); and heap-sort (see Section 9.4.2). In this chapter, we will present four other sorting algorithms, called *merge-sort*, *quick-sort*, *bucket-sort*, and *radix-sort*, and then discuss the advantages and disadvantages of the various algorithms in Section 12.4.

12.1.1   Divide-and-Conquer

The first two algorithms we describe in this chapter, merge-sort and quick-sort, use recursion in an algorithmic design pattern called *divide-and-conquer*. We have already seen the power of recursion in describing algorithms in an elegant manner (see Chapter 5). The divide-and-conquer pattern consists of the following three steps:

1. *Divide:* If the input size is smaller than a certain threshold (say, one or two elements), solve the problem directly using a straightforward method and return the solution so obtained. Otherwise, divide the input data into two or more disjoint subsets.
2. *Conquer:* Recursively solve the subproblems associated with the subsets.
3. *Combine:* Take the solutions to the subproblems and merge them into a solution to the original problem.

Using Divide-and-Conquer for Sorting

We first describe the merge-sort algorithm at a high level, without focusing on whether the data is an array or linked list. (We will soon give concrete implementations for each.) To sort a sequence S with n elements using the three divide-and-conquer steps, the merge-sort algorithm proceeds as follows:

1. *Divide:* If S has zero or one element, return S immediately; it is already sorted. Otherwise (S has at least two elements), remove all the elements from S and put them into two sequences, S_1 and S_2, each containing about half of the elements of S; that is, S_1 contains the first $\lfloor n/2 \rfloor$ elements of S, and S_2 contains the remaining $\lceil n/2 \rceil$ elements.
2. *Conquer:* Recursively sort sequences S_1 and S_2.
3. *Combine:* Put the elements back into S by merging the sorted sequences S_1 and S_2 into a sorted sequence.

In reference to the divide step, we recall that the notation $\lfloor x \rfloor$ indicates the *floor* of x, that is, the largest integer k, such that $k \leq x$. Similarly, the notation $\lceil x \rceil$ indicates the *ceiling* of x, that is, the smallest integer m, such that $x \leq m$.

We can visualize an execution of the merge-sort algorithm by means of a binary tree T, called the ***merge-sort tree***. Each node of T represents a recursive invocation (or call) of the merge-sort algorithm. We associate with each node v of T the sequence S that is processed by the invocation associated with v. The children of node v are associated with the recursive calls that process the subsequences S_1 and S_2 of S. The external nodes of T are associated with individual elements of S, corresponding to instances of the algorithm that make no recursive calls.

Figure 12.1 summarizes an execution of the merge-sort algorithm by showing the input and output sequences processed at each node of the merge-sort tree. The step-by-step evolution of the merge-sort tree is shown in Figures 12.2 through 12.4.

This algorithm visualization in terms of the merge-sort tree helps us analyze the running time of the merge-sort algorithm. In particular, since the size of the input sequence roughly halves at each recursive call of merge-sort, the height of the merge-sort tree is about $\log n$ (recall that the base of log is 2 if omitted).

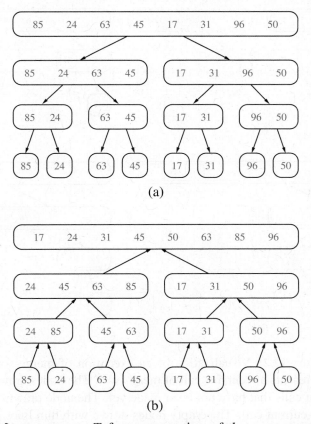

Figure 12.1: Merge-sort tree T for an execution of the merge-sort algorithm on a sequence with 8 elements: (a) input sequences processed at each node of T; (b) output sequences generated at each node of T.

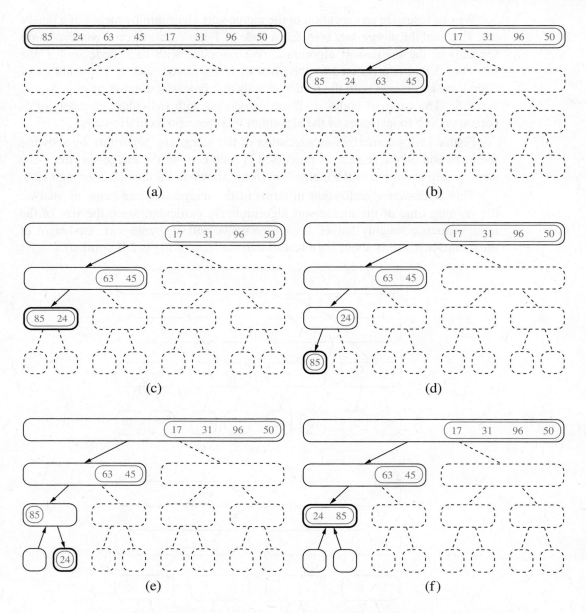

Figure 12.2: Visualization of an execution of merge-sort. Each node of the tree represents a recursive call of merge-sort. The nodes drawn with dashed lines represent calls that have not been made yet. The node drawn with thick lines represents the current call. The empty nodes drawn with thin lines represent completed calls. The remaining nodes (drawn with thin lines and not empty) represent calls that are waiting for a child call to return. (Continues in Figure 12.3.)

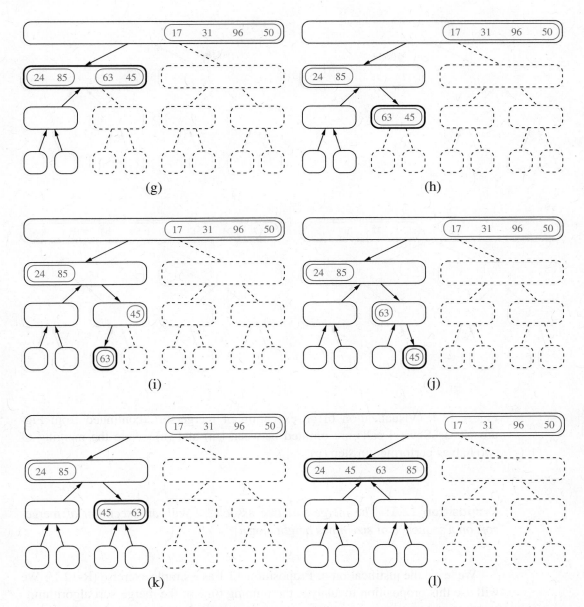

Figure 12.3: Visualization of an execution of merge-sort. (Combined with Figures 12.2 and 12.4.)

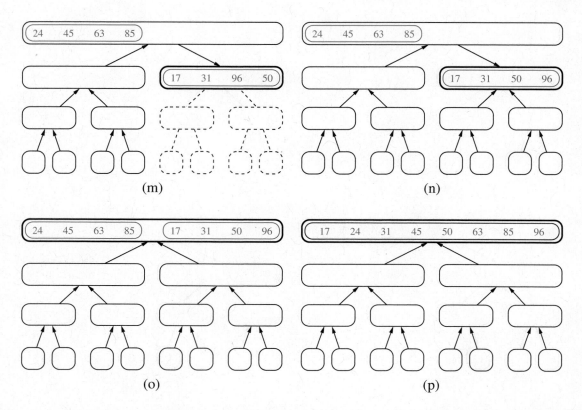

Figure 12.4: Visualization of an execution of merge-sort (continued from Figure 12.3). Several calls are omitted between (m) and (n). Note the merging of two halves performed in step (p).

Proposition 12.1: *The merge-sort tree associated with an execution of merge-sort on a sequence of size n has height* $\lceil \log n \rceil$.

We leave the justification of Proposition 12.1 as a simple exercise (R-12.1). We will use this proposition to analyze the running time of the merge-sort algorithm.

Having given an overview of merge-sort and an illustration of how it works, let us consider each of the steps of this divide-and-conquer algorithm in more detail. Dividing a sequence of size n involves separating it at the element with index $\lceil n/2 \rceil$, and recursive calls can be started by passing these smaller sequences as parameters. The difficult step is combining the two sorted sequences into a single sorted sequence. Thus, before we present our analysis of merge-sort, we need to say more about how this is done.

12.1.2 Array-Based Implementation of Merge-Sort

We begin by focusing on the case when a sequence of items is represented with an array. The merge method (Code Fragment 12.1) is responsible for the subtask of merging two previously sorted sequences, S_1 and S_2, with the output copied into S. We copy one element during each pass of the while loop, conditionally determining whether the next element should be taken from S_1 or S_2. The divide-and-conquer merge-sort algorithm is given in Code Fragment 12.2.

We illustrate a step of the merge process in Figure 12.5. During the process, index i represents the number of elements of S_1 that have been copied to S, while index j represents the number of elements of S_2 that have been copied to S. Assuming S_1 and S_2 both have at least one uncopied element, we copy the smaller of the two elements being considered. Since $i + j$ objects have been previously copied, the next element is placed in $S[i + j]$. (For example, when $i + j$ is 0, the next element is copied to $S[0]$). If we reach the end of one of the sequences, we must copy the next element from the other.

```
1   /** Merge contents of arrays S1 and S2 into properly sized array S. */
2   public static <K> void merge(K[ ] S1, K[ ] S2, K[ ] S, Comparator<K> comp) {
3     int i = 0, j = 0;
4     while (i + j < S.length) {
5       if (j == S2.length || (i < S1.length && comp.compare(S1[i], S2[j]) < 0))
6         S[i+j] = S1[i++];          // copy ith element of S1 and increment i
7       else
8         S[i+j] = S2[j++];          // copy jth element of S2 and increment j
9     }
10  }
```

Code Fragment 12.1: An implementation of the merge operation for a Java array.

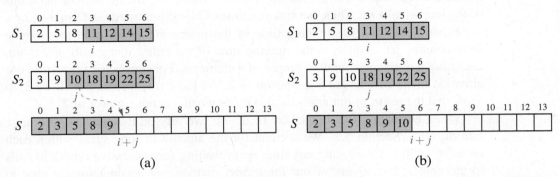

Figure 12.5: A step in the merge of two sorted arrays for which $S_2[j] < S_1[i]$. We show the arrays before the copy step in (a) and after it in (b).

```
1   /** Merge-sort contents of array S. */
2   public static <K> void mergeSort(K[ ] S, Comparator<K> comp) {
3     int n = S.length;
4     if (n < 2) return;                              // array is trivially sorted
5     // divide
6     int mid = n/2;
7     K[ ] S1 = Arrays.copyOfRange(S, 0, mid);         // copy of first half
8     K[ ] S2 = Arrays.copyOfRange(S, mid, n);         // copy of second half
9     // conquer (with recursion)
10    mergeSort(S1, comp);                            // sort copy of first half
11    mergeSort(S2, comp);                            // sort copy of second half
12    // merge results
13    merge(S1, S2, S, comp);              // merge sorted halves back into original
14  }
```

Code Fragment 12.2: An implementation of the recursive merge-sort algorithm for a Java array (using the merge method defined in Code Fragment 12.1).

We note that methods merge and mergeSort rely on use of a Comparator instance to compare a pair of generic objects that are presumed to belong to a total order. This is the same approach we introduced when defining priority queues in Section 9.2.2, and when studying implementing sorted maps in Chapters 10 and 11.

12.1.3 The Running Time of Merge-Sort

We begin by analyzing the running time of the merge algorithm. Let n_1 and n_2 be the number of elements of S_1 and S_2, respectively. It is clear that the operations performed inside each pass of the while loop take $O(1)$ time. The key observation is that during each iteration of the loop, one element is copied from either S_1 or S_2 into S (and that element is considered no further). Therefore, the number of iterations of the loop is $n_1 + n_2$. Thus, the running time of algorithm merge is $O(n_1 + n_2)$.

Having analyzed the running time of the merge algorithm used to combine subproblems, let us analyze the running time of the entire merge-sort algorithm, assuming it is given an input sequence of n elements. For simplicity, we restrict our attention to the case where n is a power of 2. We leave it to an exercise (R-12.3) to show that the result of our analysis also holds when n is not a power of 2.

When evaluating the merge-sort recursion, we rely on the analysis technique introduced in Section 5.2. We account for the amount of time spent within each recursive call, but excluding any time spent waiting for successive recursive calls to terminate. In the case of our mergeSort method, we account for the time to divide the sequence into two subsequences, and the call to merge to combine the two sorted sequences, but we exclude the two recursive calls to mergeSort.

A merge-sort tree T, as portrayed in Figures 12.2 through 12.4, can guide our analysis. Consider a recursive call associated with a node v of the merge-sort tree T. The divide step at node v is straightforward; this step runs in time proportional to the size of the sequence for v, based on the use of slicing to create copies of the two list halves. We have already observed that the merging step also takes time that is linear in the size of the merged sequence. If we let i denote the depth of node v, the time spent at node v is $O(n/2^i)$, since the size of the sequence handled by the recursive call associated with v is equal to $n/2^i$.

Looking at the tree T more globally, as shown in Figure 12.6, we see that, given our definition of "time spent at a node," the running time of merge-sort is equal to the sum of the times spent at the nodes of T. Observe that T has exactly 2^i nodes at depth i. This simple observation has an important consequence, for it implies that the overall time spent at all the nodes of T at depth i is $O(2^i \cdot n/2^i)$, which is $O(n)$. By Proposition 12.1, the height of T is $\lceil \log n \rceil$. Thus, since the time spent at each of the $\lceil \log n \rceil + 1$ levels of T is $O(n)$, we have the following result:

Proposition 12.2: *Algorithm merge-sort sorts a sequence S of size n in $O(n \log n)$ time, assuming two elements of S can be compared in $O(1)$ time.*

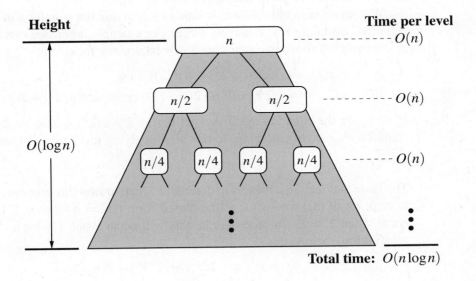

Figure 12.6: A visual analysis of the running time of merge-sort. Each node represents the time spent in a particular recursive call, labeled with the size of its subproblem.

12.1.4   Merge-Sort and Recurrence Equations ⋆

There is another way to justify that the running time of the merge-sort algorithm is $O(n \log n)$ (Proposition 12.2). Namely, we can deal more directly with the recursive nature of the merge-sort algorithm. In this section, we will present such an analysis of the running time of merge-sort, and in so doing, introduce the mathematical concept of a ***recurrence equation*** (also known as ***recurrence relation***).

Let the function $t(n)$ denote the worst-case running time of merge-sort on an input sequence of size n. Since merge-sort is recursive, we can characterize function $t(n)$ by means of an equation where the function $t(n)$ is recursively expressed in terms of itself. In order to simplify our characterization of $t(n)$, let us restrict our attention to the case when n is a power of 2. (We leave the problem of showing that our asymptotic characterization still holds in the general case as an exercise.) In this case, we can specify the definition of $t(n)$ as

$$t(n) = \begin{cases} b & \text{if } n \le 1 \\ 2t(n/2) + cn & \text{otherwise.} \end{cases}$$

An expression such as the one above is called a recurrence equation, since the function appears on both the left- and right-hand sides of the equal sign. Although such a characterization is correct and accurate, what we really desire is a big-Oh type of characterization of $t(n)$ that does not involve the function $t(n)$ itself. That is, we want a ***closed-form*** characterization of $t(n)$.

We can obtain a closed-form solution by applying the definition of a recurrence equation, assuming n is relatively large. For example, after one more application of the equation above, we can write a new recurrence for $t(n)$ as

$$\begin{aligned} t(n) &= 2(2t(n/2^2) + (cn/2)) + cn \\ &= 2^2 t(n/2^2) + 2(cn/2) + cn = 2^2 t(n/2^2) + 2cn. \end{aligned}$$

If we apply the equation again, we get $t(n) = 2^3 t(n/2^3) + 3cn$. At this point, we should see a pattern emerging, so that after applying this equation i times, we get

$$t(n) = 2^i t(n/2^i) + icn.$$

The issue that remains, then, is to determine when to stop this process. To see when to stop, recall that we switch to the closed form $t(n) = b$ when $n \le 1$, which will occur when $2^i = n$. In other words, this will occur when $i = \log n$. Making this substitution, then, yields

$$\begin{aligned} t(n) &= 2^{\log n} t(n/2^{\log n}) + (\log n)cn \\ &= nt(1) + cn \log n \\ &= nb + cn \log n. \end{aligned}$$

That is, we get an alternative justification of the fact that $t(n)$ is $O(n \log n)$.

12.1.5 Alternative Implementations of Merge-Sort

Sorting Linked Lists

The merge-sort algorithm can easily be adapted to use any form of a basic queue as its container type. In Code Fragment 12.3, we provide such an implementation, based on use of the LinkedQueue class from Section 6.2.3. The $O(n \log n)$ bound for merge-sort from Proposition 12.2 applies to this implementation as well, since each basic operation runs in $O(1)$ time when implemented with a linked list. We show an example execution of this version of the merge algorithm in Figure 12.7.

```
 1  /** Merge contents of sorted queues S1 and S2 into empty queue S. */
 2  public static <K> void merge(Queue<K> S1, Queue<K> S2, Queue<K> S,
 3                                                  Comparator<K> comp) {
 4    while (!S1.isEmpty() && !S2.isEmpty()) {
 5      if (comp.compare(S1.first(), S2.first()) < 0)
 6        S.enqueue(S1.dequeue());              // take next element from S1
 7      else
 8        S.enqueue(S2.dequeue());              // take next element from S2
 9    }
10    while (!S1.isEmpty())
11      S.enqueue(S1.dequeue());                // move any elements that remain in S1
12    while (!S2.isEmpty())
13      S.enqueue(S2.dequeue());                // move any elements that remain in S2
14  }
15
16  /** Merge-sort contents of queue. */
17  public static <K> void mergeSort(Queue<K> S, Comparator<K> comp) {
18    int n = S.size();
19    if (n < 2) return;                        // queue is trivially sorted
20    // divide
21    Queue<K> S1 = new LinkedQueue<>();        // (or any queue implementation)
22    Queue<K> S2 = new LinkedQueue<>();
23    while (S1.size() < n/2)
24      S1.enqueue(S.dequeue());                // move the first n/2 elements to S1
25    while (!S.isEmpty())
26      S2.enqueue(S.dequeue());                // move remaining elements to S2
27    // conquer (with recursion)
28    mergeSort(S1, comp);                      // sort first half
29    mergeSort(S2, comp);                      // sort second half
30    // merge results
31    merge(S1, S2, S, comp);                   // merge sorted halves back into original
32  }
```

Code Fragment 12.3: An implementation of merge-sort using a basic queue.

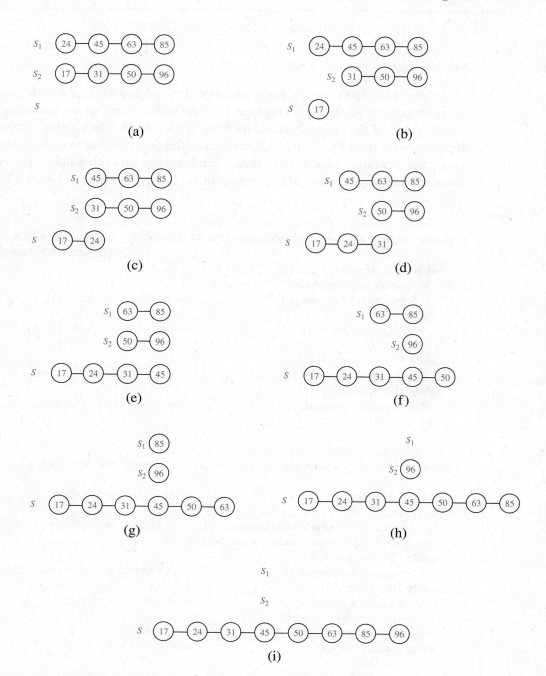

Figure 12.7: Example of an execution of the merge algorithm, as implemented in Code Fragment 12.3 using queues.

A Bottom-Up (Nonrecursive) Merge-Sort

There is a nonrecursive version of array-based merge-sort, which runs in $O(n \log n)$ time. It is a bit faster than recursive merge-sort in practice, as it avoids the extra overheads of recursive calls and temporary memory at each level. The main idea is to perform merge-sort bottom-up, performing the merges level by level going up the merge-sort tree. Given an input array of elements, we begin by merging every successive pair of elements into sorted runs of length two. We merge these runs into runs of length four, merge these new runs into runs of length eight, and so on, until the array is sorted. To keep the space usage reasonable, we deploy a second array that stores the merged runs (swapping input and output arrays after each iteration). We give a Java implementation in Code Fragment 12.4, using the built-in method System.arraycopy to copy a range of cells between two arrays. A similar bottom-up approach can be used for sorting linked lists. (See Exercise C-12.30.)

```java
1    /** Merges in[start..start+inc−1] and in[start+inc..start+2*inc−1] into out. */
2    public static <K> void merge(K[ ] in, K[ ] out, Comparator<K> comp,
3                                                        int start, int inc) {
4        int end1 = Math.min(start + inc, in.length);           // boundary for run 1
5        int end2 = Math.min(start + 2 * inc, in.length);       // boundary for run 2
6        int x=start;                                           // index into run 1
7        int y=start+inc;                                       // index into run 2
8        int z=start;                                           // index into output
9        while (x < end1 && y < end2)
10           if (comp.compare(in[x], in[y]) < 0)
11               out[z++] = in[x++];                            // take next from run 1
12           else
13               out[z++] = in[y++];                            // take next from run 2
14       if (x < end1) System.arraycopy(in, x, out, z, end1 − x);     // copy rest of run 1
15       else if (y < end2) System.arraycopy(in, y, out, z, end2 − y); // copy rest of run 2
16   }
17   /** Merge-sort contents of data array. */
18   public static <K> void mergeSortBottomUp(K[ ] orig, Comparator<K> comp) {
19       int n = orig.length;
20       K[ ] src = orig;                          // alias for the original
21       K[ ] dest = (K[ ]) new Object[n];         // make a new temporary array
22       K[ ] temp;                                // reference used only for swapping
23       for (int i=1; i < n; i *= 2) {            // each iteration sorts all runs of length i
24           for (int j=0; j < n; j += 2*i)        // each pass merges two runs of length i
25               merge(src, dest, comp, j, i);
26           temp = src; src = dest; dest = temp;  // reverse roles of the arrays
27       }
28       if (orig != src)
29           System.arraycopy(src, 0, orig, 0, n); // additional copy to get result to original
30   }
```

Code Fragment 12.4: An implementation of the nonrecursive merge-sort algorithm.

12.2   Quick-Sort

The next sorting algorithm we discuss is called *quick-sort*. Like merge-sort, this algorithm is also based on the *divide-and-conquer* paradigm, but it uses this technique in a somewhat opposite manner, as all the hard work is done *before* the recursive calls.

High-Level Description of Quick-Sort

The quick-sort algorithm sorts a sequence S using a simple recursive approach. The main idea is to apply the divide-and-conquer technique, whereby we divide S into subsequences, recur to sort each subsequence, and then combine the sorted subsequences by a simple concatenation. In particular, the quick-sort algorithm consists of the following three steps (see Figure 12.8):

1. *Divide:* If S has at least two elements (nothing needs to be done if S has zero or one element), select a specific element x from S, which is called the *pivot*. As is common practice, choose the pivot x to be the last element in S. Remove all the elements from S and put them into three sequences:
   - L, storing the elements in S less than x
   - E, storing the elements in S equal to x
   - G, storing the elements in S greater than x
   Of course, if the elements of S are distinct, then E holds just one element—the pivot itself.
2. *Conquer:* Recursively sort sequences L and G.
3. *Combine:* Put back the elements into S in order by first inserting the elements of L, then those of E, and finally those of G.

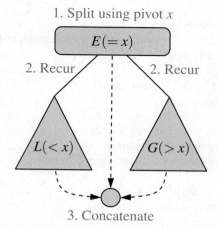

Figure 12.8: A visual schematic of the quick-sort algorithm.

Like merge-sort, the execution of quick-sort can be visualized by means of a binary recursion tree, called the ***quick-sort tree***. Figure 12.9 summarizes an execution of the quick-sort algorithm by showing the input and output sequences processed at each node of the quick-sort tree. The step-by-step evolution of the quick-sort tree is shown in Figures 12.10, 12.11, and 12.12.

Unlike merge-sort, however, the height of the quick-sort tree associated with an execution of quick-sort is linear in the worst case. This happens, for example, if the sequence consists of n distinct elements and is already sorted. Indeed, in this case, the standard choice of the last element as pivot yields a subsequence L of size $n - 1$, while subsequence E has size 1 and subsequence G has size 0. At each call of quick-sort on subsequence L, the size decreases by 1. Hence, the height of the quick-sort tree is $n - 1$.

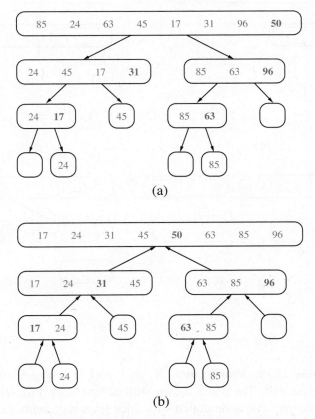

Figure 12.9: Quick-sort tree T for an execution of the quick-sort algorithm on a sequence with 8 elements: (a) input sequences processed at each node of T; (b) output sequences generated at each node of T. The pivot used at each level of the recursion is shown in bold.

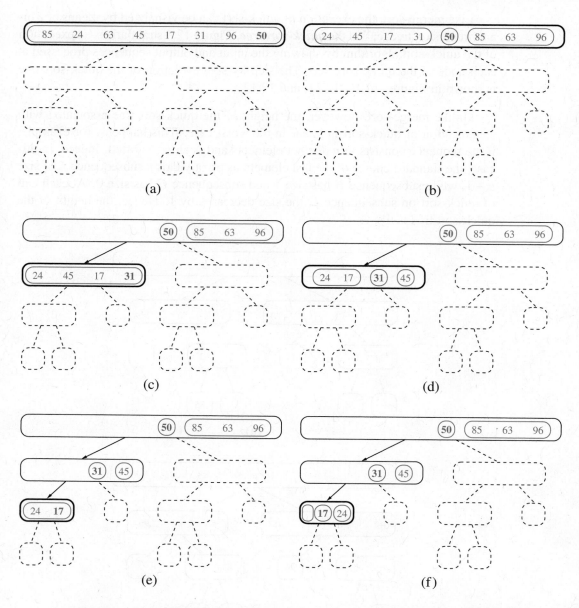

Figure 12.10: Visualization of quick-sort. Each node of the tree represents a recursive call. The nodes drawn with dashed lines represent calls that have not been made yet. The node drawn with thick lines represents the running call. The empty nodes drawn with thin lines represent terminated calls. The remaining nodes represent suspended calls (that is, active calls that are waiting for a child call to return). Note the divide steps performed in (b), (d), and (f). (Continues in Figure 12.11.)

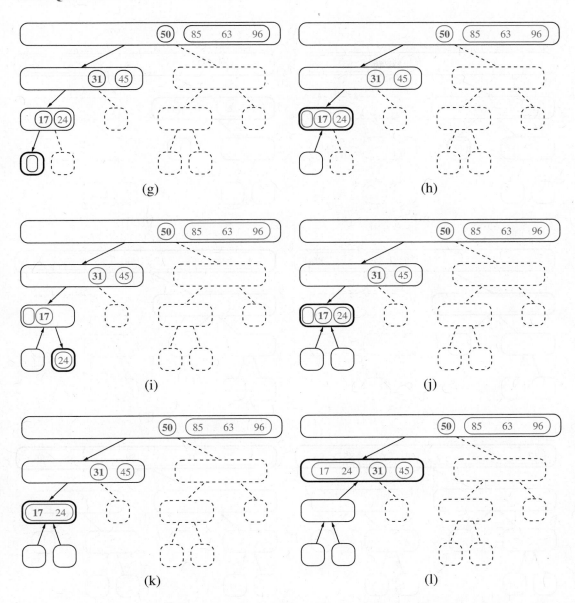

Figure 12.11: Visualization of an execution of quick-sort. Note the concatenation step performed in (k). (Continues in Figure 12.12.)

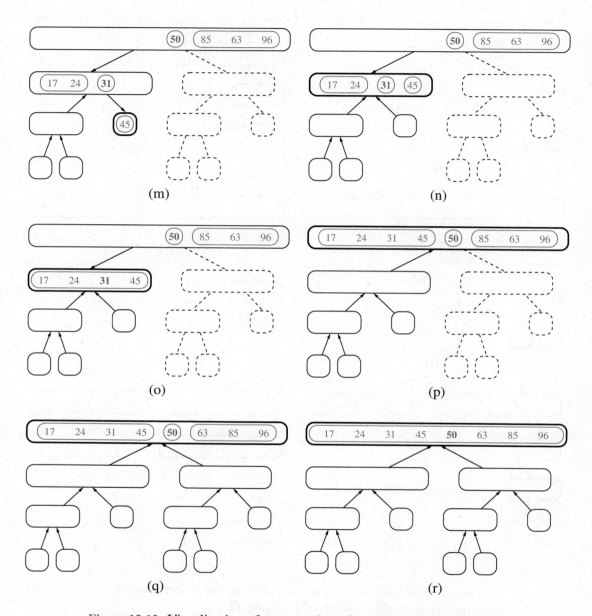

Figure 12.12: Visualization of an execution of quick-sort. Several calls between (p) and (q) have been omitted. Note the concatenation steps performed in (o) and (r). (Continued from Figure 12.11.)

Performing Quick-Sort on General Sequences

In Code Fragment 12.5, we give an implementation of the quick-sort algorithm that works on any sequence type that operates as a queue. This particular version relies on the LinkedQueue class from Section 6.2.3; we provide a more streamlined implementation of quick-sort using an array-based sequence in Section 12.2.2.

Our implementation chooses the first item of the queue as the pivot (since it is easily accessible), and then it divides sequence S into queues L, E, and G of elements that are respectively less than, equal to, and greater than the pivot. We then recur on the L and G lists, and transfer elements from the sorted lists L, E, and G back to S. All of the queue operations run in $O(1)$ worst-case time when implemented with a linked list.

```java
1   /** Quick-sort contents of a queue. */
2   public static <K> void quickSort(Queue<K> S, Comparator<K> comp) {
3     int n = S.size();
4     if (n < 2) return;                         // queue is trivially sorted
5     // divide
6     K pivot = S.first();                       // using first as arbitrary pivot
7     Queue<K> L = new LinkedQueue<>();
8     Queue<K> E = new LinkedQueue<>();
9     Queue<K> G = new LinkedQueue<>();
10    while (!S.isEmpty()) {                      // divide original into L, E, and G
11      K element = S.dequeue();
12      int c = comp.compare(element, pivot);
13      if (c < 0)                               // element is less than pivot
14        L.enqueue(element);
15      else if (c == 0)                         // element is equal to pivot
16        E.enqueue(element);
17      else                                     // element is greater than pivot
18        G.enqueue(element);
19    }
20    // conquer
21    quickSort(L, comp);                        // sort elements less than pivot
22    quickSort(G, comp);                        // sort elements greater than pivot
23    // concatenate results
24    while (!L.isEmpty())
25      S.enqueue(L.dequeue());
26    while (!E.isEmpty())
27      S.enqueue(E.dequeue());
28    while (!G.isEmpty())
29      S.enqueue(G.dequeue());
30  }
```

Code Fragment 12.5: Quick-sort for a sequence S implemented as a queue.

Running Time of Quick-Sort

We can analyze the running time of quick-sort with the same technique used for merge-sort in Section 12.1.3. Namely, we can identify the time spent at each node of the quick-sort tree T and sum up the running times for all the nodes.

Examining Code Fragment 12.5, we see that the divide step and the final concatenation of quick-sort can be implemented in linear time. Thus, the time spent at a node v of T is proportional to the **input size** $s(v)$ of v, defined as the size of the sequence handled by the call of quick-sort associated with node v. Since subsequence E has at least one element (the pivot), the sum of the input sizes of the children of v is at most $s(v) - 1$.

Let s_i denote the sum of the input sizes of the nodes at depth i for a particular quick-sort tree T. Clearly, $s_0 = n$, since the root r of T is associated with the entire sequence. Also, $s_1 \leq n - 1$, since the pivot is not propagated to the children of r. More generally, it must be that $s_i < s_{i-1}$ since the elements of the subsequences at depth i all come from distinct subsequences at depth $i - 1$, and at least one element from depth $i - 1$ does not propagate to depth i because it is in a set E (in fact, one element from *each node* at depth $i - 1$ does not propagate to depth i).

We can therefore bound the overall running time of an execution of quick-sort as $O(n \cdot h)$ where h is the overall height of the quick-sort tree T for that execution. Unfortunately, in the worst case, the height of a quick-sort tree is $n - 1$, as observed in Section 12.2. Thus, quick-sort runs in $O(n^2)$ worst-case time. Paradoxically, if we choose the pivot as the last element of the sequence, this worst-case behavior occurs for problem instances when sorting should be easy—if the sequence is already sorted.

Given its name, we would expect quick-sort to run quickly, and it often does in practice. The best case for quick-sort on a sequence of distinct elements occurs when subsequences L and G have roughly the same size. In that case, as we saw with merge-sort, the tree has height $O(\log n)$ and therefore quick-sort runs in $O(n \log n)$ time; we leave the justification of this fact as an exercise (R-12.12). More so, we can observe an $O(n \log n)$ running time even if the split between L and G is not as perfect. For example, if every divide step caused one subsequence to have one-fourth of those elements and the other to have three-fourths of the elements, the height of the tree would remain $O(\log n)$ and thus the overall performance $O(n \log n)$.

We will see in the next section that introducing randomization in the choice of a pivot will makes quick-sort essentially behave in this way on average, with an expected running time that is $O(n \log n)$.

12.2.1   Randomized Quick-Sort

One common method for analyzing quick-sort is to assume that the pivot will always divide the sequence in a reasonably balanced manner. However, we feel such an assumption would presuppose knowledge about the input distribution that is typically not available. For example, we would have to assume that we will rarely be given "almost" sorted sequences to sort, which are actually common in many applications. Fortunately, this assumption is not needed in order for us to match our intuition to quick-sort's behavior.

In general, we desire some way of getting close to the best-case running time for quick-sort. The way to get close to the best-case running time, of course, is for the pivot to divide the input sequence S almost equally. If this outcome were to occur, then it would result in a running time that is asymptotically the same as the best-case running time. That is, having pivots close to the "middle" of the set of elements leads to an $O(n \log n)$ running time for quick-sort.

Picking Pivots at Random

Since the goal of the partition step of the quick-sort method is to divide the sequence S with sufficient balance, let us introduce randomization into the algorithm and pick as the pivot a ***random element*** of the input sequence. That is, instead of picking the pivot as the first or last element of S, we pick an element of S at random as the pivot, keeping the rest of the algorithm unchanged. This variation of quick-sort is called ***randomized quick-sort***. The following proposition shows that the expected running time of randomized quick-sort on a sequence with n elements is $O(n \log n)$. This expectation is taken over all the possible random choices the algorithm makes, and is independent of any assumptions about the distribution of the possible input sequences the algorithm is likely to be given.

Proposition 12.3: *The expected running time of randomized quick-sort on a sequence S of size n is $O(n \log n)$.*

Justification: Let S be a sequence with n elements and let T be the binary tree associated with an execution of randomized quick-sort on S. First, we observe that the running time of the algorithm is proportional to the number of comparisons performed. We consider the recursive call associated with a node of T and observe that during the call, all comparisons are between the pivot element and another element of the input of the call. Thus, we can evaluate the total number of comparisons performed by the algorithm as $\sum_{s \in S} C(x)$, where $C(x)$ is the number of comparisons involving x as a nonpivot element. Next, we will show that for every element $x \in S$, the expected value of $C(x)$ is $O(\log n)$. Since the expected value of a sum is the sum of the expected values of its terms, an $O(\log n)$ bound on the expected value of $C(x)$ implies that randomized quick-sort runs in expected $O(n \log n)$ time.

To show that the expected value of $C(x)$ is $O(n \log n)$ for any x, we fix an arbitrary element x and consider the path of nodes in the tree T associated with recursive calls for which x is part of the input sequence. (See Figure 12.13.) By definition, $C(x)$ is equal to that path length, as x will take part in one nonpivot comparison per level of the tree until it is chosen as the pivot or is the only element that remains.

Let n_d denote the input size for the node of that path at depth d of tree T, for $0 \le d \le C(x)$. Since all elements are in the initial recursive call, $n_0 = n$. We know that the input size for any recursive call is at least one less than the size of its parent, and thus that $n_{d+1} \le n_d - 1$ for any $d < C(x)$. In the worst case, this implies that $C(x) \le n-1$, as the recursive process stops if $n_d = 1$ or if x is chosen as the pivot.

We can show the stronger claim that the expected value of $C(x)$ is $O(\log n)$ based on the random selection of a pivot at each level. The choice of pivot at depth d of this path is considered "good" if $n_{d+1} \le 3n_d/4$. The choice of a pivot will be good with probability at least $1/2$, as there are at least $n_d/2$ elements in the input that, if chosen as pivot, will result in at least $n_d/4$ elements begin placed in each subproblem, thereby leaving x in a group with at most $3n_d/4$ elements.

We conclude by noting that there can be at most $\log_{4/3} n$ such good pivot choices before x is isolated. Since a choice is good with probability at least $1/2$, the expected number of recursive calls before achieving $\log_{4/3} n$ good choices is at most $2\log_{4/3} n$, which implies that $C(x)$ is $O(\log n)$. ∎

With a more rigorous analysis, we can show that the running time of randomized quick-sort is $O(n \log n)$ with *high probability*. (See Exercise C-12.55.)

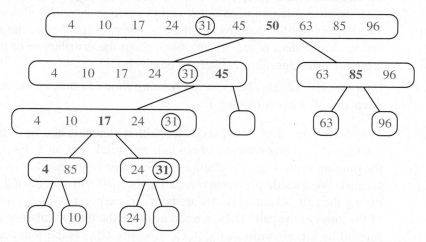

Figure 12.13: An illustration of the analysis of Proposition 12.3 for an execution of randomized quick-sort. We focus on element $x = 31$, which has value $C(x) = 3$, as it is the nonpivot element in a comparison with 50, 45, and 17. By our notation, $n_0 = 10$, $n_1 = 6$, $n_2 = 5$, and $n_3 = 2$, and the pivot choices of 50 and 17 are good.

12.2.2 Additional Optimizations for Quick-Sort

An algorithm is *in-place* if it uses only a small amount of memory in addition to that needed for the original input. Our implementation of heap-sort, from Section 9.4.2, is an example of such an in-place sorting algorithm. Our implementation of quick-sort from Code Fragment 12.5 does not qualify as in-place because we use additional containers L, E, and G when dividing a sequence S within each recursive call. Quick-sort of an array-based sequence can be adapted to be in-place, and such an optimization is used in most deployed implementations.

Performing the quick-sort algorithm in-place requires a bit of ingenuity, however, for we must use the input sequence itself to store the subsequences for all the recursive calls. We show algorithm quickSortInPlace, which performs in-place quick-sort of an array, in Code Fragment 12.6. In-place quick-sort modifies the input sequence using element swapping and does not explicitly create subsequences. Instead, a subsequence of the input sequence is implicitly represented by a range of positions specified by a leftmost index a and a rightmost index b. The divide

```
1    /** Sort the subarray S[a..b] inclusive. */
2    private static <K> void quickSortInPlace(K[ ] S, Comparator<K> comp,
3                                                       int a, int b) {
4        if (a >= b) return;          // subarray is trivially sorted
5        int left = a;
6        int right = b−1;
7        K pivot = S[b];
8        K temp;                      // temp object used for swapping
9        while (left <= right) {
10           // scan until reaching value equal or larger than pivot (or right marker)
11           while (left <= right && comp.compare(S[left], pivot) < 0) left++;
12           // scan until reaching value equal or smaller than pivot (or left marker)
13           while (left <= right && comp.compare(S[right], pivot) > 0) right−−;
14           if (left <= right) {     // indices did not strictly cross
15               // so swap values and shrink range
16               temp = S[left]; S[left] = S[right]; S[right] = temp;
17               left++; right−−;
18           }
19       }
20       // put pivot into its final place (currently marked by left index)
21       temp = S[left]; S[left] = S[b]; S[b] = temp;
22       // make recursive calls
23       quickSortInPlace(S, comp, a, left − 1);
24       quickSortInPlace(S, comp, left + 1, b);
25   }
```

Code Fragment 12.6: In-place quick-sort for an array S. The entire array can be sorted as quickSortInPlace(S, comp, 0, S.length−1).

step is performed by scanning the array simultaneously using local variables left, which advances forward, and right, which advances backward, swapping pairs of elements that are in reverse order, as shown in Figure 12.14. When these two indices pass each other, the division step is complete and the algorithm completes by recurring on these two sublists. There is no explicit "combine" step, because the concatenation of the two sublists is implicit to the in-place use of the original list.

It is worth noting that if a sequence has duplicate values, we are not explicitly creating three sublists L, E, and G, as in our original quick-sort description. We instead allow elements equal to the pivot (other than the pivot itself) to be dispersed across the two sublists. Exercise R-12.11 explores the subtlety of our implementation in the presence of duplicate keys, and Exercise C-12.34 describes an in-place algorithm that strictly partitions into three sublists L, E, and G.

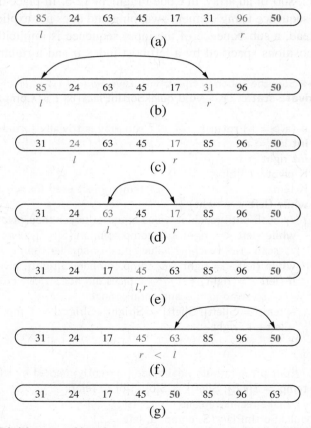

Figure 12.14: Divide step of in-place quick-sort, using index l as shorthand for identifier left, and index r as shorthand for identifier right. Index l scans the sequence from left to right, and index r scans the sequence from right to left. A swap is performed when l is at an element as large as the pivot and r is at an element as small as the pivot. A final swap with the pivot, in part (f), completes the divide step.

Although the implementation we describe in this section for dividing the sequence into two pieces is in-place, we note that the complete quick-sort algorithm needs space for a stack proportional to the depth of the recursion tree, which in this case can be as large as $n - 1$. Admittedly, the expected stack depth is $O(\log n)$, which is small compared to n. Nevertheless, a simple trick lets us guarantee the stack size is $O(\log n)$. The main idea is to design a nonrecursive version of in-place quick-sort using an explicit stack to iteratively process subproblems (each of which can be represented with a pair of indices marking subarray boundaries). Each iteration involves popping the top subproblem, splitting it in two (if it is big enough), and pushing the two new subproblems. The trick is that when pushing the new subproblems, we should first push the larger subproblem and then the smaller one. In this way, the sizes of the subproblems will at least double as we go down the stack; hence, the stack can have depth at most $O(\log n)$. We leave the details of this implementation as an exercise (P-12.59).

Pivot Selection

Our implementation in this section blindly picks the last element as the pivot at each level of the quick-sort recursion. This leaves it susceptible to the $\Theta(n^2)$-time worst case, most notably when the original sequence is already sorted, reverse sorted, or nearly sorted.

As described in Section 12.2.1, this can be improved upon by using a randomly chosen pivot for each partition step. In practice, another common technique for choosing a pivot is to use the median of tree values, taken respectively from the front, middle, and tail of the array. This **median-of-three** heuristic will more often choose a good pivot and computing a median of three may require lower overhead than selecting a pivot with a random number generator. For larger data sets, the median of more than three potential pivots might be computed.

Hybrid Approaches

Although quick-sort has very good performance on large data sets, it has rather high overhead on relatively small data sets. For example, the process of quick-sorting a sequence of eight elements, as illustrated in Figures 12.10 through 12.12, involves considerable bookkeeping. In practice, a simple algorithm like insertion-sort (Section 7.6) will execute faster when sorting such a short sequence.

It is therefore common, in optimized sorting implementations, to use a hybrid approach, with a divide-and-conquer algorithm used until the size of a subsequence falls below some threshold (perhaps 50 elements); insertion-sort can be directly invoked upon portions with length below the threshold. We will further discuss such practical considerations in Section 12.4, when comparing the performance of various sorting algorithms.

12.3   Studying Sorting through an Algorithmic Lens

Recapping our discussions on sorting to this point, we have described several methods with either a worst case or expected running time of $O(n \log n)$ on an input sequence of size n. These methods include merge-sort and quick-sort, described in this chapter, as well as heap-sort (Section 9.4.2). In this section, we will study sorting as an algorithmic problem, addressing general issues about sorting algorithms.

12.3.1   Lower Bound for Sorting

A natural first question to ask is whether we can sort any faster than $O(n \log n)$ time. Interestingly, if the computational primitive used by a sorting algorithm is the comparison of two elements, this is in fact the best we can do—comparison-based sorting has an $\Omega(n \log n)$ worst-case lower bound on its running time. (Recall the notation $\Omega(\cdot)$ from Section 4.3.1.) To focus on the main cost of comparison-based sorting, let us only count comparisons, for the sake of a lower bound.

Suppose we are given a sequence $S = (x_0, x_1, \ldots, x_{n-1})$ that we wish to sort, and assume that all the elements of S are distinct (this is not really a restriction since we are deriving a lower bound). We do not care if S is implemented as an array or a linked list, for the sake of our lower bound, since we are only counting comparisons. Each time a sorting algorithm compares two elements x_i and x_j (that is, it asks, "is $x_i < x_j$?"), there are two outcomes: "yes" or "no." Based on the result of this comparison, the sorting algorithm may perform some internal calculations (which we are not counting here) and will eventually perform another comparison between two other elements of S, which again will have two outcomes. Therefore, we can represent a comparison-based sorting algorithm with a decision tree T (recall Example 8.5). That is, each internal node v in T corresponds to a comparison and the edges from position v to its children correspond to the computations resulting from either a "yes" or "no" answer. It is important to note that the hypothetical sorting algorithm in question probably has no explicit knowledge of the tree T. The tree simply represents all the possible sequences of comparisons that a sorting algorithm might make, starting from the first comparison (associated with the root) and ending with the last comparison (associated with the parent of an external node).

Each possible initial order, or **permutation**, of the elements in S will cause our hypothetical sorting algorithm to execute a series of comparisons, traversing a path in T from the root to some external node. Let us associate with each external node v in T, then, the set of permutations of S that cause our sorting algorithm to end up in v. The most important observation in our lower-bound argument is that each external node v in T can represent the sequence of comparisons for at most one permutation of S. The justification for this claim is simple: If two different permutations P_1 and P_2 of S are associated with the same external node, then there are at least two objects x_i and x_j, such that x_i is before x_j in P_1 but x_i is after x_j in P_2. At the same time, the output associated with v must be a specific reordering of S, with either x_i or x_j appearing before the other. But if P_1 and P_2 both cause the sorting algorithm to output the elements of S in this order, then that implies there is a way to trick the algorithm into outputting x_i and x_j in the wrong order. Since this cannot be allowed by a correct sorting algorithm, each external node of T must be associated with exactly one permutation of S. We use this property of the decision tree associated with a sorting algorithm to prove the following result:

Proposition 12.4: *The running time of any comparison-based algorithm for sorting an n-element sequence is $\Omega(n \log n)$ in the worst case.*

Justification: The running time of a comparison-based sorting algorithm must be greater than or equal to the height of the decision tree T associated with this algorithm, as described above. (See Figure 12.15.) By the argument above, each external node in T must be associated with one permutation of S. Moreover, each permutation of S must result in a different external node of T. The number of permutations of n objects is $n! = n(n-1)(n-2)\cdots 2\cdot 1$. Thus, T must have at least $n!$ external nodes. By Proposition 8.7, the height of T is at least $\log(n!)$. This immediately justifies the proposition, because there are at least $n/2$ terms that are greater than or equal to $n/2$ in the product $n!$; hence,

$$\log(n!) \geq \log\left(\left(\frac{n}{2}\right)^{\frac{n}{2}}\right) = \frac{n}{2}\log\frac{n}{2},$$

which is $\Omega(n \log n)$. ■

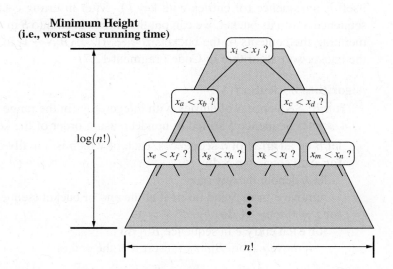

Figure 12.15: Visualizing the lower bound for comparison-based sorting.

12.3.2   Linear-Time Sorting: Bucket-Sort and Radix-Sort

In the previous section, we showed that $\Omega(n \log n)$ time is necessary, in the worst case, to sort an n-element sequence with a comparison-based sorting algorithm. A natural question to ask, then, is whether there are other kinds of sorting algorithms that can be designed to run asymptotically faster than $O(n \log n)$ time. Interestingly, such algorithms exist, but they require special assumptions about the input sequence to be sorted. Even so, such scenarios often arise in practice, such as when sorting integers from a known range or sorting character strings, so discussing them is worthwhile. In this section, we will consider the problem of sorting a sequence of entries, each a key-value pair, where the keys have a restricted type.

Bucket-Sort

Consider a sequence S of n entries whose keys are integers in the range $[0, N-1]$, for some integer $N \geq 2$, and suppose that S should be sorted according to the keys of the entries. In this case, it is possible to sort S in $O(n+N)$ time. It might seem surprising, but this implies, for example, that if N is $O(n)$, then we can sort S in $O(n)$ time. Of course, the crucial point is that, because of the restrictive assumption about the format of the elements, we can avoid using comparisons.

The main idea is to use an algorithm called **bucket-sort**, which is not based on comparisons, but on using keys as indices into a bucket array B that has cells indexed from 0 to $N-1$. An entry with key k is placed in the "bucket" $B[k]$, which itself is a sequence (of entries with key k). After inserting each entry of the input sequence S into its bucket, we can put the entries back into S in sorted order by enumerating the contents of the buckets $B[0], B[1], \ldots, B[N-1]$ in order. We describe the bucket-sort algorithm in Code Fragment 12.7.

Algorithm bucketSort(S):
> *Input:* Sequence S of entries with integer keys in the range $[0, N-1]$
> *Output:* Sequence S sorted in nondecreasing order of the keys
> let B be an array of n sequences, each of which is initially empty
> **for** each entry e in S **do**
>> let k denote the key of e
>> remove e from S and insert it at the end of bucket (sequence) $B[k]$
>
> **for** $i = 0$ to $n-1$ **do**
>> **for** each entry e in sequence $B[i]$ **do**
>>> remove e from $B[i]$ and insert it at the end of S

Code Fragment 12.7: Bucket-sort.

It is easy to see that bucket-sort runs in $O(n+N)$ time and uses $O(n+N)$ space. Hence, bucket-sort is efficient when the range N of values for the keys is small compared to the sequence size n, say $N = O(n)$ or $N = O(n\log n)$. Still, its performance deteriorates as N grows compared to n.

An important property of the bucket-sort algorithm is that it works correctly even if there are many different elements with the same key. Indeed, we described it in a way that anticipates such occurrences.

Stable Sorting

When sorting key-value pairs, an important issue is how equal keys are handled. Let $S = ((k_0, v_0), \ldots, (k_{n-1}, v_{n-1}))$ be a sequence of such entries. We say that a sorting algorithm is **stable** if, for any two entries (k_i, v_i) and (k_j, v_j) of S such that $k_i = k_j$ and (k_i, v_i) precedes (k_j, v_j) in S before sorting (that is, $i < j$), entry (k_i, v_i) also precedes entry (k_j, v_j) after sorting. Stability is important for a sorting algorithm because applications may want to preserve the initial order of elements with the same key.

Our informal description of bucket-sort in Code Fragment 12.7 guarantees stability as long as we ensure that all sequences act as queues, with elements processed and removed from the front of a sequence and inserted at the back. That is, when initially placing elements of S into buckets, we should process S from front to back, and add each element to the end of its bucket. Subsequently, when transferring elements from the buckets back to S, we should process each $B[i]$ from front to back, with those elements added to the end of S.

Radix-Sort

One of the reasons that stable sorting is so important is that it allows the bucket-sort approach to be applied to more general contexts than to sort integers. Suppose, for example, that we want to sort entries with keys that are pairs (k, l), where k and l are integers in the range $[0, N-1]$, for some integer $N \geq 2$. In a context such as this, it is common to define an order on these keys using the **lexicographic** (dictionary) convention, where $(k_1, l_1) < (k_2, l_2)$ if $k_1 < k_2$ or if $k_1 = k_2$ and $l_1 < l_2$ (see page 363). This is a pairwise version of the lexicographic comparison function, which can be applied to equal-length character strings, or to tuples of length d.

The **radix-sort** algorithm sorts a sequence S of entries with keys that are pairs, by applying a stable bucket-sort on the sequence twice; first using one component of the pair as the key when ordering and then using the second component. But which order is correct? Should we first sort on the k's (the first component) and then on the l's (the second component), or should it be the other way around?

To gain intuition before answering this question, we consider the following example.

Example 12.5: *Consider the following sequence S (we show only the keys):*

$$S = ((3,3),(1,5),(2,5),(1,2),(2,3),(1,7),(3,2),(2,2)).$$

If we sort S stably on the first component, then we get the sequence

$$S_1 = ((1,5),(1,2),(1,7),(2,5),(2,3),(2,2),(3,3),(3,2)).$$

If we then stably sort this sequence S_1 using the second component, we get the sequence

$$S_{1,2} = ((1,2),(2,2),(3,2),(2,3),(3,3),(1,5),(2,5),(1,7)),$$

which is unfortunately not a sorted sequence. On the other hand, if we first stably sort S using the second component, then we get the sequence

$$S_2 = ((1,2),(3,2),(2,2),(3,3),(2,3),(1,5),(2,5),(1,7)).$$

If we then stably sort sequence S_2 using the first component, we get the sequence

$$S_{2,1} = ((1,2),(1,5),(1,7),(2,2),(2,3),(2,5),(3,2),(3,3)),$$

which is indeed sequence S lexicographically ordered.

So, from this example, we are led to believe that we should first sort using the second component and then again using the first component. This intuition is exactly right. By first stably sorting by the second component and then again by the first component, we guarantee that if two entries are equal in the second sort (by the first component), then their relative order in the starting sequence (which is sorted by the second component) is preserved. Thus, the resulting sequence is guaranteed to be sorted lexicographically every time. We leave to a simple exercise (R-12.19) the determination of how this approach can be extended to triples and other d-tuples of numbers. We can summarize this section as follows:

Proposition 12.6: *Let S be a sequence of n key-value pairs, each of which has a key $(k_1, k_2, \ldots, k_d)$, where k_i is an integer in the range $[0, N-1]$ for some integer $N \geq 2$. We can sort S lexicographically in time $O(d(n+N))$ using radix-sort.*

Radix-sort can be applied to any key that can be viewed as a composite of smaller pieces that are to be sorted lexicographically. For example, we can apply it to sort character strings of moderate length, as each individual character can be represented as an integer value. (Some care is needed to properly handle strings with varying lengths.)

12.4 Comparing Sorting Algorithms

At this point, it might be useful for us to take a moment and consider all the algorithms we have studied in this book to sort an n-element sequence.

Considering Running Time and Other Factors

We have studied several methods, such as insertion-sort and selection-sort, that have $O(n^2)$-time behavior in the average and worst case. We have also studied several methods with $O(n \log n)$-time behavior, including heap-sort, merge-sort, and quick-sort. Finally, the bucket-sort and radix-sort methods run in linear time for certain types of keys. Certainly, the selection-sort algorithm is a poor choice in any application, since it runs in $O(n^2)$ time even in the best case. But, of the remaining sorting algorithms, which is the best?

As with many things in life, there is no clear "best" sorting algorithm from the remaining candidates. There are trade-offs involving efficiency, memory usage, and stability. The sorting algorithm best suited for a particular application depends on the properties of that application. In fact, the default sorting algorithm used by computing languages and systems has evolved greatly over time. We can offer some guidance and observations, therefore, based on the known properties of the "good" sorting algorithms.

Insertion-Sort

If implemented well, the running time of ***insertion-sort*** is $O(n+m)$, where m is the number of ***inversions*** (that is, the number of pairs of elements out of order). Thus, insertion-sort is an excellent algorithm for sorting small sequences (say, less than 50 elements), because insertion-sort is simple to program, and small sequences necessarily have few inversions. Also, insertion-sort is quite effective for sorting sequences that are already "almost" sorted. By "almost," we mean that the number of inversions is small. But the $O(n^2)$-time performance of insertion-sort makes it a poor choice outside of these special contexts.

Heap-Sort

Heap-sort, on the other hand, runs in $O(n \log n)$ time in the worst case, which is optimal for comparison-based sorting methods. Heap-sort can easily be made to execute in-place, and is a natural choice on small- and medium-sized sequences, when input data can fit into main memory. However, heap-sort tends to be outperformed by both quick-sort and merge-sort on larger sequences. A standard heap-sort does not provide a stable sort, because of the swapping of elements.

Quick-Sort

Although its $O(n^2)$-time worst-case performance makes **quick-sort** susceptible in real-time applications where we must make guarantees on the time needed to complete a sorting operation, we expect its performance to be $O(n \log n)$ time, and experimental studies have shown that it outperforms both heap-sort and merge-sort on many tests. Quick-sort does not naturally provide a stable sort, due to the swapping of elements during the partitioning step.

For decades quick-sort was the default choice for a general-purpose, in-memory sorting algorithm. Quick-sort was included as the qsort sorting utility provided in C language libraries, and was the basis for sorting utilities on Unix operating systems for many years. It has long been the standard algorithm for sorting arrays of primitive type in Java. (We discuss sorting of object types below.)

Merge-Sort

Merge-sort runs in $O(n \log n)$ time in the worst case. It is quite difficult to make merge-sort run in-place for arrays, and without that optimization the extra overhead of allocate a temporary array, and copying between the arrays is less attractive than in-place implementations of heap-sort and quick-sort for sequences that can fit entirely in a computer's main memory. Even so, merge-sort is an excellent algorithm for situations where the input is stratified across various levels of the computer's memory hierarchy (e.g., cache, main memory, external memory). In these contexts, the way that merge-sort processes runs of data in long merge streams makes the best use of all the data brought as a block into a level of memory, thereby reducing the total number of memory transfers.

The GNU sorting utility (and most current versions of the Linux operating system) relies on a multiway merge-sort variant. **Tim-sort** (designed by Tim Peters) is a hybrid approach that is essentially a bottom-up merge-sort that takes advantage of initial runs in the data while using insertion-sort to build additional runs. Tim-sort has been the standard sorting algorithm in Python since 2003, and it has become the default algorithm for sorting arrays of object types, as of Java SE 7.

Bucket-Sort and Radix-Sort

Finally, if an application involves sorting entries with small integer keys, character strings, or d-tuples of keys from a discrete range, then **bucket-sort** or **radix-sort** is an excellent choice, for it runs in $O(d(n+N))$ time, where $[0, N-1]$ is the range of integer keys (and $d = 1$ for bucket sort). Thus, if $d(n+N)$ is significantly "below" the $n \log n$ function, then this sorting method should run faster than even quick-sort, heap-sort, or merge-sort.

12.5   Selection

As important as it is, sorting is not the only interesting problem dealing with a total order relation on a set of elements. There are a number of applications in which we are interested in identifying a single element in terms of its rank relative to the sorted order of the entire set. Examples include identifying the minimum and maximum elements, but we may also be interested in, say, identifying the *median* element, that is, the element such that half of the other elements are smaller and the remaining half are larger. In general, queries that ask for an element with a given rank are called *order statistics*.

Defining the Selection Problem

In this section, we discuss the general order-statistic problem of selecting the kth smallest element from an unsorted collection of n comparable elements. This is known as the *selection* problem. Of course, we can solve this problem by sorting the collection and then indexing into the sorted sequence at index $k - 1$. Using the best comparison-based sorting algorithms, this approach would take $O(n \log n)$ time, which is obviously an overkill for the cases where $k = 1$ or $k = n$ (or even $k = 2$, $k = 3$, $k = n - 1$, or $k = n - 5$), because we can easily solve the selection problem for these values of k in $O(n)$ time. Thus, a natural question to ask is whether we can achieve an $O(n)$ running time for all values of k (including the interesting case of finding the median, where $k = \lfloor n/2 \rfloor$).

12.5.1   Prune-and-Search

We can indeed solve the selection problem in $O(n)$ time for any value of k. Moreover, the technique we use to achieve this result involves an interesting algorithmic design pattern. This design pattern is known as *prune-and-search* or *decrease-and-conquer*. In applying this design pattern, we solve a given problem that is defined on a collection of n objects by pruning away a fraction of the n objects and recursively solving the smaller problem. When we have finally reduced the problem to one defined on a constant-sized collection of objects, we then solve the problem using some brute-force method. Returning back from all the recursive calls completes the construction. In some cases, we can avoid using recursion, in which case we simply iterate the prune-and-search reduction step until we can apply a brute-force method and stop. Incidentally, the binary search method described in Section 5.1.3 is an example of the prune-and-search design pattern.

12.5.2   Randomized Quick-Select

In applying the prune-and-search pattern to finding the kth smallest element in an unordered sequence of n elements, we describe a simple and practical algorithm, known as *randomized quick-select*. This algorithm runs in $O(n)$ *expected* time, taken over all possible random choices made by the algorithm; this expectation does not depend whatsoever on any randomness assumptions about the input distribution. We note though that randomized quick-select runs in $O(n^2)$ time in the *worst case*, the justification of which is left as an exercise (R-12.25). We also provide an exercise (C-12.56) for modifying randomized quick-select to define a *deterministic* selection algorithm that runs in $O(n)$ *worst-case* time. The existence of this deterministic algorithm is mostly of theoretical interest, however, since the constant factor hidden by the big-Oh notation is relatively large in that case.

Suppose we are given an unsorted sequence S of n comparable elements together with an integer $k \in [1, n]$. At a high level, the quick-select algorithm for finding the kth smallest element in S is similar to the randomized quick-sort algorithm described in Section 12.2.1. We pick a "pivot" element from S at random and use this to subdivide S into three subsequences L, E, and G, storing the elements of S less than, equal to, and greater than the pivot, respectively. In the prune step, we determine which of these subsets contains the desired element, based on the value of k and the sizes of those subsets. We then recur on the appropriate subset, noting that the desired element's rank in the subset may differ from its rank in the full set. Pseudocode for randomized quick-select is shown in Code Fragment 12.8.

Algorithm quickSelect(S, k):
   Input: Sequence S of n comparable elements, and an integer $k \in [1, n]$
   Output: The kth smallest element of S
   if $n == 1$ **then**
      return the (first) element of S.
   pick a random (pivot) element x of S and divide S into three sequences:
      • L, storing the elements in S less than x
      • E, storing the elements in S equal to x
      • G, storing the elements in S greater than x
   if $k \le |L|$ **then**
      return quickSelect(L, k)
   else if $k \le |L| + |E|$ **then**
      return x {each element in E is equal to x}
   else
      return quickSelect($G, k - |L| - |E|$)   {note the new selection parameter}

Code Fragment 12.8: Randomized quick-select algorithm.

12.5.3 Analyzing Randomized Quick-Select

Showing that randomized quick-select runs in $O(n)$ time requires a simple probabilistic argument. The argument is based on the ***linearity of expectation***, which states that if X and Y are random variables and c is a number, then

$$E(X+Y) = E(X) + E(Y) \qquad \text{and} \qquad E(cX) = cE(X),$$

where we use $E(\mathcal{Z})$ to denote the expected value of the expression $\mathcal{Z}$.

Let $t(n)$ be the running time of randomized quick-select on a sequence of size n. Since this algorithm depends on random events, its running time, $t(n)$, is a random variable. We want to bound $E(t(n))$, the expected value of $t(n)$. Say that a recursive call of our algorithm is "good" if it partitions S so that the size of each of L and G is at most $3n/4$. Clearly, a recursive call is good with probability at least $1/2$. Let $g(n)$ denote the number of consecutive recursive calls we make, including the present one, before we get a good one. Then we can characterize $t(n)$ using the following ***recurrence equation***:

$$t(n) \leq bn \cdot g(n) + t(3n/4),$$

where $b \geq 1$ is a constant. Applying the linearity of expectation for $n > 1$, we get

$$E(t(n)) \leq E(bn \cdot g(n) + t(3n/4)) = bn \cdot E(g(n)) + E(t(3n/4)).$$

Since a recursive call is good with probability at least $1/2$, and whether a recursive call is good or not is independent of its parent call being good, the expected value of $g(n)$ is at most the expected number of times we must flip a fair coin before it comes up "heads." That is, $E(g(n)) \leq 2$. Thus, if we let $T(n)$ be shorthand for $E(t(n))$, then we can write the case for $n > 1$ as

$$T(n) \leq T(3n/4) + 2bn.$$

To convert this relation into a closed form, let us iteratively apply this inequality assuming n is large. So, for example, after two applications,

$$T(n) \leq T((3/4)^2 n) + 2b(3/4)n + 2bn.$$

At this point, we should see that the general case is

$$T(n) \leq 2bn \cdot \sum_{i=0}^{\lceil \log_{4/3} n \rceil} (3/4)^i.$$

In other words, the expected running time is at most $2bn$ times a geometric sum whose base is a positive number less than 1. Thus, by Proposition 4.5, $T(n)$ is $O(n)$.

Proposition 12.7: *The expected running time of randomized quick-select on a sequence S of size n is $O(n)$, assuming two elements of S can be compared in $O(1)$ time.*

12.6   Exercises

Reinforcement

R-12.1 Give a complete justification of Proposition 12.1.

R-12.2 In the merge-sort tree shown in Figures 12.2 through 12.4, some edges are drawn as arrows. What is the meaning of a downward arrow? How about an upward arrow?

R-12.3 Show that the running time of the merge-sort algorithm on an n-element sequence is $O(n\log n)$, even when n is not a power of 2.

R-12.4 Is our array-based implementation of merge-sort given in Section 12.1.2 stable? Explain why or why not.

R-12.5 Is our linked-list-based implementation of merge-sort (Code Fragment 12.3) stable? Explain why or why not.

R-12.6 An algorithm that sorts key-value entries by key is said to be ***straggling*** if any time two entries e_i and e_j have equal keys, but e_i appears before e_j in the input, then the algorithm places e_i after e_j in the output. Describe a change to the merge-sort algorithm in Section 12.1 to make it straggling.

R-12.7 Suppose we are given two n-element sorted sequences A and B each with distinct elements, but potentially some elements that are in both sequences. Describe an $O(n)$-time method for computing a sequence representing the union $A \cup B$ (with no duplicates) as a sorted sequence.

R-12.8 Give pseudocode descriptions for the retainAll and removeAll methods of the set ADT, assuming we use sorted sequences to implement sets.

R-12.9 Suppose we modify the deterministic version of the quick-sort algorithm so that, instead of selecting the last element in an n-element sequence as the pivot, we choose the element at index $\lfloor n/2 \rfloor$. What is the running time of this version of quick-sort on a sequence that is already sorted?

R-12.10 Consider a modification of the deterministic version of the quick-sort algorithm where we choose the element at index $\lfloor n/2 \rfloor$ as our pivot. Describe the kind of sequence that would cause this version of quick-sort to run in $\Omega(n^2)$ time.

R-12.11 Suppose the method quickSortInPlace is executed on a sequence with duplicate elements. Prove that the algorithm still correctly sorts the input sequence. What happens in the partition step when there are elements equal to the pivot? What is the running time of the algorithm if all the input elements are equal?

R-12.12 Show that the best-case running time of quick-sort on a sequence of size n with distinct elements is $\Omega(n\log n)$.

R-12.13 If the outermost while loop of our implementation of quickSortInPlace (line 9 of Code Fragment 12.6) were changed to use condition left < right, instead of condition left <= right, there would be a flaw. Explain the flaw and give a specific input sequence on which such an implementation fails.

R-12.14 If the conditional at line 14 of our quickSortInPlace implementation of Code Fragment 12.6 were changed to use condition left $<$ right, instead of condition left $<=$ right, there would be a flaw. Explain the flaw and give a specific input sequence on which such an implementation fails.

R-12.15 Following our analysis of randomized quick-sort in Section 12.2.1, show that the probability that a given input element x belongs to more than $2 \log n$ subproblems in size group i is at most $1/n^2$.

R-12.16 Of the $n!$ possible inputs to a given comparison-based sorting algorithm, what is the absolute maximum number of inputs that could be correctly sorted with just n comparisons?

R-12.17 Jonathan has a comparison-based sorting algorithm that sorts the first k elements of a sequence of size n in $O(n)$ time. Give a big-Oh characterization of the biggest that k can be.

R-12.18 Is the bucket-sort algorithm in-place? Why or why not?

R-12.19 Describe a radix-sort method for lexicographically sorting a sequence S of triplets (k,l,m), where k, l, and m are integers in the range $[0, N-1]$, for $N \geq 2$. How could this scheme be extended to sequences of d-tuples $(k_1, k_2, \ldots, k_d)$, where each k_i is an integer in the range $[0, N-1]$?

R-12.20 Suppose S is a sequence of n values, each equal to 0 or 1. How long will it take to sort S with the merge-sort algorithm? What about quick-sort?

R-12.21 Suppose S is a sequence of n values, each equal to 0 or 1. How long will it take to sort S stably with the bucket-sort algorithm?

R-12.22 Given a sequence S of n values, each equal to 0 or 1, describe an in-place method for sorting S.

R-12.23 Give an example input that requires merge-sort and heap-sort to take $O(n \log n)$ time to sort, but insertion-sort runs in $O(n)$ time. What if you reverse this list?

R-12.24 What is the best algorithm for sorting each of the following: general comparable objects, long character strings, 32-bit integers, double-precision floating-point numbers, and bytes? Justify your answer.

R-12.25 Show that the worst-case running time of quick-select on an n-element sequence is $\Omega(n^2)$.

Creativity

C-12.26 Describe and analyze an efficient method for removing all duplicates from a collection A of n elements.

C-12.27 Augment the PositionalList class (see Section 7.3) to support a method named sort that sorts the elements of a list by relinking existing nodes; you are not to create any new nodes. You may use your choice of sorting algorithm.

C-12.28 Linda claims to have an algorithm that takes an input sequence S and produces an output sequence T that is a sorting of the n elements in S.

    a. Give an algorithm, isSorted, that tests in $O(n)$ time if T is sorted.

    b. Explain why the algorithm isSorted is not sufficient to prove a particular output T to Linda's algorithm is a sorting of S.

    c. Describe what additional information Linda's algorithm could output so that her algorithm's correctness could be established on any given S and T in $O(n)$ time.

C-12.29 Augment the PositionalList class (see Section 7.3) to support a method named merge with the following behavior. If A and B are PositionalList instances whose elements are sorted, the syntax A.merge(B) should merge all elements of B into A so that A remains sorted and B becomes empty. Your implementation must accomplish the merge by relinking existing nodes; you are not to create any new nodes.

C-12.30 Implement a bottom-up merge-sort for a collection of items by placing each item in its own queue, and then repeatedly merging pairs of queues until all items are sorted within a single queue.

C-12.31 Modify our in-place quick-sort implementation of Code Fragment 12.6 to be a *randomized* version of the algorithm, as discussed in Section 12.2.1.

C-12.32 Consider a version of deterministic quick-sort where we pick as our pivot the median of the d last elements in the input sequence of n elements, for a fixed, constant odd number $d \geq 3$. What is the asymptotic worst-case running time of quick-sort in this case?

C-12.33 Another way to analyze randomized quick-sort is to use a ***recurrence equation***. In this case, we let $T(n)$ denote the expected running time of randomized quick-sort, and we observe that, because of the worst-case partitions for good and bad splits, we can write

$$T(n) \leq \frac{1}{2} \left(T(3n/4) + T(n/4) \right) + \frac{1}{2} \left(T(n-1) \right) + bn,$$

where bn is the time needed to partition a list for a given pivot and concatenate the result sublists after the recursive calls return. Show, by induction, that $T(n)$ is $O(n \log n)$.

C-12.34 Our high-level description of quick-sort describes partitioning the elements into three sets L, E, and G, having keys less than, equal to, or greater than the pivot, respectively. However, our in-place quick-sort implementation of Code Fragment 12.6 does not gather all elements equal to the pivot into a set E. An alternative strategy for an in-place, three-way partition is as follows. Loop through the elements from left to right maintaining indices a, b, and c and the invariant that elements with index i such that $0 \leq i < a$ are strictly less than the pivot, those with $a \leq i < b$ are equal to the pivot, and those with index $b \leq i < c$ are strictly greater than the pivot; elements with index $c \leq i < n$ are yet unclassified. In each pass of the loop, classify one additional element, performing a constant number of swaps as needed. Implement an in-place quick-sort using this strategy.

C-12.35 Suppose we are given an n-element sequence S such that each element in S represents a different vote for president, where each vote is given as an integer representing a particular candidate, yet the integers may be arbitrarily large (even if the number of candidates is not). Design an $O(n\log n)$-time algorithm to see who wins the election S represents, assuming the candidate with the most votes wins.

C-12.36 Consider the voting problem from Exercise C-12.35, but now suppose that we know the number $k < n$ of candidates running, even though the integer IDs for those candidates can be arbitrarily large. Describe an $O(n\log k)$-time algorithm for determining who wins the election.

C-12.37 Consider the voting problem from Exercise C-12.35, but now suppose the integers 1 to k are used to identify $k < n$ candidates. Design an $O(n)$-time algorithm to determine who wins the election.

C-12.38 Show that any comparison-based sorting algorithm can be made to be stable without affecting its asymptotic running time.

C-12.39 Suppose we are given two sequences A and B of n elements, possibly containing duplicates, on which a total order relation is defined. Describe an efficient algorithm for determining if A and B contain the same set of elements. What is the running time of this method?

C-12.40 Given an array A of n integers in the range $[0, n^2 - 1]$, describe a simple method for sorting A in $O(n)$ time.

C-12.41 Let $S_1, S_2, \ldots, S_k$ be k different sequences whose elements have integer keys in the range $[0, N - 1]$, for some parameter $N \geq 2$. Describe an algorithm that produces k respective sorted sequences in $O(n + N)$ time, where n denotes the sum of the sizes of those sequences.

C-12.42 Given a sequence S of n elements, on which a total order relation is defined, describe an efficient method for determining whether there are two equal elements in S. What is the running time of your method?

C-12.43 Let S be a sequence of n elements on which a total order relation is defined. Recall that an ***inversion*** in S is a pair of elements x and y such that x appears before y in S but $x > y$. Describe an algorithm running in $O(n\log n)$ time for determining the ***number*** of inversions in S.

C-12.44 Let S be a sequence of n integers. Describe a method for printing out all the pairs of inversions in S in $O(n + k)$ time, where k is the number of such inversions.

C-12.45 Let S be a random permutation of n distinct integers. Argue that the expected running time of insertion-sort on S is $\Omega(n^2)$. (Hint: Note that half of the elements ranked in the top half of a sorted version of S are expected to be in the first half of S.)

C-12.46 Let A and B be two sequences of n integers each. Given an integer m, describe an $O(n\log n)$-time algorithm for determining if there is an integer a in A and an integer b in B such that $m = a + b$.

C-12.47 Given two sets A and B represented as sorted sequences, describe an efficient algorithm for computing $A \oplus B$, which is the set of elements that are in A or B, but not in both.

C-12.48 Given a set of n integers, describe and analyze a fast method for finding the $\lceil \log n \rceil$ integers closest to the median.

C-12.49 Bob has a set A of n nuts and a set B of n bolts, such that each nut in A has a unique matching bolt in B. Unfortunately, the nuts in A all look the same, and the bolts in B all look the same as well. The only kind of a comparison that Bob can make is to take a nut-bolt pair (a,b), such that a is in A and b is in B, and test it to see if the threads of a are larger, smaller, or a perfect match with the threads of b. Describe and analyze an efficient algorithm for Bob to match up all of his nuts and bolts.

C-12.50 Our quick-select implementation can be made more space-efficient by initially computing only the *counts* for sets L, E, and G, and creating only the new subset that will be needed for recursion. Implement such a version.

C-12.51 Describe an in-place version of the quick-select algorithm in pseudocode, assuming that you are allowed to modify the order of elements.

C-12.52 Show how to use a deterministic $O(n)$-time selection algorithm to sort a sequence of n elements in $O(n \log n)$-***worst-case*** time.

C-12.53 Given an unsorted sequence S of n comparable elements, and an integer k, give an $O(n \log k)$-expected-time algorithm for finding the $O(k)$ elements that have rank $\lceil n/k \rceil$, $2\lceil n/k \rceil$, $3\lceil n/k \rceil$, and so on.

C-12.54 Space aliens have given us a method, alienSplit, that can take a sequence S of n integers and partition S in $O(n)$ time into sequences $S_1, S_2, \ldots, S_k$ of size at most $\lceil n/k \rceil$ each, such that the elements in S_i are less than or equal to every element in S_{i+1}, for $i = 1, 2, \ldots, k-1$, for a fixed number, $k < n$. Show how to use alienSplit to sort S in $O(n \log n / \log k)$ time.

C-12.55 Show that randomized quick-sort runs in $O(n \log n)$ time with probability at least $1 - 1/n$, that is, with ***high probability***, by answering the following:

a. For each input element x, define $C_{i,j}(x)$ to be a 0/1 random variable that is 1 if and only if element x is in $j+1$ subproblems that have size s such that $(3/4)^{i+1}n < s \le (3/4)^i n$. Argue why we need not define $C_{i,j}$ for $j > n$.

b. Let $X_{i,j}$ be an independent 0/1 random variable that is 1 with probability $1/2^j$, and let $L = \lceil \log_{4/3} n \rceil$. Argue that $\sum_{i=0}^{L-1} \sum_{j=0}^{n} C_{i,j}(x) \le \sum_{i=0}^{L-1} \sum_{j=0}^{n} X_{i,j}$.

c. Show that the expected value of $\sum_{i=0}^{L-1} \sum_{j=0}^{n} X_{i,j}$ is $(2 - 1/2^n)L$.

d. Show that the probability that $\sum_{i=0}^{L} \sum_{j=0}^{n} X_{i,j} > 4L$ is at most $1/n^2$, using the ***Chernoff bound*** that states that if X is the sum of a finite number of independent 0/1 random variables, having expected value $\mu > 0$, then $\Pr(X > 2\mu) < (4/e)^{-\mu}$, where $e = 2.71828128\ldots$.

e. Argue that randomized quick-sort runs in $O(n \log n)$ time with probability at least $1 - 1/n$.

C-12.56 We can make the quick-select algorithm deterministic, by choosing the pivot of an n-element sequence as follows:

> Partition the set S into $\lceil n/5 \rceil$ groups of size 5 each (except possibly for one group). Sort each little set and identify the median element in this set. From this set of $\lceil n/5 \rceil$ "baby" medians, apply the selection algorithm recursively to find the median of the baby medians. Use this element as the pivot and proceed as in the quick-select algorithm.

Show that this deterministic quick-select algorithm runs in $O(n)$ time by answering the following questions (please ignore floor and ceiling functions if that simplifies the mathematics, for the asymptotics are the same either way):

a. How many baby medians are less than or equal to the chosen pivot? How many are greater than or equal to the pivot?

b. For each baby median less than or equal to the pivot, how many other elements are less than or equal to the pivot? Is the same true for those greater than or equal to the pivot?

c. Argue why the method for finding the deterministic pivot and using it to partition S takes $O(n)$ time.

d. Based on these estimates, write a recurrence equation to bound the worst-case running time $t(n)$ for this selection algorithm (note that in the worst case there are two recursive calls—one to find the median of the baby medians and one to recur on the larger of L and G).

e. Using this recurrence equation, show by induction that $t(n)$ is $O(n)$.

C-12.57 Suppose we are interested in dynamically maintaining a set S of integers, which is initially empty, while supporting the following two operations:

> add(v): Adds value v to set S.
>
> median( ): Returns the current median value of the set. For a set with even cardinality, we define the median as the average of the two most central values.

We will store each element of the set in one of two priority queues: a min-oriented priority queue, Q^+, of all elements greater than or equal to the current median value, and a max-oriented priority queue, Q^-, of all elements less than the current median value.

a. Explain how to perform the operation median( ) in $O(1)$ time given such a representation.

b. Explain how to perform the operation S.add(k) in $O(\log n)$ time, where n is the current cardinality of the set, while maintaining such a representation.

C-12.58 As a generalization of the previous problem, revisit Exercise C-11.45, which involves performing general selection queries on a dynamic set of values.

Projects

P-12.59 Implement a nonrecursive, in-place version of the quick-sort algorithm, as described at the end of Section 12.2.2.

P-12.60 Experimentally compare the performance of in-place quick-sort and a version of quick-sort that is not in-place.

P-12.61 Perform a series of benchmarking tests on a version of merge-sort and quick-sort to determine which one is faster. Your tests should include sequences that are "random" as well as "almost" sorted.

P-12.62 Implement deterministic and randomized versions of the quick-sort algorithm and perform a series of benchmarking tests to see which one is faster. Your tests should include sequences that are very "random" looking as well as ones that are "almost" sorted.

P-12.63 Implement an in-place version of insertion-sort and an in-place version of quick-sort. Perform benchmarking tests to determine the range of values of n where quick-sort is on average better than insertion-sort.

P-12.64 Design and implement a version of the bucket-sort algorithm for sorting a list of n entries with integer keys taken from the range $[0, N-1]$, for $N \geq 2$. The algorithm should run in $O(n+N)$ time.

P-12.65 Implement an animation of one of the sorting algorithms described in this chapter, illustrating key properties of the algorithm in an intuitive manner.

P-12.66 Design and implement two versions of the bucket-sort algorithm in Java, one for sorting an array of **byte** values and one for sorting an array of **short** values. Experimentally compare the performance of your implementations with that of the method, java.util.Arrays.sort.

Chapter Notes

Knuth's classic text on *Sorting and Searching* [61] contains an extensive history of the sorting problem and algorithms for solving it. Huang and Langston [49] show how to merge two sorted lists in-place in linear time. The standard quick-sort algorithm is due to Hoare [45]. Several optimizations for quick-sort are described by Bentley and McIl-roy [15]. More information about randomized algorithms can be found in the book by Motwani and Raghavan [75]. The quick-sort analysis given in this chapter is a combination of the analysis given in an earlier Java edition of this book and the analysis of Kleinberg and Tardos [57]. Exercise C-12.33 is due to Littman. Gonnet and Baeza-Yates [38] analyze and compare experimentally several sorting algorithms. The term "prune-and-search" comes originally from the computational geometry literature (such as in the work of Clarkson [22] and Megiddo [70]). The term "decrease-and-conquer" is from Levitin [66].

Chapter

13

Text Processing

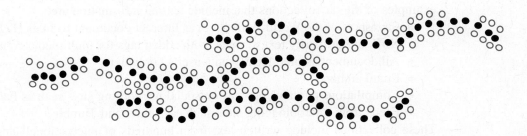

Contents

13.1 Abundance of Digitized Text

Despite the wealth of multimedia information, text processing remains one of the dominant functions of computers. Computers are used to edit, store, and display documents, and to transport files over the Internet. Furthermore, digital systems are used to archive a wide range of textual information, and new data is being generated at a rapidly increasing pace. A large corpus can readily surpass a petabyte of data (which is equivalent to a thousand terabytes, or a million gigabytes). Common examples of digital collections that include textual information are:

- Snapshots of the World Wide Web, as Internet document formats HTML and XML are primarily text formats, with added tags for multimedia content
- All documents stored locally on a user's computer
- Email archives
- Compilations of status updates on social networking sites such as Facebook
- Feeds from microblogging sites such as Twitter and Tumblr

These collections include written text from hundreds of international languages. Furthermore, there are large data sets (such as DNA) that can be viewed computationally as "strings" even though they are not language.

In this chapter, we explore some of the fundamental algorithms that can be used to efficiently analyze and process large textual data sets. In addition to having interesting applications, text-processing algorithms also highlight some important algorithmic design patterns.

We begin by examining the problem of searching for a pattern as a substring of a larger piece of text, for example, when searching for a word in a document. The pattern-matching problem gives rise to the ***brute-force method***, which is often inefficient but has wide applicability. We continue by describing more efficient algorithms for solving the pattern-matching problem, and we examine several special-purpose data structures that can be used to better organize textual data in order to support more efficient runtime queries.

Because of the massive size of textual data sets, the issue of compression is important, both in minimizing the number of bits that need to be communicated through a network and to reduce the long-term storage requirements for archives. For text compression, we can apply the ***greedy method***, which often allows us to approximate solutions to hard problems, and for some problems (such as in text compression) actually gives rise to optimal algorithms.

Finally, we introduce ***dynamic programming***, an algorithmic technique that can be applied in certain settings to solve a problem in polynomial time, which appears at first to require exponential time to solve. We demonstrate the application on this technique to the problem of finding partial matches between strings that may be similar but not perfectly aligned. This problem arises when making suggestions for a misspelled word, or when trying to match related genetic samples.

13.1.1 Notations for Character Strings

When discussing algorithms for text processing, we use character strings as a model for text. Character strings can come from a wide variety of sources, including scientific, linguistic, and Internet applications. Indeed, the following are examples of such strings:

$$S = \text{"CGTAAACTGCTTTAATCAAACGC"}$$
$$T = \text{"http://www.wiley.com"}$$

The first string, S, comes from DNA applications, and the second string, T, is the Internet address (URL) for the publisher of this book.

To allow fairly general notions of a string in our algorithm descriptions, we only assume that characters of a string come from a known ***alphabet***, which we denote as Σ. For example, in the context of DNA, there are four symbols in the standard alphabet, $\Sigma = \{A, C, G, T\}$. This alphabet Σ can, of course, be a subset of the ASCII or Unicode character sets, but it could also be something more general. Although we assume that an alphabet has a fixed finite size, denoted as $|\Sigma|$, that size can be nontrivial, as with Java's treatment of the Unicode alphabet, which allows more than a million distinct characters. We therefore consider the impact of $|\Sigma|$ in our asymptotic analysis of text-processing algorithms.

Java's String class provides support for representing an ***immutable*** sequence of characters, while its StringBuilder class supports ***mutable*** character sequences (see Section 1.3). For much of this chapter, we rely on the more primitive representation of a string as a **char** array, primarily because it allows us to use the standard indexing notation $S[i]$, rather than the String class's more cumbersome syntax, S.charAt(i).

In order to discuss pieces of a string, we denote as a ***substring*** of an n-character string P a string of the form $P[i]P[i+1]P[i+2] \cdots P[j]$, for some $0 \le i \le j \le n-1$. To simplify the notation for referring to such substrings in prose, we let $P[i..j]$ denote the substring of P from index i to index j inclusive. We note that string is technically a substring of itself (taking $i = 0$ and $j = n-1$), so if we want to rule this out as a possibility, we must restrict the definition to ***proper*** substrings, which require that either $i > 0$ or $j < n-1$. We use the convention that if $i > j$, then $P[i..j]$ is equal to the ***null string***, which has length 0.

In addition, in order to distinguish some special kinds of substrings, let us refer to any substring of the form $P[0..j]$, for $0 \le j \le n-1$, as a ***prefix*** of P, and any substring of the form $P[i..n-1]$, for $0 \le i \le n-1$, as a ***suffix*** of P. For example, if we again take P to be the string of DNA given above, then "CGTAA" is a prefix of P, "CGC" is a suffix of P, and "TTAATC" is a (proper) substring of P. Note that the null string is a prefix and a suffix of any other string.

13.2   Pattern-Matching Algorithms

In the classic *pattern-matching* problem, we are given a *text* string of length n and a *pattern* string of length $m \leq n$, and must determine whether the pattern is a substring of the text. If so, we may want to find the lowest index within the text at which the pattern begins, or perhaps *all* indices at which the pattern begins.

The pattern-matching problem is inherent to many behaviors of Java's String class, such as text.contains(pattern) and text.indexOf(pattern), and is a subtask of more complex string operations such as text.replace(pattern, substitute) and text.split(pattern).

In this section, we present three pattern-matching algorithms, with increasing levels of sophistication. Our implementations report the index that begins the leftmost occurrence of the pattern, if found. For a failed search, we adopt the conventions of the indexOf method of Java's String class, returning -1 as a sentinel.

13.2.1   Brute Force

The *brute-force* algorithmic design pattern is a powerful technique for algorithm design when we have something we wish to search for or when we wish to optimize some function. When applying this technique in a general situation, we typically enumerate all possible configurations of the inputs involved and pick the best of all these enumerated configurations.

In applying this technique to design a brute-force pattern-matching algorithm, we derive what is probably the first algorithm that we might think of for solving the problem—we simply test all the possible placements of the pattern relative to the text. An implementation of this algorithm is shown in Code Fragment 13.1.

```
1  /** Returns the lowest index at which substring pattern begins in text (or else −1).*/
2  public static int findBrute(char[ ] text, char[ ] pattern) {
3    int n = text.length;
4    int m = pattern.length;
5    for (int i=0; i <= n − m; i++) {          // try every starting index within text
6      int k = 0;                              // k is index into pattern
7      while (k < m && text[i+k] == pattern[k]) // kth character of pattern matches
8        k++;
9      if (k == m)                             // if we reach the end of the pattern,
10       return i;                             // substring text[i..i+m-1] is a match
11   }
12   return −1;                                // search failed
13 }
```

Code Fragment 13.1: An implementation of the brute-force pattern-matching algorithm. (We use character arrays rather than strings to simplify indexing notation.)

Performance

The analysis of the brute-force pattern-matching algorithm could not be simpler. It consists of two nested loops, with the outer loop indexing through all possible starting indices of the pattern in the text, and the inner loop indexing through each character of the pattern, comparing it to its potentially corresponding character in the text. Thus, the correctness of the brute-force pattern-matching algorithm follows immediately from this exhaustive search approach.

The running time of brute-force pattern matching in the worst case is not good, however, because we can perform up to m character comparisons for each candidate alignment of the pattern within the text. Referring to Code Fragment 13.1, we see that the outer **for** loop is executed at most $n - m + 1$ times, and the inner **while** loop is executed at most m times. Thus, the worst-case running time of the brute-force method is $O(nm)$.

Example 13.1: *Suppose we are given the text string*

$$\text{text} = \texttt{"abacaabaccabacabaabb"}$$

and the pattern string

$$\text{pattern} = \texttt{"abacab"}$$

Figure 13.1 illustrates the execution of the brute-force pattern-matching algorithm on this selection of text and pattern.

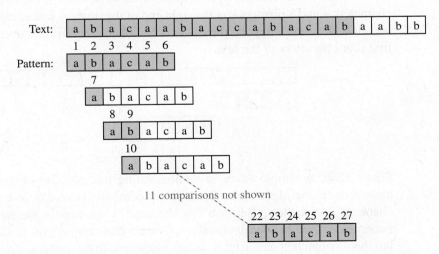

Figure 13.1: Example run of the brute-force pattern-matching algorithm. The algorithm performs 27 character comparisons, indicated above with numerical labels.

13.2.2   The Boyer-Moore Algorithm

At first, it might seem that it is always necessary to examine every character in the text in order to locate a pattern as a substring or to rule out its existence. But this is not always the case. The **Boyer-Moore** pattern-matching algorithm, which we will study in this section, can sometimes avoid examining a significant fraction of the character in the text. In this section, we will describe a simplified version of the original algorithm by Boyer and Moore.

The main idea of the Boyer-Moore algorithm is to improve the running time of the brute-force algorithm by adding two potentially time-saving heuristics. Roughly stated, these heuristics are as follows:

Looking-Glass Heuristic: When testing a possible placement of the pattern against the text, perform the comparisons against the pattern from right-to-left.

Character-Jump Heuristic: During the testing of a possible placement of the pattern within the text, a mismatch of character text[i]=c with the corresponding character pattern[k] is handled as follows. If c is not contained anywhere in the pattern, then shift the pattern completely past text[i] = c. Otherwise, shift the pattern until an occurrence of character c gets aligned with text[i].

We will formalize these heuristics shortly, but at an intuitive level, they work as an integrated team to allow us to avoid comparisons with whole groups of characters in the text. In particular, when a mismatch is found near the right end of the pattern, we may end up realigning the pattern beyond the mismatch, without ever examining several characters of the text preceding the mismatch. For example, Figure 13.2 demonstrates a few simple applications of these heuristics. Notice that when the characters e and i mismatch at the right end of the original placement of the pattern, we slide the pattern beyond the mismatched character, without ever examining the first four characters of the text.

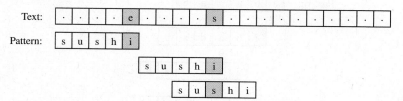

Figure 13.2: A simple example demonstrating the intuition of the Boyer-Moore pattern-matching algorithm. The original comparison results in a mismatch with character e of the text. Because that character is nowhere in the pattern, the entire pattern is shifted beyond its location. The second comparison is also a mismatch, but the mismatched character s occurs elsewhere in the pattern. The pattern is then shifted so that its last occurrence of s is aligned with the corresponding s in the text. The remainder of the process is not illustrated in this figure.

The example of Figure 13.2 is rather basic, because it only involves mismatches with the last character of the pattern. More generally, when a match is found for that last character, the algorithm continues by trying to extend the match with the second-to-last character of the pattern in its current alignment. That process continues until either matching the entire pattern, or finding a mismatch at some interior position of the pattern.

If a mismatch is found, and the mismatched character of the text does not occur in the pattern, we shift the entire pattern beyond that location, as originally illustrated in Figure 13.2. If the mismatched character occurs elsewhere in the pattern, we must consider two possible subcases depending on whether its last occurrence is before or after the character of the pattern that was mismatched. Those two cases are illustrated in Figure 13.3.

In the case of Figure 13.3(b), we slide the pattern only one unit. It would be more productive to slide it rightward until finding another occurrence of mismatched character text[i] in the pattern, but we do not wish to take time to search

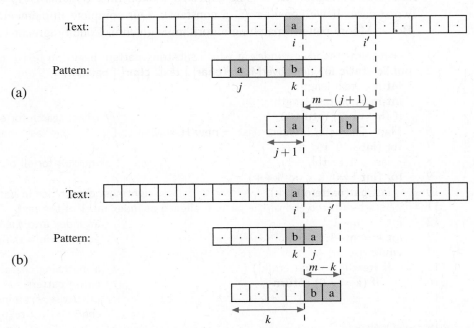

Figure 13.3: Additional rules for the character-jump heuristic of the Boyer-Moore algorithm. We let i represent the index of the mismatched character in the text, k represent the corresponding index in the pattern, and j represent the index of the last occurrence of text[i] within the pattern. We distinguish two cases: (a) $j < k$, in which case we shift the pattern by $k - j$ units, and thus, index i advances by $m - (j + 1)$ units; (b) $j > k$, in which case we shift the pattern by one unit, and index i advances by $m - k$ units.

for another occurrence. The efficiency of the Boyer-Moore algorithm relies on quickly determining where a mismatched character occurs elsewhere in the pattern. In particular, we define a function $last(c)$ as

- If c is in the pattern, $last(c)$ is the index of the last (rightmost) occurrence of c in the pattern. Otherwise, we conventionally define $last(c) = -1$.

If we assume that the alphabet is of fixed, finite size, and that characters can be converted to indices of an array (for example, by using their character code), the last function can be easily implemented as a lookup table with worst-case $O(1)$-time access to the value $last(c)$. However, the table would have length equal to the size of the alphabet (rather than the size of the pattern), and time would be required to initialize the entire table.

We prefer to use a hash table to represent the last function, with only those characters from the pattern occurring in the map. The space usage for this approach is proportional to the number of distinct alphabet symbols that occur in the pattern, and thus $O(\max(m, |\Sigma|))$. The expected lookup time remains $O(1)$ (as does the worst-case, if we consider $|\Sigma|$ a constant). Our complete implementation of the Boyer-Moore pattern-matching algorithm is given in Code Fragment 13.2.

```java
 1  /** Returns the lowest index at which substring pattern begins in text (or else −1).*/
 2  public static int findBoyerMoore(char[ ] text, char[ ] pattern) {
 3    int n = text.length;
 4    int m = pattern.length;
 5    if (m == 0) return 0;                            // trivial search for empty string
 6    Map<Character,Integer> last = new HashMap<>();   // the 'last' map
 7    for (int i=0; i < n; i++)
 8      last.put(text[i], −1);                         // set −1 as default for all text characters
 9    for (int k=0; k < m; k++)
10      last.put(pattern[k], k);                       // rightmost occurrence in pattern is last
11    // start with the end of the pattern aligned at index m−1 of the text
12    int i = m−1;                                     // an index into the text
13    int k = m−1;                                     // an index into the pattern
14    while (i < n) {
15      if (text[i] == pattern[k]) {                   // a matching character
16        if (k == 0) return i;                        // entire pattern has been found
17        i−−;                                         // otherwise, examine previous
18        k−−;                                         // characters of text/pattern
19      } else {
20        i += m − Math.min(k, 1 + last.get(text[i])); // case analysis for jump step
21        k = m − 1;                                   // restart at end of pattern
22      }
23    }
24    return −1;                                       // pattern was never found
25  }
```

Code Fragment 13.2: An implementation of the Boyer-Moore algorithm.

The correctness of the Boyer-Moore pattern-matching algorithm follows from the fact that each time the method makes a shift, it is guaranteed not to "skip" over any possible matches. For $\mathsf{last}(c)$ is the location of the ***last*** occurrence of c in the pattern. In Figure 13.4, we illustrate the execution of the Boyer-Moore pattern-matching algorithm on an input string similar to Example 13.1.

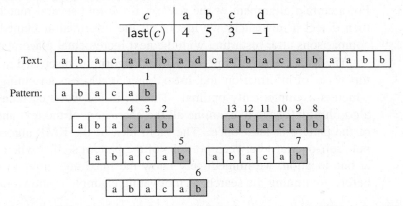

Figure 13.4: An illustration of the Boyer-Moore pattern-matching algorithm, including a summary of the $\mathsf{last}(c)$ function. The algorithm performs 13 character comparisons, which are indicated with numerical labels.

Performance

If using a traditional lookup table, the worst-case running time of the Boyer-Moore algorithm is $O(nm + |\Sigma|)$. The computation of the last function takes $O(m + |\Sigma|)$ time, although the dependence on $|\Sigma|$ is removed if using a hash table. The actual search for the pattern takes $O(nm)$ time in the worst case—the same as the brute-force algorithm. An example that achieves the worst case for Boyer-Moore is

$$\text{text} = \overbrace{aaaaaa\cdots a}^{n}$$
$$\text{pattern} = b\overbrace{aa\cdots a}^{m-1}$$

The worst-case performance, however, is unlikely to be achieved for English text; in that case, the Boyer-Moore algorithm is often able to skip large portions of text. Experimental evidence on English text shows that the average number of comparisons done per character is 0.24 for a five-character pattern string.

We have actually presented a simplified version of the Boyer-Moore algorithm. The original algorithm achieves worst-case running time $O(n + m + |\Sigma|)$ by using an alternative shift heuristic for a partially matched text string, whenever it shifts the pattern more than the character-jump heuristic. This alternative shift heuristic is based on applying the main idea from the Knuth-Morris-Pratt pattern-matching algorithm, which we discuss next.

13.2.3   The Knuth-Morris-Pratt Algorithm

In examining the worst-case performances of the brute-force and Boyer-Moore pattern-matching algorithms on specific instances of the problem, such as that given in Example 13.1, we should notice a major inefficiency (at least in the worst case). For a certain alignment of the pattern, if we find several matching characters but then detect a mismatch, we ignore all the information gained by the successful comparisons after restarting with the next incremental placement of the pattern.

The Knuth-Morris-Pratt (or "KMP") algorithm, discussed in this section, avoids this waste of information and, in so doing, it achieves a running time of $O(n+m)$, which is asymptotically optimal. That is, in the worst case any pattern-matching algorithm will have to examine all the characters of the text and all the characters of the pattern at least once. The main idea of the KMP algorithm is to precompute self-overlaps between portions of the pattern so that when a mismatch occurs at one location, we immediately know the maximum amount to shift the pattern before continuing the search. A motivating example is shown in Figure 13.5.

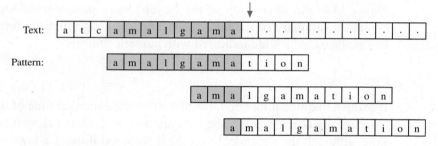

Figure 13.5: A motivating example for the Knuth-Morris-Pratt algorithm. If a mismatch occurs at the indicated location, the pattern could be shifted to the second alignment, without explicit need to recheck the partial match with the prefix ama. If the mismatched character is not an l, then the next potential alignment of the pattern can take advantage of the common a.

The Failure Function

To implement the KMP algorithm, we will precompute a ***failure function***, f, that indicates the proper shift of the pattern upon a failed comparison. Specifically, the failure function $f(k)$ is defined as the length of the longest prefix of the pattern that is a suffix of the substring pattern[1..k] (note that we did ***not*** include pattern[0] here, since we will shift at least one unit). Intuitively, if we find a mismatch upon character pattern[k+1], the function $f(k)$ tells us how many of the immediately preceding characters can be reused to restart the pattern. Example 13.2 describes the value of the failure function for the example pattern from Figure 13.5.

Example 13.2: *Consider the pattern* "amalgamation" *from Figure 13.5. The Knuth-Morris-Pratt (KMP) failure function, $f(k)$, for the string P is as shown in the following table:*

k	0	1	2	3	4	5	6	7	8	9	10	11
$P[k]$	a	m	a	l	g	a	m	a	t	i	o	n
$f(k)$	0	0	1	0	0	1	2	3	0	0	0	0

Implementation

Our implementation of the KMP pattern-matching algorithm is shown in Code Fragment 13.3. It relies on a utility method, computeFailKMP, discussed on the next page, to compute the failure function efficiently.

The main part of the KMP algorithm is its **while** loop, each iteration of which performs a comparison between the character at index j in the text and the character at index k in the pattern. If the outcome of this comparison is a match, the algorithm moves on to the next characters in both (or reports a match if reaching the end of the pattern). If the comparison failed, the algorithm consults the failure function for a new candidate character in the pattern, or starts over with the next index in the text if failing on the first character of the pattern (since nothing can be reused).

```
1  /** Returns the lowest index at which substring pattern begins in text (or else −1).*/
2  public static int findKMP(char[ ] text, char[ ] pattern) {
3    int n = text.length;
4    int m = pattern.length;
5    if (m == 0) return 0;                          // trivial search for empty string
6    int[ ] fail = computeFailKMP(pattern);         // computed by private utility
7    int j = 0;                                     // index into text
8    int k = 0;                                     // index into pattern
9    while (j < n) {
10     if (text[j] == pattern[k]) {                 // pattern[0..k] matched thus far
11       if (k == m − 1) return j − m + 1;          // match is complete
12       j++;                                       // otherwise, try to extend match
13       k++;
14     } else if (k > 0)
15       k = fail[k−1];                             // reuse suffix of P[0..k-1]
16     else
17       j++;
18   }
19   return −1;                                     // reached end without match
20 }
```

Code Fragment 13.3: An implementation of the KMP pattern-matching algorithm. The computeFailKMP utility method is given in Code Fragment 13.4.

Constructing the KMP Failure Function

To construct the failure function, we use the method shown in Code Fragment 13.4, which is a "bootstrapping" process that compares the pattern to itself as in the KMP algorithm. Each time we have two characters that match, we set $f(j) = k + 1$. Note that since we have $j > k$ throughout the execution of the algorithm, $f(k-1)$ is always well defined when we need to use it.

```
1   private static int[ ] computeFailKMP(char[ ] pattern) {
2     int m = pattern.length;
3     int[ ] fail = new int[m];              // by default, all overlaps are zero
4     int j = 1;
5     int k = 0;
6     while (j < m) {                        // compute fail[j] during this pass, if nonzero
7       if (pattern[j] == pattern[k]) {      // k + 1 characters match thus far
8         fail[j] = k + 1;
9         j++;
10        k++;
11      } else if (k > 0)                    // k follows a matching prefix
12        k = fail[k−1];
13      else                                 // no match found starting at j
14        j++;
15    }
16    return fail;
17  }
```

Code Fragment 13.4: An implementation of the computeFailKMP utility in support of the KMP pattern-matching algorithm. Note how the algorithm uses the previous values of the failure function to efficiently compute new values.

Performance

Excluding the computation of the failure function, the running time of the KMP algorithm is clearly proportional to the number of iterations of the **while** loop. For the sake of the analysis, let us define $s = j - k$. Intuitively, s is the total amount by which the pattern has been shifted with respect to the text. Note that throughout the execution of the algorithm, we have $s \leq n$. One of the following three cases occurs at each iteration of the loop.

- If $\text{text}[j] = \text{pattern}[k]$, then j and k each increase by 1, thus s is unchanged.
- If $\text{text}[j] \neq \text{pattern}[k]$ and $k > 0$, then j does not change and s increases by at least 1, since in this case s changes from $j - k$ to $j - f(k-1)$; note that this is an addition of $k - f(k-1)$, which is positive because $f(k-1) < k$.
- If $\text{text}[j] \neq \text{pattern}[k]$ and $k = 0$, then j increases by 1 and s increases by 1, since k does not change.

Thus, at each iteration of the loop, either j or s increases by at least 1 (possibly both); hence, the total number of iterations of the **while** loop in the KMP pattern-matching algorithm is at most $2n$. Achieving this bound, of course, assumes that we have already computed the failure function for the pattern.

The algorithm for computing the failure function runs in $O(m)$ time. Its analysis is analogous to that of the main KMP algorithm, yet with a pattern of length m compared to itself. Thus, we have:

Proposition 13.3: *The Knuth-Morris-Pratt algorithm performs pattern matching on a text string of length n and a pattern string of length m in $O(n+m)$ time.*

The correctness of this algorithm follows from the definition of the failure function. Any comparisons that are skipped are actually unnecessary, for the failure function guarantees that all the ignored comparisons are redundant—they would involve comparing the same matching characters over again.

In Figure 13.6, we illustrate the execution of the KMP pattern-matching algorithm on the same input strings as in Example 13.1. Note the use of the failure function to avoid redoing one of the comparisons between a character of the pattern and a character of the text. Also note that the algorithm performs fewer overall comparisons than the brute-force algorithm run on the same strings (Figure 13.1).

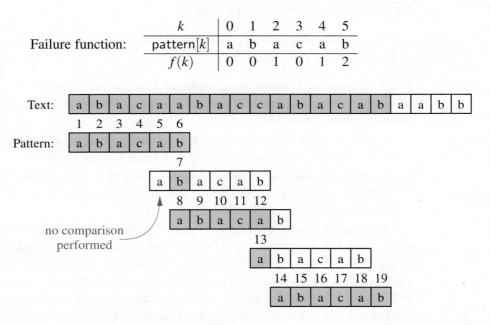

Figure 13.6: An illustration of the KMP pattern-matching algorithm. The primary algorithm performs 19 character comparisons, which are indicated with numerical labels. (Additional comparisons would be performed during the computation of the failure function.)

13.3   Tries

The pattern-matching algorithms presented in Section 13.2 speed up the search in a text by preprocessing the pattern (to compute the *last* function in the Boyer-Moore algorithm or the *failure* function in the Knuth-Morris-Pratt algorithm). In this section, we take a complementary approach, namely, we present string searching algorithms that preprocess the text, rather than the pattern. This approach is suitable for applications in which many queries are performed on a fixed text, so that the initial cost of preprocessing the text is compensated by a speedup in each subsequent query (for example, a website that offers pattern matching in Shakespeare's *Hamlet* or a search engine that offers Web pages containing the term *Hamlet*).

A *trie* (pronounced "try") is a tree-based data structure for storing strings in order to support fast pattern matching. The main application for tries is in information retrieval. Indeed, the name "trie" comes from the word "re*trie*val." In an information retrieval application, such as a search for a certain DNA sequence in a genomic database, we are given a collection S of strings, all defined using the same alphabet. The primary query operations that tries support are pattern matching and *prefix matching*. The latter operation involves being given a string X, and looking for all the strings in S that being with X.

13.3.1   Standard Tries

Let S be a set of s strings from alphabet Σ such that no string in S is a prefix of another string. A *standard trie* for S is an ordered tree T with the following properties (see Figure 13.7):

- Each node of T, except the root, is labeled with a character of Σ.
- The children of an internal node of T have distinct labels.
- T has s leaves, each associated with a string of S, such that the concatenation of the labels of the nodes on the path from the root to a leaf v of T yields the string of S associated with v.

Thus, a trie T represents the strings of S with paths from the root to the leaves of T. Note the importance of assuming that no string in S is a prefix of another string. This ensures that each string of S is uniquely associated with a leaf of T. (This is similar to the restriction for prefix codes with Huffman coding, as described in Section 13.4.) We can always satisfy this assumption by adding a special character that is not in the original alphabet Σ at the end of each string.

An internal node in a standard trie T can have anywhere between 1 and $|\Sigma|$ children. There is an edge going from the root r to one of its children for each character that is first in some string in the collection S. In addition, a path from the root of T to an internal node v at depth k corresponds to a k-character prefix

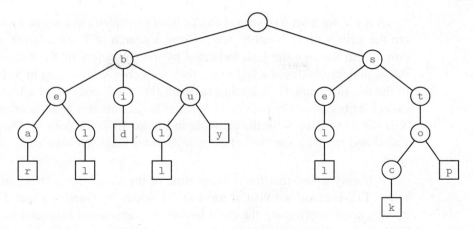

Figure 13.7: Standard trie for the strings {bear, bell, bid, bull, buy, sell, stock, stop}.

$X[0..k-1]$ of a string X of S. In fact, for each character c that can follow the prefix $X[0..k-1]$ in a string of the set S, there is a child of v labeled with character c. In this way, a trie concisely stores the common prefixes that exist among a set of strings.

As a special case, if there are only two characters in the alphabet, then the trie is essentially a binary tree, with some internal nodes possibly having only one child (that is, it may be an improper binary tree). In general, although it is possible that an internal node has up to $|\Sigma|$ children, in practice the average degree of such nodes is likely to be much smaller. For example, the trie shown in Figure 13.7 has several internal nodes with only one child. On larger data sets, the average degree of nodes is likely to get smaller at greater depths of the tree, because there may be fewer strings sharing the common prefix, and thus fewer continuations of that pattern. Furthermore, in many languages, there will be character combinations that are unlikely to naturally occur.

The following proposition provides some important structural properties of a standard trie:

Proposition 13.4: *A standard trie storing a collection S of s strings of total length n from an alphabet Σ has the following properties:*

- *The height of T is equal to the length of the longest string in S.*
- *Every internal node of T has at most $|\Sigma|$ children.*
- *T has s leaves.*
- *The number of nodes of T is at most $n+1$.*

The worst case for the number of nodes of a trie occurs when no two strings share a common nonempty prefix; that is, except for the root, all internal nodes have one child.

A trie T for a set S of strings can be used to implement a set or map whose keys are the strings of S. Namely, we perform a search in T for a string X by tracing down from the root the path indicated by the characters in X. If this path can be traced and terminates at a leaf node, then we know X is a string in S. For example, in the trie in Figure 13.7, tracing the path for "bull" ends up at a leaf. If the path cannot be traced or the path can be traced but terminates at an internal node, then X is not a string in S. In the example in Figure 13.7, the path for "bet" cannot be traced and the path for "be" ends at an internal node. Neither such word is in the set S.

It is easy to see that the running time of the search for a string of length m is $O(m \cdot |\Sigma|)$, because we visit at most $m + 1$ nodes of T and we spend $O(|\Sigma|)$ time at each node determining the child having the subsequent character as a label. The $O(|\Sigma|)$ upper bound on the time to locate a child with a given label is achievable, even if the children of a node are unordered, since there are at most $|\Sigma|$ children. We can improve the time spent at a node to be $O(\log |\Sigma|)$ or expected $O(1)$, by mapping characters to children using a secondary search table or hash table at each node, or by using a direct lookup table of size $|\Sigma|$ at each node, if $|\Sigma|$ is sufficiently small (as is the case for DNA strings). For these reasons, we typically expect a search for a string of length m to run in $O(m)$ time.

From the discussion above, it follows that we can use a trie to perform a special type of pattern matching, called **word matching**, where we want to determine whether a given pattern matches one of the words of the text exactly. Word matching differs from standard pattern matching because the pattern cannot match an arbitrary substring of the text—only one of its words. To accomplish this, each word of the original document must be added to the trie. (See Figure 13.8.) A simple extension of this scheme supports prefix-matching queries. However, arbitrary occurrences of the pattern in the text (for example, the pattern is a proper suffix of a word or spans two words) cannot be efficiently performed.

To construct a standard trie for a set S of strings, we can use an incremental algorithm that inserts the strings one at a time. Recall the assumption that no string of S is a prefix of another string. To insert a string X into the current trie T, we trace the path associated with X in T, creating a new chain of nodes to store the remaining characters of X when we get stuck. The running time to insert X with length m is similar to a search, with worst-case $O(m \cdot |\Sigma|)$ performance, or expected $O(m)$ if using secondary hash tables at each node. Thus, constructing the entire trie for set S takes expected $O(n)$ time, where n is the total length of the strings of S.

There is a potential space inefficiency in the standard trie that has prompted the development of the **compressed trie**, which is also known (for historical reasons) as the **Patricia trie**. Namely, there are potentially a lot of nodes in the standard trie that have only one child, and the existence of such nodes is a waste. We discuss the compressed trie next.

0	1	2	3	4	5	6	7	8	9	10	11	12	13	14	15	16	17	18	19	20	21	22
s	e	e		a		b	e	a	r	?		s	e	l	l		s	t	o	c	k	!

23	24	25	26	27	28	29	30	31	32	33	34	35	36	37	38	39	40	41	42	43	44	45
	s	e	e		a		b	u	l	l	?		b	u	y		s	t	o	c	k	!

46	47	48	49	50	51	52	53	54	55	56	57	58	59	60	61	62	63	64	65	66	67	68
	b	i	d		s	t	o	c	k	!		b	i	d		s	t	o	c	k	!	

69	70	71	72	73	74	75	76	77	78	79	80	81	82	83	84	85	86	87	88
h	e	a	r		t	h	e		b	e	l	l	?		s	t	o	p	!

(a)

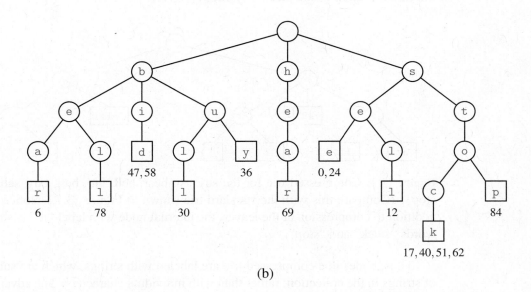

(b)

Figure 13.8: Word matching with a standard trie: (a) text to be searched (articles and prepositions, which are also known as *stop words*, excluded); (b) standard trie for the words in the text, with leaves augmented with indications of the index at which the given work begins in the text. For example, the leaf for the word "stock" notes that the word begins at indices 17, 40, 51, and 62 of the text.

13.3.2 Compressed Tries

A *compressed trie* is similar to a standard trie but it ensures that each internal node in the trie has at least two children. It enforces this rule by compressing chains of single-child nodes into individual edges. (See Figure 13.9.) Let T be a standard trie. We say that an internal node v of T is *redundant* if v has one child and is not the root. For example, the trie of Figure 13.7 has eight redundant nodes. Let us also say that a chain of $k \geq 2$ edges,

$$(v_0, v_1)(v_1, v_2) \cdots (v_{k-1}, v_k),$$

is *redundant* if:

- v_i is redundant for $i = 1, \ldots, k-1$.
- v_0 and v_k are not redundant.

We can transform T into a compressed trie by replacing each redundant chain $(v_0, v_1) \cdots (v_{k-1}, v_k)$ of $k \geq 2$ edges into a single edge (v_0, v_k), relabeling v_k with the concatenation of the labels of nodes $v_1, \ldots, v_k$.

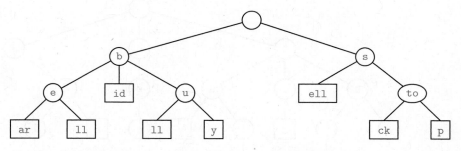

Figure 13.9: Compressed trie for the strings {bear, bell, bid, bull, buy, sell, stock, stop}. (Compare this with the standard trie shown in Figure 13.7.) Notice that, in addition to compression at the leaves, the internal node with label "to" is shared by words "stock" and "stop".

Thus, nodes in a compressed trie are labeled with strings, which are substrings of strings in the collection, rather than with individual characters. The advantage of a compressed trie over a standard trie is that the number of nodes of the compressed trie is proportional to the number of strings and not to their total length, as shown in the following proposition (compare with Proposition 13.4).

Proposition 13.5: *A compressed trie storing a collection S of s strings from an alphabet of size d has the following properties:*

- *Every internal node of T has at least two children and most d children.*
- *T has s leaves nodes.*
- *The number of nodes of T is $O(s)$.*

The attentive reader may wonder whether the compression of paths provides any significant advantage, since it is offset by a corresponding expansion of the node labels. Indeed, a compressed trie is truly advantageous only when it is used as an ***auxiliary*** index structure over a collection of strings already stored in a primary structure, and is not required to actually store all the characters of the strings in the collection.

Suppose, for example, that the collection S of strings is an array of strings $S[0]$, $S[1]$, ..., $S[s-1]$. Instead of storing the label X of a node explicitly, we represent it implicitly by a combination of three integers (i, j, k), such that $X = S[i][j..k]$; that is, X is the substring of $S[i]$ consisting of the characters from the jth to the kth inclusive. (See the example in Figure 13.10. Also compare with the standard trie of Figure 13.8.)

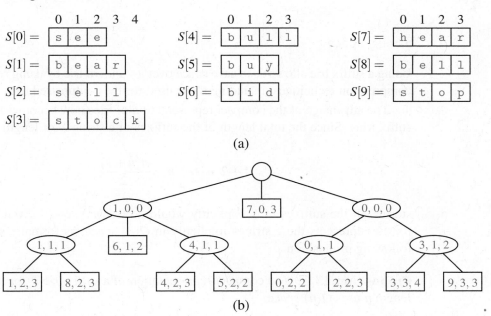

Figure 13.10: (a) Collection S of strings stored in an array. (b) Compact representation of the compressed trie for S.

This additional compression scheme allows us to reduce the total space for the trie itself from $O(n)$ for the standard trie to $O(s)$ for the compressed trie, where n is the total length of the strings in S and s is the number of strings in S. We must still store the different strings in S, of course, but we nevertheless reduce the space for the trie.

Searching in a compressed trie is not necessarily faster than in a standard tree, since there is still need to compare every character of the desired pattern with the potentially multicharacter labels while traversing paths in the trie.

13.3.3   Suffix Tries

One of the primary applications for tries is for the case when the strings in the collection S are all the suffixes of a string X. Such a trie is called the **suffix trie** (also known as a **suffix tree** or **position tree**) of string X. For example, Figure 13.11a shows the suffix trie for the eight suffixes of string "minimize." For a suffix trie, the compact representation presented in the previous section can be further simplified. Namely, the label of each vertex is a pair "j..k" indicating the string $X[j..k]$. (See Figure 13.11b.) To satisfy the rule that no suffix of X is a prefix of another suffix, we can add a special character, denoted with $, that is not in the original alphabet Σ at the end of X (and thus to every suffix). That is, if string X has length n, we build a trie for the set of n strings $X[j..n-1]\$$, for $j = 0, \ldots, n-1$.

Saving Space

Using a suffix trie allows us to save space over a standard trie by using several space compression techniques, including those used for the compressed trie.

The advantage of the compact representation of tries now becomes apparent for suffix tries. Since the total length of the suffixes of a string X of length n is

$$1 + 2 + \cdots + n = \frac{n(n+1)}{2},$$

storing all the suffixes of X explicitly would take $O(n^2)$ space. Even so, the suffix trie represents these strings implicitly in $O(n)$ space, as formally stated in the following proposition.

Proposition 13.6: *The compact representation of a suffix trie T for a string X of length n uses $O(n)$ space.*

Construction

We can construct the suffix trie for a string of length n with an incremental algorithm like the one given in Section 13.3.1. This construction takes $O(|\Sigma|n^2)$ time because the total length of the suffixes is quadratic in n. However, the (compact) suffix trie for a string of length n can be constructed in $O(n)$ time with a specialized algorithm, different from the one for general tries. This linear-time construction algorithm is fairly complex, however, and is not reported here. Still, we can take advantage of the existence of this fast construction algorithm when we want to use a suffix trie to solve other problems.

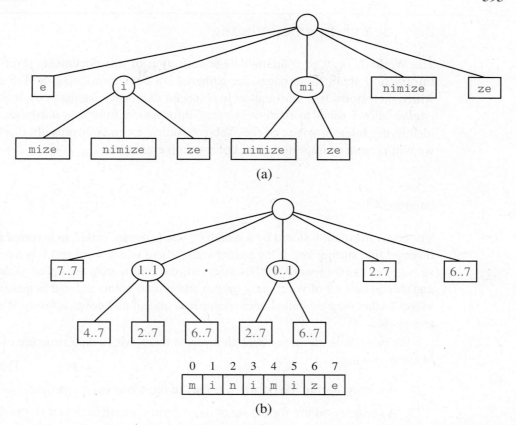

Figure 13.11: (a) Suffix trie T for the string $X =$ "minimize". (b) Compact representation of T, where pair $j..k$ denotes the substring $X[j..k]$ in the reference string.

Using a Suffix Trie

The suffix trie T for a string X can be used to efficiently perform pattern-matching queries on text X. Namely, we can determine whether a pattern is a substring of X by trying to trace a path associated with P in T. P is a substring of X if and only if such a path can be traced. The search down the trie T assumes that nodes in T store some additional information, with respect to the compact representation of the suffix trie:

> If node v has label j..k and Y is the string of length y associated with the path from the root to v (included), then $X[k-y+1..k] = Y$.

This property ensures that we can compute the start index of the pattern in the text when a match occurs in $O(m)$ time.

13.3.4   Search Engine Indexing

The World Wide Web contains a huge collection of text documents (Web pages). Information about these pages are gathered by a program called a *Web crawler*, which then stores this information in a special dictionary database. A Web *search engine* allows users to retrieve relevant information from this database, thereby identifying relevant pages on the Web containing given keywords. In this section, we will present a simplified model of a search engine.

Inverted Files

The core information stored by a search engine is a map, called an *inverted index* or *inverted file*, storing key-value pairs (w, L), where w is a word and L is a collection of pages containing word w. The keys·(words) in this map are called *index terms* and should be a set of vocabulary entries and proper nouns as large as possible. The values in this map are called *occurrence lists* and should cover as many Web pages as possible.

We can efficiently implement an inverted index with a data structure consisting of the following:

1. An array storing the occurrence lists of the terms (in no particular order).
2. A compressed trie for the set of index terms, where each leaf stores the index of the occurrence list of the associated term.

The reason for storing the occurrence lists outside the trie is to keep the size of the trie data structure sufficiently small to fit in internal memory. Instead, because of their large total size, the occurrence lists have to be stored on disk.

With our data structure, a query for a single keyword is similar to a word-matching query (Section 13.3.1). Namely, we find the keyword in the trie and we return the associated occurrence list.

When multiple keywords are given and the desired output are the pages containing *all* the given keywords, we retrieve the occurrence list of each keyword using the trie and return their intersection. To facilitate the intersection computation, each occurrence list should be implemented with a sequence sorted by address or with a map, to allow efficient set operations.

In addition to the basic task of returning a list of pages containing given keywords, search engines provide an important additional service by *ranking* the pages returned by relevance. Devising fast and accurate ranking algorithms for search engines is a major challenge for computer researchers and electronic commerce companies.

13.4 Text Compression and the Greedy Method

In this section, we will consider the important task of *text compression*. In this problem, we are given a string X defined over some alphabet, such as the ASCII or Unicode character sets, and we want to efficiently encode X into a small binary string Y (using only the characters 0 and 1). Text compression is useful in any situation where we wish to reduce bandwidth for digital communications, so as to minimize the time needed to transmit our text. Likewise, text compression is useful for storing large documents more efficiently, so as to allow a fixed-capacity storage device to contain as many documents as possible.

The method for text compression explored in this section is the *Huffman code*. Standard encoding schemes, such as ASCII, use fixed-length binary strings to encode characters (with 7 or 8 bits in the traditional or extended ASCII systems, respectively). The Unicode system was originally proposed as a 16-bit fixed-length representation, although common encodings reduce the space usage by allowing common groups of characters, such as those from the ASCII system, with fewer bits. The Huffman code saves space over a fixed-length encoding by using short code-word strings to encode high-frequency characters and long code-word strings to encode low-frequency characters. Furthermore, the Huffman code uses a variable-length encoding specifically optimized for a given string X over any alphabet. The optimization is based on the use of character *frequencies*, where we have, for each character c, a count $f(c)$ of the number of times c appears in the string X.

To encode the string X, we convert each character in X to a variable-length code-word, and we concatenate all these code-words in order to produce the encoding Y for X. In order to avoid ambiguities, we insist that no code-word in our encoding be a prefix of another code-word in our encoding. Such a code is called a *prefix code*, and it simplifies the decoding of Y to retrieve X. (See Figure 13.12.) Even with this restriction, the savings produced by a variable-length prefix code can be significant, particularly if there is a wide variance in character frequencies (as is the case for natural language text in almost every written language).

Huffman's algorithm for producing an optimal variable-length prefix code for X is based on the construction of a binary tree T that represents the code. Each edge in T represents a bit in a code-word, with an edge to a left child representing a "0" and an edge to a right child representing a "1". Each leaf v is associated with a specific character, and the code-word for that character is defined by the sequence of bits associated with the edges in the path from the root of T to v. (See Figure 13.12.) Each leaf v has a *frequency*, $f(v)$, which is simply the frequency in X of the character associated with v. In addition, we give each internal node v in T a frequency, $f(v)$, that is the sum of the frequencies of all the leaves in the subtree rooted at v.

(a)

Character	a	b	d	e	f	h	i	k	n	o	r	s	t	u	v
Frequency	9	5	1	3	7	3	1	1	1	4	1	5	1	2	1	1

(b)

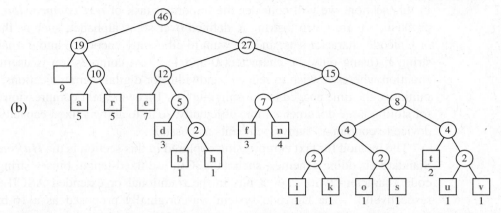

Figure 13.12: An illustration of an example Huffman code for the input string $X =$ "a fast runner need never be afraid of the dark": (a) frequency of each character of X; (b) Huffman tree T for string X. The code for a character c is obtained by tracing the path from the root of T to the leaf where c is stored, and associating a left child with 0 and a right child with 1. For example, the code for "r" is 011, and the code for "h" is 10111.

13.4.1 The Huffman Coding Algorithm

The Huffman coding algorithm begins with each of the d distinct characters of the string X to encode being the root node of a single-node binary tree. The algorithm proceeds in a series of rounds. In each round, the algorithm takes the two binary trees with the smallest frequencies and merges them into a single binary tree. It repeats this process until only one tree is left. (See Code Fragment 13.5.)

Each iteration of the **while** loop in Huffman's algorithm can be implemented in $O(\log d)$ time using a priority queue represented with a heap. In addition, each iteration takes two nodes out of Q and adds one in, a process that will be repeated $d - 1$ times before exactly one node is left in Q. Thus, this algorithm runs in $O(n + d\log d)$ time. Although a full justification of this algorithm's correctness is beyond our scope here, we note that its intuition comes from a simple idea—any optimal code can be converted into an optimal code in which the code-words for the two lowest-frequency characters, a and b, differ only in their last bit. Repeating the argument for a string with a and b replaced by a character c, gives the following:

Proposition 13.7: *Huffman's algorithm constructs an optimal prefix code for a string of length n with d distinct characters in $O(n + d\log d)$ time.*

Algorithm Huffman(X):

   Input: String X of length n with d distinct characters

   Output: Coding tree for X

   Compute the frequency $f(c)$ of each character c of X.

   Initialize a priority queue Q.

   for each character c in X **do**

      Create a single-node binary tree T storing c.

      Insert T into Q with key $f(c)$.

   while Q.size( ) > 1 **do**

      Entry $e_1 = Q$.removeMin( ) with e_1 having key f_1 and value T_1.

      Entry $e_2 = Q$.removeMin( ) with e_2 having key f_2 and value T_2.

      Create a new binary tree T with left subtree T_1 and right subtree T_2.

      Insert T into Q with key $f_1 + f_2$.

   Entry $e = Q$.removeMin( ) with e having tree T as its value.

   return tree T

Code Fragment 13.5: Huffman coding algorithm.

13.4.2 The Greedy Method

Huffman's algorithm for building an optimal encoding is an example application of an algorithmic design pattern called the ***greedy method***. This design pattern is applied to optimization problems, where we are trying to construct some structure while minimizing or maximizing some property of that structure.

The general formula for the greedy-method pattern is almost as simple as that for the brute-force method. In order to solve a given optimization problem using the greedy method, we proceed by a sequence of choices. The sequence starts from some well-understood starting condition, and computes the cost for that initial condition. The pattern then asks that we iteratively make additional choices by identifying the decision that achieves the best cost improvement from all of the choices that are currently possible. This approach does not always lead to an optimal solution.

But there are several problems that it does work for, and such problems are said to possess the ***greedy-choice*** property. This is the property that a global optimal condition can be reached by a series of locally optimal choices (that is, choices that are each the current best from among the possibilities available at the time), starting from a well-defined starting condition. The problem of computing an optimal variable-length prefix code is just one example of a problem that possesses the greedy-choice property.

13.5   Dynamic Programming

In this section, we will discuss the ***dynamic-programming*** algorithmic design pattern. This technique is similar to the divide-and-conquer technique (Section 12.1.1), in that it can be applied to a wide variety of different problems. Dynamic programming can often be used to produce polynomial-time algorithms to solve problems that seem to require exponential time. In addition, the algorithms that result from applications of the dynamic programming technique are usually quite simple, often needing little more than a few lines of code to describe some nested loops for filling in a table.

13.5.1   Matrix Chain-Product

Rather than starting out with an explanation of the general components of the dynamic programming technique, we begin by giving a classic, concrete example. Suppose we are given a collection of n two-dimensional matrices for which we wish to compute the mathematical product

$$A = A_0 \cdot A_1 \cdot A_2 \cdots A_{n-1},$$

where A_i is a $d_i \times d_{i+1}$ matrix, for $i = 0, 1, 2, \ldots, n-1$. In the standard matrix multiplication algorithm (which is the one we will use), to multiply a $d \times e$-matrix B times an $e \times f$-matrix C, we compute the product, A, as

$$A[i][j] = \sum_{k=0}^{e-1} B[i][k] \cdot C[k][j].$$

This definition implies that matrix multiplication is associative, that is, it implies that $B \cdot (C \cdot D) = (B \cdot C) \cdot D$. Thus, we can parenthesize the expression for A any way we wish and we will end up with the same answer. However, we will not necessarily perform the same number of primitive (that is, scalar) multiplications in each parenthesization, as is illustrated in the following example.

Example 13.8: *Let B be a 2×10-matrix, let C be a 10×50-matrix, and let D be a 50×20-matrix. Computing $B \cdot (C \cdot D)$ requires $2 \cdot 10 \cdot 20 + 10 \cdot 50 \cdot 20 = 10400$ multiplications, whereas computing $(B \cdot C) \cdot D$ requires $2 \cdot 10 \cdot 50 + 2 \cdot 50 \cdot 20 = 3000$ multiplications.*

The ***matrix chain-product*** problem is to determine the parenthesization of the expression defining the product A that minimizes the total number of scalar multiplications performed. As the example above illustrates, the differences between parenthesizations can be dramatic, so finding a good solution can result in significant speedups.

Defining Subproblems

One way to solve the matrix chain-product problem is to simply enumerate all the possible ways of parenthesizing the expression for A and determine the number of multiplications performed by each one. Unfortunately, the set of all different parenthesizations of the expression for A is equal in number to the set of all different binary trees that have n leaves. This number is exponential in n. Thus, this straightforward ("brute-force") algorithm runs in exponential time, for there are an exponential number of ways to parenthesize an associative arithmetic expression.

We can significantly improve the performance achieved by the brute-force algorithm, however, by making a few observations about the nature of the matrix chain-product problem. The first is that the problem can be split into **subproblems**. In this case, we can define a number of different subproblems, each of which is to compute the best parenthesization for some subexpression $A_i \cdot A_{i+1} \cdots A_j$. As a concise notation, we use $N_{i,j}$ to denote the minimum number of multiplications needed to compute this subexpression. Thus, the original matrix chain-product problem can be characterized as that of computing the value of $N_{0,n-1}$. This observation is important, but we need one more in order to apply the dynamic programming technique.

Characterizing Optimal Solutions

The other important observation we can make about the matrix chain-product problem is that it is possible to characterize an optimal solution to a particular subproblem in terms of optimal solutions to its subproblems. We call this property the **subproblem optimality** condition.

In the case of the matrix chain-product problem, we observe that, no matter how we parenthesize a subexpression, there has to be some final matrix multiplication that we perform. That is, a full parenthesization of a subexpression $A_i \cdot A_{i+1} \cdots A_j$ has to be of the form $(A_i \cdots A_k) \cdot (A_{k+1} \cdots A_j)$, for some $k \in \{i, i+1, \ldots, j-1\}$. Moreover, for whichever k is the correct one, the products $(A_i \cdots A_k)$ and $(A_{k+1} \cdots A_j)$ must also be solved optimally. If this were not so, then there would be a global optimal that had one of these subproblems solved suboptimally. But this is impossible, since we could then reduce the total number of multiplications by replacing the current subproblem solution by an optimal solution for the subproblem. This observation implies a way of explicitly defining the optimization problem for $N_{i,j}$ in terms of other optimal subproblem solutions. Namely, we can compute $N_{i,j}$ by considering each place k where we could put the final multiplication and taking the minimum over all such choices.

Designing a Dynamic Programming Algorithm

We can therefore characterize the optimal subproblem solution, $N_{i,j}$, as

$$N_{i,j} = \min_{i \leq k < j} \{N_{i,k} + N_{k+1,j} + d_i d_{k+1} d_{j+1}\},$$

where $N_{i,i} = 0$, since no work is needed for a single matrix. That is, $N_{i,j}$ is the minimum, taken over all possible places to perform the final multiplication, of the number of multiplications needed to compute each subexpression plus the number of multiplications needed to perform the final matrix multiplication.

Notice that there is a ***sharing of subproblems*** going on that prevents us from dividing the problem into completely independent subproblems (as we would need to do to apply the divide-and-conquer technique). We can, nevertheless, use the equation for $N_{i,j}$ to derive an efficient algorithm by computing $N_{i,j}$ values in a bottom-up fashion, and storing intermediate solutions in a table of $N_{i,j}$ values. We can begin simply enough by assigning $N_{i,i} = 0$ for $i = 0, 1, \ldots, n-1$. We can then apply the general equation for $N_{i,j}$ to compute $N_{i,i+1}$ values, since they depend only on $N_{i,i}$ and $N_{i+1,i+1}$ values that are available. Given the $N_{i,i+1}$ values, we can then compute the $N_{i,i+2}$ values, and so on. Therefore, we can build $N_{i,j}$ values up from previously computed values until we can finally compute the value of $N_{0,n-1}$, which is the number that we are searching for. A Java implementation of this ***dynamic programming*** solution is given in Code Fragment 13.6; we use techniques from Section 3.1.5 for working with a two-dimensional array in Java.

```
1  public static int[ ][ ] matrixChain(int[ ] d) {
2    int n = d.length − 1;                        // number of matrices
3    int[ ][ ] N = new int[n][n];                 // n-by-n matrix; initially zeros
4    for (int b=1; b < n; b++)                    // number of products in subchain
5      for (int i=0; i < n − b; i++) {            // start of subchain
6        int j = i + b;                           // end of subchain
7        N[i][j] = Integer.MAX_VALUE;             // used as 'infinity'
8        for (int k=i; k < j; k++)
9          N[i][j] = Math.min(N[i][j], N[i][k] + N[k+1][j] + d[i]*d[k+1]*d[j+1]);
10     }
11   return N;
12 }
```

Code Fragment 13.6: Dynamic programming algorithm for the matrix chain-product problem.

Thus, we can compute $N_{0,n-1}$ with an algorithm that consists primarily of three nested loops (the third of which computes the min term). Each of these loops iterates at most n times per execution, with a constant amount of additional work within. Therefore, the total running time of this algorithm is $O(n^3)$.

13.5.2 DNA and Text Sequence Alignment

A common text-processing problem, which arises in genetics and software engineering, is to test the similarity between two text strings. In a genetics application, the two strings could correspond to two strands of DNA, for which we want to compute similarities. Likewise, in a software engineering application, the two strings could come from two versions of source code for the same program, for which we want to determine changes made from one version to the next. Indeed, determining the similarity between two strings is so common that the Unix and Linux operating systems have a built-in program, named `diff`, for comparing text files.

Given a string $X = x_0x_1x_2 \cdots x_{n-1}$, a *subsequence* of X is any string that is of the form $x_{i_1}x_{i_2} \cdots x_{i_k}$, where $i_j < i_{j+1}$; that is, it is a sequence of characters that are not necessarily contiguous but are nevertheless taken in order from X. For example, the string $AAAG$ is a subsequence of the string $CG\underline{A}T\underline{AA}TT\underline{G}A\underline{G}A$.

The DNA and text similarity problem we address here is the ***longest common subsequence*** (LCS) problem. In this problem, we are given two character strings, $X = x_0x_1x_2 \cdots x_{n-1}$ and $Y = y_0y_1y_2 \cdots y_{m-1}$, over some alphabet (such as the alphabet $\{A, C, G, T\}$ common in computational genomics) and are asked to find a longest string S that is a subsequence of both X and Y. One way to solve the longest common subsequence problem is to enumerate all subsequences of X and take the largest one that is also a subsequence of Y. Since each character of X is either in or not in a subsequence, there are potentially 2^n different subsequences of X, each of which requires $O(m)$ time to determine whether it is a subsequence of Y. Thus, this brute-force approach yields an exponential-time algorithm that runs in $O(2^n m)$ time, which is very inefficient. Fortunately, the LCS problem is efficiently solvable using ***dynamic programming***.

The Components of a Dynamic Programming Solution

As mentioned above, the dynamic programming technique is used primarily for ***optimization*** problems, where we wish to find the "best" way of doing something. We can apply the dynamic programming technique in such situations if the problem has certain properties:

Simple Subproblems: There has to be some way of repeatedly breaking the global optimization problem into subproblems. Moreover, there should be a way to parameterize subproblems with just a few indices, like i, j, k, and so on.

Subproblem Optimization: An optimal solution to the global problem must be a composition of optimal subproblem solutions.

Subproblem Overlap: Optimal solutions to unrelated subproblems can contain subproblems in common.

Applying Dynamic Programming to the LCS Problem

Recall that in the LCS problem, we are given two character strings, X and Y, of length n and m, respectively, and are asked to find a longest string S that is a subsequence of both X and Y. Since X and Y are character strings, we have a natural set of indices with which to define subproblems—indices into the strings X and Y. Let us define a subproblem, therefore, as that of computing the value $L_{j,k}$, which we will use to denote the length of a longest string that is a subsequence of both the first j characters of X and the first k characters of Y, that is of prefixes $X[0..j-1]$ and $Y[0..k-1]$. If either $j = 0$ or $k = 0$, then $L_{j,k}$ is trivially defined as 0.

When both $j \geq 1$ and $k \geq 1$, this definition allows us to rewrite $L_{j,k}$ recursively in terms of optimal subproblem solutions. This definition depends on which of two cases we are in. (See Figure 13.13.)

- $x_{j-1} = y_{k-1}$. In this case, we have a match between the last character of $X[0..j-1]$ and the last character of $Y[0..k-1]$. We claim that this character belongs to a longest common subsequence of $X[0..j-1]$ and $Y[0..k-1]$. To justify this claim, let us suppose it is not true. There has to be some longest common subsequence $x_{a_1}x_{a_2}\ldots x_{a_c} = y_{b_1}y_{b_2}\ldots y_{b_c}$. If $x_{a_c} = x_{j-1}$ or $y_{b_c} = y_{k-1}$, then we get the same sequence by setting $a_c = j - 1$ and $b_c = k - 1$. Alternately, if $x_{a_c} \neq x_{j-1}$ and $y_{b_c} \neq y_{k-1}$, then we can get an even longer common subsequence by adding $x_{j-1} = y_{k-1}$ to the end. Thus, a longest common subsequence of $X[0..j-1]$ and $Y[0..k-1]$ ends with x_{j-1}. Therefore, we set

$$L_{j,k} = 1 + L_{j-1,k-1} \quad \text{if } x_{j-1} = y_{k-1}.$$

- $x_{j-1} \neq y_{k-1}$. In this case, we cannot have a common subsequence that includes both x_{j-1} and y_{k-1}. That is, we can have a common subsequence end with x_{j-1} or one that ends with y_{k-1} (or possibly neither), but certainly not both. Therefore, we set

$$L_{j,k} = \max\{L_{j-1,k}, L_{j,k-1}\} \quad \text{if } x_{j-1} \neq y_{k-1}.$$

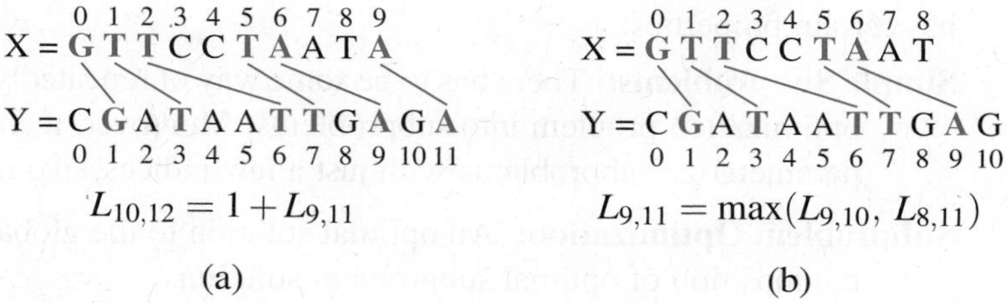

```
      0 1 2 3 4 5 6 7 8 9
X = G T T C C T A A T A


Y = C G A T A A T T G A G A
    0 1 2 3 4 5 6 7 8 9 10 11
```
$$L_{10,12} = 1 + L_{9,11}$$

(a)

```
      0 1 2 3 4 5 6 7 8
X = G T T C C T A A T


Y = C G A T A A T T G A G
    0 1 2 3 4 5 6 7 8 9 10
```
$$L_{9,11} = \max(L_{9,10}, L_{8,11})$$

(b)

Figure 13.13: The two cases in the longest common subsequence algorithm for computing $L_{j,k}$ when $j, k \geq 1$: (a) $x_{j-1} = y_{k-1}$; (b) $x_{j-1} \neq y_{k-1}$.

The LCS Algorithm

The definition of $L_{j,k}$ satisfies subproblem optimization, for we cannot have a longest common subsequence without also having longest common subsequences for the subproblems. Also, it uses subproblem overlap, because a subproblem solution $L_{j,k}$ can be used in several other problems (namely, the problems $L_{j+1,k}$, $L_{j,k+1}$, and $L_{j+1,k+1}$). Turning this definition of $L_{j,k}$ into an algorithm is actually quite straightforward. We create an $(n+1) \times (m+1)$ array, L, defined for $0 \le j \le n$ and $0 \le k \le m$. We initialize all entries to 0, in particular so that all entries of the form $L_{j,0}$ and $L_{0,k}$ are zero. Then, we iteratively build up values in L until we have $L_{n,m}$, the length of a longest common subsequence of X and Y. We give a Java implementation of this algorithm in Code Fragment 13.7.

```
1   /** Returns table such that L[j][k] is length of LCS for X[0..j−1] and Y[0..k−1]. */
2   public static int[ ][ ] LCS(char[ ] X, char[ ] Y) {
3     int n = X.length;
4     int m = Y.length;
5     int[ ][ ] L = new int[n+1][m+1];
6     for (int j=0; j < n; j++)
7       for (int k=0; k < m; k++)
8         if (X[j] == Y[k])             // align this match
9           L[j+1][k+1] = L[j][k] + 1;
10        else                          // choose to ignore one character
11          L[j+1][k+1] = Math.max(L[j][k+1], L[j+1][k]);
12    return L;
13  }
```

Code Fragment 13.7: Dynamic programming algorithm for the LCS problem.

The running time of the algorithm of the LCS algorithm is easy to analyze, for it is dominated by two nested **for** loops, with the outer one iterating n times and the inner one iterating m times. Since the if-statement and assignment inside the loop each requires $O(1)$ primitive operations, this algorithm runs in $O(nm)$ time. Thus, the dynamic programming technique can be applied to the longest common subsequence problem to improve significantly over the exponential-time brute-force solution to the LCS problem.

The LCS method of Code Fragment 13.7 computes the length of the longest common subsequence (stored as $L_{n,m}$), but not the subsequence itself. Fortunately, it is easy to extract the actual longest common subsequence if given the complete table of $L_{j,k}$ values computed by the LCS method. The solution can be reconstructed back to front by reverse engineering the calculation of length $L_{n,m}$. At any position $L_{j,k}$, if $x_j = y_k$, then the length is based on the common subsequence associated with length $L_{j-1,k-1}$, followed by common character x_j. We can record x_j as part of the sequence, and then continue the analysis from $L_{j-1,k-1}$. If $x_j \ne y_k$, then we can move to the larger of $L_{j,k-1}$ and $L_{j-1,k}$. We continue this process until reaching some $L_{j,k} = 0$ (for example, if j or k is 0 as a boundary case). A Java implementation of this strategy is given in Code Fragment 13.8. This method constructs a longest common subsequence in $O(n+m)$ additional time, since each pass of the **while** loop decrements either j or k (or both). An illustration of the algorithm for computing the longest common subsequence is given in Figure 13.14.

```
1   /** Returns the longest common substring of X and Y, given LCS table L. */
2   public static char[ ] reconstructLCS(char[ ] X, char[ ] Y, int[ ][ ] L) {
3     StringBuilder solution = new StringBuilder( );
4     int j = X.length;
5     int k = Y.length;
6     while (L[j][k] > 0)                            // common characters remain
7       if (X[j−1] == Y[k−1]) {
8         solution.append(X[j−1]);
9         j−−;
10        k−−;
11      } else if (L[j−1][k] >= L[j][k−1])
12        j−−;
13      else
14        k−−;
15    // return left-to-right version, as char array
16    return solution.reverse( ).toString( ).toCharArray( );
17  }
```

Code Fragment 13.8: Reconstructing the longest common subsequence.

	0	1	2	3	4	5	6	7	8	9	10	11	12
0	0	0	0	0	0	0	0	0	0	0	0	0	0
1	0	0	1	1	1	1	1	1	1	1	1	1	1
2	0	0	1	1	2	2	2	2	2	2	2	2	2
3	0	0	1	1	2	2	2	3	3	3	3	3	3
4	0	1	1	1	2	2	2	3	3	3	3	3	3
5	0	1	1	1	2	2	2	3	3	3	3	3	3
6	0	1	1	1	2	2	2	3	4	4	4	4	4
7	0	1	1	2	2	3	3	3	4	4	5	5	5
8	0	1	1	2	2	3	4	4	4	4	5	5	6
9	0	1	1	2	3	3	4	5	5	5	5	5	6
10	0	1	1	2	3	4	4	5	5	5	6	6	6

$$\begin{array}{c} \;0\;1\;2\;3\;4\;5\;6\;7\;8\;9 \\ X = G\,T\,T\,C\,C\,T\,A\,A\,T\,A \end{array}$$

$$\begin{array}{c} Y = C\,G\,A\,T\,A\,A\,T\,T\,G\,A\,G\,A \\ \;\;0\;1\;2\;3\;4\;5\;6\;7\;8\;9\;10\,11 \end{array}$$

Figure 13.14: Illustration of the algorithm for constructing a longest common subsequence from the array L. A diagonal step on the highlighted path represents the use of a common character (with that character's respective indices in the sequences highlighted in the margins).

13.6 Exercises

Reinforcement

R-13.1 List the prefixes of the string $P =$"aaabbaaa" that are also suffixes of P.

R-13.2 What is the longest (proper) prefix of the string "cgtacgttcgtacg" that is also a suffix of this string?

R-13.3 Draw a figure illustrating the comparisons done by brute-force pattern matching for the text "aaabaadaabaaa" and pattern "aabaaa".

R-13.4 Repeat the previous problem for the Boyer-Moore algorithm, not counting the comparisons made to compute the last(c) function.

R-13.5 Repeat Exercise R-13.3 for the Knuth-Morris-Pratt algorithm, not counting the comparisons made to compute the failure function.

R-13.6 Compute a map representing the last function used in the Boyer-Moore pattern-matching algorithm for characters in the pattern string:

"the quick brown fox jumped over a lazy cat".

R-13.7 Compute a table representing the Knuth-Morris-Pratt failure function for the pattern string "cgtacgttcgtac".

R-13.8 Draw a standard trie for the following set of strings:

{ abab, baba, ccccc, bbaaaa, caa, bbaacc, cbcc, cbca }.

R-13.9 Draw a compressed trie for the strings given in the previous problem.

R-13.10 Draw the compact representation of the suffix trie for the string:

"minimize minime".

R-13.11 Draw the frequency array and Huffman tree for the following string:

"dogs do not spot hot pots or cats".

R-13.12 What is the best way to multiply a chain of matrices with dimensions that are $10 \times 5, 5 \times 2, 2 \times 20, 20 \times 12, 12 \times 4$, and 4×60? Show your work.

R-13.13 In Figure 13.14, we illustrate that GTTTAA is a longest common subsequence for the given strings X and Y. However, that answer is not unique. Give another common subsequence of X and Y having length six.

R-13.14 Show the longest common subsequence array L for the two strings:

$$X = \text{"skullandbones"}$$
$$Y = \text{"lullabybabies"}$$

What is a longest common subsequence between these strings?

Creativity

C-13.15 Describe an example of a text T of length n and a pattern P of length m such that the brute-force pattern-matching algorithm achieves a running time that is $\Omega(nm)$.

C-13.16 Adapt the brute-force pattern-matching algorithm so as to implement a method findLastBrute(T,P) that returns the index at which the *rightmost* occurrence of pattern P within text T, if any.

C-13.17 Redo the previous problem, adapting the Boyer-Moore pattern-matching algorithm to implement a method findLastBoyerMoore(T,P).

C-13.18 Redo Exercise C-13.16, adapting the Knuth-Morris-Pratt pattern-matching algorithm appropriately to implement a method findLastKMP(T,P).

C-13.19 Give a justification of why the computeFailKMP method (Code Fragment 13.4) runs in $O(m)$ time on a pattern of length m.

C-13.20 Let T be a text of length n, and let P be a pattern of length m. Describe an $O(n + m)$-time method for finding the longest prefix of P that is a substring of T.

C-13.21 Say that a pattern P of length m is a **circular** substring of a text T of length $n > m$ if P is a (normal) substring of T, or if P is equal to the concatenation of a suffix of T and a prefix of T, that is, if there is an index $0 \le k < m$, such that $P = T[n - m + k..n - 1] + T[0..k - 1]$. Give an $O(n + m)$-time algorithm for determining whether P is a circular substring of T.

C-13.22 The Knuth-Morris-Pratt pattern-matching algorithm can be modified to run faster on binary strings by redefining the failure function as:

$$f(k) = \text{the largest } j < k \text{ such that } P[0..j - 1]\widehat{p}_j \text{ is a suffix of } P[1..k],$$

where $\widehat{p}_j$ denotes the complement of the jth bit of P. Describe how to modify the KMP algorithm to be able to take advantage of this new failure function and also give a method for computing this failure function. Show that this method makes at most n comparisons between the text and the pattern (as opposed to the $2n$ comparisons needed by the standard KMP algorithm given in Section 13.2.3).

C-13.23 Modify the simplified Boyer-Moore algorithm presented in this chapter using ideas from the KMP algorithm so that it runs in $O(n + m)$ time.

C-13.24 Let T be a text string of length n. Describe an $O(n)$-time method for finding the longest prefix of T that is a substring of the reversal of T.

C-13.25 Describe an efficient algorithm to find the longest palindrome that is a suffix of a string T of length n. Recall that a **palindrome** is a string that is equal to its reversal. What is the running time of your method?

C-13.26 Give an efficient algorithm for deleting a string from a standard trie and analyze its running time.

C-13.27 Give an efficient algorithm for deleting a string from a compressed trie and analyze its running time.

C-13.28 Describe an algorithm for constructing the compact representation of a suffix trie, given its noncompact representation, and analyze its running time.

C-13.29 Create a class that implements a standard trie for a set of strings. The class should have a constructor that takes a list of strings as an argument, and the class should have a method that tests whether a given string is stored in the trie.

C-13.30 Create a class that implements a compressed trie for a set of strings. The class should have a constructor that takes a list of strings as an argument, and the class should have a method that tests whether a given string is stored in the trie.

C-13.31 Create a class that implements a prefix trie for a string. The class should have a constructor that takes a string as an argument, and a method for pattern matching on the string.

C-13.32 Given a string X of length n and a string Y of length m, describe an $O(n+m)$-time algorithm for finding the longest prefix of X that is a suffix of Y.

C-13.33 Describe an efficient greedy algorithm for making change for a specified value using a minimum number of coins, assuming there are four denominations of coins (called quarters, dimes, nickels, and pennies), with values 25, 10, 5, and 1, respectively. Argue why your algorithm is correct.

C-13.34 Give an example set of denominations of coins so that a greedy change-making algorithm will not use the minimum number of coins.

C-13.35 In the ***art gallery guarding*** problem we are given a line L that represents a long hallway in an art gallery. We are also given a set $X = \{x_0, x_1, \ldots, x_{n-1}\}$ of real numbers that specify the positions of paintings in this hallway. Suppose that a single guard can protect all the paintings within distance at most 1 of his or her position (on both sides). Design an algorithm for finding a placement of guards that uses the minimum number of guards to guard all the paintings with positions in X.

C-13.36 Anna has just won a contest that allows her to take n pieces of candy out of a candy store for free. Anna is old enough to realize that some candy is expensive, while other candy is relatively cheap, costing much less. The jars of candy are numbered 0, 1, ..., $m-1$, so that jar j has n_j pieces in it, with a price of c_j per piece. Design an $O(n+m)$-time algorithm that allows Anna to maximize the value of the pieces of candy she takes for her winnings. Show that your algorithm produces the maximum value for Anna.

C-13.37 Implement a compression and decompression scheme that is based on Huffman coding.

C-13.38 Design an efficient algorithm for the matrix chain multiplication problem that outputs a fully parenthesized expression for how to multiply the matrices in the chain using the minimum number of operations.

C-13.39 A native Australian named Anatjari wishes to cross a desert carrying only a single water bottle. He has a map that marks all the watering holes along the way. Assuming he can walk k miles on one bottle of water, design an efficient algorithm for determining where Anatjari should refill his bottle in order to make as few stops as possible. Argue why your algorithm is correct.

C-13.40 Given a sequence $S = (x_0, x_1, \ldots, x_{n-1})$ of numbers, describe an $O(n^2)$-time algorithm for finding a longest subsequence $T = (x_{i_0}, x_{i_1}, \ldots, x_{i_{k-1}})$ of numbers, such that $i_j < i_{j+1}$ and $x_{i_j} > x_{i_{j+1}}$. That is, T is a longest decreasing subsequence of S.

C-13.41 Let P be a convex polygon, a ***triangulation*** of P is an addition of diagonals connecting the vertices of P so that each interior face is a triangle. The ***weight*** of a triangulation is the sum of the lengths of the diagonals. Assuming that we can compute lengths and add and compare them in constant time, give an efficient algorithm for computing a minimum-weight triangulation of P.

C-13.42 Give an efficient algorithm for determining if a pattern P is a subsequence (not substring) of a text T. What is the running time of your algorithm?

C-13.43 Define the ***edit distance*** between two strings X and Y of length n and m, respectively, to be the number of edits that it takes to change X into Y. An edit consists of a character insertion, a character deletion, or a character replacement. For example, the strings `"algorithm"` and `"rhythm"` have edit distance 6. Design an $O(nm)$-time algorithm for computing the edit distance between X and Y.

C-13.44 Write a program that takes two character strings (which could be, for example, representations of DNA strands) and computes their edit distance, based on your algorithm from the previous exercise.

C-13.45 Let X and Y be strings of length n and m, respectively. Define $B(j,k)$ to be the length of the longest common substring of the suffix $X[n-j..n-1]$ and the suffix $Y[m-k..m-1]$. Design an $O(nm)$-time algorithm for computing all the values of $B(j,k)$ for $j = 1, \ldots, n$ and $k = 1, \ldots, m$.

C-13.46 Let three integer arrays, A, B, and C, be given, each of size n. Given an arbitrary integer k, design an $O(n^2 \log n)$-time algorithm to determine if there exist numbers, a in A, b in B, and c in C, such that $k = a + b + c$.

C-13.47 Give an $O(n^2)$-time algorithm for the previous problem.

Projects

P-13.48 Perform an experimental analysis of the efficiency (number of character comparisons performed) of the brute-force and KMP pattern-matching algorithms for varying-length patterns.

P-13.49 Perform an experimental analysis of the efficiency (number of character comparisons performed) of the brute-force and Boyer-Moore pattern-matching algorithms for varying-length patterns.

P-13.50 Perform an experimental comparison of the relative speeds of the brute-force, KMP, and Boyer-Moore pattern-matching algorithms. Document the relative running times on large text documents that are then searched using varying-length patterns.

P-13.51 Experiment with the efficiency of the indexOf method of Java's String class and develop a hypothesis about which pattern-matching algorithm it uses. Describe your experiments and your conclusions.

P-13.52 A very effective pattern-matching algorithm, developed by Rabin and Karp [54], relies on the use of hashing to produce an algorithm with very good expected performance. Recall that the brute-force algorithm compares the pattern to each possible placement in the text, spending $O(m)$ time, in the worst case, for each such comparison. The premise of the Rabin-Karp algorithm is to compute a hash function, $h(\cdot)$, on the length-m pattern, and then to compute the hash function on all length-m substrings of the text. The pattern P occurs at substring, $T[j..j+m-1]$, only if $h(P)$ equals $h(T[j..j+m-1])$. If the hash values are equal, the authenticity of the match at that location must then be verified with the brute-force approach, since there is a possibility that there was a coincidental collision of hash values for distinct strings. But with a good hash function, there will be very few such false matches.

The next challenge, however, is that computing a good hash function on a length-m substring would presumably require $O(m)$ time. If we did this for each of $O(n)$ possible locations, the algorithm would be no better than the brute-force approach. The trick is to rely on the use of a ***polynomial hash code***, as originally introduced in Section 10.2.1, such as

$$(x_0a^{m-1} + x_1a^{m-2} + \cdots + x_{n-2}a + x_{m-1}) \bmod p$$

for a substring $(x_0, x_1, \ldots, x_{m-1})$, randomly chosen a, and large prime p. We can compute the hash value of each successive substring of the text in $O(1)$ time each, by using the following formula

$$h(T[j+1..j+m]) = (a \cdot h(T[j..j+m-1]) - x_ja^m + x_{j+m}) \bmod p.$$

Implement the Rabin-Karp algorithm and evaluate its efficiency.

P-13.53 Implement the simplified search engine described in Section 13.3.4 for the pages of a small Web site. Use all the words in the pages of the site as index terms, excluding stop words such as articles, prepositions, and pronouns.

P-13.54 Implement a search engine for the pages of a small Web site by adding a page-ranking feature to the simplified search engine described in Section 13.3.4. Your page-ranking feature should return the most relevant pages first. Use all the words in the pages of the site as index terms, excluding stop words, such as articles, prepositions, and pronouns.

P-13.55 Use the LCS algorithm to compute the best sequence alignment between some DNA strings, which you can get online from GenBank.

P-13.56 Develop a spell-checker that uses edit distance (see Exercise C-13.43) to determine which correctly spelled words are closest to a misspelling.

Chapter Notes

The KMP algorithm is described by Knuth, Morris, and Pratt in their journal article [62], and Boyer and Moore describe their algorithm in a journal article published the same year [17]. In their article, however, Knuth et al. [62] also prove that the Boyer-Moore algorithm runs in linear time. More recently, Cole [23] shows that the Boyer-Moore algorithm makes at most $3n$ character comparisons in the worst case, and this bound is tight. All of the algorithms discussed above are also discussed in the book chapter by Aho [4], albeit in a more theoretical framework, including the methods for regular-expression pattern matching. The reader interested in further study of string pattern-matching algorithms is referred to the book by Stephen [84] and the book chapters by Aho [4], and Crochemore and Lecroq [26]. The trie was invented by Morrison [74] and is discussed extensively in the classic *Sorting and Searching* book by Knuth [61]. The name "Patricia" is short for "Practical Algorithm to Retrieve Information Coded in Alphanumeric" [74]. McCreight [68] shows how to construct suffix tries in linear time. Dynamic programming was developed in the operations research community and formalized by Bellman [12].

Chapter

14

Graph Algorithms

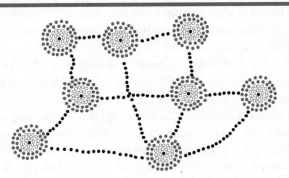

Contents

14.1 Graphs

A ***graph*** is a way of representing relationships that exist between pairs of objects. That is, a graph is a set of objects, called vertices, together with a collection of pairwise connections between them, called edges. Graphs have applications in modeling many domains, including mapping, transportation, computer networks, and electrical engineering. By the way, this notion of a "graph" should not be confused with bar charts and function plots, as these kinds of "graphs" are unrelated to the topic of this chapter.

Viewed abstractly, a ***graph*** G is simply a set V of ***vertices*** and a collection E of pairs of vertices from V, called ***edges***. Thus, a graph is a way of representing connections or relationships between pairs of objects from some set V. Incidentally, some books use different terminology for graphs and refer to what we call vertices as ***nodes*** and what we call edges as ***arcs***. We use the terms "vertices" and "edges."

Edges in a graph are either ***directed*** or ***undirected***. An edge (u,v) is said to be ***directed*** from u to v if the pair (u,v) is ordered, with u preceding v. An edge (u,v) is said to be ***undirected*** if the pair (u,v) is not ordered. Undirected edges are sometimes denoted with set notation, as $\{u,v\}$, but for simplicity we use the pair notation (u,v), noting that in the undirected case (u,v) is the same as (v,u). Graphs are typically visualized by drawing the vertices as ovals or rectangles and the edges as segments or curves connecting pairs of ovals and rectangles. The following are some examples of directed and undirected graphs.

Example 14.1: *We can visualize collaborations among the researchers of a certain discipline by constructing a graph whose vertices are associated with the researchers themselves, and whose edges connect pairs of vertices associated with researchers who have coauthored a paper or book. (See Figure 14.1.) Such edges are undirected because coauthorship is a* **symmetric** *relation; that is, if A has coauthored something with B, then B necessarily has coauthored something with A.*

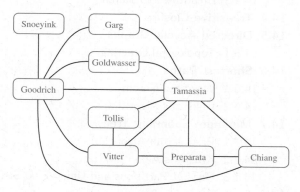

Figure 14.1: Graph of coauthorship among some authors.

Example 14.2: *We can associate with an object-oriented program a graph whose vertices represent the classes defined in the program, and whose edges indicate inheritance between classes. There is an edge from a vertex v to a vertex u if the class for v inherits from the class for u. Such edges are directed because the inheritance relation only goes in one direction (that is, it is* **asymmetric***).*

If all the edges in a graph are undirected, then we say the graph is an ***undirected graph***. Likewise, a ***directed graph***, also called a ***digraph***, is a graph whose edges are all directed. A graph that has both directed and undirected edges is often called a ***mixed graph***. Note that an undirected or mixed graph can be converted into a directed graph by replacing every undirected edge (u, v) by the pair of directed edges (u, v) and (v, u). It is often useful, however, to keep undirected and mixed graphs represented as they are, for such graphs have several applications, as in the following example.

Example 14.3: *A city map can be modeled as a graph whose vertices are intersections or dead ends, and whose edges are stretches of streets without intersections. This graph has both undirected edges, which correspond to stretches of two-way streets, and directed edges, which correspond to stretches of one-way streets. Thus, in this way, a graph modeling a city map is a mixed graph.*

Example 14.4: *Physical examples of graphs are present in the electrical wiring and plumbing networks of a building. Such networks can be modeled as graphs, where each connector, fixture, or outlet is viewed as a vertex, and each uninterrupted stretch of wire or pipe is viewed as an edge. Such graphs are actually components of much larger graphs, namely the local power and water distribution networks. Depending on the specific aspects of these graphs that we are interested in, we may consider their edges as undirected or directed, for, in principle, water can flow in a pipe and current can flow in a wire in either direction.*

The two vertices joined by an edge are called the ***end vertices*** (or ***endpoints***) of the edge. If an edge is directed, its first endpoint is its ***origin*** and the other is the ***destination*** of the edge. Two vertices u and v are said to be ***adjacent*** if there is an edge whose end vertices are u and v. An edge is said to be ***incident*** to a vertex if the vertex is one of the edge's endpoints. The ***outgoing edges*** of a vertex are the directed edges whose origin is that vertex. The ***incoming edges*** of a vertex are the directed edges whose destination is that vertex. The ***degree*** of a vertex v, denoted $\deg(v)$, is the number of incident edges of v. The ***in-degree*** and ***out-degree*** of a vertex v are the number of the incoming and outgoing edges of v, and are denoted $\text{indeg}(v)$ and $\text{outdeg}(v)$, respectively.

Example 14.5: *We can study air transportation by constructing a graph G, called a* **flight network**, *whose vertices are associated with airports, and whose edges are associated with flights. (See Figure 14.2.) In graph G, the edges are directed because a given flight has a specific travel direction. The endpoints of an edge e in G correspond respectively to the origin and destination of the flight corresponding to e. Two airports are adjacent in G if there is a flight that flies between them, and an edge e is incident to a vertex v in G if the flight for e flies to or from the airport for v. The outgoing edges of a vertex v correspond to the outbound flights from v's airport, and the incoming edges correspond to the inbound flights to v's airport. Finally, the in-degree of a vertex v of G corresponds to the number of inbound flights to v's airport, and the out-degree of a vertex v in G corresponds to the number of outbound flights.*

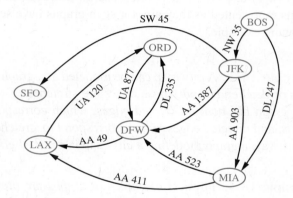

Figure 14.2: Example of a directed graph representing a flight network. The end-points of edge UA 120 are LAX and ORD; hence, LAX and ORD are adjacent. The in-degree of DFW is 3, and the out-degree of DFW is 2.

The definition of a graph refers to the group of edges as a ***collection***, not a *set*, thus allowing two undirected edges to have the same end vertices, and for two directed edges to have the same origin and the same destination. Such edges are called ***parallel edges*** or ***multiple edges***. A flight network can contain parallel edges (Example 14.5), such that multiple edges between the same pair of vertices could indicate different flights operating on the same route at different times of the day. Another special type of edge is one that connects a vertex to itself. Namely, we say that an edge (undirected or directed) is a ***self-loop*** if its two endpoints coincide. A self-loop may occur in a graph associated with a city map (Example 14.3), where it would correspond to a "circle" (a curving street that returns to its starting point).

With few exceptions, graphs do not have parallel edges or self-loops. Such graphs are said to be ***simple***. Thus, we can usually say that the edges of a simple graph are a ***set*** of vertex pairs (and not just a collection). Throughout this chapter, we will assume that a graph is simple unless otherwise specified.

A *path* is a sequence of alternating vertices and edges that starts at a vertex and ends at a vertex such that each edge is incident to its predecessor and successor vertex. A *cycle* is a path that starts and ends at the same vertex, and that includes at least one edge. We say that a path is *simple* if each vertex in the path is distinct, and we say that a cycle is *simple* if each vertex in the cycle is distinct, except for the first and last one. A *directed path* is a path such that all edges are directed and are traversed along their direction. A *directed cycle* is similarly defined. For example, in Figure 14.2, (BOS, NW 35, JFK, AA 1387, DFW) is a directed simple path, and (LAX, UA 120, ORD, UA 877, DFW, AA 49, LAX) is a directed simple cycle. Note that a directed graph may have a cycle consisting of two edges with opposite direction between the same pair of vertices, for example (ORD, UA 877, DFW, DL 335, ORD) in Figure 14.2. A directed graph is *acyclic* if it has no directed cycles. For example, if we were to remove the edge UA 877 from the graph in Figure 14.2, the remaining graph is acyclic. If a graph is simple, we may omit the edges when describing path P or cycle C, as these are well defined, in which case P is a list of adjacent vertices and C is a cycle of adjacent vertices.

Example 14.6: *Given a graph G representing a city map (see Example 14.3), we can model a couple driving to dinner at a recommended restaurant as traversing a path though G. If they know the way, and do not accidentally go through the same intersection twice, then they traverse a simple path in G. Likewise, we can model the entire trip the couple takes, from their home to the restaurant and back, as a cycle. If they go home from the restaurant in a completely different way than how they went, not even going through the same intersection twice, then their entire round trip is a simple cycle. Finally, if they travel along one-way streets for their entire trip, we can model their night out as a directed cycle.*

Given vertices u and v of a (directed) graph G, we say that u *reaches* v, and that v is *reachable* from u, if G has a (directed) path from u to v. In an undirected graph, the notion of *reachability* is symmetric, that is to say, u reaches v if an only if v reaches u. However, in a directed graph, it is possible that u reaches v but v does not reach u, because a directed path must be traversed according to the respective directions of the edges. A graph is *connected* if, for any two vertices, there is a path between them. A directed graph $\vec{G}$ is *strongly connected* if for any two vertices u and v of $\vec{G}$, u reaches v and v reaches u. (See Figure 14.3 for some examples.)

A *subgraph* of a graph G is a graph H whose vertices and edges are subsets of the vertices and edges of G, respectively. A *spanning subgraph* of G is a subgraph of G that contains all the vertices of the graph G. If a graph G is not connected, its maximal connected subgraphs are called the *connected components* of G. A *forest* is a graph without cycles. A *tree* is a connected forest, that is, a connected graph without cycles. A *spanning tree* of a graph is a spanning subgraph that is a tree. (Note that this definition of a tree is somewhat different from the one given in Chapter 8, as there is not necessarily a designated root.)

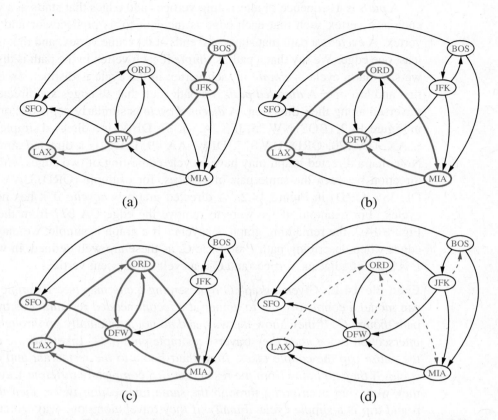

Figure 14.3: Examples of reachability in a directed graph: (a) a directed path from BOS to LAX is highlighted; (b) a directed cycle (ORD, MIA, DFW, LAX, ORD) is highlighted; its vertices induce a strongly connected subgraph; (c) the subgraph of the vertices and edges reachable from ORD is highlighted; (d) the removal of the dashed edges results in a directed acyclic graph.

Example 14.7: *Perhaps the most talked about graph today is the Internet, which can be viewed as a graph whose vertices are computers and whose (undirected) edges are communication connections between pairs of computers on the Internet. The computers and the connections between them in a single domain, like wiley.com, form a subgraph of the Internet. If this subgraph is connected, then two users on computers in this domain can send email to one another without having their information packets ever leave their domain. Suppose the edges of this subgraph form a spanning tree. This implies that, if even a single connection goes down (for example, because someone pulls a communication cable out of the back of a computer in this domain), then this subgraph will no longer be connected.*

In the propositions that follow, we explore a few important properties of graphs.

Proposition 14.8: *If G is a graph with m edges and vertex set V, then*

$$\sum_{v \ in \ V} deg(v) = 2m.$$

Justification: An edge (u, v) is counted twice in the summation above; once by its endpoint u and once by its endpoint v. Thus, the total contribution of the edges to the degrees of the vertices is twice the number of edges. ∎

Proposition 14.9: *If G is a directed graph with m edges and vertex set V, then*

$$\sum_{v \ in \ V} indeg(v) = \sum_{v \ in \ V} outdeg(v) = m.$$

Justification: In a directed graph, an edge (u, v) contributes one unit to the out-degree of its origin u and one unit to the in-degree of its destination v. Thus, the total contribution of the edges to the out-degrees of the vertices is equal to the number of edges, and similarly for the in-degrees. ∎

We next show that a simple graph with n vertices has $O(n^2)$ edges.

Proposition 14.10: *Let G be a simple graph with n vertices and m edges. If G is undirected, then $m \le n(n-1)/2$, and if G is directed, then $m \le n(n-1)$.*

Justification: Suppose that G is undirected. Since no two edges can have the same endpoints and there are no self-loops, the maximum degree of a vertex in G is $n-1$ in this case. Thus, by Proposition 14.8, $2m \le n(n-1)$. Now suppose that G is directed. Since no two edges can have the same origin and destination, and there are no self-loops, the maximum in-degree of a vertex in G is $n-1$ in this case. Thus, by Proposition 14.9, $m \le n(n-1)$. ∎

There are a number of simple properties of trees, forests, and connected graphs.

Proposition 14.11: *Let G be an undirected graph with n vertices and m edges.*

- *If G is connected, then $m \ge n-1$.*
- *If G is a tree, then $m = n-1$.*
- *If G is a forest, then $m \le n-1$.*

14.1.1   The Graph ADT

A graph is a collection of vertices and edges. We model the abstraction as a combination of three data types: Vertex, Edge, and Graph. A Vertex is a lightweight object that stores an arbitrary element provided by the user (e.g., an airport code); we assume the element can be retrieved with the getElement( ) method. An Edge also stores an associated object (e.g., a flight number, travel distance, cost), which is returned by its getElement( ) method.

The primary abstraction for a graph is the Graph ADT. We presume that a graph can be either **undirected** or **directed**, with the designation declared upon construction; recall that a mixed graph can be represented as a directed graph, modeling edge $\{u,v\}$ as a pair of directed edges (u,v) and (v,u). The Graph ADT includes the following methods:

numVertices( ): Returns the number of vertices of the graph.

vertices( ): Returns an iteration of all the vertices of the graph.

numEdges( ): Returns the number of edges of the graph.

edges( ): Returns an iteration of all the edges of the graph.

getEdge(u, v): Returns the edge from vertex u to vertex v, if one exists; otherwise return null. For an undirected graph, there is no difference between getEdge(u, v) and getEdge(v, u).

endVertices(e): Returns an array containing the two endpoint vertices of edge e. If the graph is directed, the first vertex is the origin and the second is the destination.

opposite(v, e): For edge e incident to vertex v, returns the other vertex of the edge; an error occurs if e is not incident to v.

outDegree(v): Returns the number of outgoing edges from vertex v.

inDegree(v): Returns the number of incoming edges to vertex v. For an undirected graph, this returns the same value as does outDegree(v).

outgoingEdges(v): Returns an iteration of all outgoing edges from vertex v.

incomingEdges(v): Returns an iteration of all incoming edges to vertex v. For an undirected graph, this returns the same collection as does outgoingEdges(v).

insertVertex(x): Creates and returns a new Vertex storing element x.

insertEdge(u, v, x): Creates and returns a new Edge from vertex u to vertex v, storing element x; an error occurs if there already exists an edge from u to v.

removeVertex(v): Removes vertex v and all its incident edges from the graph.

removeEdge(e): Removes edge e from the graph.

14.2 Data Structures for Graphs

In this section, we introduce four data structures for representing a graph. In each representation, we maintain a collection to store the vertices of a graph. However, the four representations differ greatly in the way they organize the edges.

- In an ***edge list***, we maintain an unordered list of all edges. This minimally suffices, but there is no efficient way to locate a particular edge (u, v), or the set of all edges incident to a vertex v.

- In an ***adjacency list***, we additionally maintain, for each vertex, a separate list containing those edges that are incident to the vertex. This organization allows us to more efficiently find all edges incident to a given vertex.

- An ***adjacency map*** is similar to an adjacency list, but the secondary container of all edges incident to a vertex is organized as a map, rather than as a list, with the adjacent vertex serving as a key. This allows more efficient access to a specific edge (u, v), for example, in $O(1)$ expected time with hashing.

- An ***adjacency matrix*** provides worst-case $O(1)$ access to a specific edge (u, v) by maintaining an $n \times n$ matrix, for a graph with n vertices. Each slot is dedicated to storing a reference to the edge (u, v) for a particular pair of vertices u and v; if no such edge exists, the slot will store null.

A summary of the performance of these structures is given in Table 14.1.

Method	Edge List	Adj. List	Adj. Map	Adj. Matrix
numVertices( )	$O(1)$	$O(1)$	$O(1)$	$O(1)$
numEdges( )	$O(1)$	$O(1)$	$O(1)$	$O(1)$
vertices( )	$O(n)$	$O(n)$	$O(n)$	$O(n)$
edges( )	$O(m)$	$O(m)$	$O(m)$	$O(m)$
getEdge(u, v)	$O(m)$	$O(\min(d_u, d_v))$	$O(1)$ exp.	$O(1)$
outDegree(v) inDegree(v)	$O(m)$	$O(1)$	$O(1)$	$O(n)$
outgoingEdges(v) incomingEdges(v)	$O(m)$	$O(d_v)$	$O(d_v)$	$O(n)$
insertVertex(x)	$O(1)$	$O(1)$	$O(1)$	$O(n^2)$
removeVertex(v)	$O(m)$	$O(d_v)$	$O(d_v)$	$O(n^2)$
insertEdge(u, v, x)	$O(1)$	$O(1)$	$O(1)$ exp.	$O(1)$
removeEdge(e)	$O(1)$	$O(1)$	$O(1)$ exp.	$O(1)$

Table 14.1: A summary of the running times for the methods of the graph ADT, using the graph representations discussed in this section. We let n denote the number of vertices, m the number of edges, and d_v the degree of vertex v. Note that the adjacency matrix uses $O(n^2)$ space, while all other structures use $O(n+m)$ space.

14.2.1 Edge List Structure

The ***edge list*** structure is possibly the simplest, though not the most efficient, representation of a graph G. All vertex objects are stored in an unordered list V, and all edge objects are stored in an unordered list E. We illustrate an example of the edge list structure for a graph G in Figure 14.4.

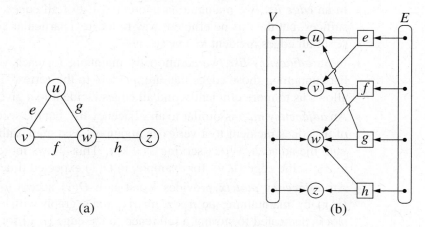

Figure 14.4: (a) A graph G; (b) schematic representation of the edge list structure for G. Notice that an edge object refers to the two vertex objects that correspond to its endpoints, but that vertices do not refer to incident edges.

To support the many methods of the Graph ADT (Section 14.1), we assume the following additional features of an edge list representation. Collections V and E are represented with doubly linked lists using our LinkedPositionalList class from Chapter 7.

Vertex Objects

The vertex object for a vertex v storing element x has instance variables for:

- A reference to element x, to support the getElement( ) method.
- A reference to the position of the vertex instance in the list V, thereby allowing v to be efficiently removed from V if it were removed from the graph.

Edge Objects

The edge object for an edge e storing element x has instance variables for:

- A reference to element x, to support the getElement( ) method.
- References to the vertex objects associated with the endpoint vertices of e. These will allow for constant-time support for methods endVertices(e) and opposite(v, e).
- A reference to the position of the edge instance in list E, thereby allowing e to be efficiently removed from E if it were removed from the graph.

Performance of the Edge List Structure

The performance of an edge list structure in fulfilling the graph ADT is summarized in Table 14.2. We begin by discussing the space usage, which is $O(n+m)$ for representing a graph with n vertices and m edges. Each individual vertex or edge instance uses $O(1)$ space, and the additional lists V and E use space proportional to their number of entries.

In terms of running time, the edge list structure does as well as one could hope in terms of reporting the number of vertices or edges, or in producing an iteration of those vertices or edges. By querying the respective list V or E, the numVertices and numEdges methods run in $O(1)$ time, and by iterating through the appropriate list, the methods vertices and edges run respectively in $O(n)$ and $O(m)$ time.

The most significant limitations of an edge list structure, especially when compared to the other graph representations, are the $O(m)$ running times of methods getEdge(u, v), outDegree(v), and outgoingEdges(v) (and corresponding methods inDegree and incomingEdges). The problem is that with all edges of the graph in an unordered list E, the only way to answer those queries is through an exhaustive inspection of all edges.

Finally, we consider the methods that update the graph. It is easy to add a new vertex or a new edge to the graph in $O(1)$ time. For example, a new edge can be added to the graph by creating an Edge instance storing the given element as data, adding that instance to the positional list E, and recording its resulting Position within E as an attribute of the edge. That stored position can later be used to locate and remove this edge from E in $O(1)$ time, and thus implement the method removeEdge(e).

It is worth discussing why the removeVertex(v) method has a running time of $O(m)$. As stated in the graph ADT, when a vertex v is removed from the graph, all edges incident to v must also be removed (otherwise, we would have a contradiction of edges that refer to vertices that are not part of the graph). To locate the incident edges to the vertex, we must examine all edges of E.

Method	Running Time
numVertices( ), numEdges( )	$O(1)$
vertices( )	$O(n)$
edges( )	$O(m)$
getEdge(u, v), outDegree(v), outgoingEdges(v)	$O(m)$
insertVertex(x), insertEdge(u, v, x), removeEdge(e)	$O(1)$
removeVertex(v)	$O(m)$

Table 14.2: Running times of the methods of a graph implemented with the edge list structure. The space used is $O(n+m)$, where n is the number of vertices and m is the number of edges.

14.2.2 Adjacency List Structure

The adjacency list structure for a graph adds extra information to the edge list structure that supports direct access to the incident edges (and thus to the adjacent vertices) of each vertex. Specifically, for each vertex v, we maintain a collection $I(v)$, called the ***incidence collection*** of v, whose entries are edges incident to v. In the case of a directed graph, outgoing and incoming edges can be respectively stored in two separate collections, $I_{out}(v)$ and $I_{in}(v)$. Traditionally, the incidence collection $I(v)$ for a vertex v is a list, which is why we call this way of representing a graph the ***adjacency list*** structure.

We require that the primary structure for an adjacency list maintain the collection V of vertices in a way so that we can locate the secondary structure $I(v)$ for a given vertex v in $O(1)$ time. This could be done by using a positional list to represent V, with each Vertex instance maintaining a direct reference to its $I(v)$ incidence collection; we illustrate such an adjacency list structure of a graph in Figure 14.5. If vertices can be uniquely numbered from 0 to $n-1$, we could instead use a primary array-based structure to access the appropriate secondary lists.

The primary benefit of an adjacency list is that the collection $I(v)$ (or more specifically, $I_{out}(v)$) contains exactly those edges that should be reported by the method outgoingEdges(v). Therefore, we can implement this method by iterating the edges of $I(v)$ in $O(\deg(v))$ time, where $\deg(v)$ is the degree of vertex v. This is the best possible outcome for any graph representation, because there are $\deg(v)$ edges to be reported.

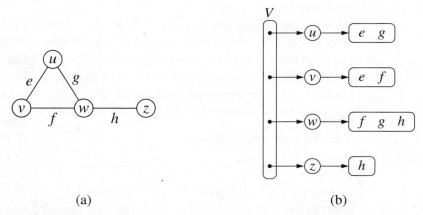

(a)   (b)

Figure 14.5: (a) An undirected graph G; (b) a schematic representation of the adjacency list structure for G. Collection V is the primary list of vertices, and each vertex has an associated list of incident edges. Although not diagrammed as such, we presume that each edge of the graph is represented with a unique Edge instance that maintains references to its endpoint vertices, and that E is a list of all edges.

Performance of the Adjacency List Structure

Table 14.3 summarizes the performance of the adjacency list structure implementation of a graph, assuming that the primary collection V and E, and all secondary collections $I(v)$ are implemented with doubly linked lists.

Asymptotically, the space requirements for an adjacency list are the same as an edge list structure, using $O(n+m)$ space for a graph with n vertices and m edges. It is clear that the primary lists of vertices and edges use $O(n+m)$ space. In addition, the sum of the lengths of all secondary lists is $O(m)$, for reasons that were formalized in Propositions 14.8 and 14.9. In short, an undirected edge (u,v) is referenced in both $I(u)$ and $I(v)$, but its presence in the graph results in only a constant amount of additional space.

We have already noted that the outgoingEdges(v) method can be achieved in $O(\deg(v))$ time based on use of $I(v)$. For a directed graph, this is more specifically $O(\text{outdeg}(v))$ based on use of $I_{\text{out}}(v)$. The outDegree(v) method of the graph ADT can run in $O(1)$ time, assuming collection $I(v)$ can report its size in similar time. To locate a specific edge for implementing getEdge(u, v), we can search through either $I(u)$ and $I(v)$ (or for a directed graph, either $I_{\text{out}}(u)$ or $I_{\text{in}}(v)$). By choosing the smaller of the two, we get $O(\min(\deg(u),\deg(v)))$ running time.

The rest of the bounds in Table 14.3 can be achieved with additional care. To efficiently support deletions of edges, an edge (u,v) would need to maintain a reference to its positions within both $I(u)$ and $I(v)$, so that it could be deleted from those collections in $O(1)$ time. To remove a vertex v, we must also remove any incident edges, but at least we can locate those edges in $O(\deg(v))$ time.

Method	Running Time
numVertices( ), numEdges( )	$O(1)$
vertices( )	$O(n)$
edges( )	$O(m)$
getEdge(u, v)	$O(\min(\deg(u),\deg(v)))$
outDegree(v), inDegree(v)	$O(1)$
outgoingEdges(v), incomingEdges(v)	$O(\deg(v))$
insertVertex(x), insertEdge(u, v, x)	$O(1)$
removeEdge(e)	$O(1)$
removeVertex(v)	$O(\deg(v))$

Table 14.3: Running times of the methods of a graph implemented with the adjacency list structure. The space used is $O(n+m)$, where n is the number of vertices and m is the number of edges.

14.2.3 Adjacency Map Structure

In the adjacency list structure, we assume that the secondary incidence collections are implemented as unordered linked lists. Such a collection $I(v)$ uses space proportional to $O(\deg(v))$, allows an edge to be added or removed in $O(1)$ time, and allows an iteration of all edges incident to vertex v in $O(\deg(v))$ time. However, the best implementation of getEdge(u, v) requires $O(\min(\deg(u), \deg(v)))$ time, because we must search through either $I(u)$ or $I(v)$.

We can improve the performance by using a hash-based map to implement $I(v)$ for each vertex v. Specifically, we let the opposite endpoint of each incident edge serve as a key in the map, with the edge structure serving as the value. We call such a graph representation an ***adjacency map***. (See Figure 14.6.) The space usage for an adjacency map remains $O(n + m)$, because $I(v)$ uses $O(\deg(v))$ space for each vertex v, as with the adjacency list.

The advantage of the adjacency map, relative to an adjacency list, is that the getEdge(u, v) method can be implemented in ***expected*** $O(1)$ time by searching for vertex u as a key in $I(v)$, or vice versa. This provides a likely improvement over the adjacency list, while retaining the worst-case bound of $O(\min(\deg(u), \deg(v)))$.

In comparing the performance of adjacency map to other representations (see Table 14.1), we find that it essentially achieves optimal running times for all methods, making it an excellent all-purpose choice as a graph representation.

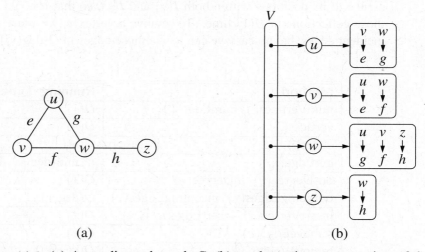

(a)   (b)

Figure 14.6: (a) An undirected graph G; (b) a schematic representation of the adjacency map structure for G. Each vertex maintains a secondary map in which neighboring vertices serve as keys, with the connecting edges as associated values. As with the adjacency list, we presume that there is also an overall list E of all Edge instances.

14.2.4 Adjacency Matrix Structure

The **adjacency matrix** structure for a graph G augments the edge list structure with a matrix A (that is, a two-dimensional array, as in Section 3.1.5), which allows us to locate an edge between a given pair of vertices in *worst-case* constant time. In the adjacency matrix representation, we think of the vertices as being the integers in the set $\{0, 1, \ldots, n-1\}$ and the edges as being pairs of such integers. This allows us to store references to edges in the cells of a two-dimensional $n \times n$ array A. Specifically, the cell $A[i][j]$ holds a reference to the edge (u, v), if it exists, where u is the vertex with index i and v is the vertex with index j. If there is no such edge, then $A[i][j] = $ null. We note that array A is symmetric if graph G is undirected, as $A[i][j] = A[j][i]$ for all pairs i and j. (See Figure 14.7.)

The most significant advantage of an adjacency matrix is that any edge (u, v) can be accessed in worst-case $O(1)$ time; recall that the adjacency map supports that operation in $O(1)$ *expected* time. However, several operation are less efficient with an adjacency matrix. For example, to find the edges incident to vertex v, we must presumably examine all n entries in the row associated with v; recall that an adjacency list or map can locate those edges in optimal $O(\deg(v))$ time. Adding or removing vertices from a graph is problematic, as the matrix must be resized.

Furthermore, the $O(n^2)$ space usage of an adjacency matrix is typically far worse than the $O(n + m)$ space required of the other representations. Although, in the worst case, the number of edges in a **dense** graph will be proportional to n^2, most real-world graphs are **sparse**. In such cases, use of an adjacency matrix is inefficient. However, if a graph is dense, the constants of proportionality of an adjacency matrix can be smaller than that of an adjacency list or map. In fact, if edges do not have auxiliary data, a boolean adjacency matrix can use one bit per edge slot, such that $A[i][j] = $ true if and only if associated (u, v) is an edge.

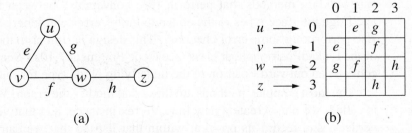

(a)   (b)

Figure 14.7: (a) An undirected graph G; (b) a schematic representation of the auxiliary adjacency matrix structure for G, in which n vertices are mapped to indices 0 to $n-1$. Although not diagrammed as such, we presume that there is a unique Edge instance for each edge, and that it maintains references to its endpoint vertices. We also assume that there is a secondary edge list (not pictured), to allow the edges( ) method to run in $O(m)$ time, for a graph with m edges.

14.2.5 Java Implementation

In this section, we provide an implementation of the Graph ADT, based on the **adjacency map** representation, as described in Section 14.2.3. We use positional lists to represent each of the primary lists V and E, as originally described in the edge list representation. Additionally, for each vertex v, we use a hash-based map to represent the secondary incidence map $I(v)$.

To gracefully support both undirected and directed graphs, each vertex maintains two different map references: outgoing and incoming. In the directed case, these are initialized to two distinct map instances, representing $I_{out}(v)$ and $I_{in}(v)$, respectively. In the case of an undirected graph, we assign both outgoing and incoming as aliases to a single map instance.

Our implementation is organized as follows. We assume definitions for Vertex, Edge, and Graph interfaces, although for the sake of brevity, we do not include those definitions in the book (they are available online). We then define a concrete AdjacencyMapGraph class, with nested classes InnerVertex and InnerEdge to implement the vertex and edge abstractions. These classes use generic parameters V and E to designate the element type stored respectively at vertices and edges.

We begin in Code Fragment 14.1, with the definitions of the InnerVertex and InnerEdge classes (although in reality, those definitions should be nested within the following AdjacencyMapGraph class). Note well how the InnerVertex constructor initializes the outgoing and incoming instance variables depending on whether the overall graph is undirected or directed.

Code Fragments 14.2 and 14.3 contain the core implementation of the class AdjacencyMapGraph. A graph instance maintains a boolean variable that designates whether the graph is directed, and it maintains the vertex list and edge list. Although not shown in these code fragments, our implementation includes private validate methods that perform type conversions between the public Vertex and Edge interface types to the concrete InnerVertex and InnerEdge classes, while also performing some error checking. This design is similar to the validate method of the LinkedPositionalList class (see Code Fragment 7.10 of Section 7.3.3), which converts an outward Position to the underlying Node type for that class.

The most complex methods are those that modify the graph. When insertVertex is called, we must create a new InnerVertex instance, add that vertex to the list of vertices, and record its position within that list (so that we can efficiently delete it from the list if the vertex is removed from the graph). When inserting an edge (u, v), we must also create a new instance, add it to the edge list, and record its position, yet we must also add the new edge to the outgoing adjacency map for vertex u, and the incoming map for vertex v. Code Fragment 14.3 contains code for removeVertex as well; the implementation of removeEdge is not included, but is available in the online version of the code.

```
1   /** A vertex of an adjacency map graph representation. */
2   private class InnerVertex<V> implements Vertex<V> {
3     private V element;
4     private Position<Vertex<V>> pos;
5     private Map<Vertex<V>, Edge<E>> outgoing, incoming;
6     /** Constructs a new InnerVertex instance storing the given element. */
7     public InnerVertex(V elem, boolean graphIsDirected) {
8       element = elem;
9       outgoing = new ProbeHashMap<>();
10      if (graphIsDirected)
11        incoming = new ProbeHashMap<>();
12      else
13        incoming = outgoing;                  // if undirected, alias outgoing map
14    }
15    /** Returns the element associated with the vertex. */
16    public V getElement() { return element; }
17    /** Stores the position of this vertex within the graph's vertex list. */
18    public void setPosition(Position<Vertex<V>> p) { pos = p; }
19    /** Returns the position of this vertex within the graph's vertex list. */
20    public Position<Vertex<V>> getPosition() { return pos; }
21    /** Returns reference to the underlying map of outgoing edges. */
22    public Map<Vertex<V>, Edge<E>> getOutgoing() { return outgoing; }
23    /** Returns reference to the underlying map of incoming edges. */
24    public Map<Vertex<V>, Edge<E>> getIncoming() { return incoming; }
25  } //------------ end of InnerVertex class ------------
26
27  /** An edge between two vertices. */
28  private class InnerEdge<E> implements Edge<E> {
29    private E element;
30    private Position<Edge<E>> pos;
31    private Vertex<V>[ ] endpoints;
32    /** Constructs InnerEdge instance from u to v, storing the given element. */
33    public InnerEdge(Vertex<V> u, Vertex<V> v, E elem) {
34      element = elem;
35      endpoints = (Vertex<V>[ ]) new Vertex[ ]{u,v};  // array of length 2
36    }
37    /** Returns the element associated with the edge. */
38    public E getElement() { return element; }
39    /** Returns reference to the endpoint array. */
40    public Vertex<V>[ ] getEndpoints() { return endpoints; }
41    /** Stores the position of this edge within the graph's vertex list. */
42    public void setPosition(Position<Edge<E>> p) { pos = p; }
43    /** Returns the position of this edge within the graph's vertex list. */
44    public Position<Edge<E>> getPosition() { return pos; }
45  } //------------ end of InnerEdge class ------------
```

Code Fragment 14.1: InnerVertex and InnerEdge classes (to be nested within the AdjacencyMapGraph class). Interfaces Vertex<V> and Edge<E> are not shown.

```java
1   public class AdjacencyMapGraph<V,E> implements Graph<V,E> {
2     // nested InnerVertex and InnerEdge classes defined here...
3     private boolean isDirected;
4     private PositionalList<Vertex<V>> vertices = new LinkedPositionalList<>();
5     private PositionalList<Edge<E>> edges = new LinkedPositionalList<>();
6     /** Constructs an empty graph (either undirected or directed). */
7     public AdjacencyMapGraph(boolean directed) { isDirected = directed; }
8     /** Returns the number of vertices of the graph */
9     public int numVertices() { return vertices.size(); }
10    /** Returns the vertices of the graph as an iterable collection */
11    public Iterable<Vertex<V>> vertices() { return vertices; }
12    /** Returns the number of edges of the graph */
13    public int numEdges() { return edges.size(); }
14    /** Returns the edges of the graph as an iterable collection */
15    public Iterable<Edge<E>> edges() { return edges; }
16    /** Returns the number of edges for which vertex v is the origin. */
17    public int outDegree(Vertex<V> v) {
18      InnerVertex<V> vert = validate(v);
19      return vert.getOutgoing().size();
20    }
21    /** Returns an iterable collection of edges for which vertex v is the origin. */
22    public Iterable<Edge<E>> outgoingEdges(Vertex<V> v) {
23      InnerVertex<V> vert = validate(v);
24      return vert.getOutgoing().values();  // edges are the values in the adjacency map
25    }
26    /** Returns the number of edges for which vertex v is the destination. */
27    public int inDegree(Vertex<V> v) {
28      InnerVertex<V> vert = validate(v);
29      return vert.getIncoming().size();
30    }
31    /** Returns an iterable collection of edges for which vertex v is the destination. */
32    public Iterable<Edge<E>> incomingEdges(Vertex<V> v) {
33      InnerVertex<V> vert = validate(v);
34      return vert.getIncoming().values();  // edges are the values in the adjacency map
35    }
36    public Edge<E> getEdge(Vertex<V> u, Vertex<V> v) {
37    /** Returns the edge from u to v, or null if they are not adjacent. */
38      InnerVertex<V> origin = validate(u);
39      return origin.getOutgoing().get(v);  // will be null if no edge from u to v
40    }
41    /** Returns the vertices of edge e as an array of length two. */
42    public Vertex<V>[] endVertices(Edge<E> e) {
43      InnerEdge<E> edge = validate(e);
44      return edge.getEndpoints();
45    }
```

Code Fragment 14.2: AdjacencyMapGraph class definition. (Continues in Code Fragment 14.3.) The validate(v) and validate(e) methods are available online.

```
46    /** Returns the vertex that is opposite vertex v on edge e. */
47    public Vertex<V> opposite(Vertex<V> v, Edge<E> e)
48                                              throws IllegalArgumentException {
49      InnerEdge<E> edge = validate(e);
50      Vertex<V>[ ] endpoints = edge.getEndpoints( );
51      if (endpoints[0] == v)
52        return endpoints[1];
53      else if (endpoints[1] == v)
54        return endpoints[0];
55      else
56        throw new IllegalArgumentException("v is not incident to this edge");
57    }
58    /** Inserts and returns a new vertex with the given element. */
59    public Vertex<V> insertVertex(V element) {
60      InnerVertex<V> v = new InnerVertex<>(element, isDirected);
61      v.setPosition(vertices.addLast(v));
62      return v;
63    }
64    /** Inserts and returns a new edge between u and v, storing given element. */
65    public Edge<E> insertEdge(Vertex<V> u, Vertex<V> v, E element)
66                                              throws IllegalArgumentException {
67      if (getEdge(u,v) == null) {
68        InnerEdge<E> e = new InnerEdge<>(u, v, element);
69        e.setPosition(edges.addLast(e));
70        InnerVertex<V> origin = validate(u);
71        InnerVertex<V> dest = validate(v);
72        origin.getOutgoing( ).put(v, e);
73        dest.getIncoming( ).put(u, e);
74        return e;
75      } else
76        throw new IllegalArgumentException("Edge from u to v exists");
77    }
78    /** Removes a vertex and all its incident edges from the graph. */
79    public void removeVertex(Vertex<V> v) {
80      InnerVertex<V> vert = validate(v);
81      // remove all incident edges from the graph
82      for (Edge<E> e : vert.getOutgoing( ).values( ))
83        removeEdge(e);
84      for (Edge<E> e : vert.getIncoming( ).values( ))
85        removeEdge(e);
86      // remove this vertex from the list of vertices
87      vertices.remove(vert.getPosition( ));
88    }
89  }
```

Code Fragment 14.3: AdjacencyMapGraph class definition (continued from Code Fragment 14.2). We omit the removeEdge method, for brevity.

14.3   Graph Traversals

Greek mythology tells of an elaborate labyrinth that was built to house the mon-strous Minotaur, which was part bull and part man. This labyrinth was so complex that neither beast nor human could escape it. No human, that is, until the Greek hero, Theseus, with the help of the king's daughter, Ariadne, decided to implement a *graph traversal* algorithm. Theseus fastened a ball of thread to the door of the labyrinth and unwound it as he traversed the twisting passages in search of the monster. Theseus obviously knew about good algorithm design, for, after finding and defeating the beast, Theseus easily followed the string back out of the labyrinth to the loving arms of Ariadne.

Formally, a *traversal* is a systematic procedure for exploring a graph by exam-ining all of its vertices and edges. A traversal is efficient if it visits all the vertices and edges in time proportional to their number, that is, in linear time.

Graph traversal algorithms are key to answering many fundamental questions about graphs involving the notion of *reachability*, that is, in determining how to travel from one vertex to another while following paths of a graph. Interesting problems that deal with reachability in an undirected graph G include the following:

- Computing a path from vertex u to vertex v, or reporting that no such path exists.
- Given a start vertex s of G, computing, for every vertex v of G, a path with the minimum number of edges between s and v, or reporting that no such path exists.
- Testing whether G is connected.
- Computing a spanning tree of G, if G is connected.
- Computing the connected components of G.
- Identifying a cycle in G, or reporting that G has no cycles.

Interesting problems that deal with reachability in a directed graph $\vec{G}$ include the following:

- Computing a directed path from vertex u to vertex v, or reporting that no such path exists.
- Finding all the vertices of $\vec{G}$ that are reachable from a given vertex s.
- Determine whether $\vec{G}$ is acyclic.
- Determine whether $\vec{G}$ is strongly connected.

In the remainder of this section, we will present two efficient graph traversal algorithms, called *depth-first search* and *breadth-first search*, respectively.

14.3.1 Depth-First Search

The first traversal algorithm we consider in this section is ***depth-first search*** (DFS). Depth-first search is useful for testing a number of properties of graphs, including whether there is a path from one vertex to another and whether or not a graph is connected.

Depth-first search in a graph G is analogous to wandering in a labyrinth with a string and a can of paint without getting lost. We begin at a specific starting vertex s in G, which we initialize by fixing one end of our string to s and painting s as "visited." The vertex s is now our "current" vertex. In general, if we call our current vertex u, we traverse G by considering an arbitrary edge (u, v) incident to the current vertex u. If the edge (u, v) leads us to a vertex v that is already visited (that is, painted), we ignore that edge. If, on the other hand, (u, v) leads to an unvisited vertex v, then we unroll our string, and go to v. We then paint v as "visited," and make it the current vertex, repeating the computation above. Eventually, we will get to a "dead end," that is, a current vertex v such that all the edges incident to v lead to vertices already visited. To get out of this impasse, we roll our string back up, backtracking along the edge that brought us to v, going back to a previously visited vertex u. We then make u our current vertex and repeat the computation above for any edges incident to u that we have not yet considered. If all of u's incident edges lead to visited vertices, then we again roll up our string and backtrack to the vertex we came from to get to u, and repeat the procedure at that vertex. Thus, we continue to backtrack along the path that we have traced so far until we find a vertex that has yet unexplored edges, take one such edge, and continue the traversal. The process terminates when our backtracking leads us back to the start vertex s, and there are no more unexplored edges incident to s.

The pseudocode for a depth-first search traversal starting at a vertex u (see Code Fragment 14.4) follows our analogy with string and paint. We use recursion to implement the string analogy, and we assume that we have a mechanism (the paint analogy) to determine whether a vertex or edge has been previously explored.

Algorithm DFS(G, u):

    Input: A graph G and a vertex u of G

    Output: A collection of vertices reachable from u, with their discovery edges

    Mark vertex u as visited.

    for each of u's outgoing edges, $e = (u, v)$ **do**

        if vertex v has not been visited **then**

            Record edge e as the discovery edge for vertex v.

            Recursively call DFS(G, v).

Code Fragment 14.4: The DFS algorithm.

Classifying Graph Edges with DFS

An execution of depth-first search can be used to analyze the structure of a graph, based upon the way in which edges are explored during the traversal. The DFS process naturally identifies what is known as the ***depth-first search tree*** rooted at a starting vertex s. Whenever an edge $e = (u,v)$ is used to discover a new vertex v during the DFS algorithm of Code Fragment 14.4, that edge is known as a ***discovery edge*** or ***tree edge***, as oriented from u to v. All other edges that are considered during the execution of DFS are known as ***nontree edges***, which take us to a previously visited vertex. In the case of an undirected graph, we will find that all nontree edges that are explored connect the current vertex to one that is an ancestor of it in the DFS tree. We will call such an edge a ***back edge***. When performing a DFS on a directed graph, there are three possible kinds of nontree edges:

- ***back edges***, which connect a vertex to an ancestor in the DFS tree
- ***forward edges***, which connect a vertex to a descendant in the DFS tree
- ***cross edges***, which connect a vertex to a vertex that is neither its ancestor nor its descendant

An example application of the DFS algorithm on a directed graph is shown in Figure 14.8, demonstrating each type of nontree edge. An example application of the DFS algorithm on an undirected graph is shown in Figure 14.9.

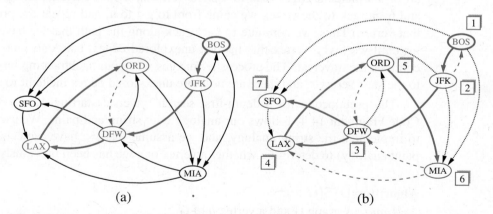

(a)   (b)

Figure 14.8: An example of a DFS in a directed graph, starting at vertex (BOS): (a) intermediate step, where, for the first time, a considered edge leads to an already visited vertex (DFW); (b) the completed DFS. The tree edges are shown with thick blue lines, the back edges are shown with dashed blue lines, and the forward and cross edges are shown with dotted black lines. The order in which the vertices are visited is indicated by a label next to each vertex. The edge (ORD,DFW) is a back edge, but (DFW,ORD) is a forward edge. Edge (BOS,SFO) is a forward edge, and (SFO,LAX) is a cross edge.

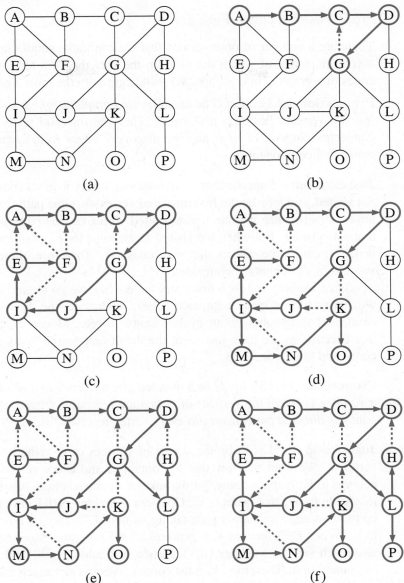

Figure 14.9: Example of depth-first search traversal on an undirected graph starting at vertex *A*. We assume that a vertex's adjacencies are considered in alphabetical order. Visited vertices and explored edges are highlighted, with discovery edges drawn as solid lines and nontree (back) edges as dashed lines: (a) input graph; (b) path of tree edges, traced from A until back edge (G,C) is examined; (c) reaching F, which is a dead end; (d) after backtracking to I, resuming with edge (I,M), and hitting another dead end at O; (e) after backtracking to G, continuing with edge (G,L), and hitting another dead end at H; (f) final result.

Properties of a Depth-First Search

There are a number of observations that we can make about the depth-first search algorithm, many of which derive from the way the DFS algorithm partitions the edges of a graph G into groups. We will begin with the most significant property.

Proposition 14.12: *Let G be an undirected graph on which a DFS traversal starting at a vertex s has been performed. Then the traversal visits all vertices in the connected component of s, and the discovery edges form a spanning tree of the connected component of s.*

Justification: Suppose there is at least one vertex w in s's connected component not visited, and let v be the first unvisited vertex on some path from s to w (we may have $v = w$). Since v is the first unvisited vertex on this path, it has a neighbor u that was visited. But when we visited u, we must have considered the edge (u, v); hence, it cannot be correct that v is unvisited. Therefore, there are no unvisited vertices in s's connected component.

Since we only follow a discovery edge when we go to an unvisited vertex, we will never form a cycle with such edges. Therefore, the discovery edges form a connected subgraph without cycles, hence a tree. Moreover, this is a spanning tree because, as we have just seen, the depth-first search visits each vertex in the connected component of s.   ∎

Proposition 14.13: *Let $\vec{G}$ be a directed graph. Depth-first search on $\vec{G}$ starting at a vertex s visits all the vertices of $\vec{G}$ that are reachable from s. Also, the DFS tree contains directed paths from s to every vertex reachable from s.*

Justification: Let V_s be the subset of vertices of $\vec{G}$ visited by DFS starting at vertex s. We want to show that V_s contains s and every vertex reachable from s belongs to V_s. Suppose now, for the sake of a contradiction, that there is a vertex w reachable from s that is not in V_s. Consider a directed path from s to w, and let (u, v) be the first edge on such a path taking us out of V_s, that is, u is in V_s but v is not in V_s. When DFS reaches u, it explores all the outgoing edges of u, and thus must also reach vertex v via edge (u, v). Hence, v should be in V_s, and we have obtained a contradiction. Therefore, V_s must contain every vertex reachable from s.

We prove the second fact by induction on the steps of the algorithm. We claim that each time a discovery edge (u, v) is identified, there exists a directed path from s to v in the DFS tree. Since u must have previously been discovered, there exists a path from s to u, so by appending the edge (u, v) to that path, we have a directed path from s to v.   ∎

Note that since back edges always connect a vertex v to a previously visited vertex u, each back edge implies a cycle in G, consisting of the discovery edges from u to v plus the back edge (u, v).

Running Time of Depth-First Search

In terms of its running time, depth-first search is an efficient method for traversing a graph. Note that DFS is called at most once on each vertex (since it gets marked as visited), and therefore every edge is examined at most twice for an undirected graph, once from each of its end vertices, and at most once in a directed graph, from its origin vertex. If we let $n_s \le n$ be the number of vertices reachable from a vertex s, and $m_s \le m$ be the number of incident edges to those vertices, a DFS starting at s runs in $O(n_s + m_s)$ time, provided the following conditions are satisfied:

- The graph is represented by a data structure such that creating and iterating through the outgoingEdges(v) takes $O(\deg(v))$ time, and the opposite(v, e) method takes $O(1)$ time. The adjacency list structure is one such structure, but the adjacency matrix structure is not.

- We have a way to "mark" a vertex or edge as explored, and to test if a vertex or edge has been explored in $O(1)$ time. We discuss ways of implementing DFS to achieve this goal in the next section.

Given the assumptions above, we can solve a number of interesting problems.

Proposition 14.14: *Let G be an undirected graph with n vertices and m edges. A DFS traversal of G can be performed in $O(n + m)$ time, and can be used to solve the following problems in $O(n + m)$ time:*

- *Computing a path between two given vertices of G, if one exists.*
- *Testing whether G is connected.*
- *Computing a spanning tree of G, if G is connected.*
- *Computing the connected components of G.*
- *Computing a cycle in G, or reporting that G has no cycles.*

Proposition 14.15: *Let $\vec{G}$ be a directed graph with n vertices and m edges. A DFS traversal of $\vec{G}$ can be performed in $O(n + m)$ time, and can be used to solve the following problems in $O(n + m)$ time:*

- *Computing a directed path between two given vertices of $\vec{G}$, if one exists.*
- *Computing the set of vertices of $\vec{G}$ that are reachable from a given vertex s.*
- *Testing whether $\vec{G}$ is strongly connected.*
- *Computing a directed cycle in $\vec{G}$, or reporting that $\vec{G}$ is acyclic.*

The justification of Propositions 14.14 and 14.15 is based on algorithms that use slightly modified versions of the DFS algorithm as subroutines. We will explore some of those extensions in the remainder of this section.

14.3.2 DFS Implementation and Extensions

We will begin by providing a Java implementation of the depth-first search algorithm. We originally described the algorithm with pseudocode in Code Fragment 14.4. In order to implement it, we must have a mechanism for keeping track of which vertices have been visited, and for recording the resulting DFS tree edges. For this bookkeeping, we use two auxiliary data structures. First, we maintain a set, named known, containing vertices that have already been visited. Second, we keep a map, named forest, that associates, with a vertex v, the edge e of the graph that is used to discover v (if any). Our DFS method is presented in Code Fragment 14.5.

```java
1  /** Performs depth-first search of Graph g starting at Vertex u. */
2  public static <V,E> void DFS(Graph<V,E> g, Vertex<V> u,
3                  Set<Vertex<V>> known, Map<Vertex<V>,Edge<E>> forest) {
4    known.add(u);                           // u has been discovered
5    for (Edge<E> e : g.outgoingEdges(u)) {  // for every outgoing edge from u
6      Vertex<V> v = g.opposite(u, e);
7      if (!known.contains(v)) {
8        forest.put(v, e);                   // e is the tree edge that discovered v
9        DFS(g, v, known, forest);           // recursively explore from v
10     }
11   }
12 }
```

Code Fragment 14.5: Recursive implementation of depth-first search on a graph, starting at a designated vertex u. As an outcome of a call, visited vertices are added to the known set, and discovery edges are added to the forest.

Our DFS method does not make any assumption about how the Set or Map instances are implemented; however, the $O(n+m)$ running-time analysis of the previous section does presume that we can "mark" a vertex as explored or test the status of a vertex in $O(1)$ time. If we use hash-based implementations of the set and map structure, then all of their operations run in $O(1)$ *expected* time, and the overall algorithm runs in $O(n+m)$ time with very high probability. In practice, this is a compromise we are willing to accept.

If vertices can be numbered from $0, \ldots, n-1$ (a common assumption for graph algorithms), then the set and map can be implemented more directly as a lookup table, with a vertex label used as an index into an array of size n. In that case, the necessary set and map operations run in worst-case $O(1)$ time. Alternatively, we can "decorate" each vertex with the auxiliary information, either by leveraging the generic type of the element that is stored with each vertex, or by redesigning the Vertex type to store additional fields. That would allow marking operations to be performed in $O(1)$-time, without any assumption about vertices being numbered.

Reconstructing a Path from *u* to *v*

We can use the basic DFS method as a tool to identify the (directed) path leading from vertex *u* to *v*, if *v* is reachable from *u*. This path can easily be reconstructed from the information that was recorded in the forest of discovery edges during the traversal. Code Fragment 14.6 provides an implementation of a secondary method that produces an ordered list of vertices on the path from *u* to *v*, if given the map of discovery edges that was computed by the original DFS method.

To reconstruct the path, we begin at the *end* of the path, examining the forest of discovery edges to determine what edge was used to reach vertex *v*. We then determine the opposite vertex of that edge and repeat the process to determine what edge was used to discover it. By continuing this process until reaching *u*, we can construct the entire path. Assuming constant-time lookup in the forest map, the path reconstruction takes time proportional to the length of the path, and therefore, it runs in $O(n)$ time (in addition to the time originally spent calling DFS).

```
1  /** Returns an ordered list of edges comprising the directed path from u to v. */
2  public static <V,E> PositionalList<Edge<E>>
3  constructPath(Graph<V,E> g, Vertex<V> u, Vertex<V> v,
4               Map<Vertex<V>,Edge<E>> forest) {
5    PositionalList<Edge<E>> path = new LinkedPositionalList<>( );
6    if (forest.get(v) != null) {           // v was discovered during the search
7      Vertex<V> walk = v;                   // we construct the path from back to front
8      while (walk != u) {
9        Edge<E> edge = forest.get(walk);
10       path.addFirst(edge);               // add edge to *front* of path
11       walk = g.opposite(walk, edge);     // repeat with opposite endpoint
12     }
13   }
14   return path;
15 }
```

Code Fragment 14.6: Method to reconstruct a directed path from *u* to *v*, given the trace of discovery from a DFS started at *u*. The method returns an ordered list of vertices on the path.

Testing for Connectivity

We can use the basic DFS method to determine whether a graph is connected. In the case of an undirected graph, we simply start a depth-first search at an arbitrary vertex and then test whether known.size( ) equals *n* at the conclusion. If the graph is connected, then by Proposition 14.12, all vertices will have been discovered; conversely, if the graph is not connected, there must be at least one vertex *v* that is not reachable from *u*, and that will not be discovered.

For directed graph, $\vec{G}$, we may wish to test whether it is ***strongly connected***, that is, whether for every pair of vertices u and v, both u reaches v and v reaches u. If we start an independent call to DFS from each vertex, we could determine whether this was the case, but those n calls when combined would run in $O(n(n+m))$. However, we can determine if $\vec{G}$ is strongly connected much faster than this, requiring only two depth-first searches.

We begin by performing a depth-first search of our directed graph $\vec{G}$ starting at an arbitrary vertex s. If there is any vertex of $\vec{G}$ that is not visited by this traversal, and is not reachable from s, then the graph is not strongly connected. If this first depth-first search visits each vertex of $\vec{G}$, we need to then check whether s is reachable from all other vertices. Conceptually, we can accomplish this by making a copy of graph $\vec{G}$, but with the orientation of all edges reversed. A depth-first search starting at s in the reversed graph will reach every vertex that could reach s in the original. In practice, a better approach than making a new graph is to reimplement a version of the DFS method that loops through all ***incoming*** edges to the current vertex, rather than all ***outgoing*** edges. Since this algorithm makes just two DFS traversals of $\vec{G}$, it runs in $O(n+m)$ time.

Computing All Connected Components

When a graph is not connected, the next goal we may have is to identify all of the ***connected components*** of an undirected graph, or the ***strongly connected components*** of a directed graph. We will begin by discussing the undirected case.

If an initial call to DFS fails to reach all vertices of a graph, we can restart a new call to DFS at one of those unvisited vertices. An implementation of such a comprehensive DFSComplete method is given in Code Fragment 14.7. It returns a map that represents a ***DFS forest*** for the entire graph. We say this is a forest rather than a tree, because the graph may not be connected.

Vertices that serve as roots of DFS trees within this forest will not have discovery edges and will not appear as keys in the returned map. Therefore, the number of connected components of the graph g is equal to g.numVertices() − forest.size().

```
1  /** Performs DFS for the entire graph and returns the DFS forest as a map. */
2  public static <V,E> Map<Vertex<V>,Edge<E>> DFSComplete(Graph<V,E> g) {
3    Set<Vertex<V>> known = new HashSet<>();
4    Map<Vertex<V>,Edge<E>> forest = new ProbeHashMap<>();
5    for (Vertex<V> u : g.vertices())
6      if (!known.contains(u))
7        DFS(g, u, known, forest);              // (re)start the DFS process at u
8    return forest;
9  }
```

Code Fragment 14.7: Top-level method that returns a DFS forest for an entire graph.

We can further determine which vertices are in which component, either by examining the structure of the forest that is returned, or by making a minor modification to the core DFS method to tag each vertex with a component number when it is first discovered. (See Exercise C-14.43.)

Although the DFSComplete method makes multiple calls to the original DFS method, the total time spent by a call to DFSComplete is $O(n+m)$. For an undirected graph, recall from our original analysis on page 635 that a single call to DFS starting at vertex s runs in time $O(n_s + m_s)$ where n_s is the number of vertices reachable from s, and m_s is the number of incident edges to those vertices. Because each call to DFS explores a different component, the sum of $n_s + m_s$ terms is $n+m$.

The situation is more complex for finding strongly connected components of a directed graph. The $O(n+m)$ total bound for a call to DFSComplete applies to the directed case as well, because when restarting the process, we proceed with the existing set of known vertices. This ensures that the DFS subroutine is called once on each vertex, and therefore that each outgoing edge is explored only once during the entire process.

As an example, consider again the graph of Figure 14.8. If we were to start the original DFS method at vertex ORD, the known set of vertices would become { ORD, DFW, SFO, LAX, MIA }. If restarting the DFS method at vertex BOS, the outgoing edges to vertices SFO and MIA would not result in further recursion, because those vertices are marked as known.

However, the forest returned by a single call to DFSComplete does not represent the strongly connected components of the graph. There exists an approach for computing those components in $O(n+m)$ time, making use of two calls to DFSComplete, but the details are beyond the scope of this book.

Detecting Cycles with DFS

For both undirected and directed graphs, a cycle exists if and only if a ***back edge*** exists relative to the DFS traversal of that graph. It is easy to see that if a back edge exists, a cycle exists by taking the back edge from the descendant to its ancestor and then following the tree edges back to the descendant. Conversely, if a cycle exists in the graph, there must be a back edge relative to a DFS (although we do not prove this fact here).

Algorithmically, detecting a back edge in the undirected case is easy, because all edges are either tree edges or back edges. In the case of a directed graph, additional modifications to the core DFS implementation are needed to properly categorize a nontree edge as a back edge. When a directed edge is explored leading to a previously visited vertex, we must recognize whether that vertex is an ancestor of the current vertex. This can be accomplished, for example, by maintaining another set, with all vertices upon which a recursive call to DFS is currently active. We leave details as an exercise (C-14.42).

14.3.3 Breadth-First Search

The advancing and backtracking of a depth-first search, as described in the previous section, defines a traversal that could be physically traced by a single person exploring a graph. In this section, we will consider another algorithm for traversing a connected component of a graph, known as a ***breadth-first search*** (BFS). The BFS algorithm is more akin to sending out, in all directions, many explorers who collectively traverse a graph in coordinated fashion.

A BFS proceeds in rounds and subdivides the vertices into ***levels***. BFS starts at vertex s, which is at level 0. In the first round, we paint as "visited," all vertices adjacent to the start vertex s; these vertices are one step away from the beginning and are placed into level 1. In the second round, we allow all explorers to go two steps (i.e., edges) away from the starting vertex. These new vertices, which are adjacent to level 1 vertices and not previously assigned to a level, are placed into level 2 and marked as "visited." This process continues in similar fashion, terminating when no new vertices are found in a level.

A Java implementation of BFS is given in Code Fragment 14.8. We follow a convention similar to that of DFS (Code Fragment 14.5), maintaining a known set of vertices, and storing the BFS tree edges in a map. We illustrate a BFS traversal in Figure 14.10.

```java
1  /** Performs breadth-first search of Graph g starting at Vertex u. */
2  public static <V,E> void BFS(Graph<V,E> g, Vertex<V> s,
3                    Set<Vertex<V>> known, Map<Vertex<V>,Edge<E>> forest) {
4    PositionalList<Vertex<V>> level = new LinkedPositionalList<>();
5    known.add(s);
6    level.addLast(s);                       // first level includes only s
7    while (!level.isEmpty()) {
8      PositionalList<Vertex<V>> nextLevel = new LinkedPositionalList<>();
9      for (Vertex<V> u : level)
10       for (Edge<E> e : g.outgoingEdges(u)) {
11         Vertex<V> v = g.opposite(u, e);
12         if (!known.contains(v)) {
13           known.add(v);
14           forest.put(v, e);               // e is the tree edge that discovered v
15           nextLevel.addLast(v);           // v will be further considered in next pass
16         }
17       }
18     level = nextLevel;                     // relabel 'next' level to become the current
19   }
20 }
```

Code Fragment 14.8: Implementation of breadth-first search on a graph, starting at a designated vertex s.

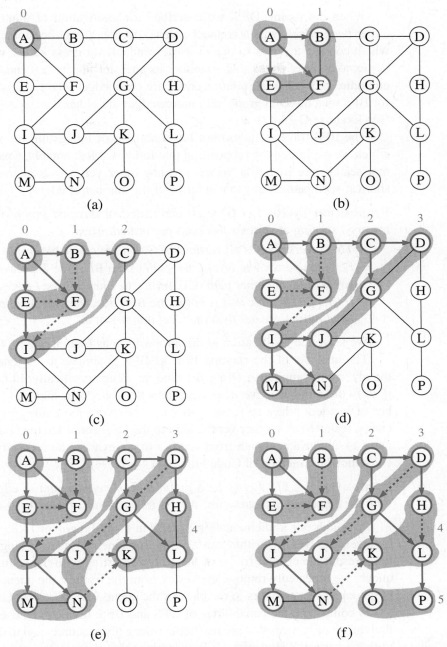

Figure 14.10: Example of breadth-first search traversal, where the edges incident to a vertex are considered in alphabetical order of the adjacent vertices. The discovery edges are shown with solid lines and the nontree (cross) edges are shown with dashed lines: (a) starting the search at A; (b) discovery of level 1; (c) discovery of level 2; (d) discovery of level 3; (e) discovery of level 4; (f) discovery of level 5.

When discussing DFS, we described a classification of nontree edges being either **back edges**, which connect a vertex to one of its ancestors, **forward edges**, which connect a vertex to one of its descendants, or **cross edges**, which connect a vertex to another vertex that is neither its ancestor nor its descendant. For BFS on an undirected graph, all nontree edges are cross edges (see Exercise C-14.46), and for BFS on a directed graph, all nontree edges are either back edges or cross edges (see Exercise C-14.47).

The BFS traversal algorithm has a number of interesting properties, some of which we explore in the proposition that follows. Most notably, a path in a breadth-first search tree rooted at vertex s to any other vertex v is guaranteed to be the shortest such path from s to v in terms of the number of edges.

Proposition 14.16: *Let G be an undirected or directed graph on which a BFS traversal starting at vertex s has been performed. Then*

- *The traversal visits all vertices of G that are reachable from s.*
- *For each vertex v at level i, the path of the BFS tree T between s and v has i edges, and any other path of G from s to v has at least i edges.*
- *If (u,v) is an edge that is not in the BFS tree, then the level number of v can be at most 1 greater than the level number of u.*

We leave the justification of this proposition as Exercise C-14.49.

The analysis of the running time of BFS is similar to the one of DFS, with the algorithm running in $O(n+m)$ time, or more specifically, in $O(n_s + m_s)$ time if n_s is the number of vertices reachable from vertex s, and $m_s \leq m$ is the number of incident edges to those vertices. To explore the entire graph, the process can be restarted at another vertex, akin to the DFSComplete method of Code Fragment 14.7. The actual path from vertex s to vertex v can be reconstructed using the constructPath method of Code Fragment 14.6

Proposition 14.17: *Let G be a graph with n vertices and m edges represented with the adjacency list structure. A BFS traversal of G takes $O(n+m)$ time.*

Although our implementation of BFS in Code Fragment 14.8 progresses level by level, the BFS algorithm can also be implemented using a single FIFO queue to represent the current fringe of the search. Starting with the source vertex in the queue, we repeatedly remove the vertex from the front of the queue and insert any of its unvisited neighbors to the back of the queue. (See Exercise C-14.50.)

In comparing the capabilities of DFS and BFS, both can be used to efficiently find the set of vertices that are reachable from a given source, and to determine paths to those vertices. However, BFS guarantees that those paths use as few edges as possible. For an undirected graph, both algorithms can be used to test connectivity, to identify connected components, or to locate a cycle. For directed graphs, the DFS algorithm is better suited for certain tasks, such as finding a directed cycle in the graph, or in identifying the strongly connected components.

14.4 Transitive Closure

We have seen that graph traversals can be used to answer basic questions of reachability in a directed graph. In particular, if we are interested in knowing whether there is a path from vertex u to vertex v in a graph, we can perform a DFS or BFS traversal starting at u and observe whether v is discovered. If representing a graph with an adjacency list or adjacency map, we can answer the question of reachability for u and v in $O(n+m)$ time (see Propositions 14.15 and 14.17).

In certain applications, we may wish to answer many reachability queries more efficiently, in which case it may be worthwhile to precompute a more convenient representation of a graph. For example, the first step for a service that computes driving directions from an origin to a destination might be to assess whether the destination is reachable. Similarly, in an electricity network, we may wish to be able to quickly determine whether current flows from one particular vertex to another. Motivated by such applications, we introduce the following definition. The ***transitive closure*** of a directed graph $\vec{G}$ is itself a directed graph $\vec{G}^*$ such that the vertices of $\vec{G}^*$ are the same as the vertices of $\vec{G}$, and $\vec{G}^*$ has an edge (u,v), whenever $\vec{G}$ has a directed path from u to v (including the case where (u,v) is an edge of the original $\vec{G}$).

If a graph is represented as an adjacency list or adjacency map, we can compute its transitive closure in $O(n(n+m))$ time by making use of n graph traversals, one from each starting vertex. For example, a DFS starting at vertex u can be used to determine all vertices reachable from u, and thus a collection of edges originating with u in the transitive closure.

In the remainder of this section, we explore an alternative technique for computing the transitive closure of a directed graph that is particularly well suited for when a directed graph is represented by a data structure that supports $O(1)$-time lookup for the getEdge(u, v) method (for example, the adjacency-matrix structure). Let $\vec{G}$ be a directed graph with n vertices and m edges. We compute the transitive closure of $\vec{G}$ in a series of rounds. We initialize $\vec{G}_0 = \vec{G}$. We also arbitrarily number the vertices of $\vec{G}$ as $v_1, v_2, \ldots, v_n$. We then begin the computation of the rounds, beginning with round 1. In a generic round k, we construct directed graph $\vec{G}_k$ starting with $\vec{G}_k = \vec{G}_{k-1}$ and adding to $\vec{G}_k$ the directed edge (v_i, v_j) if directed graph $\vec{G}_{k-1}$ contains both the edges (v_i, v_k) and (v_k, v_j). In this way, we will enforce a simple rule embodied in the proposition that follows.

Proposition 14.18: *For $i = 1, \ldots, n$, directed graph $\vec{G}_k$ has an edge (v_i, v_j) if and only if directed graph $\vec{G}$ has a directed path from v_i to v_j, whose intermediate vertices (if any) are in the set $\{v_1, \ldots, v_k\}$. In particular, $\vec{G}_n$ is equal to $\vec{G}^*$, the transitive closure of $\vec{G}$.*

Proposition 14.18 suggests a simple algorithm for computing the transitive closure of $\vec{G}$ that is based on the series of rounds to compute each $\vec{G}_k$. This algorithm is known as the **Floyd-Warshall algorithm**, and its pseudocode is given in Code Fragment 14.9. We illustrate an example run of the Floyd-Warshall algorithm in Figure 14.11.

Algorithm FloydWarshall($\vec{G}$):

    Input: A directed graph $\vec{G}$ with n vertices
    Output: The transitive closure $\vec{G}^*$ of $\vec{G}$

    let $v_1, v_2, \ldots, v_n$ be an arbitrary numbering of the vertices of $\vec{G}$
    $\vec{G}_0 = \vec{G}$
    for $k = 1$ to n **do**
        $\vec{G}_k = \vec{G}_{k-1}$
        for all i, j in $\{1, \ldots, n\}$ with $i \neq j$ and $i, j \neq k$ **do**
            if both edges (v_i, v_k) and (v_k, v_j) are in $\vec{G}_{k-1}$ **then**
                add edge (v_i, v_j) to $\vec{G}_k$ (if it is not already present)
    return $\vec{G}_n$

Code Fragment 14.9: Pseudocode for the Floyd-Warshall algorithm. This algorithm computes the transitive closure $\vec{G}^*$ of G by incrementally computing a series of directed graphs $\vec{G}_0, \vec{G}_1, \ldots, \vec{G}_n$, for $k = 1, \ldots, n$.

From this pseudocode, we can easily analyze the running time of the Floyd-Warshall algorithm assuming that the data structure representing G supports methods getEdge and insertEdge in $O(1)$ time. The main loop is executed n times and the inner loop considers each of $O(n^2)$ pairs of vertices, performing a constant-time computation for each one. Thus, the total running time of the Floyd-Warshall algorithm is $O(n^3)$. From the description and analysis above we may immediately derive the following proposition.

Proposition 14.19: *Let $\vec{G}$ be a directed graph with n vertices, and let $\vec{G}$ be represented by a data structure that supports lookup and update of adjacency information in $O(1)$ time. Then the Floyd-Warshall algorithm computes the transitive closure $\vec{G}^*$ of $\vec{G}$ in $O(n^3)$ time.*

Performance of the Floyd-Warshall Algorithm

Asymptotically, the $O(n^3)$ running time of the Floyd-Warshall algorithm is no better than that achieved by repeatedly running DFS, once from each vertex, to compute the reachability. However, the Floyd-Warshall algorithm matches the asymptotic bounds of the repeated DFS when a graph is dense, or when a graph is sparse but represented as an adjacency matrix. (See Exercise R-14.13.)

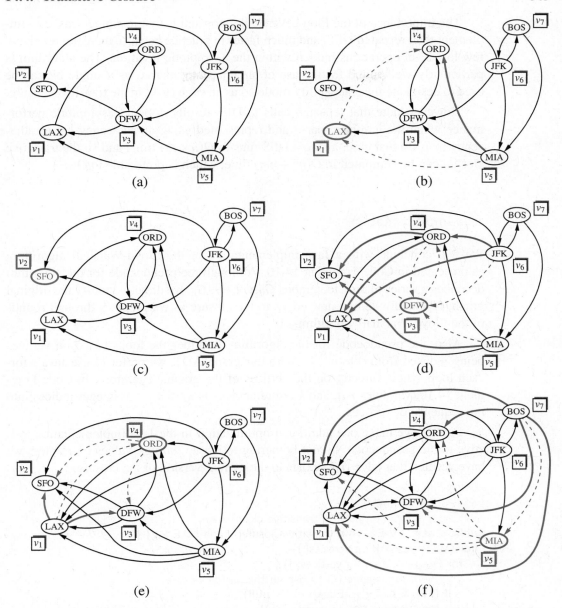

Figure 14.11: Sequence of directed graphs computed by the Floyd-Warshall algorithm: (a) initial directed graph $\vec{G} = \vec{G}_0$ and numbering of the vertices; (b) directed graph $\vec{G}_1$; (c) $\vec{G}_2$; (d) $\vec{G}_3$; (e) $\vec{G}_4$; (f) $\vec{G}_5$. Note that $\vec{G}_5 = \vec{G}_6 = \vec{G}_7$. If directed graph $\vec{G}_{k-1}$ has the edges (v_i, v_k) and (v_k, v_j), but not the edge (v_i, v_j), in the drawing of directed graph $\vec{G}_k$, we show edges (v_i, v_k) and (v_k, v_j) with dashed lines, and edge (v_i, v_j) with a thick line. For example, in (b) existing edges (MIA,LAX) and (LAX,ORD) result in new edge (MIA,ORD).

The importance of the Floyd-Warshall algorithm is that it is much easier to implement than repeated DFS, and much faster in practice because there are relatively few low-level operations hidden within the asymptotic notation. The algorithm is particularly well suited for the use of an adjacency matrix, as a single bit can be used to designate the reachability modeled as an edge (u,v) in the transitive closure.

However, note that repeated calls to DFS results in better asymptotic performance when the graph is sparse and represented using an adjacency list or adjacency map. In that case, a single DFS runs in $O(n+m)$ time, and so the transitive closure can be computed in $O(n^2 + nm)$ time, which is preferable to $O(n^3)$.

Java Implementation

We will conclude with a Java implementation of the Floyd-Warshall algorithm, as presented in Code Fragment 14.10. Although the pseudocode for the algorithm describes a series of directed graphs $\vec{G}_0, \vec{G}_1, \ldots, \vec{G}_n$, we directly modify the original graph, repeatedly adding new edges to the closure as we progress through rounds of the Floyd-Warshall algorithm.

Also, the pseudocode for the algorithm describes the loops based on vertices being indexed from 0 to $n-1$. With our graph ADT, we prefer to use Java's for-each loop syntax directly on the vertices of the graph. Therefore, in Code Fragment 14.10, variables i, j, and k are references to vertices, not integer indices into the sequence of vertices.

Finally, we make one additional optimization in the Java implementation, relative to the pseudocode, by not bothering to iterate through values of j unless we have verified that edge (i,k) exists in the current version of the closure.

```
1   /** Converts graph g into its transitive closure. */
2   public static <V,E> void transitiveClosure(Graph<V,E> g) {
3     for (Vertex<V> k : g.vertices())
4       for (Vertex<V> i : g.vertices())
5         // verify that edge (i,k) exists in the partial closure
6         if (i != k && g.getEdge(i,k) != null)
7           for (Vertex<V> j : g.vertices())
8             // verify that edge (k,j) exists in the partial closure
9             if (i != j && j != k && g.getEdge(k,j) != null)
10              // if (i,j) not yet included, add it to the closure
11              if (g.getEdge(i,j) == null)
12                g.insertEdge(i, j, null);
13  }
```

Code Fragment 14.10: Java implementation of the Floyd-Warshall algorithm.

14.5 Directed Acyclic Graphs

Directed graphs without directed cycles are encountered in many applications. Such a directed graph is often referred to as a ***directed acyclic graph***, or **DAG**, for short. Applications of such graphs include the following:

- Prerequisites between courses of an academic program.
- Inheritance between classes of an object-oriented program.
- Scheduling constraints between the tasks of a project.

We will explore this latter application further in the following example:

Example 14.20: *In order to manage a large project, it is convenient to break it up into a collection of smaller tasks. The tasks, however, are rarely independent, because scheduling constraints exist between them. (For example, in a house building project, the task of ordering nails obviously precedes the task of nailing shingles to the roof deck.) Clearly, scheduling constraints cannot have circularities, because they would make the project impossible. (For example, in order to get a job you need to have work experience, but in order to get work experience you need to have a job.) The scheduling constraints impose restrictions on the order in which the tasks can be executed. Namely, if a constraint says that task a must be completed before task b is started, then a must precede b in the order of execution of the tasks. Thus, if we model a feasible set of tasks as vertices of a directed graph, and we place a directed edge from u to v whenever the task for u must be executed before the task for v, then we define a directed acyclic graph.*

14.5.1 Topological Ordering

The example above motivates the following definition. Let $\vec{G}$ be a directed graph with n vertices. A ***topological ordering*** of $\vec{G}$ is an ordering $v_1, \ldots, v_n$ of the vertices of $\vec{G}$ such that for every edge (v_i, v_j) of $\vec{G}$, it is the case that $i < j$. That is, a topological ordering is an ordering such that any directed path in $\vec{G}$ traverses vertices in increasing order. Note that a directed graph may have more than one topological ordering. (See Figure 14.12.)

Proposition 14.21: *$\vec{G}$ has a topological ordering if and only if it is acyclic.*

Justification: The necessity (the "only if" part of the statement) is easy to demonstrate. Suppose $\vec{G}$ is topologically ordered. Assume, for the sake of a contradiction, that $\vec{G}$ has a cycle consisting of edges $(v_{i_0}, v_{i_1}), (v_{i_1}, v_{i_2}), \ldots, (v_{i_{k-1}}, v_{i_0})$. Because of the topological ordering, we must have $i_0 < i_1 < \cdots < i_{k-1} < i_0$, which is clearly impossible. Thus, $\vec{G}$ must be acyclic.

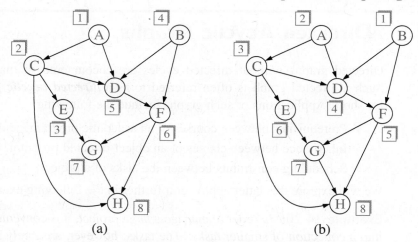

Figure 14.12: Two topological orderings of the same acyclic directed graph.

We now argue the sufficiency of the condition (the "if" part). Suppose $\vec{G}$ is acyclic. We will give an algorithmic description of how to build a topological ordering for $\vec{G}$. Since $\vec{G}$ is acyclic, $\vec{G}$ must have a vertex with no incoming edges (that is, with in-degree 0). Let v_1 be such a vertex. Indeed, if v_1 did not exist, then in tracing a directed path from an arbitrary start vertex, we would eventually encounter a previously visited vertex, thus contradicting the acyclicity of $\vec{G}$. If we remove v_1 from $\vec{G}$, together with its outgoing edges, the resulting directed graph is still acyclic. Hence, the resulting directed graph also has a vertex with no incoming edges, and we let v_2 be such a vertex. By repeating this process until the directed graph becomes empty, we obtain an ordering $v_1, \ldots, v_n$ of the vertices of $\vec{G}$. Because of the construction above, if (v_i, v_j) is an edge of $\vec{G}$, then v_i must be deleted before v_j can be deleted, and thus, $i < j$. Therefore, $v_1, \ldots, v_n$ is a topological ordering. ∎

Proposition 14.21's justification suggests an algorithm for computing a topological ordering of a directed graph, which we call ***topological sorting***. We present a Java implementation of the technique in Code Fragment 14.11, and an example execution of the algorithm in Figure 14.13. Our implementation uses a map, named inCount, to map each vertex v to a counter that represents the current number of incoming edges to v, excluding those coming from vertices that have previously been added to the topological order. As was the case with our graph traversals, a hash-based map only provides $O(1)$ expected time access to its entries, rather than worst-case time. This could easily be converted to worst-case time if vertices could be indexed from 0 to $n-1$, or if we store the count as a field of the vertex instance.

As a side effect, the topological sorting algorithm of Code Fragment 14.11 also tests whether the given directed graph $\vec{G}$ is acyclic. Indeed, if the algorithm terminates without ordering all the vertices, then the subgraph of the vertices that have not been ordered must contain a directed cycle.

```
1   /** Returns a list of verticies of directed acyclic graph g in topological order. */
2   public static <V,E> PositionalList<Vertex<V>> topologicalSort(Graph<V,E> g) {
3     // list of vertices placed in topological order
4     PositionalList<Vertex<V>> topo = new LinkedPositionalList<>();
5     // container of vertices that have no remaining constraints
6     Stack<Vertex<V>> ready = new LinkedStack<>();
7     // map keeping track of remaining in-degree for each vertex
8     Map<Vertex<V>, Integer> inCount = new ProbeHashMap<>();
9     for (Vertex<V> u : g.vertices()) {
10      inCount.put(u, g.inDegree(u));           // initialize with actual in-degree
11      if (inCount.get(u) == 0)                 // if u has no incoming edges,
12        ready.push(u);                          // it is free of constraints
13    }
14    while (!ready.isEmpty()) {
15      Vertex<V> u = ready.pop();
16      topo.addLast(u);
17      for (Edge<E> e : g.outgoingEdges(u)) {  // consider all outgoing neighbors of u
18        Vertex<V> v = g.opposite(u, e);
19        inCount.put(v, inCount.get(v) − 1);     // v has one less constraint without u
20        if (inCount.get(v) == 0)
21          ready.push(v);
22      }
23    }
24    return topo;
25  }
```

Code Fragment 14.11: Java implementation for the topological sorting algorithm. (We show an example execution of this algorithm in Figure 14.13.)

Proposition 14.22: *Let $\vec{G}$ be a directed graph with n vertices and m edges, using an adjacency list representation. The topological sorting algorithm runs in $O(n+m)$ time using $O(n)$ auxiliary space, and either computes a topological ordering of $\vec{G}$ or fails to include some vertices, which indicates that $\vec{G}$ has a directed cycle.*

Justification: The initial recording of the n in-degrees uses $O(n)$ time based on the inDegree method. Say that a vertex u is **visited** by the topological sorting algorithm when u is removed from the ready list. A vertex u can be visited only when inCount.get(u) is 0, which implies that all its predecessors (vertices with outgoing edges into u) were previously visited. As a consequence, any vertex that is on a directed cycle will never be visited, and any other vertex will be visited exactly once. The algorithm traverses all the outgoing edges of each visited vertex once, so its running time is proportional to the number of outgoing edges of the visited vertices. In accordance with Proposition 14.9, the running time is $(n+m)$. Regarding the space usage, observe that containers topo, ready, and inCount have at most one entry per vertex, and therefore use $O(n)$ space. ∎

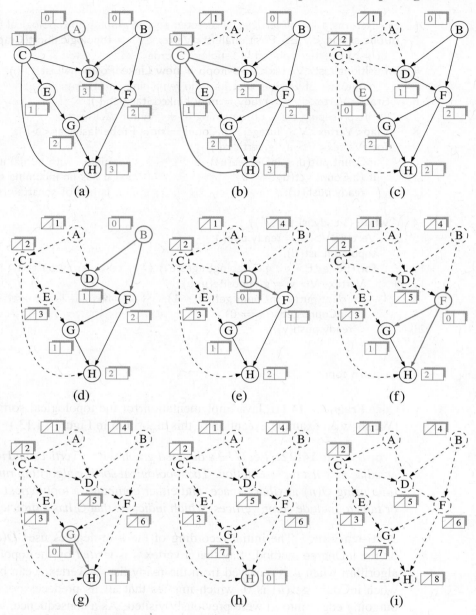

Figure 14.13: Example of a run of algorithm topologicalSort (Code Fragment 14.11). The label near a vertex shows its current inCount value, and its eventual rank in the resulting topological order. The highlighted vertex is one with inCount equal to zero that will become the next vertex in the topological order. Dashed lines denote edges that have already been examined, which are no longer reflected in the inCount values.

14.6   Shortest Paths

As we saw in Section 14.3.3, the breadth-first search strategy can be used to find a path with as few edges as possible from some starting vertex to every other vertex in a connected graph. This approach makes sense in cases where each edge is as good as any other, but there are many situations where this approach is not appropriate.

For example, we might want to use a graph to represent the roads between cities, and we might be interested in finding the fastest way to travel cross-country. In this case, it is probably not appropriate for all the edges to be equal to each other, for some inter-city distances will likely be much larger than others. Likewise, we might be using a graph to represent a computer network (such as the Internet), and we might be interested in finding the fastest way to route a data packet between two computers. In this case, it again may not be appropriate for all the edges to be equal to each other, for some connections in a computer network are typically much faster than others (for example, some edges might represent low-bandwidth connections, while others might represent high-speed, fiber-optic connections). It is natural, therefore, to consider graphs whose edges are not weighted equally.

14.6.1   Weighted Graphs

A **weighted graph** is a graph that has a numeric (for example, integer) label $w(e)$ associated with each edge e, called the **weight** of edge e. For $e = (u, v)$, we let notation $w(u, v) = w(e)$. We show an example of a weighted graph in Figure 14.14.

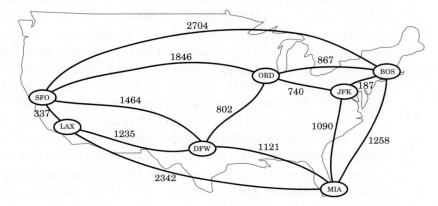

Figure 14.14: A weighted graph whose vertices represent major U.S. airports and whose edge weights represent distances in miles. This graph has a path from JFK to LAX of total weight 2,777 (going through ORD and DFW). This is the minimum-weight path in the graph from JFK to LAX.

Defining Shortest Paths in a Weighted Graph

Let G be a weighted graph. The ***length*** (or weight) of a path is the sum of the weights of the edges of P. That is, if $P = ((v_0, v_1), (v_1, v_2), \ldots, (v_{k-1}, v_k))$, then the length of P, denoted $w(P)$, is defined as

$$w(P) = \sum_{i=0}^{k-1} w(v_i, v_{i+1}).$$

The ***distance*** from a vertex u to a vertex v in G, denoted $d(u, v)$, is the length of a minimum-length path (also called ***shortest path***) from u to v, if such a path exists.

People often use the convention that $d(u, v) = \infty$ if there is no path at all from u to v in G. Even if there is a path from u to v in G, however, if there is a cycle in G whose total weight is negative, the distance from u to v may not be defined. For example, suppose vertices in G represent cities, and the weights of edges in G represent how much money it costs to go from one city to another. If someone were willing to actually pay us to go from say JFK to ORD, then the "cost" of the edge (JFK,ORD) would be negative. If someone else were willing to pay us to go from ORD to JFK, then there would be a negative-weight cycle in G and distances would no longer be defined. That is, anyone could now build a path (with cycles) in G from any city A to another city B that first goes to JFK and then cycles as many times as he or she likes from JFK to ORD and back, before going on to B. The existence of such paths would allow us to build arbitrarily low negative-cost paths (and, in this case, make a fortune in the process). But distances cannot be arbitrarily low negative numbers. Thus, any time we use edge weights to represent distances, we must be careful not to introduce any negative-weight cycles.

Suppose we are given a weighted graph G, and we are asked to find a shortest path from some vertex s to each other vertex in G, viewing the weights on the edges as distances. In this section, we explore efficient ways of finding all such shortest paths, if they exist. The first algorithm we discuss is for the simple, yet common, case when all the edge weights in G are nonnegative (that is, $w(e) \geq 0$ for each edge e of G); hence, we know in advance that there are no negative-weight cycles in G. Recall that the special case of computing a shortest path when all weights are equal to one was solved with the BFS traversal algorithm presented in Section 14.3.3.

There is an interesting approach for solving this ***single-source*** problem based on the ***greedy-method*** design pattern (Section 13.4.2). Recall that in this pattern we solve the problem at hand by repeatedly selecting the best choice from among those available in each iteration. This paradigm can often be used in situations where we are trying to optimize some cost function over a collection of objects. We can add objects to our collection, one at a time, always picking the next one that optimizes the function from among those yet to be chosen.

14.6.2 Dijkstra's Algorithm

The main idea in applying the greedy-method pattern to the single-source shortest-path problem is to perform a "weighted" breadth-first search starting at the source vertex s. In particular, we can use the greedy method to develop an algorithm that iteratively grows a "cloud" of vertices out of s, with the vertices entering the cloud in order of their distances from s. Thus, in each iteration, the next vertex chosen is the vertex outside the cloud that is closest to s. The algorithm terminates when no more vertices are outside the cloud (or when those outside the cloud are not connected to those within the cloud), at which point we have a shortest path from s to every vertex of G that is reachable from s. This approach is a simple, but nevertheless powerful, example of the greedy-method design pattern. Applying the greedy method to the single-source, shortest-path problem, results in an algorithm known as ***Dijkstra's algorithm***.

Edge Relaxation

Let us define a label $D[v]$ for each vertex v in V, which we use to approximate the distance in G from s to v. The meaning of these labels is that $D[v]$ will always store the length of the best path we have found ***so far*** from s to v. Initially, $D[s] = 0$ and $D[v] = \infty$ for each $v \neq s$, and we define the set C, which is our "***cloud***" of vertices, to initially be the empty set. At each iteration of the algorithm, we select a vertex u not in C with smallest $D[u]$ label, and we pull u into C. (In general, we will use a priority queue to select among the vertices outside the cloud.) In the very first iteration we will, of course, pull s into C. Once a new vertex u is pulled into C, we update the label $D[v]$ of each vertex v that is adjacent to u and is outside of C, to reflect the fact that there may be a new and better way to get to v via u. This update operation is known as a ***relaxation*** procedure, for it takes an old estimate and checks if it can be improved to get closer to its true value. The specific edge relaxation operation is as follows:

> **Edge Relaxation:**
> $$\textbf{if } D[u] + w(u, v) < D[v] \textbf{ then}$$
> $$D[v] = D[u] + w(u, v)$$

Algorithm Description and Example

We give the pseudocode for Dijkstra's algorithm in Code Fragment 14.12, and illustrate several iterations of Dijkstra's algorithm in Figures 14.15 through 14.17.

Algorithm ShortestPath(G, s):

Input: A directed or undirected graph G with nonnegative edge weights, and a distinguished vertex s of G.

Output: The length of a shortest path from s to v for each vertex v of G.

Initialize $D[s] = 0$ and $D[v] = \infty$ for each vertex $v \neq s$.

Let a priority queue Q contain all the vertices of G using the D labels as keys.

while Q is not empty **do**

    {pull a new vertex u into the cloud}

    u = value returned by Q.removeMin()

    for each edge (u, v) such that v is in Q **do**

        {perform the ***relaxation*** procedure on edge (u, v)}

        if $D[u] + w(u, v) < D[v]$ **then**

            $D[v] = D[u] + w(u, v)$

            Change the key of vertex v in Q to $D[v]$.

return the label $D[v]$ of each vertex v

Code Fragment 14.12: Pseudocode for Dijkstra's algorithm, solving the single-source shortest-path problem for an undirected or directed graph.

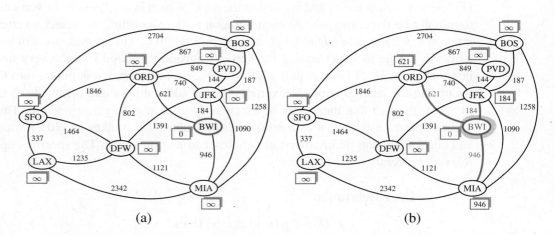

(a)   (b)

Figure 14.15: An example execution of Dijkstra's shortest-path algorithm on a weighted graph. The start vertex is BWI. A box next to each vertex v stores the label $D[v]$. The edges of the shortest-path tree are drawn as thick arrows, and for each vertex u outside the "cloud" we show the current best edge for pulling in u with a thick line. (Continues in Figure 14.16.)

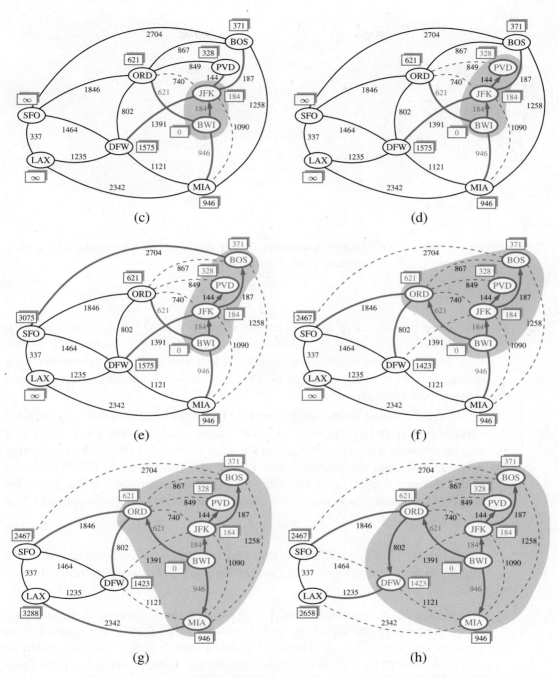

Figure 14.16: An example execution of Dijkstra's shortest-path algorithm on a weighted graph. (Continued from Figure 14.15; continues in Figure 14.17.)

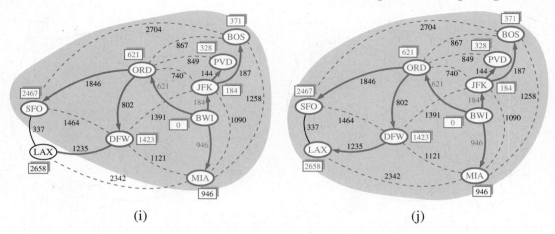

(i)   (j)

Figure 14.17: An example execution of Dijkstra's shortest-path algorithm on a weighted graph. (Continued from Figure 14.16.)

Why It Works

The interesting aspect of the Dijkstra algorithm is that, at the moment a vertex u is pulled into C, its label $D[u]$ stores the correct length of a shortest path from v to u. Thus, when the algorithm terminates, it will have computed the shortest-path distance from s to every vertex of G. That is, it will have solved the single-source shortest-path problem.

It is probably not immediately clear why Dijkstra's algorithm correctly finds the shortest path from the start vertex s to each other vertex u in the graph. Why is it that the distance from s to u is equal to the value of the label $D[u]$ at the time vertex u is removed from the priority queue Q and added to the cloud C? The answer to this question depends on there being no negative-weight edges in the graph, for it allows the greedy method to work correctly, as we show in the proposition that follows.

Proposition 14.23: *In Dijkstra's algorithm, whenever a vertex v is pulled into the cloud, the label $D[v]$ is equal to $d(s, v)$, the length of a shortest path from s to v.*

Justification: Suppose that $D[v] > d(s, v)$ for some vertex v in V, and let z be the ***first*** vertex the algorithm pulled into the cloud C (that is, removed from Q) such that $D[z] > d(s, z)$. There is a shortest path P from s to z (for otherwise $d(s, z) = \infty = D[z]$). Let us therefore consider the moment when z is pulled into C, and let y be the first vertex of P (when going from s to z) that is not in C at this moment. Let x be the predecessor of y in path P (note that we could have $x = s$). (See Figure 14.18.) We know, by our choice of y, that x is already in C at this point.

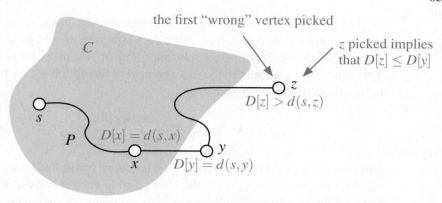

Figure 14.18: A schematic illustration for the justification of Proposition 14.23.

Moreover, $D[x] = d(s,x)$, since z is the *first* incorrect vertex. When x was pulled into C, we tested (and possibly updated) $D[y]$ so that we had at that point

$$D[y] \le D[x] + w(x,y) = d(s,x) + w(x,y).$$

But since y is the next vertex on the shortest path from s to z, this implies that

$$D[y] = d(s,y).$$

But we are now at the moment when we are picking z, not y, to join C; hence,

$$D[z] \le D[y].$$

It should be clear that a subpath of a shortest path is itself a shortest path. Hence, since y is on the shortest path from s to z,

$$d(s,y) + d(y,z) = d(s,z).$$

Moreover, $d(y,z) \ge 0$ because there are no negative-weight edges. Therefore,

$$D[z] \le D[y] = d(s,y) \le d(s,y) + d(y,z) = d(s,z).$$

But this contradicts the definition of z; hence, there can be no such vertex z. ∎

The Running Time of Dijkstra's Algorithm

In this section, we analyze the time complexity of Dijkstra's algorithm. We denote with n and m the number of vertices and edges of the input graph G, respectively. We assume that the edge weights can be added and compared in constant time. Because of the high level of the description we gave for Dijkstra's algorithm in Code Fragment 14.12, analyzing its running time requires that we give more details on its implementation. Specifically, we should indicate the data structures used and how they are implemented.

Let us first assume that we are representing the graph G using an adjacency list or adjacency map structure. This data structure allows us to step through the vertices adjacent to u during the relaxation step in time proportional to their number. Therefore, the time spent in the management of the nested **for** loop, and the number of iterations of that loop, is

$$\sum_{u \text{ in } V_G} \text{outdeg}(u),$$

which is $O(m)$ by Proposition 14.9. The outer **while** loop executes $O(n)$ times, since a new vertex is added to the cloud during each iteration. This still does not settle all the details for the algorithm analysis, however, for we must say more about how to implement the other principal data structure in the algorithm—the priority queue Q.

Referring back to Code Fragment 14.12 in search of priority queue operations, we find that n vertices are originally inserted into the priority queue; since these are the only insertions, the maximum size of the queue is n. In each of n iterations of the **while** loop, a call to removeMin is made to extract the vertex u with smallest D label from Q. Then, for each neighbor v of u, we perform an edge relaxation, and may potentially update the key of v in the queue. Thus, we actually need an implementation of an ***adaptable priority queue*** (Section 9.5), in which case the key of a vertex v is changed using the method replaceKey(e, k), where e is the priority queue entry associated with vertex v. In the worst case, there could be one such update for each edge of the graph. Overall, the running time of Dijkstra's algorithm is bounded by the sum of the following:

- n insertions into Q.
- n calls to the removeMin method on Q.
- m calls to the replaceKey method on Q.

If Q is an adaptable priority queue implemented as a heap, then each of the above operations run in $O(\log n)$, and so the overall running time for Dijkstra's algorithm is $O((n+m)\log n)$. Note that if we wish to express the running time as a function of n only, then it is $O(n^2 \log n)$ in the worst case.

Let us now consider an alternative implementation for the adaptable priority queue Q using an unsorted sequence. (See Exercise P-9.52.) This, of course, requires that we spend $O(n)$ time to extract the minimum element, but it affords very fast key updates, provided Q supports location-aware entries (Section 9.5.1). Specifically, we can implement each key update done in a relaxation step in $O(1)$ time—we simply change the key value once we locate the entry in Q to update. Hence, this implementation results in a running time that is $O(n^2 + m)$, which can be simplified to $O(n^2)$ since G is simple.

Comparing the Two Implementations

We have two choices for implementing the adaptable priority queue with location-aware entries in Dijkstra's algorithm: a heap implementation, which yields a running time of $O((n+m)\log n)$, and an unsorted sequence implementation, which yields a running time of $O(n^2)$. Since both implementations would be fairly simple to code, they are about equal in terms of the programming sophistication needed. These two implementations are also about equal in terms of the constant factors in their worst-case running times. Looking only at these worst-case times, we prefer the heap implementation when the number of edges in the graph is small (that is, when $m < n^2/\log n$), and we prefer the sequence implementation when the number of edges is large (that is, when $m > n^2/\log n$).

Proposition 14.24: *Given a weighted graph G with n vertices and m edges, such that the weight of each edge is nonnegative, and a vertex s of G, Dijkstra's algorithm can compute the distance from s to all other vertices of G in the better of $O(n^2)$ or $O((n+m)\log n)$ time.*

We note that an advanced priority queue implementation, known as a **Fibonacci heap**, can be used to implement Dijkstra's algorithm in $O(m+n\log n)$ time.

Programming Dijkstra's Algorithm in Java

Having given a pseudocode description of Dijkstra's algorithm, let us now present Java code for performing Dijkstra's algorithm, assuming we are given a graph whose edge elements are nonnegative integer weights. Our implementation of the algorithm is in the form of a method, shortestPathLengths, that takes a graph and a designated source vertex as parameters. (See Code Fragment 14.13.) It returns a map, named cloud, storing the shortest-path distance $d(s,v)$ for each vertex v that is reachable from the source. We rely on our HeapAdaptablePriorityQueue developed in Section 9.5.2 as an adaptable priority queue.

As we have done with other algorithms in this chapter, we rely on hash-based maps to store auxiliary data (in this case, mapping v to its distance bound $D[v]$ and its adaptable priority queue entry). The expected $O(1)$-time access to elements of these dictionaries could be converted to worst-case bounds, either by numbering vertices from 0 to $n-1$ to use as indices into an array, or by storing the information within each vertex's element.

The pseudocode for Dijkstra's algorithm begins by assigning $D[v] = \infty$ for each v other than the source; we rely on the special value Integer.MAX_VALUE in Java to provide a sufficient numeric value to model infinity. However, we avoid including vertices with this "infinite" distance in the resulting cloud that is returned by the method. The use of this numeric limit could be avoided altogether by waiting to add a vertex to the priority queue until after an edge that reaches it is relaxed. (See Exercise C-14.62.)

```java
 1  /** Computes shortest-path distances from src vertex to all reachable vertices of g. */
 2  public static <V> Map<Vertex<V>, Integer>
 3  shortestPathLengths(Graph<V,Integer> g, Vertex<V> src) {
 4    // d.get(v) is upper bound on distance from src to v
 5    Map<Vertex<V>, Integer> d = new ProbeHashMap<>();
 6    // map reachable v to its d value
 7    Map<Vertex<V>, Integer> cloud = new ProbeHashMap<>();
 8    // pq will have vertices as elements, with d.get(v) as key
 9    AdaptablePriorityQueue<Integer, Vertex<V>> pq;
10    pq = new HeapAdaptablePriorityQueue<>();
11    // maps from vertex to its pq locator
12    Map<Vertex<V>, Entry<Integer,Vertex<V>>> pqTokens;
13    pqTokens = new ProbeHashMap<>();
14
15    // for each vertex v of the graph, add an entry to the priority queue, with
16    // the source having distance 0 and all others having infinite distance
17    for (Vertex<V> v : g.vertices()) {
18      if (v == src)
19        d.put(v,0);
20      else
21        d.put(v, Integer.MAX_VALUE);
22      pqTokens.put(v, pq.insert(d.get(v), v));           // save entry for future updates
23    }
24    // now begin adding reachable vertices to the cloud
25    while (!pq.isEmpty()) {
26      Entry<Integer, Vertex<V>> entry = pq.removeMin();
27      int key = entry.getKey();
28      Vertex<V> u = entry.getValue();
29      cloud.put(u, key);                                 // this is actual distance to u
30      pqTokens.remove(u);                                // u is no longer in pq
31      for (Edge<Integer> e : g.outgoingEdges(u)) {
32        Vertex<V> v = g.opposite(u,e);
33        if (cloud.get(v) == null) {
34          // perform relaxation step on edge (u,v)
35          int wgt = e.getElement();
36          if (d.get(u) + wgt < d.get(v)) {               // better path to v?
37            d.put(v, d.get(u) + wgt);                    // update the distance
38            pq.replaceKey(pqTokens.get(v), d.get(v));    // update the pq entry
39          }
40        }
41      }
42    }
43    return cloud;          // this only includes reachable vertices
44  }
```

Code Fragment 14.13: Java implementation of Dijkstra's algorithm for computing the shortest-path distances from a single source. We assume that *e*.getElement() for edge *e* represents the weight of that edge.

Reconstructing a Shortest-Path Tree

Our pseudocode description of Dijkstra's algorithm in Code Fragment 14.12 and our implementation in Code Fragment 14.13 compute the value $D[v]$, for each vertex v, that is the length of a shortest path from the source vertex s to v. However, those forms of the algorithm do not explicitly compute the actual paths that achieve those distances. Fortunately, it is possible to represent shortest paths from source s to every reachable vertex in a graph using a compact data structure known as a *shortest-path tree*. This is possible because if a shortest path from s to v passes through an intermediate vertex u, it must begin with a shortest path from s to u.

We next demonstrate that a shortest-path tree rooted at source s can be reconstructed in $O(n+m)$ time, given the $D[v]$ values produced by Dijkstra's algorithm using s as the source. As we did when representing the DFS and BFS trees, we will map each vertex $v \neq s$ to a parent u (possibly, $u = s$), such that u is the vertex immediately before v on a shortest path from s to v. If u is the vertex just before v on a shortest path from s to v, it must be that

$$D[u] + w(u,v) = D[v].$$

Conversely, if the above equation is satisfied, then a shortest path from s to u followed by the edge (u,v) is a shortest path to v.

Our implementation in Code Fragment 14.14 reconstructs a tree based on this logic, testing all *incoming* edges to each vertex v, looking for a (u,v) that satisfies the key equation. The running time is $O(n+m)$, as we consider each vertex and all incoming edges to those vertices. (See Proposition 14.9.)

```
1   /**
2    * Reconstructs a shortest-path tree rooted at vertex s, given distance map d.
3    * The tree is represented as a map from each reachable vertex v (other than s)
4    * to the edge e = (u,v) that is used to reach v from its parent u in the tree.
5    */
6   public static <V> Map<Vertex<V>,Edge<Integer>>
7   spTree(Graph<V,Integer> g, Vertex<V> s, Map<Vertex<V>,Integer> d) {
8     Map<Vertex<V>, Edge<Integer>> tree = new ProbeHashMap<>( );
9     for (Vertex<V> v : d.keySet( ))
10      if (v != s)
11        for (Edge<Integer> e : g.incomingEdges(v)) { // consider INCOMING edges
12          Vertex<V> u = g.opposite(v, e);
13          int wgt = e.getElement( );
14          if (d.get(v) == d.get(u) + wgt)
15            tree.put(v, e);                               // edge is is used to reach v
16        }
17    return tree;
18  }
```

Code Fragment 14.14: Java method that reconstructs a single-source shortest-path tree, based on knowledge of the shortest-path distances.

14.7   Minimum Spanning Trees

Suppose we wish to connect all the computers in a new office building using the least amount of cable. We can model this problem using an undirected, weighted graph G whose vertices represent the computers, and whose edges represent all the possible pairs (u,v) of computers, where the weight $w(u,v)$ of edge (u,v) is equal to the amount of cable needed to connect computer u to computer v. Rather than computing a shortest-path tree from some particular vertex v, we are interested instead in finding a tree T that contains all the vertices of G and has the minimum total weight over all such trees. Algorithms for finding such a tree are the focus of this section.

Problem Definition

Given an undirected, weighted graph G, we are interested in finding a tree T that contains all the vertices in G and minimizes the sum

$$w(T) = \sum_{(u,v) \text{ in } T} w(u,v).$$

A tree, such as this, that contains every vertex of a connected graph G is said to be a *spanning tree*, and the problem of computing a spanning tree T with smallest total weight is known as the *minimum spanning tree* (or *MST*) problem.

The development of efficient algorithms for the minimum spanning tree problem predates the modern notion of computer science itself. In this section, we discuss two classic algorithms for solving the MST problem. These algorithms are both applications of the *greedy method*, which, as was discussed briefly in the previous section, is based on choosing objects to join a growing collection by iteratively picking an object that minimizes some cost function. The first algorithm we discuss is the Prim-Jarník algorithm, which grows the MST from a single root vertex, much in the same way as Dijkstra's shortest-path algorithm. The second algorithm we discuss is Kruskal's algorithm, which "grows" the MST in clusters by considering edges in nondecreasing order of their weights.

In order to simplify the description of the algorithms, we assume, in the following, that the input graph G is undirected (that is, all its edges are undirected) and simple (that is, it has no self-loops and no parallel edges). Hence, we denote the edges of G as unordered vertex pairs (u,v).

Before we discuss the details of these algorithms, however, let us give a crucial fact about minimum spanning trees that forms the basis of the algorithms.

A Crucial Fact about Minimum Spanning Trees

The two MST algorithms we discuss are based on the greedy method, which in this case depends crucially on the following fact. (See Figure 14.19.)

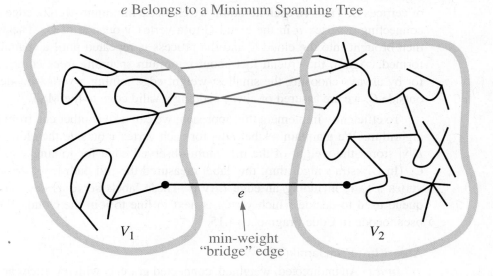

Figure 14.19: An illustration of the crucial fact about minimum spanning trees.

Proposition 14.25: *Let G be a weighted connected graph, and let V_1 and V_2 be a partition of the vertices of G into two disjoint nonempty sets. Furthermore, let e be an edge in G with minimum weight from among those with one endpoint in V_1 and the other in V_2. There is a minimum spanning tree T that has e as one of its edges.*

Justification: Let T be a minimum spanning tree of G. If T does not contain edge e, the addition of e to T must create a cycle. Therefore, there is some edge $f \neq e$ of this cycle that has one endpoint in V_1 and the other in V_2. Moreover, by the choice of e, $w(e) \leq w(f)$. If we remove f from $T \cup \{e\}$, we obtain a spanning tree whose total weight is no more than before. Since T was a minimum spanning tree, this new tree must also be a minimum spanning tree. ■

In fact, if the weights in G are distinct, then the minimum spanning tree is unique; we leave the justification of this less crucial fact as an exercise (C-14.64). In addition, note that Proposition 14.25 remains valid even if the graph G contains negative-weight edges or negative-weight cycles, unlike the algorithms we presented for shortest paths.

14.7.1 Prim-Jarník Algorithm

In the Prim-Jarník algorithm, we grow a minimum spanning tree from a single cluster starting from some "root" vertex s. The main idea is similar to that of Dijkstra's algorithm. We will begin with some vertex s, defining the initial "cloud" of vertices C. Then, in each iteration, we choose a minimum-weight edge $e = (u, v)$, connecting a vertex u in the cloud C to a vertex v outside of C. The vertex v is then brought into the cloud C and the process is repeated until a spanning tree is formed. Again, the crucial fact about minimum spanning trees comes into play, for by always choosing the smallest-weight edge joining a vertex inside C to one outside C, we are assured of always adding a valid edge to the MST.

To efficiently implement this approach, we can take another cue from Dijkstra's algorithm. We maintain a label $D[v]$ for each vertex v outside the cloud C, so that $D[v]$ stores the weight of the minimum observed edge for joining v to the cloud C. (In Dijkstra's algorithm, this label measured the full path length from starting vertex s to v, including an edge (u, v).) These labels serve as keys in a priority queue used to decide which vertex is next in line to join the cloud. We give the pseudocode in Code Fragment 14.15.

Algorithm PrimJarnik(G):

> *Input:* An undirected, weighted, connected graph G with n vertices and m edges
> *Output:* A minimum spanning tree T for G

> Pick any vertex s of G
> $D[s] = 0$
> **for** each vertex $v \neq s$ **do**
> $\quad D[v] = \infty$
> Initialize $T = \emptyset$.
> Initialize a priority queue Q with an entry $(D[v], v)$ for each vertex v.
> For each vertex v, maintain connect(v) as the edge achieving $D[v]$ (if any).
> **while** Q is not empty **do**
> $\quad$ Let u be the value of the entry returned by Q.removeMin( ).
> $\quad$ Connect vertex u to T using edge connect(e).
> $\quad$ **for** each edge $e' = (u, v)$ such that v is in Q **do**
> $\quad\quad$ {check if edge (u, v) better connects v to T}
> $\quad\quad$ **if** $w(u, v) < D[v]$ **then**
> $\quad\quad\quad D[v] = w(u, v)$
> $\quad\quad\quad$ connect(v) = e'.
> $\quad\quad\quad$ Change the key of vertex v in Q to $D[v]$.
> **return** the tree T

Code Fragment 14.15: The Prim-Jarník algorithm for the MST problem.

Analyzing the Prim-Jarník Algorithm

The implementation issues for the Prim-Jarník algorithm are similar to those for Dijkstra's algorithm, relying on an adaptable priority queue Q (Section 9.5.1). We initially perform n insertions into Q, later perform n extract-min operations, and may update a total of m priorities as part of the algorithm. Those steps are the primary contributions to the overall running time. With a heap-based priority queue, each operation runs in $O(\log n)$ time, and the overall time for the algorithm is $O((n+m)\log n)$, which is $O(m\log n)$ for a connected graph. Alternatively, we can achieve $O(n^2)$ running time by using an unsorted list as a priority queue.

Illustrating the Prim-Jarník Algorithm

We illustrate the Prim-Jarník algorithm in Figures 14.20 and 14.21.

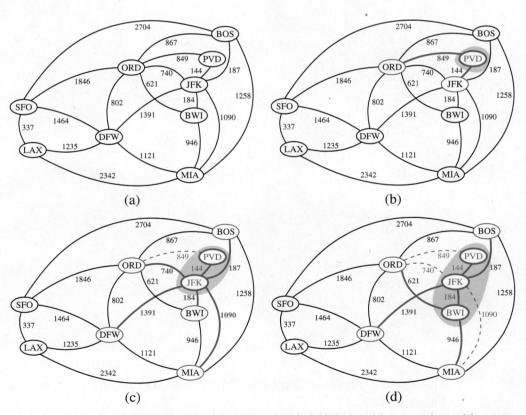

Figure 14.20: An illustration of the Prim-Jarník MST algorithm, starting with vertex PVD. (Continues in Figure 14.21.)

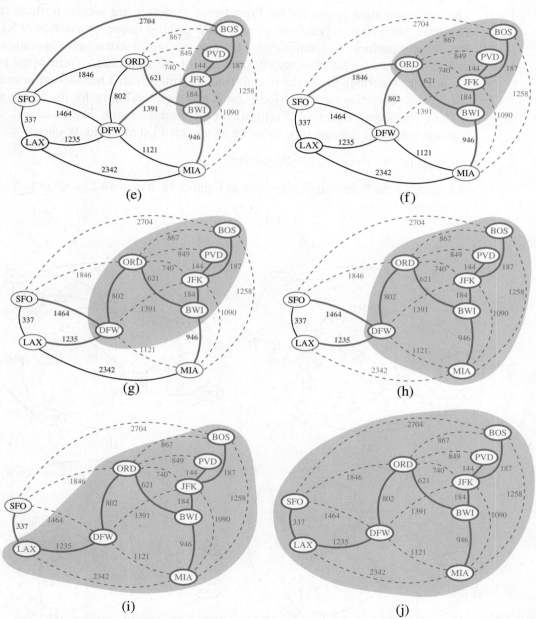

Figure 14.21: An illustration of the Prim-Jarník MST algorithm. (Continued from Figure 14.20.)

14.7.2 Kruskal's Algorithm

In this section, we will introduce *Kruskal's algorithm* for constructing a minimum spanning tree. While the Prim-Jarník algorithm builds the MST by growing a single tree until it spans the graph, Kruskal's algorithm maintains many smaller trees in a *forest*, repeatedly merging pairs of trees until a single tree spans the graph.

Initially, each vertex is in its own cluster. The algorithm then considers each edge in turn, ordered by increasing weight. If an edge e connects vertices in two different clusters, then e is added to the set of edges of the minimum spanning tree, and the two trees are merged with the addition of e. If, on the other hand, e connects two vertices in the same cluster, then e is discarded. Once the algorithm has added enough edges to form a spanning tree, it terminates and outputs this tree as the minimum spanning tree.

We give pseudocode for Kruskal's MST algorithm in Code Fragment 14.16 and we show an example of this algorithm in Figures 14.22, 14.23, and 14.24.

Algorithm Kruskal(G):

    Input: A simple connected weighted graph G with n vertices and m edges
    Output: A minimum spanning tree T for G
  for each vertex v in G **do**
    Define an elementary cluster $C(v) = \{v\}$.
  Initialize a priority queue Q to contain all edges in G, using the weights as keys.
  $T = \emptyset$ $\{T$ will ultimately contain the edges of an MST$\}$
  while T has fewer than $n - 1$ edges **do**
    (u,v) = value returned by Q.removeMin()
    Let $C(u)$ be the cluster containing u, and let $C(v)$ be the cluster containing v.
    if $C(u) \neq C(v)$ **then**
      Add edge (u,v) to T.
      Merge $C(u)$ and $C(v)$ into one cluster.
  return tree T

      Code Fragment 14.16: Kruskal's algorithm for the MST problem.

As was the case with the Prim-Jarník algorithm, the correctness of Kruskal's algorithm is based upon the crucial fact about minimum spanning trees from Proposition 14.25. Each time Kruskal's algorithm adds an edge (u,v) to the minimum spanning tree T, we can define a partitioning of the set of vertices V (as in the proposition) by letting V_1 be the cluster containing v and letting V_2 contain the rest of the vertices in V. This clearly defines a disjoint partitioning of the vertices of V and, more importantly, since we are extracting edges from Q in order by their weights, e must be a minimum-weight edge with one vertex in V_1 and the other in V_2. Thus, Kruskal's algorithm always adds a valid minimum spanning tree edge.

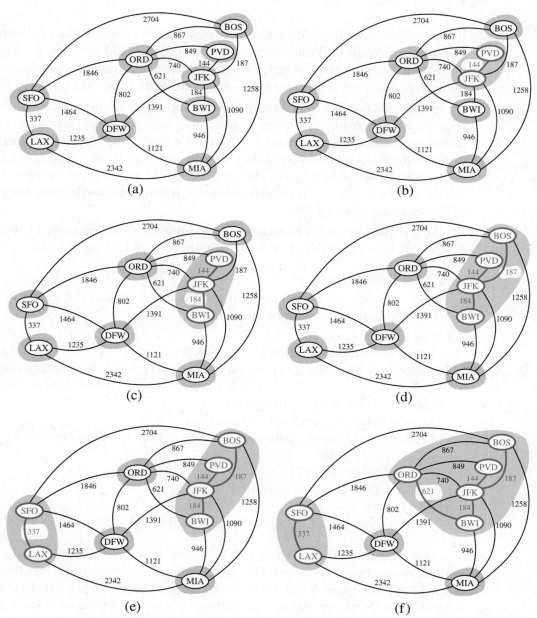

Figure 14.22: Example of an execution of Kruskal's MST algorithm on a graph with integer weights. We show the clusters as shaded regions and we highlight the edge being considered in each iteration. (Continues in Figure 14.23.)

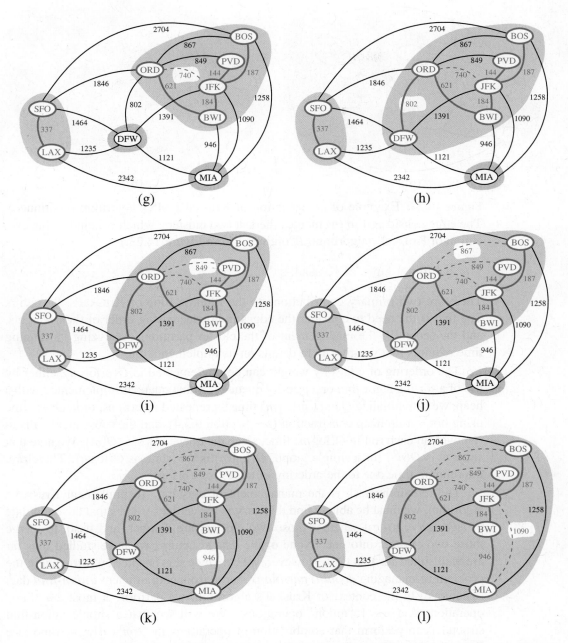

Figure 14.23: An example of an execution of Kruskal's MST algorithm. Rejected edges are shown dashed. (Continues in Figure 14.24.)

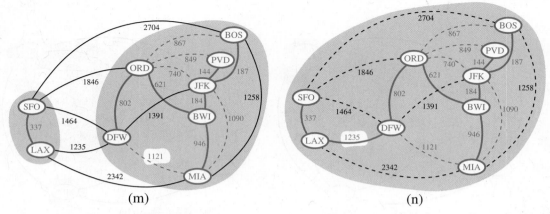

Figure 14.24: Example of an execution of Kruskal's MST algorithm (continued). The edge considered in (n) merges the last two clusters, which concludes this execution of Kruskal's algorithm. (Continued from Figure 14.23.)

The Running Time of Kruskal's Algorithm

There are two primary contributions to the running time of Kruskal's algorithm. The first is the need to consider the edges in nondecreasing order of their weights, and the second is the management of the cluster partition. Analyzing its running time requires that we give more details on its implementation.

The ordering of edges by weight can be implemented in $O(m \log m)$, either by use of a sorting algorithm or a priority queue Q. If that queue is implemented with a heap, we can initialize Q in $O(m \log m)$ time by repeated insertions, or in $O(m)$ time using bottom-up heap construction (see Section 9.3.4), and the subsequent calls to removeMin each run in $O(\log m)$ time, since the queue has size $O(m)$. We note that since m is $O(n^2)$ for a simple graph, $O(\log m)$ is the same as $O(\log n)$. Therefore, the running time due to the ordering of edges is $O(m \log n)$.

The remaining task is the management of clusters. To implement Kruskal's algorithm, we must be able to find the clusters for vertices u and v that are endpoints of an edge e, to test whether those two clusters are distinct, and if so, to merge those two clusters into one. None of the data structures we have studied thus far are well suited for this task. However, we conclude this chapter by formalizing the problem of managing ***disjoint partitions***, and introducing efficient ***union-find*** data structures. In the context of Kruskal's algorithm, we perform at most $2m$ "find" operations and $n-1$ "union" operations. We will see that a simple union-find structure can perform that combination of operations in $O(m + n \log n)$ time (see Proposition 14.26), and a more advanced structure can support an even faster time.

For a connected graph, $m \geq n - 1$; therefore, the bound of $O(m \log n)$ time for ordering the edges dominates the time for managing the clusters. We conclude that the running time of Kruskal's algorithm is $O(m \log n)$.

Java Implementation

Code Fragment 14.17 presents a Java implementation of Kruskal's algorithm. The minimum spanning tree is returned in the form of a list of edges. As a consequence of Kruskal's algorithm, those edges will be reported in nondecreasing order of their weights.

Our implementation assumes use of a Partition class for managing the cluster partition. An implementation of the Partition class is presented in Section 14.7.3.

```java
1  /** Computes a minimum spanning tree of graph g using Kruskal's algorithm. */
2  public static <V> PositionalList<Edge<Integer>> MST(Graph<V,Integer> g) {
3    // tree is where we will store result as it is computed
4    PositionalList<Edge<Integer>> tree = new LinkedPositionalList<>();
5    // pq entries are edges of graph, with weights as keys
6    PriorityQueue<Integer, Edge<Integer>> pq = new HeapPriorityQueue<>();
7    // union-find forest of components of the graph
8    Partition<Vertex<V>> forest = new Partition<>();
9    // map each vertex to the forest position
10   Map<Vertex<V>,Position<Vertex<V>>> positions = new ProbeHashMap<>();
11
12   for (Vertex<V> v : g.vertices())
13     positions.put(v, forest.makeGroup(v));
14
15   for (Edge<Integer> e : g.edges())
16     pq.insert(e.getElement(), e);
17
18   int size = g.numVertices();
19   // while tree not spanning and unprocessed edges remain...
20   while (tree.size() != size - 1 && !pq.isEmpty()) {
21     Entry<Integer, Edge<Integer>> entry = pq.removeMin();
22     Edge<Integer> edge = entry.getValue();
23     Vertex<V>[] endpoints = g.endVertices(edge);
24     Position<Vertex<V>> a = forest.find(positions.get(endpoints[0]));
25     Position<Vertex<V>> b = forest.find(positions.get(endpoints[1]));
26     if (a != b) {
27       tree.addLast(edge);
28       forest.union(a,b);
29     }
30   }
31
32   return tree;
33 }
```

Code Fragment 14.17: Java implementation of Kruskal's algorithm for the minimum spanning tree problem. The Partition class is discussed in Section 14.7.3.

14.7.3 Disjoint Partitions and Union-Find Structures

In this section, we consider a data structure for managing a **partition** of elements into a collection of disjoint sets. Our initial motivation is in support of Kruskal's minimum spanning tree algorithm, in which a forest of disjoint trees is maintained, with occasional merging of neighboring trees. More generally, the disjoint partition problem can be applied to various models of discrete growth.

We formalize the problem with the following model. A partition data structure manages a universe of elements that are organized into disjoint sets (that is, an element belongs to one and only one of these sets). Unlike with the Set ADT, we do not expect to be able to iterate through the contents of a set, nor to efficiently test whether a given set includes a given element. To avoid confusion with such notions of a set, we will refer to the sets of our partition as **clusters**. However, we will not require an explicit structure for each cluster, instead allowing the organization of clusters to be implicit. To differentiate between one cluster and another, we assume that at any point in time, each cluster has a designated element that we refer to as the **leader** of the cluster.

Formally, we define the methods of a **partition ADT** using positions, each of which stores an element x. The partition ADT supports the following methods.

makeCluster(x): Creates a singleton cluster containing new element x and returns its position.

union(p, q): Merges the clusters containing positions p and q.

find(p): Returns the position of the leader of the cluster containing position p.

Sequence Implementation

A simple implementation of a partition with a total of n elements uses a collection of sequences, one for each cluster, where the sequence for a cluster A stores element positions. Each position object stores a reference to its associated element x, and a reference to the sequence storing p, since this sequence is representing the cluster containing p's element. (See Figure 14.25.)

With this representation, we can easily perform the makeCluster(x) and find(p) operations in $O(1)$ time, allowing the first position in a sequence to serve as the "leader." Operation union(p, q) requires that we join two sequences into one and update the cluster references of the positions in one of the two. We choose to implement this operation by removing all the positions from the sequence with smaller size, and inserting them in the sequence with larger size. Each time we take a position from the smaller cluster A and insert it into the larger cluster B, we update the cluster reference for that position to now point to B. Hence, the operation union(p, q) takes time $O(\min(n_p, n_q))$, where n_p (resp. n_q) is the cardinality of the

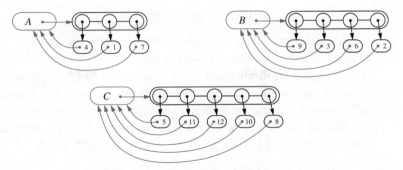

Figure 14.25: Sequence-based implementation of a partition consisting of three clusters: $A = \{1,4,7\}$, $B = \{2,3,6,9\}$, and $C = \{5,8,10,11,12\}$.

cluster containing position p (resp. q). Clearly, this time is $O(n)$ if there are n elements in the partition universe. However, we next present an amortized analysis that shows this implementation to be much better than appears from this worst-case analysis.

Proposition 14.26: *When using the sequence-based partition implementation, performing a series of k makeCluster, union, and find operations on an initially empty partition involving at most n elements takes $O(k+n\log n)$ time.*

Justification: We use the accounting method and assume that one cyber-dollar can pay for the time to perform a find operation, a makeCluster operation, or the movement of a position object from one sequence to another in a union operation. In the case of a find or makeCluster operation, we charge the operation itself 1 cyber-dollar. In the case of a union operation, we assume that 1 cyber-dollar pays for the constant-time work in comparing the sizes of the two sequences, and that we charge 1 cyber-dollar to each position that we move from the smaller cluster to the larger cluster. Clearly, the 1 cyber-dollar charged for each find and makeCluster operation, together with the first cyber-dollar collected for each union operation, accounts for a total of k cyber-dollars.

Consider, then, the number of charges made to positions on behalf of union operations. The important observation is that each time we move a position from one cluster to another, the size of that position's cluster at least doubles. Thus, each position is moved from one cluster to another at most $\log n$ times; hence, each position can be charged at most $O(\log n)$ times. Since we assume that the partition is initially empty, there are $O(n)$ different elements referenced in the given series of operations, which implies that the total time for moving elements during the union operations is $O(n\log n)$. ∎

A Tree-Based Partition Implementation ⋆

An alternative data structure for representing a partition uses a collection of trees to store the n elements, where each tree is associated with a different cluster. In particular, we implement each tree with a linked data structure whose nodes serve as the position objects. (See Figure 14.26.) We view each position p as being a node having an instance variable, element, referring to its element x, and an instance variable, parent, referring to its parent node. By convention, if p is the *root* of its tree, we set p's parent reference to itself.

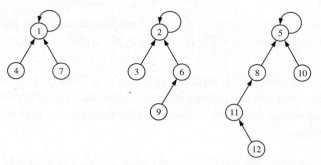

Figure 14.26: Tree-based implementation of a partition consisting of three clusters: $A = \{1,4,7\}$, $B = \{2,3,6,9\}$, and $C = \{5,8,10,11,12\}$.

With this partition data structure, operation find(p) is performed by walking up from position p to the root of its tree, which takes $O(n)$ time in the worst case. Operation union(p, q) can be implemented by making one of the trees a subtree of the other. This can be done by first locating the two roots, and then in $O(1)$ additional time by setting the parent reference of one root to point to the other root. See Figure 14.27 for an example of both operations.

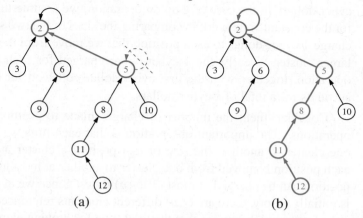

$$(a) \qquad\qquad\qquad (b)$$

Figure 14.27: Tree-based implementation of a partition: (a) operation union(p, q); (b) operation find(p), where p denotes the position object for element 12.

At first, this implementation may seem to be no better than the sequence-based data structure, but we add the following two simple heuristics to make it run faster.

Union-by-Size: With each position p, store the number of elements in the subtree rooted at p. In a union operation, make the root of the smaller cluster become a child of the other root, and update the size field of the larger root.

Path Compression: In a find operation, for each position q that the find visits, reset the parent of q to the root. (See Figure 14.28.)

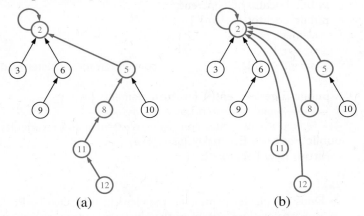

(a)   (b)

Figure 14.28: Path-compression heuristic: (a) path traversed by operation find on element 12; (b) restructured tree.

A surprising property of this data structure, when implemented using the union-by-size and path-compression heuristics, is that performing a series of k operations involving n elements takes $O(k \log^* n)$ time, where $\log^* n$ is the **log-star** function, which is the inverse of the **tower-of-twos** function. Intuitively, $\log^* n$ is the number of times that one can iteratively take the logarithm (base 2) of a number before getting a number smaller than 2. Table 14.4 shows a few sample values.

minimum n	2	$2^2 = 4$	$2^{2^2} = 16$	$2^{2^{2^2}} = 65,536$	$2^{2^{2^{2^2}}} = 2^{65,536}$
$\log^* n$	1	2	3	4	5

Table 14.4: Some values of $\log^* n$ and critical values for its inverse.

Proposition 14.27: *When using the tree-based partition representation with both union-by-size and path compression, performing a series of k makeCluster, union, and find operations on an initially empty partition involving at most n elements takes $O(k \log^* n)$ time.*

Although the analysis for this data structure is rather complex, its implementation is quite straightforward. We conclude with a Java implementation of the structure, given in Code Fragment 14.18.

```
1   /** A Union-Find structure for maintaining disjoint sets. */
2   public class Partition<E> {
3     //--------------- nested Locator class -------------
4     private class Locator<E> implements Position<E> {
5       public E element;
6       public int size;
7       public Locator<E> parent;
8       public Locator(E elem) {
9         element = elem;
10        size = 1;
11        parent = this;              // convention for a cluster leader
12      }
13      public E getElement( ) { return element; }
14    } //--------- end of nested Locator class ---------
15    /** Makes a new cluster containing element e and returns its position. */
16    public Position<E> makeCluster(E e) {
17      return new Locator<E>(e);
18    }
19    /**
20     * Finds the cluster containing the element identified by Position p
21     * and returns the Position of the cluster's leader.
22     */
23    public Position<E> find(Position<E> p) {
24      Locator<E> loc = validate(p);
25      if (loc.parent != loc)
26        loc.parent = (Locator<E>) find(loc.parent); // overwrite parent after recursion
27      return loc.parent;
28    }
29    /** Merges the clusters containing elements with positions p and q (if distinct). */
30    public void union(Position<E> p, Position<E> q) {
31      Locator<E> a = (Locator<E>) find(p);
32      Locator<E> b = (Locator<E>) find(q);
33      if (a != b)
34        if (a.size > b.size) {
35          b.parent = a;
36          a.size += b.size;
37        } else {
38          a.parent = b;
39          b.size += a.size;
40        }
41    }
42  }
```

Code Fragment 14.18: Java implementation of a Partition class using union-by-size and path compression. We omit the validate method due to space limitation.

14.8 Exercises

Reinforcement

R-14.1 Draw a simple undirected graph G that has 12 vertices, 18 edges, and 3 connected components.

R-14.2 If G is a simple undirected graph with 12 vertices and 3 connected components, what is the largest number of edges it might have?

R-14.3 Draw an adjacency matrix representation of the undirected graph shown in Figure 14.1.

R-14.4 Draw an adjacency list representation of the undirected graph shown in Figure 14.1.

R-14.5 Draw a simple, connected, directed graph with 8 vertices and 16 edges such that the in-degree and out-degree of each vertex is 2. Show that there is a single (nonsimple) cycle that includes all the edges of your graph, that is, you can trace all the edges in their respective directions without ever lifting your pencil. (Such a cycle is called an ***Euler tour***.)

R-14.6 Suppose we represent a graph G having n vertices and m edges with the edge list structure. Why, in this case, does the insertVertex method run in $O(1)$ time while the removeVertex method runs in $O(m)$ time?

R-14.7 Give pseudocode for performing the operation insertEdge(u, v, x) in $O(1)$ time using the adjacency matrix representation.

R-14.8 Repeat Exercise R-14.7 for the adjacency list representation, as described in the chapter.

R-14.9 Can edge list E be omitted from the adjacency matrix representation while still achieving the time bounds given in Table 14.1? Why or why not?

R-14.10 Can edge list E be omitted from the adjacency list representation while still achieving the time bounds given in Table 14.3? Why or why not?

R-14.11 Would you use the adjacency matrix structure or the adjacency list structure in each of the following cases? Justify your choice.

    a. The graph has 10,000 vertices and 20,000 edges, and it is important to use as little space as possible.

    b. The graph has 10,000 vertices and 20,000,000 edges, and it is important to use as little space as possible.

    c. You need to answer the query getEdge(u, v) as fast as possible, no matter how much space you use.

R-14.12 In order to verify that all of its nontree edges are back edges, redraw the graph from Figure 14.8b so that the DFS tree edges are drawn with solid lines and oriented downward, as in a standard portrayal of a tree, and with all nontree edges drawn using dashed lines.

R-14.13 Explain why the DFS traversal runs in $O(n^2)$ time on an n-vertex simple graph that is represented with the adjacency matrix structure.

R-14.14 A simple undirected graph is ***complete*** if it contains an edge between every pair of distinct vertices. What does a depth-first search tree of a complete graph look like?

R-14.15 Recalling the definition of a complete graph from Exercise R-14.14, what does a breadth-first search tree of a complete graph look like?

R-14.16 Let G be an undirected graph whose vertices are the integers 1 through 8, and let the adjacent vertices of each vertex be given by the table below:

vertex	adjacent vertices
1	(2, 3, 4)
2	(1, 3, 4)
3	(1, 2, 4)
4	(1, 2, 3, 6)
5	(6, 7, 8)
6	(4, 5, 7)
7	(5, 6, 8)
8	(5, 7)

Assume that, in a traversal of G, the adjacent vertices of a given vertex are returned in the same order as they are listed in the table above.

a. Draw G.
b. Give the sequence of vertices of G visited using a DFS traversal starting at vertex 1.
c. Give the sequence of vertices visited using a BFS traversal starting at vertex 1.

R-14.17 Bob loves foreign languages and wants to plan his course schedule for the following years. He is interested in the following nine language courses: LA15, LA16, LA22, LA31, LA32, LA126, LA127, LA141, and LA169. The course prerequisites are:

- LA15: (none)
- LA16: LA15
- LA22: (none)
- LA31: LA15
- LA32: LA16, LA31
- LA126: LA22, LA32
- LA127: LA16
- LA141: LA22, LA16
- LA169: LA32

In what order can Bob take these courses, respecting the prerequisites?

R-14.18 Compute a topological ordering for the directed graph drawn with solid edges in Figure 14.3d.

R-14.19 Draw the transitive closure of the directed graph shown in Figure 14.2.

R-14.20 If the vertices of the graph from Figure 14.11 are ordered as (JFK, LAZ, MIA, BOS, ORD, SFO, DFW), in what order would edges be added to the transitive closure during the Floyd-Warshall algorithm?

R-14.21 How many edges are in the transitive closure of a graph that consists of a simple directed path of n vertices?

R-14.22 Given an n-node complete binary tree T, rooted at a given position, consider a directed graph $\vec{G}$ having the nodes of T as its vertices. For each parent-child pair in T, create a directed edge in $\vec{G}$ from the parent to the child. Show that the transitive closure of $\vec{G}$ has $O(n \log n)$ edges.

R-14.23 Draw a simple, connected, weighted graph with 8 vertices and 16 edges, each with unique edge weights. Identify one vertex as a "start" vertex and illustrate a running of Dijkstra's algorithm on this graph.

R-14.24 Show how to modify the pseudocode for Dijkstra's algorithm for the case when the graph is directed and we want to compute shortest directed paths from the source vertex to all the other vertices.

R-14.25 Draw a simple, connected, undirected, weighted graph with 8 vertices and 16 edges, each with unique edge weights. Illustrate the execution of the Prim-Jarník algorithm for computing the minimum spanning tree of this graph.

R-14.26 Repeat the previous problem for Kruskal's algorithm.

R-14.27 There are eight small islands in a lake, and the state wants to build seven bridges to connect them so that each island can be reached from any other one via one or more bridges. The cost of constructing a bridge is proportional to its length. The distances between pairs of islands are given in the following table.

	1	2	3	4	5	6	7	8
1	-	240	210	340	280	200	345	120
2	-	-	265	175	215	180	185	155
3	-	-	-	260	115	350	435	195
4	-	-	-	-	160	330	295	230
5	-	-	-	-	-	360	400	170
6	-	-	-	-	-	-	175	205
7	-	-	-	-	-	-	-	305
8	-	-	-	-	-	-	-	-

Find which bridges to build to minimize the total construction cost.

R-14.28 Describe the meaning of the graphical conventions used in Figure 14.9 illustrating a DFS traversal. What do the line thicknesses signify? What do the arrows signify? How about dashed lines?

R-14.29 Repeat Exercise R-14.28 for Figure 14.8 that illustrates a directed DFS traversal.

R-14.30 Repeat Exercise R-14.28 for Figure 14.10 that illustrates a BFS traversal.

R-14.31 Repeat Exercise R-14.28 for Figure 14.11 illustrating the Floyd-Warshall algorithm.

R-14.32 Repeat Exercise R-14.28 for Figure 14.13 that illustrates the topological sorting algorithm.

R-14.33 Repeat Exercise R-14.28 for Figures 14.15 and 14.16 illustrating Dijkstra's algorithm.

R-14.34 Repeat Exercise R-14.28 for Figures 14.20 and 14.21 that illustrate the Prim-Jarník algorithm.

R-14.35 Repeat Exercise R-14.28 for Figures 14.22 through 14.24 that illustrate Kruskal's algorithm.

R-14.36 George claims he has a fast way to do path compression in a partition structure, starting at a position p. He puts p into a list L, and starts following parent pointers. Each time he encounters a new position, q, he adds q to L and updates the parent pointer of each node in L to point to q's parent. Show that George's algorithm runs in $\Omega(h^2)$ time on a path of length h.

Creativity

C-14.37 Give a Java implementation of the removeEdge(e) method for our adjacency map implementation of Section 14.2.5, making sure your implementation works for both directed and undirected graphs. Your method should run in $O(1)$ time.

C-14.38 Suppose we wish to represent an n-vertex graph G using the edge list structure, assuming that we identify the vertices with the integers in the set $\{0, 1, \ldots, n-1\}$. Describe how to implement the collection E to support $O(\log n)$-time performance for the getEdge(u, v) method. How are you implementing the method in this case?

C-14.39 Let T be the spanning tree rooted at the start vertex produced by the depth-first search of a connected, undirected graph G. Argue why every edge of G not in T goes from a vertex in T to one of its ancestors, that is, it is a ***back edge***.

C-14.40 Our solution to reporting a path from u to v in Code Fragment 14.6 could be made more efficient in practice if the DFS process ended as soon as v is discovered. Describe how to modify our code base to implement this optimization.

C-14.41 Let G be an undirected graph with n vertices and m edges. Describe an $O(n+m)$-time algorithm for traversing each edge of G exactly once in each direction.

C-14.42 Implement an algorithm that returns a cycle in a directed graph $\vec{G}$, if one exists.

C-14.43 Write a method, components(G), for undirected graph G, that returns a dictionary mapping each vertex to an integer that serves as an identifier for its connected component. That is, two vertices should be mapped to the same identifier if and only if they are in the same connected component.

C-14.44 Say that a maze is ***constructed correctly*** if there is one path from the start to the finish, the entire maze is reachable from the start, and there are no loops around any portions of the maze. Given a maze drawn in an $n \times n$ grid, how can we determine if it is constructed correctly? What is the running time of this algorithm?

C-14.45 Computer networks should avoid single points of failure, that is, network vertices that can disconnect the network if they fail. We say an undirected, connected graph G is **biconnected** if it contains no vertex whose removal would divide G into two or more connected components. Give an algorithm for adding at most n edges to a connected graph G, with $n \geq 3$ vertices and $m \geq n - 1$ edges, to guarantee that G is biconnected. Your algorithm should run in $O(n + m)$ time.

C-14.46 Explain why all nontree edges are cross edges, with respect to a BFS tree constructed for an undirected graph.

C-14.47 Explain why there are no forward nontree edges with respect to a BFS tree constructed for a directed graph.

C-14.48 Show that if T is a BFS tree produced for a connected graph G, then, for each vertex v at level i, the path of T between s and v has i edges, and any other path of G between s and v has at least i edges.

C-14.49 Justify Proposition 14.16.

C-14.50 Provide an implementation of the BFS algorithm that uses a FIFO queue, rather than a level-by-level formulation, to manage vertices that have been discovered until the time when their neighbors are considered.

C-14.51 A graph G is **bipartite** if its vertices can be partitioned into two sets X and Y such that every edge in G has one end vertex in X and the other in Y. Design and analyze an efficient algorithm for determining if an undirected graph G is bipartite (without knowing the sets X and Y in advance).

C-14.52 An **Euler tour** of a directed graph $\vec{G}$ with n vertices and m edges is a cycle that traverses each edge of $\vec{G}$ exactly once according to its direction. Such a tour always exists if $\vec{G}$ is connected and the in-degree equals the out-degree of each vertex in $\vec{G}$. Describe an $O(n + m)$-time algorithm for finding an Euler tour of such a directed graph $\vec{G}$.

C-14.53 A company named RT&T has a network of n switching stations connected by m high-speed communication links. Each customer's phone is directly connected to one station in his or her area. The engineers of RT&T have developed a prototype video-phone system that allows two customers to see each other during a phone call. In order to have acceptable image quality, however, the number of links used to transmit video signals between the two parties cannot exceed 4. Suppose that RT&T's network is represented by a graph. Design an efficient algorithm that computes, for each station, the set of stations it can reach using no more than 4 links.

C-14.54 The time delay of a long-distance call can be determined by multiplying a small fixed constant by the number of communication links on the telephone network between the caller and callee. Suppose the telephone network of a company named RT&T is a tree. The engineers of RT&T want to compute the maximum possible time delay that may be experienced in a long-distance call. Given a tree T, the *diameter* of T is the length of a longest path between two nodes of T. Give an efficient algorithm for computing the diameter of T.

C-14.55 Tamarindo University and many other schools worldwide are doing a joint project on multimedia. A computer network is built to connect these schools using communication links that form a tree. The schools decide to install a file server at one of the schools to share data among all the schools. Since the transmission time on a link is dominated by the link setup and synchronization, the cost of a data transfer is proportional to the number of links used. Hence, it is desirable to choose a "central" location for the file server. Given a tree T and a node v of T, the *eccentricity* of v is the length of a longest path from v to any other node of T. A node of T with minimum eccentricity is called a *center* of T.

    a. Design an efficient algorithm that, given an n-node tree T, computes a center of T.

    b. Is the center unique? If not, how many distinct centers can a tree have?

C-14.56 Say that an n-vertex directed acyclic graph $\vec{G}$ is **compact** if there is some way of numbering the vertices of $\vec{G}$ with the integers from 0 to $n-1$ such that $\vec{G}$ contains the edge (i, j) if and only if $i < j$, for all i, j in $[0, n-1]$. Give an $O(n^2)$-time algorithm for detecting if $\vec{G}$ is compact.

C-14.57 Let $\vec{G}$ be a weighted directed graph with n vertices. Design a variation of Floyd-Warshall's algorithm for computing the lengths of the shortest paths from each vertex to every other vertex in $O(n^3)$ time.

C-14.58 Design an efficient algorithm for finding a **longest** directed path from a vertex s to a vertex t of an acyclic weighted directed graph $\vec{G}$. Specify the graph representation used and any auxiliary data structures used. Also, analyze the time complexity of your algorithm.

C-14.59 An independent set of an undirected graph $G = (V, E)$ is a subset I of V such that no two vertices in I are adjacent. That is, if u and v are in I, then (u, v) is not in E. A **maximal independent set** M is an independent set such that, if we were to add any additional vertex to M, then it would not be independent any more. Every graph has a maximal independent set. (Can you see this? This question is not part of the exercise, but it is worth thinking about.) Give an efficient algorithm that computes a maximal independent set for a graph G. What is this method's running time?

C-14.60 Give an example of an n-vertex simple graph G that causes Dijkstra's algorithm to run in $\Omega(n^2 \log n)$ time when its implemented with a heap.

C-14.61 Give an example of a weighted directed graph $\vec{G}$ with negative-weight edges, but no negative-weight cycle, such that Dijkstra's algorithm incorrectly computes the shortest-path distances from some start vertex s.

C-14.62 Our implementation of shortestPathLengths in Code Fragment 14.13 relies on use of "infinity" as a numeric value, to represent the distance bound for vertices that are not (yet) known to be reachable from the source. Reimplement that method without such a sentinel, so that vertices, other than the source, are not added to the priority queue until it is evident that they are reachable.

C-14.63 Consider the following greedy strategy for finding a shortest path from vertex *start* to vertex *goal* in a given connected graph.

    1: Initialize *path* to *start*.
    2: Initialize set *visited* to {*start*}.
    3: If *start*=*goal*, return *path* and exit. Otherwise, continue.
    4: Find the edge (*start,v*) of minimum weight such that *v* is adjacent to *start* and *v* is not in *visited*.
    5: Add *v* to *path*.
    6: Add *v* to *visited*.
    7: Set *start* equal to *v* and go to step 3.

Does this greedy strategy always find a shortest path from *start* to *goal*? Either explain intuitively why it works, or give a counterexample.

C-14.64 Show that if all the weights in a connected weighted graph G are distinct, then there is exactly one minimum spanning tree for G.

C-14.65 An old MST method, called **Barůvka's algorithm**, works as follows on a graph G having n vertices and m edges with distinct weights:

    Let T be a subgraph of G initially containing just the vertices in V.
    while T has fewer than $n - 1$ edges **do**
        for each connected component C_i of T **do**
            Find the lowest-weight edge (u,v) in E with u in C_i and v not in C_i.
            Add (u,v) to T (unless it is already in T).
    return T

Prove that this algorithm is correct and that it runs in $O(m \log n)$ time.

C-14.66 Let G be a graph with n vertices and m edges such that all the edge weights in G are integers in the range $[1, n]$. Give an algorithm for finding a minimum spanning tree for G in $O(m \log^* n)$ time.

C-14.67 Consider a diagram of a telephone network, which is a graph G whose vertices represent switching centers, and whose edges represent communication lines joining pairs of centers. Edges are marked by their bandwidth, and the bandwidth of a path is equal to the lowest bandwidth among the path's edges. Give an algorithm that, given a network and two switching centers a and b, outputs the maximum bandwidth of a path between a and b.

C-14.68 NASA wants to link n stations spread over the country using communication channels. Each pair of stations has a different bandwidth available, which is known a priori. NASA wants to select $n - 1$ channels (the minimum possible) in such a way that all the stations are linked by the channels and the total bandwidth (defined as the sum of the individual bandwidths of the channels) is maximum. Give an efficient algorithm for this problem and determine its worst-case time complexity. Consider the weighted graph $G = (V, E)$, where V is the set of stations and E is the set of channels between the stations. Define the weight $w(e)$ of an edge e in E as the bandwidth of the corresponding channel.

C-14.69 Inside the Castle of Asymptopia there is a maze, and along each corridor of the maze there is a bag of gold coins. The amount of gold in each bag varies. A noble knight, named Sir Paul, will be given the opportunity to walk through the maze, picking up bags of gold. He may enter the maze only through a door marked "ENTER" and exit through another door marked "EXIT." While in the maze he may not retrace his steps. Each corridor of the maze has an arrow painted on the wall. Sir Paul may only go down the corridor in the direction of the arrow. There is no way to traverse a "loop" in the maze. Given a map of the maze, including the amount of gold in each corridor, describe an algorithm to help Sir Paul pick up the most gold.

C-14.70 Suppose you are given a *timetable*, which consists of:

- A set $\mathcal{A}$ of n airports, and for each airport a in $\mathcal{A}$, a minimum connecting time $c(a)$.
- A set $\mathcal{F}$ of m flights, and the following, for each flight f in $\mathcal{F}$:
  - Origin airport $a_1(f)$ in $\mathcal{A}$
  - Destination airport $a_2(f)$ in $\mathcal{A}$
  - Departure time $t_1(f)$
  - Arrival time $t_2(f)$

Describe an efficient algorithm for the flight scheduling problem. In this problem, we are given airports a and b, and a time t, and we wish to compute a sequence of flights that allows one to arrive at the earliest possible time in b when departing from a at or after time t. Minimum connecting times at intermediate airports must be observed. What is the running time of your algorithm as a function of n and m?

C-14.71 Suppose we are given a directed graph $\vec{G}$ with n vertices, and let M be the $n \times n$ adjacency matrix corresponding to $\vec{G}$.

  a. Let the product of M with itself (M^2) be defined, for $1 \le i, j \le n$, as follows:

$$M^2(i, j) = M(i, 1) \odot M(1, j) \oplus \cdots \oplus M(i, n) \odot M(n, j),$$

   where "$\oplus$" is the boolean **or** operator and "$\odot$" is boolean **and**. Given this definition, what does $M^2(i, j) = 1$ imply about the vertices i and j? What if $M^2(i, j) = 0$?

  b. Suppose M^4 is the product of M^2 with itself. What do the entries of M^4 signify? How about the entries of $M^5 = (M^4)(M)$? In general, what information is contained in the matrix M^p?

  c. Now suppose that $\vec{G}$ is weighted and assume the following:

   1: for $1 \le i \le n, M(i,i) = 0$.
   2: for $1 \le i, j \le n, M(i, j) = weight(i, j)$ if (i, j) is in E.
   3: for $1 \le i, j \le n, M(i, j) = \infty$ if (i, j) is not in E.

   Also, let M^2 be defined, for $1 \le i, j \le n$, as follows:

$$M^2(i, j) = \min\{M(i, 1) + M(1, j), \dots, M(i, n) + M(n, j)\}.$$

   If $M^2(i, j) = k$, what may we conclude about the relationship between vertices i and j?

C-14.72 Karen has a new way to do path compression in a tree-based union/find partition data structure starting at a position p. She puts all the positions that are on the path from p to the root in a set S. Then she scans through S and sets the parent pointer of each position in S to its parent's parent pointer (recall that the parent pointer of the root points to itself). If this pass changed the value of any position's parent pointer, then she repeats this process, and goes on repeating this process until she makes a scan through S that does not change any position's parent value. Show that Karen's algorithm is correct and analyze its running time for a path of length h.

Projects

P-14.73 Use an adjacency matrix to implement a class supporting a simplified graph ADT that does not include update methods. Your class should include a constructor method that takes two collections—a collection V of vertex elements and a collection E of pairs of vertex elements—and produces the graph G that these two collections represent.

P-14.74 Implement the simplified graph ADT described in Exercise P-14.73, using the edge list structure.

P-14.75 Implement the simplified graph ADT described in Exercise P-14.73, using the adjacency list structure.

P-14.76 Extend the class of Exercise P-14.75 to support the update methods of the graph ADT.

P-14.77 Design an experimental comparison of repeated DFS traversals versus the Floyd-Warshall algorithm for computing the transitive closure of a directed graph.

P-14.78 Develop a Java implementation of the Prim-Jarník algorithm for computing the minimum spanning tree of a graph.

P-14.79 Perform an experimental comparison of two of the minimum spanning tree algorithms discussed in this chapter (Kruskal and Prim-Jarník). Develop an extensive set of experiments to test the running times of these algorithms using randomly generated graphs.

P-14.80 One way to construct a *maze* starts with an $n \times n$ grid such that each grid cell is bounded by four unit-length walls. We then remove two boundary unit-length walls, to represent the start and finish. For each remaining unit-length wall not on the boundary, we assign a random value and create a graph G, called the *dual*, such that each grid cell is a vertex in G and there is an edge joining the vertices for two cells if and only if the cells share a common wall. The weight of each edge is the weight of the corresponding wall. We construct the maze by finding a minimum spanning tree T for G and removing all the walls corresponding to edges in T. Write a program that uses this algorithm to generate mazes and then solves them. Minimally, your program should draw the maze and, ideally, it should visualize the solution as well.

P-14.81 Write a program that builds the routing tables for the nodes in a computer network, based on shortest-path routing, where path distance is measured by hop count, that is, the number of edges in a path. The input for this problem is the connectivity information for all the nodes in the network, as in the following example:

241.12.31.14: 241.12.31.15 241.12.31.18 241.12.31.19

which indicates three network nodes that are connected to 241.12.31.14, that is, three nodes that are one hop away. The routing table for the node at address A is a set of pairs (B, C), which indicates that, to route a message from A to B, the next node to send to (on the shortest path from A to B) is C. Your program should output the routing table for each node in the network, given an input list of node connectivity lists, each of which is input in the syntax as shown above, one per line.

Chapter Notes

The depth-first search method is a part of the "folklore" of computer science, but Hopcroft and Tarjan [46, 87] are the ones who showed how useful this algorithm is for solving several different graph problems. Knuth [60] discusses the topological sorting problem. The simple linear-time algorithm that we describe for determining if a directed graph is strongly connected is due to Kosaraju. The Floyd-Warshall algorithm appears in a paper by Floyd [34] and is based upon a theorem of Warshall [94].

The first known minimum spanning tree algorithm is due to Barůvka [9], and was published in 1926. The Prim-Jarník algorithm was first published in Czech by Jarník [51] in 1930 and in English in 1957 by Prim [79]. Kruskal published his minimum spanning tree algorithm in 1956 [63]. The reader interested in further study of the history of the minimum spanning tree problem is referred to the paper by Graham and Hell [41]. The current asymptotically fastest minimum spanning tree algorithm is a randomized method of Karger, Klein, and Tarjan [53] that runs in $O(m)$ expected time. Dijkstra [30] published his single-source, shortest-path algorithm in 1959. The running time for the Prim-Jarník algorithm, and also that of Dijkstra's algorithm, can actually be improved to be $O(n \log n + m)$ by implementing the queue Q with either of two more sophisticated data structures, the "Fibonacci Heap" [36] or the "Relaxed Heap" [32].

To learn about different algorithms for drawing graphs, please see the book chapter by Tamassia and Liotta [85] and the book by Di Battista, Eades, Tamassia and Tollis [29]. The reader interested in further study of graph algorithms is referred to the books by Ahuja, Magnanti, and Orlin [7], Cormen, Leiserson, Rivest and Stein [25], Mehlhorn [72], and Tarjan [88], and the book chapter by van Leeuwen [90].

Chapter

15 Memory Management and B-Trees

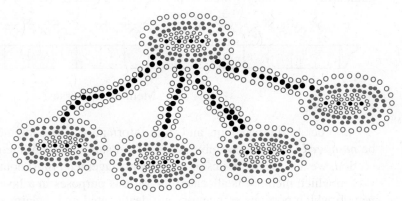

Contents

15.1   Memory Management

Computer memory is organized into a sequence of *words*, each of which typically consists of 4, 8, or 16 bytes (depending on the computer). These memory words are numbered from 0 to $N - 1$, where N is the number of memory words available to the computer. The number associated with each memory word is known as its *memory address*. Thus, the memory in a computer can be viewed as basically one giant array of memory words, as portrayed in Figure 15.1.

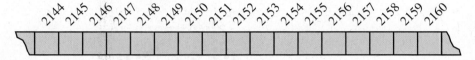

Figure 15.1: Memory addresses.

In order to run programs and store information, the computer's memory must be *managed* so as to determine what data is stored in what memory cells. In this section, we discuss the basics of memory management, most notably describing the way in which memory is allocated for various purposes in a Java program, and the way in which portions of memory are deallocated and reclaimed, when no longer needed.

15.1.1   Stacks in the Java Virtual Machine

A Java program is typically compiled into a sequence of byte codes that serve as "machine" instructions for a well-defined model—the *Java Virtual Machine* (*JVM*). The definition of the JVM is at the heart of the definition of the Java language itself. By compiling Java code into the JVM byte codes, rather than the machine language of a specific CPU, a Java program can be run on any computer that has a program that can emulate the JVM.

Stacks have an important application to the runtime environment of Java programs. A running Java program (more precisely, a running Java thread) has a private stack, called the *Java method stack* or just *Java stack* for short, which is used to keep track of local variables and other important information on methods as they are invoked during execution. (See Figure 15.2.)

More specifically, during the execution of a Java program, the Java Virtual Machine (JVM) maintains a stack whose elements are descriptors of the currently active (that is, nonterminated) invocations of methods. These descriptors are called *frames*. A frame for some invocation of method "fool" stores the current values of the local variables and parameters of method fool, as well as information on method "cool" that called fool and on what needs to be returned to method "cool".

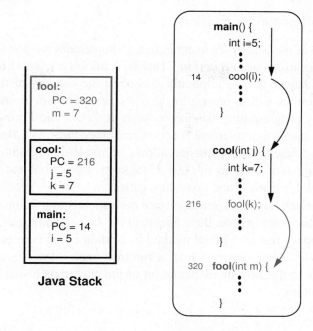

Figure 15.2: An example of a Java method stack: method fool has just been called by method cool, which itself was previously called by method main. Note the values of the program counter, parameters, and local variables stored in the stack frames. When the invocation of method fool terminates, the invocation of method cool will resume its execution at instruction 217, which is obtained by incrementing the value of the program counter stored in the stack frame.

Keeping Track of the Program Counter

The JVM keeps a special variable, called the ***program counter***, to maintain the address of the statement the JVM is currently executing in the program. When a method "cool" invokes another method "fool", the current value of the program counter is recorded in the frame of the current invocation of cool (so the JVM will know where to return to when method fool is done). At the top of the Java stack is the frame of the ***running method***, that is, the method that currently has control of the execution. The remaining elements of the stack are frames of the ***suspended methods***, that is, methods that have invoked another method and are currently waiting for it to return control to them upon its termination. The order of the elements in the stack corresponds to the chain of invocations of the currently active methods. When a new method is invoked, a frame for this method is pushed onto the stack. When it terminates, its frame is popped from the stack and the JVM resumes the processing of the previously suspended method.

Implementing Recursion

One of the benefits of using a stack to implement method invocation is that it allows programs to use *recursion*. That is, it allows a method to call itself, as discussed in Chapter 5. We implicitly described the concept of the call stack and the use of frames within our portrayal of *recursion traces* in that chapter. Interestingly, early programming languages, such as Cobol and Fortran, did not originally use call stacks to implement function and procedure calls. But because of the elegance and efficiency that recursion allows, all modern programming languages, including the modern versions of classic languages like Cobol and Fortran, utilize a runtime stack for method and procedure calls.

Each box of a recursion trace corresponds to a frame of the Java method stack. At any point in time, the contents of the Java method stack corresponds to the chain of boxes from the initial method invocation to the current one.

To better illustrate how a runtime stack allows recursive methods, we refer back to the Java implementation of the classic recursive definition of the factorial function,

$$n! = n(n-1)(n-2)\cdots 1,$$

with the code originally given in Code Fragment 5.1, and the recursion trace in Figure 5.1. The first time we call method factorial(n), its stack frame includes a local variable storing the value n. The method recursively calls itself to compute $(n-1)!$, which pushes a new frame on the Java runtime stack. In turn, this recursive invocation calls itself to compute $(n-2)!$, etc. The chain of recursive invocations, and thus the runtime stack, only grows up to size $n+1$, with the most deeply nested call being factorial(0), which returns 1 without any further recursion. The runtime stack allows several invocations of the factorial method to exist simultaneously. Each has a frame that stores the value of its parameter n as well as the value to be returned. When the first recursive call eventually terminates, it returns $(n-1)!$, which is then multiplied by n to compute $n!$ for the original call of the factorial method.

The Operand Stack

Interestingly, there is actually another place where the JVM uses a stack. Arithmetic expressions, such as $((a+b)*(c+d))/e$, are evaluated by the JVM using an *operand stack*. A simple binary operation, such as $a+b$, is computed by pushing a on the stack, pushing b on the stack, and then calling an instruction that pops the top two items from the stack, performs the binary operation on them, and pushes the result back onto the stack. Likewise, instructions for writing and reading elements to and from memory involve the use of pop and push methods for the operand stack. Thus, the JVM uses a stack to evaluate arithmetic expressions in Java.

15.1.2   Allocating Space in the Memory Heap

We have already discussed (in Section 15.1.1) how the Java Virtual Machine allocates a method's local variables in that method's frame on the Java runtime stack. The Java stack is not the only kind of memory available for program data in Java, however.

Dynamic Memory Allocation

Memory for an object can also be allocated dynamically during a method's execution, by having that method utilize the special **new** operator built into Java. For example, the following Java statement creates an array of integers whose size is given by the value of variable k:

   int[ ] items = **new** int[k];

The size of the array above is known only at runtime. Moreover, the array may continue to exist even after the method that created it terminates. Thus, the memory for this array cannot be allocated on the Java stack.

The Memory Heap

Instead of using the Java stack for this object's memory, Java uses memory from another area of storage—the ***memory heap*** (which should not be confused with the "heap" data structure presented in Chapter 9). We illustrate this memory area, together with the other memory areas, in a Java Virtual Machine in Figure 15.3. The storage available in the memory heap is divided into ***blocks***, which are contiguous array-like "chunks" of memory that may be of variable or fixed sizes.

   To simplify the discussion, let us assume that blocks in the memory heap are of a fixed size, say, 1,024 bytes, and that one block is big enough for any object we might want to create. (Efficiently handling the more general case is actually an interesting research problem.)

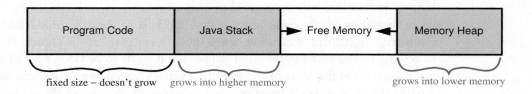

Figure 15.3: A schematic view of the layout of memory addresses in the Java Virtual Machine.

Memory Allocation Algorithms

The Java Virtual Machine definition requires that the memory heap be able to quickly allocate memory for new objects, but it does not specify the algorithm that should be used to do this. One popular method is to keep contiguous "holes" of available free memory in a linked list, called the *free list*. The links joining these holes are stored inside the holes themselves, since their memory is not being used. As memory is allocated and deallocated, the collection of holes in the free lists changes, with the unused memory being separated into disjoint holes divided by blocks of used memory. This separation of unused memory into separate holes is known as *fragmentation*. The problem is that it becomes more difficult to find large continuous chunks of memory, when needed, even though an equivalent amount of memory may be unused (yet fragmented).

Two kinds of fragmentation can occur. *Internal fragmentation* occurs when a portion of an allocated memory block is unused. For example, a program may request an array of size 1000, but only use the first 100 cells of this array. A runtime environment can not do much to reduce internal fragmentation. *External fragmentation*, on the other hand, occurs when there is a significant amount of unused memory between several contiguous blocks of allocated memory. Since the runtime environment has control over where to allocate memory when it is requested (for example, when the **new** keyword is used in Java), the runtime environment should allocate memory in a way to try to reduce external fragmentation.

Several heuristics have been suggested for allocating memory from the heap so as to minimize external fragmentation. The *best-fit algorithm* searches the entire free list to find the hole whose size is closest to the amount of memory being requested. The *first-fit algorithm* searches from the beginning of the free list for the first hole that is large enough. The *next-fit algorithm* is similar, in that it also searches the free list for the first hole that is large enough, but it begins its search from where it left off previously, viewing the free list as a circularly linked list (Section 3.3). The *worst-fit algorithm* searches the free list to find the largest hole of available memory, which might be done faster than a search of the entire free list if this list were maintained as a priority queue (Chapter 9). In each algorithm, the requested amount of memory is subtracted from the chosen memory hole and the leftover part of that hole is returned to the free list.

Although it might sound good at first, the best-fit algorithm tends to produce the worst external fragmentation, since the leftover parts of the chosen holes tend to be small. The first-fit algorithm is fast, but it tends to produce a lot of external fragmentation at the front of the free list, which slows down future searches. The next-fit algorithm spreads fragmentation more evenly throughout the memory heap, thus keeping search times low. This spreading also makes it more difficult to allocate large blocks, however. The worst-fit algorithm attempts to avoid this problem by keeping contiguous sections of free memory as large as possible.

15.1.3   Garbage Collection

In some languages, like C and C++, the memory space for objects must be explicitly deallocated by the programmer, which is a duty often overlooked by beginning programmers and is the source of frustrating programming errors even for experienced programmers. The designers of Java instead placed the burden of memory management entirely on the runtime environment.

As mentioned above, memory for objects is allocated from the memory heap and the space for the instance variables of a running Java program are placed in its method stacks, one for each running thread (for the simple programs discussed in this book there is typically just one running thread). Since instance variables in a method stack can refer to objects in the memory heap, all the variables and objects in the method stacks of running threads are called ***root objects***. All those objects that can be reached by following object references that start from a root object are called ***live objects***. The live objects are the active objects currently being used by the running program; these objects should ***not*** be deallocated. For example, a running Java program may store, in a variable, a reference to a sequence S that is implemented using a doubly linked list. The reference variable to S is a root object, while the object for S is a live object, as are all the node objects that are referenced from this object and all the elements that are referenced from these node objects.

From time to time, the Java virtual machine (JVM) may notice that available space in the memory heap is becoming scarce. At such times, the JVM can elect to reclaim the space that is being used for objects that are no longer live, and return the reclaimed memory to the free list. This reclamation process is known as ***garbage collection***. There are several different algorithms for garbage collection, but one of the most used is the ***mark-sweep algorithm***.

The Mark-Sweep Algorithm

In the mark-sweep garbage collection algorithm, we associate a "mark" bit with each object that identifies whether that object is live. When we determine at some point that garbage collection is needed, we suspend all other activity and clear the mark bits of all the objects currently allocated in the memory heap. We then trace through the Java stacks of the currently running threads and we mark all the root objects in these stacks as "live." We must then determine all the other live objects— the ones that are reachable from the root objects.

To do this efficiently, we can perform a depth-first search (see Section 14.3.1) on the directed graph that is defined by objects referencing other objects. In this case, each object in the memory heap is viewed as a vertex in a directed graph, and the reference from one object to another is viewed as a directed edge. By performing a directed DFS from each root object, we can correctly identify and mark each live object. This process is known as the "mark" phase.

Once this process has completed, we then scan through the memory heap and reclaim any space that is being used for an object that has not been marked. At this time, we can also optionally coalesce all the allocated space in the memory heap into a single block, thereby eliminating external fragmentation for the time being. This scanning and reclamation process is known as the "sweep" phase, and when it completes, we resume running the suspended program. Thus, the mark-sweep garbage collection algorithm will reclaim unused space in time proportional to the number of live objects and their references plus the size of the memory heap.

Performing DFS In-Place

The mark-sweep algorithm correctly reclaims unused space in the memory heap, but there is an important issue we must face during the mark phase. Since we are reclaiming memory space at a time when available memory is scarce, we must take care not to use extra space during the garbage collection itself. The trouble is that the DFS algorithm, in the recursive way we have described it in Section 14.3.1, can use space proportional to the number of vertices in the graph. In the case of garbage collection, the vertices in our graph are the objects in the memory heap; hence, we probably don't have this much memory to use. So our only alternative is to find a way to perform DFS in-place rather than recursively.

The main idea for performing DFS in-place is to simulate the recursion stack using the edges of the graph (which in the case of garbage collection correspond to object references). When we traverse an edge from a visited vertex v to a new vertex w, we change the edge (v, w) stored in v's adjacency list to point back to v's parent in the DFS tree. When we return back to v (simulating the return from the "recursive" call at w), we can now switch the edge we modified to point back to w. Of course, we need to have some way of identifying which edge we need to change back. One possibility is to number the references going out of v as 1, 2, and so on, and store, in addition to the mark bit (which we are using for the "visited" tag in our DFS), a count identifier that tells us which edges we have modified.

Using a count identifier requires an extra word of storage per object. This extra word can be avoided in some implementations, however. For example, many implementations of the Java virtual machine represent an object as a composition of a reference with a type identifier (which indicates if this object is an Integer or some other type) and as a reference to the other objects or data fields for this object. Since the type reference is always supposed to be the first element of the composition in such implementations, we can use this reference to "mark" the edge we changed when leaving an object v and going to some object w. We simply swap the reference at v that refers to the type of v with the reference at v that refers to w. When we return to v, we can quickly identify the edge (v, w) we changed, because it will be the first reference in the composition for v, and the position of the reference to v's type will tell us the place where this edge belongs in v's adjacency list.

15.2 Memory Hierarchies and Caching

With the increased use of computing in society, software applications must manage extremely large data sets. Such applications include the processing of online financial transactions, the organization and maintenance of databases, and analyses of customers' purchasing histories and preferences. The amount of data can be so large that the overall performance of algorithms and data structures sometimes depends more on the time to access the data than on the speed of the CPU.

15.2.1 Memory Systems

In order to accommodate large data sets, computers have a ***hierarchy*** of different kinds of memories, which vary in terms of their size and distance from the CPU. Closest to the CPU are the internal registers that the CPU itself uses. Access to such locations is very fast, but there are relatively few such locations. At the second level in the hierarchy are one or more memory ***caches***. This memory is considerably larger than the register set of a CPU, but accessing it takes longer. At the third level in the hierarchy is the ***internal memory***, which is also known as ***main memory*** or ***core memory***. The internal memory is considerably larger than the cache memory, but also requires more time to access. Another level in the hierarchy is the ***external memory***, which usually consists of disks, CD drives, DVD drives, and/or tapes. This memory is very large, but it is also very slow. Data stored through an external network can be viewed as yet another level in this hierarchy, with even greater storage capacity, but even slower access. Thus, the memory hierarchy for computers can be viewed as consisting of five or more levels, each of which is larger and slower than the previous level. (See Figure 15.4.) During the execution of a program, data is routinely copied from one level of the hierarchy to a neighboring level, and these transfers can become a computational bottleneck.

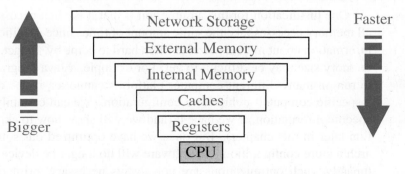

Figure 15.4: The memory hierarchy.

15.2.2   Caching Strategies

The significance of the memory hierarchy on the performance of a program depends greatly upon the size of the problem we are trying to solve and the physical characteristics of the computer system. Often, the bottleneck occurs between two levels of the memory hierarchy—the one that can hold all data items and the level just below that one. For a problem that can fit entirely in main memory, the two most important levels are the cache memory and the internal memory. Access times for internal memory can be as much as 10 to 100 times longer than those for cache memory. It is desirable, therefore, to be able to perform most memory accesses in cache memory. For a problem that does not fit entirely in main memory, on the other hand, the two most important levels are the internal memory and the external memory. Here the differences are even more dramatic, for access times for disks, the usual general-purpose external-memory device, are typically as much as $100,000$ to $1,000,000$ times longer than those for internal memory.

To put this latter figure into perspective, imagine there is a student in Baltimore who wants to send a request-for-money message to his parents in Chicago. If the student sends his parents an email message, it can arrive at their home computer in about five seconds. Think of this mode of communication as corresponding to an internal-memory access by a CPU. A mode of communication corresponding to an external-memory access that is $500,000$ times slower would be for the student to walk to Chicago and deliver his message in person, which would take about a month if he can average 20 miles per day. Thus, we should make as few accesses to external memory as possible.

Most algorithms are not designed with the memory hierarchy in mind, in spite of the great variance between access times for the different levels. Indeed, all of the algorithm analyses thus far described in this book have assumed that all memory accesses are equal. This assumption might seem, at first, to be a great oversight—and one we are only addressing now in the final chapter—but there are good reasons why it is actually a reasonable assumption to make.

One justification for this assumption is that it is often necessary to assume that all memory accesses take the same amount of time, since specific device-dependent information about memory sizes is often hard to come by. In fact, information about memory size may be difficult to get. For example, a Java program that is designed to run on many different computer platforms cannot easily be defined in terms of a specific computer architecture configuration. We can certainly use architecture-specific information, if we have it (and we will show how to exploit such information later in this chapter). But once we have optimized our software for a certain architecture configuration, our software will no longer be device-independent. Fortunately, such optimizations are not always necessary, primarily because of the second justification for the equal-time memory-access assumption.

Caching and Blocking

Another justification for the memory-access equality assumption is that operating system designers have developed general mechanisms that allow most memory accesses to be fast. These mechanisms are based on two important *locality-of-reference* properties that most software possesses:

- **Temporal locality**: If a program accesses a certain memory location, then there is increased likelihood that it accesses that same location again in the near future. For example, it is common to use the value of a counter variable in several different expressions, including one to increment the counter's value. In fact, a common adage among computer architects is that a program spends 90% of its time in 10% of its code.

- **Spatial locality**: If a program accesses a certain memory location, then there is increased likelihood that it soon accesses other locations that are near this one. For example, a program using an array may be likely to access the locations of this array in a sequential or near-sequential manner.

Computer scientists and engineers have performed extensive software profiling experiments to justify the claim that most software possesses both of these kinds of locality of reference. For example, a nested for loop used to repeatedly scan through an array will exhibit both kinds of locality.

Temporal and spatial localities have, in turn, given rise to two fundamental design choices for multilevel computer memory systems (which are present in the interface between cache memory and internal memory, and also in the interface between internal memory and external memory).

The first design choice is called *virtual memory*. This concept consists of providing an address space as large as the capacity of the secondary-level memory, and of transferring data located in the secondary level into the primary level, when they are addressed. Virtual memory does not limit the programmer to the constraint of the internal memory size. The concept of bringing data into primary memory is called *caching*, and it is motivated by temporal locality. By bringing data into primary memory, we are hoping that it will be accessed again soon, and we will be able to respond quickly to all the requests for this data that come in the near future.

The second design choice is motivated by spatial locality. Specifically, if data stored at a secondary-level memory location ℓ is accessed, then we bring into primary-level memory a large block of contiguous locations that include the location ℓ. (See Figure 15.5.) This concept is known as *blocking*, and it is motivated by the expectation that other secondary-level memory locations close to ℓ will soon be accessed. In the interface between cache memory and internal memory, such blocks are often called *cache lines*, and in the interface between internal memory and external memory, such blocks are often called *pages*.

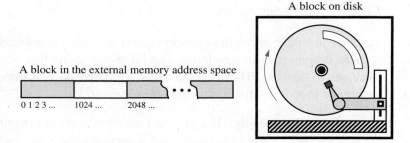

Figure 15.5: Blocks in external memory.

When implemented with caching and blocking, virtual memory often allows us to perceive secondary-level memory as being faster than it really is. There is still a problem, however. Primary-level memory is much smaller than secondary-level memory. Moreover, because memory systems use blocking, any program of substance will likely reach a point where it requests data from secondary-level memory, but the primary memory is already full of blocks. In order to fulfill the request and maintain our use of caching and blocking, we must remove some block from primary memory to make room for a new block from secondary memory in this case. Deciding which block to evict brings up a number of interesting data structure and algorithm design issues.

Caching in Web Browsers

For motivation, we will consider a related problem that arises when revisiting information presented in Web pages. To exploit temporal locality of reference, it is often advantageous to store copies of Web pages in a *cache* memory, so these pages can be quickly retrieved when requested again. This effectively creates a two-level memory hierarchy, with the cache serving as the smaller, quicker internal memory, and the network being the external memory. In particular, suppose we have a cache memory that has m "slots" that can contain Web pages. We assume that a Web page can be placed in any slot of the cache. This is known as a *fully associative* cache.

As a browser executes, it requests different Web pages. Each time the browser requests such a Web page p, the browser determines (using a quick test) if p is unchanged and currently contained in the cache. If p is contained in the cache, then the browser satisfies the request using the cached copy. If p is not in the cache, however, the page for p is requested over the Internet and transferred into the cache. If one of the m slots in the cache is available, then the browser assigns p to one of the empty slots. But if all the m cells of the cache are occupied, then the computer must determine which previously viewed Web page to evict before bringing in p to take its place. There are, of course, many different policies that can be used to determine the page to evict.

Page Replacement Algorithms

Some of the better-known page replacement policies include the following (see Figure 15.6):

- **First-in, first-out (FIFO)**: Evict the page that has been in the cache the longest, that is, the page that was transferred to the cache furthest in the past.

- **Least recently used (LRU)**: Evict the page whose last request occurred furthest in the past.

In addition, we can consider a simple and purely random strategy:

- **Random**: Choose a page at random to evict from the cache.

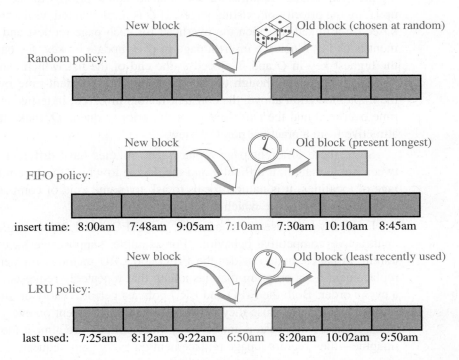

Figure 15.6: The Random, FIFO, and LRU page replacement policies.

The Random strategy is one of the easiest policies to implement, for it only requires a random or pseudorandom number generator. The overhead involved in implementing this policy is an $O(1)$ additional amount of work per page replacement. Moreover, there is no additional overhead for each page request, other than to determine whether a page request is in the cache or not. Still, this policy makes no attempt to take advantage of any temporal locality exhibited by a user's browsing.

The FIFO strategy is quite simple to implement, as it only requires a queue Q to store references to the pages in the cache. Pages are enqueued in Q when they are referenced by a browser, and then are brought into the cache. When a page needs to be evicted, the computer simply performs a dequeue operation on Q to determine which page to evict. Thus, this policy also requires $O(1)$ additional work per page replacement. Also, the FIFO policy incurs no additional overhead for page requests. Moreover, it tries to take some advantage of temporal locality.

The LRU strategy goes a step further than the FIFO strategy, for the LRU strategy explicitly takes advantage of temporal locality as much as possible, by always evicting the page that was least-recently used. From a policy point of view, this is an excellent approach, but it is costly from an implementation point of view. That is, its way of optimizing temporal and spatial locality is fairly costly. Implementing the LRU strategy requires the use of an adaptable priority queue Q that supports updating the priority of existing pages. If Q is implemented with a sorted sequence based on a linked list, then the overhead for each page request and page replacement is $O(1)$. When we insert a page in Q or update its key, the page is assigned the highest key in Q and is placed at the end of the list, which can also be done in $O(1)$ time. Even though the LRU strategy has constant-time overhead, using the implementation above, the constant factors involved, in terms of the additional time overhead and the extra space for the priority queue Q, make this policy less attractive from a practical point of view.

Since these different page replacement policies have different trade-offs between implementation difficulty and the degree to which they seem to take advantage of localities, it is natural for us to ask for some kind of comparative analysis of these methods to see which one, if any, is the best.

From a worst-case point of view, the FIFO and LRU strategies have fairly unattractive competitive behavior. For example, suppose we have a cache containing m pages, and consider the FIFO and LRU methods for performing page replacement for a program that has a loop that repeatedly requests $m + 1$ pages in a cyclic order. Both the FIFO and LRU policies perform badly on such a sequence of page requests, because they perform a page replacement on every page request. Thus, from a worst-case point of view, these policies are almost the worst we can imagine—they require a page replacement on every page request.

This worst-case analysis is a little too pessimistic, however, for it focuses on each protocol's behavior for one bad sequence of page requests. An ideal analysis would be to compare these methods over all possible page-request sequences. Of course, this is impossible to do exhaustively, but there have been a great number of experimental simulations done on page-request sequences derived from real programs. Based on these experimental comparisons, the LRU strategy has been shown to be usually superior to the FIFO strategy, which is usually better than the Random strategy.

15.3 External Searching and B-Trees

Consider the problem of maintaining a large collection of items that does not fit in main memory, such as a typical database. In this context, we refer to the secondary-memory blocks as *disk blocks*. Likewise, we refer to the transfer of a block between secondary memory and primary memory as a *disk transfer*. Recalling the great time difference that exists between main memory accesses and disk accesses, the main goal of maintaining such a collection in external memory is to minimize the number of disk transfers needed to perform a query or update. We refer to this count as the *I/O complexity* of the algorithm involved.

Some Inefficient External-Memory Representations

A typical operation we would like to support is the search for a key in a map. If we were to store n items unordered in a doubly linked list, searching for a particular key within the list requires n transfers in the worst case, since each link hop we perform on the linked list might access a different block of memory.

We can reduce the number of block transfers by storing the sequence in an array. A sequential search of an array can be performed using only $O(n/B)$ block transfers because of spatial locality of reference, where B denotes the number of elements that fit into a block. This is because the block transfer when accessing the first element of the array actually retrieves the first B elements, and so on with each successive block. It is worth noting that the bound of $O(n/B)$ transfers is only achieved when using an array of primitives in Java. For an array of objects, the array stores the sequence of references; the actual objects that are referenced are not necessarily stored near each other in memory, and so there may be n distinct block transfers in the worst case.

If a sequence is stored in *sorted* order within an array, a binary search performs $O(\log_2 n)$ transfers, which is a nice improvement. But we do not get significant benefit from block transfers because each query during a binary search is likely in a different block of the sequence. As usual, update operations are expensive for a sorted array.

Since these simple implementations are I/O inefficient, we should consider the logarithmic-time internal-memory strategies that use balanced binary trees (for example, AVL trees or red-black trees) or other search structures with logarithmic average-case query and update times (for example, skip lists or splay trees). Typically, each node accessed for a query or update in one of these structures will be in a different block. Thus, these methods all require $O(\log_2 n)$ transfers in the worst case to perform a query or update operation. But we can do better! We can perform map queries and updates using only $O(\log_B n) = O(\log n / \log B)$ transfers.

15.3.1 (a,b) Trees

To reduce the number of external-memory accesses when searching, we can represent our map using a multiway search tree (Section 11.5.1). This approach gives rise to a generalization of the $(2,4)$ tree data structure known as the (a,b) tree.

An (a,b) tree is a multiway search tree such that each node has between a and b children and stores between $a-1$ and $b-1$ entries. The algorithms for searching, inserting, and removing entries in an (a,b) tree are straightforward generalizations of the corresponding ones for $(2,4)$ trees. The advantage of generalizing $(2,4)$ trees to (a,b) trees is that a parameterized class of trees provides a flexible search structure, where the size of the nodes and the running time of the various map operations depends on the parameters a and b. By setting the parameters a and b appropriately with respect to the size of disk blocks, we can derive a data structure that achieves good external-memory performance.

Definition of an (a,b) Tree

An (a,b) *tree*, where parameters a and b are integers such that $2 \le a \le (b+1)/2$, is a multiway search tree T with the following additional restrictions:

***Size Property*:** Each internal node has at least a children, unless it is the root, and has at most b children.

***Depth Property*:** All the external nodes have the same depth.

Proposition 15.1: *The height of an (a,b) tree storing n entries is $\Omega(\log n / \log b)$ and $O(\log n / \log a)$.*

Justification: Let T be an (a,b) tree storing n entries, and let h be the height of T. We justify the proposition by establishing the following bounds on h:

$$\frac{1}{\log b} \log(n+1) \le h \le \frac{1}{\log a} \log \frac{n+1}{2} + 1.$$

By the size and depth properties, the number n'' of external nodes of T is at least $2a^{h-1}$ and at most b^h. By Proposition 11.6, $n'' = n+1$. Thus,

$$2a^{h-1} \le n+1 \le b^h.$$

Taking the logarithm in base 2 of each term, we get

$$(h-1)\log a + 1 \le \log(n+1) \le h \log b.$$

An algebraic manipulation of these inequalities completes the justification. ∎

Search and Update Operations

We recall that in a multiway search tree T, each node w of T holds a secondary structure $M(w)$, which is itself a map (Section 11.5.1). If T is an (a,b) tree, then $M(w)$ stores at most b entries. Let $f(b)$ denote the time for performing a search in a map, $M(w)$. The search algorithm in an (a,b) tree is exactly like the one for multiway search trees given in Section 11.5.1. Hence, searching in an (a,b) tree T with n entries takes $O(\frac{f(b)}{\log a} \log n)$ time. Note that if b is considered a constant (and thus a is also), then the search time is $O(\log n)$.

The main application of (a,b) trees is for maps stored in external memory. Namely, to minimize disk accesses, we select the parameters a and b so that each tree node occupies a single disk block (so that $f(b) = 1$ if we wish to simply count block transfers). Providing the right a and b values in this context gives rise to a data structure known as the B-tree, which we will describe shortly. Before we describe this structure, however, let us discuss how insertions and removals are handled in (a,b) trees.

The insertion algorithm for an (a,b) tree is similar to that for a $(2,4)$ tree. An overflow occurs when an entry is inserted into a b-node v, which becomes an illegal $(b+1)$-node. (Recall that a node in a multiway tree is a d-node if it has d children.) To remedy an overflow, we split node w by moving the median entry of w into the parent of w and replacing w with a $\lceil (b+1)/2 \rceil$-node w' and a $\lfloor (b+1)/2 \rfloor$-node w''. We can now see the reason for requiring $a \leq (b+1)/2$ in the definition of an (a,b) tree. Note that as a consequence of the split, we need to build the secondary structures $M(w')$ and $M(w'')$.

Removing an entry from an (a,b) tree is similar to what was done for $(2,4)$ trees. An underflow occurs when a key is removed from an a-node w, distinct from the root, which causes w to become an illegal $(a-1)$-node. To remedy an underflow, we perform a transfer with a sibling of w that is not an a-node or we perform a fusion of w with a sibling that is an a-node. The new node w' resulting from the fusion is a $(2a-1)$-node, which is another reason for requiring $a \leq (b+1)/2$.

Table 15.1 shows the performance of a map realized with an (a,b) tree.

Method	Running Time
get	$O\left(\frac{f(b)}{\log a} \log n \right)$
put	$O\left(\frac{g(b)}{\log a} \log n \right)$
remove	$O\left(\frac{g(b)}{\log a} \log n \right)$

Table 15.1: Time bounds for an n-entry map realized by an (a,b) tree T. We assume the secondary structure of the nodes of T support search in $f(b)$ time, and split and fusion operations in $g(b)$ time, for some functions $f(b)$ and $g(b)$, which can be made to be $O(1)$ when we are only counting disk transfers.

15.3.2   B-Trees

A version of the (a,b) tree data structure, which is the best-known method for maintaining a map in external memory, is called the "B-tree." (See Figure 15.7.) A **B-tree of order** d is an (a,b) tree with $a = \lceil d/2 \rceil$ and $b = d$. Since we discussed the standard map query and update methods for (a,b) trees above, we restrict our discussion here to the I/O complexity of B-trees.

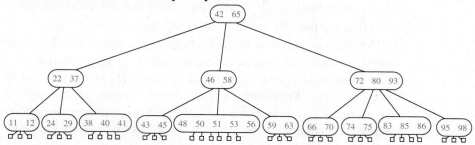

Figure 15.7: A B-tree of order 6.

An important property of B-trees is that we can choose d so that the d children references and the $d-1$ keys stored at a node can fit compactly into a single disk block, implying that d is proportional to B. This choice allows us to assume that a and b are also proportional to B in the analysis of the search and update operations on (a,b) trees. Thus, $f(b)$ and $g(b)$ are both $O(1)$, for each time we access a node to perform a search or an update operation, we need only perform a single disk transfer.

As we have already observed above, each search or update requires that we examine at most $O(1)$ nodes for each level of the tree. Therefore, any map search or update operation on a B-tree requires only $O(\log_{\lceil d/2 \rceil} n)$, that is, $O(\log n / \log B)$, disk transfers. For example, an insert operation proceeds down the B-tree to locate the node in which to insert the new entry. If the node would **overflow** (to have $d+1$ children) because of this addition, then this node is **split** into two nodes that have $\lfloor (d+1)/2 \rfloor$ and $\lceil (d+1)/2 \rceil$ children, respectively. This process is then repeated at the next level up, and will continue for at most $O(\log_B n)$ levels.

Likewise, if a remove operation results in a node **underflow** (to have $\lceil d/2 \rceil - 1$ children), then we move references from a sibling node with at least $\lceil d/2 \rceil + 1$ children or we perform a **fusion** operation of this node with its sibling (and repeat this computation at the parent). As with the insert operation, this will continue up the B-tree for at most $O(\log_B n)$ levels. The requirement that each internal node have at least $\lceil d/2 \rceil$ children implies that each disk block used to support a B-tree is at least half full. Thus, we have the following:

Proposition 15.2: *A B-tree with n entries has I/O complexity $O(\log_B n)$ for search or update operation, and uses $O(n/B)$ blocks, where B is the size of a block.*

15.4   External-Memory Sorting

In addition to data structures, such as maps, that need to be implemented in external memory, there are many algorithms that must also operate on input sets that are too large to fit entirely into internal memory. In this case, the objective is to solve the algorithmic problem using as few block transfers as possible. The most classic domain for such external-memory algorithms is the sorting problem.

Multiway Merge-Sort

An efficient way to sort a set S of n objects in external memory amounts to a simple external-memory variation on the familiar merge-sort algorithm. The main idea behind this variation is to merge many recursively sorted lists at a time, thereby reducing the number of levels of recursion. Specifically, a high-level description of this ***multiway merge-sort*** method is to divide S into d subsets $S_1, S_2, \ldots, S_d$ of roughly equal size, recursively sort each subset S_i, and then simultaneously merge all d sorted lists into a sorted representation of S. If we can perform the merge process using only $O(n/B)$ disk transfers, then, for large enough values of n, the total number of transfers performed by this algorithm satisfies the following recurrence equation:

$$t(n) = d \cdot t(n/d) + cn/B,$$

for some constant $c \geq 1$. We can stop the recursion when $n \leq B$, since we can perform a single block transfer at this point, getting all of the objects into internal memory, and then sort the set with an efficient internal-memory algorithm. Thus, the stopping criterion for $t(n)$ is

$$t(n) = 1 \quad \text{if } n/B \leq 1.$$

This implies a closed-form solution that $t(n)$ is $O((n/B)\log_d(n/B))$, which is

$$O((n/B)\log(n/B)/\log d).$$

Thus, if we can choose d to be $\Theta(M/B)$, where M is the size of the internal memory, then the worst-case number of block transfers performed by this multiway merge-sort algorithm will be quite low. For reasons given in the next section, we choose

$$d = (M/B) - 1.$$

The only aspect of this algorithm left to specify, then, is how to perform the d-way merge using only $O(n/B)$ block transfers.

15.4.1 Multiway Merging

In a standard merge-sort (Section 12.1), the merge process combines two sorted sequences into one by repeatedly taking the smaller of the items at the front of the two respective lists. In a d-way merge, we repeatedly find the smallest among the items at the front of the d sequences and place it as the next element of the merged sequence. We continue until all elements are included.

In the context of an external-memory sorting algorithm, if main memory has size M and each block has size B, we can store up to M/B blocks within main memory at any given time. We specifically choose $d = (M/B) - 1$ so that we can afford to keep one block from each input sequence in main memory at any given time, and to have one additional block to use as a buffer for the merged sequence. (See Figure 15.8.)

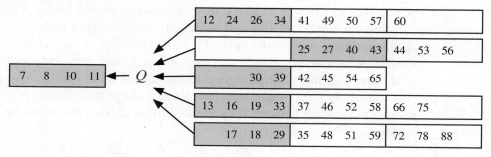

Figure 15.8: A d-way merge with $d = 5$ and $B = 4$. Blocks that currently reside in main memory are shaded.

We maintain the smallest unprocessed element from each input sequence in main memory, requesting the next block from a sequence when the preceding block has been exhausted. Similarly, we use one block of internal memory to buffer the merged sequence, flushing that block to external memory when full. In this way, the total number of transfers performed during a single d-way merge is $O(n/B)$, since we scan each block of list S_i once, and we write out each block of the merged list S' once. In terms of computation time, choosing the smallest of d values can trivially be performed using $O(d)$ operations. If we are willing to devote $O(d)$ internal memory, we can maintain a priority queue identifying the smallest element from each sequence, thereby performing each step of the merge in $O(\log d)$ time by removing the minimum element and replacing it with the next element from the same sequence. Hence, the internal time for the d-way merge is $O(n \log d)$.

Proposition 15.3: *Given an array-based sequence S of n elements stored in external memory, we can sort S with $O((n/B) \log(n/B) / \log(M/B))$ block transfers and $O(n \log n)$ internal computations, where M is the size of the internal memory and B is the size of a block.*

15.5 Exercises

Reinforcement

R-15.1 Julia just bought a new computer that uses 64-bit integers to address memory cells. Argue why Julia will never in her life be able to upgrade the main memory of her computer so that it is the maximum-size possible, assuming that you have to have distinct atoms to represent different bits.

R-15.2 Consider an initially empty memory cache consisting of four pages. How many page misses does the LRU algorithm incur on the following page request sequence: $(2,3,4,1,2,5,1,3,5,4,1,2,3)$?

R-15.3 Consider an initially empty memory cache consisting of four pages. How many page misses does the FIFO algorithm incur on the following page request sequence: $(2,3,4,1,2,5,1,3,5,4,1,2,3)$?

R-15.4 Consider an initially empty memory cache consisting of four pages. What is the maximum number of page misses that the random algorithm incurs on the following page request sequence: $(2,3,4,1,2,5,1,3,5,4,1,2,3)$? Show all of the random choices the algorithm made in this case.

R-15.5 Describe, in detail, algorithms for adding an item to, or deleting an item from, an (a,b) tree.

R-15.6 Suppose T is a multiway tree in which each internal node has at least five and at most eight children. For what values of a and b is T a valid (a,b) tree?

R-15.7 For what values of d is the tree T of the previous exercise an order-d B-tree?

R-15.8 Draw the result of inserting, into an initially empty order-7 B-tree, entries with keys $(4,40,23,50,11,34,62,78,66,22,90,59,25,72,64,77,39,12)$, in this order.

Creativity

C-15.9 Describe an efficient external-memory algorithm for removing all the duplicate entries in an array list of size n.

C-15.10 Describe an external-memory data structure to implement the stack ADT so that the total number of disk transfers needed to process a sequence of k push and pop operations is $O(k/B)$.

C-15.11 Describe an external-memory data structure to implement the queue ADT so that the total number of disk transfers needed to process a sequence of k enqueue and dequeue operations is $O(k/B)$.

C-15.12 Describe an external-memory version of the PositionalList ADT (Section 7.3), with block size B, such that an iteration of a list of length n is completed using $O(n/B)$ transfers in the worst case, and all other methods of the ADT require only $O(1)$ transfers.

C-15.13 Change the rules that define red-black trees so that each red-black tree T has a corresponding $(4, 8)$ tree, and vice versa.

C-15.14 Describe a modified version of the B-tree insertion algorithm so that each time we create an overflow because of a split of a node w, we redistribute keys among all of w's siblings, so that each sibling holds roughly the same number of keys (possibly cascading the split up to the parent of w). What is the minimum fraction of each block that will always be filled using this scheme?

C-15.15 Another possible external-memory map implementation is to use a skip list, but to collect consecutive groups of $O(B)$ nodes, in individual blocks, on any level in the skip list. In particular, we define an *order-d B-skip list* to be such a representation of a skip list structure, where each block contains at least $\lceil d/2 \rceil$ list nodes and at most d list nodes. Let us also choose d in this case to be the maximum number of list nodes from a level of a skip list that can fit into one block. Describe how we should modify the skip-list insertion and removal algorithms for a B-skip list so that the expected height of the structure is $O(\log n / \log B)$.

C-15.16 Describe how to use a B-tree to implement the Partition ADT (Section 14.7.3) so that the union and find operations each use at most $O(\log n / \log B)$ disk transfers.

C-15.17 Suppose we are given a sequence S of n elements with integer keys such that some elements in S are colored "blue" and some elements in S are colored "red." In addition, say that a red element e *pairs* with a blue element f if they have the same key value. Describe an efficient external-memory algorithm for finding all the red-blue pairs in S. How many disk transfers does your algorithm perform?

C-15.18 Consider the page caching problem where the memory cache can hold m pages, and we are given a sequence P of n requests taken from a pool of $m + 1$ possible pages. Describe the optimal strategy for the offline algorithm and show that it causes at most $m + n/m$ page misses in total, starting from an empty cache.

C-15.19 Describe an efficient external-memory algorithm that determines whether an array of n integers contains a value occurring more than $n/2$ times.

C-15.20 Consider the page caching strategy based on the *least frequently used* (LFU) rule, where the page in the cache that has been accessed the least often is the one that is evicted when a new page is requested. If there are ties, LFU evicts the least frequently used page that has been in the cache the longest. Show that there is a sequence P of n requests that causes LFU to miss $\Omega(n)$ times for a cache of m pages, whereas the optimal algorithm will miss only $O(m)$ times.

C-15.21 Suppose that instead of having the node-search function $f(d) = 1$ in an order-d B-tree T, we have $f(d) = \log d$. What does the asymptotic running time of performing a search in T now become?

Projects

P-15.22 Write a Java class that simulates the best-fit, worst-fit, first-fit, and next-fit algorithms for memory management. Determine experimentally which method is the best under various sequences of memory requests.

P-15.23 Write a Java class that implements all the methods of the sorted map ADT by means of an (a, b) tree, where a and b are integer constants passed as parameters to a constructor.

P-15.24 Implement the B-tree data structure, assuming a block size of 1024 and integer keys. Test the number of "disk transfers" needed to process a sequence of map operations.

Chapter Notes

The reader interested in the study of the architecture of hierarchical memory systems is referred to the book chapter by Burger et al. [20] or the book by Hennessy and Patterson [44]. The mark-sweep garbage collection method we describe is one of many different algorithms for performing garbage collection. We encourage the reader interested in further study of garbage collection to examine the book by Jones and Lins [52]. Knuth [61] has very nice discussions about external-memory sorting and searching. The handbook by Gonnet and Baeza-Yates [38] compares the performance of a number of different sorting algorithms, many of which are external-memory algorithms. B-trees were invented by Bayer and McCreight [11] and Comer [24] provides a very nice overview of this data structure. The books by Mehlhorn [71] and Samet [81] also have nice discussions about B-trees and their variants. Aggarwal and Vitter [3] study the I/O complexity of sorting and related problems, establishing upper and lower bounds. Goodrich et al. [40] study the I/O complexity of several computational geometry problems. The reader interested in further study of I/O-efficient algorithms is encouraged to examine the survey paper of Vitter [91].

Bibliography

[1] H. Abelson, G. J. Sussman, and J. Sussman, *Structure and Interpretation of Computer Programs*. Cambridge, MA: MIT Press, 2nd ed., 1996.

[2] G. M. Adel'son-Vel'skii and Y. M. Landis, "An algorithm for the organization of information," *Doklady Akademii Nauk SSSR*, vol. 146, pp. 263–266, 1962. English translation in *Soviet Math. Doklady*, vol. 3, pp. 1259–1262.

[3] A. Aggarwal and J. S. Vitter, "The input/output complexity of sorting and related problems," *Commun. ACM*, vol. 31, pp. 1116–1127, 1988.

[4] A. V. Aho, "Algorithms for finding patterns in strings," in *Handbook of Theoretical Computer Science* (J. van Leeuwen, ed.), vol. A. Algorithms and Complexity, pp. 255–300, Amsterdam: Elsevier, 1990.

[5] A. V. Aho, J. E. Hopcroft, and J. D. Ullman, *The Design and Analysis of Computer Algorithms*. Reading, MA: Addison-Wesley, 1974.

[6] A. V. Aho, J. E. Hopcroft, and J. D. Ullman, *Data Structures and Algorithms*. Reading, MA: Addison-Wesley, 1983.

[7] R. K. Ahuja, T. L. Magnanti, and J. B. Orlin, *Network Flows: Theory, Algorithms, and Applications*. Englewood Cliffs, NJ: Prentice Hall, 1993.

[8] K. Arnold, J. Gosling, and D. Holmes, *The Java Programming Language*. The Java Series, Upper Saddle River, NJ: Prentice Hall, 4th ed., 2006.

[9] O. Barůvka, "O jistem problemu minimalnim," *Praca Moravske Prirodovedecke Spolecnosti*, vol. 3, pp. 37–58, 1926. (in Czech).

[10] R. Bayer, "Symmetric binary B-trees: Data structure and maintenance," *Acta Informatica*, vol. 1, no. 4, pp. 290–306, 1972.

[11] R. Bayer and McCreight, "Organization of large ordered indexes," *Acta Inform.*, vol. 1, pp. 173–189, 1972.

[12] R. E. Bellman, *Dynamic Programming*. Princeton, NJ: Princeton University Press, 1957.

[13] J. L. Bentley, "Programming pearls: Writing correct programs," *Communications of the ACM*, vol. 26, pp. 1040–1045, 1983.

[14] J. L. Bentley, "Programming pearls: Thanks, heaps," *Communications of the ACM*, vol. 28, pp. 245–250, 1985.

[15] J. L. Bentley and M. D. McIlroy, "Engineering a sort function," *Software—Practice and Experience*, vol. 23, no. 11, pp. 1249–1265, 1993.

[16] G. Booch, *Object-Oriented Analysis and Design with Applications*. Redwood City, CA: Benjamin/Cummings, 1994.

[17] R. S. Boyer and J. S. Moore, "A fast string searching algorithm," *Communications of the ACM*, vol. 20, no. 10, pp. 762–772, 1977.

[18] G. Brassard, "Crusade for a better notation," *SIGACT News*, vol. 17, no. 1, pp. 60–64, 1985.

[19] T. Budd, *An Introduction to Object-Oriented Programming*. Reading, MA: Addison-Wesley, 1991.

[20] D. Burger, J. R. Goodman, and G. S. Sohi, "Memory systems," in *The Computer Science and Engineering Handbook* (A. B. Tucker, Jr., ed.), ch. 18, pp. 447–461, CRC Press, 1997.

[21] S. Carlsson, "Average case results on heapsort," *BIT*, vol. 27, pp. 2–17, 1987.

[22] K. L. Clarkson, "Linear programming in $O(n3^{d^2})$ time," *Inform. Process. Lett.*, vol. 22, pp. 21–24, 1986.

[23] R. Cole, "Tight bounds on the complexity of the Boyer-Moore pattern matching algorithm," *SIAM J. Comput.*, vol. 23, no. 5, pp. 1075–1091, 1994.

[24] D. Comer, "The ubiquitous B-tree," *ACM Comput. Surv.*, vol. 11, pp. 121–137, 1979.

[25] T. H. Cormen, C. E. Leiserson, R. L. Rivest, and C. Stein, *Introduction to Algorithms*. Cambridge, MA: MIT Press, 3rd ed., 2009.

[26] M. Crochemore and T. Lecroq, "Pattern matching and text compression algorithms," in *The Computer Science and Engineering Handbook* (A. B. Tucker, Jr., ed.), ch. 8, pp. 162–202, CRC Press, 1997.

[27] S. Crosby and D. Wallach, "Denial of service via algorithmic complexity attacks," in *Proc. 12th Usenix Security Symp.*, pp. 29–44, 2003.

[28] S. A. Demurjian, Sr., "Software design," in *The Computer Science and Engineering Handbook* (A. B. Tucker, Jr., ed.), ch. 108, pp. 2323–2351, CRC Press, 1997.

[29] G. Di Battista, P. Eades, R. Tamassia, and I. G. Tollis, *Graph Drawing*. Upper Saddle River, NJ: Prentice Hall, 1999.

[30] E. W. Dijkstra, "A note on two problems in connexion with graphs," *Numerische Mathematik*, vol. 1, pp. 269–271, 1959.

[31] E. W. Dijkstra, "Recursive programming," *Numerische Mathematik*, vol. 2, no. 1, pp. 312–318, 1960.

[32] J. R. Driscoll, H. N. Gabow, R. Shrairaman, and R. E. Tarjan, "Relaxed heaps: An alternative to Fibonacci heaps with applications to parallel computation," *Commun. ACM*, vol. 31, pp. 1343–1354, 1988.

[33] D. Flanagan, *Java in a Nutshell*. O'Reilly, 5th ed., 2005.

[34] R. W. Floyd, "Algorithm 97: Shortest path," *Communications of the ACM*, vol. 5, no. 6, p. 345, 1962.

[35] R. W. Floyd, "Algorithm 245: Treesort 3," *Communications of the ACM*, vol. 7, no. 12, p. 701, 1964.

[36] M. L. Fredman and R. E. Tarjan, "Fibonacci heaps and their uses in improved network optimization algorithms," *J. ACM*, vol. 34, pp. 596–615, 1987.

[37] E. Gamma, R. Helm, R. Johnson, and J. Vlissides, *Design Patterns: Elements of Reusable Object-Oriented Software*. Reading, MA: Addison-Wesley, 1995.

[38] G. H. Gonnet and R. Baeza-Yates, *Handbook of Algorithms and Data Structures*. Addison-Wesley, 1991.

[39] G. H. Gonnet and J. I. Munro, "Heaps on heaps," *SIAM J. Comput.*, vol. 15, no. 4, pp. 964–971, 1986.

[40] M. T. Goodrich, J.-J. Tsay, D. E. Vengroff, and J. S. Vitter, "External-memory computational geometry," in *Proc. 34th Annu. IEEE Sympos. Found. Comput. Sci.*, pp. 714–723, 1993.

[41] R. L. Graham and P. Hell, "On the history of the minimum spanning tree problem," *Annals of the History of Computing*, vol. 7, no. 1, pp. 43–57, 1985.

[42] L. J. Guibas and R. Sedgewick, "A dichromatic framework for balanced trees," in *Proc. 19th Annu. IEEE Sympos. Found. Comput. Sci.*, Lecture Notes Comput. Sci., pp. 8–21, Springer-Verlag, 1978.

[43] Y. Gurevich, "What does $O(n)$ mean?," *SIGACT News*, vol. 17, no. 4, pp. 61–63, 1986.

[44] J. Hennessy and D. Patterson, *Computer Architecture: A Quantitative Approach*. San Francisco: Morgan Kaufmann, 2nd ed., 1996.

[45] C. A. R. Hoare, "Quicksort," *The Computer Journal*, vol. 5, pp. 10–15, 1962.

[46] J. E. Hopcroft and R. E. Tarjan, "Efficient algorithms for graph manipulation," *Communications of the ACM*, vol. 16, no. 6, pp. 372–378, 1973.

[47] C. S. Horstmann and G. Cornell, *Core Java*, vol. I–Fundamentals. Upper Saddle River, NJ: Prentice Hall, 8th ed., 2008.

[48] C. S. Horstmann and G. Cornell, *Core Java*, vol. II–Advanced Features. Upper Saddle River, NJ: Prentice Hall, 8th ed., 2008.

[49] B.-C. Huang and M. Langston, "Practical in-place merging," *Communications of the ACM*, vol. 31, no. 3, pp. 348–352, 1988.

[50] J. JáJá, *An Introduction to Parallel Algorithms*. Reading, MA: Addison-Wesley, 1992.

[51] V. Jarník, "O jistem problemu minimalnim," *Praca Moravske Prirodovedecke Spolecnosti*, vol. 6, pp. 57–63, 1930. (in Czech).

[52] R. Jones and R. Lins, *Garbage Collection: Algorithms for Automatic Dynamic Memory Management*. John Wiley and Sons, 1996.

[53] D. R. Karger, P. Klein, and R. E. Tarjan, "A randomized linear-time algorithm to find minimum spanning trees," *Journal of the ACM*, vol. 42, pp. 321–328, 1995.

[54] R. M. Karp and M. O. Rabin, "Efficient randomized pattern-matching algorithms," *IBM J. Res. Develop.*, vol. 31, no. 2, pp. 249–260, 1987.

[55] R. M. Karp and V. Ramachandran, "Parallel algorithms for shared memory machines," in *Handbook of Theoretical Computer Science* (J. van Leeuwen, ed.), pp. 869–941, Amsterdam: Elsevier/The MIT Press, 1990.

[56] P. Kirschenhofer and H. Prodinger, "The path length of random skip lists," *Acta Informatica*, vol. 31, pp. 775–792, 1994.

[57] J. Kleinberg and É. Tardos, *Algorithm Design*. Reading, MA: Addison-Wesley, 2006.

[58] A. Klink and J. Wälde, "Efficient denial of service attacks on web application platforms." 2011.

[59] D. E. Knuth, "Big omicron and big omega and big theta," in *SIGACT News*, vol. 8, pp. 18–24, 1976.

[60] D. E. Knuth, *Fundamental Algorithms*, vol. 1 of *The Art of Computer Programming*. Reading, MA: Addison-Wesley, 3rd ed., 1997.

[61] D. E. Knuth, *Sorting and Searching*, vol. 3 of *The Art of Computer Programming*. Reading, MA: Addison-Wesley, 2nd ed., 1998.

[62] D. E. Knuth, J. H. Morris, Jr., and V. R. Pratt, "Fast pattern matching in strings," *SIAM J. Comput.*, vol. 6, no. 1, pp. 323–350, 1977.

[63] J. B. Kruskal, Jr., "On the shortest spanning subtree of a graph and the traveling salesman problem," *Proc. Amer. Math. Soc.*, vol. 7, pp. 48–50, 1956.

[64] R. Lesuisse, "Some lessons drawn from the history of the binary search algorithm," *The Computer Journal*, vol. 26, pp. 154–163, 1983.

[65] N. G. Leveson and C. S. Turner, "An investigation of the Therac-25 accidents," *IEEE Computer*, vol. 26, no. 7, pp. 18–41, 1993.

[66] A. Levitin, "Do we teach the right algorithm design techniques?," in *30th ACM SIGCSE Symp. on Computer Science Education*, pp. 179–183, 1999.

[67] B. Liskov and J. Guttag, *Abstraction and Specification in Program Development*. Cambridge, MA/New York: The MIT Press/McGraw-Hill, 1986.

[68] E. M. McCreight, "A space-economical suffix tree construction algorithm," *Journal of Algorithms*, vol. 23, no. 2, pp. 262–272, 1976.

[69] C. J. H. McDiarmid and B. A. Reed, "Building heaps fast," *Journal of Algorithms*, vol. 10, no. 3, pp. 352–365, 1989.

[70] N. Megiddo, "Linear programming in linear time when the dimension is fixed," *J. ACM*, vol. 31, pp. 114–127, 1984.

[71] K. Mehlhorn, *Data Structures and Algorithms 1: Sorting and Searching*, vol. 1 of *EATCS Monographs on Theoretical Computer Science*. Heidelberg, Germany: Springer-Verlag, 1984.

[72] K. Mehlhorn, *Data Structures and Algorithms 2: Graph Algorithms and NP-Completeness*, vol. 2 of *EATCS Monographs on Theoretical Computer Science*. Heidelberg, Germany: Springer-Verlag, 1984.

[73] K. Mehlhorn and A. Tsakalidis, "Data structures," in *Algorithms and Complexity* (J. van Leeuwen, ed.), vol. A of *Handbook of Theoretical Computer Science*, pp. 303–334, Amsterdam: Elsevier, 1990.

[74] D. R. Morrison, "PATRICIA—practical algorithm to retrieve information coded in alphanumeric," *Journal of the ACM*, vol. 15, no. 4, pp. 514–534, 1968.

[75] R. Motwani and P. Raghavan, *Randomized Algorithms*. New York, NY: Cambridge University Press, 1995.

[76] Oracle Corporation, "Collections framework enhancements in Java SE 7." `http://docs.oracle.com/javase/7/docs/technotes/guides/collections/changes7.html`. Accessed online, December 2013.

[77] T. Papadakis, J. I. Munro, and P. V. Poblete, "Average search and update costs in skip lists," *BIT*, vol. 32, pp. 316–332, 1992.

[78] P. V. Poblete, J. I. Munro, and T. Papadakis, "The binomial transform and its application to the analysis of skip lists," in *Proceedings of the European Symposium on Algorithms (ESA)*, pp. 554–569, 1995.

[79] R. C. Prim, "Shortest connection networks and some generalizations," *Bell Syst. Tech. J.*, vol. 36, pp. 1389–1401, 1957.

[80] W. Pugh, "Skip lists: a probabilistic alternative to balanced trees," *Commun. ACM*, vol. 33, no. 6, pp. 668–676, 1990.

[81] H. Samet, *The Design and Analysis of Spatial Data Structures*. Reading, MA: Addison-Wesley, 1990.

[82] R. Schaffer and R. Sedgewick, "The analysis of heapsort," *Journal of Algorithms*, vol. 15, no. 1, pp. 76–100, 1993.

[83] D. D. Sleator and R. E. Tarjan, "Self-adjusting binary search trees," *J. ACM*, vol. 32, no. 3, pp. 652–686, 1985.

[84] G. A. Stephen, *String Searching Algorithms*. World Scientific Press, 1994.

[85] R. Tamassia and G. Liotta, "Graph drawing," in *Handbook of Discrete and Computational Geometry* (J. E. Goodman and J. O'Rourke, eds.), ch. 52, pp. 1163–1186, CRC Press LLC, 2nd ed., 2004.

[86] R. Tarjan and U. Vishkin, "An efficient parallel biconnectivity algorithm," *SIAM J. Comput.*, vol. 14, pp. 862–874, 1985.

[87] R. E. Tarjan, "Depth first search and linear graph algorithms," *SIAM J. Comput.*, vol. 1, no. 2, pp. 146–160, 1972.

[88] R. E. Tarjan, *Data Structures and Network Algorithms*, vol. 44 of *CBMS-NSF Regional Conference Series in Applied Mathematics*. Philadelphia, PA: Society for Industrial and Applied Mathematics, 1983.

[89] A. B. Tucker, Jr., *The Computer Science and Engineering Handbook*. CRC Press, 1997.

[90] J. van Leeuwen, "Graph algorithms," in *Handbook of Theoretical Computer Science* (J. van Leeuwen, ed.), vol. A. Algorithms and Complexity, pp. 525–632, Amsterdam: Elsevier, 1990.

[91] J. S. Vitter, "Efficient memory access in large-scale computation," in *Proc. 8th Sympos. Theoret. Aspects Comput. Sci.*, Lecture Notes Comput. Sci., Springer-Verlag, 1991.

[92] J. S. Vitter and W. C. Chen, *Design and Analysis of Coalesced Hashing*. New York: Oxford University Press, 1987.

[93] J. S. Vitter and P. Flajolet, "Average-case analysis of algorithms and data structures," in *Algorithms and Complexity* (J. van Leeuwen, ed.), vol. A of *Handbook of Theoretical Computer Science*, pp. 431–524, Amsterdam: Elsevier, 1990.

[94] S. Warshall, "A theorem on boolean matrices," *Journal of the ACM*, vol. 9, no. 1, pp. 11–12, 1962.

[95] J. W. J. Williams, "Algorithm 232: Heapsort," *Communications of the ACM*, vol. 7, no. 6, pp. 347–348, 1964.

[96] D. Wood, *Data Structures, Algorithms, and Performance*. Addison-Wesley, 1993.